3e

Physics Galaxy

Volume I

Mechanics

Ashish Arora
Mentor & Founder
PHYSICS GALAXY

World's largest encyclopedia of online video courses for High School Students preparing for
* JEE Main * JEE Advanced * NEET * NSEP/INPhO/IPhO

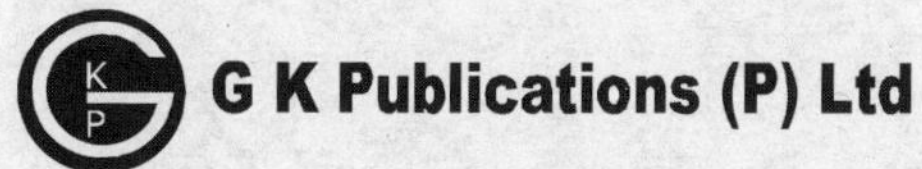

First Edition : December, 2000

Second Edition : May, 2016

Revised Edition : March, 2023

Title : Physics Galaxy : Vol.1 - Mechanics (3rd edition)

Language : English

Author's Name : Ashish Arora

Typeset & Published by :

Career Launcher Infrastructure (P) Ltd.

A-45, Mohan Cooperative Industrial Area, Near Mohan Estate Metro Station, New Delhi - 110044

Marketed by :

G.K. Publications (P) Ltd.

Plot No. 63, Sector-27A, Near Sector - 28 Metro Station, Faridabad, Haryana-121003

ISBN : **978-93-94168-51-0**

Printer's Details : Printed in India, New Delhi.

For product information :

Visit ***www.gkpublications.com*** or email to ***gkp@gkpublications.com***

Dedicated

to

My Parents, Son, Daughter

and

My beloved wife

In his teaching career since 1992 Ashish Arora personally mentored more than 10000 IITians and students who reached global heights in various career and profession chosen. It is his helping attitude toward students with which all his students remember him in life for his contribution in their success and keep connections with him live. Below is the list of some of the successful students in International Olympiad personally taught by him.

NAVNEET LOIWAL	***International GOLD Medal in IPhO-2000 at LONDON***, Also secured **AIR-4** in **IIT JEE 2000** PROUD FOR INDIA : Navneet Loiwal was the first Indian Student who won first International GOLD Medal for our country in International Physics Olympiad.
DUNGRA RAM CHOUDHARY	**AIR-1** in **IIT JEE 2002**
HARSHIT CHOPRA	***National Gold Medal in INPhO-2002*** and got **AIR-2** in **IIT JEE-2002**
KUNTAL LOYA	A Girl Student got position **AIR-8** in **IIT JEE 2002**
LUV KUMAR	***National Gold Medal in INPhO-2003*** and got **AIR-3** in **IIT JEE-2003**
RAJHANS SAMDANI	***National Gold Medal in INPhO-2003*** and got **AIR-5** in **IIT JEE-2003**
SHANTANU BHARDWAJ	***International SILVER Medal in IPhO-2002 at INDONESIA***
SHALEEN HARLALKA	***International GOLD Medal in IPhO-2003 at CHINA*** and got **AIR-46** in **IIT JEE-2003**
TARUN GUPTA	***National GOLD Medal in INPhO-2005***
APEKSHA KHANDELWAL	***National GOLD Medal in INPhO-2005***
ABHINAV SINHA	***Hon'ble Mension Award in APhO-2006*** **at** ***KAZAKHSTAN***
RAMAN SHARMA	***International GOLD Medal in IPhO-2007*** **at** ***IRAN*** and got **AIR-20** in **IIT JEE-2007**
PRATYUSH PANDEY	***International SILVER Medal in IPhO-2007*** **at** ***IRAN*** and got **AIR-85 in IIT JEE-2007**
GARVIT JUNIWAL	***International GOLD Medal in IPhO-2008*** **at** ***VIETNAM*** and got **AIR-10** in **IIT JEE-2008**
ANKIT PARASHAR	***National GOLD Medal in INPhO-2008***
HEMANT NOVAL	***National GOLD Medal in INPhO-2008*** and got **AIR-25** in **IIT JEE-2008**
ABHISHEK MITRUKA	***National GOLD Medal in INPhO-2009***
SARTHAK KALANI	***National GOLD Medal in INPhO-2009***
ASTHA AGARWAL	***International SILVER Medal in IJSO-2009*** **at** ***AZERBAIJAN***
RAHUL GURNANI	***International SILVER Medal in IJSO-2009*** **at** ***AZERBAIJAN***
AYUSH SINGHAL	***International SILVER Medal in IJSO-2009*** **at** ***AZERBAIJAN***
MEHUL KUMAR	***International SILVER Medal in IPhO-2010*** **at** ***CROATIA*** and got **AIR-19** in **IIT JEE-2010**
ABHIROOP BHATNAGAR	***National GOLD Medal in INPhO-2010***
AYUSH SHARMA	***International Double GOLD Medal in IJSO-2010*** at ***NIGERIA***
AASTHA AGRAWAL	***Hon'ble Mension Award in APhO-2011*** at ***ISRAEL*** and got **AIR-93** in **IIT JEE 2011**
ABHISHEK BANSAL	***National GOLD Medal in INPhO-2011***
SAMYAK DAGA	***National GOLD Medal in INPhO-2011***
SHREY GOYAL	***National GOLD Medal in INPhO-2012*** and secured **AIR-24** in **IIT JEE 2012**
RAHUL GURNANI	***National GOLD Medal in INPhO-2012***
JASPREET SINGH JHEETA	***National GOLD Medal in INPhO-2012***
DIVYANSHU MUND	***National GOLD Medal in INPhO-2012***
SHESHANSH AGARWAL	***International SILVER Medal in IAO-2012 at KOREA***
SWATI GUPTA	***International SILVER Medal in IJSO-2012 at IRAN***
PRATYUSH RAJPUT	***International SILVER Medal in IJSO-2012 at IRAN***
SHESHANSH AGARWAL	***International BRONZE Medal in IOAA-2013 at GREECE***
SHESHANSH AGARWAL	***International GOLD Medal in IOAA-2014 at ROMANIA***
SHESHANSH AGARWAL	***International SILVER Medal in IPhO-2015 at INDIA*** and secured **AIR-58** in **JEE(Advanced)-2015**
VIDUSHI VARSHNEY	***International SILVER Medal in IJSO-2015 at SOUTH KOREA***
AMAN BANSAL	**AIR-1 in JEE Advanced 2016**
KUNAL GOYAL	**AIR-3 in JEE Advanced 2016**
GOURAV DIDWANIA	**AIR-9 in JEE Advanced 2016**
DIVYANSH GARG	***International SILVER Medal in IPhO-2016 at SWITZERLAND***
NALIN KHANDELWAL	**AIR-1 in NEET 2019**
MRIDUL AGARWAL	**AIR-1 in JEE Advanced 2021**

ABOUT THE AUTHOR

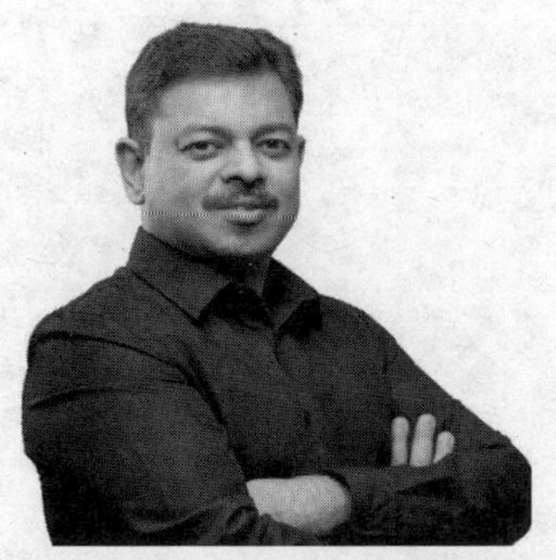

The complexities of Physics have given nightmares to many, but the homegrown genius of Jaipur- Ashish Arora has helped millions of students to live their dreams by decoding it.

Newton Law of Gravitation and Faraday's Magnetic induction force apply perfectly well with this unassuming genius. A Pied Piper of students, his webportal https://www.physicsgalaxy.com, The world's largest encyclopedia of video lectures on high school Physics possesses strong gravitational pull and magnetic attraction for students who want to make it big in life.

Ashish Arora, gifted with rare ability to train masterminds, has mentored over 10,000 IITians and Medicos in his past over three decades of teaching sojourn including lots of students made it to Top 100 in IIT-JEE/JEE(Advance) including multiple times AIR-1 and many in Top-10. Apart from that, he has also groomed hundreds of students for cracking International Physics Olympiad. No wonder his student Navneet Loiwal brought laurel to the country by becoming the first Indian to win a Gold medal at the 2000 - International Physics Olympiad in London (UK).

His special ability to simplify the toughest of the Physics theorems and applications rates him as one among the best Physics teachers in the world. With this, Arora simply defies the logic that perfection comes with age. Even at 18 when he started teaching Physics while pursuing engineering, he was as engaging as he is now. Experience, besides graying his hair, has just widened his horizon.

Now after encountering all tribes of students - some brilliant and some not-so-intelligent - this celebrated teacher has embarked upon a noble mission to make the entire galaxy of Physics inform of his webportal PHYSICSGALAXY.COM to serve and help global students in the subject. Today students from 183 countries are connected with this webportal. On any topic of physics students can post their queries in INTERACT tab of the webportal on which many global experts with Ashish Arora reply to several queries posted online by students.

Dedicated to global students of middle and high school level, his website *www.physicsgalaxy.com* also has teaching sessions dubbed in American accent and subtitles in 87 languages. For students in India preparing for JEE & NEET, his online courses will be available soon on PHYSICSGALAXY.COM.

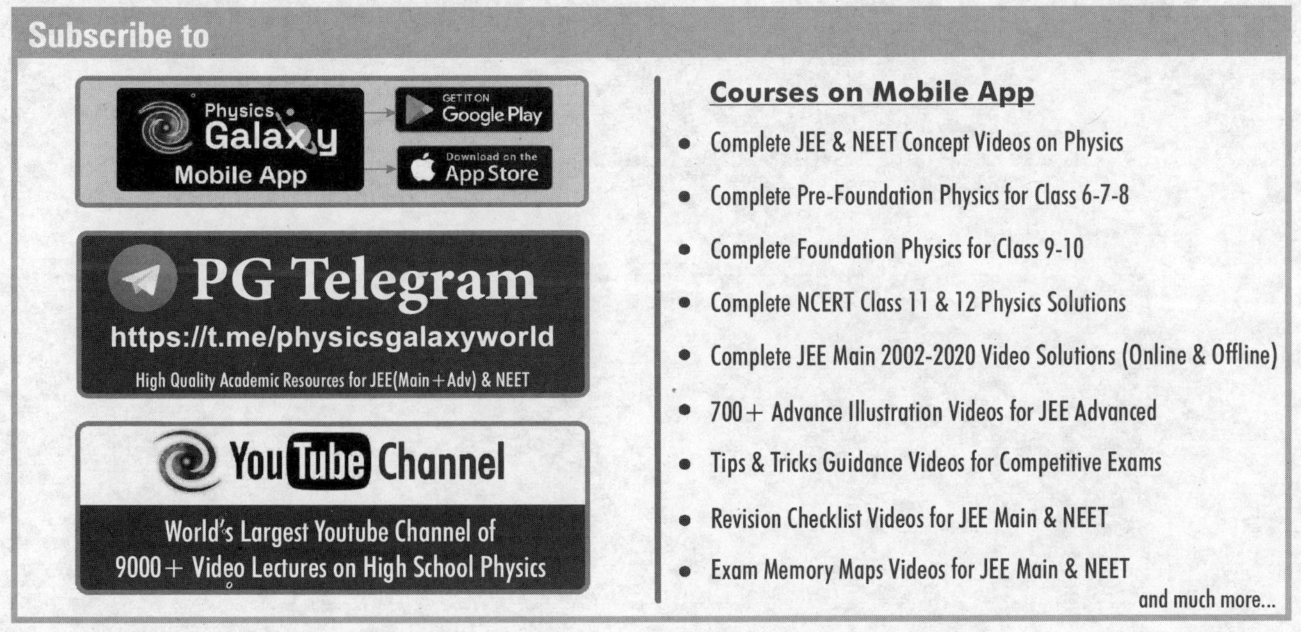

FOREWORD

It has been pleasure for me to follow the progress Er. Ashish Arora has made in teaching and professional career. In the last about three decades he has actively contributed in developing several new techniques for teaching & learning of Physics and driven important contribution to Science domain through nurturing young students and budding scientists. Physics Galaxy is one such example of numerous efforts he has undertaken.

The third edition of Physics Galaxy provides a good coverage of various topics of Mechanics, Thermodynamics and Waves, Optics & Modern Physics and Electricity & Magnetism through dedicated volumes and many new questions included. It would be an important resource for students appearing in competitive examination for seeking admission in engineering and medical streams.

The structure of book is logical and the presentation is innovative. Importantly the book covers some of the concepts on the basis of realistic experiments and examples. The book has been written in an informal style to help students learn faster and more interactively with better diagrams and visual appeal of the content. Each chapter has variety of theoretical and numerical problems to test the knowledge acquired by students. The book also includes solution to all practice exercises with several new illustrations and problems for deeper learning.

I am sure the book will widen the horizons of knowledge in Physics and will be found very useful by the students for developing in-depth understanding of the subject.

Date : May 10, 2024

Prof. Sandeep Sancheti
Ph. D. (U.K.), B.Tech. FIETE, FIE (I), SMIEEE

Vice-Chancellor (Provost) Marwadi University, Rajkot
Member Executive Council, Association of Commonwealth Universities, London
Former President, AIU, New Delhi
Former Vice-Chancellor, SRMIST, Chennai
Former President, Manipal University, Jaipur
Former-Director NIT Surathkal, NIT New Delhi, NIT Trichy,
NIT Calicut, SPA Delhi; Former-Mentor Director NIT Goa,
NIT Sikkim, NIT Puducherry
Former-Member JEE Apex Board (JAB), MHRD, GoI
Former-Chairman, Central Counselling Board (CCB), AIEEE, MHRD, GoI
Former-Chairman, Direct Admission of Students Abroad (DASA), MHRD, GoI

PREFACE

For a science student, Physics is the most important subject, unlike to other subjects it requires logical reasoning and high imagination of brain. Without improving the level of physics it is very difficult to achieve a goal in the present age of competitions. To score better, one does not require hard working at least in physics. It just requires a simple understanding and approach to think a physical situation. Actually physics is the surrounding of our everyday life. All the six parts of general physics-Mechanics, Heat, Sound, Light, Elcctromagnetism and Modern Physics are the constituents of our surroundings. If you wish to make the concepts of physics strong, you should try to understand core concepts of physics in practical approach rather than theoretical. Whenever you try to solve a physics problem, first create a hypothetical approach rather than theoretical. Whenever you try to solve a physics problem, first create a hypothetical world in your imagination about the problem and try to think psychologically, what the next step should be, the best answer would be given by your brain psychology. For making physics strong in all respects and you should try to merge and understand all the concepts with the brain psychologically.

The book PHYSICS GALAXY is designed in a totally different and friendly approach to develop the physics concepts psychologically. The book is presented in four volumes, which covers almost all the core branches of general physics. First volume covers Mechanics. It is the most important part of physics. The things you will learn in this book will form a major foundation for understanding of other sections of physics as mechanics is used in all other branches of physics as a core fundamental. In this book every part of mechanics is explained in a simple and interactive experimental way. The book is divided in seven major chapters, covering the complete kinematics and dynamics of bodies with both translational and rotational motion then gravitation and complete fluid statics and dynamics is covered with several applications.

The best way of understanding physics is the experiments and this methodology I am using in my lectures and I found that it helps students a lot in concept visualization. In this book I have tried to translate the things as I used in lectures. After every important section there are several solved examples included with simple and interactive explanations. It might help a student in a way that the student does not require to consult any thing with the teacher. Everything is self explanatory and in simple language.

One important factor in preparation of physics I wish to highlight that most of the student after reading the theory of a concept start working out the numerical problems. This is not the efficient way of developing concepts in brain. To get the maximum benefit of the book students should read carefully the whole chapter at least three or four times with all the illustrative examples and with more stress on some illustrative examples included in the chapter. Practice exercises included after every theory section in each chapter is for the purpose of in-depth understanding of the applications of concepts covered. Illustrative examples are explaining some theoretical concept in the form of an example. After a thorough reading of the chapter students can start thinking on discussion questions and start working on numerical problems.

Exercises given at the end of each chapter are for circulation of all the concepts in mind. There are two sections, first is the discussion questions, which are theoretical and help in understanding the concepts at root level. Second section is of conceptual MCQs which helps in enhancing the theoretical thinking of students and building logical skills in the chapter. Third section of numerical MCQs helps in the developing scientific and analytical application of concepts. Fourth section of advance MCQs with one or more options correct type questions is for developing advance and comprehensive thoughts. Last section is the Unsolved Numerical Problems which includes some simple problems and some tough problems which require the building fundamentals of physics from basics to advance level problems which are useful in preparation of NSEP, INPhO or IPhO.

In this third edition of the book I have included many new questions and solutions in different exercises at practice, conceptual, numerical and advance MCQs to support students who are dependent on their self study and not getting access to teachers for their preparation.

This book has taken a shape just because of motivational inspiration by my mother in 1997 when I just thought to write something for my students. She always motivated and was on my side whenever I thought to develop some new learning methodology for my students.

I don't have words for my best friend my wife Anuja for always being together with me to complete this book in the unique style and format.

I would like to pay my gratitude to Sh. Dayashankar Prajapati in assisting me to complete the task in Design Labs of PHYSICSGALAXY.COM and presenting the book in totally new format of third edition.

At last but the most important person, my father who has devoted his valuable time in finally presenting the book in such a format and a simple language, thanks is a very small word for his dedication in building the base structure of this book.

In this third edition I have tried my best to make this book error free but owing to the nature of work, inadvertently, there is possibility of errors left untouched. I shall be grateful to the readers, if they point out me regarding errors and oblige me by giving their valuable and constructive suggestions via emails for further improvement of the book.

Date : May 10, 2024

Ashish Arora

PHYSICSGALAXY.COM

B-80, Model Town, Malviya Nagar, Jaipur-302017

e-mails: ashisharora@physicsgalaxy.com

ashash12345@gmail.com

CONTENTS

Chapter 3 *Work, Energy and Power* 149-218

Chapter 4 *Linear Momentum and its Conservation* 219-286

Chapter 6 Gravitation 355-429

ANSWERS & SOLUTIONS

Kinematics

1

FEW WORDS FOR STUDENTS

This chapter introduces you to a simple description of motion: One-dimensional or motion along a straight line and Two-dimensional or motion in a plane. A thorough mastery of these idea is necessary for understanding the following chapters, which discuss the laws and behaviour of motional bodies. As a matter of fact, most chapters in this book will make some use of the contents of this introduction to motion.

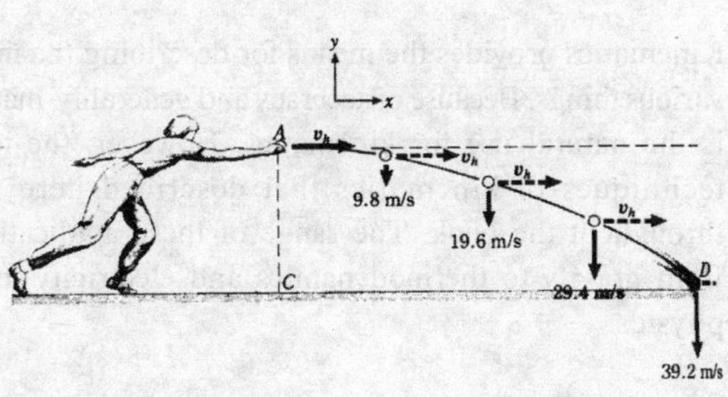

CHAPTER CONTENTS

COVER APPLICATION

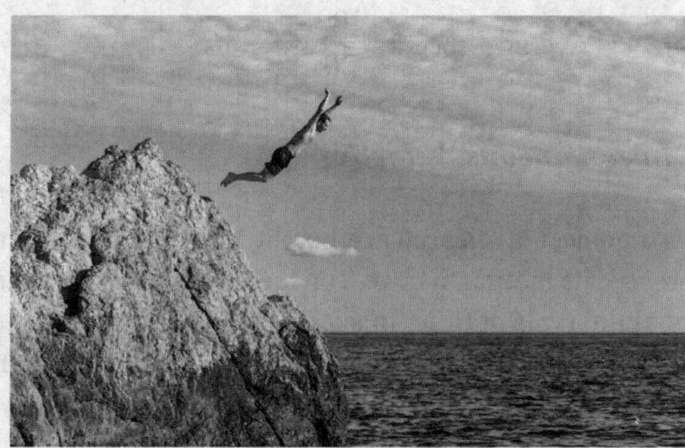

Figure (a)

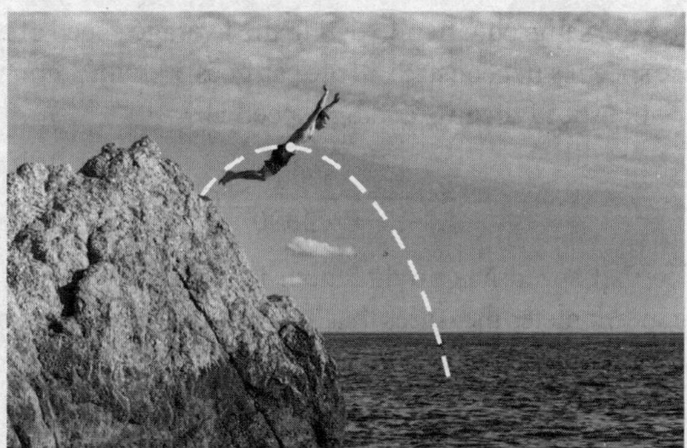

Figure (b)

Figure-(a) shows a diver jumping off from a cliff having some extended projection. The diver has to be experienced enough to jump in such a way that he should not land on the rocks. Figure-(b) shows the trajectory of motion of centre of mass of the diver's body. The initial velocity of jump and the angle θ is such that the horizontal range of projectile motion at sea level lands in the water. The diver may not have mathematical approach but with experience of diving he is able to interpret correct initial speed and angle to achieve the successful dive.

A large part of our everyday experience, as well as our scientific experience, concerns things that move. For this reason, the study of motion is one of the most basic studies in physics. The study of motion is divided into two parts, Kinematics and Dynamics. Kinematics describes the positions and motions of objects in space as a function of time but does not consider the causes of motion. The study of the causes of motion are called dynamics.

Kinematics provides the means for describing the motions of various things. Because of accuracy and generality, mathematics is the natural use for kinematics. However, the ideas and techniques of kinematics that described here are used throughout the book. The range of these applications runs from gravity to thermodynamics and electricity to modern physics.

We begin our study of kinematics by considering motion in only one dimension or rectilinear motion. The advantage of this is the introduction of all the necessary concepts in their simplest form. In further sections we will learn how to apply these concepts to two dimensional motion.

1.1 Speed

When you say that a car is moving at a speed of 20 meters per second (20 m/s), everyone knows what you mean; the car will go 20 m in 1 s provided it maintains this speed. In 0.5 s the car will go $0.5 \times 20 = 10$ m, and in 2 s it will go $2 \times 20 = 40$ m. In general, the distance a car travels if its speed does not change is

$$\text{Distance traveled} = \text{speed} \times \text{time taken}$$

Solving for speed, we find

$$\text{Speed} = \frac{\text{Distance traveled}}{\text{time taken}}$$

We use the same equation to define the average speed of a car whose speed is not constant. If the car goes 5 km in 3 hrs, with a variable speed then its average speed is

$$\text{Average speed} = \frac{5000}{3 \times 3600} = 0.463 \text{ m/s}$$

Notice that speed has no direction. It is a scalar quantity. A car's speedometer measures that how fast the car is going but it tells us nothing about the direction of travel.

1.2 Average Velocity

In everyday conversation, we use the terms speed and velocity interchangeably. In physics, however, these two quantities have different meanings. Velocity of an object includes the direction of motion with the magnitude, unlike to speed which has only the magnitude (scalar). As velocity is a vector quantity, an object's average speed is often not equal to its average velocity, even in magnitude. Now we come to an exact definition of velocity.

Refer to figure-1.1. An object is carried from point A to point B through the path shown by dashed curve. The displacement from A to B is shown as the vector $\boldsymbol{r}$ between the two points. As shown, the displacement is $|\boldsymbol{r}|$ towards E30°N and is a vector quantity. We define the average velocity of the object as it is carried from A to B by

$$\text{Average velocity} = \frac{\text{displacement vector}}{\text{time taken}}$$

$$\bar{v} = \frac{r}{t} \quad \dots(1.1)$$

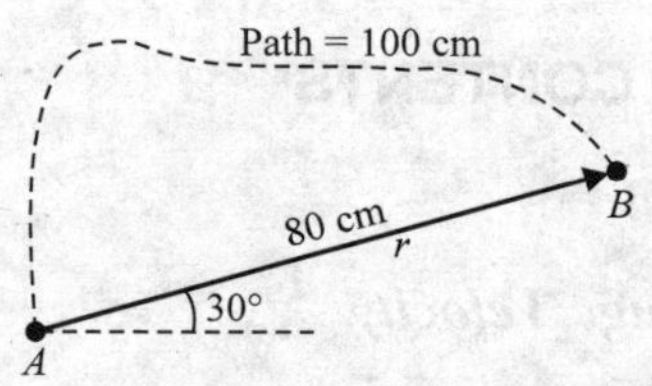

Figure 1.1

Here bar above the v is used to indicate that this is an average velocity. The direction of $\bar{v}$ is same as the displacement vector.

Let us take a numerical example. In the figure shown the distance of straight line from A to B is 80 cm and an object takes 20 s to go from A to B through 100 cm path, then we have

$$\text{Average velocity} = \frac{80}{20} = 4 \text{ cm/s E30°N}$$

However the average speed is

$$\text{Average speed} = \frac{100}{20} = 5 \text{ cm/s}$$

1.3 Instantaneous Velocity

When an object is released at a height, it falls under gravity. If we observe its motion, it covers unequal (increasing) distances in equal intervals of time. In such cases we say the velocity of the object is increasing, such a velocity at a single point is called the instantaneous velocity.

As the object is released, its direction of velocity is clear i.e. downward, in the direction of its motion. Look at figure-1.2. To find the velocity of the object roughly during its fall at point C, we consider the small section of path $AB(\Delta r)$. If object covers this distance in duration Δt the average velocity of the object from A to B is

$$\bar{v} = \frac{\Delta r}{\Delta t} \quad \ldots (1.2)$$

This is not the exact velocity at C as velocity is continuously increasing. If we make the duration Δt smaller, the point A and B will be much closer to C and the average velocity of the ball will be quite closer to the ball's actual velocity at C. If the duration is so small that we can write $\Delta t \to 0$, then A and B will be so close to C that the average velocity, we compute is almost exactly equal to the velocity at C. We call the velocity at C the instantaneous velocity at that point and represent it by v. Mathematically we can define the instantaneous velocity as

$$\vec{v} = \lim_{\Delta t \to 0} \frac{\overrightarrow{\Delta r}}{\Delta t} = \frac{\overrightarrow{dr}}{dt} \quad \ldots (1.3)$$

The symbol $\lim\limits_{\Delta t \to 0}$ is read "in the limiting case where Δt tends to zero." It represents mathematically the experimental procedure in which Δt is made so small that the average velocity between A and B becomes essentially the instantaneous velocity at C. This is represented mathematically in differential form as

$$\vec{v} = \frac{\overrightarrow{dr}}{dt}$$

There is one more interesting relation between instantaneous velocity and speed. When we make Δt very small, the object cannot change its direction of motion appreciably during the time it takes go to from A to B. As a result, the straight line distance from A to B equals the path length covered by the object as it goes from A to B. Therefore, because the path length and the displacement have the same magnitude, the instantaneous velocity and the speed at C also have the same magnitude. Thus we see that the magnitude of the instantaneous velocity at a point is equal to the speed at that point.

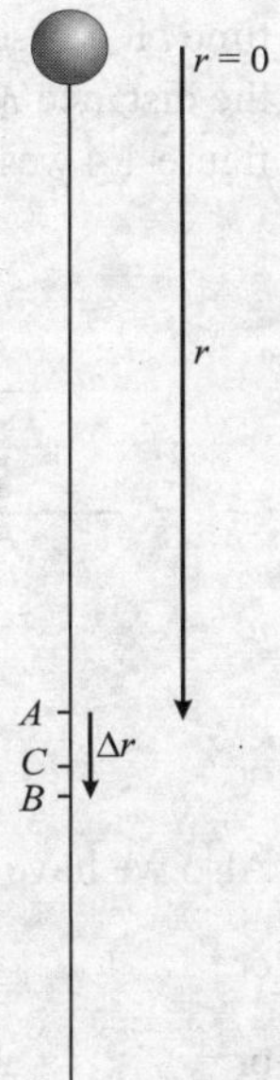

Figure 1.2

The historical definition of instantaneous velocity is : *"The velocity of the particle at an instant of its journey"*. If we define the instantaneous velocity of a particle from the point of view of a practical situation of motion of a particle, the situation would be somewhat different and might be more accurate.

In fact velocity is the rate of change of position of the particle and it is not possible to evaluate the rate at which position changes at *an instant*, because at an instant the position of particle does not change. To evaluate the instantaneous velocity we consider an elemental distance dx in the neighborhood of that instant at which we are required to evaluate the instantaneous velocity. If this distance dx is covered by the particle in time dt, it shows that the average velocity of the particle in the small duration dt is dx/dt. This dt is the duration in the neighborhood of the time instant $t = t$. (say from $t = t$ to $t = t + dt$). Now this velocity dx/dt can be said as instantaneous velocity at time $t = t$.

This Instantaneous velocity can be written as

$$v = \frac{dx}{dt} \quad \text{[Time derivative of displacement]}$$

Instantaneous velocity of a particle in its motion can be a constant or may vary with time and displacement. We consider some examples for understanding the numerical concepts associated with kinematics problems with uniform motion i.e. with constant speed motion.

 # Illustrative Example 1.1

Road distance from Jaipur to Ajmer is 135 km. How long can one afford to stop for lunch if he can drive at an average speed of 72 kph on the highway, if he has to reach in 2½ hr.

Solution

Total time taken from Jaipur to Ajmer for non-stop driving is $= \frac{135}{72} = 1$ hr 52.5 min

Extra time available for lunch is = 2 hr 30 min – 1 hr 52.5 min = 37.5 mins.

 # Illustrative Example 1.2

A 10 hr tour is made at an average speed of 40 kph. If during the first half of the distance the average speed of the bus was 30 kph, what was the average speed for the second half of the trip ?

Solution

Total distance the bus covered is = 40 kph × 10 hr = 400 km

For first half bus speed was 30 kph, thus time taken to cover 200 km is $= \frac{200}{30} = 6.66$ hr.

Thus bus covered remaining 200 km during 3.37 hr, its average speed is $= \frac{200}{3.37} = 60$ kph

Illustrative Example 1.3

A carrier train, when it is 100 km away from the station, going at a constant speed of 70 kph towards the station. At this instant a fast bird from its engine flies towards the station at 100 kph net speed. When the bird gets to the station, it turns back and flies again towards the train, when it reaches engine, it again turns and heads towards the station. If bird keeps on flying in such a manner, find the distance travelled by the bird before train reaches the station ? How many trips, it made in this duration between station and the train ?

Solution

Time taken by the train to reach the station is $= \dfrac{100}{70} = 1.43$ hr

In this duration bird travels a distance = 100 × 1.43 = 143 km.

As here distance travelled by the bird is continuously reducing after each trip, time of successive trips is also reducing. When train is just approaching the station, the trip length is negligible or tends to zero and hence time of trip is also negligible or tends to zero, thus theoretically it takes infinite trips.

Illustrative Example 1.4

An athlete starts running along a circular track of 50 m radius at a speed 5 m/s in the clockwise direction for 40 s. Then the athlete reverses direction and runs in the anticlockwise direction at 3 m/s for 100 s. At the end, how far around the track is the runner from the starting point ?

Solution

During first run she covers a distance 5 × 40 = 200 m and in its second opposite run, she covers a distance 3 × 100 = 300 m. Thus at the end she is 100 m away from her starting point in anticlockwise direction as shown in figure-1.3.

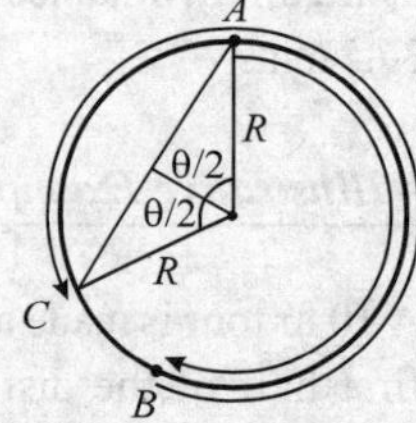

Figure 1.3

The displacement of the runner from the starting point A is given by vector AC. It is calculated as

The angle subtended by the arc AC at centre is

$$\theta = \frac{arc\ AC}{\text{radius}} = \frac{100}{50} = 2\ \text{rad} = 114.6°$$

Length of cord AC is given by

$$l_{AC} = 2R \sin\frac{\theta}{2} = 2 \times 50 \times \sin 57.3° = 84.15\ \text{m}.$$

Illustrative Example 1.5

A steamer going downstream overcame a raft at a point P. 1 hr later it turned back and after some time passed the raft at a distance 6 km from the point P. Find the speed of river if speed of river relative to water remains constant.

Solution

Let u and v kph be the velocities of the steamer and the river flow. When steamer is going downstream, its velocity is $(u + v)$ kph due to river flow.

During 1 hr, distances travelled by the steamer and raft are $(u + v)$ km and u km respectively.

Now when steamer returns (say from point M), its velocity become $(v - u)$ kph as it in upstream direction, and say after time t it crosses the raft at point Q, which is 6 km from P, then the distance MQ is $(v - u)t$ km and PM is $(u + ut)$ km. From figure-1.4 we have

$$u + v = u + ut + (v - u)t$$

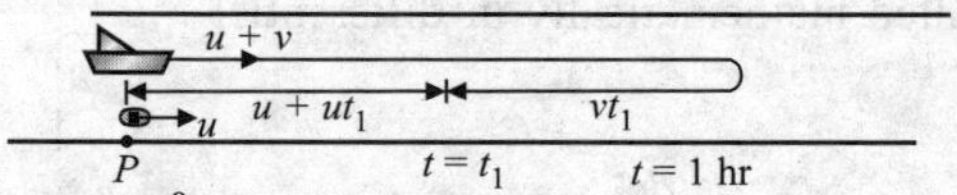

Figure 1.4

or $\quad t = 1$ hr.

Also we have $\quad u + ut = 6$

or $\quad 2u = 6$

or $\quad u = 3$ kph

Illustrative Example 1.6

Two ships, 1 and 2, move with constant velocities 3 m/s and 4 m/s along two mutually perpendicular straight tracks toward the intersection point O. At the moment $t = 0$ the ships were located at the distances 120 m and 200 m from the point O. How soon will the distance between the ships become the shortest and what is it equal to ?

Solution

At an intermediate time instant t, let the positions of the ships 1 and 2 are $(120 - 3t)$ and $(200 - 4t)$ respectively as shown in figure-1.5. At this instant distance between them is

$$l = \sqrt{(120 - 3t)^2 + (200 - 4t)^2}$$

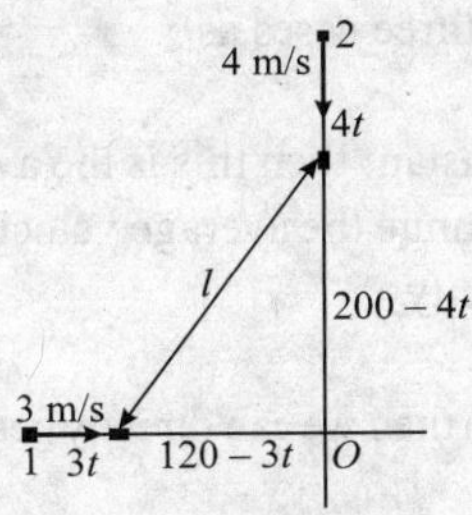

Figure 1.5

This distance l is minimum at some instant say at $t = t_0$, it is given by using the concept of maxima-minima, it leads to find $\frac{dl}{dt} = 0$, which gives us t_0.

$$\frac{dl}{dt} = \frac{2(120-3t).(-3)+2(200-4t).(-4)}{2\sqrt{(120-3t)^2+(200-4t)^2}} = 0$$

or $\quad 25\,t - 1160 = 0$

or $\quad t = \frac{1160}{25} = 46.4 \text{ s} = t_0$

The shortest distance between the ships now is given by

$$l_{min} = \sqrt{(120-3\times46.4)^2+(200-4\times46.4)^2} = 24 \text{ m}$$

Practice Exercise 1.1

(i) Two bicycle riders made a 30 km trip in the same time. Cyclist *A* travelled non-stop at an average speed of 20 kph. Another cyclist *B* travelled with a lunch break of 20 min. What was the average speed of *B* for the actual riding ?

[25.75 kph]

(ii) The light speed is 3.0×10^8 m/s, and the sound speed is 340 m/s. Find the value of count *N*, if "A child start counting after every second, he sees a bomb blast 1 km away and stops when he hear its blast sound."

[3]

(iii) Two cars travelling in parallel lanes at 90 kph and 72 kph. Assuming each car to be 5 m long, find the time taken during the overtake and the total road distance used for the overtake.

[2 s, 55 m]

(iv) A point traversed half the distance with a velocity v_0. The remaining part of the distance was covered with velocity v_1 for half the time, and with velocity v_2 for the other half of the time. Find the mean velocity of the point averaged over the whole time of the motion.

[$2v_0(v_1 + v_2)/(2v_0 + v_1 + v_2)$]

(v) From point *A* located on a highway as shown in figure-1.6, one has to reach by car as soon as possible to point *B* located in the field at a distance *l* from the highway. It is given that the car velocity decreases in the field η time than on the highway. At what distance from the point *D* car must turn off the highway into the field for minimum time ?

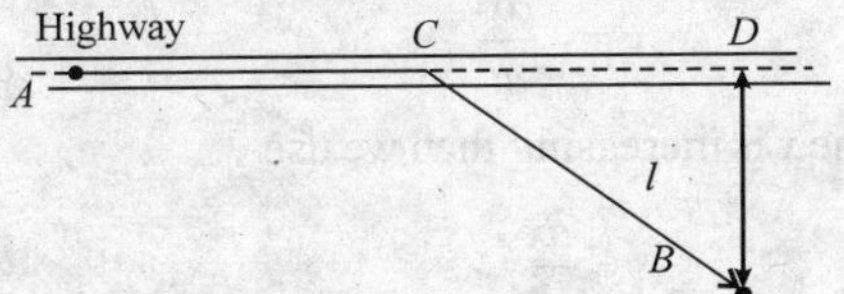

Figure 1.6

[$\frac{l}{\sqrt{\eta^2-1}}$]

(vi) Two junglemen are standing at the two opposite banks of a river of width '*l*' facing each other. One of them starts beating a drum and sound reaches to the other one after time t_1 he starts. Then second one starts beating the drum and now first one hear the sound after time t_2. Calculate the velocity of sound relative to air and the velocity of wind, if it is blowing from first bank to the other bank at right angle to the river flow.

[$\frac{l}{2}(\frac{1}{t_1}+\frac{1}{t_2})$, $\frac{l}{2}(\frac{1}{t_1}-\frac{1}{t_2})$]

(vii) A rectangular reservoir has a 1 km difference between its sides. Two fishermen simultaneously leave one vertex of the rectangle for a point located at the opposite vertex. One fisherman crosses the reservoir in a boat, the other walks along the bank. Find the size of the reservoir if each of them has a speed of 4 km/hr and one of them arrives half an hour earlier than the other.

[3 km × 4 km]

(viii) A car is moving at a constant speed of 40 km/hr along a straight road which heads towards a large vertical wall and make a sharp 90° turn by the side of the wall. A fly flying at a constant speed of 100 km/hr, starts from the wall towards the car at an instant when the car is 20 km away, flies until it reaches the glass pane of the car and returns to the wall at the same speed. It continues to fly between the car and the wall till the car makes the 90° turn. (a) What is the total distance the fly has traveled during this period ? (b) How many trips has it made between the car and the wall ?

Ans. [50 km, ∞]

1.4 Variation in Instantaneous Velocity

As we have discussed that instantaneous velocity of a particle can be a constant or may vary with time or displacement. In vector form representation, depending on the variation, sign of velocity vector changes as

If with time x is decreasing then we use

$$v = -\frac{dx}{dt}$$

If with time x is increasing then we use

$$v = \frac{dx}{dt}$$

The concept of instantaneous velocity is useful in solving problems, when velocity of a given object is not constant. For example we consider an example of evaluating average velocity, there are some cases in which one of the two data (displacement and time taken) is not give so it should be evaluated from the other information given in the problems. As there are two possible situations, which are discussed here

(a) Displacement is not given and only initial and final time instant (t_2 and t_1) are given.

In any case the instantaneous velocity of a particle can be given in either of the three forms.

(i) v = constant, (ii) $v = f(x)$ [depends on displacement], (iii) $v = f(t)$ [depend on time]
In each case we can put v as dx/dt and then by integrating the differential equation $v = dx/dt$ we can get the required data.

Case (i) : If v = constant, then this is the average velocity as if velocity does not change, the average velocity remains same as instantaneous velocity.

Case (ii) : If $v = f(x)$ then we use $\frac{dx}{dt} = f(x)$

$\Rightarrow \frac{dx}{f(x)} = dt$ and on integrating $\int_0^{x_1} \frac{dx}{f(x)} = \int_0^{t} dt$, we get the value of x_1 and similarly by changing the limits we can get x_2 also. Here lower limits correspond to the starting point, when $t = 0$, $x = 0$ and the upper limits correspond when the time is t_1, and particle's coordinate will be $x = x_1$.

Case (iii) : If $v = f(t)$ then we can directly get $x_2 - x_1$ by integrating $\int_{x_1}^{x_2} dx = \int_{t_1}^{t_2} f(t)\, dt$.

Here lower limits correspond to the position, when particle is at $x = x_1$ and time is $t = t_1$ and the upper limits correspond when the time is t_2, and particle's coordinate will be $x = x_2$.

(b) If time duration is not given, only x_1 and x_2 are given

Again we can take three cases as

Case (i) : If v = constant then this is the average velocity as if velocity does not change the average velocity remains same as instantaneous velocity.

Case (ii) : If $v = f(x)$ then we can directly get $t_2 - t_1$ by integrating

$$\int_{x_1}^{x_2} \frac{dx}{f(x)} = \int_{t_1}^{t_2} dt.$$

Here limits of integration are corresponding to the position of particle at times t_1 and t_2

Case (iii) : If $v = f(t)$ then by integrating $\int_0^{x_2} dx = \int_0^{t_1} f(t)\, dt$. We get the value of t_1 and similarly by changing the limits we can get t_2 also.

> Web Reference at www.physicsgalaxy.com
>
> **Age Group -** High School Physics | Age 17-19 Years
> **Section -** MECHANICS
> **Topic -** Motion in One Dimensions
> **Module Numbers -** 1, 2, 3 and 4

1.5 Acceleration

In previous section, we have discussed the motion of a car. Its velocity may change or it may remains constant. We have defined the instantaneous velocity, which gives an idea about how fast the position of an object changes with time. Similarly it is reasonable to define a term which gives an idea about how velocity of an object changes with time, it is termed as acceleration. In a given duration of the motion of an object average acceleration and instantaneous acceleration can be defined as

$$\text{Average Acceleration} = \frac{\text{Total change in velocity}}{\text{time taken}} = \frac{\Delta \vec{v}}{\Delta t}$$

As if a particle is moving with initial velocity $\vec{u}$ and after time t its final velocity becomes $\vec{v}$, we have its average acceleration is

$$a = \frac{v-u}{t}$$

$$\text{Hence Instantaneous Acceleration} = \lim_{\Delta t \to 0} \frac{\Delta \vec{v}}{\Delta t} = \frac{dv}{dt}$$

[Time derivative of velocity]

In some cases when velocity changes, we must define the

acceleration of the object. Velocity may increase or decrease depending on the case of problem. When acceleration of an object is positive, the velocity of it is increasing but if it is negative, it will be decreasing. In this particular case, we say that the body has decelerated, but deceleration is an obsolete term and it is more precise to use the term acceleration with the appropriate sign to show the direction and behavior of the motion.

In differential form instantaneous acceleration can be given in three ways as it is the time derivative of velocity and the second derivative of displacement as

$$a = \frac{dv}{dt} = \frac{d^2r}{dt^2} \qquad \ldots(1.4)$$

One more form can be generated as

$$a = \frac{dv}{dt} \times \frac{dx}{dx} = \frac{dx}{dt} \times \frac{dv}{dx} = v\frac{dv}{dx} \qquad \ldots(1.5)$$

These forms are speed equations to obtain the different parameters related to motion of an accelerated particle (both uniformly accelerated and non-uniformly accelerated).

1.6 Speed Equations

"Speed Equations are used for solving the problems of kinematics."

In general we use three differential form of equations for problems of kinematics as

(i) $v = \frac{dx}{dt}$

(ii) $a = \frac{dv}{dt}$

(iii) $a = v\frac{dv}{dx}$

Equation-(i), we've already discussed in section 1.2, it can be used whenever the velocity of a particle is given as a function of time or displacement. To understand the practical importance of equation (ii) and (iii), we discuss an illustrative example.

 # Illustrative Example 1.7

A particle at origin starts towards positive direction of x-axis, with an acceleration a. This acceleration can be defined in three ways; (a) a = constant; (b) $a = f(x)$; and (c) $a = f(t)$. Find the velocity of the particle as a function of time. Also find velocity of the particle when it is at a displacement x from origin. Given that the velocity of the particle at $t = 0$ is $v = u$.

Solution

Here we first use equation-(ii) as $a = \frac{dv}{dt}$

or $$dv = a\,dt$$

On integrating we'll have $$\int_u^v dv = \int_0^t a\,dt$$

Here lower limits of integration corresponds to the starting position that at $t = 0$, velocity is $v = u$ and upper limits correspond to a general time $t = t$ when velocity becomes v.

$$v - u = \int_0^t a\,dt \qquad \ldots(1.6)$$

If a is a function of time we can integrate above expression and if it is a constant, it will give us

$$v = u + at \qquad \ldots(1.7)$$

This equation is the standard speed equation. no-(1) and it is only applicable for constant acceleration cases.

Now we use equation-(iii) as

$$a = v\frac{dv}{dx}$$

$$v\,dv = a\,dx$$

On integration we'll have

$$\int_u^v v\,dv = \int_0^s a\,dx$$

$$v^2 - u^2 = 2\int_0^s a\,dx \qquad \ldots(1.8)$$

If a is a function of displacement we can integrate the expression and if a is a constant it results

$$v^2 = u^2 + 2as \qquad \ldots(1.9)$$

This equation is standard speed equation no-2 and it is only applicable for constant acceleration cases.

From equations-(1.7), putting the value of v in equation-(1.9), we get

$$(u + at)^2 = u^2 + 2as$$

On solving $$s = ut + \frac{1}{2}at^2 \qquad \ldots(1.10)$$

This equation relates to displacement of the particle with the time of motion. Equations-(1.7), (1.9) and (1.10) are valid only for constant acceleration cases. If acceleration in a case is not constant, we go for the differential forms of speed equations.

For the cases of constant acceleration, we also have a fourth derived speed equation, which gives the distance traveled by the object in n^{th} second after start. It is derived from equation-(1.10), which gives the total displacement from start to t^{th} second. For n^{th} second displacement, we can write

$$s_n = [u\,(n) - \frac{1}{2}\,a\,(n)^2] - [u\,(n-1) - \frac{1}{2}\,a\,(n-1)^2]$$

$$s_n = u + \frac{1}{2}\,a\,(2n-1) \qquad \text{...(1.11)}$$

Web Reference at www.physicsgalaxy.com

Age Group - High School Physics | Age 17-19 Years
Section - MECHANICS
Topic - Motion in One Dimensions
Module Numbers - 5, 6, 7 and 8

1.7 Uniformly Accelerated Motion

A simple type of motion is motion with constant acceleration. When an object moves with constant acceleration, the acceleration is equal to the average acceleration. For problems related to motion of objects with constant accelerations we use the four speed equations

$$v = u + at$$

$$v^2 = u^2 + 2as$$

$$s = ut + \frac{1}{2}\,at^2$$

$$s_n = u + \frac{1}{2}\,a\,(2n-1)$$

In Numerical problems of kinematics of constant acceleration motion, we use some short-cut techniques to find the required parameters, based on these speed equation. Next we discuss these techniques with some examples.

 # Illustrative Example 1.8

A driver travelling at 90 kph applied the brakes for 5 s. If the braking acceleration was 2 m/s^2, what was her final speed ?

Solution

Before braking the initial speed of car is

$$u = 90 \text{ kph} = 90 \times \frac{5}{18} = 25 \text{ m/s}$$

Retardation produced by brakes is $a = -2$ m/s^2

When brakes are applied, car start retarding. After 5.0 s final speed of car is given by

$$v = u + at$$

or $$= 25 - 2 \times 5 = 15 \text{ m/s}$$

 # Illustrative Example 1.9

A slowly moving flatcar is 12.0 m long passing a point at straight road at 10 kph. A boy beside the road near to that point tosses rocks onto the moving flatcar at the rate of one per second. (a) If the first rock just hits the front edge of the car, how many rocks will fall onto that car ? (b) How many rocks will fall onto that car if the car begins to accelerate at 0.5 m/s^2, just as the first rock hits the car ?

Solution

(a) Speed of flatcar is = 10 kph = 2.78 m/s.
As the flatcar is 12.0 m in length, total time it takes to cross the point is $= \frac{12}{2.78} = 4.31$ s

As first rock hits the front edge of the car, let us take this time $t = 0$, thus in 4.0 s, five rocks will hit the car and fifth will fall on road.

(b) If car begins to accelerate at 0.5 m/s^2, time taken to cross the point is given by

$$s = ut + \frac{1}{2}\,at^2$$

or $$12 = 2.78\,t + \frac{1}{2}\,(0.5)\,t^2$$

or $$t^2 + 11.12\,t - 48 = 0$$

or $$t = 3.32 \text{ s}$$

or $$t = -28.88 \text{ s}$$

As time here can not be negative, it takes 3.32 seconds to cross the point, hence four rocks will fall on it.

 # Illustrative Example 1.10

In a car race, car A takes a time of t sec less than car B at the finish and passes the finishing point with a velocity v more than the car B. Assuming that the cars start from rest and travel with constant accelerations a_1 and a_2 respectively, show that $v = \sqrt{a_1 a_2}\,t$.

Solution

In car race, cars starts from rest and accelerates with constant accelerations. Here we'll discuss an important concept of uniformly accelerated motion. If a body starts from rest i.e. with zero initial velocity and accelerates with an acceleration a. After travelling a distance s, its velocity can be given by speed equation

$$v^2 = u^2 + 2as$$

As we have $u = 0$,

$$v = \sqrt{2as} \quad \ldots \text{(A)}$$

For the time taken to travel this distance s, we use second speed equation as

Here again we have $u = 0$,

$$s = \frac{1}{2}at^2$$

or

$$t = \sqrt{\frac{2s}{a}}$$

Similarly if a body starts with an initial velocity u and retards with deceleration a, if after travelling a distance s, its final speed becomes zero, we have

Using

$$v^2 = u^2 - 2as \quad \ldots \text{(B)}$$

Here we have $v = 0$, thus

$$u = \sqrt{2as}$$

Similarly the time it will take can be directly given as

$$t = \sqrt{\frac{2s}{a}}$$

In above cases students should note that to apply the results given in equations-(A) and (B), either initial or final velocity of the body must be zero and it should be uniformly accelerated.

In the question above car A starts with acceleration a_1 and car B with acceleration a_2. If car B reaches the finishing point at time T and with speed u, car A will reach at time $T - t$ and with speed $u + v$ as given in the question.

As both the cars starts from rest and covers same distance, say s, we have

For car A

$$v + u = \sqrt{2a_1 s}$$

and

$$T - t = \sqrt{\frac{2s}{a_1}}$$

For car B

$$u = \sqrt{2a_2 s}$$

and

$$T = \sqrt{\frac{2s}{a_2}}$$

From above equations eliminating the terms of u and T, we get

$$v = \sqrt{2a_1 s} - \sqrt{2a_2 s}$$

and

$$t = \sqrt{\frac{2s}{a_2}} - \sqrt{\frac{2s}{a_1}}$$

Dividing the above equations, we get

$$v = \sqrt{a_1 a_2}\ t$$

 # Illustrative Example 1.11

A car and a truck move in the same straight line at the same instant of time from the same point. The car moves with a constant velocity of 40 m/s and truck starts with a constant acceleration of 4 m/s^2. Find the time t that elapses before the truck catches the car. Find also the greatest distance between them prior to it and the time at which this occurs.

Solution

After time t from start, the position of car from start is

$$s_1 = 40\,t$$

and the position of truck from start is

$$s_2 = \frac{1}{2}(4)\,t^2$$

When truck catches the car

$$s_2 = s_1$$

or

$$40\,t = 2\,t^2$$

or

$$t = 20 \text{ s}$$

Before this the distance between them is

$$s = s_1 - s_2$$

or

$$s = 40\,t - 2\,t^2$$

This distance is maximum when $\frac{ds}{dt} = 0$, (using maxima-minima), which gives

$$\frac{ds}{dt} = 40 - 4\,t = 0$$

or

$$t = 10 \text{ s}$$

At $t = 10$ s, distance between them will be maximum, which is given as

$$s_{max} = 40\,(10) - 2\,(10)^2 = 200 \text{ m}$$

 # Illustrative Example 1.12

A driver travelling at 30 kph sees the light turn red at the intersection. If his reaction time is 0.6 s, and the car can decelerate at 4.5 m/s^2, find the stopping distance of the car. What would the stopping distance be if the car were moving at 90 kph.

Solution

Initial speed of car is = 30 kph = 8.3 m/s.

Reaction time of driver is 0.6 s, it is the duration she takes to put the brakes on and in this duration car travels with the uniform speed.

The distance travelled by the car during her reaction time is = $8.34 \times 0.6 = 5$ m.

Now after travelling 5 m, car start decelerating at 4.5 m/s^2. As final velocity of the car is zero, when it comes to rest, we have for its initial velocity $u = \sqrt{2as}$.

The distance travelled by the car before coming to rest can be given as $s = \dfrac{u^2}{2a} = \dfrac{(8.34)^2}{2 \times 4.5} = 7.71$ m

Total stopping distance is = 5 + 7.71 = 12.71 m.

If initial speed of car were 90 kph or 25 m/s, the distance travelled by car during reaction time of driver will become $25 \times 0.6 = 15$ m and the second distance will change as $s = \dfrac{(25)^2}{2 \times 4.5} = 69.45$ m.

Total stopping distance is = 15 + 69.45 = 84.45 m

Web Reference at www.physicsgalaxy.com

Age Group - High School Physics | Age 17-19 Years
Section - MECHANICS
Topic - Motion in One Dimensions
Module Numbers - 9, 10, 11, 12 and 13

Practice Exercise 1.2

(i) A bike starts from rest and accelerates at 4 m/s^2 for 5.0 s. It then moves at constant velocity for 25.0 s, and then decelerates at 2.0 m/s^2 until it stops. Find the total distance that the motorcycle has moved.

[650 m]

(ii) Fiat Siena can accelerate from 0 to 48 kph in 3.6 s and from 0 to 96 kph in 10.2 s Also, under constant acceleration from rest it crosses the 0.4 km marker at a speed of 140 kph. (a) Calculate the average acceleration needed get the speed 48 kph. (b) Calculate the average acceleration during the time it requires to go from 48 to 96 kph. (c) What constant acceleration would be required to get a speed of 140 kph over the 0.4 km run starting from rest ?

[(a) 3.7 m/s^2, (b) 2.01 m/s^2, (c) 1.89 m/s^2]

(iii) Two friends start bikes from one corner of a square field of edge L towards the diagonally opposite corner in the same time t. They both start from the same place and take different routes. One travels along the diagonal with constant acceleration a, and the other accelerates momentarily and then travels along the edge of the field with constant speed v. What is the relationship between a and v ?

[$a = \dfrac{v^2}{\sqrt{2}L}$]

(iv) A truck travelling along a straight road at a constant speed of 72 kph passes a car at time $t = 0$ moving much slower. At the instant the truck passes the car, the car starts accelerating at constant 1 m/s^2 and overtake the truck 0.6 km further down the road, from where the car moves uniformly. Find the distance between them at time $t = 50$ s.

[300 m]

(v) A motorcycle and a car start from rest at the same place at the same time and they travel in the same direction. The cycle accelerates uniformly at 1 m/s^2 upto a speed of 36 kph and the car at 0.5 m/s^2 upto a speed of 54 kph. Calculate the time and the distance at which the car overtakes the cycle.

[35 s, 300 m]

(vi) A driver, having a definite reaction time is capable of stopping his car over a distance of 30 m on seeing a red traffic signal, when the speed of the car is 72 kph and over a distance of 10 m when the speed is 36 kph. Find the distance over a distance over which he can stop the car if it were running at a speed of 54 kph. Assume that his reaction time and the deceleration of the car remains same in all the three cases.

[18.75 m]

(vii) A point moving with constant acceleration from A to B in the straight line AB has velocities u and v at A and B respectively. Find its velocity at C, the mid point of AB. Also show that if the time from A to C is twice that from C to B, then $v = 7u$.

[$\sqrt{\dfrac{u^2 + v^2}{2}}$]

(viii) A train is targeted to run from Delhi to Pune at an average speed of 80 kph but due to repairs of track looses 2 hrs in the first part of the journey. If then accelerates at a rate of 20 kph^2 till the speed reaches 100 kph. Its speed is now maintained till the end of the journey. If the train now reaches station in time, find the distance from when it started accelerating ?

[840 km]

(ix) A train of length 350 m starts moving rectilinearly with constant acceleration 3×10^{-2} m/s^2; $t = 30$ s after the start the locomotive headlight is switched on (event-1) and $T = 60$ s after that event the tail signal light is switched on (event-2). Find the distance between these events in the reference frames fixed to the train and to the Earth. How and at what constant velocity V relative to the Earth must a certain reference frame F move for the two events to occur in it at the same point ?

Ans. [242 m, 4.03 m/s]

(x) Two cars traveling towards each other on a straight road at velocity 10 m/s and 12 m/s respectively. When they are 150 m apart, both drivers apply their brakes and each car decelerates at 2 m/s^2 until it stops. How far apart will they be when they have both come to a stop ?

Ans. [89 m]

(xi) Two bodies move in the same straight line at the same instant of time from the same origin. The first body moves with a constant velocity of 40 m/s and second starts with a constant acceleration of 4 m/s^2. Find the time t that elapses before the second catches the first body. Find also the greatest distance between them prior to it and the time at which this occurs.

Ans. [20 s, 200 mts]

1.8 Free Fall

We are all familiar to falling objects - for example, a paperweight that is accidentally knocked off the edge of a desk. Often in describing the motion of the paperweight, we may neglect air resistance. If air resistance has a negligible effect on a falling object, then it is valid to assume that the object's acceleration is entirely due to gravity. In this case the motion is called free-fall. Treating the motion of the paperweight as free-fall it is a valid approximation as long as it does not fall too far. Even for short falls, this approximation is not satisfied for an object such as a feather or a flat piece of paper.

Galileo Galilei made several experiments and studies of free-fall and determined that the acceleration due to gravity is constant and is same for different objects. The magnitude of this acceleration is represented by the symbol g. Although g varies slightly from place to place on the earth's surface, but the value that is accurate for our use is

$$g = 9.8 \text{ m/s}^2 \qquad \ldots(1.12)$$

Numerical problems of free fall utilize the four speed equations, replacing the value of a by g.

$$v = u - gt \qquad \ldots(1.13)$$

$$v^2 = u^2 - 2gh \qquad \ldots(1.14)$$

$$h = ut - \frac{1}{2} gt^2 \qquad \ldots(1.15)$$

$$h_n = u + \frac{g}{2}(2n-1) \qquad \ldots(1.16)$$

Using the above equation, we now take some examples for better understanding of concepts associated with freely falling objects.

Illustrative Example 1.13

If a body travels half its total path in the last second of its fall from rest, find the time and height of its fall. Take $g = 10$ m/s^2

Solution

If H be the total height the body falls from rest, total time to fall is $t = \sqrt{\frac{2H}{g}}$

It is given that the body falls $H/2$ distance in time $(t-1)$, thus we have $t - 1 = \sqrt{\frac{2(H/2)}{g}}$

or from above equations, eliminating t, we have

$$\sqrt{\frac{2H}{g}} - \sqrt{\frac{H}{g}} = 1$$

or $$\sqrt{\frac{H}{g}}(\sqrt{2}-1) = 1$$

or $$\sqrt{\frac{H}{g}} = \frac{1}{0.414}$$

or $$H = 58 \text{ m}$$

Total time of fall is $$t = \sqrt{\frac{2H}{g}} = \sqrt{\frac{116}{10}} = 3.4 \text{ s}$$

Illustrative Example 1.14

A person sitting on the top of a tall building is dropping balls at regular intervals of one second. Find the positions of the 3rd, 4th and 5th ball when the 6th ball is being dropped. Take $g = 10$ m/s^2

Solution

When 6th ball is being dropped, the positions of the other (previously fallen) balls can be calculated by using the time of falling of each ball till this instant.

For 5th ball, it was dropped just one second before. Thus it has fallen a distance $= \frac{1}{2} gt^2 = 5$ m.

For 4th ball, it was dropped two second before this instant. It has fallen a distance $= \frac{1}{2}(10)2^2 = 20$ m.

For 3rd ball, it was dropped two second before this instant. Its depth is $= \frac{1}{2}(10)3^2 = 45$ m.

Illustrative Example 1.15

A small parachute dropped from a 30 m high cliff falls freely under gravity for 1.0 s and then attains a terminal velocity 1.2 m/s. 20.0 s later a stone is dropped from the cliff. Will the stone catch up with the parachute before it reaches the ground ? (Take $g = 10$ m/s^2)

Solution

Distance fallen by the parachute in first 1.0 s is

$$= \frac{1}{2}gt^2 = \frac{1}{2}(10)(1)^2 = 5 \text{ m}$$

Rest of the height 30 – 5 = 25 m, it covers with uniform speed 1.2 m/s. Thus time taken by the parachute to reach the ground is $= \frac{25}{1.2} = 20.84$ s.

Total time taken by the parachute to reach the ground is $= 1 + 20.84$ s $= 21.84$ s.

Stone is dropped after 20.0 s. Time taken to reach ground is

$$= \sqrt{\frac{2H}{g}} = \sqrt{\frac{2 \times 30}{10}} = 2.45 \text{ s}$$

Total time taken by stone from the time of dropping the parachute is $20 + 2.45 = 22.45$ s

It is clear that stone requires time longer than the parachute requires. Thus stone will not catch the parachute.

Illustrative Example 1.16

A balloon is going up with a uniform speed 20 m/s. It was at a height of 100 m from ground, when a stone is dropped from its basket. Find the time taken by the stone to reach the ground and the height of the balloon from the ground, when stone hits the ground. (Take $g = 10$ m/s^2)

Solution

As balloon is going up, when stone is dropped, it will also has the same upward speed of 20 m/s. So it will first go up retarded by gravity and fall back towards ground. The practical situation is shown in figure-1.7.

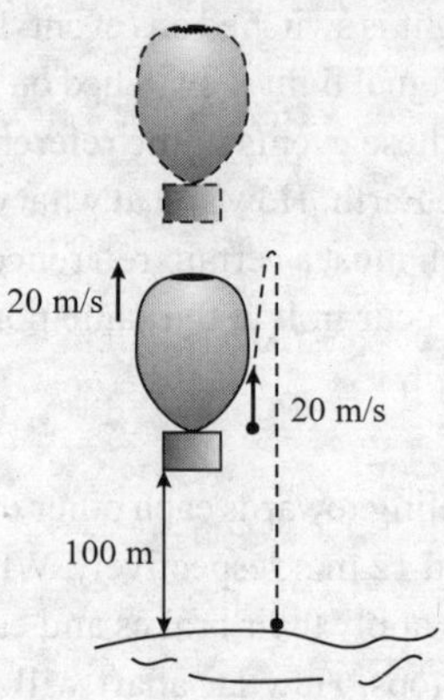

Figure 1.7

Here to find time we use second speed equation for free fall motion

$$h = ut - \frac{1}{2}gt^2$$

From figure, here we take $u = 20$ m/s and $h = -100$ m

We have $\quad -100 = 20\,t - \frac{1}{2}(10)\,t^2$

Solving, it gives $\quad t = 6.89$ s or $t = -2.89$ s

Thus stone will take 6.89 s to reach the ground and it will follow the path shown in figure by dotted line.

In this duration, balloon ascends a height

$$= 20 \times 6.89 = 137.8 \text{ m}$$

Height of balloon from ground at the instant, stone hitting the ground is $= 100 + 137.8 = 237.8$ m.

Illustrative Example 1.17

From the foot of a tower 90 m high, a stone is thrown up so as to reach the top of the tower. Two second later another stone is dropped from the top of the tower. Find when and where two stones meet. (Take $g = 10$ m/s^2)

Solution

First stone is thrown so as to reach the top of the tower, so its initial velocity is

$$u = \sqrt{2gH}$$

$$= \sqrt{2 \times 10 \times 90} = 42.5 \text{ m/s}$$

Let us take the time $t = t_0$, when the two stones meet at a height h above the foot of the tower. The first stone is travelled a height h in the duration t_0 and the second stone has fallen a distance $(90 - h)$ in time $(t_0 - 2)$. From speed equations, we have

For first stone $\quad h = 42.5\,t_0 - \frac{1}{2}(10)\,t_0^2$

For second stone

$$90-h=\frac{1}{2}(10)(t_0-2)^2$$

Adding above two equation,

$$22.5\,t_0=70$$

or $$t_0=3.11\text{ s}$$

Thus height h is given as

$$h=42.5\,(3.11)-\frac{1}{2}(10)(3.11)^2$$

$$=83.82\text{ m}$$

Illustrative Example 1.18

A girl is standing in an elevator that is moving upward at a velocity of 5 m/s and acceleration 2 m/s^2, when she drops her handbag. If she was originally holding the bag at a height of 1.5 m above the elevator floor, how long will it take the bag to hit the floor.

Solution

In such problems, generally called elevator problems we can use the concept of relative acceleration. Here we solve the problem with respect to elevator or we assume that we are observing from inside of elevator. The concept of relative motion is discussed in detail in section 1.11 of this chapter. That much of detail is not required here.

Imagine the situation, if you are standing in an elevator accelerating up with an acceleration a. If you are holding a box in your hand, it is also accelerating up with the same acceleration. If you release it free, it falls with acceleration g towards the elevator floor, which is coming up with acceleration a. Here we can say that the approach acceleration of box towards the elevator floor is $(g+a)$, and we assume that elevator floor is at rest and box is going down with respect to floor with this acceleration called relative acceleration. Similarly if elevator is going down, we take relative acceleration $(g-a)$.

In this problem, elevator is going up with a velocity 5 m/s, and an acceleration 2 m/s^2, when the bag is dropped. Bag's relative velocity with respect to elevator floor is zero as both at that instant have the same velocity but relative acceleration of the bag is taken as $10+2=12$ m/s^2.

The distance fallen by the bag is 1.5 m, as we are assuming elevator is at rest.

Thus time required is $=\sqrt{\dfrac{2H}{a}}=\sqrt{\dfrac{2\times1.5}{12}}=0.5$ s

NOTE : If we carefully imagine the situation from outside the elevator, bag has covered the actual distance less than 1.5 m. The situation will be more clear in mind with the next two example.

Illustrative Example 1.19

A truck starts from rest with an acceleration of 1.5 m/s^2 while a car 150 m behind starts from rest with an acceleration of 2 m/s^2. How long will it take before both the truck and car side by side, and how much distance is traveled by each ?

Solution

If we take truck at rest, then with respect to truck the relative acceleration of car is $2-1.5=0.5$ m/s^2. Now car has to travel 150 m with initial velocity zero, hence it takes time

$$=\sqrt{\frac{2\times150}{0.5}}=24.5\text{ sec.}$$

Distance traveled by car in 24.5 sec is

$$=\frac{1}{2}at^2=\frac{1}{2}\times2\times(24.5)^2=600\text{ m}$$

Distance traveled by truck in 24.5 sec is

$$=600-150=450\text{ m}$$

Illustrative Example 1.20

An elevator car whose floor to ceiling distance is equal to 2.7 m starts ascending with constant acceleration 1.2 m/s^2. Two seconds after the start a bolt begins falling from the ceiling of the car. Find :

(a) the time after which bolt hits the floor of the elevator.

(b) the net displacement and distance traveled by the bolt, with respect to earth. (Take $g=9.8$ m/s^2)

Solution

(a) If we consider elevator at rest, then relative acceleration of the bolt is

$$a_r=9.8+1.2=11\text{ m/s}^2$$

Initial velocity of the bolt is 2.4 m/s and it is getting retarded with 11 m/s^2. With respect to elevator initial velocity of bolt is 0 and it has to travel 2.7 m with 11 m/s^2. Thus time taken can be directly given as

$$t=\sqrt{\frac{2s}{a}}=\sqrt{\frac{2\times2.7}{11}}=0.7\text{ seconds}$$

(b) Velocity of the elevator after 2 sec is

$$v=at=1.2\times2=2.4\text{ m/s upwards.}$$

In 0.7 seconds distance traveled by the elevator is

$$l = 2.4 \times 0.7 + 0.5 \times 1.2 \times 0.49$$

$$= 1.98 \text{ m}$$

The final displacement of the bolt is 2.7 – 1.98 = 0.72 m.

We can observe the actual motion of the bolt, it is shown in figure-1.8. It first goes up and then gets back down and hit the floor of the elevator at a distance 0.72 m below the starting point. To find the distance we find the distance it travels before coming to rest at the topmost point of its trajectory. At the time of detachment of the bolt, its velocity is 2.4 m/s.

So its distance up to the top $= \dfrac{u^2}{2g} = \dfrac{(2.4)^2}{19.6} = 0.293$ m

Total distance traveled by the bolt is $= 0.293 \times 2 + 0.72 = 1.31$ m

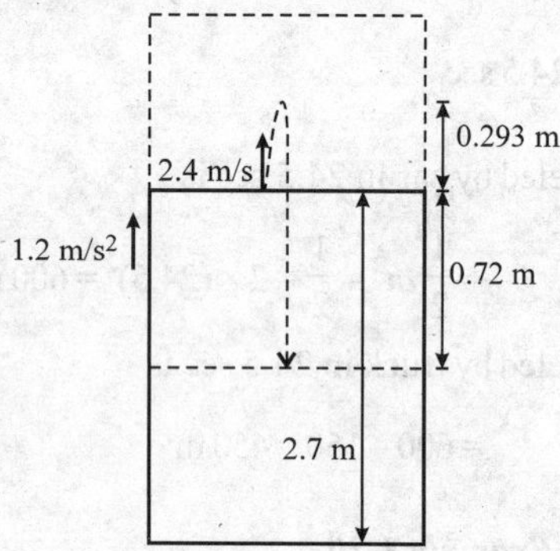

Figure 1.8

Web Reference at www.physicsgalaxy.com

Age Group - High School Physics | Age 17-19 Years

Section - MECHANICS

Topic - Motion in One Dimensions

Module Numbers - 14, 15, 16, 17 and 18

Practice Exercise 1.3

(i) A ball is allowed to slip from rest down a smooth incline plane, and the distances are marked every 2.0 s. If the second mark is made 1.6 m from the starting point, where are the first and fourth marks ?

[0.4 m, 6.4 m]

(ii) Water drops from the nozzle of a shower into the stall floor 176.4 m below. The drops fall at regular interval of time, the first drop striking the floor at the instant the fourth drop begins to fall. Find the location of the individual drops when a drop strikes the floor. Take $g = 9.8$ m/s^2.

[78.4 m, 19.6 m]

(iii) A particle is projected vertically upward from the ground at time $t = 0$ and reaches a height h at $t = T$. Show that the greatest height of the particle is $(gT^2 + 2h)^2/8gT^2$.

(iv) A circus artist maintains four balls in motion making each in turn to rise to a height of 5 m from his hand. Calculate the velocity with which he projects the balls. Where will the other three balls be at the instant when the fourth one is just leaving his hand ? Take $g = 10$ m/s^2.

[10 m/s, 3.75 m, 5.0 m, 3.75 m]

(v) A dog sees a flowerpot sail up and then back down past a window 5 ft high. If the total time the pot is in sight is 1.0 sec, find the height above the window that the pot rises. Take $g = 32$ ft/s^2.

[1/16 ft]

(vi) A ball projected vertically upwards from A, the top of a tower reaches the ground in t_1 seconds. If it is projected vertically downwards from A with the same velocity, it reaches the ground in t_2 seconds. If it falls freely from A, show that it would reach the ground in $\sqrt{t_1 t_2}$ seconds.

(vii) Jimmy is doing an experiment to measure the height of a tall building. He drops a watermelon from the roof the building. 3.0 s later he hears the watermelon splash sound. What height of the building he had calculated. Take speed of sound 340 m/s and air resistance on water melon can be neglected. Take $g = 10$ m/s^2.

[40.7 m]

(viii) You are on the roof of your school building 60 m, high. You see your physics teacher 1.6 m tall walking directly towards the building at 2 m/s. You wish to throw an egg vertically down at a speed 5 m/s on to your teacher's head. Where should your teacher be when you throw the egg. Neglect air resistance. Take $g = 10$ m/s^2.

[6 m away from school building]

(ix) A student goes to the a 100 m high floor of Kutubmeenar at Delhi. To verify the law of gravity, he starts from a window with zero initial velocity, with a stopwatch in his hand. After 3.0 s, Batman comes to the same floor and jumps to save the boy. What must be his initial velocity so that he'll just be able to save the boy. Assume free fall for both boy and Batman before he catches the boy. Take $g = 10$ m/s^2.

[60.5 m/s]

(x) From the top of a tall building (height 27.3 m), a boy throws an apple upward, which strikes ground after 16 s. Take $g = 9.8$ m/s^2, find the speed of apple with which it was thrown and the maximum height reached by it.

Ans. [76.8 m/s, 327.45 m]

(xi) A rocket is fired vertically from rest and ascends with constant net vertical acceleration of 30 m/s^2 for 1 minute. Its fuel is then all used up and it continues as a free particle in the gravitational field of the earth. Find :

(a) Maximum height reached;

(b) The total time elapsed from take off until the rocket strikes the Earth. Take $g = 10$ m/s^2.

Ans. [447.84 s]

1.9 Graphical Interpretation of Motion

We now switch over to algebraic definition of displacement, velocity and acceleration with a graphical interpretation. Graphical analysis of motion sometimes appears to be easier in solving complex numerical problems of kinematics, and because of this we take this section more carefully and cautiously.

1.9.1 Displacement Versus Time Graphs

It is a general tendency in a plot to take the independent variable (generally time) on the x-axis, or abscissa and the dependent variable on the y-axis, or ordinate. Generally displacement *vs* time graphs of the moving particle (or body) helps in interpretation of velocity and its behavior whether motion is uniformly accelerated (positive or negative) or non-accelerated (uniform velocity).

We have the differential relation in velocity and displacement as $v = dx/dt$

It shows that velocity is given by the slope (tan θ) of the x *vs* t curve. This slope relation reveals that if x *vs* t curve is a straight line than it implies that the slope of the curve is a constant and hence it represents the uniform velocity motion. (Shown in figure-1.9(a)). If it is a horizontal straight line, it represents zero slope hence particle is at rest. (Shown in figure-1.9(b)).

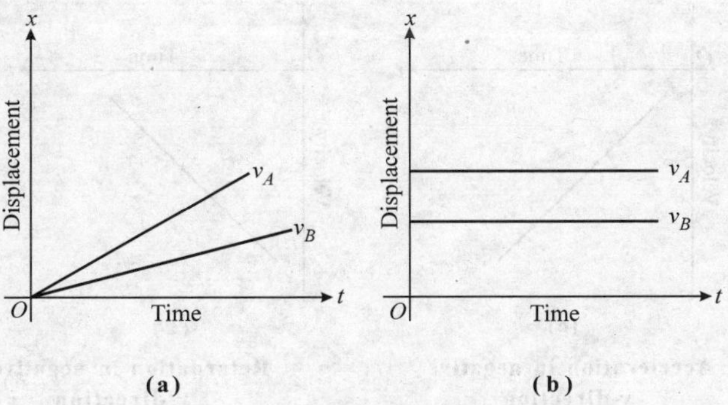

Figure 1.9

If x *vs* t graph is not a straight line, it means that it is a non-uniform motion. If slope of the curve (tangent) is an acute angle, means it is positive and particle is moving in positive direction of x-axis or away from origin and by observation we can check whether slope is increasing or decreasing with time (shown in figure-1.10(a)). If we find the slope of the curve at two instants t_1 and t_2, as shown in figure-1.10(a), we see that slope at time t_2 is less than slope at time t_1. It shows that the velocity of the particle is decreasing, hence the curve represents the decelerated (negative acceleration) motion. If we have a look at figure-1.10(b), again slope is decreasing with time, but in this case slope is obtuse (i.e. negative), hence particle is moving in the direction of negative x-axis or towards origin. Similarly curves shown in figure-1.11(a) and 1.11(b) represents the accelerated motion, away from the origin and towards origin respectively.

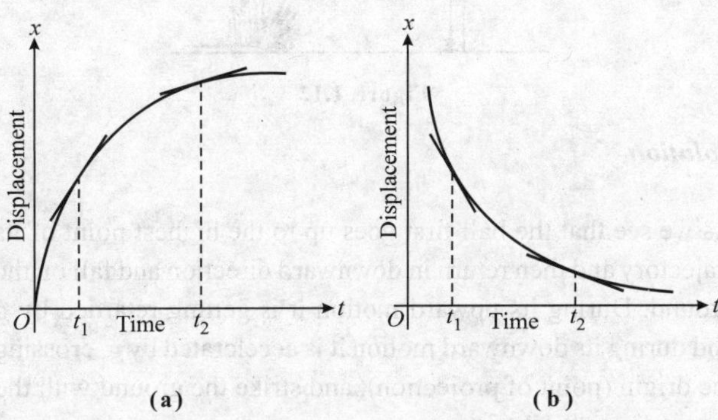

Deceleration away from origin **Deceleration towards origin**

Figure 1.10

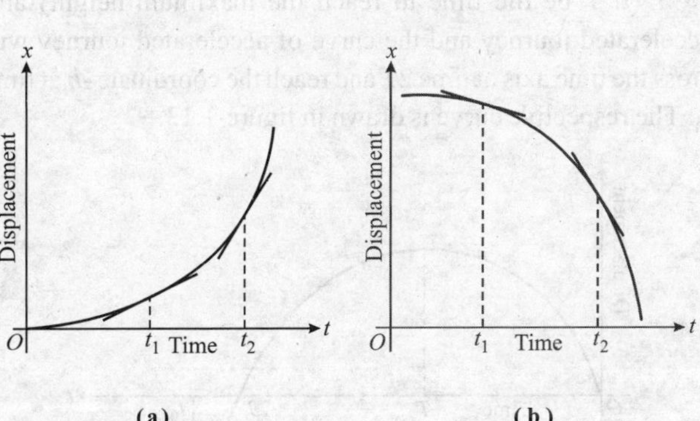

Acceleration away from origin **Acceleration towards origin**

Figure 1.11

In all the above graphs, curves are drawn above the time axis. It shows that all the time particle's x-coordinate is positive. When particle moves on negative x-direction, or to the left of origin, curve is drawn below the time axis as x-coordinate of the particle become negative. To explain this, we take up an illustrative example.

Illustrative Example 1.21

Consider the child standing on the top of a tower of height h, shown in figure-1.12. He throws the ball up and the ball follows the trajectory as shown in figure. Draw the displacement versus time graph of the ball's motion during its flight. Take vertically upwards direction as positive x-axis.

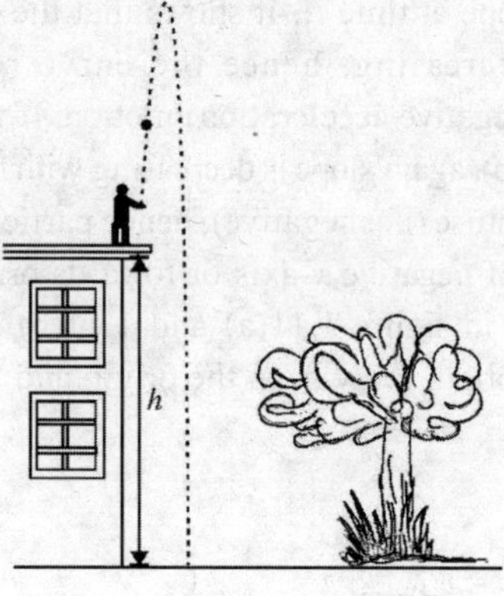

Figure 1.12

Solution

As we see that the ball first goes up to the highest point of its trajectory and then return in downward direction and fall on the ground. During its upward motion it is getting retarded by g and during its downward motion it is accelerated by g, crossing the origin (point of projection), and strike the ground with the x-coordinate "$-h$".

The graph is drawn in two parts-retarded journey from $t = 0$ to $t = T$ (if T be the time to reach the maximum height) and accelerated journey and the curve of accelerated journey will cross the time axis at time $2T$ and reach the coordinate $-h$ at time t_0. The respective curve is drawn in figure-1.13.

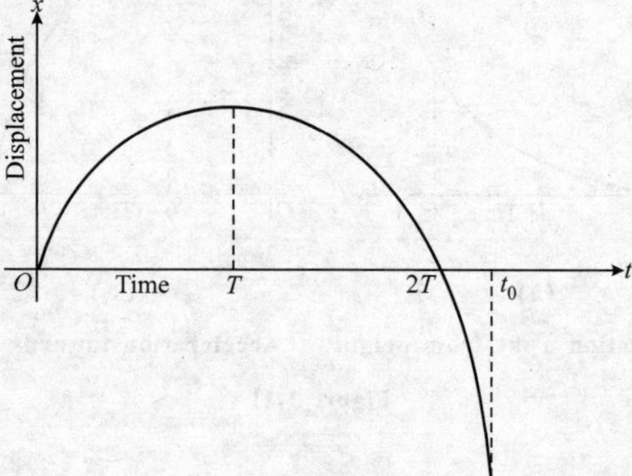

Figure 1.13

1.9.2 Velocity Versus Time Graphs

Velocity-Time curves give the information about the acceleration, whether it is uniform or non-uniform. As we know that the acceleration is time derivative of velocity

$$a = dv/dt.$$

Acceleration can be represented by the slope of the velocity-time curve. If velocity-time curve is a straight line, means that the acceleration of the motion is uniform, and if it is not a straight line it will belong to a non-uniform acceleration. The acceleration is decreasing or increasing and it can be judged by observing the slope of the curve at two or more instants.

Consider the graph shown in figure-1.14. It represents the motion of a particle moving non-uniformly in a straight line. Here from $t = 0$ to $t = t_1$, particle moves with constant acceleration. From $t = t_1$ to $t = t_2$, it moves with uniform velocity and then with variable acceleration. After time $t = t_2$, the acceleration at any instant (say t) can be found by the slope of the curve at that instant.

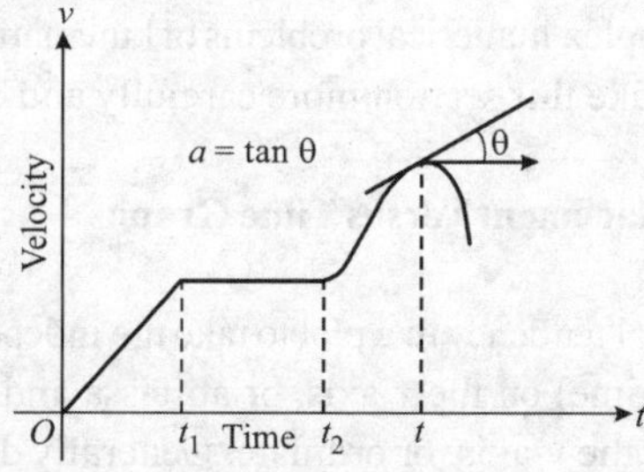

Figure 1.14

Different possible velocity time curves for uniform acceleration are shown in figure-1.15.

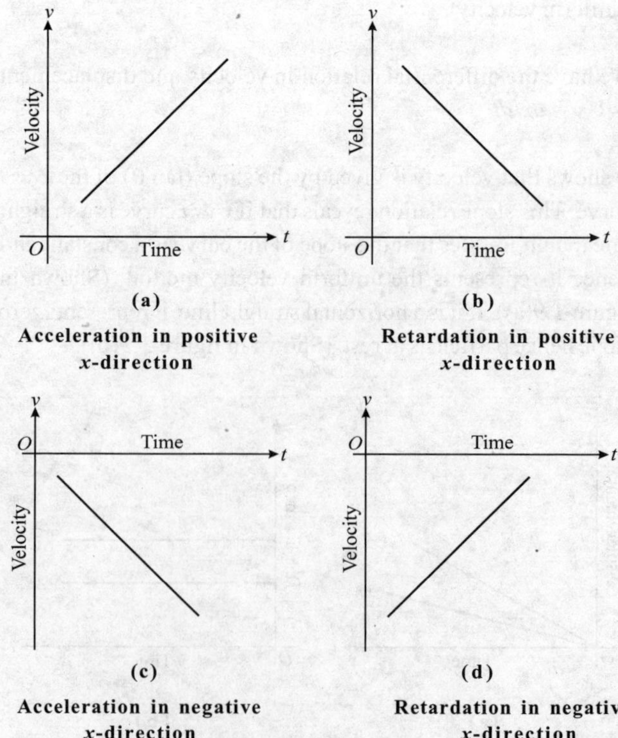

Figure 1.15

The direction of the particle's velocity (towards positive x-direction or negative x-direction) determines the location of the curve, above the time axis or below the time axis. Figure-1.15 shows the velocity-time curves for different uniformly accelerated motions.

Illustrative Example 1.22

Draw the velocity-time graph for the case explained in example 1.21.

Solution

Respective graph is shown in figure-1.16. As the ball first goes up (retardation in positive x-direction), then it falls down (acceleration in negative x-direction).

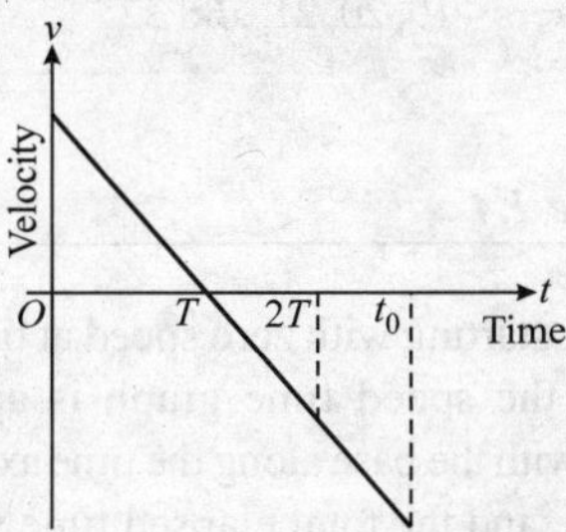

Figure 1.16

There is one more utility of velocity-time graph. It can be used to evaluate the distance and displacement of the particle in a given duration. As we know in general terms displacement is the produce of velocity and time, this can be given by the area under the velocity-time graph. Figure-1.17 shows a velocity-time graph of a particle's motion. The portions of the curve above time axis represent the motion of the particle in positive x-direction and the portions of the curve below the time axis represent the reverse motion in negative x-direction. To calculate the total displacement and the distance traveled by the particle in its motion, we find the area s_1, s_2 and s_3. Here area s_1 and s_3 are the distances traveled by the particle in positive x-direction and s_2 is the distance traveled in negative x-direction. Hence

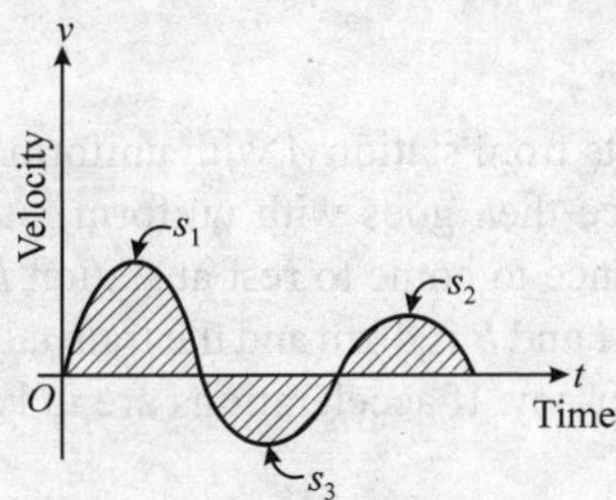

Figure 1.17

Total displacement $= s_1 + s_2 - s_3$

Total distance $= s_1 + s_2 + s_3$

Several types of numerical problems become easy to solve by graphical method. For explaining this we take an example.

Illustrative Example 1.23

A car starting from rest, first moves with an acceleration of 5 m/s^2 for sometime and after moving with a uniform speed for some time starts decelerating at the same rate to come to rest in a total time of 25 sec. If the average velocity of the car over the whole journey is 20 m/s, for how long does it move with a uniform speed ?

Solution

Whole journey of car is divided into three parts, acceleration, uniform motion and retardation. As acceleration and retardation are same, with equal final and initial velocities, the distances covered in first and last period will be same. Let the time durations for the three parts be t_1, t_2 and t_1 and let the distances covered be s_1, s_2 and s_1. We also assume that the maximum velocity of the car in its journey is v. The respective velocity-time graph is shown in figure-1.18

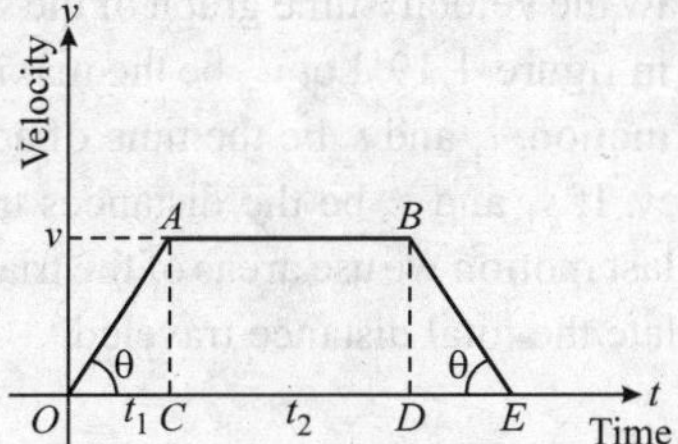

Figure 1.18

Average Velocity of car is

$$\bar{v} = \frac{\text{Total Displacement}}{\text{Time taken}}$$

$$\frac{2s_1 + s_2}{25} = 20 \text{ m/s}$$

$$2s_1 + s_2 = 500 \text{ m} \qquad \ldots (1.17)$$

s_1 and s_2 can be taken by evaluating the areas of triangle OAC and rectangle $ABCD$ as

Area of triangle OAC is $s_1 = \frac{1}{2} v t_1$

[v is the maximum velocity of the car]

Area of rectangle $ABCD$ is $s_2 = v t_2$

As acceleration and retardation are 5 m/s^2. We have slope of lines OA and BE.

$$\tan\theta = \frac{v}{t_1} = 5 \qquad \ldots (1.18)$$

From equation-(1.17) $vt_1 + vt_2 = 500$ ...(1.19)

From equations-(1.18) and (1.19) $t_1^2 + t_1 t_2 = 100$ ...(1.20)

Total time of motion is 25 s $2t_1 + t_2 = 25$ ...(1.21)

On solving equations-(1.20) and (1.21), we get $t_1 = 5$ and 20, using (1.21) we get $t_2 = 15$ and -15, negative time here does not have any significance, hence we take $t_2 = 15$ s, the duration for which the car moves with uniform velocity.

 # Illustrative Example 1.24

A car accelerates from rest at a constant rate α for sometime after which it decelerates at a constant rate β to come to rest. If the total time lapse is t seconds, evaluate (i) the maximum velocity reached and (ii) the total distance traveled.

Solution

Such type of problems, in which first acceleration and then retardation takes place become very short, by using graphical method. We draw the velocity-time graph of the situation given and it is given in figure-1.19. Let v_m be the maximum velocity attained in the motion, t_1 and t_2 be the time of accelerated and retarded journey. If s_1 and s_2 be the distances traveled by the car in first and last motion we use areas of the triangle shown in figure to calculate the total distance traveled.

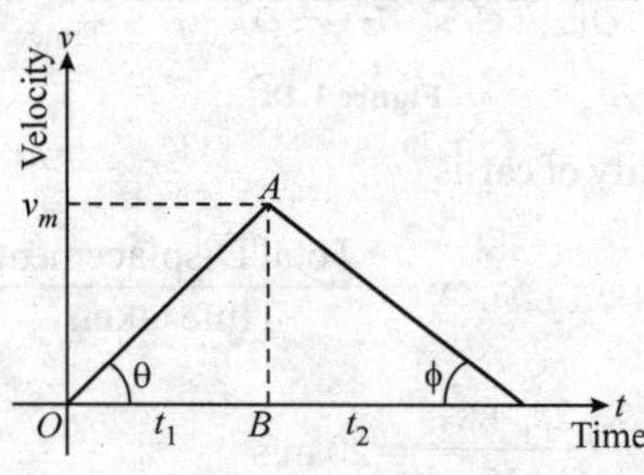

Figure 1.19

Acceleration of car in first motion is

$$\alpha = \tan\theta = \frac{v_m}{t_1}$$

Retardation of car in last motion is

$$\beta = \tan\phi = \frac{v_m}{t_2}$$

and $$t_1 + t_2 = t$$

or $$\frac{v_m}{\alpha} + \frac{v_m}{\beta} = t$$

or $$v_m = \frac{\alpha\beta t}{\alpha + \beta}$$

Displacement of car = area of the triangle

$$= \frac{1}{2} v_m t = \frac{\alpha\beta t^2}{2(\alpha + \beta)}$$

Similar to velocity-time graphs, we can plot acceleration-time graphs. Acceleration-time graphs are not of much utility in solving numerical problems, so acceleration-time graphs are not being given here. Students are advised to plot these graphs in their note-book, with reference to velocity-time graphs given in the previous section.

Web Reference at www.physicsgalaxy.com
Age Group - High School Physics | Age 17-19 Years
Section - MECHANICS
Topic - Motion in One Dimensions
Module Numbers - 19, 20, 21, and 22

Practice Exercise 1.4

(i) A truck driver, starting with zero speed at time zero, drove in such a way that the speed time graph is approximately an isosceles triangle with the base along the time axis. The maximum speed was 30 m/s, and the total elapsed time was 50.0 s. What distance did he travel.

[750 m]

(ii) Figure-1.20 shows displacement-time graph of a particle. Find the time during motion such that the average velocity of the particle during that period is zero.

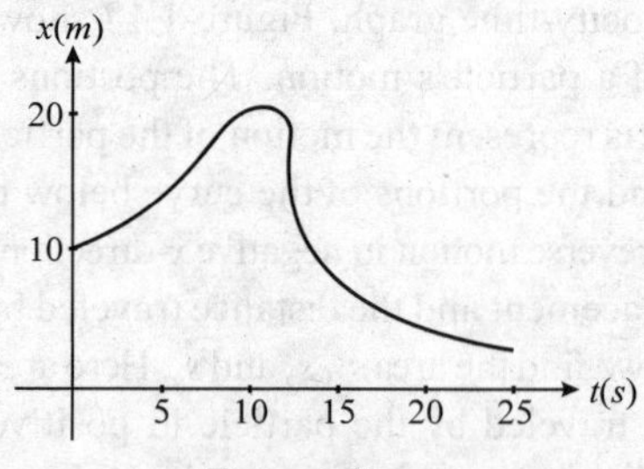

Figure 1.20

[15.0 s]

(iii) A train starts from station A with uniform acceleration a_1 for some distance then goes with uniform retardation a_2 for some more distance to come to rest at station B. The distance between station A and B is 4 km and the train takes 4 minutes to complete this journey. If accelerations are in km per minutes^2 unit, show that :

$$\frac{1}{a_1} + \frac{1}{a_2} = 2$$

(iv) Between two stations a train accelerates uniformly at first, then moves with constant speed and finally retards uniformly.

If the ratios of time taken are 1 : 8 : 1 and the greatest speed is 60 km/hr, find the average speed over the whole journey.

[54 kph]

(v) A particle starts from rest and traverses a distance s with a uniform acceleration and then moves uniformly with the acquired velocity over a further distance 2 s. Finally it comes to rest after moving through a further distance 3 s under uniform retardation. Assuming the entire path is a straight line, find the ratio of the average speed over the journey to the maximum speed on the way.

[3/5]

(vi) A particle starts with an initial velocity u towards + x direction with an acceleration a after time t_1, it starts retarding with another acceleration a', comes to an instantaneous stop and returns. It reaches its initial position at time t_2. Draw the approximate time dependence plots for particle's displacement and velocity.

(vii) A particle moves in a straight line. Figure-1.21 shows the distance traversed by the particle as a function of time t. Using the graph, find (a) the average velocity of the point during the time of motion. (b) the maximum velocity. (c) the time $t = t_0$ at which the instantaneous velocity is equal to the mean velocity averaged over the first t_0 seconds.

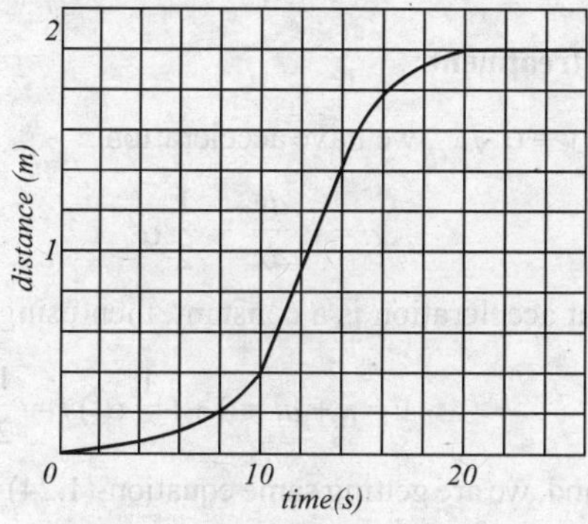

Figure 1.21

[(a) 10 cm/s, (b) 25 cm/s, (c) 16 s]

(viii) The velocity of a particle that moves in the positive X-direction varies with its position, as shown in figure-1.22. Find its acceleration in m/s^2 when $x = 6$ m.

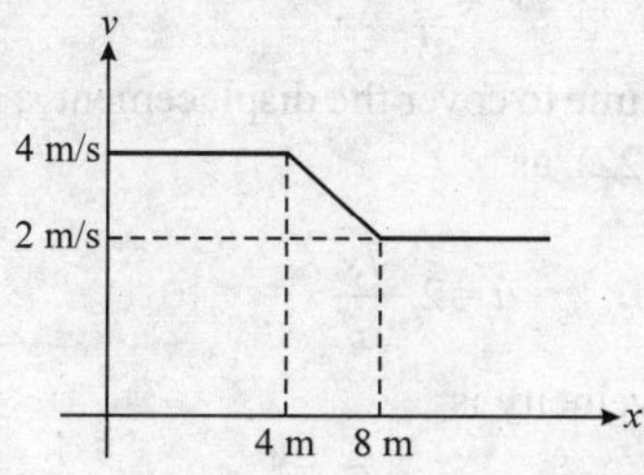

Figure 1.22

[– 1.5 m/s^2]

(ix) The acceleration vs time of a particle moving along $+x$ direction is shown in figure-1.23. It starts at $t = 0$, from rest. Draw the position-time graph for the motion.

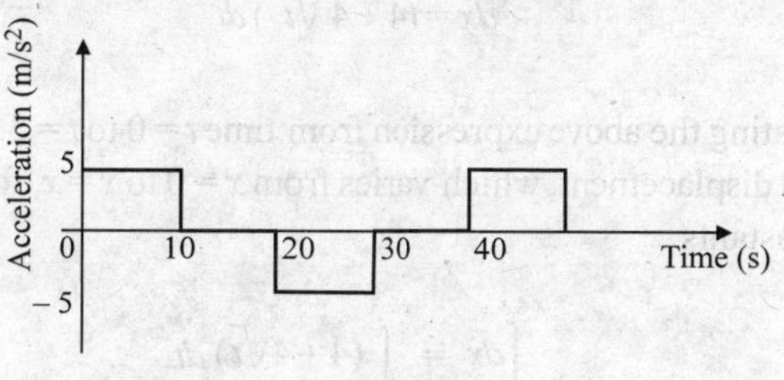

Figure 1.23

1.10 Motion with Time and Displacement Dependence

In previous sections we've already discussed that instantaneous velocity and acceleration need not be a constant in motion of a body moving in a straight line. These may depend on time or displacement and acceleration can also be given as a function of instantaneous speed of the particle. Speed equations for uniform acceleration can not be applied to solve such cases. Whenever function of acceleration or velocity is given, we must use calculus to solve the differential speed equations already discussed in section-1.6. To understand the concepts related to variation in instantaneous velocity and acceleration we take some illustrative and numerical examples.

 # Illustrative Example 1.25

Instantaneous velocity of a particle moving in a straight line is given as $v = (4 + 4\sqrt{t}\,)$ m/s. For the first five second of motion. Then after velocity of it becomes a constant. Find the acceleration of the particle at time t = 3.0 s and its displacement till this instant.

Solution

As we know that acceleration of a particle is time derivative of its instantaneous velocity.

For it we use
$$a = \frac{dv}{dt} = \frac{d}{dt}(4 + 4\sqrt{t}\,)$$

or
$$a = \frac{2}{\sqrt{t}}$$

and at time t = 3.0 s, acceleration is

$$a = \frac{2}{\sqrt{3}} \text{ m/s}^2$$

To find displacement, we know that velocity is the time derivative of displacement, we have to integrate velocity using differential speed equation as

$$v = \frac{dx}{dt} = 4 + 4\sqrt{t}$$

or $$dx = (4 + 4\sqrt{t})\, dt$$

Integrating the above expression from time $t = 0$ to $t = 3.0$ s, we get the displacement, which varies from $x = 0$ to $x = x$, for these time instants.

$$\int_{x=0}^{x=x} dx = \int_{x=0}^{x=3} (4 + 4\sqrt{t})\, dt$$

or $$x = [4t + \frac{8}{3} t^{3/2}]_0^3$$

or $$= [12 + 13.85] = 25.85 \text{ m}$$

 # Illustrative Example 1.26

Instantaneous velocity of an object varies with time as $v = \alpha - \beta t^2$. Find its position and acceleration as a function of time. Also find the object's maximum positive displacement from the origin.

Solution

Similar to the previous example, for acceleration we use

$$a = \frac{dv}{dt} = \frac{d}{dt}(\alpha - \beta t^2) = -2\beta t$$

For displacement we use

$$v = \frac{dx}{dt} = \alpha - \beta t^2$$

or $$dx = (\alpha - \beta t^2)\, dt$$

Integrating within proper limits, we have

$$\int_0^x dx = \int_0^t (\alpha - \beta t^2)\, dt$$

or $$x = \alpha t - \frac{1}{3} bt^3$$

 # Illustrative Example 1.27

The velocity of a particle moving in the positive direction of the x axis varies as $v = \alpha\sqrt{x}$, where α is a positive constant. Taking at $t = 0$, the particle was at point $x = 0$, find:

(a) The velocity and the acceleration of the particle as a function of time.

(b) The average velocity of the particle averaged over the time that it takes to cover first s metres of the path.

Solution

(a) As we've explained earlier, if velocity or acceleration of a particle is given as a function of distance or time, we use calculus. As here

$$\frac{dx}{dt} = \alpha\sqrt{x}$$

$$\frac{dx}{\sqrt{x}} = \alpha\, dt$$

On integrating $$\int_0^x \frac{dx}{\sqrt{x}} = \int_0^t \alpha\, dt$$

$$x = \frac{1}{4}\alpha^2 t^2 \quad \text{...(1.22)}$$

This gives us the displacement of the particle as a function of time. On differentiating we get velocity as a function of time, as

$$v = \frac{dx}{dt} = \frac{1}{2}\alpha^2 t \quad \text{...(1.23)}$$

Acceleration as $$a = \frac{dv}{dt} = \frac{1}{2}\alpha^2 \quad \text{...(1.24)}$$

Equation-(1.24) shows that the acceleration of the particle is a constant, it implies that here we can also use speed equation for constant accelerations as an alternative treatment.

Alternative treatment :

As we have $v = \alpha\sqrt{x}$, we have acceleration

$$a = v\frac{dv}{dx} = \frac{1}{2}\alpha^2$$

It shows that acceleration is a constant, then using

$$v = u + at = 0 + (\frac{1}{2}\alpha^2)\, t = \frac{1}{2}\alpha^2 t$$

In this method, we are getting same equation-(1.24) in a shorter way and for such cases students are advised to check whether the acceleration is constant or not. If it is not a constant, proceed with calculus.

(b) Average velocity in covering first s metre of the path is

$$\bar{v} = \frac{s}{t}$$

Where t is the time to cover the displacement s. It can be given by equation-(1.22), as

$$t = 2\frac{\sqrt{s}}{\alpha}$$

Thus average velocity is

$$\bar{v} = \frac{\alpha\sqrt{s}}{2}$$

Illustrative Example 1.28

A point moves rectilinearly with deceleration which depends on the velocity v of the particle as $a = k\sqrt{v}$, where k is a positive constant. At the initial moment the velocity of the point is equal to v_0. What distance will it cover before it stops, and what time it will take to cover that distance.

Solution

In the problem it is clear that acceleration here is not constant and it depends on velocity. It means, we should use calculus as

$$v\frac{dv}{dx} = -k\sqrt{v}$$

$$\sqrt{v}\,dv = -k\,dx$$

On integrating $\displaystyle\int_{v_0}^{v}\sqrt{v}\,dv = -\int_0^x k\,dx$

$$\frac{2}{3}(v_0^{3/2} - v^{3/2}) = kx$$

Substituting $v = 0$ and $x = s$

$$s = \frac{2v_0^{3/2}}{3k}$$

To find the time taken to come to rest, we use $a = dv/dt$, as

$$\frac{dv}{dt} = -k\sqrt{v}$$

$$\frac{dv}{\sqrt{v}} = -k\,dt$$

On integrating $\displaystyle\int_{v_0}^{v}\frac{dv}{\sqrt{v}} = -\int_0^t k\,dt$

$$2(\sqrt{v_0} - \sqrt{v}) = kt$$

Substituting $v = 0$ and $t = T$

$$T = \frac{2\sqrt{v_0}}{k}$$

Illustrative Example 1.29

An object moves such that is acceleration is given as $a = 3 - 2t$. Find the initial speed of the object such that the particle will have the same x-coordinate at $t = 5.0$ s as it had at $t = 0$. Also find the object's velocity at $t = 5.0$ s.

Solution

To find the instantaneous velocity of the object we use

$$a = \frac{dv}{dt} = 3 - 2t$$

or $$dv = (3 - 2t)\,dt$$

If the initial velocity of the object is taken as v_0, we integrate the above expression from time 0 to t and corresponding velocities from v_0 to v.

$$\int_{v_0}^{v} dv = \int_0^t (3 - 2t)\,dt$$

or $$v - v_0 = 3t - t^2$$

or $$v = v_0 + 3t - t^2$$

For displacement, we write

$$\frac{dx}{dt} = v_0 + 3t - t^2$$

or $$dx = (v_0 + 3t - t^2)dt$$

As it is given that at $t = 0$ and $t = 5.0$ s, object's displacement are equal say $x = 0$, then we have

$$\int_0^0 dx = \int_0^5 (v_0 + 3t - t^2)\,dt$$

or $$0 = \left[v_0t + \frac{3}{2}t^2 - \frac{1}{3}t^3\right]_0^5$$

or $$v_0(5) + \frac{3}{2}(5)^2 - \frac{1}{3}(5)^3 = 0$$

or $$v_0 = 0.832 \text{ m/s}$$

Now we have object's instantaneous velocity as

$$v = 0.832 + 3t - t^2$$

At $t = 5.0$ s, instantaneous velocity can be given as

$$v = 0.832 + 3(5) - (5)^2 = -9.17 \text{ m/s}$$

Practice Exercise 1.5

(i) The displacement x of a particle moving in one dimension, under the action of a constant force is related to the time t by the equation :

$$t = \sqrt{x} + 3$$

where x is in metres and t is in seconds. Find the displacement of the particle when its velocity is zero.

[0]

(ii) Instantaneous velocity of a particle moving in $+x$ direction is given as $v = \dfrac{3}{x^2 + 2}$. At $t = 0$, particle starts from origin. Find the average velocity of the particle between the two points

$P(x=2)$ and $Q(x=4)$ of its motion path.

[0.264 m/s]

(iii) A car moves rectilinearly from station A to the next stop B with an acceleration varying according to the law $a = b - cx$ where b and c are positive constants and x is its distance from station A. Find the distance between these stations if car stops at station B and its starts from rest from A.

[$2\ b/c$]

(iv) A particle moves along a straight line such that its displacement at any time t is given by $x = t^3 - 6t^2 + 3t + 4$. What is the velocity of the particle when its acceleration is zero ?

[– 9 m/s]

(v) A radius vector of a point varies with time t as

$$\vec{r} = \vec{b}t\,(1 - \alpha t)$$

where b is a constant vector and α is a positive factor. Find :

(a) The velocity $\vec{v}$ and the acceleration $\vec{a}$ of the particle as a functions of time.

(b) The time interval Δt taken by the particle to return to the initial position, and the distance s covered during that time.

[$\vec{b}(1 - 2\alpha t)$, $-2\alpha\vec{b}$, $1/\alpha$, $b/2\alpha$]

(vi) A box is thrown with velocity v_0 on top of a rough table of length l. Assume friction on the object is such that during its motion, its acceleration is given as $a = -kv$, where k is a positive constant. Find the velocity of the box when it leaves the edge of the table. Also find the time after which it falls off the edge.

[$v = v_0 - kl$, $t = \frac{1}{k}\ ln\left(\frac{v_0}{v_0 - kl}\right)$]

(vii) A particle start revolution with initial speed u in a circular path of radius R. During revolution it is retarded due to friction and its acceleration is given as $a = -cv^2$. Find the speed of the particle after completing one revolution.

[$u\ e^{-2\pi RC}$]

1.11 Relative Motion

To understand the concept of relative motion we must know first - What is a reference frame ?

A reference frame is a platform where observer is situated or the space with respect to which all measurements are taken. For better understanding we explain it on the basis of following example.

Consider the carriage train on rails A and a farmer B shown in figure-1.24, let the train move with a velocity $\vec{V}_A$ and the farmer with the velocity $\vec{V}_B$ on train.

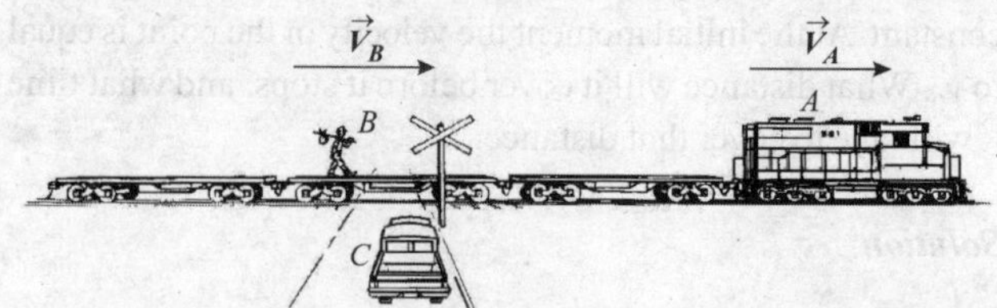

Figure 1.24

Here the velocity of farmer as measured by an observer in the earth or car C (driver) is given as -

$$\vec{V}_{BC} = \vec{V}_B + \vec{V}_A \qquad \ldots(1.25)$$

This is the velocity of B with respect to C. Here reference frame of farmer is the train and that of observer is earth. Always remember that the velocity of an object (farmer) with respect to earth will be velocity of the object (farmer) on its frame (train) added to the velocity of the reference frame of the object.

Now consider the situation shown in figure-1.25. It is similar to previous case, but the difference is in observer. Now observer is moving (lorry driver) with the velocity $\vec{V}_C$.

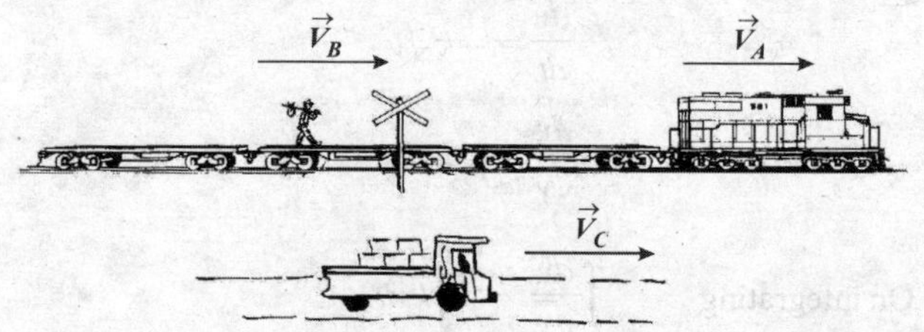

Figure 1.25

In this case the velocity of farmer as observed by lorry driver is given as

$$\vec{V}_{BC} = \vec{V}_B + \vec{V}_A - \vec{V}_C \qquad \ldots(1.26)$$

This gives the velocity of B with respect to C. It is clear from equation-(1.26) that if observer is also moving on earth, with respect to itself, all the stationary objects on earth will appear to be moving in backward direction with the same velocity with which it is moving and because of it in equation-(1.26), we've subtracted $\vec{V}_C$ from the velocity of B with respect to earth.

Now we'll discuss some of the applications concerned to the relative motion, as given below

Web Reference at www.physicsgalaxy.com
Age Group - High School Physics | Age 17-19 Years
Section - MECHANICS
Topic - Concept of Relative Motion
Module Numbers - 1, 2, 3, and 4

1.11.1 River Flow Cases

Consider a river shown in figure-1.26(a), let the flow velocity of current be $\vec{U}_f$ and a swimmer jumps into the river from a point A, from one bank of the river as shown, in a direction perpendicular to the direction of current.

Due to the flow velocity of river the swimmer is drifted along the river by a distance BC and the net velocity of the swimmer will be $\vec{V}_R$ as shown along the direction AC.

If we find the components of velocity of swimmer along and perpendicular to the flow, these are :

Velocity along the river $V_x = U_f$

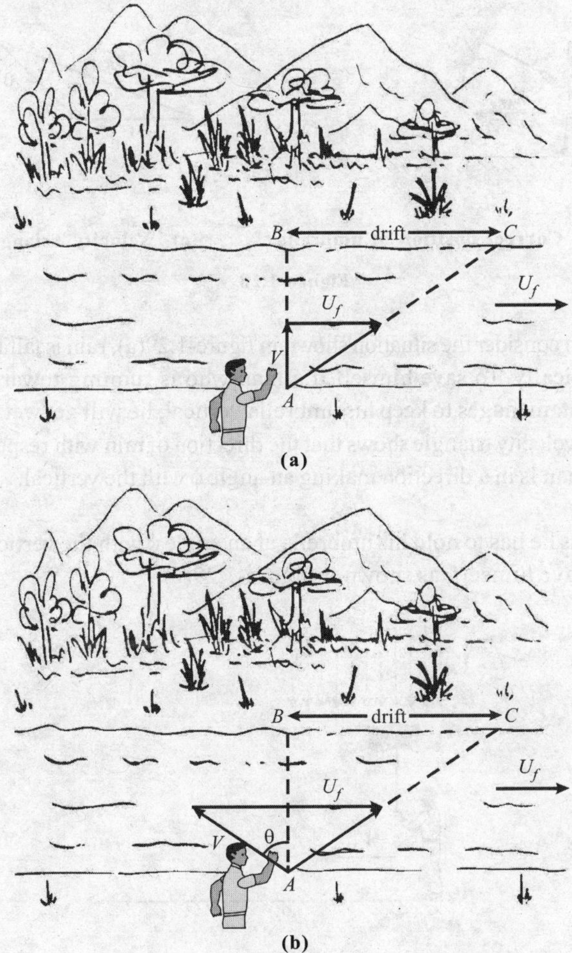

Figure 1.26

Velocity perpendicular to the river $V_y = V$

The net speed directly can be given by the velocity triangle as $\sqrt{V^2 + U_f^2}$

Here time taken to cross the river is $t = \dfrac{d}{V_y}$

As the swimmer crosses the river with the velocity V_y only, velocity V_x is only used to drift the motion of the swimmer due to current in the river.

The drift carried along the river flow is : x = drift speed (V_x) × time taken to cross the river (t)

$$= U_f \frac{d}{V}$$

Now consider the case when the swimmer jumps from the point A into the river making an angle θ with the normal to the current direction, as shown in figure-1.26(b). Due to this the net velocity of the swimmer with respect to earth given by velocity triangle in figure, is given as :

$$\vec{V}_{net} = \vec{V} + \vec{U}_f \quad \text{...(1.27)}$$

The velocity component along the river is

$$V_x = U_f - V\sin\theta$$

The velocity component in a direction perpendicular to the current is

$$V_y = V\cos\theta$$

The resultant velocity with which the swimmer will cross the river is

$$V_R = \sqrt{V_x^2 + V_y^2}$$

The time taken by the swimmer to cross the river is

$$t = \frac{d}{V_y} = \frac{d}{V\cos\theta}$$

The drift carried along the river is

$$x = V_x \cdot t = (U_f - V\sin\theta) \times \frac{d}{V\cos\theta}$$

If we are required to minimize the drift or the question is asked to find the angle θ at which the swimmer will swim such that the drift will be minimized, we put $\dfrac{dx}{d\theta} = 0$, which gives a value of θ at which if the swimmer will swim, drift will be minimum.

Similarly if the swimmer will jump in the downstream direction at the angle θ with the normal to current flow, corresponding velocity triangle is as shown in figure-1.27.

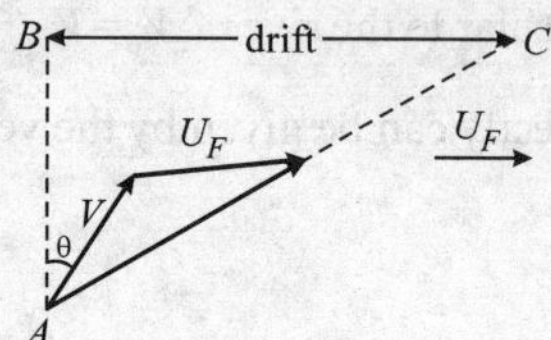

Figure 1.27

In this case we have velocity component along the river

$$V_x = U_f + V\sin\theta$$

Velocity component normal to the current flow is

$$V_y = V\cos\theta$$

Hence time taken to cross the river is

$$t = \frac{d}{V_y} = \frac{d}{V\cos\theta}$$

The drift along the river flow is

$$x = (U_f + V\sin\theta) \times \frac{d}{V\cos\theta}$$

Web Reference at www.physicsgalaxy.com

Age Group - High School Physics | Age 17-19 Years
Section - MECHANICS
Topic - Concept of Relative Motion
Module Numbers - 5, 6, 7, 8 and 9

1.11.2 Rainfall Cases

When rainfall occurs, the direction of rain drops falling on ground is different from the rain direction, measured by a moving observer. If velocity of rain drops is $\vec{V}_R$ and $\vec{V}_M$ and if the velocity of a moving man on a straight road, the velocity of the rain drops as observed by man can be given as

Velocity of rain with respect to man is

$$\vec{V}_{RM} = \vec{V}_R - \vec{V}_M \qquad \dots (1.28)$$

If we consider the situation shown in figure-1.28, when rainfall starts at an angle θ from the vertical with a velocity $\vec{V}_R$ and a man is running on straight road with a velocity $\vec{V}_M$ towards right, the velocity of raindrops observed by man can be given by forming the velocity triangle shown in figure.

Here $\vec{V}_{RM}$ is the rain velocity observed by the man.

Velocity triangle in figure-1.28(c) shows that the direction of velocity of rain with respect to man is at an angle φ with the vertical. Psychologically it appears that man should hold his umbrella directed against the rain fall direction, as shown in figure-1.28(a). But it is not the correct position, because rain drops are coming toward man in a different direction (ϕ from vertical). Always remember that to save himself man should hold the umbrella in the direction against the relative velocity of the rain with respect to him. Figure-1.28(b) shows the correct holding position.

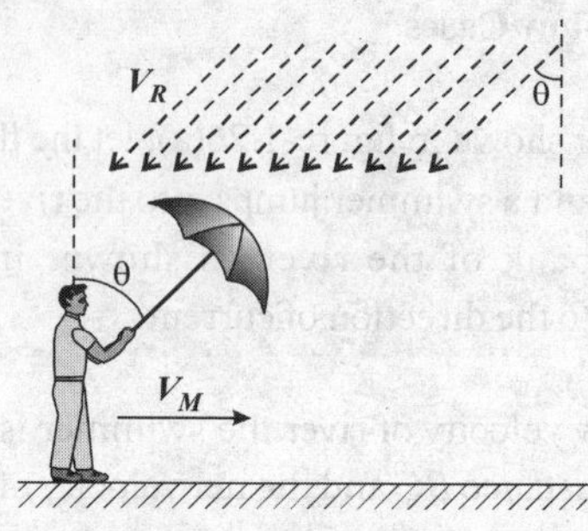

(a) Wrong position of umbrella

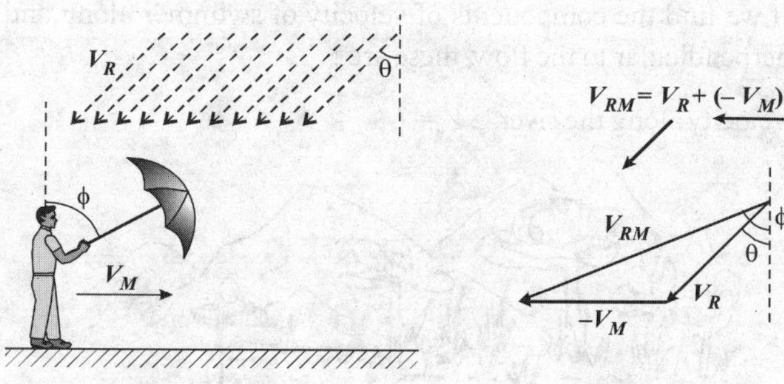

(b) Correct position of umbrella (c) Velocity Triangle

Figure 1.28

Next consider the situation shown in figure-1.29(a), rain is falling vertically. To save himself if a man who is running towards right, manages to keep his umbrella vertical, he will get wet as the velocity triangle shows that the direction of rain with respect to man is in a direction making an angle ϕ with the vertical.

Thus he has to hold his umbrella at an angle ϕ with the vertical to save himself, as shown in figure-1.29(b).

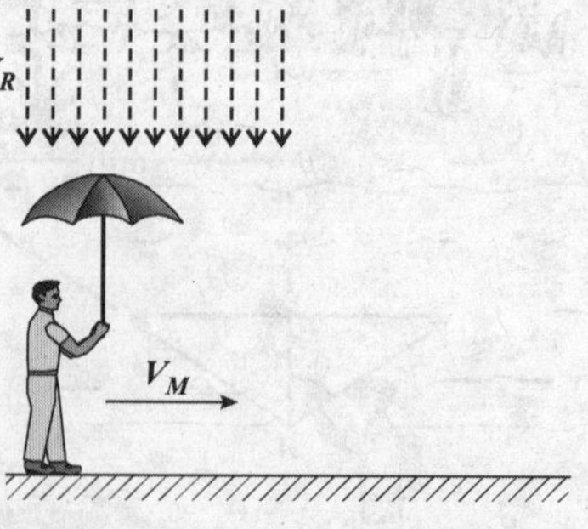

(a) Wrong position of umbrella

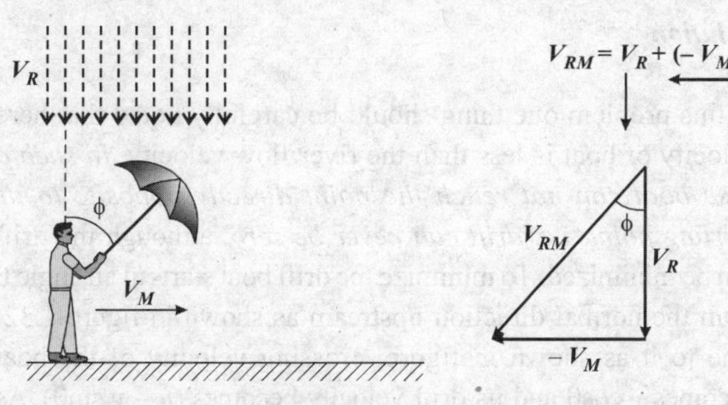

(b) Correct position of umbrella (c) Velocity Triangle

Figure 1.29

Again consider the open car shown in figure-1.30(a), we are required to find the velocity with which if the car is moving, no drops will fall on the driver. Figure-1.30(b) shows such a situation. If car is running at a speed $\vec{V}_C$ such that direction $\vec{V}_{RC}$ (velocity of rain with respect to car) is in a direction shown in figure-1.30(b), such that the rain drop which is just touching the top edge of the glasspane will follow the dotted path shown in figure, hence the driver will be saved.

Analysis is shown in velocity triangle, the velocity of the car in this situation can be given as

$$V_C = V_R \tan\theta$$

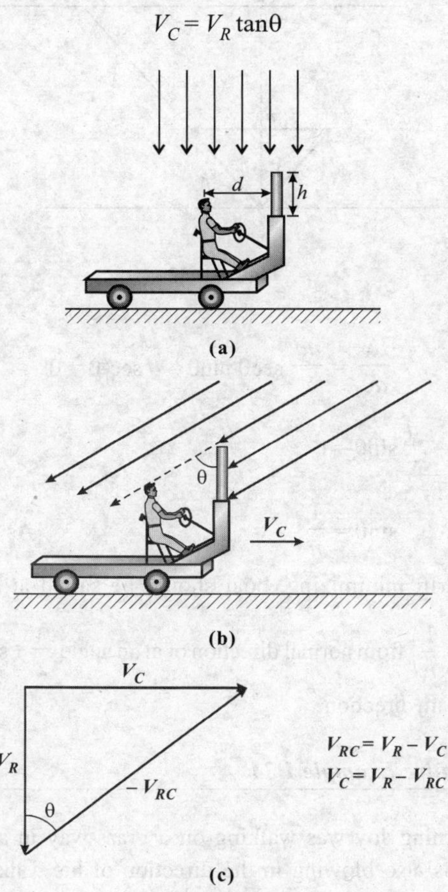

Figure 1.30

$$V_C = V_R\left(\frac{d}{h}\right)$$

There can be several cases and numerical problems based on the above discussion. We'll discuss some more similar and different cases in following examples.

 # Illustrative Example 1.30

A man standing on a road has to hold his umbrella at 30° with the vertical to keep the rain away. He throws the umbrella and starts running at 10 km/hr. He finds that rain drop are hitting his head vertically. Find the speed of raindrops with respect to (a) road (b) the moving man.

Solution

Given that the velocity of rain drops with respect to road is making an angle 30° with the vertical, and the velocity of the man is 10 kph, also the velocity of rain drops with respect to man is vertical.

We have

$$\vec{V}_{RM} = \vec{V}_R - \vec{V}_M$$

Hence $$\vec{V}_R = \vec{V}_{RM} + \vec{V}_M$$

The situation is shown in velocity triangle in figure-1.31.

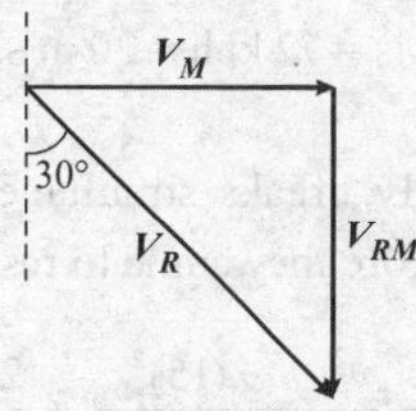

Figure 1.31

It shows clearly that $V_R = V_M \operatorname{cosec}\theta = 10 \times 2 = 20$ kph

and $V_{RM} = V_M \cos\theta = 10 \times \frac{\sqrt{3}}{2} = 5\sqrt{3}$ kph

 # Illustrative Example 1.31

A river 400 m wide is flowing at a rate of 2.0 m/s. A boat is sailing at a velocity of 10.0 m/s with respect to the water, in a direction perpendicular to the river. (a) Find the time taken by the boat to reach the opposite bank. (b) How far from the point directly opposite to the starting point does the boat reach the opposite bank ?

Solution

As it is given that boat is sailing in a direction normal to current. Crossing velocity of boat is = 10 m/s

So time taken by the boat to reach the other bank is

$$= \frac{400}{10} = 40\text{ s}$$

Drift due to flow of river is = Drift velocity × time to cross the river

Here boat is sailing in normal direction so drift velocity is the river current velocity

Thus, drift is $\qquad x = 2.0 \times 40 = 80\text{ m}$

Illustrative Example 1.32

Two trains, one travelling at 54 kph and the other at 72 kph, are headed towards each other on a level track. When they are two kilometers apart, both drivers simultaneously apply their brakes. If their brakes produces equal retardation in both the trains at a rate of 0.15 m/s^2, determine whether there is a collision or not.

Solution

Speed of first train is = 54 kph = 15 m/s

Speed of second train is = 72 kph = 20 m/s

As both drivers apply breaks simultaneously the distance travelled by trains before they come to rest is calculated as

$$s_1 = \frac{v_1^2}{2a} = \frac{(15)^2}{2 \times 0.15} = \frac{225}{0.3} = 750\text{ m}$$

$$s_2 = \frac{v_2^2}{2a} = \frac{(20)^2}{2 \times 0.15} = \frac{400}{0.3} = 1333.34\text{ m}$$

Total distance $= s_1 + s_2 = 750 + 1333.34 = 2083.33$ m

As this distance is more than 2 km, trains will collide.

Illustrative Example 1.33

A boat moves relative to water with a velocity which is n times less than the river flow velocity. At what angle to the stream direction must the boat move to minimize drifting ?

Solution

In this problem one thing should be carefully noted that here velocity of boat is less than the river flow velocity. *In such a case boat can not reach the point directly opposite to its starting point, i.e. drift can never be zero*, although the drift can be minimized. To minimize the drift boat starts at an angle θ from the normal direction upstream as shown in figure-1.32. Due to it as shown in figure, crossing velocity of the boat becomes $v\cos\theta$ and its drift velocity becomes $(u - v\sin\theta)$. As here u is always more than $v\sin\theta$, drift can never be zero.

Time taken to cross the river is

$$t = \frac{d}{v\cos\theta}$$

In this duration drift BC is

$$x = (u - v\sin\theta) \times \frac{d}{v\cos\theta} = \frac{ud}{v}\sec\theta - d\tan\theta$$

This drift x is minimum when $\frac{dx}{d\theta} = 0$, according to maxima-minima.

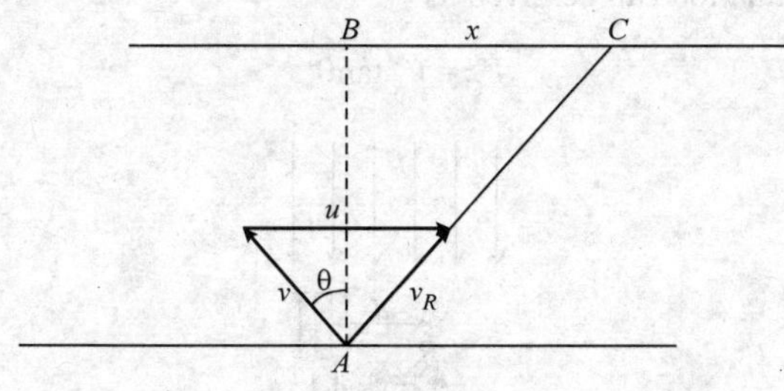

Figure 1.32

$$\text{Thus} \qquad \frac{dx}{d\theta} = \frac{ud}{v}\sec\theta\tan\theta - d\sec^2\theta = 0$$

$$\text{or} \qquad \frac{u}{v}\sin\theta = 1$$

$$\text{or} \qquad \sin\theta = \frac{1}{n} \qquad \left[\text{As } v = \frac{u}{n}\right]$$

So for drift minimizing, boat should be sailed at an angle $\theta = \sin^{-1}\left(\frac{1}{n}\right)$ from normal direction or at an angle $\frac{\pi}{2} + \sin^{-1}\left(\frac{1}{n}\right)$ from stream direction.

Illustrative Example 1.34

One morning Joy was walking on a grass-way in a garden. Wind was also blowing in the direction of his walking with speed u. He suddenly saw his friend Kim walking on the parallel grass-way at a distance x away. Both stopped as they saw each other when they were directly opposite on their ways at a distance x. Joy shouted "*Hi Kim*". Find the time after which Kim would have heard his greeting. Sound speed in still air is v.

Solution

The situation is shown in figure-1.33. When Joy shouted, the sound which is going directly toward Kim will not reach her as due to wind drift is added to it. The sound which is going in the direction at an angle θ, to their line joining will reach to Kim as when drift is added to it as shown in figure, the resultant is in the direction of their line joining.

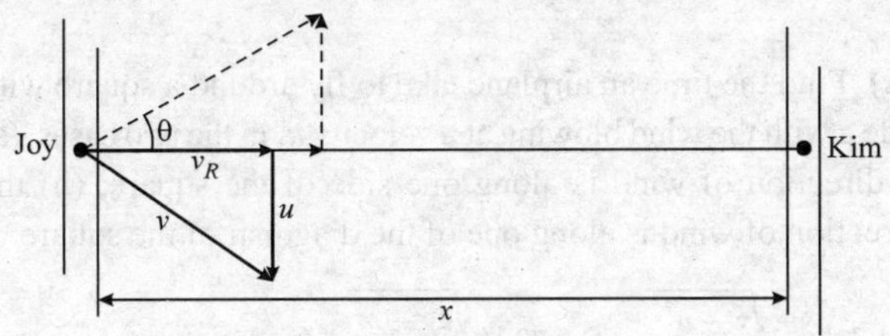

Figure 1.33

The resultant velocity of sound is

$$v_R = \sqrt{v^2 - u^2}$$

Time taken by sound to reach Kim is

$$t = \frac{x}{\sqrt{v^2 - u^2}}$$

 # Illustrative Example 1.35

Two swimmers leave point A on one bank of the river to reach point B lying right across on the other bank. One of them crosses the river along the straight line AB while the other swims at right angles to the stream and then walks the distance that he has been carried away by the stream to get to point B. What was the velocity u of her walking if both swimmers reached the destination simultaneously ? The stream velocity is 2 km/hr and the velocity of each swimmer with respect to water is 2.5 km/hr.

Solution

Let us take velocity of swimmer with respect to water is v and that of river current is v_r. Figure-1.34 shows the situation. The swimmer which crosses the river along the straight line AB, has to swim in upstream direction such that its resultant velocity becomes toward AB as shown in figure. If the width of river is assumed to be d, then

Resultant velocity of first swimmer is $v_1 = \sqrt{v^2 - v_r^2}$

Time taken by her to cross the river is

$$t = \frac{d}{\sqrt{v^2 - v_r^2}} = \frac{d}{\sqrt{2.5^2 - 2^2}} = \frac{d}{1.5} \text{ hr}$$

Second swimmer if swims along AB, she is drifted towards point C, due to river flow as shown in figure-1.34 and then she has to walk down to reach point B with velocity u.

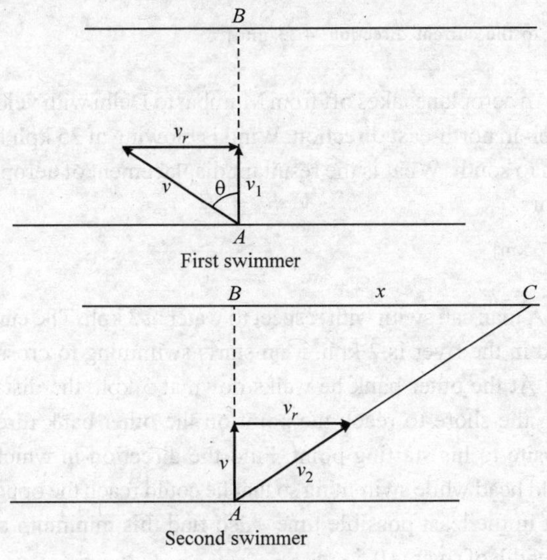

Figure 1.34

Here crossing velocity of second swimmer is v, as its is swimming along normal direction.

Time taken to cross the river by her is

$$t_1 = \frac{d}{v} = \frac{d}{2.5} \text{ hr}$$

Her drift due to river flow is

$$x = v_r \times \frac{d}{v}$$

Time taken to reach point B by walking is

$$t_2 = \frac{x}{u} = \frac{v_r d}{uv} = \frac{2 \times d}{u \times 2.5} = \frac{d}{1.25u} \text{ hr}$$

Given that both the swimmers reach the destination simultaneously, so we have

$$t = t_1 + t_2$$

or $$\frac{d}{1.5} = \frac{d}{2.5} + \frac{d}{1.25u}$$

or $$u = 3.0 \text{ kph}$$

Web Reference at www.physicsgalaxy.com

Age Group - High School Physics | Age 17-19 Years

Section - MECHANICS

Topic - Concept of Relative Motion

Module Numbers - 10, 11, 12, 13, 14, 15, 16 and 17

Practice Exercise 1.6

(i) The river 500 m wide is flowing with a current of 4 kph. A boat starts from one bank of the river wishes to cross the river at right angle to stream direction. Boatman can row the boat at 8 kph. In which direction he should row the boat. What time he'll take to cross the river ?

[120° to the current direction, 4.33 min]

(ii) An aeroplane takes off from Mumbai to Delhi with velocity 50 kph in north-east direction. Wind is blowing at 25 kph from north to south. What is the resultant displacement of aeroplane in 2 hrs.

[73.67 km]

(iii) A man can swim with respect to water at 3 kph. The current speed in the river is 2 kph. Man starts swimming to cross the river. At the other bank he walks down at 5 kph, the distance along the shore to reach the point on the other bank directly opposite to his starting point. Find the direction in which he should head while swimming so that he could reach the opposite point in the least possible time. Also find this minimum time. The width of river is 0.5 km.

[$\sin^{-1}$ (3/7) from the normal direction, 12.65 min]

(iv) Two boats, *A* and *B*, move away from a buoy anchored at the middle of a river along the mutually perpendicular straight lines, the boat *A* along the river, and the boat *B* across the river. Having moved off an equal distance from the buoy the boats returned. Find the ratio of times of motion of boats t_a / t_b if the velocity of each boat with respect to water is 1.2 times greater than the stream velocity.

[1.8]

(v) A man running on a horizontal road at 8 km/hr finds the rain falling vertically. He increase the speed to 12 km/hr and finds that the drops make angle 30° with the vertical. Find the speed and the direction of the rain with respect to the road.

[$4\sqrt{7}$ kph]

(vi) Two particles *A* and *B* are approaching each other on a straight line, the former with a uniform velocity of 25 m/s and other with 15 m/s, when they are 225 m apart forces are simultaneously applied to both of them. The deceleration given by the force to the *B* increases linearly with time by 0.3 m/s^2 every second, while the *A* is given a uniform deceleration. (a) What must be the minimum deceleration of the *A* so that the particles do not collide ? (b) What is the time taken by the particles to come to stop ?

[2.5 m/s^2, 10.0 s]

(vii) A body starts from rest at *A* and moves with uniform acceleration a in a straight line. *T* seconds after, a second body starts from *A* and moves with uniform velocity *V* in the same line. Prove that the second body will be ahead of the first for a time $\frac{2}{a}\sqrt{V(V-2aT)}$.

(viii) An aeroplane has to go from a point *A* to another point *B*, 500 km away due 30° east of north. *A* wind is blowing due north at a speed of 20 m/s. The air speed of the plane is 150 m/s. (a) find the direction in which the pilot should head the plane to reach the point *B*. (b) find the time taken by the plane to go from *A* to *B*.

[(a) $\sin^{-1}$ (1/15) east of direction *AB*, (b) 50 min]

(ix) Find the time an airplane take to fly around a square with side a with the wind blowing at a velocity *u*, in the two cases, (a) If direction of wind is along one side of the square; (b) the direction of wind is along one of the diagonal of the square ?

[(a) $2a\left(\frac{v+\sqrt{v^2-u^2}}{v^2-u^2}\right)$, (b) $2\sqrt{2}\,a\left(\frac{\sqrt{2v^2-u^2}}{v^2-u^2}\right)$]

(x) A man swimming in a river from a point *A* on one bank has to reach a point *C* on other bank, which is at a distance *l* from the point *B*, directly opposite to *A* on other bank. River width is *d* and the current velocity is u_0. Find the minimum speed of swimmer relative to still water with which he should swim.

[$\frac{u_0 d}{\sqrt{l^2+d^2}}$]

1.12 Motion in Two Dimension

Now we change our kinematics analysis from one dimension to two dimensions. In previous sections, we've discussed about the motion of an object along a straight line. Now we discuss, what happens when a particle moves in a plane. Have a look at figure-1.35, which shows a particle moving in *X-Y* plane, along a two dimensional path, known as trajectory of the particle. We discuss the motion of the particle between two points of the curve *A* and *B*. If the particle is moving along the curve and its velocity at an instant is *v* at an intermediate position of particle at point *P*. In two dimensional motion, direction of velocity of a particle is always tangential to

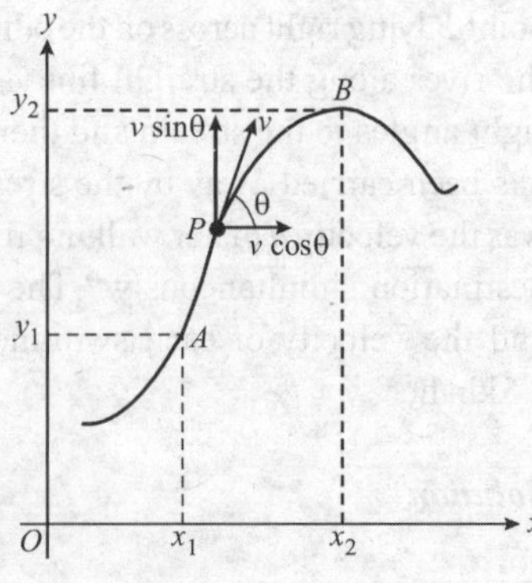

Figure 1.35

its trajectory curve. As the particle moves from point $A(x_1, y_1)$ to point $B(x_2, y_2)$. Its projection on x-axis changes from x_1 to x_2, and its projection on y-axis changes from y_1 to y_2. The velocities of the projections of the particle along x and y direction can be found by resolving the velocity of the particle in x and y direction.

If along the curve particle moves a distance dr in time dt, we define $v = dr/dt$. Similarly, when particle moves dr along the curve, its x-coordinate changes by dx and y-coordinate changes by dy. Thus the velocity projections can be written as

$$v_x = \frac{dx}{dt} = v\cos\theta \qquad \ldots(1.29a)$$

and $$v_y = \frac{dy}{dt} = v\sin\theta \qquad \ldots(1.29b)$$

In standard unit vector notification we can write the instantaneous velocity of particle as

$$\vec{v} = v_x\,\hat{i} + v_y\,\hat{j}$$

Squaring and adding equations-(1.29) and (1.30), gives net velocity of the particle as

$$v = \sqrt{v_x^2 + v_y^2} \qquad \ldots(1.30)$$

Dividing above equations will give the angle formed by the trajectory with the positive x-direction or the slope angle of the trajectory as

$$\tan\theta = \frac{v_y}{v_x}$$

or $$\theta = \tan^{-1}\frac{v_y}{v_x} \qquad \ldots(1.31)$$

1.12.1 Acceleration in Two Dimensional Motion

Acceleration is defined as the rate of change of velocity. As velocity is a vector quantity it has both magnitude and direction, and in two dimensional motion, magnitude of velocity or and as well as direction can be changed, hence acceleration can exist, either only magnitude of velocity changes, or only direction changes, or both will change. The acceleration which accounts for the change in magnitude of the velocity is known as tangential acceleration and the acceleration which accounts for the change in direction of the velocity is known as normal acceleration. Total or net acceleration of the particle is given by the vector sum of the two accelerations, tangential and normal accelerations. This topic will be discussed in detail in next chapter. Here we'll discuss about the projections of the total acceleration in x and y directions, a_x and a_y.

The total or net acceleration of a particle moving in two dimensions, can be resolved in two mutually perpendicular directions x and y and these two projections termed as a_x and a_y, and mathematically these can be given as

$$a_x = \frac{dv_x}{dt} = v_x\frac{dv_x}{dx} = \frac{d^2x}{dt^2} \qquad \ldots(1.32)$$

and $$a_y = \frac{dv_y}{dt} = v_y\frac{dv_y}{dy} = \frac{d^2y}{dt^2} \qquad \ldots(1.33)$$

From equations-(1.32) and (1.33), total acceleration is given as

$$\vec{a}_{\text{net}} = a_x\,\hat{i} + a_y\,\hat{j}$$

The magnitude of which is given as

$$a_{\text{net}} = \sqrt{a_x^2 + a_y^2} \qquad \ldots(1.34)$$

If we find the direction of net acceleration vector is given as

$$\varphi = \tan^{-1}\frac{a_y}{a_x}$$

Students should note that this direction is different than the direction of net velocity i.e. θ, we found earlier. In further chapters we discuss this direction in more detail.

1.12.2 Trajectory of a Particle in Two Dimension

Path traced by a moving particle in space is called trajectory of the particle, as in one dimensional motion the trajectory of a particle is straight line. In two dimensional motion the trajectory of a moving particle will be a two dimensional curve e.g. circle, ellipse, parabola, hyperbola, spiral, cycloid and so many more paths, including random paths. Shape of trajectory is decided by the forces acting on the particle, for a specific shape a particular type of force or a group of forces are required. This we'll discuss after the chapter of forces. When a coordinate system is associated with a particle's motion, the curve equation in which the particle moves $[y = f(x)]$ is called equation of trajectory. It is just giving us the relation among x and y coordinates of the particle (locus of particle).

To find equation of trajectory of a particle there are several methods but the simple way is to find first x and y coordinates of the particle as a function of time and eliminate the time factor. We discuss few examples of basic two dimensional motions and trajectory of particle in two dimensions.

 # Illustrative Example 1.36

A particle is moving in XY plane such that its velocity in x-direction remains constant at 5 m/s and its velocity in y-direction varies with time as $v = 3\,t$ m/s, where t is time in seconds. Find :

(a) Speed of particle after time $t = 10$ s.

(b) Direction of motion of particle at that time.

(c) Acceleration of particle at $t = 5$ s and its direction.

(d) Displacement of particle at this instant.

(e) Equation of trajectory of particle if it starts at time $t = 0$ from rest at origin.

Solution

(a) At time $t = 10$ s particle velocity in x and y directions are

$$v_x = 5 \text{ m/s}$$

and $$v_y = 3\,(10) = 30 \text{ m/s}$$

Magnitude of instantaneous velocity is

$$v = \sqrt{v_x^2 + v_y^2} = \sqrt{(5)^2 + (30)^2}$$

$$= 30.41 \text{ m/s}$$

(b) As we know that the direction of motion of particle is along the instantaneous velocity of it thus we have the inclination of particle's velocity from horizontal is

$$\theta = \tan^{-1}\left(\frac{v_y}{v_x}\right) = \tan^{-1}\left(\frac{30}{5}\right) = 80.53°$$

(c) Acceleration of particle in x and y directions are

$$a_x = \frac{d}{dt}(v_x) = 0 \qquad [\text{As } v_x = 5 \text{ m/s constant}]$$

and $$a_y = \frac{d}{dt}(v_y) = 3 \text{ m/s}^2 \qquad [\text{As } v_y = 3t \text{ m/s}]$$

Thus net acceleration of particle is constant and is given as

$$a = \sqrt{a_x^2 + a_y^2} = 3 \text{ m/s}^2$$

(d) To find displacement of particle in x and y direction, we used respective velocities as, we have In x-direction particle velocity is constant $v_x = 5$ m/s, thus

Displacement of particle along x-direction is

$$x = v_x t = 5\,t = 5(5) = 25 \text{ m}$$

In y-direction particle velocity is given as

$$v_y = 3t \text{ m/s} \quad \text{thus we have}$$

$$\frac{dy}{dt} = 3t$$

or $$dy = 3t\,dt$$

Integrating within proper limits, we have

$$\int_0^y dy = \int_0^t 3t\,dt$$

or $$y = \left[\frac{3}{2}t^2\right]_0^t = \frac{3}{2}t^2 = \frac{3}{2}(5)^2 = 37.5 \text{ m}$$

Note that here acceleration in y-direction is constant and is $a_y = 3$ m/s^2, so this can be obtained directly using speed equations as

$$y = \frac{1}{2}a_y t^2 = \frac{1}{2}(3)(5)^2 = 37.5 \text{ m}$$

Thus displacement of particle from starting point (origin) is

$$\vec{r} = 25\,\hat{i} + 37.5\,\hat{j} = 45.07\,\underline{|56.31°}\text{ m}$$

(e) For finding equation of trajectory we should require x and y coordinates of particle as a function of time, and here we have

$$x = 5t \qquad \text{...(1.35a)}$$

$$y = \frac{3}{2}t^2 \qquad \text{...(1.35b)}$$

Eliminating t from equations-(1.35a) and (1.35b), we have

$$y = \frac{3}{50}x^2 \qquad \text{...(1.36)}$$

Equation-(1.36) gives the equation of trajectory of the particle.

 # Illustrative Example 1.37

A car starts moving from rest on a horizontal ground such that the position vector of car with respect to its starting point is given as $\vec{r} = bt\,\hat{i} + ct^2\,\hat{j}$, where a and b are positive constants, and $\hat{i}$ and $\hat{j}$ are the unit vectors along two perpendicular direction (x and y axes) intersect at the starting point of car (origin). Find :

(a) The equation of the trajectory of car $y = f(x)$.

(b) The angle between direction of velocity and acceleration of car as a function of time $\theta = f(t)$.

(c) Average velocity of car over first t seconds of motion.

Solution

(a) From position vector we can write the x and y coordinates of the car as

$$x = bt \qquad \text{...(1.37a)}$$

and $$y = ct^2 \qquad \text{...(1.37b)}$$

Eliminating t from equations-(1.37a) and (1.37b), we get

$$y = \frac{c}{b^2}x^2$$

(b) From equations-(1.37a) and (1.37b), velocity components of car in x and y direction are

$$v_x = b \quad \text{and} \quad v_y = 2\,ct$$

In vector form velocity of car can be written as

$$\vec{v} = b\,\hat{i} + 2\,ct\,\hat{j}$$

Its magnitude is $\quad v = \sqrt{b^2 + 4c^2t^2}$

Acceleration of car in x and y direction are

$$a_x = 0 \quad \text{and} \quad a_y = 2\,c$$

In vector form acceleration of car is

$$\vec{a} = 2\,c\,\hat{j}$$

Its magnitude is $\quad a = 2\,c$

To find angle between vector v and vector $\boldsymbol{a}$, we take dot product of the two vectors. If θ is the angle between the two at a general time instant t, we have

$$\vec{a} \cdot \vec{v} = av\cos\theta$$

or $$(2\,c\,\hat{j}) \cdot (b\,\hat{i} + 2\,ct\,\hat{j}) = (2\,b)\left(\sqrt{b^2 + 4c^2t^2}\right)\cos\theta$$

or $$\cos\theta = \frac{2ct}{\sqrt{b^2 + 4c^2t^2}}$$

(c) Average velocity of car in first t seconds can be given as

$$<v> = \frac{\text{displacement vector at time } t}{t}$$

Thus, we have $$<\vec{v}> = \frac{\vec{r}}{t} = \frac{bt\,\hat{i} + ct^2\,\hat{j}}{t} = b\,\hat{i} + ct\,\hat{j}$$

 # Illustrative Example 1.38

A point moves in the XY plane according to the law $x = kt$ and $y = kt\,(1 - \alpha t)$, where k and α are positive constants, and t is time. Find:

(a) The equation of trajectory of the particle.

(b) The time t_0 after start at $t = 0$ when the direction between velocity and acceleration of particle becomes 45°.

Solution

(a) Equation of trajectory can be directly obtained by eliminating t from x and y coordinates of the point, so we have

$$y = x\left(1 - \frac{\alpha}{k}x\right)$$

(b) Velocity and acceleration vector of the point can be given as

$$\vec{v} = k\,\hat{i} + k(1 - 2\alpha t)\,\hat{j}$$

Its magnitude is $\quad v = k\sqrt{2 + 4\alpha^2t^2 - 4\alpha t}$

and $$\vec{a} = -\,2k\alpha\,\hat{j}$$

Its magnitude is $\quad a = 2k\alpha$

As at time t_0 the angle between vector $\boldsymbol{a}$ and vector $\boldsymbol{v}$ is 45°, we have from dot product

$$\vec{a} \cdot \vec{v} = av\cos(45°)$$

or $$(-\,2k\alpha\,\hat{j}) \cdot [k\,\hat{i} + k(1 - 2\alpha t_0)\,\hat{j}]$$
$$= (2\,k\alpha)\left(k\sqrt{2 + 4\alpha^2t_0^2 - 4\alpha t_0}\right)\frac{1}{\sqrt{2}}$$

Solving we get $\quad t_0 = \dfrac{1}{\alpha}$

Web Reference at www.physicsgalaxy.com

Age Group - High School Physics | Age 17-19 Years

Section - MECHANICS

Topic - Motion in Two Dimensions

Module Numbers - 1, 2, 3, 4 and 5

Practice Exercise 1.7

(i) The coordinates of a bird flying in the xy-plane are $x = 2 - \alpha t$ and $y = \beta t^2$, where $\alpha = 3.6$ m/s and $\beta = 1.8$ m/s^2. Calculate the velocity and acceleration vectors and their magnitude as a functions of time. Also find the magnitude and direction of bird's velocity and acceleration at $t = 3.0$ s. From the given data can you find whether at this instant, bird is speeding up, speeding down or it is taking a turn. If so in which direction.

[$\sqrt{12.96 + 12.96t^2}$ m/s, 3.6 m/s^2, 11.38 m/s, 3.6 m/s^2]

(ii) On a smooth horizontal platform a mass of 2 kg is dragged with a horizontal force of 10 Nt. On platform there are so many holes spreaded on its surface below which there is an air blower which exerts a force on block in upward direction depending on its height above the platform as $\vec{F} = 20\,(2 - h)$ N, where h is the height of the block above the platform. Let at $t = 0$ block starts from rest from origin of coordinate system shown. Find the equation of trajectory of the block during its motion. Consider x-axis along the motion of particle and y-axis in vertical up direction.

[$2\sqrt{x} = \sin^{-1}(y - 1) - \dfrac{3\pi}{2}$]

(iii) A ball is thrown straight up in air with an initial velocity u. Air exerts a force on it in horizontal direction which produces an acceleration depending on its height from ground as $a_x = ah^2$.

Find the displacement of ball from the projection point as a function of time.

$[r = \sqrt{x_t^2 + y_t^2}$ where $x_t = \frac{au^2t^4}{12} + \frac{ag^2t^6}{120} - \frac{augt^5}{20}$, $y_t = ut - \frac{1}{2}gt^2]$

(iv) A boy releases a toy plane from the top of a high hill of height H. Hill is so high that gravity varies with height from ground as $g = g_0\left(1 - \frac{2h}{R}\right)$, where h is the height from ground and R is the radius of earth. The engine of toy plane accelerates it in horizontal direction with acceleration $a_x = bt^2$. Find the position from the foot of hill where the plane lands and the time after which it lands.

$$\left[\frac{bR^2}{48g_0^2}\left[\ln\left(\frac{R+\sqrt{2RH-H^2}}{R-H}\right)\right]^4, \sqrt{\frac{R}{2g_0}}\ln\left(\frac{R+\sqrt{2RH-H^2}}{R-H}\right)\right]$$

(v) The position vector of a particle P with respect to a stationary point O changes with time according to the law $\vec{r} = \vec{b}\sin\omega t + \vec{c}\cos\omega t$ where $\vec{b}$ and $\vec{c}$ are constant vectors with $\boldsymbol{b} \perp \boldsymbol{c}$ and ω is a positive constant. Find the equation of the path of the particle $y = f(x)$, assuming x and y axes to coincide with the direction of the vector $\vec{b}$ and $\vec{c}$ respectively and to have the origin at the point O.

Ans. $\left[\frac{x^2}{b^2} + \frac{y^2}{c^2} = 1\right]$

(vi) The motion of a particle restricted to move in a two dimensional plane is given by

$$x = 2\cos\pi t$$

and $$y = 1 - 4\cos 2\pi t$$

where x and y are in metres and t is in seconds. Show that the path of the particle is a part of parabola $y = 5 - 2x^2$. Find the velocity and the acceleration of particle at $t = 0$ and $t = 1.5$s.

Ans. [0, 158.98 m/s^2, 6.2 m/s, 157.75 m/s^2]

1.13 Projectile Motion

It is one of the most important application of two dimensional motion. In this chapter, we will discuss all the properties and numerical aspects related to projectile motion.

Motion of a body after its projection is known as projectile motion. It can be of several types e.g. in presence of an external force or in free space or in influence of a force field governing some particular laws etc. In this section we will mainly discuss the projectile motion under influence of gravity and its applications in absence of air friction.

Consider figure-1.36, which shows a trajectory of a projectile thrown from the origin with an initial velocity u at an angle θ to the horizontal.

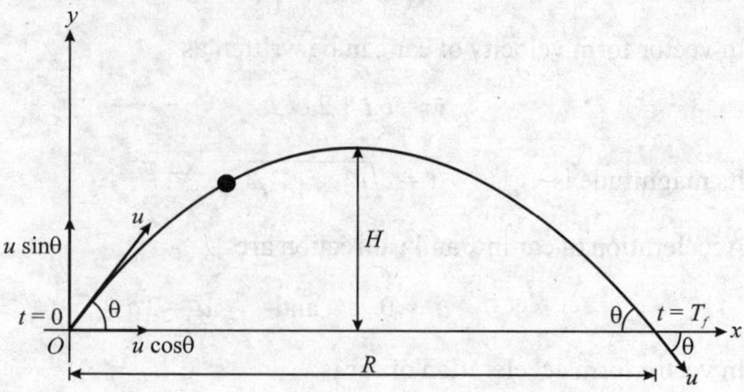

Figure 1.36

To analyze the motion we resolve the motion of the body in two separate one dimensional motions. One along x-direction and other along y-direction. We resolve the initial velocity in two corresponding directions

The horizontal component of the initial velocity is

$$u_x = u\cos\theta$$

The vertical component is

$$u_y = u\sin\theta$$

In the whole motion there is only one force acting on the body i.e. the force of gravity due to which it has only one acceleration in y-direction "$-g$".

If we consider the horizontal projection of the body during flight, it will run with a constant velocity from the starting point O to the point where the projectile will hit the ground. In y-direction motion particle starts with the velocity $u\sin\theta$ and retarded by g. It goes up to a maximum height H and then it returns to the ground. If these two motions are combined, it results the trajectory shown in figure-1.35.

If the body is projected at time $t = 0$, it will fall on the ground at time $t = T_f$ known as time of flight, the value of which can be given as

Using $$s = ut - \frac{1}{2}gt^2$$

We take $$0 = u\sin\theta\, T_f - \frac{1}{2}g T_f^2$$

$$T_f = \frac{2u\sin\theta}{g} \qquad \ldots(1.38)$$

When the particle is at the topmost point of its trajectory its vertical component of velocity is zero and as H be the maximum height, at which it will have only the horizontal component of velocity

We get $v^2 = u^2 - 2gs$

$$0 = (u \sin\theta)^2 - 2gH$$

$$H = \frac{u^2 \sin^2\theta}{2g} \quad \dots(1.39)$$

The horizontal distance to which the body travels during its flight is known as the horizontal range, which can be evaluated to be the distance traveled by the horizontal projection of the body in the duration time of flight.

The horizontal range of projectile is

$$R = u\cos\theta \times T_f$$

$$R = \frac{u^2 \sin 2\theta}{g} \quad \dots(1.40)$$

From equation-(1.40), it is clear that the horizontal range of projectile depends on the angle of projection θ, as θ varies, range will change and range will accordingly be maximum when the factor sin2θ will be have a maximum value. Thus the maximum range is

$$R = \frac{u^2}{g}$$

When $\sin 2\theta = 1$

If range is not maximum, then R depends on sin2θ, and there can be two values of θ at which sin2θ has a single value for $(0 < \theta < 90°)$. This implies when range is not maximum and there will always be two values of angles of projections, at which we get the same ranges, if u is same in both the cases. These two angles are known as complementary angles as to be $\theta_1 + \theta_2 = 90°$. (Figure-1.37)

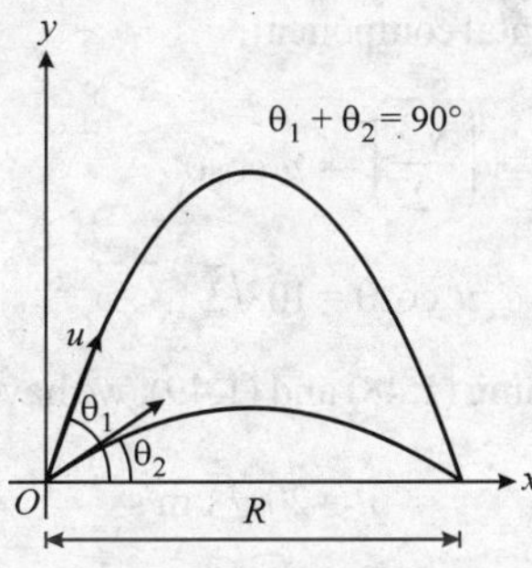

Figure 1.37

When a body is projected at $t = 0$, then at time $t = t$, the velocity projections of the particle in x and y directions are $v \cos\varphi$ and $v \sin\varphi$, respectively as shown in figure-1.37, if velocity at time t is v and it is making an angle φ with the positive direction of x-axis.

In x-direction velocity component is

$$v_x = u \cos\theta \quad \text{(Remains constant as } a_x = 0)$$

In y-direction velocity component is

$$v_y = u \sin\theta - gt \quad \text{(Retarded by } a_y = -g)$$

In vectorial form velocity of the particle in projectile motion as a function of time is given as

$$\vec{v} = (u \cos\theta)\,\hat{i} + (u \sin\theta - gt)\,\hat{j} \quad \dots(1.41)$$

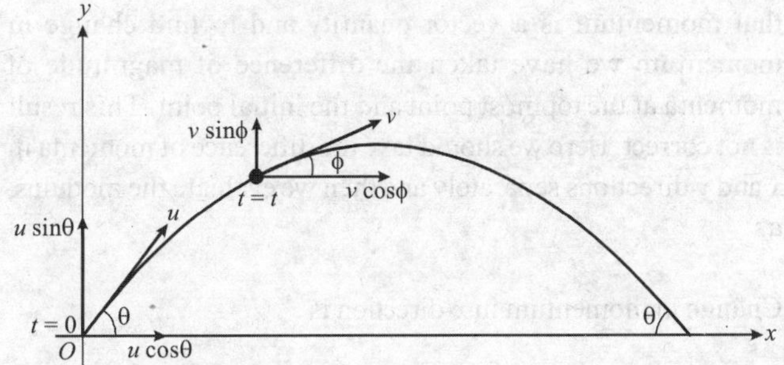

Figure 1.38

Its magnitude at time t is

$$v = \sqrt{u^2 + g^2t^2 - 2ugt \sin\theta} \quad \dots(1.42)$$

During motion we can also find the projectile coordinate at a general time $t = t$ as

Its x-coordinate is $x = u \cos\theta \,.\, t$ (As $a_x = 0$) ...(1.43)

As particle moves in x-direction with constant velocity $u \cos\theta$

Its y-coordinate is $y = u\sin\theta \,.\, t - \frac{1}{2} g \,.\, t^2$ ...(1.44)

As in y-direction, particle's initial velocity is $u \sin\theta$ and is retarded by g.

Eliminate t between equations-(1.43) and (1.44), we get the relation in x and y.

$$y = x \tan\theta - \frac{gx^2}{2u^2 \cos^2\theta} \quad \dots(1.45)$$

It is the equation of the path of trajectory in the coordinate system where x-direction is along horizontal and y-direction is along vertical. This trajectory path equation is very useful in solving numerical problems. Let us take few examples on basic projectile motion.

Illustrative Example 1.39

A projectile is thrown from a point on ground with an initial speed u and at an elevation θ, to the horizontal. Find the change in momentum of the particle, when it reaches the topmost point of its trajectory.

Solution

As we all know that during projectile motion the horizontal component of the velocity of the particle remains constant, $u\cos\theta$, so at its topmost point its vertical component of the velocity is zero and it will have only $u\cos\theta$. At the initial point of trajectory, velocity of the particle was u. Thus change in momentum can be given as $(mu\cos\theta - mu)$. But it is to be noted that momentum is a vector quantity and to find change in momentum we have taken the difference of magnitude of momenta at the topmost point and the initial point. This result is not correct. Here we should take the difference of momenta in x and y directions separately and then we evaluate the modulus, as

Change in momentum in x-direction is

$$\Delta p_x = mu\cos\theta - mu\cos\theta = 0$$

Change in momentum in y-direction is

$$\Delta p_y = 0 - mu\sin\theta$$

Thus net change in momentum is

$$\Delta p = -\, mu\sin\theta$$

Magnitude of change in momentum is

$$\Delta p = mu\sin\theta$$

 # Illustrative Example 1.40

A body projected with the same velocity at two different angles covers the same horizontal distance R. If T_{f_1} and T_{f_2} are the two times of flight, prove that $R = \frac{1}{2} g T_{f_1} T_{f_2}$.

Solution

As it is given that the range of the two projectile are same, thus these must be thrown at complimentary angles. If one is thrown at θ, other must be at $\frac{\pi}{2} - \theta$. Thus time of flight for the two projectile we have are

$$T_{f_1} = \frac{2u\sin\theta}{g} \quad \text{and} \quad T_{f_2} = \frac{2u\cos\theta}{g}$$

Multiplying the two we get

$$T_{f_1} T_{f_2} = \frac{4u^2\sin\theta\cos\theta}{g^2} \qquad \ldots(1.46)$$

Range of projectile we have

$$R = \frac{2u^2\sin\theta}{g} \qquad \ldots(1.47)$$

From equations-(1.46) and (1.47), we get

$$R = \frac{1}{2} g T_{f_1} T_{f_2}$$

 # Illustrative Example 1.41

A student and his friend while experimenting for projectile motion with a stop-watch, taken some approximate readings. As one throws a stone in air at some angle, other observes that after 2.0 s it is moving at an angle 30° to the horizontal and after 1.0 s, it is travelling horizontally. Determine the magnitude and the direction of initial velocity of the stone.

Solution

Let we take u is the initial velocity and α be the projection angle. It is given that at $t = 3.0$ s, stone is at maximum height. Thus we have half of time of flight is 3.0 s.

$$\frac{u\sin\theta}{g} = 3$$

or $$u\sin\theta = 30 \qquad \ldots(1.48)$$

If we take v be the velocity of the stone at $t = 2.0$ s, when it is making an angle 30° with the horizontal, we have

$$v\cos 30° = u\cos\theta$$

and $$v\sin 30° = u\sin\theta - g(2)$$

or $$v\left(\frac{1}{2}\right) = 30 - 20 = 10$$

or $$v = 20 \text{ m/s}$$

Now from horizontal component

$$v\left(\frac{\sqrt{3}}{2}\right) = u\cos\theta$$

or $$u\cos\theta = 10\sqrt{3} \qquad \ldots(1.49)$$

Squaring and adding (1.48) and (1.49), we have

$$u = 20\sqrt{3} \text{ m/s}$$

Dividing $$\tan\theta = \sqrt{3}$$

or $$\theta = 60°$$

 # Illustrative Example 1.42

A cannon fires successively two shells with velocity 250 m/s. The first at an angle 60° and the second at the angle 45° to the horizontal, the azimuth being the same. Find the time interval between their firing so that the two shells collide in air. Assume no air friction.

Solution

Figure-1.39 shows the corresponding situation. Let the two shells collide at point A (x, y). If we take t_1 and t_2 be the durations of the shells from shot to reaching the point A, for first and second shell respectively. We have x and y coordinate of A for the two shells

$$x = u\cos\theta\, t_1 = u\cos\varphi\, t_2 \qquad \ldots(1.50)$$

$$y = u\sin\theta\, t_1 - \frac{1}{2}gt_1^2 = u\sin\theta\, t_2 - \frac{1}{2}gt_2^2 \qquad \ldots(1.51)$$

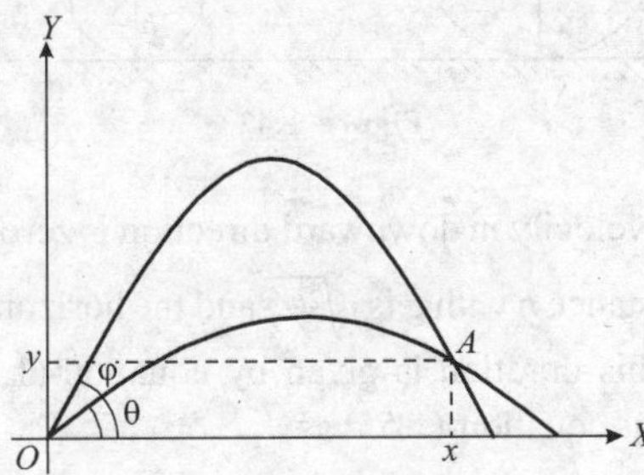

Figure 1.39

From equation-(1.50) $\quad t_1 = \dfrac{\cos\varphi}{\cos\theta}t_2 \qquad \ldots(1.52)$

Substituting this value in equation-(1.51), we get

$$u\sin\theta\frac{\cos\varphi}{\cos\theta}t_2 - \frac{1}{2}g\left(\frac{\cos\varphi}{\cos\theta}t_2\right)^2 = u\sin\theta\, t_2 - \frac{1}{2}gt_2^2$$

On solving, we get $\quad t_2 = \dfrac{2u\cos\theta\sin(\theta-\varphi)}{g(\cos^2\varphi - \cos^2\theta)}$

Using value of in (1.52) we get

$$t_1 = \frac{2u\cos\varphi\sin(\theta-\varphi)}{g(\cos^2\varphi - \cos^2\theta)}$$

Time difference in firing, leading to the collision of the shells is $\Delta t = t_1 - t_2$

or $\quad \Delta t = \dfrac{2u\sin(\theta-\varphi)}{g(\cos\varphi + \cos\theta)} = 11$ seconds

 # Illustrative Example 1.43

A particle is thrown over a triangle from one end of a horizontal base and grazing the vertex falls on the other end of the base. If α and β be the base angles and θ be the angle of projection, prove that $\tan\theta = \tan\alpha + \tan\beta$.

Solution

The situation is shown in figure-1.40.

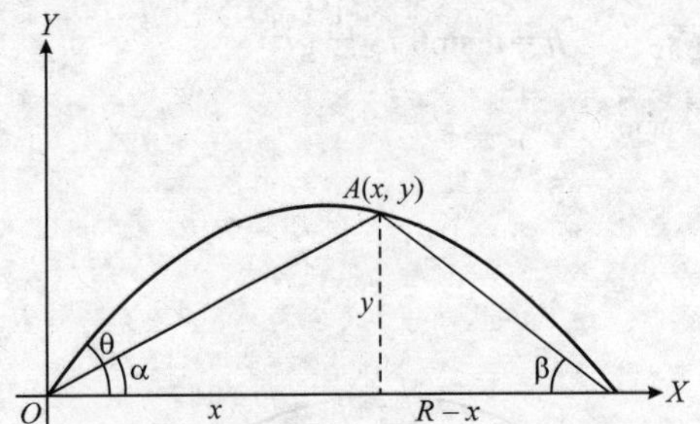

Figure 1.40

From figure, we have

$$\tan\alpha + \tan\beta = \frac{y}{x} + \frac{y}{R-x} \quad [R \text{ is the range of projectile}]$$

$$\tan\alpha + \tan\beta = \frac{yR}{x(R-x)} \qquad \ldots(1.53)$$

Equation of trajectory is

$$y = x\tan\theta - \frac{gx^2}{2u^2\cos^2\theta}$$

$$y = x\tan\theta\left(1 - \frac{gx}{2u^2\cos\theta\sin\theta}\right)$$

$$y = x\tan\theta\left(1 - \frac{x}{R}\right) \qquad \ldots(1.54)$$

$$\tan\theta = \frac{yR}{x(R-x)}$$

From equations-(1.53) and (1.54), we have

$$\tan\theta = \tan\alpha + \tan\beta$$

 # Illustrative Example 1.44

A stone is projected from the point of a ground in such a direction so as to hit a bird on the top of a telegraph post of height h and then attain the maximum height $2h$ above the ground. If at the instant of projection, the bird were to fly away horizontally with a uniform speed, find the ratio between the horizontal velocities of the bird and the stone, if the stone still hits the bird while descending.

Solution

Let θ be the angle of projection and u be the velocity of projection. Situation is shown in figure-1.41. It is given that the maximum height of the projectile is $2h$, we have

$$u\sin\theta = \sqrt{4gh}$$

If time taken by the projectile to reach points A and B are t_1 and t_2, then t_1 and t_2 are the roots of the equation

$$h = u\sin\theta\, t - \frac{1}{2}gt^2$$

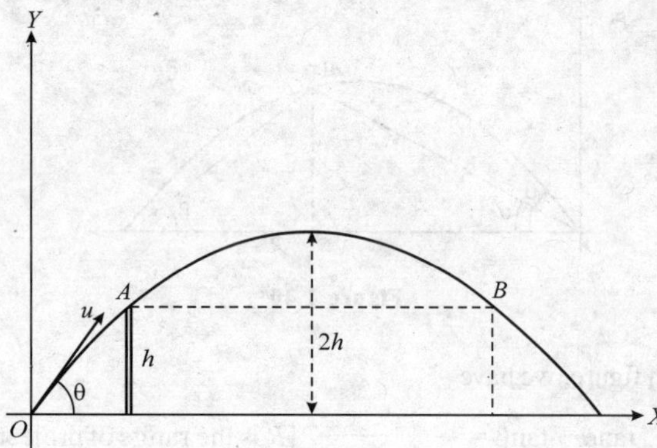

Figure 1.41

$$\frac{1}{2}gt^2 - u\sin\theta + h = 0$$

Solving $$t = \frac{u\sin\theta}{g} \pm \frac{\sqrt{u\sin\theta - 2gh}}{g}$$

Using $$t = \sqrt{\frac{4h}{g}} \pm \sqrt{\frac{2h}{g}}$$

Thus we have $$t_1 = \sqrt{\frac{4h}{g}} - \sqrt{\frac{2h}{g}}$$

and $$t_2 = \sqrt{\frac{4h}{g}} + \sqrt{\frac{2h}{g}}$$

Now the distance AB can be written as

$$v\, t_2 = u\cos\theta\,(t_2 - t_1)$$

Ratio of horizontal velocities

$$\frac{v}{u\cos\theta} = \frac{t_2 - t_1}{t_2} = \frac{2}{\sqrt{2}+1}$$

Illustrative Example 1.45

The radius of the front and rear wheels of a carriage are a and b, and c is the distance between the front and rear axles. A particle of dust driven from the highest point of the rear wheel is observed to alight on the highest point of the front wheel. Find the velocity of the carriage.

Solution

If v is the velocity of the carriage then the velocity of the top of the wheel is $2v$ as the wheels are in pure rolling (refer concept of pure rolling in chapter-5). The dust particle leaves from the topmost point of the rear wheel hence its velocity is $2v$. But with respect to the carriage it is v. It lands on the topmost point of the front wheel, as shown in figure-1.42. It travels horizontal distance $\sqrt{c^2 - (b-a)^2}$ in the duration it falls by $(2b - 2a)$. Whenever a body is thrown horizontally and if it covers distance R in the duration it falls by h, you can use

$$R = u\sqrt{\frac{2h}{g}} \qquad \dots(1.55)$$

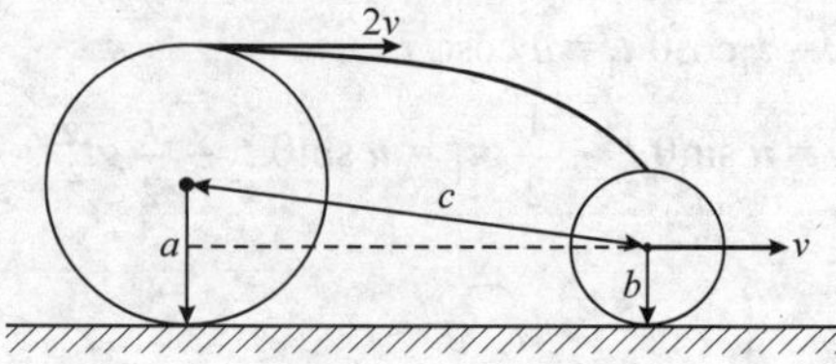

Figure 1.42

As its initial velocity in downward direction is zero, time taken to cover a distance h with g is $\sqrt{2h/g}$ and the horizontal distance covered in this duration is given by equation-(1.51). In this problem we us equation-(1.55) as

$$\sqrt{c^2 - (b-a)^2} = v\sqrt{\frac{4(b-a)}{g}}$$

$$v = \sqrt{\frac{(c+b-a)(c+a-b)g}{4(b-a)}}$$

Web Reference at www.physicsgalaxy.com

Age Group - High School Physics | Age 17-19 Years
Section - MECHANICS
Topic - Motion in Two Dimensions
Module Numbers - 6, 7, 8, 9, 10, 11 and 12

Practice Exercise 1.8

(i) A stone is thrown from the top of a tower of height 50 m with a velocity of 30 m per second at an angle of 30° above the horizontal. Find (a) the time during which the stone will be in air, (b) the distance from the tower base to where the stone will hit the ground, (c) the speed with which the stone will hit the ground, (d) the angle formed by the trajectory of the stone with the horizontal at the point of hit.

[(a) 5.0 s, (b) $75\sqrt{3}$ m, (c) 43.58 m/s, (d) $\tan^{-1}\left(\frac{7}{3\sqrt{3}}\right)$]

(ii) A stone is thrown up from the top of a tower 20 m with a velocity of 24 m/s at an elevation of 30° above the horizontal. Find the horizontal distance from the foot of the tower to the point at which the stone hits the ground. Take $g = 10$ m/s^2

[73.37 m]

(iii) Two bodies are thrown at the same time and in opposite directions and with an equal velocity v_0 at angles α_1 and α_2 to the horizon. What is the velocity with which the bodies move relative to each other ? What will be the distance between the bodies be after time t elapses ?

[$2v_0 \sin\left(\frac{\alpha_2-\alpha_1}{2}\right)$, $2V_0 t \sin\left(\frac{\alpha_2-\alpha_1}{2}\right)$]

(iv) A ball rolls down from the top of a staircase with some horizontal speed u. If the height and width of the steps are h and b respectively, then show that ball will just strike the edge of nth step if $n = \frac{2hu^2}{gb^2}$.

(v) A boat is moving directly away from a gun on the shore with speed v_1. The gun fires a shell with speed v_2 at an angle of elevation α and hits the boat. Prove that the distance of the boat from the gun at the moment it is fired is given by :

$$\frac{2v_2 \sin\alpha}{g}(v_2\cos\alpha - v_1)$$

(vi) Two bodies were thrown simultaneously from the same point one, straight up, and the other, at angle $\theta = 60°$ to the horizontal. The initial velocity of each body is equal to $v_0 = 25$ m/s. Neglecting the air drag, find the distance between the bodies $t = 1.70$ s later. Take $g = 10$ m/s^2.

[22 m]

(vii) Two particles are projected from a point at the same instant with velocities whose horizontal and vertical components are u_1, v_1 and u_2, v_2 respectively. Prove that the interval between their passing through the other common point of their path is

$$\frac{2(v_1u_2 - v_2u_1)}{g(u_1+u_2)}$$

(viii) A ball is thrown from a point in level with and at a horizontal distance r from the top of a tower of height h. How must the speed and angle of the projection of the ball be related to r in order that the ball may just go grazing past the top edge of the tower ? At what horizontal distance x from the foot of the tower does the ball hit the ground ? For a given speed of projection, obtain an equation for finding the angle of projection so that x is at a minimum.

[$rg = u^2 \sin 2\theta$, $\frac{u\cos\theta}{g}\{(u^2\sin^2\theta + 2gh)^{1/2} - u\sin\theta\}$]

(ix) In a "Ram Leela" stage show an unhappy guy from audience throws an rotten egg at Rawana. The egg travels a horizontal distance of 15 m in 0.75 s before hitting the Rawana's face 1.7 m above the stage. The egg is thrown at 2.0 m above the horizontal floor with an initial velocity 30° above the horizontal. (a) Find the initial and final velocities of egg . (b) How high is the stage above the floor. Take $g = 10$ m/s^2.

[(a) $\frac{40}{\sqrt{3}}$ m/s, 20.40 m/s, (b) 6.15 m]

(x) A machine gun is mounted on the top of a tower of height 100 m. At what angle should the gun be inclined to cover a maximum range on the ground below ? The muzzle velocity of the bullet is 150 m/s. Take $g = 10$ m/s^2.

[46.3°]

1.13.1 Projectile Motion on Inclined Plane

Till now we were discussing the simple projectile motion and its properties when it is thrown on a straight horizontal plane. Now we switch it onto the case when a projectile is made on an inclined plane shown in figure-1.43.

Figure-1.43 shows an inclined plane at an angle α and a particle is projected at an angle θ with the direction of plane with initial velocity u. In such cases we take our reference x and y axes in the direction along and perpendicular to the inclined as shown.

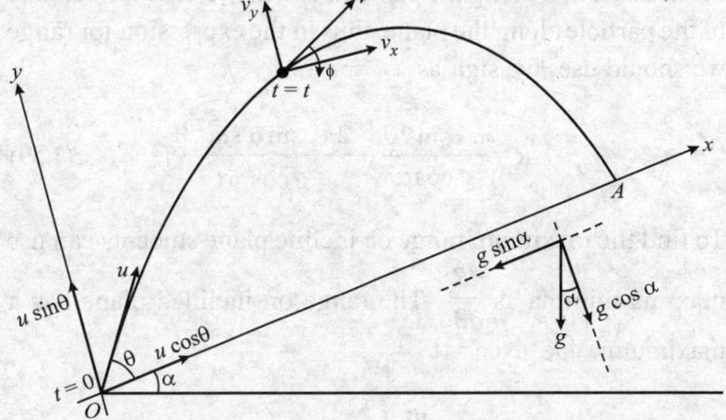

Figure 1.43

Unlike to the previous case, here the x-component of the velocity of the projectile will also be retarded by a $g\sin\alpha$. Now y-component of the velocity is retarded by $g\cos\alpha$ instead of g. As shown here g is resolved in two directions.

As here y-direction component is retarded by $g\cos\alpha$, to find the time of flight and maximum height, we can use equations-(1.38) and (1.39), replacing g by $g\cos\alpha$,

Time of flight on inclined plane projectile is

$$T_f = \frac{2u\sin\theta}{g\cos\alpha} \quad \ldots(1.56)$$

Maximum height of the projectile with respect to inclined plane is

$$H = \frac{u^2 \sin^2 \theta}{2g\cos\alpha} \quad \dots(1.57)$$

For evaluation of range on inclined plane we cannot use the previous relation of equation-(1.40), just by replacing g by $g \cos\alpha$, as here we also have

$$a_x = -g \sin\alpha.$$

Now we again find the distance traveled by the particle along x-direction in the duration time of flight is

$$R = u \sin\theta \,.\, T_f - \frac{1}{2} g \sin\alpha \,.\, T_f^2$$

On substituting the value of T_f here, we get

$$R = \frac{u^2 \sin 2\theta}{g\cos\alpha} - \frac{2u^2 \sin\alpha \sin^2\theta}{g\cos^2\alpha} \quad \dots(1.58)$$

Students are advised not to apply the expression of range on inclined in equation-(1.58), as a standard result, it should be processed and evaluated according to the numerical problem. Above results we've derived for the projectile thrown up an inclined plane. If projectile is thrown down an inclined plane, the acceleration along the plane $\sin\alpha$ will increase the velocity of the particle along the plane, thus in the expression for range we should use +ve sign as

$$R = \frac{u^2 \sin 2\theta}{g\cos\alpha} + \frac{2u^2 \sin\alpha \sin^2\theta}{g\cos^2\alpha} \quad \dots(1.59)$$

To find the maximum range on incline plane students can use maxima-minima as $\frac{dR}{d\theta}$. The range on inclined plane has a maximum value given as

$$R = \frac{u^2}{g(1 \pm \sin\alpha)} \quad \dots(1.60)$$

In equation-(1.60), +ve sign is used for projectile up the plane and -ve sign is used for projectile down the plane. The above result is left for student as an exercise to be evaluated. Students should also evaluate the angle at which projectile must be thrown to get this maximum range on inclined plane.

Illustrative Example 1.46

A ball is dropped from a height h above a point on an inclined plane, with angle of inclination θ. The ball make an elastic collision with the surface and rebounds off the plane. Determine the distance from the point of first impact to the point where ball hit the plane second time.

Solution

The situation is shown in figure-1.44. We take the point of first impact as the origin of our reference. Direction along the plane will be the x-axis and the direction perpendicular to the plane will be the y-axis. It is given that the ball rebounds elastically and implies that no change in kinetic energy of the ball before and after the collision. The ball rebounds with the same velocity with which it will strike the plane after falling a distance h, which is $u = \sqrt{2gh}$. After rebound, the horizontal component of velocity $u \sin\theta$ will be accelerated by $g \sin\theta$ and the vertical component of the velocity $u \cos\theta$ will be retarded by $g \cos\theta$.

Here time of flight from first impact to the second impact is given as

$$T_f = \frac{2u_y}{a_y} = \frac{2u\cos\theta}{g\cos\theta} = \frac{2u}{g}$$

In this duration the distance traveled by the horizontal component is

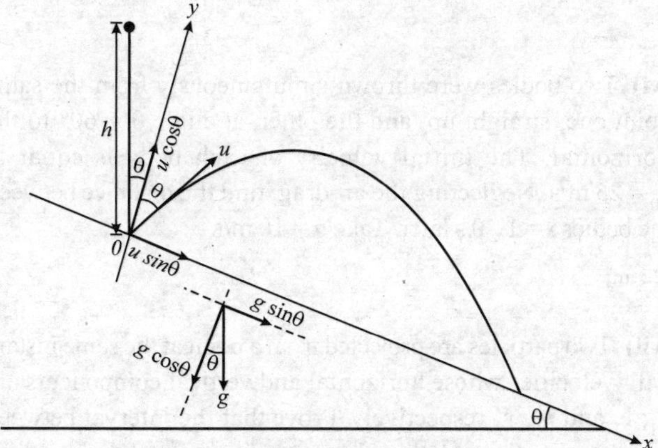

Figure 1.44

$$R = u \sin\theta \,.\, \frac{2u}{g} + \frac{1}{2} g \sin\theta \,.\left(\frac{2u}{g}\right)^2 = \frac{4u^2 \sin\theta}{g}$$

$$= 8\, h \sin\theta \qquad [\text{As } u = \sqrt{2gh}\,]$$

Illustrative Example 1.47

A projectile is thrown with a speed u, at an angle θ to an inclined plane of inclination β. Find the angle θ at which the projectile is thrown such that it strikes the inclined plane (i) normally (ii) horizontally.

Solution

(i) If it strikes the plane normally as shown in figure-1.45, we can say that at the time of striking particle's x-component of velocity is zero ($v_x = 0$).

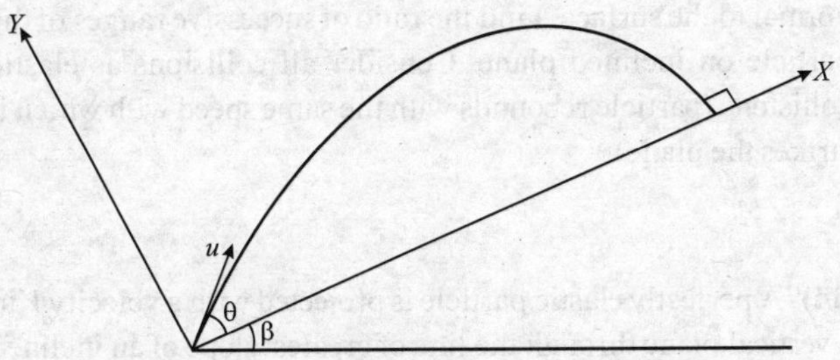

Figure 1.45

Here we have time of flight of particle is

$$T_f = \frac{2u\sin\theta}{g\cos\beta}$$

Thus from speed equation in x-direction, we have

$$0 = u\cos\theta - g\sin\beta\left(\frac{2u\sin\theta}{g\cos\beta}\right)$$

or $\cot\theta = 2\tan\beta$

or $\theta = \cot^{-1}(2\tan\beta)$

(ii) As it strikes inclined plane horizontally as show in figure-1.46, we can say that it is the maximum height of the projectile and half of the range as seen from ground plane. If R is the range of projectile on inclined plane, we have

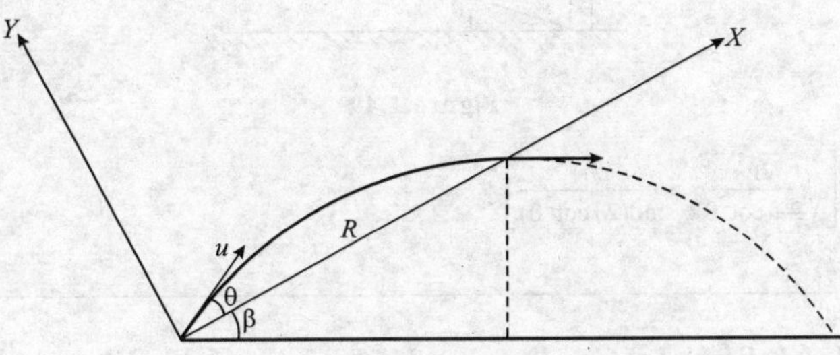

Figure 1.46

$$R\sin\beta = \frac{u^2\sin^2(\theta+\beta)}{2g} \quad \ldots(1.61a)$$

$$R\cos\beta = \frac{u^2\sin 2(\theta+\beta)}{g}\times\frac{1}{2} \quad \ldots(1.61b)$$

Dividing equations-(1.61a) and (1.61b), we get

$$\tan\beta = \frac{\sin^2(\theta+\beta)}{\sin 2(\theta+\beta)}$$

or $\tan\beta = \frac{1}{2}\tan(\theta+\beta)$

or $\theta = \tan^{-1}(2\tan\beta) - \beta$

Illustrative Example 1.48

A child throws a ball so as to clear a wall of height h and at a distance x from it. Find the minimum speed required for clearing the wall.

Solution

If we join the wall top edge with the point of projection as shown in figure-1.47, the distance is $\sqrt{h^2+x^2}$. If we consider this as incline plane of inclination $\alpha = \tan^{-1}\left(\frac{h}{x}\right)$, this must be the maximum range on incline plane. If particle is thrown with a speed u, we must have to clear the wall

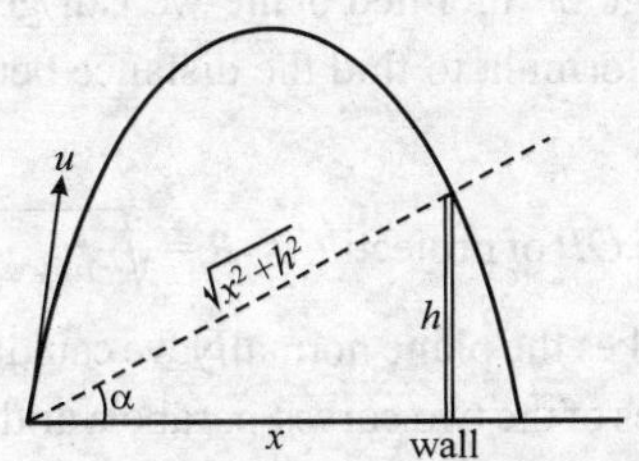

Figure 1.47

$$R_{max} = \frac{u^2}{g(1+\sin\alpha)} \geq \sqrt{h^2+x^2}$$

or $\quad u \geq g\left(h+\sqrt{h^2+x^2}\right) \quad \left[\text{As } \sin\alpha = \frac{h}{\sqrt{h^2+x^2}}\right]$

1.13.2 Use of Co-ordinate Geometry For Projectile Problems

Sometime it is convenient to use co-ordinate geometry to solve the projectile problems. For example consider a projectile thrown at an angle θ with an inclined plane OP of inclination α. If we observe this projectile from ground plane it seems to complete the parabola OAB, but due to inclined plane it strikes at point A having coordinate (x_1, y_1) in ground frame shown in figure-1.48.

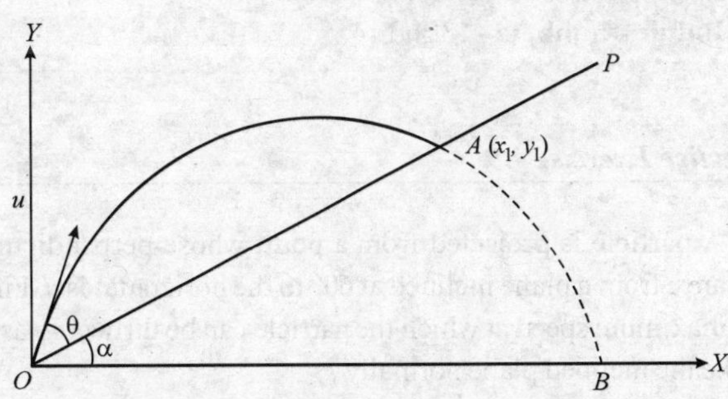

Figure 1.48

In ground frame the equation of parabola OAB is written as the equation of trajectory of projectile hauled at an angel $(\theta + \alpha)$ with the horizontal, as

$$y = x\tan(\theta+\alpha) - \frac{gx^2}{2u^2\cos^2(\theta+\alpha)} \qquad \dots(1.62)$$

The equation of the straight line OP (inclined plane) in this frame is

$$y = x\tan\alpha \qquad \dots(1.63)$$

Here A is the point where the two curves intersects, thus on solving equations-(1.62) and (1.63) simultaneously, we can get the coordinates of intersection point A (x_1, y_1). Now if we wish to find the range on inclined plane we can get it directly by using distance formula to find the distance between points O and A.

Range on plane OP of projectile is $R = \sqrt{x_1^2 + y_1^2}$

If projectile strikes the plane normally we can directly have the product of slopes of the two curves-parabola and line of greatest slope of inclined plane as – 1. In above example we have the slope of parabola at A is

$$m_1 = \frac{dy}{dx}(x_1, y_1) = \tan(\theta+\alpha) - \frac{gx_1}{u^2\cos(\alpha+\alpha)}$$

The slope of line OP is

$$m_2 = \tan\alpha$$

If projectile strikes the inclined plane normally at A, we have

$$m_1 \times m_2 = -1$$

Solving above relation we can get the required parameters.

Web Reference at www.physicsgalaxy.com

Age Group - High School Physics | Age 17-19 Years
Section - MECHANICS
Topic - Motion in Two Dimensions
Module Numbers - 13 and 14

Practice Exercise 1.9

(i) A particle is projected from a point whose perpendicular distance from a plane inclined at 60° to the horizontal is d. Find the maximum speed at which the particle can be thrown so as to strike the inclined plane normally.

$[u < \left[\sqrt{\frac{1}{2}dg(\sqrt{13}-1)}\right]]$

(ii) From an inclined plane a particle is thrown in a direction normal to the surface. Find the ratio of successive ranges of the particle on inclined plane. Consider all collisions as elastic collisions (particle rebounds with the same speed with which it strikes the plane)

[1 : 3 : 5]

(iii) A perfectly elastic particle is projected with a velocity V in a vertical plane through the line of greatest slope of an inclined plane of elevation α. If after striking the plane, the particle rebounds vertically, Find the time it takes to return to the point of projection.

$[\frac{6V}{g\sqrt{(1+8\sin^2\alpha)}}]$

(iv) A particle is thrown in horizontal direction with speed u from a point P, the top of a tower shown in figure-1.49 at a vertical height h above the inclined plane of inclination θ. Find the speed with which the particle is thrown so that it strikes the plane normally. Also find the distance from the foot of the tower where the particle will strike.

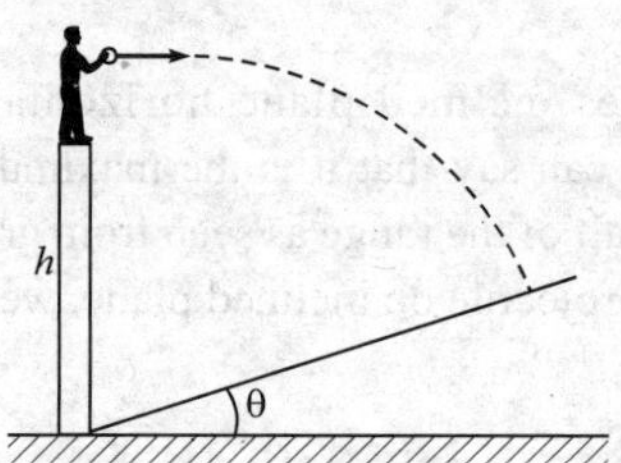

Figure 1.49

$[\left[\sqrt{\frac{2gh}{2+\cot^2\theta}}, \frac{2h}{\sin\theta(2+\cot^2\theta)}\right]]$

1.14 Simple Constrained Motion of Bodies and Particles in Two Dimensions

In previous section, we have discussed projectile motion. The best way to deal with the projectile motion is to solve the motion independently in horizontal and perpendicular directions. For horizontal plane projectile motion, the horizontal component of the velocity remains constant and the vertical component of it is retarded by the acceleration "g".

Similar to projectile motion, there can be several two dimensional motions, in which the laws of motion can be separately applied to x and y directions and later on the developed relations can be linked for getting the required parameters. Sometime x and y directional motion or any two directions of the motion are related by some specific rule, we call such rules as constraint rules.

These rules relate one direction of motion of an object with some other direction of the same object or some other object also. We take few illustrative examples to explain the concept of constraint motion.

Illustrative Example 1.49

Figure-1.50 shows a rod of length l resting on a wall and the floor. Its lower end A is pulled towards left with a constant velocity u. Find the velocity of the other end B downward when the rod makes an angle θ with the horizontal.

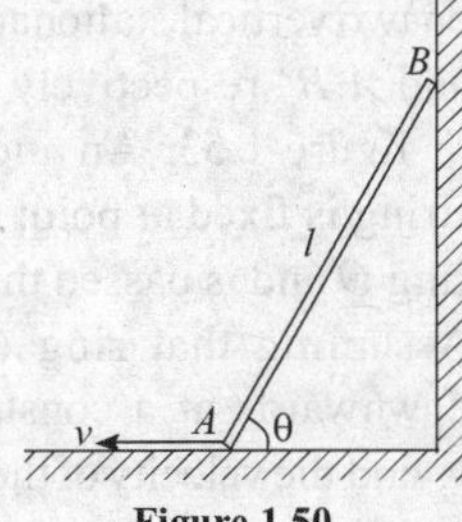

Figure 1.50

Solution

In such type of problems, when velocity of one part of a body is given and that of other is required or in cases, when relation in two velocities is required, we first find the relation between the two displacements then differentiate with respect to time. Here if the distance from the corner to the point A is x and that up to B is y. Now the left velocity of point A can be given as

$$v = \frac{dx}{dt}$$

and that of B can be given as

$$v_B = -\frac{dy}{dt} \quad \text{[– sign indicates, } y \text{ decreasing]}$$

If we relate x and y as

$$x^2 + y^2 = l^2$$

Differentiating with respect to t

$$2x\frac{dx}{dt} + 2y\frac{dy}{dt} = 0$$

$$x\,v = yv_B$$

$$v_B = v\,\frac{x}{y} = v\cot\theta$$

Alternative

In cases when the relation between two points of a rigid body is required, we can make use of the fact that in a rigid body the distance between two points always remains same. Thus the relative velocity of one point of an object with respect to any other point of the same object in the direction of line joining them will always remain zero, as their separation always remains constant.

Here in above example the distance between the points A and B of the rod always remains constant, thus, the two points must have same velocity components in the direction of their line joining i.e. along the length of the rod.

If point B is moving down with velocity v_B, its component along the length of the rod is $v_B \sin\theta$. Similarly the velocity component of point A along the length of rod is $v\cos\theta$. Thus we have

$$v_B \sin\theta = v\cos\theta$$

or $$v_B = v\cot\theta$$

Illustrative Example 1.50

In the arrangement shown in figure-1.51, the ends A and B of an inextensible string move downwards with uniform speed u. Pulleys A and B are fixed. Find the speed with which the mass M moves upwards.

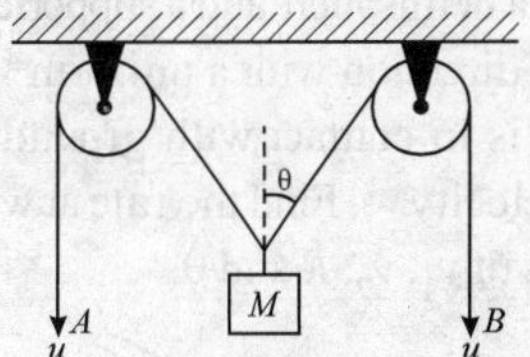

Figure 1.51

Solution

Here again we use the same concept which we have applied in the previous problem. If the distance of mass M from the ceiling is y and the distance of M from each pulley is x and the distance between the two pulleys is l. Then u will be the rate at which x is decreasing. If v is the velocity of M upward, it is the rate at which y is decreasing. Thus we have

$$u = -\frac{dx}{dt} \quad \text{and} \quad v = -\frac{dy}{dt}$$

Now we find the relation in x and y as

$$x^2 + \frac{l^2}{4} = y^2$$

On differentiating with respect to t

$$2x\frac{dx}{dt} = 2y\,\frac{dy}{dt}$$

$$xu = yv$$

$$v = u\,\frac{dx}{dt} = u\sec\theta$$

Alternative

Here also we can use the previous alternative method. As length of the string during motion remains constant (inextensible string), we can state that the velocity components of all the points on a string along the length of string must remains same.

Here as pulley and the string in contact with it is going up with velocity v, its component along and the string is $v \cos\theta$ and the ends of string A and B are going down with velocity u, we must have

$$v \cos\theta = u$$

or $$v = u \sec\theta$$

NOTE : Here students should note that although in both of these examples, alternative method seems to be more easy and simple but, in so many problems it becomes difficult or complex to think. In so many cases it is helpful but students are advised to capture both the concepts in head for instant applications.

 # Illustrative Example 1.51

Figure-1.52 shows a hemisphere and a supported rod. Hemisphere is moving in right direction with a uniform velocity v_2 and the end of rod which is in contact with ground is moving in left direction with a velocity v_1. Find the rate at which the angle θ is changing in terms of v_1, v_2, R and θ.

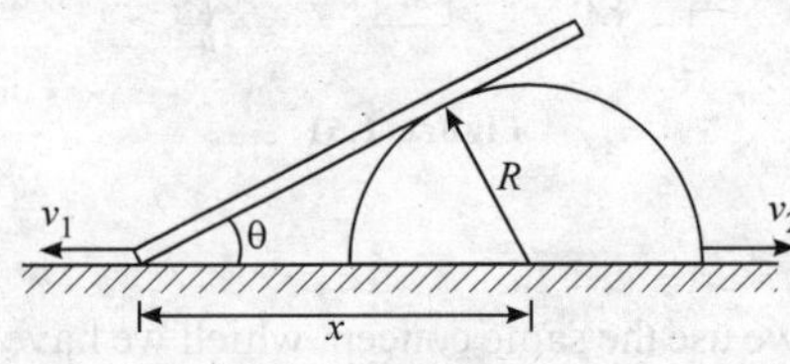

Figure 1.52

Solution

Here x is the separation between centre of hemisphere and the end of rod. Rate of change of x can be taken as the relative velocity of end of rod and hemisphere centre i.e. $(v_1 + v_2)$. We are required to find the rate of change of θ and rate of change of x we know, so we have to develop a relation between x and θ, which is given as

$$x = R \operatorname{cosec}\theta$$

Differentiating with respect to time we get

$$\frac{dx}{dt} = -R \operatorname{cosec}\theta \cot\theta \frac{d\theta}{dt}$$

or $$\frac{d\theta}{dt} = -\frac{(v_1 + v_2)\sin^2\theta}{R\cos\theta}$$

Web Reference at www.physicsgalaxy.com

Age Group - High School Physics | Age 17-19 Years
Section - MECHANICS
Topic - Constrained Motion
Module Numbers - 1, 2, 3, 4 and 5

Practice Exercise 1.10

(i) In example-1.49 find the velocity of the mid point of the rod in terms of its length l, v and θ.

[$\frac{v}{2} \operatorname{cosec}\theta$]

(ii) Two rings O and O' are put on two vertical stationary rods AB and $A'B'$ respectively as shown in figure-1.53. An inextensible string is fixed at point A' and on ring O and is passed through O'. Assuming that ring O' moves downwards at a constant speed v, find the velocity of the ring O in terms of α.

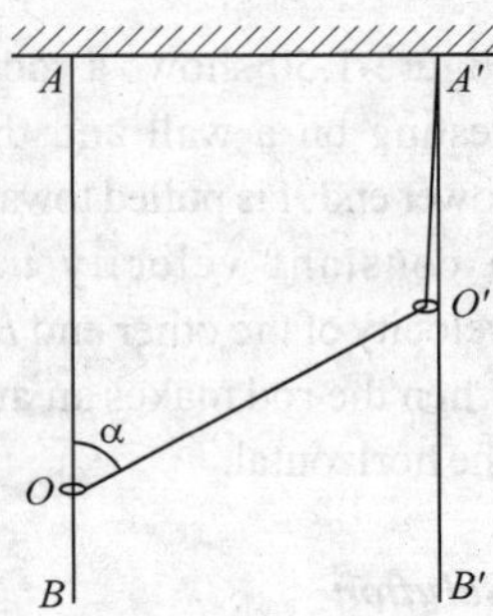

Figure 1.53

[$\frac{v(1-\cos\alpha)}{\cos\alpha}$]

(iii) An aircraft is descending to land at an airport in the morning. The aircraft is landing to the east, so that pilot has the sun in his eyes. The aircraft has a speed v and is descending at an angle α, and the sun is at an angle β above the horizon. Find the speed with which the aircraft's shadow moves over the ground.

[$v(\cos\alpha + \sin\alpha \cot\beta)$]

(iv) Figure-1.54 shows a small mass m hanging over a pulley. The other end of the thread is being pulled in horizontal direction with a uniform speed u. Find the speed with which the mass ascend at the instant the string makes an angle θ with the horizontal.

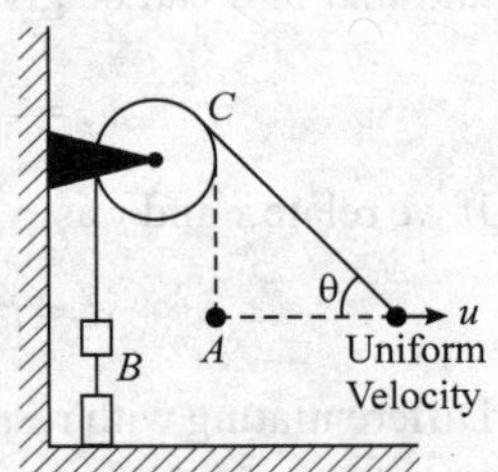

Figure 1.54

[$u \cos\theta$]

(v) A man of height 1.2 m walks away from a lamp hanging at a height of 4.0 m above ground level. If the man walks with a speed of 2.8 m/s, determine the speed of the tip of man's shadow.

[4.0 m/s]

(vi) Find the speed of the box-3, if box-1 and box-2 are moving with speeds v_1 and v_2 as shown in figure-1.55 when the string makes an angle θ_1 and θ_2 with the horizontal at its left and right end.

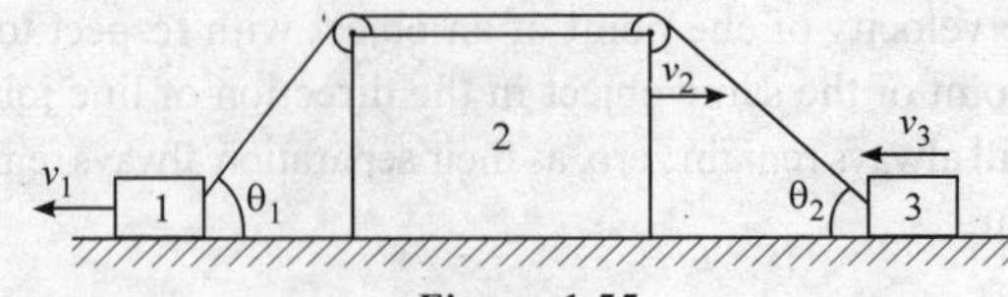

Figure 1.55

[$\frac{(v_1 + v_2)\cos\theta_1}{\cos\theta_2} - v_2$]

(vii) A ring A which can slide on a smooth wire is connected to one end of a string as shown in figure-1.56. Other end of the string is connected to a hanging mass B. Find the speed with the ring when the string makes an angle θ with the wire and mass B is going down with a velocity v.

[$v \sec\theta$]

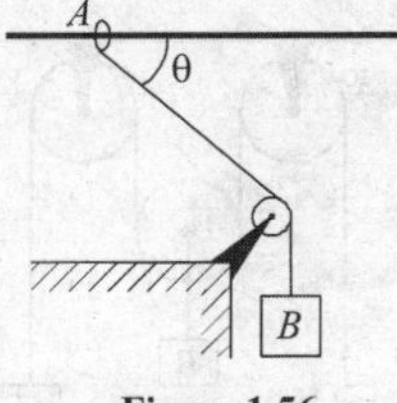

Figure 1.56

1.14.1 Pulley Constraints

The problems in which few bodies are connected with one or more strings and strings are passed through pulleys, some of which are fixed and some are movable. In such problems, we develop constraint rules in different ways, sometime by observation and sometime by some special technique. In coming section we will discuss such type of things. These are mainly used in next chapter, for finding acceleration of different bodies of a system.

First we start our analysis with simple cases of pulleys. Consider the situation shown in figure-1.57. Two bodies are connected with a string which passes over a pulley at the corner of a table. Here if string is inextensible, we can directly state that the displacement of A in downward direction is equal to the displacement of B in horizontal direction on table, and if displacements of A and B are equal in equal time, their speeds and acceleration magnitude must also be equal.

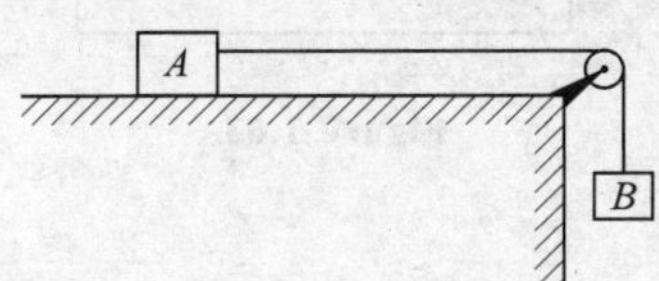

Figure 1.57

Similarly consider the situation shown in figure-1.58. Two masses are hanging from a pulley with a string. Here if mass A is heavy, it goes down and B goes up by same distance. Thus here also the displacement, speed and acceleration magnitude of the two are equal.

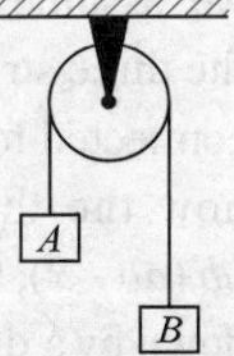

Figure 1.58

In all such cases it is not necessary that the two blocks move with equal speed and acceleration. It occurs only when pulleys are fixed like in above examples pulleys are fixed at a table corner or tied with a string to the ceiling. Now consider the case shown in figure-1.59(a). Two masses A and B are tied to strings and arranged in the situation shown. Here mass B is connected to a movable pulley Y supported by a string which passes over a fixed pulley X and to which mass A is connected.

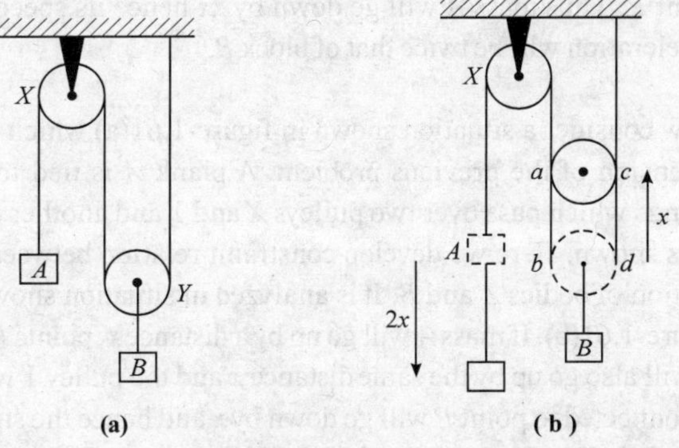

Figure 1.59

To analyze the motions of A and B, you should look carefully at analysis shown in figure-1.59(b). If mass B goes up by a distance x, we can observe that the string lengths ab and cd are slack, due to the weight of block A, this length ($ab + cd = 2x$) will go on this side and block A will descend by a distance $2x$. As in equal time duration A has travelled a distance twice that of B, thus its speed and acceleration must also be twice that of B.

In such cases it is not necessary that block B will go up. It may also be possible that B will go down and A will go up with twice the speed and acceleration, it depends on the masses of the two objects. We can only develop the relation in accelerations of blocks, we cannot comment on its direction without knowing their masses. This we will discuss in detail in next chapter.

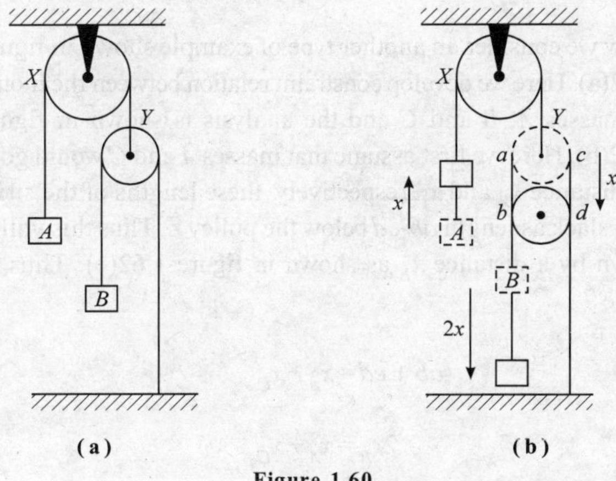

Figure 1.60

Here we consider few more examples of pulley constraints. Consider the situation shown in figure-1.60(a). In this case we find relation in acceleration of masses A and B. Let we analyze the motion of A and B as shown in figure-1.60(b). If we consider that mass B is going up by a distance x, pulley Y which is attached to the same string will go down by the same distance x. Due to this the string which is connected to mass A will now have free lengths ab and cd ($ab = cd = x$) which will go on the side of mass A due to its weight as the other end is fixed at point P. Thus mass A will go down by $2x$ hence its speed and acceleration will be twice that of block B.

Now consider a situation shown in figure-1.61(a) which is an extension of the previous problem. A plank A is tied to two strings which pass over two pulleys X and Y and another mass B as shown. Here we develop constraint relation between the motion of bodies A and B. It is analyzed in situation shown in figure-1.61(b). If mass A will go up by a distance x, points P and Q will also go up by the same distance x and the pulley Y which is connected to point P will go down by x and hence the strings lengths ab and cd ($ab = cd = x$) which become free plus the length x due to movement of Q upward will go on the side of mass B, hence it will go down by a distance $3x$. Thus its speed and acceleration are thrice that of mass A.

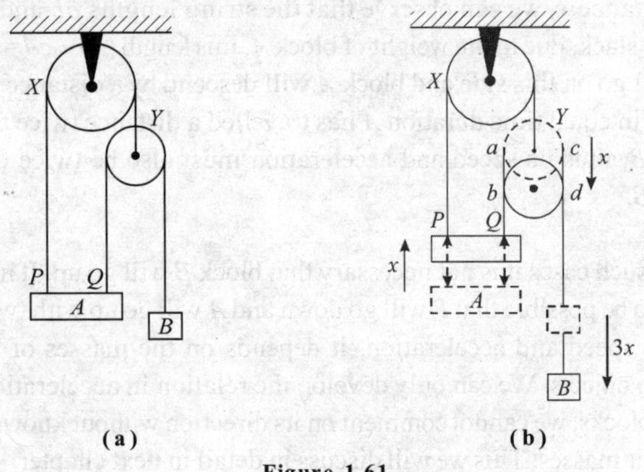

Figure 1.61

Now we consider an another type of example shown in figure-1.62(a). Here we develop constraint relation between the motion of masses A, B and C and the analysis is shown in figure-1.62(b). Here we first assume that masses A and C would go up by distance x_A and x_C respectively, these lengths of the string will slack as length ab-cd below the pulley Z, Thus this will go down by a distance x_B as shown in figure-1.62(b). Thus we have

$$ab + cd = x_A + x_C$$

or $$2x_B = x_A + x_C$$

Differentiating w.r.t. time, we get

$$2v_B = v_A + v_C \qquad \dots(1.64)$$

Differentiating again w.r.t. time

$$2a_B = a_A + a_C \qquad \dots(1.65)$$

Equations-(1.64) and (1.65) are the constraint relations for motion of masses A, B and C.

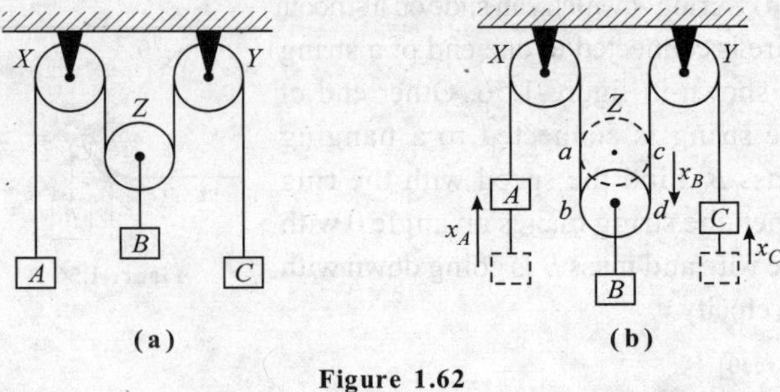

Figure 1.62

Now we consider few advance cases in following examples.

Illustrative Example 1.52

Consider the situation of block pulley arrangement shown in figure-1.63. A plank is connected to three strings and an electric motor M is fitted on to it and a string is wound on it according to the arrangement shown in figure. Given that the string is winding on shaft of motor at a speed v. Find the speed with which the plank would be going up.

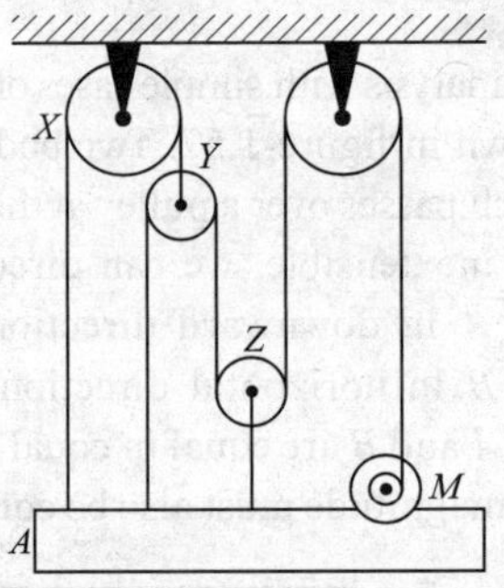

Figure 1.63

Solution

The analysis of the situation is shown in figure-1.64. Here first we assume that the plank goes up by a distance x. Obviously the three strings ab, cd and ef slack by a distance x which are connected to the plank at points a, c and e. Now we analyze how the three slack lengths are adjusted. Due to slack ab ($ab = x$), this length will go on side of pulley Y and it will go down by a distance x. Due to this string 2 will also slack by an additional distance gh and ij ($gh = ij = x$) with slack cd and all these slack lengths in string 2 ($cd + gh + ij = 3x$) will go on side of pulley Z. Due to slack ef, pulley Z has to go up by a distance x and this will further slack the string 2 by kl and mn ($kl = mn = x$) hence the total slack in string 2 is ($cd + gh + ij + kl + mn = 5x$) plus x due to the displacement of motor up by a distance x, thus it is $6x$. As it is given that motor is winding at a speed v, to make all the strings tight, we must have that the string length wound on motor shaft must be $6x$ in the duration plank goes up by x.

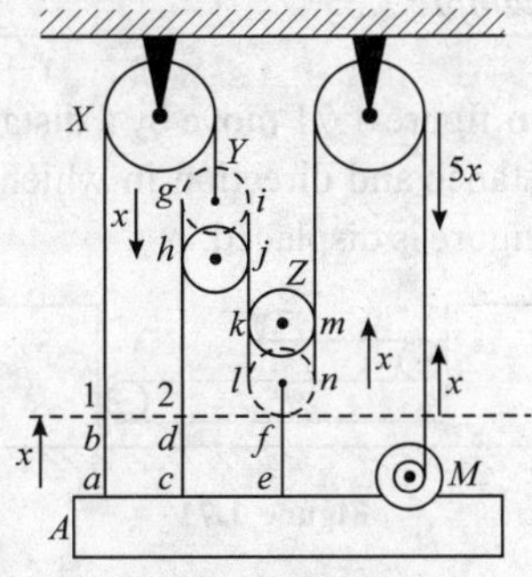

Figure 1.64

Thus the speed with which the plank is going up must be $v/6$.

Illustrative Example 1.53

Figure-1.65 shows a system of four pulleys with two masses A and B. Find, at an instant :

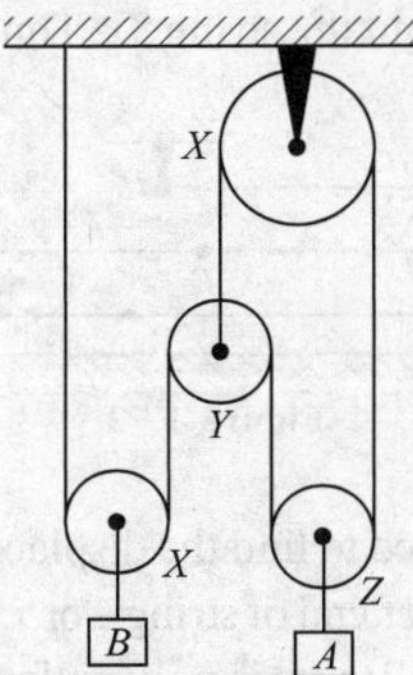

Figure 1.65

(a) Speed of block A when the block B is going up at 1 m/s and pulley Y is going up at 2 m/s.

(b) Acceleration of block A if block B is going up at 3 m/s^2 and pulley Y is going down at 1 m/s^2.

Solution

(a) Here the analysis of the situation is shown in figure-1.66. If we assume that block B and along with it pulley X goes up by a distance x, it will result a slack of length ab and cd ($ab + cd = 2x$) in string 1.

Simultaneously if we assume that the pulley Y goes up by a distance y, it results a compensation of the slackened length by ef and gh ($ef + gh = 2y$) and due to it the same string connected to pulley Y goes up by a distance y. Thus to the left of pulley Z, string has a slack length $(2x - 2y)$ and on to right of its slack length is y, which is due to upward motion of pulley Y. Thus total slack above the pulley Z will become $(2x - 2y + y = 2x - y)$. Thus pulley Z has to go down by a distance $\dfrac{2x-y}{2}$ to tighten all the strings.

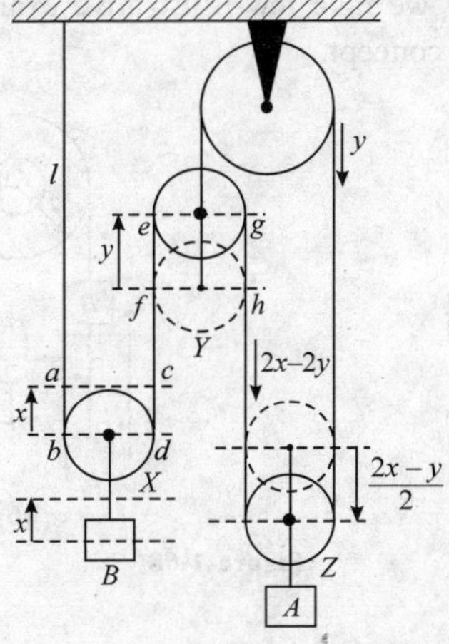

Figure 1.66

Thus speed of pulley Z or block A is

$$v_A = \frac{2v_B - v_y}{2} = 0$$

Hence block A will be at rest at this instant.

(b) Here it is given that the block B is going up and pulley Y is going down, here we are leaving the analysis for students to develop the constrained relation for the motion of block B, pulley Y and pulley Z (or block A). Finally you must get

$$a_A = \frac{2a_B - a_y}{2} = 3.5 \text{ m/s}^2$$

1.14.2 Step Pulley Constraints

In one pulley if two or more discs of different radii are connected as shown in figure-1.67, these are called step pulleys.

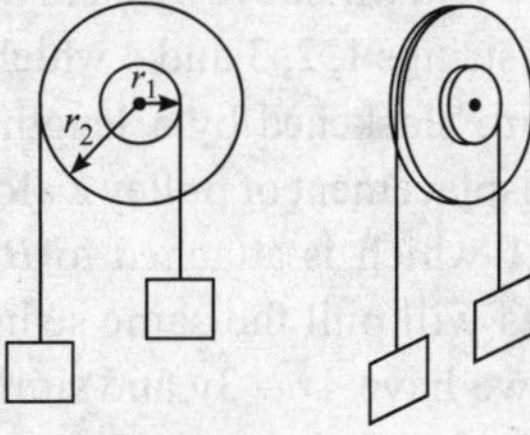

Figure 1.67

Now are discuss about the constrained relation between acceleration of objects connected with a step pulley. Consider the example shown in figure-1.68(a). If we consider that block A goes down by x, pulley rotates clockwise by an angle $\theta = x/r$ as shown in figure-1.68(b), due to this block B will go up by a distance $y = 2r \times \theta = 2x$. Thus if block A is having some acceleration or velocity then block B will have velocity or acceleration $2r/r$ i.e. twice that of A. If radius of inner and outer disc are r_1 and r_2, then acceleration of block B will be r_2/r_1 times that of A. Now we take few illustrative examples to better understand the concept.

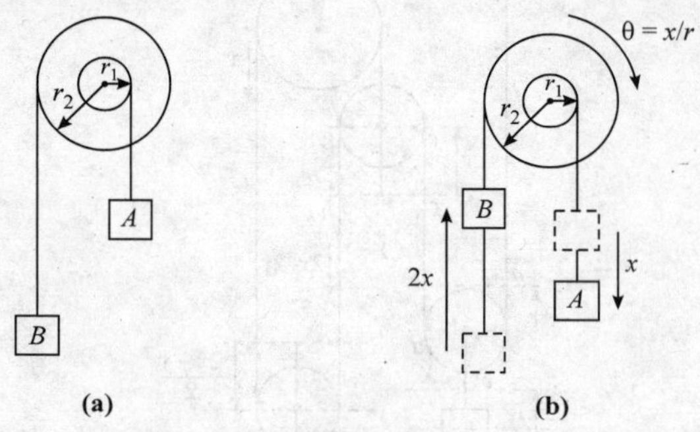

Figure 1.68

Illustrative Example 1.54

Block C shown in figure-1.69 is going down at acceleration 2 m/s^2. Find the acceleration of blocks A and B.

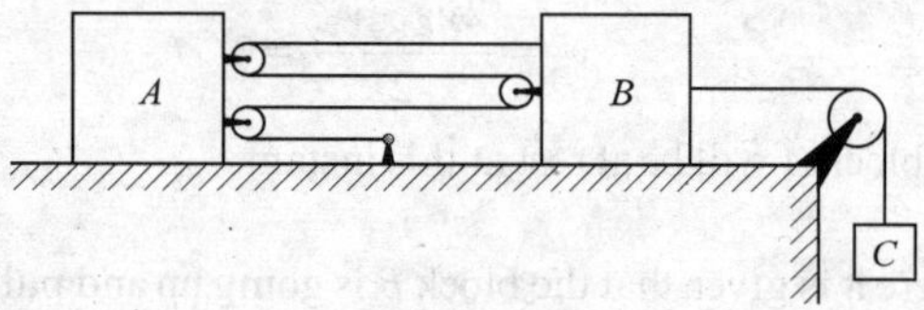

Figure 1.69

Solution

The analysis is shown in figure-1.70. As block B and C are connected by a string there accelerations must be same hence we can directly state

$$a_B = 2 \text{ m/s}^2$$

Block A is also constrained to move with block B, with pulleys X, Y and Z. As shown in figure, we assume if block B and C moves by a distance y, A will move by x and due to this the parts (like length ab) of strings 1, 2, 3 and 4 which are passing over pulleys X and Y are slackened by a length $4x$. This will be tightened by the displacement of pulley Z along with the block B and the string 1 which is attached to B at point d, by a distance y and this will pull the same string by $3y$ (like the length cd). Thus we have $4x = 3y$ and similarly we have the constrained relation for blocks A and B as :

$$a_A = \frac{3}{4}\, a_B = 1.5 \text{ m/s}^2$$

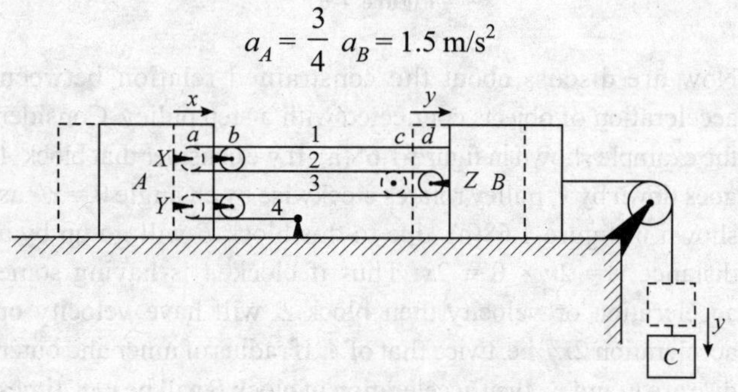

Figure 1.70

Illustrative Example 1.55

Block A shown in figure-1.71 move by a distance 3 m toward left. Find the distance and direction in which the point P on string shown in figure is displaced.

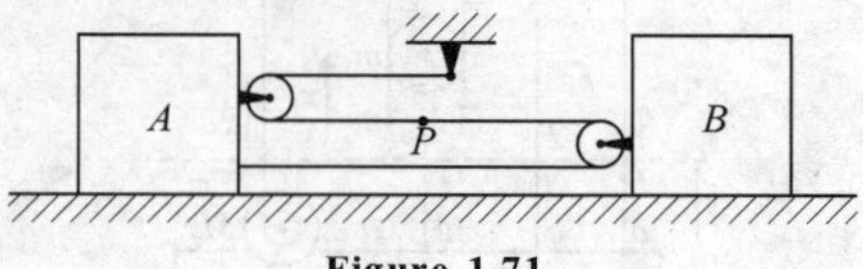

Figure 1.71

Solution

Analysis of the problem is shown in figure-1.72. If the block A moves towards left by a distance x, the string lengths $ab + cd + ef = 3x$ will be pulled towards right and to provide this length block B has to move toward left by a distance y such that the string lengths on the two sides of the pulley Y (twice of ab) i.e. $2y$ will slack to tight the string $3x$. Thus we have $3x = 2y$.

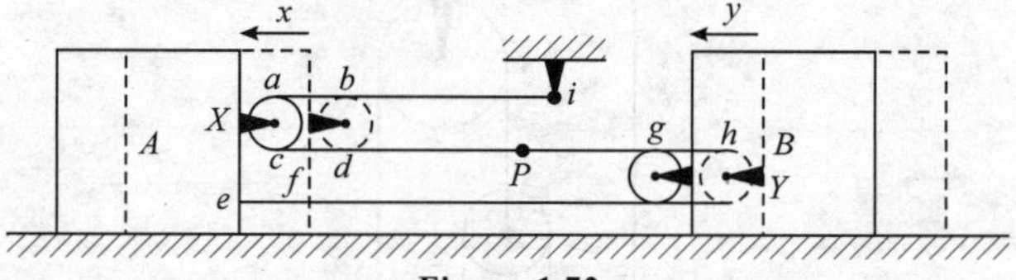

Figure 1.72

As here we are required to find the displacement of the point P, we can start from either end of string e or i. If we start from i, we can see that from i to P there is only pulley X which pulleys the thread by a distance $2x$, thus P will move toward left by $2x$.

Alternatively we can start from e. As we can see that from e to P there is only pulley Y, which slacks the string by $2y$ and point e is pulled toward left by a distance x, thus point P will move toward left by a distance $2y - x$, which is again $2x$. Thus the displacement of point P is twice of x which is 6 m.

Illustrative Example 1.56

Consider the situation shown in figure-1.73(a). Find the constraint relation for velocities of blocks A and B.

Solution

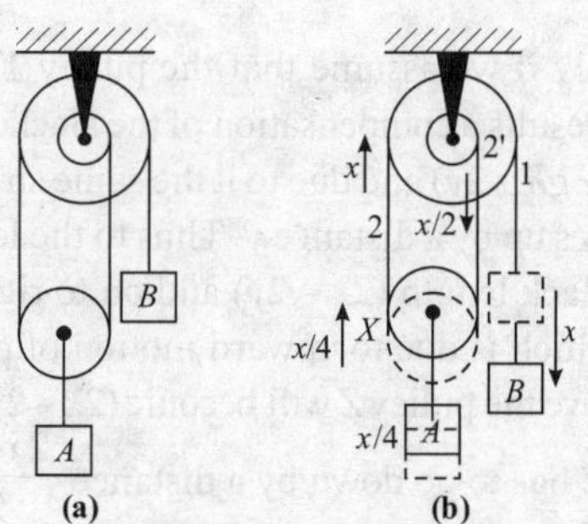

Figure 1.73

We start our analysis from block B as shown in figure-1.73(b). If it is assumed to go down by a distance x, string 2 will go up by the same distance x and due to this thread 2' will go down by $x/2$ as the ratio of the two radii is 1/2. Thus the reduction in length of the string 2 + 2' is $x/2$ as from side 2 it is going up by x and from side 2' it is coming down by $x/2$. So pulley X has to go up by a distance $x/4$ to slack the string 2 + 2' by $x/2$ which is to be reduced. Thus block A along with the pulley X will go up by $x/4$ and the same constrained relation exists for velocities and acceleration of blocks A and B. Thus the velocity constrained relation between A and B is

$$v_A = \frac{v_B}{9}$$

Illustrative Example 1.57

Consider the situation shown in figure-1.74(a). A string connected to block B is passing through two movable pulleys X and Y and wound on the smaller disc of a step pulley. Another block A attached to the pulley X. Analyze the constrained motion of blocks A and B. (Step pulley radii ratio = 1:3)

Solution

The analysis of the situation is shown in figure-1.74(b). Here it is important to note that pulley Y is connected to one side of the step pulley thus displacement of this pulley must be accounted while determining the constrained relation of block A and B.

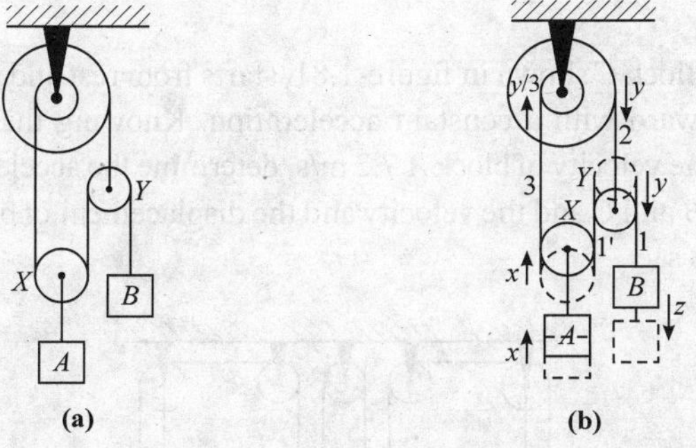

Figure 1.74

Let us assume that block A goes up by a distance x and pulley Y goes down by a distance y. If pulley Y comes down by y, thread 3 will go up by a distance $y/3$ (as $r_1/r_2 = 1/3$). As pulley Y comes down by y, strings 1 and 1' will slack by y and as block A and pulley X goes up by x, string 3 will slack by $(x - y/3)$ and string 1' will slack by $(x + y)$. As string 3, 1 and 1' are the parts of same string, thus total slack in this string is tightened by vertical down displacement of the block B. Thus displacement of block B downward is (say z)

$$z = x - \frac{y}{3} + x + y + y = 2x + \frac{5y}{3}$$

Thus if the velocities of block A, B and pulley Y are v_A, v_B and y_Y then we have

$$v_B = 2v_A + \frac{5}{3}v_Y$$

Several times such cases occurs when direct relation between velocity and acceleration of the blocks does not exist and we have to include the motion of pulleys.

Illustrative Example 1.58

If block B shown in figure-1.75(a) is going down with acceleration 5 m/s^2, find the acceleration of the block A. All pulleys and strings are ideal. Radii ratio for the two step pulleys are 1 : 3 : 5 and 1 : 2.

Solution

The analysis of the situation is shown in figure-1.75(b).

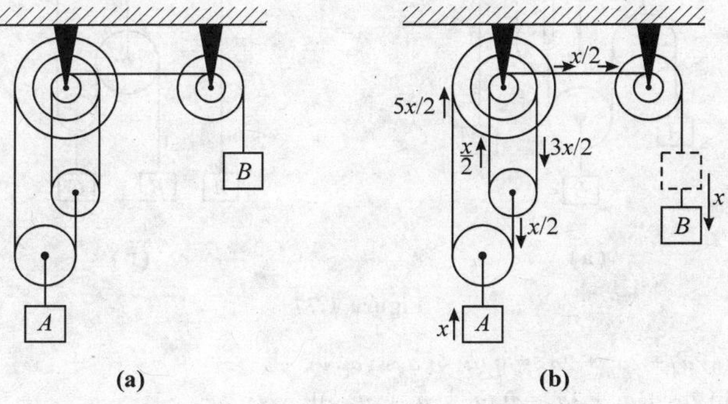

Figure 1.75

Here we start our analysis from block B. Let us assume that it goes down by a distance x, due to this string 2 will shift to the right by $x/2$ and hence thread 3 will go up by same $x/2$. The string 4 goes down by $3x/2$ and string 6 goes up by $5x/2$. Now the total slack in string 3 + 4 is $(3x/2 - x/2 = x)$, thus pulley X will go down by $x/2$ and hence string 5 also go down by $x/2$. Now the total reduction in length of string 5 + 6 is $(5x/2 - x/2 = 2x)$, thus pulley Y will go up by a distance x to provide the reduction $2x$ hence block A will also go up by x. Thus blocks A and B both are moving with same velocity and acceleration.

NOTE : Here students must be careful about the string length analysis that no string should remain slack after final displacement of all the objects (masses and pulleys).

Practice Exercise 1.11

(i) Figure-1.76 shows a pulley over which a string passes and connected to two masses A and B. Pulley moves up with a velocity v_P and mass B is also going up at a velocity v_B. Find the velocity of mass A if :

(a) $v_P = 5$ m/s and $v_B = 10$ m/s,

(b) $v_P = 5$ m/s and $v_B = -20$ m/s.

[(a) 0 m/s, (b) 30 m/s]

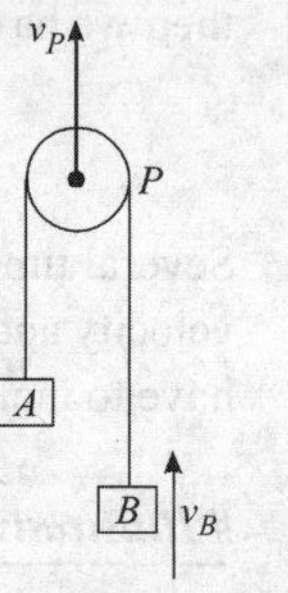

Figure 1.76

(ii) Find the relation in acceleration of the three masses shown in figure-1.77(a) and 1.77(b).

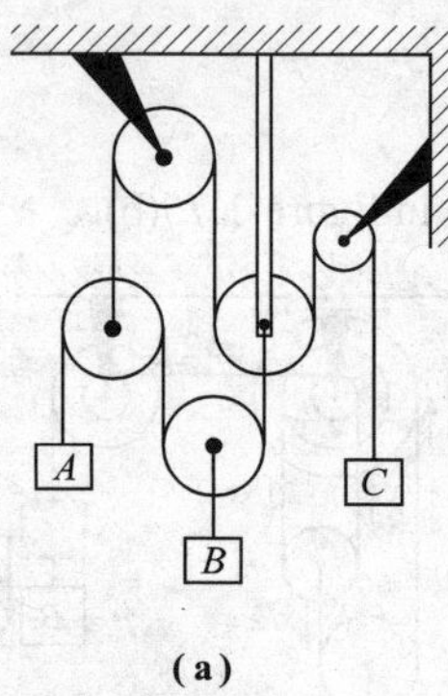

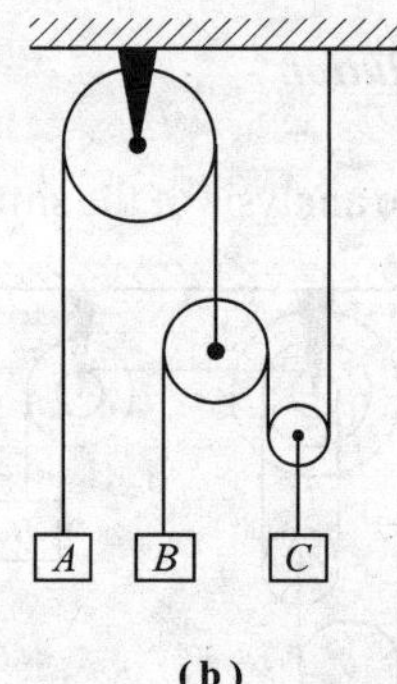

Figure 1.77

[(a) $a_A + 2a_B + 2a_C = 0$ ($a_A\downarrow$; $a_B\downarrow$; $a_C\downarrow$),
(b) $2a_A + a_B + 2a_C = 0$ ($a_A\downarrow$; $a_B\downarrow$; $a_C\downarrow$)]

(iii) Figure-1.78(a) and 1.78(b) shows a system of two masses A and B and a motor M. Find the relation in velocities of mass A and B, if the motor winding speed is v.

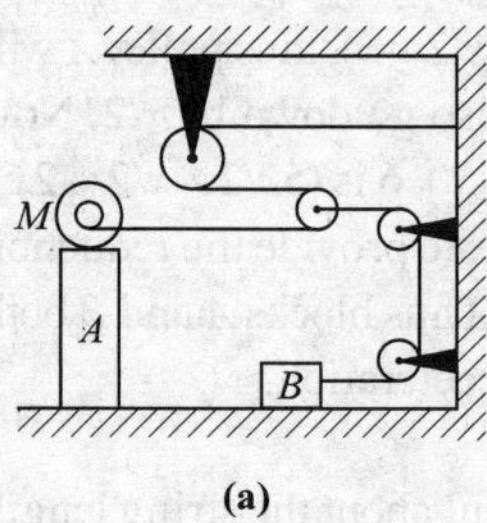

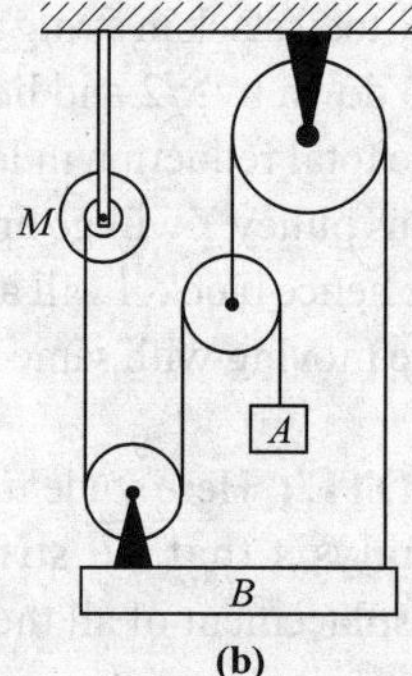

Figure 1.78

[(a) $2v_B + v_A = v$ ($v_A\rightarrow$; $v_A\rightarrow$) (b) $4v_B + v_A = v$ ($v_B\uparrow$; $v_A\uparrow$)]

(iv) Find the Relation among velocities of the blocks shown in figure-1.79(a) and 1.79(b), moving under the given constraints.

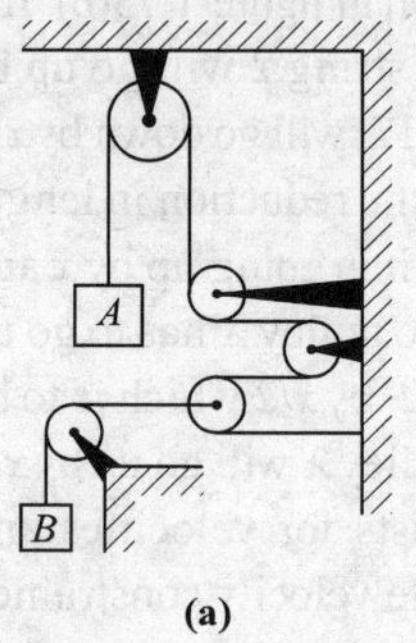

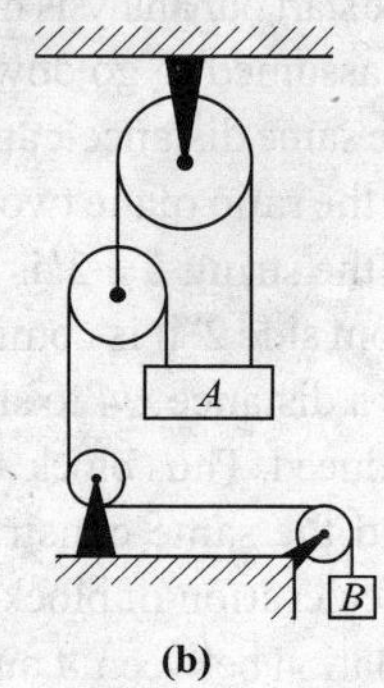

Figure 1.79

[(a) $2v_B = v_A$ ($v_B\uparrow$; $v_A\downarrow$) (b) $3v_A = v_B$ ($v_A\uparrow$; $v_B\downarrow$)]

(v) Block B shown in figure-1.80, moves downward with a constant velocity of 20 cm/s. At $t = 0$, block A is moving upward with a constant acceleration, and its velocity is 3 cm/s. If at $t = 3$ s blocks C has moved 27 cm to the right, determine the velocity of block C at $t = 0$ and the acceleration of A and C.

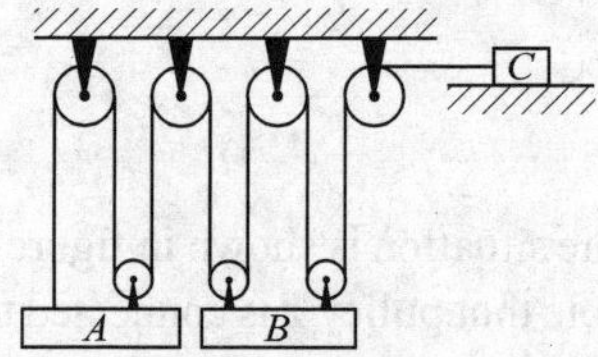

Figure 1.80

[$a_A = 20$ cm/s$^2\uparrow$; $a_C = 60$ cm/s$^2\rightarrow$; $v_C = 71$ cm/sec $\leftarrow$]

(vi) Block C shown in figure-1.81, starts from rest and moves downward with a constant acceleration. Knowing that after 12 s the velocity of block A 7.2 m/s, determine the acceleration of A, B and C and the velocity and the displacement of block B after 8 s.

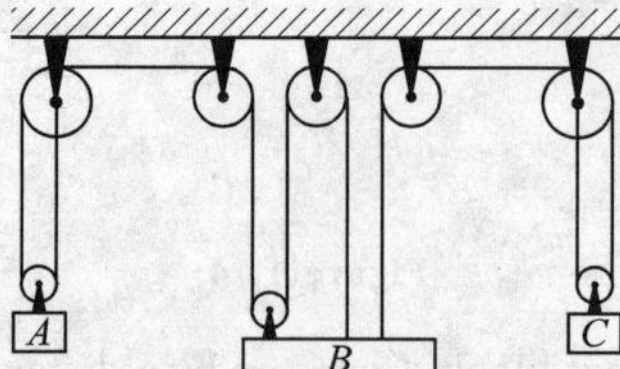

Figure 1.81

[$a_C = 2$ m/s$^2\downarrow$; $a_B = 4$ m/s$^2\uparrow$; $a_A = 6$ m/s$^2\downarrow$; $v_B = 32$ m/s $\uparrow$; $s_B = 128$ m$\uparrow$]

(vii) The system shown in figure-1.82 starts from rest, and each block moves with a constant acceleration. If the relative acceleration of block C with respect to block B is 6 m/s^2 upward and the relative acceleration of block D with respect to block A is 11 m/s^2 downward, determine the velocity of block C after 3 s from starts.

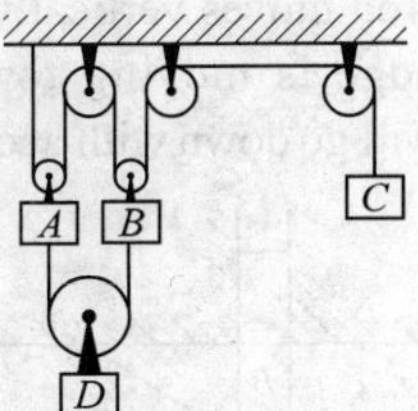

Figure 1.82

[57 m/s ↓]

1.14.3 Wedge Constraints

Till now we've discussed the motion of blocks connected by strings governed by pulleys connected in several ways possible. Here we will discuss the relation between the motion of two or more bodies which are in contact and responsible for motion of bodies.

First we consider a very simple case shown in figure-1.83(a). Here a triangular block of mass M is free to move on ground and m is free to move on inclined surface of M. Here M is constrained to move only along horizontal ground and m is also constrained to move only along the inclined surface of M relative to it. Here if M is going toward left with speed v_1 (say), and if on its inclined surface m is going down with speed v_2, then we can state that the net speed of M is v_1 but m is also moving to the left along with M, thus its net speed is given by vector sum of the two v_1 and v_2 as shown in figure-1.83(b).

$$v_m = \sqrt{v_1^2 + v_2^2 + 2v_1v_2\cos\theta}$$

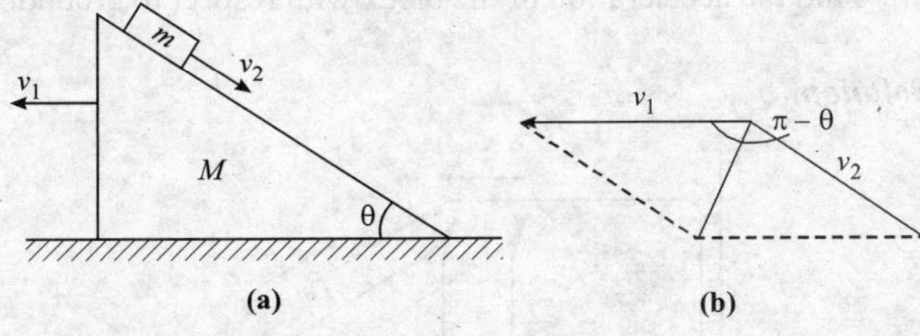

Figure 1.83

Same can also be evaluated by using the velocity components in horizontal and vertical directions of small mass m. Here it is going along the incline with a velocity v_2 relative to M and it is also moving with M toward left with velocity v_1, thus we have

Horizontal velocity of m relative to ground is

$$v_x = v_2\cos\theta - v_1$$

Vertical velocity of m relative to ground is

$$v_y = v_2\sin\theta$$

Net velocity of m is

$$v_m = \sqrt{v_1^2 + v_y^2} = \sqrt{v_1^2 + v_y^2 + 2v_1v_2\cos\theta}$$

Now consider the situation shown in figure-1.84. Here block A and B are constrained to move on their contact surface as well as horizontal ground and vertical wall. Here as B goes down, A will move to the left. If B goes down by a distance x, A will move toward left by a distance $x\cot\theta$. Thus if velocity and acceleration of B are v and a downward, velocity and acceleration A will be $v\cos\theta$ and $a\cot\theta$ toward left.

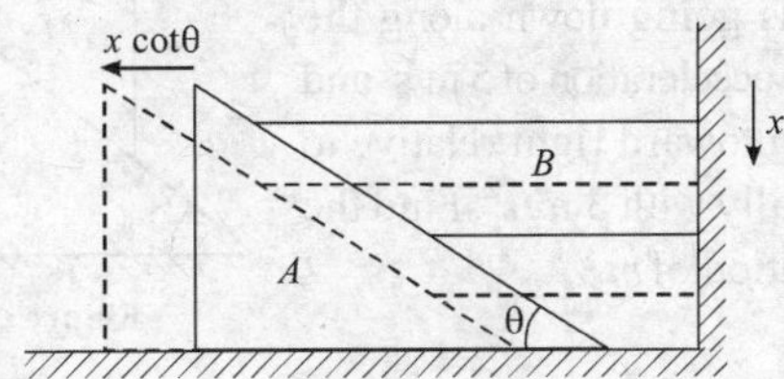

Figure 1.84

Now we modify the situation slightly as shown in figure-1.85(a). Here block C will remain at rest and block A will move toward left when system is released. Due to motion of A toward left B will go down as well as move to the left as it is constrained to move on the incline surface of C. If this is moving down by a distance x, then it must move toward left by $x\cot\theta_1$. Now if we talk about motion of A, it must move to left by $x\cot\theta_1 + x\cot\theta_2$ as shown in figure-1.85(b).

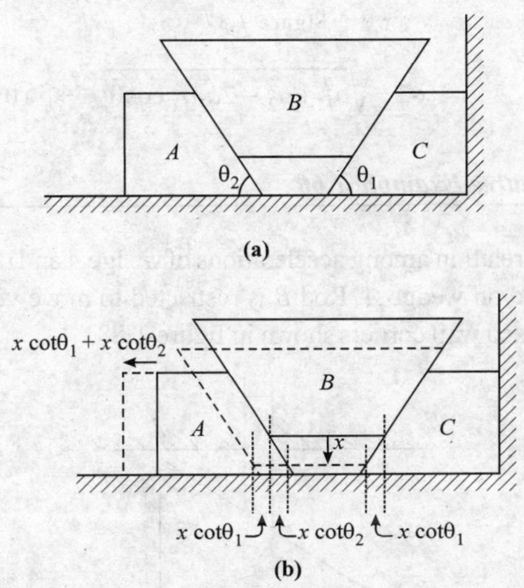

Figure 1.85

Block A moves to left by $x\cot\theta_1$ along with block B as it is moving left by $x\cot\theta_1$ and as we have discussed in previous example if B is only moving down (not moving left) the displacement of A would be $x\cot\theta_2$ and as it is having both motions, block A will go left by $x\cot\theta_1$ (due to left motion of B) plus $x\cot\theta_2$ (due to vertical down motion of B).

Now we consider few examples on the same concept of wedge constraints. In several problems we will deal the constrained relation of motion of blocks which are constrained to move along some wedge planes as well as connected to some pulleys. In such problems we must be very careful about the constrained relation of motion of blocks and wedges as these relations are developed by using both concepts of wedge constraints and pulley constraints.

Illustrative Example 1.59

In the situation shown in figure-1.86, if mass M is going down along the incline at an acceleration of 5 m/s^2 and m is moving toward right relative to M horizontally with 3 m/s^2. Find the net acceleration of m.

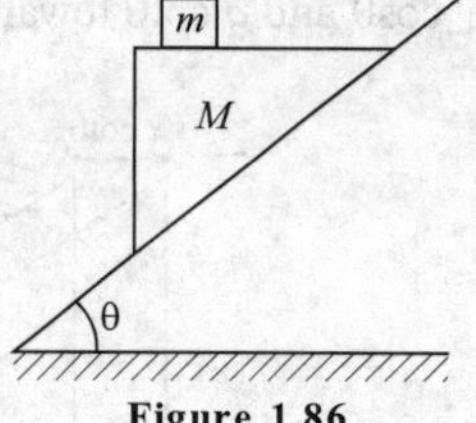

Figure 1.86

Solution

As m is also moving down along the incline with M, we can find the net acceleration of m using vector addition of the two acceleration in m, shown in figure-1.87. Thus we have

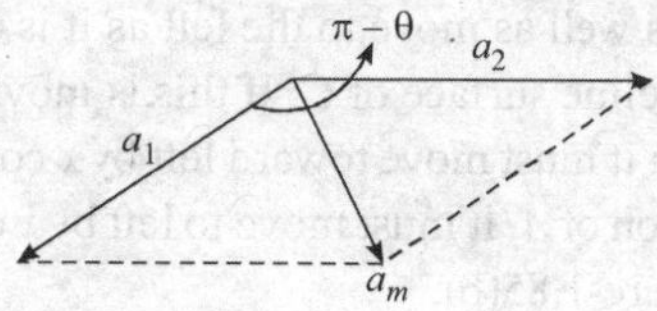

Figure 1.87

$$a_m = \sqrt{a_1^2 + a_2^2 - 2a_1a_2 \cos\theta} = 4.35 \text{ m/s}^2$$

Illustrative Example 1.60

Find the relation among accelerations of wedge A and the rod B supported on wedge A. Rod B is restricted to move vertically by two fixed wall corners shown in figure-1.88.

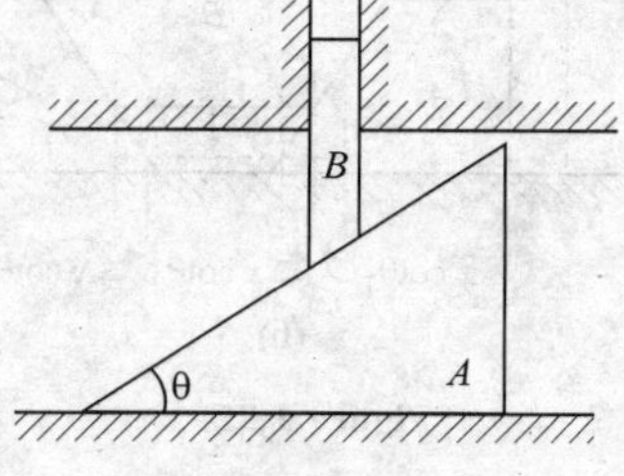

Figure 1.88

Solution

Here we can observe that the rod is restricted to move only in vertical direction and wedge can move along horizontal plane only. Here if wedge moves toward right by a distance x, figure-1.89 shows that the rod moves vertically down by a distance $x \tan\theta$. Thus if wedge is moving toward right with an acceleration a_1, rod will go down with acceleration a_2, given as

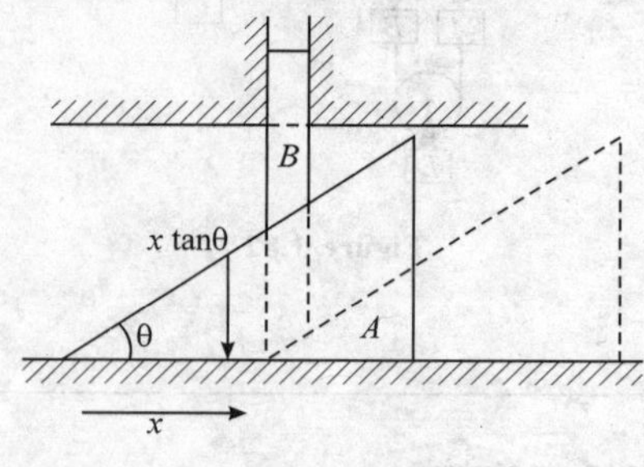

Figure 1.89

$$a_2 = a_1 \tan\theta$$

Illustrative Example 1.61

Figure-1.90 shown a block A constrained to slide along the incline plane of the wedge B shown. Block A is attached with a string which passes through three ideal pulleys and connected to the wedge B. If wedge is pulled toward right with an acceleration a_1.

(a) Find the acceleration of the block with respect to wedge.

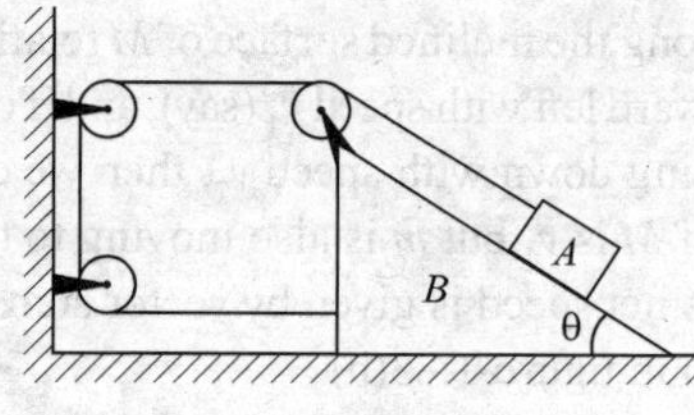

Figure 1.90

(b) Find the acceleration of the block with respect to ground.

Solution

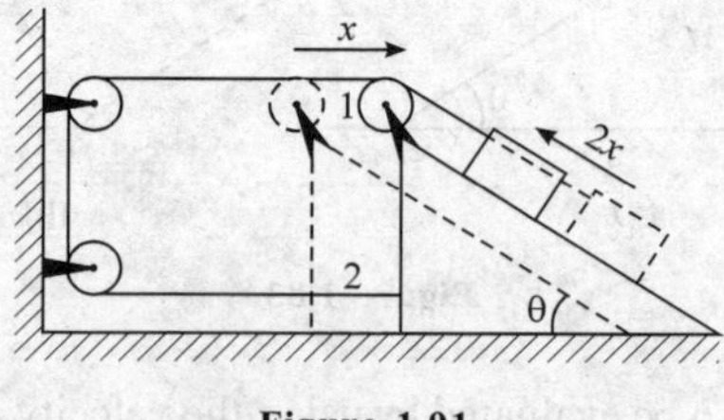

Figure 1.91

The analysis of the situation is shown in figure-1.91. If the wedge is pulled toward right by a distance x, we can see that the string portions 1 and 2 are increased toward left of it which is of length $2x$. By the same length the block A will move up the inclined plane relative to the wedge, thus if the acceleration of the wedge toward right is a_1, the acceleration of the block A relative to wedge will be $2a_1$. Now the acceleration of block A relative to ground can be obtained by vector sum of its acceleration and that of wedge, which is given as

$$a_A = [a_1^2 + 4a_1^2 - 4a_1^2 \cos\theta]^{1/2}$$

or $$= a_1\sqrt{5 - 4\cos\theta}$$

Web Reference at www.physicsgalaxy.com

Age Group - High School Physics | Age 17-19 Years
Section - MECHANICS
Topic - Constrained Motion
Module Numbers - 10, 11, 12 and 13

Practice Exercise 1.12

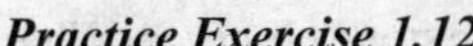

(i) Find the relation among the acceleration of blocks A and B constrained to move along the inclined surfaces of the fixed wedge shown in figure-1.92.

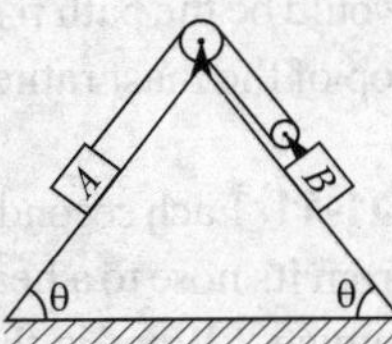

Figure 1.92

$[a_A = 2\,a_B]$

(ii) If the wedge A shown in figure-1.93, is moving toward left with acceleration 3 m/s², find the net acceleration of block B which is constrained to slide along the wedge surface. ($\theta = 30°$)

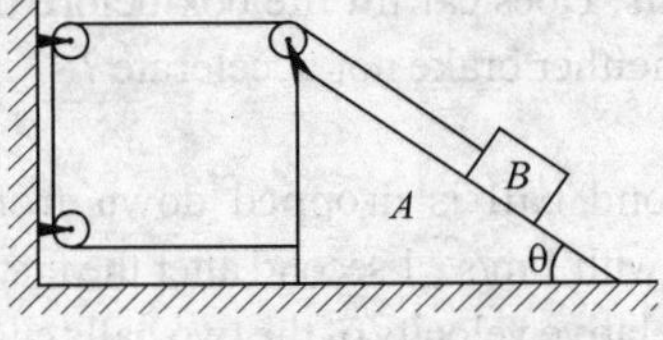

Figure 1.93

$[\left(3\sqrt{5 - 2\sqrt{3}}\right) \text{m/s}^2]$

(iii) Find the speed of the block B when the wedges A and C are moving toward each other with speed v and the strings connected to block make and angle θ with the vertical, as shown in figure-1.94.

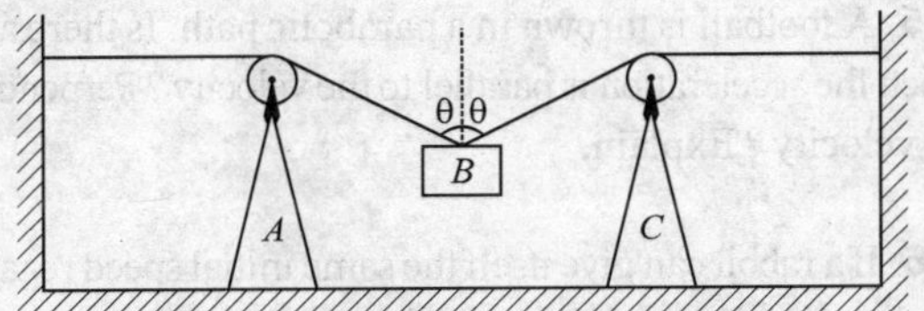

Figure 1.94

$[v_B = \dfrac{v(1 - \sin\theta)}{\cos\theta}]$

(iv) Find the acceleration of the block B as shown in figure-1.95(a) and (b) relative to the block A and relative to ground if the block A is moving toward left with acceleration a.

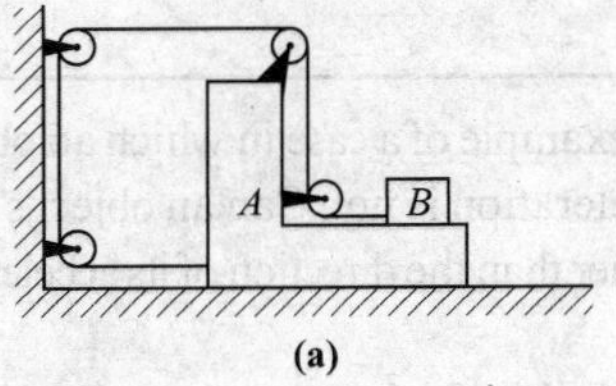

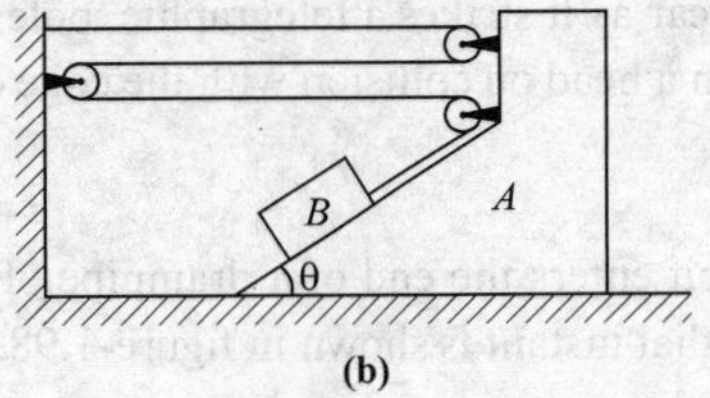

Figure 1.95

[(a) $a_{BA} = 2a$, $a_{BG} = a$, (b) $a_{BA} = 3a$, $a_{BG} = a\sqrt{10 + 6\cos\theta}$]

(v) If the point P on string shown in figure-1.96 is pulled down with a velocity v, find the velocity of the block A connected to another string passing over a step pulley with radii ratio 1 : 2.

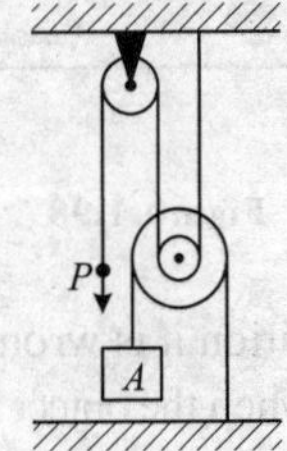

Figure 1.96

$[v]$

(vi) Find the constrained relation among the acceleration of blocks A, B and C for the situation shown in figure-1.97. Ratio of radii of step pulley is given as 1 : 2.

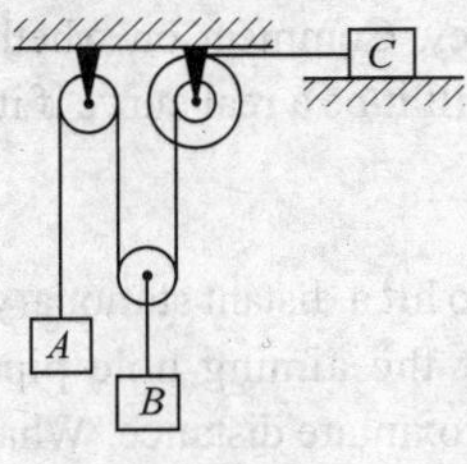

Figure 1.97

$[2a_A + a_C = 4a_B\ (a_A\uparrow;\ a_C\leftarrow;\ a_B\downarrow)]$

Advance Illustrations Videos at www.physicsgalaxy.com

Age Group - Advance Illustrations
Section - Mechanics
Topic - Kinematics
Illustrations - 64 In-depth Illustrations Videos

* * * * *

Discussion Question

Q1-1 Give an example of a case in which an object's velocity is zero but its acceleration is not. Can an object's velocity ever be in a direction other than the direction of its acceleration ? Explain.

Q1-2 Sketch graphs of velocity and acceleration as a function of time for a car as it strikes a telegraphic pole. Repeat for a billiard ball in a head on collision with the edge of the billiard table.

Q1-3 A rabbit enters the end of a drainpipe of length L. Its motion from that instant is shown in figure-1.98. Describe the motion in words.

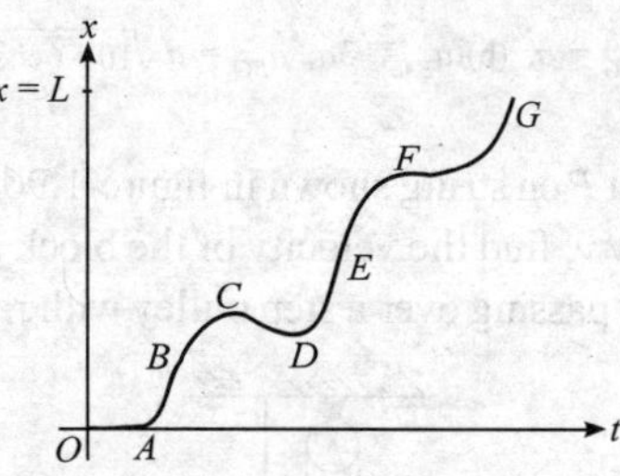

Figure 1.98

Q1-4 Under what condition it is wrong to say that an object's acceleration is negative when the object is thrown upward. Does the sign of the acceleration depend at all on the direction. Can an object's acceleration be positive when the object is slowing down ?

Q1-5 The distance-time curve for a hypothetical journey has the shape of an equilateral triangle with one side along the time axis. Discuss the velocity and acceleration necessary to bring about such a journey. Comment on whether or not this is a realistic journey. Will it be a real curve if it is a displacement-time curve.

Q1-6 If you want to hit a distant stationary object with a rifle, you have to adjust the aiming hole pipe for the mark of corresponding approximate distance. What is the need for it. Why don't you use a single adjustment for firing objects at different distances.

Q1-7 A person standing on the edge of a cliff at some height above the ground below throws one ball straight up with initial speed u and then throws another ball straight down with the same initial speed. Which ball, if either, has the larger speed when it hits the ground ? Neglect air resistance.

Q1-8 An airplane on flood relief mission has to drop a sack of rice exactly in the centre of a circle on the ground while flying at a predetermined height and speed. What is so difficult about that ? Don't it just drop the sack when it is directly above the circle.

Q1-9 A car's speedometer is correctly calibrated for tires of a specific size. If larger diameter tires are substituted, what will be the effect on the speedometer reading ?

Q1-10 If an observer is in a boat accelerating with a constant acceleration, observes a stone dropped from rest from the top of a mast. What would be the path of the stone observed. What would be the path if stone had been thrown downward from the top of the mast rather than dropped from rest.

Q1-11 Each second a rabbit moves half the remaining distance from its nose to a head of lettuce. Does the rabbit ever get to the lettuce ? What is the limiting value of the rabbit's velocity ? Draw graphs showing the rabbit's position and average velocity versus time.

Q1-12 Assume that a car is moving behind a loaded truck. Both moving with the same uniform velocity. A box from the top of the truck falls. Does car hit the box before the box hits the road, if driver neither brake nor accelerate ?

Q1-13 A second ball is dropped down from an elevator accelerating up with 1 m/s^2, 1 second after the first ball is dropped. How does the relative velocity of the two balls change with time. How the ratio v_1/v_2 change with time.

Q1-14 A ball is thrown from above the athlete's shoulder level. To get a maximum range on the ground, it should be thrown at an angle less than 45°. Explain why ? Give an example in which the required angle for getting the maximum rang is more than 45°.

Q1-15 A football is thrown in a parabolic path. Is there a point at which the acceleration is parallel to the velocity ? Perpendicular to the velocity ? Explain.

Q1-16 If a rabbit can give itself the same initial speed regardless of the direction in which it jumps, how is the maximum vertical height to which it can jump related to its maximum horizontal range ?

Q1-17 Look at the situation shown in figure-1.99. A fireman fires his shot aiming to a monkey, who falls at the time of shot. So the shot has passed the highest point of its trajectory and is descending when it hits the monkey, which is still in air. At the instant, the shot was at the highest point of its trajectory, was the monkey's height above the ground the same, lower, or higher than that of the shot. Explain your answer.

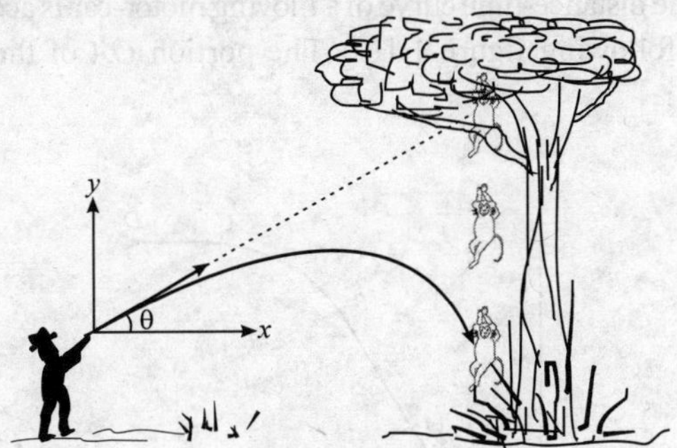

Figure 1.99

Q1-18 If you are on the west bank of a river that is flowing north with a speed 4 m/s. Your swimming speed relative to the water is 5 m/s, and the river is 60 m wide. What is your path relative to earth that allows you to cross the river in the shortest time ? Explain your reasoning.

* * * * *

Conceptual MCQs Single Option Correct

1-1 For a particle moving along a straight line, the displacement x depends on time t as $x = At^3 + Bt^2 + Ct + D$. The ratio of its initial velocity to its initial acceleration depends on :

(A) A & C (B) B & C
(C) C (D) C and D

1-2 For the displacement time graph shown in figure-1.100, the ratio of the speeds during the first two seconds and the next four seconds is :

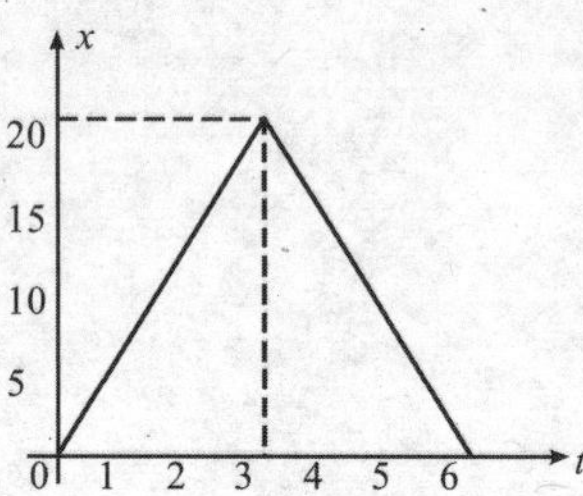

Figure 1.100

(A) 1 : 1 (B) 1 : 2
(C) 2 : 1 (D) 3 : 2

1-3 From the top of a tower, a stone A is thrown upwards and a stone B is thrown downwards with the same speed. The velocity of stone A, on colliding with the ground is :

(A) Greater than the velocity of B
(B) Less than the velocity of B
(C) The velocities of stones A and B will be same
(D) Both the stones will fall on the earth at the same time

1-4 Two cars C_1 and C_2 are moving on parallel roads in the same direction with velocity v. The relative velocity of C_1 w.r.t. C_2 is :

(A) Directed towards C_2 (B) Directed towards C_1
(C) Zero (D) $2v$

1-5 A ball dropped from a height reaches the same height after elastic impact with a glass floor. If the event is continued, the velocity-time graph is shown by the adjoining figure :

(A) 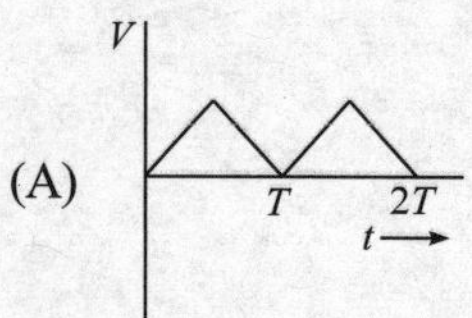

(B) 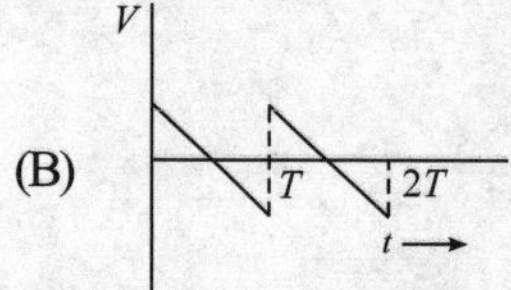

(C) 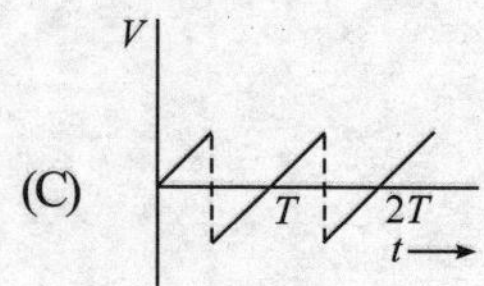

(D) 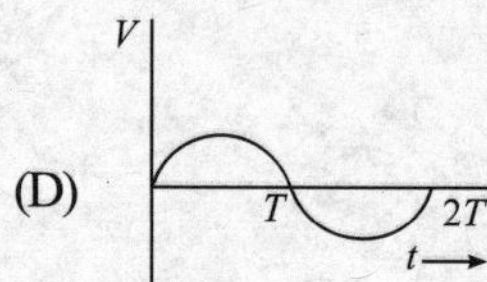

1-6 The distance-time curve of a moving motor-car is according to the following figure-1.101. The portion OA of the curve shows :

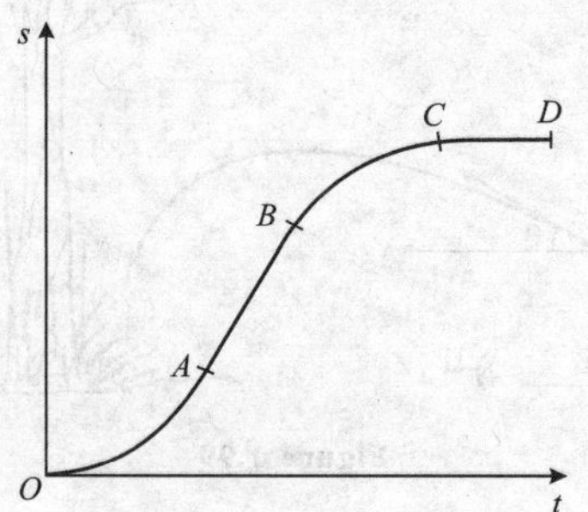

Figure 1.101

(A) Accelerated motion (B) Retarted motion
(C) Uniform motion (D) State of rest

1-7 In the above figure, the portion AB of the curve shows :

(A) Accelerated motion (B) Retarted motion
(C) Uniform motion (D) State of rest

1-8 In the above figure, portion BC of the curve shows :

(A) Accelerated motion (B) Retarted motion
(C) Uniform motion (D) State of rest

1-9 Two particles start from rest simultaneously and are equally accelerated throughout the motion, the relative velocity of one with respect to other is :

(A) Zero
(B) Non zero and directed parallel to acceleration
(B) Non zero and directed opposite to acceleration
(D) Directed perpendicular to the acceleration

1-10 The following graph shows the speed of a body which is :

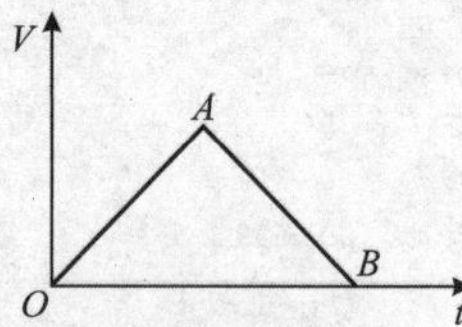

Figure 1.102

(A) Projected upwards with some velocity in vertical plane
(B) Having only constant accelerated motion
(C) Having only the constant retardation
(D) A perfectly elastic ball falling from a height on a friction less and hard floor

1-11 If a particle is moving along positive x-axis and its acceleration and x-coordinate graph is shown-1.103. Then the slope of v-x graph between $x = 0$ to $x = 10$ m

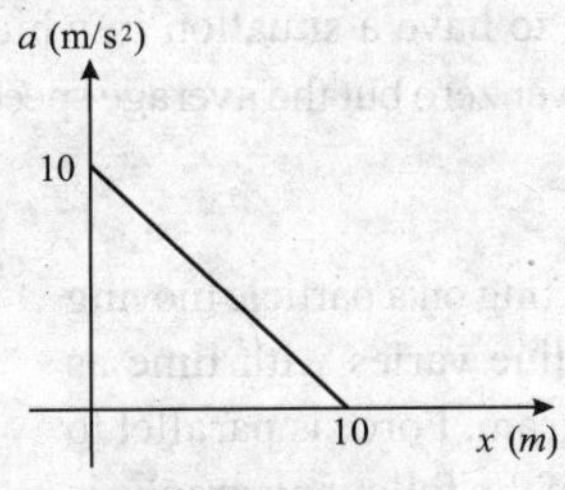

Figure 1.103

(A) increases
(B) decreases
(C) constant
(D) first increases then decreases

1-12 The distance travelled by the moving body is :
(A) The area between the speed time graph and time axis.
(B) The area between the speed time graph and speed axis
(C) The area between the distance time graph and time axis
(D) The area between the distance time graph and distance axis

1-13 The diagram shows the velocity-time graph for a particle moving in a straight line. The sum of the two shaded areas represents :
(A) The increase in displacement of the particle
(B) The average velocity of the particle
(C) The average acceleration of the particle
(D) The distance moved by the particle

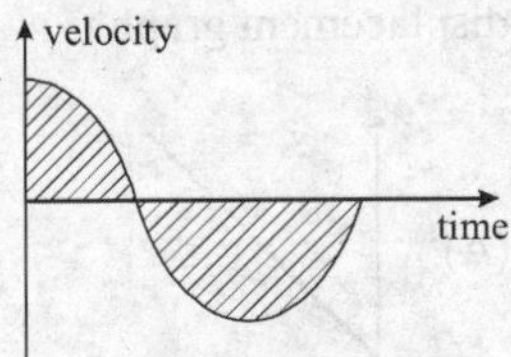

Figure 1.104

1-14 Forces proportional to AB, BC & $2\,CA$ act along the sides of triangle ABC in order, their resultant represented in magnitude and direction as :
(A) CA (B) AC
(C) BC (D) CB

1-15 A particle moves as shown in the following figure-1.105 :

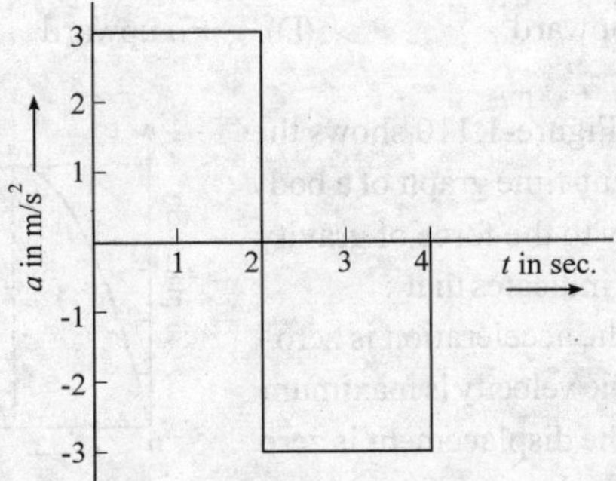

Figure 1.105

From the above curve the correct velocity-time graph for the interval of 4 seconds will be :

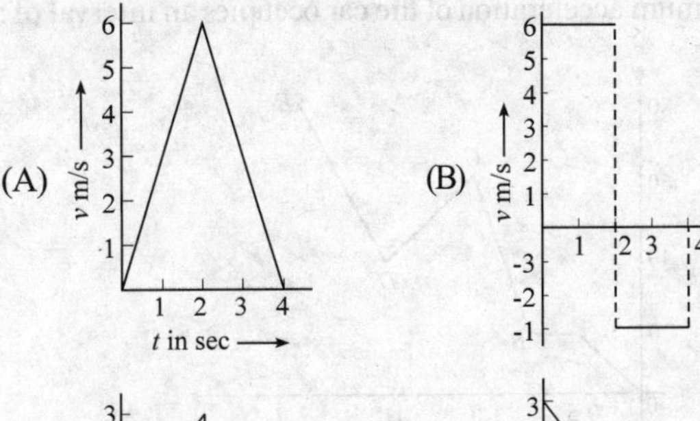

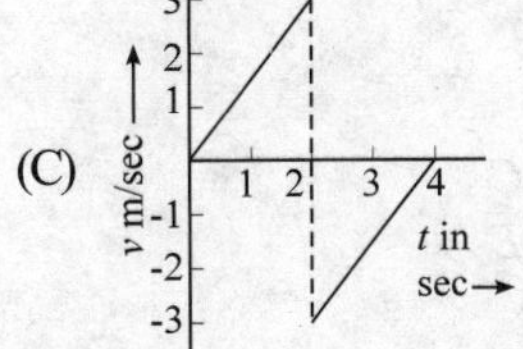

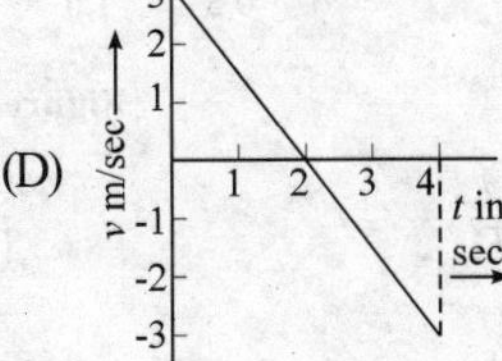

1-16 The following figure-1.106 shows the velocity-time graph of a body. According to this, at the point B :
(A) The force is zero
(B) The force is in the direction of the motion
(C) The force is in opposite direction of the motion
(D) It is only the gravitational force

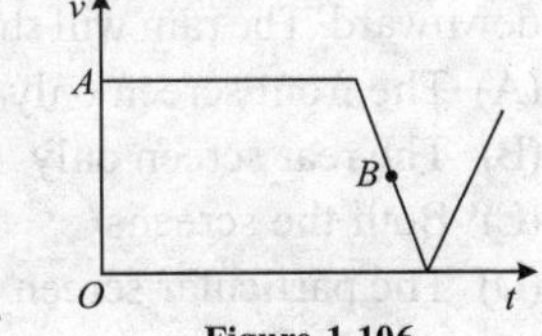

Figure 1.106

1-17 A bullet is fired in a horizontal direction from a tower while a stone is simultaneously dropped from the same point then :
(A) The bullet and the stone will reach the ground simultaneously
(B) The stone will reach earlier
(C) The bullet will reach earlier
(D) None of these

1-18 Which graph in the following figure best represents the variation of velocity with time of a ball which bounces vertically on a hard surface, from the moment when it rebounds from the surface ?

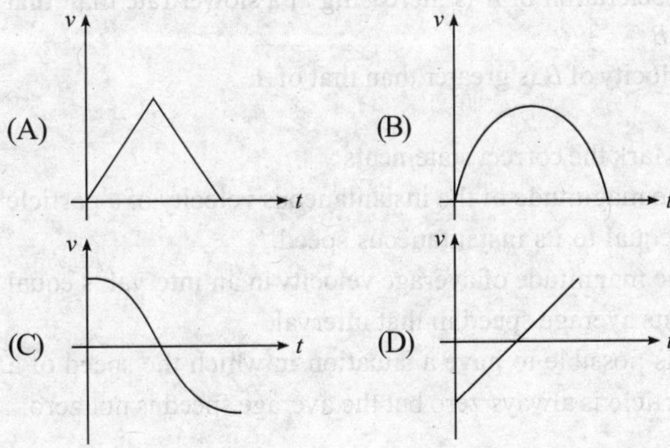

1-19 The variation in the speed of a car during its two hour journey is shown in the graph of the figure-1.107. The magnitude of the maximum acceleration of the car occupies an interval of :

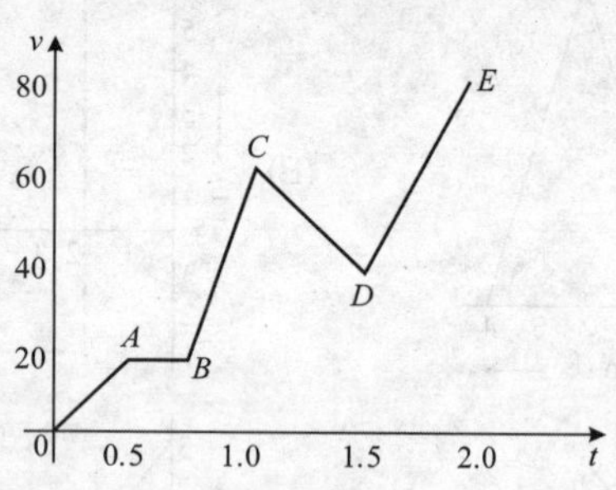

Figure 1.107

(A) OA (B) BC
(C) CD (D) DE

1-20 A car which has front and rear glass screens almost vertical is moving on a road when rain drops are falling vertically downward. The rain will strike :
(A) The front screen only
(B) The rear screen only
(C) Both the screens
(D) The particular screen depending upon the velocity

1-21 A river is flowing from north to south at a speed of 0.3 kph. A man on the west bank of the river, capable of swimming 1 kph in still water, wants to swim across the river in the shortest time. He should in a direction :
(A) Due east (B) 30° north of east
(C) 30° west of north (D) 60° north of east

1-22 A time-velocity graph of two vehicles A and B starting from rest at the same time is given in the figure-1.108. The statement that can be deduced correctly from the graph is :

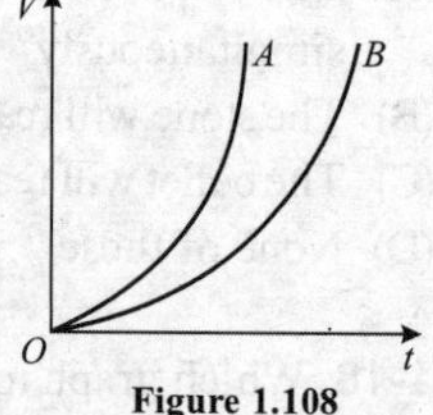

Figure 1.108

(A) Acceleration of A is greater than that of B
(B) Acceleration of B is greater than that of A
(C) Acceleration of A is increasing at a slower rate than that of B
(D) Velocity of B is greater than that of A.

1-23 Mark the correct statements :
(A) The magnitude of the instantaneous velocity of a particle is equal to its instantaneous speed.
(B) The magnitude of average velocity in an interval is equal to its average speed in that interval.
(C) It is possible to have a situation in which the speed of a particle is always zero but the average speed is not zero.
(D) It is possible to have a situation in which the speed of a particle is never zero but the average speed in an interval is zero.

1-24 The force acting on a particle moving along a straight line varies with time as shown in the diagram. Force is parallel to velocity. Which of the following graphs is best representative of its speed and time graphs :

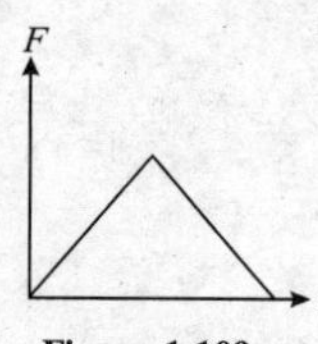

Figure 1.109

(A)
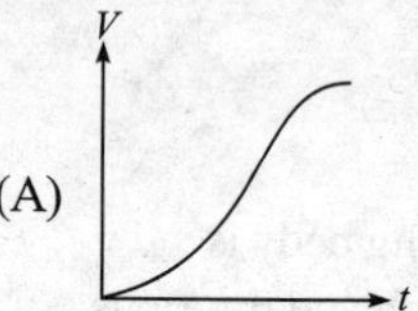

(B)
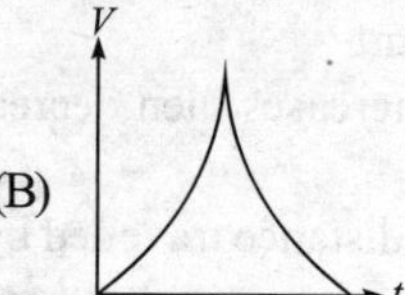

(C)
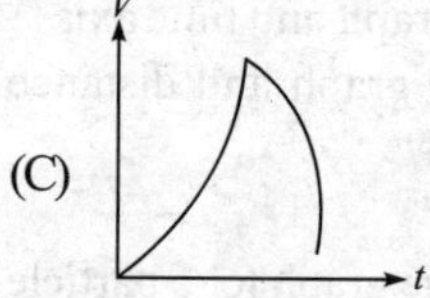

(D)
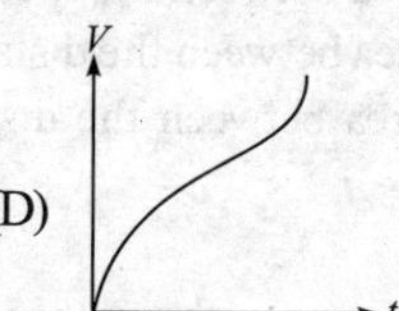

1-25 An object is dropped from rest. Its velocity versus displacement graph is :

(A)
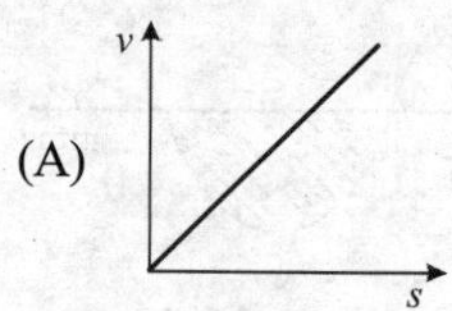

(B)
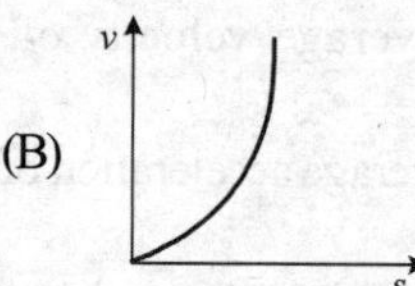

(C)
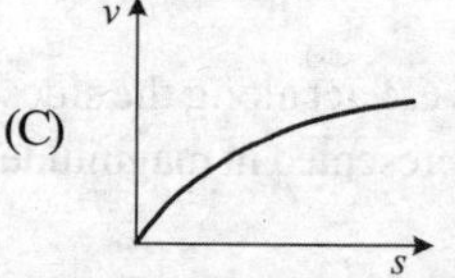

(D)
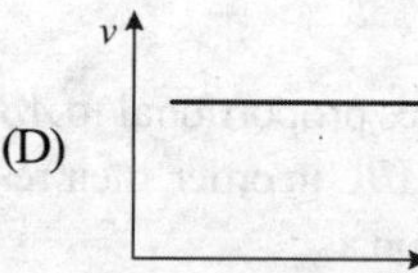

1-26 A stone is dropped from a balloon rising with acceleration a. The acceleration of the stone relative to the balloon is :
(A) g downward (B) $g + a$ downward
(C) $g - a$ upward (D) $g + a$ upward

1-27 The Figure-1.110 shows the displacement-time graph of a body subject only to the force of gravity. This graph indicates that :

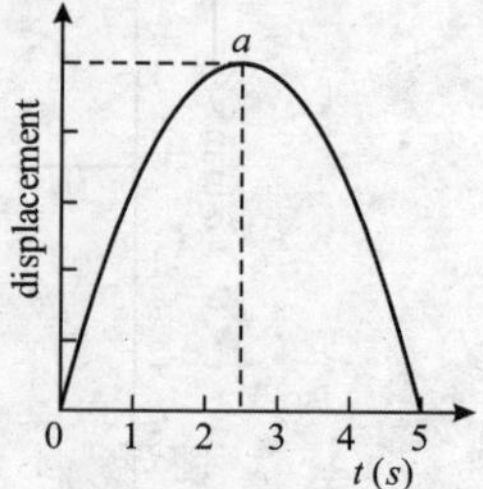

Figure 1.110

(A) At A, the acceleration is zero
(B) At A, the velocity is maximum
(C) At A, the displacement is zero
(D) The acceleration is constant for all times shown

1-28 Two particle are projected simultaneously in the same vertical plane from the same point, with different speeds u_1 and u_2, making angles θ_1 and θ_2 respectively with the horizontal, such that $u_1 \cos\theta_1 = u_2 \cos\theta_2$. The path followed by one, as seen by the other (as long as both are in flight) is :

(A) A horizontal straight line
(B) A vertical straight line
(C) A parabola
(D) A straight line making an angle $|\theta_1 - \theta_2|$ with the horizontal.

1-29 A ball is projected vertically up with an initial velocity. Which of the following graphs represents the KE of the ball?

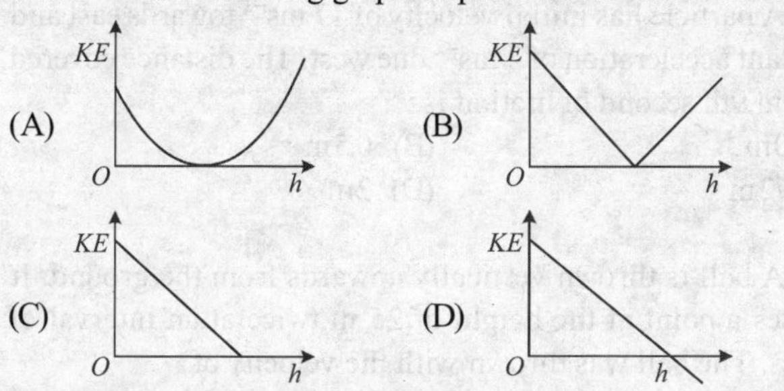

1-30 The velocity of a particle moving in straight line is given by the graph shown here. Then its acceleration is best represented by :

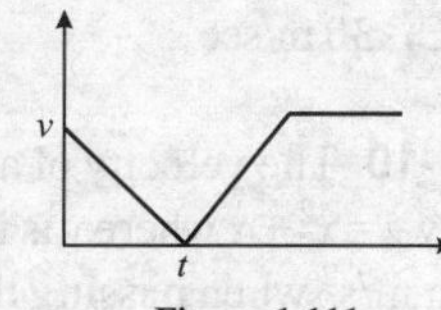
Figure 1.111

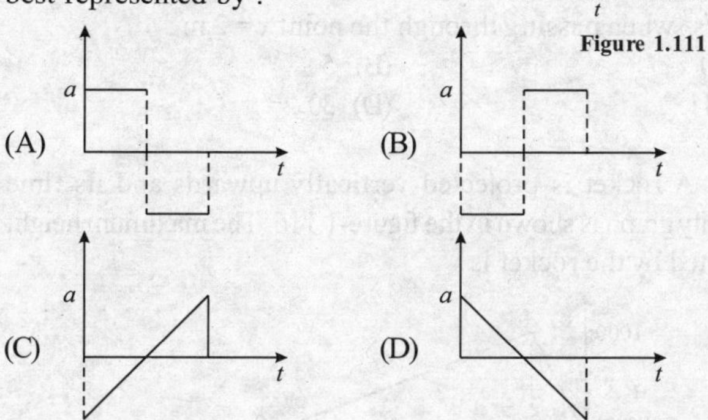

1-31 A ball is thrown up with a certain velocity at an angle θ to the horizontal. The kinetic energy KE of the ball varies with horizontal displacement x as :

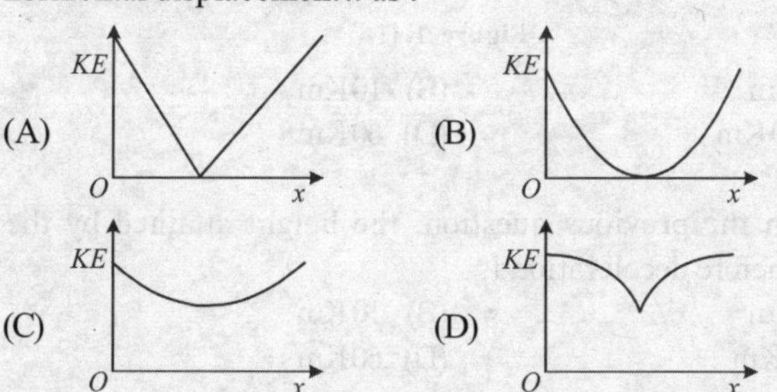

1-32 A small object is dropped from the top of a building and falls to the ground. As it falls, accelerating due to gravity, it passes window. It has speed v_1 at the top of the window and speed v_2 at the bottom of the window, at what point does it have a speed $\frac{v_1 + v_2}{2}$? Neglect the air resistance.

(A) It depends on the height of the window or its distance from the top of the building.
(B) Above the centre point of the window
(C) Below the centre point of the window
(D) At the centre point of the window

1-33 Acceleration vs time graph is shown in the figure for a particle moving along a straight line. The particle is initially at rest. Find the time instant(s) when the particle comes to rest?

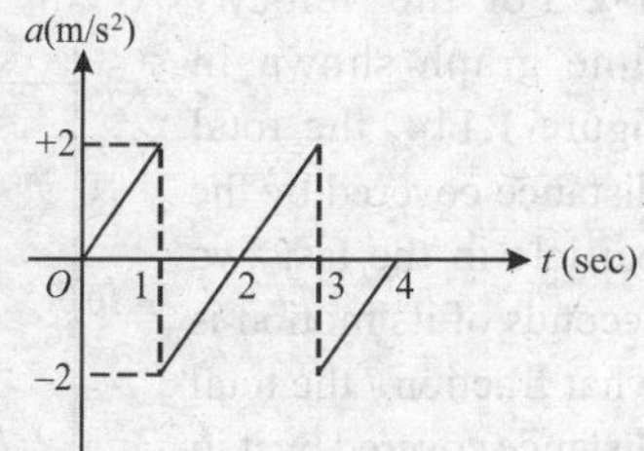
Figure 1.112

(A) $t = 0, 1, 2, 3, 4$
(B) $t = 0, 2, 4$
(C) $t = 1, 3$
(D) None of these

1-34 A toy car is moving on a closed track whose curved portions are semicircles of radius 1 m. The shown below graph describes the variation of speed of the car with distance moved by it (starting from point P). The time t required for the car to complete one lap is equal to $6K$ second. Find K : (Take $\pi ln\, 2 \approx 2$)

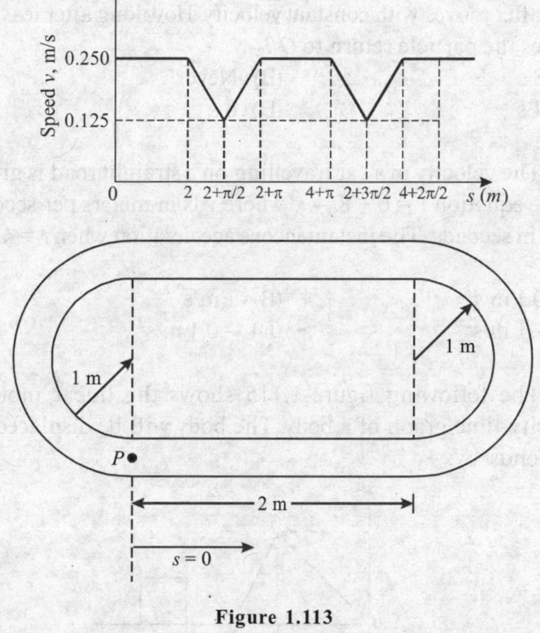
Figure 1.113

(A) 4
(B) 8
(C) 12
(D) 16

1-35 Which of the following sets of displacements might be capable of returning a car to its starting point ?

(A) 4, 6, 8 and 15 km
(B) 10, 30, 50 and 120 km
(C) 5, 10, 30 and 50 km
(D) 40, 50, 75 and 200 km

* * * * *

Numerical MCQs Single Options Correct

1-1 A particle starts moving in + ve x direction with initial velocity of 10 ms^{-1} with a uniform acceleration of magnitude 2 ms^{-2} but directed in – ve x direction. What is the distance traversed by the particle in 12 seconds :

(A) –24 m (B) 24 m
(C) 70 m (D) 74 m

1-2 For the velocity time graph shown in figure-1.114, the total distance covered by the particle in the last two seconds of its motion is what fraction f the total distance covered by it in all the seven seconds ?

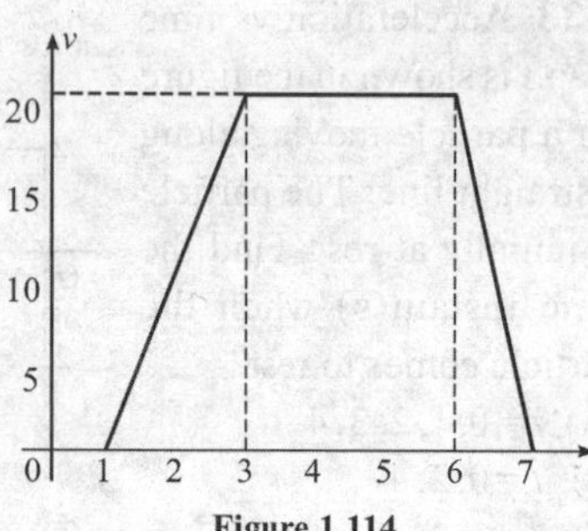

Figure 1.114

(A) 1/2
(B) 2/3
(C) 1/4
(D) 1/3

1-3 A particle moves in a straight line and passes through O, a fixed point on the line, with a velocity of 6 ms^{-1}. The particle moves with a constant retardation of 2 ms^{-2} for 4 seconds and thereafter moves with constant velocity. How long after leaving O does the particle return to O ?

(A) 8 s (B) Never
(C) 4 s (D) 6 s

1-4 The velocity of a car travelling on a straight road is given by the equation $v = 6 + 8t - t^2$ where v is in meters per second and t in seconds. The instantaneous acceleration when $t = 4.5$ s is :

(A) 0.1 m/s^2 (B) 1 m/s^2
(C) –1 m/s^2 (D) –0.1 m/s^2

1-5 The following figure-1.115 shows the linear motion velocity-time graph of a body. The body will be displaced in 5 seconds by:

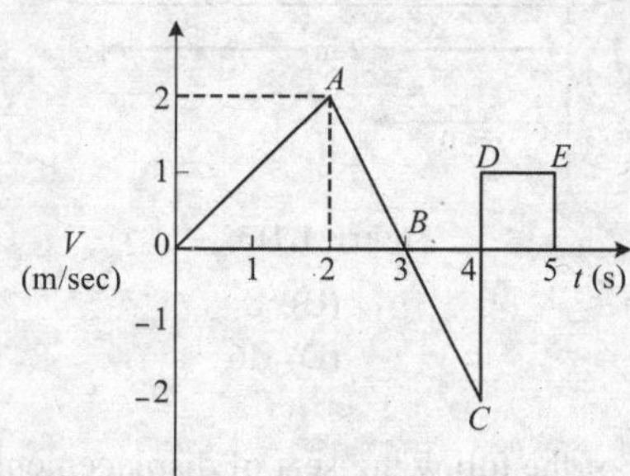

Figure 1.115

(A) 2m (B) 3m
(C) 4m (D) 5m

1-6 In the above question, the acceleration in the portion OA of the curve will be :

(A) Zero (B) 2 m/sec^2
(C) 1 m/sec^2 (D) 0.5 m/sec^2

1-7 In the above question, which portion of the curve will have zero acceleration :

(A) OA (B) AB
(B) CD (D) DE

1-8 A particle has initial velocity of 17 ms^{-1} towards east and constant acceleration of 2 ms^{-2} due west. The distance covered by it in 9th second of motion is :

(A) 0m (B) 0.5 m
(C) 72 m (D) 2m

1-9 A ball is thrown vertically upwards from the ground. It crosses a point at the height of 25 m twice at an interval of 4 secs. The ball was thrown with the velocity of

(A) 20 m/sec (B) 25 m/sec
(C) 30 m/sec (D) 35 m/sec

1-10 The velocity of a particle moving on the x-axis is given by $v = x^2 + x$ where v is in m/s and x is in m. Find its acceleration in m/s^2 when passing through the point $x = 2$ m :

(A) 0 (B) 5
(C) 11 (D) 30

1-11 A rocket is projected vertically upwards and its time velocity graph is shown in the figure-1.116. The maximum height attained by the rocket is :

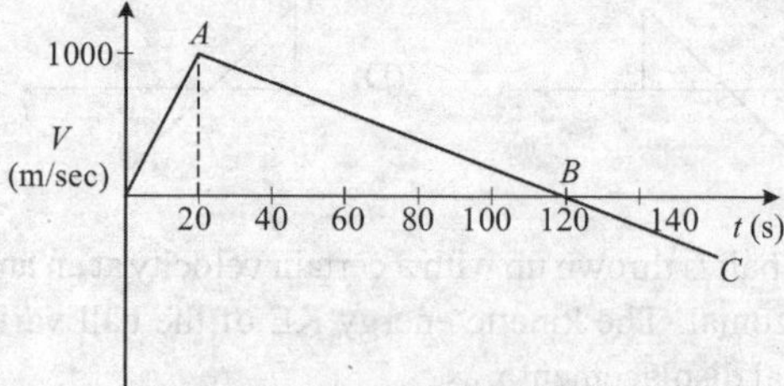

Figure 1.116

(A) 1 Km (B) 10 Km
(C) 100 Km (D) 60 Km

1-12 In the previous question, the height attained by the rocket before deceleration is :

(A) 1 Km (B) 10 Km
(C) 20 Km (D) 60 Km

1-13 In the previous question, the mean velocity of the rocket reaching the maximum height is :

(A) 100 m/sec (B) 50 m/sec
(C) 500 m/sec (D) 25/3 m/sec

1-14 In the above question, the acceleration of the rocket is :

(A) 50 m/sec^2 (B) 100 m/sec^2
(C) 500 m/sec^2 (D) 10 m/sec^2

1-15 The engine of a motor cycle can produce a maximum acceleration 5 m/s^2. It s brakes can produce a maximum retardation 10 m/s^2. What is the minimum time in which it can cover a distance of 1.5 km ?

(A) 5 s (B) 10 s
(C) 15 s (D) 30 s

1-16 Two balls are dropped from the same point after an interval of 1 s. If acceleration due to gravity is 10 m/s^2, what will be their separation 3 seconds after the release of first ball ?

(A) 5m (B) 10m
(C) 25m (D) 30m

1-17 The following figure-1.117 shows the time and applied force graph for a body. What will be the momentum gained by the body in 6 seconds :

(A) Zero
(B) 60 N-s
(C) 30 N-s
(D) 40 N-s

Figure 1.117

1-18 A person throws balls into the air one after the other at an interval of one second. The next ball is thrown when the velocity of the ball thrown earlier is zero. To what height the ball rise :

(A) 5m (B) 10m
(C) 20m (D) 40m

1-19 A body starts from rest and moves for n seconds with uniform acceleration a, its velocity after n seconds is v. The displacement of the body in last 3 seconds is :

(A) $\frac{v(6n-9)}{2n}$ (B) $\frac{2v(6n-9)}{n}$

(C) $\frac{2v(2n+1)}{n}$ (D) $\frac{2v(n-1)}{n}$

1-20 The displacement-time graph for two particle A and B are straight lines inclined at angles of 30º and 90º with the time axis. The ratio of the velocities V_A and V_B is :

(A) 1 : 2
(B) $1:\sqrt{3}$
(C) $\sqrt{3}:1$
(D) 1 : 3

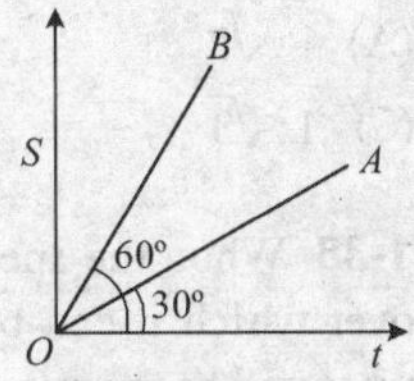

Figure 1.118

1-21 A particle has an initial velocity of 9 m/s due east and a constant acceleration of 2 m/s^2 due west. The distance covered by the particle in the fifth second of its motion is :

(A) 0 (B) 0.5m
(C) 2m (D) None of these

1-22 The velocity-time graph of a linear motion is shown below. The distance from the origin after 8 seconds is :

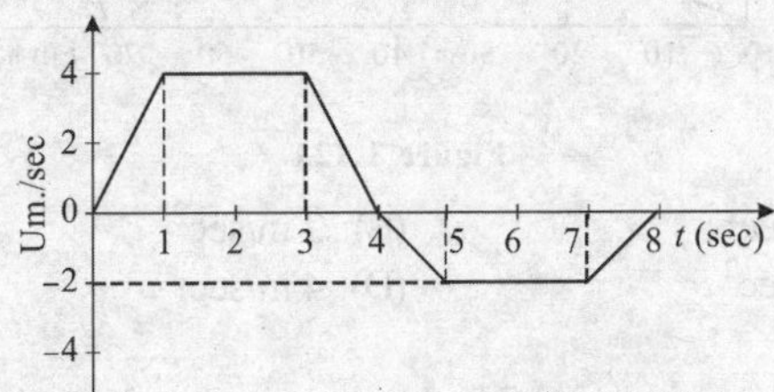

Figure 1.119

(A) 18m (B) 16m
(C) 8m (D) 6m

1-23 Water drops fall at regular intervals from a roof. At an instant when a drop is about to leave the roof, the separations between 3 successive drops below the roof are in the ratio :

(A) 1 : 2 : 3 (B) 1 : 4 : 9
(C) 1 : 3 : 5 (D) 1 : 5 : 13

1-24 A body is in straight line motion with an acceleration given by $a = 32 - 4v$. The initial conditions are at $t = 0$, $v = 4$. Find the velocity when $t = ln\,2$:

(A) 15/2 (B) 17/2
(C) 23/4 (D) 31/4

1-25 A particle is moving in a circle or radius r centred at O with constant speed v. The change in velocity in moving from P to Q ($\angle POQ = 40º$) is :

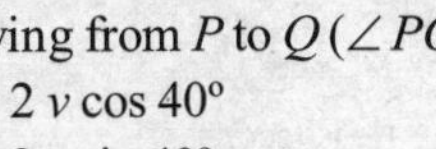

(A) $2v\cos 40º$
(B) $2v\sin 40º$
(C) $2v\cos 20º$
(D) $2v\sin 20º$

Figure 1.120

1-26 A car accelerates from rest at constant rate for the first 10 s and covers a distance x. It covers a distance y in the next 10 s at the same acceleration. Which of the following is true ?

(A) $x = 3y$ (B) $y = 3x$
(C) $x = y$ (D) $y = 2x$

1-27 A particle starts from rest and moves with acceleration a which varies with time t as $a = kt$ where k is a constant. The displacement s of the particle at time t is

(A) $\frac{1}{2}kt^2$ (B) $\frac{1}{2}at^2$

(C) $\frac{1}{6}at^2$ (D) None

1-28 The following shows the time-velocity graph for a moving object. The maximum acceleration will be :

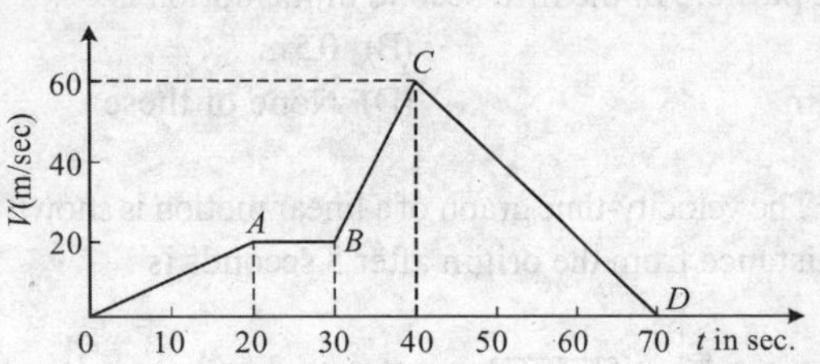

Figure 1.121

(A) 1 m/sec^2 (B) 2 m/sec^2
(C) 3 m/sec^2 (D) 4 m/sec^2

1-29 In the above question the magnitude of retardation will be :

(A) 1 m/sec^2 (B) 2 m/sec^2
(C) 3 m/sec^2 (D) 4 m/sec^2

1-30 A rocket is fired vertically upwards and moves with net acceleration of 10 m/s^2. After 1 min the fuel is exhausted. The time taken by it to reach the highest point after the fuel is exhausted will be :

(A) 10 sec (B) 20 sec
(C) 30 sec (D) 60 sec

1-31 In the following velocity-time graph of a body, the distance and displacement travelled by the body in 5 seconds in meters will be :

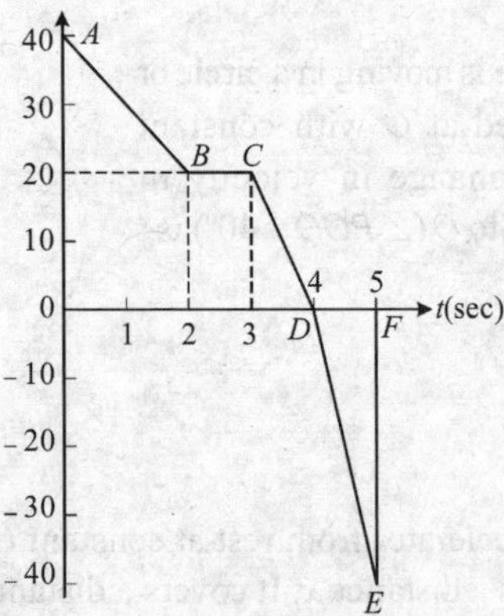

Figure 1.122

(A) 70, 110 (B) 110, 70
(C) 40, 70 (D) 90, 50

1-32 The displacement x of a body varies with time t as $x = -\frac{2}{3}t^2 + 16t + 2$. The body will come to rest after :

(A) 6 s (B) 12 s
(C) 18 s (D) 20 s

1-33 A particle moves in a straight line. The displacement x of the particle varies with time as $x = 2 - 5t + 6t^2$. Then the initial velocity of the particle is :

(A) 2 m/s (B) -5 m/s
(C) 6 m/s (D) -3 m/s

1-34 A parachutist drops freely from an aeroplane for 10 s before the parachute opens out. Then the descends with a net retardation of 2.5 m/s^2. If he bails out the plane at a height of 2495 m and g = 10 m/s^2, his velocity on reaching the ground will be:

(A) 2.5 m/s (B) 7.5 m/s
(C) 5 m/s (D) 10 m/s

1-35 The acceleration of a particle starting from rest, varies with time according to the relation $a = kt + c$. The velocity of the particle after time t will be :

(A) $kt^2 + ct$ (B) $\frac{1}{2}kt^2 + ct$
(C) $\frac{1}{2}(kt^2 + ct)$ (D) $kt^2 + \frac{1}{2}ct$

1-36 The variation of velocity of a particle moving along a straight line is illustrated in the following figure-1.123. The distance covered by the particle in 4 seconds is :

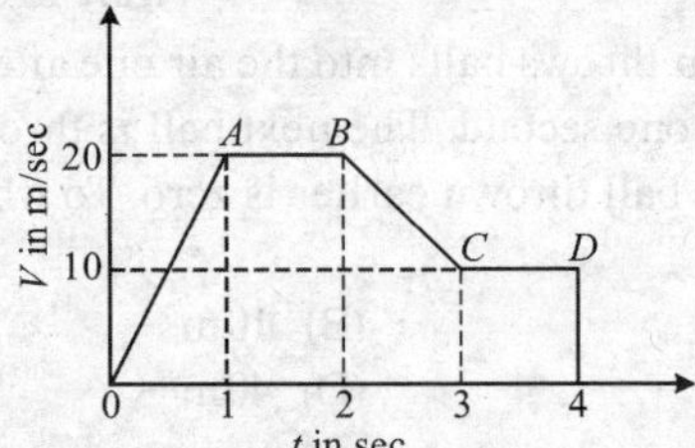

Figure 1.123

(A) 60 m (B) 25 m
(C) 55 m (D) 30 m

1-37 When an object is shot from the bottom of a long smooth inclined plane kept at an angle 60° with horizontal, it can travel a distance x_1 along the plane. But when the inclination is decreased to 30° and the same object is shot with the same velocity, it can travel x_2 distance. Then $x_1 : x_2$ will be :

(A) $1 : \sqrt{2}$ (B) $\sqrt{2} : 1$
(C) $1 : \sqrt{3}$ (D) $1 : 2\sqrt{3}$

1-38 When the speed of the car is v, the minimum distance over which it can be stopped is x. If the speed becomes nv, what will be the minimum distance over which it can be stopped during same time :

(A) x/n (B) nx
(C) x/n^2 (D) n^2x

1-39 The following figure-1.124 shows the velocity-time graph of a moving body along a straight line.

The displacement and distance travelled in six seconds be respectively given as :

(A) 8 m, 16 m
(B) 16 m, 8 m
(C) 16 m, 16 m
(D) 8 m, 8 m

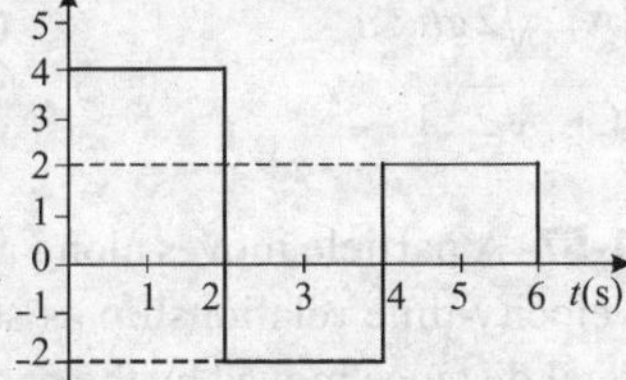

Figure 1.124

1-40 A particle is moving in a straight line with initial velocity u and uniform acceleration f. If the sum of the distances travelled in t^{th} and $(t+1)^{th}$ seconds is 100 cm, then its velocity after t seconds, in cm/s, is :

(A) 20 (B) 30
(C) 50 (D) 80

1-41 The following figure-1.125 shows the velocity-time graph of a train. The total distance travelled by the train is :

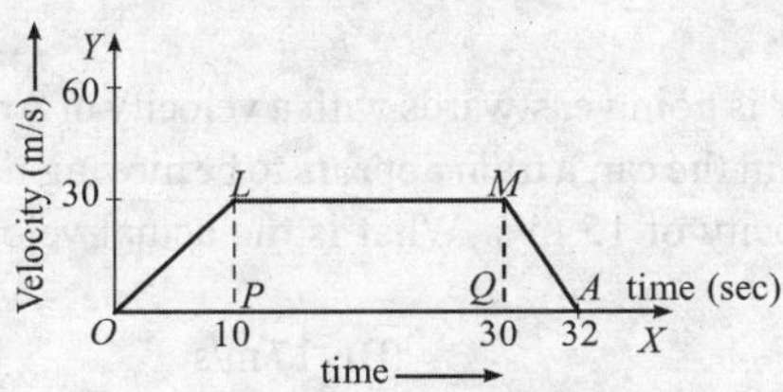

Figure 1.125

(A) 780 m (B) 1200 m
(C) 660 m (D) 1500 m

1-42 A stone falls from rest. The total distance covered by it in the last second of its motion is equal to the distance covered in the first three seconds of its motion. How long does the stone remains in the air ?

(A) 4 s (B) 5 s
(C) 6 s (D) 7 s

1-43 The figure-1.126 shows the acceleration versus time graph of a train. If it starts from rest, the distance it travels before it comes to rest is :

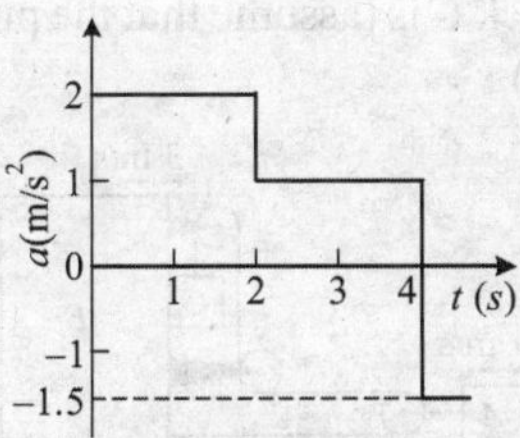

Figure 1.126

(A) 30 m (B) 26 m
(C) 13 m (D) 40 m

1-44 A particle moving on a straight line ultimately comes to rest ? What is the angle between its initial velocity and acceleration ?

(A) Zero (B) $\pi/4$
(C) $\pi/2$ (D) π

1-45 On a two lane road a car A is travelling with a speed of $v = 5\ ms^{-1}$. Two car B and C approach car A in opposite direction with a speed $u = 10\ ms^{-1}$ each. At a certain instant when the B and C are equidistant from A each being $l = 1500$ m, B decides to overtake A before C does. What minimum acceleration of car B is required to avoid an accident with C :

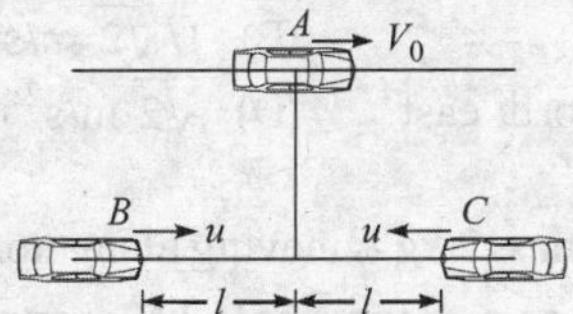

Figure 1.127

(A) $-0.2\ ms^{-2}$ (B) $-1/15\ ms^{-2}$
(C) $0.2\ ms^{-2}$ (D) $1/15\ ms^{-2}$

1-46 Two cars get closer by 8 m every second while traveling in the opposite directions. They get closer by 0.8 m while traveling in the same directions. What are the speeds of the two cars ?

(A) 4 m/s and 4.4 m/s (B) 4.4 m/s and 3.6 m/s
(C) 4 m/s and 3.6 m/s (D) 4 m/s and 3 m/s

1-47 A train 200 m long moving at constant acceleration crosses a bridge 300 m long. It enters the bridge with a speed of 3 m/s and leaves it with a speed of 5 m/s. What is the time taken to cross the bridge ?

(A) 25 s (B) 75 s
(C) 125 s (D) 150 s

1-48 A ball is dropped from the top of a tower 100 m high. Simultaneously another ball is thrown upwards with a speed of 50 m/s. After what time do they cross each other :

(A) 1 s (B) 2 s
(C) 3 s (D) 4 s

1-49 A truck travelling due north at 20 m/s turns east and travels at the same speed. What is the change in velocity :

(A) 40 m/s north east (B) $20\sqrt{2}$ m/s south east
(C) $20\sqrt{2}$ m/s south west (D) $20\sqrt{2}$ m/s north west

1-50 If the velocity v of a particle moving along a straight line decreases linearly with its position coordinates s from 50 m/s to a value approaching zero at $s = 100$ m, the time it takes to reach the 100 m position will be :

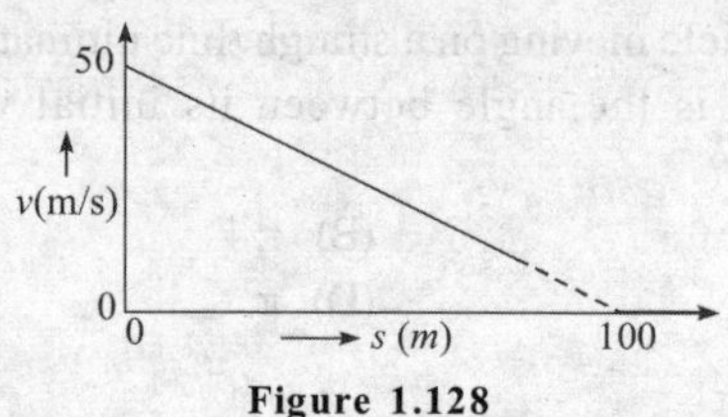

Figure 1.128

(A) 10 s (B) 5 s
(C) Infinity (D) 0.5 s

1-51 A particle is moving at a speed of 5 m/s along east. After 10 s its velocity changes and becomes 5 m/s along north. What is the average acceleration during this interval ?

(A) 0 (B) $1/\sqrt{2}$ m/s^2 north west
(C) $1/\sqrt{2}$ ms^2 north east (D) $\sqrt{2}$ m/s^2 north east

1-52 A body of mass 2 kg is moving along north-east direction with a speed $\sqrt{2}$ m/s. A force of 0.2 N is applied on the body due west for 10 sec. The final velocity of the body is :

(A) 1 m/s due north (B) 1 m/s due east
(C) 2 m/s due north (D) 2 m/s due east

1-53 A person moves 30 m north, then 20 m east and finally $30\sqrt{2}$ m south-west. This displacement from the original position is :

(A) 14 m south west (B) 20 m south
(C) 10 m west (D) 15 m east

1-54 A river is flowing with a speed of 1 km/hr. A swimmer wants to go to point '*C*' starting from '*A*'. He swims with a speed of 5 km/hr, at an angle θ w.r.t. the river. If $AB = BC = 400$ m. Then the value of θ is :

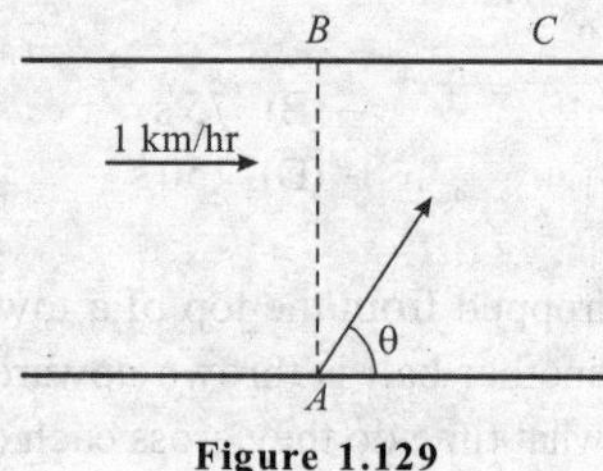

Figure 1.129

(A) 37º (B) 30º
(C) 53º (D) 45º

1-55 A blind person after walking 10 steps in one direction, each of length 80 cm, turns randomly to the left or to right by 90º. After walking a total of 40 steps, the maximum displacement of the person from its starting point can be :

(A) 30m (B) $16\sqrt{2}$ m
(C) $8\sqrt{2}$ m (D) 0m

1-56 A person standing on the roof of a house of height h throws a particle vertically downwards and other particle in a horizontal direction with the same speed u. The ratio of speeds of the particles on reaching the earth is :

(A) $\sqrt{2gh} : u$ (B) 1 : 2
(C) $\sqrt{2} : 1$ (D) 1 : 1

1-57 A particle moves along a horizontal straight line with a velocity-time relationship as shown in the figure-1.130. The total distance moved by the particle is :

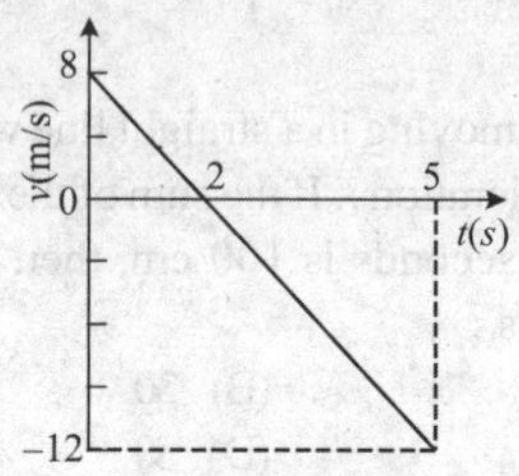

Figure 1.130

(A) 39m (B) 13m
(C) 26m (D) 2.6m

1-58 A car is going eastwards with a velocity of 8 m/s. To the passengers in the car, a train appears to be moving north wards with a velocity of 15 m/s. What is the actual velocity of the train :

(A) 7 m/s (B) 17 m/s
(C) 23 m/s (D) None of these

1-59 Rain is falling vertically downwards with a velocity of 3 kph. a man walks in the rain with a velocity of 4 kph. The rain drops will fall on the man with a velocity of :

(A) 1 kph (B) 3 kph
(C) 4 kph (D) 5 kph

1-60 A man walks in rain with a velocity of 5 kph. The rain drops strike at him at an angle of 45º with the horizontal. The downward velocity of the rain drops will be :

(A) 5 kph (B) 4 kph
(C) 3 kph (D) 1 kph

1-61 The velocities of *A* and *B* are marked in the figure-1.131. The velocity of block *C* is (assume that the pulleys are ideal and string inextensible) :

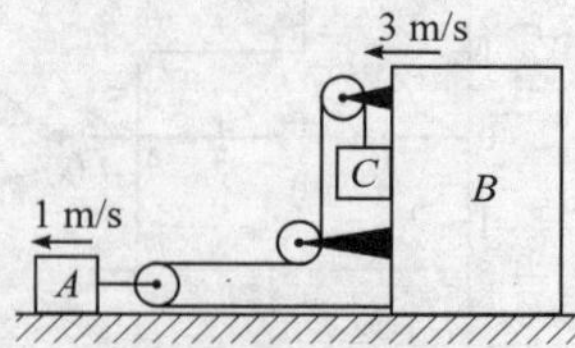

Figure 1.131

(A) 5 m/s (B) 2 m/s
(C) 3 m/s (D) 4 m/s

1-62 If θ is the angle between the velocity and acceleration of a projectile at a point of its path, its value when the projectile is at the highest point is :

(A) 0º (B) 180º
(C) 90º (D) 45º

1-63 If the angle of projection θ corresponds to horizontal range being equal to the maximum height then tanθ equals :

(A) 1 (B) $1/\sqrt{3}$
(C) $\sqrt{3}$ (D) 4

1-64 A thief is running away on a straight road in a jeep moving with a speed of 9 m/s. A police man chases him on a motor cycle moving at a speed of 10 m/s. If the instantaneous separation of the jeep from the motorcycle is 100 m, how long will it take for the police man to catch the thief?

(A) 1 s (B) 19 s
(C) 90 s (D) 100 s

1-65 Two cars are moving in the same direction with a speed of 30 kph. They are separated from each other by 5 km. Third car moving in the opposite direction meets the two cars after an interval of 4 minutes. What is the speed of the third car ?

(A) 30 kph (B) 35 kph
(C) 40 kph (D) 45 kph

1-66 A particle is projected upwards with a velocity of 110 m/s at an angle of 60º with the vertical. Find the time when the particle will move perpendicular to its initial direction, taking $g = 10$ m/s^2 :

(A) 10 seconds (B) 22 seconds
(C) 5 seconds (D) $10\sqrt{3}$ seconds

1-67 The horizontal range of a projectile is R and the maximum height attained by it is H. A strong wind now begins to blow in the direction of the motion of the projectile, giving it a constant horizontal acceleration = $g/2$. Under the same conditions of projection, the horizontal range of the projectile will now be :

(A) $R + \frac{H}{2}$ (B) $R + H$
(C) $R + \frac{3H}{2}$ (D) $R + 2H$

1-68 Two particles, one with constant velocity 50 m/s and the other with uniform acceleration 10 m/s^2, start moving simultaneously from the same place in the same direction. They will be at a distance of 125 m from each other after :

(A) 5 sec (B) $5(1+\sqrt{2})$ sec
(C) 10 sec (D) $10(\sqrt{2}+1)$ sec

1-69 A stone is dropped from an aeroplane which is rising with acceleration 5 ms^{-2}. If the acceleration of the stone relative to the aeroplane be f, then the following is (are) true :

(A) $f = 5$ ms^{-2} downward (B) $f = 5$ ms^{-2} upward
(C) $f = 15$ ms^{-2} upward (D) $f = 15$ ms^{-2} downward

1-70 A ball is thrown vertically upwards in air. If the air resistance can not be neglected (Assume it be directly proportional to velocity) then the acceleration of the ball at the highest point will be :

(A) 0 (B) g
(C) $>g$ (D) $<g$

1-71 If $y = x - x^2$ is the of the path of a projectile, then which of the following is **incorrect** :

(A) Range = 1 m (B) Maximum height = 0.25 m
(C) Time of flight = 0.5 sec. (D) Angle of projection = 45º

1-72 A rocket is fired upwards. Its velocity versus time graph is shown in the figure-1.132. The maximum height reached by the rocket is :

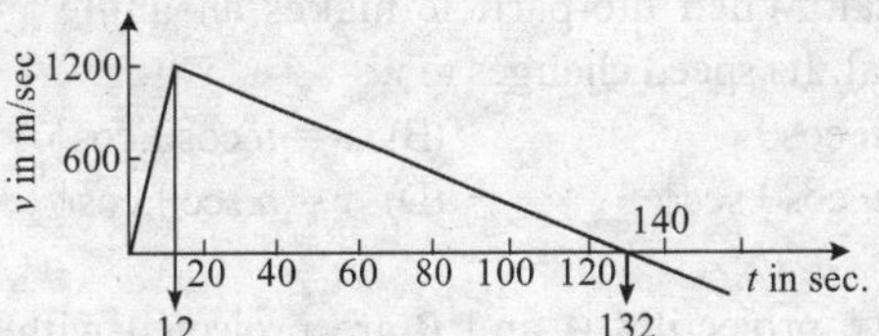

Figure 1.132

(A) 7.1 km (B) 79.2 km
(C) 72 km (D) Infinite

1-73 A person walks up a stalled escalator in 90 s. When standing on the same escalator, now moving, he is carried in 60 s. The time it would take him to walk up the moving escalator will be :

(A) 27 s (B) 72 s
(C) 18 s (D) 36 s

1-74 An object is thrown horizontally from a tower H meter high with a velocity of $\sqrt{2gH}$ m/s. Its velocity on striking the ground will be :

(A) $\sqrt{2gH}$ (B) $\sqrt{6gH}$
(C) $2\sqrt{gH}$ (D) $2\sqrt{2gH}$

1-75 A train travels from one station to another at a speed of 40 km/hour and returns to the first station at the speed of 60 km/hour. Calculate the average speed and average velocity of the train :

(A) 48 km/hr, zero (B) 36 km/hr, zero
(C) 24 km/hr, 24 km/hr (D) None of these

1-76 A motor car is going due north at a speed of 50 km/h. It makes a 90° left turn without changing the speed. The change in the velocity of the car is about :

(A) 50 km/h towards west

(B) $50\sqrt{2}$ km/h towards south-west

(C) 70 km/h towards north-west

(D) Zero

1-77 A bird flies for 4 sec with a velocity of $|t-2|$ m/s in a straight line, where t = time in seconds. It covers a distance of :

(A) 2m (B) 4m

(C) 6m (D) 8m

1-78 Three particles A, B and C are thrown from the top of a tower with the same speed. A is thrown straight up, B is thrown straight down and C is thrown horizontally. They hit the ground with speeds v_A, v_B and v_C respectively :

(A) $v_A = v_B = v_C$ (B) $v_A > v_B > v_C$

(C) $v_A = v_B > v_C$ (D) $v_A > v_B = v_C$

1-79 A particle is thrown with a speed u at an angle θ with the horizontal. When the particle makes an angle ϕ with the horizontal. Its speed changes to v :

(A) $v = u\cos\theta$ (B) $v = u\cos\theta.\cos\phi$

(C) $v = u\cos\theta.\sec\phi$ (D) $v = u\sec\theta.\cos\phi$

1-80 Two projectiles A and B are projected with angle of projection 15° for the projectile A and 45° for the projectile B. If R_A and R_B be the horizontal range for the two projectiles, then :

(A) $R_A < R_B$

(B) $R_A = R_B$

(C) $R_A > R_B$

(D) The information is insufficient to decide the relation of R_A with R_B.

1-81 In the arrangement shown in the figure-1.133 if v_1 and v_2 are instantaneous velocities of masses m_1 and m_2, respectively, and angle $ACB = 2\theta$ at the instant then :

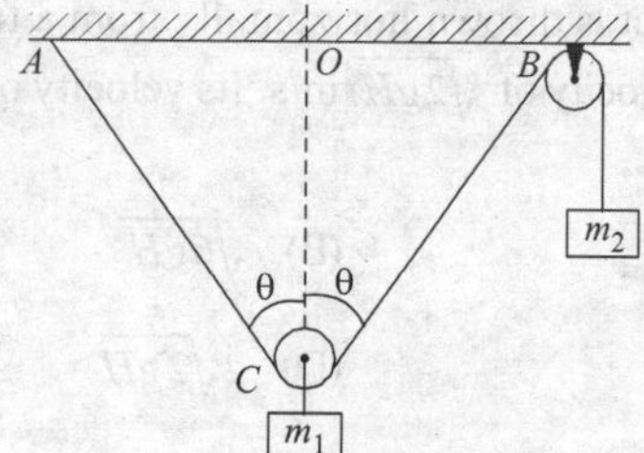

Figure 1.133

(A) $\theta = \cos^{-1}\frac{v_2}{2v_1}$ (B) $\theta = \cos^{-1}\frac{v_1}{2v_2}$

(C) $\theta = \tan^{-1}\frac{v_1}{2v_2}$ (D) $\theta = \sin^{-1}\frac{v_1}{v_2}$

1-82 A man rows a boat with a speed of 18 km/hr in northwest direction. The shoreline makes an angle of 15° south of west. Obtain the component of the velocity of the boat along the shoreline :

(A) 9 km/hr (B) $18\frac{\sqrt{3}}{2}$ km/hr

(C) 18 cos 15° km/hr (D) 18 cos 75° km/hr

1-83 A bullet is fired from a gun falls at a distance half of its maximum range. The angle of projection of the bullet can be :

(A) 15° (B) 30°

(C) 60° (D) 75°

1-84 A bus is beginning to move with an acceleration of 1 m/s^2. A boy who is 48 m behind the bus starts running at 10 m/s. The time(s) at which the boy can catch the bus :

(A) 8 s (B) 10 s

(C) 12 s (D) 14 s.

1-85 An experiment on the take-off performance of an aeroplane shows that the acceleration varies as shown in the figure-1.134, and that it takes 12 s to take off from a rest position. The distance along the runway covered by the aeroplane is :

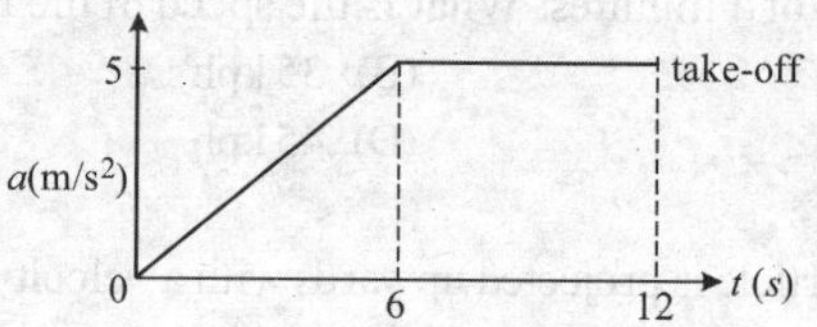

Figure 1.134

(A) 210m (B) 2100m

(C) 21000m (D) 1200m

1-86 Wind is blowing in the north direction at speed of 2 m/s which causes the rain to fall at some angle with the vertical. With what velocity should a cyclist drive so that the rain appears vertical to him :

(A) 2 m/s south (B) 2 m/s north

(C) 4 m/s west (D) 4 m/s south

1-87 A particle has a velocity u towards east at t = 0. Its acceleration is towards west and is constant. Let x_A and x_B be the magnitude of displacement in the first 10 seconds and the next 10 seconds :

(A) $x_A < x_B$

(B) $x_A = x_B$

(C) $x_A > x_B$

(D) The information is insufficient to decide the relation of x_A with x_B.

1-88 A particle thrown up vertically reaches its highest point in time t_1 and returns to the ground in further time t_2. The air resistance exerts a constant force on the particle opposite to its direction of motion

(A) $t_1 > t_2$
(B) $t_1 = t_2$
(C) $t_1 < t_2$
(D) may be (A) or (C) depending on the ratio of the force of air resistance to the weight of the particle.

1-89 Three particles start from origin at the same time with a velocity 2 ms^{-1} along positive x-axis, the second with a velocity 6 ms^{-1} along negative y-axis. Find the velocity of the third particle along $x = y$ line so that the three particles may always lie in a straight line :

(A) $-3\sqrt{3}$ m/s
(B) $3\sqrt{2}$ m/s
(C) $-3\sqrt{2}$ m/s
(D) $2\sqrt{2}$ m/s

1-90 A car 2 m long and 3 m wide is moving at 13 m/sec when a bullet hits it in a direction making an angle $\theta = \tan^{-1} 3/4$ with the car as seen from the street. The bullet enters one edge of the corner and passes out at the diagonally opposite corner. Neglecting any interaction between bullet and car find the time for the bullet to cross the car :

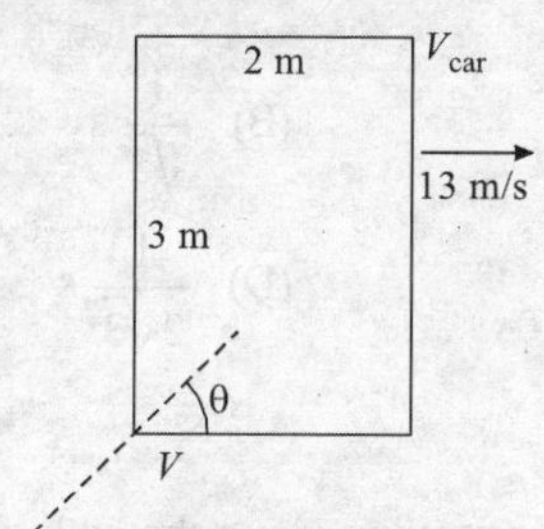

Figure 1.135

(A) 0.25 s
(B) 1.3 s
(C) 0.15 s
(D) 0.6 s

1-91 Rain is falling with a speed of 4 m/s in a direction making an angle of 30° with vertical towards south. What should be the magnitude & direction of velocity of cyclist to hold his umbrella exactly vertical, so that rain does not wet him :

(A) 2 m/s towards north
(B) 4 m/s towards south
(C) 2 m/s towards south
(D) 4 m/s towards north

1-92 The greatest acceleration or deceleration that a train may have is a. The minimum time in which the train can get from one station to the next at a distance s is :

(A) $\sqrt{\dfrac{s}{a}}$
(B) $\sqrt{\dfrac{2s}{a}}$
(C) $\dfrac{1}{2}\sqrt{\dfrac{s}{a}}$
(D) $2\sqrt{\dfrac{s}{a}}$

1-93 A car of mass = m = 1000 kg is moving with constant speed v = 100 m/s on a parabolic shaped bridge $AFOE$ of span $l = 40\ m$ and height $h = 20\ m$ as shown in the figure-1.136. Then the net force applied by the bridge on the car when the car is at point F, is :

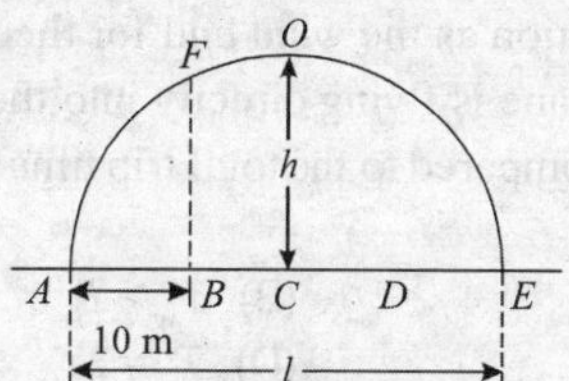

Figure 1.136

(A) $5000\sqrt{\dfrac{5}{2}}N$
(B) $\dfrac{5000}{\sqrt{2}}N$
(C) $\dfrac{10000}{\sqrt{2}}N$
(D) $5000\sqrt{\dfrac{2}{5}}N$

1-94 A block B is suspended from a cable that is attached to the block at E, wraps around three pulleys and is tied to the back of a truck D. If the truck starts from rest when x_D is zero and moves forward with a constant acceleration of $a_p = 3/2$ m/s^2, if the speed of the block at the instant $x_D = 3\ m$ is :

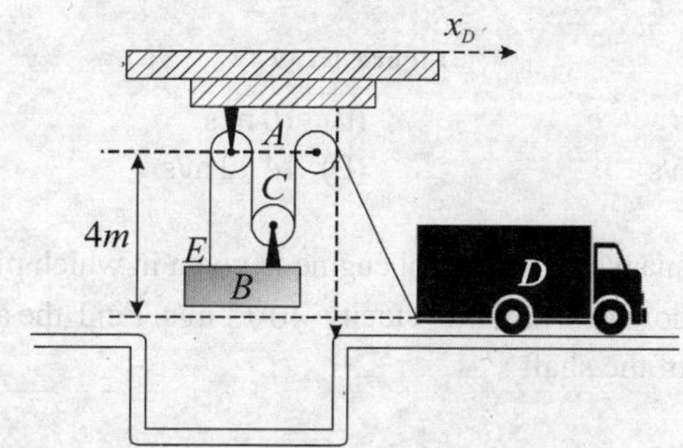

Figure 1.137

(A) $\dfrac{1}{5}$ m/s
(B) $\dfrac{2}{5}$ m/s
(C) $\dfrac{3}{5}$ m/s
(D) 1 m/s

1-95 A particle is projected at an angle 60° with horizontal with a speed of 10 $\sqrt{3}$ m/s from point A as shown. At the same time the sufficient long wedge is made to move with constant velocity of 10 $\sqrt{3}$ towards right as shown in figure-1.138. The time in second after which particle will hit the wedge will be. (g = 10 m/s^2)

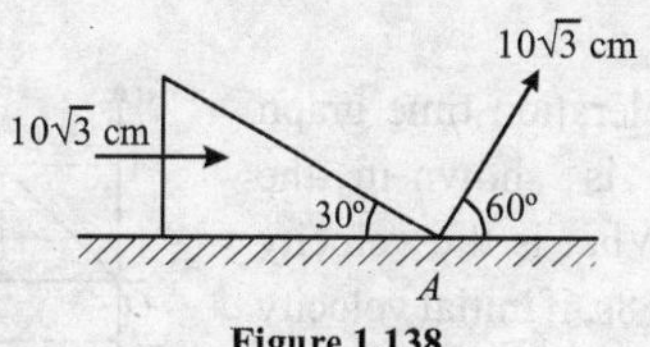

Figure 1.138

(A) 1 s
(B) 2 s
(C) 3 s
(D) it will never collide on the wedge

1-96 An airplane flies northward from town A to town B and then back again. There is a steady wind blowing towards the north so that for the first stage of the trip, the airplane is flying in the same direction as the wind and for the return trip of the journey, the airplane is flying directly into the wind. The total trip time T_w, as compared to the total trip time in the absence of any wind T_0 :

(A) $T_w = T_0$ (B) $T_w > T_0$
(C) $T_w < T_0$ (D) $T_w = 2T_0$

1-97 In the arrangement of rigid links of equal length l, they can freely rotate about the joined ends as shown in the figure-1.139. If the end U is pulled horizontally with constant speed 20 m/s, find the approximate speed of end P when the angle SUT is 90º.

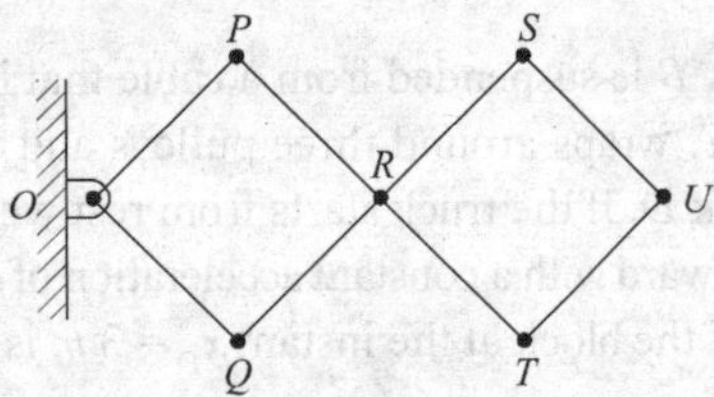

Figure 1.139

(A) 5 m/s (B) 10 m/s
(C) 7.1 m/s (D) 14.12 m/s

1-98 A snapshot of a petrol engine is given in which piston is moving downwards with velocity $40\sqrt{3}$ m/s. Find the angular velocity of the shaft :

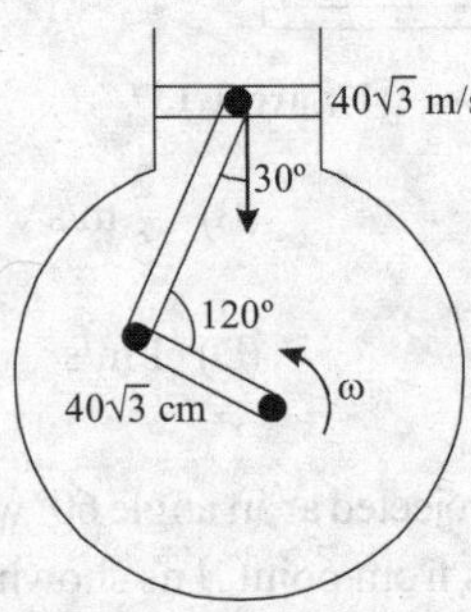

Figure 1.140

(A) 400 rad/s (B) 300 rad/s
(C) 200 rad/s (D) 500 rad/s

1-99 The acceleration time graph of a particle is shown in the figure-1.141. What is the velocity of particle at $t = 8$s, if initial velocity of particle is 3 m/s? (Assume motion is 1 dimension)

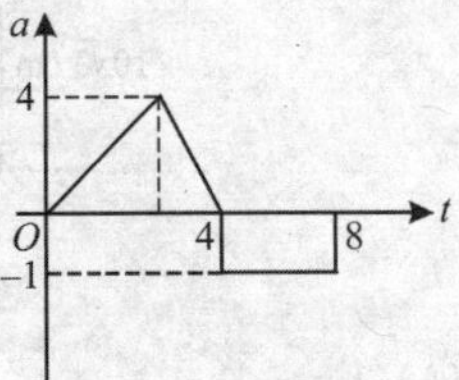

Figure 1.141

(A) 4 m/s (B) 5 m/s
(C) 6 m/s (D) 7 m/s

1-100 A particle is moving on a circular path of radius R with uniform angular speed ω. The magnitude of average velocity of particle during time $t = 0$ to $t = \dfrac{2\pi}{2\omega}$:

(A) $\dfrac{\sqrt{3}}{2}\dfrac{\omega R}{\pi}$ (B) $\dfrac{3}{2}\dfrac{\omega R}{\pi}$

(C) $\dfrac{3\sqrt{3}}{2}\dfrac{\omega R}{\pi}$ (D) $\dfrac{2}{3}\dfrac{\omega R}{\pi}$

1-101 A particle is thrown at time $t = 0$ with a velocity of 10 m/s at an angle of 60° with the horizontal from a point on an incline plane, making an angle of 30° with the horizontal. The time when the velocity of the projectile becomes parallel to the incline is :

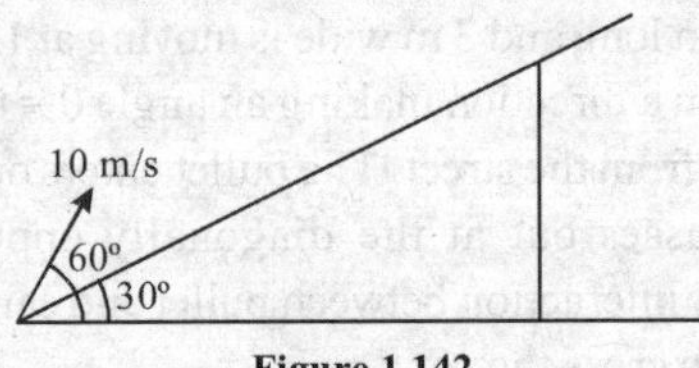

Figure 1.142

(A) $\dfrac{2}{\sqrt{3}}$ s (B) $\dfrac{1}{\sqrt{3}}$ s

(C) $\sqrt{3}$ s (D) $\dfrac{1}{2\sqrt{3}}$ s

1-102 A particle is moving along the path given by $y = \dfrac{C}{6}t^6$ (where C is a positive constant). The relation between the acceleration (a) and the velocity (v) of the particle at $t = 5$ s is :

(A) $5a = v$ (B) $a = 5v$
(C) $a = \sqrt{v}$ (D) $a = v$

1-103 Three particles are projected in air with the minimum possible speeds, such that the first goes from A to B, the second goes from B to C and the third goes from C to A. Points A and C are at the same vertical level. The two inclines make the same angle α with the horizontal as shown. Then the relation among the projection speeds of the three particles is :

(A) $u_3 = u_1 + u_2$ (B) $u_3^2 = 2u_1u_2$

(C) $\dfrac{1}{u_3} = \dfrac{1}{u_1} + \dfrac{1}{u_2}$ (D) $u_3^2 = u_1^2 + u_2^2$

1-104 A particle moving in the positive x-direction has initial velocity v_0. The particle undergoes retardation kv^2, where v is its instantaneous velocity. The velocity of the particle as a function of time is given by :

(A) $v = v_0/(1 + kv_0t)$ (B) $v = \frac{2v_0}{1+kt}$

(C) $v = \frac{v_0}{kt}$ (D) $v = \frac{v_0}{(1+k^2v_0^2t)}$

1-105 A particle is projected with a speed u in air at angle θ with the horizontal. The particle explodes at the highest point of its path into two equal fragments, one of the fragments moving up straight with a speed u. The difference in time in which the two particle fall on the ground is (Assume it is at a height H at the time of explosion)

(A) $\frac{2u}{g}$ (B) $\frac{u}{g}\sqrt{u^2 - 2gH}$

(B) $\frac{1}{2g}\sqrt{u^2 + 2gH}$ (D) $\frac{2}{g}\sqrt{u^2 + 2gH}$

1-106 In the figure shown a river of width 4 km is flowing with the speed of 5 km/h. A swimmer whose swimming speed relative to the water is 4 km/h, starts swimming from a point A on a bank. On the other bank B is a point which is directly opposite to A. What minimum distance (in km) the swimmer will have to walk on the other bank to reach the point B.

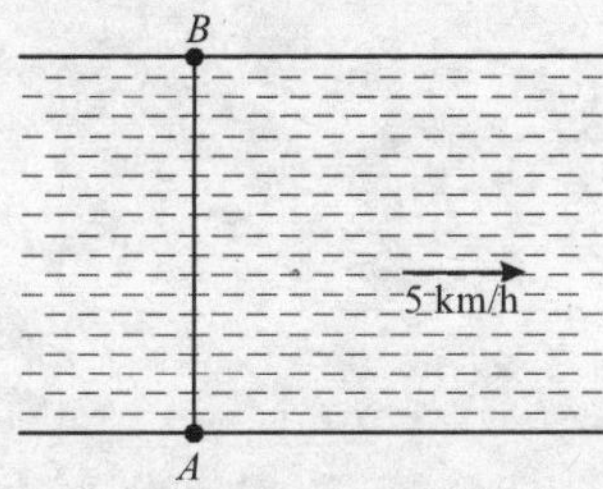

Figure 1.143

(A) 2 (B) 3
(C) 4 (D) 5

1-107 If block A starts from rest at $t = 0$ & begins to move towards right with 2 m/s^2 & simultaneously C moves towards right with constant velocity of 4 m/s. Velocity of block B at $t = 5$ sec will be :

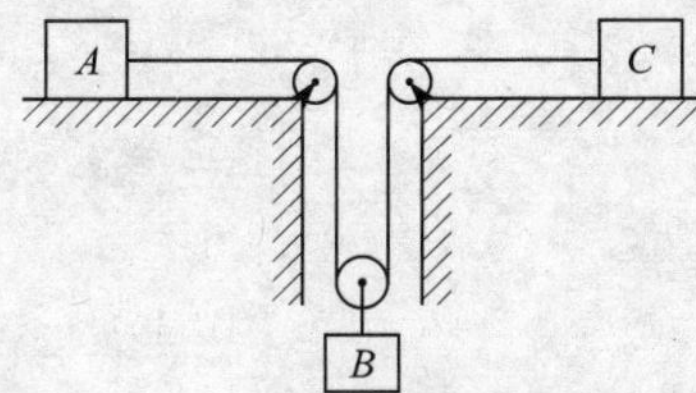

Figure 1.144

(A) 2 m/s (B) 3 m/s
(C) 4 m/s (D) None

1-108 In the pulley system shown the two upper pulleys are fastened together to form single unit. The cable is wrapped around the smaller pulley with its end secured to the pulleys so that it cannot slip. Determine the upward acceleration of block B if A has downward acceleration of 2 m/s^2 :

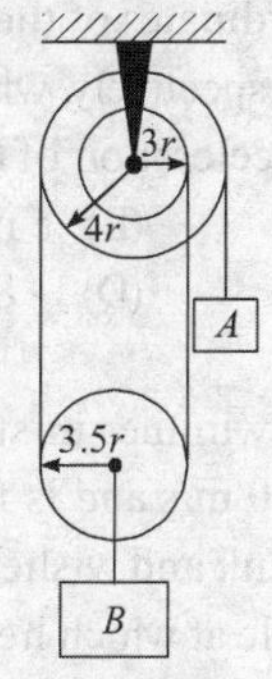

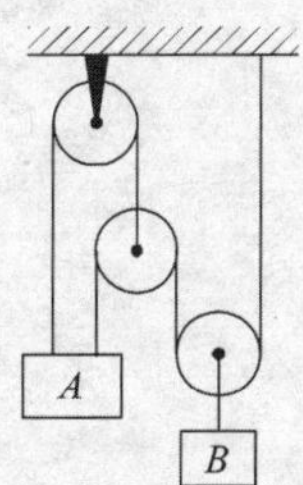

Figure 1.145

(A) 16 m/s^2 (B) 8 m/s^2
(C) 0.5 m/s^2 (D) 0.25 m/s^2

1-109 Knowing that block B starts to move downward with a constant velocity of 18 cm/sec, the velocity of block A will be :

Figure 1.146

(A) 27 cm/s (B) 12 cm/s
(C) 36 cm/s (D) 9 cm/s

1-110 If velocity of block B in the given arrangement is 300 mm/sec towards right. Then velocity of A will be :

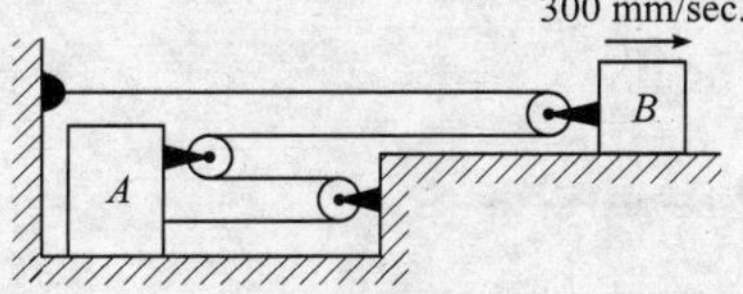

Figure 1.147

(A) 200 mm/sec (B) 100 mm/sec
(C) 450 mm/sec (D) 150 mm/sec

1-111 Find range of projectile which is projected perpendicular to the incline plane with velocity 20 m/s as shown in figure-1.148 :

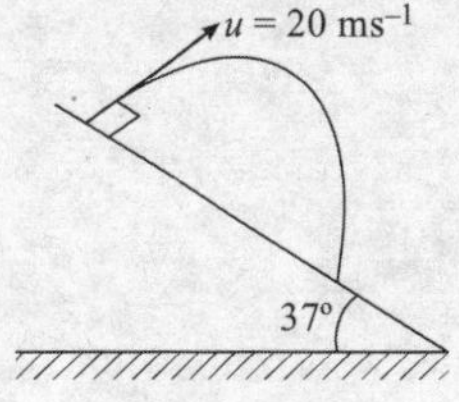

Figure 1.148

(A) 75 m (B) 40 m
(C) 45 m (D) 50 m

1-112 The x and y coordinates of the particle at any time are $x = 5t - 2t^2$ and $y = 10t$ respectively, where x and y are in meters and t in seconds. The acceleration of the particle at $t = 2$ s is :
(A) 0 (B) 5 m/s^2
(C) -4 m/s^2 (D) -8 m/s^2

1-113 The speed of a swimmer in still water is 20 m/s. The speed of river water is 10 m/s and is flowing due east. If he is standing on the south bank and wishes to cross the river along the shortest path the angle at which he should make his strokes w.r.t. north is given by :
(A) 30° west (B) 0°
(C) 60° west (D) 45° west

1-114 A projectile is fired from the surface of the earth with a velocity of 5 ms^{-1} and angle θ with the horizontal. Another projectile fired from another planet with a velocity of 3 ms^{-1} at the same angle follows a trajectory which is identical with the trajectory of the projectile fired from the earth. The value of the acceleration due to gravity on the planet is (in ms^{-2}) is (given g = 9.8 ms^{-2}) :
(A) 3.5 (B) 5.9
(C) 16.3 (D) 110.8

1-115 A particle is moving such that its position coordinates (x, y) are (2 m, 3 m) at time $t = 0$, (6 m, 7 m) at time $t = 2$ s and (13 m, 14 m) at time $t = 5$ s. Average velocity vector ($\vec{V}_{av}$) from $t = 0$ to $t = 5$ s is :
(A) $\frac{1}{5}(13\hat{i} + 14\hat{j})$ (B) $\frac{7}{3}(\hat{i} + \hat{j})$
(C) $2(\hat{i} + \hat{j})$ (D) $\frac{11}{5}(\hat{i} + \hat{j})$

* * * * *

Advance MCQs with One or More Options Correct

1-1 The displacement x of a particle as a function of time t is shown in following figure-1.149. The figure indicates :

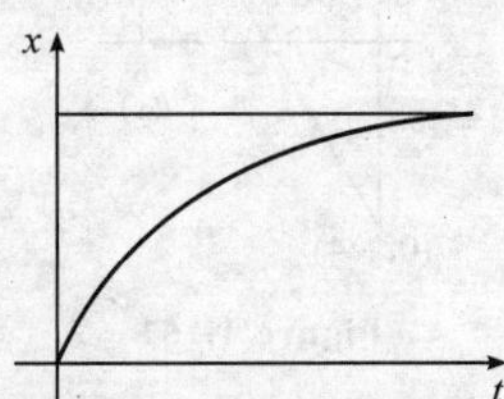

Figure 1.149

(A) The particle starts with a certain velocity, but the motion is retarded and finally particle stops
(B) The velocity of particle is constant through out
(C) The acceleration of the particle is constant throughout
(D) The particle starts with a constant velocity, the motion is accelerated :

1-2 A particle is projected vertically upwards with a velocity u from a point O. When it returns to the point of projection :
(A) Its average velocity is zero
(B) Its displacement is zero
(C) Its average speed is $u/2$
(D) Its average speed is u

1-3 An object may have :
(A) Varying speed without having varying velocity.
(B) Varying velocity without having varying speed.
(C) Non zero acceleration without having varying velocity.
(D) Non zero acceleration without having varying speed.

1-4 Choose the correct statement(s) :
(A) We can have a motion having zero displacement and nonzero average speed.
(B) Average velocity is half the sum of its initial and final velocity.
(C) Total displacement is equal to product of average velocity and time.
(D) Acceleration of a particle is positive if it is moving in negative direction with decreasing speed.

1-5 Choose the correct statement(s) :
(A) If a particle moving in a straight line has a negative acceleration then this always meant that the speed is decreasing.
(B) If speed of a particle moving in straight line changes, it must have non-zero acceleration.
(C) Acceleration of a particle is negative if it is moving in +ve direction with decreasing speed.
(D) Rate of change of speed is magnitude of acceleration at any instant.

1-6 Figure shows some velocity versus time graphs :

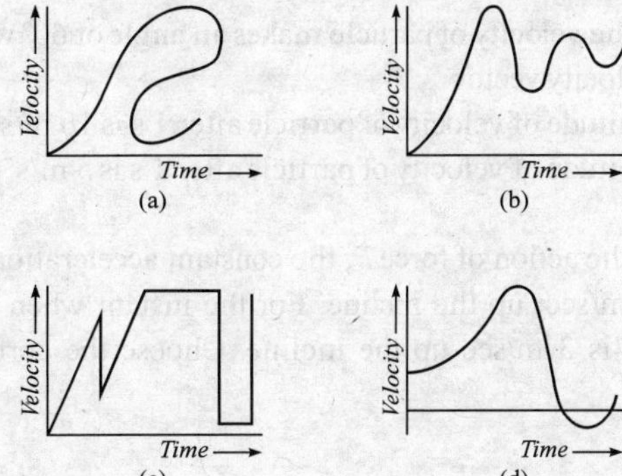

Only some of these can be realised in practice. These are :
(A) Figure-(a) (B) Figure-(b)
(C) Figure-(c) (D) Figure-(d)

1-7 Man A sitting in a car moving with 54 km/hr observes another man B in front of car crossing perpendicularly the road of width 15 m in 3 s :
(A) Speed of man B is $5\sqrt{10}$ m/s
(B) Speed of man B is 5 ms^{-1}
(C) Actual direction of motion of B is at an angle of $\tan^{-1}\left(\frac{1}{3}\right)$ with direction of motion of car
(D) Actual direction of motion of B is at an angle of $\tan^{-1}(3)$ with direction opposite to the direction of motion of car

1-8 A motor boat is to reach at a point 30° upstream on other side of a river flowing with velocity 5 m/s. Velocity of motor boat with respect to water is $5\sqrt{3}$ m/sec. The driver should steer the boat at an angle of :
(A) 30° up w.r.t. the line of destination from the starting point
(B) 60° up w.r.t. normal to the bank
(C) 120° w.r.t. stream direction
(D) None of these

1-9 The position of a particle moving in a straight line is given by

$$x = 3t^3 - 18t^2 + 36t$$

Here, x is in m and t in second. Then
(A) direction of velocity and acceleration both change at $t = 2$s
(B) the distance travelled by particle is equal to magnitude of displacement for $t = 0$ to $t = 5$s
(C) the speed of particle is decreasing in $t = 0$ to $t = 2$s then it is increasing for $t > 2$
(D) the magnitudes of velocity and acceleration are equal at $t = 0$

1-10 A particle is projected at an angle = 30° with the horizontal, with a velocity of 10 m/s then

(A) after 2 s the velocity of particle makes an angle of 60° with initial velocity vector
(B) after 1 s the velocity of particle makes an angle of 60° with initial velocity vector
(C) the magnitude of velocity of particle after 1 s is 10 m/s
(D) the magnitude of velocity of particle after 1 s is 5 m/s

1-11 Under the action of force P, the constant acceleration of block B is 6 m/sec² up the incline. For the instant when the velocity of B is 3 m/sec up the incline. Choose the correct option(s)

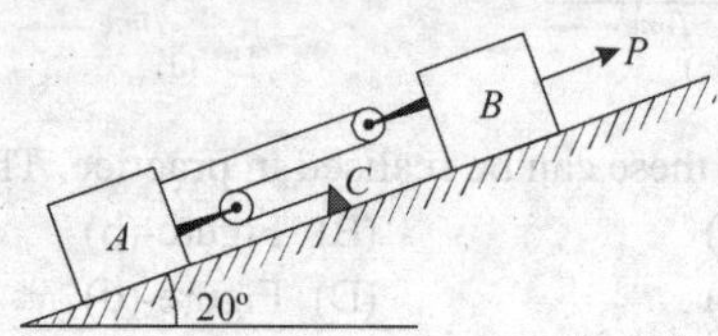

Figure 1.150

(A) Velocity of B relative to A is 1 m/s
(B) Acceleration of B relative to A is 2 m/s²
(C) The velocity of point C of the cable (in ground frame) is 4 m/s
(D) Velocity of B relative to A is 2 m/s

1-12 A particle moves with constant speed v along a regular hexagon $ABCDEF$ in the same order. Then the magnitude of the average velocity for its motion from A to :

(A) F is $v/5$ (B) D is $v/3$
(C) C is $v\sqrt{3}/2$ (D) B is v

1-13 A particle has initial velocity 10 m/s. It moves due to constant retarding force along the line of velocity which produces a retardation of 5 m/s². Then :

(A) The maximum displacement in the direction of initial velocity is 10 m
(B) The distance travelled in first 3 seconds is 7.5 m
(C) The distance travelled in first 3 seconds is 12.5 m
(D) The distance travelled in first 3 seconds is 17.5 m

1-14 If a particle is moving along a straight line and following is the graph showing acceleration varying with time then choose correct statement(s). At $t = 0, x = 0$ and $v_0 = 7\ \text{ms}^{-1}$:

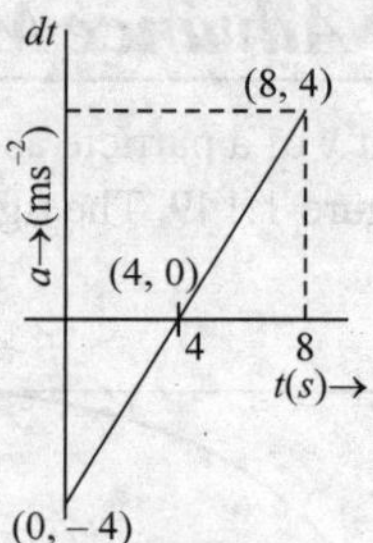

Figure 1.151

(A) Its displacement can never become zero
(B) Its velocity can never become zero
(C) Its displacement can become zero
(D) Its velocity can become zero

1-15 A particle moving along a straight line with uniform acceleration has velocities 7 m/s at A and 17 m/s at C. B is the mid point of AC. Then :

(A) The velocity at B is 12 m/s
(B) The average velocity between A and B is 10 m/s
(C) The ratio of the time to go from A to B to that from B to C is 3 : 2
(D) The average velocity between B and C is 15 m/s

1-16 The string shown in the figure-1.152 is passing over small smooth pulley rigidly attached to trolley A. If speed of trolley is constant and equal to V_A. Speed and magnitude of acceleration of block B at the instant shown in figure is :

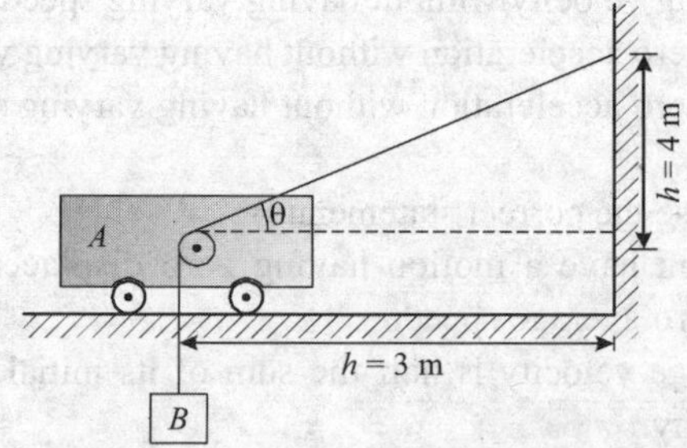

Figure 1.152

(A) $V_B = V_A, a_B = 0$ (B) $a_B = 0$
(C) $a_B = \frac{3}{5} v_A$ (D) $a_B = \frac{16 v_A^2}{125}$

* * * * *

Unsolved Numerical Problems for Preparation of NSEP, INPhO & IPhO

For detailed preparation of INPhO and IPhO students can refer advance study material on www.physicsgalaxy.com

1-1 A ball is released from rest. If it takes 1 second to cross the last 20 m before hitting the ground, find the height from which it was dropped.

Ans. [31.25 m]

1-2 The accelerator of a train can produce uniform acceleration 0.25 m/s^2 and its brake can produce retardation 0.5 m/s^2. What is the shortest time in which the train can travel two stations 8 km apart, if it stops at both stations ? What is the maximum speed attained and for how long does the train move with uniform velocity ?

Ans. [5 min 10 sec, 186 km/hr, Zero]

1-3 An insect is moving on a groove whose displacement is given as $x = 6t^2 - 8 + 40 \cos \pi t$, where x and t are expressed in metres and seconds. Find the position, velocity and acceleration of insect at time $t = 6$ s.

Ans. [248 m, 72 m/s, – 383 m/s^2]

1-4 Two cars, A and B, are traveling in the same direction with velocities v_a and v_b respectively. When car A is at a distance d behind car B, the brakes on A are applied, causing a deceleration at a rate a. Show that to prevent a collision between A and B it is necessary that :

$$v_A - v_B = \sqrt{2ad}$$

1-5 A motorboat starts from rest with an acceleration given by the law $a = \frac{c}{(x+4)^2}$ m/s^2, where c is a positive constant. Given that the velocity of the boat when its displacement is 8 m is 4 m/s. Find:

(a) The magnitude of c.

(b) The position of the boat when its speed was 4.5 m/s.

(c) The maximum velocity of the boat.

Ans. [48 m^3/s^2, 21.6 m, 4.9 m/s]

1-6 The acceleration of a particle is given by the relation as $a = -kv^{5/2}$, where k is a constant. The particle starts at $x = 0$ with a velocity of 16 m/s, and when $x = 6$, the velocity is observed to be 4 m/s. Find the velocity of particle when $x = 5$ m and the time at which the velocity of the particle is 9 m/s.

Ans. [4.76 m/s, 0.3425 s]

1-7 In a given steam jet, the velocity of the steam at the mouth of jet is $v_0 = 3.6$ m/s. The velocity of the steam at a distance x from jet is given as $v = \frac{0.18\, v_0}{x}$. Find the acceleration of the air at $x = 2$ m and the time required for the air to flow from $x = 1$ m to $x = 3$ m.

Ans. [– 0.0525 m/s^2, 6.17 s]

1-8 Figure-1.153 shows three blocks A, B and C connected by a cable and system of pulleys. The block B is pulled downward with a constant velocity of 7.5 cm/s. At $t = 0$, block A starts moving downward from rest with a constant acceleration. It is given that the velocity of block A after travelling 20 cm is 30 cm/s, find the change in position, velocity and the acceleration of block C at this instant.

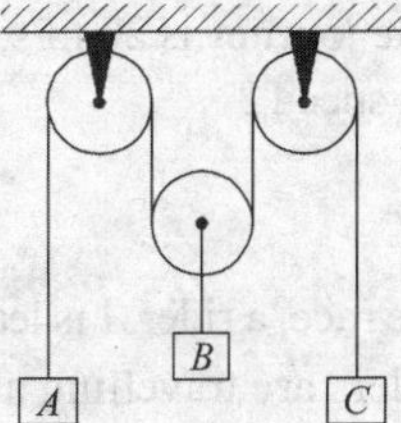

Figure 1.153

Ans. [40 cm, 45 cm/s, 2.25 cm/s^2]

1-9 A traffic police officer observes a fast moving car. Due to over speed officer starts his bike, accelerates uniformly to 90 kph in 8 s, and maintaining a constant velocity of 90 kph, overtakes the car 42 s after the car passed him. If he overtakes the car after 18 s from the instant he starts, find the distance the officer travelled before overtaking and the speed of car.

Ans. [0.5 km, 42.9 kph]

1-10. A steel ball is dropped from the roof of a building. A man standing in front of a 1 m high window in the building notes that the ball takes 0.1 s to fall from the top to bottom of the window. The ball continues to fall and strikes the ground. On striking the ground, the ball gets rebounded with the same speed with which it hits the ground. If the ball reappears at the bottom of the windows 2 s after passing the bottom of the window on the way down, find the height of the building.

Ans. [21.004 m]

1-11 A particle starts from a point A, starting of curve and travels along the solid curve shown in figure-1.154. Find approximately the position B of the particle such that the average velocity between the positions A and B has the same direction as the instantaneous velocity at B.

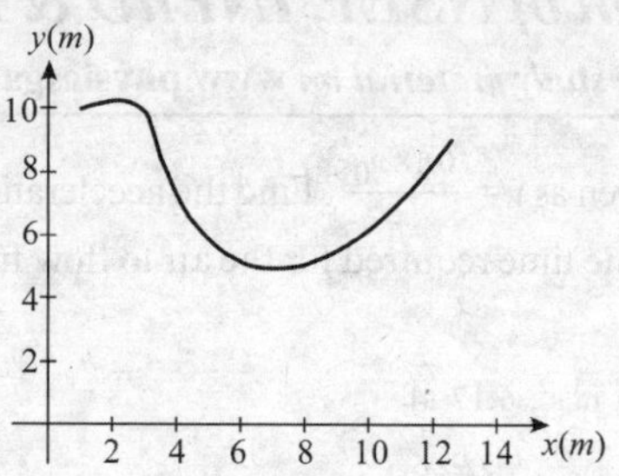

Figure 1.154

Ans. [(5 m, 6 m)]

1-12 A car, starting from rest, first moves with an acceleration of 5 m/s^2 for sometime and then, after moving with a uniform speed for some time, starts decelerating at the same rate to come to rest in a total time of 25 sec. If the average velocity of the car over the whole journey is 20 m/s, for how long does it move with a uniform speed ?

Ans. [15 sec]

1-13 In a motorcycle race, a rider A is leading another rider B by 36 m and both riders are travelling at a constant speed of 170 kph. At $t = 0$ both starts accelerating at a constant rate. It is given that after 8 s, B overtakes A and at this instant speed of A is 220 kph. Find the accelerations of the two riders.

Ans. [1.74 m/s^2, 2.86 m/s^2]

1-14 Two friends A and B are standing a distance x apart in an open field and wind is blowing in a direction perpendicular to the line joining AB. A beats a drum and finds a time lag between seeing and hearing the drum beating by A. Find this time lag.

Ans. [$\frac{x}{\sqrt{v^2 - u^2}}$]

1-15 Two blocks A and B are shown in figure-1.155. Block A moves to the left with a constant velocity of 6 m/s. Find :

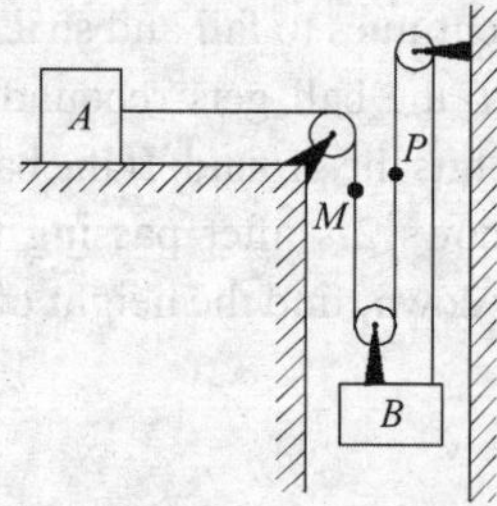

Figure 1.155

(a) Velocity of the block B.

(b) Velocity of the point P of the string.

(c) Relative velocity of the point M of the cable with respect to the point P.

Ans. [2 m/s up, 2 m/s down, 8 m/s up]

1-16 In figure-1.156 block A starts from rest and moves upward with a constant acceleration. After 8 s the relative velocity of block B with respect to A is 0.6 m/s. Find the accelerations of blocks A and B. Also find the velocity of block B after 6 s.

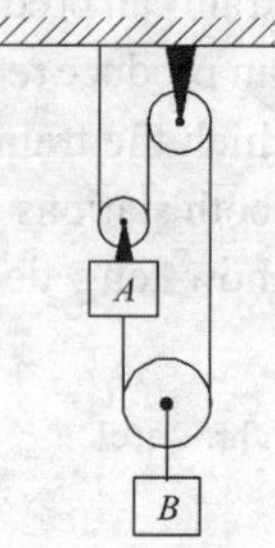

Figure 1.156

Ans. [5 cm/s^2 up, 2.5 cm/s^2 down, 15 cm/s down]

1-17 A man of height 1.2 meters walks away from a lamp hanging at a height of 4 metres above ground level. If the man walks with a speed of 2.8 m/s, determine the speed of the tip of man's shadow.

Ans. [4 m/s]

1-18 A particle moves in a straight line with the velocity curve shown in figure-1.157. Draw approximate acceleration vs time and displacement vs time curves. Consider $x = 0$ at $t = 0$.

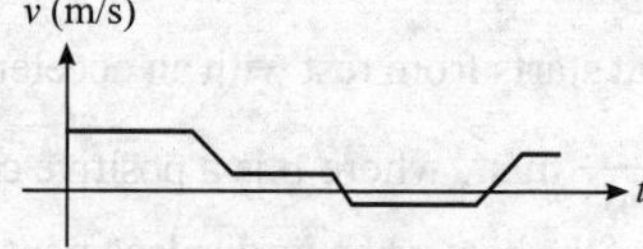

Figure 1.157

1-19 A point mass starts moving in a straight line with a constant acceleration a. At a time t_1 after the beginning of motion the acceleration changes sign, remaining the same in magnitude. Determine the time t from the beginning of motion in which the point mass returns to the initial position.

Ans. [$t_1(2 + \sqrt{2})$]

1-20 A car C_1 travelling at a uniform speed of 75 kph passed another car C_2 at rest beside the track. Two minutes later C_2 starts and accelerates uniformly until its speed increases to 100 kph, then it maintains the speed. After 12 minutes from the instant C_1 passes C_2, C_2 is 800 m ahead of C_1. Find when and where C_2 overtakes C_1 and the acceleration of C_2.

Ans. [10.1 min, 12.6 km, 0.443 m/s^2]

1-21 A helicopter takes off along the vertical with an acceleration $a = 3\ m/s^2$ and zero initial velocity. In a certain time t_1, the pilot switches off the engine. At the point of take off, the sound dies away in a time $t_2 = 30$ sec. Determine the velocity of the helicopter at the moment when its engine is switched off assuming that velocity of sound is 320 m/s.

Ans. [80 m/s]

1-22 Two bodies move in a straight line towards each other at initial velocities v_1 and v_2 and with constant acceleration a_1 and a_2 directed against the corresponding velocities at the initial instant. What must be the maximum initial separation between the bodies for which they meet during the motion ?

Ans. [$\frac{(v_1 + v_2)^2}{2(a_1 + a_2)}$]

1-23 Block B shown in figure-1.158 moves to the right with a constant velocity of 30 cm/s. Find :

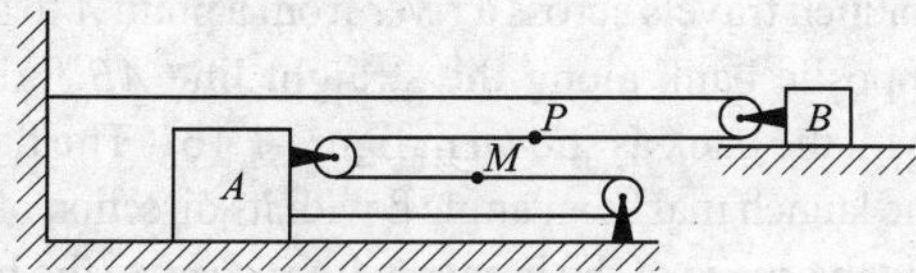

Figure 1.158

(a) The velocity of block A.

(b) The velocity of the point P of the string.

(c) The velocity of the point M of the string.

(d) The relative velocity of the point P of the string with respect to the block A.

Ans. [(a) 20 cm/s right, (b) 60 cm/s right, (c) 20 cm/s left, (d) 40 cm/s right]

1-24 At $t = 0$, block B in figure-1.158 starts moving with a velocity 15 cm/s and with a constant acceleration. It is observed that after block A travels 24 cm to the right its velocity is 6 cm/s. Find :

(a) The accelerations of A and B,

(b) The acceleration of point M of the string.

Ans. [(a) 1.33 m/s^2 left, 2 cm/s^2 left, (b) 1.33 m/s^2 right]

1-25 A stone is dropped from the top of a cliff of height h. "n" seconds later, a second stone is projected downwards from the same cliff with a vertically downward velocity u. Show that the two stones will reach the bottom of the cliff together, if

$$8h\,(u - gn)^2 = gn^2\,(2u - gn)^2$$

What can you say about the limiting value of "n" ?

Ans. [$\sqrt{\frac{2h}{g}}$]

1-26 How long will a plane take to fly around a square with side a with the wind blowing at a velocity u, in the two cases (a) the direction of the wind coincides with one of the sides (b) the direction of the wind coincides with one diagonal of the square. The velocity of the plane in still air is $v > u$.

Ans. [(a) $\frac{2a(v + \sqrt{v^2 - u^2})}{v^2 - u^2}$, (b) $\frac{4a\sqrt{(v^2 - u^2/2)}}{v^2 - u^2}$]

1-27 The motion of an insect on a table is given as $x = 4t - 2\sin t$ and $y = 4 - 2\cos t$, where x and y are in metres and t is in seconds. Find the magnitude of minimum and maximum velocities attained by the insect.

Ans. [2 m/s, 6 m/s]

1-28 Two motor cars start from A simultaneously and reach B after 2 hrs. The first car traveled half the distance at a speed of $v_1 = 30$ km/hr and the other half at a speed of 60 km/hr. The second car covered the entire distance with a constant acceleration. At what instant of time, where the speeds of both the vehicles same ? Will one of them overtake the other enroute ?

Ans. [0.75 hr, 1.5 hr, no overtaking]

1-29 A body of mass m is thrown straight up with a velocity u_0. Find the velocity u' with which the body comes down if the air drag equals cu^2 where c is a constant and u is the velocity of the body.

Ans. [$u' = \frac{u_0}{\left(1 + \frac{cu_0^2}{mg}\right)^{1/2}}$]

1-30 In a village Shyam bats for hitting two points A and B on a staircase with his goli from the position P shown in figure-1.159. Find the velocities required for P to hit A and B.

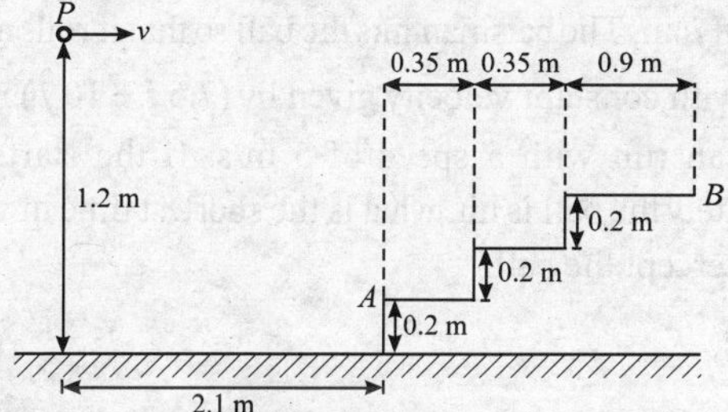

Figure 1.159

Ans. [4.65 m/s, 10.6 m/s]

1-31 A ship moves along the equator to the east with velocity $v_0 = 30$ km/hr. The south eastern wind blows at an angle $\varphi = 60°$ to the equator with velocity $v = 15$ km/hr. Find the wind velocity v' relative to the ship and the angle φ' between the equator and the wind direction in the reference frame fixed to the ship.

Ans. [39.4 km/hr, 19°]

1-32 Point A moves uniformly with velocity v so that the vector v is continually "*aimed*" at point B, which in its turn moves rectilinearly and uniformly with velocity $u < v$. At the initial moment of time $v \perp u$ and the points are separated by a distance l. How soon the points converge ?

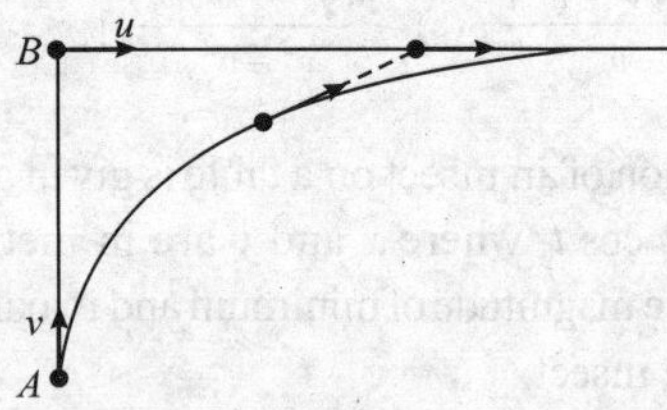

Figure 1.160

Ans. $[\frac{vl}{v^2 - u^2}]$

1-33 The speed of a train increases at a constant rate from zero to v and then remains constant for an interval and finally decreases to zero at a constant rate β. If l be the total distance described, prove that the total time taken is :

$$\frac{l}{v} + \frac{v}{2}\left(\frac{1}{\alpha} + \frac{1}{\beta}\right)$$

1-34 The position vector $\vec{r}$ of a moving particle at time t after the start of the motion is given by $\vec{r} = (5 + 20\,t)\,\hat{i} + (95 + 10\,t - 5\,t^2)\,\hat{j}$. At the $t = T$, the particle is moving at right angles to its initial direction of motion. Find the value of T and the distance of the particle from its initial position at this time.

Ans. [5 s, 125 m]

1-35 On a cricket field, the batsman is at the origin of coordinates and a fielder stands in position given as $(46\,\hat{i} + 28\,\hat{j})$m. The batsman hits the ball so that it rolls along the ground with constant velocity given by $(7.5\,\hat{i} + 10\,\hat{j})$ m/s. The fielder can run with a speed of 5 m/s. If the starts to run immediately the ball is hit, what is the shortest time in which he could intercept the ball.

Ans. [4 s]

1-36 Two steel balls fall freely on an elastic slab. The first ball is dropped from a height h_1 and the second from a height h_2 $(h_2 < h_1)$ T sec after the first ball. After the passage of time T, the velocities of the balls coincide in magnitude and direction. Determine the time T and the time interval during which the velocities of the two balls will be equal assuming that the balls do not collide.

Ans. $[\frac{2\sqrt{2}(\sqrt{h_1} - \sqrt{h_2})}{\sqrt{g}}]$

1-37 A motor boat, with its engine on in a running river and blown over by a horizontal wind is observed to travel at 20 kph in a direction 53° East of North. The velocity of the boat with its engine on in still water & blown over by the horizontal wind is 4 kph Eastward and the velocity of the boat with its engine on over the running river, in the absence of wind is 8 kph due south. Find :

(a) The velocity of the boat in magnitude and direction, over still water in the absence of wind.

(b) The velocity of the wind in magnitude and direction.

Ans. [23.32 kph, 59° SOW]

1-38 A particle moves from rest in a straight line with alternate acceleration and retardation of magnitudes a and a' respectively during equal intervals of time t. Find the space it has described at the end of 2 n such intervals.

Ans. $[nt^2\ \{a + \frac{1}{2}(a - a')(2n - 1)\}]$

1-39 A launch travels across a river from a point A to a point B on the opposite bank along the straight line AB forming an angle α with the bank as shown in figure-1.161. The flag on the mast of the launch makes an angle β with its direction of motion. Determine the speed of the launch with respect to the bank. Let u be the velocity of wind blowing in the direction perpendicular to the current.

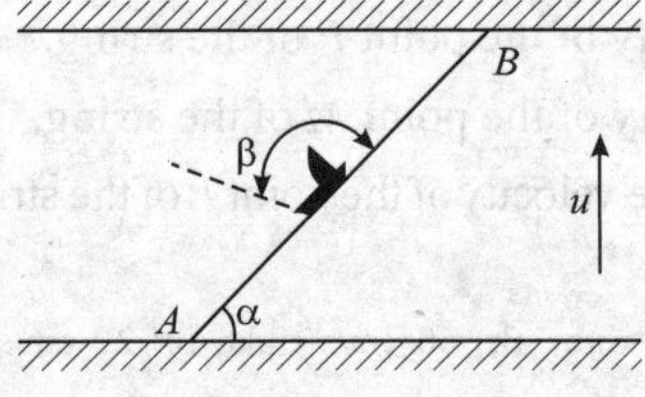

Figure 1.161

Ans. $[u \sin(\alpha + \beta - \pi/2) \sin\beta]$

1-40 A particle moves for total time T sec in a straight line in three consecutive parts such that its acceleration during the first, second and third parts is in the ratio 1 : 2 : 7. The distances covered in the first and the third parts are a and b meters while the time taken for each of the is t seconds. Find the average velocity of the particle during the second part.

Ans. $[\frac{a+b}{2t} + 3\left(\frac{a-b}{4t}\right)]$

1-41 Two particles are simultaneously thrown at an elevation 45°, towards each other from points A and B, roofs of two high buildings. Their velocities of projection are 14 m/s and 2 m/s respectively. Horizontal and vertical separation between points A and B is 22 m and 9 m respectively. Calculate the minimum separation between the particle in the process of their motion.

Ans. [6 m]

1-42 A ball is projected directly upward with an initial speed v_0, bounces elastically from a roof inclined at an angle 45° as shown in figure-1.162 and then it strikes a table at a horizontal distance 2 D from its starting point. Find v_0.

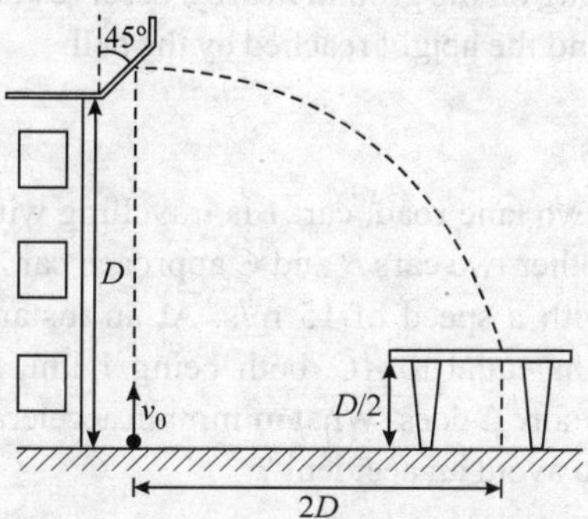

Figure 1.162

Ans. [$\sqrt{6gD}$]

1-43 The current velocity of a river grows in proportion to the distance from its bank and reaches the maximum value v_0 in the middle. Near the banks the velocity is zero. A boat is moving along the river in such a manner that it is always perpendicular to the current and the speed of the boat in still water is u. Find the distance through which the boat crossing the river will be carried away by the current if the width of the river is c. Also determine the trajectory of the boat.

Ans. [$\frac{cv}{4u}$, $y^2 = \frac{ucx}{v_0}$]

1-44 A vertical wind screen of a car is made up of two parts, as shown in figure-1.163, where the upper one A is 25 cm vertically long and covers the 5 cm of the lower piece B. The upper one is hinged at the top so that it can be opened outward, inclining to the vertical. The car is running on the horizontal road at 60 km/hr in the rain which is falling vertically at 20 km/hr. Find the maximum angle, through which the upper part A can be opened outward, such that the rain drops do not enter the car.

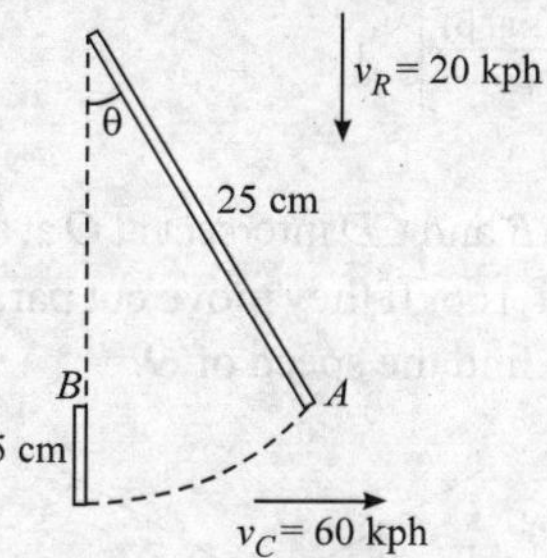

Figure 1.163

Ans. [59°]

1-45 A hunter is riding an elephant of height 4 m moving in a straight line with uniform speed of 2 m/s. He sights a deer running with a speed V in front at a distance of $4\sqrt{5}$ m moving perpendicular to the direction of motion of the elephant. If hunter can throw his spear with a speed of 10 m/s relative to the elephant, then at what angle θ to its direction of motion must he throw his spear horizontally for a successful hit. Find also the speed V of the deer.

Ans. [37°, 6 m/s]

1-46 A swimmer wishes to cross a 500 m wide river flowing at a rate 5 km/hr. His speed with respect to water is 3 km/hr. (a) If he heads in a direction making an angle θ with the flow, he takes to cross the river. (b) Find the shortest possible time to cross the river.

Ans. [(a) 10/sinθ, (b) 10 mins]

1-47 Two particles 1 and 2 move with constant velocities v_1 and v_2. At the initial moment their radius vectors are equal to r_1 and r_2. How must these four vectors be interrelated for the particles to collide ?

Ans. [$\frac{r_2 - r_1}{|r_1 - r_2|} = \frac{v_1 - v_2}{|v_1 - v_2|}$]

1-48 A stone is thrown from ground level so as to just clear a wall 4 m high at a distance of 4 m and falls at a distance of 14 m from the wall. Find the magnitude and direction of the velocity of the ball.

Ans. [$\sqrt{182}$ m/s]

1-49 A bomber plane is moving horizontally in a straight line 594 km/hour in the same straight line. When the fighter is 300 m behind, he fires his guns which are then horizontal. If the bullets have a muzzle velocity of 3348 km/hour relative to the fighter at what distance below the line of sight and at what angle will the bullet hit the bomber ? Neglect air resistance and wind effects. Given that the velocity of the fighter plane is 720 km/hour.

Ans. [0.474 m, 0.9°]

1-50 A man in a row boat must get from Point A to point B on the opposite bank of the river as shown in figure-1.164. The distance $BC = a$. The width of the river $AC = b$. At what minimum speed u relative to the still water should the boat travel to reach the point B ? The velocity of flow of the river is v_0.

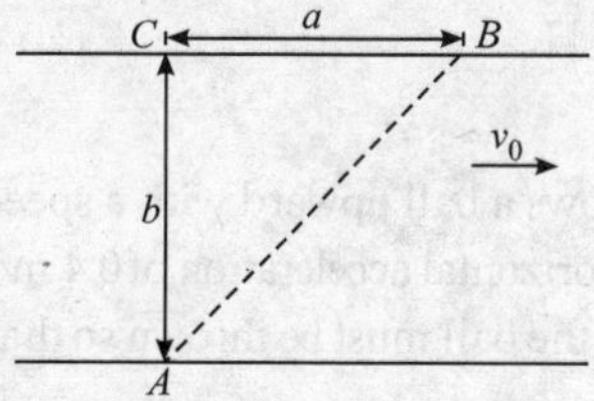

Figure 1.164

Ans. [$\frac{v_0 b}{\sqrt{a^2 + b^2}}$]

1-51 A is projected from origin with an initial velocity $v_0 = 700$ cm/s in a direction 37° above the horizontal as shown in figure-1.165. Another ball B, 300 cm from origin on a line 37° above the horizontal is released from rest at the instant A starts. (a) How far will B have fallen when it is hit by A ? (b) In what direction A moving when it hits B ?

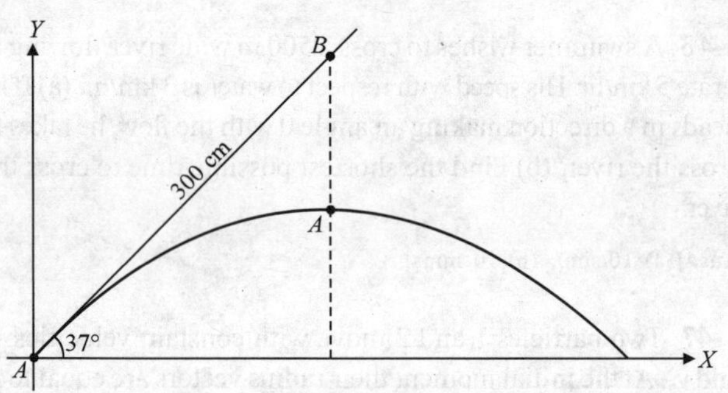

Figure 1.165

Ans. [90 cm, horizontal]

1-52 An aeroplane files horizontally at a height h at a speed v. An anti aircraft gun fires a shell at the plane when it is vertically above the gun. Show that the minimum muzzle velocity required to hit the plane is $\sqrt{v^2 + 2gh}$ at an angle $\tan^{-1}\dfrac{\sqrt{2gh}}{v}$.

1-53 A ball is projected at an angle of 30° above with the horizontal from the top of a tower and strikes the ground in 5 s at an angle of 45° with the horizontal. Find the height of the tower and the speed with which it was projected.

Ans. [$50(\sqrt{3} - 1)$ m/s, $125(2 - \sqrt{3})$ m]

1-54 Two boys simultaneously aim their guns at a bird sitting on a tower. The first boy releases his shot with a speed of 100 m/s at an angle of projection of 30°. The second boy is ahead of the first by a distance of 50 m and releases his shot with a speed of 80 m/s. How must he aim his gun so that both the shots hit the bird simultaneously ? What is the distance of the foot of the tower from the two boys and the height of the tower ? With what velocities and when do the two shots hit the bird ?

Ans. [$\theta = \sin^{-1}\left(\dfrac{5}{8}\right)$]

1-55 A boy throws a ball upward with a speed of 12 m/s. The wind imparts a horizontal acceleration of 0.4 m/s^2. At what angle θ to the vertical, the ball must be thrown so that it returns to the point of release.

Ans. [$\tan^{-1}\left(\dfrac{1}{25}\right)$]

1-56 A student is standing on the open platform of a moving train at a speed of 10 m/s. The student throws a ball into the air along a path that, he judges to make an initial angle of 60° with the horizontal and to be in line with the track. The professor, who is standing on the ground nearby, observes the ball to rise vertically. Find the height reached by the ball.

Ans. [15 m]

1-57 On a two lane road, car A is travelling with a speed of 10 m/s and other two cars B and C approach car A in opposite directions with a speed of 15 m/s. At an instant, when the distance AB is equal to AC, both being 1 km, B decides to overtake A before C does. What minimum acceleration of car B is required to avoid an accident ?

Ans. [1 m/s^2]

1-58 A particle moves in the plane x y with constant acceleration a directed along the negative y-axis. The equation of motion of the particle has the form $y = k_1 x - k_2 x^2$, where k_1 and k_2 are positive constants. Find the velocity of the particle at the origin of coordinates.

Ans. [$\sqrt{(k_1^2 + 1)\dfrac{a}{2k_2}}$]

1-59 A gardener shower jet is placed at a distance d from the wall of a building. If R is the maximum range of the jet that is produced when the bowl is connected to the nose of a fire engine, show that the portion of the wall that is hit by the jet of water is bounded by a parabola whose height is $\dfrac{(R^2 - d^2)}{2R}$ and breadth is $2\sqrt{R^2 - d^2}$.

1-60 A perfectly elastic ball is thrown from the foot of a plane whose inclination to horizontal is β. If after striking the plane at a distance R from the point of projection it rebounds and retraces its former path, find the velocity of projection.

Ans. [$u = \left[\dfrac{gR(1 + 3\sin^2\beta)}{2\sin\beta}\right]^{1/2}$]

1-61 Two lines AB and CD intersect at O at an inclination α, as shown in figure-1.166. If they move out parallel to themselves with the speed v, find the speed of O.

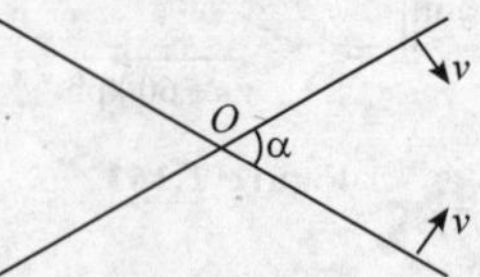

Figure 1.166

Ans. [v cosec $\dfrac{\alpha}{2}$]

1-62 A gun of muzzle speed v_0 is situated at height h above a horizontal plane. Prove that the angle at which it must be fired so as to achieve the greatest range on the plane is given by -

$$\theta = \frac{1}{2}\cos^{-1}\left(\frac{gh}{v_0^2 + gh}\right)$$

1-63 A shell is fired from a gun from the bottom of a hill along its slope. The slope of the hill is $\alpha = 30°$, and the angle of the barrel to the horizontal $\beta = 60°$. The initial velocity v of the shell is 21 m/sec. Find the distance from the gun to the point at which the shell falls.

Ans. [30 m]

1-64 The maximum range of a particle with a certain speed on a horizontal plane is R. Find its maximum range when projected on an inclined plane with inclination 30°.

Ans. [$2R/3$]

1-65 A projectile aimed at a mark which is in the horizontal plane through the point of projection falls a cm short of it when the elevation is α and goes b cm too far when the elevation is β. Show that if the velocity of projection is same in all the cases, the proper elevation is

$$\frac{1}{2}\sin^{-1}\left(\frac{b\sin 2\alpha + a\sin 2\beta}{a+b}\right)$$

1-66 A boy sitting at the rear end of a railway compartment of a train, running at a constant acceleration on horizontal rails throws towards the fore end of the compartment with a muzzle velocity of 20 m/sec at an angle 37° above the horizontal, when the train is running at a speed of 10 m/sec. If the same boy catches the ball without moving from his seat and at the same height of projection, find the speed of the train at the instant of his catching the ball.

Ans. [41.99 m/sec]

1-67 There is an inclined surface of inclination θ. A smooth groove is cut into it forming an angle α with AB as shown in figure-1.167. A steel ball is free to slide a long the groove. If the ball is released from the point O. Find the speed when it comes to A.

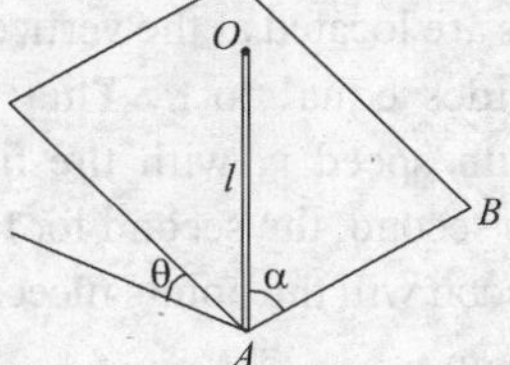

Figure 1.167

Ans. [$\sqrt{2gl\sin\theta\sin\alpha}$]

1-68 To a person travelling due East with velocity u, the wind appears to blow from an angle α North of East. When he starts travelling due North with velocity $2u$, the wind appears to blow from an angle β North of East. Find the true direction of the wind.

Ans. [θ WOS where $\tan\theta = \frac{1+2\cot\alpha}{2+\tan\beta}$]

1-69 A guided missile is fired to strike an object at the same level 38 km away. It may be assumed that it rises vertically 1.5 km and then for the remainder of the flight it follows a parabolic path at an elevation of 45°. Calculate its velocity at the beginning of its parabolic path.

Ans. [2177 km/h]

1-70 A train takes 2 minutes to acquire its full speed 60 kph from rest and 1 minute to come to rest from the full speed. If somewhere in between two stations 1 km of the track be under repair and the limited speed on this part be fixed to 20 kph, find the late running of the train on account of this repair work, assuming otherwise normal at running of the train between the stations.

Ans. [2 min 40 sec]

1-71 A boy is trying to hit a bird sitting on a wall 10 m high with a stone. Just before being hit by the stone, the bird flies away horizontally with a velocity of 5 m/s. The stone further goes up to a maximum height of 5 m and then hits the bird. Determine the initial velocity of stone and angle of projection.

Ans. [73°75; 17.87 m/s]

1-72 Particle P and Q of mass 20 gms and 40 gms respectively are simultaneously projected from points A and B on the ground. The initial velocities of P and Q make 45° and 135° angles respectively with the horizontal as shown in the figure-1.168. Each particle has an initial speed of 49 m /s. The separation AB is 245 m. Both particles travel in the same vertical plane and undergo a collision. After the collision P retraces its path. Determine the position of Q when it hits the ground. How much time after the collision does the particle Q take to reach the ground. Take $g = 9.8$ m/s^2.

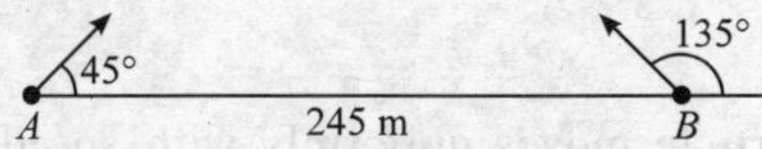

Figure 1.168

Ans. [122.5 m, 3.53 sec]

1-73 Two shots are projected from a gun at the top of a hill with the same velocity u at angles of projection α and β

respectively. If the shots strike the horizontal ground through the foot of the hill at the same point, show that the height h of the hill above the plane is given by :

$$h = \frac{2u^2(1 - \tan\alpha \tan\beta)}{g(\tan\alpha + \tan\beta)^2}$$

1-74 A point moves in the plane xy according to the law $x = a \sin \omega t$, $y = a(a - \cos \omega t)$, where a and ω are positive constants. Find :

(a) The distance s traversed by the point during the time T;

(b) The angle between the point's velocity and acceleration vectors.

Ans. [(a) $a\omega\tau$ (b) $\frac{\pi}{2}$]

1-75 Two towers AB and CD are situated at a distance d apart, as shown in figure-1.169. AB is 20 m high and CD is 30 m high from the ground. An object of mass m is thrown from the top of AB horizontally with a velocity of 10 m/s towards CD. Simultaneously another object of mass 2 m is thrown from the top of CD at an angle of 60° to the horizontal towards AB with the same magnitude of initial velocity as that of the first object. The two objects move in the same vertical plane, collide in mid air and stick to each other (i) calculate the distance d between the towers and (ii) find the position where the objects hit the ground.

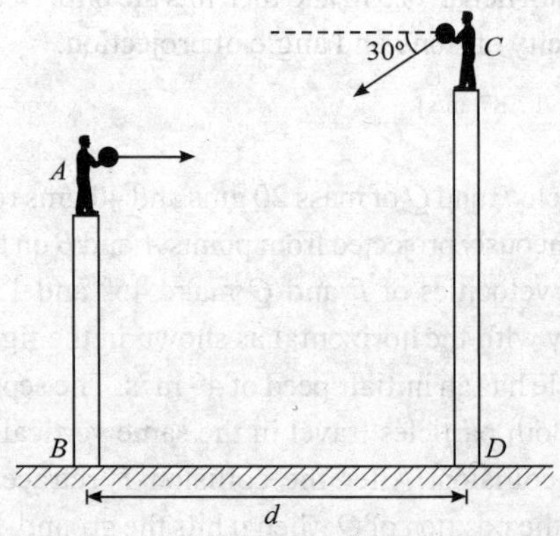

Figure 1.169

Ans. [$10\sqrt{3}$ m, $20\frac{\sqrt{3}}{3}$ m]

1-76 A particle moves uniformly with speed v along a parabolic path $y = kx^2$, where k is a positive constant. Find the acceleration of the particle at the point $x = 0$.

Ans. [2 kv^2]

1-77 A particle is projected up an inclined plane of inclination β at an elevation α to the horizon. Show that (a) $\tan\alpha = \cot\beta + 2\tan\beta$, if particle strikes the plane at right angles; (b) $\tan\alpha = 2\tan\beta$, if the particle strikes the plane horizontally.

1-78 Two bodies were thrown simultaneously from the same point one straight up, and the other at an angle θ_0 with the horizontal. The initial speed of each body is equal to v_0. Neglecting the air drag, find the distance between the bodies after time t.

Ans. [$v_0 t\sqrt{2(1 - \sin\theta_0)}$]

1-79 A particle move in a plane according to the law $v = v_0\boldsymbol{i} + b\omega\cos\omega t\boldsymbol{j}$. If the particle is at the origin at $t = 0$, find the equation of its path, $y = f(x)$ and its distance from the origin at $t = 3\omega/2$.

Ans. [$y = b\sin\left(\omega\frac{x}{v_0}\right)$, $\sqrt{\frac{9}{4}v_0^2\omega^2 + b^2\sin^2\left(\frac{3}{2}\omega^2\right)}$]

1-80 Two swimmers start a race. One who reaches the point C first on the other bank wins the race. A makes his strokes in a direction of 37° to the river flow with velocity 5 kph relative to water. B makes his strokes in a direction 127° to the river flow with same relative velocity. River is flowing with speed of 2 kph and is 100 m wide. Who will win the race ? Compute the time taken by A and B to reach the point C if the speeds of A and B on the ground are 8 kph and 6 kph respectively.

Ans. [B wins, time of A = 165 s, time of B = 150 s]

1-81 Two particles are simultaneously projected in the same vertical plane from the same point with velocities u and v at angles α and β with horizontal. Show that :

(a) The line joining them moves parallel to itself.

(b) The time that elapses when their velocities are parallel is

$$\frac{uv\sin(\alpha - \beta)}{g(v\cos\beta - u\cos\alpha)}$$

(c) The time that elapses between their transits through the other common point is

$$\frac{2uv\sin(\alpha - \beta)}{g(v\cos\beta + u\cos\alpha)}$$

1-82 Three points are located at the vertices of an equilateral triangle whose sides equal to a. They all start moving simultaneously with speed v, with the first point heading continually for the second, the second for third, and the third for the first. How soon will the points meet and where ?

Ans. [$2a/3v$, at centroid]

* * * * *

Forces & Newton's Laws of Motion 2

FEW WORDS FOR STUDENTS

In the last chapters you learned to describe motion. In this chapter we discuss the underlying causes of motion, which are summed up in Newton's three laws. These laws enable us to describe the future or past of the motion of a body if we know the forces acting on it. In some cases you will see that these laws require some modification for analization of the problem situation.

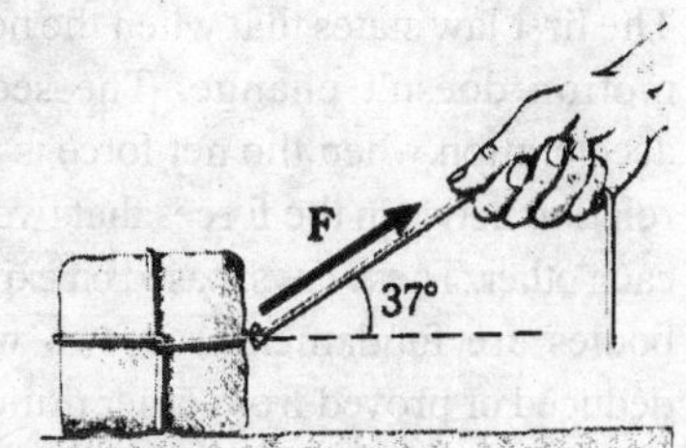

CHAPTER CONTENTS

COVER APPLICATION

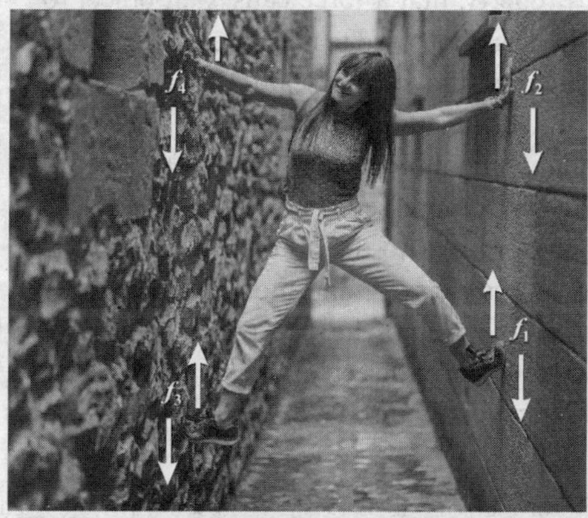

Figure (a)

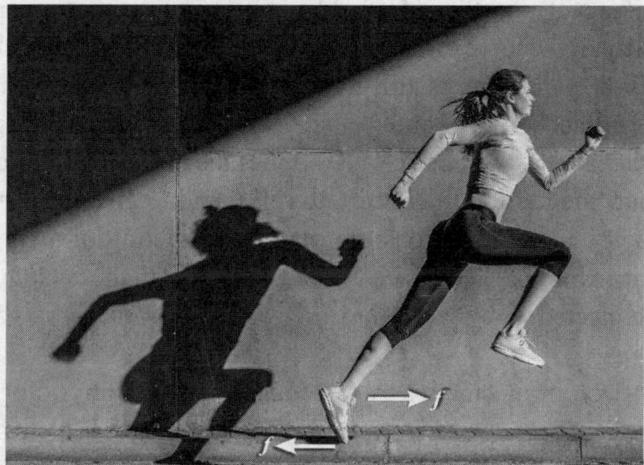

Figure (b)

Figure-(a) shows a girl holding her body at rest with support of two walls by pressing with her hands and shoes. The friction acting on the two walls is balancing the weight of her body due to which she is able to keep herself at rest. For sufficient friction, she has to push the walls with a minimum force so as to have sufficient normal reaction at four contacts to keep friction balancing her weight. Figure-(b) shows a running girl who can accelerate only because of the friction acting on her body at her shoe. Friction increases with normal contact force so if while running she takes slight jump, the normal reaction will be more and it will impart more friction and higher acceleration on body so she will be able to run faster.

How a body moves is determined by the interactions of that body with its environment. These interactions are called forces. In preceding chapters we studied kinematics, the language for describing motion. Now we are ready to think about what makes bodies move the way they do. Here we'll use the kinematics relations with two new concepts, force and mass, to analyze the principle of dynamics. These principles can be wrapped up in a neat package of three statements called Newton's laws of motion. The first law states that when the net force on a body is zero, its motion doesn't change. The second law relates force to acceleration when the net force is not zero. The third law is a relation between the forces that two interacting bodies exert on each other. These laws, based on experimental studies of moving bodies are fundamental in two ways. First, they cannot be deduced or proved from other principles. Second, they make it possible to understand most familiar kinds of motion. Newton's laws are universal, however, they require modification at very high speed (close to the speed of light) and for very small sizes (as within an atom).

The concept of force gives us a quantitative description of the interaction between two bodies or between a body and its environment. When a force involves direct contact between two bodies, we call it a contact force. Contact forces include the pushes or pulls you exert with your hand, the force of a rope pulling on a block to which it is tied, and the friction force that the ground exerts on a ball player sliding into home. There are also long range forces, that act even when the bodies are separated by some distance (small or may be large). Anyone can experience a common long range force if he ever plays with a pair of magnets. Gravitational attraction is also a long range force.

2.1 Force and Superposition

To lift a pail of water and to hold it in his hand a man must apply to the pail the force of the hand, he feels the force with which he pulls the pail upwards, this force is equal to the one with which the pail acts on his hand in the downward direction. When a worker pushes a loaded cart he applies the force of his hands to impart the motion to the cart, to roll it and to give the cart its velocity. In these actions the man has a feeling of a certain strain in his body. The force we have spoken of in these examples is connected with that felling.

However, in mechanics by force is not meant a physiological felling. What is understood by force in mechanics is a physical cause changing the state of motion of bodies and resulting from an interaction of two bodies. Thus, a physical force in mechanics should by no means be confused with the felling of strain. For instance, a worker pushing a cart acts upon the cart with a certain force and this action is accompanied with a feeling of strain in his muscles, however the motion of the cart is governed by a certain law connected with the magnitude of the force applied by the worker to the cart and not with his felling. If the same force is applied to the cart by another body for example, by a tractor, the motion of the cart will be the same.

As discussed above in everyday language, a force is a push or a pull. From common experience, we can point out four properties of force :

(a) Since a push or a pull has both magnitude and direction, we expect that force is a vector quantity.

(b) Forces occur in pairs. If object A exerts a force on object B, then B also exerts a force on A. For example, when a bat strikes a ball, the bat exerts a force on the ball but the ball exerts a force on the bat also. In the example discussed in previous para, when a worker exerts a force on a cart, it results strains in his muscles.

(c) A force can cause an object to accelerate. If you kick a football, the ball's velocity changes while your foot is in contact with it.

(d) A force can deform an object. As you can see from figure-2.1, the ball when hits the floor, is deformed by the contact force exerted on it by the floor. The floor is deformed too, but since it is harder than the ball, its deformation is not as noticeable.

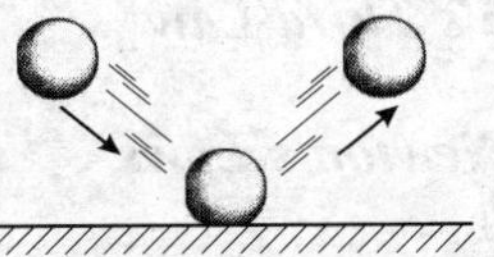

Figure 2.1

The last property, that a force causes an object to be deformed, is often used to measure a force. This is the principle of a spring scale. A spring scale consists of a spring, usually contained in a housing, and a point which indicates the amount the spring is stretched or compressed. The magnitude of this force is proportional to the amount the spring is stretched or compressed, and the direction of the force is along the spring. The scale may be calibrated to read in Newtons or directly in kg to measure the weight of an object (figure-2.2)

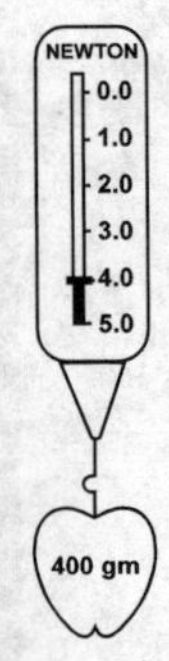

Figure 2.2

Web Reference of Video Lectures at www.physicsgalaxy.com

Age Group - High School Physics | Age 17-19 Years
Section - MECHANICS
Topic - Forces and Newton's Laws of Motion
Module Numbers - 1, 2, and 3

2.2 Newton's First Law

"Everybody continues in its state of rest, or in uniform motion in a straight line unless it is compelled to change that state by forces impressed upon it."

This law is often called the law of inertia, because inertia means resistance to a change, and the law states that an object naturally tends to maintain whatever velocity it happens to have, including zero velocity.

If an object is in a state of rest or in uniform motion in a straight line, then its acceleration is zero. Thus the first law can be stated in an another way as - If no forces are exerted on an object, the object's acceleration is zero. Thus if we find that if the body is at rest at the start, it remains at rest, if it is initially moving, it continues to move in the same direction with constant speed. These results show that in Newton's first law, zero net force is equivalent to no force at all. This is just the principle of superposition of forces.

When a body is acted on by no forces, or by several forces such that their vector sum is zero, we say that the body is in equilibrium. In equilibrium, a body is either at rest (static equilibrium) or moving in a straight line with constant velocity (dynamic equilibrium). But for a body in equilibrium, the net force on it is zero

$$\Sigma \vec{F} = 0 \qquad \ldots (2.1)$$

For this to be true, each component of the net force must be zero, so

$$\Sigma F_x = 0 \quad \text{and} \quad \Sigma F_y = 0 \qquad \ldots (2.2)$$

We are assuming that the body can be represented adequately as a point particle and the above conditions represent its translational equilibrium i.e. no straight line motion. There is one more type of equilibrium called rotational equilibrium, which will be discussed in later part of the chapter.

2.3 Newton's Second Law

In discussing Newton's first law, we have seen that when a body is acted on by no force or zero net force, it moves with constant velocity and zero acceleration. But what happens when the net force is not zero ? For example, in figure-2.3 (a) we apply a constant horizontal force to a sliding box on a smooth plane in the same direction the box is moving. Then $\overline{F}$ is constant and in the same direction as v. We find that during the time the force is acting, the velocity of the box changes at a constant rate that is box moves with constant acceleration.

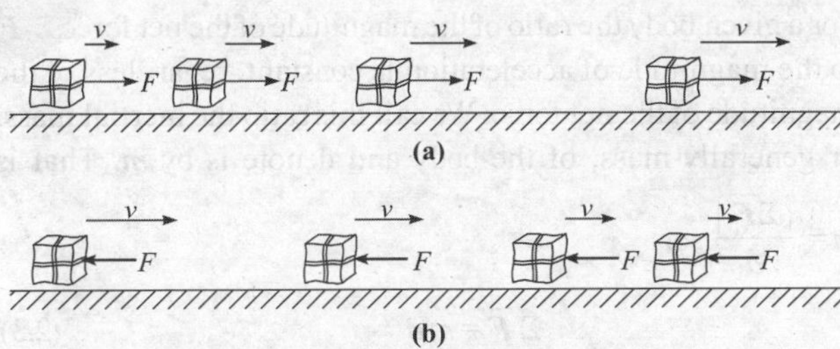

Figure 2.3

Similar application can be shown by the example in figure-2.3 (b), if force $\vec{F}$ acts on the body in opposition to the direction of its velocity $\vec{v}$, the velocity of the box reduces at a constant rate.

We conclude that the presence of a net force acting on a body causes the body to accelerate. The direction of the acceleration is the same as that of the net force. If the magnitude of the net force is constant, then so is the magnitude of the acceleration.

These conclusions about net force and acceleration also apply to a body moving along a curved path. For example, figure-2.4 shows a ball moving in a horizontal circle on an ice surface of negligible friction. A string attaching the ball to the center exerts a force of constant magnitude toward the centre of the circle. The result is acceleration that is constant in magnitude and directed toward the centre of the circle. The speed of the ball here remains constant as we'll discuss in further chapters that the force acting in a direction perpendicular to velocity can only be able to change the direction of velocity. It cannot change the magnitude of velocity.

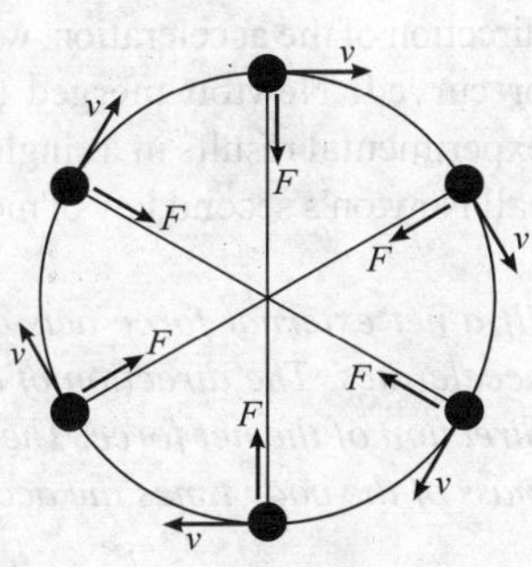

Figure 2.4

Figure-2.5 shows the relationship between the force and the acceleration. We apply a constant horizontal force on the disc on a frictionless horizontal surface, it accelerates with a constant acceleration. If we change the magnitude of the net force, the acceleration changes in the same proportion. Doubling the net force doubles the acceleration, halving the force halves the acceleration and so on.

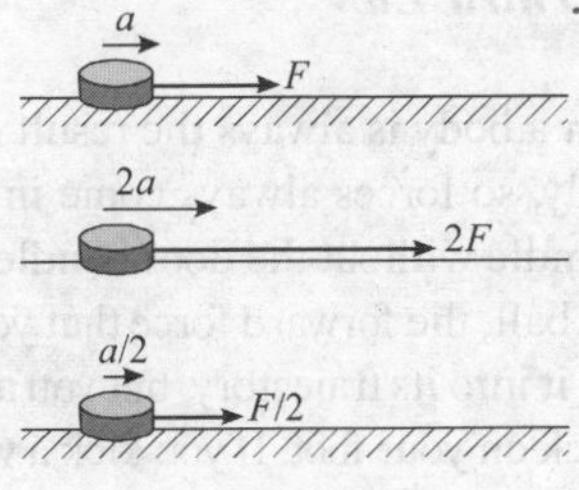

Figure 2.5

For a given body the ratio of the magnitude of the net force $\Sigma \vec{F}$ to the magnitude of acceleration is constant, regardless of the magnitude of the net force. We call this ratio the inertial mass, or generally mass, of the body and denote is by m. That is

$m = \dfrac{|\Sigma \vec{F}|}{a}$, or

$$\Sigma \vec{F} = m\vec{a} \quad \ldots (2.3)$$

Here we have to be careful to state that the net force on a body is what causes that body to accelerate. Experiment shows that if a combination of forces $\vec{F}_1$, $\vec{F}_2$, $\vec{F}_3$, ... is applied to a body, the body will have the same acceleration (magnitude and direction) as when only a single force is applied, if that single force is equal to the vector sum $\vec{F}_1 + \vec{F}_2 + \vec{F}_3 + ...$ In other words, the principle of superposition of forces also holds true when the net force is not zero and the body is accelerating.

Equation-(2.3) relates the magnitude of the net force on a body to the magnitude of the acceleration that it produces. We have also seen that the direction of the net force is the same as the direction of the acceleration, whether the body's path is straight or curved. Newton merged up all these relationships and experimental results in a single concise statement that we now call Newton's second law of motion :

"If a net external force acts on a body of mass m, the body accelerates. The direction of acceleration is the same as the direction of the net force. The net force vector is equal to the mass of the body times the acceleration of the body."

Symbolically it can be represented by equation-(2.3). Usually, we will use it in component form, with a separate equation for each component of force and the corresponding acceleration.

$$\Sigma F_x = ma_x; \quad \Sigma F_y = ma_y; \quad \Sigma F_z = ma_z$$

This set of component equations is equivalent to the single vector equation-(2.3). Each component of total force equals the mass times the corresponding component of acceleration.

The other important point, towards which the Newton's second law refers is external forces. By this we mean forces exerted on the body by other bodies in its environment. It's impossible for a body to affect its own motion by exerting a force on itself.

2.4 Newton's Third Law

A force acting on a body is always the result of its interaction with another body, so forces always come in pairs. You can't pull on a door handle without the door handle pulling back on you. If you kick a ball, the forward force that your foot exerts on the ball launches it into its trajectory, but you also feel the force the ball exerts back on your foot. If you kick a wall, the pain you feel is due to the force that the wall exerts on your foot.

In every case the force that you exert on the other body is in the opposite direction to the force that body exerts on you. Whenever two bodies interact, the two forces that they exerts on each other are always equal in magnitude and opposite in direction. This is called Newton's third law of motion. In words it can be expressed as

"To every action there is always opposed an equal reaction, or the mutual actions of two bodies upon each other are always directed towards the other one. These two forces have the same magnitude but are opposite in direction. These two forces act on different bodies."

Look at the figure-2.6, a child kicks a bowl. Here also we can analyze the concept of "*action-reaction*". The child kicks the bowl with a force give by $\vec{F}_{A\,on\,B}$ and its reaction is the force with which the bowl reacts the foot of the child $\vec{F}_{B\,on\,A}$. But in more precise way we can consider either force as the "action" and the other as the "reaction". We often say simply that the force always act in pairs and are equal and opposite, meaning that they have equal magnitudes and opposite directions.

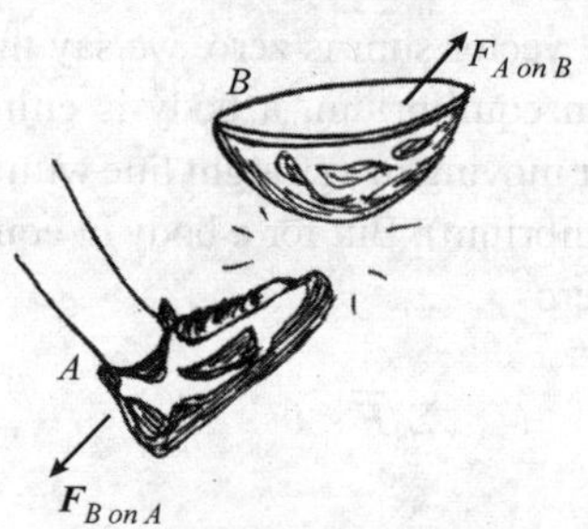

Figure 2.6

In figure-2.6 the action and reaction forces are contact forces that are present only when the two bodies are touching. But Newton's third law also applies to long range forces that do not require physical contact, such as the force of gravitational attraction or the electrostatic interaction between two charged bodies. A cork ball exerts an upward gravitational force on the earth that is equal in magnitude to the downward gravitational force the earth exerts on the ball. When you drop the ball in gravity, both the ball and the earth accelerate towards each other. The net force on each body has the same magnitude, but the earth's acceleration is microscopically small because its mass is so great.

2.5 Using Newton's Laws

Newton's three laws of motion contain all the basic principles we need to solve a wide variety of problems in mechanics. These laws are very simple in form, but the process of applying them to specific situation can pose real challenges. In this part of the chapter we'll discuss the techniques and methods of solving typical problems concerned with the application of Newton's Laws of motion.

In a given problem Newton's laws are applied for the objects given in the problem. In a specific problem, first we are required to choose a body and then we find the number of forces acting on it, and all the forces are drawn on the body, considering it as a point mass. The resulting diagram is known as free body diagram (*FBD*). Here be careful that in free body diagram, we are required to show only those forces which are acting on the body, from its surroundings, *do not include those forces which are applied by the body*. Before learning how to draw free body diagram, and its equations of motion, we'll discuss about some specific forces and their properties.

2.5.1 External and Internal Forces

Whenever a force acts on a body, it changes the motion of the body. As the motion of a body or bodies is concerned there can be two type of forces - External and Internal forces. External forces are those which act from outside of the system, only action acts on the system, reaction of these forces are not utilized by the system. Internal forces are those which are developed within the system bodies, hence both action and reaction of these force are in the system. If we consider a situation, shown in figure-2.7, box A is placed over box B, and a force F is applied on box A.

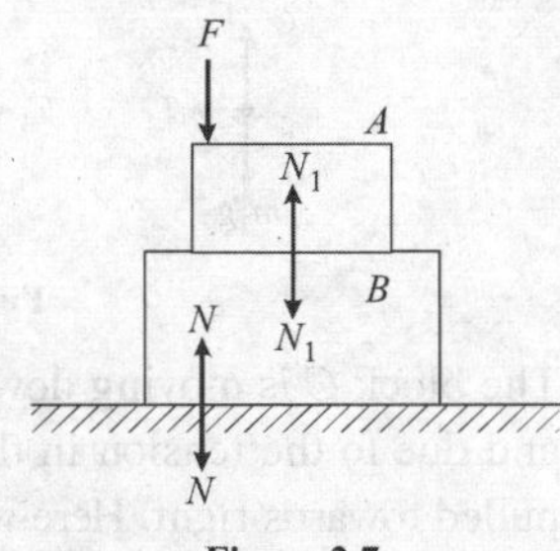

Figure 2.7

Here system includes two blocks, A and B, and the force F which is acting from outside of the system is an external force and the normal contact force between the two blocks is the internal force of this system. Now we'll discuss properties and applications for some important forces.

2.5.2 Normal Contact Force

It is also called as normal reaction between two surfaces. It always acts in a direction perpendicular to the contact surface. Have a look at the following situations and the normal reactions shown in the free body diagrams of the respective objects in figure-2.8. We note here that in parts (c) and (e), the normal reaction on a spherical or cylindrical object always passes through the centre of the object as the contact surface is tangential to the object.

Also note in part (b), where the rod is in contact with the ground, the contact surface is that of ground as there is only one point of rod in contact, hence, normal reaction is perpendicular to the surface of ground, on rod upward and on ground downward. Similarly if we consider the contact of the rod and the edge of the box, the surface in contact is that of the rod, hence normal reaction is perpendicular to its surface and on box it is in opposite direction (action-reaction).

In part (d), a box is supported by two side edges of corners. The normal reaction at the contacts is perpendicular to the surfaces of the sides of box. If box rotates along the sides, the normal reactions remains perpendicular to these surfaces.

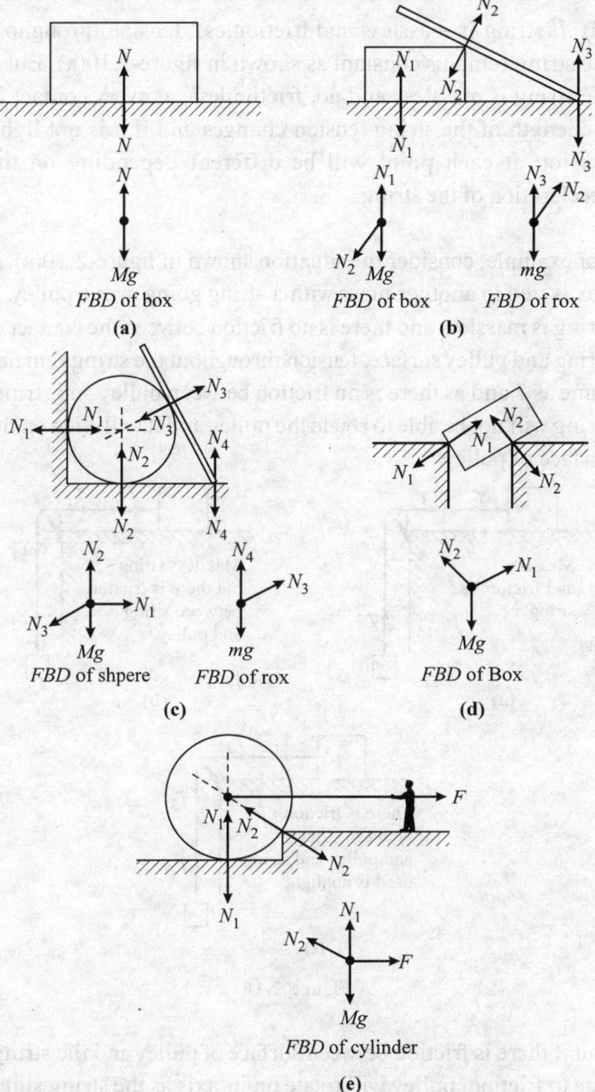

Figure 2.8

2.5.3 Tension in a String

It is an inter molecular force between the atoms of a string, which acts or reacts when the string is stretched There are some important points to remember about the tension in a string, which are helpful in drawing free body diagram of the bodies in a system. These are

(i) Force of tension act on a body in the direction away from the point of contact or tied ends of the string. For example consider figure-2.9. A man pulls a box with a string. The tension in string acts on the box towards right or in the direction away from the tied point and on the man it is again away from it. The way of showing the direction of tension is shown in figure.

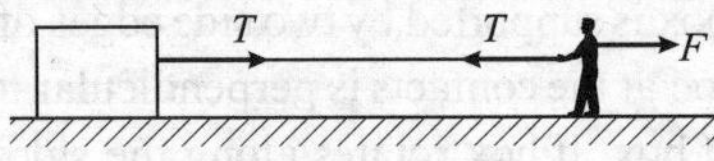

Figure 2.9

(ii) If string is massless and frictionless, tension throughout the string remains constant as shown in figure-2.10(a). But if the string is massless and not frictionless, at every contact in the length of the string tension changes and if it is not light, tension at each point will be different depending on the acceleration of the string.

For example, consider the situation shown in figure-2.10(a). A box is tied to another mass with a string going over a pulley. If string is massless and there is no friction between the contact of string and pulley surface, tension throughout the string remains same as T and as there is no friction between pulley and string, string will not be able to rotate the pulley and it will slide on the surface of pulley.

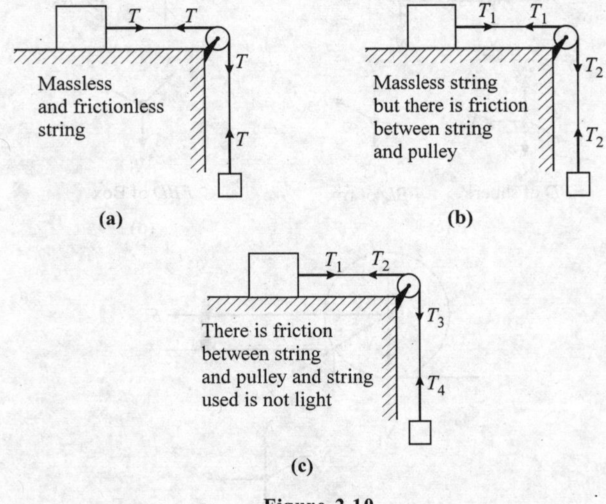

Figure 2.10

But if there is friction between surface of pulley and the string, due to friction, pulley will rotate on its axis as the string slides on it. In this case due to friction between pulley and the string, tensions in string on two sides of the pulley will be different as shown in figure-2.10(b). If string has a mass, it will accelerate and tension at each point will be different on the string as shown in figure-2.10(c). How this tension can be obtained, we will explain in further sections.

(iii) If a force is directly applied on a string, as say a child is pulling a tied string from the other end with some force, the tension in the string will be equal to the applied force, irrespective of the motion of the pulling agent. In figure-2.9, the man is applying a force F on string, thus the tension in string will be equal to this force, irrespective of whether the box will move or not, man will move or not.

Above three points are very useful in application of Newton's laws to different situations. For better understanding of the above points, we consider a situation shown in figure-2.11

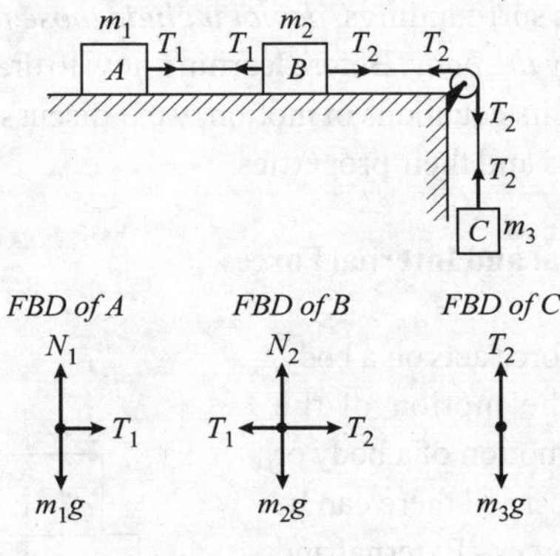

Figure 2.11

The block C is moving down due to the force of gravity on it and due to the tension in the string, blocks A and B are also pulled towards right. Here we assume that the strings used are massless and frictionless, thus in a string tension will not change. Let us regard tension in the string between A and B as T_1 and in the other string as T_2. As we have discussed that the direction of the tension on a body is always away from the point of contact or tied ends, the respective directions are shown in figure. String is passing over the pulley, thus at the contacts of pulley it experiences two T_2, one towards left and other downwards.

The respective free body diagrams for the blocks A, B and C are also shown in the figure, which represent the forces acting on the blocks, independent of the others.

We take one more example for the similar situation, shown in figure-2.12. The respective free body diagrams are also shown. Here the important thing is, in the free body diagram of bigger block. M. Two tensions T_1 are shown, one towards left and other downward. Actually these forces are acting on the pulley P attached to the block M at its upper right corner. As pulley P is rigidly attached to it, all forces on pulley can be considered as acting on the block M.

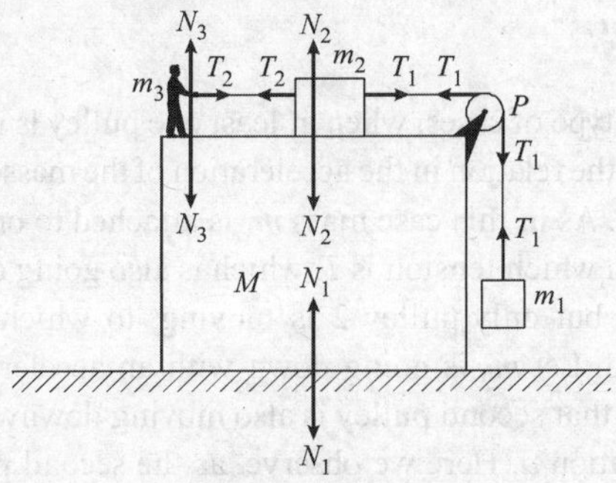

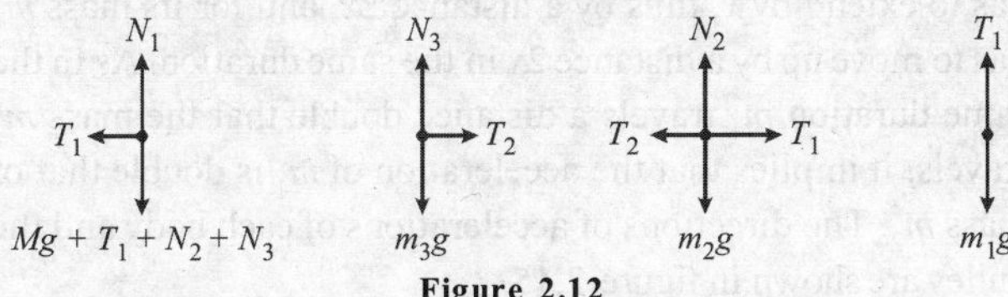

Free Body Diagrams of Masses M, m_3, m_2 and m_1

Figure 2.12

Another important thing to be noted for further use is the tension T_2 in the second string, the man is holding. *This tension is equal to the force applied by the man holding it.*

2.5.4 Application of Forces in Newton's Second Law

If some forces are acting on a body, then the resultant of all the forces $\vec{F}$ is equal to the product of mass of the body and the acceleration produced in it. Thus

$$\vec{F} = m\,\vec{a} \qquad \ldots(2.4)$$

If a body is at rest, known as state of equilibrium, we say resultant of all the forces acting on it are equal to zero. Thus

$$\vec{F} = 0 \qquad \ldots(2.5)$$

For solving a given problem on Newton's Laws, firstly the forces acting on each of the bodies of the system given are analyzed and then free body diagram of each body is drawn independently.

In each free body diagram all the forces are generally resolved in two mutually perpendicular directions, one of which must be along the relative motion of the body on its reference surface. If body is in equilibrium, then the resolving direction must be in the direction of tendency of motion of the body. The direction in which the body is moving we apply equation-(2.4) and for the direction normal to it, in which there is no motion of the body we use equation-(2.5).

For better understanding of above concept, we take some examples.

Illustrative Example 2.1

Find the acceleration of masses m_1 and m_2 connected by an inextensible string, shown in figure-2.13(a). The string and pulley are assumed to be massless and frictionless.

Solution

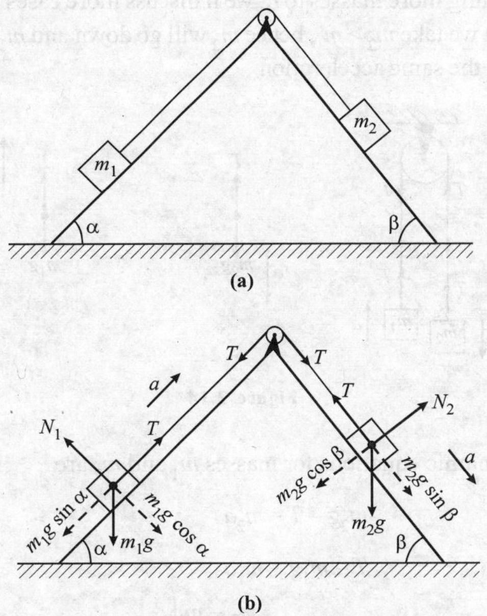

Figure 2.13

Respective free body diagrams are shown in figure-2.13(b). Here we assume that the mass m_2 is going down the incline plane with an acceleration a, hence mass m_1 will go up the incline with the same acceleration as they are connected by an inextensible string.

Here we resolve forces in free body diagrams along the incline and normal to it, as we have discussed that one of the direction of resolution must be along the motion of the body. The dynamic equation for motion of the masses m_1 and m_2 are given below.

For mass m_2 in the direction of motion

$$m_2 g \sin\beta - T = m_2 a \qquad \ldots(2.6)$$

Normal to the direction of motion

$$N_2 = m_2 g \cos\beta \qquad \ldots(2.7)$$

For mass m_1 in the direction of motion

$$T - m_1 g \sin\alpha = m_1 a \qquad \ldots(2.8)$$

Normal to the direction of motion

$$N_1 = m_1 g \cos\alpha \qquad \ldots(2.9)$$

Adding equations-(2.6) and (2.8), we get

$$m_2 g \sin\beta - m_1 g \sin\alpha = (m_2 + m_1)a$$

or

$$a = \frac{m_2 \sin\beta - m_1 \sin\alpha}{m_2 + m_1}\, g$$

Atwood's Machine: It is a simple pulley supporting two masses connected with a string as shown in figure-2.14. There can be several variations in it by increasing number of pulleys and adding more masses to it, we'll discuss more cases further. Here let we take $m_2 > m_1$, hence m_2 will go down and m_1 will go up with the same acceleration.

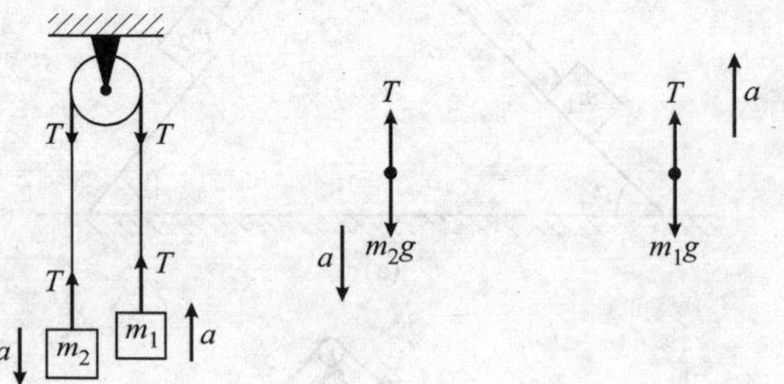

Figure 2.14

The dynamic equations for masses m_1 and m_2 are

$$m_2g - T = m_2a$$

$$T - m_1g = m_1a$$

Solving we get $$a = \frac{m_2 - m_1}{m_1 + m_2}g \qquad \ldots(2.10)$$

and $$T = \frac{(2m_1m_2)g}{m_1 + m_2} \qquad \ldots(2.11)$$

Above two results are very useful as intermediate results in several problems.

Now we take another example of a modified Atwood's machine, with a movable pulley.

 # Illustrative Example 2.2

A situation is shown in figure-2.15, Find the acceleration of masses m_1 and m_2 mass of pulley is m_p. Consider the string going over the pulley is massless and frictionless.

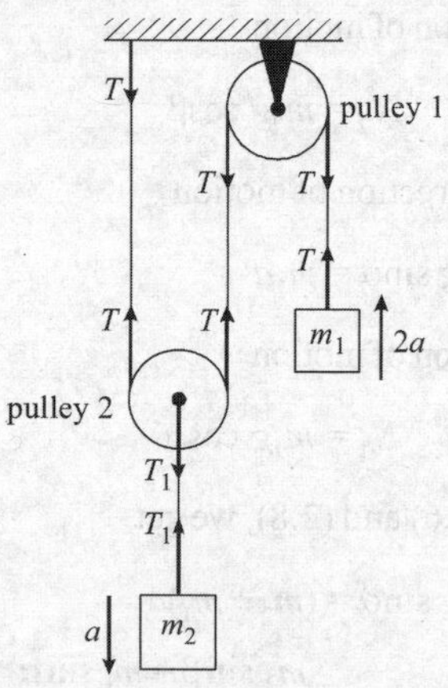

Figure 2.15

Solution

In such type of cases, when at least one pulley is moving, first we find the relation in the acceleration of the masses, which are moving. As in this case mass m_1 is attached to one end of the string in which tension is T, which is also going over both the pulley's but only pulley 2 is moving, to which mass m_2 is attached. Let m_2 is going down with an acceleration a, this implies that second pulley is also moving downward with the acceleration a. Here we observe, as the second pulley moves down say by a distance x, string on both sides of this pulley has to extend by x, thus by a distance $2x$, and for its mass m_1 has to move up by a distance $2x$ in the same duration. As in the same duration m_1 travels a distance double that the mass m_2 travels, it implies that the acceleration of m_1 is double that of mass m_2. The directions of accelerations of each body and the pulley are shown in figure-2.15.

The dynamic equation of each object is

Motion equation for mass m_1 is

$$T - m_1g = m_1(2a) \qquad \ldots(2.12)$$

Motion equation for mass m_2 is

$$m_2g - T_1 = m_2a \qquad \ldots(2.13)$$

Motion equation for pulley is

$$T_1 + m_pg - 2T = m_pa \qquad \ldots(2.14)$$

Multiplying equation-(2.12) by 2 and adding with equation-(2.13) and (2.14)

$$m_2g + m_pg - 2m_1g = (4m_1 + m_P + m_2)a$$

or $$a = \frac{m_2 + m_P - 2m_1}{4m_1 + m_P + m_2}g$$

In above case if pulleys are considered as massless, we have $m_P = 0$, thus directly from equation-(2.14), it gives $T_1 = 2T$ and the acceleration a can be given as

$$a = \frac{m_2 - 2m_1}{4m_1 + m_2}g$$

 # Illustrative Example 2.3

Find the acceleration of masses m_1 and m_2, moving down the smooth incline plane. The string and the pulley are massless and frictionless.

Solution

As discussed in previous problem, by observation we can say that if acceleration of m_1 down the plane is a, then acceleration of m_2, vertically up will be $2a$. As it is also given that pulleys are massless, the tension in second string can be taken as $2T$, if T is the tension in the first string, shown in figure-2.16.

Here we can directly write the dynamic equations of motion of the two masses m_1 and m_2 as

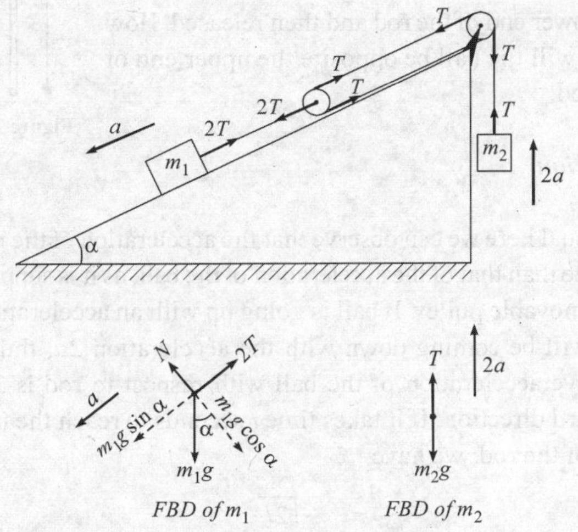

Figure 2.16

Motion equation for mass m_1 is

$$m_1 g \sin\alpha - 2T = m_1 a \quad \ldots(2.15)$$

Motion equation for mass m_2 is

$$T - m_2 g = m_2(2a) \quad \ldots(2.16)$$

Multiplying equation-(2.16) by 2 and adding to equation-(2.15), we get

$$a = \frac{m_1 \sin\alpha - 2m_2}{m_1 + 4m_2}$$

Illustrative Example 2.4

A toy truck of mass M is moving towards left with an acceleration a_1 as shown in figure-2.17. It is connected to a mass m_1 with a massless and frictionless string, going over a movable massless pulley, to which another mass m_2 is connected. Find the force acting on the truck towards left and the accelerations of masses m_1 and m_2.

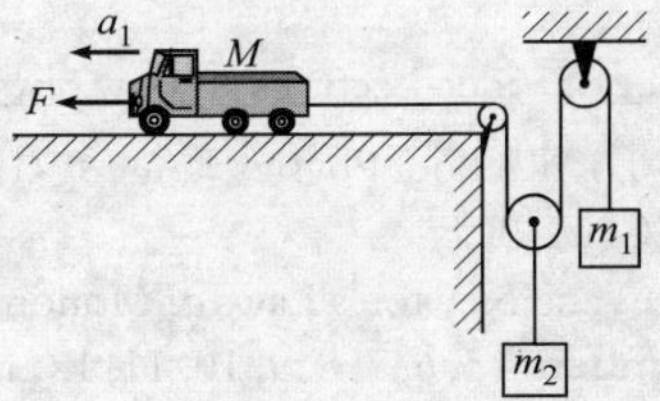

Figure 2.17

Solution

Useful forces acting on the bodies are shown in the diagram in figure-2.18. The direction of accelerations initially we have assumed are also shown. As we have explained earlier that if a movable pulley is present, first we are required to find the relation in accelerations of the bodies. Here it is given that truck is moving towards left with acceleration a_1, for m_1 and m_2 we assume that they are moving down and up with acceleration a_3 and a_2 respectively.

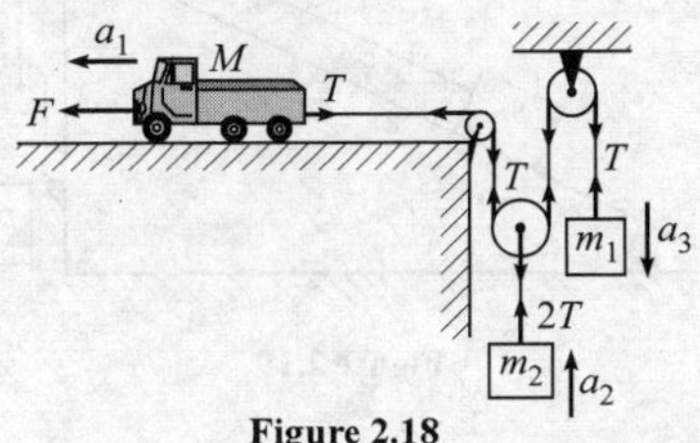

Figure 2.18

Let we consider if mass m_2 moves up by a distance x_2, pulley attached to it will also move up by x_2, which will result a slackness of $2x_2$ in the string attached to truck and m_1. If in the same duration truck moves by x_1 and mass m_1 moves down by x_3, we have $x_1 + x_3 = 2x_2$. Same relation we have among the acceleration of the respective bodies as

$$a_1 + a_3 = 2a_2 \quad \ldots(2.17)$$

According to the forces shown in figure-2.18 and the force of gravity, we can write the dynamic equations of the three bodies as

For Truck $\quad F - T = Ma_1 \quad \ldots(2.18)$

For mass m_1 $\quad m_1 g - T = m_1 a_3 \quad \ldots(2.19)$

For mass m_2 $\quad 2T - m_2 g = m_2 a_2 \quad \ldots(2.20)$

Subtracting equation-(2.18) from (2.19), we get

$$m_1 a_3 - Ma_1 = m_1 g - F$$

or

$$a_3 = \frac{m_1 g - F + Ma_1}{m_1} \quad \ldots(2.21)$$

From equation-(2.17)

$$a_2 = \frac{a_1}{2} + \frac{m_1 g - F + Ma_1}{2m_1} \quad \ldots(2.22)$$

Adding the above equations-(2.18), (2.19) and (2.20), we get

$$F + m_1 g - m_2 g = Ma_1 + m_1 a_3 + m_2 a_2$$

or

$$F = m_2 g - m_1 g + Ma_1 + m_1 a_3 + m_2 a_2$$

Where a_2 and a_3 are given by the equation-(2.21) and (2.22)

Illustrative Example 2.5

Find the acceleration of the body of mass m_2 in the arrangement shown in figure-2.19, if the mass m_2 is η times great as the mass m_1 and the angle that the inclined plane forms with the horizontal is equal to θ. The masses of the pulleys and threads, as well as the friction, are assumed to be negligible.

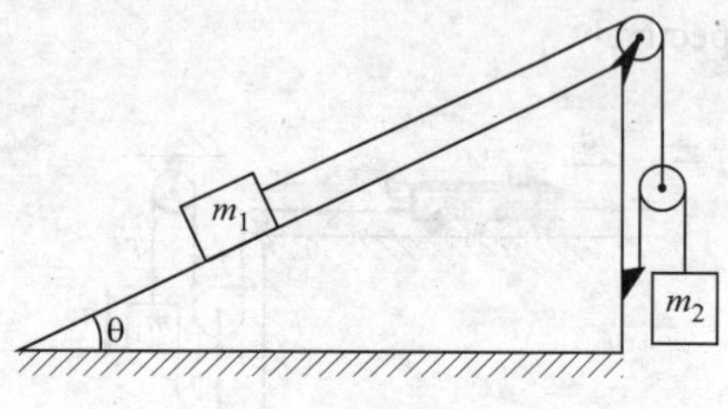

Figure 2.19

Solution

Here the small pulley is movable and by observation we can say that the acceleration of m_2 is double that of m_1. So we assume if m_1 is moving up the inclined plane with an acceleration a, the acceleration of mass m_2 going down is $2a$. The free body diagrams of m_1 and m_2 are shown in figure-2.20.

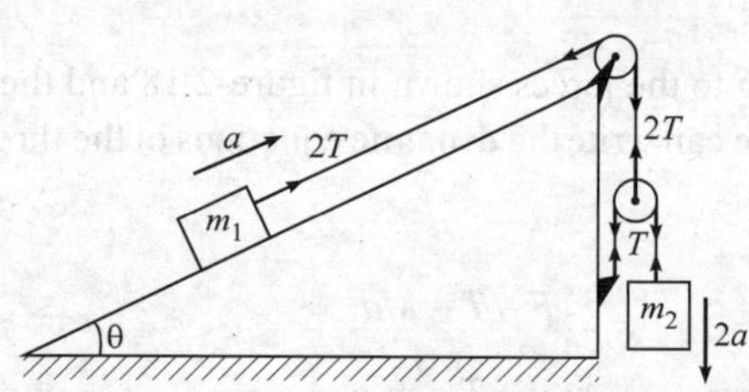

Figure 2.20

The dynamic equations can be written as

For mass m_1, $\quad 2T - m_1 g\sin\theta = m_1 a \quad$ ... (2.23)

For mass m_2, $\quad m_2 g - T = m_2(2a) \quad$ ... (2.24)

Multiplying equation-(2.24) by 2 and adding to equation-(2.23)

$$2m_2 g - m_1 g\sin\theta = (m_1 + 4m_2)a$$

$$a = \frac{2m_2 g - m_1 g\sin\theta}{m_1 + 4m_2}$$

$$a = \frac{2g[2\eta - \sin\theta]}{4\eta + 1} \quad [\text{As } m_2 = \eta m_1]$$

Illustrative Example 2.6

In the arrangement shown in figure-2.21, the mass of ball is η times as great as that of the rod the length of the rod is l. The masses of the pulleys and the threads, as well as the friction, are negligible. The ball is set on the same level as the lower end of the rod and then released. How soon will the ball be opposite the upper end of the rod.

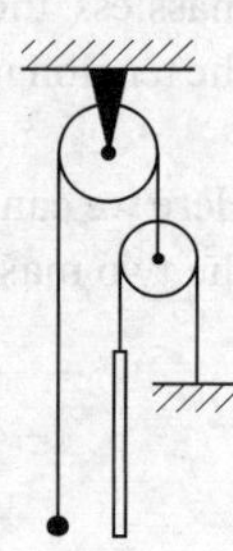

Figure 2.21

Solution

As usual here we can observe that the acceleration of the rod is double than that of the acceleration of the ball, as it is supported by a movable pulley. If ball is going up with an acceleration a, rod will be coming down with the acceleration $2a$, thus the relative acceleration of the ball with respect to rod is $3a$ in upward direction. If it takes time t seconds to reach the upper end of the rod, we have

$$t = \sqrt{\frac{2l}{3a}} \quad \text{... (2.25)}$$

Let mass of ball be m and that of rod is M, the dynamic equations of these are

For rod $\quad Mg - T = M(2a) \quad$ ... (2.26)

For ball $\quad 2T - mg = ma \quad$ ... (2.27)

Multiplying equation-(2.26) by 2 and adding to equation-(2.27)

$$2\,Mg - mg = (4M + m)a$$

or
$$a = \frac{2\,Mg - mg}{4\,M + m}$$

or
$$a = \left(\frac{2-\eta}{\eta+4}\right)g \quad [\text{As } m = \eta M]$$

From equation-(2.25), we have

$$t = \sqrt{\frac{2l(\eta+4)}{3g(2-\eta)}}$$

Web Reference of Video Lectures at www.physicsgalaxy.com

Age Group - High School Physics | Age 17-19 Years

Section - MECHANICS

Topic - Forces and Newton's Laws of Motion

Module Numbers - 5, 6, 7, 8, 9, 10, 11, 12, 13 and 14

Practice Exercise 2.1

(i) Find the tensions in the two cords and the accelerations of the blocks in figure-2.22 if friction is negligible. The pulleys are massless and frictionless, m_1 = 200 gm, m_2 = 500 gm and m_3 = 400 gm. Take g = 10 m/s^2.

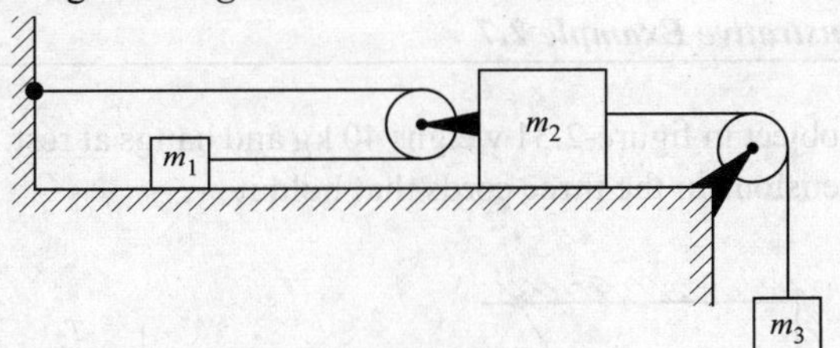

Figure 2.22

[0.94 N, 3.06 N, 4.7 m/s^2, 2.35 m/s^2, 2.35 m/s^2]

(ii) Two blocks with masses m_1 = 3 kg and m_2 = 4 kg are touching each other on a frictionless table, as shown in figure-2.23. If the force shown acting on m_1 is 5 N (a) What is the acceleration of the two blocks and (b) How hard does m_1 push against m_2 ?

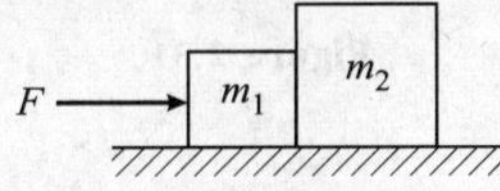

Figure 2.23

[0.714 m/s^2, 2.85 N]

(iii) The masses of blocks A and B in figure-2.24 are 20 kg and 10 kg, respectively. The blocks are initially at rest on the floor and are connected by a massless string passing over a massless and frictionless pulley. An upward force F is applied to the pulley. Find the acceleration a_1 and a_2 of the two blocks A and B when F is (a) 124 N (b) 294 N (c) 424 N.

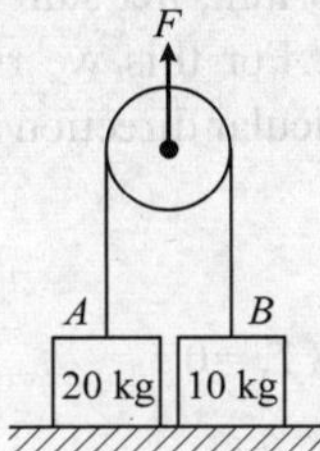

Figure 2.24

[(a) 0,0 (b) 0, 4.7 m/s^2, (c) 0.6 m/s^2, 11.2 m/s^2]

(iv) The three blocks in figure-2.25 are released from rest and accelerate at the rate of 5 m/s^2. If M = 4 kg, what is the magnitude of the frictional force on the block that slides horizontally ?

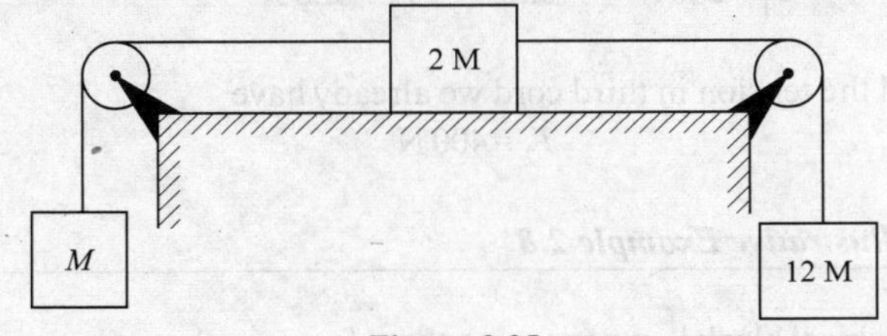

Figure 2.25

[140 N]

(v) Find the acceleration of the block A and B shown in figure-2.26 (a) and (b)

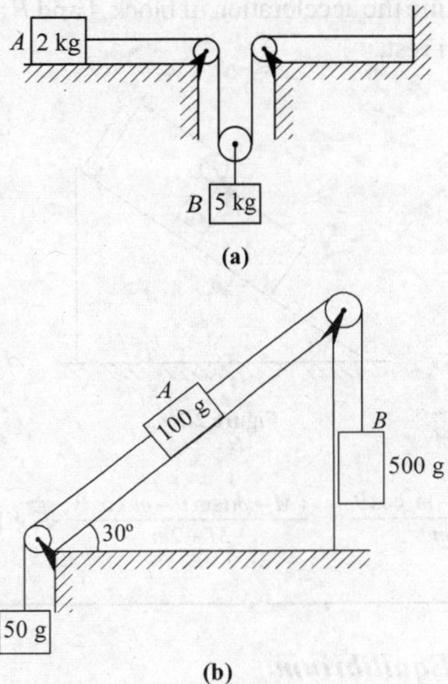

Figure 2.26

[(a) $10g/13$ forward, $5g/13$ downward, (b) $8g/13$ downward]

(vi) A block of mass M is pulled along a horizontal frictionless surface by a rope of mass m, as shown in figure-2.27. A horizontal force F is applied to one end of the rope. (a) Find the force the rope exerts on the block, and (b) the tension in the rope at its midpoint.

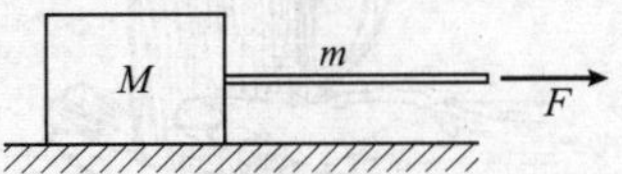

Figure 2.27

$$\left[\frac{MF}{M+m}, \frac{(M+m/2)F}{M+m}\right]$$

(vii) Two masses m and 2 m are connected by a mass less string which passes over a light frictionless pulley shown in figure-2.28. The masses are initially held with equal lengths of the strings on either side of the pulley. Find the velocity of the masses at the instant the lighter mass moves up a distance of 6.54 mts. This string is suddenly cut at that instant. Calculate the time taken by each mass to reach the ground. Take g = 9.8 m/s^2.

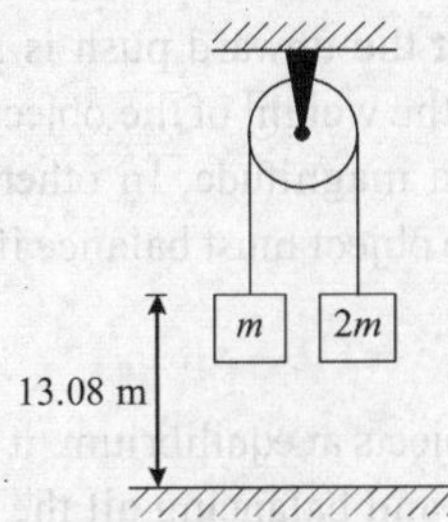

Figure 2.28

[3.27 m/s^2, 6.54 m/s, 2.78 s, 2/3 s]

(viii) A block A of mass M on an inclined surface and a small weight B of mass m is attached to a string as shown in figure-2.29. Determine the acceleration of block A and B after system is released from rest.

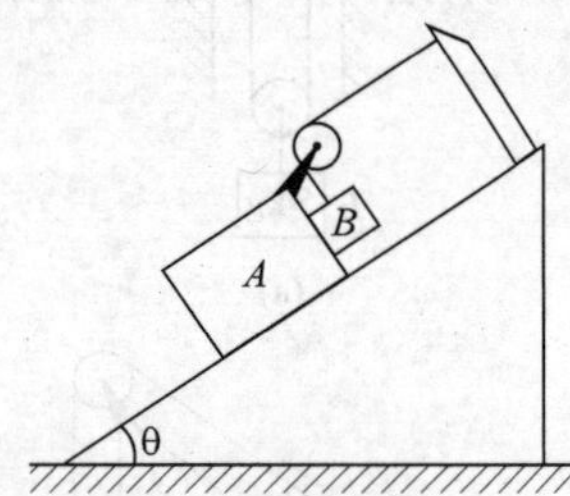

Figure 2.29

$$\left[\frac{(M+m)\sin\theta - m\cos\theta}{M+2m}g,\ \frac{(M+m)\sin\theta - m\cos\theta}{M+2m}\sqrt{2g}\right]$$

2.6 Static Equilibrium

An important part of physics has to do with objects and systems that are at rest and remain at rest, which is known as static equilibrium. In this section we discover that two basic conditions must be satisfied if an object it to remain at rest. Also we'll discuss how to use these conditions to different situations.

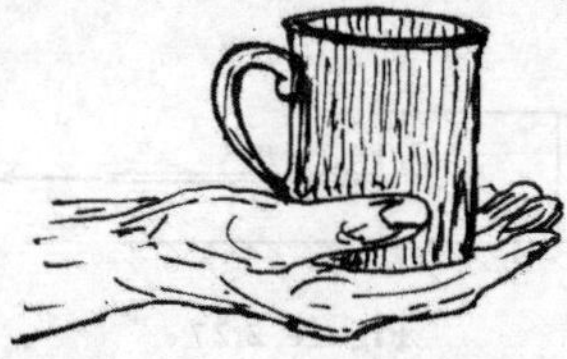

Figure 2.30

To start with static equilibrium consider figure-2.30, an object supported by a hand. We all know why the object does not fall, but we'll first examine this simple situation in detail so that we may easily understand more complicated situations.

What are the forces acting on the object ? We know that if we release, it will fall. This shows that a force is puling downward on it, the force of gravity. To support the object, the hand must push it upward. Let the upward push is P. As the object is a motionless, means the weight of the object Mg and the upward push P are equal in magnitude. In other words, the vertical forces acting on the object must balance if equilibrium is to be achieved.

In the analysis of objects at equilibrium, it is helpful to sketch a free body diagram, and balancing all the forces acting on the body in two perpendicular directions, in which the forces are resolved. This is the first condition of equilibrium, stated as-

"The vector sum of all the forces acting on a body is equal to zero."

We take few examples to explain the concept of static equilibrium.

Illustrative Example 2.7

The object in figure-2.31 weighs 40 kg and hangs at rest. Find the tensions in the three cords that hold it.

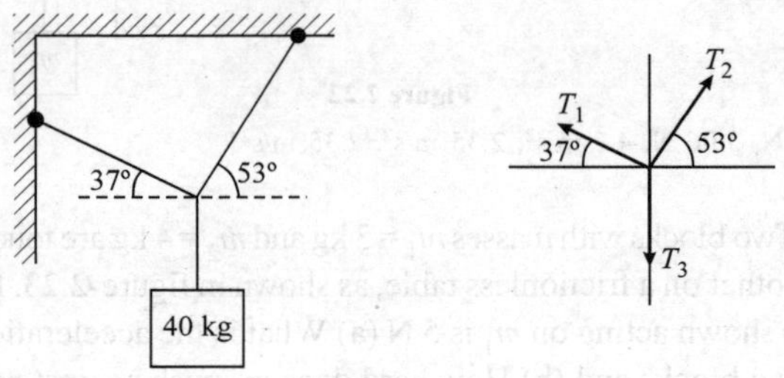

Figure 2.31

Solution

Because the object is at equilibrium, the vector sum of the forces acting directly on it must be zero. There are only two such forces, the tension in the lower cord and the pull of gravity, 400 N. Therefore, the tension in the lower cord must be 400 N. It is the tension that supports the object.

Figure-2.31 shows the junction where the three cords meet. As the system is in equilibrium, net sum of all the forces at the junction must be zero. For this we resolve the tensions in horizontal and perpendicular direction as

In horizontal direction

$$0.6\,T_2 - 0.8\,T_1 = 0 \qquad \ldots (2.28)$$

In vertical direction

$$0.6\,T_1 + 0.8\,T_2 - 400 = 0 \qquad \ldots (2.29)$$

On solving the above equations we get

$$T_1 = 240\text{ N} \quad \text{and} \quad T_2 = 320\text{ N}$$

and the tension in third cord we already have

$$T_2 = 400\text{ N}$$

Illustrative Example 2.8

A cubical block is experiencing three forces as shown in figure 2.32. Find the friction force acting on the block if it is at rest.

Given that $F_1 = 30$ N; $F_2 = 50$ N and $F_3 = 42$ N.

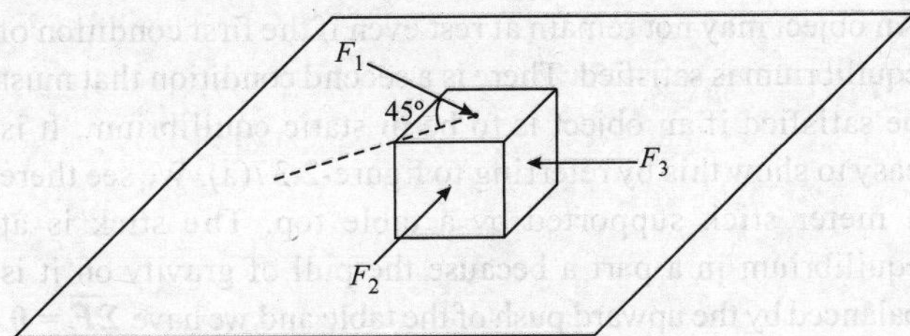

Figure 2.32

Solution

As shown in figure force F_1 is having three components, one along vertical $(F/\sqrt{2})$, other along force $F_2\left(\frac{F}{\sqrt{2}} \times \frac{1}{\sqrt{2}}\right)$ and one against $F_3\left(\frac{F}{\sqrt{2}} \times \frac{1}{\sqrt{2}}\right)$. Here the net horizontal force acting on the block is given by

$$F_{net} = \sqrt{(F_2 + F/\sqrt{4})^2 + (F_3 - F/\sqrt{4})^2}$$

or $$= \sqrt{(50+15)^2 + (42-15)^2} = 70.384 \text{ N}$$

As it is given that block is in static equilibrium, thus sum of all horizontal forces acting on it is must be zero. Sum of given external horizontal forces is 70.384 N and is in a direction $\theta = \tan^{-1}(65/67)$ from the direction of force F_3. We can state that friction force acting on block must be exactly opposing this force so as to keep the block in static equilibrium.

 # Illustrative Example 2.9

A chain of mass m is attached at two points A and B of two fixed walls as shown in figure-2.33. Due to its weight a sag is there in the chain such that at point A and B it makes an angle θ with the normal to the wall. Find the tension in the chain at : (Assume tension is always along the length of chain)

(a) Point A and B

(b) Mid point of the chain

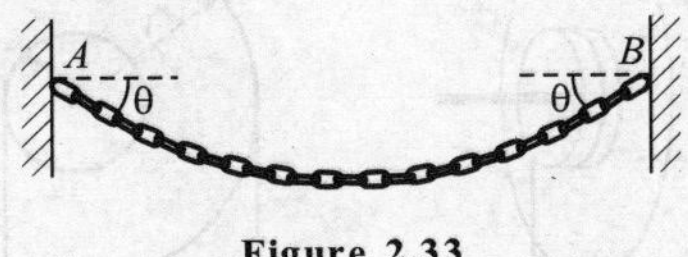

Figure 2.33

Solution

(a) Let the tension in the chain at point A and B is T, so at these point chain will pull the wall hinges with the same force and wall hinges will also exert same force on chain in tangential direction as shown in figure-2.34.

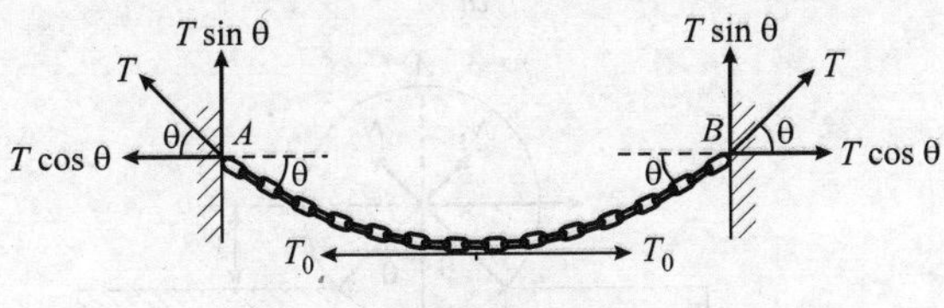

Figure 2.34

Now for vertical equilibrium of chain we have

$$2T\sin\theta = mg$$

or $$T = \frac{1}{2} mg \operatorname{cosec}\theta$$

(b) Let tension at the mid point of chain is T_0. It must be along horizontal direction as at mid point slope is zero. For horizontal equilibrium of chain we can state that at every point horizontal component of the tension in the chain must be equal as no other external force is acting on it in horizontal direction. Thus we have

$$T_0 = T\cos\theta$$

or $$= \frac{1}{2} mg \cot\theta$$

 # Illustrative Example 2.10

Figure-2.35 shows a cylinder A of mass M which is resting on two smooth edges, one fixed and other is that of a block of B. At an instant block B is pulled toward left with a constant speed v. Find the force exerted by the cylinder on the fixed edge after some time when the distance between the two edges will become $x = \sqrt{2}R$. At $t = 0$ the distance between the two edges was zero.

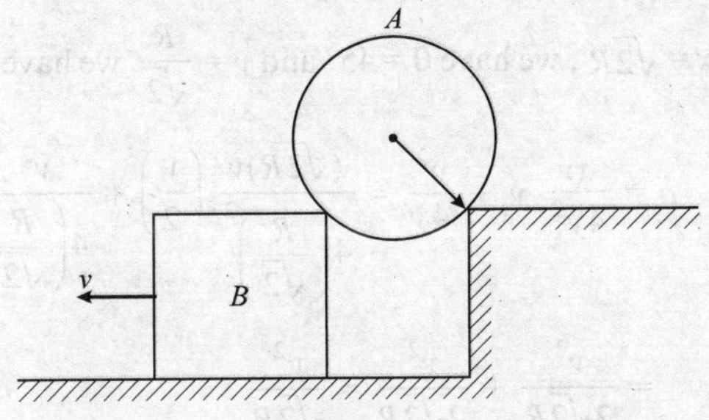

Figure 2.35

Solution

Analysis of the situation is shown in figure-2.36. If we consider the distance of block B from the fixed edge is x at an instant t, we have

$$v = \frac{dx}{dt}$$

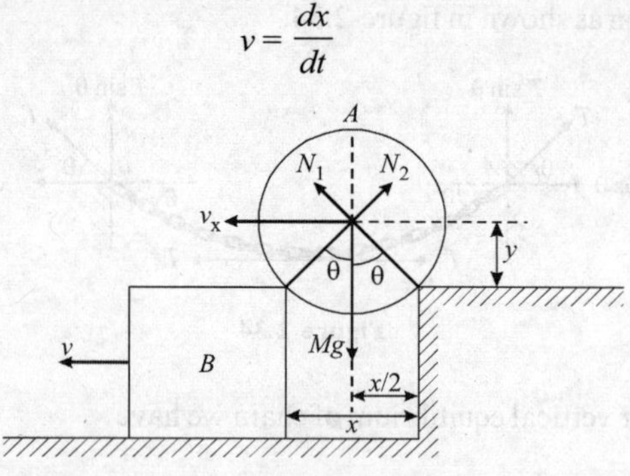

Figure 2.36

We can see from figure that the centre of cylinder A is at a distance $x/2$ from the fixed edge, thus its horizontal velocity is always $v/2$ and remains constant. As in horizontal direction there is no acceleration we can state that the two normal forces acting on the cylinder due to two edges remains same in magnitude as there is no horizontal net force on it. For vertical motion of the cylinder we can write.

$$\frac{x^2}{4} + y^2 = R^2$$

differentiating with respect to time

$$\frac{x}{2}\frac{dx}{dt} + 2y\frac{dy}{dt} = 0$$

or $$\frac{x}{2}v - 2yv_y = 0 \qquad [v_y = -\frac{dy}{dt}]$$

or $$v_y = \frac{x}{4y}v$$

Differentiating again with respect to time

$$a_y = -\frac{x}{4y^2}\frac{dy}{dt}v + \frac{v}{4y}\frac{dx}{dt}$$

For cylinder equation of motion in vertical direction is

$$Mg - 2N\cos\theta = Ma_y \qquad [\text{As } N_1 = N_2 = N]$$

When $x = \sqrt{2}R$, we have $\theta = 45°$ and $y = \frac{R}{\sqrt{2}}$ we have

$$a_y = \frac{xv}{4y^2}v_y + \frac{v^2}{4y} = \frac{(\sqrt{2}R)v}{4\left(\frac{R}{\sqrt{2}}\right)^2}\left(\frac{v}{2}\right) + \frac{v^2}{4\left(\frac{R}{\sqrt{2}}\right)}$$

$$= \frac{v^2}{2\sqrt{2}R} + \frac{v^2}{2\sqrt{2}R} = \frac{v^2}{\sqrt{2}R}$$

Thus we have $$Mg - \sqrt{2}\,N = \frac{Mv^2}{\sqrt{2}R}$$

or $$N = \frac{Mg}{\sqrt{2}} - \frac{Mv^2}{2R}$$

2.6.1 Torque

An object may not remain at rest even if the first condition of equilibrium is satisfied. There is a second condition that must be satisfied if an object is to be in static equilibrium. It is easy to show this by referring to figure-2.37(a). We see there a meter stick supported by a table top. The stick is at equilibrium in a part a because the pull of gravity on it is balanced by the upward push of the table and we have $\Sigma\vec{F} = \mathbf{0}$.

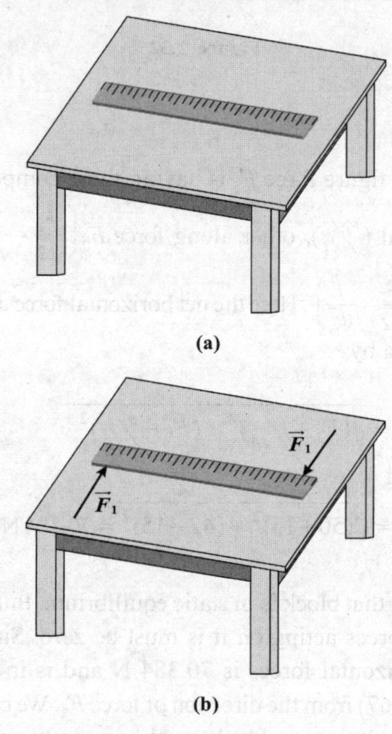

Figure 2.37

Now consider what happens when you push near its two ends with equal but oppositely directed forces $\vec{F}_1$ and $-\vec{F}_1$ as shown in figure-2.37(b), the meter stick does not remain at rest. Even though $\vec{F}_1$ balances $-\vec{F}_1$ and therefore the condition $\Sigma\vec{F} = \mathbf{0}$ is satisfied, the stick begins to rotate. There must be another condition, one involving rotation, that must be satisfied if the object is to be in equilibrium. We will discuss second condition for equilibrium in the next section. First, however, we must discuss how forces cause rotation.

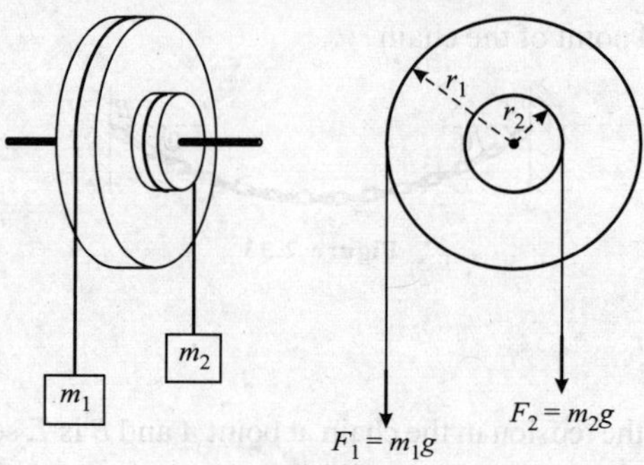

Figure 2.38

To learn how forces and rotations are related, we can perform the experiment shown in figure-2.38. We see there a wheel that consists of two disks cemented together. It is free to rotate on a stationary axle that we call the axis, or pivot, of rotation. By hanging objects from the two cords, we can determine the turning effect of a force. The force $\vec{F}_2$ tries to turn the wheel clockwise, while $\vec{F}_1$ tries to turn the wheel counterclockwise. By experimenting with different radii r_1 and r_2 for the two disks, we find that the two turning effects balance whenever

$$F_1 r_1 = F_2 r_2$$

The above relation, product of force and the radii, is known as torque. Torque is the physical quantity which measures the turning effect of a force on a body. Its magnitude is given by the product of the force and the perpendicular distance from the axis of rotation or pivot. In above case it is simply the product of force and the radii.

We can learn more about turning effects from figure-2.39. A meter stick pivoted at its center is subjected to two forces F_1 and F_2 as shown. F_1 is acting in a direction perpendicular to the rod, to the left of pivot and F_2 is acting at an angle θ to the rod, to the right of the pivot. The force F_1 has a tendency of rotating the rod in clockwise direction and F_2 will tend it to rotate in anticlockwise direction.

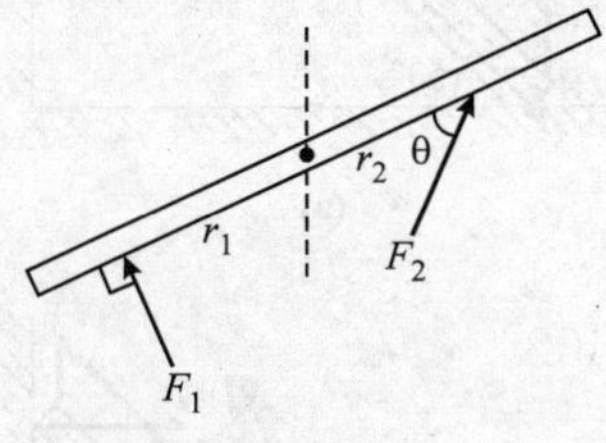

Figure 2.39

Here torque provided by forces F_1 is

$$\tau_1 = F_1 \times r_1$$

and torque provided by force F_2 is

$$\tau_2 = F_2 \times r_2 \sin\theta$$

τ_1 and τ_2 are the turning effects of the forces F_1 and F_2 on the rod. The rod will rotate in the direction of the torque whichever is higher.

One important point should be noted that *"When the line of force goes through the pivot, or axis of rotation, the torque due to the force about the pivot is zero."*

Now we know how to express the turning effect of a force in terms of torque, we can state the second condition for static equilibrium. Experiments show that, for an object to remain motionless, the clockwise torques acting on it must be balanced by the counterclockwise torques or for an object to be in equilibrium, the sum of all the torques acting on it must be zero.

Illustrative Example 2.11

In figure-2.40(a), we see a beam of length L pivoted at one end and supporting a 200 kg object at the other end. Find the tension T in the supporting cable that runs upward to the ceiling. Assume that the weight of the beam is negligible. Take $g = 10\ \text{m/s}^2$

Solution

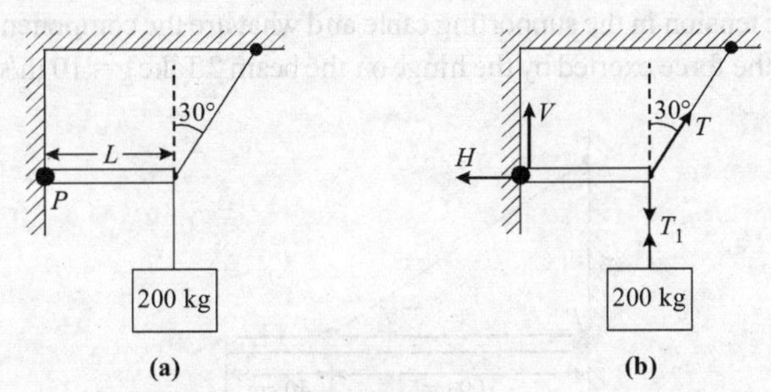

Figure 2.40

The lower cord supports the 200 kg object, thus the tension in it is 2000 N. First we isolate the beam as the object for discussion. Its free body diagram is shown in figure-2.40(b). Be careful that here we are not drawing the free body diagram by taking the object as a point. Here we also don't know about the force which the hinge exerts on the beam, we represent this force in a general way by giving its x and y components, as H and V. Now we apply the two conditions of equilibrium on it.

The translational equilibrium of beam, we write force equations :

$$T\sin(30^\circ) = H \qquad \ldots(2.30)$$

$$T\cos(30^\circ) + V = 2000 \qquad \ldots(2.31)$$

The rotational equilibrium of beam, we write torque equations about the pivot P. In case of hinged objects, it is convenient to choose the hinged point as axis of rotation. In next section we we'll discuss that we have a wider choice. As we consider the axis of rotation at P, the forces H and V have zero torque about P as the lines of H and V passes through P, hence perpendicular distance of H and V from P is zero.

We find torque due to T by its components. The component $T\sin(30°)$ again passes through the point P, so its torque is equal to zero, but due to $T\cos(30°)$, it is in anticlockwise direction. Due to weight of the hanging mass, the torque at P is in clockwise direction, thus for equilibrium, we have

$$T\cos(30°)\times L = Mg\times L$$

or $$T=\frac{2000}{\cos(30°)}$$

$$=2310\text{ N}$$

If we wish to find the force exerted by the hinge on the rod from equations-(2.30) & (2.31), we have

$$H=1155\text{ N} \quad \text{and} \quad V=0$$

Illustrative Example 2.12

For the uniform 5 kg beam shown in figure-2.41(a), how large is the tension in the supporting cable and what are the components of the force exerted by the hinge on the beam ? Take $g = 10\text{ m/s}^2$.

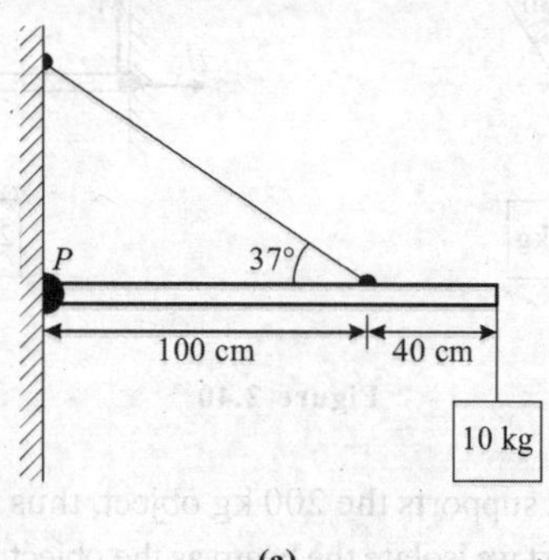

(a)

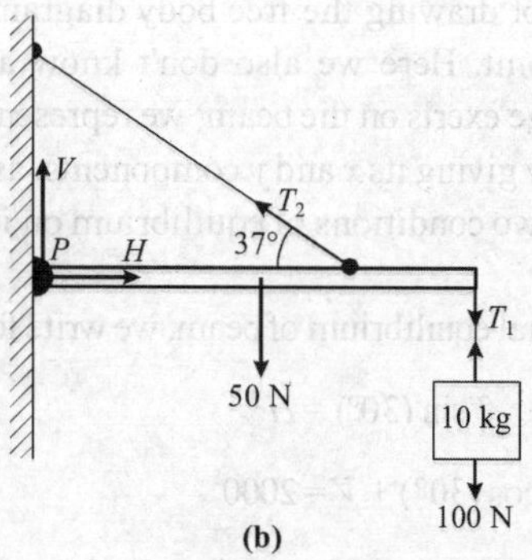

(b)

Figure 2.41

Solution

We first isolate the beam and draw the free body diagram shown in figure-2.41(b). Notice that the weight of the beam, 50 N, is taken as acting at the beam's centre of mass. Further we have replaced the tension in the cable by its components, as the application of torque is simpler with components. Here we can eliminate the torques of force components at the wall, H and V, by taking point P as pivot. We have

$$\Sigma\tau=0 \quad\Rightarrow\quad T_2\sin(37°)\times 1.0-50\times 0.7-100\times 1.4=0$$

$$\Sigma F_x=0 \;\Rightarrow\quad H-T_2\cos(37°)=0$$

$$\Sigma F_y=0 \;\Rightarrow\quad V+T_2\sin(37°)-50-100=0$$

On solving the equations we get

$$T_2=291.66\text{ N};\quad H=233.33\text{ N} \quad\text{and}\quad V=-25\text{ N}$$

Here V comes with a negative sign, it implies that the direction of vertical force from hinge on beam shown in figure-2.41(b) is opposite to that the actual one, it is acting in downward direction on the beam.

Illustrative Example 2.13

The uniform 20 kg ladder hinged at the bottom in figure-2.42(a), leans against a smooth wall. If a 40 kg person stands on the ladder shown, how large are the forces at the wall the ground. Take $g = 10\text{ m/s}^2$.

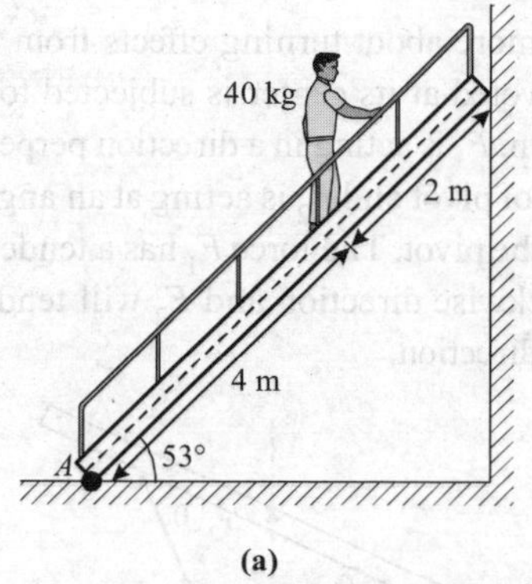

(a)

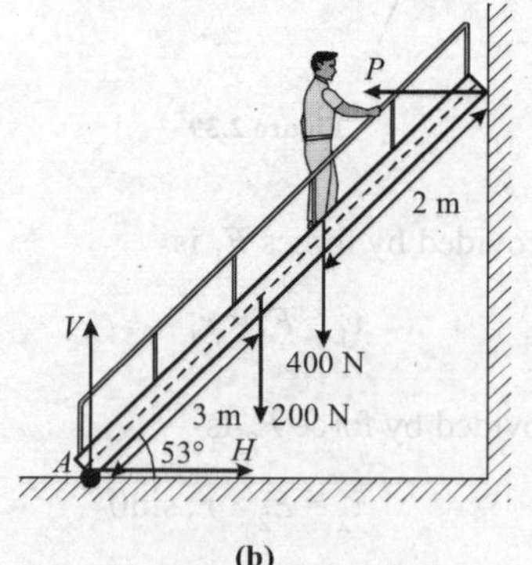

(b)

Figure 2.42

Solution

Consider figure-2.42(b), all the forces acting on the ladder are shown. For horizontal and vertical equilibrium, we use

In x-dir $\qquad H-P=0$

In y-dir $\qquad V-200-400=0$

On solving we get $V = 600$ N

For rotational equilibrium about point A, we have $\Sigma\,\tau = 0$, which can be given as

$$P(6)(0.8) - 200(3)(0.6) - 400(4)(0.6) = 0$$

On solving it gives $P = H = 275$ N

Illustrative Example 2.14

Calculate the force P required to cause the block of weight $W_2 = 200$ N just to slide under the block of weight $W_1 = 100$ N shown in figure-2.43. What is the tension in the string AB and the normal forces acting between the blocks and that applied by ground on W_2 ? Surfaces of the blocks in contact are rough and the frictional force between the two blocks is 25 N and that between lower block and ground is 75 N. Take $g = 10$ m/s^2.

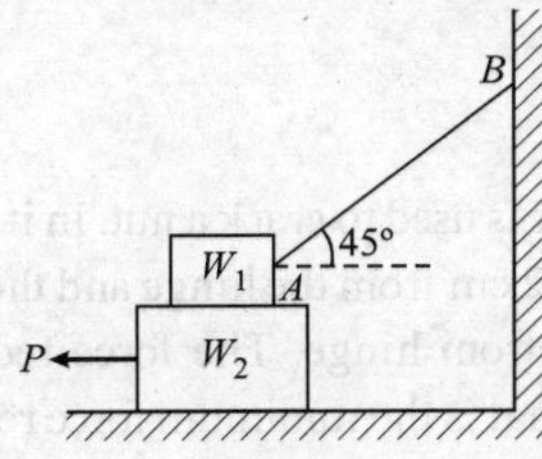

Figure 2.43

Solution

Free body diagrams of the blocks W_1 and W_2 are shown in figure-2.44. When W_2 just slides, we can state that the system is in limiting equilibrium and forces are just balanced to slide. For equilibrium of blocks we have for block W_2

$$P = f_1 + f_2 = 100 \text{ N}$$

and $$N_1 = W_2 + N_2$$

and for block W_1

$$N_2 + \frac{T}{\sqrt{2}} = W_1$$

and $$f_1 = \frac{T}{\sqrt{2}} = 25 \text{ N}$$

$\Rightarrow$ $$T = 25\sqrt{2} \text{ N}$$

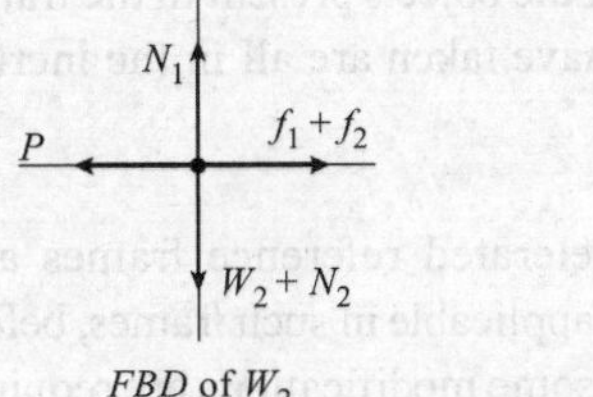

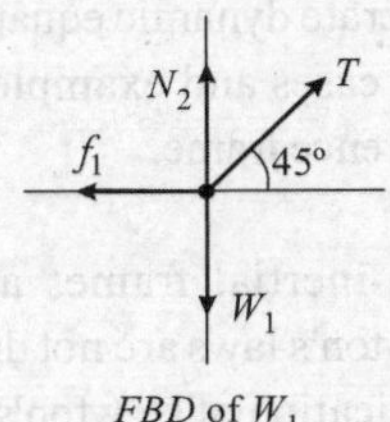

Figure 2.44

from above equations we get

$$N_2 = 75 \text{ N}$$

and $$N_1 = 275 \text{ N}$$

Illustrative Example 2.15

Figure-2.45 shows a platform on which a man of mass M is standing and holding a string passing over a system of ideal pulleys. Another mass m is hanging as shown in figure. Find the force man has to exert to maintain the equilibrium of system. Also find the force exerted by platform on man.

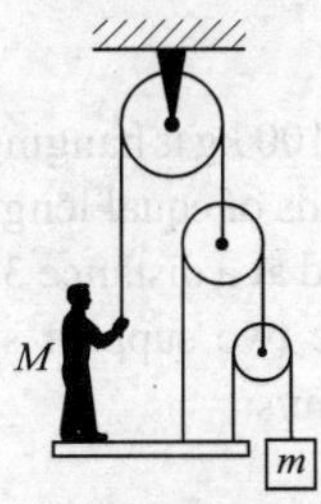

Figure 2.45

Solution

If tension in string which the man is holding is T, the tension in the string to which the mass m is connected is $T/4$ which must balance mg. Thus we have

$$T = 4\text{ mg} = \text{force exerted by man on string}$$

If the force, which platform is exerting on man is N, for equilibrium of man we must have

$$N + T = Mg$$

or $$N = Mg - 4\text{ mg}$$

Practice Exercise 2.2

(i) Three equal masses are suspended from frictionless pulleys as shown in figure-2.46. If the weight w_2 in figure is 400 N, what must be the values of the weights w_1 and w_3.

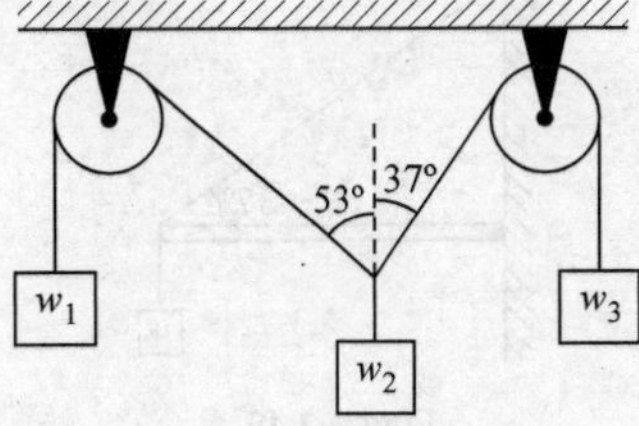

Figure 2.46

[240 N, 320 N]

(ii) In figure-2.47 the tension in the diagonal string is 60 N. Find the magnitudes of the horizontal forces F_1 and F_2 the must be applied to hold the system in the position shown in figure-2.48. What is the weight of the suspended block.

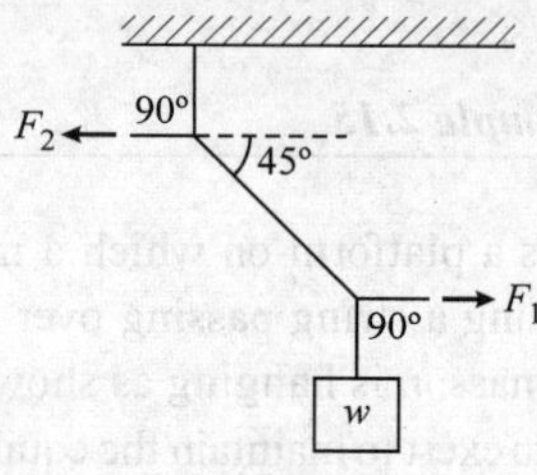

Figure 2.47

[42.4 N each, 42.4 N]

(iii) A 1 m rod of mass 100 kg is hanging from two inextensible support strings at its ends of equal lengths. If an another mass of 20 kg is placed on rod at a distance 30 cm from the left end, find the tension in the two support strings, if rod remains horizontal. Take $g = 10\ m/s^2$

[560 N, 640 N]

(iv) Find the tension in each cord in figure-2.48, if the weight of the suspended block is w.

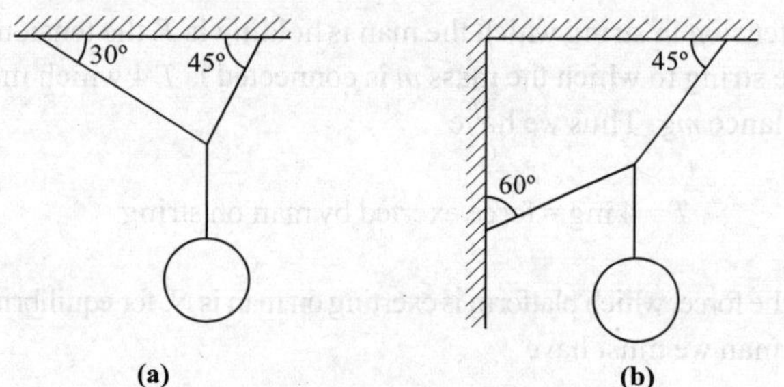

Figure 2.48

[(a) $\dfrac{2w}{1+\sqrt{3}}, \dfrac{\sqrt{6}w}{1+\sqrt{3}}$; (b) $\dfrac{2w}{\sqrt{3}-1}, \dfrac{\sqrt{6}w}{\sqrt{3}-1}$]

(v) A horizontal uniform boom that weighs 200 N and is 5 m long supports a load of 1000 N, as shown in figure-2.49. Find all the forces acting on the boom.

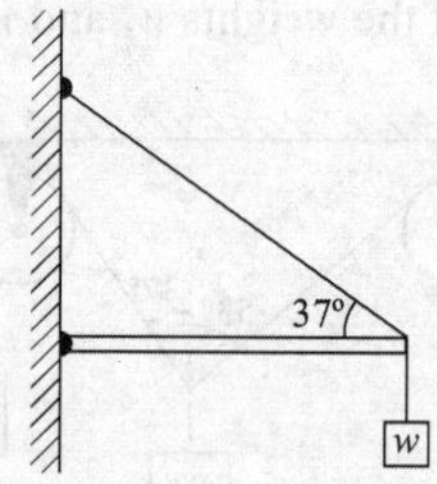

Figure 2.49

[T = 1833.33 N, H = 1466.67 N, V = 100 N]

(vi) A step pulley system is shown in figure-2.50. Find the relation in masses m and M for which the system remain in equilibrium. Assume string will not slide over the pulleys. $\left(\dfrac{r_1}{r_2} = \dfrac{1}{2}, \dfrac{r_3}{r_4} = \dfrac{3}{4}\right)$

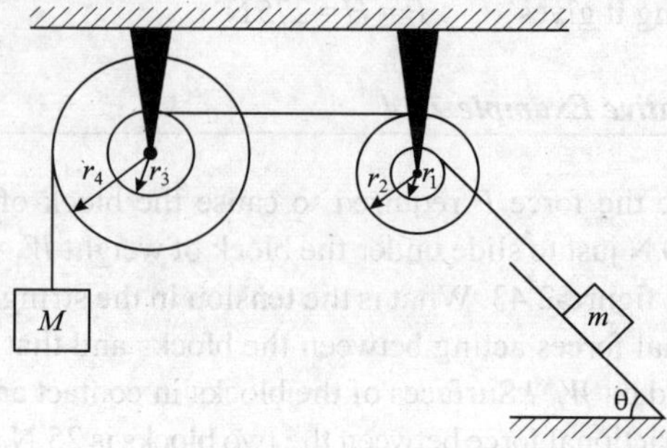

Figure 2.50

$\left[\dfrac{M}{m} = \dfrac{3}{8}\sin\theta\right]$

(vii) A nut cracker is used to crack a nut. In it nut is held in two arms at a distance 2 cm from the hinge and the handle of it is at a distance 25 cm from hinge. The force required to crack a walnut is 30 N. What is the minimum force required to crack it with the nut cracker.

[2.4 N]

2.7 Pseudo Force

In previous sections we've discussed about external and internal forces. Pseudo force is always treated as an external force for a system. Before understanding the concept of a pseudo force, we have to make our concepts clear about reference frames as pseudo force is a frame dependent quantity. In general reference frames are classified in two broad categories - Inertial and Non-inertial reference frames.

2.7.1 Inertial and Non-inertial Reference Frames

Inertial frames are those which do not have any acceleration, that is either the frame at rest or it is moving with a uniform speed. In such frames we can directly apply Newton's laws and generate dynamic equations of the objects present in the frame. The cases and examples we have taken are all in the inertial reference frame.

Non-inertial frames are accelerated reference frames and Newton's laws are not directly applicable in such frames, before application of Newton's laws, some modifications are required to solve a problem, if such frames are present.

2.7.2 Requirement of Pseudo Force

Consider the situation shown in figure-2.51. A block of mass 10 kg is placed on a smooth table resting on ground. A child is standing on the table and there is sufficient friction present between table and the shoes of child so that child will not slip.

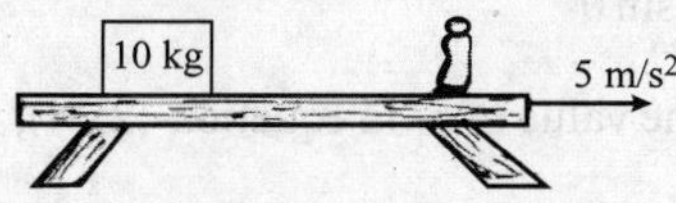

Figure 2.51

If we push the table with some acceleration, say 5 m/s^2. The child will not slip on the table but there is no friction between block and the table, so block remains at rest and table will slide under the block.

If child observes the block, it appears to him that block is going backward with the same acceleration 5 m/s^2 in backward direction, because table is at rest with respect to the child. (As earth is moving but it appears to be at rest with respect to us). Here child observes that a 10 kg mass is moving with an acceleration 5 m/s^2 with respect to table and hence a force $10 \times 5 = 50$ N is acting on the 10 kg block in backward direction. This force is known as Pseudo Force. Actually there is no force acting on the block, it only appears to be acting on it, if it is observed from the table, the non-inertial frame. Due to this force, whatever acceleration is produced in the block is also with respect to the table only. But be careful in applying the pseudo force on an object, take care of these points

Apply a pseudo force on an object if and only if it is placed on another object (non-inertial frame) accelerating with respect to some inertial reference frame (i.e. earth).

The direction of pseudo force must be opposite to the direction of acceleration of the non-inertial frame.

The magnitude of pseudo force is the product of mass of the body and acceleration of the non-inertial frame.

Applying pseudo force is convenient to solve the problem as after application of a pseudo force on a body, all equations and results associated with it become relative to the respective non-inertial frame. For better understanding, we take some examples for it.

 # Illustrative Example 2.16

Figure-2.52 shows a box of mass m is placed on a wedge of mass M on a smooth surface. How much force F is required to be applied on M so that during motion m remains at rest on its surface.

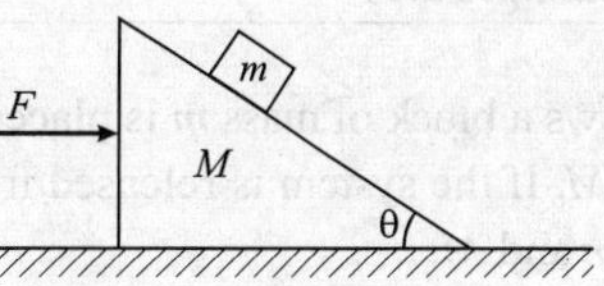

Figure 2.52

Solution

The force acting on the bodies m and M are shown in figure-2.53 along with free body diagrams of mass m and M. As the two bodies move together, we can find the acceleration of system towards right directly as

$$a = \frac{F}{m + M}$$

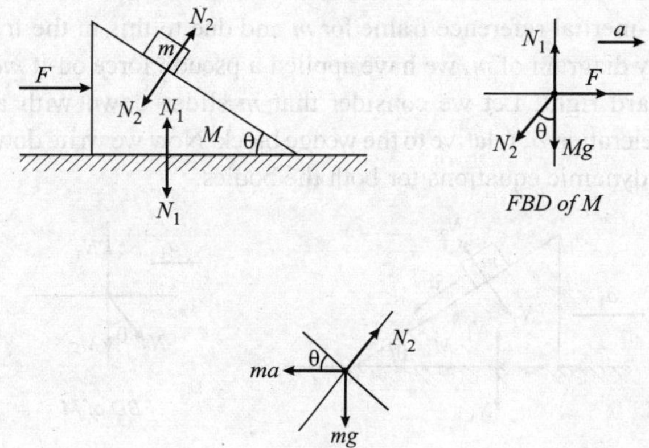

Figure 2.53

Here the condition is, the small block of mass m should remain at rest on the incline surface of the wedge block. Look at the *FBD* of m in figure-2.53, the force acting on it towards left ma is the pseudo force on it as its reference frame is the wedge block. As wedge block is moving with an acceleration, we consider m relative to it. Now with respect to wedge block m is at rest or in equilibrium, we can balance all the forces along the tendency of motion of body (i.e. inclined plane) and perpendicular to it shown in *FBD* of it.

For m to be at rest, from *FBD* of m, along the plane

$$mg \sin\theta = ma \cos\theta$$

or $$a = g \tan\theta$$

or $$\frac{F}{m + M} = g \tan\theta$$

or $$F = (m + M) g \tan\theta$$

Illustrative Example 2.17

Figure-2.54 shows a block of mass m is placed on an inclined wedge of mass M. If the system is released from rest find the acceleration of m and M.

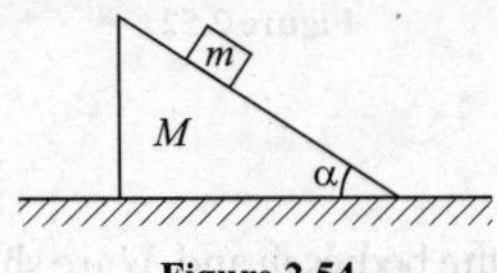

Figure 2.54

Solution

Figure-2.55 shows the forces acting on the bodies and the free body diagrams of M and m. Due to the normal reaction N_1 acting on M, it moves towards left and m slides downward. As M slides in left direction, with an acceleration a_1, it becomes a non-inertial reference frame for m and due to this in the free body diagram of m, we have applied a pseudo force on it ma_1 toward right. Let we consider that m slides down with an acceleration a_2 relative to the wedge block. Now we write down the dynamic equations for both the bodies.

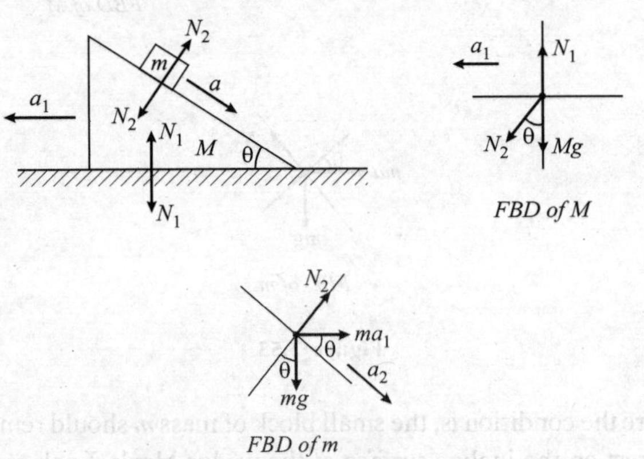

Figure 2.55

Motion equation for M with respect to earth

Along the plane

$$N_2 \sin\theta = Ma_1 \quad \text{...(2.32)}$$

Perpendicular to the plane

$$N_1 = Mg + N_2 \cos\theta \quad \text{...(2.33)}$$

Motion equation for m with respect to M

Along the plane

$$mg \sin\theta + ma_1 \cos\theta = ma_2 \quad \text{...(2.34)}$$

Perpendicular to the plane

$$N_2 = mg \cos\theta - ma_1 \sin\theta \quad \text{...(2.35)}$$

From equations-(2.32) and (2.35) we have

$$\frac{Ma_1}{\sin\theta} = mg \cos\theta - ma_1 \sin\theta$$

or
$$a_1 = \frac{mg\cos\theta}{\dfrac{M}{\sin\theta} + m\sin\theta} = \frac{mg\sin\theta\cos\theta}{M + m\sin^2\theta} \quad \text{...(2.36)}$$

Substituting the value of a_1 in equation-(2.34), we get

$$a_2 = g\sin\theta + \frac{mg\sin\theta\cos^2\theta}{M + m\sin^2\theta} \quad \text{...(2.37)}$$

Equation-(2.36) gives the acceleration of M but equation-(2.37) gives the acceleration of m with respect to M. The net acceleration of m, is the vector addition of a_1 and a_2, as m is also moving with a_1 toward left along with M.

Net acceleration of m can be obtained by the vector sum shown in figure-2.56.

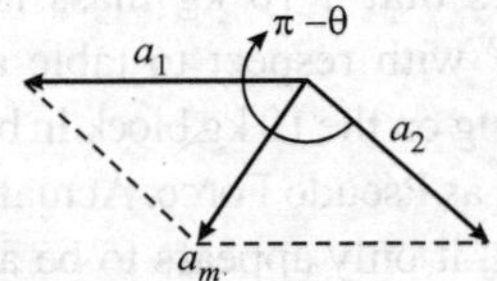

Figure 2.56

$$a_m = [a_1^2 + a_2^2 - 2a_1a_2 \cos\theta]^{1/2}$$

Illustrative Example 2.18

Figure-2.57 shows a large block of mass M, supporting two small mass m_1 and m_2, connected by a light, frictionless thread. A force F is acting on M, such that the block m_1 is sliding down, with an acceleration a_1. Find the force F applied on M and also the acceleration of M. Assuming all surfaces are frictionless.

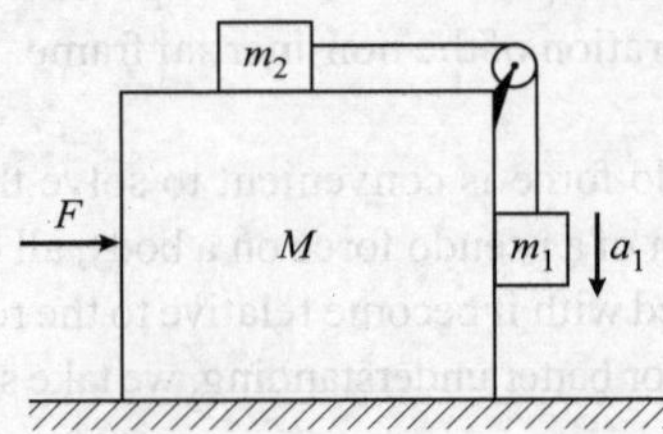

Figure 2.57

Solution

Figure-2.58 shows the forces acting on bodies and free body diagrams of M, m_1 and m_2. Now we take the acceleration of the mass M is a on floor and as a_1 is given for m_1 downward, m_2 will also move forward with a_1, relative to M. For solving, we write the dynamic equations for masses.

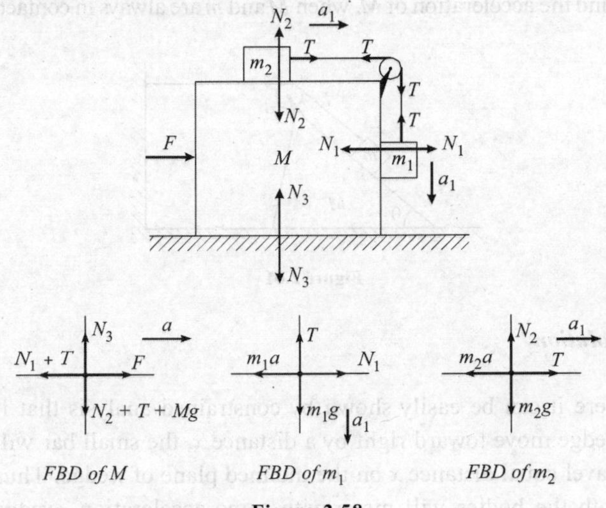

Figure 2.58

Motion equations for mass M

Along the motion

$$F - N_1 - T = Ma \qquad \ldots(2.38)$$

Normal to the motion

$$N_3 = N_2 + T + Mg \qquad \ldots(2.39)$$

Motion equations for mass m_1

Along the motion

$$m_1g - T = m_1a_1 \qquad \ldots(2.40)$$

Normal to the motion

$$N_1 = m_1a \qquad \ldots(2.41)$$

Motion equation for mass m_2

Along the motion

$$T - m_2a = m_2a_1 \qquad \ldots(2.42)$$

Normal to the motion

$$N_2 = m_2g \qquad \ldots(2.43)$$

Adding equation-(2.40) and (2.42), we get

$$m_1g - m_2a = (m_1 + m_2)a_1$$

or
$$a = \frac{m_1}{m_2}g - \left(1 + \frac{m_1}{m_2}\right)a_1$$

Now adding equation-(2.38), (2.42) and (2.43), we get

$$F - m_1a - m_2a = Ma + m_2a_1$$

or
$$F = m_1a + (M + m_2)a + m_2a_1$$

Substituting the value of a in above expression we get

$$F = (m_1 + M + m_2)\left(\frac{m_1}{m_2}g - a_1 - \frac{m_1}{m_2}a_1\right) + m_2a_1$$

$$= m_1g + \frac{(M + m_1)m_1}{m_2}(g - a_1) - (M + 2m_1)a_1$$

2.7.3 Concept of a Weighing Machine

When any body is placed on the platform of a weighing machine, a normal reaction exist between the body and the weighing machine. A weighing machine is calibrated to measure the normal reaction acting on the platform of the machine by the body placed over it in units of kilogram force (kgf). 1 kgf is the weight of 1kg body on earth surface which is equal to 9.8N. If the body is at rest the forces acting on it are balanced so the upward normal reaction on body is balancing its weight so machine will measure the weight of the body in kgf.

If a weighing machine is placed in an elevator which is accelerating upward then in *FBD* of the body placed over it there will be two forces - its weight in downward direction and normal reaction in upward direction. As the body is also accelerating upward we can say that normal reaction is more than its weight so weighing machine will measure a reading which is more than the actual weight of body. Similarly we can show that if elevator is accelerating down then the reading of weighing machine will be less than the weight of the body.

2.7.4 Concept of a Spring Balance

A spring balance is used to measure the tension in the string in which the spring balance is connected. It is generally calibrated to measure tension in units of *kgf*. When a body is hung from a spring balance and in static equilibrium, the tension in string connected to body is equal to the weight of body which elongates the spring balance to some extent and the pointer on spring balance reads the value of tension on the calibrated scale attached to it. Similar to the case of a weighing machine if a body hanging from a spring balance is kept in an elevator which is accelerating upward then the reading of spring balance will be more than the actual weight of the body as for upward acceleration tension in string attached to body will be more than the weight for upward acceleration and if elevator is accelerating downward its reading will be less than the actual weight of the body.

Illustrative Example 2.19

Find the weight shown by the weighing machine on which a man of mass m is standing at rest relative to it as shown in figure-2.59. M is released from rest.

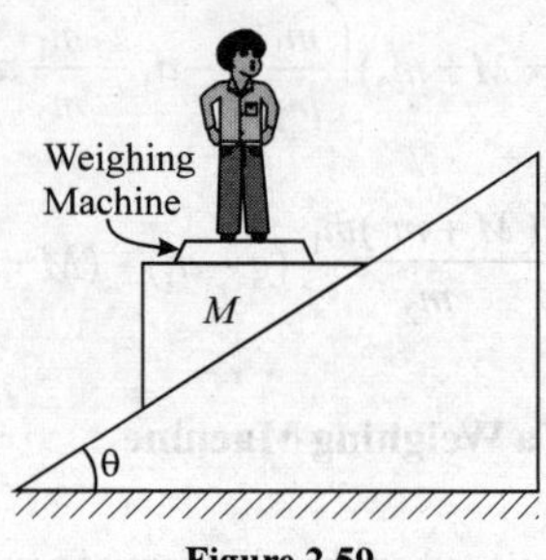

Figure 2.59

Solution

If the wedge is in free fall, its acceleration must be $g\sin\theta$. Here we are required to find the weight shown by the weighing machine i.e. the normal force acting between man and the weighing machine. For it we solve the problem in the reference frame of the wedge. The force acting on man in the reference of wedge block are shown in figure-2.60.

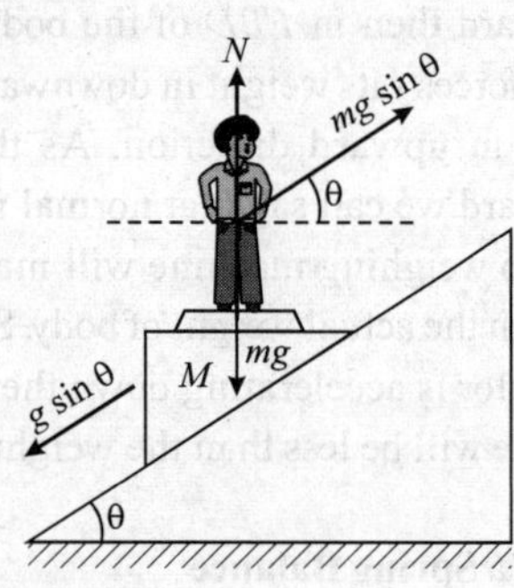

Figure 2.60

With respect to wedge frame, man will experience a pseudo force $mg\sin\theta$ as shown opposite to the acceleration of the wedge. Now for equilibrium of man relative to wedge we have

$$N + mg\sin^2\theta = mg$$

$$\Rightarrow \quad N = mg - mg\sin^2\theta = mg\cos^2\theta$$

$$\Rightarrow \quad \text{reading} = \frac{N}{g} = m\cos^2\theta$$

Illustrative Example 2.20

In the figure-2.61 a bar of mass m is on the smooth inclined face of the wedge of mass M, the inclination to the horizontal being θ. The wedge is resting on a smooth horizontal plane. Assuming the pulley to be smooth and the string is light and inextensible. Find the acceleration of M, when M and m are always in contact.

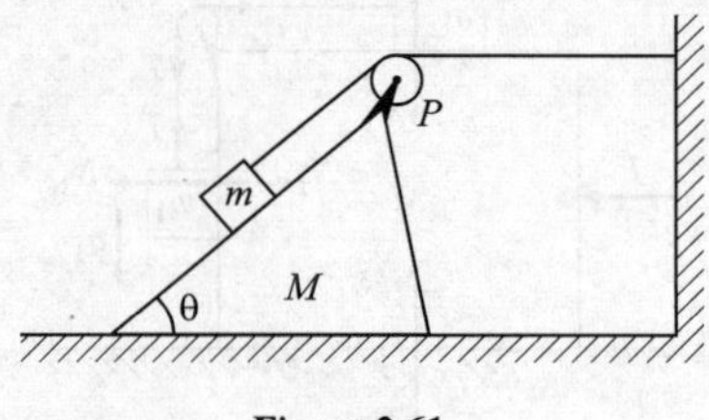

Figure 2.61

Solution

Here it can be easily shown by constrained analysis that if wedge move toward right by a distance x, the small bar will travel equal distance x on the inclined plane of wedge. Thus both the bodies will move with same acceleration, wedge towards right on earth and bar downward along incline on wedge. As bar is taken on wedge, a non inertial frame, a pseudo force is applied on bar towards left as shown in its free body diagram. Now we write down the motion equations of m and M according to forces shown in their *FBDs* in figure-2.62.

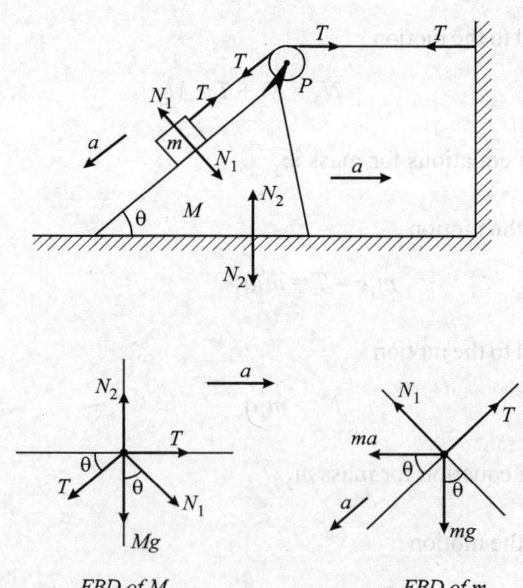

Figure 2.62

Motion equation for M

Along the plane

$$T + N_1\sin\theta - T\cos\theta = Ma \qquad \ldots(2.44)$$

Its vertical motion equations will not be used here as, no motion of it is in vertical direction.

Motion equation for m

Along the plane

$$ma\cos\theta + mg\sin\theta - T = ma \quad \dots (2.45)$$

Normal to plane

$$N_1 + ma\sin\theta = mg\cos\theta \quad \dots (2.46)$$

Substituting the value of T_1 and N_1 from equations (2.45) and (2.46) in equation (2.44), we get

$$a = \frac{mg\sin\theta}{M + 2m(1-\cos\theta)}$$

Alternative Treatment

The problems of above category can also be solved in earth frame (without using pseudo force) as follows but still it is advisable to consider acceleration of wedge in earth frame a_1 and that of bar relative to wedge a_2. Now while drawing *FBD*, be careful about the resolution of forces. At the time of solving problem in earth frame it is favourable to resolve force along horizontal and vertical direction and to write the equations of motion in horizontal and vertical direction. The respective *FBDs* are shown in figure-2.63.

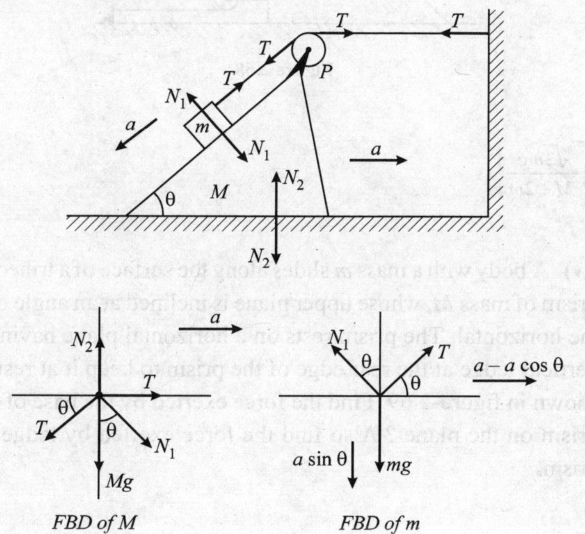

Figure 2.63

Equations of motion for mass M will remain same as equation-(2.44)

$$T + N_1\sin\theta - T\cos\theta = Ma \quad \dots (2.47)$$

Motion equation for m are (now written in horizontal and vertical direction relative to earth)

$$T\cos\theta - N\sin\theta = m(a - a\cos\theta) \quad \dots (2.48)$$

and $$mg - T\sin\theta - N\cos\theta = ma\sin\theta \quad \dots (2.49)$$

Solving equations-(2.47), (2.48) and (2.49) we get the same result

$$a = \frac{mg\sin\theta}{M + 2m(1-\cos\theta)}$$

NOTE : Be careful while solving the problem in earth frame that you should consider acceleration of mass relative to its surface (accelerating) but write the equations in horizontal and vertical directions relative to earth (ground).

 # Illustrative Example 2.21

Figure-2.64 shows a block of mass M supporting a bar of mass m through a pulley system. If system is released from rest, find the acceleration of block M and the tension in the strings.

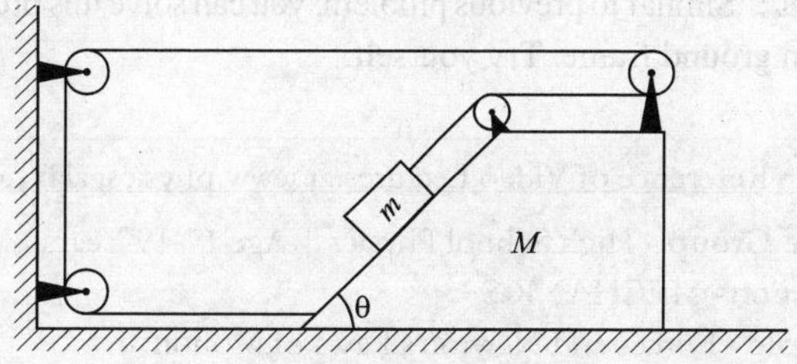

Figure 2.64

Solution

The forces acting on block M and bar m are shown in figure-2.65. Here first we can easily develop the constrained relation among the acceleration of mass M and m. We can observe that if M moves towards left with acceleration a, bar m will move down on inclined surface of M with an acceleration $2a$ relative to it. The free body diagrams of the masses are also shown in figure-2.65.

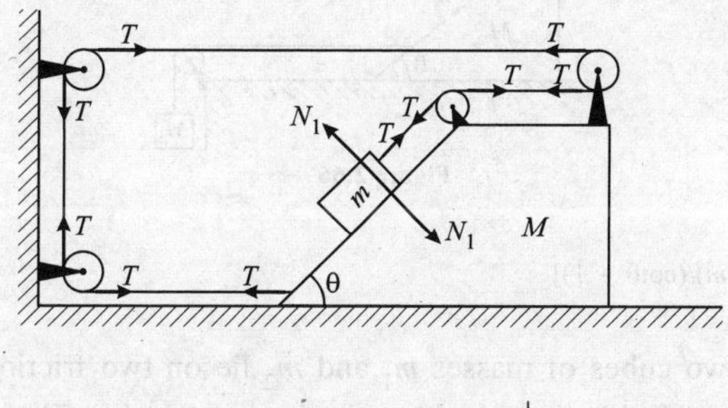

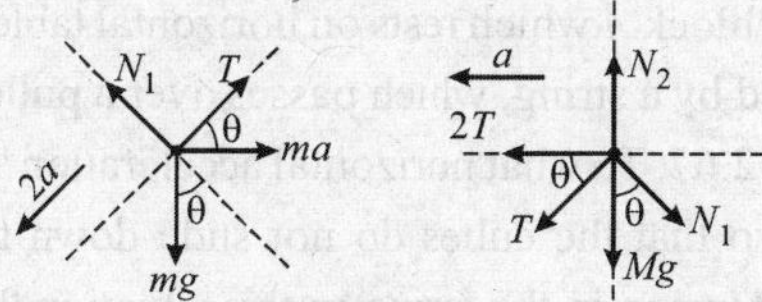

Figure 2.65

The equation of motion for M is

$$2T + T\cos\theta - N_1\sin\theta = Ma$$

The equations of motion for m are

$$mg\sin\theta - T - ma\cos\theta = 2ma$$

and $N_1 = mg\cos\theta + ma\sin\theta$

On solving above equations we get

$$a = \frac{2mg\sin\theta}{M + m(5 + 4\cos\theta)}$$

and $T = \dfrac{mg\sin\theta(M + m + 2m\cos\theta)}{M + m(5 + 4\cos\theta)}$

NOTE : Similar to previous problem, you can solve this problem also in ground frame. Try yourself.

Web Reference of Video Lectures at www.physicsgalaxy.com
Age Group - High School Physics | Age 17-19 Years
Section - MECHANICS
Topic - Forces and Newton's Laws of Motion
Module Numbers - 17, 18, 19, 20, 21, and 22

Practice Exercise 2.3

(i) Find the mass M_1 of the hanging block shown in figure-2.66, which will prevent the smaller block from slipping over the triangular block. All the surfaces are frictionless and the strings and the pulleys are light.

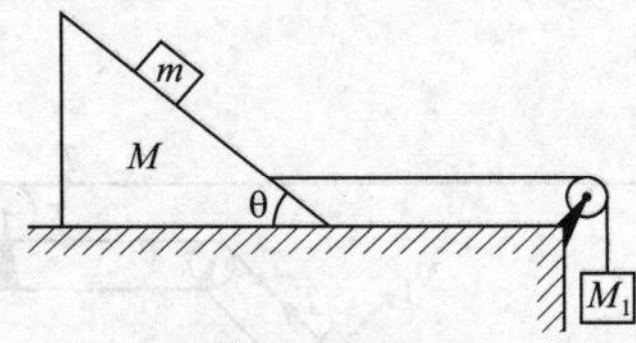

Figure 2.66

[$(M + m)/(\cot\theta - 1)$]

(ii) Two cubes of masses m_1 and m_2 lie on two frictionless slopes of the block A which rests on horizontal table. The cubes are connected by a string, which passes over a pulley as shown in the figure-2.67. To what horizontal acceleration "f" the block accelerates so that the cubes do not slide down the planes ? What is the tension in the string in this situation ?

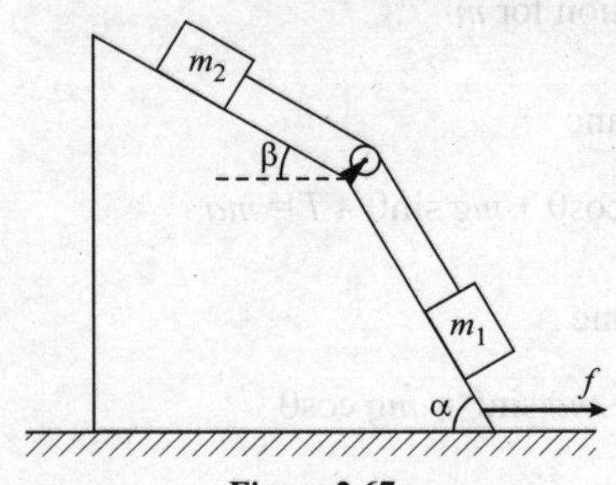

Figure 2.67

[$f = g\left(\dfrac{m_1\sin\alpha + m_2\sin\beta}{m_1\cos\alpha + m_2\cos\beta}\right)$, $T = \dfrac{m_1 m_2 g\sin(\alpha - \beta)}{m_1\cos\alpha + m_2\cos\beta}$]

(iii) In the arrangement shown in figure-2.68 the masses of the wedge M and the body m are known. There is no friction at any of the surfaces. The mass of the pulleys and thread is negligible. Find the acceleration of the body m relative to the horizontal surface on which the wedge slides.

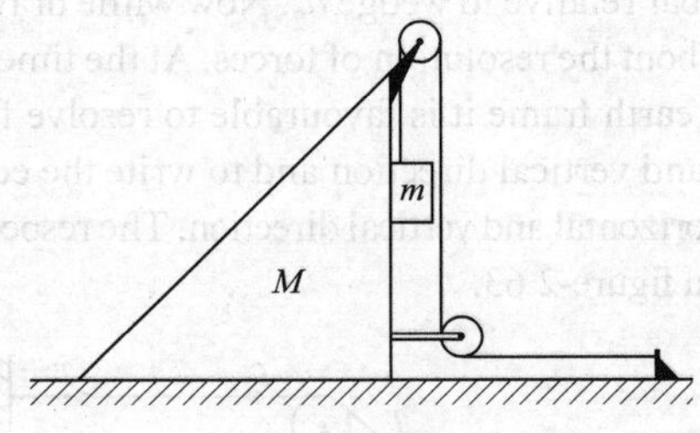

Figure 2.68

[$\left[\dfrac{\sqrt{2}mg}{M + 2m}\right]$]

(iv) A body with a mass m slides along the surface of a trihedral prism of mass M, whose upper plane is inclined at an angle α to the horizontal. The prism rests on a horizontal plane having a vertical ledge at the rear edge of the prism to keep it at rest as shown in figure-2.69. Find the force exerted by the base of the prism on the plane ? Also find the force exerted by ledge on prism.

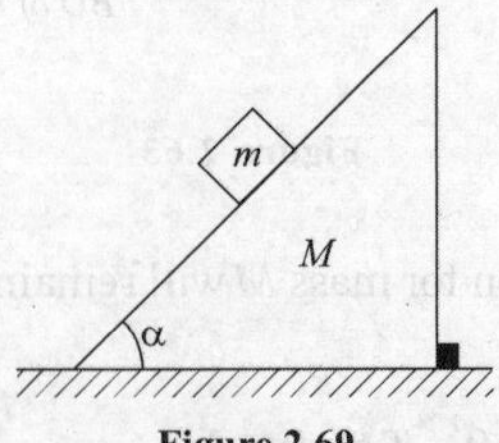

Figure 2.69

[$Mg + mg\cos^2\alpha$, $mg\sin\alpha\cos\alpha$]

(v) Find the acceleration of the mass m shown in figure-2.70.

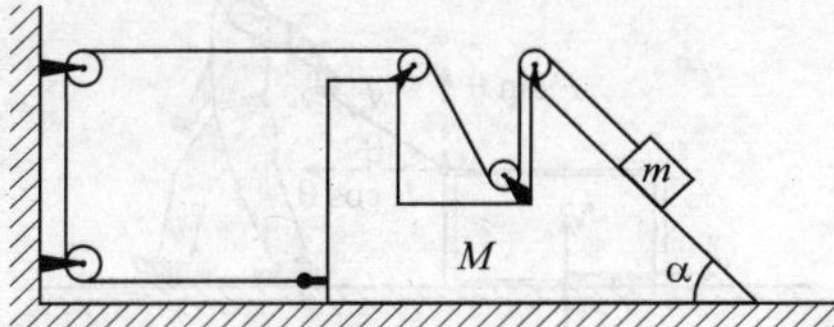

Figure 2.70

$$\left[\frac{2mg\sin\alpha\sqrt{5-4\cos\alpha}}{M+m(5-4\cos\alpha)}\right]$$

(vi) If the man manages to keep himself at rest on platform, as shown in figure-2.71. Find the acceleration of the system masses m and M. All pulleys, platform and string are light and frictionless. Also find the force man has to exert on string in this situation.

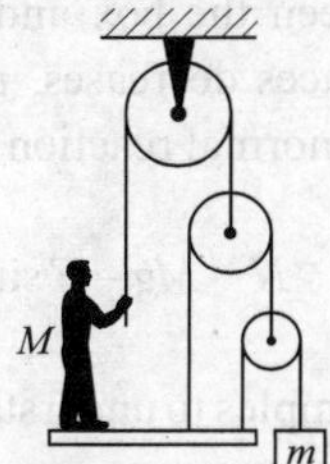

Figure 2.71

$$\left[\frac{7m-M}{49m+M}g,\ \frac{32mM}{49m+M}\cdot g\right]$$

2.8 Friction

Before we start with the problems based on applications of Newton's laws, let us discuss friction because friction forces play an important part in nearly all application of Newton's laws.

There are three major categories of friction forces :

1. Viscous friction or wet friction forces occur when objects move through gases and liquids. The most common example is air friction, which acts when we run, we throw an object in air.

2. Rolling friction forces arise as, for example, a rubber tire rolls on pavement, primarily because the tire deforms as the wheel rolls. The sliding of molecules against each other within the rubber causes energy to be lost.

3. Sliding friction forces occur when the two surfaces in contact with each other oppose the sliding of one surface over the other.

It is the third type of friction that is our main concern in this section.

Consider the experiment shown in figure-2.72. If someone pulls lightly the box shown with a horizontal force, it does not move. Apparently, the tabletop also pushes horizontally on the box with an equal and opposite force f. This equal force which is preventing the box to slide, is the friction f, opposing the box to slide and it is directed parallel to the sliding surface.

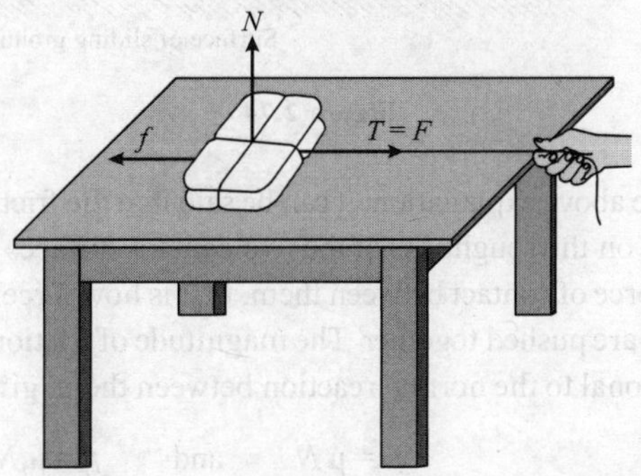

Figure 2.72

If we slowly increase the force with which we are pulling the box, as shown in figure-2.73, graph shows that the friction force increases with our force upto a certain critical value, f_L, the box suddenly begins to move, and as soon as it starts moving, a smaller force is required to maintain its motion as in motion friction is reduced. The friction value from 0 to f_L is known as static friction, which balances the external force on the body and prevent it from sliding. The value f_L is the maximum limit up to which the static friction acts is known as limiting friction, after which body starts sliding and friction reduces to kinetic friction. (figure-2.73)

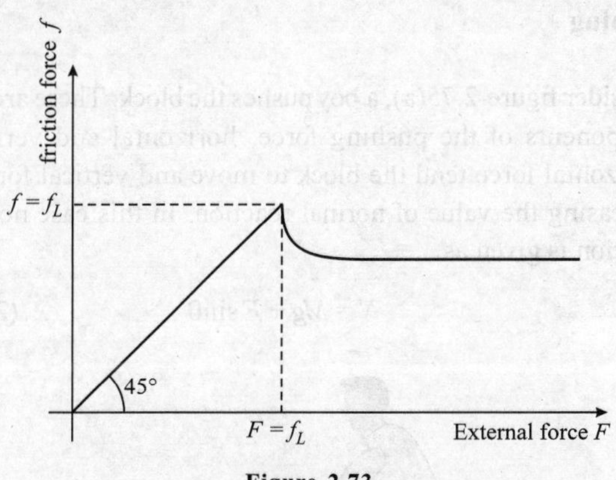

Figure 2.73

The main reason behind this behaviour is shown in figure-2.74. As you see, the surfaces in contact are far from smooth. Even highly polished surfaces look like this when observed at high magnification. The jagged points from one surface penetrate those of the other surface, and this causes the surfaces to resist sliding. Once sliding has begun, however, the surfaces do not have time to "settle down" onto each other completely. As a result, less force is required to keep then moving than to start the motion.

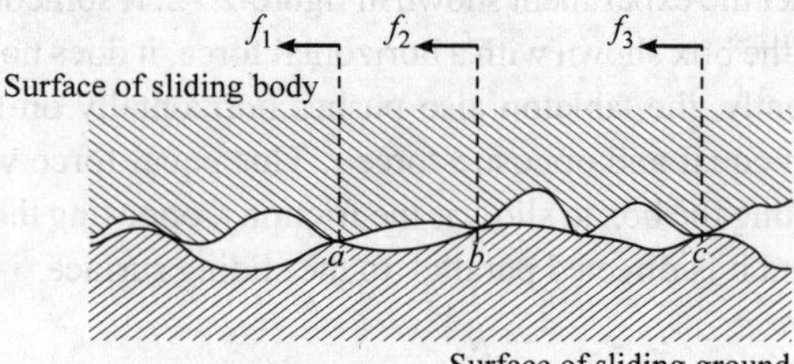

Figure 2.74

From the above explanation, it can be said that the friction force depends on the roughness of the two contact surfaces and also on the force of contact between them, that is how forcefully two surfaces are pushed together. The magnitude of friction force is proportional to the normal reaction between them, given as

$$f_L = \mu_s N \quad \text{and} \quad f_k = \mu_k N$$

Here μ_s and μ_k are called static and kinetic coefficients of friction, respectively. The factors μ_s and μ_k are depending on what the surfaces are made of and how clean and dry they are. Although friction forces are dependent on the roughness of the surfaces, there are two approximate statements about friction can be given as (1) at low speeds, f_k does not change much with speed as one surface slides over the other, and (2) for given surfaces and a normal reaction between them, the values of static and kinetic friction is independent of the area of the contact between surfaces.

2.8.1. Pulling on a Rough Surface is Always Easier Than Pushing

Consider figure-2.75(a), a boy pushes the block. There are two components of the pushing force, horizontal and vertical. Horizontal force tend the block to move and vertical force is increasing the value of normal reaction. In this case normal reaction is given as

$$N = Mg + F\sin\theta \qquad \dots(2.50)$$

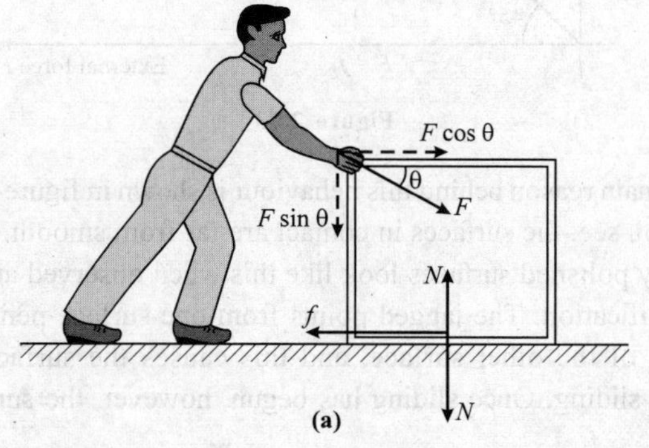

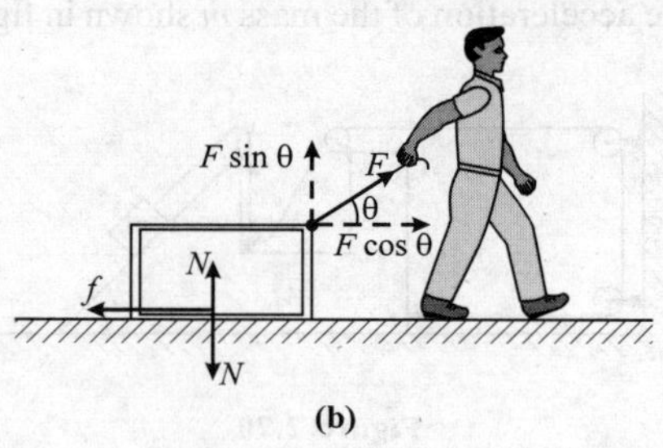

Figure 2.75

As N increases, the limiting friction $f_L = \mu_s N$ also increases and hence it is difficult to push the object. But unlike to this case in figure-2.75(b), a boy pulls a box with a rope, here again there are two components of the tension in the rope, horizontal and vertical. Horizontal force is tending the box to move but here the vertical force is in upwards direction, which decreases the normal reaction between the box and the floor. As normal reaction between surfaces decreases, it is easier to slide the object in this case, the normal reaction is given as

$$N = Mg - F\sin\theta \qquad \dots(2.51)$$

We now take some examples to understand the above concepts regarding friction in a better way.

Illustrative Example 2.22

A 100 kg load is uniformly moved over a horizontal plane by a force F applied at an angle 30° to the horizontal. Find this force if the coefficient of friction between the load and the plane is 0.3. Take $g = 10\ \text{m/s}^2$

Solution

As shown in figure-2.76, F is the pulling force due to which the normal reaction between the load and the ground decreases, which will also decrease the friction. The normal reaction at the bottom contact is given as

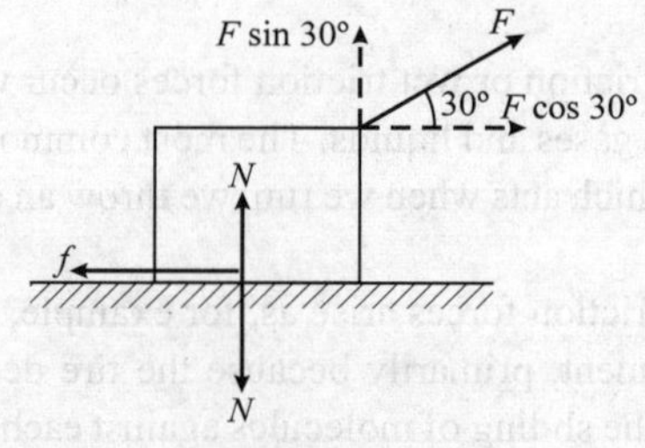

Figure 2.76

$$N = Mg - F\sin 30°$$

or $$= 1000 - \frac{1}{2}F$$

As it is given that the load moves uniformly, net sum of forces in the direction of motion must be zero. Thus

$$F\cos 30° = \mu N$$

or $$\frac{\sqrt{3}}{2}F = 0.3 \times (1000 - \frac{1}{2}F)$$

or $$F = \frac{300 \times 2}{\sqrt{3}+1} = 219.6\,\text{N}$$

Illustrative Example 2.23

Consider the situation shown in figure-2.77, the block *B* moves on a frictionless surface, while the coefficient of friction between *A* and the surface on which it moves is 0.2. Find the acceleration with which the masses move and also the tension in the strings. Take g = 10 m/s^2

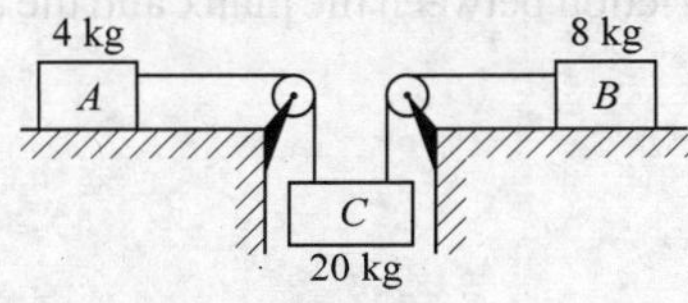

Figure 2.77

Solution

Let a be the acceleration with which the masses move and T_1 and T_2 be the tensions in left and right strings. Friction on mass *A* is $\mu mg = 8$ N. Then we have equations of motion of masses *A*, *B* and *C* are

For mass *A* $$T_1 - 8 = 4a \qquad \ldots(2.52)$$

For mass *B* $$T_2 = 8a \qquad \ldots(2.53)$$

For mass *C* $$200 - T_1 - T_2 = 20a \qquad \ldots(2.54)$$

Adding the above three equations, we get

$$32a = 192$$

or $$a = 6\,\text{m/s}^2$$

From equatons-(2.52) and (2.53), we have

$$T_1 = 48\,\text{N}$$

and $$T_2 = 32\,\text{N}$$

Illustrative Example 2.24

A small body starts sliding down an inclined plane of inclination θ, whose base length is equal to *l*. The coefficient of friction between the body and the surface is μ. If the angle θ is varied keeping *l* constant, at what angle will the time of sliding be least ?

Solution

When body slides down as shown in figure-2.78 its acceleration can be given as

$$a = g\sin\theta - \mu g\cos\theta$$

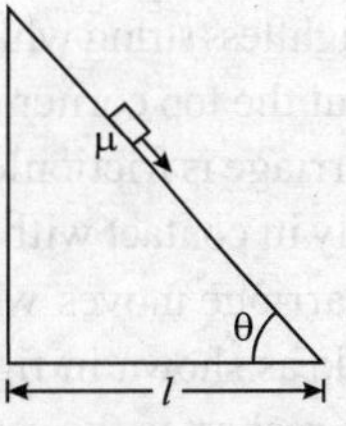

Figure 2.78

The length of incline travelled by the body is *l* secθ, thus the time taken by the body to come down is

$$t = \sqrt{\frac{2l\sec\theta}{a}}$$

or $$= \sqrt{\frac{2l\sec\theta}{g\sin\theta - \mu g\cos\theta}}$$ as

Time will be least when $\frac{dt}{d\theta} = 0$, thus we have

$$\cos^2\theta - \sin^2\theta + 2\mu\sin\theta\cos\theta = 0$$

$$\cos 2\theta + \mu\sin 2\theta = 0$$

or $$\tan 2\theta = -\frac{1}{\mu}$$

Illustrative Example 2.25

A block slides down an inclined plane of slope angle θ with constant velocity. It is then projected up the same plane with an initial velocity v_0. How far up the incline will it move before coming to rest ?

Solution

As block slides with uniform velocity, its weight component *mg* sinθ is balanced by friction between its surface and ground. Thus we have

$$mg\sin\theta = \mu mg\cos\theta$$

or $$\mu = \tan\theta$$

When it is projected up with a velocity v_0, it will be retarded by both, $g \sin\theta$ and friction and as friction is equal to force of gravity, it will now be retarded by $2g \sin\theta$, hence the distance covered by the particle along the plane is

$$s = \frac{v_0^2}{2a} = \frac{v_0^2}{4g \sin\theta}$$

Illustrative Example 2.26

Two blocks of masses m_1 and m_2 respectively are connected by an inextensible and weightless string which passes over a smooth and light pulley fixed at the top corner of a long carriage. The upper surface of the carriage is frictionless and the body A rests on it. B hangs vertically in contact with the rough vertical side of the carriage. The carriage moves with an acceleration $g/7$ towards right hand side as shown in figure-2.79. If the blocks remain stationary with respect to the carriage and $m_1 = 7.5\ m_2$, calculate the coefficient of friction between the block B and vertical side of the carriage.

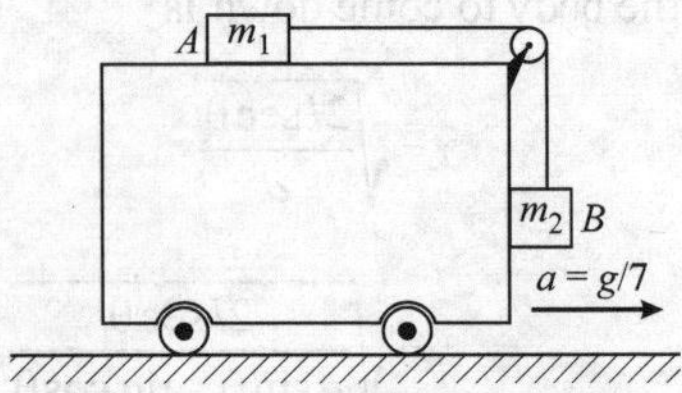

Figure 2.79

Solution

In this problem the reference frame of masses m_1 and m_2, the carriage is moving with an acceleration $a = g/7$. On both the masses there will be a pseudo force when these are observed with respect to the carriage. Pseudo force on m_1 in backward direction tend to pull the mass m_2 upward. In this case friction on m_2 will act in downward direction. We solve the situation using the figure-2.80, which shows all the forces acting on the bodies except gravity and pseudo forces.

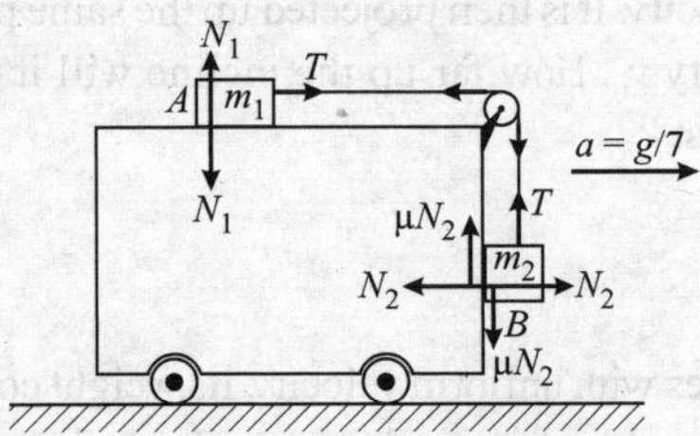

Figure 2.80

As the masses m_1 and m_2 are at rest with respect to carriage, we must have sum of all the forces acting on it are zero. Thus we have

For mass m_1 $\quad T = m_1 a \quad \ldots(2.55)$

For mass m_2 $\quad T = m_2 g + \mu m_2 a \quad \ldots(2.56)$

Solving equations-(2.55) and (2.56), we have

$$\mu = \frac{m_1 - 7m_2}{m_2} = 0.5 \quad [\text{As } m_1 = 7.5\, m_2]$$

Illustrative Example 2.27

A plank of mass m_1 with a bar of mass m_2 placed on it lies on a smooth horizontal plane. A horizontal force growing with time t as $F = kt$ (k is a constant) is applied to the bar. Find how the acceleration of the plank and of the bar depend on t, if the coefficient of friction between the plank and the bar is equal to μ.

Solution

As force is proportional to time, initially this force will be less than frictional force hence the bar and the plank will move together. After some time when the frictional force is less than applied force, then both the blocks will move with different accelerations. Thus initially combined acceleration of the system will be

$$a = \frac{F}{m_1 + m_2} = \frac{kt}{m_1 + m_2}$$

After some time when the applied force exceeds frictional force, m_2 starts sliding on m_1. Let us take the acceleration of m_1 is a_1 on ground and that of m_2 is a_2 on the surface of m_1. Consider the forces acting on the two bodies shown in figure-2.81.

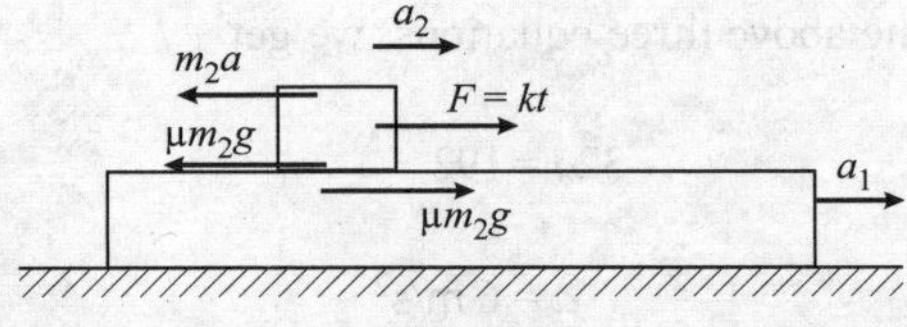

Figure 2.81

When m_2 starts sliding over the plank, friction on it will oppose its motion with respect to plank, so $\mu m_2 g$ will act in backward direction and its reaction on the plank is in forward direction which will move the plank with acceleration a_1 as it is the only force acting on plank, which can be given as

$$a_1 = \frac{\mu m_2 g}{m_1}$$

As plank is accelerated, it becomes a noninertial frame for m_2, with respect to it a pseudo force m_2a_1 is applied on the bar. As it is sliding with acceleration a_2 with respect to plank, we have its motion equation as

$$F - \mu m_2 g - m_2 a_1 = m_2 a_2$$

or
$$a_2 = \frac{kt}{m_2} - \mu g - a_1$$

This acceleration a_2 of bar is with respect to plank, hence net acceleration of bar is $a_2 + a_1$. Thus the net acceleration of bar is

$$a_{bar} = a_2 + a_1 = \frac{kt}{m_2} - \mu g$$

Now one more thing is to be calculated, the time instant when bar start sliding on plank. It is the instant when the acceleration of bar with respect to plank a_2 is just started or zero or when the external force on bar just balances the friction plus pseudo force on it. Let us take this instant is t_1, it can be given as at time t_1

$$kt_1 = m_2 a_1 + \mu m_2 g$$

or
$$t_1 = \frac{\mu m_2 g(m_1 + m_2)}{m_1 k}$$

Illustrative Example 2.28

A bar of mass m is placed on a triangular block of mass M as shown in figure-2.82. The friction coefficient between the two surface is μ and ground is smooth. Find the minimum and maximum horizontal force F required to be applied on block so that the bar will not slip on the inclined surface of block.

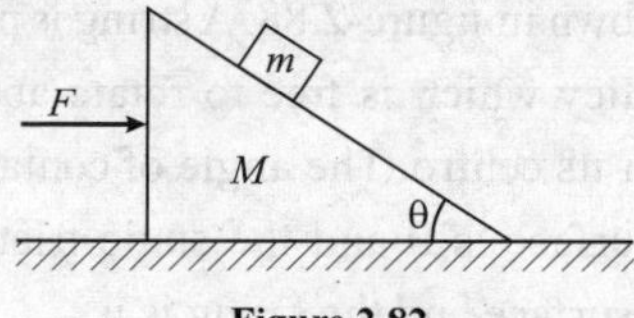

Figure 2.82

Solution

Here if both the masses are moving together, acceleration of the system will be $\frac{F}{M+m}$. If we observe the mass m relative to M, it experiences a pseudo force ma toward left. Along the incline it experiences two forces, $mg \sin\theta$ downward and $ma \cos\theta$ upward. If $mg \sin\theta$ is more than $ma \cos\theta$, it has a tendency of slipping downward so friction on it will act in upward direction. Here if block m is in equilibrium on inclined surface, we must have

$$mg \sin\theta - ma \cos\theta \le \mu(mg \cos\theta + ma \sin\theta)$$

or
$$a \ge \frac{\sin\theta - \mu\cos\theta}{\cos\theta + \mu\sin\theta} g$$

or
$$F \ge \frac{\sin\theta - \mu\cos\theta}{\cos\theta + \mu\sin\theta}(M+m)g \quad \ldots(2.57)$$

If force is more than the value obtained in equation-(2.57), $ma \cos\theta$ will increase on m and the static friction on it will decrease. At $a = g \tan\theta$ [when $F = (M+m)g \tan\theta$], we know that the force $mg \sin\theta$ will be balanced by $ma \cos\theta$ at this acceleration no friction will act on it. If applied force will increase beyond this value, $ma \cos\theta$ will exceed $mg \sin\theta$ and friction starts acting in downward direction.

Web Reference of Video Lectures at www.physicsgalaxy.com

Age Group - High School Physics | Age 17-19 Years
Section - MECHANICS
Topic - Friction
Module Numbers - 1, 2, 3, 4, 5, 6, 7 and 8

Practice Exercise 2.4

(i) A child pushes a box that has mass m up an incline plane at an angle α above the horizontal. The coefficients of friction between the incline and the box are μ_s and μ_k. The force applied by the child is horizontal. (a) If μ_s is greater than some critical value, the child cannot start the box moving up the incline, no matter how hard he pushes. Calculate this critical value of μ_s. (b) Assume that μ_s is less than this critical value. What magnitude of force must the child apply to keep the box moving up the plane at constant speed.

[$\cot\alpha$, $\frac{mg(\sin\alpha + \mu_k \cos\alpha)}{\cos\alpha - \mu_k \sin\alpha}$]

(ii) Calculate the force P required to cause the block of weight W_1 = 200 N just to slide under the block of weight W_2 = 100 N shown in figure-2.83. What is the tension in the string AB ? Coefficient of friction μ = 0.25 for all surfaces in contact.

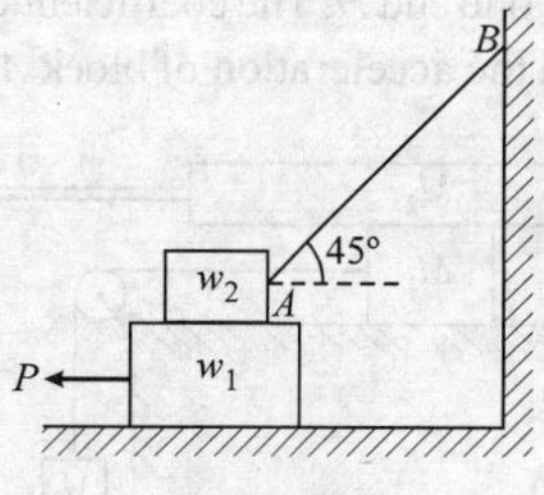

Figure 2.83

[90 N, $20\sqrt{2}$ N]

(iii) Figure-2.84 shows a man of mass M standing on a board of mass m. What minimum force is required to exert on string to slide the board. The friction coefficient between board and floor is μ and there is sufficient friction between man and board so that man does not slip.

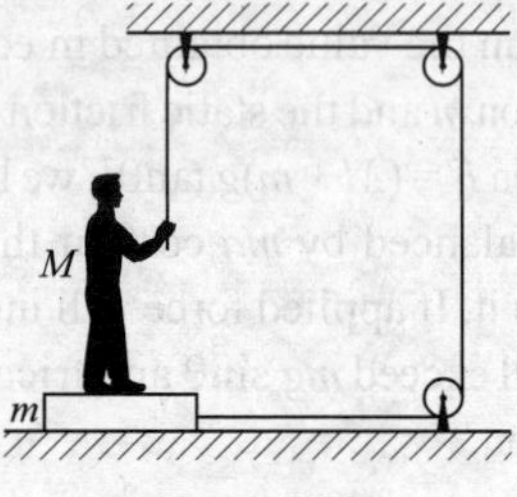

Figure 2.84

$[\frac{\mu(M+m)g}{1+\mu}]$

(iv) A uniform ladder AB of length 3 metres and weight 20 kg rests with the end A against rough vertical wall and the end B on level round. If the wall and the ground are equally rough and the coefficient of friction is 0.5, find the limiting position of equilibrium. Take $g = 10\ m/s^2$.

[37° with horizontal]

(v) Figure-2.85 shows a block B of mass m, cart C of mass M, and the coefficient of static friction between the block and the cart is μ. Neglect frictional between wheels and axles and the rotational effects of the wheels. Determine the minimum value of F which must be applied on B such that it will not slide.

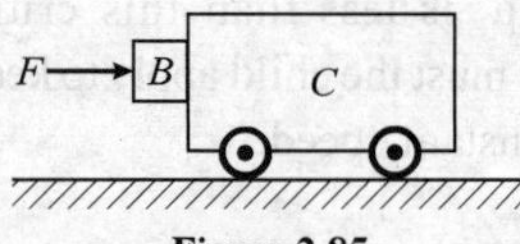

Figure 2.85

$[\frac{mg}{\mu}\left(1+\frac{m}{M}\right)]$

(vi) In figure-2.86, the block A of mass M_1 rests on a rough horizontal surface. The coefficient of friction between the block and the surface is μ. A uniform plank B, of mass M_2 rests on A. B is prevented from moving by connecting it to a light rod R which is hinged at one end H. The coefficient of friction between A and B is μ. Find the acceleration of block A and C.

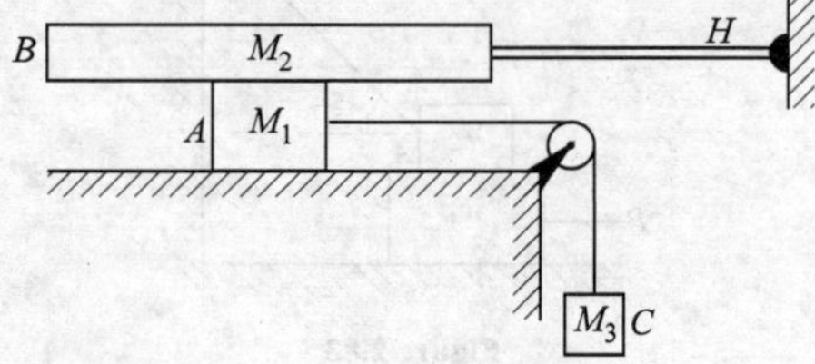

Figure 2.86

$[\frac{M_3g - \mu g(M_1+2M_2)}{(M_1+M_3)}]$

(vii) In the arrangement shown in figure-2.87 the masses of the wedge M and the body m are known. The appreciable friction exists only between the wedge and the body m, the friction coefficient being μ. The masses of the pulleys and thread is negligible. Find the acceleration of the body m relative to the horizontal surface on which the wedge slides.

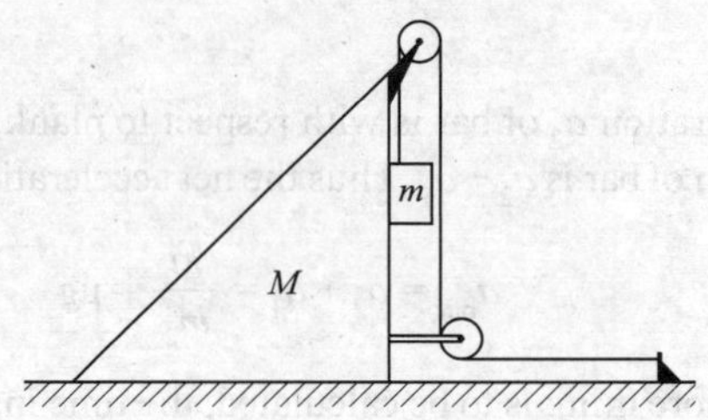

Figure 2.87

$[\frac{\sqrt{2g}}{(2+\mu+M/m)}]$

2.8.2 Friction Between Pulley and String

The part of dynamics we've covered we were mainly dealing with ideal pulleys and strings which are massless and frictionless. If we consider the friction between the string and the surface of pulley over which it is passing, the tension on the two sides of the string must be different. To develop the relation in the two tensions we take a simple illustration.

A situation is shown in figure-2.88. A string is passing over the surface of a pulley which is free to rotate about the axle O passing through its centre. The angle of contact of the string on the pulley surface is θ and the static friction coefficient between pulley surface and the string is μ.

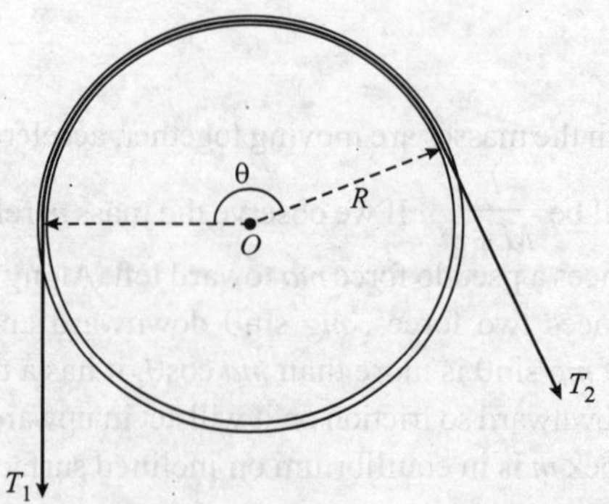

Figure 2.88

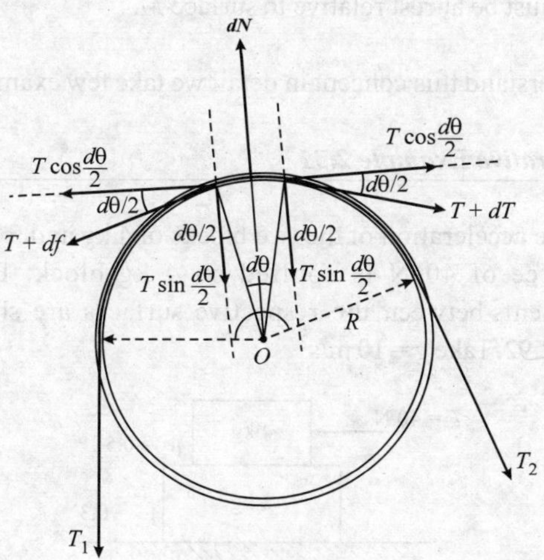

Figure 2.89

If the tension on right part of string is T_2 and if it is more than that in left part (i.e. T_1), it will have a sliding tendency toward right and on string friction will act in the direction of T_1, so as to balance T_2 (as string is massless)

As the difference in T_1 and T_2 increases, friction acting on string will increase till it reaches limiting friction and then the string starts slipping over the pulley. Now we develop a relation in the two tension when the string just starts slipping over pulley. Analysis is shown in figure-2.89. We consider a small element of the string in contact with pulley surface. Let the tension (tangentially acting) toward left is T and that toward right is $T + dT$. The excess tension dT on right is cause of friction toward left, if it is df, we must have

$$dT = df = \mu dN \quad \text{[At the time of slipping]}$$

And here dN can be obtained by our conventional method as

$$dN = 2(T + dT)\sin\frac{d\theta}{2} = T\,d\theta$$

or $$dT = \mu\, T\, d\theta$$

or $$\frac{dT}{T} = \mu\, d\theta$$

Integrating with the proper limits

$$\int_{T=T_1}^{T=T_2} \frac{dT}{T} = \int_0^\theta \mu\, d\theta$$

or $$\ln\left(\frac{T_2}{T_1}\right) = \mu\,\theta$$

or $$T_2 = T_1 e^{\mu\theta} \qquad \dots(2.58)$$

To understand the applications of this relation we take few examples.

Illustrative Example 2.29

Figure-2.90 shows a cylinder mounted on an horizontal axle. A massless string is wound on it two and a half turn and connected to two masses m and $2\,m$. If the system is in limiting equilibrium, find the coefficient of friction between the string and the pulley surface.

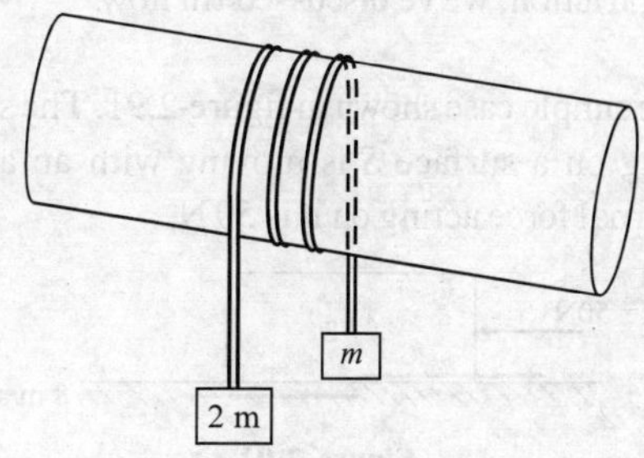

Figure 2.90

Solution

If the system is in equilibrium, the tensions in the two hanging parts of the string will be mg and $2mg$ respectively. From equation-(2.58) we have

$$2mg = mg\, e^{\mu(5\pi)} \quad \text{[As the angle of contact} = 5\pi]$$

or $$\mu = \frac{1}{5\pi}\ln(2)$$

Illustrative Example 2.30

Two masses m_1 kg and m_2 kg passes over an atwoods machine. Find the ratio of masses m_1 and m_2 so that string passing over the pulley will just start slipping over its surface. The friction coefficient between the string and pulley surface is 0.2.

Solution

For a simple atwood's machine we can write for the two masses

$$m_1 g - T_1 = m_1 a$$

and $$T_2 - m_2 g = m_2 a$$

and if string starts slipping, we have

$$T_1 = T_2 e^{\mu\pi}$$

or $$m_1(g - a) = m_2(g + a)\, e^{\mu\pi}$$

If string just slips, we can use $a = 0$, thus we have

$$\frac{m_1}{m_2} = e^{0.2\pi}$$

2.8.3 Conditions For Sliding

There are several cases of dynamics in which a student get confused to check whether there is sliding between two given surfaces or not. In this section we will mainly discuss the conditions under which sliding takes place but again the basis of judgement will remain same, the fundamentals of static, kinetic and limiting friction, we've discussed till now.

Consider the simple case shown in figure-2.91. The shown block of mass 4 kg on a surface S is moving with an acceleration 8 m/s^2. External force acting on it is 50 N.

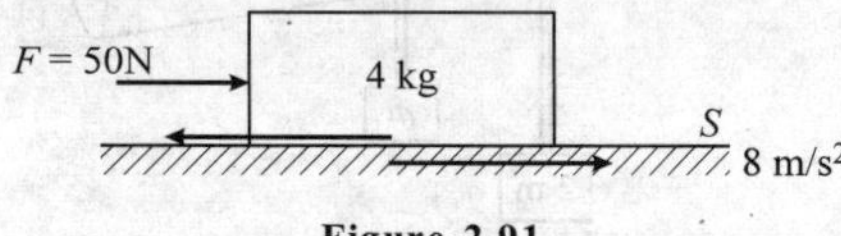

Figure 2.91

The friction coefficient given between the two surfaces is 0.5. If we will write the dynamics equation for this mass, we have

$$F - f = ma$$

or $$50 - f = 4(8)$$

or $$f = 18\text{ N}$$

If we find the friction force acting on the block using friction coefficient we get

$$f = \mu mg = 20\text{ N}$$

How it is possible ? It shows that if block is sliding on the surface, friction on it must be 20 N but analytical calculation shows that it is 18 N. It implies that either the given data is with some error or we are not interpreting the correct situation. Yes it is ! actually here on calculations we find the friction acting on the block is less than limiting or kinetic friction, it straight forward implies that block is not sliding on the surface it is placed so we can state that the block along with the surface S is moving with the acceleration 8 m/s^2.

What we have discussed its reverse is also true. If we initially assume that block is sliding on S, we use friction as 20 N, we get acceleration of the block

$$50 - 20 = 4\,(a)$$

or $$a = 7.5\text{ m/s}^2$$

Which is less than that given in the situation. This means that the accelerating force is more than that we are using which is possible only when friction is less than 20 N, which implies the block must be at rest relative to surface M.

To understand this concept in detail we take few examples.

 # *Illustrative Example 2.31*

Find the acceleration of the two blocks of 4 kg and 5 kg mass if a force of 40 N is applied on 4 kg block. Friction coefficients between the respective surfaces are shown in figure-2.92. Take $g = 10$ m/s^2

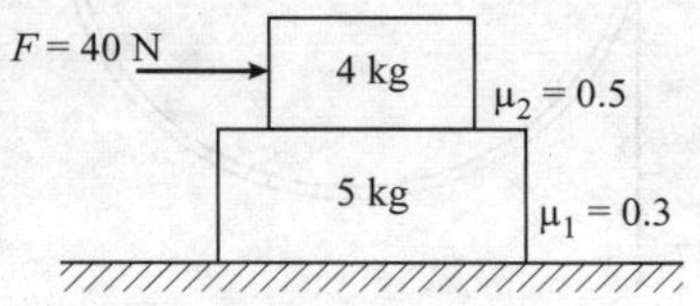

Figure 2.92

Solution

In such type of problems we have to check first whether there is a sliding between 4 kg and 5 kg block or not. We first assume that there is no sliding between the two blocks and the two are moving together on the surface. In this case friction on 5 kg block will be opposing and is sliding friction

$$f_1 = \mu\,(m_1 + m_2)g = 27\text{ N}$$

On 4 kg friction f_2 will be opposing but it must be static friction as 4 kg is not sliding on 5 kg block we assume initially. On 5 kg block f_2 is acting in opposite direction as shown in figure-2.93. If the two are moving together again be careful, we are only assuming that two are moving together this, f_2 will be an internal force of the system and the two blocks will move with an acceleration

$$a = \frac{40 - 27}{9} = \frac{13}{9}\text{ m/s}^2$$

Figure 2.93

Now if we consider 4 kg block only we have

$$40 - f_2 = 4 \times \frac{13}{9}$$

or $$f_2 = 40 - \frac{52}{9} = 34.22\text{ N}$$

The maximum possible value of f_2 can be $\mu_2 m_1 g = 20$ N and the above found value is more than this. It implies that the block 4 kg can never be at rest relative to 5 kg block.

NOTE : If in above case if the value of f_2 obtained could be less than 20 N, it would imply that this is the value of static friction and both are moving together. (check next example)

Here we have checked and found that there is slipping between 4 kg and 5 kg block, thus the friction between 4 kg and 5 kg block must be 20 N. But here if 20 N is acting on 5 kg block it is insufficient to displace the 5 kg block as the limiting friction at the bottom of 5 kg is 27 N thus it will remain at rest and 4 kg block only will move with acceleration

$$a = \frac{40-20}{4} = 5 \text{ m/s}^2$$

Illustrative Example 2.32

Solve previous problem again if $\mu_1 = 0.1$ and $\mu_2 = 0.8$,

Solution

Again we start our analysis by assuming that both the blocks are moving together. Their acceleration will be

$$a = \frac{40-9}{9} = \frac{31}{9} \text{ m/s}^2 \quad [\text{As here } f_1 = \mu (m_1 + m_2) g = 9 \text{ N}]$$

For 4 kg block we have

$$40 - f_2 = 4 \times \frac{31}{9}$$

or $$f_2 = 26.22 \text{ N}$$

Here the maximum possible value of f_2 will be $\mu m_1 g = 32$ N, which is more than that value found above. It implies that here f_2 is the static friction force as it is less than limiting value hence both the blocks are moving together with acceleration $31/9 = 3.44 \text{ m/s}^2$.

Illustrative Example 2.33

Find the maximum possible force which can be applied to the 8 kg block shown in figure-2.94 to move both the blocks together if bottom surface is (a) frictionless; (b) having friction coefficient 0.3. Take $g = 10 \text{ m/s}^2$

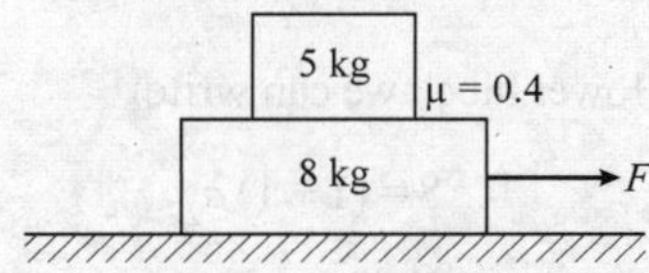

Figure 2.94

Solution

(a) If bottom surface is frictionless and we assume both are moving together, acceleration of the combined mass will be

$$a = \frac{F}{13} \text{ m/s}^2$$

Force of friction between the two blocks will be acting as shown in figure-2.95. Here it is important to note the direction of friction acting on the two blocks. As first 8 kg is pulled friction will oppose it and on 5 kg it is in opposite (forward) direction which will drive it to move in same direction.

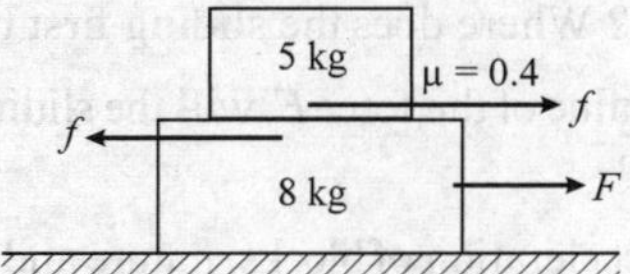

Figure 2.95

Now as F increases f will also increase but not beyond $\mu mg = 20$ N. The two blocks can move together till f will become equal to 20 N. At this instant we have

$$f = 5 \times \frac{F}{13} = 20 \text{ N}$$

or $$F = 52 \text{ N} \quad [\text{maximum value}]$$

Thus when F exceed 52 N, f will tend to exceed 20 N but it can not go slipping between the two surface starts.

(b) If ground has a friction coefficient 0.3, the friction acting on 8 kg block will be 39 N if it slide on applying external force F as shown in figure-2.96. If we assume that both the blocks are moving together, acceleration of the two will be given as

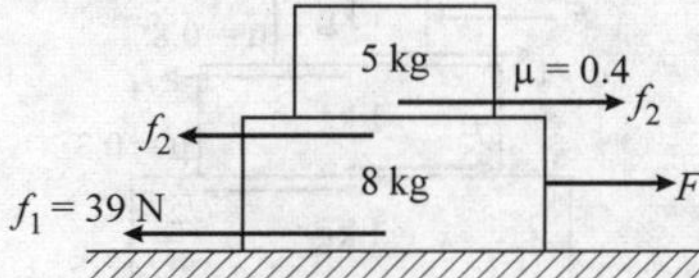

Figure 2.96

$$a = \frac{F-39}{13} \text{ m/s}^2$$

If we consider 5 kg block only, friction f_2 is the only force acting on it. The maximum possible value of f_2 will be $\mu mg = 20$ N. If F is increased f_2 will also increase but slipping between the two blocks will not start till its value will reach 20 N. Thus for 5 kg block

$$f = 20 = 5 \times \frac{F-39}{13}$$

or $$F = 91 \text{ N}$$

Illustrative Example 2.34

In the situation of three blocks shown in figure-2.97.

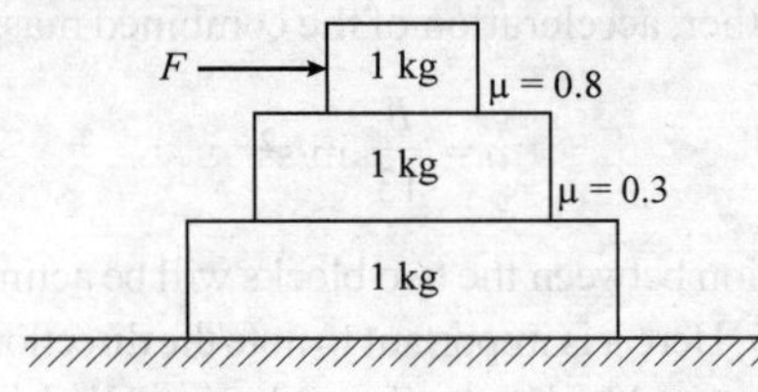

Figure 2.97

(a) For what maximum value of force F, can all the three blocks move together ? Where does the sliding first begins.

(b) For what value of the force F, will the sliding starts at other rough surface ?

(c) Find the acceleration of blocks, nature and value of friction forces at rough surfaces for following value of force F. Take $g = 10\ \text{m/s}^2$

(i) 3 N (ii) 15 N

Solution

(a) When the force F starts acting, the friction forces acting on the three blocks are as shown in figure-2.98. The limiting values of the two friction forces is

$$f_{1L} = 0.8\,(10) = 8\ \text{N} \quad \text{and} \quad f_{2L} = 0.3\,(20) = 6\ \text{N}$$

as bottom surface is frictionless and if we assume that the three blocks are moving together, acceleration of the system will be

$$a = \frac{F}{3}\ \text{m/s}^2$$

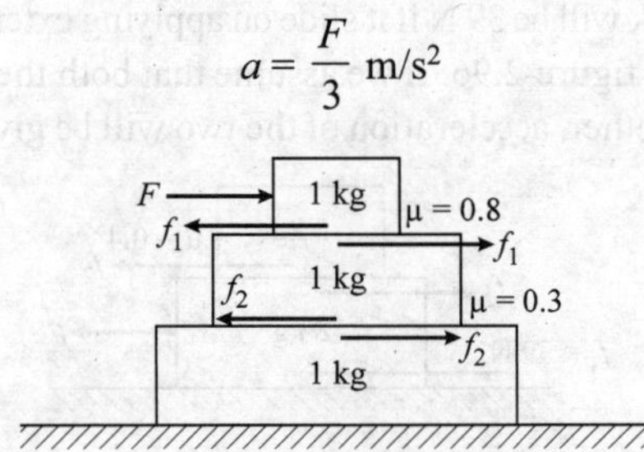

Figure 2.98

Considering lowermost block, it is experiences f_{2L}, we have

$$f_{2L} = 1 \times \frac{F}{3}$$

or $$F = 18\ \text{N}$$

This implies that the sliding between lower and middle block take place when applied force exceeds 18 N. Now we check for the sliding between middle and the top block. For this we consider the motion of middle block, assuming that no sliding at the lower surface, we have

$$f_{1L} - f_2 = \frac{F}{3}$$

As we have $f_2 = \dfrac{F}{3}$, we have

$$f_{1L} = \frac{2F}{3}$$

or $$F = 12\ \text{N}$$

Thus sliding at the top surface take place when the applied force exceeds 12 N which is less than the force required to start sliding at the lower surface. So this is the maximum force which can be applied to move the three blocks together and when force increases sliding first start at the upper surface.

(b) Now when force exceeds 12 N at upper surface friction becomes sliding friction and sliding starts and at this moment and for higher values of F friction at the upper surface will be constant and is equal to 8 N. If we write the equation of motion for the middle and lower block together, we have

$$8 - f_2 = 1 \times a$$

and $$f_2 = 1 \times a$$

Solving we get $$a = 4\ \text{m/s}^2$$

Now from the equation of lower block we have $f_2 = 4$ N which is less than its limiting value, thus sliding at this surface can never take place.

(c) (i) If applied force is $F = 3$ N, no sliding takes place at any of the surface and the three blocks move together with acceleration $F/3 = 1\ \text{m/s}^2$, the magnitude of friction at lower and upper surface remain same, we obtained in part (a) as

$$f_1 = \frac{2F}{3} = 2\ \text{N} \quad \text{and} \quad f_2 = \frac{F}{3} = 1\ \text{N}$$

(ii) If applied force is $F = 15$ N, sliding at upper surface starts and as we have discussed in part (b) that lower and middle block will always move together. For upper block we can write

$$15 - 8 = 1 \times a_1$$

or $$a_1 = 7\ \text{m/s}^2$$

For middle and lower block we can write

$$8 = (1 + 1)\,a_2$$

or $$a_2 = 4\ \text{m/s}^2$$

Friction at the upper surface will be sliding friction 8 N and at the lower surface it is static friction 4 N which we've obtained in part (b) and it can also be given as

$$f_2 = 1 \times 4 = 4\text{ N} \quad \text{[For lower block]}$$

Illustrative Example 2.35

In the situation shown in figure-2.99.

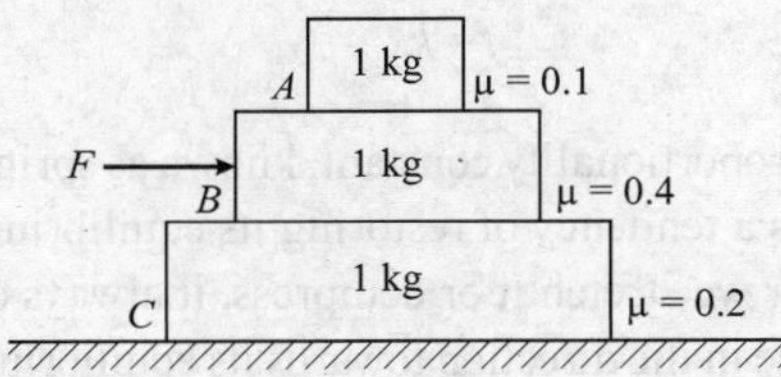

Figure 2.99

(a) For what minimum value of the force *F* will the system or any part of it start to move ?

(b) Find the values of force *F* when slipping starts between (i) *A* and *B* and (ii) *B* and *C*. Take $g = 10\text{ m/s}^2$

Solution

The limiting values of the friction at the three surfaces are given as

At the top surface $f_{3L} = 0.1\,(10) = 1$ N, at the middle surface $f_{2L} = 0.4\,(20) = 8$ N and at the bottom surface $f_{1L} = 0.2\,(30) = 6$ N.

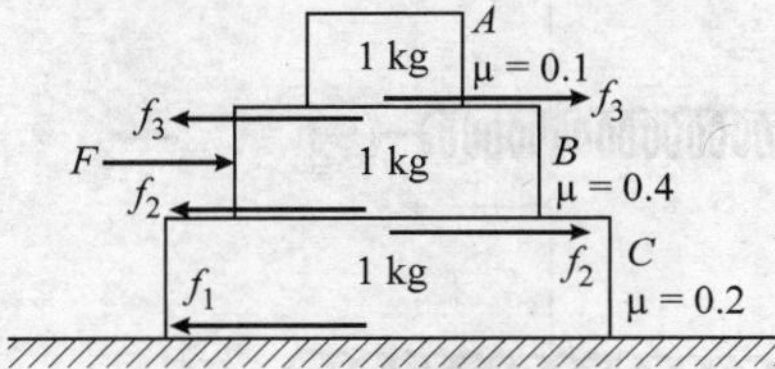

Figure 2.100

If the three blocks are moving together (if system slides at the bottom surface only), acceleration of the system will be given as

$$a = \frac{(F-6)}{3}\text{ m/s}^2$$

If system does not slide at the bottom surface also $a = 0$, thus $F = 6$ N. As the limiting friction at the middle surface is 8 N, no sliding takes place anywhere unless *F* exceeds 6 N.

(b) As we have discussed that the system starts sliding at the bottom surface when *F* exceeds 6 N. Sliding between blocks *A* and *B* takes place when f_3 will approach its limiting value of 1 N and sliding between *B* and *C* takes place when f_2 will approach its limiting value of 8 N. Now for checking the sliding condition for surface between *B* and *C* we write equations for the three blocks as

$$F - f_{2L} - f_3 = 1 \times a$$

and $$f_3 = 1 \times a$$

and $$f_{2L} - f_{1L} = 1 \times a$$

Solving we get $\quad a = 2\text{ m/s}^2;\ f_3 = 2\text{ N} \quad \text{and} \quad F = 12\text{ N}$

Here we found $f_3 = 2$ N, which is more than its limiting value of 1 N which is not possible. It implies that before sliding starts between *B* and *C*, sliding between *A* and *B* is started. Now to check the sliding between *A* and *B* we again write equations for the three blocks as

$$F - f_2 - f_{3L} = 1 \times a$$

and $$f_{3L} = 1 \times a$$

and $$f_2 - f_{1L} = 1 \times a$$

Solving we get $\quad a = 1\text{ m/s}^2;\ f_2 = 7\text{ N} \quad \text{and} \quad F = 9\text{ N}$

Thus when force *F* becomes 9 N, sliding between *A* and *B* starts first. Now to check when sliding between *B* and *C* will start we again write equation of the three blocks taking friction at the upper surface as sliding friction as

$$F - f_{2L} - f_{3L} = 1 \times a_1$$

and $$f_{3L} = 1 \times a$$

and $$f_{2L} - f_{1L} = 1 \times a_1$$

Here we are assuming that the upper block already started sliding with acceleration *a* and the sliding between *B* and *C* is just started and at this instant both are accelerating with acceleration a_1.

Solving we get

$$a = 1\text{ m/s}^2;\ a_1 = 2\text{ m/s}^2 \quad \text{and} \quad F = 11\text{ N}$$

Thus sliding between *B* and *C* is started when applied force *F* exceeds 11 N.

Web Reference of Video Lectures at www.physicsgalaxy.com

Age Group - High School Physics | Age 17-19 Years
Section - MECHANICS
Topic - Friction
Module Numbers - 9, 10 and 11

Practice Exercise 2.5

(i) Find the acceleration of the two blocks shown in figure-2.101. Take $g = 10\ m/s^2$.

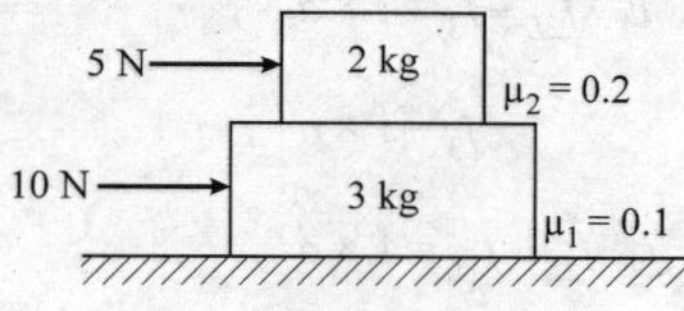

Figure 2.101

[2 m/s², 2 m/s²]

(ii) In the situation shown in figure-2.102, (a) What minimum force will make any part for whole system move. (b) For the following values of force, find the acceleration of two blocks, nature and value of friction at the two surfaces 2 N and 6 N. Take $g = 10\ m/s^2$.

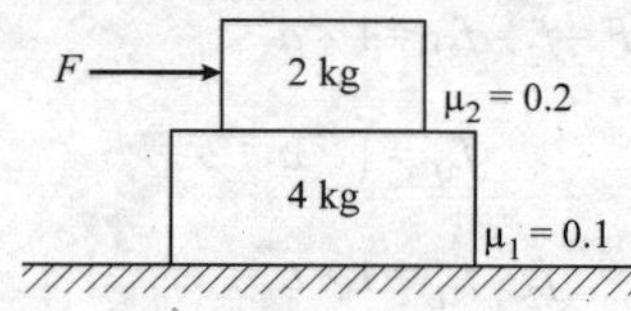

Figure 2.102

[(a) 4 N, (b) 1 m/s², 0]

(iii) In previous question if force acts on the lower block, (a) Where does the sliding begins first. (b) What is the minimum force at which any part of system starts sliding. (c) At what value of force F will the sliding starts at the other surfaces. (d) For the following values of F, find the acceleration of the two blocks, nature and value of friction at both rough surfaces -3 N, 12 N, 24 N. Take $g = 10\ m/s^2$.

[(a) lower; (b) 6 N; (c) 18 N; (d) 0 m/s², 3 N, 0 N, 1 m/s², 6 N, 2 N, 3.5 m/s², 2 m/s², 6 N, 4 N]

(iv) In the situation shown in figure-2.103, (a) for what maximum value of force F can all three blocks move together. (b) Find the value of force F at which sliding starts at other rough surfaces. (c) Find acceleration of all blocks, nature and value of friction force for following value of force F – 10 N, 18 N and 25 N. Take $g = 10\ m/s^2$.

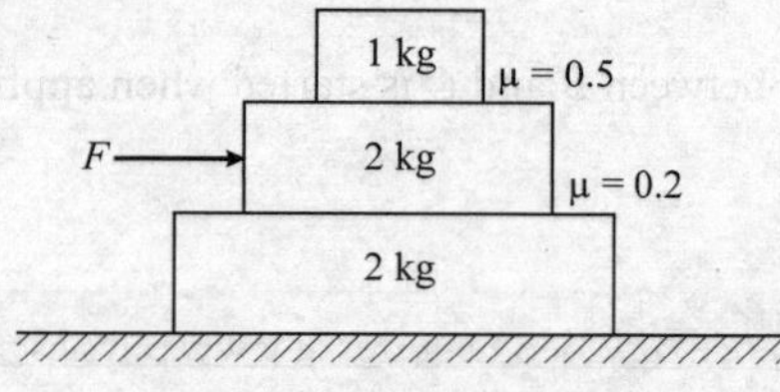

Figure 2.103

[(a) 15 N (b) 21 N (c) (2 m/s², 2 m/s², 2 m/s²), (3 m/s², 4 m/s², 4 m/s²), (3 m/s², 7 m/s², 5 m/s²]

2.9 *Spring Force*

We know that the more force we apply to a spring, the more it stretches. For a spring that obeys Hooke's law, the extension of the spring is proportional to the applied force. Figure-2.104 shows a spring in its equilibrium length. If we stretch it by a distance x from its equilibrium position, it applies a restoring force F, towards its equilibrium position, which is proportional to x, given by

$$f = kx \qquad \ldots(2.59)$$

Here k is a proportionality constant, known as spring constant. A spring has a tendency of restoring its equilibrium position, thus whether we stretch it or compress, it always opposes the external force in the direction towards its equilibrium position.

One more point is to be noted that a spring applies the restoring force equally at both of its ends, doesn't matter whether an end is fixed or not.

As shown in figure-2.104, an end of the spring is fixed to wall and other is pulled by applying a force. As the restoring force is directly proportional to the stretch of compression in it, for stretching it by x, we apply a force F on it and for stretching it to double the length to $2x$, we have to apply a force double of the previous value.

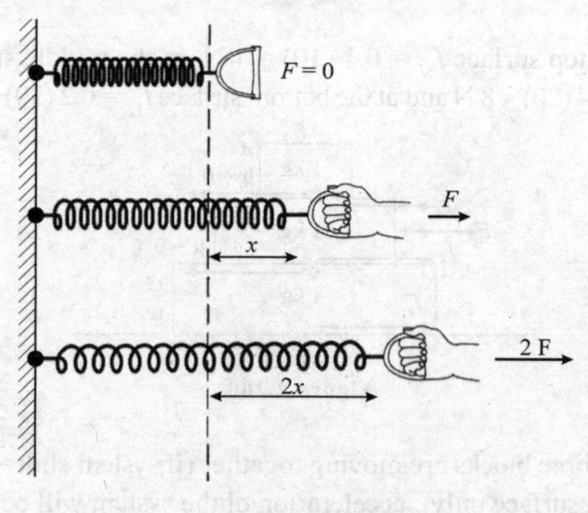

Figure 2.104

We take few examples of dynamics, which includes the concept of spring force.

2.9.1 Force Constant of a Spring

In previous section we have discussed about the force exerted by a spring when stretched or compressed. The spring exerts a force due to its elastic properties. When a spring is stretched or compressed from its natural (relaxed) state, its potential energy increases and the work done in stretching or compressing is stored in it in the form of its elastic potential energy. As every system tend to retain its minimum energy state for greater stability, spring tries to restore its natural state, hence applies the restoring force on the external agent pulling or pushing the spring. Already we know that the restoring force which is proportional to the deformation length of the spring as $F = kx$, where k is the force constant of the spring which depends on the spring shape, material and its elastic properties. If we cut a spring in two equal halves, what will be the k for each part of the spring ? Or if two springs of force constants k_1 and k_2 are connected in series, what will be the equivalent force constant of the spring.

For answering above questions, we must know how k depends on length and shape of spring. First we discuss different configurations of spring combinations.

Springs in Series : Look at figure-2.105. Two light springs of force constants k_1 and k_2 are connected in series and a mass m is hanging from them. Other end of the spring is rigidly connected to the ceiling.

Figure 2.105

We know that the stretch in a spring is proportional to the tension in it. As springs are light, in both the springs, tension remains same as mg. Thus if x_1 and x_2 are the stretch in the two springs, we have tension in them.

$$k_1x_1 = k_2x_2 = mg \qquad ...(2.60)$$

If k_{eq} is considered as the equivalent force constant of the combined spring, we have

$$k_{eq}(x_1 + x_2) = mg \qquad ...(2.61)$$

Substituting the value of x_1 and x_2 from equation-(2.60) to equation-(2.61), we get

$$\frac{1}{k_{eq}} = \frac{1}{k_1} + \frac{1}{k_2} \qquad ...(2.62)$$

Equation-(2.62) can be generalized for more than two springs connected in series as

$$\frac{1}{k_{eq}} = \frac{1}{k_1} + \frac{1}{k_2} + \frac{1}{k_3} + ... \qquad ...(2.63)$$

Where k_1, k_2, k_3, ... are the spring force constants of the respected springs.

Springs in Parallel : As shown in figure-2.106, if two springs are connected in parallel and a mass m is hanging from the combination than both the springs are stretched by equal amounts say x and for equilibrium of mass m we have

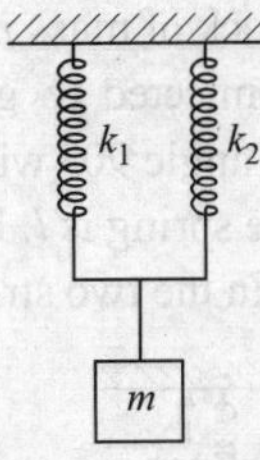

Figure 2.106

$$k_1x + k_2x = mg \qquad ...(2.64)$$

If k_{eq} be the equivalent force constant of the combination, we have

$$k_{eq}x = mg \qquad ...(2.65)$$

From equations-(2.64) and (2.65), we have

$$k_{eq} = k_1 + k_2 \qquad ...(2.66)$$

Above equation can be generalized for more than two springs as

$$k_{eq} = k_1 + k_2 + k_3 + ... \qquad ...(2.67)$$

Parts of a Spring : If a spring of force constant k of length l is cut in two parts say of l_1 and l_2, let us assume that new force constants are k_1 and k_2 for the two parts. If we connect these two parts in series, the equivalent force constant must be initial k. Thus we have

$$\frac{1}{k_{eq}} = \frac{1}{k_1} + \frac{1}{k_2} \qquad ...(2.68)$$

According to the molecular properties of a spring, the force constant of a part of the spring is inversely proportional to its length, which gives us

$$k_1 = \frac{c}{l_1} \quad \text{and} \quad k_2 = \frac{c}{l_2} \qquad ...(2.69)$$

Where c is a positive constant. Substituting the above values of new force constants k_1 and k_2 in equation-(2.68), we get

$$\frac{1}{k_{eq}} = \frac{l_1}{c} + \frac{l_2}{c}$$

or $$c = \frac{l}{k_{eq}}$$

Using value of c in equation-(2.69), we have

$$k_1 = \frac{k_{eq}l}{l_1} \quad \text{and} \quad k_2 = \frac{k_{eq}l}{l_2} \qquad ...(2.70)$$

Illustrative Example 2.36

Figure-2.107 shows a block of mass m attached to a spring of force constant k and connected to ground by two string of equal lengths making an angle 90° with each other. In relaxed state natural length of the spring is l. In the situation shown in figure, find the tensions in the two strings.

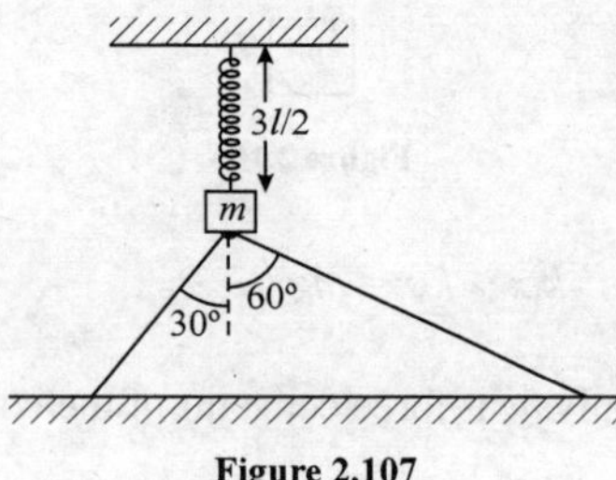

Figure 2.107

Solution

As the natural length of spring is l, and in the situation shown in figure-2.108, its length is $3l/2$. Thus the spring is stretched by a distance $l/2$ hence it exerts a restoring force on block $k(l/2)$ upward as shown in figure-2.108, which shows also the tensions acting on the block along the directions of the strings. As the block is in equilibrium, we can balance all the forces acting on it along horizontal and vertical directions.

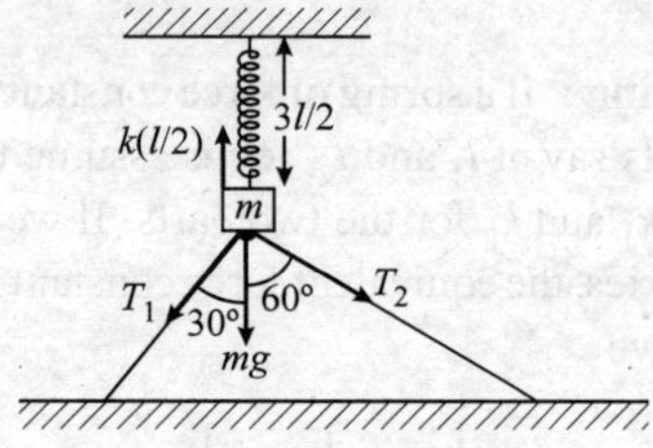

Figure 2.108

Along horizontal direction

$$T_1 \sin 30° = T_2 \sin 60°$$

or $$T_1 = \sqrt{3}\, T_2 \qquad \ldots (2.71)$$

Along vertical direction

$$k\left(\frac{l}{2}\right) = mg + T_1 \cos 30° + T_2 \cos 60°$$

or $$\sqrt{3}\, T_1 + T_2 = kl - 2\,\text{mg} \qquad \ldots (2.72)$$

Substituting value of T_1 from equation-(2.71) to (2.72), we get

$$4T_2 = kl - 2\,\text{mg}$$

$$T_2 = \frac{1}{4}\,(kl - 2\,\text{mg})$$

From equation-(2.71), we have

$$T_1 = \frac{\sqrt{3}}{4}\,(kl - 2\,\text{mg})$$

Illustrative Example 2.37

Figure-2.109 shows a block A on a smooth surface attached with a spring of force constant k to the ceiling. In this state spring is in its natural length l. The block A is connected with a massless and frictionless string to another identical mass B hanging over a light and smooth pulley. Find the distance moved by A before it leaves contact with the ground.

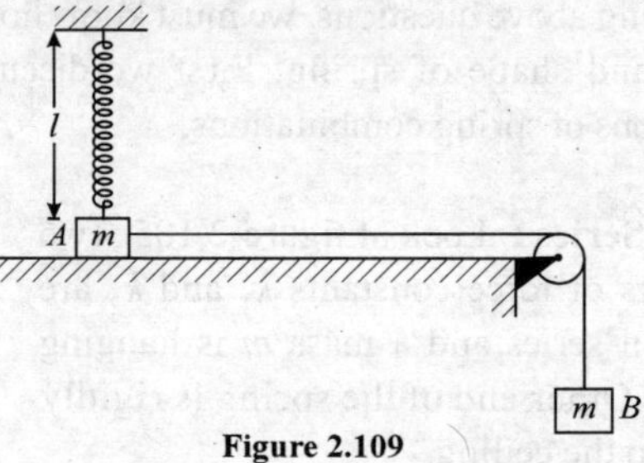

Figure 2.109

Solution

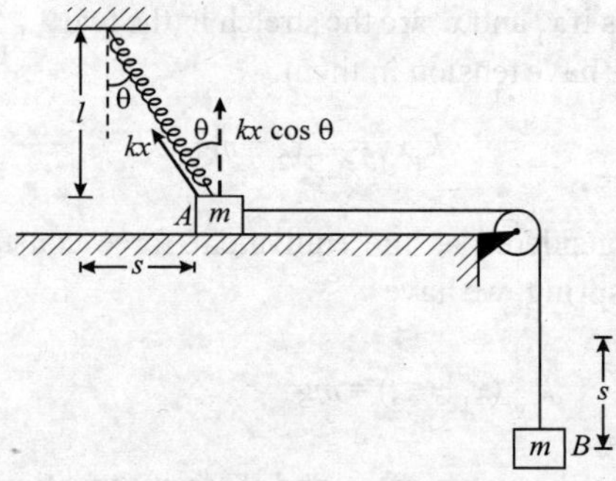

Figure 2.110

Due to weight of block B, it moves down and pulls the block A now as both the block A and B move, spring gets stretched and becomes inclined as its lower end is attached to the block A. It will break off from the ground below it when the vertical component of the spring force on block A will balance its weight mg. Let it happens when A moves by a distance s as shown in figure-2.110.

At this instant let the spring be inclined at an angle θ with the vertical. If the stretch in the spring at this instant is x, then it is given as

$$x = l \sec\theta - l$$

or $$= l\,(\sec\theta - 1) \qquad \ldots (2.73)$$

If mass A breaks off from ground below it, we have

$$kx\cos\theta = mg \quad \ldots(2.74)$$

From equations-(2.73) and (2.74), substituting the value of x, we get

$$kl(\sec\theta - 1)\cos\theta = mg$$

or $$kl(1-\cos\theta) = mg$$

or $$\cos\theta = 1 - \frac{mg}{kl}$$

or $$\tan\theta = \frac{[k^2l^2 - (kl-mg)^2]^{\frac{1}{2}}}{kl - mg}$$

At this instant the distance travelled by masses A and B is given by

$$s = l\tan\theta$$

or $$s = l\frac{[k^2l^2 - (kl-mg)^2]^{\frac{1}{2}}}{kl - mg}$$

Illustrative Example 2.38

When a mass M hangs from a spring of length l, it stretches the spring by a distance x. Now the spring is cut in two parts of lengths $l/3$ and $2l/3$, and the two springs thus formed are connected to a straight rod of mass M which is horizontal in the configuration shown in figure-2.111. Find the stretch in each of the spring.

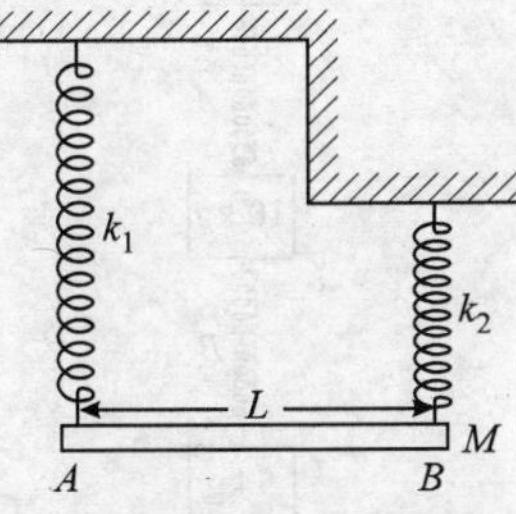

Figure 2.111

Solution

As it given that the mass M stretches the original spring by a distance x, we have

$$kx = Mg$$

or $$k = \frac{Mg}{x} \quad \ldots(2.75)$$

The new force constants of the two springs can be given by using equation-(2.70) as

$$k_1 = 3k \quad \text{and} \quad k_2 = \frac{3k}{2}$$

Let we take the stretch in the two springs be x_1 and x_2, we have for the equilibrium of the rod

$$k_1x_1 + k_2x_2 = Mg$$

or $$2kx_1 + \frac{3k}{2}x_2 = Mg$$

From equation-(2.75), we have

$$x_1 + \frac{x_2}{2} = \frac{x}{3} \quad \ldots(2.76)$$

As the rod is horizontal and in static equilibrium, we have net torque acting on the rod about any point on it must be zero. Thus we have torque on it about end A are

$$k_2x_2L = Mg\frac{L}{2}$$

or $$x_2 = \frac{Mg}{2k_2}$$

$$= \frac{Mg}{3k} = \frac{x}{3}$$

Using this value of x_2 in equation-(2.76), we have $x_1 = \frac{x}{6}$

This can also be directly obtained by using torque zero about point B on the rod as

$$k_1x_1L = Mg\frac{L}{2}$$

or $$x_1 = \frac{Mg}{2k_1}$$

$$= \frac{Mg}{6k} = \frac{x}{6}$$

Illustrative Example 2.39

Find the stretch in the springs shown in figure-2.112. The respective data are given in the figure. The friction and masses in pulleys are negligible.

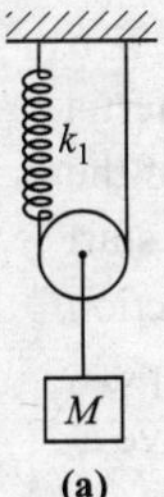

(a)

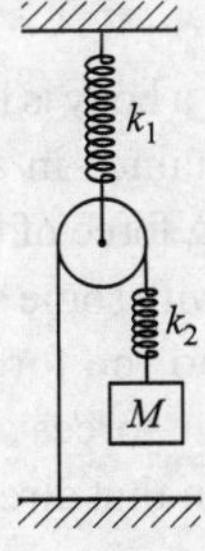

(b)

Figure 2.112

Solution

(a) As mass M is in equilibrium, the tension in the string with which it is hanging will be Mg. As pulley is massless the tension in the upper string must be half of the lower string, $Mg/2$. The stretch in the spring must be such that the restoring force in the string is equal to the tension in it. Thus we have

$$k_1 x = \frac{Mg}{2}$$

or $$x_1 = \frac{Mg}{2k_1}$$

(b) Here again mass M is in equilibrium, thus the tension in the string connected to it must be equal to Mg and hence the restoring force in the lower spring will also be Mg. If x_1 be the extension in this spring, we have

$$k_1 x_1 = Mg$$

or $$x_1 = \frac{Mg}{k_1}$$

As pulley is light, the tension in upper string must be twice that of the lower string, 2 Mg which is equal to the restoring force in the upper spring. If x_2 is the extension in the upper spring, we have

$$k_2 x_2 = 2\,Mg$$

or $$x_2 = \frac{2\,Mg}{k_2}$$

Web Reference of Video Lectures at www.physicsgalaxy.com

Age Group - High School Physics | Age 17-19 Years

Section - MECHANICS

Topic - Forces & Newton's Laws of Motion

Module Numbers - 15 and 16

2.10 Breaking of Supports

Whenever a body is in equilibrium, due to inertia it is maintained in a state of rest. If any of the supporting force of body is removed, body start from rest with some acceleration in the direction opposite to the force applied by the support, as all other forces acting on body will have a resultant in that direction.

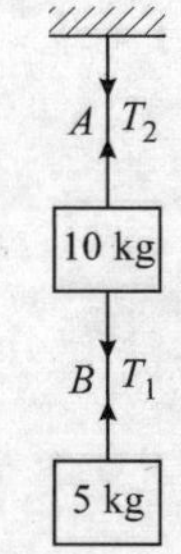

Figure 2.113

We discuss the situation with an example shown in figure-2.113. Two masses 5 kg and 10 kg are hanging in equilibrium with the strings A and B. If tensions in the strings A and B are T_1 and T_2 respectively, then we have

$$T_1 = 5\,g = 50\text{ N}$$

$$T_2 = 15\,g = 150\text{ N}$$

If at some instant we break string B, tension T_1 become zero instantaneously and block will start falling from rest under gravity and 10 kg block, as it is still in equilibrium, T_2 will instantly change to 10 N to balance its weight.

If instead of string B, we break the string A, tension T_2 becomes zero and both the blocks will start falling with acceleration g. Now T_1 is just an internal force for the system of two blocks and as there is no interaction between the two blocks and both are falling under gravity T_1 will also instantly become zero.

Now to understand the concept in a better way we slightly modify the situation of previous example. Instead of strings, we use springs as shown in figure-2.114. Initially the blocks are in equilibrium,. If spring B breaks, its tension will instantly become zero as we are using ideal springs (massless/inertialess), but due to inertia initially 10 kg mass will not move from its initial position, so tension in upper spring will not change instantly hence it will accelerate in upward direction with acceleration given as

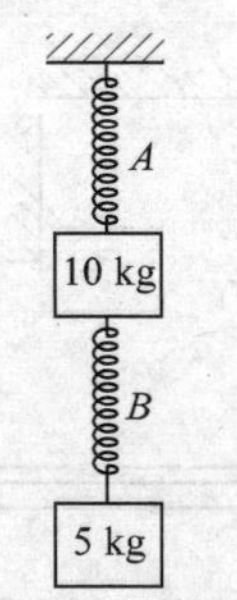

Figure 2.114

$$a = \frac{T_2 - m_2}{m}$$

or $$a = \frac{150-100}{10} = 5\text{ m/s}^2$$

If spring A breaks tension in spring A will instantly become zero, but as due to inertia 5 kg and 10 kg blocks will start moving from rest. As initially just after breaking of spring A the two masses are at rest, tension in spring B will not change at this instant which is $T = 5\text{ g} = 50$ N. Thus at this instant (just after spring A is cut) acceleration of 10 kg mass is

$$a_1 = \frac{10g - kx}{10} = \frac{100+50}{10} = 15 \text{ m/s}^2$$

and that of 5 kg mass is

$$a_2 = \frac{5g - kx}{5} = \frac{50-50}{5} = 0 \text{ m/s}^2$$

We take few more example to understand this concept in a better way.

Illustrative Example 2.40

Find the readings of spring balances S_1, S_2 and S_3 of the springs shown in figure-2.115(a). If the string snaps at point A find the readings of the three spring balances just after the string snaps. All pulleys and strings are ideal.

Solution

Force analysis of the situation is shown in figure-2.115(b). Let the tension in the string A is T_1 and that in string B is T_2 and that in C is T_3. So for equilibrium of the two masses, it is obvious that $T_1 = 200$ N, $T_2 = 400$ N and $T_3 = 150$ N. So initial readings of the springs must be 40 kg, 20 kg and 15 kg respectively.

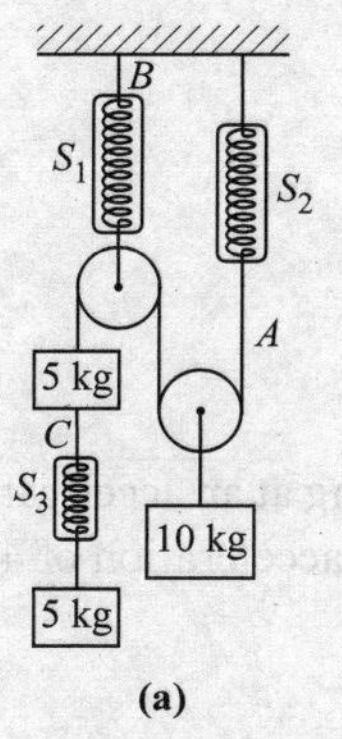

(a)

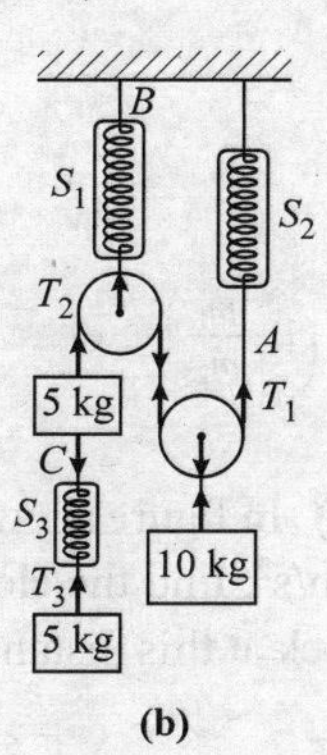

(b)

Figure 2.115

When the string A snaps, tension in this string will instantly become zero and hence as upper pulley is ideal the tension in string B will also become zero instantly, so readings of the balance S_1 and S_2 will be zero just after string A snaps. After breaking of string A masses will start falling from rest from their initial position, thus due to inertia of 5 kg and 15 kg the stretch in balance S_3 will not change instantly thus its reading will remain same as 15 kg.

Illustrative Example 2.41

(a) Find the acceleration of the three masses shown in figure-2.116(a) and the extension in the spring. The force constant of the spring is 100 N/m. Assume all strings and pullies are ideal.

(b) Find the acceleration of the masses A and B just after the string snaps at P.

(c) Find the acceleration of the masses A and B just after the string snaps at P but in this case the spring is replaced by a string. Take $g = 10$ m/s².

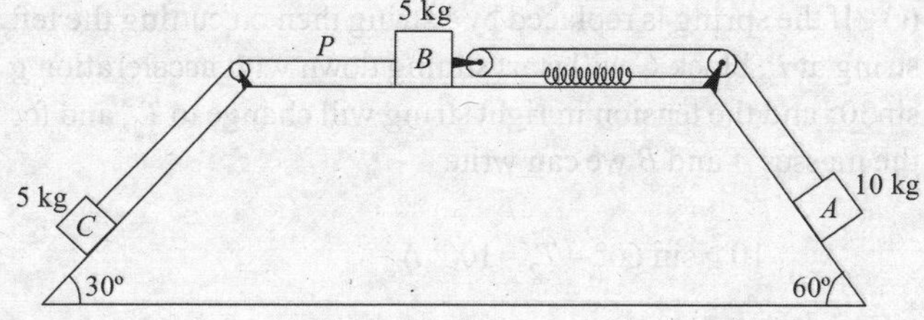

Figure 2.116(a)

Solution

(a) Constrain motion of the block shows that if 5 kg masses are moving with an acceleration a, 10 kg will move with $2a$. The force diagram of the masses is shown in figure-2.116(b).

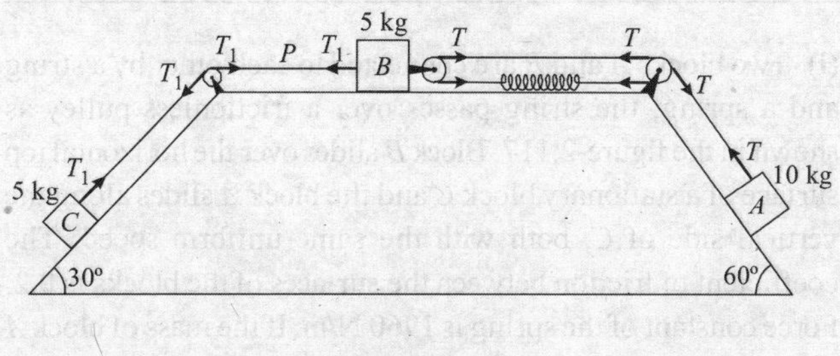

Figure 2.116(b)

Now we write equations of motion for the three blocks as

$$10g \sin 60° - T = 10(2a)$$

$$2T - T_1 = 5a$$

$$T_1 - 5g \sin 30° = 5a$$

Solving we get $\quad a = \frac{1}{2}(1 - 4\sqrt{3}) \text{ m/s}^2$

and $\quad T = 10(4\sqrt{3} - 1)$ N

(b) If string snaps at point P, tension in this string will instantly become zero but due to inertia of the blocks A and B, the extension of the spring will not change instantly thus tension in this string will remain same.

The acceleration of block A will remain same $2a$ as no change is there in the forces acting on it but the acceleration of block B will change as one of the force acting on it disappears (tension T_1), thus its new acceleration is

$$2T = 5a_1$$

or $$a_1 = \frac{2T}{5} = 4(4\sqrt{3} - 1)\ \text{m/s}^2$$

(c) If the spring is replaced by a string then on cutting the left string at P, block C will start sliding down with acceleration $g \sin 30°$ and the tension in right string will change to T_2, and for the masses A and B we can write

$$10\, g \sin 60° - T_2 = 10(2a)$$

and $$2T_2 = 5a$$

Solving we get $$a = \frac{20\sqrt{3}}{9}\ \text{m/s}^2$$

and $$T_2 = \frac{50}{9}(4\sqrt{3} - 1)\ \text{N}$$

Practice Exercise 2.6

(i) Two blocks A and B are connected to each other by a string and a spring; the string passes over a frictionless pulley as shown in the figure-2.117. Block B slides over the horizontal top surface of a stationary block C and the block A slides along the vertical side of C, both with the same uniform speed. The coefficient of friction between the surfaces of the blocks is 0.2. Force constant of the spring is 1960 N/m. If the mass of block A is 2 kg, calculate the mass of block B and the extension in the spring. Take $g = 9.8\ \text{m/s}^2$.

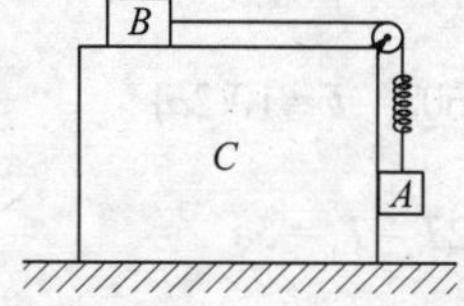

Figure 2.117

[10 kg. 1 cm]

(ii) A smooth semicircular wire track of radius R is fixed in a vertical plane as shown in figure-2.118. One end of a massless spring of natural length $3R/4$ is attached to the lower point O of the wire track. A small ring of mass $m = 1$ kg, which can slide on the track, is attached to the other end of the spring. The ring is held stationary at point P such that the spring makes an angle of 60° with the vertical. The spring constant $K = mg/R$. Consider the ring to be smooth (ii) draw free body diagram of the ring and (ii) determine the tangential acceleration of the ring and the normal reaction acting on it. Take $g = 10\ \text{m/s}^2$.

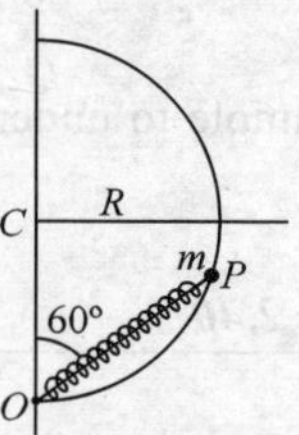

Figure 2.118

[$25\frac{\sqrt{3}}{4}$ m/s², 3.75 N]

(iii) Find the acceleration of masses m_1, m_2 and m_3 shown in figure-2.119 just after the string is cut at point A.

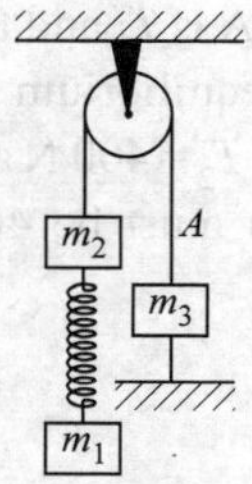

Figure 2.119

[0, $\left(1 + \frac{m_1}{m_2}\right)g$, g]

(iv) In figure shown if 2 kg block is moving at an acceleration 2 m/s², find the elongation in spring and acceleration of 4 kg block at this instant. Take $g = 10\ \text{m/s}^2$.

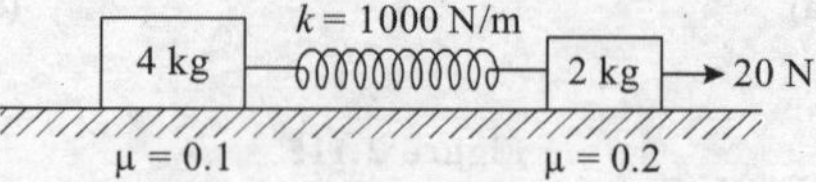

Figure 2.120

[0.012 m, 2 m/s²]

* * * * *

Discussion Question

Q2-1 Objects on the moon weigh only about one sixth as much as they do on earth, you would almost certainly be able to lift a heavy person. Could you easily stop him if he was running at a fast rate across the moon's surface ?

Q2-2 A ball is thrown from the edge of a high cliff. No matter what the angle at which it is thrown, because of air resistance the ball will eventually end up moving vertically downward. Justify this statement.

Q2-3 Suppose you are riding in a car at constant velocity when the driver suddenly slams on the brakes so that you are "*pushed*" forward. Was this "*push*" exerted on you by some other object. Discuss about this "*push*" in different frame of references, with respect to car and with respect to earth.

Q2-4 A block with mass m is supported by a cord C from the ceiling, and a similar cord D is attached to the bottom of the block. Explain this : if you give a sudden jerk to D, it will break; but if you pull on D steadily, C will break.

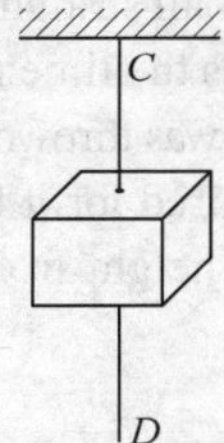

Figure 2.121

Q2-5 A spring scale is used to weight beans on an elevator. How will the readings for a given amount of beans change when the elevator is (a) going down with constant velocity, (b) moving with a constant downward acceleration less than g, (c) moving upward with a constant velocity, (d) accelerating upward with an acceleration a. What happens in above cases if we use a beam balance.

Q2-6 A bird alights on a stretched telegraph wire. Does this change the tension in the wire ? If so, by an amount less than, equal to, or greater than the weight of the bird ?

Q2-7 Is there any directional relation between the net force on an object and the object's velocity ? If so, what is that relation ?

Q2-8 A horse is urged to pull a wagon the horse refuses to try, citing Newton's third laws as a defense: the pull of the horse on the wagon is equal to but opposite the pull of the wagon on the horse. "If I can never exert a greater force on the wagon than it exerts on me, how can I ever start the wagon moving ?" Asks the horse. How would you reply ?

Q2-9 A coin is put on a long play record. The player is started but, before the final speed of rotation is reached, the coin flies off. Explain why ?

Q2-10 "In a tug-of-war one team slowly gives way to the other. Work is done by losing team on winning team" Is it true.

Q2-11 You are an astronaut in the lounge of an orbiting space station and you remove the cover from a long thin jar containing a single olive. Describe several ways to remove the olive from the jar.

Q2-12 If you stand facing forward during a bus or subway ride, why does a quick deceleration topple you forward and a quick increase in speed throw you backward ? Why do you have better balance if you face toward the side of the bus or subway train ?

Q2-13 When an object is thrown in air, does it travel a greater horizontal distance while climbing to its maximum height or while descending from its maximum height back to the ground ? Or is the horizontal distance travelled the same for both ?

Q2-14 Two 2 kg weight are attached to spring balance as shown in figure-2.122. What is the reading of the scale ?

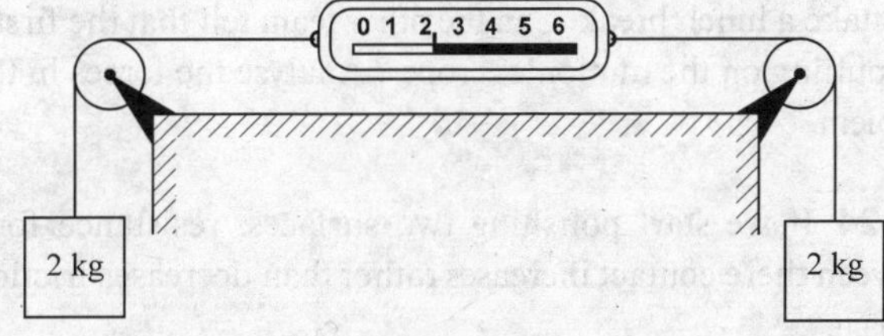

Figure 2.122

Q2-15 An elevator is supported by a single cable. There is no counterweight. The elevator receives passengers at the ground floor and takes them to the top floor, where they disembark. New passengers enter and are taken down to the ground floor. During this round trip, when is the tension in the cable equal to the weight of the elevator plus passengers ? When greater ? When less ?

Q2-16 Under what conditions could unequal masses by strung over a pulley without the pulley having any tendency to turn ?

Q2-17 The sun is directly below us at midnight, in line with the earth's centre. Are we then heavier at midnight, due to the sun's gravitational force on us, than we are at noon ? Explain.

Q2-18 A block rests on an inclined plane with enough friction to prevent its sliding down, to start the block moving, is it easier to push it up the plane, down the plane, or sideways ? Discuss all the three cases in detail.

Q2-19 A soda water bottle is falling freely. Where the bubbles in the water will go.

Q2-20 In a tug of war, three men pull on a rope to the left at A and three men pull to the right at B with forces of equal magnitude. Then a 5 *lb* weight is hung from the centre of the rope. (a) Can the men get the rope AB to be horizontal ? (b) If not, explain. If so, determine the magnitudes of the forces at A and B required to do this.

Q2-21 Air is thrown on a sail attached to a boat from an electric fan placed on the boat. Will the boat start moving ?

Q2-22 A massless rope is strung over a frictionless pulley. A monkey holds onto one end of the rope, and a mirror, having the same weight as the monkey, is attached to the other end of the rope at the monkey's level. Can the monkey get away from its image seen in the mirror (a) by climbing up the rope, (b) by climbing down the rope, or (c) by releasing the rope ?

Q2-23 Two teams of students are having a tug-of-war. The rope passes through a small hole fence that separates the two teams. Neither team can see the other. Both teams pull mightily, but neither budges. As lunch time approaches the members of one team decide to tie their end of the rope to a stout tree while they take a lunch break. Can the other team tell that the first is not pulling on the motionless rope ? Analyse the forces in this problem.

Q2-24 If we start polishing two surfaces, resistance force between there contact increases rather than decreases friction. Explain.

Q2-25 Why do tires grip the road better on level ground than they do when going uphill or downhill ?

Q2-26 A box, heavier than you is placed on a rough floor. The coefficient of static friction between the box and the floor is the same as that between your shoes and the floor. Can you displace the box across the floor.

Q2-27 "The path of a projectile under gravity is a parabola because it has no horizontal acceleration", Discuss the above statement.

Q2-28 A heavy iron ball is taken into space where it is weightless. Will it hurt to kick this football since it is weightless ?

Q2-29 When you tighten a nut on a bolt, how are you increasing the frictional force ?

Q2-30 Suppose that you drop a marble of mass m into a jar of honey. As the marble sinks, its speed is effectively constant. What is the net force on the marble as it sinks ? What are the magnitude and direction of the forces exerted by the honey ?

Q2-31 Could you weigh yourself on a scale whose maximum reading is less than your weight ? If so, how ?

Q2-32 A ladder is resting against a wall and a person climbs up the ladder. Is the ladder more likely to slip out at the bottom as the person climbs closer to the top of the ladder ? Explain.

Q2-33 A man sits in a chair that is suspended from a rope. The rope passes over a pulley suspended from the ceiling, and the man holds the other end of the rope in his hands. What is the tension in the rope, and what force does the chair exert on the man ?

Q2-34 What happens to a baseball that is fired downward through air at twice its terminal speed does it speed up, slow down, or continue to move with its initial speed ?

Q2-35 You throw a baseball straight upward. If air resistance is not neglected, how does the time required for the ball to go from the height at which it was thrown up to its maximum height compare to the time required for it to fall from its maximum height back down to the height from which it was thrown ? Explain your answer.

Q2-36 A car at rest is struck from the rear by a second car. The injuries incurred by the two drivers are of distinctly different character. Explain.

Q2-37 There is more water in a beaker placed in the pan of a spring balance. If we dip our finger in this water without touching the bottom of the beaker, then what would be the effect on the reading of the balance ?

Q2-38 A ball is suspended by a cord from the ceiling of a motor car. What will be the effect on the position of the ball if (i) car is moving with constant velocity on horizontal road. (ii) accelerated on horizontal road. (iii) retarding on horizontal road. (iv) car is turning towards right (v) car is moving on an inclined plane with constant velocity. (vi) accelerating on incline plane with g $\sin\theta$, where θ is the angle of incline. (vii) accelerating up the incline with g $\sin\theta$.

Q2-39 In a box car a helium filled balloon is tied to the floor with a string. Car is moving on a horizontal road. If suddenly breaks are applied, what happens to the balloon. Will it jerked forward, backward or remain at rest.

* * * * *

Conceptual MCQs Single Option Correct

2-1 Let a_1 & a_2 are the accelerations of A & B. Let b_1 & b_2 the accelerations of C & D relative to the wedges A and B respectively, choose the right relation. (directions of a_1, a_2, b_1 & b_2 are shown in figure below) :

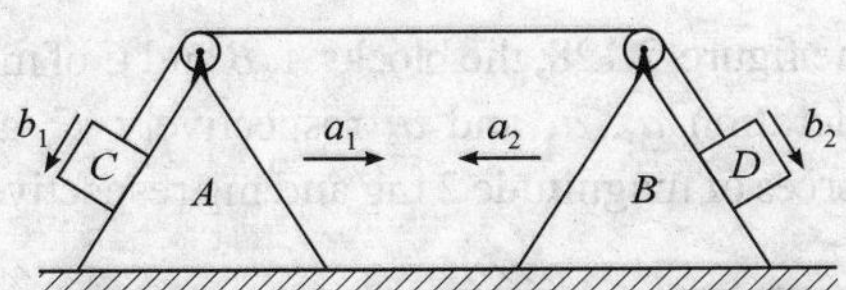

Figure 2.123

(A) $a_1 - a_2 + b_1 - b_2 = 0$ (B) $a_1 + a_2 - b_1 - b_2 = 0$
(C) $a_1 + a_2 + b_1 + b_2 = 0$ (D) $a_1 + b_2 = a_2 + b_1$.

2-2 While walking on ice, one should take small steps to avoid slipping. This is because smaller steps ensure :
(A) Larger friction (B) Smaller friction
(C) Larger normal force (D) Smaller normal force

2-3 In the arrangement shown in figure-2.124 pulley A and B are massless and the thread is inextensible. Mass of pulley C is equal to m. If friction in all the pulleys is negligible, then :

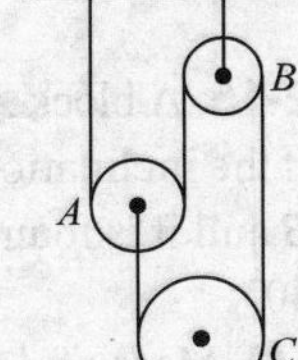

Figure 2.124

(A) Tension in thread is equal to 1/2 mg
(B) Acceleration of pulley C is equal to $g/2$ (downward)
(C) Acceleration of pulley A is equal to $g/2$ (upward)
(D) Acceleration of pulley A is equal to 2 g (upward)

2-4 A ball is dropped vertically from height d above the ground. It hits the ground and bounces up vertically to a height $d/2$. Neglecting subsequent motion and air resistance, its velocity v varies with height h above the ground as :

(A) 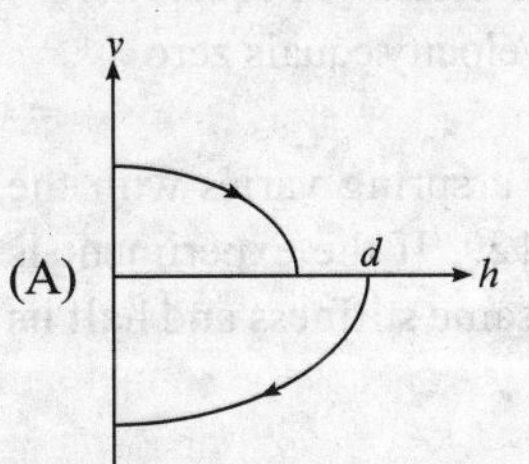

(B) 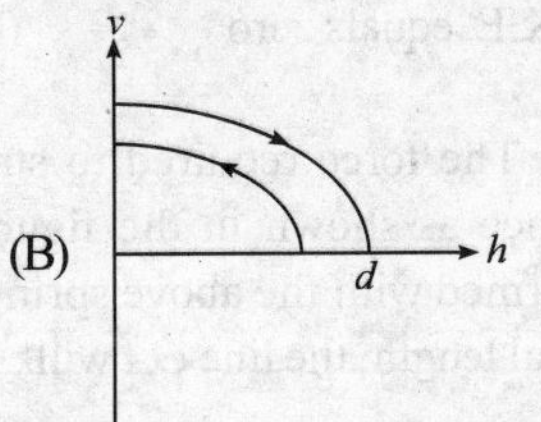

(C) 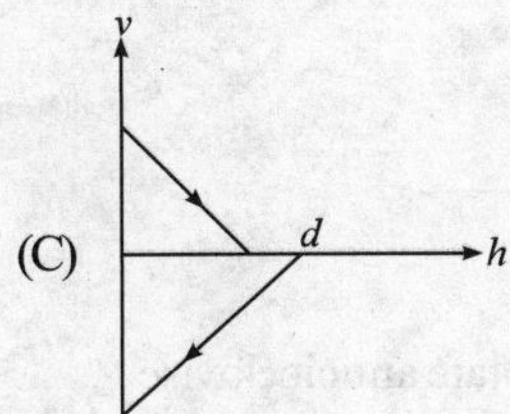

(D) 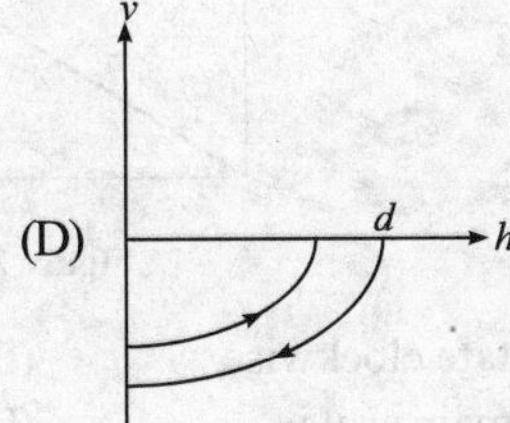

2-5 A bicycle moves on a horizontal road with some positive acceleration. The force of friction exerted by the road on the front and rear wheels are F_1 and F_2 respectively :
(A) Both F_1 and F_2 act in the forward direction
(B) Both F_1 and F_2 act in the reverse direction
(C) F_1 acts in the forward direction, F_2 act in the reverse direction
(D) F_2 acts in the forward direction, F_1 act in the reverse direction

2-6 Consider the situation shown in figure-2.125. The wall is smooth but the surfaces of A and B in contact are rough. The friction on B due to A in equilibrium :
(A) Is upward
(B) Is downward
(C) Is zero
(D) The system cannot remain in equilibrium

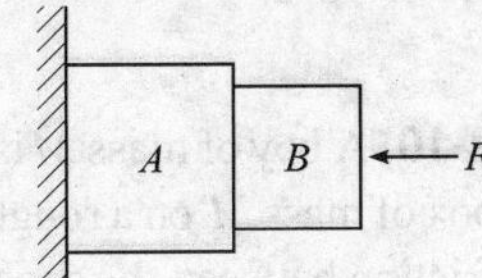

Figure 2.125

2-7 A block is about to slide down an inclined plane when its inclination to the horizontal is θ. If now a 5 kg weight is attached on the block :
(A) It is still about to slide down the plane
(B) It will not slide down the plane unless the inclination is increased
(C) It will not slide down the plane unless the inclination is decreased
(D) It will never slide down whatever be the inclination

2-8 Two objects A and B are thrown upward simultaneously with the same speed. The mass of A is greater than the mass of B. Suppose the air exerts a constant and equal force of resistance on the two bodies :
(A) The two bodies will reach the same height
(B) A will go higher that B
(C) B will go higher than A
(D) Any of the above three may happen depending on the speed with which the objects are thrown

2-9 Block A is placed on block B, whose mass is greater than that of A. There is friction between the blocks, while the ground is smooth. A horizontal force P, increasing linearly with time, begins to act on A. The acceleration a_1 and a_2 of A and B respectively are plotted against time (t). Choose the correct graph :

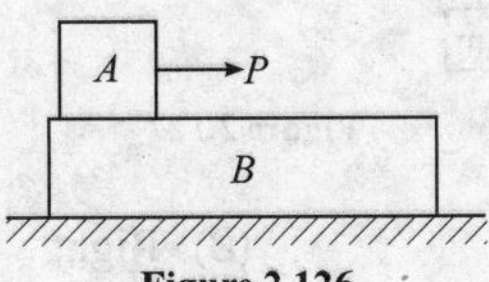

Figure 2.126

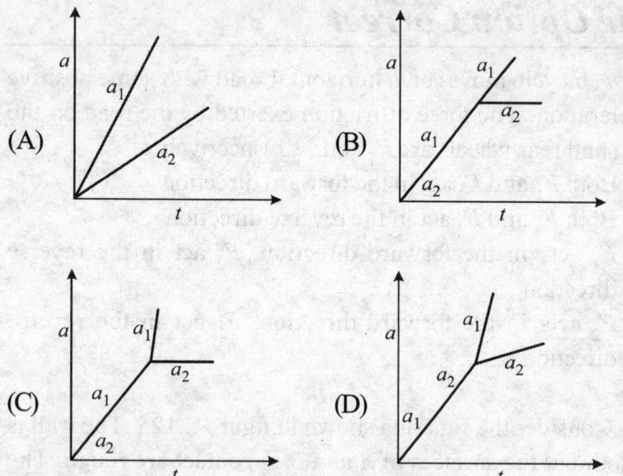

2-10 A boy of mass M is applying a horizontal force to slide a box of mass M' on a rough horizontal surface. The coefficient of friction between the shoes of the boy and the floor is μ and that between the box and the floor is μ'. In which of the following cases it is certainly not possible to slide the box ?

(A) $\mu < \mu', M < M'$ (B) $\mu > \mu', M < M'$
(C) $\mu < \mu', M > M'$ (D) $\mu > \mu', M > M'$

2-11 A block rests on a rough plane whose inclination θ to the horizontal can be varied. Which of the following graphs indicates how the frictional force F between the block and the plane varies as θ is increased ?

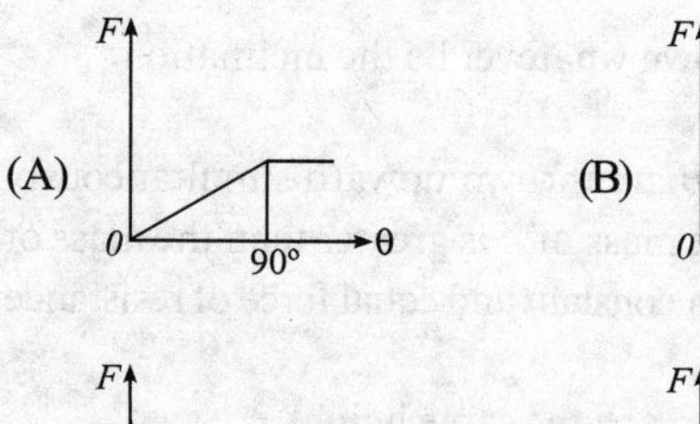
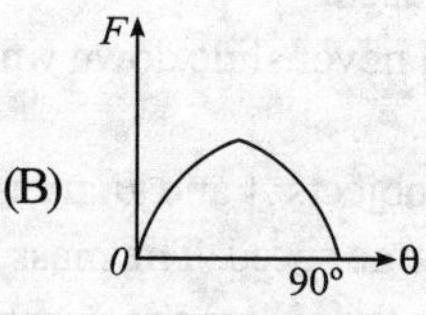
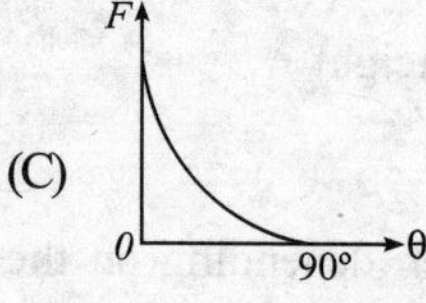
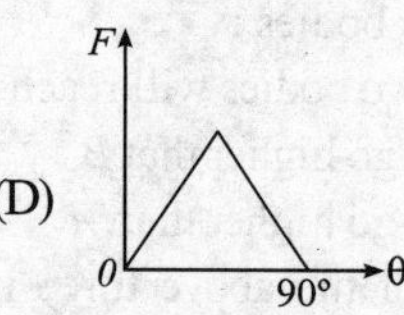

2-12 In the balance machine, shown in the figure-2.127 which arm will move downward ?

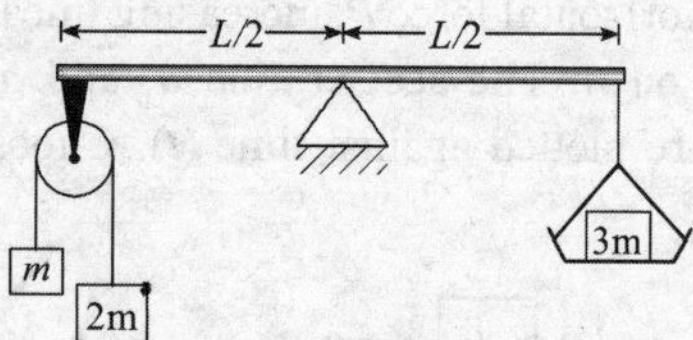

Figure 2.127

(A) Left (B) Right
(C) None (D) Cannot be said

2-13 In a situation the contact force by a rough horizontal surface on a body placed on it has constant magnitude. If the angle between this force and the vertical is decreased, the frictional force between the surface and the body will :

(A) Increase (B) Decrease
(C) Remain the same (D) May increase or decrease

2-14 In the figure-2.128, the blocks A, B and C of mass m each have acceleration a_1, a_2 and a_3 respectively. F_1 and F_2 are external forces of magnitude 2 mg and mg respectively :

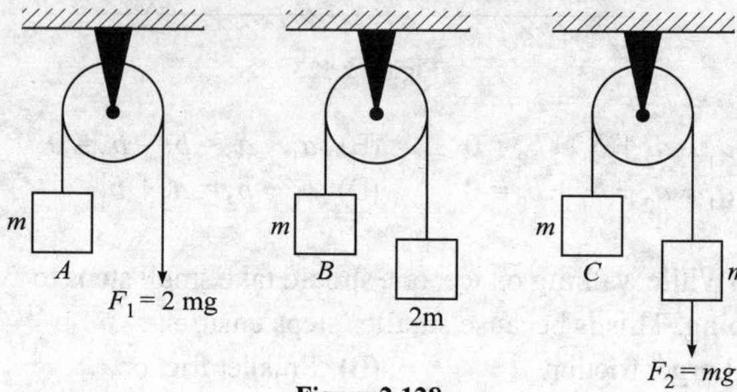

Figure 2.128

(A) $a_1 = a_2 = a_3$ (B) $a_1 > a_3 > a_2$
(C) $a_1 = a_2, a_2 > a_3$ (D) $a_1 > a_2, a_2 = a_3$

2-15 A block A kept on an inclined surface just begins to slide if the inclination is 30°. The block is replaced by another block B and it is found that it just begins to slide if the inclination is 40° :

(A) Mass of A > mass of B (B) Mass of A < mass of B
(C) Mass of A = mass of B (D) All the three are possible.

2-16 When the force of constant magnitude always act perpendicular to the motion of a particle then :

(A) Velocity is constant (B) Acceleration is constant
(C) K.E. is constant (D) None of these

2-17 Essential characteristic of equilibrium is :

(A) Momentum equal zero (B) Acceleration equals zero
(C) K.E. equals zero (D) Velocity equals zero

2-18 The force required to stretch a spring varies with the distance as shown in the figure-2.129. If the experiment is performed with the above spring of same stiffness and half its natural length, the line OA will :

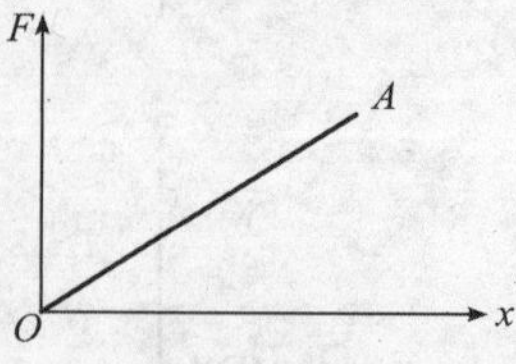

Figure 2.129

(A) Rotate clockwise (B) Rotate anticlockwise
(C) Remain as it is (D) Become double in length

2-19 A person standing on the floor of an elevator drops a coin. The coin reaches the floor of the elevator in a time t_1 if the elevator is stationary and in time t_2 if it is moving uniformly. Then :

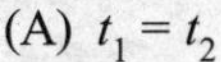

(A) $t_1 = t_2$

(B) $t_1 < t_2$

(C) $t_1 > t_2$

(D) $t_1 < t_2$ or $t_1 > t_2$ depending on whether the lift if going up or down.

2-20 A scooter starting from rest moves with a constant acceleration for a time Δt_1, then with a constant velocity for the next Δt_2 and finally with a constant deceleration for the next Δt_3 to come to rest. A 500 N man sitting on the scooter behind the driver manages to stay at rest with respect to the scooter without touching any other part. The force exerted by the seat on the man is :

(A) 500 N throughout the journey

(B) Less than 500 N throughout the journey

(C) More than 500 N throughout the journey

(D) > 500 N for time Δt_1 and Δt_3 and 500 N for Δt_2

2-21 A block of mass m is supported by a string passing through a smooth peg as shown in the figure-2.130. Variation of tension in the string T as a function of θ best represented by (here the total length of the string is varied) :

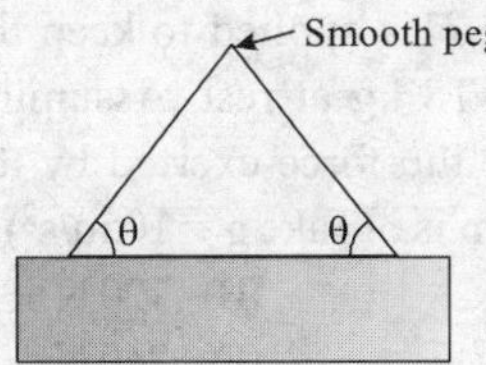

Figure 2.130

(A)
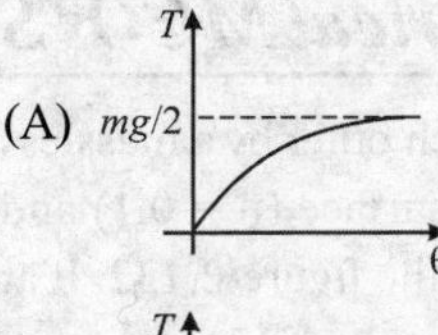

(B)
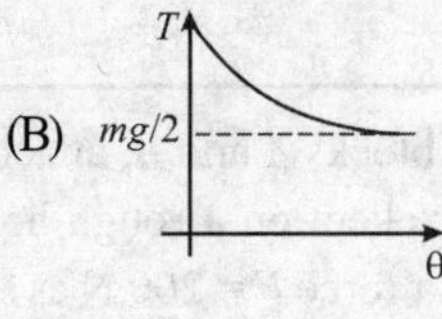

(C)
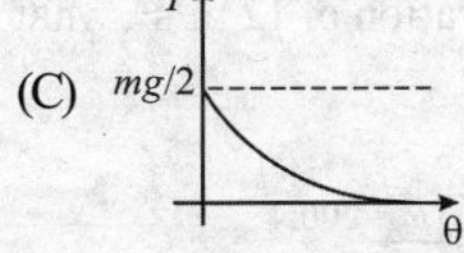

(D)
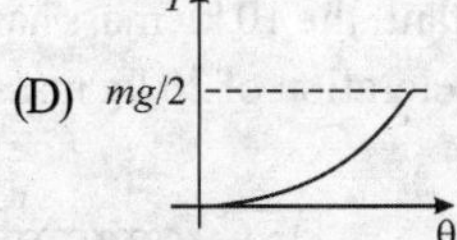

2-22 A metal block of mass m is placed on a smooth metallic plane in support with string as shown in diagram. If, after long time due to corrosion, the contact surface becomes rough with coefficient of friction μ, then friction force acting on the block will be :

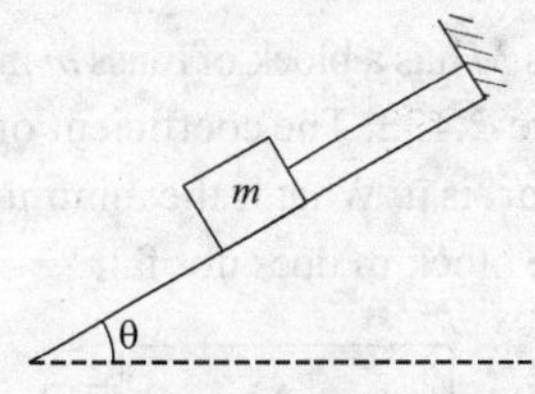

Figure 2.131

(A) μmg cos θ

(B) mg sin θ

(C) mg

(D) None

2-23 In an imaginary atmosphere, the air exerts a small force F on any particle in the direction of the particle's motion. A particle of mass 'm' projected upward takes a time t_1 in reaching the maximum height and t_2 in the return journey to the original point then :

(A) $t_1 < t_2$

(B) $t_1 > t_2$

(C) $t_1 = t_2$

(D) The relation between t_1 and t_2 depends on the mass of the particle

* * * * *

Numerical MCQs Single Options Correct

2-1 Two blocks *A* and *B*, attached to each other by a massless spring, are kept on a rough horizontal surface ($\mu = 0.1$) and pulled by a force $F = 200$ N as shown in the figure-2.132. If at some instant, the 10 kg mass has acceleration of 12 m/s^2, what is the acceleration of 20 kg mass ?

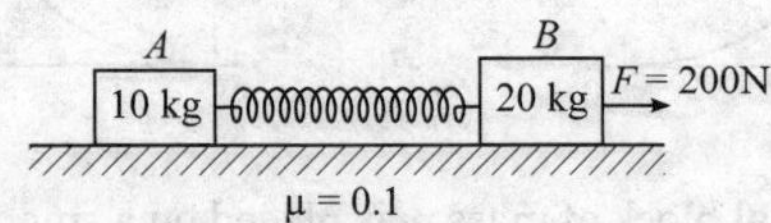

Figure 2.132

(A) 2.5 m/s^2 (B) 4.0 m/s^2
(C) 3.6 m/s^2 (D) 1.2 m/s^2

2-2 A cart of mass *M* has a block of mass *m* in contact with it as shown in the figure-2.133. The coefficient of friction between the block and the cart is μ. What is the minimum acceleration of the cart so that the block m does not fall ?

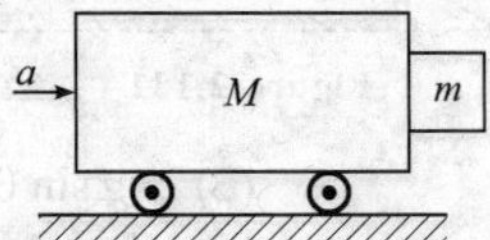

Figure 2.133

(A) μg (B) g/μ
(C) μ/g (D) $M\mu g/m$

2-3 A body of mass *m* is kept stationary on a rough inclined plane of angle of inclination θ. The magnitude of force acting on the body by the inclined plane is equal to :

(A) mg (B) $mg \sin\theta$
(C) $mg \cos\theta$ (D) None

2-4 Two blocks *A* (1 kg) and *B* (2 kg) are connected by a string passing over a smooth pulley as shown in the figure-2.134. *B* rests on rough horizontal surface and *A* rest on *B*. The coefficient of friction between *A* & *B* is the same as that between *B* and the horizontal surface. The minimum horizontal force *F* required to move *A* to the left is 25 N. The coefficient of friction is : ($g = 10$ m/s^2)

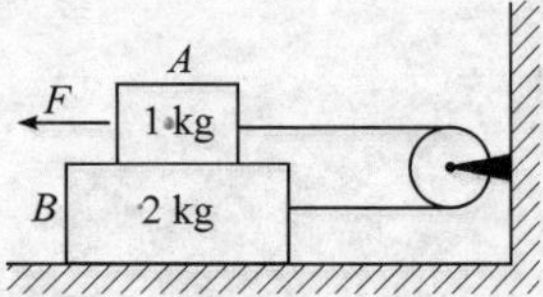

Figure 2.134

(A) 0.67 (B) 0.5
(C) 0.4 (D) 0.25

2-5 A particle moving on the inside of a smooth sphere of radius *r* describing a horizontal circle at a distance *r*/2 below the centre of the sphere. What is its speed ?

(A) $\sqrt{5gr}$ (B) $\sqrt{4gr/3}$
(C) $\sqrt{3gr/2}$ (D) $\sqrt{\sqrt{3}gr}$

2-6 In the system of pulleys shown what should be the value of m_1 such that 100 gm remains at rest : (Take $g = 10$ m/s^2)

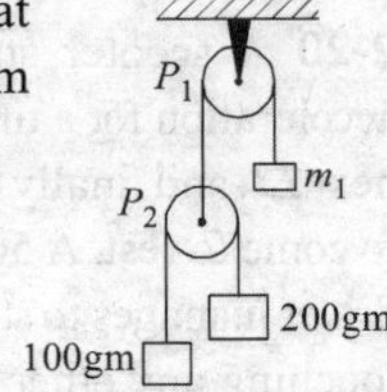

Figure 2.135

(A) 180 gm
(B) 160 gm
(C) 100 gm
(D) 200 gm

2-7 A body of mass *M* is kept on a rough horizontal surface (friction coefficient = μ). A person is trying to pull the body by applying a horizontal force but the body is not moving. The force by the surface on *A* is *F* where :

(A) $F = Mg$ (B) $F = \mu Mg$
(C) $Mg \le F \le Mg\sqrt{1+\mu^2}$ (D) $Mg \ge F \ge Mg\sqrt{1-\mu^2}$

2-8 In the figure-2.136 at the free end of the light string, a force *F* is applied to keep the suspended mass of 18 kg at rest. Assuming pulley is light then the force exerted by the ceiling on the system is : (Take $g = 10$ m/s^2)

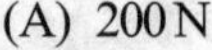

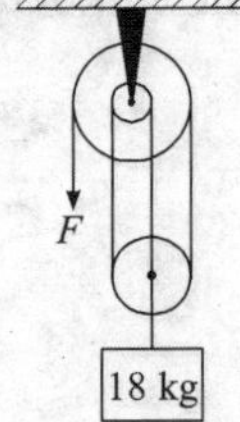

Figure 2.136

(A) 200 N (B) 120 N
(C) 180 N (D) 240 N

2-9 A ball weighing 10 gm hits a hard surface vertically with a speed of 5 m/s and rebounds with the same speed. The ball remains in contact with the surface for (0.01) s. The average force exerted by the surface on the ball is :

(A) 100 N (B) 10 N
(C) 1 N (D) 150 N

2-10 The pulleys in the diagram are all smooth and light. The acceleration of *A* is a upwards and the acceleration of *C* is *f* downwards. The acceleration of *B* is :

(A) $\frac{1}{2}(f-a)$ up

(B) $\frac{1}{2}(a+f)$ down

(C) $\frac{1}{2}(a+f)$ up

(D) $\frac{1}{2}(a-f)$ up

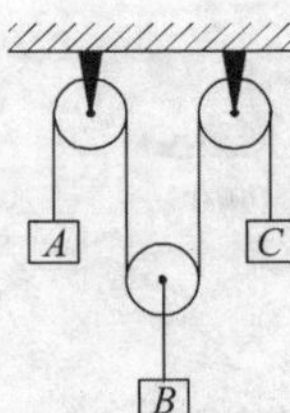

Figure 2.137

2-11 In the system shown, the initial acceleration of the wedge of mass $5M$ is (there is no friction anywhere) :

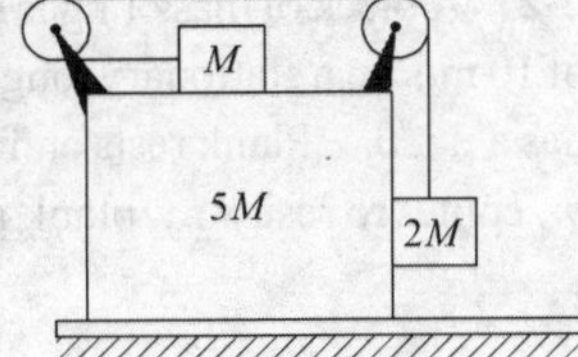

Figure 2.138

(A) Zero
(B) $2g/23$
(C) $3g/23$
(D) None

2-12 Find the acceleration of 3 kg mass when acceleration of 2kg mass is $2ms^{-2}$ as shown in figure-2.139 :

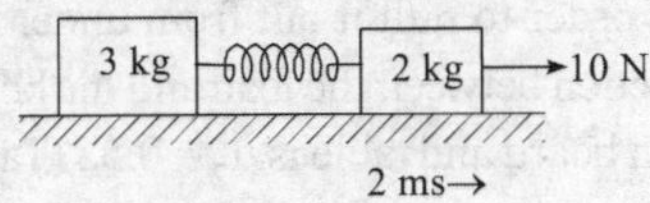

Figure 2.139

(A) $3ms^{-2}$ (B) $2ms^{-2}$
(C) $0.5ms^{-2}$ (D) Zero

2-13 Force F is applied on upper pulley. If $F = 30\,t$ where t is time in second. Find the time when m_1 loses contact with floor : (Take $g = 10\ m/s^2$)

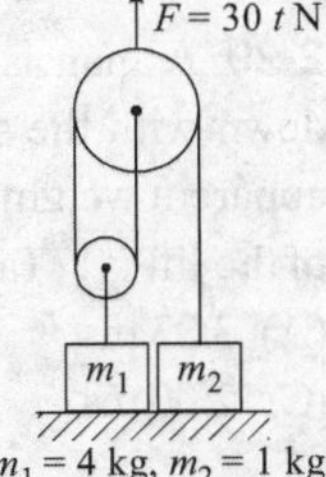

Figure 2.140

(A) 1 sec
(B) 1.66 sec
(C) 2 sec
(D) None of these

2-14 A varying horizontal force $F = bt$ acts on a block of mass m kept on a smooth horizontal surface. An identical block is kept on the first block. The coefficient of friction between the block is μ. The time after which the relative sliding between the block takes place is :

(A) $2\ mg/b$ (B) $2\ \mu mg$
(C) $\mu mg/b$ (D) None of these

2-15 The system shown is just on the verge of slipping. The co-efficient of static friction between the block and the table top is :

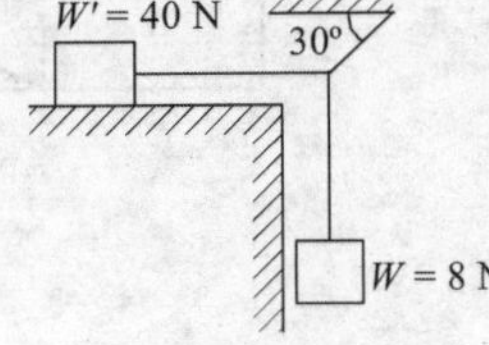

Figure 2.141

(A) 0.5
(B) 0.95
(C) 0.15
(D) 0.35

2-16 A body is moving down a long inclined plane of angle of inclination θ. The coefficient of friction between the body and the plane varies as $\mu = 0.1\ x$, where x is the distance moved down the plane. The body will have the maximum velocity when it has travelled a distance x given by :

(A) $x = 10 \tan\theta$ (B) $x = 5 \tan\theta$
(C) $\sqrt{2} \cot\theta$ (D) $x = \dfrac{\sqrt{10}}{\cot\theta}$

2-17 A block A kept on a rough plate (OO_1) with coefficient of static friction $\mu_s = 0.75$ & coefficient of kinetic friction $\mu_k = 0.5$. The plate is leaning with horizontal at an angle $\theta = \tan^{-1}(\mu_s)$. If the plate is further tilted slightly then the acceleration of block will be :

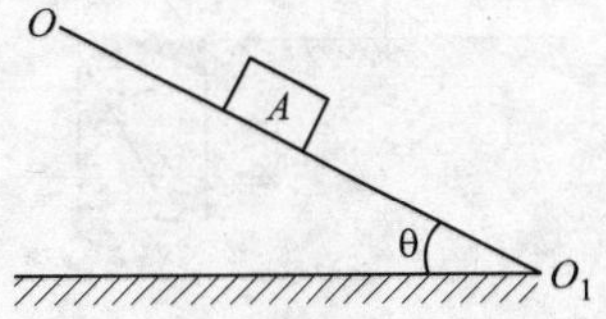

Figure 2.142

(A) $1.5\ m/s^2$ (B) $2\ m/s^2$
(C) $2.5\ m/s^2$ (D) None of these

2-18 For a particle rotating in a vertical circle with uniform speed, the maximum and minimum tension in the string are in the ratio 5 : 3. If the radius of vertical circle is 2 m, the speed of revolving body is :

(A) $\sqrt{5}$ m/s (B) $4\sqrt{5}$ m/s
(C) 5 m/s (D) 10 m/s

2-19 Block M slides down on frictionless incline as shown. The minimum friction coefficient so that m does not slide with respect to M would be :

(A) $\dfrac{1}{4}$

(B) $\dfrac{1}{2}$

(C) $\dfrac{3}{4}$

(D) None of these

Figure 2.143

2-20 A force $F = Be^{-Ct}$ acts on a particle whose mass is m and whose velocity is 0 at $t = 0$. It's terminal velocity is :

(A) $\dfrac{C}{mB}$ (B) $\dfrac{B}{mC}$

(C) $\dfrac{BC}{m}$ (D) $-\dfrac{B}{mC}$

2-21 Neglecting friction and mass of pulley, what is the acceleration of mass B ?

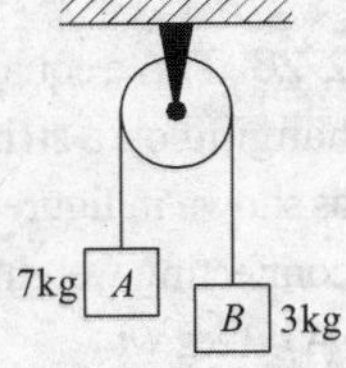

Figure 2.144

(A) $g/3$
(B) $5g/2$
(C) $2g/3$
(D) $2g/5$

2-22 Two bodies of mass m and $4m$ are attached by a string shown in the figure-2.145. The body of mass m hanging from a string of length l is executing simple harmonic motion with amplitude A while other body is at rest on the surface. The minimum coefficient of friction between the mass $4m$ and the horizontal surface must be to keep it at rest is :

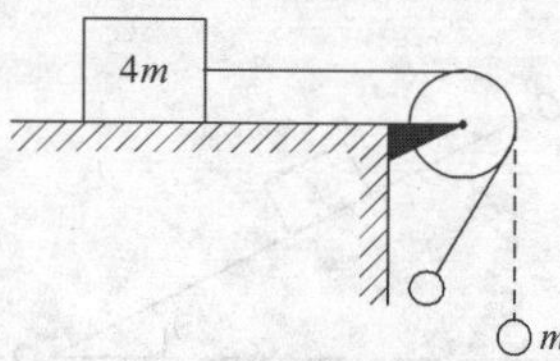

Figure 2.145

(A) $\frac{1}{4}\left(1-\frac{A^2}{l^2}\right)$ (B) $\frac{1}{4}\left(1+\frac{A^2}{l^2}\right)$

(C) $\frac{1}{4}\frac{A}{l}\cos\theta$ (D) $\frac{1}{4}$

2-23 A spring of force constant k is cut into two pieces such that one piece is double the length of the other. Then the long piece will have a force constant of :

(A) (2/3)k (B) (3/2)k
(C) 3k (D) 6k

2-24 A man of mass m stands on a frame of mass M. He pulls on a light rope, which passes over a pulley. The other end of the rope is attached to the frame. For the system to be in equilibrium, what force must the man exert on the rope ?

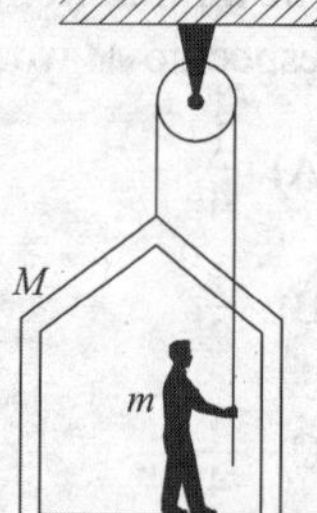

Figure 2.146

(A) $\frac{(M+m)g}{2}$
(B) $(M+m)g$
(C) $(M-m)g$
(D) $(M+2m)g$

2-25 A car starts from rest to cover a distance s. The coefficient of friction between the road and the tyres is μ. The minimum time in which the car can cover the distance is proportional to :

(A) μ (B) $\sqrt{\mu}$
(C) $1/\mu$ (D) $1/\sqrt{\mu}$

2-26 Three equal weights of mass 3 kg each are hanging on a string passing over a fixed pulley as shown in figure-2.147. The tension in the string connecting weight B and C is : (Take $g = 10\text{ m/s}^2$)

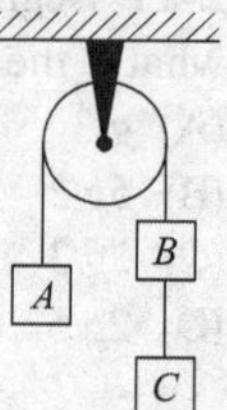

Figure 2.147

(A) 1 kg wt
(B) 2 kg wt
(C) 3 kg wt
(D) 4 kg wt

2-27 A block of mass 1 kg is horizontally thrown with a velocity of 10 m/s on a stationary long plank of mass 2 kg whose surface has a $\mu = 0.5$. Plank rests on frictionless surface. The time when m_1 comes to rest w.r.t. plank is :

(A) 2 s (B) $\frac{3}{4}$ s
(C) $\frac{4}{3}$ s (D) 1 s

2-28 A board of mass $m = 1$ kg lies on a table and a weight of $M = 2$ kg on the board. What minimum force F must be applied on the board in order to pull it out from under the load ? The coefficient of friction between the load and the board is $\mu_1 = 0.25$ and that between board and table is $\mu_2 = 0.5$: (Take $g = 10\text{ m/s}^2$)

(A) 7.5 N
(B) 15 N
(C) 22.5 N
(D) 30 N

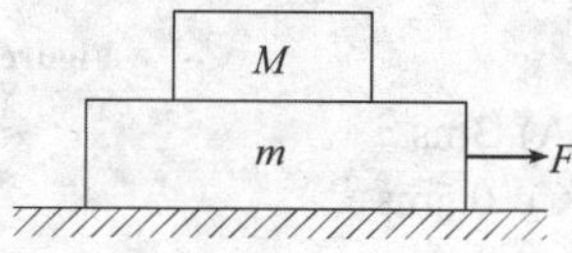

Figure 2.148

2-29 A man is standing in a lift which goes up and comes down with the same constant acceleration. If the ratio of the apparent weights in the two cases is 2 : 1, then the acceleration of the lift is : (Take $g = 10\text{ m/s}^2$)

(A) 3.33 ms^{-2} (B) 2.50 ms^{-2}
(C) 2.00 ms^{-2} (D) 1.67 ms^{-2}

2-30 A block of unknown mass is at rest on a rough, horizontal surface. A horizontal force F is applied to the block. The graph in the figure-2.149 shows the acceleration of the block with respect to the applied force. The mass of the block is :

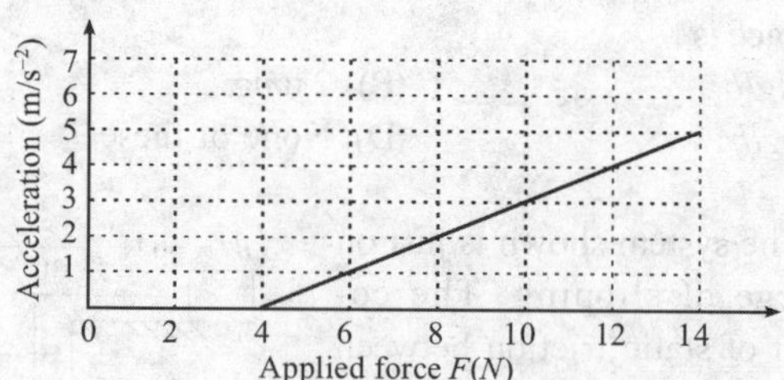

Figure 2.149

(A) 1.0 kg (B) 0.1 kg
(C) 2.0 kg (D) 0.2 kg

2-31 In the shown mass pulley system, pulleys and string are massless. The one end of the string is pulled by the force $F = mg$. The acceleration of the block will be :

(A) $g/2$
(B) 0
(C) g
(D) $3g$

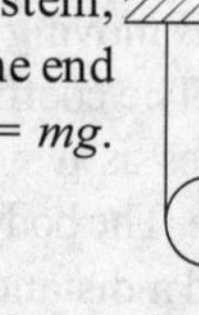
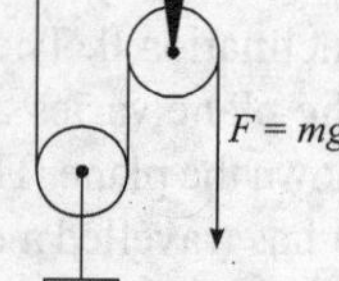

Figure 2.150

2-32 A block is given certain upward velocity along the incline of elevation α. The time of ascent to upper point was found to be half the time of descent to initial point. The co-efficient of friction between block and incline is :

(A) $0.5 \tan \alpha$ (B) $0.3 \tan \alpha$
(C) $0.6 \tan \alpha$ (D) $0.2 \tan \alpha$

2-33 Consider the shown arrangement the coefficient of friction between the two blocks is 0.5. There is no friction between 4 kg block and horizontal surface. If a horizontal force of 12 N is applied on 2 kg block as shown in figure-2.151, acceleration of 4 kg block would be : (Take $g = 10 \text{ m/s}^2$) :

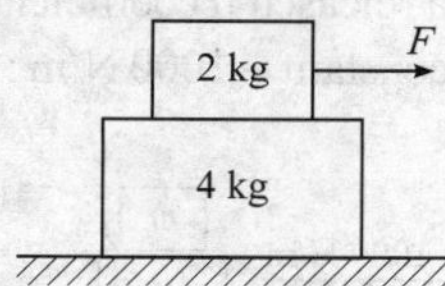

Figure 2.151

(A) 2.5 m/s^2 (B) 2 m/s^2
(C) 5 m/s^2 (D) None of these

2-34 A 40 kg slab rests on a frictionless floor. A 10 kg block rests on top of the slab as shown in the figure-2.152. The coefficient of static friction between the block and slab is 0.60 and coefficient of kinetic friction is 0.40. The 10 kg block is acted upon by a horizontal force of 100 N. The resulting acceleration of slab will be : (Take $g = 10 \text{ m/s}^2$)

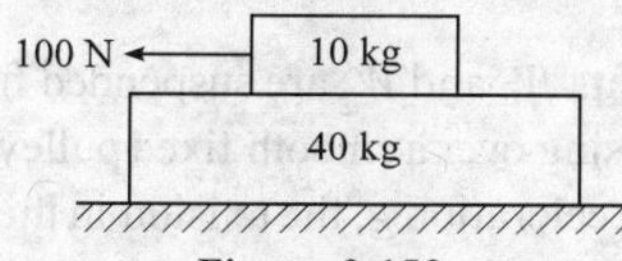

Figure 2.152

(A) 1 m/s^2 (B) 1.47 m/s^2
(C) 1.52 m/s^2 (D) 6.1 m/s^2

2-35 A load attached to the end of a spring and in equilibrium produces 9 cm extension of spring. If the spring is cut into three equal parts and one end of each is fixed at '*O*' and other ends are attached to the same load, the extension in cm of the combination in equilibrium now is :

(A) 1 (B) 3
(C) 6 (D) 9

2-36 A heavy spherical ball is constrained in a frame as shown in figure-2.153. The inclined surface is smooth. The maximum acceleration with which the frame can move without causing the ball to leave the frame :

(A) $g/2$
(B) $g\sqrt{3}$
(C) $\frac{g}{\sqrt{3}}$
(D) $g\sqrt{2}$

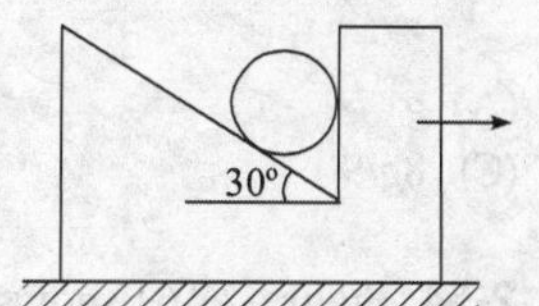

Figure 2.153

2-37 Find the reading of spring balance as shown in figure-2.154. Assume that mass *M* is in equilibrium :

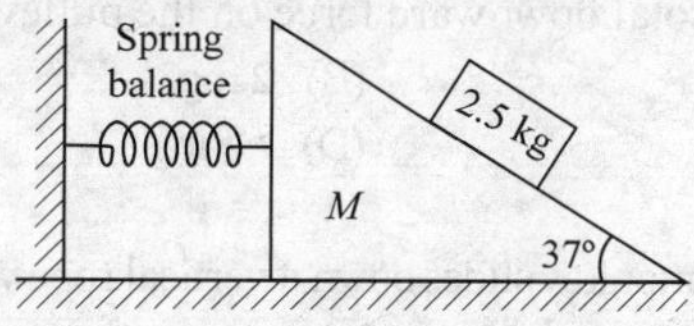

Figure 2.154

(A) 8 N (B) 9 N
(C) 12 N (D) Zero

2-38 For what value of *M* will the masses be in equilibrium. Masses are placed on fixed wedge :

(A) 5 kg
(B) 4 kg
(C) 3.75 kg
(D) 3 kg

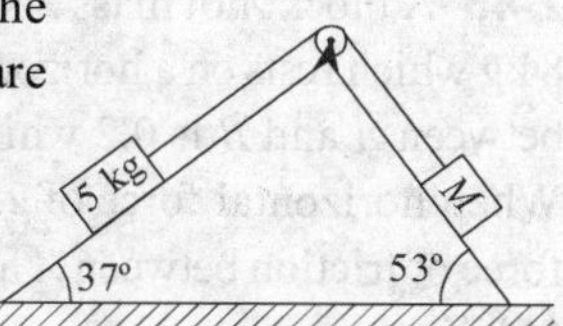

Figure 2.155

2-39 A body of mass *m* starts sliding down an incline of 30° from rest. The body comes to rest just when it reaches the bottom. If the top half of the plane is perfectly smooth and the lower half is rough, find the force of friction :

(A) $\frac{mg}{4}$ (B) $\frac{mg}{\sqrt{3}}$
(C) mg (D) $\frac{mg}{\sqrt{2}}$

2-40 A mass of 0.5 kg is just able to slide down the slope of an inclined rough surface when the angle of inclination is 60°. The minimum force necessary to pull the mass up the incline along the line of greatest slope is : (Take $g = 10 \text{ m/s}^2$)

(A) 20 N (B) 9 N
(C) 100 N (D) 1 N

2-41 Minimum force required to keep a block of mass 1 kg at rest against a rough vertical wall is *P*. If a force *P*/2 is applied then the acceleration of the block will be : (Take $g = 10 \text{ m/s}^2$)

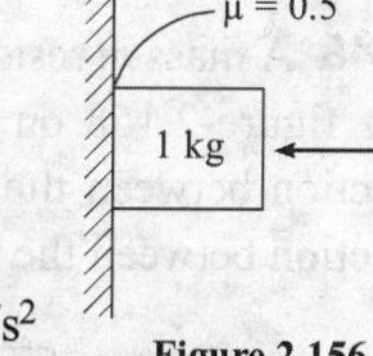

Figure 2.156

(A) 5 m/s^2 (B) 2.5 m/s^2
(C) 2 m/s^2 (D) 0.9 m/s^2

2-42 A 60 kg body is pushed with just enough force to start it moving across a floor and the same force continues to act afterwards. The co-efficient of static and kinetic friction are 0.5 & 0.4 respectively. The acceleration of the body is : (Take $g = 10 \text{ m/s}^2$)

(A) 6 m/s^2 (B) 1 m/s^2
(C) 2.5 m/s^2 (D) 3.8 m/s^2

2-43 A particle of small mass m is joined to a very heavy body by a light sting passing over a light pulley. Both bodies are free to move. The total downward force on the pulley is :

(A) mg (B) 2 mg
(C) 4 mg (D) >> mg

2-44 A 20 kg monkey slides down a vertical rope with a constant acceleration of 7 ms^{-2}. If $g = 10\ ms^{-2}$, what is the tension in the rope ?

(A) 140 N (B) 100 N
(C) 60 N (D) 30 N

2-45 A block A of mass 2 kg rests on another block B of mass 8 kg which rests on a horizontal floor. The coefficient of friction between A and B is 0.2 while that between B and floor is 0.5. When horizontal force of 25 N is applied on the block B, the force of friction between A and B is : (Take $g = 10\ m/s^2$)

(A) Zero (B) 3.9 N
(C) 5.0 N (D) 49 N

2-46 A man slides down a light rope whose breaking strength is η times his weight ($\eta < 1$). What should be his maximum acceleration so that the rope just breaks ?

(A) ηg (B) $g(1-\eta)$
(C) $\frac{g}{1+\eta}$ (D) $\frac{g}{2-\eta}$

2-47 A string of negligible mass going over a clamped pulley of mass m supports a block of mass M as shown in the figure-2.157. The force on the pulley by the clamp is given :

(A) $\sqrt{2}\,Mg$
(B) $\sqrt{2}\,mg$
(C) $\sqrt{(M+m)^2+m^2}\ g$
(D) $\sqrt{(M+m)^2+M^2}\ g$

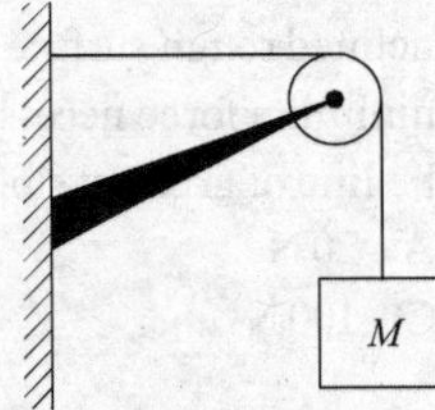

Figure 2.157

2-48 A mass m rests under the action of a force F as shown in the figure-2.158 on a horizontal surface. The coefficient of friction between the mass and the surface is μ. The force of friction between the mass and the surface is :

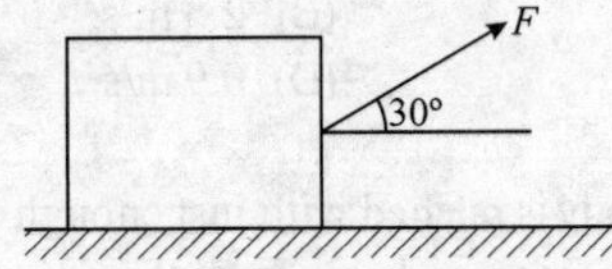

Figure 2.158

(A) μmg (B) $\mu[mg+\frac{F}{2}]$
(C) $\frac{F\sqrt{3}}{2}$ (D) $\mu[mg-\frac{F}{2}]$

2-49 A block of mass 0.1 kg is held against a wall by applying a horizontal force of 5 N on the block. If the coefficient of friction between the block and the wall is 0.5, the magnitude of the frictional force acting on the block is : (Take $g = 9.8\ m/s^2$)

(A) 0.49 N (B) 0.98 N
(C) 2.5 N (D) 4.9 N

2-50 A block of mass $M = 4$ kg is kept on a smooth horizontal plane. A bar of mass $m = 1$ kg is kept on it. They are connected to a spring as shown & the spring is compressed. Then what is the maximum compression in the spring for which the bar will not slip on the block when released if coefficient of friction between them is 0.2 & spring constant = 1000 N/m : (Take $g = 10\ m/s^2$)

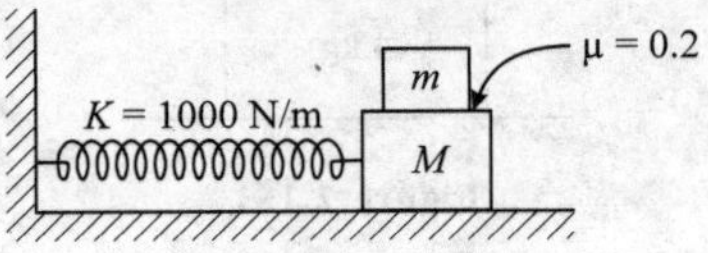

Figure 2.159

(A) 1 cm (B) 1 m
(C) 1.25 cm (D) 10 cm

2-51 If Newton is redefined as the force of attraction between two masses (each of 1 Kg) 1 meter apart, the value of G is :

(A) 10 N $Kg^{-2}\ m^2$ (B) 0.1 N $Kg^{-2}\ m^2$
(C) 1 N $Kg^{-2}\ m^2$ (D) 100 N $Kg^{-2}\ m^2$

2-52 Two weights W_1 and W_2 are suspended from the ends of a light string passing over a smooth fixed pulley. If the pulley is pulled up with acceleration g, the tension in the string will be :

(A) $\frac{4W_1W_2}{W_1+W_2}$ (B) $\frac{2W_1W_2}{W_1+W_2}$
(C) $\frac{W_1-W_2}{W_1+W_2}$ (D) $\frac{W_1W_2}{2(W_1+W_2)}$

2-53 Three weights are hanging over a smooth fixed pulley as shown in the figure-2.160. What is the tension in the string connecting weights B and C ?

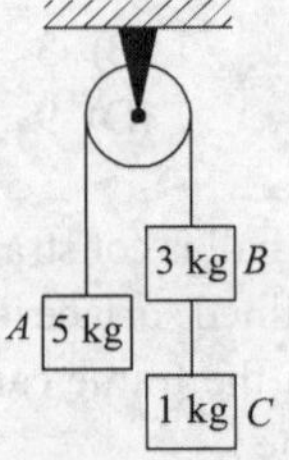

Figure 2.160

(A) g (B) $g/9$
(C) $8g/9$ (D) $10g/9$

2-54 Figure-2.161 shows a wooden block on a horizontal plane at a rest being acted upon by three forces : $F_1 = 10$ N, $F_2 = 2$ N and friction. If F_1 is removed the resultant force acting on the block will be :

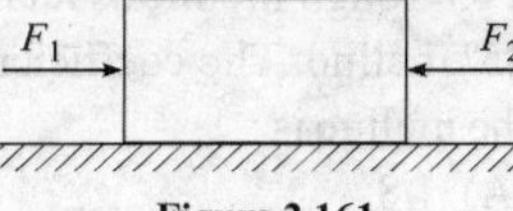

Figure 2.161

(A) 2 N towards left
(B) 2 N towards right
(C) 0 N
(D) Cannot be determined

2-55 Figure-2.162 shows a wedge of mass 2 kg resting on a frictionless floor. A block of mass 1 kg is kept on the wedge and the wedge is given an acceleration of 5 m/sec² towards right. Then :

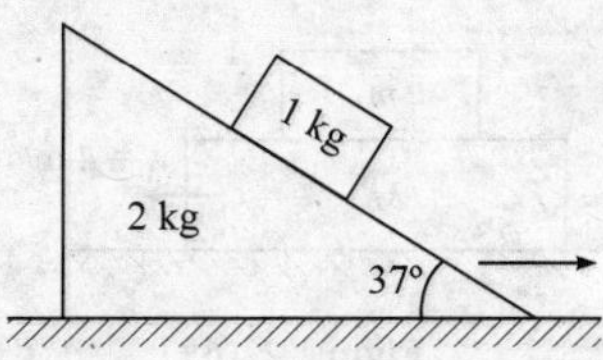

Figure 2.162

(A) Block will remain stationary w.r.t. wedge.
(B) The block will have an acceleration of 1 m/sec² w.r.t. the wedge.
(C) Normal reaction on the block is 11 N.
(D) Net force acting on the wedge is 4 N.

2-56 A man drags an m kg crate across a floor by pulling on a rope inclined at angle θ above the horizontal. If the coefficient of static friction between the floor and crate is μ_s then the tension required in the rope to start the crate moving is :

(A) $\dfrac{\mu_s mg}{(\sin\theta - \mu_s \cos\theta)}$ (B) $\dfrac{\mu_s mg}{(\sin\theta + \mu_s \cos\theta)}$

(C) $\dfrac{\mu_s mg}{(\cos\theta - \mu_s \sin\theta)}$ (D) $\dfrac{\mu_s mg}{(\cos\theta + \mu_s \sin\theta)}$

2-57 If the coefficient of kinetic friction be μ_k in above question then the initial acceleration of the crate will be :

(A) $\left[\left(\dfrac{T}{mg}\right)(\cos\theta + \mu_k \sin\theta) + \mu_k\right]g$

(B) $\left[\left(\dfrac{T}{mg}\right)(\cos\theta + \mu_k \sin\theta) - \mu_k\right]g$

(C) $\left[\left(\dfrac{T}{mg}\right)(\sin\theta + \mu_k \cos\theta) - \mu_k\right]g$

(D) $\left[\left(\dfrac{T}{mg}\right)(\sin\theta + \mu_k \cos\theta) + \mu_k\right]g$

2-58 A block of mass 2 kg is given a push horizontally and then the block starts sliding over a horizontal plane. The graph shows the velocity time graph of the motion. The co-efficient of sliding friction between the plane and the block is :

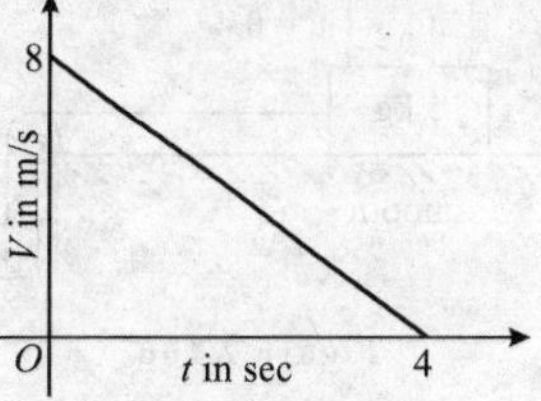

Figure 2.163

(A) 0.02 (B) 0.2
(C) 0.04 (D) 0.4

2-59 A force of 100 N is applied on a block of mass 3 kg as shown in the figure-2.164. The coefficient of friction between the surface and the block is 0.25. The frictional force acting on the block is : (Take $g = 10$ m/s²)

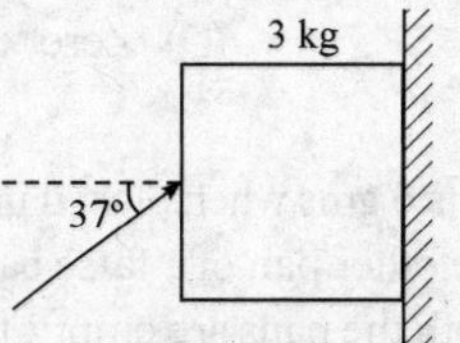

Figure 2.164

(A) 15 N downwards (B) 25 N upwards
(C) 20 N downwards (D) 30 N upwards

2-60 A block of mass 1 kg is kept on a horizontal surface in a truck. The coefficient of static friction between the block and the surface is 0.6. If the acceleration of truck is 5 m/s², then frictional force acting on the block is :

(A) 2 N (B) 3 N
(C) 5 N (D) 6 N

2-61 A block of mass M on a horizontal smooth surface is pulled by a load of mass $\dfrac{M}{2}$ by means of a rope AB and string BC as shown in the figure-2.165. The length & mass of the rope AB are L and $\dfrac{M}{2}$ respectively and BC is massless. As the block is pulled from $AB = L$ to $AB = 0$ its acceleration changes from :

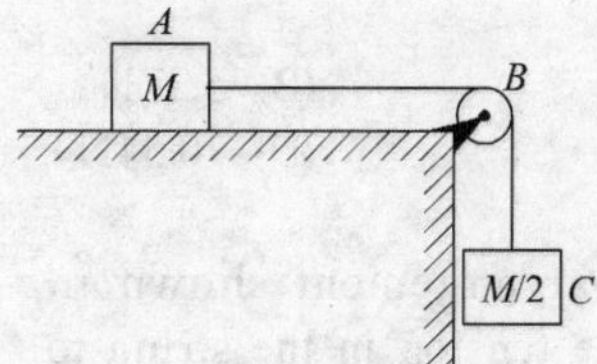

Figure 2.165

(A) $\dfrac{3g}{4}$ to g (B) $\dfrac{g}{4}$ to $\dfrac{g}{2}$

(C) $\dfrac{g}{4}$ to g (D) $\dfrac{3g}{2}$ to $2g$

2-62 What should be the maximum value of M so that the 4 kg block does not slip over the 5 kg block : (Take $g = 10$ m/s^2)

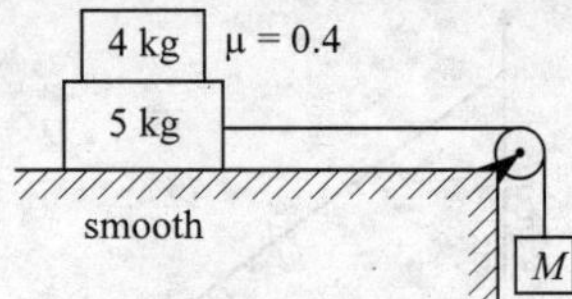

Figure 2.166

(A) 12 kg (B) 8 kg
(C) 10 kg (D) 6 kg

2-63 The direction of three forces 1 N, 2 N and 3 N acting at a point are parallel to the sides of an equilateral triangle taken in order. The magnitude of their resultant is :

(A) $\sqrt{3}$ N (B) $\frac{\sqrt{3}}{2}$ N
(C) $\frac{3}{2}$ N (D) Zero

2-64 A body weighs 6 gms when placed in one pan and 24 gms when placed on the other pan of a false balance. If the beam is horizontal when both the pans are empty, the true weight of the body is :

(A) 13 gm (B) 12 gm
(C) 15.5 gm (D) 15 gm

2-65 A 20 kg block placed on a level frictionless surface is attached to a cord which passes over two small frictionless pulleys, as shown in figure-2.167, to a hanging block originally at rest 1 m above the floor. If the hanging block strikes the floor 2 s after the system is released, the weight of the hanging block is :

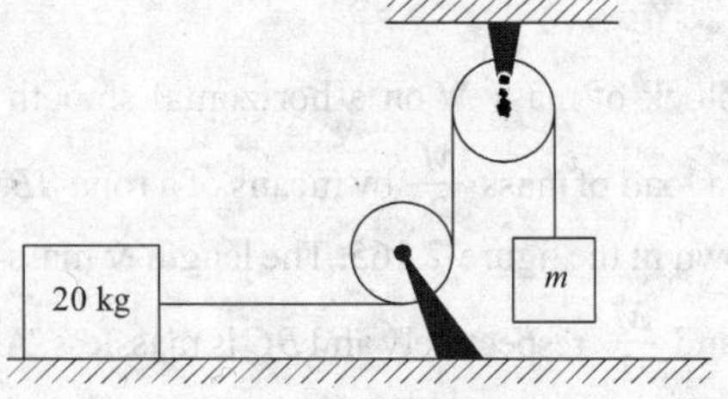

Figure 2.167

(A) 3.5 N (B) 5.27 N
(C) 5.4 N (D) 10.54 N

2-66 For the arrangement shown in figure-2.168, the tension in the string to prevent it from sliding down, is :

(A) 6 N
(B) 6.4 N
(C) 0.4 N
(D) None of these

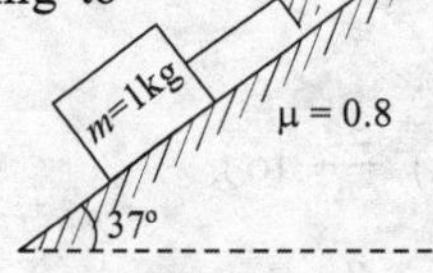

Figure 2.168

2-67 A given object takes 3 times as much time to slide down a 45° rough incline as it takes to slide down a perfectly smooth 45° incline. The coefficient of friction between the object and the incline is :

(A) 1/8 (B) 8/9
(C) $1/2\sqrt{2}$ (D) $2\sqrt{2}/3$

2-68 A stationary body of mass m is slowly lowered onto a massive platform of mass M ($M >> m$) moving at a speed $v_0 = 4$ m/s. How much will the body slide with respect to the platform ($\mu = 0.2$ and $g = 10$ m/s^2) ?

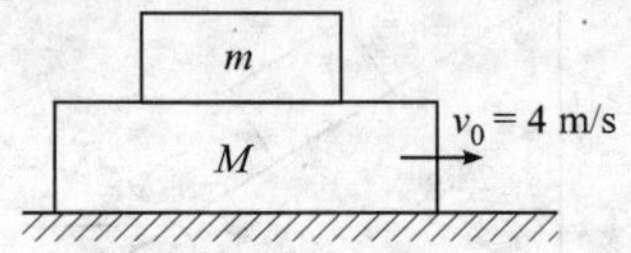

Figure 2.169

(A) 4m (B) 6m
(C) 12m (D) 8m

2-69 In the arrangement shown, the pulleys are smooth and the strings are inextensible. The acceleration of block B is :

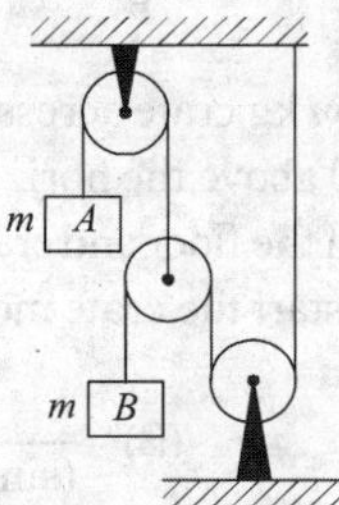

Figure 2.170

(A) $g/5$ (B) $5g/5$
(C) $2g/5$ (D) $2g/3$

2-70 An empty plastic box of mass 9 kg is found to accelerate up at the rate of $g/3$ when placed deep inside water. Mass of the sand that should be put inside the box so that it may accelerate down at the rate of $g/4$ is :

(A) 7 kg (B) 6 kg
(C) 9 kg (D) None of these

2-71 With what minimum acceleration mass M must be moved on frictionless surface so that m remains stick to it as shown in figure-2.171. The co-efficient of friction between M & m is μ :

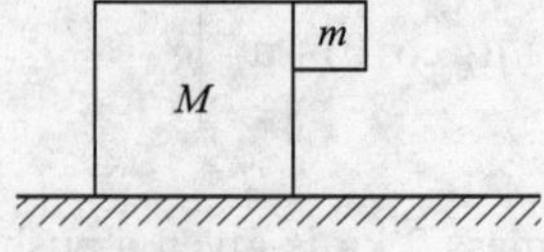

Figure 2.171

(A) μg (B) $\frac{g}{\mu}$

(C) $\frac{\mu mg}{M+m}$ (D) $\frac{\mu mg}{M}$

2-72 The coefficient of friction between 4 kg and 5 kg blocks is 0.2 and between 5 kg block and ground is 0.1 respectively. Choose the correct statements : (Take $g = 10\text{ m/s}^2$)

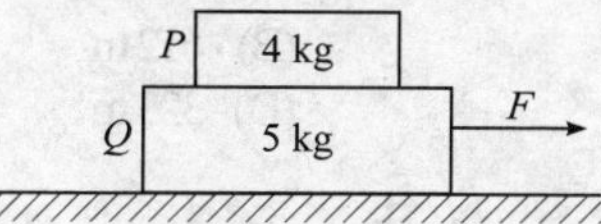

Figure 2.172

(A) Minimum force needed to cause system to move is 17 N
(B) When force is 4 N static friction at all surfaces is 4 N to keep system at rest
(C) Maximum acceleration of 4 kg block is 2 m/s^2
(D) Slipping between 4 kg and 5 kg blocks start when F is 17 N

2-73 Find the friction force between the blocks in the figure-2.173:

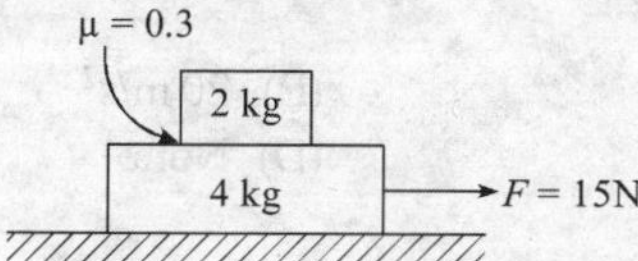

Figure 2.173

(A) 6 N (B) 18 N
(C) 5 N (D) 12 N

2-74 A pulley is attached to one arm of a balance and a string passed around it carries two masses m_1 and m_2. The pulley is provided with a clamp due to which m_1 and m_2 do not move. On removing the clamp, m_1 and m_2 start moving. How much change in counter mass has to be made to restore balance ?

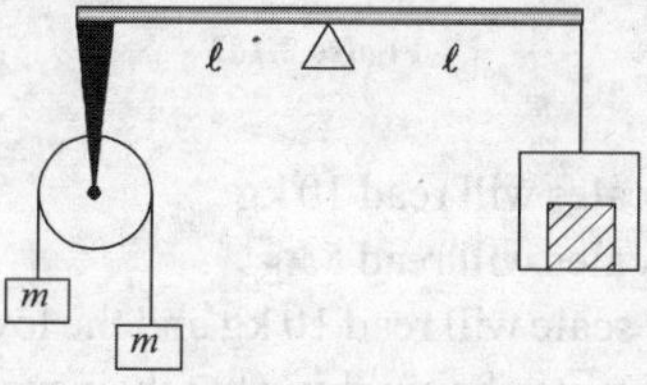

Figure 2.174

(A) $\frac{(m_1+m_2)^2}{m_1-m_2}$ (B) $\frac{(m_1-m_2)^2}{m_1+m_2}$

(C) $2m_1 - m_2$ (D) $m_1 - m_2$

2-75 Blocks A and B have masses of 2 kg and 3 kg respectively. The ground is smooth. P is an external force of 10 N. The force exerted by B on A is :

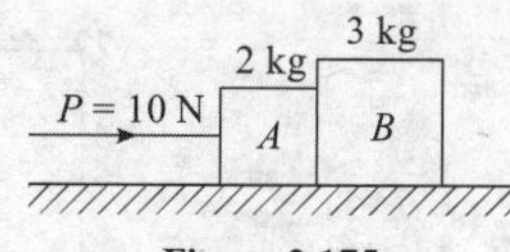

Figure 2.175

(A) 4 N
(B) 6 N
(C) 8 N
(D) 10 N

2-76 Two blocks of masses m_1 and m_2 are placed in contact with each other on a horizontal platform. The coefficient of friction between the platform and the two blocks is the same. The platform moves with an acceleration. The force of interaction between the blocks is :

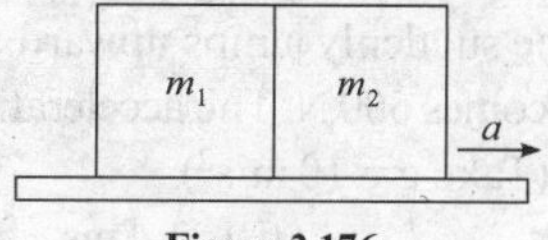

Figure 2.176

(A) Zero in all cases (B) Zero only if $m_1 = m_2$
(C) Non zero only if $m_1 > m_2$ (D) Non zero only if $m_1 < m_2$

2-77 A body of weight w_1 is suspended from the ceiling of a room through a chain of weight w_2. The ceiling pulls the chain by a force :

(A) w_1 (B) w_2

(C) $w_1 + w_2$ (D) $\frac{w_1 + w_2}{2}$

2-78 A horizontal rope of length y is pulled by a constant horizontal force F. What is the tension at a distance x from the end where the force applied ?

(A) $\frac{F(y-x)}{y}$ (B) $\frac{F.y}{y-x}$

(C) $\frac{F.y}{x}$ (D) $\frac{F.y}{y}$

2-79 A block of mass m slides in an inclined right angle trough as shown in the figure-2.177. If the coefficient of kinetic friction between the block and the material composing the trough is μ, then the acceleration of the block will be :

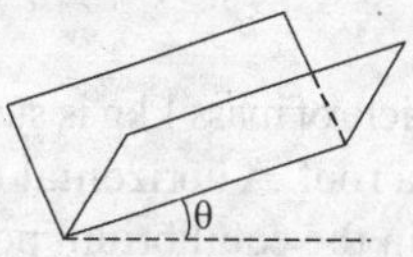

Figure 2.177

(A) $(\cos\theta - \mu\sin\theta)g$ (B) $(\sin\theta - \mu\sin\theta)g$

(C) $(\sin\theta - \mu\cos\theta)g$ (D) $(\sin\theta - \sqrt{2}\,\mu\cos\theta)g$

2-80 A ball is held at rest in position A by two light cords. The horizontal cord is now cut and the ball swings to the position B. What is the ratio of the tension in the cord in position B to that in position A originally ?

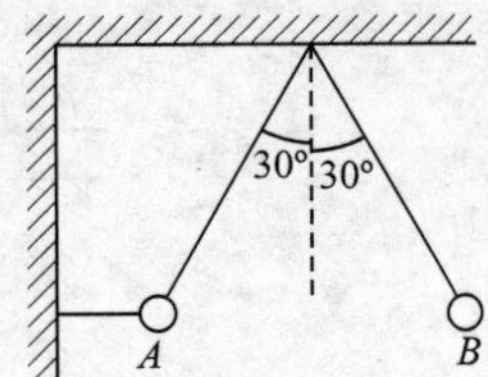

Figure 2.178

(A) 3 (B) 3/4
(C) 1/2 (D) 1

2-81 A boy standing on a weighing machine notices his weight as 400 N. When he suddenly jumps upward the weight shown by the machine becomes 600 N. The acceleration with which the boy jumps up is : (Take $g = 10\ m/s^2$)

(A) $5\ ms^{-2}$ (B) $3.4\ ms^{-2}$
(C) $6\ ms^{-2}$ (D) $9.8\ ms^{-2}$

2-82 Two masses A and B of 5 kg and 6 kg are connected by a string passing over a frictionless pulley fixed at the corner of table as shown in figure-2.179. The coefficient of friction between A and the table is 0.3. The minimum mass of C that must be placed on A to prevent it from moving is equal to : (Take $g = 10\ m/s^2$)

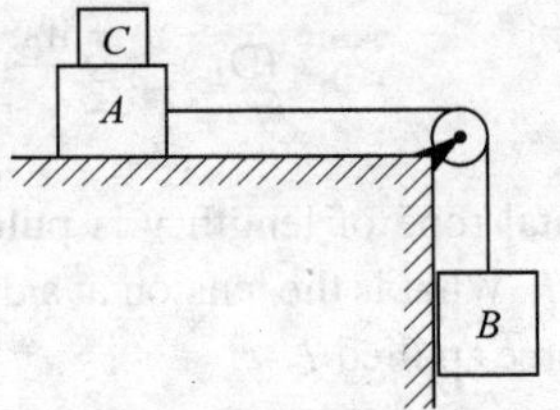

Figure 2.179

(A) 15 kg (B) 10 kg
(C) 5 kg (D) 3 kg

2-83 A heavy body of mass 25 kg is to be dragged along a horizontal plane ($\mu = 1/\sqrt{3}$). The least force required to start the body is :

(A) 25 kgf (B) 2.5 kgf
(C) 12.5 kgf (D) 50 kgf

2-84 A heavy particle of mass 1 kg is suspended from a massless string attached to a roof. A horizontal force F is applied to the particle such that in the equilibrium position the string makes an angle 30° with the vertical. The magnitude of the force F equals :

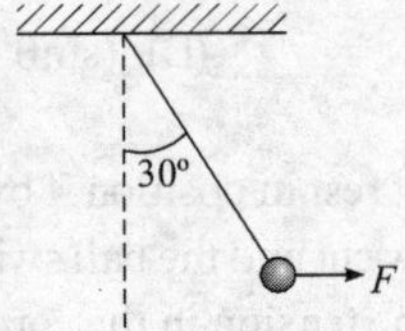

Figure 2.180

(A) 10 N (B) $10\sqrt{3}$ N
(C) 5 N (D) $10/\sqrt{3}$ N

2-85 The human body can safely stand an acceleration 9 times that due to gravity which is $10\ m/s^2$. The minimum radius of curvature with which a pilot may safely turn a plane vertically upward at the end of a dive, when the plane's speed is 720 km/hr is :

(A) 500 m (B) 612 m
(C) 475 m (D) 323 m

2-86 A 1 kg block is being pushed against a wall by a force $F = 75$ N as shown in the figure-2.181. The coefficient of friction is 0.25. The magnitude of acceleration of the block is : (Take $g = 10\ m/s^2$)

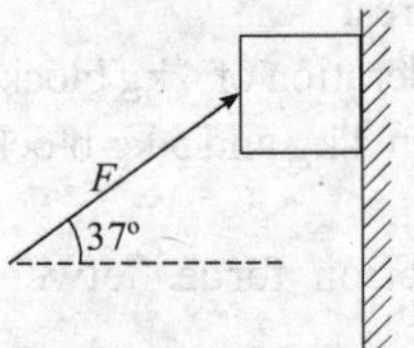

Figure 2.181

(A) $10\ m/s^2$ (B) $20\ m/s^2$
(C) $5\ m/s^2$ (D) None

2-87 A block of mass 10 kg is suspended through two light spring balances as shown in figure-2.182 :

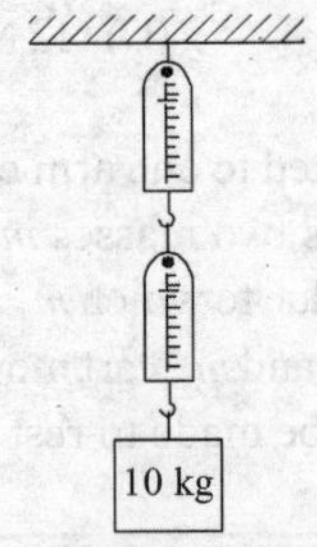

Figure 2.182

(A) Both the scales will read 10 kg
(B) Both the scales will read 5 kg
(C) The upper scale will read 10 kg and the lower zero
(D) The reading may be anything but their sum will 10 kg

2-88 Three rigid rods are joined to form an equilateral triangle ABC of side 1 m. Three particles carrying charges 20 μC each are attached to the vertices of the triangle. The whole system is at rest in an inertial frame. The resultant force on the charge particle at A has the magnitude :

(A) Zero (B) 3.6 N
(C) $3.6\sqrt{3}$ N (D) 7.2 N

2-89 A rope of length L has its mass per unit length λ varies according to the function $\lambda(x) = e^{x/L}$. The rope is pulled by a constant force of 1 N on a smooth horizontal surface. The tension in the rope at $x = L/2$ is :

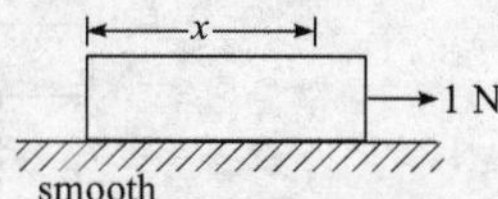

Figure 2.183

(A) 0.50 N (B) 0.38 N
(C) 0.62 N (D) None

2-90 What force must man exert on rope to keep platform in equilibrium : (Take $g = 10\ m/s^2$)

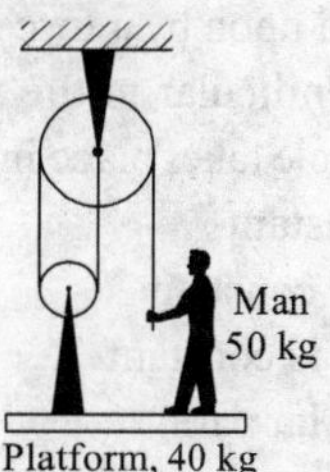

Figure 2.184

(A) 100 N (B) 200 N
(C) 300 N (D) 500 N

* * * * *

Advance MCQs with One or More Options Correct

2-1 A particle is acted upon by a force of constant magnitude which is always perpendicular to the velocity of the particle. The motion of the particle takes place in a plane. It follows that :
(A) Its velocity is constant
(B) Its acceleration is constant
(C) Its kinetic energy is constant
(D) It moves in a circular path

2-2 A reference frame attached to the earth :
(A) Is the inertial frame as motion of earth is at uniform speed.
(B) Cannot be the inertial frame because earth is revolving around the sun
(C) Is an inertial frame because Newton's Laws are applicable in this frame
(D) Cannot be the inertial frame because earth is rotating about its own axis

2-3 When a bicycle is in motion, the force of friction exerted by the ground on the two wheels in different cases is such that it acts :
(A) In the backward direction on the front wheel and in the forward direction on the rear wheel.
(B) In the forward direction on the front wheel and in the backward direction on the rear wheel.
(C) In the backward direction on both the front and on the rear wheel.
(D) In the forward direction on both the front and on the rear wheel.

2-4 A car C of mass m_1, rests on a plank of mass m_2. The plank rests on a smooth floor. The string and pulley are ideal. The car starts and moves towards the pulley with certain acceleration :

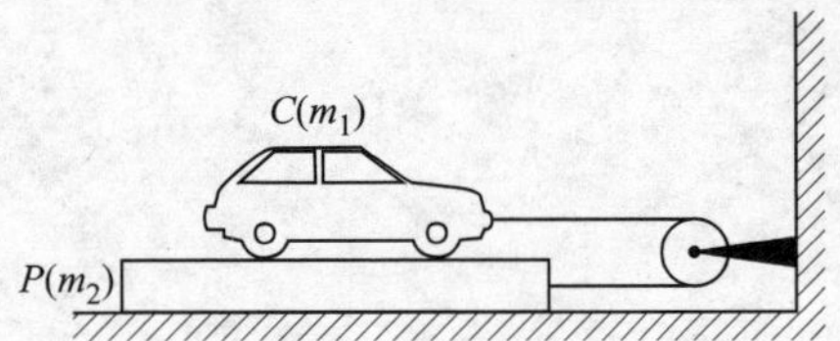

Figure 2.185

(A) If $m_1 > m_2$, the string will remain under tension
(B) If $m_1 < m_2$, the string will become slack
(C) If $m_1 = m_2$, the string will have no tension, and C and P will have accelerations of equal magnitudes
(D) C and P will have accelerations of equal magnitude if $m_1 \geq m_2$

2-5 The blocks B & C in the figure-2.186 have mass 'm' each. The strings AB & BC are light, having tensions T_1 & T_2 respectively. The system is in equilibrium with a constant horizontal force mg action on C:

(A) $\tan\theta_1 = \frac{1}{2}$
(B) $\tan\theta_2 = 1$
(C) $T_1 = \sqrt{5}$ mg
(D) $T_2 = \sqrt{2}$ mg

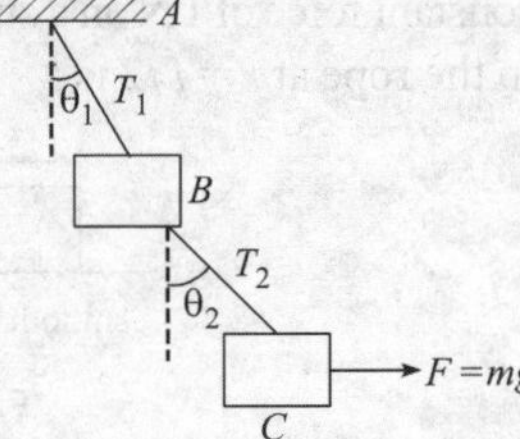

Figure 2.186

2-6 Five identical cubes each of mass 'm' are on a straight line with two adjacent faces in contact on a horizontal surface as shown in the figure-2.187. Suppose the surface is frictionless and a constant force P is applied from left to right to the end face of A, which of the following statements are correct :

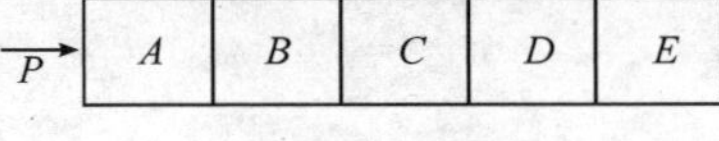

Figure 2.187

(A) The acceleration of the system is $\frac{5P}{m}$
(B) The resultant force acting on each cube is $\frac{P}{5}$
(C) The force exerted by C & D is $\frac{2P}{5}$
(D) The acceleration of the cube D is $\frac{P}{5}$ m

2-7 In the arrangement shown in the figure-2.188 if system is in equilibrium ($g = 10$ m/s^2) :
(A) Tension $T_1 = 50$ N
(B) Tension $T_1 = 500$ N
(C) Angle $\theta = 37°$
(D) Angle $\theta = 53°$

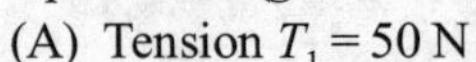
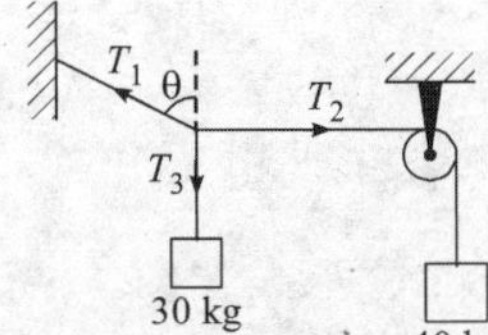

Figure 2.188

2-8 A cart with a mass $M = \frac{1}{2}$ kg is connected by a string to a weight of mass $m = 200$ g. At the initial moment the cart moves to the left along a horizontal plane at a speed $V_0 = 7$ ms^{-1}. ($g = 9.8$ ms^{-2})

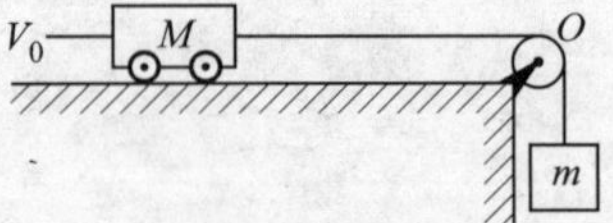

Figure 2.189

(A) The distance covered by cart in 5 s is zero
(B) After 5 s weight of mass m will be in same position
(C) The distance covered by cart in 5 s is 17.5 m
(D) None of the above

2-9 A block of weight 9.8 N is placed on a table. The smooth table surface exerts an upward force of 10 N on the block. Assume $g = 9.8\ \text{m/s}^2$:
(A) The block exerts a force of 10 N on the table
(B) The block exerts a force of 19.8 N on the table
(C) The block exerts a force of 9.8 N on the table
(D) The block has an upward acceleration.

2-10 A 10 kg block is placed on a horizontal surface whose coefficient of friction is 0.2. A horizontal force $P = 15$ N first acts on it in the eastward direction. Later, in addition to P a second horizontal force $Q = 20$ N acts on it in the northward direction : (Take $g = 10\ \text{m/s}^2$)
(A) The block will not move when only P acts, but will move when both P and Q act
(B) If the block moves, the acceleration will be $0.5\ \text{m/s}^2$
(C) When the block moves, its direction of motion will be $\tan^{-1}(13/4)$ east of north
(D) When both P and Q act, the direction of the force of friction acting on the block will be $\tan^{-1}(3/4)$ west of south

2-11 Two identical blocks are connected by a light spring. The combination is suspended at rest from a string attached to the ceiling, as shown in the figure-2.190 below. The string breaks suddenly. Immediately after the string breaks :

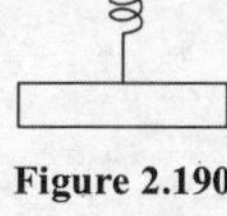
Figure 2.190

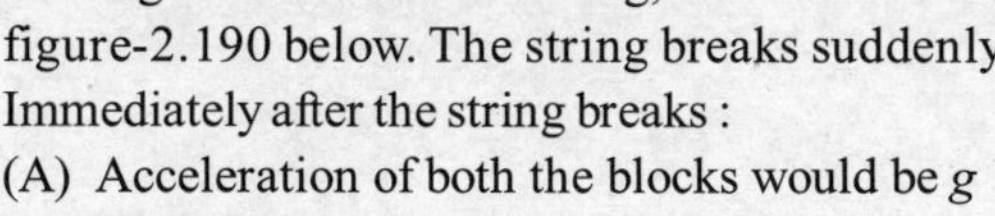
(A) Acceleration of both the blocks would be g downward
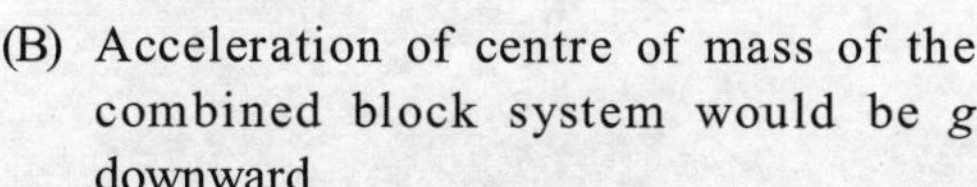
(B) Acceleration of centre of mass of the combined block system would be g downward
(C) Acceleration of upper block would be $2g$ downward
(D) Acceleration of lower block would be g upward

2-12 A block of mass m is pulled by a force of constant power P placed on a rough horizontal plane. The friction coefficient between the block and the surface is μ. Then :
(A) The maximum velocity of the block during the motion is $\dfrac{P}{\mu mg}$
(B) The maximum velocity of the block during the motion is $\dfrac{P}{2\mu mg}$
(C) The block's speed is never decreasing and finally becomes constant.
(D) The speed of the block first increases to a maximum value and then decreases.

2-13 The ring shown in the figure-2.191 is given a constant horizontal acceleration ($a_0 = g/\sqrt{3}$). Maximum deflection of the string from the vertical is θ_0, then :

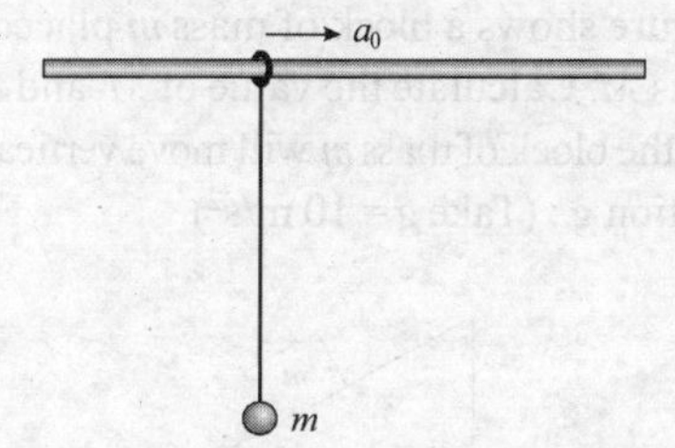

Figure 2.191

(A) $\theta_0 = 30°$
(B) $\theta_0 = 60°$
(C) at maximum deflection, tension in string is equal to mg
(D) at maximum deflection, tension in string is equal to $\dfrac{2mg}{\sqrt{3}}$

2-14 In the adjacent figure there is a cube having a smooth groove at an inclination of 30° with horizontal in its vertical face. A cylinder A of mass 2 kg can slide freely inside the grove. The cube is moving with constant horizontal acceleration a_0 parallel to the shown face, so that the slider does not have acceleration along horizontal.

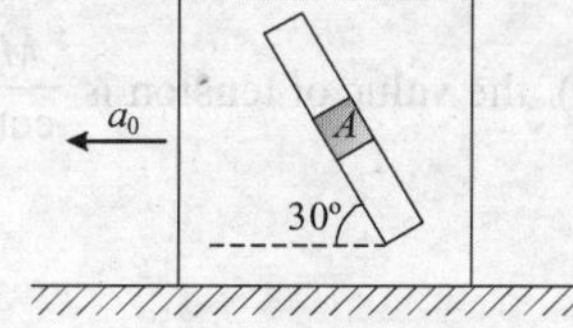

Figure 2.192

(A) The normal reaction acting on cube is zero
(B) The value of a_0 is $g\sqrt{3}$
(C) The value of a_0 is g.
(D) Acceleration of the particle in ground frame is g

2-15 Two blocks of masses m_1 and m_2 are connected through a massless inextensible string. Block of mass m_1 is placed at the fixed rigid inclined surface while the block of mass m_2 hanging at the other end of the string, which is passing through a fixed massless frictionless pulley shown in figure-2.193. The coefficient of static friction between the block and the inclined plane is 0.8. The system of masses m_1 and m_2 is released from rest. (Take $g = 10\ \text{m/s}^2$)

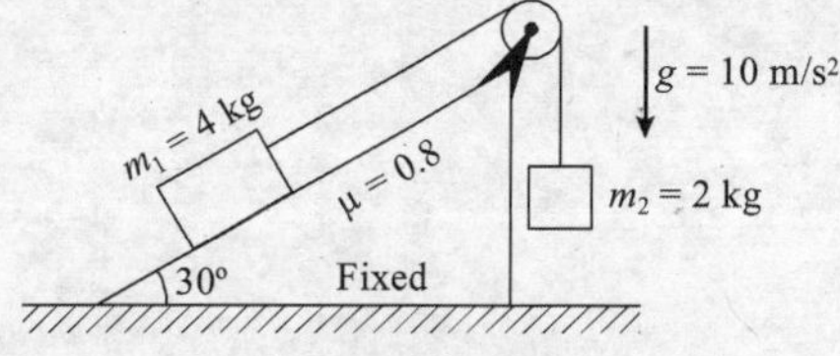

Figure 2.193

(A) the tension in the string is 20 N after releasing the system
(B) the contact force by the inclined surface on the block is along normal to the inclined surface
(C) the magnitude of contact force by the inclined surface on the block m_1 is $20\sqrt{3}$ N
(D) none of these

2-16 The figure shows a block of mass m placed on a smooth wedge of mass M. Calculate the value of M' and tension in the string, so that the block of mass m will move vertically downward with acceleration g : (Take $g = 10\ \text{m/s}^2$)

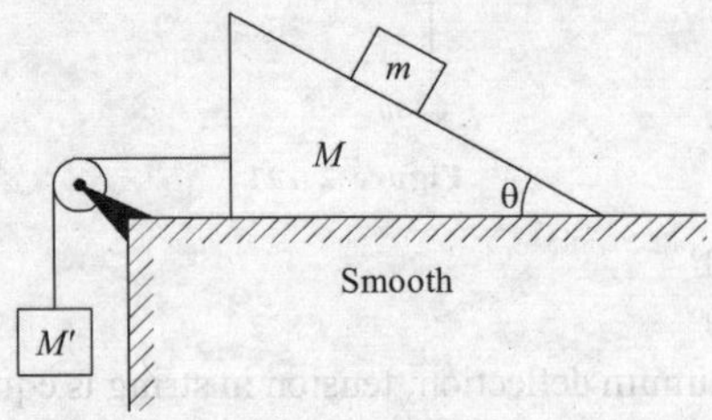

Figure 2.194

(A) the value M' is $\dfrac{M\cot\theta}{1-\cot\theta}$

(B) the value M' is $\dfrac{M\cot\theta}{1-\tan\theta}$

(C) the value of tension in the string is $\dfrac{Mg}{\tan\theta}$

(D) the value of tension is $\dfrac{Mg}{\cot\theta}$

2-17 In the figure-2.195, a man of true mass M is standing on a weighing machine placed in a cabin. The cabin is joined by a string with a body of mass m. Assuming no friction, and negligible mass of cabin and weighing machine, the measured mass of man is : (normal force between the man and the machine is proportional to the mass)

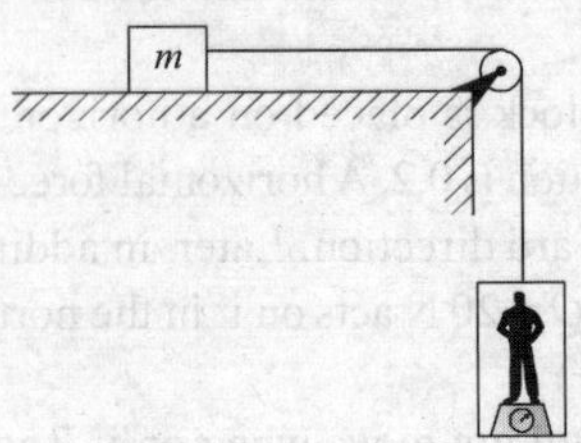

Figure 2.195

(A) Measured mass of man is $\dfrac{Mm}{(M+m)}$

(B) Acceleration of man is $\dfrac{mg}{(M+m)}$

(C) Acceleration of man is $\dfrac{mg}{(M+m)}$

(D) Measured mass of man is M

* * * * *

Unsolved Numerical Problems for Preparation of NSEP, INPhO & IPhO

For detailed preparation of INPhO and IPhO students can refer advance study material on www.physicsgalaxy.com

2-1 A packet of 150 kg is released from an airplane travelling due east at an altitude of 7200 m with a ground speed of 100 m/s. The wind applies a constant force on the packet of 300 N directed horizontally in the opposite direction to the plane's flight path. Where and when does the packet hit the ground. (with respect to the release location and time)

Ans. [38 s, 2.36 km]

2-2 A block $m = 0.5$ kg slides down a frictionless inclined plane 2 m long as shown in figure-2.196. It then slides on a rough horizontal table surface of $\mu = 0.3$ for 0.5 m. It then leaves the top of the table, which is 1.0 m high. How far from the base of the table does the block land ?

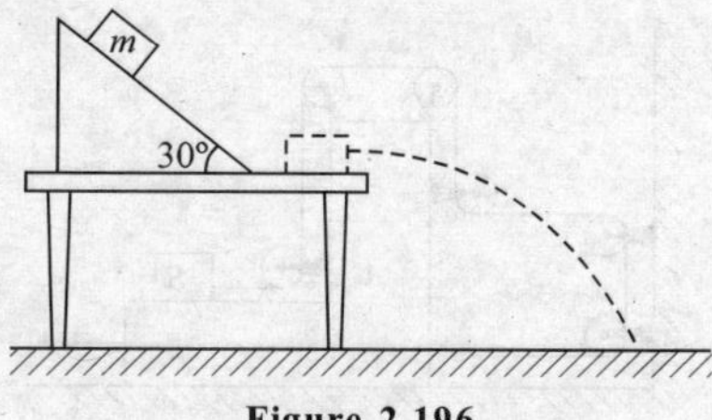

Figure 2.196

Ans. [1.85 m]

2-3 A baseball is dropped from the roof of a tall building. As the ball falls, the air exerts a drag force that varies directly with the speed as $f = qv$ is a constant. Show that the ball acquires a terminal speed. Find the speed of the falling ball as a function of time.

Ans. $[\frac{mg}{q}(1 - e^{-qt/m})]$

2-4 A block of metal weighing 2 kg is resting on a frictionless plane. It is struck by a jet releasing water at a rate of 1 kg/s and at a speed of 5 m/s. Calculate the initial acceleration of the block.

Ans. [2.5 m/s^2]

2-5 Having gone through a plank of thickness h, a bullet changed its velocity v_0. Find the time of motion of the bullet in the plank, assuming the resistance force to be proportional to the square of the velocity.

Ans. $[\frac{h(v_0 - v)}{v_0 v \log_e(v_0/v)}]$

2-6 A particle of mass M is dropped vertically into a medium that offers resistance proportional to the velocity of the particle. The buoyancy of the medium is negligible, and the resisting force per unit velocity is f. What uniform velocity will the particle finally attain ?

Ans. $[\frac{Mg}{f}]$

2-7 Consider the system of pulleys as shown in figure-2.197. Find the acceleration of the three masses m_1, m_2 and m_3. ($m_1 = 1$ kg, $m_2 = 2$ kg and $m_3 = 3$ kg)

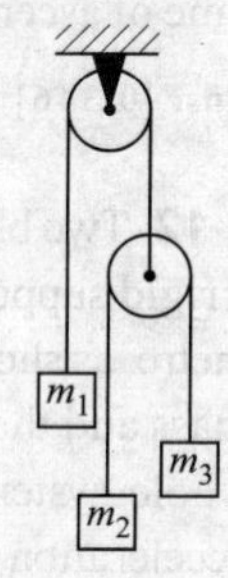

Figure 2.197

Ans. [19g/29, 17g/29, 21g/29]

2-8 A smooth ring A mass m can slide on a fixed horizontal rod. A string tied to the ring passes over a fixed pulley B and carries a block C of mass M (= $2m$) as shown in figure-2.198. At an instant the string between the ring and the pulley makes an angle α with the rod. (a) Show that, if the ring slides with a speed v, the block descends with speed $v\cos\alpha$; (b) With what acceleration will the ring start moving if the system is released from rest with $\alpha = 30°$.

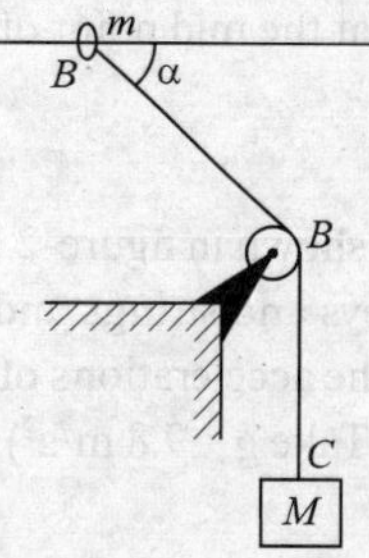

Figure 2.198

Ans. [6.78 m/s^2]

2-9 When an archer pulls on the bow string with a force of 500 N, the bow string makes angles of 53° with the arrow. What is the tension in the string.

Ans. [416.67 N]

2-10 A man with mass 85 kg stands on a platform with mass 25 kg. He pulls on the free end of a rope that runs over a pulley on the ceiling and has its other end fastened to the platform. The mass of the rope and the mass of the pulley can be neglected, and the pulley is frictionless. With what force does he have to pull so that he and the platform have an upward acceleration of 2.2 m/s^2. (Take $g = 10$ m/s^2)

Ans. [15 N, 270 N]

2-11 A body of mass 5×10^{-3} kg is launched up on a rough inclined plane making an angle of 30° with the horizontal. Obtain the coefficient of friction between the body and the plane if the time of ascent is half of the time of descent.

Ans. [0.346]

2-12 Two blocks of mass 2.9 kg and 1.9 kg are suspended from a rigid support S by two inextensible wires each of length one metre, as shown in figure-2.199. The upper wire has negligible mass and the lower wire has a uniform mass of 0.2 kg/m. The whole system of blocks, wires and support have an upward acceleration of 0.2 m/s². (Take $g = 9.8$ m/s²)

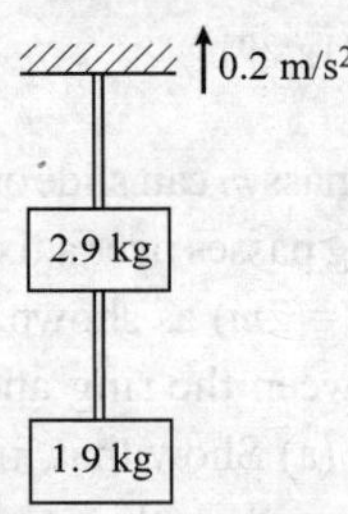

Figure 2.199

(i) Find the tension at the mid point of the lower wire.

(ii) Find the tension at the mid point of the upper wire.

Ans. [20 N, 50 N]

2-13 The two blocks shown in figure-2.200 are initially at rest. Assuming ideal pulleys and strings and neglecting friction at all the surfaces, find the accelerations of the two blocks and the tension in the cable. (Take $g = 9.8$ m/s²)

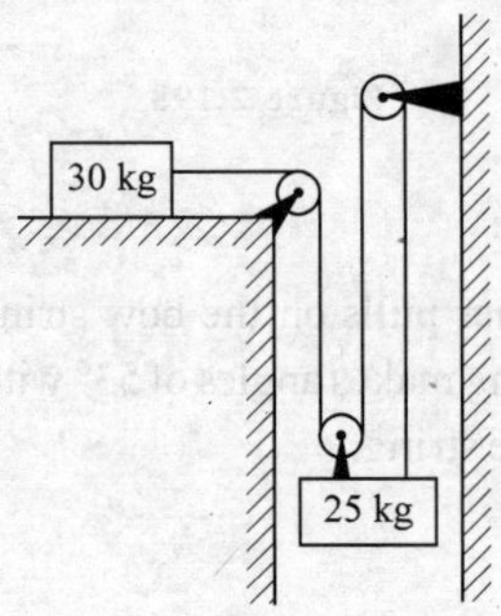

Figure 2.200

Ans. [2.49 m/s², 0.831 m/s², 74.8 N]

2-14 In the figure-2.201 shown the bigger block A has a mass of 40 kg and the upper block B is of 8 kg. The coefficients of friction between all surfaces of contact are 0.2 (static) and 0.15 (sliding). Find the acceleration of masses when set free.

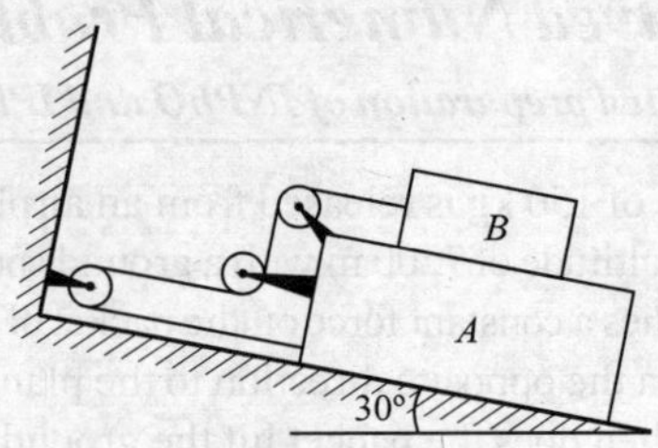

Figure 2.201

Ans. [1.6 m/s²]

2-15 Figure-2.202 shows a two block constrained motion system. Block A has a mass M and B has a mass m. If block A is pulled toward right horizontally with an external force F, find the acceleration of the block B relative to ground.

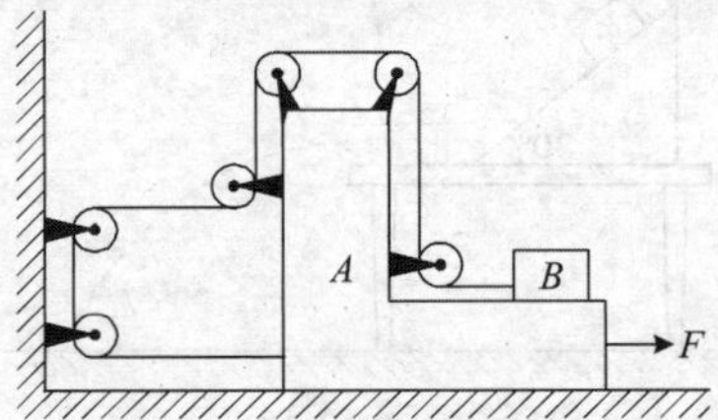

Figure 2.202

Ans. $\left[\left[a = \frac{f}{M+m}\right]\right]$

2-16 Solve the previous problem if the blocks A and B are of different shapes as shown in figure-2.203.

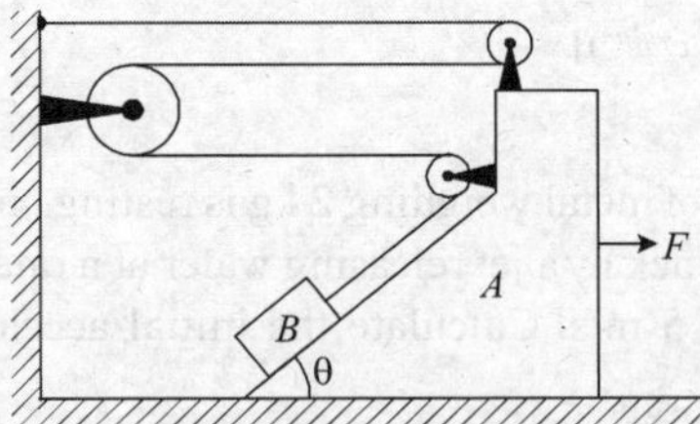

Figure 2.203

Ans. $\left[\left(\frac{F - 3mg\sin\theta}{M + 10m}\right)\sqrt{(10 - 6\cos\theta)}\right]$

2-17 At the moment $t = 0$, the force $F = kt$ is applied to a small body of mass m resting on smooth horizontal plane. The permanent direction of this force forms an angle θ with the horizontal. Find :

(i) The velocity of the body at the moment of its breaking off the plane;

(ii) The distance traversed by the body up to this moment.

Ans. $\left[\frac{mg^2}{2k}, \frac{\cos\theta}{\sin^2\theta}, \frac{m^3g^3\cos\theta}{6k^2\sin^3\theta}\right]$

2-18 A chain of length l is placed on a smooth spherical surface of radius R with one of its ends fixed at the top of the sphere. What will be the acceleration a of each element of the chain when its upper end is released ? It is assumed that the length of the chain $l < \pi R/2$.

Ans. $\left[\frac{Rg}{l}(1-\cos\frac{l}{R})\right]$

2-19 If masses of the blocks A and B shown in figure-2.204(a) and 2.204(b) are 10 kg and 5 kg respectively, find the acceleration of the two masses. Assume all pulleys and strings are ideal. (Take $g = 9.8$ m/s²)

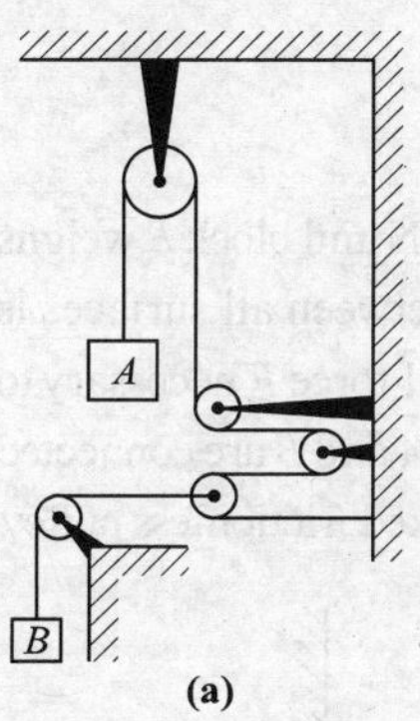

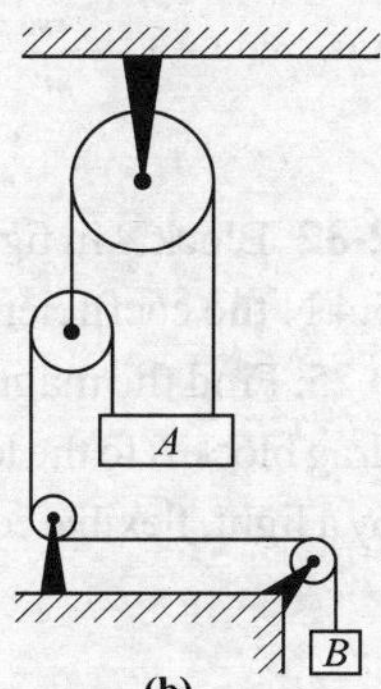

Figure 2.204

Ans. $\left[\left(\frac{20}{3}\right), \left(\frac{10}{3}\right) \text{m/s}^2, \frac{10}{11} \text{m/s}^2, \frac{30}{11} \text{m/s}^2\right]$

2-20 In the figure-2.205 shown in blocks A, B and C has masses $m_A = 5$ kg, $m_B = 5$ kg and $m_C = 10$ kg respectively, find the acceleration of the three blocks. Assume all pulleys and strings are ideal. (Take $g = 10$ m/s²)

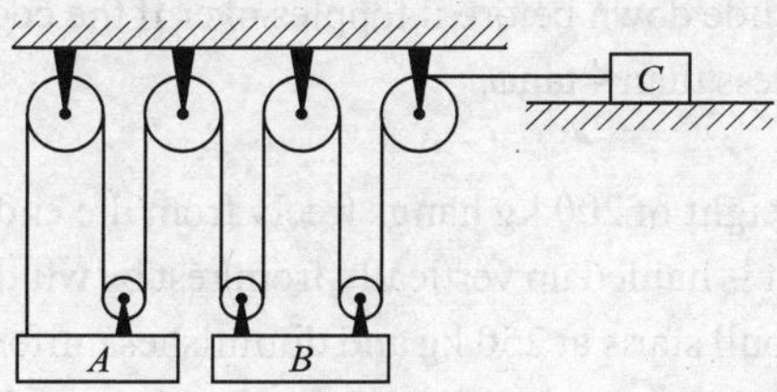

Figure 2.205

Ans. [$a_A = 1.76$ m/s² ↓ , $a_B = 0.98$ m/s² ↑ , $a_C = 1.4$ m/s² ←]

2-21 One end of a string is attached to a 6 kg mass on a smooth horizontal table. The string passes over the edge of the table and to its other end is attached a light smooth pulley. Over this pulley passes another string to the ends of which are attached masses of 4 kg and 2 kg respectively. Show that the 6 kg mass moves with an acceleration of $8g/17$.

2-22 Two blocks of masses m_1 and m_2 are kept touching each other on an inclined plane of inclination α with the horizontal. Show that (i) the force of interaction between the blocks is

$$\frac{(\mu_1 - \mu_2)m_1 m_2 g\cos\alpha}{(m_1 + m_2)}$$

and (ii) the minimum value of α at which the blocks just start sliding is

$$\alpha = \tan^{-1}\frac{\mu_1 m_1 + \mu_2 m_2}{m_1 + m_2}$$

Where μ_1 and μ_2 are the coefficients of friction between the block m_1 and the inclined plane and between the block m_2 and the inclined plane respectively.

2-23 Two blocks A and B of mass 1 kg and 2 kg respectively are connected by a string, passing over a light frictionless pulley. Both the blocks are resting on a horizontal floor and the pulley is held such that string remains just taut. At the moment $t = 0$, a force $F = 20t$ N starts acting on the pulley along vertically upward direction as shown in figure-2.206. Calculate

(a) Velocities of A when B loses contact with the floor.

(b) Height raised by the pulley upto that instant.

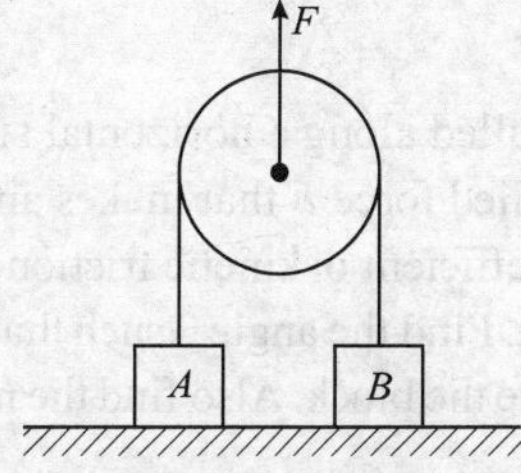

Figure 2.206

Ans. [5 m/s, 5/6 m]

2-24 A worker wishes to pile a cone of sand onto a circular area in his yard. The radius of the circle is r, and no sand is to spill onto the surrounding area. If μ is the static coefficient of friction between each layer of sand along the slope and the sand, show that the greatest volume of sand that can be stored in this manner is $\frac{1}{3}\pi\mu R^3$.

2-25 A 30 kg mass is initially at rest on the floor of a truck. The coefficient of static friction between the mass and the truck floor is 0.3 and the coefficient of kinetic friction is 0.2. Before each acceleration given below, the truck is travelling due east at constant speed. Find the magnitude and direction of the friction force acting on the mass (a) when the truck accelerates at 1.8 m/s² eastward, (b) when it accelerates at 3.8 m/s² westward. Take $g = 10$ m/s²

Ans. [54 N, 59 N]

2-26 At the moment $t = 0$ a stationary particle of mass m experiences a time-dependent force $F = kt(t' - t)$, where k is a constant vector, t' is the time during which the given force acts. Find :

(a) The momentum of the particle when the action of the force discontinued;

(b) The distance covered by particle while the force acted.

Ans. $[kt^3/6,\ dt = \frac{kt^4}{12m}]$

2-27 A disc is kept on a smooth horizontal plane with its plane parallel to horizontal plane. A groove is made in the disc as shown in the figure-2.207. The coefficient of friction between a mass m inside the groove and the surface of the groove is 2/5 and $\sin\theta = 3/5$. Find the acceleration of mass with respect to the frame of reference of the disc.

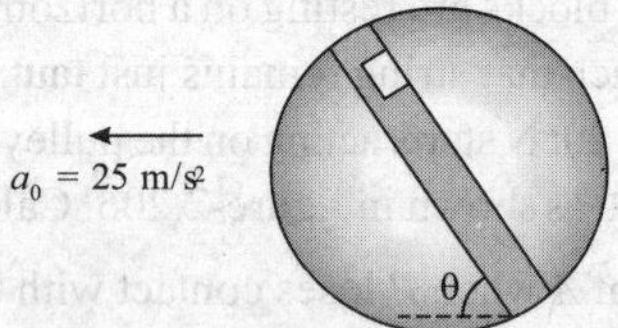

Figure 2.207

Ans. [10 m/s²]

2-28 A crate is pulled along a horizontal surface at constant velocity by an applied force F that makes an angle θ with the horizontal. The coefficient of kinetic friction between the crate and the surface is μ. Find the angle θ such that the applied force is minimum to slide the block. Also find the minimum value of this force.

Ans. $[\tan^{-1}\mu,\ \frac{mmg}{\sqrt{1+m^2}}]$

2-29 A uniform rod is made to lean between a rough vertical wall and the ground. Show that the least angle at which the rod can be leaned without slipping is given by

$$\alpha = \tan^{-1}\left(\frac{1-\mu_1\mu_2}{2\mu_2}\right)$$

where μ_1 and μ_2 stand for the coefficient of friction between (a) the rod and the wall, and (ii) the rod and the ground.

2-30 A small body was launched up an inclined plane set at an angle α against the horizontal. Find the coefficient of friction, if the time of the ascent of the body is η times less than the time of its descent.

Ans. $[k = \frac{(\eta^2-1)}{(\eta^2+1)}\tan\alpha]$

2-31 A motor-boat of mass m moves along a lake with velocity v_0. At the moment $t = 0$ the engine of the boat is shut down. Assuming the resistance of the particle to be proportional to the velocity of the boat $F = -rv$, find :

(a) How long the motorboat moved with the shutdown engine;

(b) The velocity of the motorboat as a function of the distance covered with the shutdown engine, as well as total distance covered till the complete stop.

(c) The mean velocity of the motorboat over the time interval (beginning with the moment $t = 0$), during which its velocity decreases η times.

Ans. $[\infty,\ v = v_0 - \frac{rs}{m'},\ \frac{mv_0}{r'},\ \frac{v_0(\eta-1)}{\ln(\eta)}]$

2-32 Block A in figure-2.208 weights 2.7 N and block B weighs 5.4 N the coefficient of kinetic friction between all surfaces is 0.25. Find the magnitude of the horizontal force F necessary to drag block B to the left at constant speed if A and B are connected by a light, flexible cord passing around a fixed frictionless pulley.

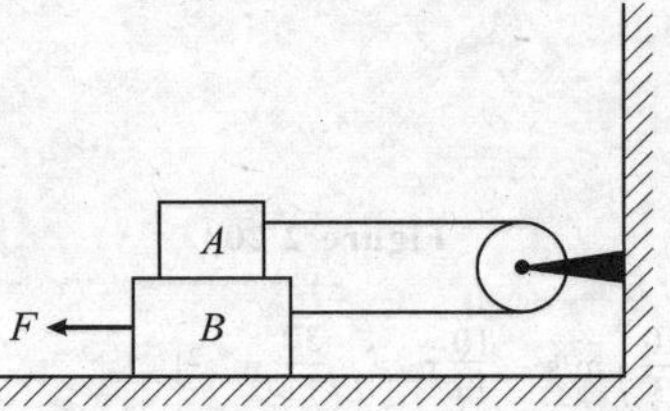

Figure 2.208

Ans. [3.38 N]

2-33 A uniform cone of half angle φ stands on a rough inclined plane. Show that as the inclination of the plane is increased the cone will slide down before it topples over if the coefficient of friction is less than $4\tan\varphi$.

2-34 A weight of 200 kg hangs freely from the end of a rope. The weight is hauled up vertically from rest by winding up the rope. The pull starts at 250 kg and diminishes uniformly at the rate of one kg per metre wound up. Find the velocity after 30 metres have been wound up. Neglect the weight of the rope.

Ans. $[\sqrt{10.5g}$ m/s]

2-35 Block A with weight $2w$, slides down an inclined plane S of slope angle 37° at a constant speed while the plank B, with weight w, rests on top of block A as shown in figure-2.209. The plank is attached by a cord to the top of the plane. If the coefficient of friction is the same between blocks A and B and between S and block A, determine its value.

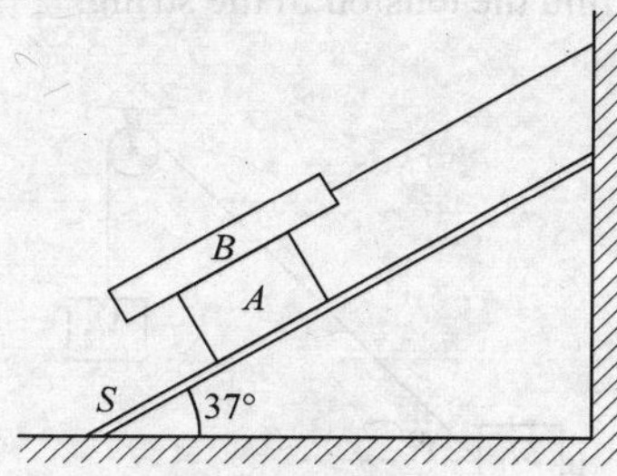

Figure 2.209

Ans. [0.375]

2-36 A small disc A is placed on an inclined plane forming an angle α with the horizontal and is imparted an initial velocity v_0. Find how the velocity of the disc depends on the angle θ, shown in figure-2.210, if the friction coefficient $\mu = \tan\alpha$ and at the initial moment $\theta = \pi/2$.

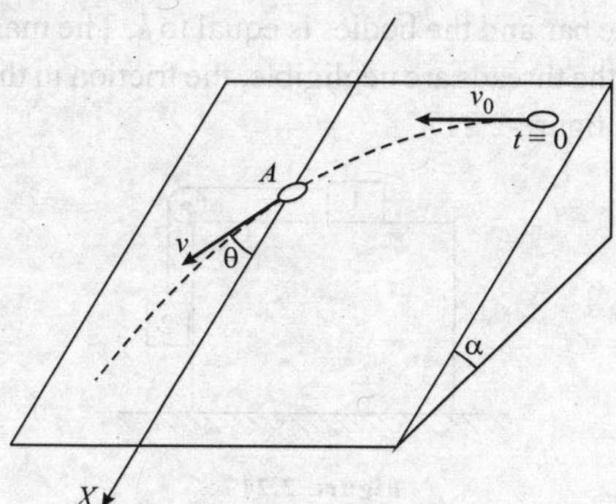

Figure 2.210

Ans. [$v = \frac{v_0}{1+\cos\varphi}$]

2-37 A horizontal plane with the coefficient of friction μ supports two bodies, a block A of mass 2 m and an electric motor with a battery fixed on another block B, all together having the mass m. A thread attached to the block A is wound on the shaft of the electric motor. The distance between the block and the electric motor is L. When the motor is switched on, the block A starts moving with constant acceleration a. How soon will the bodies collide ?

Ans. [$t = \sqrt{\frac{2L}{3a+\mu g}}$]

2-38 A fixed pulley carries a weightless thread with masses m_1 and m_2 at its ends. There is friction between the thread and the pulley. It is such that the thread starts slipping when the ratio $m_2/m_1 = \eta_0$ find :

(a) The friction coefficient

(b) The acceleration of the mass when $m_2/m_1 = \eta > \eta_0$.

Ans. [$\mu = \ln\left(\frac{\eta_0}{\pi}\right)$, $a = \frac{\eta - \eta_0}{\eta + \eta_0} g$]

2-39 A body with zero initial velocity slips from the top of an inclined plane forming an angle α with the horizontal. The coefficient of friction μ between the body and the plane increases with the distance s from the top according to the law $\mu = bs$. After what distance the body will stop.

Ans. [$\frac{2\tan\alpha}{b}$]

2-40 A thin rod of length 1 m is fixed in a vertical position inside a train, which is moving horizontally with constant acceleration 4 m/s^2. A bead can slide on the rod, and friction coefficient between them is 1/2. If the bead is released from rest at the top of the rod, find the time when it will reach at the bottom. ($g = 10$ m/s^2)

Ans. [$\frac{1}{2}$ s]

2-41 A boy of mass M stands on a platform of mass m as shown in figure-2.211, supporting two strings via a massless support S. Strings are passing over the pulleys and other ends are connected to the platform as shown. Find the acceleration of the platform and the boy if he applies a constant force T to the string he is holding, which is connected to support S.

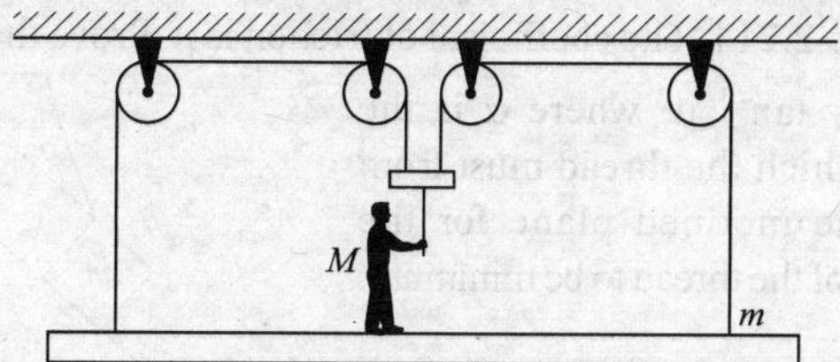

Figure 2.211

Ans. [$\frac{2T-(M+m)g}{M+m}$]

2-42 If the two blocks moves with a constant uniform speed then find coefficient of friction between the surface of the block B and the table. The spring is massless and the pulley is frictionless.

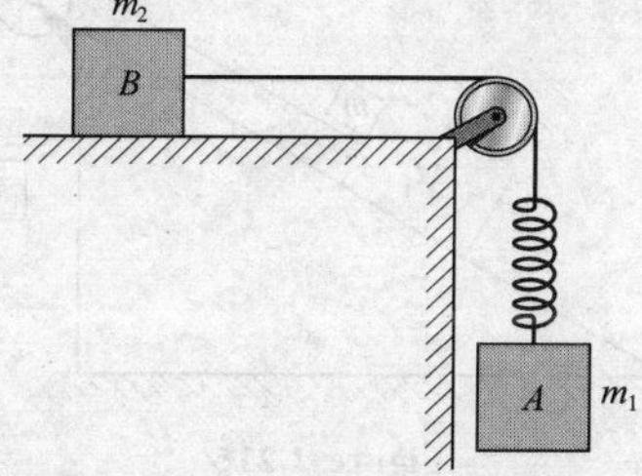

Figure 2.212

Ans. [$\frac{m_1}{m_2}$]

2-43 Block M slides down on frictionless incline as shown. The minimum friction coefficient so that m does not slide with respect to M would be $x/4$. What is the value of x.

Ans. [3]

2-44 A 12 kg monkey climbs a light rope. The rope passes over a pulley and is attached to a 16 kg bunch of bananas resting on floor. Mass and friction in the pulley are negligible so that the pulley's only effect is to reverse the direction of the rope. What is the maximum acceleration the monkey can have without lifting the bananas ? (Take $g = 10\ m/s^2$)

Ans. [10/3 m/s²]

2-45 In the figure shown-2.213 coefficient of static friction between blocks is 0.1 while floor is smooth. Find the minimum value of force F required to cause slipping between blocks. Angle of string is 53° with horizontal.

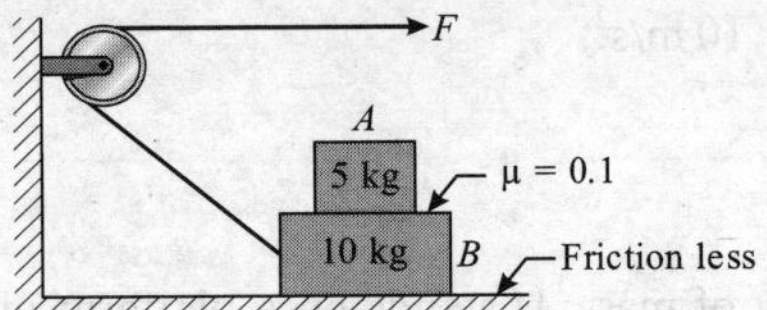

Figure 2.213

Ans. [25 N]

2-46 A bar of mass m is pulled by means of a thread up an inclined plane forming an angle θ with the horizontal as shown in figure-2.214. The coefficient of friction is μ. Prove that

(a) $\alpha = \tan^{-1}\mu$, where α is the angle which the thread must from with the inclined plane for the tension of the thread to be minimum.

(b) $T_{min} = \dfrac{mg\sin\theta + \mu mg\cos\theta}{\sqrt{1+\mu^2}}$

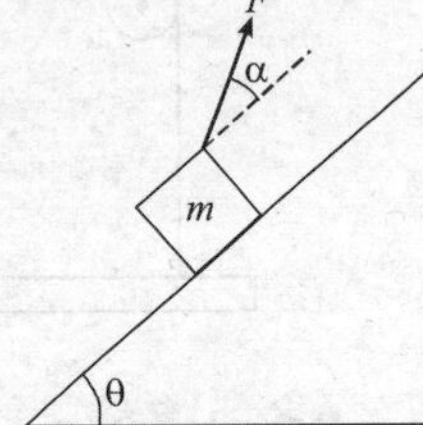

Figure 2.214

2-47 Find the mass M in the situation shown in figure-2.215 such that m remains at rest on the front surface of M_1. The coefficient of friction between the front surface of M_1 and that of m is μ.

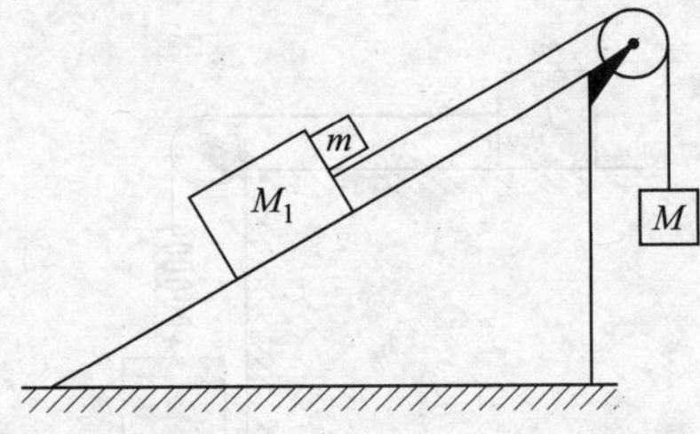

Figure 2.215

Ans. $\left[\dfrac{(m+M_1)\cos\theta}{(\mu\cos\theta + \mu\sin\theta)}\right]$

2-48 A block of mass m_1 rests on a rough horizontal plane with which its coefficient of friction is μ. A light string attached to this block passes over a light frictionless pulley and carries another block of mass m_2 as shown in figure-2.216. When the system is just about to move, find the value of μ in terms of m_1, m_2 and θ. Also find the tension in the string.

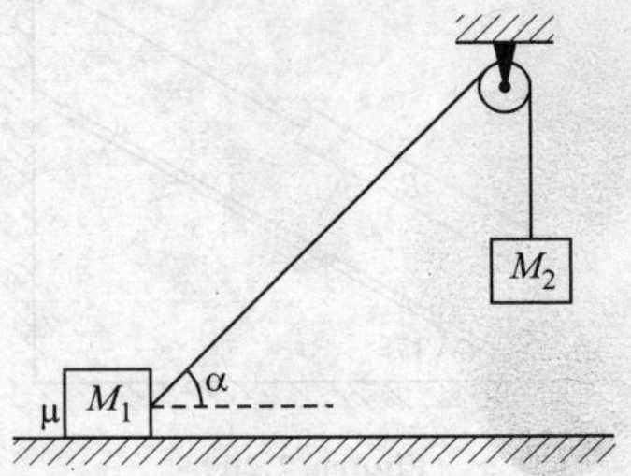

Figure 2.216

Ans. $\left[\dfrac{m_2\cos\alpha}{m_1 - m_2\sin\alpha}\right]$

2-49 With what minimum acceleration the bar A should be shifted horizontal to keep bodies 1 and 2 stationary relative to the bar ? The masses of the bodies are equal, and the coefficient of friction between the bar and the bodies is equal to k. The masses of the pulley and the threads are negligible, the friction in the pulley is absent. See figure-2.217.

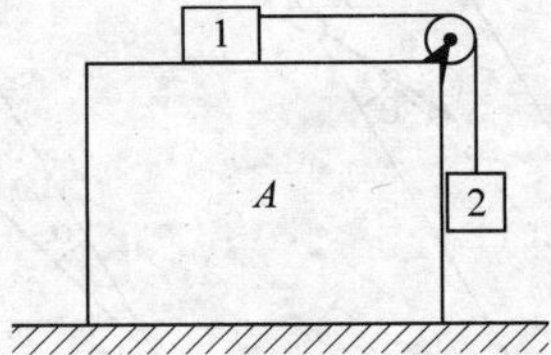

Figure 2.217

Ans. $\left[\dfrac{g(1-k)}{1+k}\right]$

2-50 Find out the value(s) of θ of the inclined plane such that the mass m remains at rest on the wedge of mass M_2 as shown in figure-2.218. Friction between the small block and the wedge plane is μ and all other surface are smooth.

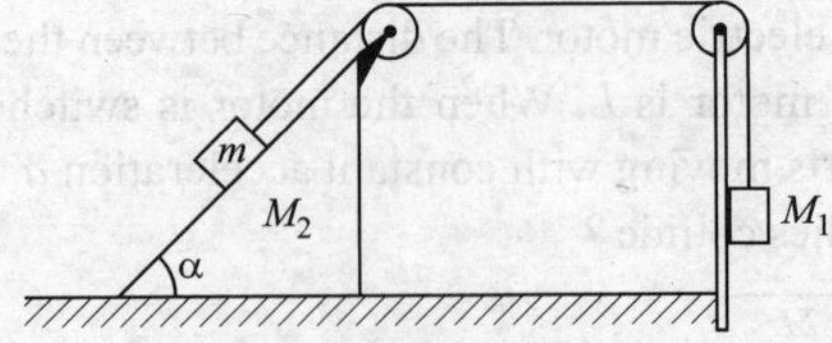

Figure 2.218

Ans. [$\sin\alpha_{max} = \dfrac{\sqrt{4p^2q^2 - 4(p^2+q^2)(r^2-p^2)} - 2qr}{2(p^2+q^2)}$,

where $p = m(g - \mu a)$, $q = m(a + \mu g)$, $r = M_1(a - g)$ and $a = \dfrac{M_1 g}{M_1 + M_2 + m}$

$\sin\alpha_{min} = \dfrac{\sqrt{4l^2k^2 - 4(l^2+k^2)(n^2-l^2)} - 2kn}{2(l^2+k^2)}$,

where $l = m(a - \mu g)$, $k = m(g + \mu a)$, $n = M_1(a - g)$ and $a = \dfrac{M_1 g}{M_1 + M_2 + m}$]

2-51 In the figure-2.219, the masses A and B are of 4 kg and 12 kg respectively. When the system is released from rest, find the time after which the block B will hit the ground.

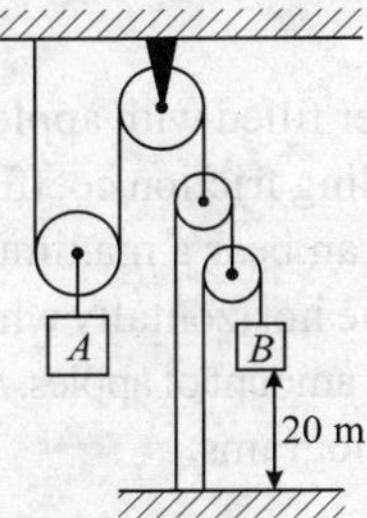

Figure 2.219

Ans. [2.05 sec]

2-52 In the figure 2.220 all the surfaces are frictionless. What force F is required to be applied on the bigger block so that m_2 and m_3 will remain at rest on it.

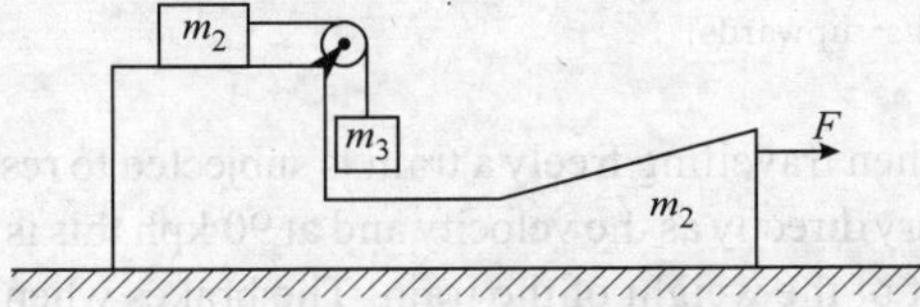

Figure 2.220

Ans. [$\frac{m_3(m_1+m_2+m_3)g}{m_2}$]

2-53 Mass of block B shown in figure-2.221 is m and that of cart C is M. Show that the maximum value of force F such that the block does not slip over the surface of C, has a magnitude

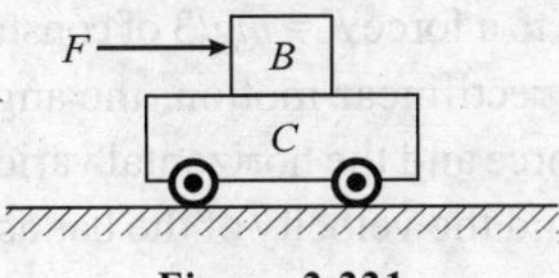

Figure 2.221

$$F_{\max} = \mu mg\left(1+\frac{m}{M}\right)$$

2-54 If a car is moving rightward with acceleration $a = g\sqrt{k}$ m/s rightward as shown in the figure-2.222. Find the value of k so that, rod maintains its orientation as shown in the figure. Neglect the friction and mass of the small rollers at A and B.

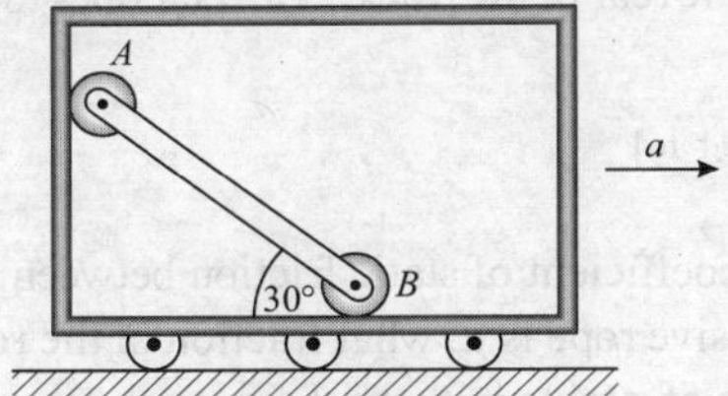

Figure 2.222

Ans. [3 m/s²]

2-55 A meter stick is hung from two spring balances A and B of equal lengths that are located at the 20 cm and 70 cm marks of the meter stick. Weights of 2.0 N are placed at the 10 cm and 40 cm marks, while a weight of 1.0 N is placed at the 90 cm mark. The weight of the uniform meter stick is 1.5 N. Determine the scale readings of the two balances A and B.

Ans. [3.8 N, 2.7 N]

2-56 A ladder is hanging from ceiling as shown in figure-2.223. Three men of masses 10 kg, 12 kg and 8 kg are climbing in such a way that man A is going down with an acceleration of 1.6 m/s² and C is rising up with an acceleration of 0.9 m/s² and man B is going up with a constant speed of 0.6 m/s. Find the tension in the string supporting the ladder.

Ans. [291.2 N]

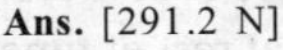

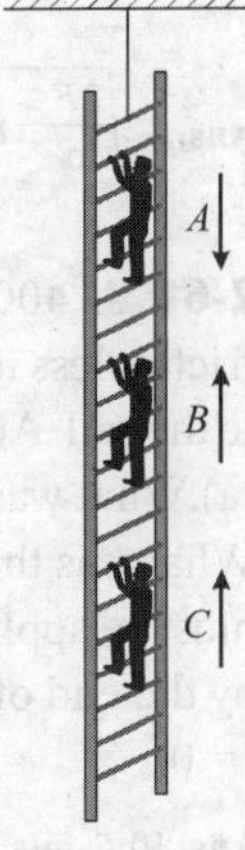

Figure 2.223

2-57 In the figure shown-2.224, a block B of mass 10 kg rests on a bracket A (shaded) of 30 kg. All the surfaces are smooth. Find the magnitude of relative acceleration (in m/s²) of bracket A (shaded) with respect to block B. (Pulley and string are ideal)

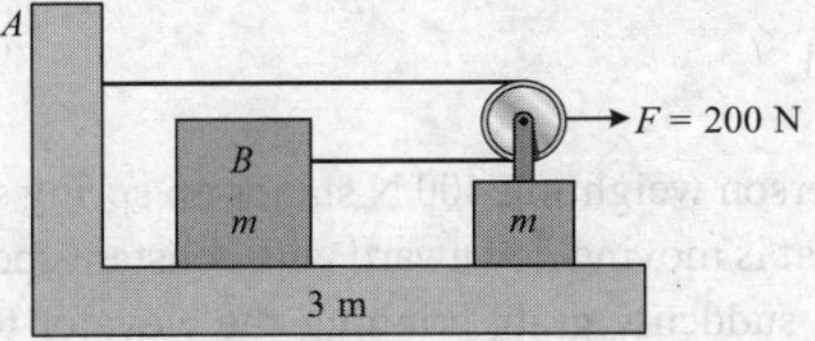

Figure 2.224

Ans. [5 m/s²]

2-58 The force which keeps a hot air balloon is the buoyant force F. Suppose a hot air balloon of mass M has a downward acceleration of magnitude a. Find the ballast mass that must be dropped from it to cause the balloon to accelerate upward with same magnitude a.

Ans. [$\frac{2Ma}{g+a}$]

2-59 A 20 kg bucket is lowered by a rope with constant velocity of 0.5 m/s. What is the tension in the rope ? A 20 kg bucket is lowered with a constant downward acceleration of 1 m/s². What is the tension in the rope ? A 10 kg bucket is raised with a constant upward acceleration with same magnitude a.

Ans. [200 N, 180 N, 220 N]

2-60 A heavy chain with a mass per unit length ρ is pulled by the constant force F along a horizontal surface consisting of a smooth section and a rough section. The chain is initially at rest on the rough surface with $x = 0$ as shown in figure-2.225. If the coefficient of kinetic friction between the chain and the rough surface is μ_k, determine the velocity v of the chain when $x = L$.

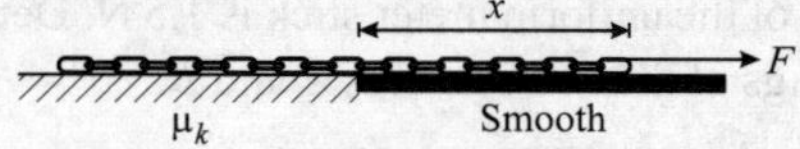

Figure 2.225

Ans. $[\sqrt{\frac{2F}{\rho} - \mu_k gL}]$

2-61 A 400 kg ice boat moves on runners on essentially frictionless ice. A steady wind blows, applying a constant force to the sail. At the end of 8.0 sec run, the acceleration is 0.5 m/s^2. (a) What was the acceleration at the beginning of the run ? (b) What was the force due to the wind ? (c) What retarding force must be applied at the end of 4.0 sec to bring the ice boat to rest by the end of the next 4 sec ? (assume boat was at rest at time $t = 0$)

Ans. [0.5 m/s^2, 200 N, 400 N]

2-62 A box is placed in the middle of the bed of a flatbed truck and is not strapped down. The coefficient μ between the bed and the box is 0.75. If the truck is travelling at a speed of 22 m/s along a horizontal street, what is the minimum stopping distance such that the box will not slide ?

Ans. [33 m]

2-63 A person weighting 400 N stands on spring scales in an elevator that is moving downward with constant speed of 4 m/s the brakes suddenly grab, bringing the elevator to a stop in 1.8 s. Describe the scale readings from just before the brakes grab until after the elevator is at rest.

Ans. [400 N, 488.89 N, 400 N]

2-64 Determine the expression for the acceleration of block A and B as shown in figure-2.226. Assume that the surface of body A are small and have well lubricated bearings. Also find the force, the pulley exerts on the clamp ?

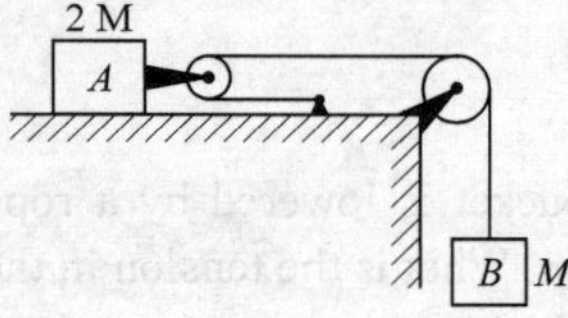

Figure 2.226

Ans. [g/3, 2g/3 $\sqrt{2}$Mg/3]

2-65 The upper portion of an inclined plane of inclination α is smooth and the lower portion is rough. A particle slides down from rest from the top and just comes to rest at the foot. If the ratio of the smooth length to rough length is $m : n$, find the coefficient of friction.

Ans. $[\frac{m+n}{n}]$

2-66 A light container filled with apples is to be dragged on a rough floor where sliding friction coefficient is 0.35. The rope used for the purpose can bear a maximum of 1100 N tension. Find the angle with the horizontally which one has to pull the rope to carry maximum amount of apples. Also find this maximum amount of apples in kilograms.

Ans. [(a) 19.3°, (b) 3329.5 N]

2-67 A simple Atwood machine composed of a single pulley and two masses m_1 and m_2 is on an elevator. When $m_1 = 44.7$ kg and $m_2 = 45.3$ kg, it takes 5.0 sec for mass m_2 to descend exactly one meter from rest relative to the elevator. What is the elevator's motion ?

Ans. [2 m/s^2 upwards]

2-68 When travelling freely a train is subjected to resistances which vary directly as the velocity and at 90 kph this is equal to 1 percent of the weight of the train. The brakes when applied create a further resistance equal to 1/16th of the weight of the train. If the brakes are suddenly applied when the velocity is 90 kph find the time and distance travelled before the train comes to rest.

Ans. [37.92 sec, 467 m]

2-69 A bar of mass m resting on a smooth horizontal plane starts moving due to a force $F = mg/3$ of constant magnitude. In the process of its rectilinear motion, the angle θ between the direction of this force and the horizontal varies as $\theta = ks$, where k is a constant. Find the velocity of the bar as a function of the angle θ.

Ans. $[\sqrt{\frac{2g}{3k}\sin\theta}]$

2-70 A 20 kg box rests on the flat floor of a truck. The coefficients of friction between box and floor are $\mu_s = 0.15$ and $\mu_k = 0.10$. The truck stops at a stop sign and then starts to move with an acceleration of 2 m/s^2. If the box is 2.2 m from the rear of the truck when the truck starts, how much time elapses before the box falls off the rear of the truck ? How far does the truck travel in this time.

Ans. [2.1 s, 4.4 m]

2-71 If the coefficient of static friction between a table and a uniform massive rope is μ, what fraction of the rope can hang over the edge of a table without the rope sliding.

Ans. $[\frac{\mu}{1+\mu}]$

2-72 Two small balls of the same size and of mass m_1 and m_2 ($m_1 > m_2$) are tied by a thin weightless thread and dropped from a balloon. Determine the tension T of the thread during the flight after the motion of the balls attained steady-state.

Ans. $[\frac{1}{2}(m_1 - m_2)g]$

2-73 A block of mass m is projected on a larger block of mass 10 m and length l with a velocity v as shown in figure-2.227. The coefficient of friction between the two blocks is μ_2 while that between the lower block and the ground is μ_1. Given that $\mu_2 > \mu_1$.

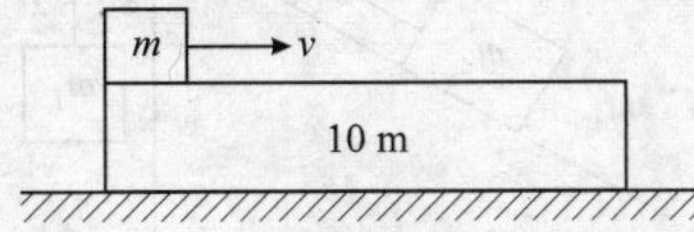

Figure 2.227

(a) Find the minimum value of v such that the mass m falls off the block of mass 10 m.

(b) If v has this minimum value, find the time taken by block m to do so.

Ans. [(a) $v_{min} = \sqrt{\frac{22(\mu_2 - \mu_1)g}{10}}$ (b) $t = \sqrt{\frac{20l}{11g(\mu_2 - \mu_1)}}$]

2-74 A block with mass m_1 is placed on an inclined plane with slope angle α and is connected to a second hanging block that has mass m_2 by a cord passing over a small, frictionless pulley as shown in figure-2.228. The coefficient of static friction is μ_s, and the coefficient of kinetic friction is μ_k. (a) Find the mass m_2 for which block m_1 moves up the plane at constant speed once it has been set in motion. (b) Find the mass m_2 for which block m_1 moves down the plane at constant speed once it has been set in motion. (c) For what range of values of m_2 will the blocks remain at rest if they are released from rest ?

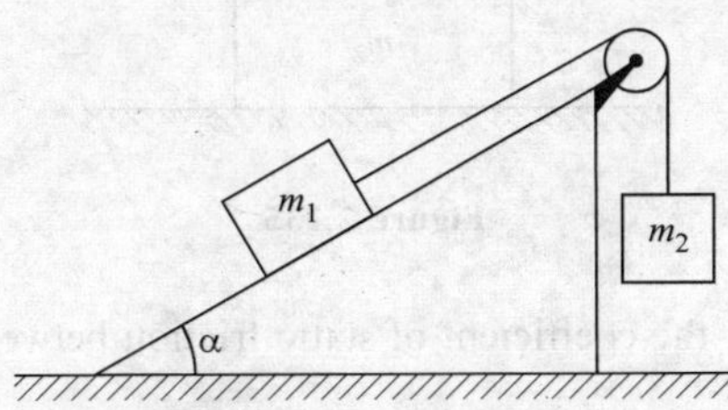

Figure 2.228

Ans. $[m_1 \sin\theta + \mu_k m_1 \cos\theta,\ m_1 \sin\theta - \mu_k m_1 \cos\theta]$

2-75 (a) Block A in figure-2.229 weighs 90 N. The coefficient of static friction between the block and the surface on which it rests is 0.3. The weight w is 15 N, and the system is in equilibrium. Find the friction force exerted on block A. (b) Find the maximum weight w for which the system will remain in equilibrium.

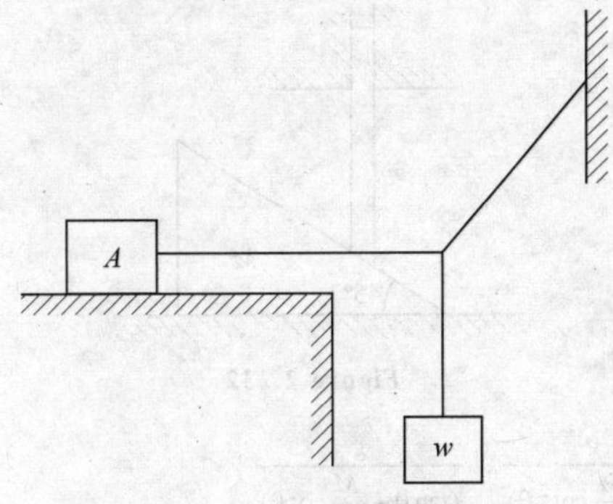

Figure 2.229

Ans. [8.66 N, 46.76 N]

2-76 A uniform rod of length L rests against a smooth roller as shown in figure-2.230. Find the friction coefficient between the ground and the lower end if the minimum angle that the rod can make with the horizontal is θ.

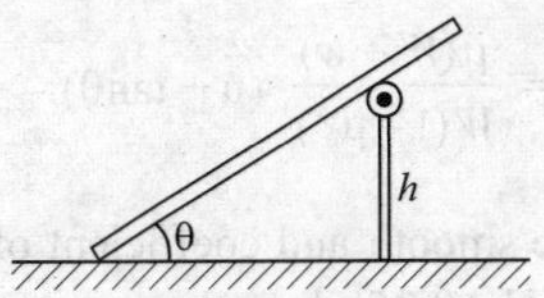

Figure 2.230

Ans. $[\frac{L\cos\theta\sin^2\theta}{2h - L\cos^2\theta\sin\theta}]$

2-77 Block A of mass m and block B of mass 2 m are placed on a fixed triangular wedge by means of a massless, inextensible string and a frictionless pulley as shown in figure-2.231. The wedge is inclined at 45° to the horizontal on both sides. The coefficient of friction between block A and wedge is 2/3 and that between the block B and the wedge is 1/3. If the system of A and B is released from rest, find (a) the acceleration of A, (b) tension in string, (c) the magnitude and direction of the force of friction acting on A.

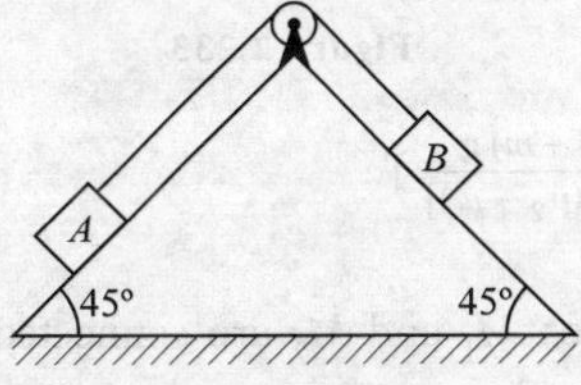

Figure 2.231

Ans. $[0,\ 2\frac{\sqrt{2}}{3}\text{mg},\ \frac{mg}{3\sqrt{2}}$ downward]

2-78 Find the acceleration of the prism of mass M and that of the bar of mass m shown in figure-2.232.

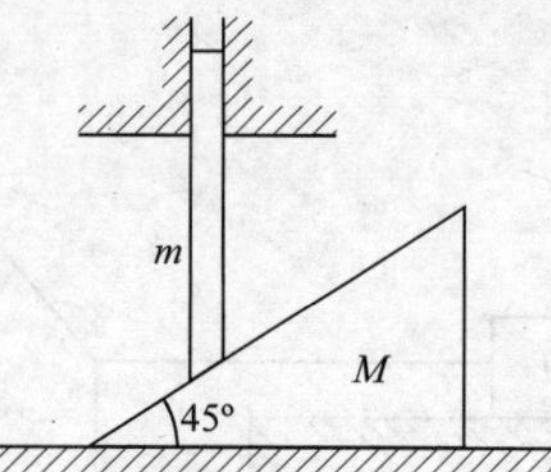

Figure 2.232

Ans. $\left[\dfrac{g}{(1+\frac{M}{m}\cot^2\theta)}, \dfrac{g}{(\tan\theta+\frac{M}{m}\cot\theta)}\right]$

2-79 (i) A uniform ladder of length L and weight w rests against a vertical wall and makes an angle θ with the horizontal ground. If the coefficient of friction at the point of contact of the ladder with the wall and ground is μ, show that the greatest height x, measured along the ladder from the foot to which a man of weight W may climb without the ladder slipping, is given by

$$\frac{x}{L}=\frac{\mu(W+w)}{W(1+\mu^2)}(\mu+\tan\theta)-\frac{w}{2W}$$

(ii) If the wall be smooth and coefficient of friction between ladder and ground be 0.25, show that

$$x=\frac{L}{4}\left(1-\frac{w}{W}\right)\tan\theta-\frac{wL}{2W}$$

2-80 Consider the situation shown in figure-2.233. Find the acceleration of the system and the tension in the strings.

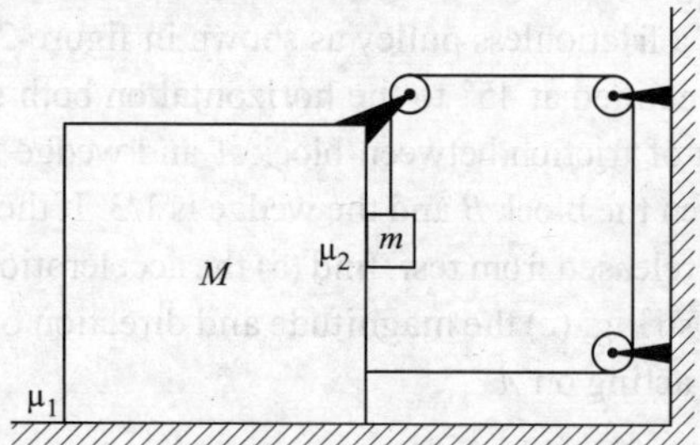

Figure 2.233

Ans. $\left[\dfrac{2m-\mu_1(M+m)g}{M+m[5+1(\mu_2-\mu_1)]}\right]$

2-81 Two masses M_1 and M_2 are connected by light string, which passes over the top of a smooth plane inclined at 30° to the horizontal, so that one mass rests on the plane and the other hangs vertically as shown in figure-2.234. It is found that M_1, hanging vertically can draw M_2 up the full length of the plane in half the time in which M_2 hanging vertically draws M_1 up. Find M_1/M_2. Assume pulley to be smooth. Initially at time $t = 0$ smooth masses $M_1 = 15$ kg and $M_2 = 10$ kg are held at rest and then they released. If after one second, the string snaps, find the further time taken for the 15 kg mass to return to its original position on the plane. Take $g = 10$ m/s²

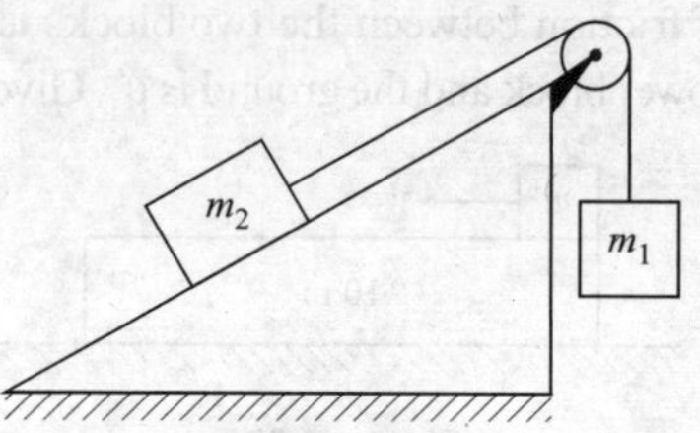

Figure 2.234

Ans. [3/2, 0.69 sec]

2-82 Two blocks, of mass m_1 and m_2, are placed as shown in figure-2.235 and placed on a frictionless horizontal surface. There is friction between the two blocks. An external force of magnitude F is applied to the top block at an angle α below the horizontal.

(a) If the two blocks move together, find their acceleration.

(b) Show that the two blocks will move together only if

$$F<\frac{\mu_s m_1(m_1+m_2)g}{m_2\cos\alpha-\mu_s(m_1+m_2)\sin\alpha}$$

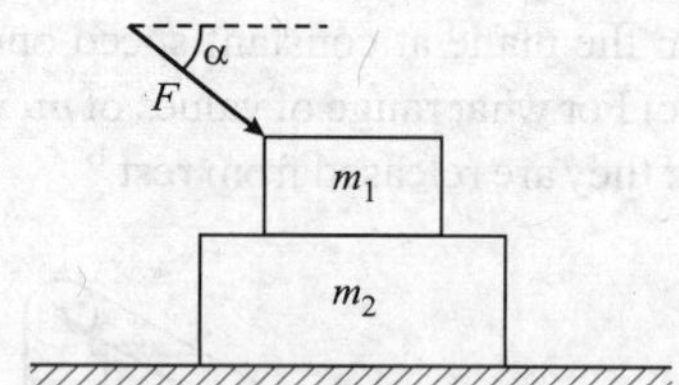

Figure 2.235

Where μ_s is the coefficient of static friction between the two blocks.

Ans. $\left[\dfrac{F\cos\alpha}{m_1+m_2}\right]$

* * * * *

3

Work, Energy and Power

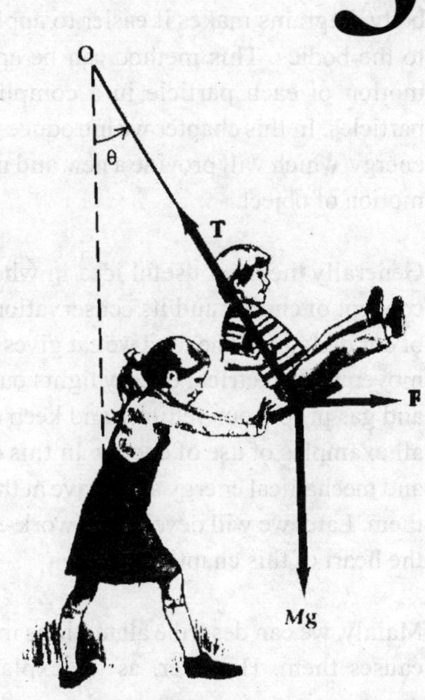

FEW WORDS FOR STUDENTS

In this chapter we introduce several important concepts in relation to work, energy and power. Most important is the section on conservation of mechanical energy, in other chapters we will describe also how the concepts we read here are applied to other forms of energy. The law of energy conservation is one of the most powerful tools available for analyzing physical situations. Further we'll see that those difficult problems, which, when solved using other methods become simpler using work and energy methods.

CHAPTER CONTENTS

COVER APPLICATION

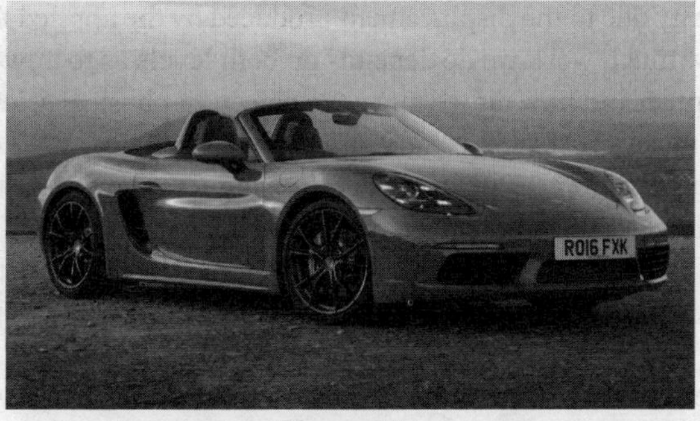

Figure-(a)

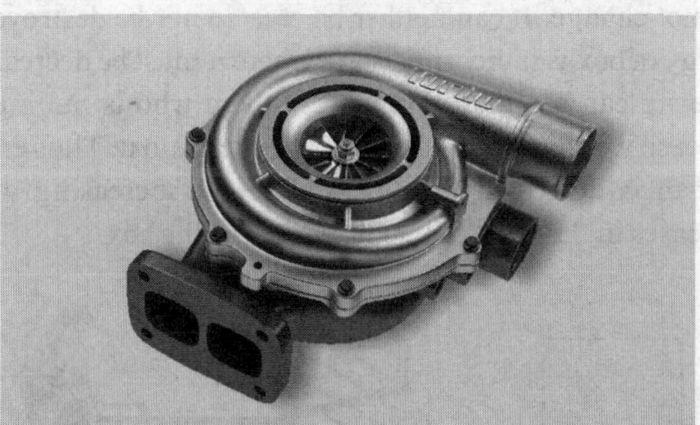

Figure-(b)

Figure-(a) shows Porsche Doppelkupplung (PDK) 718 Boxster which accelerates from 0 to 100 kph in just 4.9 seconds ! This happens because of its specific turbo charger which makes it among top rated and fastest cars in the world. Figure-(b) shows the turbo charger which gets additional compressed air from the turbocharger in the engine to produce more power and enhanced efficiency. Apart from turbo charger rest of the engine in the car is normal internal combustion engine.

In the previous chapters we have developed a straight forward method for finding the motion of a particle. Newton's second law connects the net force to the acceleration. Use of free body diagrams makes it easier to apply Newton's second law to the bodies. This method can be applied to determine the motion of each particle in a complicated system of many particles. In this chapter we introduce the concept of work and energy, which will provide a new and useful perspective on the motion of object.

Generally the most useful idea in whole of the science is the concept of energy and its conservation. Energy is a vital part of our daily life. The food we eat gives energy to our bodies for movement, electrical energy lights our homes and streets, oil and gas propel our vehicles and keep us in motion. These are all examples of use of energy. In this chapter we define work and mechanical energy and arrive at the relationships between them. Later we will develop the work-energy theorem which is the heart of this chapter.

Mainly, we can describe all motions in terms of the forces that causes them. However, as we explain in this chapter, the conservation of energy greatly simplifies the description of motion in many instances. The principle of conservation of energy is a universal concept that is important not only in mechanics but also in other branches of physics. In order to understand the concept we first discuss the concept of work and the basic relation between force, work, and energy.

3.1 Work

Have a look at figure-3.1. A man pulls a box placed on a rough floor. If man pulls the box with a force F, according to Newton's third law, the box will also pull man in opposite direction with the same force F. Friction between floor and the surface of box opposes the motion of box in forward direction. If F exceeds limiting friction, the box starts sliding. If it slides, its kinetic energy increases. As we know that the total energy of a system can not change. It can neither be created nor be destroyed. If energy of box is increasing, somewhere it must be decreasing. Here we can see that only man is there who is pulling the object so we can say that he is giving energy to it. Thus energy of man is decreasing and that of box is increasing which increases in the form of kinetic energy of the box.

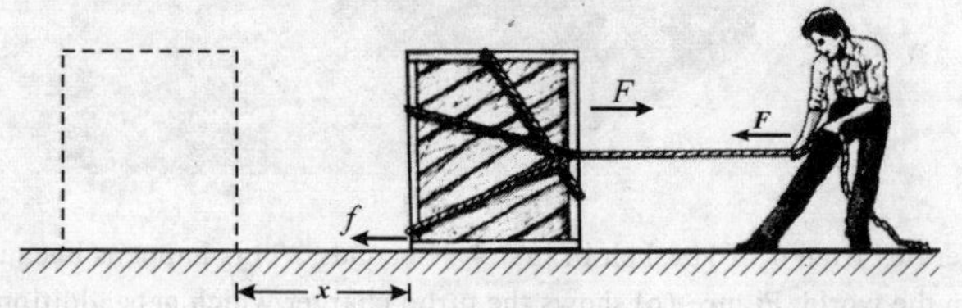

Figure 3.1

If F does not exceed limiting friction, no sliding occurs, hence no transfer of energy takes place. Here the cause of energy transfer is the displacement of box. If displacement takes place, energy is transferred and if no displacement there is no transfer of energy. This transfer of energy is known as "*Work*" and work is said to be done if and only when the applied force produces some displacement.

Whenever a force is applied to an object, it is ready to do work but work will be done only if it displaces the object. In work always at least two bodies are involved, one who is doing work (whose energy is decreasing) and the other on which work is being done (whose energy is increasing).

Consider the situation shown in figure-3.2(a). If a man punches a hard wall, the energy he wishes to transfer to wall (to do work on wall), is reflected back to his hand and he will be injured as no displacement takes place on wall, hence no work is done and obviously no energy is used by the wall. If the man makes his punch strong enough to break the wall as shown in figure-3.2(b), his hand will not be injured, the reason is the utilization of his energy by the wall (work done in breaking). As the wall breaks, displacement is produced by the force of his punch, hence energy is transferred to the wall and negligible amount of energy is reflected.

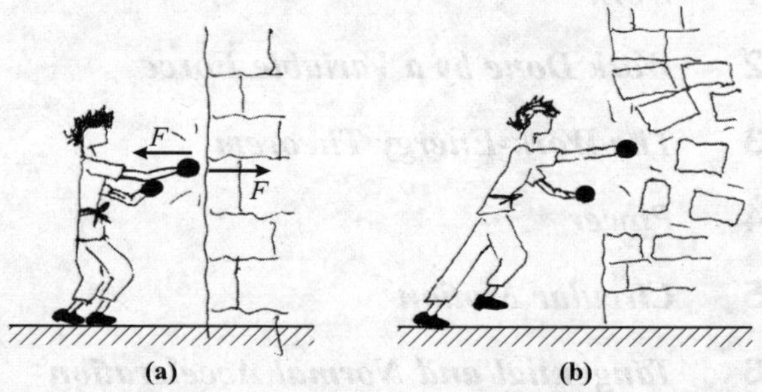

Figure 3.2

The concept of work is now clear that it is just the transfer of energy due to the displacement produced by the applied force. How much work we do depends on both levels as to how hard we push and how far we move the object. In physical sciences, the meaning of work is more precise and restricted. If we exert a constant force F on an object, causing it to move a distance parallel to F, then the work W done by the force is defined to be the product of the magnitude of the force times the distance through which it acts as the object is moved.

There are two important conditions in our definition of work. First, the force must be exerted on the object through a distance. In other words the force must move the object. Second, for work to be done the force must have a component parallel to the direction of motion. If an applied force is not along the direction of motion, we can resolve it into components parallel to and perpendicular to the displacement (figure-3.3). Only the component of force that is parallel to the displacement contributes the work. Thus, if the force F makes an angle θ with the line of motion, displaces the body by a distance x, as shown in figure, the component of force that contributes the work is $F_x = F\cos\theta$. Mathematically the work done is

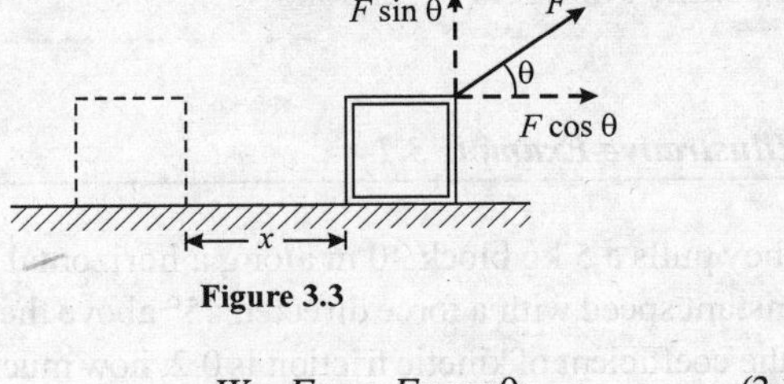

Figure 3.3

$$W = F_x x = Fx\cos\theta \qquad \ldots(3.1)$$

3.1.1 Positive and Negative Work

From equation-(3.1) we can say directly that work can be either positive or negative depending on θ, whether acute or obtuse. This can be understood theoretically with an example. Consider a boy riding a bicycle, another boy standing infront of his track tries to stop it and after some skidding he is able to stop it. The boy standing applies a force in a direction opposite to the direction of motion of bicycle due to which bicycle retards and stops. Here if we analyze the situation in mathematical form, we say force applied by the standing boy is opposite to the direction of displacement of point of application of force hence work done by standing boy is negative and the force applied by the bicycle on standing boy (due to Newton's Third Law) is in the same direction as that of displacement of point of application of force thus work done by bicycle is positive. The same situation can be discussed on the basis of energy. As bicycle is being retarded thus its kinetic energy is decreasing hence it is doing work (positive) and as the boy (which was standing) is gaining energy from bicycle, we say it is the one on which work is being done (negative work).

In all type of interactions (pair of forces) if point of application of forces is displaced, always both positive work (energy supply) and negative work (energy absorption) takes place simultaneously. The force direction which is same as that of the displacement will supply energy and its (one who is applying this force) energy decreases and the other agent or object who is applying the other force of the pair will gain energy. In this analysis the energy which decreases (in someone who is doing the work) and energy increases (in someone on which work is being done) can be in any form. It may be possible that the one who is doing work will be loosing its chemical energy and the one on which work is being done will be gaining energy in kinetic or potential or in any other form.

3.2 Work Done by a Variable Force

If the force exerted on a moving object is constant we can calculate the work by the simple application of the equation-(3.1). If the force changes after a given displacement and again changes after some further displacement, but remaining constant for that displacement, the total work can be taken as the sum of products of force and the respective displacements in each part independently.

If force is having a continuous variation with displacement as $F = f(x)$, then we find the elemental work dW which is done when force produces an elemental displacement dx, it is given as

$$dW = F \,.\, dx \qquad \ldots(3.2)$$

If total displacement is s then total work can be given by integration of the above elemental work for a displacement dx

$$W = \int dW = \int_0^s F \,.\, dx \qquad \ldots(3.3)$$

An important example of this idea is a spring that obeys Hooke's law. We know that the more force we apply to a spring the more it stretches. If force constant of a spring is k which exerts a restoring force kx where x is the stretch or compression in the spring.

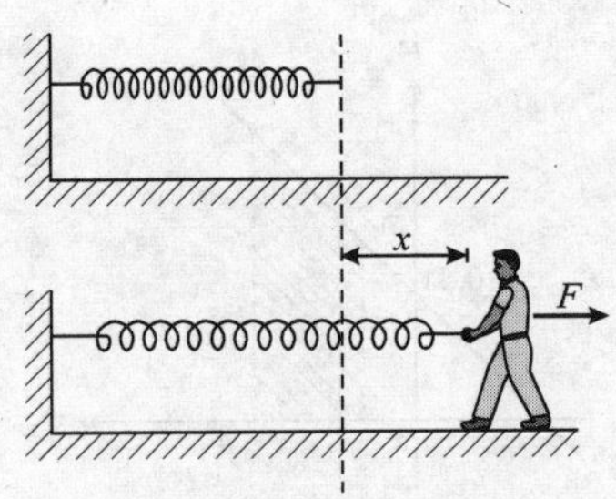

Figure 3.4

Consider the situation shown in figure-3.4. If the man stretches the spring from its equilibrium length to a new position at a displacement x. The force man has to exert, in order to balance the restoring force, is the same kx. In this process the work done by the man is

$$W = \int_0^x kx \,.\, dx$$

$$W = \frac{1}{2} kx^2 \qquad \ldots(3.4)$$

This work is done by the man on the spring so energy of man is reduced by this amount and it goes into the spring. This energy is stored in the form of elastic potential energy of the spring. When the spring is set free it shoots towards its mean position, the elastic energy is now released due to its displacement back to the initial position.

The above example shows that whenever a spring is stretched or compressed, it stores $\frac{1}{2}kx^2$ energy in it, which is released, when it moves towards the equilibrium position and during its motion towards equilibrium position we can say that now spring is doing work.

3.2.1 Graphical Analysis of Work Done by a Force

Work done by a force is given by the numerical product of force and displacement. This we can also obtain by graphical method.

In previous chapters, we've used graphical approach to find displacement from *v-t* graph, which was given by the area under the velocity-time curve as it is given by the product of the two. Similarly if force acting on a body is given as a function of displacement, the work done by the force is given by the area under force-displacement graph. For example if we consider a variable force $F = (3x + 5)$N acting on a body and if it is displaced from $x = 2$ m to $x = 4$ m. The work done can be given by the shaded area shown in figure-3.5.

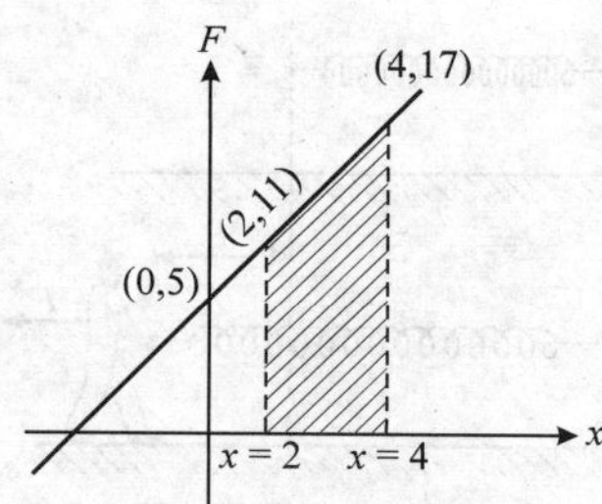

Figure 3.5

Thus we have work done by this force is

$$W = \text{area of shaded trapezium}$$

$$= \frac{1}{2} \times 2 \times (11 + 17) = 28 \text{ joule}$$

If we find the same using integration, we have

$$W = \int_2^4 (3x+5)\, dx = \left(\frac{3x^2}{2} + 5x\right)_2^4 = 28 \text{ joule}$$

Now we take few examples about understanding the concept of work and how it is evaluated.

> Web Reference of Video Lectures at www.physicsgalaxy.com
> **Age Group -** High School Physics | Age 17-19 Years
> **Section -** MECHANICS
> **Topic -** Work, Energy and Power
> **Module Numbers -** 1, 2, 3 and 4

 # Illustrative Example 3.1

A boy pulls a 5 kg block 20 m along a horizontal surface at a constant speed with a force directed 45° above the horizontal. If the coefficient of kinetic friction is 0.2, how much work does the boy do on the block ?

Solution

The forces acting on the block are shown in figure-3.6

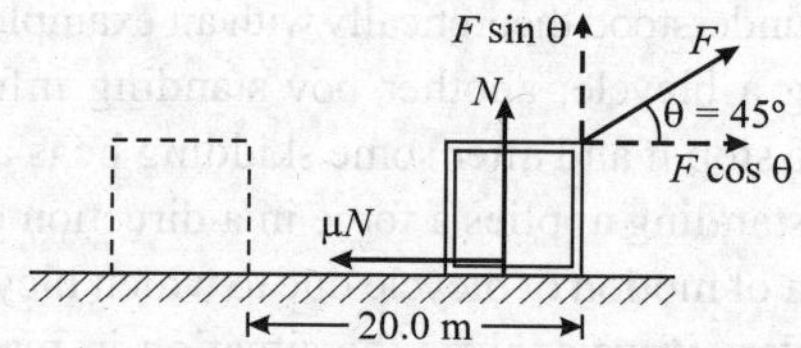

Figure 3.6

As the block moves with uniform velocity, we have

$$N + F\sin 45^\circ = mg$$

and $$F\cos 45^\circ = \mu N$$

From above equations we get

$$F = \frac{\mu mg}{\cos 45^\circ + \mu \sin 45^\circ} = 11.55 \text{N}$$

The block is pulled through a horizontal distance 20.0 m. Thus the work done is

$$W = F\cos 45^\circ \times 20.0$$

or $$= (11.55 \times 0.707) \times 20.0 = 163.32 \text{ Joule}$$

 # Illustrative Example 3.2

A body is thrown on a rough surface such that friction force acting on it is linearly varying with distance travelled by it as $f = ax + b$. Find the work done by the friction on the box if before coming to rest the box travels a distance *s*.

Solution

As the force is acting in the direction opposite to the box motion, work done by this force must be negative. As force is not constant, we use

$$W = \int_0^s f.dx$$

or $$= \int_0^s (ax + b).dx$$

or $$= \left(\frac{ax^2}{2} + bx\right)_0^s$$

$$= \frac{1}{2}as^2 + bs$$

Illustrative Example 3.3

A force varying with distance is given as $F = ae^{-bx}$ acts on a particle of mass m moving in a straight line. Find the work done on the particle in its displacement from origin to a distance d.

Solution

As the applied force varies with displacement, its work is given as $W = \int_0^d F.dx$

or here $$W = \int_0^d ae^{-bx}\, dx$$

$$= -\frac{a}{b}\left[e^{-bx}\right]_0^d = \frac{a}{b}(1 - e^{-bd})$$

Illustrative Example 3.4

A 2kg body is displaced on a rough plane with friction coefficient $\mu = 0.5$ with a variable force $F = (4x^2 + 15)$ N. Find the kinetic energy of the block after the block has travelled a distance 5 m.

Solution

As displacement of the body is in the direction of force that implies work done by the force is positive and as friction is always in the direction opposite to displacement, its work is always negative and it will always absorb energy from the body (in form of heat). Thus total work done on the body is

$$W = \int_0^5 (4x^2 + 15)\, dx - 0.5 \times 2 \times 9.8 \times 5$$

$$= 241.66 - 49 = 192.66 \text{ joule}$$

As we have discussed that the total amount of work done on an object is its net increase in energy, here it is only the kinetic energy of the block.

Illustrative Example 3.5

A body of 4 kg mass placed on a smooth horizontal surface experiences a force varying with displacement of block as shown in figure-3.7. Find the speed of the body when force ceases to act on it.

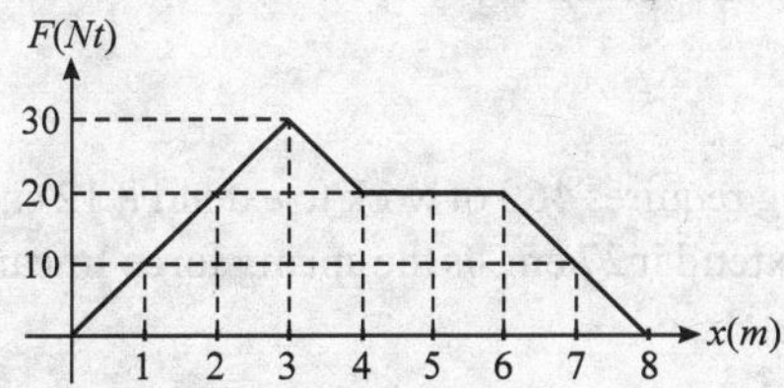

Figure 3.7

Solution

As we know work done is given by the area under *F-x* curve, we have from figure-3.7

$$W = \frac{1}{2} \times 3 \times 30 + \frac{1}{2} \times 1 \times 50 + 20 \times 2 + \frac{1}{2} \times 2 \times 20 = 130 \text{ joule}$$

Which is the gain in kinetic energy of the block as

$$\frac{1}{2}mv^2 = 130$$

or $$v = \sqrt{65} \text{ m/s}$$

Web Reference of Video Lectures at www.physicsgalaxy.com

Age Group - High School Physics | Age 17-19 Years
Section - MECHANICS
Topic - Work, Energy and Power
Module Numbers - 1, 2, 3 and 4

Practice Exercise 3.1

(i) A factory worker pushes a 25.0 kg crate downward at an angle of 30° below the horizontal a distance of 6.0 m along a level floor. (a) What magnitude of force must the worker apply to move the crate at constant velocity, if the coefficient of kinetic friction between the crate and floor is 0.3 ? (b) How much work is done on the crate by this force when the crate is pushed a distance of 6.0 m ? (c) How much work is done on the crate by friction during this displacement ? (d) How much work is done by the normal force and by gravity ? (e) What is the total work done on the crate ? Take $g = 10\ \text{m/s}^2$.

[(a) 104.74 N; (b) 544.27 J; (c) – 544.27 J, (d) 0,0; (e) 0]

(ii) Find the work a boy of weight 55 kg has to do against gravity when climbing from the bottom to the top of a 3.0 m high tree.

[1650 J]

(iii) A force of 20.0 N is required to hold a spring stretched by 5.0 cm from its equilibrium position. How much work was done in stretching the spring ?

[0.5J]

(iv) A spring requires 46 J of work to extend it 12 cm and 270 J of work to extend it 27 cm. Is the spring force linearly varying with the stretch.

[No]

(v) A force is given by $F = kx^2$, where x is in meters and $k = 10\ \text{N/m}^2$. What is the work done by this force when it acts from $x = 0$ to $x = 0.1$ m ?

[3.33×10^{-3} J]

3.3 The Work-Energy Theorem

In previous sections we've discussed about work as transfer of energy and here in this section we develop a theorem that relates the work to kinetic energy i.e. the energy of motion. This work-energy theorem provides a powerful method that connects a particle's speed with its position, no matter how complicated is the motion.

To understand this, first we consider the special case of an object moving along a straight line, say along x-axis. (figure-3.8).

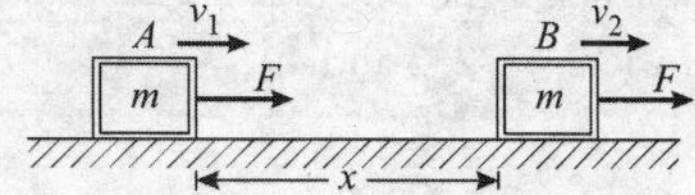

Figure 3.8

At position A the kinetic energy of the object is $\frac{1}{2}mv_1^2$. A constant force F acts on it in its direction of motion produces an acceleration F/m, which increases its velocity. Let us consider after a displacement x its velocity becomes v_2 or its kinetic energy becomes $\frac{1}{2}mv_2^2$. Its energy is increased. It is due to the work done by the external force F on the object, which we write as

$$\frac{1}{2}mv_1^2 + Fx = \frac{1}{2}mv_2^2$$

If in above case force F acts in the direction opposite to the motion of the body, the energy of object decreases as work is done by the object in overcoming the opposition of the force F, so we write our equation as

$$\frac{1}{2}mv_1^2 - Fx = \frac{1}{2}mv_2^2$$

Thus, if force is acting in the direction of motion, it will do work on object and its energy increases. If it is acting in opposition to motion of object, obviously object will do work on it and its energy decreases. We can define a general statement about the work associated and the energy of an object as

Initial kinetic energy of the object + work done on it - work done by it = Final kinetic energy

The result is called the *work-energy theorem.* The second and third terms on left hand side of the work-energy theorem can be combinedly termed as the work done by the net force, or the net work. We can think of calculating this net work by adding all the forces acting on an object to get the net force and determining the work done by the net force. Equivalently, we can determine the work done by each force separately and add these individual contributions to get the net work.

We can also rearrange the above result as

Net work = Final kinetic energy - Initial kinetic energy of the object

The above statement shows the connection between work and kinetic energy as : *"The work done by the net force acting on an object is equal to the change in the kinetic energy of that object".*

The kinetic energy increases if the net force on the object does positive work, means object displacement is in the direction of force. The kinetic energy decreases if the net force does negative work i.e. object displacement is opposite to the direction of force applied. If the net work is zero, kinetic energy does not change.

Because the net work equals the change in kinetic energy, it is often convenient to think of the net work as the measure of the kinetic energy transferred to an object. For example, if you throw a ball, the net work done on the ball is positive and the ball gains kinetic energy. Your hand has given energy to the ball. If you catch a ball, the net work done on the ball is negative and ball loses kinetic energy. In this case ball has done work on your hand or your hand has taken energy from the ball.

If we know the speed of an object at each of two points in its motion, we can evaluate the work done by the net force by using the work energy theorem, stated above. These approaches will be illustrated by the following examples.

 # Illustrative Example 3.6

A trolley-car starts from rest at the top of a hill as shown in figure-3.9 and moves down the curved track. Determine its speed as it reaches the bottom. Assume that the work done by frictional forces is negligible.

Solution

As trolley-car moves along the curved track, the only force acting on it is the force of gravity in downward direction. Thus net work done on the trolley-car by the gravity force is force multiplied by the displacement of the trolley-car in the direction of force i.e. in downward direction which is the height of the hill. Total work done on the car is its gain in kinetic energy, if speed of car at the bottom of the hill is v.

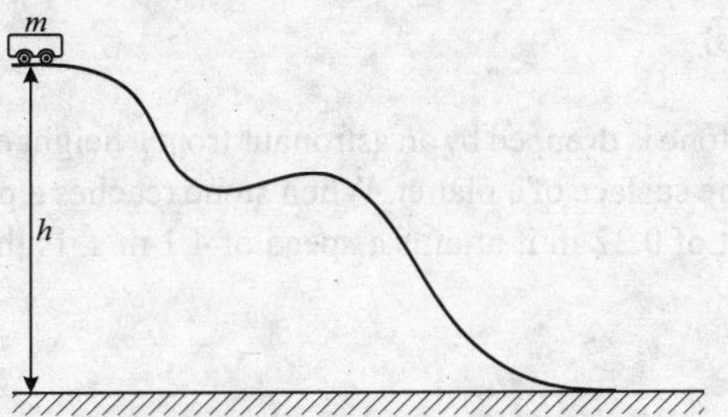

Figure 3.9

According to work-energy theorem we have

$$mg\,.\,h = \frac{1}{2}\,mv^2$$

or $$v = \sqrt{2gh}$$

 # Illustrative Example 3.7

Figure-3.10 shows a rough horizontal plane which ends in a vertical wall, to which a spring is connected, having a force constant k. Initially spring is in its relaxed state. A block of mass m starts with an initial velocity u towards the spring from a distance l_0 from the end of spring shown. When block strikes at the end of the spring, it compresses the spring and comes to rest. Find the maximum compression in the spring. The friction coefficient between the block and the floor is μ.

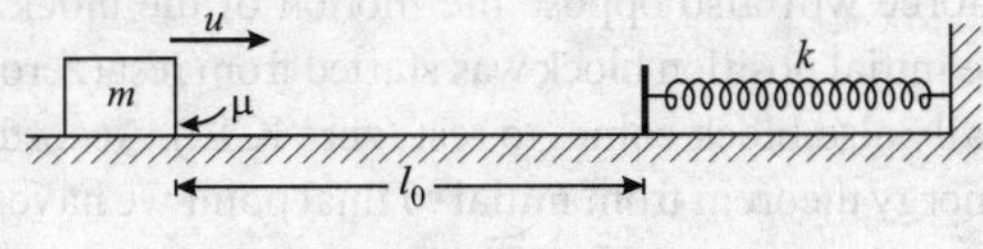

Figure 3.10

Solution

During motion of the block, friction is the only force opposing its motion before coming in contact with the spring. After starting the compression in spring, its force will also oppose the motion. Both of these forces are opposing the motion of the block thus reducing its kinetic energy. If x is the maximum compression in the spring before block comes to rest, then according to work-energy theorem we have

$$\frac{1}{2}\,mu^2 - \mu mg\,.\,(l_0 + x) - \frac{1}{2}\,kx^2 = 0$$

or $$kx^2 - 2\mu mgx + mu^2\ 2\mu mgl_0 = 0$$

or $$x = \frac{2\mu mg + [4\mu^2 m^2 g^2 - 4k(\mu^2 - 2\mu mgl)]^{1/2}}{2k}$$

[–ve sign discarded]

 # Illustrative Example 3.8

Figure-3.11 shows a rough incline at an angle θ with coefficient of friction μ. At the bottom a spring is attached with force constant k. A block of mass m is released from a position at a length l away from the spring. Write down the work-energy equations to find the maximum compression in the spring and the distance by which the block rebound up the inclined plane.

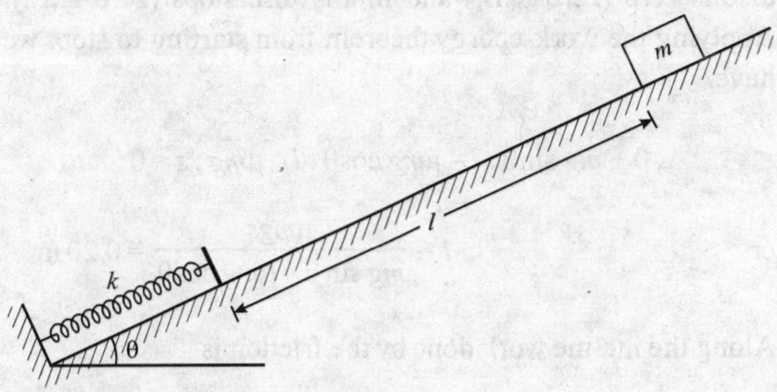

Figure 3.11

Solution

During the downward motion of the block, $mg \sin\theta$ acts on it downward along the incline and friction $\mu mg \cos\theta$ will act against the motion along the incline. Let the spring be compressed by a distance x, when block comes to rest the spring force will also oppose the motion of the block. Here from the initial position block was started from rest (zero K.E.) and finally also block comes to rest (zero K.E.). According to work-energy theorem from initial to final point we have

$$0 + mg \sin\theta \,.\, (l + x) - \mu mg \cos\theta \,.\, (l + x) - \frac{1}{2} kx^2 = 0 \quad \ldots (3.5)$$

If block rebounds a distance l' up the plane then during upward motion gravity and friction both will oppose the motion but spring force will push the block upwards hence it will give the energy to the block. Thus applying work-energy theorem from initial (compressed position) to the final position where it comes to rest, we have

$$0 + \frac{1}{2} kx^2 - mg \sin\theta \,.\, (l' + x) - \mu mg \cos\theta \,.\, (l' + x) = 0 \quad \ldots (3.6)$$

Above equations-(3.5) and (3.6) will give the maximum compression in the spring and the rebound length along the incline plane l'.

 # Illustrative Example 3.9

A disc of mass $m = 50$ gm slides with the zero initial velocity down an inclined plane set at an angle $\theta = 30°$ to the horizontal, having traversed the distance $s = 50$ cm along the horizontal plane, the disc stops. Find the work performed by the friction forces over the whole distance, assuming the friction coefficient $\mu = 0.15$ for both inclined and horizontal planes.

Solution

Let the disc slides a length l along the incline and travels 50 cm along the horizontal plane. Given that initial velocity of the disc is zero (zero K.E.) and finally disc stops (zero K.E.). Applying the work-energy theorem from starting to stop, we have.

$$0 + mg \sin\theta \,.\, l - \mu mg \cos\theta \,.\, l - \mu mg \,.\, s = 0$$

or
$$l = \frac{\mu mgs}{mg \sin\theta - \mu mg \cos\theta} = 0.20 \text{ m}$$

Along the incline work done by the friction is

$$W_{f1} = \mu mg \cos\theta \times l$$

or
$$= 0.15 \times 0.05 \times 10 \times 0.866 \times 0.2 \text{ J} = 0.013 \text{ J}$$

Along the horizontal plane work done by the friction is

$$W_{f_2} = \mu mg\, s$$

$$= 0.15 \times 0.05 \times 10 \times 0.5 = 0.037 \text{ J}$$

Net work done by the friction is negative of sum of W_{f_1} and, W_{f_2} as

$$W_f = 0.013 + 0.037 = 0.05 \text{ J}$$

Web Reference of Video Lectures at www.physicsgalaxy.com
Age Group - High School Physics | Age 17-19 Years
Section - MECHANICS
Topic - Work, Energy and Power
Module Numbers - 5 and 18

Practice Exercise 3.2

(i) A block shown in figure-3.12 slides on a semicircular frictionless track. If it starts from rest at position A, what is its speed at the point marked B ? Take $g = 10$ m/s^2.

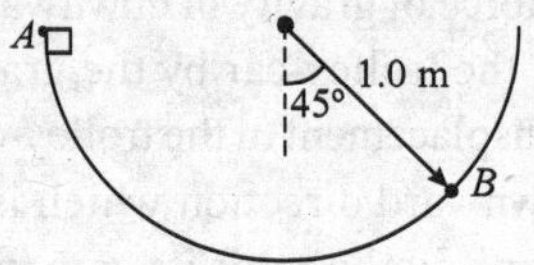

Figure 3.12

[3.76 m/s]

(ii) A stone is dropped by an astronaut from a height of 1.47 m above the surface of a planet. When stone reaches a point P at a height of 0.32 m it attains a speed of 4.1 m/s. Is the planet earth ?

[No]

(iii) A brick is placed on a vertical compressed massless spring of force constant 350 N/m attached to the ground. When the spring is released the brick is propelled upward. If the brick mass is 1.8 kg and will reach a maximum height of 3.6 m above its initial position on the compressed spring, what distance must the spring be compressed initially ? Take $g = 10$ m/s^2.

[0.608 m]

(iv) In figure-3.13, a block slides along a track from one level to a higher level, by moving through an intermediate valley. The track is frictionless until the block reaches the higher level. There a frictional force stops the block in a distance d. The block's initial speed v_0 is 6 m/s, the height difference h is 1.1 m and the coefficient of kinetic friction μ is 0.6. Find d. Take $g = 10\ m/s^2$.

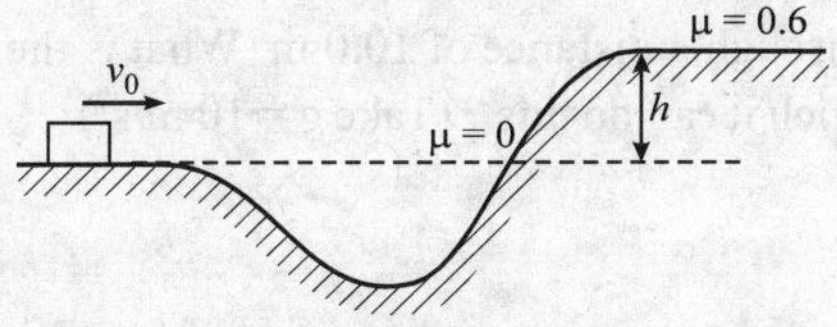

Figure 3.13

[1.167 m]

(v) A small particle slides along a track with elevated ends and a flat central part, as shown in figure-3.14. The flat part has a length 3 m. The curved portions of the track are frictionless, but for the flat part the coefficient of kinetic friction is $\mu = 0.2$. The particle is released at point A, which is at a height $h = 1.5$ m above the flat part of the track. Where does the particle finally come to rest ? Take $g = 10\ m/s^2$.

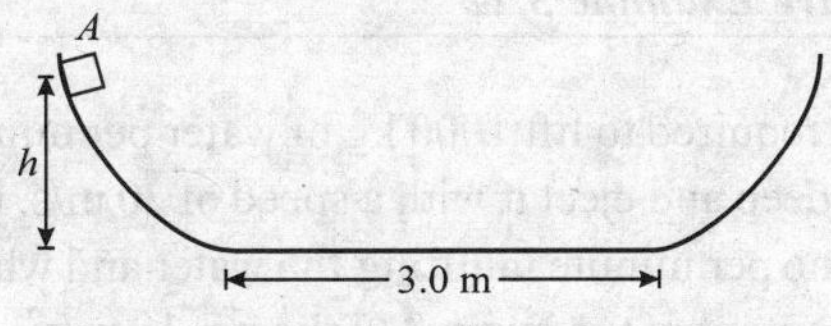

Figure 3.14

[Mid point]

Web Reference of Video Lectures at www.physicsgalaxy.com
Age Group - High School Physics | Age 17-19 Years
Section - MECHANICS
Topic - Work, Energy and Power
Module Numbers - 5 and 18

3.4 Power

When we purchase a car or jeep we are interested in the horsepower of its engine. We know that usually *an engine with large horsepower is most effective in accelerating the automobile*. Now we'll discuss the meaning of power in detail.

In many cases it is useful to know not just the total amount of work being done, but how fast the work is done. For example, if you have a machine that can provide only a certain amount of work in a day and you wish to accomplish double of that much work, then you will have to either spend two days for the job or get an additional machine. We define power as the rate at which work is being done. Its defining equation is

$$\text{Power} = \frac{\text{work done}}{\text{time taken to do work}}$$

or
$$P = \frac{\Delta W}{\Delta t} \qquad \ldots(3.7)$$

Where ΔW is the amount of work done in the time interval Δt. When work is measured in joules and t is in seconds, the unit for power is the joule per second, which is called watt. For motors and engines, power is usually measured in horsepower, where horsepower is

$$1 hp = 746\ W$$

The definition of power in equation-(3.7) applies to all types of work, whether mechanical, electrical, thermal or any other. However we can rewrite the definition in a special way for mechanical work by simply rearranging terms. When a force acts on an object so that it moves with a speed v, we can calculate the power from the force and speed. If we consider the force to be constant the work is $\Delta W = F\Delta x$, we have

$$P = \frac{F\Delta x}{\Delta t}$$

$$P = Fv \qquad \ldots(3.8)$$

The above relation is valid when we are finding average power. For overall work it can also be written as the total work on an object is equal to total change in its kinetic energy. Thus average power can be defined as

$$\text{Average Power} = \frac{\text{work done}}{\text{time taken to do work}}$$

$$= \frac{\text{Total change in kinetic energy}}{\text{Total time}}$$

If force and velocity or any of these is not a constant during motion, the rate of doing work will change with time. In such situations we define another term i.e. Instantaneous Power, power at an instant. Which is equal to rate of doing work in the very short neighborhood of an instant, given as

$$P = \frac{dW}{dt}$$

or
$$P = \frac{dK}{dt} \qquad \ldots(3.9)$$

Where dK is the change in kinetic energy of the body in time dt. If a force $\vec{F}$ is acting on the object during its motion, the elemental work done by it in the small duration dt is given as $dW = \vec{F} \cdot \overrightarrow{dx}$. Thus instantaneous power at this instant is given as

$$P = \frac{dW}{dt} = \frac{\vec{F} \cdot \overrightarrow{dx}}{dt}$$

$$P = \vec{F} \cdot \vec{v} \qquad \ldots(3.10)$$

Where v is the instantaneous velocity of the particle and dot product is used as only that component of force will contribute to power which is acting in the direction of instantaneous velocity.

Illustrative Example 3.10

A body of mass m is thrown at an angle θ to the horizontal with the initial velocity u. Find the mean power developed by gravity over the whole time of motion of the body, and the instantaneous power of gravity as a function of time.

Solution

The situation is shown in figure-3.13. Mean power of gravity over the whole time of motion can be given as

$$\text{Mean Power} = \frac{\text{Net gain in kinetic energy}}{\text{Total time of motion}}$$

As we know that in projectile motion on horizontal plane, particle strikes the ground with the same speed with which it was projected, kinetic energy of particle does not change hence from initial point to final point there is no gain in kinetic energy.

$$\text{Mean Power} = 0$$

Now we find the instantaneous power of gravity at an instant $t = t$ when particle has velocity v shown in figure-3.15. This velocity is vectorially given as

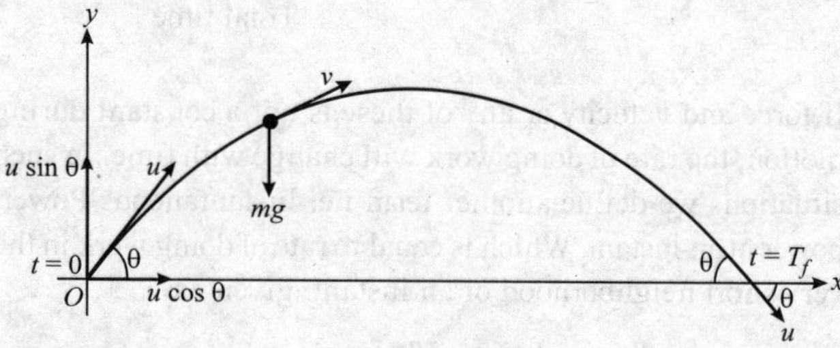

Figure 3.15

$$\vec{v} = (u\cos\theta)\,\hat{i} + (u\sin\theta - gt)\,\hat{j}$$

And vectorial force on it is

$$\vec{F} = -mg\,\hat{j}$$

Instantaneous power can be given as

$$P = \vec{F} \cdot \vec{v}$$

$$\Rightarrow \quad P = (-mg\,\hat{j}) \cdot (u\cos\theta\,\hat{i} + u\sin\theta\,\hat{j} - gt\,\hat{j})$$

$$\Rightarrow \quad P = mg\,(gt - u\sin\theta)$$

Illustrative Example 3.11

An electric motor that can develop 1.0 hp is used to lift a mass of 25 kg through a distance of 10.0 m. What is the minimum time in which it can do this ? (Take $g = 10\ \text{m/s}^2$)

Solution

If 25 kg mass is lifted to a height of 10.0 m, work done against gravity is $= mgh = 25 \times 10 \times 10 = 2500$ J

If motor is working at full power 1.0 hp or 746 Watt, it will do the required work in time t_0 seconds.

Thus we have $\quad 746 \times t_0 = 2500$

or $\quad t_0 = \dfrac{2500}{746} = 3.35$ s

Illustrative Example 3.12

A pump is required to lift 1000 kg of water per minute from a well 12 m deep and eject it with a speed of 20 m/s. How much work is done per minute in lifting the water and what must be the power output of the pump ? (Take $g = 10\ \text{m/s}^2$)

Solution

When 1000 kg of water is lifted from a 12.0 m deep well

Work required is $= mgh = 1.2 \times 10^5$ J

Work required per second is $= \dfrac{1.2 \times 10^5}{60} = 2000$ J/s

Kinetic energy gained by the water per second is

$$= \frac{1}{2}mv^2 = \frac{1}{2} \times \frac{1000}{60} \times (20)^2 = 3333.33\ \text{J/s}$$

Total work required per second by the pump is

$$= 2000 + 3333.33 = 5333.33\ \text{J/s}$$

Illustrative Example 3.13

A small body of mass m is located on a horizontal plane at the point O. The body acquires a horizontal velocity u. Find :

(a) The mean power developed by the friction force during the whole time of motion, if the friction coefficient is k.

(b) The maximum instantaneous power developed by the friction force, if the friction coefficient varies as $k = \alpha x$, where α is a constant and x is the distance from the point O.

Solution

(a) The frictional force acting on the body

$$f_r = \mu mg$$

Retardation provided by this force is

$$a = -\mu g$$

Total time taken by the body to come to rest is

$$t = \frac{u}{a}$$

or $$= \frac{u}{\mu g}$$

Total change in kinetic energy due to friction is

$$\Delta E = \frac{1}{2}\, mu^2 - 0$$

Mean power can be given as

$$\text{Mean Power} = \frac{\text{Net gain in kinetic energy}}{\text{Total time of motion}} = \frac{\Delta E}{t}$$

or $$\frac{\frac{1}{2}mu^2}{u/_{\mu g}} = \frac{1}{2}\, mu\mu g$$

(b) When friction coefficient is $k = \alpha x$, the friction force on the body when it is at a distance x from the point O is

$$f_r = \alpha xmg$$

Retardation due to this force is

$$a = -\alpha gx$$

or $$v\frac{dv}{dx} = -\alpha gx$$

or $$v\, dv = -\alpha gx\, dx$$

Integrating the above expression for velocity at a distance x from point O, gives

$$\int_u^v v\, dv = -\int_0^x \alpha gx\, dx$$

or $$v^2 = u^2 - \alpha gx^2$$

Instantaneous power due to friction force at a distance x from point O is

$$P = \boldsymbol{F}.\boldsymbol{v}$$

or $$= -\alpha mgx\sqrt{(u^2 - \alpha gx^2)} \quad \ldots(3.11)$$

This power is maximum when $\frac{dp}{dx} = 0$, thus

$$\frac{dp}{dx} = \frac{\alpha mgx}{[u^2 - \alpha gx^2]^{1/2}} \times \alpha gx - \alpha mg\,[u^2 - \alpha gx^2]^{1/2} = 0$$

or $$x = \frac{u}{\sqrt{2\alpha g}} \quad \ldots(3.12)$$

Equation-(3.12) gives the value of x at which instantaneous power is maximum. Using above value of x in equation-(3.11) gives the maximum instantaneous power as

$$P_{max} = -\alpha mg\frac{u}{\sqrt{2\alpha g}}\sqrt{u^2 - u^2/_2}$$

$$P_{max} = -\frac{1}{2}\, mu^2\sqrt{\alpha g}$$

Web Reference of Video Lectures at www.physicsgalaxy.com
Age Group - High School Physics | Age 17-19 Years
Section - MECHANICS
Topic - Work, Energy and Power
Module Numbers - 19, 20 and 21

Practice Exercise 3.3

(i) A 80 kg person expends 400 W when walking on a horizontal tracker belt at a speed of 7.2 kph. When the tracker belt is inclined without changing the speed, the person's expended power increases to 600 W. Estimate the angle of incline of the tracker belt by assuming that all of the increased output power goes into overcoming the force of gravity. Assume constant friction by tracker belt in both horizontal and inclined position. Take $g = 10\ \text{m/s}^2$.

[7.31°, 35.45°]

(ii) A bus of mass 1000 Kg has an engine which produces a constant power of 50 kW. If the resistance to motion, assumed constant is 1000 N, find the maximum speed at which the bus can travel on level road and the acceleration when it is travelling at 25 m/s. Take $g = 10\ \text{m/s}^2$

[50 m/s, 1 m/s²]

(iii) An automobile engine develops 30 hp in moving the automobile at a constant speed of 50 miles/hr. What is the average retarding force due to such things as wind resistance, internal friction, tire friction, etc. ?

[1007.1 N]

(iv) The force needed to pull the tape through an audio cassette player is 0.98 N. In operation the tape travels at a constant speed of 2.5 cm/s. The motor consumes a power of 1.8 W. What percentage of the power input to the motor is required to pull the tape at its operating speed ?

[1.36%]

(v) The power P delivered by a windmill whose blades sweep in a circle of diameter D by a wind of speed v is proportional to the square of the diameter and the cube of the wind speed. Show that this dependence on diameter and wind speed exist when 100% energy transfer takes place. Also show that

$$P = \frac{\pi}{8}\rho D^2 v^3$$

Where is ρ the density of air.

(vi) A train of mass 10^6 kg is going up an incline plane with incline 1 in 49 at a rate of 10 m/s. If the resistance due to friction be 10 N per metric ton, calculate the power of the engine. If the engine is shut off, how far will the train move before it comes to rest ? Take $g = 9.8$ m/s^2.

[2.1×10^6 W, 238.095 m]

3.5 Circular Motion

Up to this point, about motion we have studied one dimensional motion and projectile motion which is two dimensional. In this section we begin with the circular motion which is also a two dimensional motion. Some part of the terminology in this section will be useful in further chapters for describing other types of motions such as rotational motion and oscillations.

Consider a point particle moving along a circular path of radius r with constant speed v. A particle moving in this manner is said to undergo uniform circular motion. By a "*particle*" we mean an object of negligible size and constant mass. As shown in figure-3.16, if a door is opened about its hinges on the wall, points A, B and C on door are in circular motion of radii r_1, r_2 and r_3, as these points move in circular paths of the respective radii, when door is opened. But here the motion of door is not considered as a circular motion, it is a different type of motion which we will discuss in further chapters, rotational motion. In rotational motion different points (particles) of a body are in circular motion of different radii. We will discuss several concepts related to circular motion but before proceeding with our anlayzation, we've to learn first, some basic properties of circular motion.

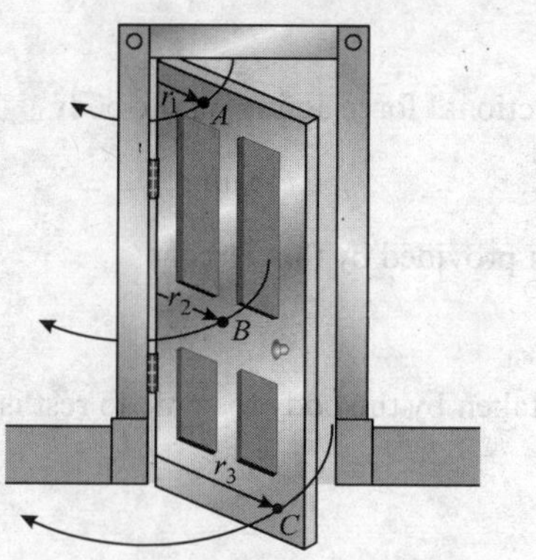

Figure 3.16

3.5.1 Angular Coordinate, Velocity and Acceleration

The quantities we use to describe the angular motion of an object about an axis (centre of circle) are the object's angular coordinate θ, angular velocity ω, and angular acceleration α. Now first we define these quantities and make them analogous with the respective linear quantities.

Angular Coordinate

The angular coordinate of a door can be measured as shown in figure-3.17. Let we consider Z-axis along the hinges and the xy plane be the plane of the ground with the x-axis along the wall. When the gate is opened, its angular coordinate is measured in anticlockwise direction from x-axis when viewed from the positive z-direction. Hence, an angle measured anticlockwise is positive and an angle measured clockwise is negative. A right hand rule gives the positive sense for θ (figure-3.18(b)). If you imagine grasping the z axis with your right hand so that your thumb points in the $+z$ direction, your fingers curl in the positive θ sense. If we consider this θ as angular displacement than your thumb (i.e. $+z$ direction) gives the direction of angular displacement vector.

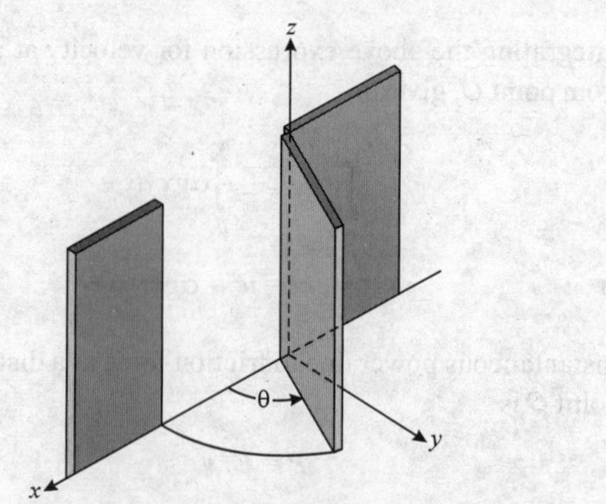

Figure 3.17

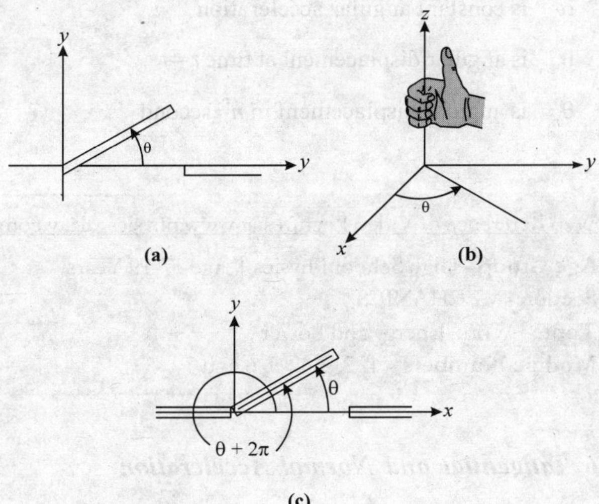

Figure 3.18

A major difference between the angular coordinate θ and the linear coordinate x is that θ is cyclic. That is, the angular coordinates θ and $\theta + 2\pi$ represent the same angular position. Generally if n is any positive or negative integer, then θ and $\theta + 2n\pi$ represent the same angular position. In general cases values of θ are adjusted so that they fall in the range from 0 to 2π or from $-\pi$ to $+\pi$.

Angular Velocity

The angular velocity is the rate of change of angular displacement. It gives the idea about how fast a given object is revolving. Analogously to linear motion, where average velocity is defined to be displacement divided by time, it is given as

$$\text{Average angular velocity} = \frac{\text{angle turned}}{\text{time taken}}$$

$$\langle\omega\rangle = \frac{\Delta\theta}{\Delta t} \quad \ldots (3.13)$$

The angular velocity is denoted by the Greek letter "ω". Units for angular velocity are radians per second, used generally.

The instantaneous angular velocity can also be defined for a revolving object, analogous with the linear instantaneous velocity as

$$\omega = \left|\frac{d\theta}{dt}\right| \quad \ldots (3.14)$$

The angular velocity is a vector quantity whose magnitude is the angular speed and direction gives the sense of revolution. Our right hand thumb rule gives the direction of revolution of object and it relates the direction with ω. As explained earlier if an object is in circular motion, rotate your fingers in the direction of revolution of the object, the direction in which your thumb points will be the direction of angular displacement and also the direction of angular velocity. See figure-3.18(b).

Angular Acceleration

It is the rate of change of angular velocity of an object. Let us discuss an example. If you revolve a bob tied with a string over your head, it moves in a horizontal circle. If you stop putting your efforts in revolution and make your hand steady. The bob slows down due to air friction and its circle becomes smaller and its angular velocity reduces. It covers less angle in large time interval and finally stops. In above motion the bob was having an angular acceleration (negative) due to air friction.

It is given as

$$\alpha = \frac{d\omega}{dt} = \frac{d^2\theta}{dt^2} \quad \ldots (3.15)$$

As its linear counterpart, acceleration can also be defined in differential form of velocity and displacement as $a = v\frac{dv}{dx}$, we also have

$$\alpha = \omega\frac{d\omega}{d\theta} \quad \ldots (3.16)$$

If we again consider the example of opening the door discussed earlier, during its motion, points A, B and C, all the three are turned by equal angles in same time interval. Thus the three points have equal angular velocities or we can say that all particles of the door have equal angular velocities, but different linear velocities.

Consider the circular motion shown in figure-3.19. A particle is revolving with a speed v in a circle of radius r. Let we consider the particle covers an angular displacement $d\theta$ in time dt. During this elemental time duration, particle covers a linear displacement dl which can be given as vdt. The linear displacement can be given in terms of angular displacement as

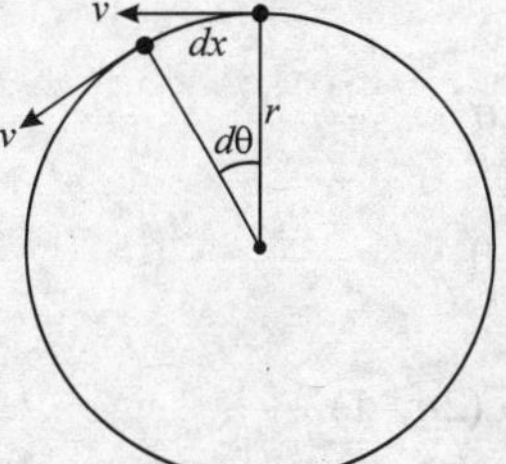

Figure 3.19

$$dl = r\,d\theta$$

or $$v\,dt = r\,d\theta$$

or $$v = r\frac{d\theta}{dt} = r\omega$$

Similarly if the object has angular acceleration , its linear acceleration in tangential direction is given as

$$a = r\alpha \qquad \ldots(3.17)$$

3.5.2 Kinematics of Circular Motion

In first chapter we have discussed about kinematics of a body in one dimensions and two dimensions. This section relate the different parameters of circular motion with time. Here we will discuss two cases, one is the motion with constant angular acceleration and other with variable angular acceleration, analogous to the linear motion.

Cases of Constant Angular Acceleration

With reference from the previous section we can say that the angular displacement, angular velocity and angular accelerations are the angular counterparts of the analogous linear displacement, velocity and accelerations.

For linear motion we use four speed equations for motion of body when it moves with constant acceleration, given as

$$v = u \pm at$$

$$s = ut \pm \frac{1}{2}at^2$$

$$v^2 = u^2 \pm 2as$$

$$s_n = u \pm \frac{1}{2}a(2n-1)$$

Analogous to the above equations, we can derive angular speed equations as

$$\omega = \omega_0 \pm \alpha t \qquad \ldots(3.18)$$

$$\theta = \omega_0 t \pm \frac{1}{2}\alpha t^2 \qquad \ldots(3.19)$$

$$\omega^2 = \omega_0^2 \pm 2\alpha\theta \qquad \ldots(3.20)$$

$$\theta_n = \omega_0 \pm \frac{1}{2}\alpha(2n-1) \qquad \ldots(3.21)$$

Where

ω_0 is initial angular velocity at $t = 0$

ω is final angular velocity at $t = t$

α is constant angular acceleration

θ is angular displacement at time $t = t$

θ_n is angular displacement in n^{th} second

> Web Reference of Video Lectures at www.physicsgalaxy.com
> **Age Group** - High School Physics | Age 17-19 Years
> **Section** - MECHANICS
> **Topic** - Work, Energy and Power
> **Module Numbers** - 1, 2, 3, 4, 5, 6 and 7

3.6 Tangential and Normal Acceleration

Acceleration is rate of change of velocity. Velocity is a vector, which can be changed by changing its magnitude or direction or both. In uniform circular motion, speed is constant but direction of velocity changes continuously. As direction of velocity changes, we say velocity is changing, hence body must have acceleration.

To understand the concept of acceleration in such cases consider the motion of a particle moving along a straight line shown in figure-3.20(a). If a force starts acting on it in its direction of motion, its speed will increase and the acceleration is given as

$$a = \frac{F}{m}$$

Now consider next situation in figure-3.20(b), the force acts at an angle θ to its motion direction. It has two components, $F\cos\theta$ acts along the direction of motion, which increases its speed and $F\sin\theta$ acts perpendicular to its motion. We know that a perpendicular force can not do work on a moving object and if no work is done no change in kinetic energy will take place due to this force and hence it is unable to change the speed of the particle. But as it is acting perpendicular to the motion, it tends to change the direction of motion as shown in figure-3.20(b) by the dashed path.

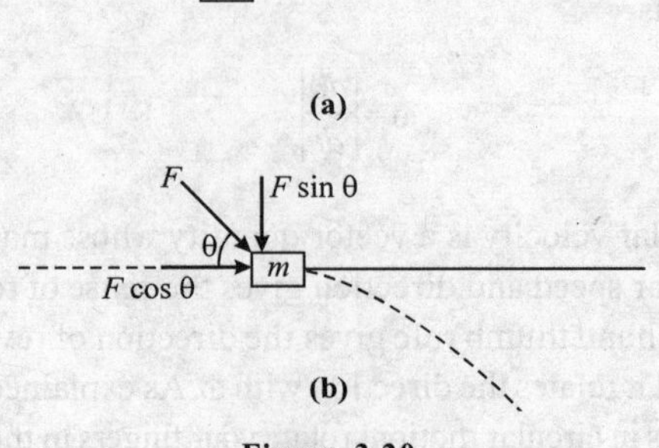

Figure 3.20

Here acceleration due to the force component along the motion direction is

$$a_t = \frac{F\cos\theta}{m} \qquad \ldots(3.22)$$

Acceleration due to the force component perpendicular to the motion direction is

$$a_N = \frac{F\sin\theta}{m} \qquad \ldots(3.23)$$

Here a_t is the acceleration responsible for change in magnitude of velocity and a_N is the acceleration responsible for change in direction of velocity. Here a_t always acts in the direction tangential to the motion of particle and is known as tangential acceleration and a_N, which changes the direction of velocity, acts in the direction of normal to the trajectory towards concave side, is known as normal acceleration or centripetal acceleration.

3.6.1 Centripetal Acceleration

In uniform circular motion the velocity is constantly changing, there must be only the centripetal or normal acceleration. The tangential acceleration here is zero as the magnitude of velocity remains constant. Let we consider an instant a particle is at position P shown in figure-3.21(a), in uniform circular motion it is moving with velocity v_P. In the short interval of time Δt, the particle moves by an angular displacement $\Delta\theta$ to another point Q. During the time interval Δt, the velocity changes by an amount $\Delta v = v_Q - v_P$. The average acceleration for this small duration is

$$\vec{a} = \frac{\overrightarrow{\Delta v}}{\Delta t} \qquad \ldots(3.24)$$

To evaluate the acceleration we translate the vectors v_P and v_Q to a common origin shown in figure-3.21(c). The change in velocity Δv is also shown. As the time interval Δt is made smaller, points P and Q are found closer together.

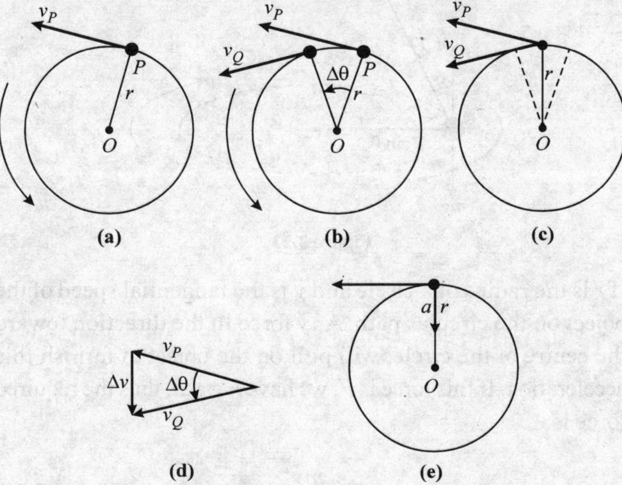

Figure 3.21

We can see that this angle is also the angle between the two velocity vectors shown in figure-3.21(d). When becomes so small that v_P and v_Q are almost parallel and their difference Δv is almost perpendicular to both of them. In the limit when Δt tends to zero, Δv is perpendicular to v. Hence the instantaneous acceleration which is in the same direction as Δv, is directed radially towards the centre of the circular path. Therefore a particle moving with constant speed around a circle is always accelerated toward the centre (figure-3.21(e)).

From figure-3.21(d), the acceleration can be easily evaluated. The magnitude of change in velocity Δv can be given as

$$\Delta v = v\,\Delta\theta \qquad \ldots(3.25)$$

[arc length = radius × angle subtended by arc]

Here $|v_P| = |v_Q| = v$, and from equation-(3.25), centripetal acceleration is

$$a = \frac{v\Delta\theta}{\Delta t} = v\,\omega$$

or

$$a = \frac{v^2}{r} \qquad [\text{As } v = r\,\omega] \qquad \ldots(3.26)$$

Whose direction is always towards the centre of the circle.

3.6.2 Normal Acceleration in a General Two Dimension Motion

Consider the motion of a particle along a two dimensional curve shown in figure-3.22. If particle is moving with a uniform speed, its tangential acceleration is zero. But here as it is moving in a curve, its velocity is changing so it will have normal acceleration, acting perpendicular to the instantaneous velocity.

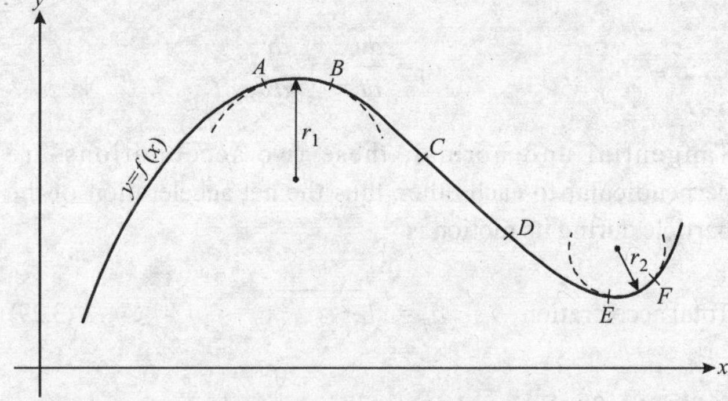

Figure 3.22

As shown in figure-3.22, different section of the curves can be considered as arcs of circles of different radii. For example when particle is moving along the section AB of the curve, it behaves like a circle of radius r_1. It experiences a normal acceleration towards its instantaneous centre of the circle. During motion between AB, the normal acceleration can be given as v_2/r_1.

When curvature is high (more bending of curve), the radius of the instantaneous circle will be small and acceleration of the particle will be large like in section EF of curve shown in figure-3.22 and when curvature is small (less bending of curve), the radius of the instantaneous circle will be large and acceleration of the particle will be small. In flat parts of the curve, like in section CD of the curve, radius of curvature is infinite thus normal acceleration is zero.

If the equation of trajectory of the particle (equation of curve) is given or evaluated, we can find the radius of curvature of the instantaneous circle by using the formula

$$R = \frac{\left[1+\left(\frac{dy}{dx}\right)^2\right]^{3/2}}{\left|\frac{d^2y}{dx^2}\right|} \qquad \ldots(3.27)$$

Above formula can be obtained by solving the equation of trajectory and the equation of normal at the point where radius of curvature is required. This radius of curvature can be used to find the instantaneous normal acceleration of the particle, given as

$$a_N = \frac{v^2}{R} \qquad \ldots(3.28)$$

Here v is the instantaneous speed of the particle. If speed is also varying then particle will also has instantaneous tangential acceleration, given as

$$a_t = \frac{dv}{dt} = v\frac{dv}{dx}$$

Tangential and normal, these two accelerations are perpendicular to each other, thus the net acceleration of the particle during its motion is

$$\text{Total acceleration} \qquad a_T = \sqrt{a_t^2 + a_N^2} \qquad \ldots(3.29)$$

In chapter-2, while studying motion in two dimension, we have resolved the total acceleration of the particle along x and y directions as a_x and a_y and the total acceleration was given as

$$a_T = \sqrt{a_x^2 + a_y^2} \qquad \ldots(3.30)$$

We can use either of equations-(3.29) and (3.30) to find the total acceleration of a particle in two dimensional motion.

Web Reference of Video Lectures at www.physicsgalaxy.com

Age Group - High School Physics | Age 17-19 Years
Section - MECHANICS
Topic - Circular Motion
Module Numbers - 8, 9, 10, 11, 12, and 13

3.6.3 Force Required For Circular Motion

According to Newton's first law, a net force must act on an object if the object is accelerated or to be deflected from straight line motion. This force which is responsible for circular motion of an object is known as centripetal force, due to which centripetal acceleration acts on the object. Without centripetal force it is impossible for a particle to move in circular path. For example, a car taking a circular turn on a road will slip from the track if the track is too slippery to provide the required friction force at the wheel. In this case friction in inwards direction is acting as a centripetal force.

Again consider an example of a conical pendulum shown in figure-3.23. A simple pendulum is revolved in a horizontal circle as shown. During horizontal circular motion it is in equilibrium along vertical direction as its weight is balanced by the vertical component of the tension in the thread. The horizontal component of the tension in string is acting along radially inward direction which is acting as centripetal force in this case and due to which the direction of velocity changes continuously.

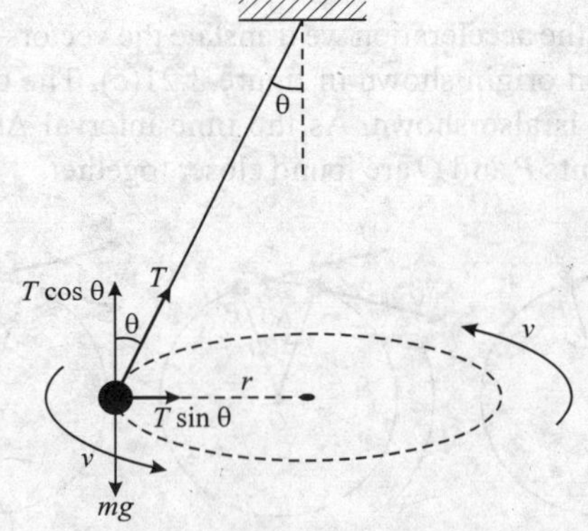

Figure 3.23

If r is the radius of a circle and v is the tangential speed of the object on the circular path. Any force in the direction toward the centre of the circle, will pull on the object to furnish this acceleration. If this force is F, we have $F = ma$, thus the required force is

$$F = \frac{mv^2}{r} \qquad \ldots(3.31)$$

All objects that travel in a circle (or an arc of a circle) require a centripetal force. The earth is pulled toward the sun by gravitational attraction. This pull behaves like the required centripetal force and is responsible for earth to circle the sun. Similarly moon and other satellites circle the earth because of earth's gravitational attraction. In further sections and examples, we will get more clarification of centripetal forces.

One important point is to be noticed that centripetal force does no work. To do a non zero work, a force should have a component in the direction of motion or a component of displacement of particle should be in the direction of applied force, whereas the motion exist only in the tangential direction to the circle. Therefore no work is done by it. It only changes the direction of motion.

3.6.4 Concept of Centrifugal Force

In doing problems involving uniform circular motion, we should have a tendency to include an extra outward force of magnitude mv^2/R to "*make the body in radial equilibrium*". This outward force is usually called centrifugal force. Actually this concept is wrong. Most important about this is the body is not in equilibrium, it is in motion around its circular path. Its velocity is constantly changing in direction, so it accelerates and not in equilibrium. Other thing is that if there were an additional outward force to balance the inward force, there would then be no net inward force to cause the circular motion and the body would move in a straight line, not in a circle.

For example, we consider a car with passengers going around a circular path on a level road tends to slide to the outside of the turn, it appears to be due to centrifugal force. But such a passenger is in an accelerating non-inertial frame of reference in which Newton's first and second laws don't apply.

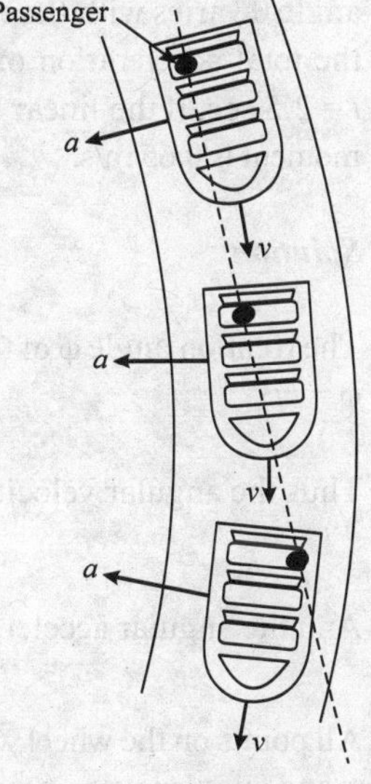

Figure 3.24

With respect to car the explanation is true as with respect to passenger car is at rest but it is accelerating inward with v^2/R, thus passengers experience a pseudo force in outward direction mv^2/R, with respect to car, due to which they tend to collide with the outward wall of the car. But what really happens is shown in figure-3.24, when seen from an inertial frame of reference (earth) is that the passenger tends to keep moving in a straight line and the outer side of the car moving in circular path turns into the passenger as car turns.

Thus in an inertial frame of reference there is no such thing like centrifugal force.

In problems of circular motion, we can use centrifugal force but only with reference to the body in circular motion only. Consider the circular motion of a stone revolving in a circular path tied with a string. Tension in string is acting toward center of the circle. If we consider the situation with reference to the body, its speed is zero and it is pulled towards the centre. As it is not moving towards the centre, or it is in radial equilibrium, we can say that a force must be acting on the body in outward direction which is balancing the tension in string or the centripetal force. This is the centrifugal force, of which magnitude must be equal to mv^2/R. This is applied in radially outward direction as shown in figure-3.25.

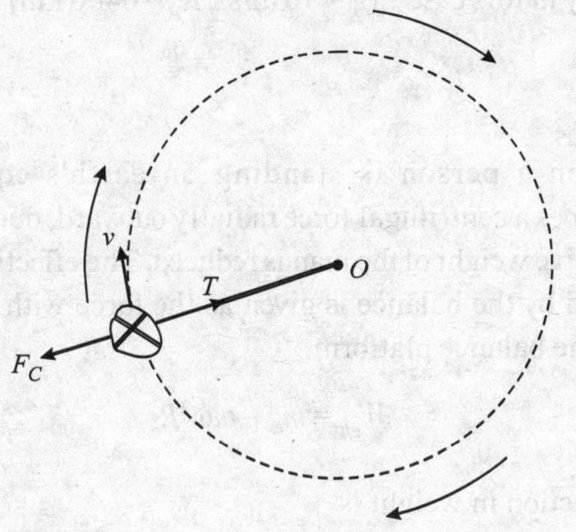

Figure 3.25

$$\text{Centrifugal force} \qquad F_C = T = \frac{mv^2}{R} \qquad \ldots(3.32)$$

Now we take few examples to discuss the above concept of circular motion and forces involved.

Illustrative Example 3.14

A stone with a mass of 0.9 kg is attached to one end of a string 0.8 m long. The string will break if its tension exceeds 500 N. The stone is whirled in a horizontal circle on a frictionless table top. The other end of the string is kept fixed. Find the maximum speed of the stone, it can attain without breaking the string.

Solution

It is given that tensile strength of string is = 500 N

When the stone of 0.9 kg is whirled in a circle of radius 0.8 m, it experiences a centrifugal force given as

$$\frac{mv^2}{l} = \frac{0.9v^2}{0.8}$$

The string will break, when this force become equal to 500 N, thus we have

$$\frac{0.9v^2}{0.8} = 500$$

or $$v = \sqrt{\frac{500 \times 8}{9}} = 21.081$$

Illustrative Example 3.15

A person stands on a spring balance at the equator. (a) How much is the reduction in weight as measured by the balance. (b) If the speed of earth's rotation is changed such that the balance reading is half of its true weight, what will be the length of the day in this case ? ($g = 10$ m/s^2, $R_e = 6400$ km)

Solution

(a) When a person is standing on earth's equator, it experiences a centrifugal force radially outward, due to which the effective weight of the man is reduced. The effective weight measured by the balance is given as the force with which he pushes the balance platform.

$$W_{eff} = mg - m\omega^2 R_e$$

The reduction in weight is

$$W_{net} - W_{eff} = m\omega^2 R_e$$

(b) If the balance reading becomes mg/2, we have

$$\frac{mg}{2} = mg - m\omega^2 R_e$$

or $$\omega = \sqrt{\frac{g}{2R_e}} = 8.83 \times 10^{-4} \text{ rad/s}$$

Thus the length of the day is now

$$T = \frac{2\pi}{\omega} = \frac{2 \times 3.14}{8.83 \times 10^{-4}} = 7112.12 \text{ s} = 1 \text{ hr } 58 \text{ min}$$

Illustrative Example 3.16

What is the radius of curvature of the parabola traced out by the projectile in which a particle is projected with a speed u at an angle θ with the horizontal, at a point where the velocity of particle makes an angle $\theta/2$ with the horizontal.

Solution

At the point on particle's trajectory where particle's velocity makes an angle $\theta/2$ with the horizontal, we can use the slope of trajectory as

$$\frac{dy}{dx} = \tan\left(\frac{\theta}{2}\right)$$

From equation of trajectory we have

$$y = x\tan\theta - \frac{gx^2}{2u^2\cos^2\theta}$$

or $$\frac{dy}{dx} = \tan\theta - \frac{gx}{u^2\cos^2\theta}$$

or $$\frac{d^2y}{dx^2} = -\frac{g}{u^2\cos^2\theta}$$

We have for radius of curvature at a point on trajectory

$$R = \frac{\left[1 + \left(\frac{dy}{dx}\right)^2\right]^{3/2}}{\left|\frac{d^2y}{dx^2}\right|} = \frac{(1 + \tan^2 \theta/2)^{3/2}}{\left(\frac{g}{u^2\cos^2\theta}\right)}$$

or $$= \frac{u^2 \sec^3 \theta/2 \cos^2\theta}{g}$$

Illustrative Example 3.17

A wheel rotates around a stationary axis so that the rotation angle θ varies with times as $\varphi = kt^2$ where $k = 0.2$ rad/s^2. Find the total acceleration of the point at the rim at the moment $t = 2.5$ sec, if the linear velocity of the point at the rim at this moment is 0.65 m/s.

Solution

The rotation angle φ of the wheel is given a function of time as $\varphi = kt^2$

Thus the angular velocity of the wheel is $\omega = \frac{d\varphi}{dt} = 2kt$

And the angular acceleration of wheel is $\alpha = \frac{d^2\varphi}{dt^2} = 2k$

All points on the wheel will have the same angular acceleration α and angular velocity ω but linear acceleration and velocities are different.

Linear acceleration (tangential) of a point on the rim of wheel is

$$a = R\alpha = 2kR$$

Normal acceleration (centripetal) of that point is

$$a_N = \omega^2 R = 4k^2t^2R$$

If v is the speed of a point on the rim then

$$v = R\omega$$

or $$= 2ktR$$

or $$R = \frac{v}{2kt}$$

Using this value of R in tangential and normal acceleration, we have

$$a = \frac{v}{t} \quad \text{and} \quad a_N = 2kvt$$

Total acceleration of this point is

$$a_T = \sqrt{a^2 + a_N^2}$$

or $$= \sqrt{\left(\frac{v^2}{t^2}\right) + 4k^2v^2t^2}$$

or $$= \left[\frac{(0.065)^2}{(2.5)^2} + 4(0.2)^2(0.65)^2(2.5)^2\right]^{1/2}$$

or $$= 0.7 \text{ m/s}^2$$

 # Illustrative Example 3.18

A stone is thrown horizontally with a velocity of 10 m/s. Find the radius of curvature of its trajectory at the end of 3 seconds after motion began. ($g = 10$ m/s^2)

Solution

The radius of curvature of a trajectory can be given directly by the expression given in equation-(3.27)

As stone is thrown horizontally, we have equation of trajectory as -

$$y = -\frac{gx^2}{2u^2}$$

Which gives $$\frac{dy}{dx} = \frac{gx}{u^2} \quad \text{and} \quad \frac{d^2y}{dx^2} = \frac{g}{u^2}$$

After 3 sec of projection horizontally, stone's x-coordinate is $x = 10 \times 3 = 30$ m/s

and at $x = 30$ m, $$\frac{dy}{dx} = \frac{30g}{u^2} \quad \text{and} \quad \frac{d^2y}{dx^2} = \frac{1}{10}$$

Radius of curvature at $x = 30$ m is

$$R = \frac{\left[1 + \left(\frac{dy}{dx}\right)^2\right]^{3/2}}{\left|\frac{d^2y}{dx^2}\right|} = \frac{[1+(3)^2]^{3/2}}{\frac{1}{10}}$$

or $$= 100\sqrt{10} \text{ m}$$

Web Reference of Video Lectures at www.physicsgalaxy.com

Age Group - High School Physics | Age 17-19 Years
Section - MECHANICS
Topic - Circular Motion
Module Numbers - 15, 16, 17, 18, 19 and 20

Practise Exercise 3.4

(i) A particle is revolving in a circular path of radius 500 m at a speed 30 m/s. It is increasing its speed at the rate of 2 m/s^2. What is its acceleration ?

[2.69 m/s^2]

(ii) A solid body starts rotating about a stationary axis with an angular acceleration $\beta = at$. How soon after the beginning of rotation will the total acceleration vector of a general point on the body form an angle α with its velocity vector ?

[$\left[\left(\frac{4\tan\alpha}{a}\right)^{1/3}\right]$]

(iii) A solid body rotates with angular retardation about a stationary axis with an angular retardation $\beta = k\sqrt{\omega}$, where ω is its angular velocity of the body at an instant. Find the average angular speed of body averaged over the whole time of rotation if at the initial moment of time its angular velocity was equal to ω_0.

[$\omega_0/3$]

(iv) A solid body starts from test rotating about a stationary axis with an angular acceleration $\alpha = \alpha_0 \cos\theta$, where α_0 is a constant vector and θ is an angle of rotation from the initial position. Find the angular velocity of the body as a function of the angle θ.

[$\sqrt{2\alpha_0 \sin\theta}$]

3.7 Vertical Circular Motion of a Pendulum Bob

Consider a bob attached to a string tied at a pivot shown in figure-3.26. If the bob is given a horizontal velocity it moves in a vertical circle. This situation forms the basis of a wide category of problems. Different type of cases can be made depending on the projection speed of the bob. We will discuss this situation in detail for different speeds of projections.

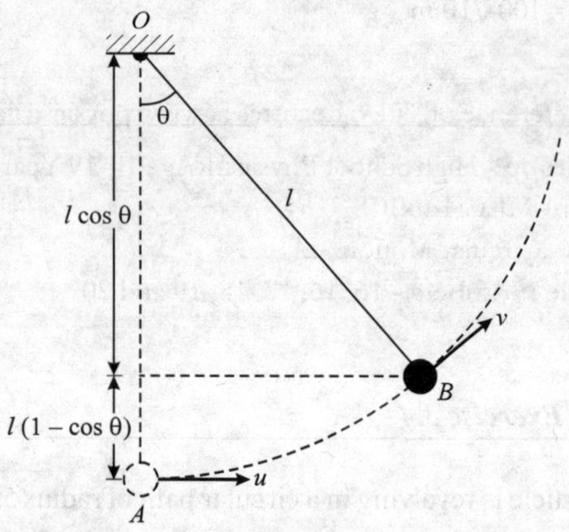

Figure 3.26

If the bob is given an initial speed u as shown in figure-3.26, it starts following the circular path shown by dashed line. As it moves up, due to gravity, its speed decreases. When it is at an angular displacement θ from the initial position, we can find its speed by energy conservation as

At points A and B, we have

$$\frac{1}{2}mu^2 = \frac{1}{2}mv^2 + mgh$$

or $$v = \sqrt{u^2 - 2gh}$$

Where $$h = l(1 - \cos\theta) \qquad \ldots(3.33)$$

Thus $$v = \sqrt{u^2 - 2gl(1-\cos\theta)} \qquad \ldots(3.34)$$

Equation-(3.34) gives the velocity of bob during circular motion, at an angular displacement θ from the initial position.

If initial velocity u, imparted to the bob is very small than after traversing a small angular amplitude it will return back as velocity is not sufficient to make the complete revolution and it will start oscillations. Let the angular amplitude be $\theta = \alpha$, at which its velocity becomes zero. Angle α can be obtained from equation-(3.34) by substituting $v = 0$ in it as

$$0 = \sqrt{u^2 - 2gl(1-\cos\alpha)}$$

or $$u^2 - 2gl + 2gl\cos\alpha = 0$$

or $$\cos\alpha = \frac{2gl - u^2}{2gl} \qquad \ldots(3.35)$$

During circular motion tension in the string is also varying. See figure-3.27, when the bob is at an angular position θ, there are two forces acting on it. Tension T toward centre of circle and mg in downward direction. The net force toward the center of circle is $(T - mg\cos\theta)$, which is acting as the required centripetal force. Thus when the bob is at an angular displacement θ, we have

$$T - mg\cos\theta = \frac{mv^2}{l}$$

or $$T = mg\cos\theta + \frac{mv^2}{l}$$

Substituting the value of v from equation-(3.34), we get

$$T = \frac{mu^2}{l} - 2mg + 3mg\cos\theta \qquad \ldots(3.36)$$

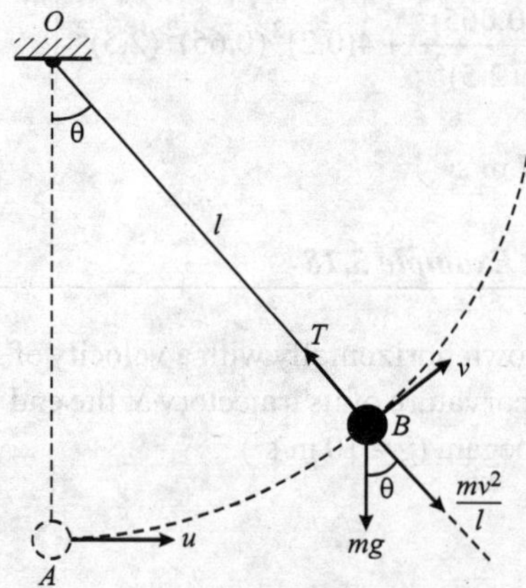

Figure 3.27

Equation-(3.36) gives the tension in thread when it makes an angle θ with the downward normal. Sometimes it is possible that tension in thread becomes zero during revolution. It can not occur in lower half of the circle but it can be possible when particle is making revolution in upper half of the circle. If it happens at an angle $\theta = \varphi$ then it can be evaluated from equation-(3.36) as

$$0 = \frac{mu^2}{l} - 2mg + 3mg\cos\varphi$$

or $$u^2 - 2gl + 3gl\cos\varphi = 0$$

or $$\cos\varphi = \frac{2gl - u^2}{3gl} \qquad \ldots(3.37)$$

Equations-(3.35) and (3.37) are very useful in describing the circular motion of the bob, on the basis of initial projection velocity of it. Let us discuss some cases of projection of it which may be helpful in solving different type of problems related to vertical circular motion.

3.7.1 Projection Cases

Case-I : If projection velocity is $u = \sqrt{2gl}$

From equation-(3.35), $\cos\alpha = 0$ or $\alpha = \frac{\pi}{2}$

From equation-(3.37), $\cos\varphi = 0$ or $\varphi = \frac{\pi}{2}$

It shows that the velocity of bob and tension in thread becomes zero simultaneously at an angular displacement $\frac{\pi}{2}$, or when thread becomes horizontal. Thus particle will oscillate in lower half of the circle, as shown in figure-3.28.

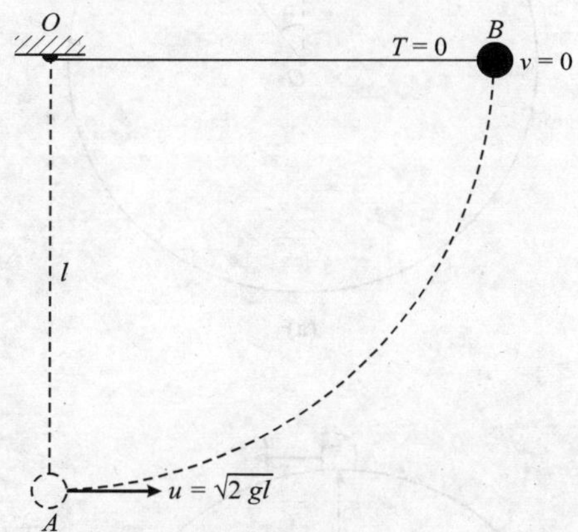

Figure 3.28

If projection velocity is less than $\sqrt{2gl}$, from equation-(3.35) and (3.37) it is clear that φ will be more than α, thus tension in string will never become zero and velocity of the bob will be zero at an angle $\theta < \frac{\pi}{2}$ and particle will oscillate in lower half of the circle with angular amplitude α.

Case-II : If projection velocity is $u = \sqrt{4gl}$

From equation-(3.35), $\cos\alpha = -1$ or $\alpha = \pi$

From equation-(3.37), $\cos\varphi = -\frac{2}{3}$ or $\varphi = 131.8°$

Which shows that initial velocity of bob is sufficient to carry the bob to highest point but tension in thread becomes zero at 131.8° and afterward it will no longer be in circular motion. As soon as thread will slack, particle becomes free to move and it will follow the projectile path as shown in figure-3.29(a). If instead of thread we use a light rod for our purpose as shown in figure-3.29(b), it cannot slack during revolution and particle is now able to move to the topmost point of the circle (as $\alpha = \pi$). When it reaches the topmost point its velocity becomes zero but due to its inertia, it will fall in forward direction and completes the circle.

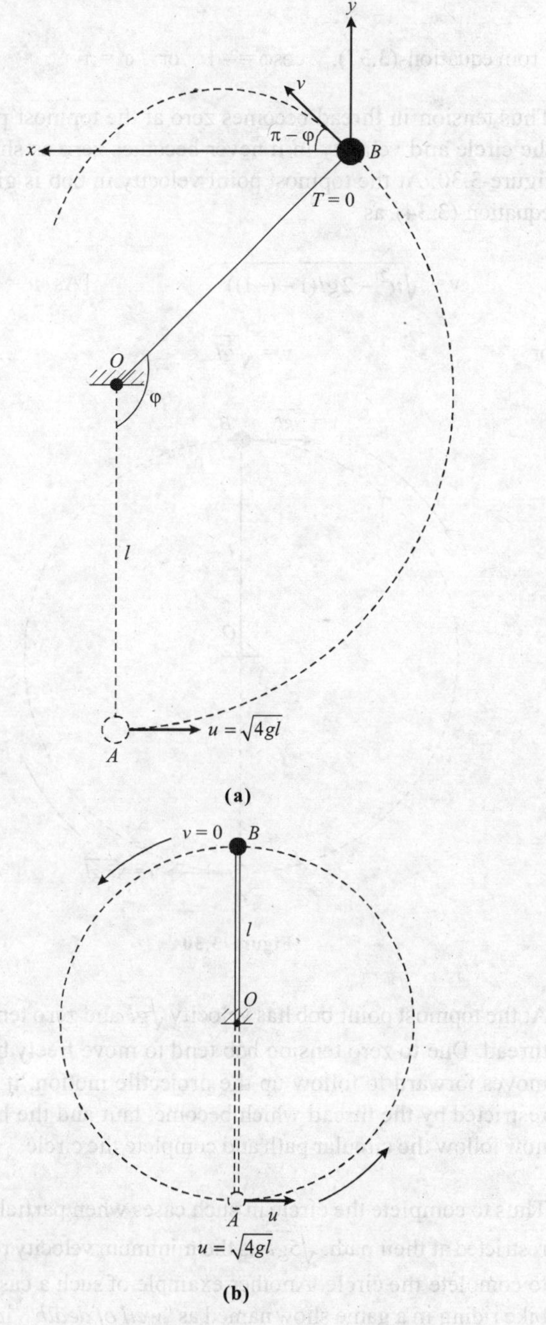

Figure 3.29

Thus in cases when particle is restricted to move along the

circular path, $\sqrt{4gl}$ is the sufficient velocity for the particle at the bottom most point to complete the circle. If particle is not restricted to its path, it will leave the path at an angle 131.8°.

Case-III : If projection velocity is

$$u = \sqrt{5gl}$$

From equation-(3.35), $\cos\alpha = -\frac{3}{2}$ or α does not exist.

From equation-(3.37), $\cos\varphi = -1$ or $\varphi = \pi$

Thus tension in thread becomes zero at the topmost point of the circle and velocity in it never becomes zero as shown in figure-3.30. At the topmost point velocity in bob is given by equation-(3.34), as

$$v = \sqrt{u^2 - 2gl(1-(-1))} \qquad [\text{As } u = \sqrt{5gl}\,]$$

or

$$v = \sqrt{gl} \qquad \dots(3.38)$$

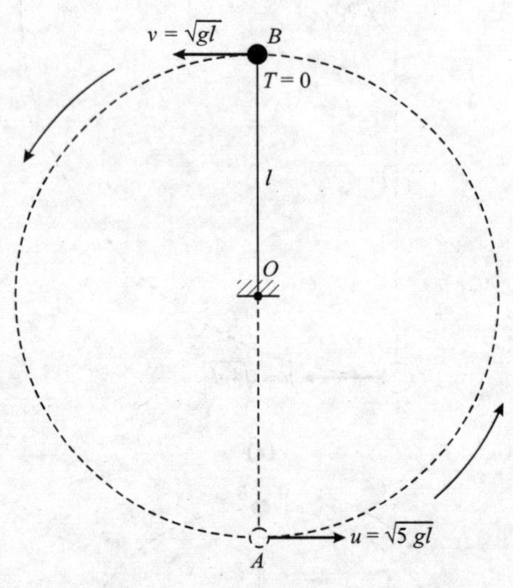

Figure 3.30

At the topmost point bob has velocity $\sqrt{gl}$ and zero tension in thread. Due to zero tension bob tend to move freely but as it moves forward to follow up the projectile motion, it will be restricted by the thread which become, taut and the bob will now follow the circular path and complete the circle.

Thus to complete the circle in such cases when particle is not restricted at their path, $\sqrt{5gl}$ is the minimum velocity required to complete the circle. Another example of such a case is the bike riding in a game show named as "*well of death*", in which a motorcyclist rides the bike in a vertical circle at a speed more than $\sqrt{5gR}$ at the bottommost point. At the top for contact not to be broken the velocity must be more than $\sqrt{gR}$.

3.7.2 Motion of a Body Outside a Spherical Surface

Consider the small box shown in figure-3.31, placed at the top of a spherical surface of radius R. If it is projected with initial velocity u, it moves in circular path along the spherical surface for some distance and at some point it breaks off the surface below it and follow the projectile trajectory.

First we find the velocity of the box, when it moves an angle θ from the vertical position. This can be done by using energy conservation in figure-3.31(a) at points A and B as

$$\frac{1}{2}mu^2 + mgR(1-\cos\theta) = \frac{1}{2}mv^2$$

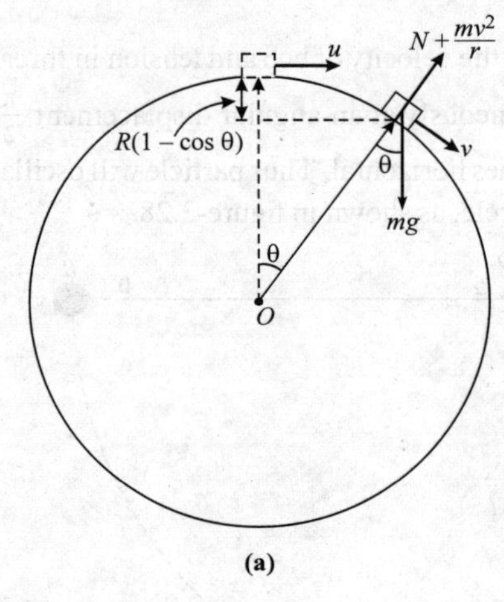

(a)

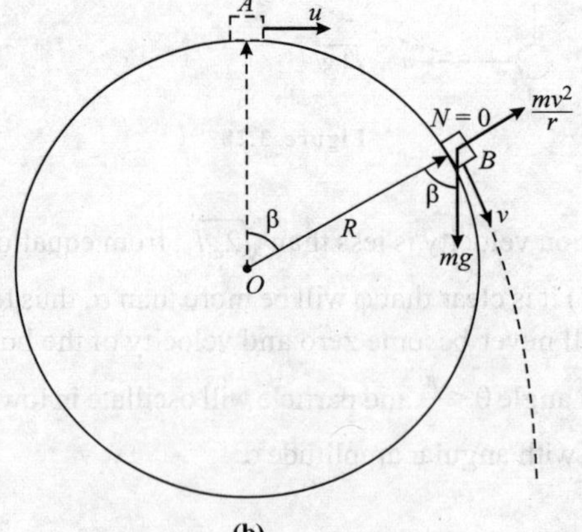

(b)

Figure 3.31

or

$$v = \sqrt{u^2 + 2gR(1-\cos\theta)} \qquad \dots(3.39)$$

During its circular motion the normal reaction acts on body in outward direction so the net force on body toward centre is $(mg\cos\theta - N)$ which provides the necessary centripetal force for circular motion. Thus we have

$$mg\cos\theta - N = \frac{mv^2}{R} \qquad \ldots(3.40)$$

Let we take an angle β when normal reaction becomes zero, as the contact between body and spherical surface breaks off as shown in figure-3.31(b). From equation-(3.40), we have

$$mg\cos\beta = \frac{mv^2}{R}$$

Substituting the value of v from equation-(3.39), we have

$$Rg\cos\beta = u^2 + 2gR(1-\cos\beta)$$

or
$$\cos\beta = \frac{2gR+u^2}{3gR} \qquad \ldots(3.41)$$

If projection velocity of the body is given, above equation gives the angle at which body leaves the spherical surface and starts projectile motion in gravity as shown in figure-3.29(a).

We now take some examples for explaining above concepts.

Illustrative Example 3.19

A 40 kg mass, hanging at the end of a rope of length l, oscillates in a vertical plane with an angular amplitude θ_0. What is the tension in the rope when it makes an angle θ with the vertical ? If the breaking strength of the rope is 80 kgf, what is the maximum angular amplitude with which the mass can oscillate without the rope breaking ?

Solution

From figure-3.32, we have

$$h = l(\cos\theta - \cos\theta_0)$$

The velocity at the angular displacement θ is given as

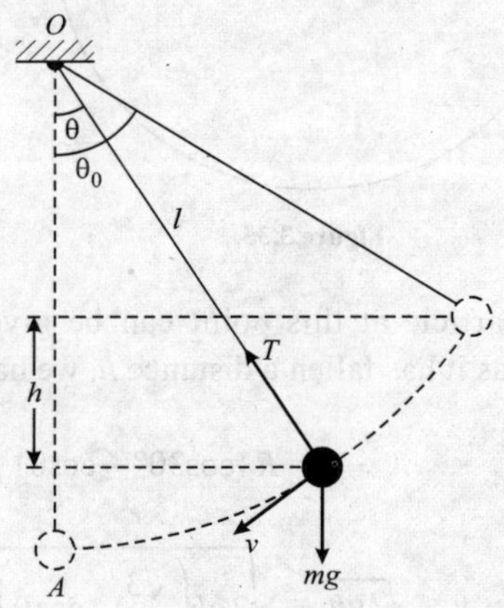

Figure 3.32

$$v = \sqrt{2gh}$$

or
$$= \sqrt{2gl(\cos\theta - \cos\theta_0)}$$

Tension at this instant in the string is given by

$$T - mg\cos\theta = \frac{mv^2}{l}$$

Substituting the value of v

or
$$T - mg\cos\theta = 2mg(\cos\theta - \cos\theta_0)$$

or
$$T = mg(3\cos\theta - 2\cos\theta_0)$$

This tension is maximum at mean position where θ = 0. Thus we have $T_{max} = 80\ kgf$

$$80 = 40(3 - 2\cos\theta_0)$$

or
$$\cos\theta_0 = \frac{1}{2}$$

or
$$\theta_0 = 60°$$

Illustrative Example 3.20

Figure-3.33 shows a loop track of radius r. A box starts sliding from a platform at a distance h above the top of the loop and goes around the loop without falling off the track. Find the minimum value of h for a successful looping. Friction is negligible at all surfaces.

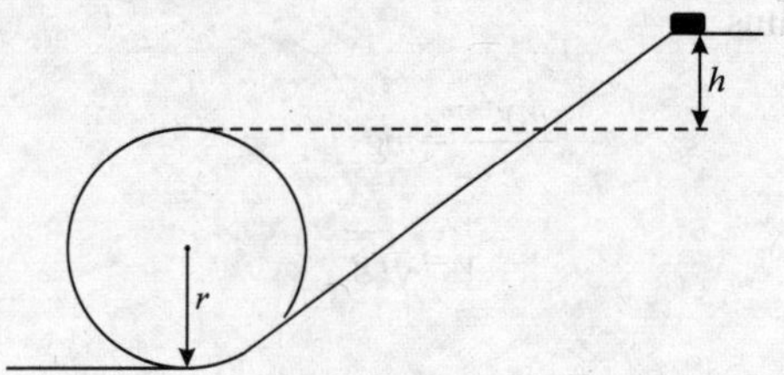

Figure 3.33

Solution

As the surfaces are frictionless, velocity of box at the bottom of the track can be given as

$$v = \sqrt{2g(h+2r)}$$

To complete the loop the box must have its speed at least $\sqrt{5gr}$ at the bottom, otherwise it will loose contact and start following the projectile parabolic trajectory. Thus we have

$$\sqrt{2g(h+2r)} = \sqrt{5gr}$$

or $$h+2r=\frac{5}{2}r$$

or $$h=\frac{r}{2}$$

Illustrative Example 3.21

Figure-3.34 shows a smooth track, a part of which is a circle of radius r. A block of mass m is pushed against a spring of spring constant k fixed at the left end and is then released. Find the initial compression of the spring so that the block presses the track with a force mg when it reaches the point P, where the radius of the track is horizontal.

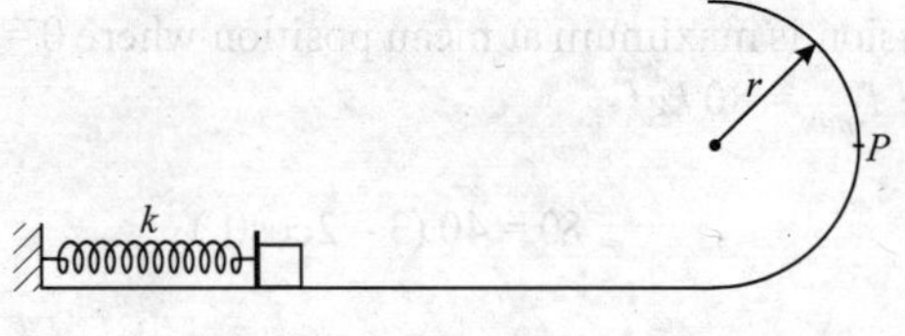

Figure 3.34

Solution

Let the initial compression of the spring is x and when the spring is released, the stored compressional energy in the spring is given to the block and it shoots on the track, which ends in a vertical circle of radius r. When mass reaches the point P, the weight of block at this point is in vertical downward direction and the block pushes the track with the only force mv^2/r.

At P the force on track should be equal to the weight of the block, thus

$$\frac{mv^2}{r}=mg$$

or $$v=\sqrt{rg}$$

Now we apply work-energy theorem from starting point of the spring to the point P for the block.

As initial kinetic energy of the block is zero and at P it is $\frac{1}{2}mv^2$, thus we have

$$0+\frac{1}{2}kx^2-mgr=\frac{1}{2}mv^2$$

or $$\frac{1}{2}kx^2-mgr=\frac{1}{2}m(rg)$$

or $$kx^2=3\,mgr$$

or $$x=\sqrt{\frac{3mgr}{k}}$$

Illustrative Example 3.22

A small box of mass m is kept on a fixed, smooth sphere of radius R at a position where the radius through the box makes an angle of 30° with the vertical. The box is released from this position. (a) What is the force exerted by the sphere on the box just after the release ? (b) Find the distance travelled by the box before it leaves contact with the sphere.

Solution

(a) At the time of release speed of box is zero. It will push the sphere only with the normal component of its weight. Along radial direction, we have

$$N=mg\cos 30°$$

or $$N=\frac{\sqrt{3}}{2}mg$$

(b) The situation is shown in figure-3.35.

Let the box loose contact with the sphere at an angle θ from the vertical. At this instant its normal reaction becomes zero, thus we have at this point

$$\frac{mv^2}{R}=mg\cos\theta$$

or $$v=\sqrt{Rg\cos\theta} \quad \ldots(3.42)$$

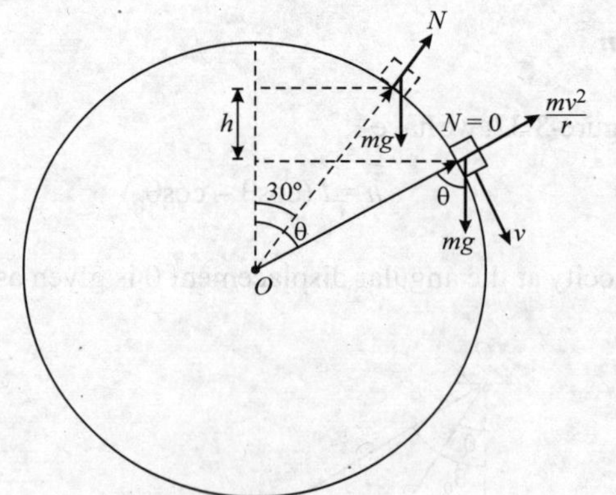

Figure 3.35

Velocity of particle at this point can be given by energy conservation as it has fallen a distance h, we have

$$h=R(\cos 30°-\cos\theta)$$

and $$v=\sqrt{2gh}=\sqrt{2gh\left(\frac{\sqrt{3}}{2}-\cos\theta\right)} \quad \ldots(3.43)$$

Equating equations-(3.42) and (3.43), we have

$$\cos\theta = \sqrt{3} - 2\cos\theta$$

or $$\cos\theta = \frac{1}{\sqrt{3}}$$

$$\theta = 54.73°$$

Angular displacement of the box before leaving the sphere is $54.73° - 30 = 24.73°$

Distance travelled by the box is

$$= \frac{24.73}{180} \times 3.14 \times R = 0.431R$$

Illustrative Example 3.23

A particle is suspended from a fixed point by a string of length 5 m. It is projected from the equilibrium position with such a velocity that the string slackens after the particle has reached a height 8 m above the lowest point. Find the velocity of the particle, just before the string slackens. Find also, to what height the particle can rise further.

Solution

As shown in figure-3.36 at point B, $T = 0$

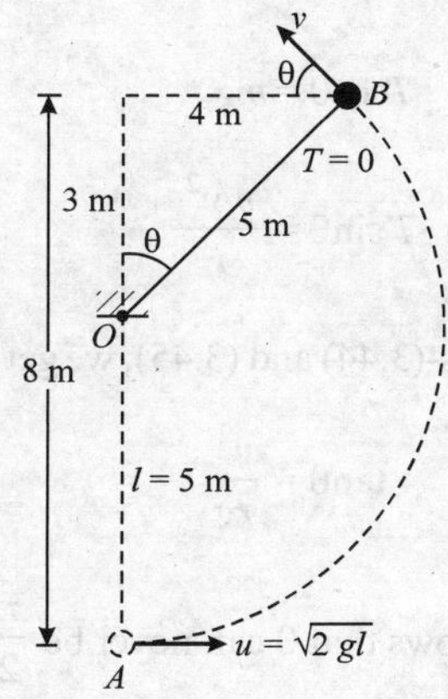

Figure 3.36

Thus we have

$$\frac{mv^2}{l} = mg\cos\theta$$

or $$v = \sqrt{gl\cos\theta} = \sqrt{29.4}$$

or $$= 5.42 \text{ m/s}$$

After point B, particle will move in a projectile trajectory with this initial velocity. Let h be the maximum height it further rises. It is given as

$$h = \frac{v^2 \sin^2\theta}{2g}$$

or $$= \frac{29.4 \times (4/5)^2}{2 \times 9.8} = 0.96 \text{ m}$$

Illustrative Example 3.24

A heavy particle hanging from a fixed point by a light inextensible string of length l is projected horizontally with speed $\sqrt{gl}$. Find the speed of the particle and the inclination of the string to the vertical at the instant of the motion when the tension in the string equal to the weight of the particle.

Solution

Given that initial velocity of projection of particle is $u = \sqrt{gl}$. The tension in the string at an angle θ from the vertical is given by equation-(3.36), as

$$T = \frac{mu^2}{l} - 2\,mg + 3\,mg\cos\theta$$

or $$T = 3\,mg\cos\theta - mg \quad [\text{As } u = \sqrt{gl}\,]$$

or $$\cos\theta = \frac{T + mg}{3mg} \quad [\text{As } T = mg]$$

At this angle the velocity is given by equation-(3.34), as

$$v = \sqrt{u^2 - 2gl(1 - \cos\theta)}$$

$$= \sqrt{gl - 2gl \times \frac{1}{3}}$$

or $$= \sqrt{\frac{gl}{3}}$$

Web Reference of Video Lectures at www.physicsgalaxy.com

Age Group - High School Physics | Age 17-19 Years
Section - MECHANICS
Topic - Circular Motion
Module Numbers - 21 to 31

Practice Exercise 3.5

(i) A ball is attached to a horizontal cord of length L whose other end is fixed, (a) If the ball is released, what will be its speed at the lowest point of its path ? (b) A peg is located a distance h directly below the point of attachment of the cord. If $h = 0.75$ L, what will be the speed of the ball when it reaches the top of its circular path about the peg ?

[$\sqrt{2gL}$, $\sqrt{gL}$]

(ii) An automatic tumble dryer has a 0.65 m diameter basket that rotates about a horizontal axis. As the basket turns, the clothes fall away from the basket's edge and tumble over. If the clothes fall away from the basket at a point 60° from the vertical what is the rate of rotation of dryer drum ? Take $g = 10$ m/s^2.

[3.92 rad/s]

(iii) A smooth circular tube is held in a vertical position. A small ball which is free to slide inside the tube is held stationary at the highest position in the tube. If the ball is slightly displaced from its position of rest, show that the force exerted by the ball on the wall of the tube is given as mg (3cosθ – 2), where m is the mass of the ball and θ is the angular displacement from highest position. Upto what value of θ, this result will remain valid.

[$\cos^{-1}(2/3)$]

(iv) A particle is suspended from a fixed point by a string of length 5 m. It is projected from the equilibrium position with such a velocity that the string slackens after the particle has reached a height 8 m above the lowest point. Find the velocity of the particle, just before the string slackens. Find also, to what height the particle can rise further. Take $g = 10$ m/s^2.

[5.42 m/s, 0.96 m]

(v) A stunt pilot in an airplane diving vertically downward at a speed of 220 kph turns vertically upward by following an approximately semicircular path with a radius of 180 m. (a) How many g's does the pilot experience due to his motion alone ? (b) By what factor does the pilot's weight appear to increase at the bottom of the dive ?

[(a) 2g (b) 3 times]

(vi) A smooth surface hemisphere is fixed on a ground as shown in figure-3.37. From the topmost point of it, a small ball starts sliding with no initial velocity. Find the distance s between the center of base circle of hemisphere and the point where particle strikes the ground.

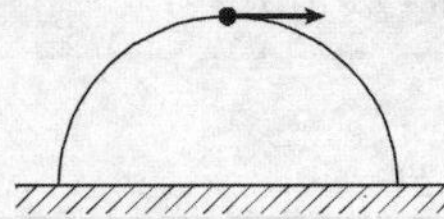

Figure 3.37

[$\frac{R}{27}[4\sqrt{23} + 5\sqrt{5}]$]

3.8 Horizontal Circular Motion

When you revolve a stone tied with a string over your head is the most common example of horizontal circular motion. In such cases gravity acts perpendicular to the circular path, hence it can not affect the speed of the path but for vertical equilibrium there must be a balancing force against gravity. Figure-3.38 shows the case we were discussing. In this case the balancing force is the vertical component of tension in string T cosθ. Here horizontal component of tension T sinθ is acting toward centre of the circle. It is the required centripetal force for circular motion.

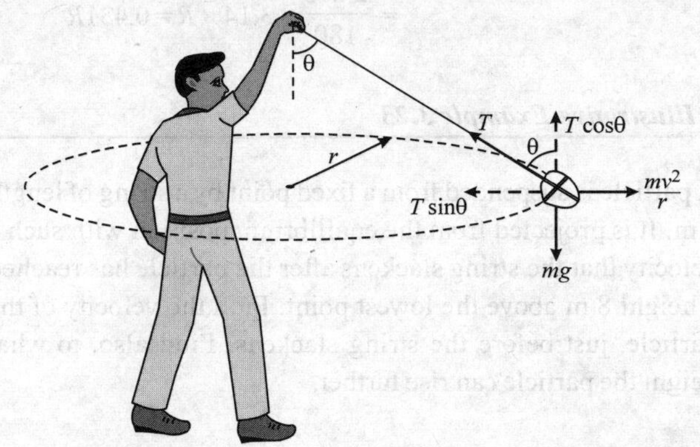

Figure 3.38

Along radial and vertical directions, we have

$$T\cos\theta = mg \qquad \ldots(3.44)$$

and

$$T\sin\theta = \frac{mv^2}{r} \qquad \ldots(3.45)$$

Dividing equations-(3.44) and (3.45), we get

$$\tan\theta = \frac{v^2}{rg} \qquad \ldots(3.46)$$

Above relation shows that θ can never be $\frac{\pi}{2}$. It can be if and only if $v \to \infty$.

Squaring and adding the above equations, we get

Tension in string $$T = m\sqrt{g^2 + \frac{v^4}{r^2}} \qquad \ldots(3.47)$$

3.8.1 Banking of Tracks

A popular example of horizontal circular motion is the effect on a two wheeler or four wheeler, while taking a turn on a circular road. Several different cases of turning can be considered. Let us discuss few of them

Case-I : Two Wheeler on a Flat Road and Banked Road

Figure-3.39 shows a two wheeler taking a turn on a curved road with radius of curvature R. During turning it experiences (with respect to himself or bike) an outward external force, the centrifugal force, which will tend to pull it in outward direction. Here the centripetal force is provided by friction between road and tyre contacts which will act in radially inward direction as shown in figure. As we know that the maximum value of friction force possible is μN, and here $N = mg$

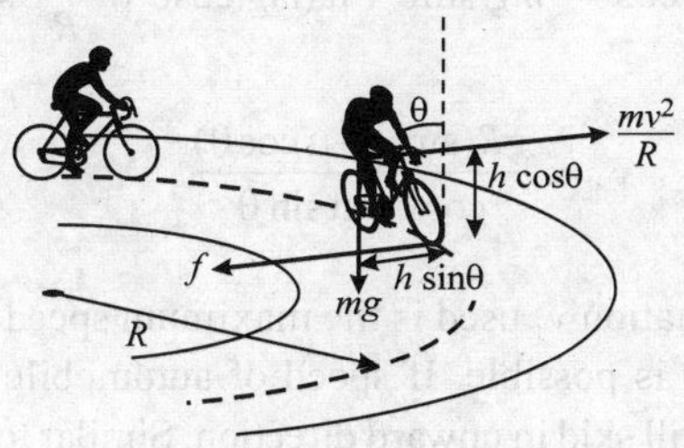

Figure 3.39

Thus for safe turning without skidding, we must have

$$\frac{mv^2}{R} < \mu mg$$

or $$v < \sqrt{\mu R g} \quad \ldots(3.48)$$

Also during a safe turn, the motorcyclist tilt himself at an angle θ, otherwise the vehicle will topple on outer side, due to the clockwise torque of mv^2/R, which can be evaluated as

$$\tau_{ck} = \frac{mv^2}{R} \times h\cos\theta \quad \ldots(3.49)$$

Where h is the height of center of mass of the bike and the rider.

This torque is balanced by the anticlockwise torque provided by mg, which can be given as

$$\tau_{ack} = mg \times h\sin\theta \quad \ldots(3.50)$$

For safe turning above two torques will balance each other. Thus

$$\frac{mv^2}{R} \times h\cos\theta = mg \times h\sin\theta$$

$$\tan\theta = \frac{v^2}{Rg}$$

or $$\theta = \tan^{-1}\frac{v^2}{Rg} \quad \ldots(3.51)$$

If angle of tilt θ, is increased beyond this value, torque of mg will become more than that of mv^2/R, and bike will topple inward and because of short angle of tilt, it will topple outward.

For several situation for safe turning, road constructors make the road banked at a suitable angle for a general speed and put a speed limit board before turn. If rider takes the turn at this speed it can be taken without tilting himself as the road is banked as shown in figure-3.40 which shows the cross section of a bike taking turn at a banked road. In this case normal reaction on bike is in the direction perpendicular to road, horizontal component of which balances the centrifugal force and vertical component balances its weight.

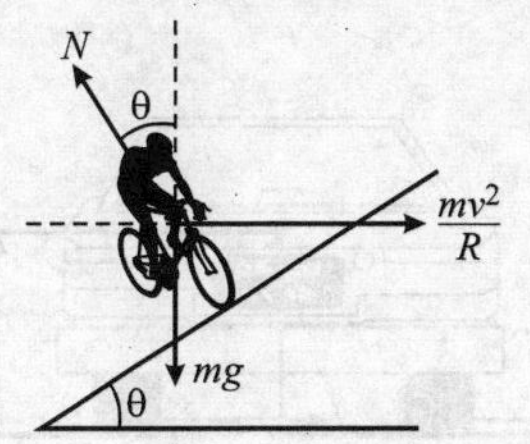

Figure 3.40

Case-II : Four Wheeler on Flat Road and Banked Road

Let us consider a four wheeler taking a turn on a flat road shown in figure-3.41(a). During turn, it experiences the centrifugal force on its centre of mass with respect to the frame of car taking the turn which is at a height h above the ground. With respect to the outer wheels contact, there is a torque of centrifugal force on it in clockwise direction given as

$$\tau_{ck} = \frac{mv^2}{R} \times h$$

The weight of automobile will also exert an anticlockwise torque on it, about the same contact, which will tend the automobile's inner wheels on ground contact. The anticlockwise torque on car due to its weight is given as

$$\tau_{ack} = mg \times \frac{l}{2}$$

Where l is the distance between the tyres of the car. If clockwise torque due to centrifugal force will exceed the anticlockwise torque, the inner wheels will loose contact with ground and the automobile will tend to overturn, as shown in figure-3.41(b). If now velocity is not decreased then also it will overturn. The maximum speed limit to which car will not overturn can be calculated by equating the two torques, given as

$$\frac{mv^2}{R} \times h = mg \times \frac{l}{2}$$

$$\Rightarrow \quad v = \sqrt{\frac{Rgl}{2h}}$$

Above expression of speed limit is the safe turning speed limit for car without overturning provided car tyres does not skid for which minimum friction is needed on road otherwise due to centrifugal force, car tyres will skid outward.

Similar to the case of two wheeler, here also we can make the road banked for safe turning. But here an additional possibility of skidding is also present. Now look at the figure-3.42, which shows the cross sectional view of the turning automobile on a banked road. The centrifugal force on it is in horizontally outward direction. We resolve this force and weight of automobile in the direction along the banked road and perpendicular to it.

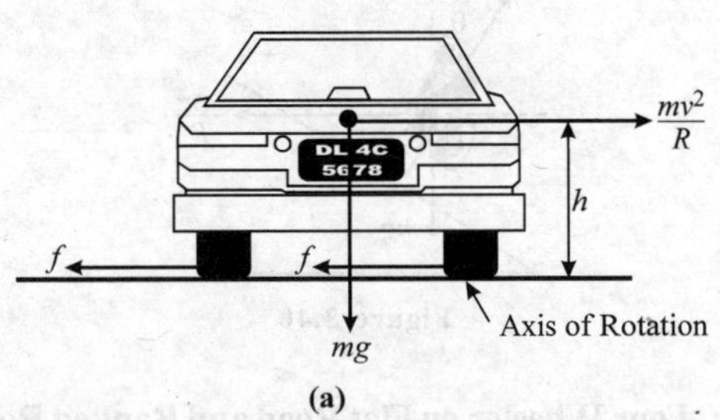

(a)

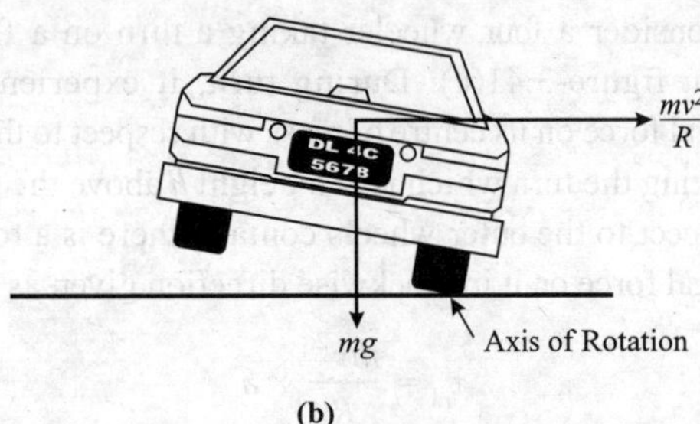

(b)

Figure 3.41

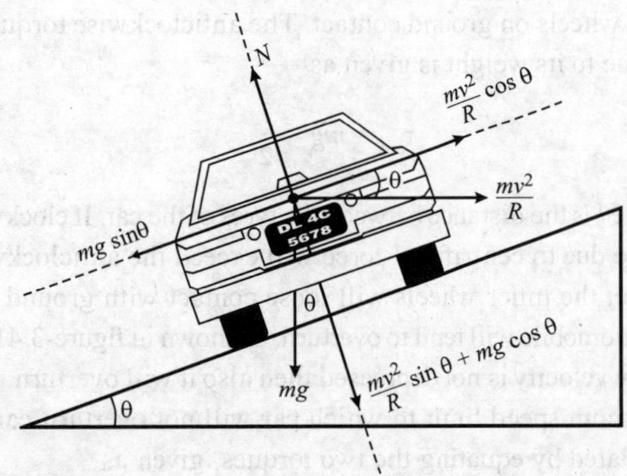

Figure 3.42

The tendency of skidding of automobile, depends on its speed. If its speed is high such that on the automobile $\frac{mv^2}{R}\cos\theta > mg\sin\theta$, it will have a tendency of skidding in upward direction and friction on vehicle acts in downward direction along the banked road and if the vehicle is moving at such a speed so that $\frac{mv^2}{R}\cos\theta$ exceeds $mg\sin\theta$ + friction on it, the automobile will skid upward. Thus maximum speed limit of automobile without skidding on banked road can be obtained by the relation given below.

$$\frac{mv_1^2}{R}\cos\theta = mg\sin\theta + \mu\left(mg\cos\theta + \frac{mv_1^2}{R}\sin\theta\right)$$

$$\Rightarrow \qquad v_1 = \sqrt{\frac{gR(\sin\theta + \mu\cos\theta)}{\cos\theta - \mu\sin\theta}}$$

In above equation v_1 used is the maximum speed up to which safe turning is possible. If speed of automobile exceed this speed v_1, it will skid in upward direction. Similar to this if speed decreases, tendency of skidding may become downward and in this situation, friction will act in upward direction. It is possible when $mg\sin\theta > \frac{mv^2}{R}\cos\theta$. If speed decreases beyond a minimum value, automobile will skid downward if the banking angle is greater than angle of respose. This minimum speed can be obtained by the relation given below.

$$mg\sin\theta = \frac{mv_2^2}{R}\cos\theta + \mu\left(mg\cos\theta + \frac{mv_2^2}{R}\sin\theta\right)$$

$$\Rightarrow \qquad v_2 = \sqrt{\frac{gR(\sin\theta - \mu\cos\theta)}{\cos\theta + \mu\sin\theta}}$$

Above relation gives the value of minimum velocity v_2 which is required for safe turning on a banked road if banking angle is greater than angle of respose. Thus for turning without skidding the automobile velocity must be between v_2 and v_1.

If the banking angle of road is less than angle of repose than car will not skid even if it is at rest so there is no lower speed limit on such a banked road for safe turning without skidding.

Let us take few examples, for the concepts circulation of horizontal circular motion.

Illustrative Example 3.25

A particle of mass m is attached to one end of a weightless and inextensible string of length L. The particle is on a smooth horizontal table. The string passes through a hole in the table and to its other end is attached a small particle of equal mass m. The system is set in motion with the first particle describing a circle on the table with constant angular velocity ω_1 and the second particle moving in the horizontal circle as a conical pendulum with constant angular velocity ω_2. Show that the length of the portions of the string on either side of the hole are in the ratio $\omega_2^2 : \omega_1^2$.

Solution

Situation is shown in figure-3.43.

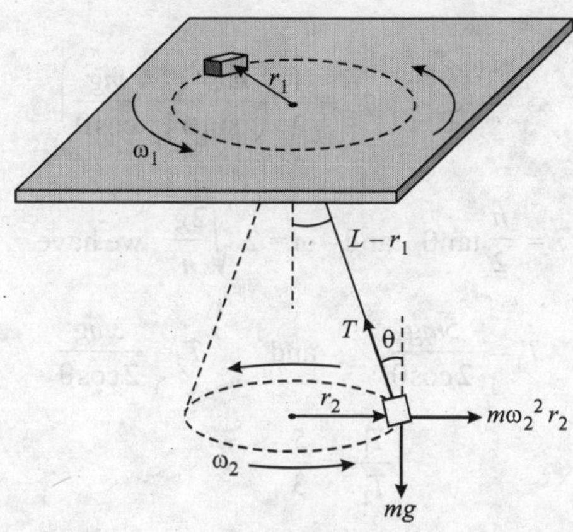

Figure 3.43

Here tension in string remains same as there is no friction between the thread and the edge of the hole in the table. For the two circular motions of upper mass and the lower mass m we have

$$T = m\omega_1^2 r_1 \qquad \dots(3.52)$$

and $$T\sin\theta = m\omega_2^2 r_2 \qquad \dots(3.53)$$

and $$T\cos\theta = mg \qquad \dots(3.54)$$

If length of the thread is taken as L, as shown in figure, radius r_2 can be given as

$$r_2 = (L - r_1)\sin\theta \qquad \dots(3.55)$$

From equations-(3.52), (3.53) and (3.55) we have

$$m\omega_1^2 r_1 = m\omega_2^2 (L - r_1)$$

or $$\frac{r_1}{(L - r_1)} = \frac{\omega_2^2}{\omega_1^2}$$

 # Illustrative Example 3.26

A particle describes a horizontal circle on the smooth inner surface of a conical funnel as shown in figure-3.44. If the height of the plane of the circle above the vertex is 9.8 cm, find the speed of the particle.

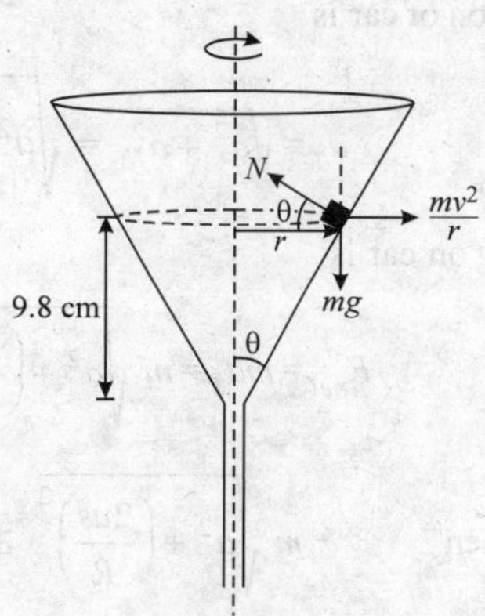

Figure 3.44

Solution

Let the speed of particle be v, with which it is revolving in a circle of radius r, where r is given as

$$r = h\tan\theta$$

Due to its circular motion we have

$$N\cos\theta = \frac{mv^2}{r} \qquad \dots(3.56)$$

or $$N\sin\theta = mg \qquad \dots(3.57)$$

Dividing above equations, we have

$$\tan\theta = \frac{rg}{v^2}$$

Substituting the value of r we get

or $$v = \sqrt{gh} = 0.98 \text{ m/s}$$

 # Illustrative Example 3.27

A car starts from rest in a circular flat road of radius R with an acceleration a. The friction coefficient between the road and the tyres is μ. Find the distance car will travel before it start skidding.

Solution

During circular motion car will skid when net force acting on it exceeds limiting friction. Here it is given that the tangential acceleration of car is a. Thus the speed of car after travelling a distance s is given as $v = \sqrt{2as}$

When speed of car is v, centripetal acceleration on it is

$$a_N = \frac{v^2}{R} = \frac{2as}{R}$$

Total acceleration of car is

$$a_T = \sqrt{a^2 + a_N^2} = \sqrt{a^2 + \left(\frac{2as}{R}\right)^2}$$

Net force acting on car is

$$F_{net} = ma_T = m\sqrt{a^2 + \left(\frac{2as}{R}\right)^2}$$

Car will skid when $\quad m\sqrt{a^2 + \left(\frac{2as}{R}\right)^2} \geq \mu mg$

or $$s = \sqrt{(u^2g^2 - a^2)\left(\frac{R^2}{4a^2}\right)}$$

Illustrative Example 3.28

A particle is attached by means of two equal strings to two points A and B in the same vertical line and describes a horizontal circle with a uniform angular speed. If the angular speed of the particle is $2\sqrt{2g/h}$ with $AB = h$, show that the ratio of the tensions of the strings is 5 : 3.

Solution

The situation is shown in figure-3.45 and the forces acting on the particle are also shown.

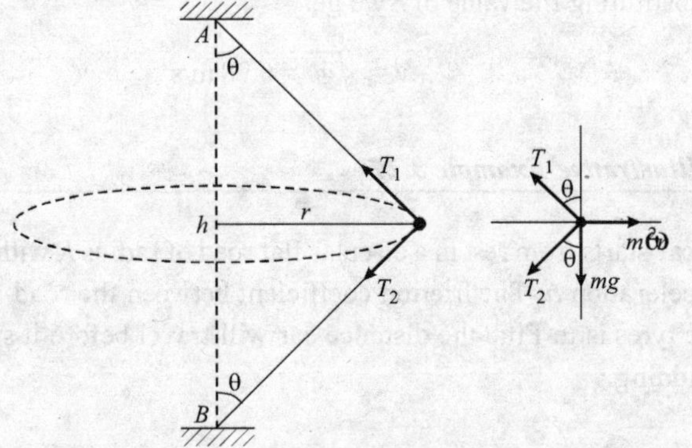

Figure 3.45

According to the vertical and radial equilibrium of the particle, we have

$$T_1 \cos\theta = T_2 \cos\theta + mg$$

or $$(T_1 - T_2)\cos\theta = mg$$

or $$T_1 - T_2 = \frac{mg}{\cos\theta} \quad \ldots (3.58)$$

and $$T_1 \sin\theta + T_2 \sin\theta = m\omega^2 r$$

or $$T_1 + T_2 = \frac{m\omega^2 r}{\sin\theta} \quad \ldots (3.59)$$

Solving equations-(3.58) and (3.59), we get

$$T_1 = \frac{1}{2}\left(\frac{m\omega^2 r}{\sin\theta} + \frac{mg}{\cos\theta}\right)$$

and $$T_2 = \frac{1}{2}\left(\frac{m\omega^2 r}{\sin\theta} - \frac{mg}{\cos\theta}\right)$$

We have $r = \frac{h}{2}\tan\theta$ and $\omega = 2\sqrt{\frac{2g}{h}}$, we have

$$T_1 = \frac{5mg}{2\cos\theta} \quad \text{and} \quad T_2 = \frac{3mg}{2\cos\theta}$$

or $$\frac{T_1}{T_2} = \frac{5}{3}$$

Illustrative Example 3.29

A hemispherical bowl of radius R is set rotating about its axis of symmetry which is kept vertical. A small block kept in the bowl rotates with the bowl without slipping on its surface. If the surface of the bowl is smooth and the angle made by the radius through the block with the vertical is θ, find the angular speed at which the bowl is rotating.

Solution

Let we take the bowl is rotating with an angular velocity ω. The block will be in a circular motion with radius $R\sin\theta$, as shown in figure-3.46. As the block is in equilibrium, we have along horizontal and vertical directions

$$N\cos\theta = mg$$

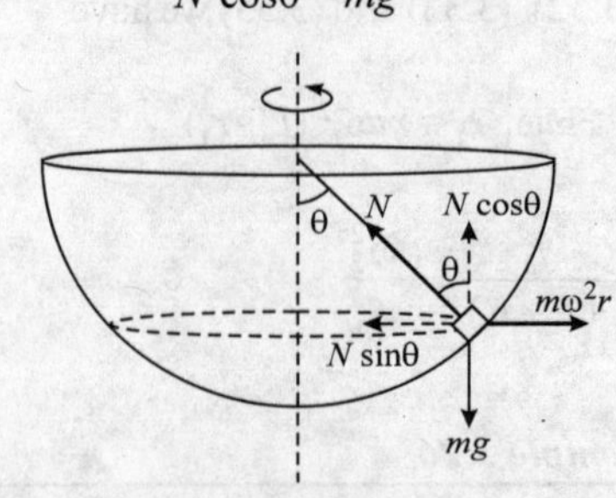

Figure 3.46

and $$N\sin\theta = m\omega^2 R\sin\theta$$

or $$N = m\omega^2 R$$

From above equations we get

$$\frac{mg}{\cos\theta} = m\omega^2 R$$

or $$\omega = \sqrt{gR\sec\theta}$$

Web Reference of Video Lectures at www.physicsgalaxy.com

Age Group - High School Physics | Age 17-19 Years
Section - MECHANICS
Topic - Circular Motion
Module Numbers - 14 and 16

Practice Exercise 3.6

(i) A space station 960 m in diameter rotates fast enough that the artificial gravity at the outer edge is 1.5 g. (a) What is the frequency of rotation ? (b) What is its period ? (c) At what distance from the center will the artificial gravity be 0.75 g ? Take $g = 10\ \text{m/s}^2$.

[0.0281 sec^{-1}, 35.52 sec, 240 m]

(ii) Calculate the angle of banking required for a curve of 200 m radius so that a car rounding the curve at 80 kph would have no tendency to skid outward or inward. Assume the surface is frictionless. Take $g = 10\ \text{m/s}^2$.

[$\tan^{-1}(0.247) \simeq 13.87°$]

(iii) A liquid is kept in a cylindrical vessel which is rotating along its axis. The liquid rises at the sides. If the radius of the vessel is 0.05 m and the speed of rotation is 2 rev. per second, find the difference in the height of the liquid at the center of the vessel and its sides ($g = 10\ \text{m/s}^2$).

[2 cm]

(iv) A sleeve A can slide freely along the smooth rod bent in the shape of a half circle of radius R as shown in figure-3.47. The system is set in rotation with a constant angular velocity ω about the vertical axis OO'. Find the angle θ corresponding to the steady position of the sleeve.

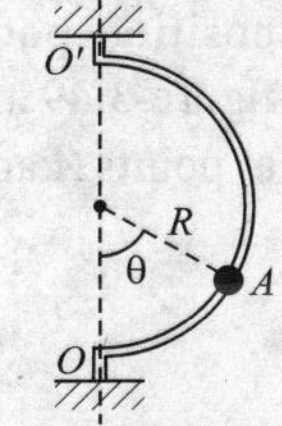

Figure 3.47

[$\theta_1 = 0$ and $\theta_2 = \cos^{-1}(g/\omega^2 R)$]

(v) A hemispherical bowl of radius $R = 0.1$ m is rotating about its own axis (which is vertical) with an angular velocity ω. A particle of mass 0.01 kg on the friction less inner surface of the bowl is also rotating with same ω. The particle is at a height h from the bottom of the bowl. (a) Obtain the relation between h and ω. What is the minimum value of ω needed in order to have a non zero value of h ? (b) It is desired to measure g using this set up, by measuring h accurately. Assuming that r and ω are known precisely, and that the least count in the measurement of h is 10^{-4} m. What is the minimum possible error Δg in the measured value of g ? $g = 9.8\ \text{m/s}^2$.

[$h = R - \frac{g}{\omega^2}$, $7\sqrt{2}$ rad/s, $9.8 \times 10^{-3}\ \text{m/s}^2$]

(vi) A smooth light horizontal rod AB can rotate about a vertical axis passing through its ends A. The rod is fitted with a small sleeve of mass m attached to the end A by a weightless spring of length l_0 and force constant k. What work must be performed to slowly get this system going and reaching the angular velocity ω ?

[$\frac{1}{2}\frac{l_0^2 m\omega^2 k(k+m\omega^2)}{(k-m\omega^2)^2}$]

3.9 Potential Energy & Conservative Force Fields

Force fields are regions in which at any point a body experiences a force under one or more conditions. The force applied by the field on body may impart or extract energy to or from the body by doing work when body is displaced in the field. If the work done against the field force is stored in system this is called interaction or potential energy of system and such a force field is called conservative force field and the forces are called conservative forces. Gravitational forces and electric forces are commonly used conservative forces.

If work done against the field force is dissipated to surrounding then such fields are called non-conservative force fields, and the forces are called non conservative forces. Friction is the most common non-conservative force we use in general cases of dynamics.

3.9.1 Relation in Force and Potential Energy

Potential energy is the stored form of energy and it is a characteristic property of conservative force fields or in a system we define potential energy only when one or more conservative forces are present. For each type of conservative force potential energy is separately defined.

In a conservative force field at every point we can define or consider potential energy of a body placed in the field and at a position far away (infinity) distance from field we assume no interaction of body with the field and this state we consider as reference zero potential energy state.

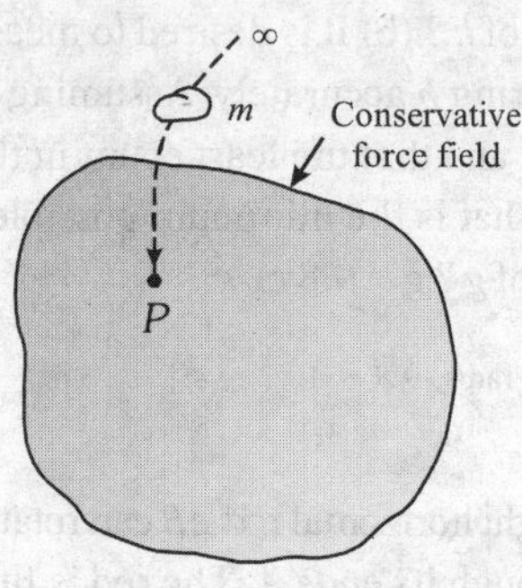

Figure 3.48

$$W_{\infty\to P} = -\int_{\infty}^{P} \overrightarrow{F(r)}\cdot\overrightarrow{dr} \quad \ldots(3.60)$$

Here $-\overrightarrow{F(r)}$ is the external force required to bring the body slowly from infinity to P so body does not gain any kinetic energy. This work done given by equation-(3.60) will be the energy gained by the force field as the force of system would be doing negative work in this process and this energy will be called as potential energy of body in the force field at point P and can be expressed as

$$U_P = -\int_{\infty}^{P} \overrightarrow{F(r)}\cdot\overrightarrow{dr} \quad \ldots(3.61)$$

Thus potential energy of a body in a system of conservative forces can also be defined as

"It is the work done in bringing the body from the state of zero potential energy to any point in space"

Using the above understanding of potential energy we can relate force acting on a body and it potential energy in conservative force fields. If on displacing a body in conservative field at a position $\vec{r}$ by a displacement dr, the change in potential energy of body is given as

$$dU = -\overrightarrow{F(r)}\cdot\overrightarrow{dr} = -F(r)\, dr \cos\theta$$

Where $F(r)\cos\theta$ is the force component along displacement. So in this situation along the position vector the component of force is given as

$$F(r)\cos\theta = -\frac{dU}{dr}$$

or $$\overrightarrow{F(r)}_{11} = -\frac{dU}{dr}\hat{r}$$

If there is a unidirectional force field in which force is varying with x-coordinate of a system and potential energy of system is given as $U(x)$ then the force on a body in this system at a position is given by

$$\overrightarrow{F(x)} = -\frac{dU_{(x)}}{dx}\hat{i} \quad \ldots(3.62)$$

3.9.2 Conservative Force in a three dimensional force field

If in a region of space potential energy of a body varies in three dimensions then force on body is represented as-

$$\vec{F} = -\nabla U \quad \ldots(3.63)$$

Where ∇ is the symbol used for 'gradient' and it is called gradient operator which shows maximum variation rate with position. This is also written as

$$\vec{F} = -\nabla U = -\text{gradient}\,(U)$$

This expression indicates that direction of force is in the direction of maximum decrease in potential energy in space and its magnitude is given by the rate of charge of potential energy with position. For a three dimensional system gradient operator is expressed as

$$\nabla \equiv \frac{\partial}{\partial x}\hat{i} + \frac{\partial}{\partial y}\hat{j} + \frac{\partial}{\partial z}\hat{k}$$

Where ∂ is partial derivative operator system bob. Thus relation in force and potential energy of a body in three dimensional space is given as

$$\vec{F} = -\nabla U = -\left(\frac{\partial U}{\partial x}\hat{i} + \frac{\partial U}{\partial y}\hat{j} + \frac{\partial U}{\partial z}\hat{k}\right) \quad \ldots(3.64)$$

3.9.3 Work done in conservative and non-conservative force fields

As already discussed that in conservative fields at every position potential energy of a body can be defined. In figure-3.49 a conservative force field is shown and for a body at points A and B potential energy is given as

$$U_A = -\int_{\infty}^{A} F(r)\cdot dr$$

and $$U_B = -\int_{\infty}^{B} F(r)\cdot dr$$

Now if the body is displaced from A to B slowly, work done against the field force is given as

$$W = -\int_{A}^{B} F(r)\cdot dr$$

This work increases the potential energy of system as no leases take place in conservative force fields so we use

$$W = -\int_A^B F(r)\cdot dr$$

$$= U_B - U_A = \left(-\int_\infty^B F(r)\cdot dr\right)$$

$$-\left(-\int_\infty^A F(r)\cdot dr\right)$$

Thus work done does not depend on path weather body is displaced along path I or II this work remain same. That is another important point about work in conservative fields we can keep always.

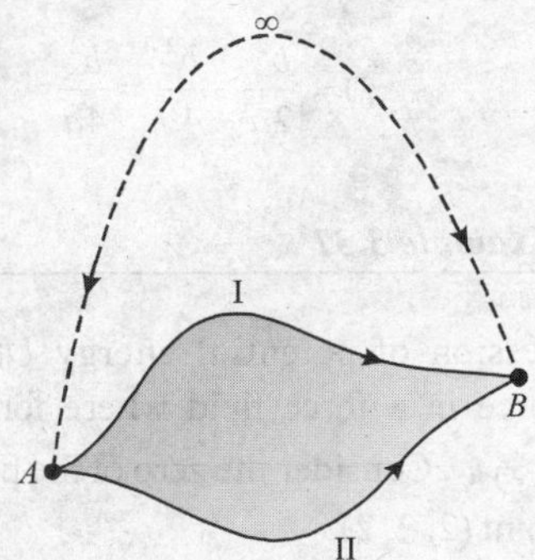

Figure 3.49

"In conservative force fields work done in displacing a body by field forces only depend upon the initial and final position of body and not on the path followed for displacement"

Also remember that the above statement is for field forces not for external forces. This will be valid for external forces if body is displaced slowly and no kinetic energy is imparted to the body.

3.9.4 State of Equilibrium and Potential Energy

In a conservative force field as discussed. The force and potential energy at a position are related as

$$\vec{F} = -\frac{dU}{dr}\vec{r} \text{ [Along position vector } r\text{]}$$

In this expression at the state of equilibrium of body we use

$$\vec{F} = 0 \Rightarrow \frac{dU}{dr} = 0 \qquad \ldots(3.64)$$

Equation-(3.64) explains the condition of equilibrium of body under conservative forces which can exist in three cases when U is constant or U is maximum or U is minimum at a position with respects to the neighbouring positions.

If we see and analyse figure-3.50 which shows variation of potential energy of a body with position in a conservative force field. The positions A, B and C are three points at which we can say that body is in equilibrium. We can also classify different states of equilibrium based on potential energy state of body. Lets discuss these states one by one.

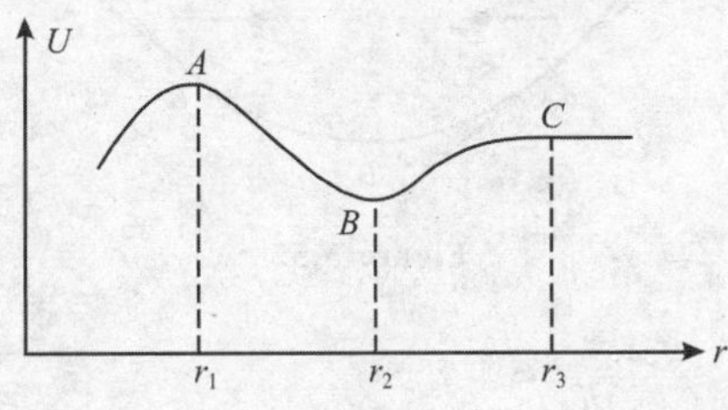

Figure 3.50

3.9.5 Unstable Equilibrium

At point A in figure-3.50 potential energy of body is maximum compared to its neghbouring points and as slope of curve at point A is zero at this point no force is acting on body so this is the state of equilibrium. If we slightly displaced the body away from A in any direction, we can see that the direction of force on body is away from A as force direction is always toward low energy states.

So in this state is body is slightly is displaced from equilibrium position, field force will push the body away from this position. Such an equilibrium state is called unstable equilibrium. Figure-3.51 shows the position of curve in neighborhood of point A and direction of force if body is displaced to $A+$ and $A-$ neghbouring positions.

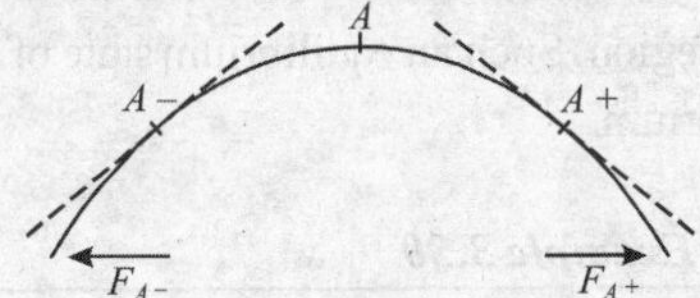

Figure 3.51

As $\vec{F} = -\frac{dU}{dr}\hat{r}$, at $A+$ position $\frac{dU}{dr}$ (slope of curve) is negative hence force on body is in positive direction and at $A-$ position $\frac{dU}{dr}$ (slope of curve) is positive hence force on body is in negative direction.

3.9.6 Stable Equilibrium

At point B in figure-3.50 potential energy of body is minimum compared to its neghbouring points and as slope of curve at B

is zero at this point no force is acting on body so it is the state of equilibrium. If from this point we slightly displace the body away from B in any direction, from figure-3.52 which is the portion of curve shown in figure-3.50, we can see that force on body will act toward point B which has a tendency to restore the equilibrium position of body at point B. Such an equilibrium position is called stable equilibrium position.

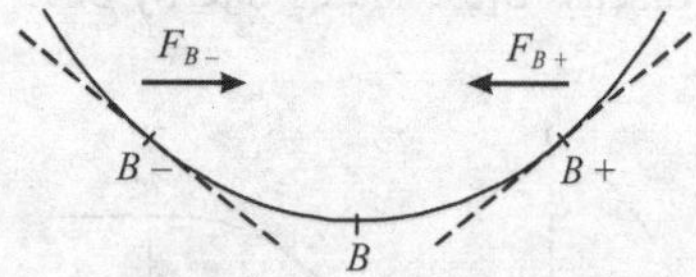

Figure 3.52

At $B+$ position $\frac{dU}{dr}$ (slope of curve) is positive hence force on body is in negative direction

At $B-$ position $\frac{dU}{dr}$ (slope of curve) is negative hence force on body is in positive direction.

The position of curve shown in figure-3.52 is called *"potential well"* in which when a particle is located at equilibrium position and slightly displaced then due to restoring force it starts oscillations about the stable equilibrium position.

3.9.7 Neutral Equilibrium :

At the points in neighborhood of point C, in figure-3.50 potential energy of body in force field is constant so slope of curve is zero and hence no force is acting on body in this region and body will remain in equilibrium if it is displaced any where in this region. Such an equilibrium state of body is called neutral equilibrium.

 # Illustrative Example 3.30

The potential energy function for the force between two atoms in a diatomic molecule is approximately given by $U(x)=\frac{a}{x^{12}}-\frac{b}{x^{6}}$, where a and b are constant and x is the distance between the atoms. Find the dissociation energy of the molecule which is given as $D=[U(x=\infty)-U_{\text{at equilibrium}}]$.

Solution

We are given with potential energy of diatomic molecule as

$$U=\frac{a}{x^{12}}-\frac{b}{x^{6}}$$

At equilibrium state of molecule we have $\frac{dU}{dx}=0$

$$\Rightarrow \quad 12ax^{-13}=6bx^{-7}$$

$$\Rightarrow \quad \frac{2a}{b}=x^{6}$$

$$\Rightarrow \quad x=\left(\frac{2a}{b}\right)^{1/6}$$

Dissociation Energy of the molecule is given as

$$D=U|_{x=\infty}-U|_{x=\left(\frac{2a}{b}\right)^{1/6}}$$

$$\Rightarrow \quad D=\frac{-a}{\left(\frac{2a}{b}\right)^{2}}+\frac{b}{\frac{2a}{b}}$$

$$\Rightarrow \quad D=\frac{b^2}{2a}-\frac{b^2}{4a}=\frac{b^2}{4a}$$

 # Illustrative Example 3.31

Find the expression of potential energy $U(x, y, z)$ for a conservative force in a force field where force is given as $\vec{F}=yz\hat{i}+xz\hat{j}+xy\hat{k}$. Consider the zero of the potential energy chosen at the point (2, 2, 2).

Solution

As the relation in Force and potential energy in a conservative force field is given as

$$\vec{F}=-\frac{\partial U}{\partial x}\hat{i}-\frac{\partial U}{\partial y}\hat{j}-\frac{\partial U}{\partial z}\hat{k}$$

By comparing the given expression of force we have

$$\frac{\partial U}{\partial x}=-yz;$$

$$\frac{\partial U}{\partial y}=-xz;$$

$$\frac{\partial U}{\partial z}=-xy;$$

Therefore $U=-xyz+C$ where C is the constant. As at (2, 2, 2), $U=0$ so we get $C=8$

Thus potential energy of the given force field is $U=(-xyz+8)$ J

 # Illustrative Example 3.32

The potential energy of a particle of mass 1kg free to move

along x-axis is given by $U(x)=\left(\frac{x^2}{2}-x\right)$ joule. If total mechanical energy of the particle is 2 J, then find the maximum speed of the particle. (Assuming only conservative force acts on particle)

Solution

The total mechanical energy of the particle at any instant is sum of kinetic and potential energy hence we use

$$KE+PE=2\text{ J}$$

$$\Rightarrow \quad \frac{1}{2}mv^2+\frac{x^2}{2}-x=2$$

$$\Rightarrow \quad v^2=2x-x^2+4$$

For max v; we use $\frac{d(v^2)}{dx}=0$

$$\Rightarrow \quad 2-2x=0$$

$$\Rightarrow \quad x=1$$

Thus maximum speed is at $x=1$, which is given as

$$v_{max}^2=2-1+4$$

$$v_{max}=\sqrt{5}\text{ ms}^{-1}$$

For general overview of Energy, Work and Circular motion, we take few Illustrative examples, which will help you to understand more concepts of the running topic.

 # Illustrative Example 3.33

A chain of mass m and radius R placed on a smooth table is revolving with a speed v about a vertical axis coinciding with the symmetry axis of the chain. Find the tension in the chain.

Solution

Situation is shown in figure-3.53. The chain is revolving at an angular speed ω, due to this each small part of the chain experiences a centrifugal force in outward direction and as ω increases, tension in chain will increase due to increase in centrifugal force.

To find tension we consider a small elemental length dl on the chain as shown in figure, which subtend an angle $d\theta$ at the center. This element (say mass = dm) experiences the centrifugal force along radially outward direction, given as

$$F_{cf}=\frac{dmv^2}{R}$$

As shown in figure, tension acts at the edges of this dl tangentially away from the element. If we resolve the two tensions along and perpendicular to the element, the components $T\cos\frac{d\theta}{2}$, will cancel

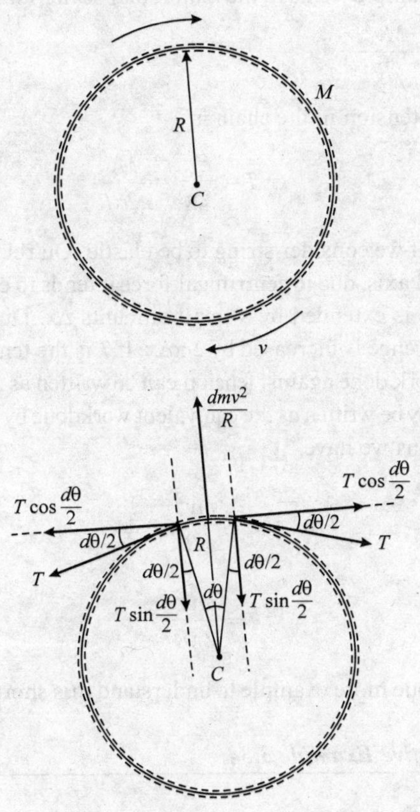

Figure 3.53

each other and the perpendicular components which are in radially inward direction, $2T\sin\frac{d\theta}{2}$ acts as centripetal force and balances the centrifugal force, thus we have

$$2T\sin\frac{\theta}{2}=\frac{dmv^2}{R}$$

As $d\theta$ is very small, we can use $\sin d\theta=d\theta$, thus

$$T\,d\theta=\left(\frac{M}{2\pi R}\times R\,d\theta\right)\times\frac{v^2}{R} \qquad \left[dm=\frac{M}{2\pi R}\times R\,d\theta\right]$$

or

$$T=\frac{Mv^2}{2\pi R}$$

Similar to this problem in further chapters of this book as well as in further volumes you will face different type of problems to find the tension in a string. For all such problems there is a short cut but illogical method also exist to get the final result. Here we explain it.

Direct Short-Cut : To find the tension in a circular chain or a ring, find the net radial scaler force (sum of the total force) acting on the chain in all directions and divide it by 2π.

In this example we have the total radial scaler force on chain is $F_{sc} = \dfrac{Mv^2}{R}$

Thus the tension in the chain is

$$T = \frac{F_{sc}}{2\pi} = \frac{Mv^2}{2\pi R}$$

Proof : If we consider string to be elastic. On relating about its central axis, due to centrifugal force it tends to expand, say its radius is extended by a small amounts Δx. Due to it, the circumference is increased by $2\pi\Delta x$. If T is the tension in the string, work done against tension can be written as $(T \times 2\pi\Delta x)$ which may be written as the equivalent workdone by centrifugal forces, thus we have

$$T \times 2\pi\Delta x = \frac{mv^2}{R} \times \Delta x$$

or
$$T = \frac{mv^2}{2\pi R}$$

We take one more example to understand this short-cut.

Illustrative Example 3.34

Figure-3.54(a) shows a cone of half angle θ on which a chain of mass m is resting with sufficient friction so that it will not slip on the surface of cone. If cone starts rotating at an angular velocity ω, find the tension developed in the chain.

Solution

Figure-3.54(b) shows the force diagram of the chain and cone.

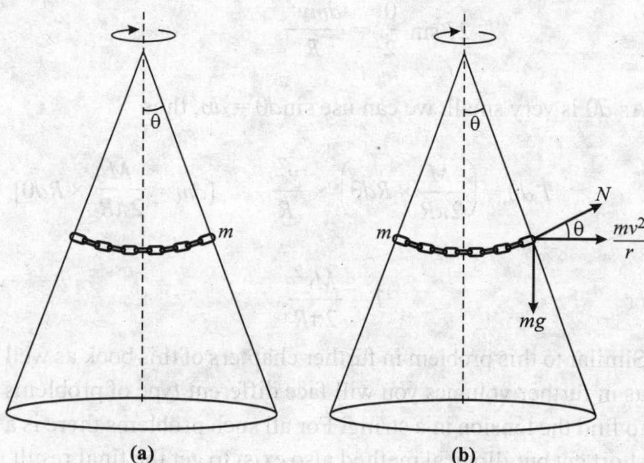

Figure 3.54

Here net radial scaler force acting on the chain is

$$F_{sc} = N\cos\theta + \frac{mv^2}{r}$$

From the condition of equilibrium of chain we have

$$N = mg\sin\theta - \frac{mv^2}{r}\cos\theta$$

Thus we have

$$F_{sc} = mg\sin\theta\cos\theta - \frac{mv^2}{r}(\cos^2\theta - 1)$$

Now the tension in the chain can be directly given as

$$T = \frac{F_{sc}}{2\pi} = \frac{m}{2\pi}\left[g\sin\theta\cos\theta - \frac{v^2}{r}(\cos^2\theta - 1)\right]$$

Illustrative Example 3.35

A uniform chain is held on a frictionless table with one third of its length hanging over the edge. If the chain has a length l and a mass m, how much work is required to pull the hanging part back on the table?

Solution

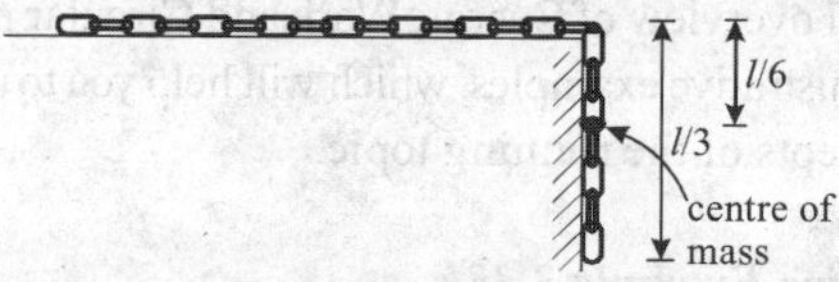

Figure 3.55

The situation is shown in figure-3.55. Here the mass of chain is distributed uniformly along the length of the chain and as the surface is smooth, we can assume that the mass of the hanging part is at its centre of mass and also that of the resting part is on the table. When it is pulled up, work is required against gravity in displacing the centre of mass of the hanging chain up by $l/6$. Hence the work required is

$$W = \frac{m}{3} \times g \times \frac{l}{6} = \frac{mgl}{18}$$

NOTE : If the surface is not smooth then you must not concentrate the distributed mass at the centre of mass.

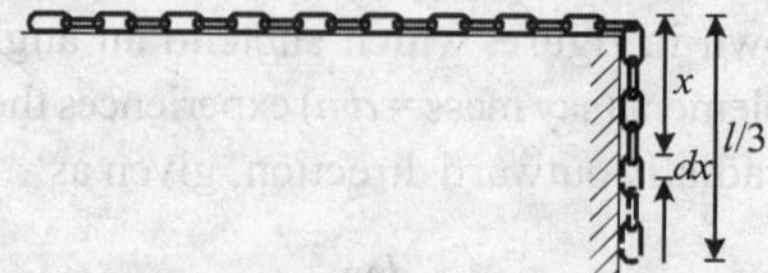

Figure 3.56

Alternatively the problem can be solved by the usual method

of finding the work as

$$W = \int F \cdot dx$$

Figure-3.56 shows the intermediate situation when the chain is being pulled. If its x length is hanging, the force of gravity on it is

$$F = \frac{m}{l}\, x\, g$$

In pulling the chain up by a length dx, work done is

$$dW = \frac{m}{l}\, xg\, dx$$

Total work done in pulling the chain completely is

$$W = \int_{l/3}^{0} \frac{m}{l}\, xg\, dx = -\frac{mgl}{19}$$

Here negative sign signifies that the work done by gravity is negative i.e. work is done against gravity.

Illustrative Example 3.36

A particle of mass m moves along a circle of radius R with a normal acceleration varying with time as $a_N = kt^2$, where k is a constant. Find the time dependence of power developed by all the forces acting on the particle and the mean value of this power averaged over the first t seconds after the beginning of the motion.

Solution

As given in the problem that normal acceleration of the particle varies with time, we have

$$a_N = \frac{v^2}{R} = kt^2$$

or $$v = \sqrt{kRt}$$

On differentiating we get the tangential acceleration of the particle as

$$a_{tan} = \frac{dv}{dt} = \sqrt{kR}$$

Thus total acceleration of the particle is

$$a_T = \sqrt{a_N^2 + a_{tan}^2}$$

The net force acting on particle is

$$F_{net} = ma_T$$

But the power is delivered to the particle by those forces only which are acting along the direction of velocity of the particle. Here it is only the tangential force. Thus power delivered by the forces is given as

$$P = ma_{tan} \times v$$

or $$= m\sqrt{kR} \times \sqrt{kR}t = mkRT$$

Average power over first t seconds of motion can be given as

$$<P> = \frac{\text{Kinetic Energy gained in first t seconds}}{t}$$

Velocity of the particle after t seconds of start is

$$v = \sqrt{kR}t$$

Kinetic energy of it is K.E.

$$= \frac{1}{2}mv^2 = \frac{1}{2}\text{mkRt}^2$$

Thus average power is

$$<P> = \frac{1}{2}\text{mkRt}$$

Illustrative Example 3.37

A system consists of two identical blocks, each of mass m, linked together by the compressed weightless spring of stiffness k, as shown in figure-3.57. The blocks are connected by a thread which is burned through at a certain moment. Find

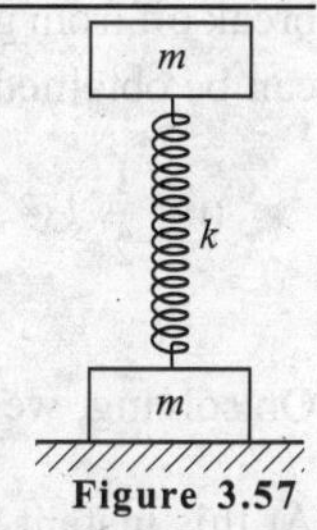

Figure 3.57

(a) At what values of initial compression, the initial compression of the spring, the lower block will bounce up after the thread has been burned through.

(b) To what height will the centre of gravity of this system will rise if the initial compression of the spring is 7 mg/k.

Solution

(a) Let the Initial compression is x in the spring from its natural length. When the thread is burned, the spring shoots towards its natural length and moves up further to a distance h, as shown in figure-3.58. This h should be at least equal to that extension in the spring which is just sufficient to break off the lower mass from ground. Thus when the upper mass reaches the point B, the restoring force on lower block will balance its weight as

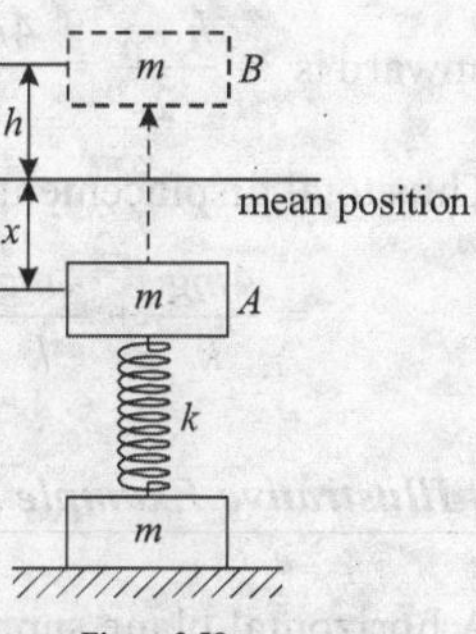

Figure 3.58

$$kh = mg$$

Applying work-energy theorem between points A and B, we get

$$0+\frac{1}{2}kx^2-mg(x+h)-\frac{1}{2}kh^2=0$$

As upper block comes to rest at B, we take $K.E.$ of block zero at B.

or $$x^2-\frac{2mg}{k}x-\frac{3m^2g^2}{k}=0 \quad \left[\text{Substituting } h=\frac{mg}{k}\right]$$

Solving, we get $x=\frac{3mg}{k}$ or $-\frac{mg}{k}$

Since x is positive, the minimum initial compression required is $=\frac{3mg}{k}$

(b) If the initial compression is $\frac{7mg}{k}$, which is greater than the above found $\frac{3mg}{k}$, the lower mass m will also moves up and the centre of mass of the system will move up, say by a maximum distance y from ground and when the lower mass break off from ground, let the upper mass has a speed v, which can be obtained by using work-energy theorem as

$$0+\frac{1}{2}kx^2-mg(x+h)-\frac{1}{2}kh^2=\frac{1}{2}mv^2 \quad \left[\text{Here } x=\frac{7mg}{k}\right]$$

On solving, we get $v=\sqrt{\frac{32m}{k}}\,g$

At this instant lower mass starts from rest, hence velocity of centre of mass is $v_{cm}=\frac{v}{2}=\sqrt{\frac{8m}{k}}\,g$

If the centre of mass further rises up by a distance y, we have

$$y=\frac{v_{cm}^2}{2g}=\frac{4mg}{k}$$

Before the break off of the displacement of centre of mass upward is $=\frac{h+x}{2}=\frac{4mg}{k}$

Thus total displacement of centre of mass upward is

$$=\frac{4mg}{k}+\frac{4mg}{k}=\frac{8mg}{k}$$

Illustrative Example 3.38

A horizontal plane supports a plank with a bar of mass 1 kg placed on it and attached by a light elastic non deformed cord of length 40 cm to a point O as shown in figure-3.59. The coefficient of friction between the bar and plank is 0.2. The plank is slowly shifted to the right until the bar starts sliding over it. It occurs at the moment when the cord deviates from the vertical by 30°. Find the work that has been performed by that moment by the friction force acting on the bar in the reference frame fixed to the plane.

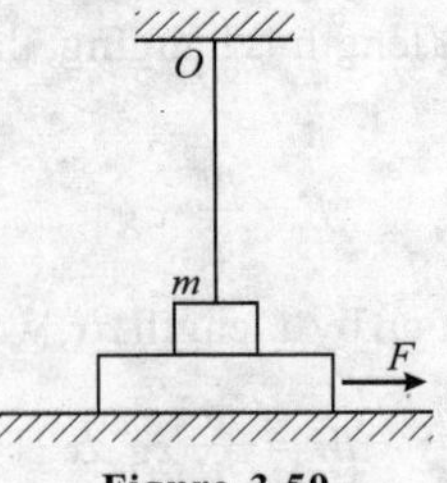

Figure 3.59

Solution

The intermediate force diagram of the system is shown in figure-3.60. We have the extension in cord at this instant is

$$x=l(\sec\theta-1)$$

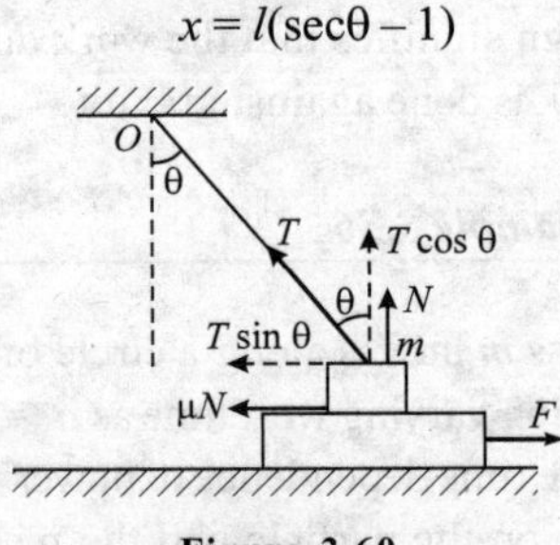

Figure 3.60

If the force constant of the cord is k, in it the tension developed is $T=kx$

The bar will start sliding when

$$kx\sin\theta=\mu N$$

At the instant the normal reaction is

$$N=mg-kx\cos\theta$$

Solving we get $$k=\frac{1}{x}\times\frac{\mu mg}{(\sin\theta+\mu\cos\theta)}$$

or $$=\frac{1}{l(\sec\theta-1)}\times\frac{\mu mg}{(\sin\theta+\mu\cos\theta)}$$

In the process as displacement is slow, the total work done is on the spring as its potential energy increases to $\frac{1}{2}kx^2$.

Thus

Work done against friction = Increment in potential energy of the spring

or $$W=\frac{1}{2}kx^2$$

or $$=\frac{1}{2}\times\frac{\mu mg}{l(\sec\theta-1)\times(\sin\theta+\mu\cos\theta)}\times l^2(\sec\theta-1)^2$$

$$\text{or} \qquad = \frac{\mu mgl(1-\cos\theta)}{2\cos\theta(\sin\theta+\mu\cos\theta)}$$

Substituting the numerical data, we get $W = 0.09$ J

Illustrative Example 3.39

A circular table with smooth horizontal surface is rotating at an angular speed ω about its axis. A groove is made on the surface along a radius and a small particle is gently placed inside the groove at a distance l from the centre. Find the speed of the particle with respect to the table as its distance from the centre becomes L.

Solution

Here the motion of the particle is constrained with in the groove along radial direction. During rotation of the table, when particle is at a distance x from the centre of the table as shown in figure-3.61, its acceleration is given as

$$a = \omega^2 x$$

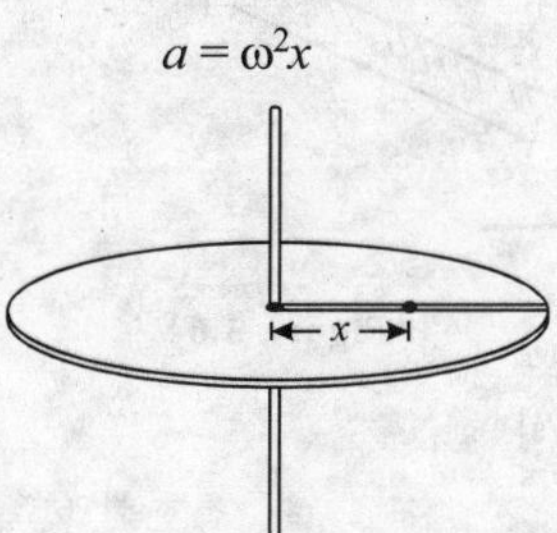

Figure 3.61

$$\text{or} \qquad v\frac{dv}{dx} = \omega^2 x$$

$$\text{or} \qquad v\,dv = \omega^2 x\,dx$$

$$\text{Integrating} \qquad \int_0^v v\,dv = \int_l^L \omega^2 x\,dx$$

$$\text{or} \qquad \left[\frac{v^2}{2}\right]_0^v = \omega^2\left[\frac{x^2}{2}\right]_l^l$$

$$\text{or} \qquad v = \omega(L^2 - l^2)^{1/2}$$

Illustrative Example 3.40

A car starts from rest, on a horizontal circular road of radius R, the tangential acceleration of the car is a. The friction coefficient between the road and the tyre is μ. Find the speed at which car will skid and also find the distance after travelling it skids.

Solution

When car starts, it has two acceleration, normal and tangential. It is given that tangential acceleration is a, and the normal acceleration towards centre is given as

$$a_N = \frac{v^2}{R}$$

Where v is the instantaneous speed of car given as

$$v = at$$

Thus, total acceleration of the car is

$$a_T = \sqrt{a^2 + a_N^2}$$

Net force acting on car is

$$F = ma_T$$

When this net force will exceed the maximum friction on car, it will skid, thus

$$m\sqrt{a^2 + \frac{v^4}{R^4}} \geq \mu mg$$

$$\text{Solving, we get} \qquad v = R^2(\mu^2 g^2 - a^2)^{1/4}$$

The distance travelled by the time it skids is

$$s = \frac{v^2}{2a} = \frac{R^4(\mu^2 g^2 - a^2)^{1/2}}{2a}$$

Illustrative Example 3.41

A small box of mass m is placed on the outer surface of a smooth fixed sphere of radius R at a point where the radius makes an angle φ with the vertical. The box is released from this position. Find the distance travelled by the box before it leaves contact with the sphere.

Solution

The situation is shown in figure-3.62. It starts falling along the circular path outside the sphere and breaks off from the surface when its contact reaction becomes zero. It happens when

$$\frac{mv^2}{R} = mg\cos\theta$$

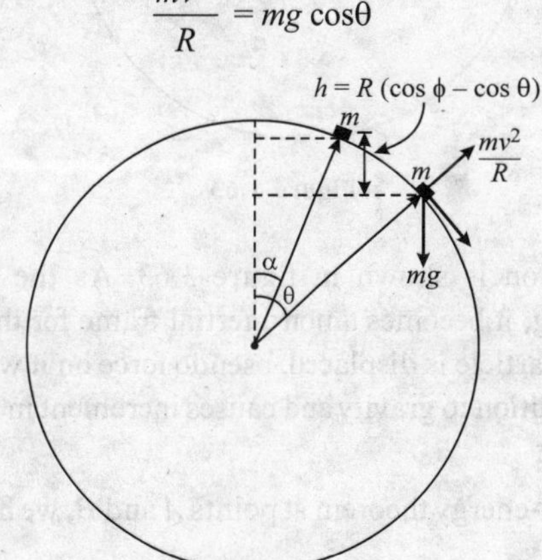

Figure 3.62

or $\qquad v = \sqrt{Rg\cos\theta}$

Where v is the instantaneous velocity of the box at an angle θ from the vertical. It can be obtained by

$$v = \sqrt{2gh} \qquad \text{[As from rest it falls a distance } h\text{]}$$

or $\qquad = \sqrt{2gR(\cos\varphi - \cos\theta)}$

Using above equations, we get

$$\sqrt{Rg\cos\theta} = \sqrt{2gR(\cos\varphi - \cos\theta)}$$

or $\qquad 3\cos\theta = 2\cos\varphi$

or $\qquad \theta = \cos^{-1}\left(\frac{2}{3}\cos\varphi\right)$

Thus distance travelled by the box before leaving the contact with the sphere is

$$s = R(\theta - \varphi)$$

or $\qquad s = R\left[\cos^{-1}\left(\frac{2}{3}\cos\varphi\right) - \varphi\right]$

Illustrative Example 3.42

A smooth sphere of radius R is moving in a straight line with an acceleration a. A particle is released from top of the sphere from rest. Find the speed of the particle when it is at an angular position θ from the initial position relative to the sphere.

Solution

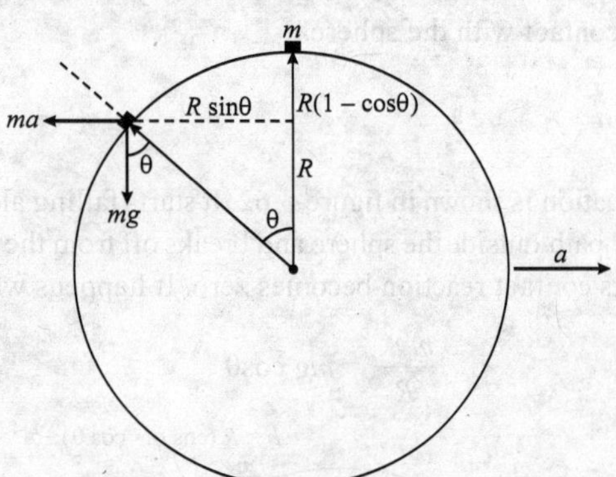

Figure 3.63

The situation is shown in figure-3.63. As the sphere is accelerating, it becomes a non-inertial frame for the particle and when particle is displaced, pseudo force on it will also do work in addition to gravity and causes increment in its kinetic energy.

Using work-energy theorem at points A and B, we have

$$0 + mgR(1 - \cos\theta) + maR\sin\theta = \frac{1}{2}mv^2$$

or $\qquad v = \sqrt{R(a\sin\theta + g(1 - \cos\theta))}$

Practice Exercise 3.7

(i) An ideal massless spring S can be compressed 1.0 m by a force of 100 N. This spring is placed at the bottom of a frictionless inclined plane which makes an angle of 30° with the horizontal as shown in figure-3.64. A 10 kg mass is released from rest at the top of the incline and is brought to rest momentarily after compressing the spring 2.0 m.

(a) Through what distance does the mass slide before coming to rest ?

(b) What is the speed of the mass just before it reaches the spring ?

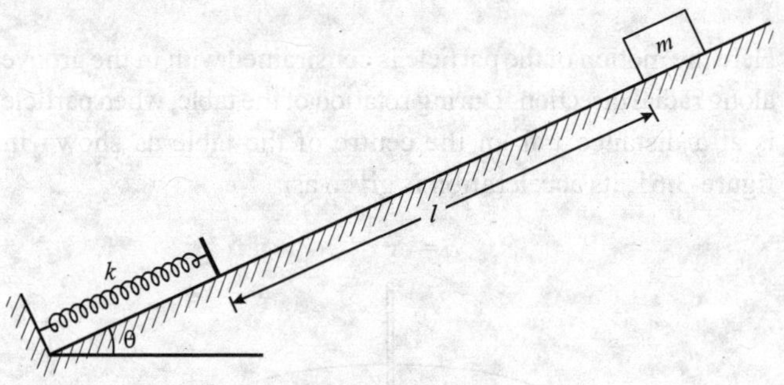

Figure 3.64

[(a) 4m, (b) $\sqrt{20}$ m/s]

(ii) A particle of mass 0.5 kg travels in a straight line with velocity $v = ax^{3/2}$ where $a = 5\ \text{m}^{-1/2}\ \text{s}^{-1}$. What is the work done by the all force during its displacement from $x = 0$ to $x = 2$m?

[50 J]

(iii) A block rests on an inclined plane as shown in figure-3.65. A spring to which it is attached via a pulley is being pulled downward with gradually increasing force. The value of μ_s is known. Find the potential energy U of the spring at the moment when the block begins to move.

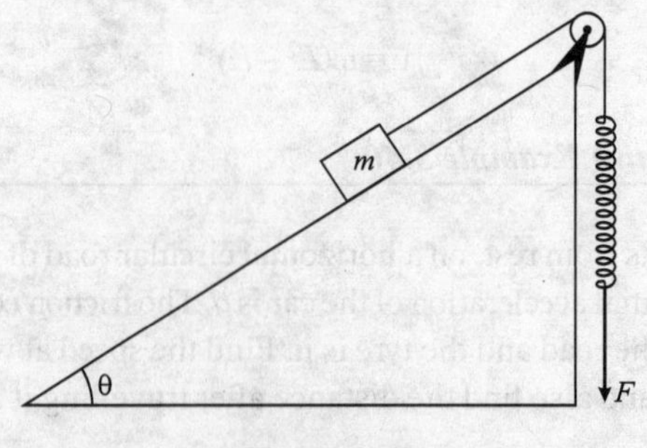

Figure 3.65

$\left[\dfrac{[mg(\sin\theta + \mu_s\cos\theta)]^2}{2k}\right]$

(iv) Force between the atoms of a diatomic molecule has its origin in the interactions between the electrons and the nuclei present in each atom. This force is conservative and associated potential energy $U(r)$ is, to a good approximation, represented by the Lennard – Jones potential.

$$U(r) = U_0\left\{\left(\frac{a}{r}\right)^{12} - \left(\frac{a}{r}\right)^{6}\right\}$$

Here r is the distance between the two atoms and U_0 and a are positive constants. Develop expression for the associated force and find the equilibrium separation between the atoms.

[$\frac{6v_0}{a}\left\{2\left(\frac{a}{r}\right)^{13} - \left(\frac{9}{r}\right)^{7}\right\}, 2^{1/6}a$]

(v) A bob tied to the end of a string of length 2 m, other end of which is fixed at a point in a vertical wall at a point O. The bob is imparted a vertical downward velocity of 5 m/s when the string is horizontal and swings in a vertical plane. Find the angular displacement of the bob from its initial position, when the string breaks. Given that the tensile strength of the string is twice the weight of the bob. Take $g = 10$ m/s^2.

[$\sin^{-1}\left(\frac{2}{3}\right)$]

(vi) In a spring gun having spring constant 100 N/m a small ball of mass 0.1 kg is put in its barrel by compressing the spring through 0.05 m. (a) Find the velocity of the ball when the spring is released. (b) Where should a box be placed on the ground so that the ball falls in it, if the ball leaves the gun horizontally at a height of 2 m above the ground. Take $g = 10$ m/s^2.

[(a) 1.58 m/s, (b) 1 m]

(vii) A chain AB of length equal to the quarter of a circle of radius R is placed on a smooth hemisphere as shown in figure-3.66. When it is released, it starts falling. Find the velocity of the chain when it falls of the end B from the hemisphere.

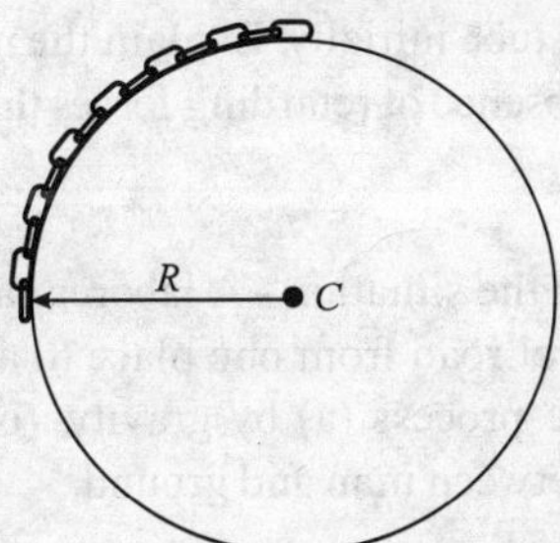

Figure 3.66

[$\left[\sqrt{gR\left(\frac{\pi}{2}+\frac{4}{\pi}\right)}\right]$]

(viii) A particle of mass m approaches a region of force starting from $r = +\infty$. The potential energy function in terms of distance r from the origin is given by,

$$U(r) = \frac{K}{2a^3}(3a^2 - r^2) \text{ for, } 0 \le r \le a$$

$$= K/r \text{ for, } r \ge a$$

(a) Derive the force $F(r)$ and determine whether it is repulsive or attractive.

(b) With what velocity should the particle start at $r = \infty$ to cross over to other side of the origin.

(c) If the velocity of the particle at $r = \infty$ is $\sqrt{\frac{2K}{am}}$, towards the origin describe the motion.

[(a) repulsive (b) $\sqrt{\frac{3K}{am}}$]

(ix) A particle moving in a straight line is acted upon by a force which performs work at a constant rate and changes its velocity from u to v over a distance x. Find the time of the motion.

[$\left[\frac{3}{2}\frac{(u+v)x}{u^2+v^2+uv}\right]$]

(x) The potential energy function of a particle in a region of space is given as $U = (2xy + yz)$J
Here x, y and z are in metre. Find the force acting on the particle at a general point $P(x, y, z)$.

[$\vec{F} = -[2y\,\hat{i} + (2x + z)\,\hat{j} + y\,\hat{k}]$]

Discussion Question

Q3-1 If you take a pail of water and turn it upside down all the water will spill out. But if you take the pail of water, attach a rope to the handle, and turn it rapidly in a vertical circle the water will not spill out when it is upside down at the top of the path why is this ? Explain it is terms of centrifugal force and also in terms of inertia.

Q3-2 Suppose you lift a suitcase from the floor to a table. Does the work you do on the suitcase depend on (a) whether you lift it straight up or along a more complicated path, (b) the time it takes, (c) the height of the table, (d) the weight of the suitcase ? Repeat the parts (a) to (d) for the power needed rather than the work.

Q3-3 When an object slides along a rough surface, the force of friction does negative work on it. Is it ever possible for friction to do positive work ? Give an example.

Q3-4 Springs A and B are identical except that A is stiffer than B. In which spring more work is done if (a) both are stretched by same amount ? (b) both are stretched by the same force ?

Q3-5 If there is a definite force and there is a finite displacement of the force, does that mean work is definitely done by the force ? Explain.

Q3-6 A rock thrown with a certain speed from the top of a cliff will enter the water below with a speed that is the same whether the rock is thrown horizontally or at any angle. Discuss.

Q3-7 If you lift a body to a height h with a force that is equal to the weight of a body, how much work is done and if you lift it with a force that is greater than the weight of a body, where does the extra energy go ?

Q3-8 A spring is kept compressed by tying its ends together tightly. It is then placed in acid and dissolved. What happened to its stored potential energy ?

Q3-9 Potential energy is energy that a body possesses by virtue of its position, while kinetic energy is that a body possesses by virtue of its speed could there be an energy that a body possesses by virtue of its acceleration ? Discuss.

Q3-10 In picking up an object from the floor and putting it on a table, we do work. However, the initial and final values of the object's kinetic energy are zero. Is there a violation of the work energy theorem here ? Explain why or why not.

Q3-11 Reply to the student's statement, "I know there is a centrifugal force acting on me when I move in circular motion in my car because I can feel the force pushing me against the side of the car".

Q3-12 An elevator descends from the top of a building and stops at the ground floor, what becomes of the energy that had been potential energy or the work of gravity ?

Q3-13 For a person to loose weight, is it more effective to exercise or to cut down on the intake of food. Give logical reason.

Q3-14 Does power needed to raise a box onto a platform depend on how fast it is raised ?

Q3-15 The displacement of a body depends on the reference frame of the observer who measures it. It follows that the work done on a body should also depend on the observer's reference frame. Suppose you drag a crate across a rough floor by pulling on it with a rope. Identify reference frames in which the work done on the crate by the rope would be (a) positive, (b) zero, and (c) negative.

Q3-16 A car is running on a road. The driver applies the brakes such that the tyres jam and car skids to stop. Its kinetic energy decreasing to zero. What type of energy increases as a result of the action ? If driver operates the brakes in such a way that there is no skidding or sliding. In this case, what type of energy increases as a result of the action ?

Q3-17 Why is it tiring to hold a heavy weight even though no work is done ?

Q3-18 If positive work is done putting a body into motion, is the work done in bringing a moving body to rest negative work ? Explain.

Q3-19 There is a vertical circular glass tube completely filled with water, except for an air bubble that is temporarily at rest at the bottom of the tube initially. Explain the motion of this air bubble. First in absence of retarding forces than in presence of them.

Q3-20 Consider the situation - A laborer carrying bricks on his head on a level road from one place to another. Find the work done in the process (a) by gravity, (b) by man (c) by frictional force between man and ground.

Q3-21 Does the work done by a force depend on the frame of reference ?

Q3-22 A lorry and a car moving with the same kinetic energy are brought to rest by the application of brakes which provide equal retarding forces. Which of them will come to rest in a shorter distance ?

Q3-23 A car accelerates from an initial speed to a greater final speed while the engine delivers constant power. Is the acceleration greater at the beginning of this process or at the end ?

Q3-24 Two protons are brought towards each other. Will the potential energy of the system decrease or increase ? If a proton and an electron be brought nearer, then ?

Q3-25 For a conservative system, what is $\frac{\Delta E}{\Delta t}$? (E is the kinetic energy of the system)

Q3-26 An automobile jack is used to lift a heavy car by exerting a force that is much smaller in magnitude than the weight of the car. Does this mean that less work is done on the car by the force exerted by the jack than if the car had been lifted directly ? Explain.

Q3-27 Raj meets Jene after several years and is immediately attracted to her. Raj has a mass 50 kg and Jene has a mass 42 kg and initially they are separated by 5 m. Is their attraction purely physical.

Q3-28 A rowboat moves in west direction upstream at 4 kph relative to water. If the current moves east at 3 kph relative to the bank, is any work being done ?

Q3-29 If we throw a stone at an angle to the horizontal, it follows a parabolic path. Another second stone is also thrown with the same speed and at the same angle alongside the first. An insect sitting on the second stone who have some idea of Mechanics, observes the path of first stone and decares that it does not have any kinetic energy at all. Who is right, you or the insect ? How does the law of conservation of energy fit into this situation (with respect to you and insect) ?

Q3-30 Work done by external forces is always equal to the gain in kinetic energy. Is it always true ?

Q3-31 In a tug of war one team is slowly giving way to the other. What work is being done and by whom ?

Q3-32 Why is it easier to climb a mountain via a zigzag trail rather than to climb straight up ?

Q3-33 "Work done in raising a box on to a platform does not depend on how fast it is raised" Justify the statement.

* * * * *

Conceptual MCQs Single Option Correct

3-1 The force acting on a body moving along x axis varies with the position of the particle as shown in the figure-3.67. The body is in stable equilibrium at :

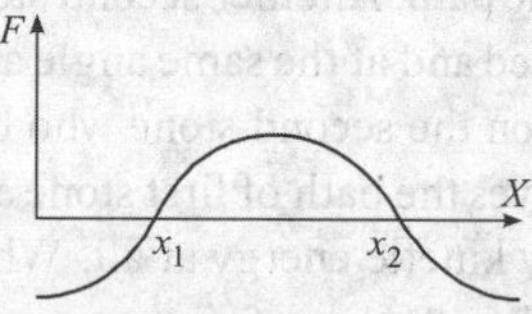

Figure 3.67

(A) $x = x_1$ (B) $x = x_2$
(C) Both x_1 and x_2 (D) Neither x_1 nor x_2

3-2 A particle of mass m is tied to a light string and rotated with a speed v along a circular path of radius r. If T = tension in the string and mg = gravitational force on the particle then the actual forces acting on the particle are :

(A) mg and T only
(B) mg, T and an additional forces of mv^2/r directed inwards
(C) mg, T and an additional forces of mv^2/r directed outwards
(D) Only a force mv^2/r directed outwards

3-3 A small block is shot into each of the four tracks as shown below. Each of the tracks risks to the same height. The speed with which the block enters the track is the same in all cases. At the highest point of the track, the normal reaction is maximum in :

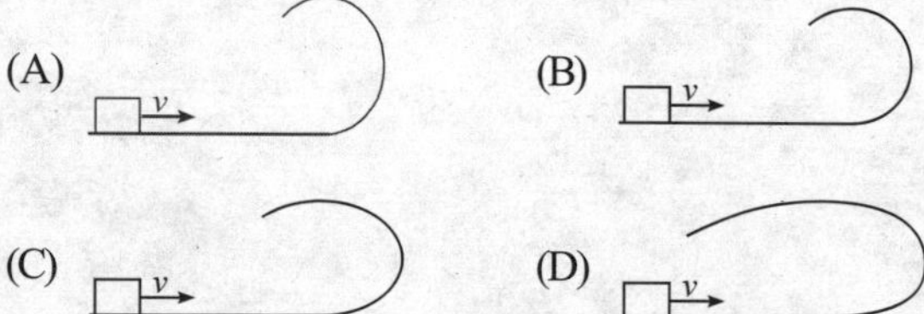

3-4 If the earth stops rotating, the apparent value of g on its surface will :

(A) Increases everywhere
(B) Decrease everywhere
(C) Remain the same everywhere
(D) Increase at some places and remain the same at some other places

3-5 A body is moved along a straight line by a machine delivering constant power. The distance moved by the body in time t is proportional to :

(A) $t^{1/2}$ (B) $t^{3/4}$
(C) $t^{3/2}$ (D) t^2

3-6 A car moves at a constant speed on a road as shown in figure-3.68. The normal force by the road on the car is N_A and N_B when it is at the points A and B respectively :

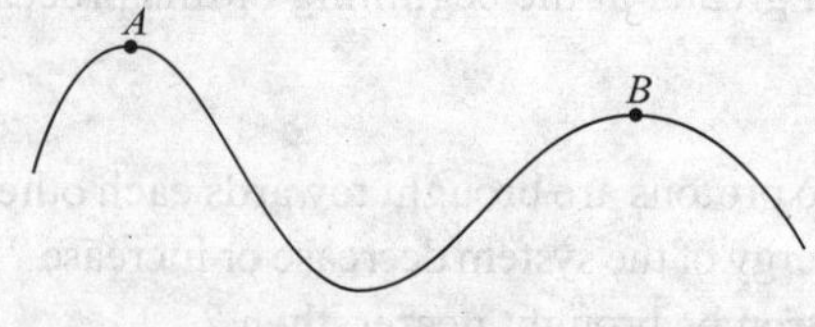

Figure 3.68

(A) $N_A = N_B$
(B) $N_A < N_B$
(C) $N_A > N_B$
(D) Insufficient information to decide the relation of N_A and N_B.

3-7 The tube AC forms a quarter circle in a vertical plane. The ball B has an area of cross-section slightly smaller than that of the tube, and can move without friction through it. B is placed at A and displaced slightly. It will :

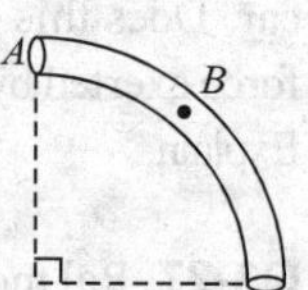

Figure 3.69

(A) Always be in contact with the inner wall of the tube
(B) Always be in contact with the outer wall of the tube
(C) Initially be in contact with the inner wall and later with the outer wall
(D) Initially be in contact with the outer wall and later with the inner wall.

3-8 A train A runs from east to west and another train B of the same mass runs from west to east at the same speed along the equator. A presses the track with a force F_1 and B presses the track with a force F_2 :

(A) $F_1 > F_2$
(B) $F_1 < F_2$
(C) $F_1 = F_2$
(D) The information is insufficient to find the relation between F_1 and F_2.

3-9 In the figure-3.70, the ball A is released from rest when the spring is at its natural (unstretched) length. For the block B, of mass M to leave contact with the ground at some stage, the minimum mass of A must be :

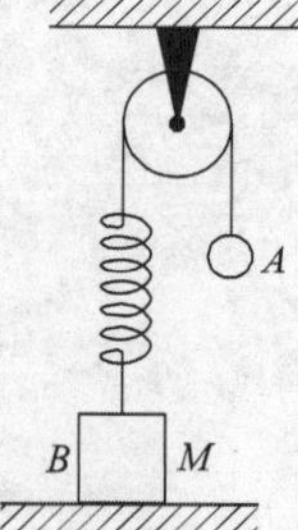

Figure 3.70

(A) 2 M
(B) M
(C) $M/2$
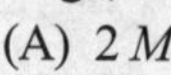
(D) A function of M and the force constant of the spring.

3-10 The figure-3.71 shows the variation of energy with the orbit radius of a body in circular planetary motion. Find the correct statement about the curves A, B and C :

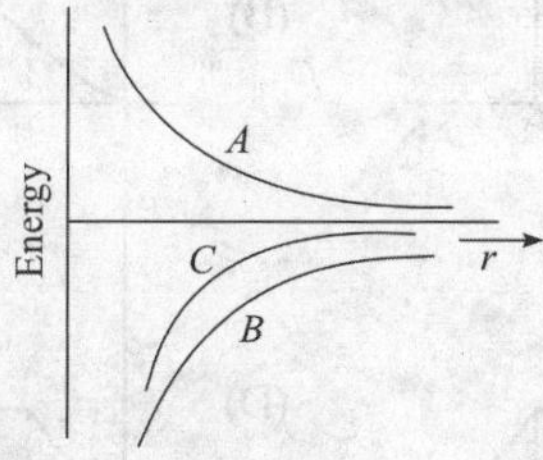

Figure 3.71

(A) A shows the kinetic energy, B the total energy and C the potential energy of the system.
(B) C shows the total energy, B the kinetic energy and A the potential energy of the system.
(C) C and A are kinetic and potential energies respectively and B is the total energy of the system.
(D) A and B are kinetic and potential energies and C is the total energy of the system.

3-11 An aircraft is travelling at constant speed in a horizontal circle with centre Q. Each diagram below shows a tail view of the aircraft, the dotted line representing the line of the wings and the circle representing the centre of gravity of the aircraft. Which one of the diagram correctly shows the force acting on the aircraft ?

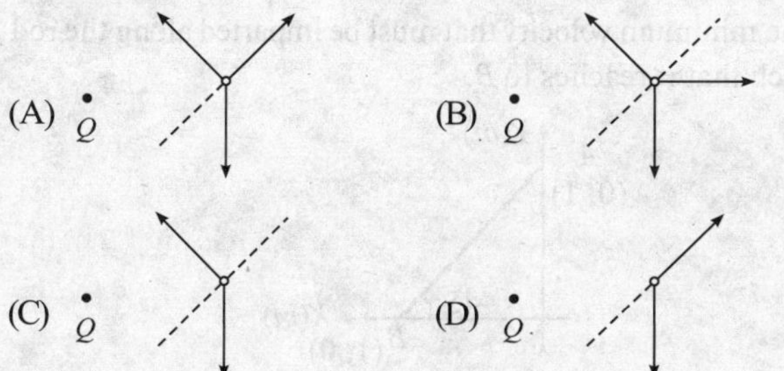

3-12 A lorry and a car moving with the same K.E. are brought to rest by applying the same retarding force. Then
(A) Lorry will come to rest in a shorter distance
(B) Car will come to rest in a shorter distance
(C) Both come to rest in same distance
(D) None of above

3-13 A rod of length L is pivoted at one end and is rotated with a uniform angular velocity in horizontal plane. Let T_1 and T_2 be the tensions at the points $L/4$ and $3L/4$ away from the pivoted ends :
(A) $T_1 > T_2$
(B) $T_2 > T_1$
(C) $T_1 = T_2$
(D) The relation between T_1 and T_2 depends on whether the rod rotates clockwise or anticlockwise.

3-14 A block of mass m slides down a smooth vertical circular track. During the motion, the block is in :
(A) Vertical equilibrium (B) Horizontal equilibrium
(C) Radial equilibrium (D) None of these.

3-15 The potential energy of a particle varies with x according to the relation $U(x) = x^2 - 4x$. The point $x = 2$ is a point of :
(A) Stable equilibrium (B) Unstable equilibrium
(C) Neutral equilibrium (D) None of above

3-16 A motor drives a body along a straight line with a constant force. The power P developed by the motor must vary with time t as :

(A) 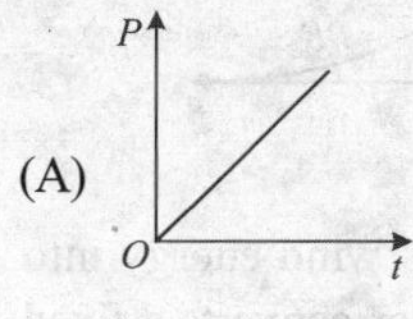

(B) 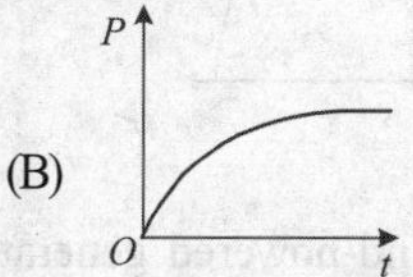

(C) 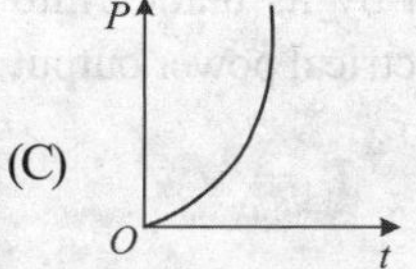

(D) 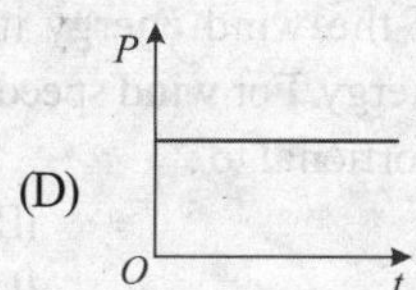

3-17 A motorcycle is going on an overbridge of radius R. The driver maintains a constant speed. As the motorcycle is ascending on the overbridge, the normal forces on it is :
(A) Increasing (B) Decreases
(C) Remains the same (D) Fluctuates.

3-18 A particle of mass 2kg starts moving in a straight line with an initial velocity of 2m/s at a constant acceleration of 2m/s^2. Then rate of change of kinetic energy :
(A) Is four times the velocity at any moment
(B) Is two times the displacement at any moment
(C) Is four times the rate of change of velocity at any moment
(D) Is constant throughout

3-19 A ball is released from the top of a tower. The ratio of work done by force of gravity in first, second and third second of the motion of ball is :
(A) 1 : 2 : 3 (B) 1 : 4 : 16
(C) 1 : 3 : 5 (D) 1 : 9 : 25

3-20 The ratio of momentum and kinetic energy of particle is inversely proportional to the time. Then this is the case of a:
(A) Uniformly accelerated motion
(B) Uniform motion
(C) Uniformly retarded motion
(D) Simple harmonic motion

3-21 A particle falls from rest under gravity. Its potential energy with respect to ground (*PE*) and its kinetic energy (*KE*) are plotted against time (*t*). Choose the correct graph :

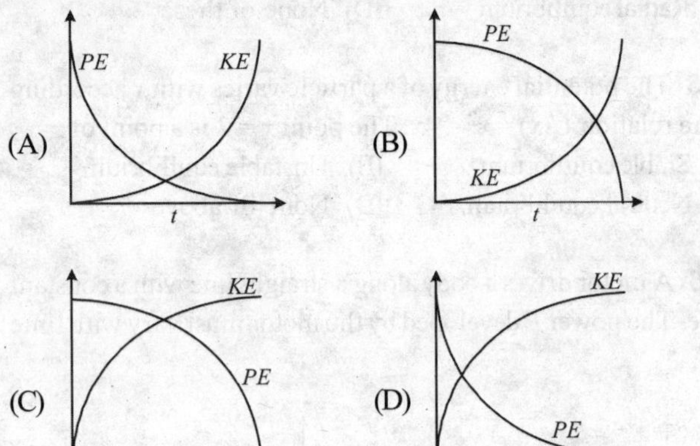

3-22 A wind-powered generator converts wind energy into electrical energy. Assume that the generator converts a fixed fractions of the wind energy intercepted by its blades into electrical energy. For wind speed *v*, the electrical power output will be proportional to :

(A) v (B) v^2

(C) v^3 (D) v^4

3-23 A particle, which is constrained to move along the x-axis, is subjected to a force in the same direction which varies with the distance *x* from the origin as $F(x) = -kx + ax^2$. Here *k* and *a* are positive constants. For $x \geq 0$, the functional form of the potential energy $U(x)$ of the particle is :

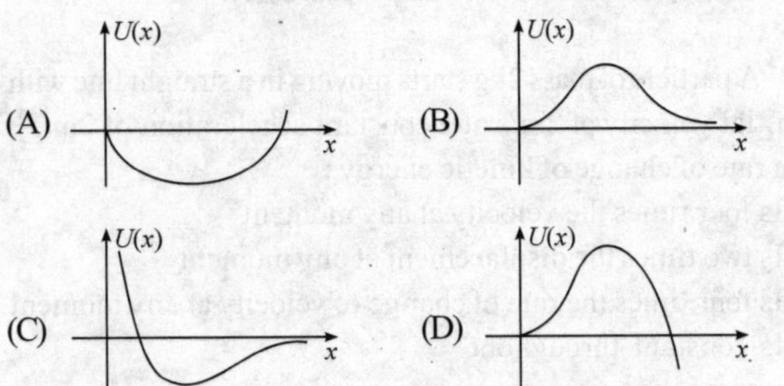

3-24 Acceleration versus time graph of a particle moving in a straight line is as shown in adjoining figure-3.72. If initially particle was at rest. Then corresponding kinetic energy versus time graph will be :

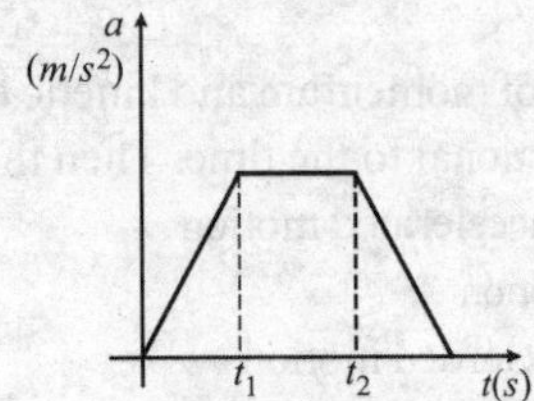

Figure 3.72

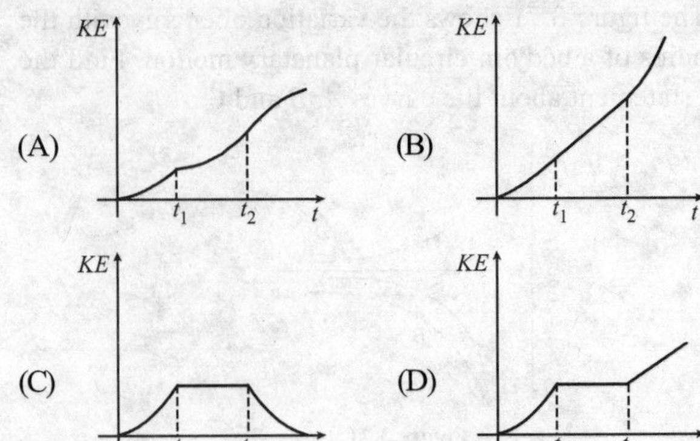

3-25 The potential energy for a force field $\vec{F}$ is given by $U(x, y) = \sin(x + y)$. The magnitude of force acting on the particle of mass *m* at $\left(0, \frac{\pi}{4}\right)$ is :

(A) 1 (B) $\sqrt{2}$

(C) $\frac{1}{\sqrt{2}}$ (D) 0

3-26 In an *XY* horizontal plane a force field $\vec{F} = -(40\ \text{N/m})(y\hat{i} + x\hat{j})$ is present where *x* and *y* are the coordinates of any point on the plane. A smooth rod *AB* is fixed in the plane as shown in the figure. A particle of mass 5 *kg* is to be released with a velocity in this force field such that it reaches to point *B*. Find the minimum velocity that must be imparted along the rod at *A* such that it reaches to *B*.

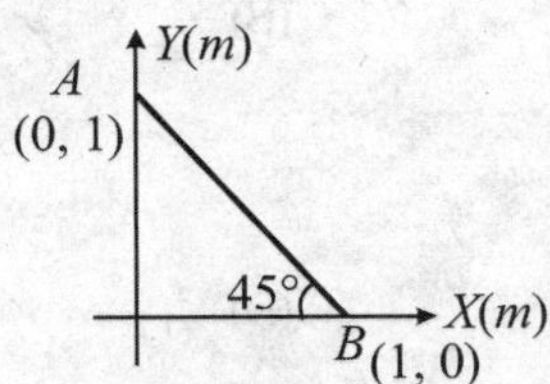

Figure 3.73

(A) 1 m/s (B) 2 m/s

(C) 3 m/s (D) 4 m/s

3-27 A ball of mass *m* is thrown upward with a velocity *v*. If air exerts an average resisting force *F*, the velocity with which the ball returns to the thrower is:

(A) $v\sqrt{\frac{mg}{mg+F}}$ (B) $v\sqrt{\frac{F}{mg+F}}$

(C) $v\sqrt{\frac{mg-F}{mg+F}}$ (D) $v\sqrt{\frac{mg+F}{mg-F}}$

3-28 A railway track is banked for a speed *v*, by making the height of the outer rail '*h*' higher than that of the inner rail. The horizontal separation between the rails is *d*. The radius of curvature of the track is 'r' : then which of the following relation is true?

(A) $\frac{h}{d} = \frac{v^2}{rg}$ (B) $\tan\left(\sin^{-1}\frac{h}{d}\right) = \frac{v^2}{rg}$

(C) $\tan^{-1}\left(\frac{h}{d}\right) = \frac{v^2}{rg}$ (D) $\frac{h}{r} = \frac{v^2}{dg}$

3-29 The kinetic energy acquired by a mass m in travelling a certain distance d, starting from rest, under the action of a force $F = kt$ is :

(A) directly proportional to t^2
(B) independent of t
(C) directly proportional to t^4
(D) directly proportional to t

3-30 A block of mass m is attached with a spring in its natural length, of spring constant k. The other end A of spring is moved with a constant acceleration 'a' away from the block as shown in the figure-3.74. Find the maximum extension in the spring. Assume that initially block and spring is at rest w.r.t ground frame :

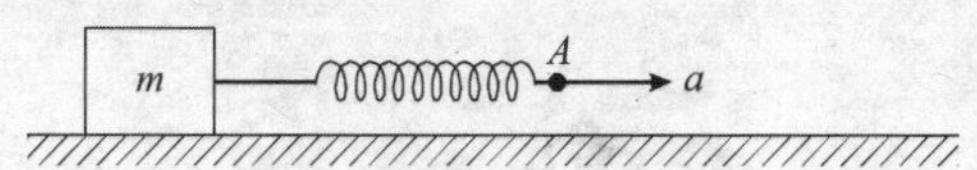

Figure 3.74

(A) $\frac{ma}{k}$ (B) $\frac{1}{2}\frac{ma}{k}$

(C) $\frac{2ma}{k}$ (D) $\frac{1}{2}\frac{4ma}{k}$

3-31 A block of 1 kg is kept on a rough surface of an elevator moving up with constant velocity of 5 m/s. In 10 second work done by normal reaction (no sliding on incline surface)

(i) from ground frame is 320 J
(ii) is equal to work done by friction force in elevator frame
(iii) is equal to work done by friction in ground frame

(A) (i) (B) (ii), (iii)
(C) (i), (ii) (D) only (iii).

3-32 A particle is projected from ground with speed u at angle θ with the horizontal. Radius of curvature of the trajectory of the particle :

(A) is not minimum at highest point
(B) is minimum at the point of projection
(C) is same at all points
(D) varies from $\frac{u^2}{g\cos\theta}$ to $\frac{u^2\cos^2\theta}{g}$

3-33 A small coin is placed on a stationary horizontal disc at a distance r from its centre. The disc starts rotating about a fixed vertical axis through its centrre with a constant angular acceleration α. Determine the number of revolutions N, accomplishes by the disc before the coin starts slipping on the disc. The coefficients of static friction between the coin and the disc is μ_g.

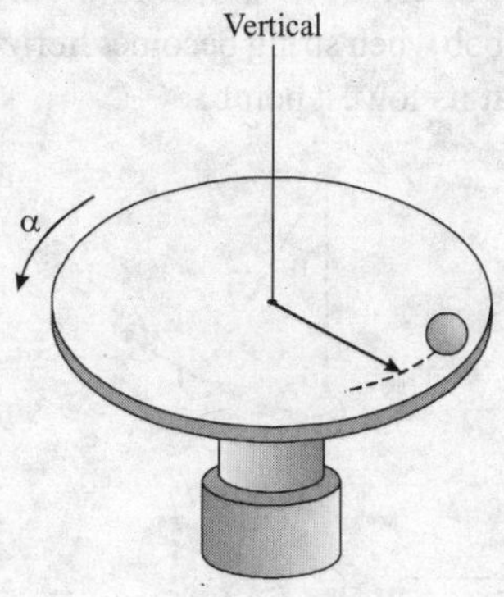

Figure 3.75

(A) $\frac{\left\{\left(\frac{\mu_s g}{r}\right)^2 + \alpha^2\right\}^{1/2}}{4\pi\alpha}$ (B) $\frac{\left\{\left(\frac{\mu_s g}{r}\right)^2 - \alpha^2\right\}^{1/2}}{4\pi\alpha}$

(C) $\frac{\left\{\left(\frac{\mu_s g}{r}\right)^2 - \alpha^2\right\}^{1/2}}{2\pi\alpha}$ (D) $\frac{\left\{\left(\frac{\mu_s g}{r}\right)^2 + \alpha^2\right\}^{1/2}}{2\pi\alpha}$

3-34 A force $\vec{F} = b\frac{-y\hat{i} + x\hat{j}}{x^2 + y^2}$ N (b is a constant) acts on a particle as it undergoes counterclockwise circular motion in a circle : $x^2 + y^2 = 16$. The work done by the force when the particle undergoes one complete revolution is (x, y are in m)

(A) Zero (B) 2π bJ
(C) 2 bJ (D) None of these

3-35 A particle moves with a speed v in a circle of radius R. The x-component of the average velocity of the particle in a half-revolution, as shown in figure-3.76, is :

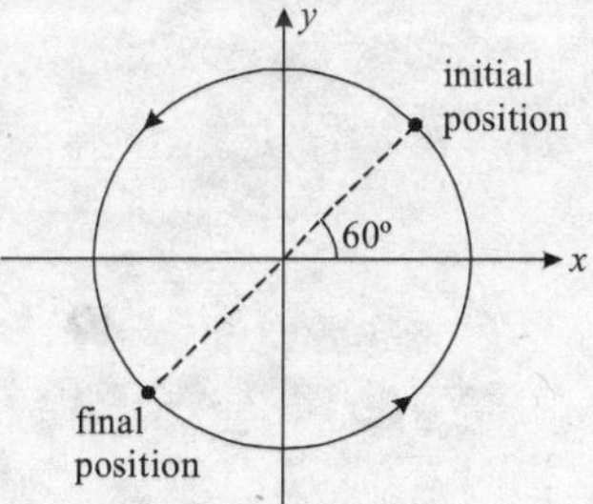

Figure 3.76

(A) $-\frac{v}{\pi}$ (B) $-\frac{v}{2\pi}$

(C) $-\frac{v}{4\pi}$ (D) $-\frac{2v}{\pi}$

3-36 An agent applies force of constant magnitude F_0 always in the tangential direction as shown in the figure-3.77. Find the speed of the bob when string becomes horizontal, assuming that it is at rest at its lowest point :

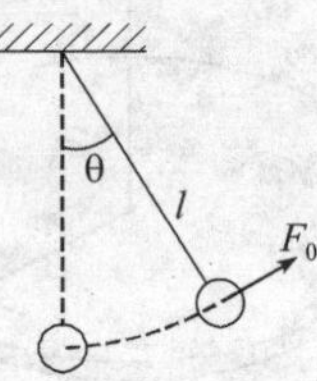

Figure-3.77

(A) $\sqrt{\frac{l}{m}(\pi F_0 - 2mg)}$ (B) $\sqrt{lg}$

(C) $\sqrt{\frac{l}{m}(\pi F_0) - 4mg}$ (D) $\sqrt{\frac{l}{m}F_0}$

3-37 A block Q of mass $2m$ is placed on a horizontal frictionless plane. A second block of mass m is placed on it and is connected to a spring of spring constant K, the two block are pulled by distance A. Block Q oscillates without slipping. The work done by the friction force on block Q when the spring regains its natural length is :

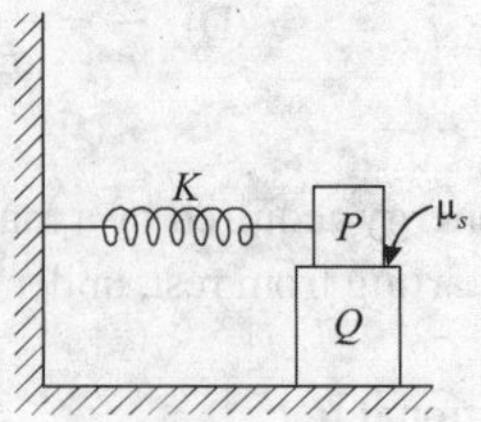

Figure 3.78

(A) $\frac{1}{3}KA^2$ (B) $\frac{2}{3}KA^2$

(C) $\frac{1}{2}KA^2$ (D) $\frac{1}{4}KA^2$

* * * * *

Numerical MCQs Single Options Correct

3-1 A man pulls a bucket of water from a depth of h from a well. If the mass of the rope and that of bucket full of water are m and M respectively, the work done by the man is :

(A) $(M+m)gh$ (B) $\left(M+\frac{m}{2}\right)gh$

(C) $\left(\frac{M+m}{2}\right)gh$ (D) $\left(\frac{M}{2}+m\right)gh$

3-2 Under the action of a force, a 2 kg body moves such that its position x as a function of time is given by $x = t^3/3$ where x is in metre and t in second. The work done by the force in the first two second is :

(A) 1600 joule (B) 160 joule
(C) 16 joule (D) 1.6 joule

3-3 A smooth ring of mass M is threaded on a string whose ends are then threaded over two smooth fixed pulleys with masses m and m' tied on to them respectively. The various portions of strings are vertical. The system is free to move. What is the condition if M alone is to remain at rest ?

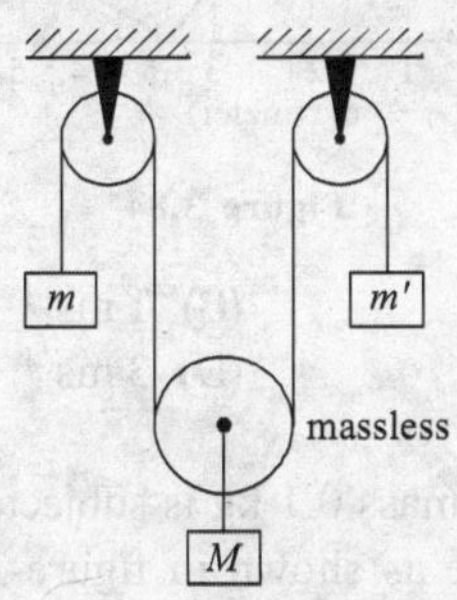

Figure 3.79

(A) $\frac{4}{M}=\frac{1}{m}+\frac{1}{m'}$ (B) $\frac{2}{M}=\frac{1}{m}+\frac{1}{m'}$

(C) $\frac{1}{M}=\frac{1}{m}+\frac{1}{m'}$ (D) $\frac{3}{M}=\frac{1}{m}+\frac{1}{m'}$

3-4 A particle is kept fixed on a turntable rotating uniformly. As seen from the ground, the particle goes in a circle, its speed is 20 cm/s and acceleration is 20 cm/s². The particle is now shifted to a new position to make the radius half of the original value. The new values of the speed and acceleration will be :

(A) 10 cm/s, 10 cm/s² (B) 10 cm/s, 80 cm/s²
(C) 40 cm/s, 10 cm/s² (D) 40 cm/s, 40 cm/s².

3-5 A cube of mass M starts at rest from point 1 at a height $4R$, where R is the radius of the circular track. The cube slides down the frictionless track and around the loop. The force which the track exerts on the cube at point 2 is :

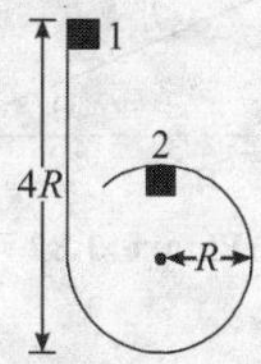

Figure 3.80

(A) $3Mg$ (B) Mg
(C) $2Mg$
(D) Cube will not reach the point 2

3-6 A block is attached to a spring of stiffness k. The other end of the spring is attached to a fixed wall. The entire system lie on a horizontal surface and the spring is in natural state. The natural length of the spring is l_0. If the block is slowly lifted up vertically to a height $\frac{5}{12}l_0$ from its initial position :

(A) The work done by the lifting force $= \frac{kl_0^2}{288}+\frac{5}{12}mgl_0$

(B) The work done by the spring force $= \frac{kl_0^2}{288}$

(C) The work done by the gravity $= \frac{5}{12}mgl_0$

(D) The work done by lifting force $= -\frac{5}{12}mgl_0+\frac{kl_0^2}{288}$

3-7 By applying a force $\vec{F} = (3xy - 5z)\hat{j} + 4z\hat{k}$ a particle is moved along the path $y = x^2$ from point (0, 0, 0) to the point (2, 4, 0). The work done by the F on the particle is :

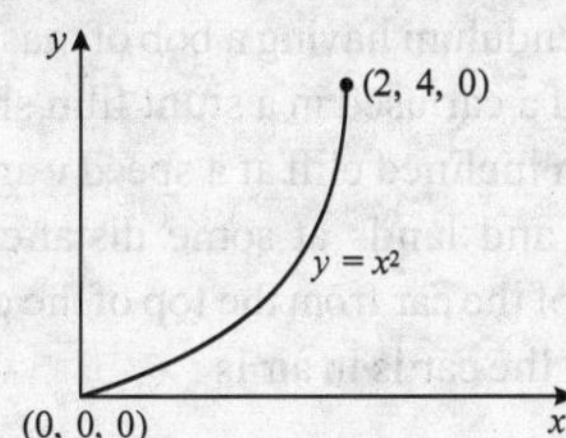

Figure 3.81

(A) $\frac{280}{5}$ (B) $\frac{140}{5}$

(C) $\frac{232}{5}$ (D) $\frac{192}{5}$

3-8 A block of mass m is placed at the top of a smooth wedge ABC. The wedge is rotated about an axis passing through C as shown in the figure-3.82. The minimum value of angular speed ω such that the block does not slip on the wedge is :

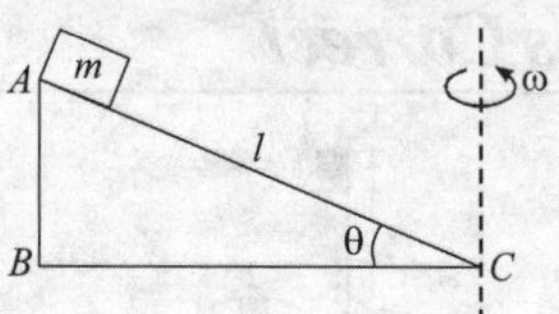

Figure 3.82

(A) 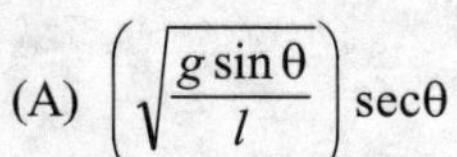 $\left(\sqrt{\dfrac{g\sin\theta}{l}}\right)\sec\theta$ (B) $\left(\sqrt{\dfrac{g}{l}}\right)\cos\theta$

(C) $\left(\sqrt{\dfrac{g}{l\cos\theta}}\right)\cos\theta$ (D) $\sqrt{\dfrac{g\sin\theta}{l}}$

3-9 The work done in moving a particle from a point (1, 1) to (2, 3) in a plane and in a force field with potential $U = \lambda(x+y)$ is :

(A) 0 (B) λ

(C) 3λ (D) -3λ

3-10 A particle of mass m is fixed to one end of a light spring of force constant k and unstretched length l. The system is rotated about the other end of the spring with an angular velocity ω, in gravity free space. The increase in length of the spring will be :

(A) 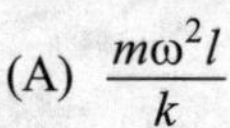 $\dfrac{m\omega^2 l}{k}$

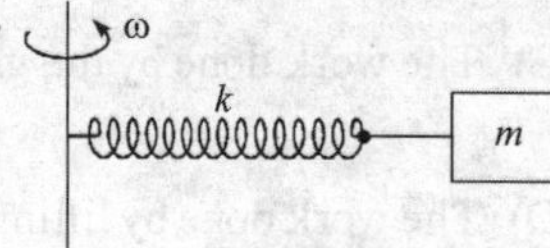

Figure 3.83

(B) $\dfrac{m\omega^2 l}{k - m\omega^2}$

(C) $\dfrac{m\omega^2 l}{k + m\omega^2}$ (D) None of these

3-11. A simple pendulum having a bob of mass m is suspended from the ceiling of a car used in a stunt film shooting. The car moves up along an inclined cliff at a speed v and makes a jump to leave the cliff and lands at some distance. Let R be the maximum height of the car from the top of the cliff. The tension in the string when the car is in air is :

(A) mg (B) $mg - \dfrac{mv^2}{R}$

(C) $mg + \dfrac{mv^2}{R}$ (D) Zero.

3-12 A spring, which is initially in its unstretched condition, is first stretched by a length x and then again by a further length x. The work done in the first case is W_1 and in the second case is W_2:

(A) $W_2 = W_1$ (B) $W_2 = 2W_1$

(C) $W_2 = 3W_1$ (D) $W_2 = 4W_1$

3-13 A particle of mass m moves from rest under the action of a constant force F which acts for two seconds. The maximum power attained is :

(A) $2Fm$ (B) $\dfrac{F^2}{m}$

(C) $\dfrac{2F}{m}$ (D) $\dfrac{2F^2}{m}$

3-14 A boy whose mass is 30 kg climbs, with a constant speed, a vertical rope of 6 m long in 10 s. The power of the boy during the climb is : (Take $g = 10\ \text{ms}^{-2}$)

(A) 60 W (B) 3000 W

(C) 180 W (D) 5 W

3-15 A body with mass 2 kg moves in one direction in the presence of a force which is described by the potential energy graph. If the body is released from rest at $x = 2$ m, then its speed when it crosses $x = 5$ m is :

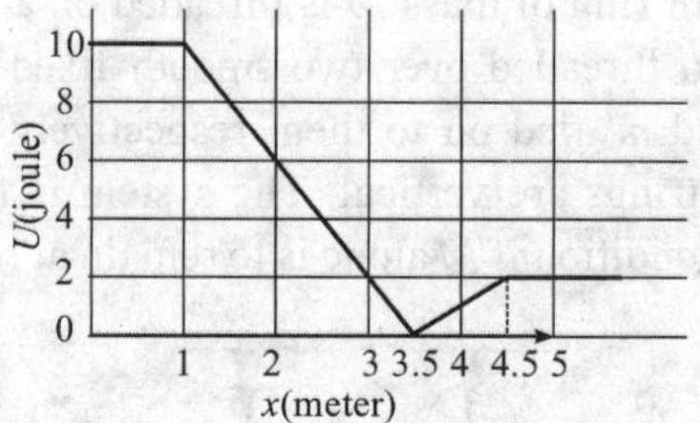

Figure 3.84

(A) Zero (B) $1\ \text{ms}^{-1}$

(C) $2\ \text{ms}^{-1}$ (D) $3\ \text{ms}^{-1}$

3-16 A particle of mass 0.1 kg is subjected to a force which varies with distance as shown in figure-3.85. If it starts its journey from rest at $x = 0$, its velocity at $x = 12$ m is :

(A) 0 m/s

(B) 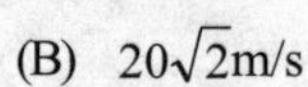 $20\sqrt{2}$ m/s

(C) $20\sqrt{3}$ m/s

(D) 40 m/s

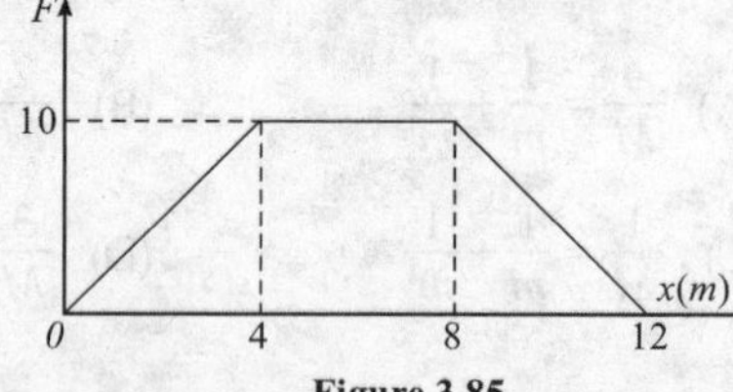

Figure 3.85

3-17 A motor is to be used to lift water from a depth of 10 m & discharging it on ground level at a speed 10 m/s. If 2 kg of water is lifted per second & the efficiency of motor is 40%. The minimum power of the motor should be nearly :

(A) 1.5 HP (B) 1 HP

(C) 0.67 HP (D) 2 HP

3-18 A small block slides with velocity $0.5\sqrt{gr}$ on the horizontal frictionless surface as shown in the figure-3.86. The block leaves the surface at point C. The angle θ in the figure is :

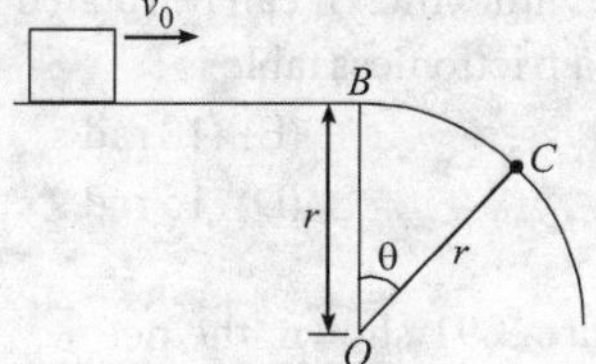

Figure 3.86

(A) $\cos^{-1}(4/9)$ (B) $\cos^{-1}(3/4)$
(C) $\cos^{-1}(1/2)$ (D) None of the above

3-19 A stone of mass 1 kg tied to a light inextensible string of length $L = 10/3$ m is whirling in a circular path of radius L in a vertical plane. If the ratio of the maximum tension in the string to the minimum tension in the string is 4 and if g is taken to be 10 m/sec^2, the speed of the stone at the highest point of the circle is :

(A) 20 m/sec (B) $10\sqrt{3}$ m/s
(C) $5\sqrt{2}$ m/sec (D) 10 m/sec

3-20 A particle of mass m is attached to one end of a string of length l while the other end is fixed to a point h above the horizontal table. The particle is made to revolve in a circle on the table so as to make p revolutions per second. The maximum value of p if the particle is to be in contact with the table will be :

(A) $2\pi\sqrt{gh}$ (B) $\sqrt{g/h}$
(C) $2\pi\sqrt{h/g}$ (D) $\frac{1}{2\pi}\sqrt{g/h}$

3-21 Two particles, each of mass m are attached to the two ends of a light string of length l which passes through a hole at the centre of a table. One particle describes a circle on the table with angular velocity ω_1 and the other describes a circle as a conical pendulum with angular velocity ω_2 below the table as shown in figure-3.87. If l_1 and l_2 are the lengths of the portion of the string above and below the table, then :

(A) $\frac{l_1}{l_2} = \frac{\omega_2^2}{\omega_1^2}$

(B) $\frac{l_1}{l_2} = \frac{\omega_1^2}{\omega_2^2}$

(C) $\frac{1}{\omega_1^2} + \frac{1}{\omega_2^2} = \frac{l}{g}$

(D) $\frac{1}{\omega_1^2} + \frac{1}{\omega_2^2} > \frac{l}{g}$

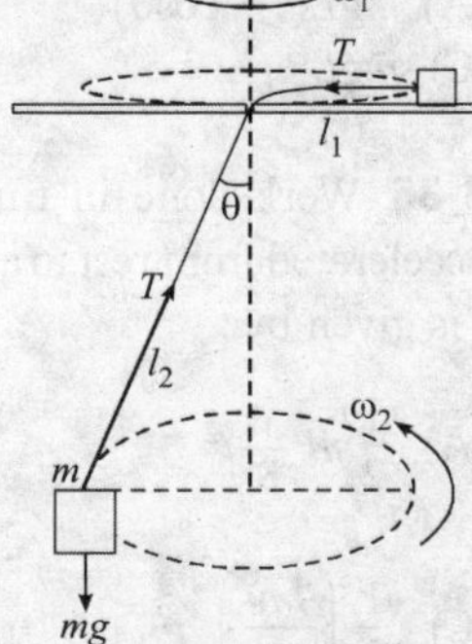

Figure 3.87

3-22 Two springs A and $B(k_A = 2k_B)$ are stretched by applying forces of equal magnitudes at the four ends. If the energy stored in A is E, that in B is :

(A) $E/2$ (B) $2E$
(C) E (D) $E/4$

3-23 A man who is running has half the kinetic energy of a boy of half his mass. The man speeds up by 1 ms^{-1} and then has the same kinetic energy as the boy. The original speed of the boy was :

(A) $\sqrt{2}$ ms^{-1} (B) $2(\sqrt{2}+1)$ ms^{-1}
(C) 2 ms^{-1} (D) $\sqrt{2}+1$ ms^{-1}

3-24 A chord is used to lower vertically a block of mass M a distance d at a constant downward acceleration of $g/4$. Then the work done by the cord on the block is :

(A) $mg\,d/4$ (B) $3\,Mg\,d/4$
(C) $-3\,Mg\,d/4$ (D) $Mg\,d$

3-25 Two blocks each of mass M are connected to the ends of a light frame as shown in figure-3.88. The frame is rotated about the vertical line of symmetry. The rod breaks if the tension in it exceeds T_0. The maximum frequency with which the frame may be rotated without breaking the rod will be :

(A) 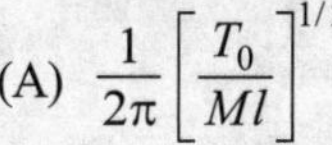 $\frac{1}{2\pi}\left[\frac{T_0}{Ml}\right]^{1/2}$

(B) 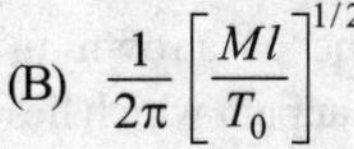 $\frac{1}{2\pi}\left[\frac{Ml}{T_0}\right]^{1/2}$

(C) 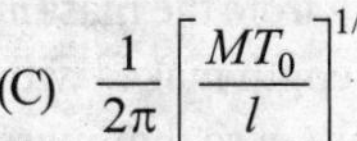 $\frac{1}{2\pi}\left[\frac{MT_0}{l}\right]^{1/2}$

(D) $\frac{1}{2\pi}\left[\frac{l}{MT_0}\right]^{1/2}$

Figure 3.88

3-26 A uniform flexible chain of mass m and length $2l$ hangs in equilibrium over a smooth horizontal pin of negligible diameter. One end of the chain is given a small vertical displacement so that the chain slips over pin. The speed of the chain when it leaves pin is :

(A) $\sqrt{3gl}$ (B) $\sqrt{2g}$
(C) $\sqrt{gl}$ (D) $\sqrt{4g}$

3-27 A block of mass 4 kg is resting on a horizontal table and a force of 10 N is applied on it in the horizontal direction. The coefficient of kinetic friction between the block and the table is 0.1. The work done in $\sqrt{20}$ s :

(A) By the applied force is 150 J
(B) By the frictional force is 60 J
(C) By the applied force and the net force are 150 J and 90 J respectively
(D) All are correct

3-28 If the block in the shown arrangement is acted upon by a constant force F for $t \geq 0$, its maximum speed will be :

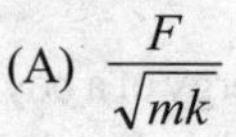

(A) $\dfrac{F}{\sqrt{mk}}$

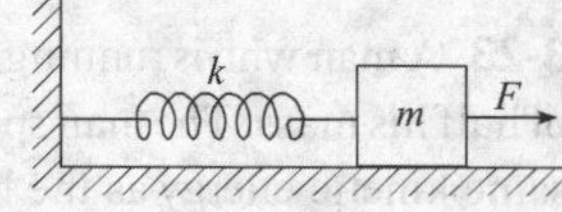

Figure 3.89

(B) $\dfrac{2F}{\sqrt{mk}}$

(C) $\dfrac{F}{\sqrt{2mk}}$ (D) $\dfrac{\sqrt{2}F}{\sqrt{mk}}$

3-29 A car of mass 500 kg is driven with acceleration 1 m/s^2 along straight level road against constant external resistance of 1000 N. When the velocity is 5 m/s the rate at which the engine is working is :

(A) 5 kW (B) 7.5 kW
(C) 2.5 kW (D) 10 kW

3-30 A particle of mass m describes a circle of radius r. The centripetal acceleration of the particle is $4/r^2$. What will be the momentum of the particle ?

(A) $2\,m/r$ (B) $2\,m/\sqrt{r}$
(C) $4\,m/\sqrt{r}$ (D) $4\,m/r$

3-31 A large mass M and a small mass m hang at two ends of a string that passes through a smooth tube as shown in figure-3.90. The mass m moves around a circular path which lies in the horizontal plane. The length of the string from the mass m to the top of the tube l and θ is the angle this length makes with the vertical. The frequency of rotation of mass m so that mass M be stationary will be :

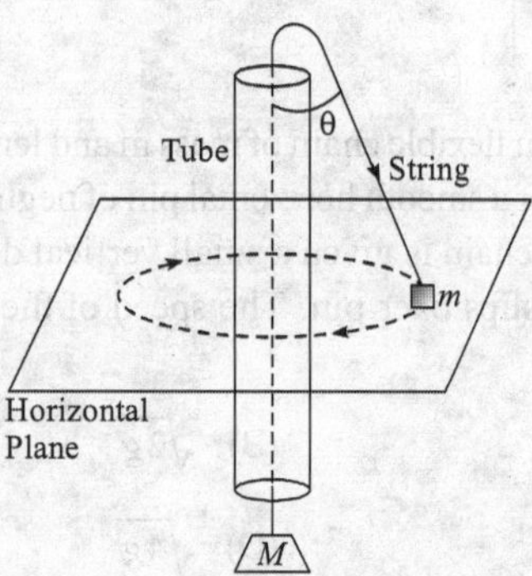

Figure 3.90

(A) $\dfrac{1}{2\pi}\sqrt{\dfrac{Mg}{ml}}$ (B) $\dfrac{1}{2\pi}\sqrt{\dfrac{ml}{Mg}}$

(C) $\dfrac{1}{2\pi}\sqrt{\dfrac{mg}{Ml}}$ (D) $\dfrac{1}{2\pi}\sqrt{\dfrac{mM}{gl}}$

3-32 The maximum tension an inextensible rope of mass density 0.1 kg m^{-1} can bear is 40 N. Length of rope is 2m. The maximum angular velocity with which it can be rotated horizontally in a circular path on a frictionless table is :

(A) $10\sqrt{2}$ rad/s (B) 18 rad/s
(C) 16 rad/s (D) 15 rad/s

3-33 In the figure-3.91 shown, the net work done by the tension when the bigger block of mass M touches the ground is :

(A) $+Mgd$
(B) $-(M+m)\,gd$
(C) $-Mgd$
(D) Zero

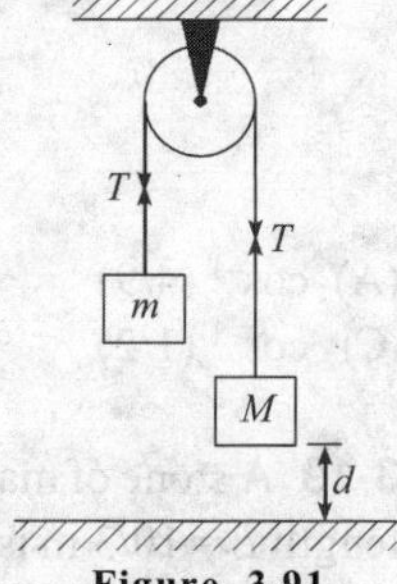

Figure 3.91

3-34 A uniform chain of length l and mass m is placed on a smooth table with one-fourth of its length hanging over the edge. The work that has to be done to pull the whole chain back onto the table is :

(A) $\dfrac{1}{4}mgl$ (B) $\dfrac{1}{8}mgl$

(C) $\dfrac{1}{16}mgl$ (D) $\dfrac{1}{32}mgl$

3-35 An object of mass m is tied to string of length L and a variable horizontal force is applied on it which starts at zero and gradually increases (it is pulled extremely slowly so that equilibrium exists at all times) until the string makes an angle θ with the vertical. Work done by the force F is :

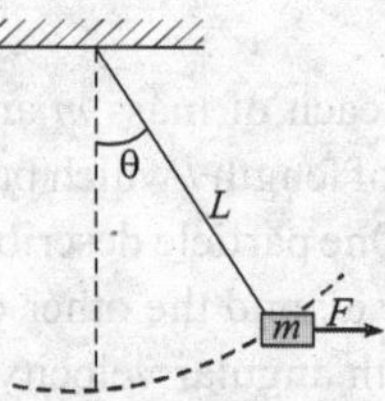

Figure 3.92

(A) $mgL(1-\cos\theta)$ (B) $FL\sin\theta$
(C) mgL (D) $FL(1+\tan\theta)$

3-36 Work done in time t on a body of mass m which is accelerated from rest to a speed v in time t_1 as a function of time t is given by :

(A) $\dfrac{1}{2}m\dfrac{v}{t_1}t^2$ (B) $m\dfrac{v}{t_1}t^2$

(C) $\dfrac{1}{2}\left(\dfrac{mv}{t_1}\right)^2 t^2$ (D) $\dfrac{1}{2}m\dfrac{v^2}{t_1^2}t^2$

3-37 A flexible chain of length $L = 20\sqrt{2}$ m and weight $W = 10$ kg is initially placed at rest on a smooth frictionless wedge surface

ABC. It is given a slight jerk on one-side so that it will start sliding on the side. Find the speed of the chain when its one end will leave the vertex of the wedge : (Take $g = 10$ m/s^2)

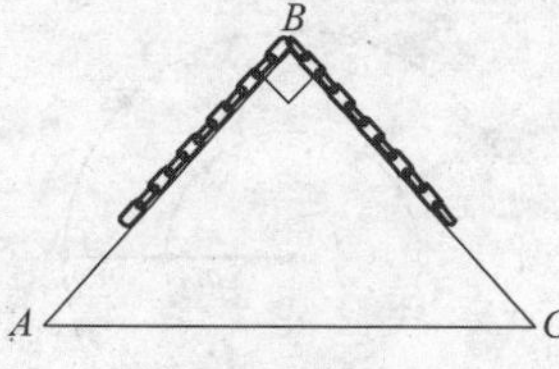

Figure 3.93

(A) $10\sqrt{2}$ m/s (B) 10 m/s
(C) 4 m/s (D) $(10\sqrt{2})^{1/2}$

3-38 A simple pendulum has a string of length l and bob of mass m. When the bob is at its lowest position, it is given the minimum horizontal speed necessary for it to move in a circular path about the point of suspension. The tension in the string at the lowest position of the bob is :
(A) 3 mg (B) 4 mg
(C) 5 mg (D) 6 mg

3-39 A block of mass 1 kg slides down a curved track from rest that is one quadrant of a circle of radius 1 m. Its speed at the bottom is 2 m/s. The work done by frictional force is :

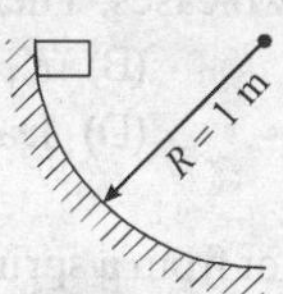

Figure 3.94

(A) 8 J (B) – 8 J
(C) 4 J (D) – 4 J

3-40 A uniform chain of length L and mass M is lying on a smooth table and one third of its length is hanging vertically down over the edge of the table. If g is acceleration due to gravity, the work required to pull the hanging part on to the table is :

(A) mgL (B) $\frac{mgL}{3}$
(C) $\frac{mgL}{9}$ (D) $\frac{mgL}{18}$

3-41 In the track shown in figure-3.95, section AB is a quadrant of a circle of 1 metre radius in vertical plane. A block is released at A and slides without friction until it reaches at B. After B it moves on a rough horizontal floor and comes to rest at D, 3 metres from B. The coefficient of friction between floor and the body will be :

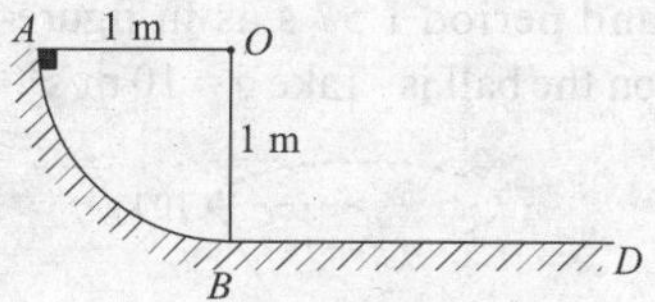

Figure 3.95

(A) 1/3 (B) 2/3
(C) 1/4 (D) 3/8

3-42 A block of mass m is attached to the two springs in vertical plane as shown in the figure-3.96. If initially both the springs are at their natural lengths. Then velocity of the block is maximum at displacement x given as :

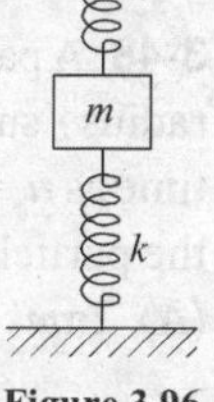

Figure 3.96

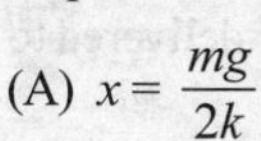
(A) $x = \frac{mg}{2k}$ (B) $x = \frac{mg}{k}$

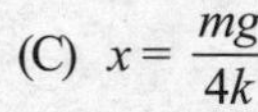
(C) $x = \frac{mg}{4k}$ (D) $x = \frac{3mg}{2k}$

x is the displacement of the block form its initial position.

3-43 A heavy particle is suspended by a string of length 1.5 m. It is given a horizontal velocity $\sqrt{57}$ m/s. Find the speed of the particle when the string becomes slack : (Take $g = 10$ m/s^2)
(A) 3 m/s (B) 1.5 m/s
(C) 2 m/s (D) 2.5 m/s

3-44 In a simple pendulum, the breaking strength of the string is double the weight of the bob. The bob is released from rest when the string is horizontal. The string breaks when it makes an angle θ with the vertical :
(A) $\theta = \cos^{-1}(1/3)$ (B) $\theta = 60°$
(C) $\theta = \cos^{-1}(2/3)$ (D) $\theta = 0$

3-45 A particle of mass m is fixed to one end of a light rigid rod of length l and rotated in a vertical circular path about its other end. The minimum speed of the particle at its highest point must be :

(A) Zero (B) $\sqrt{gl}$
(C) $\sqrt{1.5gl}$ (D) $\sqrt{2gl}$

3-46 A particle of mass 0.01 kg travels along a space curve with velocity given by $4\hat{i} + 16\hat{k}$ m/s. After some time, its velocity becomes $8\hat{i} + 20\hat{j}$ m/s due to the action of a conservative force. The work done on the particle during this interval of time is :
(A) 0.32 J (B) 6.9 J
(C) 9.6 J (D) 0.96 J

3-47 A 10 kg ball attached to the end of a rigid massless rod of length 1 m rotates at constant speed in a horizontal circle of radius 0.5 m and period 1.57 s as in figure-3.97 The force exerted by rod on the ball is : Take $g = 10 \text{ m/s}^2$.

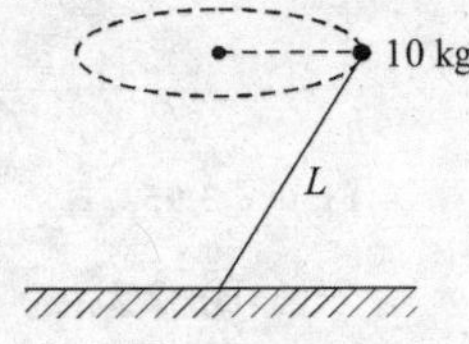

Figure 3.97

(A) 1.28N (B) 128
(C) 10N (D) 12.8N

3-48 A particle of mass m is moving in a circular path of constant radius r such that its centripetal acceleration a_c is varying with time as $a_c = k^2rt^2$, where k is a constant. The power delivered to the particle by the forces acting on it is :

(A) $2\pi mk^2r^2t$ (B) mk^2r^2t

(C) $\frac{1}{3}\ mk^4r^2t^5$ (D) 0

3-49 A ball of mass 1 kg moves inside a smooth fixed spherical shell of radius 1 m with an initial velocity $v = 5$ m/s from the bottom. What is the total force acting on the particle at point B :

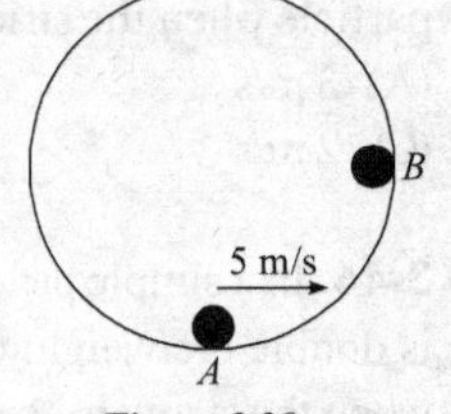

Figure 3.98

(A) 10N
(B) 25N
(C) $5\sqrt{5}$ N
(D) 5N

3-50 Two equal masses are attached to the two ends of a spring constant k. The masses are pulled out symmetrically to stretch the spring by a length x over its natural length. The work done by the spring on each mass is :

(A) $\frac{1}{2}k\,x^2$ (B) $-\frac{1}{2}k\,x^2$

(C) $\frac{1}{4}k\,x^2$ (D) $-\frac{1}{4}k\,x^2$

3-51 A small block of mass m is kept on a rough inclined surface of inclination θ fixed in a elevator. The elevator goes up with a uniform velocity v and the block does not slide on the wedge. The work done by the force of friction on the block in time t will be :

(A) Zero (B) $mgvt \cos^2\theta$
(C) $mgvt \sin^2\theta$ (D) $mgvt \sin 2\theta$

3-52 A particle of mass m_1 is fastened to one end of a string and one of m_2 to the middle point, the other end of the string being fastened to a fixed point on a smooth horizontal table. The particles are then projected, so that the two portions of the string are always in the same straight line and describes horizontal circles. Find the ratio of tensions in the two parts of the string :

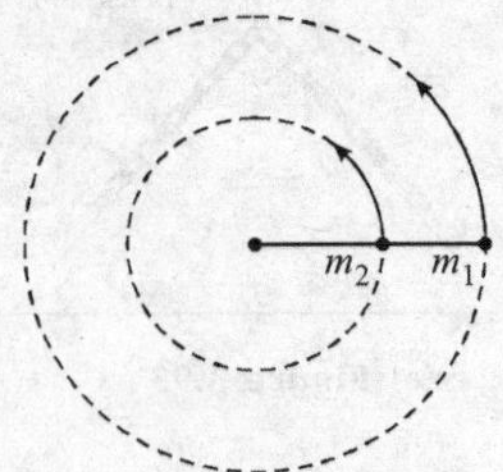

Figure 3.99

(A) $\frac{m_1}{m_1 + m_2}$ (B) $\frac{m_1 + m_2}{m_1}$

(C) $\frac{2m_1 + m_2}{2m_1}$ (D) $\frac{2m_1}{m_1 + m_2}$

3-53 A particle is released from the top of two inclined rough surfaces of height 'h' each. The angle of inclination of the two planes are 30° and 60° respectively. All other factors (e.g. coefficient of friction, mass of block etc.) are same in both the cases. Let K_1 and K_2 be the kinetic energies of the particle at the bottom of the plane in two cases. Then :

(A) $K_1 = K_2$ (B) $K_1 > K_2$
(C) $K_1 < K_2$ (D) Data insufficient

3-54 A 15 gm ball is shot from a spring gun whose spring has a force constant of 600 N/m. The spring is compressed by 5 cm. The greatest possible horizontal range of the ball for this compression is : (Take $g = 10 \text{ m/s}^2$)

(A) 6.0m (B) 12.0m
(C) 10.0m (D) 8.0m

3-55 Water is pumped from a depth of 10 m and delivered through a pipe of cross section 10^{-2} m^2 upto a height of 10 m. If it is needed to deliver a volume 0.2 m^3 per second the power required will be :

(A) 19.6kW (B) 9.8kW
(C) 39.2kW (D) 4.9kW

3-56 System shown in figure-3.100 is released from rest. Pulley and spring is massless and friction is absent everywhere. The speed of 5 kg block when 2 kg block leaves the contact with ground is : (Take force constant of spring $k = 40$ N/m and $g = 10 \text{ m/s}^2$)

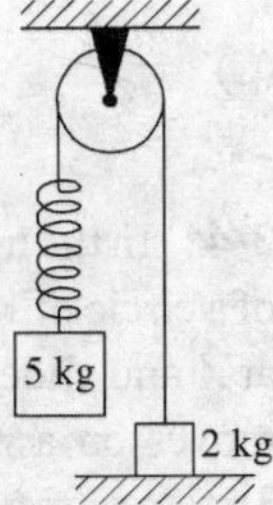

Figure 3.100

(A) $\sqrt{2}$ m/s (B) $2\sqrt{2}$ m/s
(C) 2 m/s (D) $4\sqrt{2}$ m/s

3-57 A particle of mass m is projected with velocity u at an angle α with horizontal. During the period when the particle descends from highest point to the position where its velocity vector makes an angle $\frac{\alpha}{2}$ with horizontal. Work done by gravity force is :

(A) $\frac{1}{2}mu^2\tan^2\alpha$ (B) $\frac{1}{2}m^2\tan^2\frac{\alpha}{2}$

(C) $\frac{1}{2}mu^2\cos^2\alpha\tan^2\frac{\alpha}{2}$ (D) $\frac{1}{2}mu^2\cos^2\frac{\alpha}{2}\sin^2\alpha$

3-58 Force acting on a particle is $(2\hat{i}+3\hat{j})$ N. Work done by this force is zero, when a particle is moved on the line $3y+kx=5$. Here value of k is :

(A) 2 (B) 4
(C) 6 (D) 8

3-59 A particle is given an initial speed u inside a smooth spherical shell of radius $R = 1$ m that it is just able to complete the circle. Acceleration of the particle when its velocity is vertical is :

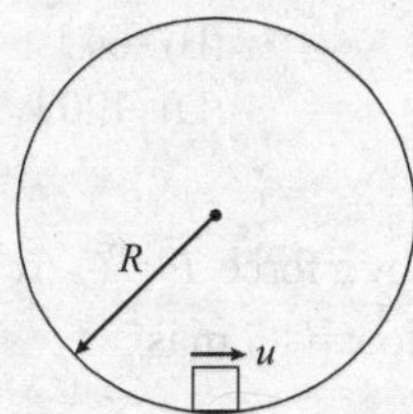

Figure 3.101

(A) $g\sqrt{10}$ (B) g
(C) $g/\sqrt{2}$ (D) $g\sqrt{6}$

3-60 Power supplied to a particle of mass 2 kg varies with time as $P = \frac{3t^2}{2}$ watt. Here t is in second. If velocity of particle at $t = 0$ is $v = 0$. The velocity of particle at time $t = 2$ s will be :

(A) 1 m/s (B) 4 m/s
(C) 2 m/s (D) $2\sqrt{2}$ m/s

3-61 An ice cube of size $a = 10$ cm is floating in a tank (base area $A = 50$ cm × 50 cm) partially filled with water. The change in gravitational potential energy, when ice melts completely is : (density of ice is 900 kg/m^3)

(A) –0.072 J (B) –0.24 J
(C) –0.016 J (D) –0.045 J

3-62 A particle moves on a rough horizontal ground with some initial velocity say v_0. If 3/4th of its kinetic energy is lost in friction in time t_0. Then coefficient of friction between the particle and the ground is :

(A) $\frac{v_0}{2g\,t_0}$ (B) $\frac{v_0}{4g\,t_0}$

(C) $\frac{3v_0}{4g\,t_0}$ (D) $\frac{v_0}{g\,t_0}$

3-63 Two particles 1 and 2 are allowed to descend on two frictionless chords OP and OQ. The ratio of the speeds of the particles 1 and 2 respectively when they reach on the circumference is :

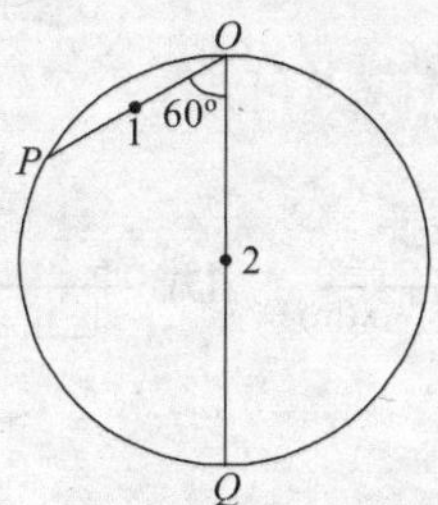

Figure 3.102

(A) $\frac{1}{4}$ (B) $\frac{1}{2}$

(C) 1 (D) $\frac{1}{2\sqrt{2}}$

3-64 An object of mass m slides down a hill of height h of arbitrary shape and after travelling a certain horizontal path stops because of friction. The friction coefficient is different for different segments for the entire path but is independent of the velocity and direction of motion. The work that a force must perform to return the object to its initial position along the same path is :

(A) mgh (B) $2\,mgh$
(C) $4\,mgh$ (D) $-\,mgh$

3-65 A block of mass m slides down a rough inclined plane of inclination θ with horizontal with zero initial velocity. The coefficient of friction between the block and the plane is μ with $\theta > \tan^{-1}(\mu)$. Magnitude of rate of work done by the force of friction at time t is :

(A) $\mu mg^2 t\sin\theta$ (B) $mg^2 t(\sin\theta - \mu\cos\theta)$
(C) $\mu mg^2 t\cos\theta(\sin\theta - \mu\cos\theta)$ (D) $\mu mg^2 t\cos\theta$

3-66 A particle is displaced from $x = -6$ m to $x = +6$ m. A force F acting on the particle during its motion is shown in figure-3.103. Graph between work done by this force (W) and displacement (x) should be :

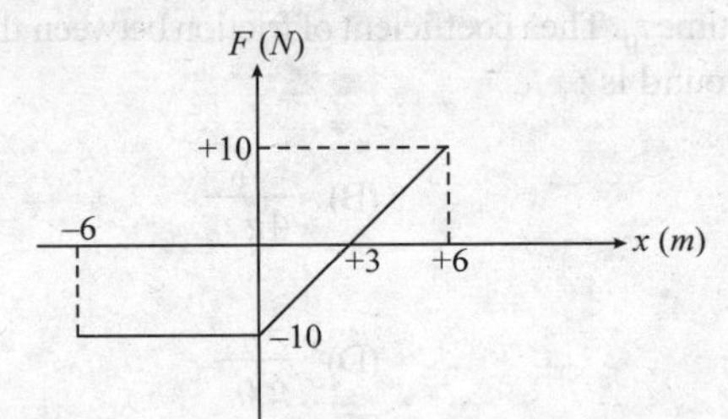

Figure 3.103

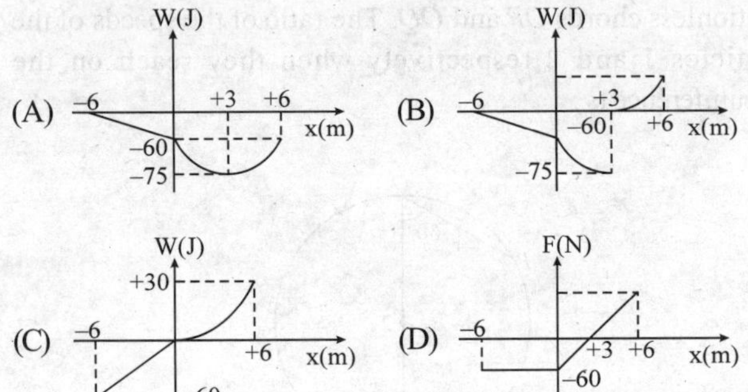

3-67 A force F acting on a body depends on its displacement S as $F \propto S^{-1/3}$. The power delivered by F will depend on displacement as :

(A) $S^{2/3}$ (B) $S^{-5/3}$

(C) $S^{1/2}$ (D) S^0

3-68 A particle is released from a height H. At certain height its kinetic energy is two times its potential energy with reference at bottom point. Height and speed of particle at that instant are :

(A) $\frac{H}{3}, \sqrt{\frac{2gH}{3}}$ (B) $\frac{H}{3}, 2\sqrt{\frac{gH}{3}}$

(C) $\frac{2H}{3}, \sqrt{\frac{2gH}{3}}$ (D) $\frac{H}{3}, \sqrt{2gH}$

3-69 Velocity-time graph of a particle of mass 2 kg moving in a straight line is as shown in figure-3.104. Work done by all the forces on the particle is :

(A) 400 J

(B) −400 J

(C) −200 J

(D) 200 J

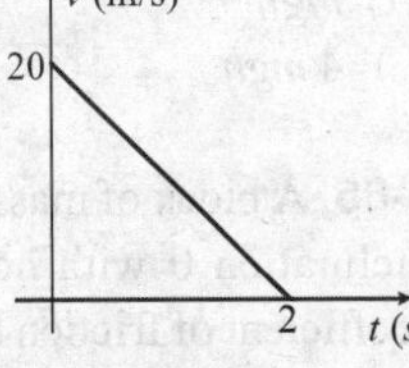

Figure 3.104

3-70 A man throws the bricks to a height of 12 m where they reach with a speed of 12 m/s. If he throws the bricks such that they just reach that height, what percentage of energy will be saved : (Take g = 9.8 m/s^2)

(A) 29% (B) 46%

(C) 38% (D) 50%

3-71 A pendulum of mass 1 kg and length l = 1 m is released from rest at angle θ = 60°. The power delivered by all the forces acting on the bob at angle θ = 30° will be : (Take g = 10 m/s^2)

(A) 13.5 watt (B) 20.4 watt

(C) 24.6 watt (D) Zero

3-72 A bead of mass 5 kg is free to slide on the horizontal rod AB. They are connected to two identical springs of natural length h ms. as shown. If initially bead was at O & M is vertically below L then, velocity of bead at point N will be :

(A) $5h$ m/s

(B) $40h/3$ m/s

(C) $8h$ m/s

(D) None of these

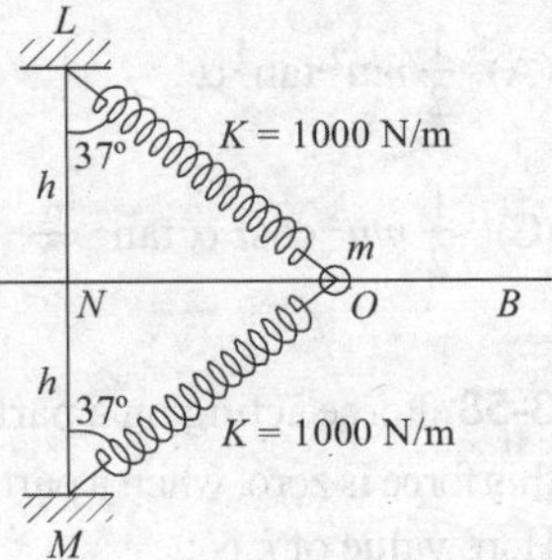

Figure 3.105

3-73 The displacement of a body of mass 2 kg varies with time t as $S = t^2 + 2t$, where S is in meters and t is in seconds. The work done by all the forces acting on the body during the time interval t = 2 s to t = 4 s is :

(A) 36 J (B) 64 J

(C) 100 J (D) 120 J

3-74 The work done by a force $\overline{F} = (-6x^3\,\hat{i})$ N in displacing a particle from x = 4 m to x = −2 m is :

(A) −240 J

(B) 360 J

(C) 420 J

(D) Will depend upon the path

3-75 A block is released from the top of a smooth inclined plane of inclination θ as shown in figure-3.106. Let v be the speed of the particle after travelling a distance s down the plane. Then which of the following will remain constant :

(A) $v^2 + 2gs \sin\theta$

(B) $v^2 - 2gs \sin\theta$

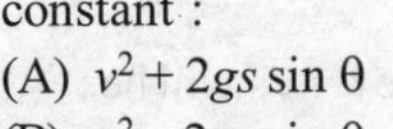

(C) $v - \sqrt{2gs}\, \sin\theta$

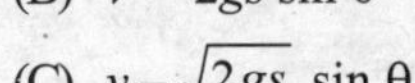

(D) $v + \sqrt{2gs}\, \sin\theta$

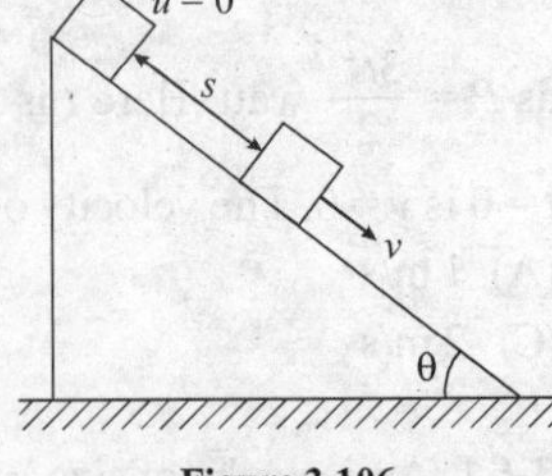

Figure 3.106

3-76 Rain drops fall from a certain height with a terminal velocity v on the ground. The viscous force is $F = 6\pi\eta r v$. Here η is coefficient of viscosity, r the radius of rain drop and v is speed. Then work done by all the forces acting on the ball till it reaches the ground is proportional to :

(A) r^7 (B) r^5

(C) r^3 (D) r^2

3-77 A constant power P is applied to a particle of mass m. The distance travelled by the particle when its velocity increases from v_1 to v_2 is (neglect friction)

(A) $\frac{3P}{m}(v_2^2 - v_1^2)$ (B) $\frac{m}{3P}(v_2 - v_1)$

(C) $\frac{m}{3P}(v_2^3 - v_1^3)$ (D) $\frac{m}{3P}(v_2^2 - v_1^2)$

3-78 A 1.5 kg block is initially at rest on a horizontal frictionless surface when a horizontal force in the positive direction of x-axis is applied to the block. The force is given by $\vec{F} = (4 - x^2)\,\hat{i}$ N, where x is in metre and the initial position of the block is $x = 0$. The maximum kinetic energy of the block between $x = 0$ and $x = 2.0$ m is :

(A) 2.33 J (B) 8.67 J

(C) 5.33 J (C) 6.67 J

3-79 The tangential acceleration of a particle in a circular motion of radius 2 m is $a_t = \alpha t$ m/s² (where α is a constant) Initially the particle as rest. Total acceleration of the particle makes 45° with the radial acceleration after 2 sec. The value of constant α is :

(A) $\frac{1}{2}$ m/s³ (B) 1 m/s³

(C) 2 m/s³ (D) Data are insufficient

3-80 A block of mass 1 kg is attached to one end of a spring of force constant $k = 20$ N/m. The other end of the spring is attached to a fixed rigid support. This spring block system is made to oscillate on a rough horizontal surface ($\mu = 0.04$). The initial displacement of the block from the equilibrium position is $a = 30$ cm. How many times the block passes from the mean position before coming to rest ? (Take $g = 10$ m/s²)

(A) 11 (B) 7

(C) 6 (D) 15

3-81 With what minimum speed v must a small ball should be pushed inside a smooth vertical tube from a height h so that it may reach the top of the tube ? Radius of the tube is R :

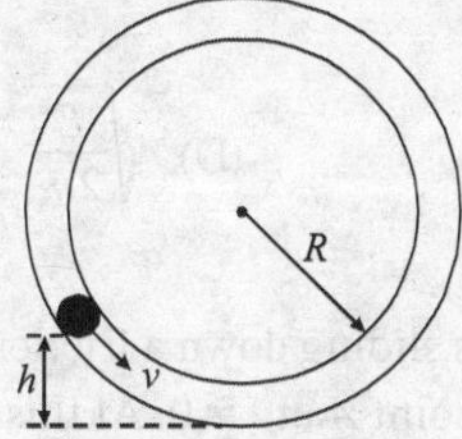

Figure 3.107

(A) $\sqrt{2g(h+2R)}$ (B) $\frac{5}{2}R$

(C) $\sqrt{g(5R-2h)}$ (D) $\sqrt{2g(2R-h)}$

3-82 A block of mass m is pulled by a constant power P placed on a rough horizontal plane. The friction coefficient between the block and the surface is μ. Maximum velocity of the block will be :

(A) $\frac{\mu P}{mg}$ (B) $\frac{\mu mg}{P}$

(C) μmgP (D) $\frac{P}{\mu mg}$

3-83 Two blocks of masses $m_1 = 1$ kg and $m_2 = 2$ kg are connected by non-deformed light spring. They are lying on a rough horizontal surface. The coefficient of friction between the blocks and the surface is 0.4. What minimum constant force F has to be applied in horizontal direction to the block of mass m_1 in order to shift the other block ? (Take $g = 10$ m/s²)

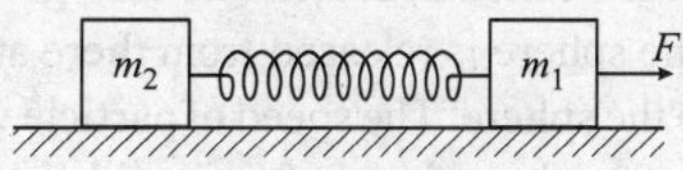

Figure 3.108

(A) 8 N (B) 15 N

(C) 10 N (D) 25 N

3-84 Force acting on a particle moving in a straight line varies with the velocity of the particle as $F = \frac{K}{v}$. Here K is a constant. The work done by this force in time t is :

(A) $\frac{K}{v^2}\cdot t$ (B) $2Kt$

(C) Kt (D) $\frac{2Kt}{v^2}$

3-85 A ball of mass m and density ρ is immersed in a liquid of density 3 ρ at a depth h and released. To what height will the ball jump up above the surface of liquid (neglect the resistance of water and air) :

(A) h (B) $h/2$

(C) $2h$ (D) $3h$

3-86 A block of mass m is attached with a massless spring of force constant k. The block is placed over a rough inclined surface for which the coefficient of friction is $\mu = \frac{3}{4}$. The minimum value of M required to move the block up the plane is (Neglect mass of string and pulley and friction in pulley) :

(A) $\frac{3}{5}m$

(B) $\frac{4}{5}m$

(C) $2m$

(D) $\frac{3}{2}m$

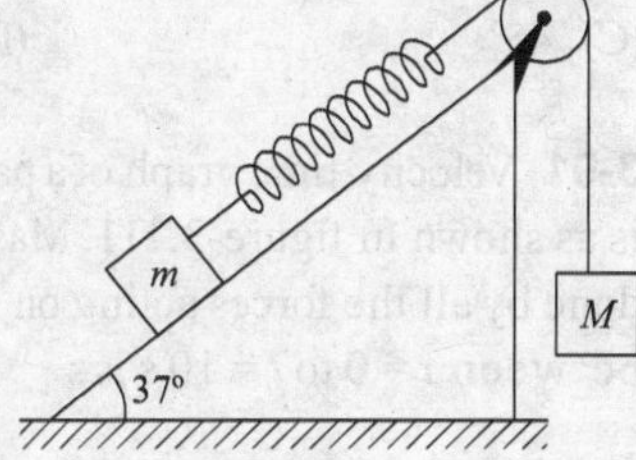

Figure 3.109

3-87 A cannon of mass $2m$ located at the base of an inclined plane shoots a shell of mass m in horizontal direction with velocity v_0. The angle of inclination of plane is 45° and the coefficient of friction between the cannon and the plane is 0.5. The height to which cannon ascends the plane as a result of recoil is :

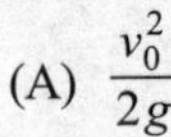

(A) $\frac{v_0^2}{2g}$ (B) $\frac{v_0^2}{12g}$

(C) $\frac{v_0^2}{6g}$ (D) $\frac{v_0^2}{g}$

3-88 A smooth sphere of radius R is made to translate in a straight line with a constant acceleration $a = g$. A particle kept on the top of the sphere is released from there at zero velocity with respect to the sphere. The speed of particle with respect to the sphere as a function of angle θ as it slides down is :

(A) $\frac{\sqrt{Rg(\sin\theta + \cos\theta)}}{2}$ (B) $\sqrt{Rg(1 + \cos\theta - \sin\theta)}$

(C) $\sqrt{4Rg\sin\theta}$ (D) $\sqrt{2Rg(1 + \sin\theta - \cos\theta)}$

3-89 A bob is suspended from a crane by a cable of length $l = 5$ m. The crane and load are moving at a constant speed v_0. The crane is stopped by a bumper and the bob on the cable swings out an angle of 60°. The initial speed v_0 is : (Take $g = 9.8$ m/s²)

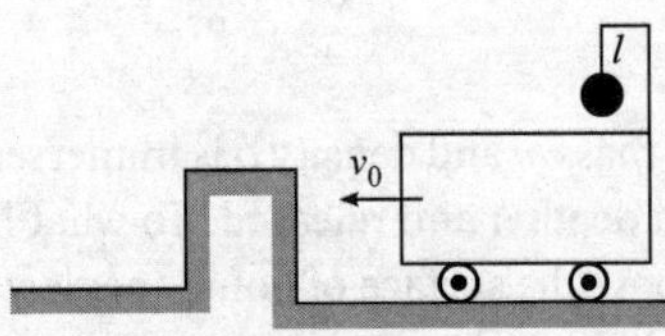

Figure 3.110

(A) 10 m/s (B) 7 m/s
(C) 4 m/s (D) 2 m/s

3-90 A car is moving in a circular horizontal track of radius 10 m with a constant speed of 10 m/s. A plumb bob is suspended from the roof of the car by a light rigid rod of length 1.00 m. The angle made by the rod with the track is :
(A) Zero (B) 30°
(C) 45° (D) 60°

3-91 Velocity-time graph of a particle moving in a straight line is as shown in figure-3.111. Mass of the particle is 2 kg. Work done by all the forces acting on the particle in time interval between $t = 0$ to $t = 10$ s is :

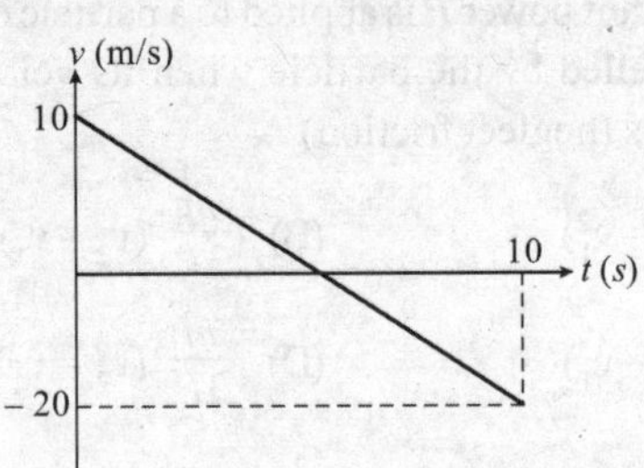

Figure 3.111

(A) 300 J (B) – 300 J
(C) 400 J (D) – 400 J

3-92 Two blocks A and B of mass m and 2 m are connected by a massless spring of force constant k. They are placed on a smooth horizontal plane. Spring is stretched by an amount x and then released. The relative velocity of the blocks when the spring comes to its natural length is :

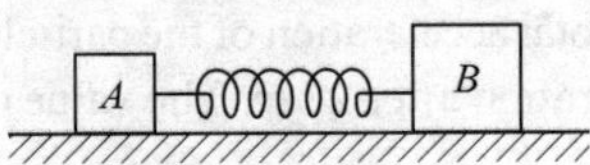

Figure 3.112

(A) $\left(\sqrt{\frac{3k}{2m}}\right)x$ (B) $\left(\sqrt{\frac{2k}{3m}}\right)x$

(C) $\sqrt{\frac{2kx}{m}}$ (D) $\sqrt{\frac{3km}{2x}}$

3-93 The potential energy of a particle of mass m is given by $U = \frac{1}{2}kx^2$ for $x < 0$ and $U = 0$ for $x \geq 0$. If total mechanical energy of the particle is E. Then its speed at $x = \sqrt{\frac{2E}{k}}$ is :

(A) Zero (B) $\sqrt{\frac{2E}{m}}$

(C) $\sqrt{\frac{E}{m}}$ (D) $\sqrt{\frac{E}{2m}}$

3-94 A particle P is sliding down a frictionless hemispherical bowl. It passes the point A at $t = 0$. At this instant of time, the horizontal component of its velocity is v. A bead Q of the same mass as P is ejected from A at $t = 0$ along the horizontal string AB, with the speed v. Friction between the bead and the string may be neglected. Let t_P and t_Q be the respective times taken by P and Q to reach the point B then :

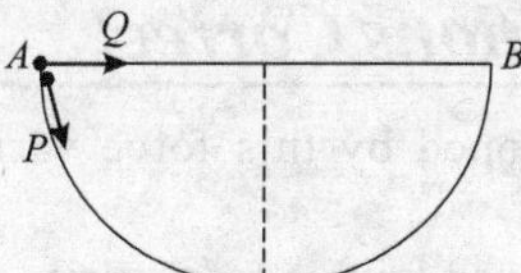

Figure 3.113

(A) $t_P < t_Q$ (B) $t_P = t_Q$

(C) $t_P > t_Q$ (D) $\frac{t_P}{t_Q} = \frac{\text{length of arc } ABC}{\text{length of chord } AB}$

3-95 A small block of mass m slides along a smooth frictionless track as shown in the figure-3.114 (i) If it starts from rest at P, what is the resultant force acting on it at Q ? (ii) At what height above the bottom of the loop should the block be released so that the force it exerts against the track at the top of the loop equals its weight :

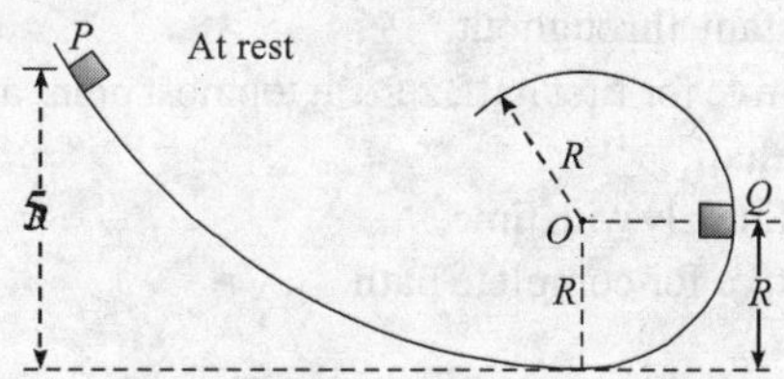

Figure 3.114

(A) $\sqrt{75}$ mg, 3R (B) $\sqrt{65}$ mg, 2R

(C) $\sqrt{75}$ mg, 2R (D) $\sqrt{65}$ mg, 3R

3-96 A stone is tied to a string of length l is whirled in a vertical circle with the other end of the string at the centre. At a certain instant of time, the stone is at its lowest position and has a speed u. The magnitude of the change in its velocity at it reaches a position where the string is horizontal is :

(A) $\sqrt{(u^2 - 2gl)}$ (B) $\sqrt{2gl}$

(C) $\sqrt{(u^2 - gl)}$ (D) $\sqrt{(2u^2 - gl)}$

3-97 A long horizontal rod has a bead which can slide along its length, and initially placed at a distance L from one end of A of the rod. The rod is set in angular motion about A with constant angular acceleration α. If the coefficient of friction between the rod and the bead is μ and gravity is neglected, then the time after which the bead starts slipping is :

(A) $\sqrt{\frac{\mu}{\alpha}}$ (B) $\frac{\mu}{\sqrt{\alpha}}$

(C) $\frac{1}{\sqrt{\mu\alpha}}$ (D) Infinitesimal

3-98 An insect crawls up a hemispherical surface very slowly (see the figure-3.115). The coefficient of friction between the insect and the surface is 1/3. If the line joining the centre of the hemispherical surface to the insect makes an angle α with the vertical, the maximum possible value of α is given by :

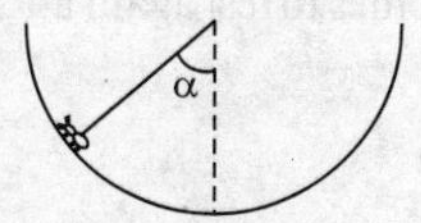

Figure 3.115

(A) $\cot \alpha = 3$ (B) $\tan \alpha = 3$

(C) $\sec \alpha = 3$ (D) $\operatorname{cosec} \alpha = 3$

3-99 An ideal spring with spring-constant k is hung from the ceiling and a block of mass M is attached to its lower end. The mass is released with the spring initially unstretched. Then the maximum extension in the spring is :

(A) 4 Mg/k (B) 2 Mg/k

(C) Mg/k (D) $Mg/2k$

3-100 A 10 kg block is released from rest at the top of a incline and brought to rest momentarily after compressing the spring by 2 metres. What is the speed of mass just before it reaches the spring :

(A) $\sqrt{20}$ m/s

(B) $\sqrt{30}$ m/s

(C) $\sqrt{10}$ m/s

(D) $\sqrt{40}$ m/s

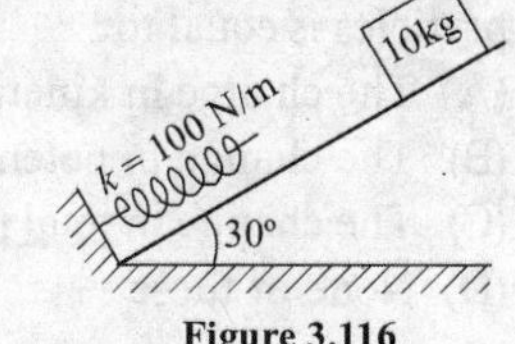

Figure 3.116

3-101 The following figure-3.117 illustrates the relation between the position of a particle and force. The work done in displacing the particle from $x = 1$ to 5 m is :

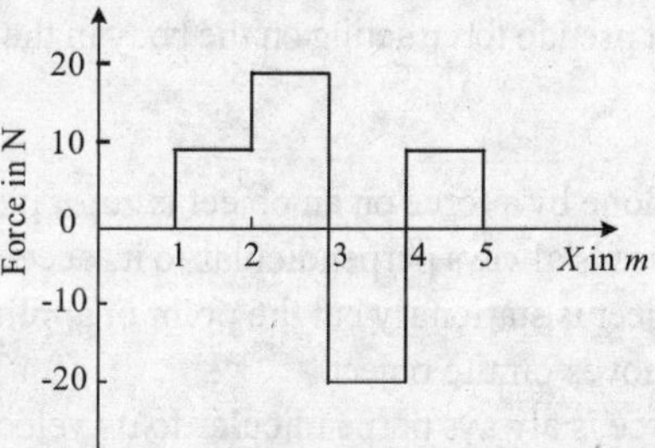

Figure 3.117

(A) 20 joules (B) 60 joules

(C) 70 joules (D) 100 joules

* * * * *

Advance MCQs with One or More Options Correct

3-1 A ball of mass m is attached to the lower end of a light vertical spring of force constant k. The upper end of the spring is fixed. The ball is released from rest with the spring at its normal length, and comes to rest again after descending through a distance x :

(A) $x = mg/k$
(B) $x = 2\,mg/k$
(C) The ball will have no acceleration at the position where it has descended through $x/2$.
(D) The ball will have an upward acceleration equal to g at its lowermost position.

3-2 A heavy particle is suspended by a string of length 60 cm from a fixed point O. It is projected horizontally with speed 4.2 m/s from its lowest position : (Take $g = 9.8$ m/s^2)

(A) The particle will rise to a maximum height of 30 cm above O.
(B) The maximum height above O reached by the particle will be less than 30 cm.
(C) When the particle reaches the maximum height it will have kinetic energy.
(D) The particle will leave the circular path while going up.

3-3 Work done by the conservative forces in a system of particles is equal to :

(A) The change in kinetic energy of the system
(B) The change in potential energy of the system
(C) The change in total mechanical energy of the system
(D) None of these

3-4 Select the correct alternative(s) :

(A) Work done by static friction is always zero.
(B) Work done by kinetic friction can be positive.
(C) Kinetic energy of a system can not be increased without applying any external force on the system.
(D) Work energy theorem is valid in non-inertial frames if we account pseudo force acting on the body in the non-inertial frame.

3-5 Work done by a force on an object is zero, if :

(A) The force is always perpendicular to its acceleration.
(B) The object is stationary but the point of application of the force moves on the object.
(C) The force is always perpendicular to its velocity.
(D) The object moves in such a way that the point of application of the force remains fixed.

3-6 A particle moves in a straight line with constant acceleration under a constant force F. Select the correct alternative(s) :

(A) Power developed by this force varies linearly with time.
(B) Power developed by this force varies parabolically with time.
(C) Power developed by this force varies linearly with displacement.
(D) Power developed by this force varies parabolically with displacement.

3-7 Kinetic energy of a particle moving in a straight line is proportional to the time t. The magnitude of the force acting on the particle is :

(A) Directly proportional to the speed of the particle.
(B) Inversely proportional to $\sqrt{t}$.
(C) Inversely proportional to the speed of the particle.
(D) Directly proportional to $\sqrt{t}$.

3-8 In projectile motion power of the gravitational force :

(A) Is constant throughout.
(B) Is negative for first half, zero at topmost point and positive for rest half.
(C) Varies linearly with time.
(D) Is positive for complete path.

3-9 A person applies a constant force $\vec{F}$ on a particle of mass m and finds that the particle moves in a circle of radius r with a uniform speed v as seen (in the plane of motion) from an inertial frame of reference. Select the correct statement.

(A) This is not possible
(B) There are other forces on the particle
(C) The resultant of the other forces is mv^2/r towards the centre
(D) The resultant of the other forces varies in magnitude as well as in direction

3-10 One end of a light spring of force constant k is fixed to a wall and the other end is tied to a block placed on a smooth horizontal surface. In a displacement, the work done by the spring is $\frac{1}{2}kx^2$. The possible case(s) may be :

(A) The spring was initially stretched by a distance x and finally was in its natural length.
(B) The spring was initially in its natural length and finally it was compressed by a distance x.
(C) The spring was initially compressed by a distance x and finally was in its natural length.
(D) The spring was initially in its natural length and finally stretched by a distance x.

3-11 A block of mass 2 kg is hanging over a smooth and light pulley through a light string. The other end of the string is pulled by a constant force $F = 40$ N. The kinetic energy of the particle increases 40 J in a given interval of time. Then : (Take $g = 10$ m/s^2)

(A) Tension in the string is 40 N.
(B) Displacement of the block in the given interval of time is 2 m.
(C) Power developed by this force varies linearly with displacement.
(D) Power developed by this force varies parabolically with displacement.

3-12 The spring is compressed by a distance a and released. The block again comes to rest when the spring is elongated by a distance b. During this :

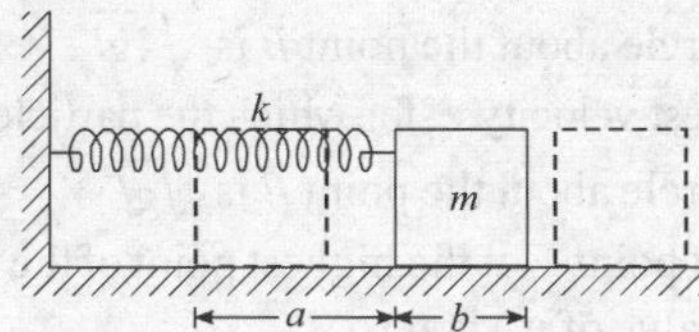

Figure 3.118

(A) Work done by the spring on the block = $\frac{1}{2}k(a+b)^2$

(B) Work done by the spring on the block = $\frac{1}{2}k(a^2-b^2)$

(C) Coefficient of friction = $\frac{k(a-b)}{2mg}$

(D) Coefficient of friction = $\frac{k(a+b)}{2mg}$

3-13 The potential energy in joules of a particle of mass 1 kg moving in a plane is given by $U = 3x + 4y$, the position coordinates of the point being x and y, measured in metres. If the particle is at rest at (6, 4), then
(A) Its acceleration is of magnitude 5 m/s^2
(B) Its velocity when it crosses the y-axis is 10 m/s
(C) It crosses the y-axis ($x = 0$) at $y = -4$
(D) It moves in a straight line passing through the origin (0, 0)

3-14 A block is suspended by an ideal spring of force constant k. If the block is pulled down by applying constant force F and if maximum displacement of block from its initial position of rest is x_0 then :
(A) Increase in energy stored in spring is kx_0^2

(B) $x_0 = \frac{3F}{2k}$

(C) $x_0 = \frac{2F}{k}$

(D) Work done by applied force F is Fx_0

3-15 For a curved track of radius R, banked at angle θ :
(A) A vehicle moving with a speed $v_0 = \sqrt{Rg\tan\theta}$ is able to negotiate the curve without calling friction into play at all
(B) A vehicle moving with any speed $v > v_0$ is able to negotiate the curve with calling friction into play.
(C) A vehicle is moving with any speed $v < v_0$ must also have the force of friction into play
(D) The minimum value of the angle of banking for a vehicle parked on the banked road can stay there without slipping, is given by $\theta = \tan^{-1}\mu_s$ (μ_s = coefficient of static friction)

3-16 A single conservative force $F(x)$ acts on a particle that moves along the x-axis. The graph of the potential energy with x is given. At $x = 5$m, the particle has a kinetic energy of 50J and its potential energy is related to position 'x' as $U = 15 + (x-3)^2$ Joule, where x is in meter. Then :

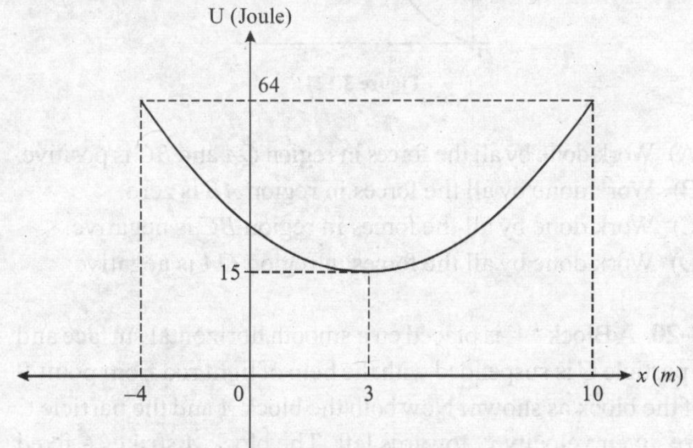

Figure 3.119

(A) The mechanical energy of system is 69 J
(B) The mechanical energy of system is 19J
(C) At $x = 3$, the kinetic energy of particle is minimum
(D) The maximum value of kinetic energy is 54 J

3-17 The potential energy of a particle of mass 1 kg in a conservative field is given as $U = (3x^2y^2 + 6x)$ J, where x and y are measured in meter. Initially particle is at (1, 1) & at rest then :
(A) Initial acceleration of particle is $6\sqrt{5}$ ms^2
(B) Work done to slowly bring the particle to origin is 9 J
(C) Work done to slowly bring the particle to origin is – 9 J
(D) If particle is left free it moves in straight line

3-18 In the adjacent figure a uniform rod of length L and mass m is kept at rest in horizontal position on an elevated edge. The value of x (consider the figure-3.120) is such that the rod will have maximum angular acceleration α as soon as it set free.

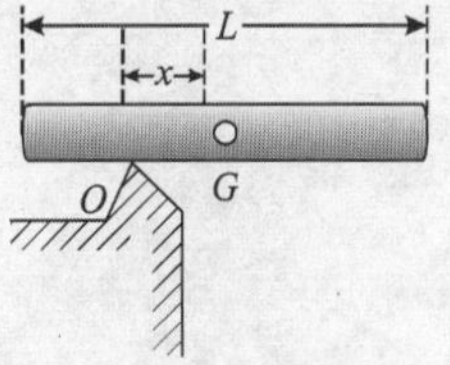

Figure 3.120

(A) x is equal to $\frac{L}{2\sqrt{3}}$ (B) α is equal to $\frac{g\sqrt{3}}{2L}$

(C) α is equal to $\frac{g\sqrt{3}}{L}$ (D) x is equal to $\frac{L}{\sqrt{3}}$

3-19 Displacement time graph of a particle moving in a straight line is as shown in figure-3.121. Select the correct alternative(s) :

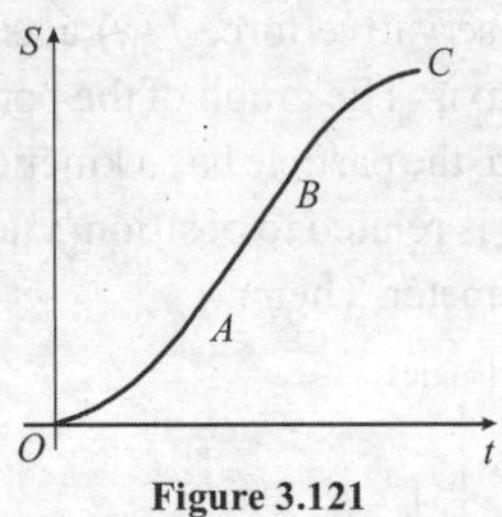

Figure 3.121

(A) Work done by all the forces in region OA and BC is positive.
(B) Work done by all the forces in region AB is zero.
(C) Work done by all the forces in region BC is negative.
(D) Work done by all the forces in region OA is negative.

3-20 A Block 'A' is placed on a smooth horizontal surface and a particle C is suspended with the help of light rod from point B of the block as shown. Now both the block A and the particle C are given velocity v_0 towards left. The block A strikes a fixed wall and suddenly stops. Then, (The rod BC is free to rotate about B)

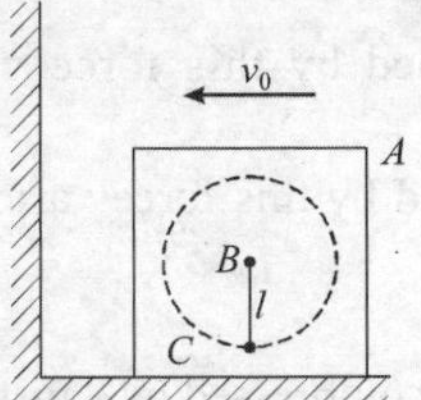

Figure 3.122

(A) The smallest velocity v_0 for which the particle C will swing in a full circle about the point B is $\sqrt{4gl}$.
(B) The smallest velocity v_0 for which the particle C will swing in a full circle about the point B is $\sqrt{gl}$.
(C) Velocity of point C at the highest point of the circle (for the smallest value of v_0) is zero.
(D) Velocity of point C at the highest point of the circle (for the smallest value of v_0) is $\sqrt{gl}$.

3-21 A man is running with a constant acceleration on a plank which is placed on a horizontal smooth surface. Then choose the correct option(s) :
(A) Work done by friction on the man is negative
(B) Work done by friction on the man is positive
(C) Work done by friction on the plank is positive
(D) Work done by friction on the plank is negative

* * * * *

Unsolved Numerical Problems for Preparation of NSEP, INPhO & IPhO

***For detailed preparation of INPhO and IPhO students can refer advance study material on* www.physicsgalaxy.com**

3-1 An astronaut with space suit has a mass of 110 kg. Climbing up a hill 7.3 m high in 7.2 sec requires the astronaut to expend a power of 200 W. Is the astronaut on the earth ?

Ans. [No]

3-2 In an amusement park passengers riding in a Air racer are revolving around a tall steel tower. At top speed all of its planes fly at 60° bank, and about 50m from the tower. In this position the support chains make an angle of 60° with the vertical. Calculate the speed of the planes.

Ans. [29.42 m/s]

3-3 A man is drawing water from a well with a bucket which leaks uniformly. The bucket when full weighs 20 kg and when it arrives the top only half the water remains. The depth of the water is 20 m. What is the work done ?

Ans. [3000 J]

3-4 A train of mass 100 metric tons is drawn up an incline of 1 in 49 at the rate of 36 kph by an engine. If the resistance due to friction be 10 N per metric ton, calculate the power of the engine. If the steam is shut off, how far will the train move before it comes to rest ?

Ans. [210 kw, 238.1 m]

3-5 An elevator has a mass of 600 kg, not including passengers. The elevator is designed to ascend at constant speed a vertical distance of 20 m in 15 sec. It is driven by a motor that can provide up to 30 hp to the elevator, what is the maximum number of passengers that can ride in the elevator ? Assume that an average passenger has a mass of 65 kg.

Ans. [17]

3-6 Consider a spring that does not obey Hooks's law. One end of the spring is held fixed. When it is stretched or compressed by an amount x, the force it exert is $F = ax - bx + cx^2$. Where a = 50 N/m, b = 150 N/m^2 and c = 5000 N/m^3. How much work must be done to stretch this spring by 1m from its unstretched length ?

Ans. [1616.67 J]

3-7 An object of mass 5 kg falls from rest through a vertical distance of 20 m and reaches a velocity of 10 m/s. How much work is done by the push of the air on the object ?

Ans. [– 750 J]

3-8 The engine of a car of mass m supplies a constant power P to the wheel to accelerate the car. Rolling friction and air resistance can be neglected. The car is initially at rest

(a) Show that the speed of the car is given as a function of time by $v = \left(\frac{2Pt}{m}\right)^{1/2}$

(b) Show that the acceleration of the car is not constant but is given as a function of time by $a = \left(\frac{P}{2mt}\right)^{1/2}$.

(c) Show that the displacement as a function of time is given by $x - x_0 = \left(\frac{8P}{9m}\right)^{1/2} t^{3/2}$.

3-9 A highway curve with a radius of 750 m is banked properly for a car traveling 120 kph. If a 1590 kg car takes the turn at a speed of 230 kph, how much sideways force must the tires exert against the road if the car does not skid ?

Ans. [6230 N]

3-10 A cyclist rides along the circumference of a circular horizontal plane of radius R, the frictional coefficient being dependent only on distance r from the centre O of the plane as $\mu = \mu_0 (1 - r/R)$, where μ_0 is a constant. Find the radius of the circle with the centre at the point along which the cyclist can ride with the maximum velocity. What is this velocity ?

Ans. [$R/2$, $\frac{1}{2}\sqrt{\mu_0 Rg}$]

3-11 The disk in a CD player does not rotate at a constant angular speed, but spins at a rate which is decided by a control unit so that the linear speed of the track being read is constant. The laser beam used to read the data on the disk starts at an inner radius of 5cm and continues to read until reaching an outer radius of 10 cm. If the disk rotates at 600 rev/min at the start, what will be its rotation rate at the end ?

Ans. [300 rev/min]

3-12 A small ball is suspended from a point O by a thread of length l. A nail is driven into the wall at a distance of $l/2$ below O, at A. The ball is drawn aside so that the thread takes up a horizontal position. At what point to the ball trajectory, will be the highest point to which it will rise ?

Ans. [$5l/6$, $50l/54$]

3-13 An amusement park ride consists of a broad short cylinder arranged so that it rotates around its vertical axis. People stand inside the cylinder with their backs to the outer wall and feel an outward push when the cylinder rotates. When the cylinder is rotating fast enough, it is tipped so that its axis of rotation is almost horizontal. If the radius of the cylinder is 4.5m, how fast must it rotate so that the riders do not fall away from the walls at the topmost position ?

Ans. [0.23 rev/sec]

3-14 A designer of race track is appointed on moon for a car race. He has to design a 1.5 km diameter circular race track assuming a speed of 240 km/hr for the type of cars used. If everything else is to stay the same in the design, by how many degrees and in which direction with respect to the horizontal designers will have to change the angle at which the track is banked on the moon as compared to the banking angle on earth ? The acceleration of gravity on the moon is 1.62 m/s^2.

Ans. [Increase by 44.5°]

3-15 The kinetic energy of a particle moving along a circle of radius r depends on distance covered s as $K = As^2$, where A is a constant. Find the force acting on the particle as a function of s.

Ans. [$2As\,[1 + (s/r)^2]^{½}$]

3-16 Two bars of masses m_1 and m_2 connected by a non deformed light spring rest on a horizontal plane. The coefficient of friction between the bars and the surface is equal to μ. What minimum constant force has to be applied in the horizontal direction to the bar of mass m_1 in order to shift the other bar ?

Ans. [$\left(m_1 + \frac{m_2}{2}\right)\mu g$]

3-17 Show that the height h to which a man of mass m can jump is given approximately by

$$h = \frac{1}{2g}\left(\frac{4sP}{m}\right)^{\frac{2}{3}}$$

where P is the maximum power, the man can use and s is the height of centre of mass of man from ground.

3-18 A string of length 1m is fixed at one end and carries a mass of 100 gm at the other end. This string makes 2/π revolution per second around a vertical axis passing through its second end. Calculate (i) the angle of inclination of a string with the vertical, (ii) the tension in the string and (iii) the linear velocity of the mass.

Ans. [52°14' , 1.6 N, 3.162 m/s]

3-19 Light airplanes are designed so that their wings can safely provide a lift force of 3.8 times the weight of the airplane. What is the maximum bank angle that a pilot can safely maintain in a constant altitude turn without threatening the safety of the airplane ?

Ans. [75°]

3-20 A stone with a mass of 0.9 kg is attached to one end of string 0.8 m along. The string will break if its tension exceeds 500 N. The stone is whirled in a horizontal circle on a frictionless table top. The other end of the string is kept fixed. Find the maximum speed of the stone which it can attain without breaking the string.

Ans. [21.08 m/sec]

3-21 The block on the loop the loop as shown in figure-3.123 slides without friction. At what height from A it starts so that it presses against the track at B with a net upward force equal to its own weight ? The radius of loop is R.

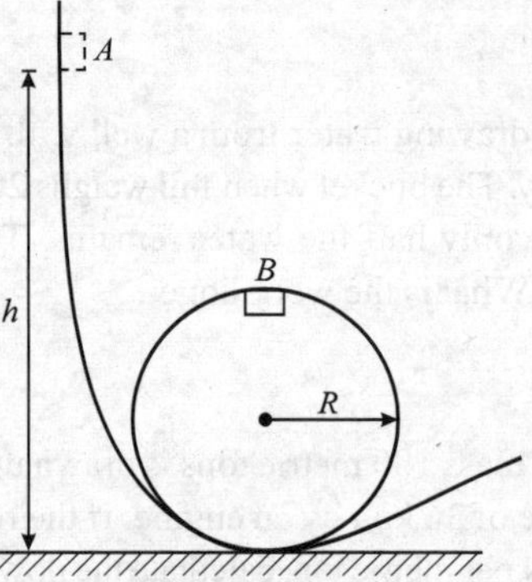

Figure 3.123

Ans. [3 R]

3-22 A body of mass m was slowly hauled up the hill by a force F which at each point was directed along a tangent to the trajectory as shown in figure-3.124. Find the work performed by this force, if the height of the hill is h, the length of its base l, and the coefficient of friction μ.

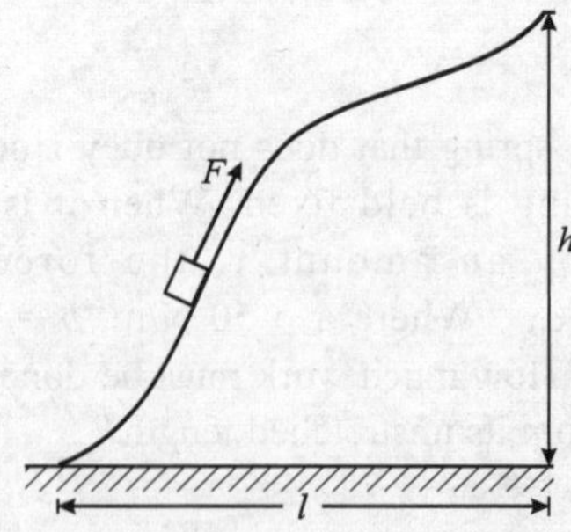

Figure 3.124

Ans. [$mg(h + \mu l)$]

3-23 An object is attracted toward the origin with a force given by $F = -\,{}^{k}\!/_{x^2}$. Calculate the work done by the force F when the object moves in the x-direction from x_1 to x_2. If $x_2 > x_1$, is the work done by F positive or negative ? You now exert a force with your hand to move the object slowly from x_1 to x_2 again while it is being acted on by the force F. How much work do you do ? If $x_2 > x_1$, is the work you do positive or negative ?

Ans. [$-2k\left[\frac{1}{x_1^3}-\frac{1}{x_2^3}\right]$, negative, $2k\left[\frac{1}{x_1^3}-\frac{1}{x_2^3}\right]$, positive]

3-24 A hemispherical bowl of radius R is rotated about its vertical axis. A small particle is kept on its inner surface where the radius makes an angle θ with the vertical. The particle rotates with the bowl without any slipping. The friction coefficient between the block and the bowl surface is μ. Find the range of the angular speed for which the block will not slip.

Ans. [$\left[\frac{g(\sin\theta-\mu\cos\theta)}{R\sin\theta(\cos\theta+\mu\sin\theta)}\right]^{1/2}$ to $\left[\frac{g(\sin\theta+\mu\cos\theta)}{R\sin\theta(\cos\theta-\mu\sin\theta)}\right]^{1/2}$]

3-25 A system consists of two springs connected in series and having the stiffness coefficients k_1 and k_2. Find the minimum work to be performed in order to stretch this system by x.

Ans. [$\frac{k_1k_2x^2}{2(k_1+k_2)}$]

3-26 Aircraft experience a lift force (due to air) that is perpendicular to the plane of the wings. A small airplane is flying at a constant speed of 280 kph. At what angle from the horizontal must the wings of the airplane be tilted for the plane to execute a horizontal turn from east to north with a turning radius of 1200 m ?

Ans. [36°]

3-27 Two identical twins, Tui and Kui are playing on a large merry go round in an amusement park. The surface of merry go round is frictionless and is turning at a constant rate of revolution as the twins ride on it. Tui, sitting 2 m from the center of the merry go round, must hold onto one of the metal posts attached to the merry go round with a horizontal force of 90 N to keep from sliding off. Kui is sitting at the edge, 4 m from the center. With what horizontal force must she hold on to keep from falling off?

Ans. [180 N]

3-28 A small block with mass m is placed inside an inverted cone that is rotating about a vertical axis such that the time for one revolution of the cone is T. The walls of the cone make an anlge β with the vertical. The coefficient of static friction between the block and the cone is μ. If the block is to remain at a constant height h above the apex of the cone, what are the maximum and minimum values of T?

Ans. [$2\pi\left(\frac{h\tan\beta}{g}\right)^{1/2}\left(\frac{\sin\beta-\mu\cos\beta}{\cos\beta+\mu\sin\beta}\right)^{1/2}$, $2\pi\left(\frac{h\tan\beta}{g}\right)^{1/2}\left(\frac{\sin\beta+\mu\cos\beta}{\cos\beta-\mu\sin\beta}\right)^{1/2}$]

3-29 An object is attracted toward the origin with a force of magnitude $F = kx^3$, where $k = 5\ \text{N/m}^3$. How much work is done by the force F when the object moves from 1m to 2 m ? Is the work positive or negative.

Ans. [18.8 J]

3-30 A designer proposes a design for an automobile crash barrier in which a 1200 kg car moving at 20 m/s crashes into a spring of negligible mass that slows the car to a stop. To avoid injuring the passengers, the acceleration of the car as it slow can be no more than 5 g. Find the required spring constant and find the distance the spring will compress slowing the car to a stop.

Ans. [7200 N/m, 8.16]

3-31 What power is required for a grinding machine, whose wheel has a radius of 20 cm and runs at 2.5 rev/s, when the tool to be sharpened is held against the wheel with a force of 180 N ? The coefficient of kinetic friction between the tool and the wheel is 0.32.

Ans. [180 W]

3-32 A particle moving along the x-axis is subjected to a force given by $F = F_0(e^{x/a} - 1)$, where F_0 and are constants. Determine an expression for the work done by this force as the particle moves from the origin to the point $x = r$.

Ans. [$F_0(e^{r/a} - a - r)$]

3-33 During 0.19 sec, a wheel rotates through an angle of 2.36 rad as a point on the periphery of the wheel moves with a constant speed of 2.87 m/s. What is the radius of the wheel ?

Ans. [0.23 m]

3-34 One end of a light string is slipped around a peg fixed in a horizontal table top, while the other end is tied to a 0.5 kg small disc. The disc is given an initial velocity of magnitude 3.4 m/s so that it moves in a horizontal circle of radius 0.75 m. The object comes to rest after 2.5 revolutions. (a) For the entire motion, what work is done by the frictional force ? (b) Assume that the magnitude of the frictional force is constant and determine the coefficient of kinetic friction at the interface. (c) Determine the tension in the string at the instant that the disc completes the first revolution. (d) How much work is done by the tension in the string ?

Ans. [–2.9 J, 0.05, 4.6 N, 0]

3-35 A ball of mass m is attached to a light string of length L and suspended vertically. A constant horizontal force, whose magnitude F equals the weight of the ball, is applied. Determine the speed of the ball as it reaches the 90° level.

Ans. [0]

3-36 A smooth table is placed horizontally and a spring of unstretched length l_0 and force constant k has one end fixed to its center. To the other end of the spring is attached a mass m which is making n revolutions per second around the center. Show that the radius r of this uniform circular motion is $kl_0 / (k - 4\pi^2 mn^2)$ and the tension T in the spring is $4\pi^2 mkl_0 n^2 / (k - 4\pi^2 mn^2)$.

3-37 Suppose that a man (60 kg) is standing in an elevator. The elevator accelerates upward from rest at 1 m/s^2 for 2 sec, then for further 10 sec, it moves with the constant velocity and then decelerates at the same rate for 2 sec. (a) For the whole motion, how much work is done by the normal force on the man by the elevator floor ? (b) By man's weight (c) What average power is delivered by the normal force for the whole motion. (d) What instantaneous power is delivered by the normal force at 7 sec ? (e) at 13 sec ?

Ans. [14 kJ, –14 kJ, 1k/W, 1.2 kW, 0.5 kW]

3-38 In an industry a 300 kg crate is dropped vertically from a packing machine onto a conveyor belt moving at 1.2 m/s. The coefficient of kinetic friction between belt and crate is 0.4. After a short time, slipping between the belt and the crate ceases and the crate then moves along with the belt. For the period of time during which the crate is being brought to rest relative to the belt, calculate, for a reference frame, (a) the kinetic energy supplied to the crate, (b) the magnitude of the kinetic frictional force acting on the crate, the magnitude of energy supplied by the motion. (c) Why are the answers to (a) and (c) different.

Ans. [216 J, 1180 N, 432 J]

3-39 A bicyclist of mass 80 kg (including the bicycle) can coast down a 3.4° hill at a steady speed of 6 kph. Pumping hard, the cyclist can descend the hill at a speed of 30 kph. Using the same power, at what speed can the cyclist climb the same hill ? Assume the force of friction is directly proportional to the speed v.

Ans. [24 kph]

3-40 An engineer is designing a spring to be placed at the bottom of an elevator shaft, if the elevator cable should break at a height h above the top of the spring, calculate the required value of the spring constant k, so that passengers undergo an acceleration of no more than 10 g when brought to rest, Let M be the total mass of the elevator and passengers.

Ans. [$99Mg/2h$]

3-41 A man finds that, on level ground, his 800 kg car accelerates from rest to 15 m/s in 10 sec and then coasts to rest from 15 m/s in 500 m. Compute the average horsepower delivered by the car.

Ans. [7650 W]

3-42 A child's 200 gm toy car is driven by an electric motor that has a constant output power. The car can climb a 20° incline at 20 cm/s and can travel on a horizontal table at 40 cm/s. The friction force retarding it is kv, where k is a constant and v is its speed. How steep in incline can it climb with a speed of 30 cm/s ?

Ans. [7.64°]

3-43 A solid body rotates about a stationary axis so that its angular velocity depends on the rotation angle φ as $\omega = \omega_0 - k\varphi$, where ω_0 and k are positive constants. At the moment $t = 0$, the angle $\varphi = 0$. Find the time dependence of (a) angular velocity (b) rotation angle.

Ans. [$\omega_0 e^{-kt}$, $\frac{\omega_0}{k}(1 - e^{-kt})$]

3-44 (a) The bob of a simple pendulum of length l is released from a point in the same horizontal line as the point of suspension and at a distance l from it. Calculate the tension in the string at the lowest point of its swing.

(b) If the string of the pendulum is catched by a nail located vertically below the point of suspension and the bob just swings around a complete circle around the nail, find the distance of the nail from the point of suspension.

(c) If the string of the pendulum is made of rubber then show that it will be stretched by 3 mg/k on reaching the bob at the lowest point. Here k is the force constant of the string.

Ans. [3 mg, 3l/5]

3-45 The resistance to motion of an automobile depends on road friction, which is almost independent of speed, and on air drag, which is proportional to speed squared. For a car with a weight of 12000 N, the total resistance force F is given by $F = 300 + 1.8\,v^2$, where F is in newtons and v is in meters per second. Calculate the power required to accelerate the car at 0.92 m/s^2 when the speed is 80 kph.

Ans. [51 kW]

3-46 One end of a light string is attached to a 1.2 kg disc which can slide with negligible friction of a 37° incline as shown in figure-3.125. The other end of the string is fixed to a point on the incline, and the disc moves in a circular path of radius 0.75 m. At the lowest position, the tension in the string is 110 N.

Determine (a) the speed of the disc at this lowest point (b) the speed of the disc at the highest point in the circle, (c) the tension in the string for this highest position.

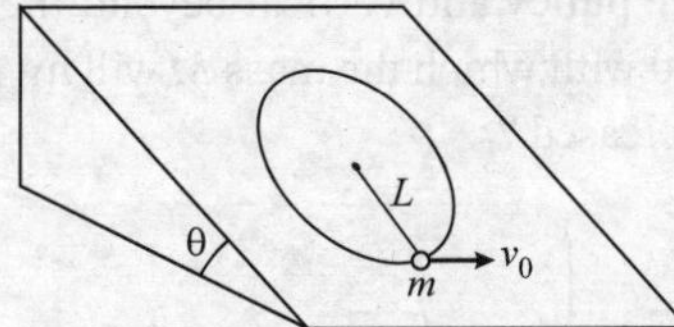

Figure 3.125

Ans. [8.015 m/s, 6.8 m/s, 66.8 N]

3-47 A particle of mass 9 kg is moving under the action of a central force whose potential energy is given by $U = 10/r$. For what energy it will orbit a circle of radius 10 m ? Calculate the time period of this motion.

Ans. [– 0.5 J, 60 π sec]

3-48 A device consists of a smooth *L*-shaped rod located in a horizontal plane and a sleeve *A* of mass *m* attached by a weightless spring to a point *B* as shown in figure-3.126. The spring length is *l* and stiffness is equal to *k* the whole system rotates with a constant angular velocity ω about a vertical axis passing through the point *O*. Find the elongation of the spring. How is the result affected by the rotation direction ?

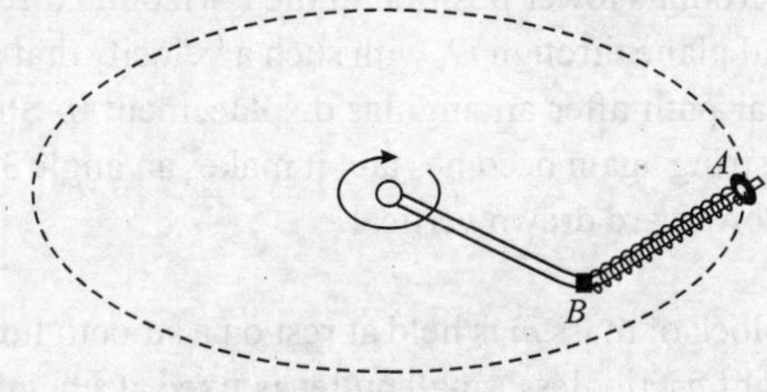

Figure 3.126

Ans. [$\Delta l = \dfrac{l}{\dfrac{k}{m\omega^2} - 1}$]

3-49 A particle *A* moves along a circle of radius $R = 50$ cm so that its radius vector *v* relative to the point *O* rotates with constant angular velocity $\omega = 0.4$ rad/s. Find its total acceleration.

Ans. [0.32 m/s^2]

3-50 A particle moves in the *XY* plane with velocity given as

$$v = ai + bxj$$

At the initial moment of time, the particle was located at the point (0, 0), find

(a) The equation of trajectory of particle.

(b) The radius of curvature of its trajectory as a function of *x*.

Ans. [$\dfrac{bx^2}{2a}$, $\dfrac{(a^2 + b^2x^2)^{3/2}}{ba^2}$]

3-51 A shell acquires the initial velocity 320 m/s, having turned complete two revolutions inside the barrel whose length is equal to 2 m. Assuming that the shell moves inside the barrel with uniform acceleration, find the angular velocity of its axial rotation at the moment when the shell escapes the barrel.

Ans. [2×10^3 m/s]

3-52 A small objects slides without friction from the height 50 cm shown in figure-3.127 and then loops the vertical loop of radius 20 cm from which a symmetrical section of angle 2α has been removed. Find the angle α such that after losing constant at *A* and flying through the air, the object will reach at point *B*.

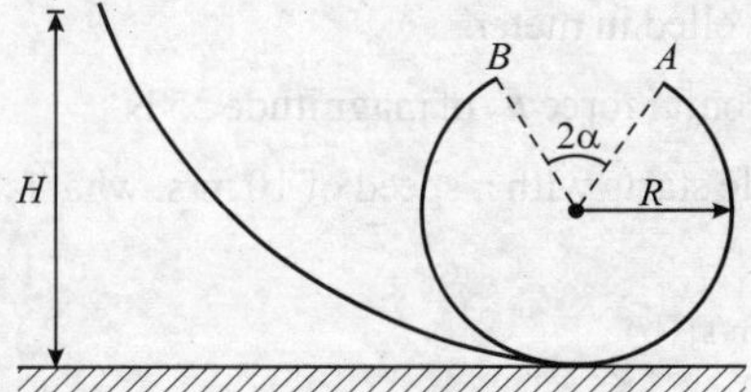

Figure 3.127

Ans. [60°]

3-53 A point moves along a circle with a velocity $v = kt$ where $k = 0.5$ m/s^2. Find the total acceleration of the point at the moment when it covered the nth fraction of the circle after the beginning of motion *n* being 0.1.

Ans. [0.8 m/s^2]

3-54 In figure-3.128(a) and 3.128(b), *AC*, *DG* and *GF* are fixed inclined planes. $BC = EF = x$ and $AB = DF = y$. A small block of mass *M* is released from rest form the point *A*. It slides down *AC* and reaches *C* with a speed V_C the same block is released from rest from point *D*. It slides down *DGF* and reaches the point F with speed V_F. The coefficients of kinetic friction between the block and both the surfaces *AC* and *GDF* are μ. Calculate V_C and V_F.

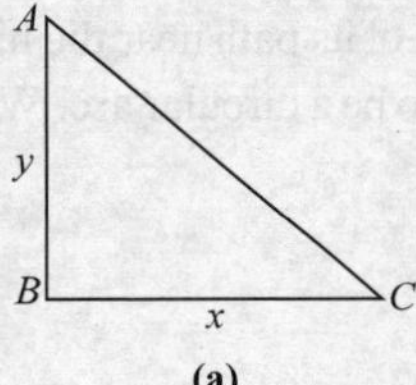

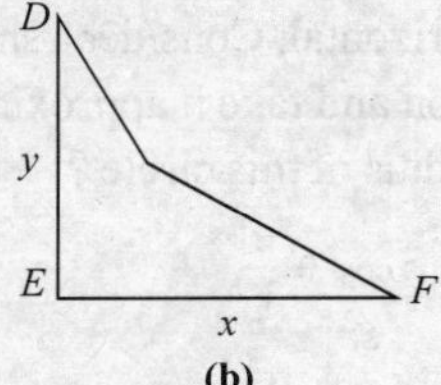

Figure 3.128

Ans. [$V_C = \sqrt{2g(y - \mu x)}$, $V_F = \sqrt{2g(y - \mu x)}$]

3-55 AB is a quarter of a smooth circular track of radius 4 m as shown in figure-3.129. A particle P of mass 5 kg moves along the track from A to B under the action of the following forces :

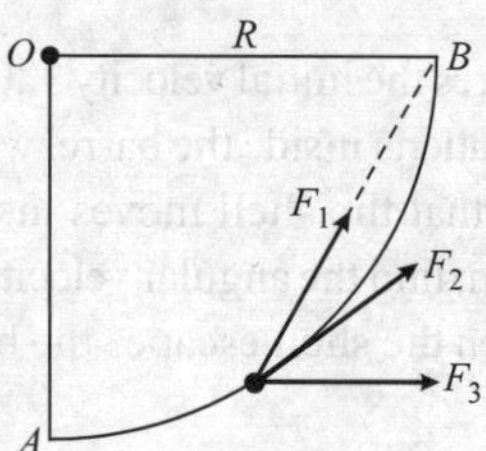

Figure 3.129

(i) A force F_1 direct always towards point B, its magnitude is content and is equal to 4 N.

(ii) A force F_2 that is directed along the instantaneous tangent to the circular track, its magnitude is $(20 - s)$ N, where s is the distance travelled in meter.

(iii) A horizontal force F_3 of magnitude 25 N.

If the particle starts with a speed of 10 m/s, what is its speed at B.

Ans. [12.85 m/s]

3-56 A 20 gm bullet pirces through a plate of mass $M_1 = 1$ kg and then comes to rest inside a second plate of mass $M_2 = 2.98$ kg as shown in figure. It is found that the two plates, initially at rest, now move with equal velocities. Find the percentage loss in the initial velocity of the bullet when it is between M_1 and M_2. Neglect any loss of material of the plates, due to action of bullet.

Ans. [25%]

3-57 A 100 ton engine is moving up a slope of gradient 5° at a speed of 100m/hr. The coefficient of friction between the engine and tails is 0.1. If the engine has an efficiency of 4% for converting heat into work, find the amount of coal the engine has to burn up in one hour (Burning of 1 kg of coal yields 50,000 Joule)

Ans. [9.15×10^3 kg]

3-58 A particle is projected with a speed u at an angle θ with the horizontal. Consider a small part of its path near the highest position and take it approximately to be a circular arc. What is the radius of this circle ?

Ans. [$\dfrac{u^2 \cos^2 \theta}{g}$]

3-59 A string with one end fixed on a rigid wall, passing over a fixed frictionless pulley at a distance of 2 m from the wall, has a point mass $M = 2$ kg attached to it at a distance of 1m from the wall as shown in figure-3.130. A mass $m = 0.5$ kg attached at the free end is held at rest so that the string is horizontal between the wall and the pulley and vertical beyond the pulley. What will be the speed with which the mass M will hit the wall when the mass m is released ?

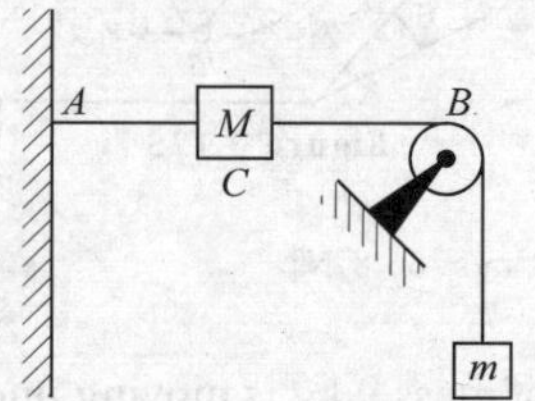

Figure 3.130

Ans. [3.36 m/s]

3-60 A particle slides down the surface of a smooth fixed sphere of radius r starting from rest at the highest point. Find where it will leave the sphere. Show that it will strike the horizontal plane through the lowest point of the sphere at a distance equal to $5[\sqrt{5} + 4\sqrt{2}](r/27)$ from the vertical diameter.

3-61 A heavy particle is suspended by a light thread, the other end of the thread being fixed to a point O. The particle is projected from its lower position in the horizontal direction in the vertical plane through O, with such a velocity that it leaves the circular path after an angular displacement θ. Show that when the string again becomes taut it makes an angle $3\theta - 360°$ with the downward drawn vertical.

3-62 A block of mass m is held at rest on a smooth horizontal floor. A light frictionless, small pulley is fixed at a height of 6m from the floor. A light inextensible string of length 16 m, connected with A passes over the pulley and another identical block B is hung from the string. Initial height of B is 5 m from the floor as shown in figure-3.131. When the system is released from rest, B starts to move vertically downwards and A slides on the floor towards right. (a) If at an instant string makes an angle θ with horizontal, calculate relation between velocity u of A and v of B. (b) Calculate v when B strikes the floor.

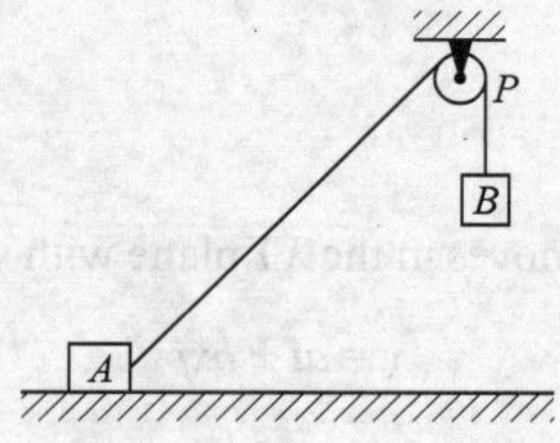

Figure 3.131

Ans. [$40/\sqrt{41}$ m/s]

3-63 A smooth rubber cord of length l whose coefficients of elasticity is k is suspended by one end from the end O as shown in figure-3.132. The other end is fitted with a catch B. A small sleeve of mass m starts from the point O. Neglecting the masses of the thread and the catch, find the maximum elongation of the cord.

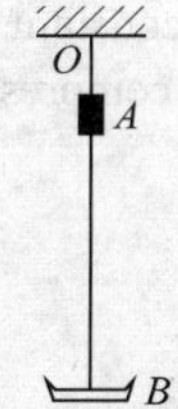

Figure 3.132

Ans. [$\frac{mg}{k}\left(1+\sqrt{1+\frac{2kl}{mg}}\right)$]

3-64 The basket in a front loading automatic clothes dryer rotates about a horizontal axis. The basket rotates so that the force exerted by the basket on clothes located at the basket's edge is zero at the top of the path. If the radius of the basket is 0.65 m, how fast must the basket turn to accomplish this ?

Ans. [0.62 rev/sec]

3-65 A small ring of mass m can slide on a smooth circular ire of radius r and center O, which is fixed in a vertical plane. From a point on the wire at a vertical distance $r/2$ above O, the ring is given a velocity $\sqrt{gr}$ along the downward tangent to the wire. Show that it will just reach the highest point of the wire. Find the reaction between the ring and the wire when the ring is at a vertical distance $r/2$ below.

Ans. [3.5 mg]

3-66 If the system is released from rest, determine the speeds of both masses after B has moved 1 m. Neglect friction and masses of the pulleys (Take $g = 10$ m/s^2)

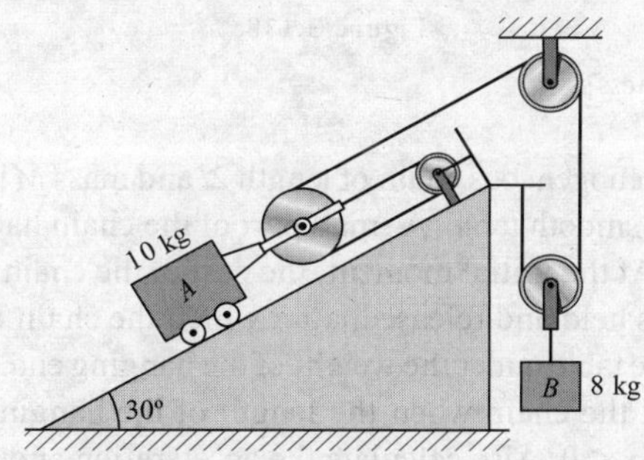

Figure 3.133

Ans. [$v_B = 2.74$ m/s, $v_A = 182$ m/s]

3-67 A chain AB of length l is loaded in a smooth horizontal tube so that its fraction of length h hangs freely and touches the surface of the table with its end B. At a certain moment, the end A of the chain is set free, with what velocity will this end of the chain slip out of the tube ?

Ans. [$\sqrt{2gh\ln(l/h)}$]

3-68 An electron with mass 9.1×10^{-31} kg moves with a speed of 2×10^6 m/s in a circle of 2.85 cm radius under the influence of magnetic field. A proton of mass 1.67×10^{-27} kg, moving in the same plane with the same speed, experiences the same centripetal force. What is the radius of the proton's orbit ?

Ans. [52.2 m]

3-69 A particle is suspended vertically from a point O by an inextensible massless string of length L as shown in figure-3.134. A vertical line AB is at a distance $L/8$ from O as is given a horizontal velocity u. At some point, its motion ceases to be circular and eventually the object passes through line AB. At the instant of crossing AB, its velocity is horizontal. Find u.

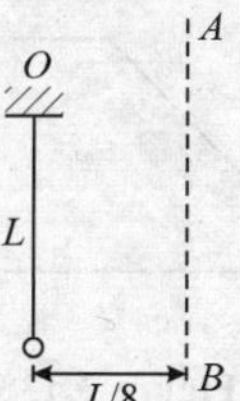

Figure 3.134

Ans. [$\sqrt{\frac{1}{2}(4+3\sqrt{3})gL}$]

3-70 A cyclist intends to cycle up a 12° hill 100m high. Assuming the mass of bicycle plus person is 78.0 kg, (a) Calculate how much work must be done against gravity. (b) If each complete revolution of the pedals moves the bike 5.10 m along its path, calculate the average force that must be exerted on the pedals tangent to their circular path. Neglect friction and other losses. The pedals turn in a circle of diameter 36cm.

Ans. [76400 J, 717 N]

3-71 A rod of length 1m and mass 0.5 kg is fixed at one end is initially hanging vertical. The other end is now raised until it makes an angle 60° with the vertical. How much work is required ?

Ans. [1.225 J]

3-72 In a vertical circle, AB is the horizontal diameter. Let AD and AE are two cords of the circle which subtend the angles θ and 2θ at the centre of the circle respectively. If a particle slides along the two cords from A to D and A to E and the ratio of the time durations it take to travel the distances AD and AE is $1 : n$ then prove that :

$$(n^2 - 1)\cos\theta = 1$$

3-73 A penny with a mass m sits on a horizontal turntable at a distance r from the axis of rotation. The turn table accelerates at a rate of α rad/s^2 from $t = 0$. The penny starts slipping at $t = t_1$. The friction coefficient on the surface of turn table and the penny is μ. Find :

(i) The direction in which it starts sliding.

(ii) The magnitude of frictional force at time $t = t_2$ ($t_2 < t_1$).

3-74 A block of mass 5 kg is suspended from the end of a vertical spring which is stretched by 10 cm under the load of the block. The block is given a sharp impulse from below so that it acquires an upwards speed of 2 m/s. How high will it rise ?

Ans. [20 cm]

3-75 A 20 kg block is originally at rest on a horizontal surface for which the coefficient of friction is 0.6. If a horizontal force F is applied such that it varies with time as shown in figure-3.135.

(i) Determine the speed of the block in 10 s.

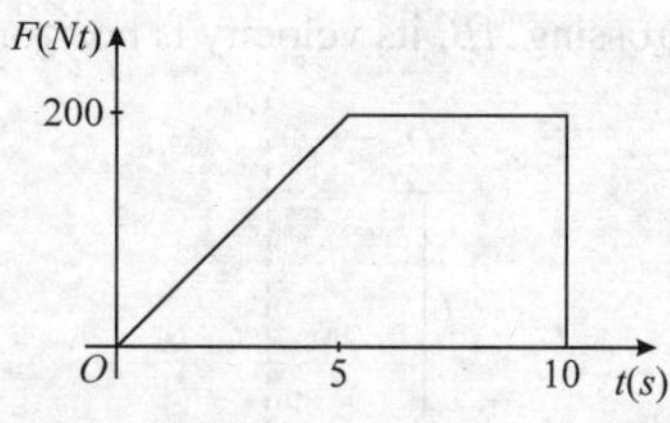

Figure 3.135

(ii) Determine the work done by this force in this duration.

(iii) Determine the work done by frictional force in this duration.

Ans. [24 m/s, 14480.4 J, 8720.4 J]

3-76 A has a mass 15 kg and B has a mass of 45 kg. They are on a rotating surface and are connected by a cord passing around the frictionless pulley as shown in the figure-3.136. If the coefficient of friction between the masses and the surface if $\mu = 0.25$.

(i) Determine the value of ω at which radial sliding will occur.

(ii) Determine how much work is done by an agent to get this angular velocity, when sliding just starts.

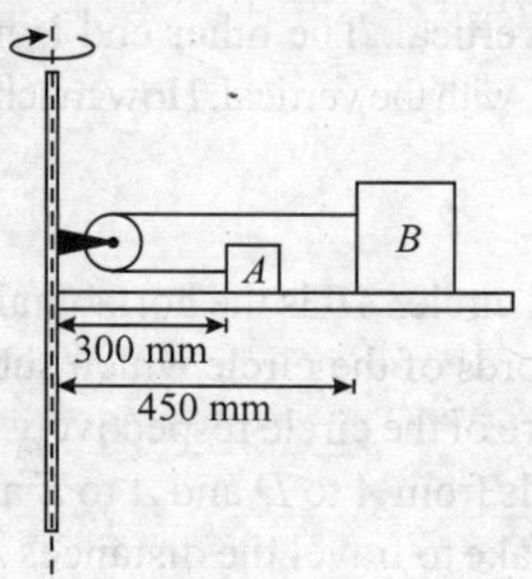

Figure 3.136

Ans. [3.1 rad/s, 50.3 J]

3-77 At a mine the end of side track is to be provided with a spring bumper. The spring must be capable of stopping a 4000 kg ore car which has a velocity of 2 m/s down the incline at a point 40 m up the incline from the point where incline starts and then coasts from there to the bumper as indicated in the figure-3.137. The track resistance remains constant at 30 kg. What should be the spring constant the level after rebounding from the point of maximum compression ?

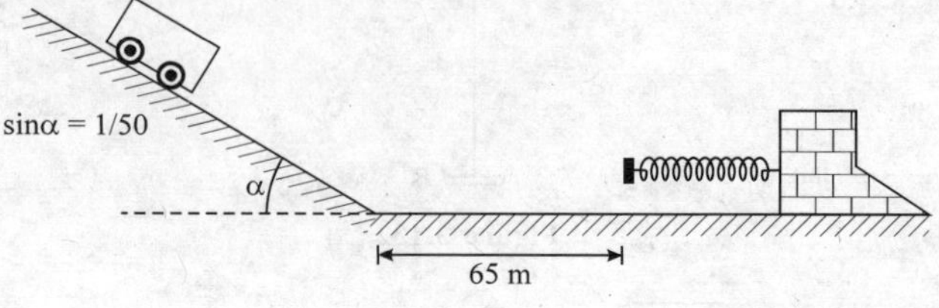

Figure 3.137

Ans. [66800 N/m, 27.34 m]

3-78 A heavy particle of mass m is in motion on a smooth surface of a hemisphere of radius R and there is no friction. At the initial instant the particle is at the topmost point A and has an initial velocity v_0. At what point will the particle leave the surface of the hemisphere ? Also determine the value of v_0 for which the particle will leave the sphere at the initial instant.

Ans. [$\theta = \cos^{-1}\left(\frac{2}{3} + \frac{v_0^2}{3gR}\right)$, $\sqrt{gR}$]

3-79 Figure-3.138 shows a rod of length 20 cm pivoted near and end and which is made to rotate in a horizontal plane with a constant angular speed. A ball of mass m is suspended by a string also of length 20 cm from the other end of the rod. If the angle θ made by the string with the vertical is 30°, find the angular speed of rotation. Take $g = 10$ m/s^2.

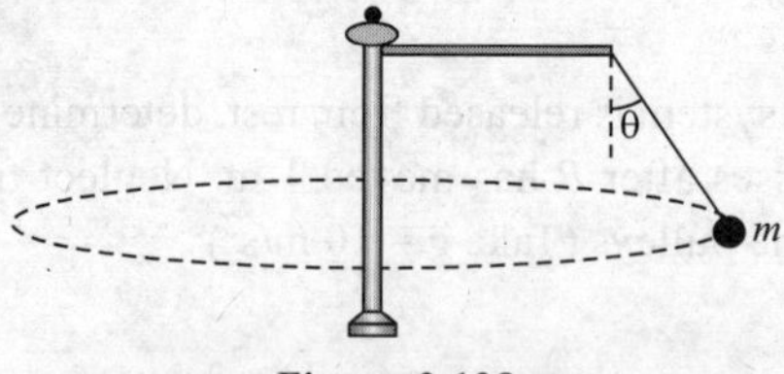

Figure 3.138

Ans. [4.4 rad/s]

3-80 A homogeneous chain of length $2l$ and mass M lies on an absolutely smooth table. A small part of the chain hangs from the table. At the initial moment, the part of the chain lying on the table is held and released, after which the chain begins to slide off the table under the weight of the hanging end. Find the velocity of the chain when the length of the hanging part is equal to $x (x < l)$. Also calculate the acceleration and the force with which it acts on the edge of the table.

Ans. [$x\sqrt{\frac{g}{2l}}$, $\frac{xg}{2l}$, $\frac{\sqrt{2}Mg}{4l^2}(2l - x)x$]

* * * * *

Linear Momentum and its Conservation 4

FEW WORDS FOR STUDENTS

We first introduced the concept of momentum in our discussion of Newton's second laws. Now we take a closer look at the concept of momentum. The laws of conservation of energy and momentum are the most important concepts used in analyzing the motion. This chapter shows you how to use them in combination and extend their range of usefulness. There are some cases when these laws are applied individually but some application require its use simultaneously to solve some specific type of complex problems. This is the cause, that you should be careful to study and capture all the relations and judgments in each step of this chapter.

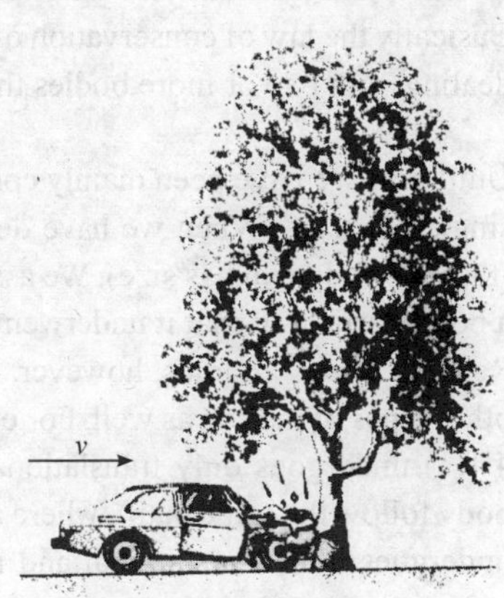

CHAPTER CONTENTS

COVER APPLICATION

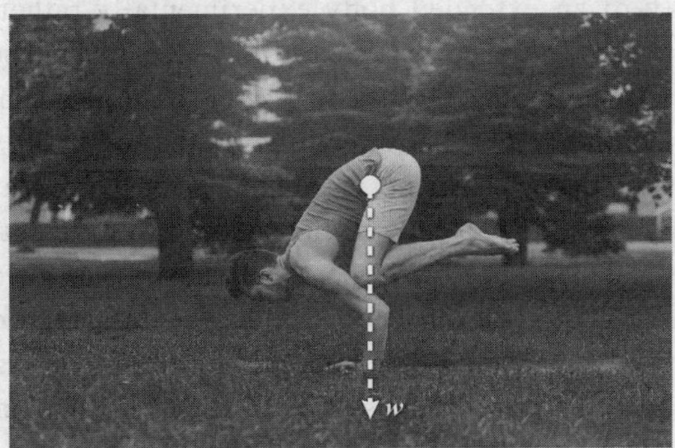

Figure-(a)

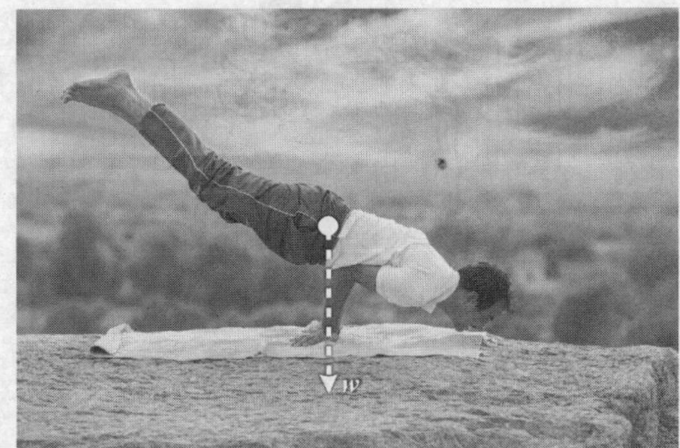

Figure-(b)

Figures-(a) and (b) shows the two yoga balancing positions which are adjusted by the practitioners in such a way that their body centre of mass is located just above the points where hands are in contact with the ground because of which there will be no torque on body due to the weight of body and body will not fall.

The law of conservation of energy, which, we discussed in the previous chapter, is one of most important conservation laws in physics. Among the other quantities found to be conserved are linear momentum, angular momentum, and electric charge. In this chapter we will discuss linear momentum and its conservation. We will also make use of the laws of conservation of linear momentum and of energy to analyze collisions. Basically the law of conservation of momentum is useful when dealing with two or more bodies that interact with each other.

Until now we have been mainly concerned with the motion of single particles. When we have dealt with an extended body (that is a body that has size). We assumed that it approximated a point particle or that it underwent only translational motion. Real "*extended*" bodies, however, can undergo rotational and other types of motion as well. For example, the diver in figure-4.1(a) undergoes only translational motion (all parts of the body follow the same path), where as the diver in figure-4.1(b) undergoes both translational and rotational motion. We will refer to motion that is not pure translation as general motion.

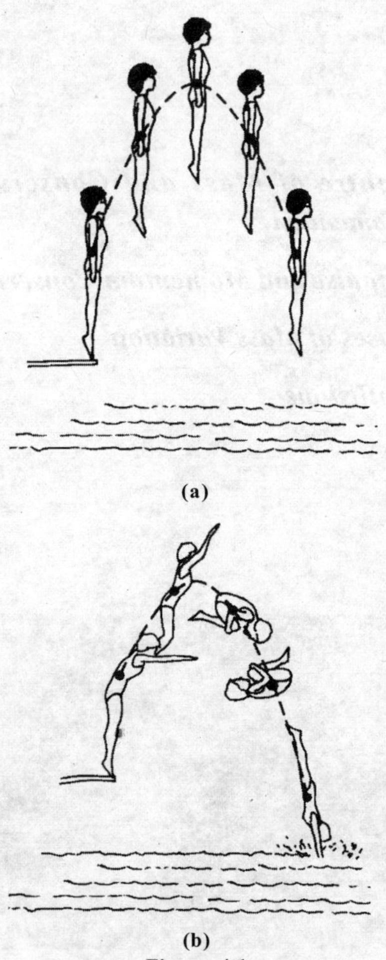

Figure 4.1

Observations of the motion of bodies indicate that even if a body rotates or there are several bodies that move relative to one another, there is one point that moves in the same path that a particle would if subjected to the same net force. This point is called the centre of mass or centre of inertia. The general motion of an extended body can be considered as the sum of the translational motion of its centre of mass plus rotational, vibrational or other type of motion about its centre of mass.

For an example, consider the motion of the centre of mass of the diver in figure-4.1(a), the centre of mass follows a parabolic path even when the diver rotates as shown in figure-4.1(b). This is the same parabolic path that a projected particle follows when acted on only by the force of gravity (that is projectile motion). Other points in the rotating diver's body follow more complicated paths.

Here we begin out study from the analyzation of centre of mass of different type of objects and it will lead to develop the relation between the Newton's second law with the concept of conservation of momentum.

4.1 Centre of Mass and Centre of Gravity

A concept similar to centre of mass is centre of gravity. The centre of gravity of a body is that point at which the force of gravity can be considered to act. Of course the force of gravity actually acts on all the different parts or particles of a body, but for purpose of determining the motion of a body as a whole we can assume that the entire weight of the body (which is the sum of the weights of all its parts) acts at the centre of gravity. Strictly speaking, there is a conceptual difference between the centre of gravity and the centre of mass, but for practical purposes they are generally the same point.

NOTE : There would be a difference between the two only if a body is large enough so that the acceleration due to gravity would be different at different parts of the body.

It is often easier to determine the centre of mass or centre of gravity of an extended body experimentally rather than analytically. To do so, we make use of the fact that if a body is suspended from any point, it will swing unless its centre of mass lies on a vertical line directly below the point from which it is suspended. If the object is two dimensional or has a plane of symmetry, it needs only be hung from two different pivot points and the respective vertical lines drawn, then the centre of mass will be at the intersection of the two lines. If the object doesn't have a plane of symmetry, the centre of mass with respect to the third dimension is found by suspending the object from at least three points that are not in a plane. For symmetrically shaped bodies such as uniform cylinders (wheels), spheres and rectangular solids, the centre of mass is located at the geometric centre of the body.

Important About Centre of Gravity

When the centre of gravity of a body is fixed so that the body's can freely turn about it, the body is in an equilibrium state for all possible positions it can occupy. This implies that *the sum of the moments of the forces of gravity of all the particles of the body about any horizontal axis passing through the centre of gravity is equal to zero.*

The notion of the centre of gravity understood as the point of application of the resultant of the forces of gravity makes sense only for the bodies whose dimensions are not very large or, more precisely, are small relative to the Earth's radius. Only in this case it allowable to regard the gravity forces acting on the particles of the body as parallel to each other. When the indicated condition is not fulfilled there is no point in variable connected with the body through which the resultant of the gravitational forces always pass. In order to illustrate what has been said we shall discuss the following example.

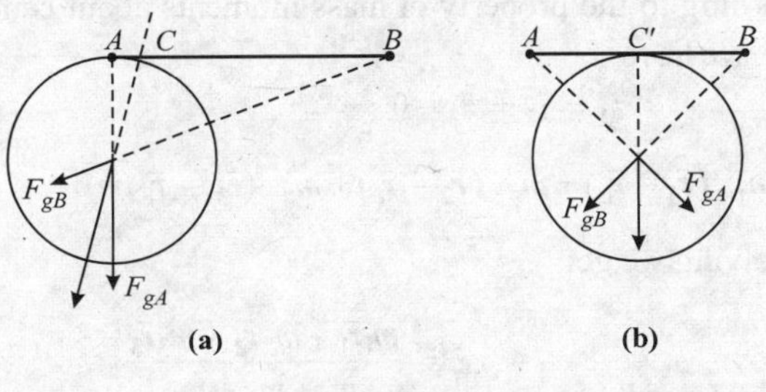

Figure 4.2

Consider a body consisting of two identical material points A and B placed at the ends of an imaginable rigid weightless rod AB of length $2R$ where R is the radius of the Earth (figure-4.2). Let us determine the positions of the lines of action of the resultant of the gravity forces for the two different cases shown in figure-4.2(a) and 4.2(b). In the former case this line passes through a point C of the rod lying near the point A. Since the distance from the point B to the centre of the Earth is $\sqrt{5}$ times the distance from the point A to the centre of the Earth and as is known from Newton's law of gravitation, the force of gravitational attraction is inversely proportional to the square of the distance, we have $CB = 5AC$, which determines the position of the point C on the axis of the rod. In the latter case it is evident that the line of action of the resultant gravity force passes through the midpoint C' of the rod. It is clear that varying the position of the rod in all possible ways we obtain different points on the axis of the rod through which the line of action of the resultant gravity force passes.

4.2 *Localization of Centre of Mass*

There are two types of system of which centre of mass can be located, (i) discrete objects system are (ii) continuous object system. As shown in figure-4.3(a) there are tow bodies of same masses m and m are separated by a distance l from each other. We can at once say by observation that the centre of mass of this system is located at the centre of the line joining the two particles. If the two masses are m_1 and m_2 ($m_1 > m_2$), then centre of mass of this system will be located at a point on the line joining and nearer to m_1 shown in figure-4.3(b). If there are three or more masses (point masses) then also the centre of mass of the all these bodies will be in the surrounding space of these bodies, shown in figure-4.3(c). Such a system is known as discrete object system, in which all the components of the system are point masses and we are required to determine the location of the centre of mass of the system.

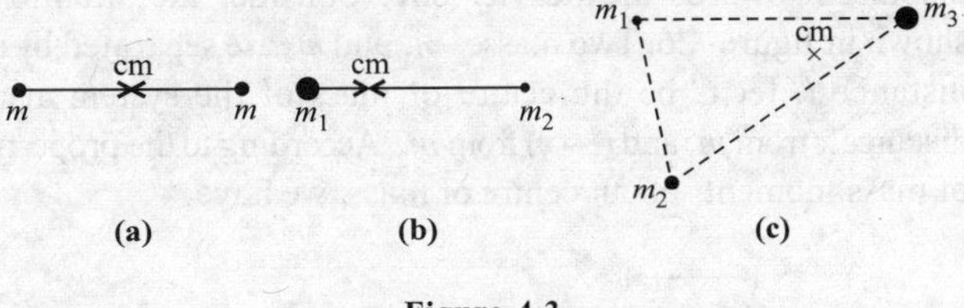

Figure 4.3

Now consider few uniform bodies shown in figure-4.4. Centre of mass of all these bodies must lie at the geometric centre of the respective bodies, as discussed earlier, but the egg shaped body shown in figure-4.4 will obviously has its centre of mass located to the left of its geometric centre. Such system in which there is only a single nonuniform body are known as continuous object systems.

To locate the centre of mass different system, we define a vector property associated with all the components of general system that is *Mass Moment* of a particle.

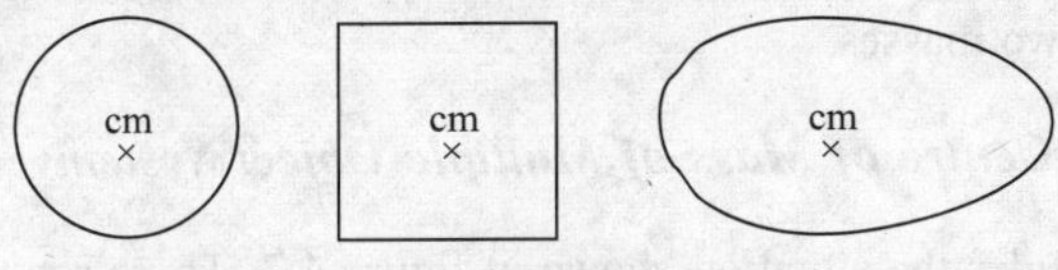

Figure 4.4

Mass Moment : It is defined as the product of mass of the particle and distance of the particle from the point about which mass moment is taken. It is a vector quantity and its direction is directed from the point about which it is taken to the particle, as shown in figure-4.5, the mass moment of particle A(mass = m) about the point P is given by z.

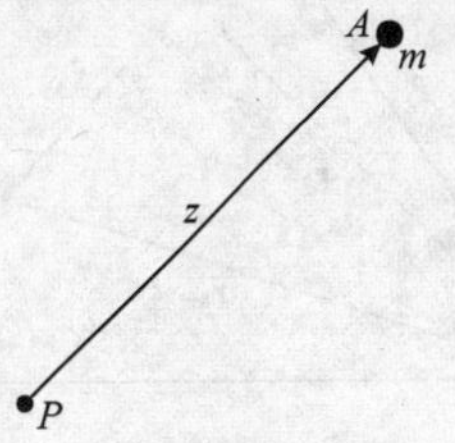

Figure 4.5

There is an important property of centre of mass associated with the mass moments of the components of the system which forms the basis of analytical determination of centre of mass of a system. The property is -"*The summation of mass moments of all the components of a system about its centre of mass is always equal to zero*". This statement is an experimentally verified property which does not require any analytical proof. It can be used as a universal property in all type of systems.

4.3 Centre of mass of a Two Body System

We've discussed that the centre of mass of two identical bodies separated by a finite distance apart lies exactly midway between them and if the two bodies are of unequal masses then it is displaced towards the heavier one. Consider the situation shown in figure-4.6. Two masses m_1 and m_2 are separated by a distance l, let C be the centre of mass of the system at a distance x from m_1 and $(l-x)$ from m_2. According to the property of mass moments about centre of mass, we have

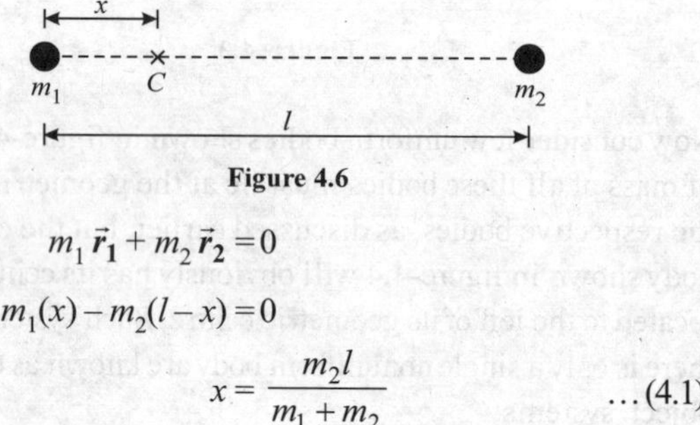

Figure 4.6

$$m_1\vec{r}_1 + m_2\vec{r}_2 = 0$$

$$m_1(x) - m_2(l-x) = 0$$

$$x = \frac{m_2 l}{m_1 + m_2} \qquad \dots(4.1)$$

Equation-(4.1) can be captured as a standard result and it can be recalled as the centre of mass of a two body system is at a distance x from one of the masses and it is equal to the product of other mass and the distance of separation over the sum of the two masses.

4.4 Centre of Mass of Multiple Object System

Consider the situation shown in figure-4.7. There are three masses in a coordinate system with respective coordinates (x_1, y_1, z_1), (x_3, y_3, z_3) and (x_2, y_2, z_2). The position vectors of these masses with respect to origin can be given as

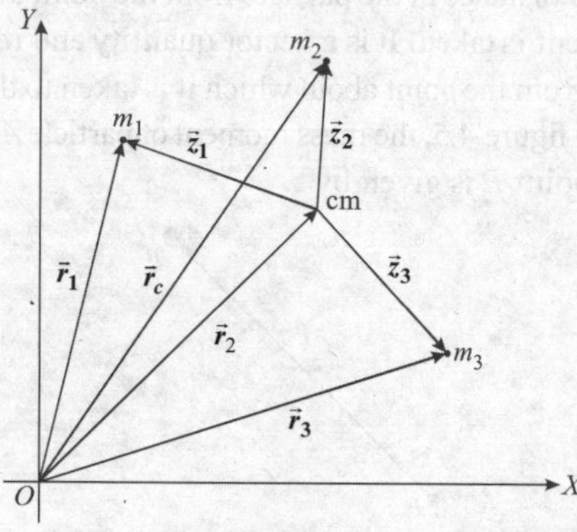

Figure 4.7

$$\vec{r}_1 = x_1\hat{i} + y_1\hat{j} + z_1\hat{k}$$

$$\vec{r}_2 = x_2\hat{i} + y_2\hat{j} + z_2\hat{k}$$

$$\vec{r}_3 = x_3\hat{i} + r_3\hat{j} + z_3\hat{k}$$

In this system, we will now locate the position of centre of mass. Let the coordinates of centre of mass be (x_c, y_c, z_c) and so the position vector of it will be

$$\vec{r}_c = x_c\hat{i} + y_c\hat{j} + z_c\hat{k}$$

The mass moments of the mass m_1, m_2 and m_3 about the centre of mass can be given as

$$\vec{z}_1 = m_1 \,.\, (\vec{r}_1 - \vec{r}_c)$$

$$\vec{z}_2 = m_2 \,.\, (\vec{r}_2 - \vec{r}_c)$$

$$\vec{z}_3 = m_3 \,.\, (\vec{r}_3 - \vec{r}_c)$$

According to the property of mass moments about centre of mass, we have

$$\vec{z}_1 + \vec{z}_2 + \vec{z}_3 = 0$$

$$m_1 \,.\, (\vec{r}_1 - \vec{r}_c) + m_2 \,.\, (\vec{r}_2 - \vec{r}_c) + m_3 \,.\, (\vec{r}_3 - \vec{r}_c) = 0$$

On solving we get

$$\vec{r}_c = \frac{m_1\vec{r}_1 + m_2\vec{r}_2 + m_3\vec{r}_3}{m_1 + m_2 + m_3} \qquad \dots(4.2)$$

This relation can also be generalized for n mass system also. Now by substituting the vector in terms of unit vector $\hat{i}$, $\hat{j}$ and $\hat{k}$ and comparing the coefficients of $\hat{i}$, $\hat{j}$ and $\hat{k}$, we get

$$x_c = \frac{m_1x_1 + m_2x_2 + m_3x_3}{m_1 + m_2 + m_3} \qquad \dots(4.3)$$

$$y_c = \frac{m_1y_1 + m_2y_2 + m_3y_3}{m_1 + m_2 + m_3} \qquad \dots(4.4)$$

$$z_c = \frac{m_1z_1 + m_2z_2 + m_3z_3}{m_1 + m_2 + m_3} \qquad \dots(4.5)$$

Equation-(4.3), (4.4) and (4.5) can also be extended to n-object system.

Equation-(4.2) gives the position vector of the centre of mass of the system with respect to the origin. The velocity of the centre of mass of the system can be given by differentiating the equation-(4.2) as

$$\vec{v}_c = \frac{m_1\vec{v}_1 + m_2\vec{v}_2 + m_3\vec{v}_3}{m_1 + m_2 + m_3} \qquad \dots(4.6)$$

Now by differentiating equation-(4.2), the acceleration of the centre of the centre of the system as

$$\vec{a}_c = \frac{m_1\vec{a}_1 + m_2\vec{a}_2 + m_3\vec{a}_3}{m_1 + m_2 + m_3} \quad \ldots(4.7)$$

Equations-(4.6) and (4.7) will be used in next section in defining the law of conservation of momentum for a system of bodies.

We now take some examples for determining the location of centre of mass of a discrete body system.

4.4.1 Displacement of Center of Mass of a System of Particles

If in a system of particles $\overrightarrow{\Delta r_1}$, $\overrightarrow{\Delta r_2}$, $\overrightarrow{\Delta r_3}$...are the displacement vectors of the particles of system having masses m_1, m_2, m_3... then the displacement vector of center of mass of this system of particles can be directly given by the vector difference using equation(4.2) as

$$\overrightarrow{\Delta r_c} = \frac{m_1\overrightarrow{\Delta r_1} + m_2\overrightarrow{\Delta r_2} + m_3\overrightarrow{\Delta r_3}}{m_1 + m_2 + m_3} \quad \ldots(4.8)$$

 # Illustrative Example 4.1

Figure-4.8 shows a rod of mass 10 kg of length 100 cm with some point masses tied to it at different positions. Find the point on the rod at which if the rod is picked over a knife edge, it will be in equilibrium about that knife edge.

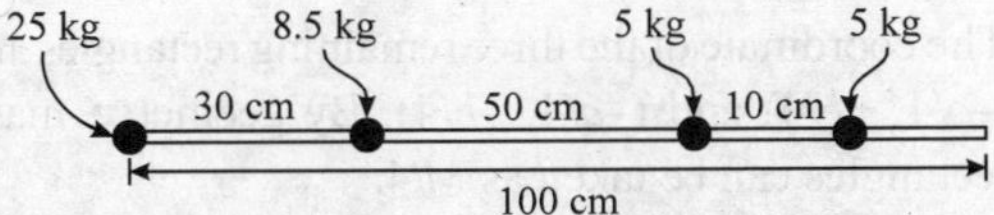

Figure 4.8

Solution

Centre of mass of the system shown in figure-4.8, will be the point, at which if we place a knife edge, system will remain in equilibrium.

To locate the centre of mass of the system, we consider an origin at the left end of the rod. With respect to this origin the position of centre of mass of the system is

$$x_c = \frac{25\times0+8.5\times30+10\times50\times80+5\times90}{53.5} = 30 \text{ cm}$$

 # Illustrative Example 4.2

Two children *A* and *B* of same mass *M* sitting on a sea-saw as shown in figure-4.9. Initially the beam is horizontal. At once child *B* throw away his cap (mass *M*/25) which falls at the point *Q*, mid point of the left half of the beam, due to this the balance of beam is disturbed. To balance it again what is the mass *m* required to be put at the point *P* on the right half of the beam.

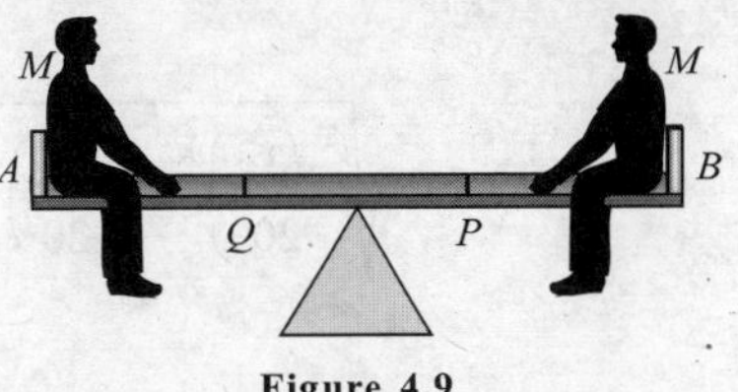

Figure 4.9

Solution

Initially the beam was horizontal because the centre of mass of the system was at the centre (pivot of sea-saw) of the system. When child *B* threw his cap to point *Q*, centre of mass of system shifts to the left of the pivot that why the balance got disturbed and beam starts rotating in anticlockwise sense. To balance it again, we must put some mass to the right of it so as to displace the centre of mass of the system again at the system centre.

If a mass *m* is put at point *P*, to bring centre of mass of the system at the centre, we have

$$M\,.\,\frac{L}{2} + \frac{M}{25}\,.\,\frac{L}{4} = \frac{24M}{25}\,.\,\frac{L}{2} + m\,.\,\frac{L}{4}$$

or $$m = 0.12\,\text{M}$$

 # Illustrative Example 4.3

Figure-4.10 shows a fixed wedge on which two blocks of masses 2 kg and 3 kg are placed on its smooth inclined surfaces. When the two blocks are released from rest, find the acceleration of centre of mass of the two blocks.

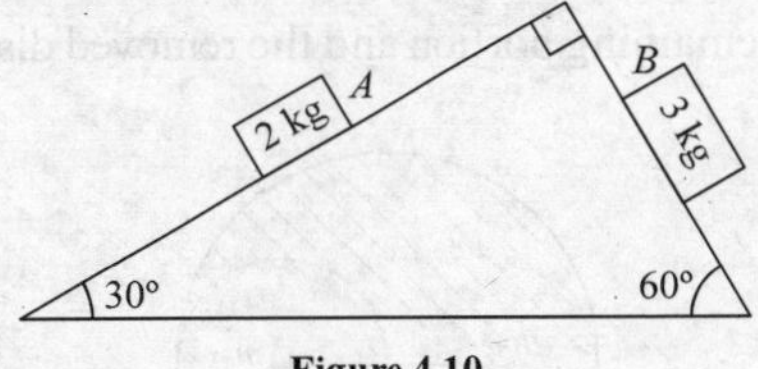

Figure 4.10

Solution

As shown in figure-4.10, blocks *A* slides with acceleration *g*/2 and block *B* slides with acceleration $\sqrt{3}g/2$. Now the acceleration of centre of mass of the system of blocks *A* and *B* can be given both in *X* and in *Y* direction as

$$a_x = \frac{3\times\sqrt{3}g/2\,.\cos60^\circ - 2\times g/2\,.\cos30^\circ}{5} = \frac{\sqrt{3}g}{20}$$

and $$a_y = \frac{3\times\sqrt{3}g/2\,.\sin60^\circ - 2\times g/2\,.\sin30^\circ}{5} = \frac{11g}{20}$$

Thus acceleration of centre of mass of the system is given as

$$a_{cm} = \sqrt{a_x^2 + a_y^2}$$

$$= \sqrt{\left(\frac{\sqrt{3}g}{20}\right)^2 + \left(\frac{11g}{20}\right)^2} = \frac{\sqrt{31}}{10}g$$

Illustrative Example 4.4

Figure-4.11 shows a circular disc of radius R from which a small disc is cut such that the periphery of the small disc touch the large disc and whose radius is $R/2$. Find the centre of mass of the remaining part of the disc.

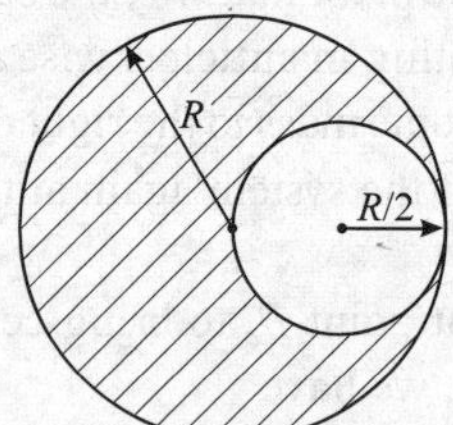

Figure 4.11

Solution

If the disc shown in figure-4.11 were complete, its centre of mass lie at its geometric centre and the centre of mass of the smaller disc, which is removed, also lie at its centre. If from the bigger disc, smaller one is removed then the centre of mass of the remaining portion will be somewhere on the left of the centre of the bigger disc. Let it be at a distance x from the centre. The analysis is shown in figure-4.12. Now the centre of mass of the remaining portion and the removed disc must be at C.

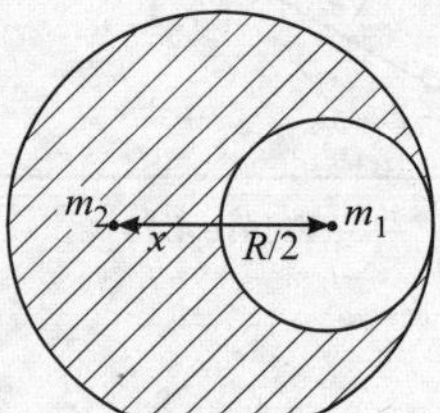

Figure 4.12

If masses of the removed disc and the remaining portion are m_1 and m_2, we have

$$m_1 = \frac{M}{\pi R^2} \times \pi \frac{R^2}{4} = \frac{M}{4}$$

$$m_2 = M - \frac{M}{4} = \frac{3M}{4}$$

Now applying the concept of centre of mass of a two body system we get the distance x at which the centre of mass of the remaining portion of the disc lie, as

$$x = \frac{m_1(x + R/2)}{m_1 + m_2}$$

$$Mx = \frac{M}{4}\left(x + \frac{R}{2}\right)$$

$$4x = x + \frac{R}{2}$$

$$x = \frac{R}{6}$$

Illustrative Example 4.5

Consider a rectangular plate of dimensions $a \times b$. If this plate is considered to be made up of four rectangles of dimensions $\frac{a}{2} \times \frac{b}{2}$ and we now remove one out of four rectangles. Find the position where the centre of mass of the remaining system will be.

Solution

The rectangular plate is shown in figure-4.13, of which one part is removed. We can find the x and y- coordinate of the centre of mass of this system, taking origin at centre of the plate. The coordinate of the three remaining rectangles are ($a/4$, $b/4$), ($-a/4$, $+b/4$) and ($-a/4$, $-b/4$). By geometry, masses of these rectangles can be taken as $M/4$.

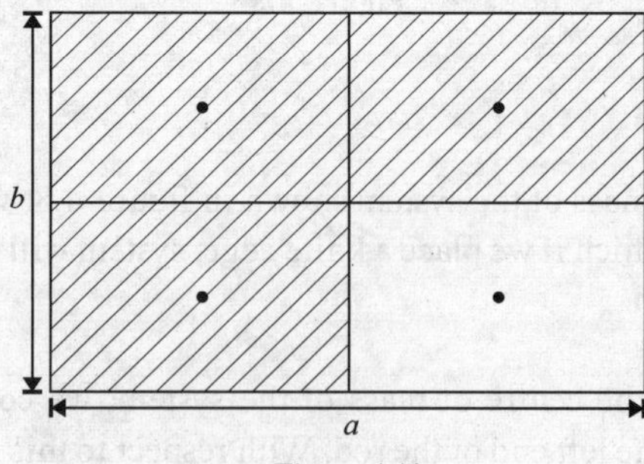

Figure 4.13

Now x-coordinate of the centre of mass :

$$x_{cm} = \frac{M/4 \cdot a/4 - M/4 \cdot a/4 - M/4 \cdot a/4}{3M/4} = -\frac{a}{12}$$

and y-coordinate of centre of mass :

$$y_{cm} = \frac{M/4 \cdot b/4 + M/4 \cdot b/4 - M/4 \cdot b/4}{3M/4} = \frac{b}{12}$$

Illustrative Example 4.6

There are two masses m_1 and m_2 are placed at a distance l apart, let the centre of mass of this system is at a point named C. If m_1 is displaced by l_1 towards C and m_2 is displaced by l_2 away from C. Find the distance, from C where new centre of mass will be located.

Solution

If m_1 and m_2 are placed at a distance l apart, there centre of mass will be located at a distance x from m_1, where

$$x = \frac{m_2 l}{m_1 + m_2}$$

If m_1 is displaced by l_1 towards C and m_2 is displaced by l_2 away from C. The new centre of mass C' now will be located at a distance x' from m_1, where

$$x' = \frac{m_2(l - l_1 + l_2)}{m_1 + m_2}$$

Displacement of centre of mass is

$$\Delta x = x + l_1 - x$$

$$= \frac{m_2(l - l_1 + l_2)}{m_1 + m_2} + l_1 - \frac{m_2 l}{m_1 + m_2}$$

$$= \frac{m_1 l_1 + m_2 l_2}{m_1 + m_2}$$

Illustrative Example 4.7

Let there are three equal masses situated at the vertices of an equilateral triangle, as shown in figure-4.14. Now particle-A starts with a velocity v_1 towards line AB, particle – B starts with a velocity v_2 towards line BC and particle – C starts with velocity v_3 towards line CA. Find the displacement of the centre of mass of the three particles A, B and C after time t. What it would be if $v_1 = v_2 = v_3$

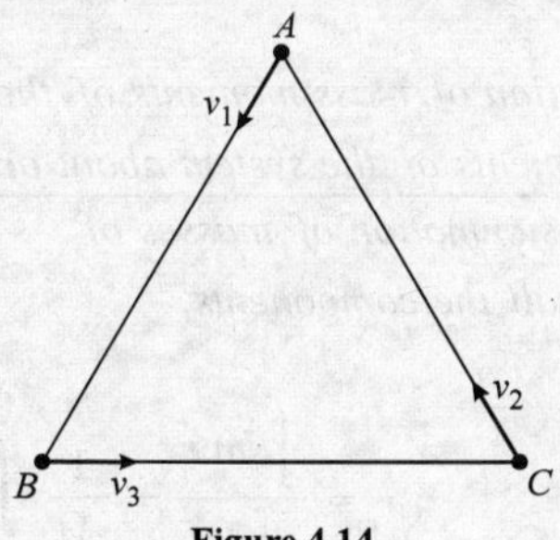

Figure 4.14

Solution

First we write the three velocities in vectorial form, taking right direction as positive x-axis and upwards as positive y-axis.

$$\vec{v}_1 = -\frac{1}{2} v_1 \hat{i} - \frac{\sqrt{3}}{2} v_1 \hat{j}$$

$$\vec{v}_2 = v_2 \hat{i}$$

$$\vec{v}_3 = -\frac{1}{2} v_3 \hat{i} + \frac{\sqrt{3}}{2} v_3 \hat{j}$$

Thus the velocity of centre of mass of the system is

$$\vec{v}_{cm} = \frac{\vec{v}_1 + \vec{v}_2 + \vec{v}_3}{3}$$

$$\vec{v}_{cm} = -\left(v_2 - \frac{1}{2}v_1 - \frac{1}{2}v_3\right)\hat{i} + \frac{\sqrt{3}}{2}(v_3 - v_1)\hat{j}$$

Which can be written as

$$\vec{v}_{cm} = v_x \hat{i} + v_y \hat{j}$$

Thus displacement of the centre of mass in time t is

$$\Delta\vec{r} = v_x t\hat{i} + v_y t\hat{j}$$

If $\qquad v_1 = v_2 = v_3 = v$

We have $\qquad \vec{v}_{cm} = 0$

Therefore no displacement of centre of mass of the system.

Practice Exercise 4.1

(i) Find the centre of mass of the disc shown in figure-4.15. A square is removed from the disc as shown.

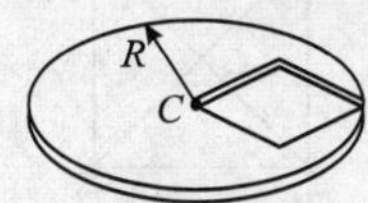

Figure 4.15

[Distance from C is $x_c = \frac{R}{2(2\pi - 1)}$]

(ii) From a gun whose barrel is inclined at an angle θ to horizontal fires 3 small balls of mass 2 kg, 5 kg and 4 kg which move in different directions as shown in figure-4.16 It is given that the centre of mass of the three shells moves in the direction of barrel of gun. Find θ.

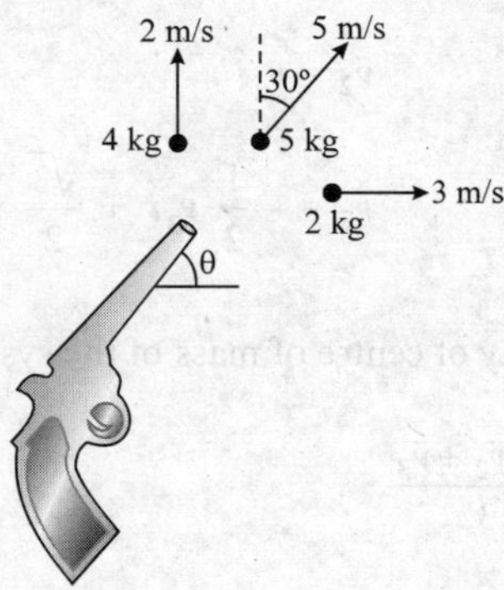

Figure 4.16

[$\theta = \tan^{-1}\left(\frac{16+25\sqrt{3}}{37}\right)$]

(iii) Three laminar objects of uniform density a square, a disc and an equilateral triangle are placed as shown in figure-4.17. Find the coordinates of centre of mass of the three bodies.

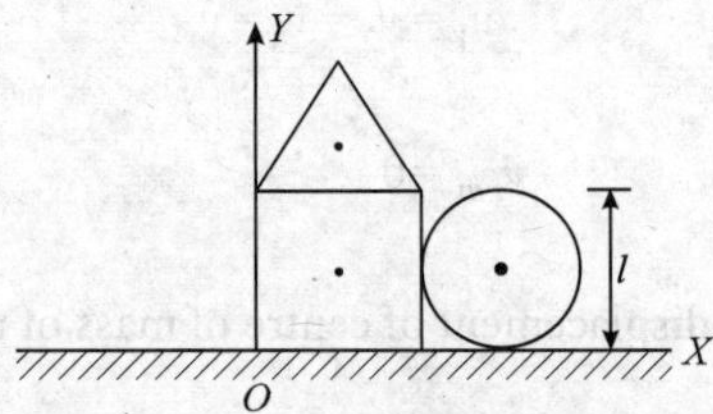

Figure 4.17

[$\left[\frac{(3\pi+\sqrt{3}+4)l}{2(4+\pi+\sqrt{3})}, \frac{(\pi+2\sqrt{3}+5)l}{2(4+\pi+\sqrt{3})}\right]$]

(iv) Four particles of masses $m_1 = 2$ kg, $m_2 = 4$ kg, $m_3 = 1$ kg and m_4 are placed at four corners of a square as shown in figure-4.18. Can mass of m_4 be adjusted in such a way that the centre of mass of system will be at the centre of the square C.

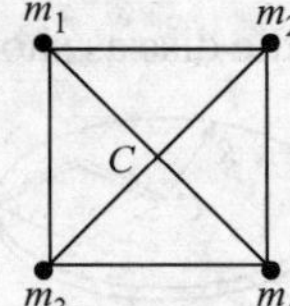

Figure 4.18

[No]

(v) Find x and y coordinates of the centre of mass of the plate shown in figure-4.19 from which a square of side 2 m is cut out.

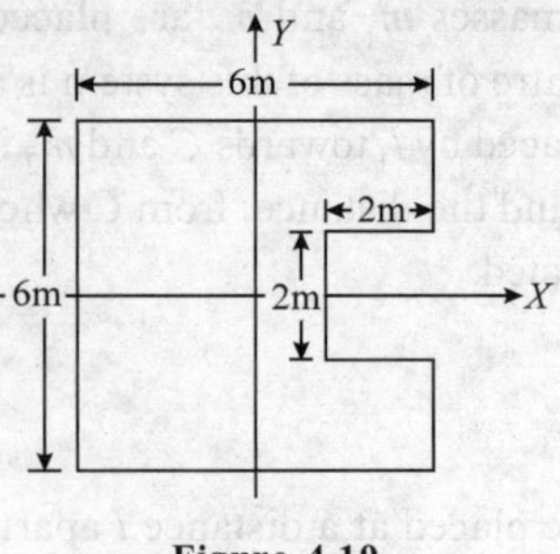

Figure 4.19

[– 0.25 m, 0]

4.5 Continuous Object System

Consider the nonuniform object shown in figure-4.20

We are required to find the position of the centre of mass of this object, in the given reference frame. For discrete object system we use the relation

$$\vec{r}_c = \frac{m_1\vec{r}_1 + m_2\vec{r}_2 + \ldots\ldots\ldots}{m_1 + m_2 + \ldots\ldots\ldots} \quad \ldots(4.8)$$

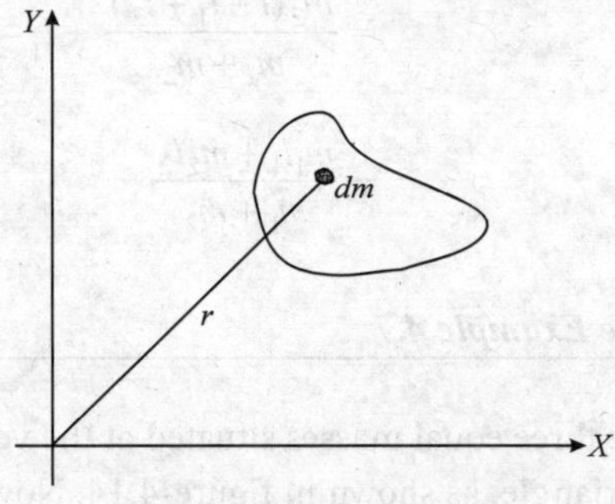

Figure 4.20

Where m_1, m_2, m_3 ...... are the components of the system, but here in a single non uniformly shaped object we have infinite components of masses dm each. Analogous to the equation-(4.8) we can define the position vector of the centre of mass of this body as given by equation-(4.8)

$$\boldsymbol{r}_c = \frac{\textit{summation of mass moments of the components of the system about origin}}{\textit{summation of masses of all the components}}$$

$$\boldsymbol{r}_c = \frac{\int dm\,\boldsymbol{r}}{\int dm} = \frac{1}{M}\int dm\,\boldsymbol{r} \quad \ldots(4.9)$$

Here *dmr* is the mass moment of one of the infinite component of the system(body) and integration is used to sum all the mass moments and hence $\vec{r}_c$ gives us the position vector of the centre of mass of the body.

This relation can also be split into separate *x*, *y* and *z* coordinates of the centre of mass of the body as

$$x_{cm} = \frac{1}{M}\int dm\, x \quad \text{and} \quad y_{cm} = \frac{1}{M}\int dm\, y$$

and $$z_{cm} = \frac{1}{M}\int dm\, z$$

Now we'll use these relation to find the centre of mass of an irregularly shaped object. Some times by observation two of the three coordinates of the centre of mass can be determined and only the third one (either of *x*, *y* or *z*) will be derived by the above relations.

For example we find the centre of mass of some standard objects, which we'll use in further numerical problems.

4.5.1 Centre of Mass of a Semicircular Ring

Figure-4.21 shows the object (semi circular ring). By observation we can say that the *x*-coordinate of the centre of mass of the ring is zero as the half ring is symmetrical on both sides of the origin. Only we are required to find the *y*-coordinate of the centre of mass.

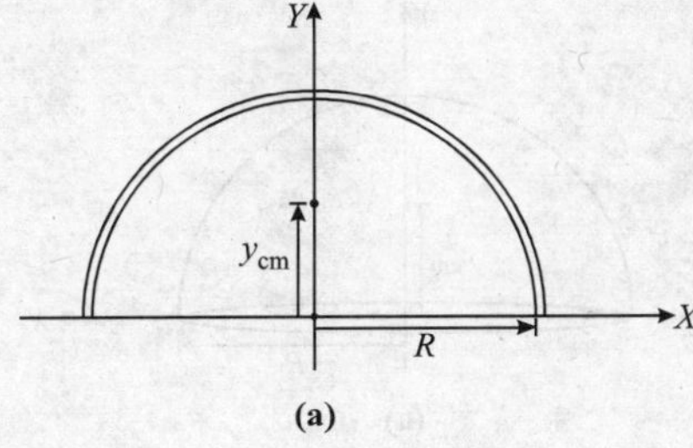

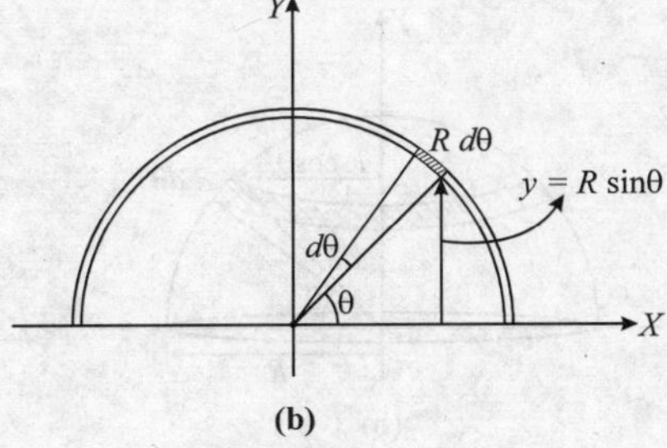

Figure 4.21

To find y_{cm} we use $$y_{cm} = \frac{1}{M}\int dm\, y \qquad \text{...(4.10)}$$

Here for *dm* we consider an elemental arc of the ring at an angle θ from the *x*-direction of angular width *d*θ. If radius of ring is *R* then its *y* coordinate will be *R* sinθ, here *dm* is given as

$$dm = \frac{M}{\pi R} \times R\, d\theta$$

So from equation-(4.10), we have

$$y_{cm} = \frac{1}{M}\int_0^{\pi} \frac{M}{\pi R} R d\theta\, R \sin\theta$$

$$= \frac{R}{\pi}\int_0^{\pi} \sin\theta\, d\theta$$

$$y_{cm} = \frac{2R}{\pi} \qquad \text{...(4.11)}$$

4.5.2 Centre of Mass of a Semicircular Disc

Figure-4.22 shows the half disc of mass *M* and radius *R*. Again here we are only required to find the *y*-coordinate of the centre of mass of this disc as centre of mass will be located on its half vertical diameter. Here to find y_{cm}, we consider a small elemental ring of mass *dm* of radius *x* on the disc which will be integrated from *0* to *R*. Here *dm* is given as

$$dm = \frac{2M}{\pi R^2}\, \pi x\, dx$$

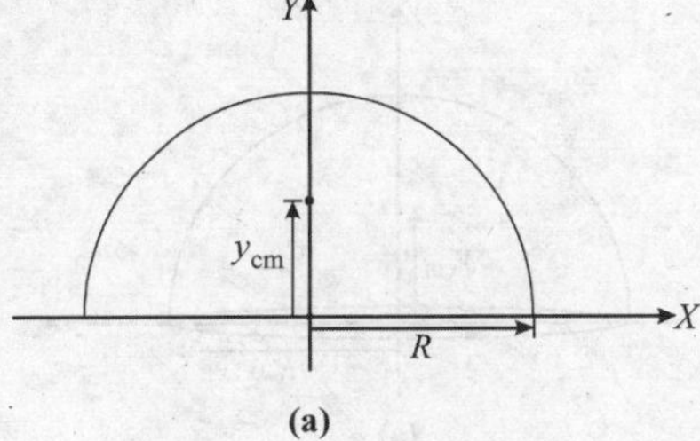

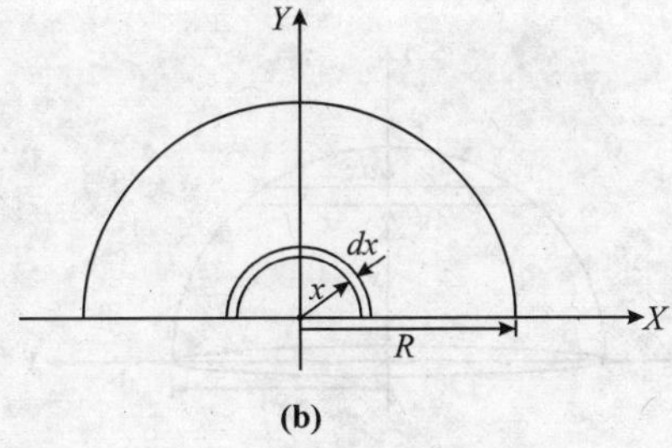

Figure 4.22

Now the y-coordinate of dm is taken as $\frac{2x}{\pi}$, as in previous section, we have derived that mass of a half ring is concentrated at $\frac{2R}{\pi}$ distance from its centre.

Here y_{cm} is given as,

$$y_{cm} = \frac{1}{M}\int_0^R dm\,\frac{2x}{\pi}$$

$$= \frac{1}{M}\int_0^R \left(\frac{2M}{\pi R^2}\pi x\,dx\right)\frac{2x}{\pi}$$

$$= \frac{4}{\pi R^2}\int_0^R x^2 dx$$

$$y_{cm} = \frac{4R}{3\pi} \qquad \ldots(4.12)$$

4.5.3 Centre of Mass of a Solid Hemisphere

Figure-4.23 shows a hemisphere of mass M and radius R. To find its centre of mass (only y-coordinate), we consider an elemental disc of width dx, mass dm at a distance x from the centre of the hemisphere. This radius of this elemental disc will be given as

$$r = \sqrt{R^2 - x^2}$$

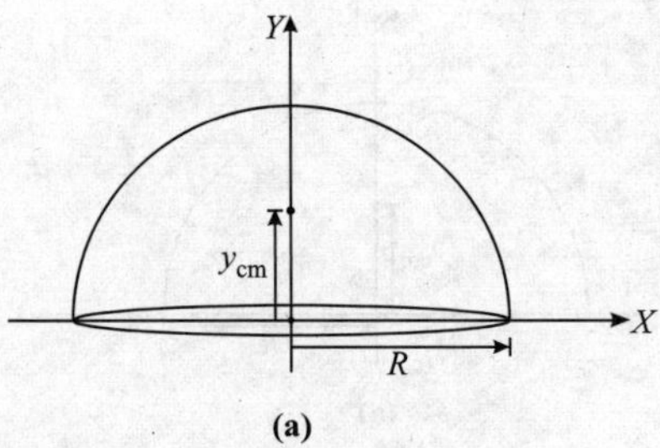

(a)

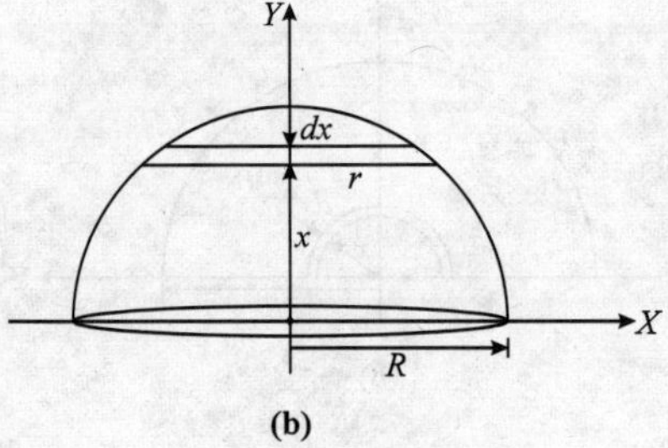

(b)

Figure 4.23

The mass dm of this disc can be given as

$$dm = \frac{3R}{2\pi R^3} \times \pi r^2 dx$$

$$= \frac{3M}{2R^3}(R^2 - x^2)\,dx$$

y_{cm} of the hemisphere is given as

$$y_{cm} = \frac{1}{M}\int_0^R dm\,x$$

$$= \frac{1}{M}\int_0^R \frac{3M}{2\pi R^3}(R^2 - x^2)\,dx\,x$$

$$= \frac{3}{2\pi R^3}\int_0^R (R^2 - x^2)x\,dx$$

$$y_{cm} = \frac{3R}{8} \qquad \ldots(4.13)$$

4.5.4 Centre of Mass of a Hollow Hemisphere

Figure-4.24 shows a hollow hemisphere of mass M and radius R. Now we consider an elemental circular strip of angular width $d\theta$ at an angular distance $d\theta$ from the base of the hemisphere. This strip will have an area

$$dS = 2\pi R\cos\theta\, Rd\theta$$

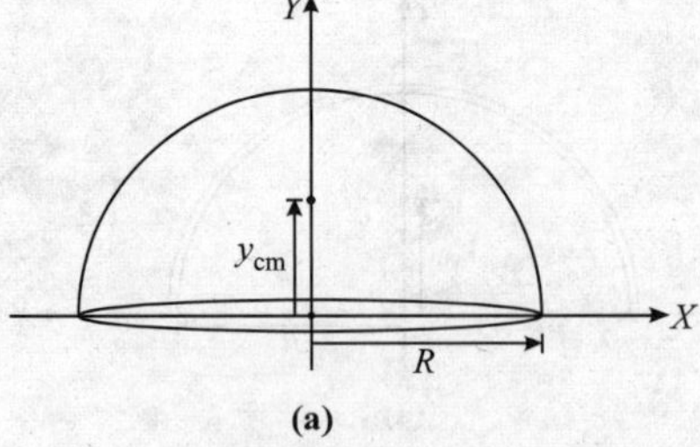

(a)

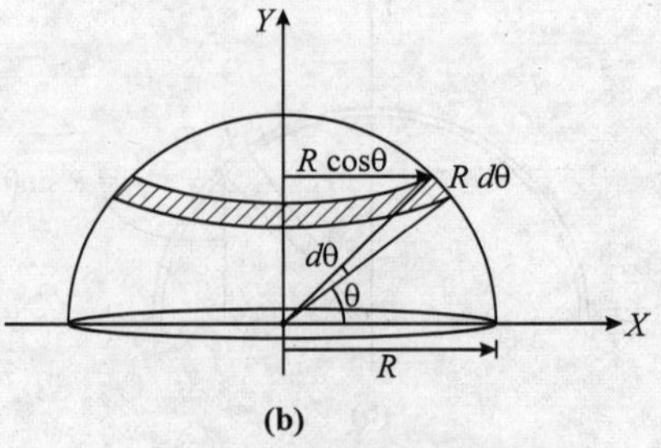

(b)

Figure 4.24

Its mass dm is given as

$$dm = \frac{M}{2\pi R^2}\,2\pi R\cos\theta\,Rd\theta$$

Here y-coordinate of this strip of mass dm can be taken as $R\sin\theta$. Now we can obtain the centre of mass of the system as

$$y_{cm} = \frac{1}{M}\int_0^{\frac{\pi}{2}} dm\,R\sin\theta$$

$$= \frac{1}{M}\int_0^{\frac{\pi}{2}} \frac{M}{2\pi R^2}$$

$$2\pi R\cos\theta\,R\,d\theta\,R\sin\theta$$

$$= R\int_0^{\frac{\pi}{2}} \sin\theta\cos\theta\,d\theta$$

$$y_{cm} = \frac{R}{2} \qquad \ldots(4.14)$$

4.5.5 Centre of Mass of a Solid Cone

Figure-4.25 shows a solid cone of mass M, height H and base radius R. Obviously the centre of mass of this cone will lie somewhere on its axis, at a height less than $H/2$. To locate the centre of mass we consider an elemental disc of width dx and radius r, at a distance x of the apex of the cone. Let the mass of this disc be dm, which can be given as

$$dm = \frac{3M}{\pi R^2 H}\times \pi r^2\,dx \quad [\text{where } r = \frac{Rx}{H}]$$

Here y_{cm} can be given as

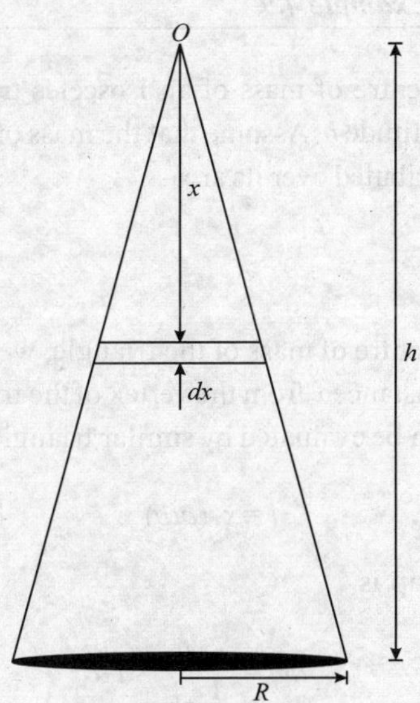

Figure 4.25

$$y_{cm} = \frac{1}{M}\int_0^H dm\,x$$

$$= \frac{1}{M}\int_0^H \frac{3M}{\pi R^2 H}\,\pi\left(\frac{Rx}{H}\right)^2 dx\,x$$

$$= \frac{3}{H^3}\int_0^H x^3\,dx$$

$$= \frac{3H}{4} \qquad \ldots(4.15)$$

4.5.6 Centre of Mass of a Hollow Cone

Figure-4.26 shows a hollow cone of mass M, height H and base radius R. To locate the centre of mass of the system, we consider the elemental strip of vertical width dx at a distance x from the apex of the cone. Here the lateral width (actual width) of the strip is dx secθ. It should be noted that in previous section we've considered a disc of actual width dx, as it was a solid sphere and its mass is distributed uniformly in its whole volume but here unlike to that case the mass is distributed only over its lateral surface area, hence in calculation of the mass of the strip, we should consider the lateral area (actual area) of the strip. Here area of the elemental strip is given as

$$dS = 2\pi r\times dx\sec\theta$$

$$[\text{Here } \sec\theta = \frac{\sqrt{R^2+H^2}}{H}]$$

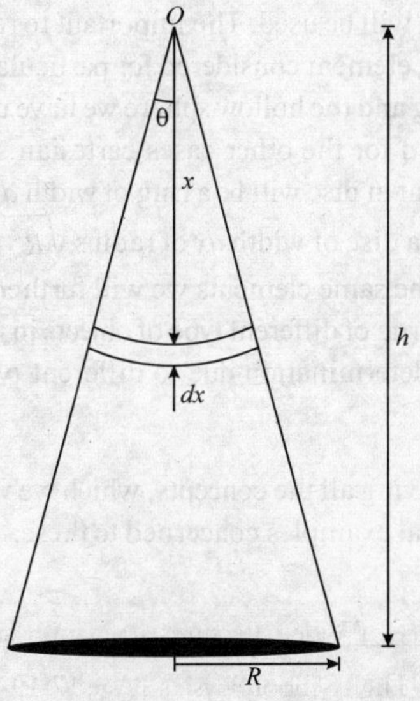

Figure 4.26

Here r is the radius of this elemental disc given by considering similar triangles as

$$\frac{r}{x}=\frac{R}{H}$$

$$r=\frac{Rx}{H}$$

Now the mass dm of the strip can be given as

$$dm=\frac{M}{\pi R\sqrt{R^2+H^2}}\times 2\pi\frac{Rx}{H}\times dx\sec\theta$$

$$=\frac{2Mx}{H^2}$$

Here the centre of mass of the cone can be given as

$$y_{cm}=\frac{1}{M}\int^{H}dm\,x$$

$$=\frac{1}{M}\int_0^H\frac{2Mx^2}{H^2}dx$$

$$=\frac{2}{H}\int_0^H x^2\,dx$$

$$y_{cm}=\frac{2H}{3}\quad\text{... (4.16)}$$

These all results from equations-(4.11) to (4.16) are the standard results which we are permitted to use directly in numerical problems. The most important thing here is the integration procedure for different type of objects used. Not only in the case of finding the centre of mass but in so many other chapters this procedure will be used. The important to remember is the corresponding element considered for particular objects as for the case of ring and the hollow sphere we have used polar form integration and for the other cases cartesian system is used, also the element in disc will be a ring of width dx of radius x, in sphere, it was a disc of width dx of radius $\sqrt{R^2-x^2}$ and so in other cases. The same elements we will further use in finding moment of inertia of different type of objects in next chapter, in electric field determination due to different type of object in Electricity.

Now for dissolving all the concepts, which we've read, we take some numerical examples concerned to these.

Web Reference of Video Lectures at www.physicsgalaxy.com

Age Group - High School Physics | Age 17-19 Years
Section - MECHANICS
Topic - System of Particles - I
Module Number - 8, 9, 10, 11, 12, 13 and 14

Illustrative Example 4.8

AB is a uniformly shaped rod of length L and cross sectional are S, but its density varies with distance from one end A of the rod as $\rho = px^2 + c$, where p and c are positive constants. Find out the distance of the centre of mass of this rod from the end A.

Solution

To find the centre of mass of the rod from the reference point A, we consider a small elemental mass dm at a distance x of width dx from end A. Here dm is given as

$$dm=\rho\times S\,.\,dx$$

$$dm=(px^2+c).\,S\,dx$$

If the distance of centre of mass from A is x_c, then

$$x_c=\frac{\int dm\,x}{\int dm}$$

$$=\frac{\int_0^L(px^3+cx)\,S\,dx}{\int_0^L(px^2+c)\,S\,dx}$$

$$=\frac{(pL^2+2c)}{(pL^2+3c)}$$

Illustrative Example 4.9

Find out the centre of mass of an isosceles triangle of base length a and altitude b. Assume that the mass of the triangle is uniformly distributed over its area.

Solution

To locate the centre of mass of the triangle, we take a strip of width dx at a distance x from the vertex of the triangle. Length of this strip can be evaluated by similar triangles as

$$l=x.\,(a/b)$$

Mass of the strip is

$$dm=\frac{M}{\frac{1}{2}ab}\times l\,dx$$

$$= \frac{2M}{ab} \cdot \frac{a}{b} x\,dx = \frac{2M}{b^2} x\,dx$$

Distance of centre of mass from the vertex of the triangle is

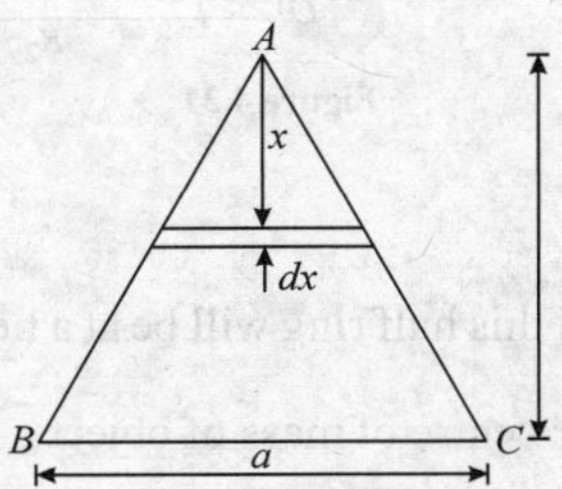

Figure 4.27

$$x_c = \frac{1}{M} \int dm\, x$$

$$= \int_0^b \frac{2x^2}{b^2} dx$$

$$= \frac{2}{3} b$$

Illustrative Example 4.10

Find out the centre of mass of a composite object shown in figure-4.28. Object consists of a cone with its base joint with the base of a hemisphere. The dimensions of the object are shown in figure. Assume uniform density of the system, find the centre of mass of this system.

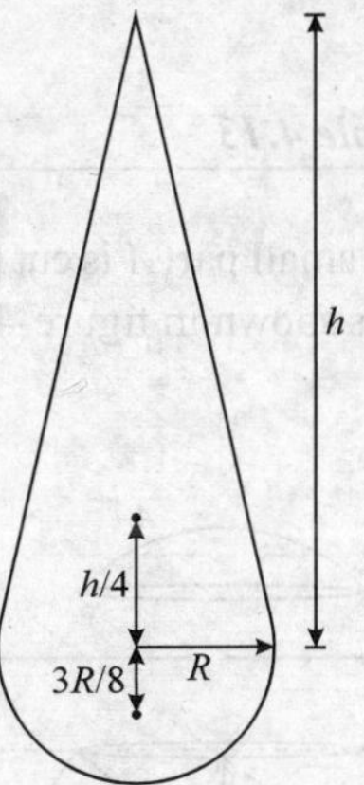

Figure 4.28

Solution

The shown object is made up of joining a solid cone and a hemisphere. We already know the location of the centre of mass of a cone and that of a hemisphere. The masses of the two are in proportion of their volume. The masses of cone and hemisphere are

Mass of cone is $\qquad m_1 = \rho \cdot \frac{1}{3} \pi R^2 h$

And that of hemisphere is

$$m_2 = \rho \cdot \frac{4}{3} \pi R^3$$

Now we apply the result of two body system to find the centre of mass of the composite body. Let l be the distance between the independent centre of the mass of the bodies cone and hemisphere, then

$$l = \frac{3R}{8} + \frac{H}{4}$$

The position of centre of mass from m_2 is

$$x = \frac{m_1 l}{m_1 + m_2}$$

Illustrative Example 4.11

A table has a heavy circular top of radius 1 m and mass 20 kg. It has four light legs of lengths 1 m fixed symmetrically on its circumference. (a) What is the maximum mass that may be placed any where on this table without toppling the table ? (b) What is the area of the table top over which any weight may be placed without toppling it ?

Solution

(a) As shown in figure-4.29, when the mass is placed on the table top such that it is outside the square, formed by the four legs (as fixed symmetrically on circumference), the table has a tendency of toppling. If the centre of mass of the table and the mass will come out of this square, the total weight of table and the mass will overturn the table about the bottom points of the legs.

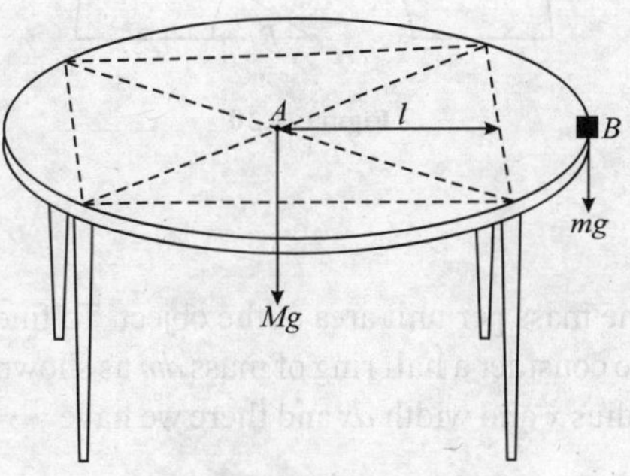

Figure 4.29

When the mass is placed at the circumference of the table, the centre of mass of the table and the mass is at a distance x (say) from the centre of the table, then

$$x = \frac{m \cdot r}{m + M} = \frac{m}{m + 20}$$

This distance x if more than or equal to $l = 1 \times \cos 45° = 0.707$ m, the table will topple, thus

$$0.707 = \frac{m}{m + 20}$$

$$0.293\, m = 14.14$$

$$m = 48.25 \text{ kg}$$

This is the maximum mass which can be placed anywhere on the table, without toppling.

(b) The area over which any weight can be placed without toppling the table is the area of the square formed by the four legs, as if any weight is placed over it, the centre of mass will remain in the square and the table will remain in equilibrium.

Side of the square is

$$= 2 \times 1 \times \sin 45° = \sqrt{2} \text{ m}$$

Thus the area of the square is

$$= [\sqrt{2}\,]^2 = 2 \text{ m}^2$$

 # Illustrative Example 4.12

Find the centre of mass of an annular half disc shown in figure-4.30.

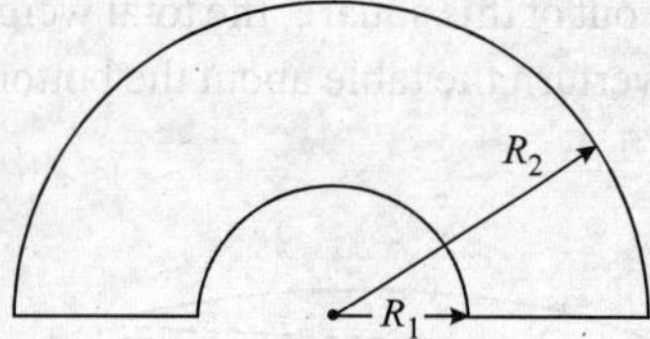

Figure 4.30

Solution

Let ρ be the mass per unit area of the object. To find its centre of mass we consider a half ring of mass dm as shown in figure-4.31 of radius x and width dx and there we have

$$dm = \rho \,.\, \pi x \, dx$$

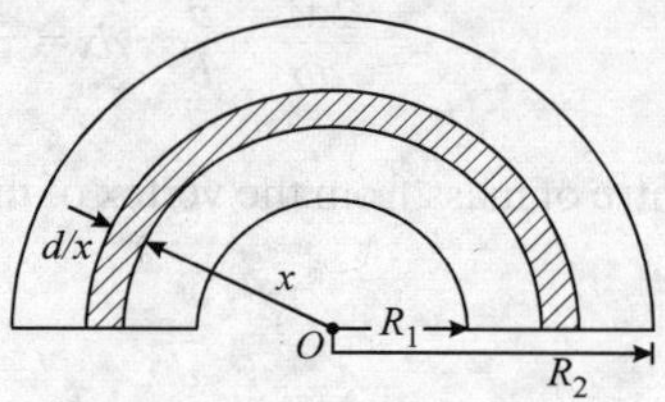

Figure 4.31

Centre of mass of this half ring will be at a height $\frac{2x}{\pi}$ from O.

Thus we have for centre of mass of object

$$y_{cm} = \frac{1}{M} \int_{R_1}^{R_2} (\rho . \pi \, x \, dx) \cdot \frac{2x}{\pi}$$

$$y_{cm} = \frac{2\rho}{\rho \frac{\pi}{2}(R_2^2 - R_1^2)} \int_{R_1}^{R_2} x^2 \, dx = \frac{4(R_2^3 - R_1^3)}{3\pi(R_2^2 - R_1^2)}$$

Alternative Solution

We can also find the centre of mass of this object by considering it to be complete half disc of radius R_2 and a smaller half disc of radius R_1 cut from it. If y_{cm} be the centre of mass of this disc we have from the mass moments.

$$\rho \cdot \frac{\pi R_1^2}{2} \times \frac{4R_1}{3\pi} + \rho \cdot \frac{\pi}{2}(R_2^2 - R_1^2) \times y_{cm} = \rho \cdot \frac{\pi R_2^2}{2} \times \frac{4R_2}{3\pi}$$

$$y_{cm} = \frac{4(R_2^3 - R_1^3)}{3\pi(R_2^2 - R_1^2)}$$

 # Illustrative Example 4.13

From a solid sphere a small part A is cut by a plane at a distance $R/2$ from the centre as shown in figure-4.32. Find the centre of mass of object A.

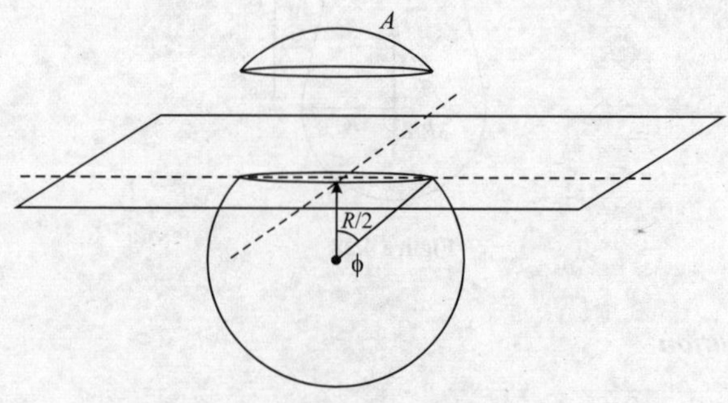

Figure 4.32

Solution

To find centre of mass of object A, we consider a small elemental disc of width dx at a distance x from the centre C as shown in figure-4.33. Radius of this elemental disc will be given as

$$r = \sqrt{R^2 - x^2}$$

Figure 4.33

If ρ be the density of substance, mass of this elemental disc will be

$$dm = \rho \,.\, \pi r^2\, dx$$

$$= \rho\pi\,(R^2 - x^2)\, dx$$

Mass of object A can be obtained as

$$M = \int_{R/2}^{R} dm$$

$$= \int_{R/2}^{R} \rho\pi(R^2 - x^2)dx$$

$$= \rho\pi\left[R^2 x - \frac{x^3}{3}\right]_{R/2}^{R}$$

$$= \rho\pi\left[\left(R^3 - \frac{R^3}{3}\right) - \left(\frac{R^3}{2} - \frac{R^3}{24}\right)\right]$$

$$M = \frac{5}{24}\,\rho\pi R^3$$

$$y_{cm} = \frac{1}{M}\int_{R/2}^{R} dm.x$$

$$= \frac{24}{5\rho\pi R^3}\int_{R/2}^{R} \rho\pi(R^2 - x^2)x\, dx$$

$$= \frac{24}{5R^3}\left[\frac{R^2x^2}{2} - \frac{x^4}{4}\right]_{R/2}^{R}$$

$$= \frac{12}{5R^3}\left[\left(R^4 - \frac{R^4}{2}\right) - \left(\frac{R^4}{4} - \frac{R^4}{32}\right)\right]$$

$$y_{cm} = \frac{27}{40}R$$

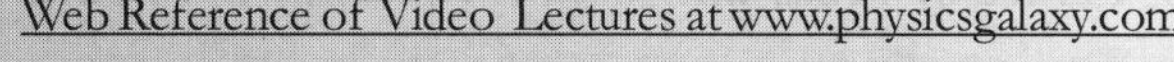

Web Reference of Video Lectures at www.physicsgalaxy.com

Age Group - High School Physics | Age 17-19 Years
Section - MECHANICS
Topic - System of Particles - I
Module Number - 15, 16 and 17

Practice Exercise 4.2

(i) Find centre of mass distance from point O of the uniform circular arc shown in figure-4.34.

$\left[\dfrac{2R\sin\left(\dfrac{\phi}{2}\right)}{\phi}\right]$

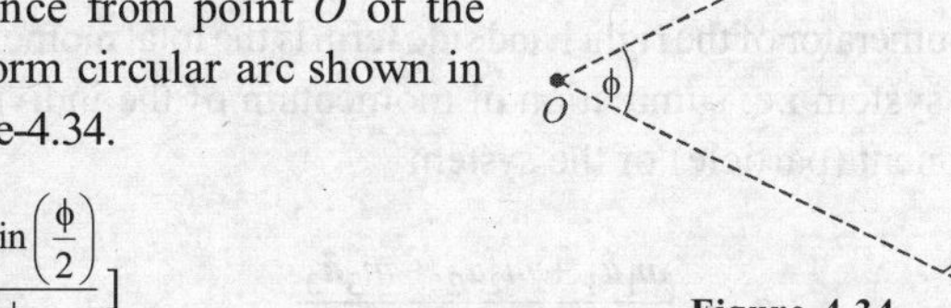

Figure 4.34

(ii) Find location distance from point O of mass center of a sector of a thin uniform plate of the shape of a sector of a circular disc of radius R as shown in figure-4.35 enclosing an angle 2θ at center.

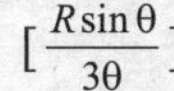

$\left[\dfrac{R\sin\theta}{3\theta}\right]$

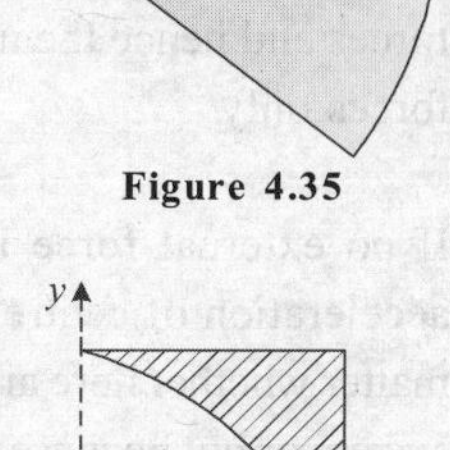

Figure 4.35

(iii) From a square plate of side a, a quarter circular disc of radius a is removed as shown in figure-4.36. Find the coordinates of centre of mass of the remaining part.

$\left[\left[\dfrac{2a}{3(4-\pi)}, \dfrac{2a}{3(4-\pi)}\right]\right]$

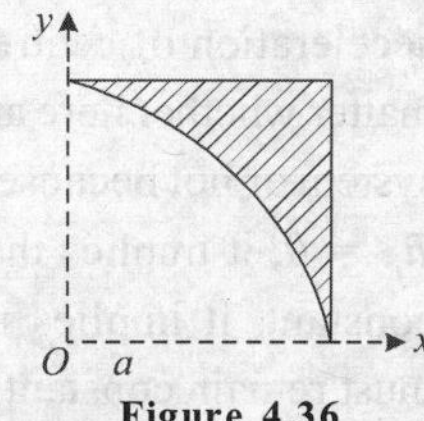

Figure 4.36

(iv) From a hemisphere of radius R a cone of base radius $R/2$ and height R is cut as shown in figure-4.37. Find the height of centre of mass of the remaining object.

$\left[\left(\dfrac{11R}{28}\right)\right]$

Figure 4.37

(v) Find centre of mass of an object (Paraboloid) which is formed by rotating a parabola $x = ky^2$ about x-axis and height of object is h as shown in figure-4.38. Assume the object is of uniform density.

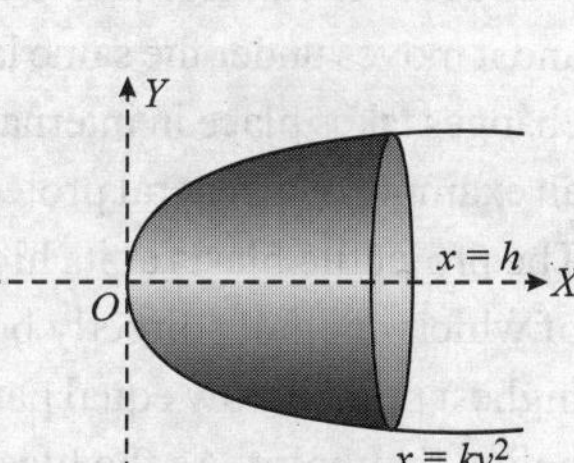

Figure 4.38

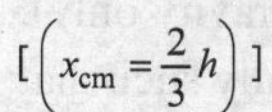

$\left[\left(x_{cm} = \dfrac{2}{3}h\right)\right]$

4.6 Centre of Mass and Conservation of Momentum

To discuss the Momentum Conservation Law first we recall few previous derived results, related to centre of mass. The velocity of the centre of mass of a system of n components is given as

$$\vec{v}_c = \frac{m_1\vec{v}_1 + m_2\vec{v}_2 + m_3\vec{v}_3}{m_1 + m_2 + m_3} \quad \ldots (4.17)$$

Here numerator of the right hand side term is the total momentum of the system i.e. summation of momentum of the individual component (particle) of the system

$$\vec{a}_c = \frac{m_1\vec{a}_1 + m_2\vec{a}_2 + m_3\vec{a}_3}{m_1 + m_2 + m_3} \quad \ldots (4.18)$$

Here numerator of the right hand side term gives the total force acting on the system. Actually it is the summation of all the forces acting on the individual component (particle) of the system but action and reaction both of an internal force must be within the system. Vector summation will cancel all internal forces and hence the numerator gives only sum of all external forces only.

If no external force is acting on a system of particles, the acceleration of centre of mass of the system will be zero, no matter whether here are accelerations in the components of the system or not because these all can be due to internal forces. If $\vec{a}_c = 0$, it implies that $\vec{v}_c$ must be a constant and if $\vec{v}_c$ is a constant, it implies that the total momentum of the system must remain constant. It leads to the principal of conservation of momentum in absence of external forces as - *"If no external force is acting on the system, net momentum of the system must remain constant"*.

This also implies if a certain constant external force is acting on a system of particles, the acceleration of centre of mass of the system is a constant and if during the motion, internal forces of the system changes or removed or new forces are produced, it can not affect the motion of the centre of mass and it moves under the same laws which were applicable before changes takes place in internal forces. To discuss it, we consider an example of a general projectile motion shown in figure-4.38. The projectile blasts at its highest point in two equal parts, out of which one falls directly below that point. As the blast at its highest point in tow equal parts, out of which one falls directly below that point. As the blast takes place only due to internal forces. It can not affect the motion of centre of mass of the projectile (as it was moving in the influence of gravity only). The other part of the projectile moves automatically such that the centre of mass of the system must be in the same parabolic trajectory as shown. At every instant the instantaneous centre of mass of the two parts of the body, will be following the same path and the other part will land at a distance $3R/2$ from the projection point at the same instant when the second part strikes the ground at $3R/2$. (Here R is the horizontal range of the projectile)

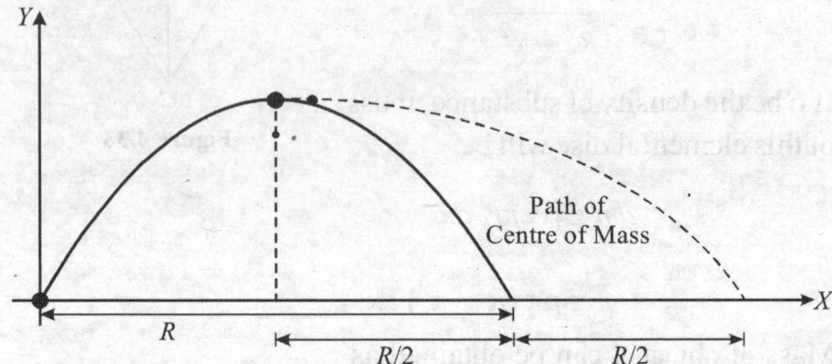

Figure 4.39

The statement of the principal of conservation of momentum can also be verified by the Newton's Second Law of motion defined as *"Momentum exerted per second on a body is equal to the applied force on it"*. Mathematically it can be written as

$$F = \frac{dp}{dt} \quad \ldots (4.19)$$

Here if we use momentum of a system of particle is constant then we get $F = 0$. There are several examples related to this identity. The most popular example was recoiling of a gun when a shot is fired (figure-4.40)

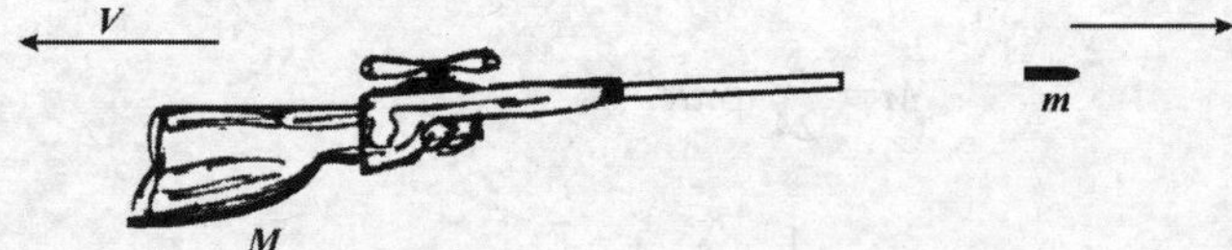

Figure 4.40

Before shot is fired, the net momentum of the system is zero and as shot is due to internal forces, the net momentum of the system after the shot must be zero as

$$MV = mv$$

Here M, V and m, v are the masses and velocities of gun and bullet respectively. Velocity V is known as the recoil velocity of the gum due to shot.

Now we take some examples concerned to it and then we further proceed to the momentum conservation in presence of external forces.

Web Reference of Video Lectures at www.physicsgalaxy.com
Age Group - High School Physics | Age 17-19 Years
Section - MECHANICS
Topic - System of Particles - II
Module Number - 1, 2, 3, 4 and 5

 # Illustration Example 4.14

A plank of mass M and length L is at rest on a frictionless floor. At one end of it a child of mass m is standing as shown in figure-4.41. If child walks towards the other end, find the distance, which the plank moves (a) till the child reaches the centre of the plank, (b) till the child reaches the other end of the plank.

Solution

The corresponding situation can be better explained with the help of figure-4.41.

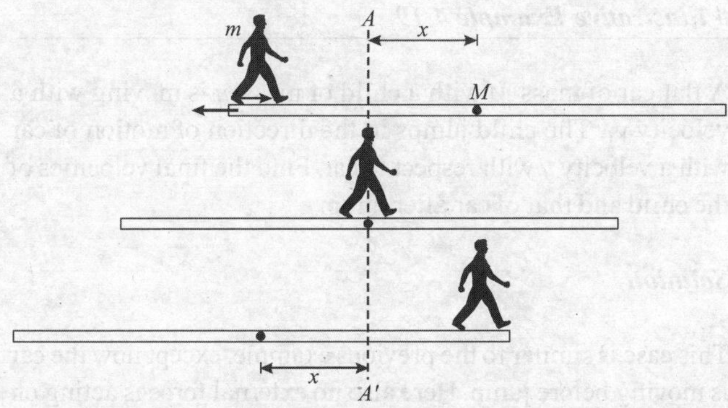

Figure 4.41

As no external force is acting on the system, the centre of mass of the system must remain stationary. The only interaction force between the child and the plank is the friction as shown in figure, due to which the child walks along the plank and the friction on plank would be in opposite direction, due to which plank moves towards left, such that the centre of mass of plank plus child remains at rest. The initial distance of the centre of mass from the centre of the plank is

$$x_c = \frac{m \, . \, L/2}{m + M}$$

Initially the centre of mass of the system is on line AA' as shown in figure. During motion of child, this centre of mass must remain at this line only. As child moves towards right, plank will move towards left such that centre of mass remains on AA'. Thus when child reaches the centre of the plank, the plank's centre also must reach the same point so that the centre of mass is at the same position. Up to this instant the plank moves by a distance x_c. Similarly when child reaches the other end plank has to move towards left further by x_c, to maintain the position of centre of mass.

 # Illustrative Example 4.15

Figure-4.42 shows a flat car of mass M on a frictionless road. A small massless wedge is fitted on it as shown. A small ball of mass m is released from the top of the wedge, it slides over it and fall in the hole at distance l from the initial position of the ball. Find the distance the flat car moves till the ball get into the hole.

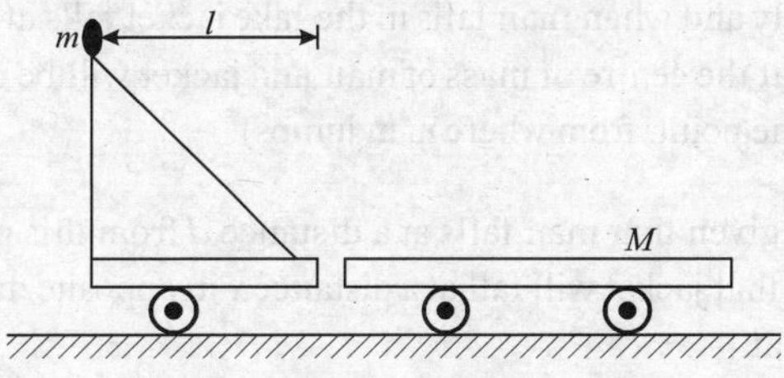

Figure 4.42

Solution

When ball falls into the hole, with respect to the flat car, ball travels a horizontal distance l. During this motion, to conserve momentum and to maintain the position of centre of mass, car moves towards left, say by a distance x. Thus, the total distance traveled by the ball towards right is $(l - x)$. As centre of mass remains at rest, the change in mass moments of the two (ball and car) about any point must be equal to zero. Hence

$$m \, . \, (l - x) = M \, . \, x$$

$$m = \frac{m \, . \, l}{M + m}$$

 # Illustrative Example 4.16

A man of mass M jumps from an aeroplane as shown in figure-4.43. He sees the hard ground below him and a lake at a distance d from the point directly below him. He immediately put off his jacket (mass = m) and throws it in a direction directly away from the lake. If he just fail to strike the ground, find distance he should walk know to pick his jacket. (Neglect air

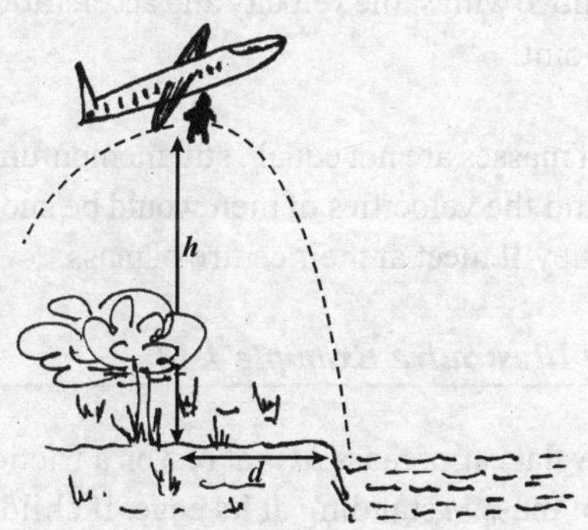

Figure 4.43

resistance and take the velocity of man at the time of jump with respect to earth is zero.)

Solution

As shown in figure-4.43, to save himself, man throws his jacket in opposite direction to the lake. According to momentum conservation he himself gets a velocity in the direction of the lake. During the motion as only gravity is the external force on the system (man plus jacket), centre of mass will not be displaced horizontally. Thus centre of mass of the system falls vertically and when man falls in the lake jacket falls at a point such that the centre of mass of man and jacket will be directly below the point, from where man jumps).

As it is given that man falls at a distance d from this point, it implies that jacket will fall at a distance x in opposite direction such that

$$m\,.\,x = M\,.\,d$$

$$x = \frac{M}{m}\,d$$

Illustration Example 4.17

Two men of same mass m hold the two ends of a rope and start pulling each other on a friction less plane. Find the position where they will meet. Is there any difference, if masses of men are not equal.

Solution

As men are standing on frictionless floor no external force is acting on them, the only force between them will be the tension in the rope. Due to tension both starts moving towards each other and as momentum of the system is conserved both will move with same velocity and acceleration and meet at their mid point.

If masses are not equal , still momentum will remain conserved and the velocities of men would be such that $m_1v_1 = m_2v_2$, and they'll meet at their centre of mass.

Illustrative Example 4.18

A flat car of mass M is at rest on a frictionless floor with a child of mass m standing at its edge. If child jumps off from the car towards right with an initial velocity u, with respect to the car, find the velocity of the car after its jump.

Solution

Let car attains a velocity v, and the net velocity of the child with respect to earth will be $u - v$, as u is its velocity with respect to car.

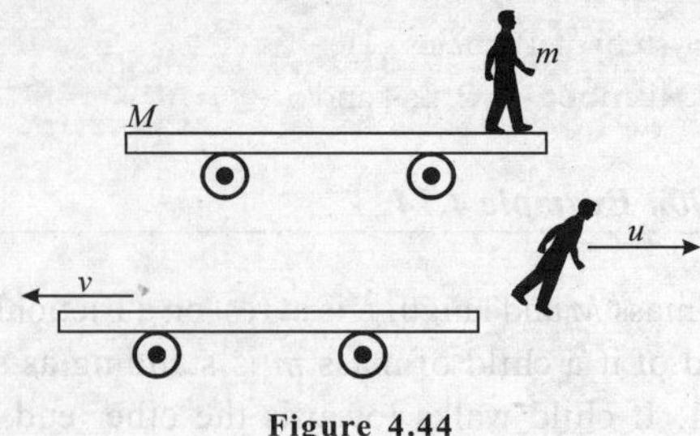

Figure 4.44

Initially, the system was at rest, thus according to momentum conservation, momentum after jump must be zero, as

$$m\,(u - v) = M\,v$$

$$v = \frac{mu}{m + M}$$

Illustrative Example 4.19

A flat car of mass M with a child of mass m is moving with a velocity v_1. The child jumps in the direction of motion of car with a velocity u with respect to car. Find the final velocities of the child and that of car after jump.

Solution

This case is similar to the previous example, except now the car is moving before jump. Here also no external force is acting on the system, hence momentum remains conserved. After jump car attains a velocity v_2 in the same direction, which is less than v_1, due to backward push of the child for jumping. After jump child attains a velocity $u + v_2$ in the direction of motion of car, with respect to ground.

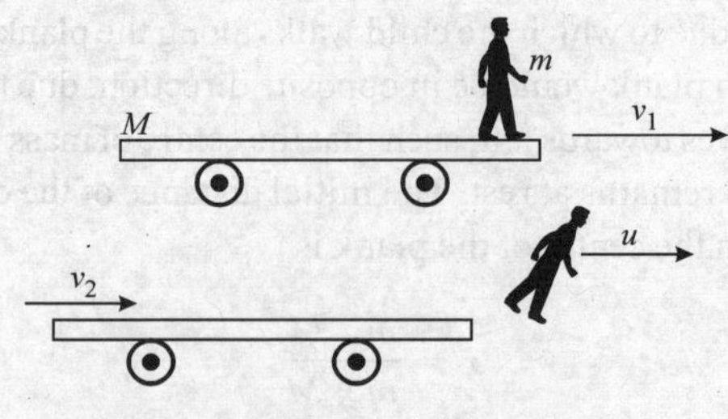

Figure 4.45

According to momentum conservation

$$(M + m)v_1 = Mv_2 + m\,(u + v_2)$$

Velocity of car after jump is

$$v_2 = \frac{(M + m)v_1 + mu}{M + m}$$

Velocity of child after jump is

$$u+v_2=\frac{(M+m)v_1+(M+2m)u}{M+m}$$

Illustrative Example 4.20

Two trucks of mass M each are moving in opposite direction on adjacent parallel tracks with same velocity u. One is carrying potatoes and other is carrying onions, bag of potatoes has a mass m_1 and bag of onions has a mass m_2 (included in the mass of truck M). When trucks get close to each other while passing, the drivers exchange a bag with the other one by throwing towards the other one. Find the final velocities of the trucks after exchange of the bags.

Solution

Here at the time of exchange of bags, momentum in the direction of individual motion remains conserved. The situation is shown in figure-4.45.

When driver of first truck carrying potatoes, throws a bag of mass m_1, in a direction perpendicular to the motion direction, towards the other truck, as shown in figure-4.46. During throw the bag has a velocity u in the direction of motion of the first truck. Similarly, when the second truck driver throws the onion bag of mass m_2, towards the first truck, it brings a momentum m_2u in the direction of the second truck. Now we conserve momentum for both the trucks independently as

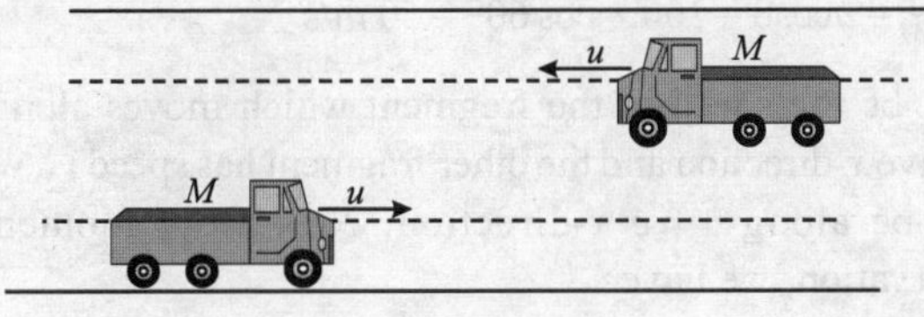

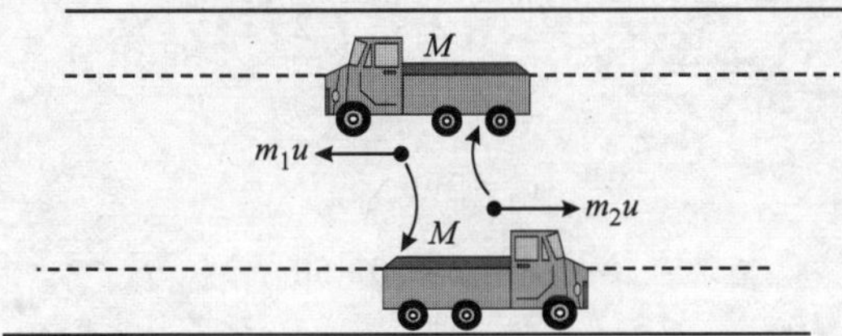

Figure 4.46

First truck carrying potatoes

$$Mu-m_1u-m_2u=(M-m_1+m_2)v_1$$

On solving, velocity of first truck after exchange is

$$v_1=\frac{Mu-m_1u-m_2u}{M-m_1+m_2}$$

Second truck carrying onions

$$Mu-m_2u-m_1u=(M-m_2+m_1)v_2$$

On solving, velocity of first truck after exchange is

$$v_2=\frac{Mu-m_1u-m_2u}{M-m_2+m_1}$$

Illustrative Example 4.21

Figure-4.47 shows two blocks of masses 5 kg and 2 kg placed on a frictionless surface and connected with a spring. An external kick gives a velocity 14 m/s to the heavier block in the direction of lighter one. Deduce (a) velocity gained by the centre of mass and (b) the separate velocities of the two blocks in the centre of mass coordinates just after the kick.

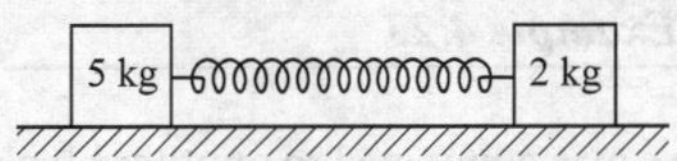

Figure 4.47

Solution

(a) Velocity of centre of mass is

$$v_{cm}=\frac{5\times14+2\times0}{5+2}=10\text{ m/s}$$

(b) Due to kick on 5 kg block, it starts moving with a velocity 14 m/s immediately, but due to inertia 2 kg block remains at rest, at that moment. Thus

Velocity of 5 kg block w. r. to centre of mass is

$$v_1=14-10=4\text{ m/s}$$

and the velocity of 2 kg block w. r. to centre of mass is

$$v_2=0-10=-10\text{ m/s}$$

Illustrative Example 4.22

Two blocks of masses m_1 and m_2 connected by a weightless spring of stiffness k rest on a smooth horizontal plane as shown in figure-4.48. Block 2 is shifted a small distance x to the left and then released. Find the velocity of centre of mass of the system after block 1 breaks off the wall.

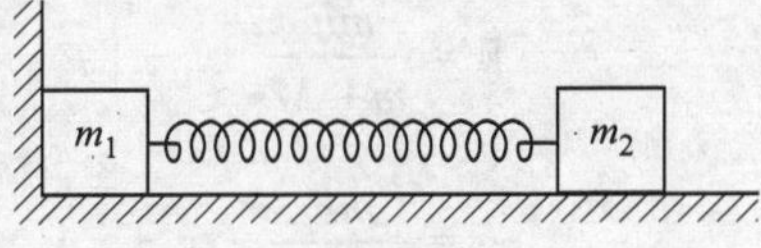

Figure 4.48

Solution

If m_2 is shifted by a distance x and released, the mass m_1 will break off from the wall when the spring, restores its natural length and m_2 will start going towards right. At the time of breaking m_1, m_2 will be going towards right, with a velocity v, which is given as

$$\frac{1}{2}kx^2 = \frac{1}{2}mv^2$$

$$v = \frac{\sqrt{k}}{m}x$$

and the velocity of centre of mass at this instant is

$$v_{cm} = \frac{m_1 \times 0 + m_2 \times v}{m_1 + m_2} = \frac{m_2}{m_1 + m_2} \cdot \frac{\sqrt{k}}{m}$$

Illustrative Example 4.23

A block of mass m is connected to another block of mass M by a massless spring of spring constant k. The blocks are kept on a smooth horizontal plane and the blocks are at rest and the spring is unstretched when a constant force F starts acting on the block of mass M to pull it. Find the maximum extension of the spring.

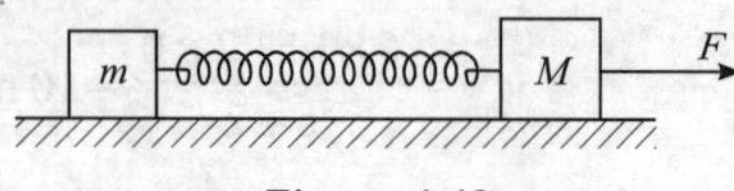

Figure 4.49

Solution

We solve the situation in the reference frame of centre of mass. As only F is the external force acting on the system, due to this force, the acceleration of the centre of mass is $F/(M+m)$. Thus with respect to centre of mass there is a Pseudo force on the two masses in opposite direction, the free body diagram of m and M with respect to centre of mass (taking centre of mass at rest) is shown in figure-4.50.

$\frac{mF}{m+M}$ kx m $\frac{MF}{m+M}$ km M F

Figure 4.50

Taking centre of mass at rest, if m moves maximum by a distance x_1 and M moves maximum by a distance x_2, then the work done by external forces (including Pseudo force) will be

$$W = \frac{mF}{m+M} \cdot x_1 + \left(F - \frac{MF}{m+M}\right) \cdot x_2$$

$$= \frac{mF}{m+M} \cdot (x_1 + x_2)$$

This work is stored in the form of potential energy of the spring as

$$U = \frac{1}{2}k(x_1 + x_2)^2$$

Thus on equating we get the maximum extension in the spring, as after this instant the spring starts contracting.

$$\frac{1}{2}k(x_1 + x_2)^2 = \frac{mF}{m+M} \cdot (x_1 + x_2)$$

$$x_{max} = x_1 + x_2 = \frac{2mF}{k(m+M)}$$

Illustrative Example 4.24

A shell is fixed from a cannon with a speed of 100 m/s at an angle 60° with the horizontal (positive x-direction). At the highest point of its trajectory, the shell explodes into two equal fragments. One of the fragments moves along the negative x-direction with a speed of 50 m/s. What is the speed of the other fragment at the time of explosion.

Solution

As we know in absence of external forces the motion of centre of mass of a body remains uneffected. Thus here the centre of mass of the two fragment will continues to follow the original projectile path.

The velocity of the shell at the highest point of trajectory is

$$v_M = u\cos\theta = 100 \times \cos 60° = 50 \text{ m/s}$$

Let v_1 be the speed of the fragment which moves along the negative x-direction and the other fragment has speed v_2, which must be along + *ve* x-direction. Now from momentum conservation, we have

$$mv = \frac{m}{2}v_1 = \frac{m}{2}v_2$$

or $$2v = v_2 - v_1$$

or $$v_2 = 2v + v_1$$

$$= 2 \times 50 + 50$$

$$= 150 \text{ m/s}$$

Illustrative Example 4.25

A shell is fired from a cannon with a speed of 100 m/s at an angle 30° with the vertical (y-direction). At the highest point of its trajectory, the shell explodes into two fragments of masses in the ratio 1 : 2. The lighter fragments moves vertically upwards with an initial speed of 200 m/s. What is the speed of the heavier fragment at the time of explosion.

Solution

The velocity of shell at the highest point is

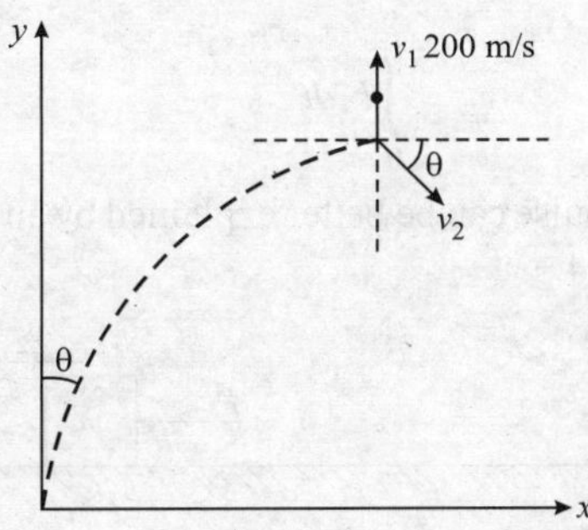

Figure 4.51

$$v = u \sin \theta$$

$$= 100 \times \sin 30°$$

$$= 50 \text{ m/s}$$

Let m be the mass of the shell. Then the mass of the lighter fragment is m/s and that of heavier fragment is 2 m/s.

Initial momentum of the shell before explosion is

$$mv = 50 \text{ m}$$

As no external forces is acting on the shell, we can conserve momentum of shell before and after its explosion.

NOTE : An external force of gravity is present here during explosion but as explosion is an instantaneous phenomenon, so due to very short duration impulse of gravity is negligible and can not cause any change in momentum. Thus in all very short duration explosions or collisions, always we ignore the presence of gravity just before and after the occurrence.

In x-direction

or $$mv = \frac{2m}{3} v_2 \cos\theta \quad \ldots (4.20)$$

and in y-direction $v_2 \cos\theta = \frac{3}{2} v$

$$0 = \frac{m}{3} v_1 - \frac{2m}{3} v_2 \sin\theta$$

or $$v_2 \sin\theta = \frac{v_1}{2} \quad \ldots (4.21)$$

Squaring and adding equations-(4.20) and (4.21), we get

$$v_2^2 = \frac{9}{4} v^2 + \frac{1}{4} v_1^1$$

$$v_2 = \frac{1}{2} \sqrt{9v^2 + v_1^2}$$

$$= \frac{1}{2} \sqrt{9 \times 2500 + 40000}$$

$$= 125 \text{ m/s}$$

Web Reference of Video Lectures at www.physicsgalaxy.com
Age Group - High School Physics | Age 17-19 Years
Section - MECHANICS
Topic - System of Particles - II
Module Number - 6, 7, 8, 9 and 10

Practice Exercise 4.3

(i) In a boat of mass 4 M and length l on a frictionless water surface. Two men A (mass = M) and B (mass 2 M) are standing on the two opposite ends. Now A travels a distance $l/4$ relative to boat towards its centre and B moves a distance $3l/4$ relative to boat and meet A. Find the distance travelled by the boat on water till A and B meet.

[$5l/28$]

(ii) A shell of mass m is fired from a gun of mass km which can recoil freely on a horizontal plane, the elevation of the gun is 45°. Find the ratio of the energy of the shell to that of the gun.

[$\frac{(2k^2+2k+1)}{k}$]

(iii) A gun in mounted on a railroad car. The mass of the car with all of its components is 80 m mass of each shell to be fired is 5 m. The muzzle velocity of the shells is 100 m/s horizontally, what is the recoil speed of the car after second shot ? Consider car to be at rest initially.

[$100\left[\frac{1}{15}+\frac{1}{16}\right]$ m/s]

(iv) A block A (mass = 4M) is placed on the top of a wedge block B of base length l (mass = 20M) as shown in figure-4.52. When the system is released from rest. Find the distance moved by the block B till the block A reaches ground. Assume all surfaces are frictionless.

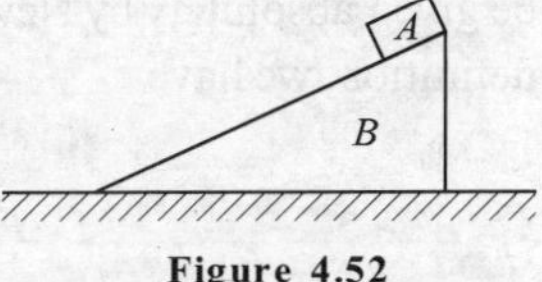

Figure 4.52

[$l/6$]

(v) A space shuttle of mass M, moving at 4000 kph relative to earth ejects a capsule backward of mass $M/5$. If speed of ejection of capsule is 120 kph relative to state of shuttle before ejection, find the final velocity of the shuttle.

[4030 kph]

(vi) An isolated particle of mass m is moving slowly in a horizontal xy plane, along x-axis, at a certain height above ground. It suddenly explodes into two fragments of masses $m/4$ and $3m/4$. An instant later, the smaller fragment is at $y = +15$ cm relative to point of explosion. Find the position of heavier fragment at this instant.

[$y = -5$ cm]

(vii) A shell at rest at origin explodes into three fragments of masses 1 kg, 2 kg and m kg. The fragments of masses 1kg and 2 kg fly off with speeds 12 m/s along x-axis and 8m/s along y-axis respectively. If $m$kg flies off with speed 40m/s then find the total mass of the shell.

[3.5 kg]

(viii) A small block of mass m starts sliding down from rest along the smooth surface of a fixed hollow hemisphere of same mass m. Find the distance of centre of mass of block and hemisphere from centre of hemisphere C when block m separates from the surface of hemisphere.

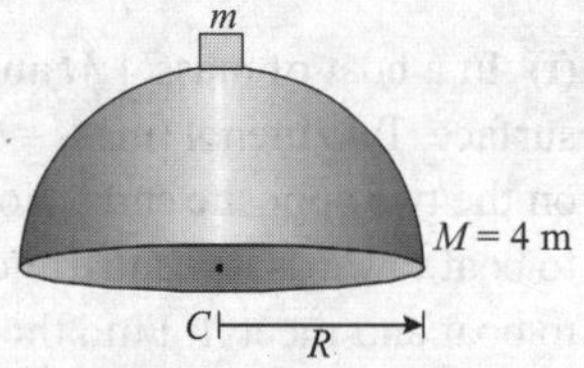

Figure 4.53

[$\sqrt{\frac{23}{75}}R$]

4.7 Impulse and Momentum Conservation

Momentum of a system is a conserved quantity. It remains conserved as energy whether external force are present or not. If external forces are absent the total momentum of a system of particles remains constant, which we've discussed in previous section. If external forces are acting on the system, still the momentum of system remains conserved, as it is neither created nor destroyed, it can only be transferred. The reasoning can be given absolutely by Newton's Second law of motion, by the definition, we have

$$F = \frac{dp}{dt}$$

$$dp = F\,dt \qquad \ldots(4.22)$$

Here dp is the change in momentum due to the applied force F for a time dt. The right hand side term $F\,dt$ is known as impulse of the force F. Impulse is the momentum imparted by the force F in the direction of the force F. Using equation-(4.22), we can find the net change in momentum of a system (or a body) due to external force. If Δp be the net change in momentum then it can be evaluated by

If a constant force F is acting for a time t then

$$\Delta p = Ft$$

If variable force is acting for a time t then

$$\Delta p = \int_0^t F\,dt$$

The concept of impulse can be better explained by an example shown in figure-4.54.

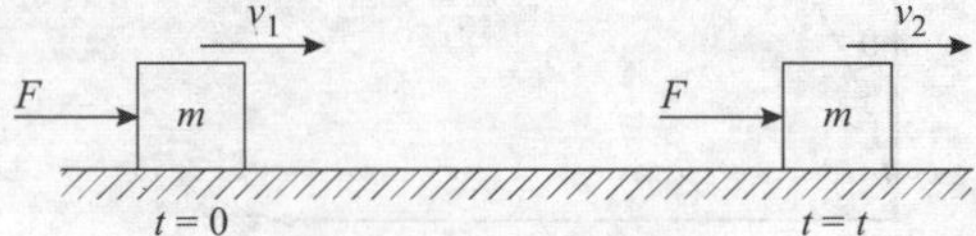

Figure 4.54

A is a block of mass m moving with a velocity v_1, at time $t = 0$ a constant force F is applied on it in the direction of velocity for a time t. Due to this force the velocity of the body increases hence momentum increases. If after time t the velocity of the body becomes v_2, then according to momentum conservation we have

Initial momentum + momentum imparted = Final momentum

$$mv_1 + Ft = mv_2 \qquad \ldots(4.23)$$

If applied force is opposite to the direction of v_1 then we'll have

$$mv_1 - Ft = mv_2 \qquad \ldots(4.24)$$

Equations-(4.23) and (4.24) are similar to the equations written for work - energy theorem as work done by the system or on the system are subtracted or added to the initial kinetic energy, gives the final kinetic energy of the system. Similar to that in initial momentum impulse due the forces acting on the system are added or subtracted, gives the final momentum of the system. If force is in the direction of the initial velocity of the particle, impulse is added to the initial momentum and if it is against the velocity, impulse is subtracted from the initial momentum

Illustrative Example 4.26

A body of mass 10 kg is pulled with a time varying horizontal force $F = 2t^2$ N on a rough surface having friction coefficient $\mu = 0.2$. Find the speed of block after 6 seconds.

Solution

We can see that block starts sliding when external force exceeds frictional force, thus we have

$$F = 2t^2 = \mu mg = 0.2 \times 10 \times 10 = 20$$

$$t^2 = 10 \Rightarrow t = \sqrt{10}\text{ s}$$

At $t = \sqrt{10}$ sec block starts sliding, then onwards its acceleration can be given as

$$a = \frac{2t^2 - 20}{10} \text{ m/s}^2$$

We require velocity at $t = 6$ sec, thus

$$dv = \left(\frac{t^2}{5} - 2\right) dt$$

or
$$\int_0^v dv = \int_{\sqrt{10}}^{6} \left(\frac{t^2}{5} - 2\right) dt$$

$$v = \left[\frac{t^3}{15} - 2t\right]_{\sqrt{10}}^{6} = \left(\frac{46}{15} - 12\right) - \left(\frac{10\sqrt{10}}{15} - 2\sqrt{10}\right)$$

$$v = \left(\frac{72}{5} - 12\right) - \left(\frac{2}{3}\sqrt{10} - 2\sqrt{10}\right)$$

$$v = \left(\frac{12}{5} + \frac{4}{3}\sqrt{10}\right) \text{ m/s}$$

Alternative Solution

As now we have studied the concept of impulses, whenever velocity of an object is required in the friction, we should go like this

Here we have $F = 2t^2$

We also have total given momentum is

$$\Delta\rho = \int (F - \mu mg)\, dt = \int_{\sqrt{10}}^{6} (2t^2 - 20)\, dt = \left[\frac{2t^3}{3} - 20t\right]_{\sqrt{10}}^{6}$$

$$= \left[(144 - 120) - \left(\frac{20\sqrt{10}}{3} - 20\sqrt{10}\right)\right]$$

$$\Delta\rho = 24 + \frac{40\sqrt{10}}{3}$$

We have $\Delta\rho = m(v_f - v_i)\, mv_f = 24 + \dfrac{40\sqrt{10}}{3}$

$$\Rightarrow \quad v_f = \left(\frac{12}{5} + \frac{4}{3}\sqrt{10}\right) \text{ m/s}$$

 # Illustrative Example 4.27

A block of A is released from rest from the top of a wedge block of height h shown in figure-4.55. If velocity of block when it reaches the bottom of inclive is v_0, find the time of sliding.

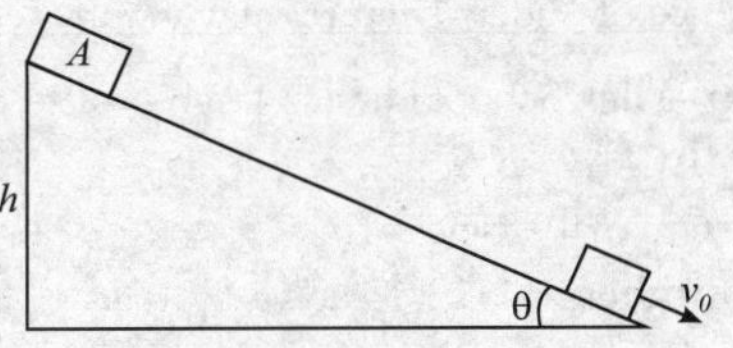

Figure 4.55

Solution

If time of contact be t, we have

$$(mg\sin\theta - \mu mg\cos\theta)\, t = mv_0$$

Also we have

$$(mg\sin\theta - \mu mg\cos\theta)\operatorname{cosec}\theta = \frac{1}{2}mv_0^2$$

Dividing the two equations we have

$$\frac{t}{h\operatorname{cosec}\theta} = \frac{2}{v_0}$$

or
$$t_0 = \frac{2h\operatorname{cosec}\theta}{v_0}$$

 # Illustrative Example 4.28

On a spring block system shown in figure-4.56, a time varying force $F = 5t$ N is applied on 2 kg mass. After 10 s, velocity of 3 kg mass is 30 m/sec, Find velocity of 2 kg mass at this instant.

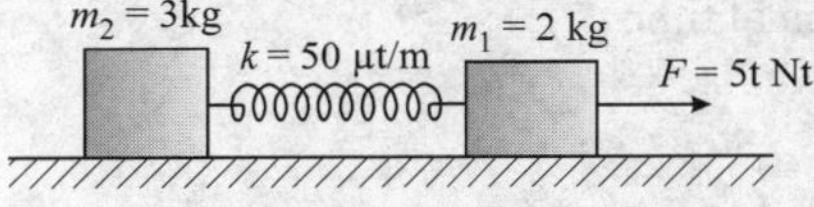

Figure 4.56

Solution

If after time t, we find velocity of centre of mass of system, we can find by using impulse moment equation. As spring force is the internal force of system, we have

$$(2+3)v_{cm} = \int_0^t 5t\, dt = \frac{5t^2}{2}$$

and at $t = 10$ s, we have

$$v_{cm} = \frac{5[10]^2/2}{5} = 50 \text{ m/sec}$$

If at this instant velocity of 2 kg mass is v_2, we have

$$v_{cm} = \frac{3 \times 30 + 2 \times v_2}{5}$$

or
$$v_2 = \frac{5 \times 50 - 3 \times 30}{2} = \frac{160}{2} = 80 \text{ m/s}$$

Web Reference of Video Lectures at www.physicsgalaxy.com
Age Group - High School Physics | Age 17-19 Years
Section - MECHANICS
Topic - System of Particles - II
Module Number - 11, 12, 13 and 14

4.8 Cases of Mass Variation

The impulse concept is very useful in studying the mass variation problems. We have discussed several cases in which the mass of the body or different bodies of a system of particles does not change, remain constant during experiment. Now we'll discuss some different kind of problems in which mass of an object also changes with time.

All the problems in which the mass of an object changes and due to which if motion of a body in a system is affected, it can be solved with the help of impulse concept and the conservation of momentum in an efficient and easier way. To understand directly the cases, read out the following example.

Illustration Example 4.29

A tank-car of mass M is at rest on a road. At $t = 0$, a force F starts acting on the tank-car and also the rain fall starts, in vertical direction, as shown in figure-4.57. The rain is falling with a velocity v_r with respect to earth and the rate of collection of water in the tank is r kg/s. Find the velocity of the tank-car as a function of time t.

Solution

In the cases of mass variation, we generally apply momentum conservation at time $t = t$ and $t = t + dy$. Figure shows, the situation at time $t = t$ and aiso at $t = t + dt$. Let at time $t = t$, mass of the car be m and its velocity as v, in the duration dt, further dm mass will be added and in this duration car gains the speed to $v + dv$.

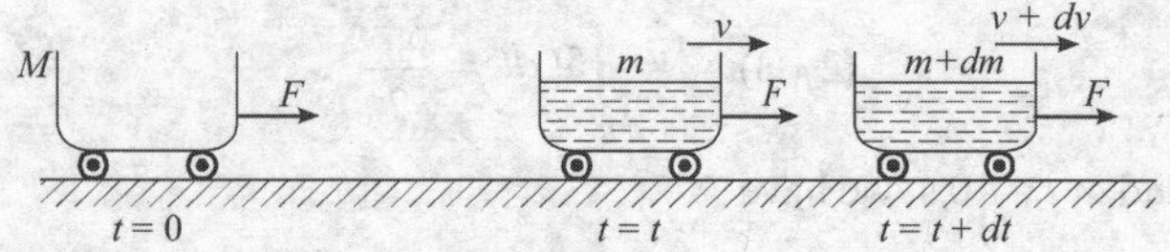

Figure 4.57

If we apply momentum conservation at time t and $t + dt$, we have

$$mv + F\,dt = (m + dm)\,(v + dv)$$

$$mv + F\,dt = mv + dmv + mdv$$

$$F\,dt = dmv + mdv$$

Here $\qquad m = M + rt$

and $\qquad dm = rdt$

Thus, we have

$$(M + rt)\,dv = (F - rv)\,dt$$

$$\frac{dv}{F - rv} = \frac{dt}{M + rt}$$

On integrating,

$$\int_0^v \frac{dv}{F - rv} = \int_0^t \frac{dt}{M + rt}$$

$$\ln\frac{F}{F - rv} = \ln\frac{M + rt}{M}$$

$$v = \frac{Frt}{Mr + r^2 t}$$

The example can be modified if we consider rain fall at an angle θ to the vertical in the direction against the velocity of the car as shown in figure-4.58. In this case, we have to add the momentum carried by the rain fall in time dt, to the car in opposite direction. Now the equation of momentum conservation will be of the form

$$mv + F\,dt - dm\,V_R \sin\theta = (m + dm)\,(v + dv)$$

Now we can separate the terms of dv and dt and then on integration gives the velocity of tank-car as a function of time.

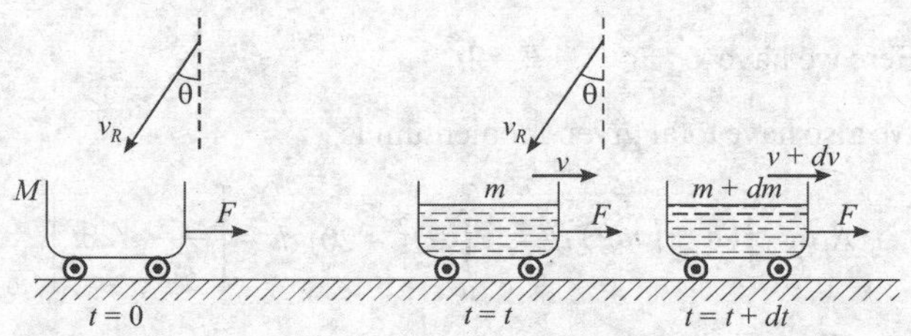

Figure 4.58

There can be many cases in which the mass of system varies with time. As discussed, "*In all the cases of mass variation, we use momentum conservation at an intermediate instant from time t to t + dt*". Read out carefully the examples given below.

Illustration Example 4.30

Let there be a tank-car filled with water, shown in figure-4.59. The initial mass of the car with water is M. At $t = 0$, a hole is made in the left wall of the car and water start spilling out from the car, with a constant velocity u with respect to the car. The rate of ejection of water is r kg/s. Find the velocity of the car as a function of time.

Solution

The corresponding situation is shown in figure-4.57.

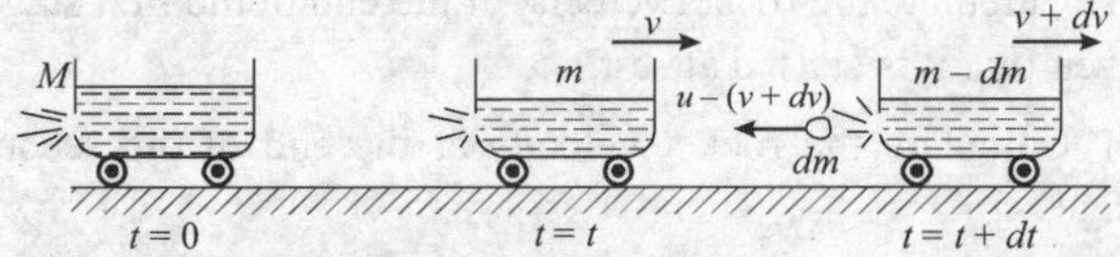

Figure 4.59

As usual, we apply conservation of linear momentum at time $t = t$ and $t = t + dt$. The equation formed is given as

$$mv = (m - dm)(v + dv) - dm(u - v - dv)$$

Here the velocity of dm after ejection is u, with respect to the car and with respect to earth, it is

$$u - (v + dv)$$

The above case can also be taken as analogous to the case of rocket propulsion. The rocket is of initial mass M, starts ejecting its fuel at a rate of r kg/s and at a relative velocity u.

Illustration Example 4.31

A cart loaded with sand moves along a horizontal floor due to a constant force F coinciding in direction with the cart's velocity vector. In the process sand spills through a hole in the bottom with a constant rate $\mu kg/s$. Find the acceleration and velocity of the cart at the moment t, if at the initial moment $t = 0$ the cart with loaded sand had the mass m_0 and its velocity was equal to zero. Friction is to be neglected.

Solution

In this problem the sand spills through a hole in the bottom of the cart. Hence, the relative velocity of the sand v_r will be zero because it will acquire the same velocity as that of the cart at the moment.

$$v_r = 0$$

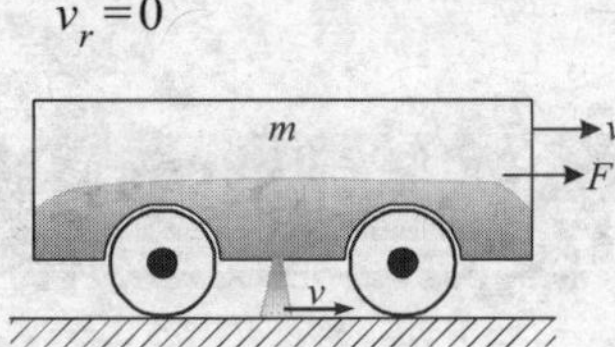

Figure 4.60

Thus, $$F_t = 0 \left(\text{as } F_t = v_r \frac{dm}{dt}\right)$$

and the net force will be F only

$$\Rightarrow \quad F_{net} = F$$

or $$m\left(\frac{dv}{dt}\right) = F \quad \ldots(4.25)$$

But here $$m = m_0 - \mu t$$

$$\Rightarrow \quad (m_0 - \mu t)\frac{dv}{dt} = F$$

or $$\int_0^v dv = \int_0^t \frac{Fdt}{m_0 - \mu t}$$

$$\Rightarrow \quad v = \frac{F}{-\mu}\left[ln(m_0 - \mu t)\right]_0^t$$

or $$v = \frac{F}{\mu}\ln\left(\frac{m_0}{m_0 - \mu t}\right)$$

From equation-(4.25), acceleration of the cart

$$a = \frac{dv}{dt} = \frac{F}{m} \quad \text{or} \quad a = \frac{F}{m_0 - \mu t}$$

Illustration Example 4.32

A plate of mass M is moved with constant velocity v against dust particles moving with velocity u in opposite direction as shown. The density of the dust is ρ and plate area is A. Find the force F required to keep the plate moving uniformly. (ρ in kg/m^3)

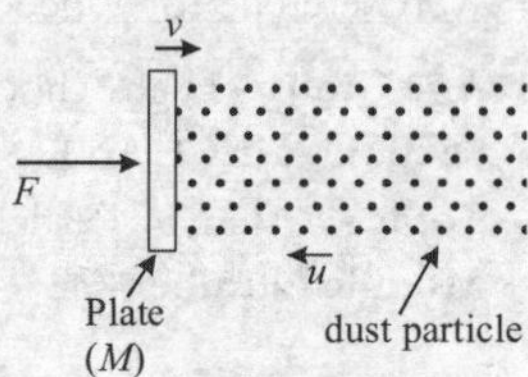

Figure 4.61

Solution

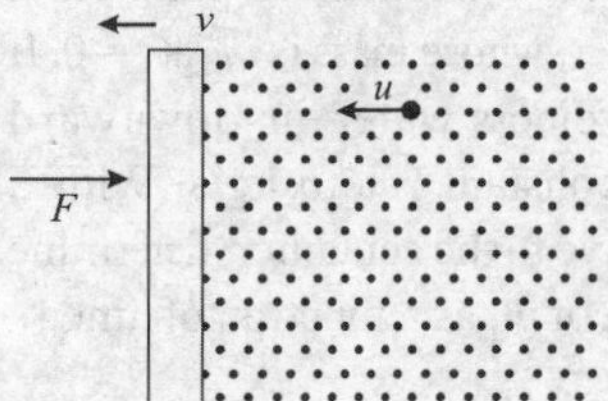

Figure 4.62

Velocity of plate relative dust = $(v + u)$ →. In time 'dt' plate comes into contact with dust particles stored in volume, $dV = Adx = A(v + u)\,dt$

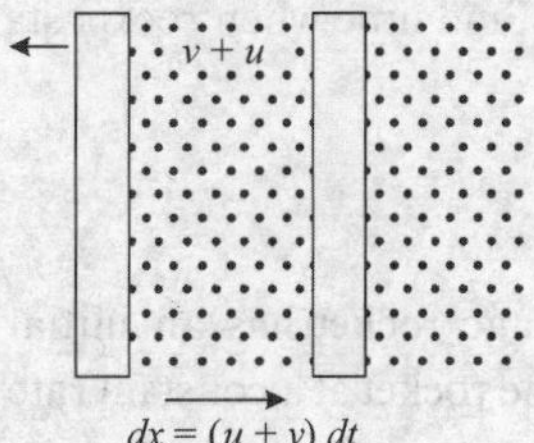

Figure 4.63

So mass of dust striking to plate in time dt is

$$dm = \rho dV = \rho A\,(v+u)dt \qquad \ldots(4.26)$$

It we consider plate + dm mass of dust as system, and apply impulse momentum equation over time dt.

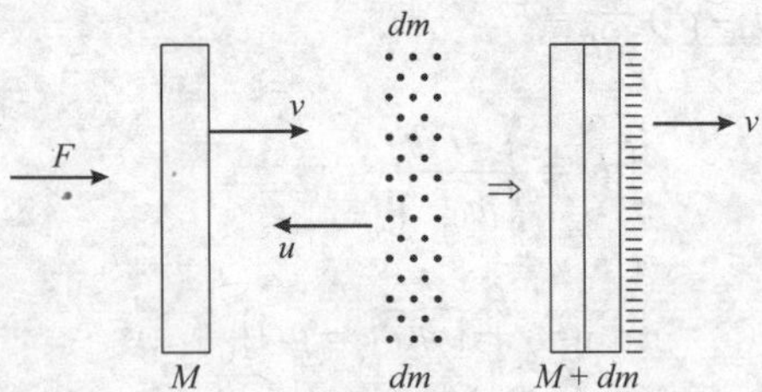

Figure 4.64

$$Fdt = (M+dm)\,v - [Mv - dmu]$$
$$Fdt = Mv + dmv - Mv + dmu$$
$$F = \frac{dm}{dt}(u+v)$$

From equation-(4.26) we have

$$F = \rho A\,(v+u)^2$$

Web Reference of Video Lectures at www.physicsgalaxy.com
Age Group - High School Physics | Age 17-19 Years
Section - MECHANICS
Topic - System of Particles - II
Module Number - 32

Practice Exercise 4.4

(i) A mass m_1 is connected by a weightless cable passing over a frictionless pulley to a container of water, whose mass is m_0 at $t = 0$. If the container ejects water in downward direction at a constant rate b kg/s. With a velocity v_0 relative to the container, determine the acceleration of m_1 as a function of time.

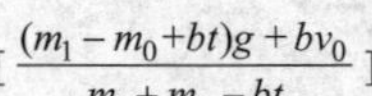

$$\left[\frac{(m_1 - m_0 + bt)g + bv_0}{m_1 + m_0 - bt}\right]$$

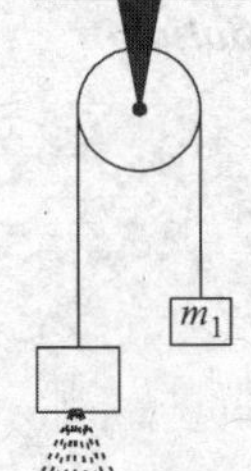

Figure 4.65

(ii) A rocket with initial mass M is launched by emitting, gas with velocity v_0 (relative to the rocket body) downwards. The mass of the gas emitted per second is k. (k is constant and obeys $kv_0 < Mg$). Find time when rocket start to lift.

$$\left[\left(\frac{M}{k} - \frac{v_0}{g}\right)\right]$$

(iii) A double stage rocket has an initial mass M_i. Gas is exhausted from the rocket at a constant rate of dm/dt and with an exhaust velocity u relative to the rocket. When the mass of the rocket reaches the value μ, the first stage of mass m of which fuel is exhausted is disengaged from the rocket and then the rocket continues to the second stage at the same rate and exhaust velocity as in the first stage, until it reaches a mass M_f.

(a) Calculate the rocket velocity at the end of the first stage, given that it is started at rest.

(b) Calculate the rocket velocity at the end of the second stage.

(c) What is the final velocity of a one stage rocket of the same initial M_i mass and the same amount of fuel ? Is it greater or less than final velocity of the double stage rocket ?

[(a) $v_1 = u \ln \frac{M_i}{\mu}$ (b) $v_2 = u \ln \frac{M_i(\mu - m)}{\mu M_f}$ (c) $v_f = u \ln \frac{M_i}{M_f + m}$, $v_2 > v_f$]

(iv) A particle of mass M is initially at rest starts moving under the action of a constant force $F\hat{i}$. It encounters the resistance of a stream of fine dust moving with velocity $-v_0\hat{i}$, which deposits matter on it at a constant rate ρ, show that its mass will be m when it has travelled a distance -

$$\frac{F - \rho v_0}{\rho^2}\left[m - M\left(1 + \ln\left|\frac{m}{M}\right|\right)\right]$$

(v) A balloon having mass 'm' is filled with gas and is held in hands of a boy. Then suddenly it get released and gas starts coming out of it with a constant rate. The velocities of the ejected gases is also constant 2m/s with respect to the balloon. Find out the velocity of the balloon when the mass of gas is reduced to half.

[2ln(2) m/s]

(vi) A railroad car of length L and mass m_0 when empty is moving freely on a horizontal track while being loaded with sand from a stationary chute at a rate $dm/dt = q$. Knowing that the car was approaching the chute a speed v_0, determine

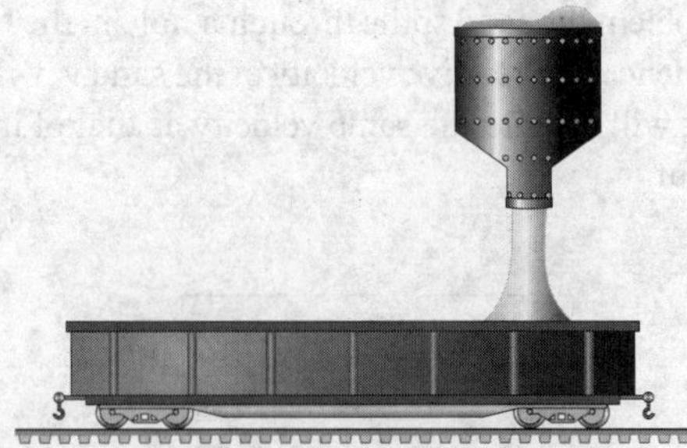

Figure 4.66

(a) The mass of the car and its load after the car has cleared the chute.

(b) The speed of the car at that time.

[(a) $m_0 e^{\left(\frac{qL}{m_0 v_0}\right)}$ (b) $v_0 e^{-\left(\frac{qL}{m_0 v_0}\right)}$]

4.9 Collisions

Collision is the transfer of momentum due to only internal forces between the particles taking part in collision. The proper definition of collision between two bodies can be written as - *"When exchange of momentum takes place between two physical bodies only due to their mutual interaction force, is defined as collision between two bodies."* As shown in figure-4.67, two bodies move in different directions interact each other at the point of intersection of their line of motion and the impulse of reaction due to their physical contact is the cause of the transfer of momentum from one body to another. We'll discuss the process in detail in further sections, now we take up a simple example of collision without physical contact.

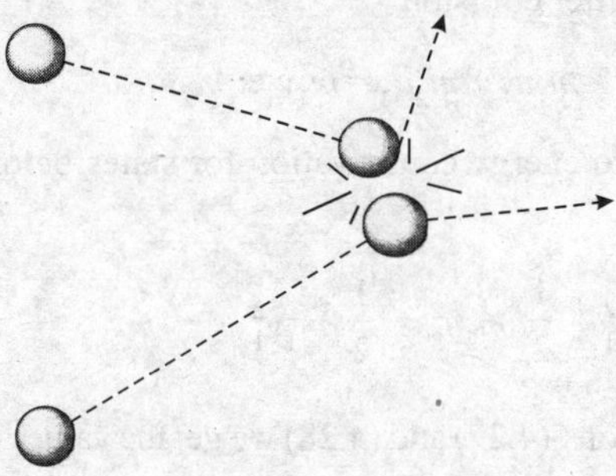

Figure 4.67

Consider two masses m_1 and m_2 with positive charges q_1 and q_2, moving with velocities u_1 and u_2 respectively, as shown in figure-4.61 initially at a large separation. In this situation if $u_1 > u_2$, the separation between the two charges will decrease and the Coulambian force of repulsion between them increases and this force will act on the two particles in opposite direction, as shown. This force accelerates the second particle and retards the first particle. This continues until the velocities of both become equal and when the velocities of both are equal the separation between them is minimum because, before this instant, velocity of first was greater than that of second and the separation was decreasing. Still the electrostatic repulsion force is acting, now as shown in figure-4.68(c) and 4.68(d), after this instant second particle's velocity further increases and that of first particle decreases and the separation starts increasing. When the two particles get separated very far, the repulsive force between them will vanish and the particles continue to move with their final velocities.

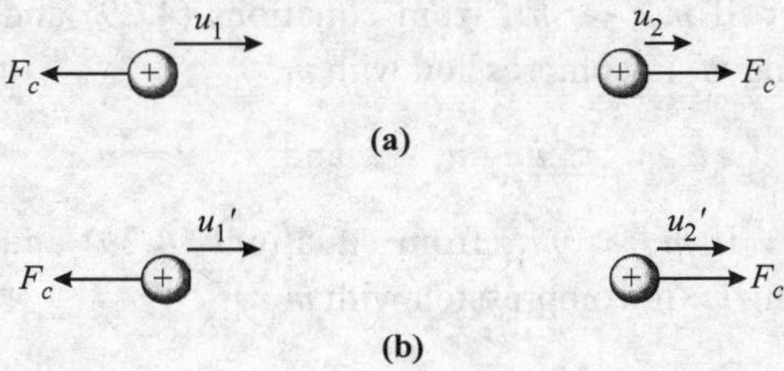

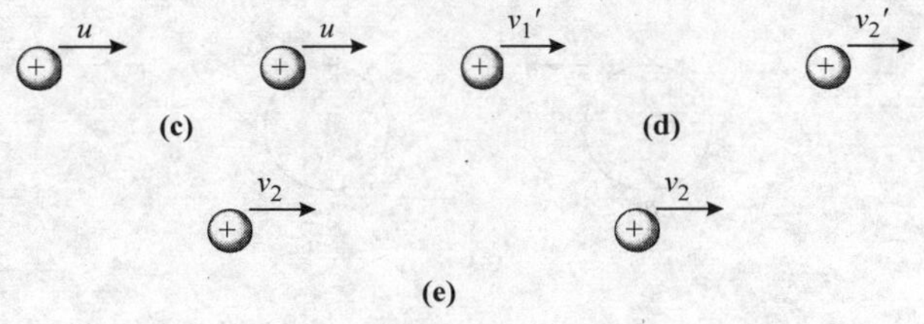

Figure 4.68

In the whole process, we can observe that no external force is acting on the two masses, so the momentum of the system must remain constant. We can observe in figure-4.68(a) to (e) that at every stage, due to electrostatic force, momentum of second particle is continuously increasing and that of first particle is decreasing but total momentum must remains constant.

We've shown that for collision physical contact is not necessary. Momentum can be transferred from one body to another by any mutual interaction force (only internal forces), doesn't matters whether there is physical contact or not. The cases of collision in which physical contact takes place are known as *"Impact"*.

Before mathematical analyzation of collision, we take up an example of impact between two bodies.

Consider two bodies of masses m_1 and m_2, moving velocities u_1 and u_2 respectively ($u_1 > u_2$) as shown in figure-4.69(a). After some time they'll come in contact as shown in figure-4.69(b). As velocity of first is more than that of second, it will push the second body and there is a normal reaction developed between the two bodies and the two will get deformed as shown in figure-4.69(c). Here this normal reaction will be the internal force responsible for acceleration of second and retardation of first body. Due to the contact reaction the velocity of first becomes u_1' and that of second becomes u_2' but if still u_1' is greater than u_2', further deformation increases and this will continue until the velocity of both will become equal. This situation is shown in figure-4.69(d). At this instant the deformation of the two bodies is maximum and no further deformation increment takes places at the velocities are equal. Further process of collision depends on the nature of the bodies as :

(i) If bodies are Elastic

If the two colliding bodies are elastic i.e. these have a tendency to restore their deformation to original shape, a restoring force f_R will act between the two bodies, which will further accelerate the second body and retards the first body and the separation of the two will start increasing, as shown in figure-4.69(f).

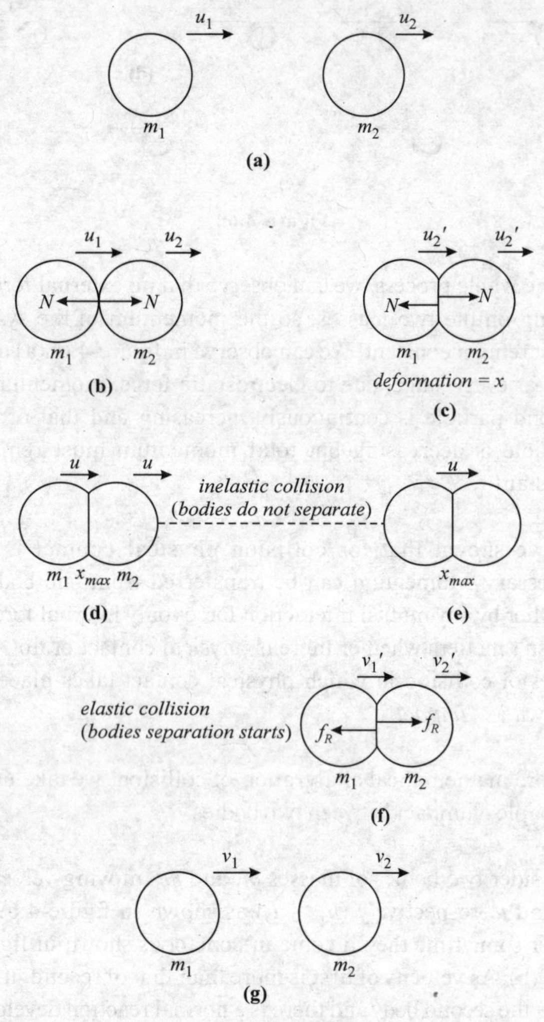

Figure 4.69

After some time the deformation is fully recovered and the bodies get separated from each other. In case of perfectly elastic bodies, the total energy in deformation is recovered as the kinetic energy of the bodies and no energy is lost.

If bodies are even partially elastic the restoring force will act and bodies gets separated out deformation is not fully recovered, some amount of energy in deformation is lost.

(ii) If Bodies are Inelastic

If the two colliding bodies are inelastic then these does not have a tendency of reformation. If the bodies get deformed, these remain in the deformed shape and the two will move with the same velocities without getting separated as shown in figure-4.69 (e). Maximum energy is lost in inelastic collision.

We will now discuss elastic, partial elastic and inelastic collision separately.

4.9.1 Elastic Collision

Figure-4.70 shows a collision of two elastic bodies moving in straight line, known as head-on collision. As we have discussed that in the process of collision no external force acts, hence the momentum of the system remains constant and in case of elastic collision, the energy stored in deformation is restored as the kinetic energy of the two bodies after separation of the bodies.

Figure 4.70

According to momentum conservation we have for states before and after collision

$$m_1u_1 + m_2u_2 = m_1v_1 + m_2v_2 \qquad \ldots(4.27)$$

According to energy conservation for states before and after collision

$$\frac{1}{2}\, m_1u_1^2 + \frac{1}{2}\, m_2u_2^2 = \frac{1}{2}\, m_1v_1^2 + \frac{1}{2}\, m_2v_2^2 \qquad \ldots(4.28)$$

From equations-(4.27) and (4.28) we get the values of velocities v_1 and v_2 after collision. Expressions for velocities v_1 and v_2 are given here, students are advised to remember the results, these are very helpful in solving a particular category of collision problems, few are given in examples

$$v_1 = \frac{m_1 - m_2}{m_1 + m_2}\, u_1 + \frac{2m_2}{m_1 + m_2}\, u_2 \qquad \ldots(4.29)$$

$$v_2 = \frac{m_2 - m_1}{m_2 + m_1}\, u_2 + \frac{2m_1}{m_2 + m_1}\, u_1 \qquad \ldots(4.30)$$

We now discuss three particular cases of head-on elastic collisions

Case-1 : If $m_1 = m_2$, we have from equation-(4.29) and (4.30)

$$v_1 = u_2 \quad \text{and} \quad v_2 = u_1$$

Thus if masses of bodies are equal, velocities after collision are interchanged. If the second particle is at rest, after collision first comes to rest and second moves with the velocity of the first.

Case-2 : If $m_1 >> m_2$, from equations-(4.29) and (4.30), neglecting m_2 in compression with m_1

$$v_1 = 2u_2 - u_1 \quad \text{and} \quad v_2 = u_2$$

Case-3 : If $m_2 >> m_1$, from equations-(4.29) and (4.30), neglecting m_1 in compression with m_2

$$v_1 = 2u_2 - u_1 \quad \text{and} \quad v_2 = u_2$$

NOTE : All velocities used in equations-(4.29) and (4.30) are used in vector form as given below

$$\vec{v}_1 = \frac{m_1 - m_2}{m_1 + m_2}\vec{u}_1 + \frac{2m_2}{m_1 + m_2}\vec{u}_2 \quad \ldots(4.31)$$

$$\vec{v}_2 = \frac{m_2 - m_1}{m_2 + m_1}\vec{u}_2 + \frac{2m_1}{m_2 + m_1}\vec{u}_1 \quad \ldots(4.32)$$

4.9.2 Partial Elastic and Inelastic Head-on Collision

In case of partial elastic and inelastic collisions, kinetic energy of the system does not remain conserved, as deformation of the bodies are not fully recovered. In such cases we can not apply kinetic energy conservation unlike to the previous case. So we have only the momentum conservation equation and there are two variables v_1 and v_2. In these case we define another term known as coefficient of restitution.

Coefficient of restitution is defined as

$$e = \frac{\text{velocity of separation after collision}}{\text{velocity of approach before collision}}$$

$$e = \frac{v_2 - v_1}{u_1 - u_2} \quad \ldots(4.33)$$

So for the case of partial or inelastic collision, we use the equations

$$m_1u_1 + m_2u_2 = m_1v_1 + m_2v_2 \quad \ldots(4.34)$$

$$v_2 - v_1 = e\,(u_1 - u_2) \quad \ldots(4.35)$$

Solving equation-(4.29) and (4.30), we get

$$v_1 = \left(\frac{m_1 - em_2}{m_2 + m_2}\right)u_1 + \frac{m_2}{m_1 + m_2}(1+e)\,u_2 \quad \ldots(4.36)$$

$$v_2 = \left(\frac{m_2 - em_1}{m_2 + m_2}\right)u_2 + \frac{m_1}{m_1 + m_2}(1+e)\,u_1 \quad \ldots(4.37)$$

Coefficient of restitution is also termed as degree of elasticity. Practically value of e varies between 0 and 1. For an ideal elastic collision $e = 1$ and for completely inelastic collision $e = 0$. Equation-(4.29) and (4.30) can also be obtained by equations-(4.33) and (4.34) by substituting $e = 1$. The equation of coefficient of restitution is applied in the direction of line of contact of the bodies. This will become clear in the next section.

Web Reference of Video Lectures at www.physicsgalaxy.com

Age Group - High School Physics | Age 17-19 Years
Section - MECHANICS
Topic - System of Particles - II
Module Number - 15, 16, 17, 18, 19, 20 and 21

Illustration Example 4.33

A ball is dropped on a floor from a height h, If coefficient of restitution is e, find the height to which the ball will rise and the time it will take to come to rest again.

Solution

The ball reaches the floor with velocity $u = \sqrt{2gh}$

If collision on the floor is elastic the ball will rebound with the same velocity u and it will reach the same height. But if the coefficient of restitution between ball and the floor is e, the ball will rebound with a less velocity v, given as

$$v = eu \quad \ldots(4.38)$$

As have v is the velocity of separation and u is the velocity of approach.

In this case the ball will rebound to a height h_1, from equations-(4.38), it is given as

$$h_1 = \frac{v^2}{2g} = e^2h \quad \ldots(4.39)$$

In downward and upward motion the acceleration of the particle is g only, thus total time of motion is the time of downward motion plus time of upward motion, as

$$t = \sqrt{\frac{2h}{g}} + \sqrt{\frac{2e^2h}{g}}$$

$$= \sqrt{\frac{2h}{g}} + e\sqrt{\frac{2h}{g}}$$

Illustrative Example 4.34

An elevator platform is going up at a speed 20 m/sec and during its upward motion a small ball of 50 gm mass falling in downward direction strikes the platform elastically at a speed. Find the speed with which the ball rebounds.

Solution

The situation is analysed in figure-4.71. There we can consider mass of platform to be very large compared to that of ball, so we have

$u_1 = 20$ m/s, $m = 50$ gm, $u_2 = 5$ m/s

Figure 4.71

$$\vec{v}_1 = \vec{u}_1 \quad \text{and} \quad \vec{v}_2 = 2\vec{u}_1 - \vec{u}_2$$

Thus rebound velocity of ball is

$$\vec{v}_2 = 2 \times 20 - (-5) = 45 \text{ m/sec upward}$$

Illustrative Example 4.35

A neutron moving at a speed v undergoes a head-on elastic collision with a mass number A at rest. Find the ratio of kinetic energies of the neutron after and before collision.

Solution

If we consider mass of a neutron to be m and the mass of nucleus of mass number A is mA then for elastic head on collision, we have

$$u_1 = v \quad \text{and} \quad u_2 = 0$$

After collision velocity of neutron is

$$v_1 = \left(\frac{1-A}{1+A}\right) v$$

Thus KE of neutron after collision is

$$k_f = \frac{1}{2} mv_1^2 = \frac{1}{2} mv^2 \left(\frac{1-A}{1+A}\right)^2$$

Thus KE of neutron before collision was

$$k_i = \frac{1}{2} mv^2$$

We require $$\frac{k_f}{k_i} = \left(\frac{1-A}{1+A}\right)^2$$

Illustrative Example 4.36

Two balls A and B each of mass m are placed on a smooth ground as shown in figure-4.72. Another ball C of mass m arranged to the right of ball B as shown. If a velocity v_1 is given to ball A in rightward direction, find no. of collisions between the balls of (a) $M < m$ and (b) $M > m$. Consider all collisions to be elastic.

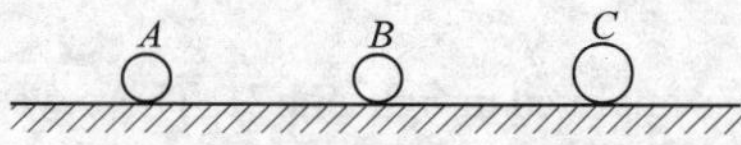

Figure 4.72

Solution

(a) First collision will be between balls A and B. Since both the balls are of same mass, after the collision A will come to rest and B will move with v_1, now it will collide to C. If after this collision, velocities of balls B and C are v_B and v_C respectively, we have

$$v_B = \left(\frac{m-M}{m+M}\right) v_1$$

$$v_C = \left(\frac{2m}{m+M}\right) v_1$$

here as we have $M < m$, $v_B < v_C$ and both are positive thus both the balls are moving forward and will not collide again, hence there are total two collision.

(b) If in second collision we have $M > m$, we get v_B negative, so ball B moves in backward direction after second collision and will strike again to ball A (which is at rest to the left of it) and come to rest and ball A will more to the left with speed v_B. Then now there are total three collision.

Web Reference of Video Lectures at www.physicsgalaxy.com

Age Group - High School Physics | Age 17-19 Years
Section - MECHANICS
Topic - System of Particles - II
Module Number - 22, 23, 24, 25 and 26

4.9.3 Two Dimensional Collisions

In the previous section we limited ourselves to one dimensional situations. However there are many common situations, such as collisions between billiard balls or air molecules, the objects move in different directions after the collision and it is necessary to consider two or three dimensions. Then the vector aspect of momentum becomes important. We first write out the general equations, simplify to two dimension and consider a specific example. As before, provided that the net external force on the system is zero, we write the conservation rule again as "*The momentum before collision equals the momentum after collision in every direction.*"

As we have discussed, two dimensional collisions, can be of three types, elastic, partial inelastic and inelastic. In every case we use to conserve momentum in two mutually perpendicular directions, say x and y. To understand two dimensional collisions, we take few Illustration examples. Go through these carefully.

Illustration Example 4.37

Two balls approaching each other along two perpendicular directions and collide at the intersection. After the collision, they stick together. If one ball has a mass of 14.5 kg and an initial speed of 11.5 m/s and the other has a mass of 17.5 kg and an initial speed of 15.5 m/s, what will be their speed and direction immediately after impact ?

Solution

The situation is shown in figure-4.73. The collision is perfectly inelastic. We can use the law of conservation of momentum to find the speed just after the collision. We must choose a coordinate system to solve the problem. For it, generally, we take one of the initial velocity direction as x-axis and then perpendicular to it as y-axis, as shown in figure-4.73. Now we write the equation of conservation of momentum in both x and y-direction.

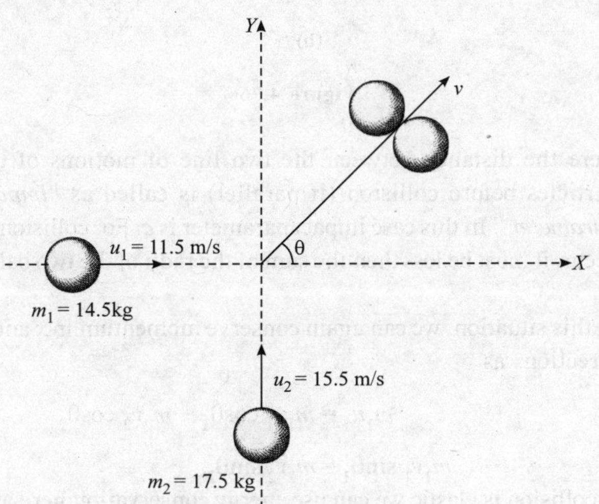

Figure 4.73

Momentum in x-direction is

$$m_1 u_1 = (m_1 + m_2)\, v \cos\theta$$

$$v \cos\theta = \frac{m_1 u_1}{m_1 + m_2} = \frac{14.5 \times 11.5}{14.5 \times 17.5} = 5.231 \text{ m/s} \qquad \ldots(4.40)$$

And in y-direction is

$$m_2 u_2 = (m_1 + m_2)\, v \sin\theta$$

$$v \sin\theta = \frac{m_2 u_2}{m_1 + m_2} = \frac{17.5 \times 15.5}{14.5 \times 17.5} = 8.48 \text{ m/s} \qquad \ldots(4.41)$$

Now squaring and adding equation-(4.40) and (4.41)

$$v = \sqrt{5.21^2 + 8.48^2} = 9.95 \text{ m/s}$$

Dividing (4.41) by (4.40)

$$\theta = \tan^{-1} \frac{8.48}{5.21} = 58.4°$$

Thus the two balls move off at an angle of 58.4° from the initial direction of travel of the 14.5 kg ball.

Consider the situation shown in figure-4.74, in which two objects collide but do not stick together after impact. The case will be either of an elastic collision or will be partial inelastic collision. Both the objects move in different directions. For solving the problem related to such cases, again we take one of the initial direction of motion as x-axis and its perpendicular as y-axis. Now we conserve momentum in x and in y directions separately.

In x-direction, we have

$$m_1 u_1 + m_2 u_2 \cos\theta = m_1 v_1 \cos\theta_1 + m_2 v_2 \cos\theta_2 \qquad \ldots(4.42)$$

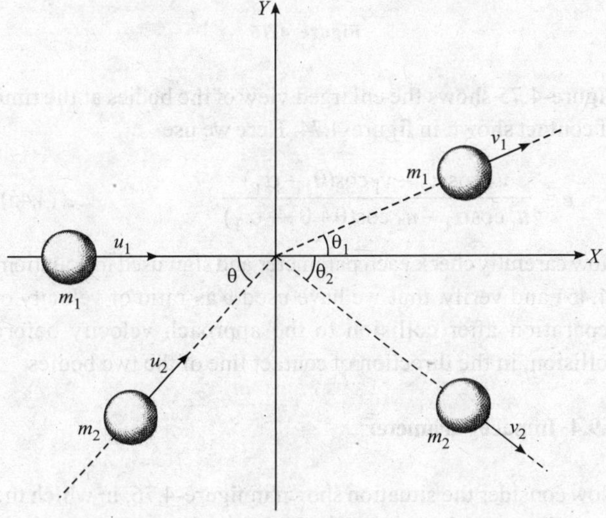

Figure 4.74

In y direction, we have

$$m_2 u_2 \sin\theta = m_1 v_1 \sin\theta_1 - m_2 v_2 \sin\theta_2 \qquad \ldots(4.43)$$

If the collision is elastic, we use

$$\frac{1}{2} m_1 u_1^2 + \frac{1}{2} m_2 u_2^2 = \frac{1}{2} m_1 v_1^2 + \frac{1}{2} m_2 v_2^2 \qquad \ldots(4.44)$$

On solving equations-(4.42), (4.43) and (4.44), we get the result required in the problem but if the collision is partially inelastic, we cannot use equation-(4.44). Instead of this equation we make use of coefficient of restitution as the ratio of velocity of separation after collision to the velocity of approach before collision, but in two dimensional case it is not as easy as we have applied in one dimensional case in equation-(4.35).

Here coefficient of restitution equation is made in the direction of line of contact of the two bodies, as shown in figure-4.75. At the time of contact of the two bodies, the contact force develops between them is along the line joining their centres.

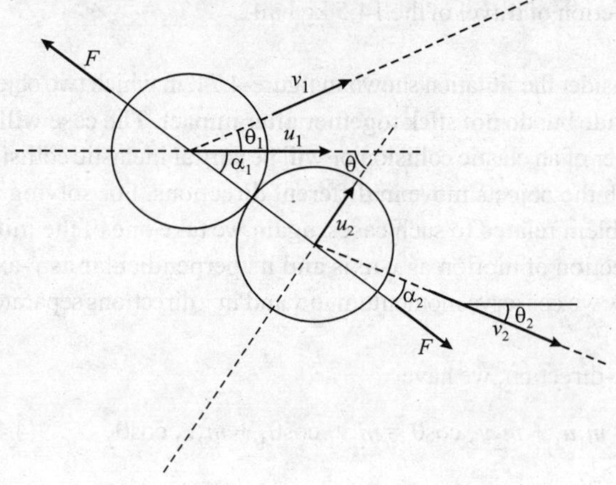

Figure 4.75

Figure-4.75 shows the enlarged view of the bodies at the time of contact shown in figure-4.74. Here we use

$$e = \frac{v_2 \cos\alpha_2 - v_1 \cos(\theta_1 + \alpha_1)}{u_1 \cos\alpha_1 - u_2 \cos(\theta + \theta_2 + \alpha_2)} \quad \ldots (4.45)$$

Now carefully check each parameter and sign used in equation-(4.45) and verify, that we have used e as ratio of velocity of separation after collision to the approach velocity before collision, in the direction of contact line of the two bodies.

4.9.4 Impact Parameter

Now consider the situation shown in figure-4.76, in which the second mass m_2 is at rest. The object m_1 with an initial velocity u_1 strikes m_2, at rest. These objects could be billiard balls, subatomic particles, whatever you like, and the two need not have the same mass. After the collision, we observe that the object 1, which was initially in motion along the x direction, diverge at an angle θ_1 and the one which was at rest, will start from the reference line at an angle θ_2. As initially m_2 was at rest, when m_1 comes in contact with it, their contact line must be at an angle θ_2, because a particle at rest, starts moving in that direction where the force acts on it. If initially m_2 was moving parallel to m_1, the direction of motion m_2 after collision will be at an angle less than θ_2.

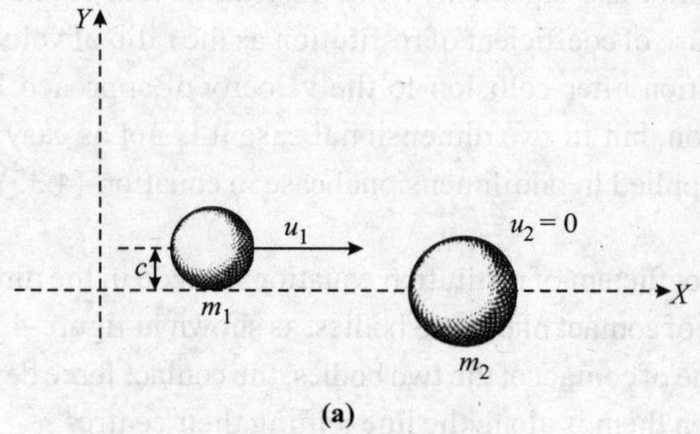

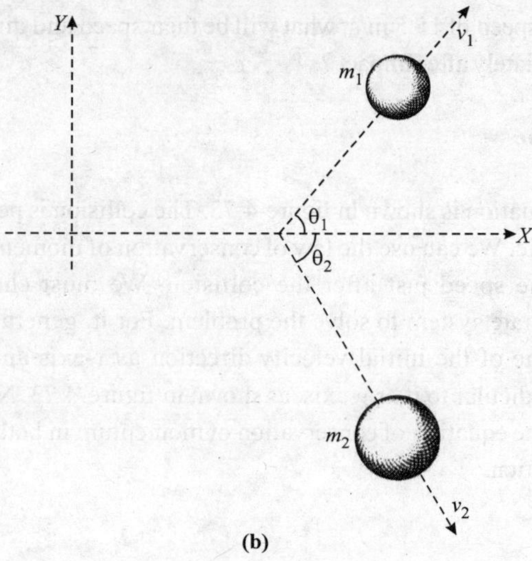

Figure 4.76

Here the distance between the two line of motions of the particles before collision (if parallel) is called as "*Impact parameter*". In this case impact parameter is c. For collision to occur, it must be less then the sum of the radii of the two balls.

In this situation, we can again conserve momentum in x and y directions as

$$m_1 u_1 = m_1 v_1 \cos\theta_1 + m_2 v_2 \cos\theta_2$$

$$m_1 v_1 \sin\theta_1 = m_2 v_2 \sin\theta_2$$

If collision is elastic we can use energy conservation here as

$$\frac{1}{2}\, m u_1^2 = \frac{1}{2}\, m_1 v_1^2 + \frac{1}{2}\, m_2 v_2^2$$

There is one important property about this type of collision, which is shown in figure-4.76 is that if $m_1 = m_2$ and m_2 is at rest and it is elastic collision than always

$$\theta_1 + \theta_2 = 90°$$

This relation can be obtained by solving above equations of momentum and energy conservation.

4.9.5 Super Elastic Collision

A super elastic collision is one in which the internal potential energy of the bodies is released in form of kinetic energy during collision. In such cases after collision the sum of final kinetic energies of the colliding bodies is more than the sum of initial kinetic energies of the bodies. The best example to describe a super elastic collision is bursting of a cracker when it collides with a body so that the internal energy released due to burst creates an impuse and increases the kinetic energy of the system. In such cases generally (in most of cases) the relative speed of separation of bodies is more than the relative speed of approach of the colliding bodies so the coefficient of restitution in such **collisions is greater than unity.**

 # Illustration Example 4.38

A ball is thrown toward a floor at an angle of incidence θ with speed u. The coefficient of restitution between floor and ball is e. Find the speed with which the ball rebounds and the angle which it makes with the normal.

Solution

The situation is shown in figure-4.77. As the ball comes toward floor its velocity has two components, along the floor $u\sin\theta$ and normal to the floor $u\cos\theta$. When ball strikes the floor, a normal reaction is developed between the ball and the floor which acts on ball in the direction away from the floor. This force is the cause of changing the value of $u\cos\theta$. If floor is smooth no force will act on ball along the floor, thus there is no change in the component $u\sin\theta$. When ball rebounds its horizontal components remains same but the normal components is changed. If ball rebounds with speed v making an angle α with the normal as shown in figure-4.68, we have along horizontal direction

$$v\sin\theta = u\sin\theta \qquad \ldots(4.46)$$

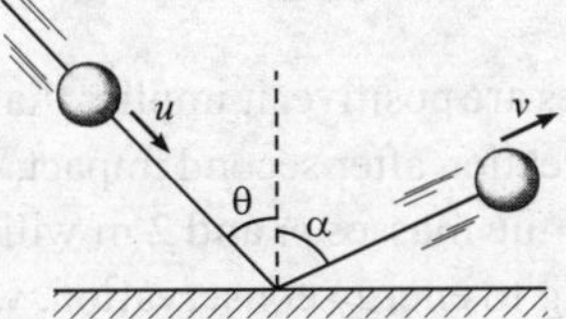

Figure 4.77

When ball is coming toward floor, its approach velocity can be given as the normal component of the ball's velocity $u\cos\theta$ and after collision its separation velocity with the floor is given as $v\cos\alpha$, thus according to the definition of coefficient of restitution, we have

$$v\cos\alpha = e\, u\cos\theta \qquad \ldots(4.47)$$

Using equations-(4.46) and (4.47), we have

Squaring and adding, we get

$$v = u\sqrt{\sin^2\theta + e^2\cos^2\theta} \qquad \ldots(4.48)$$

Dividing, we get $\quad \tan\alpha = \dfrac{1}{e}\tan\theta \qquad \ldots(4.49)$

Here from equations-(4.48) and (4.49), we can observe that if collision is perfectly elastic, $e = 1$ and it gives $v = u$ and $\alpha = \theta$. And if collision is perfectly inelastic, $e = 0$ and equation-(4.49) shows the ball does not rebound and it will slide on the smooth floor with $u\sin\theta$.

Now students should think what happens in above cases if floor is not smooth.

 # Illustration Example 4.39

Figure-4.78 shows a right angled triangular prism of mass M resting on a smooth floor. A smooth ball of mass m is coming toward its inclined surface in horizontal direction with speed u. It collides with it and slides along the surface of incline. Find the velocity of wedge and the ball just after collision.

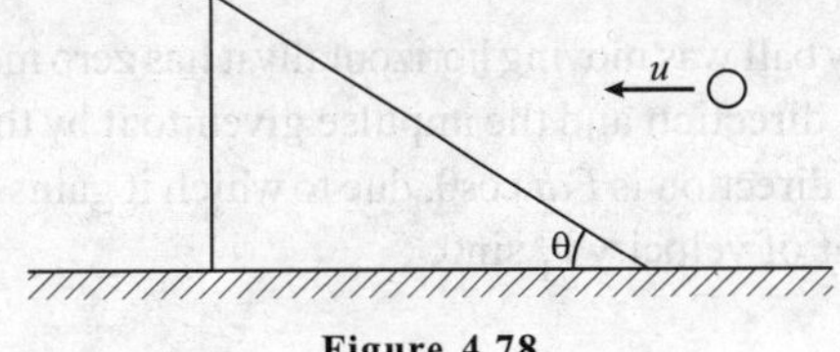

Figure 4.78

Solution

In this problem, we can conserve momentum in horizontal direction as there is no external force acting on the system along horizontal direction.

Here do not conserve momentum in vertical direction as in vertical direction there is an external force on system i.e. the normal reaction on prism by ground. If after collision ball moves up the incline plane with speed v_1 relative to prism and the prism moves toward left with speed v_2. We have

$$mu = m(v_1\cos\theta + v_2) + Mv_2 \qquad \ldots(4.50)$$

Here we can not conserve energy because ball does not rebound from the plane as it is a sort of inelastic collision. The above equation has two variables v_1 and v_2 and we don't have any other equation to solve this problem.

In such cases it is convenient to use impulse equation independent for each body of the system instead of using momentum conservation.

Look at figure-4.79. When ball collides with the incline, a normal reaction F acts on it in the direction shown in figure and on prism the same is in opposite direction.

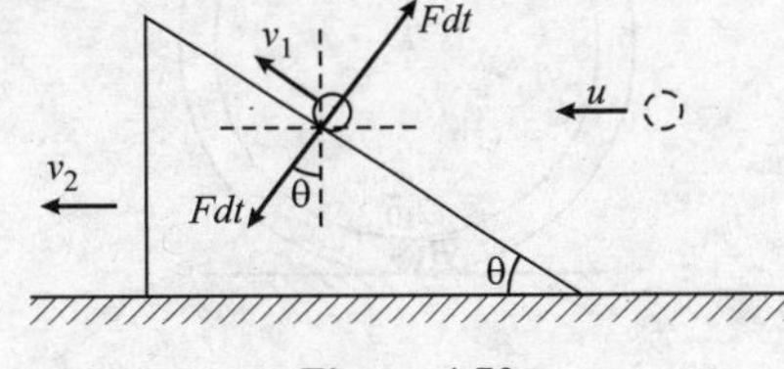

Figure 4.79

Now we write impulse equations for m and M independently.

For ball, we have along horizontal direction

$$mu - Fdt \sin\theta = m(v_1 \cos\theta + v_2) \qquad \ldots(4.51)$$

If dt is the collision duration, along horizontal direction force F imparts a momentum $Fdt \sin\theta$ to ball, as a result of which the final velocity of ball in horizontal direction becomes $(v_1\cos\theta + v_2)$.

In vertical direction, for ball we have

$$0 + Fdt \cos\theta = mv_1 \sin\theta \qquad \ldots(4.52)$$

As initially ball was moving horizontally it has zero momentum in vertical direction and the impulse given to it by the force F in vertical direction is $Fdt \cos\theta$, due to which it gains a vertical component of velocity $v_1 \sin\theta$.

Now for prism along horizontal direction, we have

$$0 + Fdt \sin\theta = Mv_2 \qquad \ldots(4.53)$$

A initially prism was at rest and $Fdt \sin\theta$ imparts a velocity v_2 to it. There is no need to write the vertical impulse equation for prism as there is no motion of it in vertical direction.

Above three equations-(4.51), (4.52) and (4.53) can be solved for velocities v_1 and v_2.

Illustrative Example 4.40

A ball of mass m is just disturbed from the top of a fixed smooth circular tube in a vertical plane and falls impinging on a ball of mass 2 m at the bottom. The coefficient of restitution is 1/2. Find the heights to which the balls rise after a second impact.

Solution

The situation is shown in figure-4.80. If u be the velocity of ball A just before impact. Then

$$u = \sqrt{2g(2a)}$$

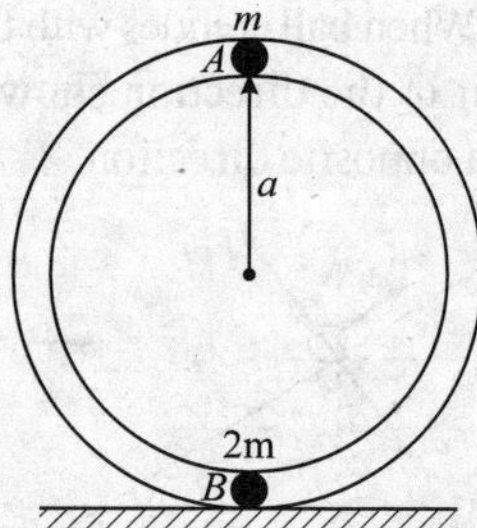

Figure 4.80

Consider the first impact between A and B. If velocities of the balls becomes v_1 and v_2 respectively, according to linear momentum conservation

$$mu + 0 = mv_1 + 2\,mv_2 \qquad \ldots(4.54)$$

Coefficient of restitution is given as

$$e = \frac{v_2 - v_1}{u} = \frac{1}{2} \qquad \ldots(4.55)$$

On solving equations-(4.54) and (4.55), we get

$$v_1 = 0 \quad \text{and} \quad v_2 = \frac{u}{2}$$

Now we consider the second impact between A and B, when ball B returns to its initial position with the same speed $u/2$. If after second impact the velocities of the two balls become v_3 and v_4. Again from linear momentum conservation and coefficient of restitution

$$2m\left(\frac{u}{2}\right) + 0 = mv_3 + 2\,mv_4 \qquad \ldots(4.56)$$

and

$$e = \frac{v_3 - v_4}{\frac{u}{2}} = \frac{1}{2} \qquad \ldots(4.57)$$

On solving equations-(4.56) and (4.57), we get

$$v_3 = \frac{u}{2} \quad \text{and} \quad v_4 = \frac{u}{4}$$

Both the velocities are positive, it implies that both masses will move in same direction after second impact. If h_1 and h_2 be the heights to which the masses m and 2 m will rise after second impact, according to energy conservation, we have

For ball of mass m

$$\frac{1}{2}\,m\left(\frac{u}{2}\right)^2 = \text{mgh}_1$$

or

$$h_1 = \frac{u^2}{8g} = \frac{a}{2}$$

For ball of mass 2 m

$$\frac{1}{2}\,(2m)\left(\frac{u}{4}\right)^2 = 2\,\text{mgh}_2$$

or

$$h_2 = \frac{u^2}{32g} = \frac{a}{8}$$

Illustrative Example 4.41

A mass $M = 1$ kg lies on a smooth horizontal base of a rough inclined plane at an angle 37° with the horizontal as shown in figure-4.81. A bullet of mass $m = 0.1$ kg is fired horizontally with a velocity $u = 110$ m/s and gets embeded in it almost immediately. The impulse imparted carries the combined mass up the incline and finally lands on the horizontal level with the horizontal base.

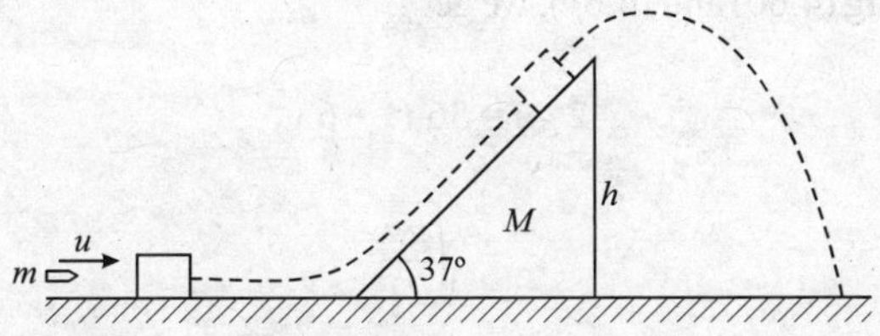

Figure 4.81

If the length of the incline is $l = 1.8$ m and the incline offers a coefficient of kinetic friction 0.5 to the sliding of the mass, find the horizontal distance from the base of the incline to the point of landing of the combined mass. Assume the contact of the incline with the horizontal plane is smooth and mass is not jerked when starts up on incline plane.

Solution

After collision the speed of the combined mass is given as

$$v = \frac{mu}{M+m}$$

or $$= 10 \text{ m/s}$$

The retardation of the body over the incline is

$$a = g\sin\theta - u\, g\cos\theta = 10 \text{ m/s}^2$$

Velocity of the block at the top of the incline is

$$v_f = \sqrt{v^2 - 2as}$$

$$= (100 - 2 \times 10 \times 1.8)^{1/2}$$

$$= 8 \text{ m/s}$$

At the point of leaving the inclined plane, the mass is at a height $h = 1.8 \times \sin 37° = \frac{5.4}{5}$ m

After leaving it lands on ground at time t, thus we have for its vertical projectile motion

$$-h = v_f \sin\theta - \frac{1}{2} gt^2$$

or $$-\frac{5.4}{5} = 8\left(\frac{3}{5}\right)t - \frac{1}{2}(10)t^2$$

Solving the above equation gives

$$t = 1.148 \text{ s}$$

In this duration the horizontal range of the mass is

$$x_2 = v_f \cos 37° \times t$$

or $$= 8\left(\frac{4}{5}\right) \times 1.148 = 7.347 \text{ m}$$

Horizontal span of incline is

$$x_1 = l\cos 37° = 1.8 \times \frac{4}{5} = 1.44 \text{ m}$$

Total horizontal distance covered by the mass is

$$s = x_1 + x_2 = 7.347 + 1.44 = 8.787 \text{ m}$$

Illustrative Example 4.42

A bead can slide on a smooth straight wire and a particle of mass m attached to the bead by a light string of length l. The particle is held in contact with the wire with string taut and as shown in figure-4.82 and then let fall. If the bead has a mass 2 m. Then when the string makes an angle θ with the wire, find the speed of the bead and the distance it slides upto this instant.

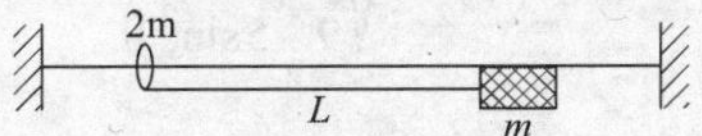

Figure 4.82

Solution

When the system is released from rest, m starts falling and due to tension in string bead starts sliding to right. Here as no external force is acting on system in horizontal direction so system centre of mass will not displace in horizontal direction.

We consider the situation when string makes an angle θ with the wire as shown in figure-4.83. Let system centre of mass is at position C shown, then initially the distance of mass m from C is $2L/3$ and when it is at angle θ from the wire its horizontal distance from C is $2/3\, L\cos\theta$. Similarly that of bead are $L/3$ and $L/3 \cos\theta$ respectively. Thus the distance it slides is

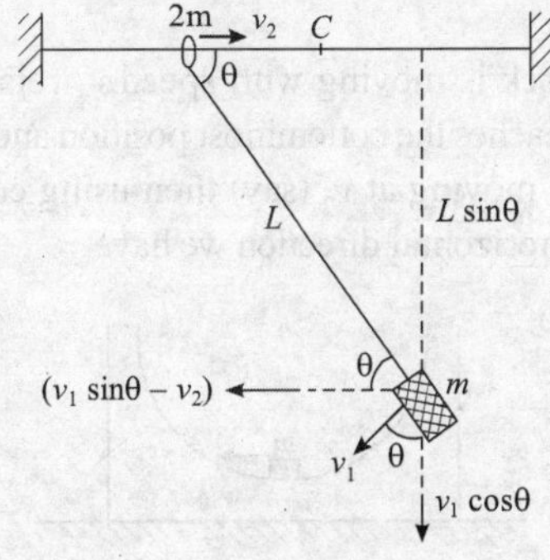

Figure 4.83

$$d_{Bead} = \frac{L}{3} - \frac{L}{3}\cos\theta = \frac{L}{3}(1 - \cos\theta)$$

If at this instant the speed of block and bead are v_1 (relative to bead) and v_2 then using work energy theorem we have

$$mgL\sin\theta = \frac{1}{2}m(v_1^2+v_2^2-2v_1v_2\sin\theta)+\frac{1}{2}(2m)v_2^2 \quad \ldots(4.58)$$

Using momentum conservation in horizontal direction as $\Sigma F_{horizontal} = 0$

$$m(v_1\sin\theta - v_2) = (2m)v_2 \quad \ldots(4.59)$$

Solving (4.58) and (4.59) we get

$$\Rightarrow \quad v_1 = \frac{3v_2}{\sin\theta}$$

$$2gL\sin\theta = v_2^2\left[1+\frac{9}{\sin^2\theta}-6\right]$$

$$\Rightarrow \quad v_2 = \sqrt{\frac{2gL\sin^3\theta}{9-5\sin^2\theta}}$$

Illustrative Example 4.43

Figure shows a block A of mass $6m$ having a smooth semicircular groove of radius a placed on a smooth horizontal surface. A block B of mass m is released from a position in grove where its radius is horizontal. Find the speed of bigger block when smaller block reaches its bottommost position.

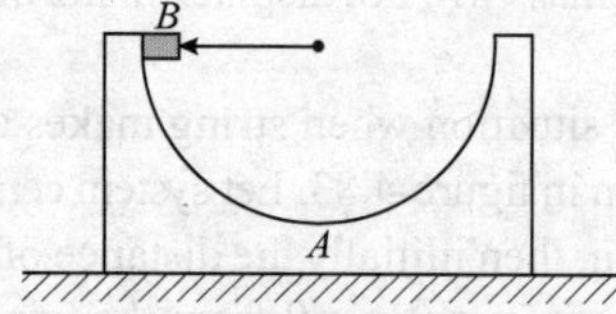

Figure 4.84

Solution

Let smaller block is moving with speed v_1 relative to bigger block when it reaches the bottommost position and at this instant bigger block is moving at v_2 (say) then using conservation of momentum in horizontal direction we have

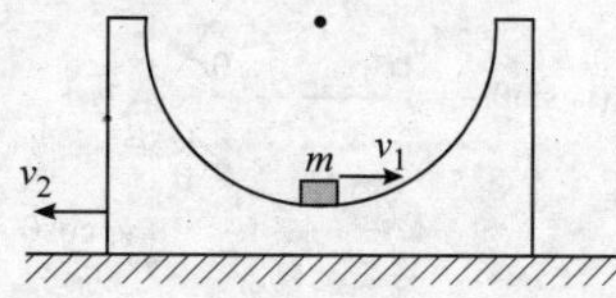

Figure 4.85

$$6mv_2 = m(v_1 - v_2) \quad \ldots(4.60)$$

Now using energy conservation

$$mga = \frac{1}{2}m(v_1-v_2)^2 + \frac{1}{2}(6m)v_2^2 \quad \ldots(4.61)$$

Solving (4.60) and (4.61), we get

$$2ga = 36v_2^2 + 6v_2^2$$

$$\Rightarrow \quad v_2 = \sqrt{\frac{ga}{21}}$$

Web Reference of Video Lectures at www.physicsgalaxy.com
Age Group - High School Physics | Age 17-19 Years
Section - MECHANICS
Topic - System of Particles - II
Module Number - 27, 28, 29, 30 and 31

Practice Exercise 4.5

(i) A piece of wood of mass 0.03 kg is dropped from the top of a building 100 m high. At the same time, a bullet of mass 0.02 kg is fired vertically upward with a velocity of 100 m/s from the ground. The bullet gets embedded in the wooden piece after striking. Find the height to which the combination rises above the building before it starts falling. Take $g = 10\text{ m/s}^2$.

[40 m]

(ii) Two balls A and B having different but unknown masses, collide elastically. A is initially at rest when B has a speed v. After collision B has a speed $v/2$ and moves at right angles to its original motion. (a) Find the direction in which ball A moves after collision. (b) Determine the speed of A.

[(a) $\tan^{-1}\left(\frac{1}{2}\right)$ from original direction, (b) $\frac{3v}{2\sqrt{5}}$ if collision is elastic.]

(iii) A ball of mass $m = 1$ kg falling vertically with a velocity $v_0 = 2$ m/s strikes a wedge of mass $M = 2$ kg kept on a smooth, horizontal surface as shown in figure-4.86. The coefficient of resitution between the ball and the wedge is $e = 1/2$. Find the velocity of the wedge and the ball immediately after collision.

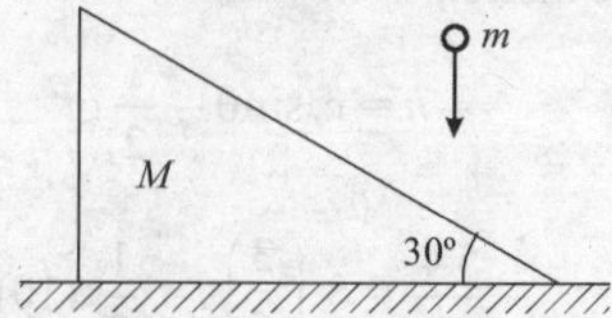

Figure 4.86

[$v_1 = \frac{1}{\sqrt{3}}\text{ ms}^{-1}$, $v_2 = \frac{2}{\sqrt{3}}\text{ ms}^{-1}$]

(iv) A body of mass M with a small box of mass m placed on it rests on a smooth horizontal surface. The box is set in motion in the horizontal direction with a velocity u as shown in figure-4.87. To what height relative to the initial level will the box rise after breaking off from the body M ? Assume all surfaces are frictionless.

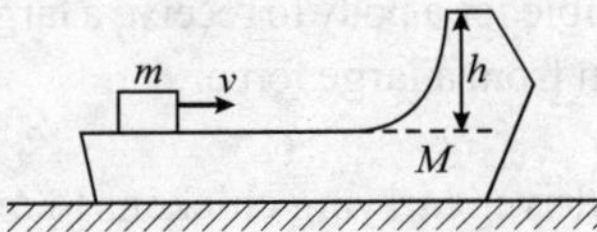

Figure 4.87

$[\frac{Mu^2}{2g(M+m)}]$

(v) Three identical balls each of mass $m = 0.5$ kg are connected with each other as shown in figure-4.88 and rest over a smooth horizontal table. At moment $t = 0$, ball B is imparted a horizontal velocity $v_0 = 9\text{ms}^{-1}$. Calculate velocity of A just before it collides with ball C.

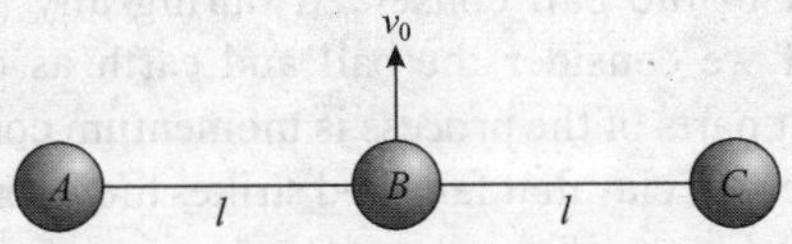

Figure 4.88

[6 ms^{-1}]

(vi) Two particles, each of mass m, are connected by a light inextensible string of length $2l$. Initially they lie on a smooth horizontal table at points A and B distant l apart. The particle at A is projected across the table with velocity u. Find the speed with which the second particle begins to move if the direction of u is :

(a) along BA,

(b) at an angle of 120° with AB

(c) perpendicular to AB.

In each case also calculate (in terms of m and u) the impulsive tension in the string.

[(a) $\frac{u}{2}$, $\frac{mu}{2}$; (b) $\frac{u\sqrt{13}}{8}$, $\frac{mu\sqrt{13}}{8}$; (c) $\frac{u\sqrt{3}}{4}$, $\frac{mu\sqrt{3}}{4}$]

(vii) A sphere of mass m_1 in motion hits directly another sphere of mass m_2 at rest and sticks to it, the total kinetic energy after collision is 2/3 of their total K.E. before collision. Find the ratio of $m_1 : m_2$.

[2 : 1]

---

* * * * *

Discussion Question

Q4-1 "A helium filled balloon has more potential energy at higher altitudes". Is the statement correct? Explain.

Q4-2 In head on collision of equal masses, the velocities are interchanged. Can velocities in a head on collision be interchanged if the masses are not equal ?

Q4-3 Explain why an egg thrown against a wall will break, while an egg thrown against a loose vertical sheet will not.

Q4-4 When a balloon filled with air released so that the air escapes, the balloon shoots off into the air. Explain. Would the same happen if the balloon were released in a vacuum ?

Q4-5 Does doubling the thrust of a rocket by doubling the rate at which mass is thrown backward double the final speed of the rocket ? Why or why not ?

Q4-6 A baseball player has a nightmare. He is accidentally locked in a railroad boxcar. Fortunately, he has his ball and bat along. To start the car moving, he stands at one end and bats the ball toward the other end. The impulse exerted by the ball as it hits the end wall, gives the car a forward motion. Since the ball always rebounds and rolls along the floor back to him, the player repeats this process over and over. Eventually the car attains a very high speed, and the player is killed as the boxcar collides with another car sitting at rest on the track. Analyze this dream and the physics concepts involved in it.

Q4-7 Can the coefficient of restitution ever be greater than 1 ?

Q4-8 Explain, on the basis of conservation of momentum, how a fish propels itself forward using its tail.

Q4-9 The shorter the impact time of an impulse, the greater the force must be for the same momentum change and hence the greater the deformation of the object on which the force acts. Explain on this basis the value of "*air bags*" which are intended to inflate during an automobile collision and reduce the possibility of fracture or death.

Q4-10 A man stretches a spring attached to the front wall of railway carriage over a distance l in a uniformly moving train. During this time the train covers a distance L. Does the work done by the man depend on the coordinate system related to the earth or the train ? The man moves opposite to the direction of motion of the train as he stretches the spring.

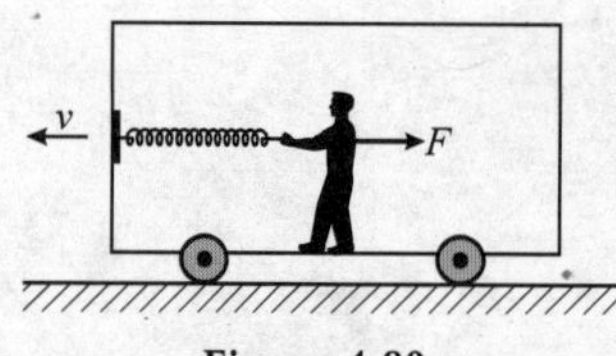

Figure 4.89

Q4-11 Is it possible for a body to receive a larger impulse from a small force than from a large force.

Q4-12 A truck driver carrying chickens to market is stopped at a weighing station. He bangs on the side of the truck to frighten the chickens so that they will fly up and make the truck lighter. Will his scheme work ? Does it make any difference if the truck is open or closed ? Explain.

Q4-13 A ball dropped onto a hard floor has a downward momentum, and after it rebounds, its momentum is upward. The ball's momentum is not conserved in the collision. Explain.

Q4-14 A ball is dropped from a height h onto a hard floor, from which it rebounds at very nearly its original speed. Is the momentum of the ball conserved during any part of this process ? If we consider the ball and earth as our system, during what parts of the process is momentum conserved ? If we use a piece of clay that falls and strikes the floor, then what will be the answers of previous questions.

Q4-15 Sometimes when extinguishing a fire on a burning ship, a fireboat will have some of its nozzles pointing away from the fire. Why ?

Q4-16 A rocket following a parabolic path through the air suddenly explodes into many pieces. What can you say about the motion of this system of pieces ?

Q4-17 A gum ball is shot at a block of wood. In which case does the gum exert the larger impulse on the block, when it sticks or when it rebounds ?

Q4-18 When the supporting stick S is jerked out from the apparatus shown in figure. The board falls down about the hinged end H. The ball B is caught by the cup C. Explain how the cup C can reach the ground before the ball, even though the ball is in free fall.

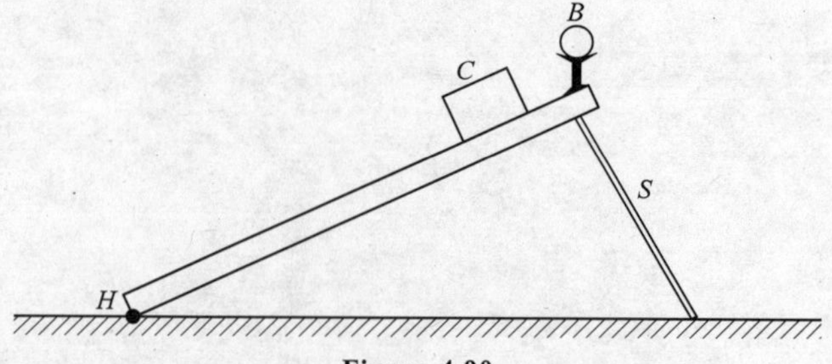

Figure 4.90

Q4-19 If only an external force can change the momentum of the centre of mass of an object, how can the internal force of an engine accelerate a car ?

Q4-20 It is said that in ancient times a rich man with a bag of gold coins was frozen to death stranded on the surface of a frozen lake. Because the ice was frictionless, he could not push himself to shore. What could he have done to save himself, had he not been so miserly ?

Q4-21 Discuss the possibility of a particular type of collision in which the particles have more kinetic energy after the collision than before. It is known as super elastic collision. Will momentum remain conserved in such a collision.

Q4-22 In a collision between two cars, which would you expect to be more damaging to the occupants, if the cars collide and remain together, or if the two rebound backward ? Explain.

Q4-23 The velocity of a bullet fired from a rifle held against the shooter's shoulder is measured very carefully. The rifle is then clamped to a massive rock so that it has no measurable recoil. How does that affect the velocity of the bullet ?

Q4-24 A high jumper clears the bar successfully. Is it possible that his centre of mass crossed the bar from below it.

Q4-25 Most of the skid marks left at the scene of an automobile accident are left by the car tires after the collision occurs. How can measuring the direction and length of these skid marks after the collision reveal whether either of the cars involved was speeding before the collision ?

Q4-26 In a head on collision between two particles, is it necessary that the particles will acquire a common velocity at least for one instant ? In oblique collision ?

Q4-27 In the early age of rocket motion it was assumed by many people that a rocket would not work in outer space because there was no air for the exhaust gases to push against. Explain why the rocket does work in outer space.

Q4-28 An hourglass with a valve that starts the flow of sand is being weighed on a sensitive balance. Compare the momentum of the sand before the valve is turned, when sand is being dropped in a steady stream from the upper to the lower half, and when all the sand is in the bottom. What are the scale readings at these three times. Does the scale read differently when the momentum of the sand is changing ?

Q4-29 A massive sphere is fitted on to a light rod. When will the rod fall faster, if it is placed vertically on end A or end B ? The end of the rod on the ground does not slip.

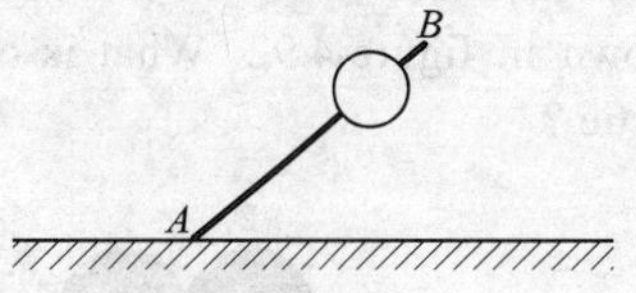

Figure 4.91

Q4-30 Explain on the basis of impulse equation, why it is unwise to hold your legs rigidly straight when you jump to the ground from a wall. How is this related to the commonly held belief that a drunken person has less chance of being injured in a fall than one who is sober ?

* * * * *

Conceptual MCQs Single Option Correct

4-1 A rocket works on the principle of conservation of :
(A) Mass (B) Kinetic energy
(C) Linear momentum (D) Angular momentum

4-2 Choose the only incorrect statement from the following :
(A) The position of the centre of mass of a system of particles does not depend upon the internal forces between particles.
(B) The centre of mass of a solid may lie outside the body of the solid.
(C) A body tied to a string is whirled in a circle with a uniform speed. If the string is suddenly cut, the angular momentum of the body will not change from its initial value.
(D) The angular momentum of a comet revolving around a massive star, remains constant over the entire orbit.

4-3 Two identical balls marked 2 and 3, in contact with each other and at rest on a horizontal frictionless table, are hit head-on by another identical ball marked 1 moving initially with a speed v as shown in figure-4.92. What is observed, if the collision is elastic ?

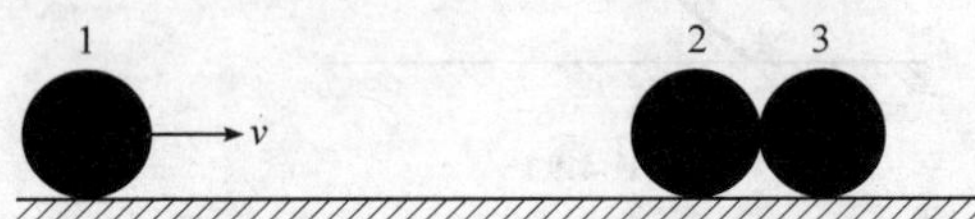

Figure 4.92

(A) Ball 1 comes to rest and balls 2 and 3 roll out with speed $\frac{v}{2}$ each
(B) Balls 1 and 2 come to rest and ball 3 rolls out with speed v
(C) Balls 1, 2 and 3 roll out with speed $\frac{v}{3}$ each
(D) Balls 1, 2 and 3 come to rest

4-4 Which one of the following is true in the case of inelastic collisions ?

	Total Energy	*Kinetic Energy*	*Momentum*
(A)	conserved	conserved	conserved
(B)	conserved	not conserved	conserved
(C)	conserved	conserved	not conserved
(D)	not conserved	not conserved	conserved

4-5 A ball is dropped from a height of 10 m. It is embedded 1 m in sand and stops. In this process :
(A) Only momentum is conserved
(B) Only kinetic energy is conserved
(C) Both momentum and kinetic energy are conserved
(D) Neither momentum nor kinetic energy is conserved

4-6 A bullet is fired from a rifle which recoils after firing. The ratio of the kinetic energy of the rifle to that of the bullet is :
(A) Zero (B) One
(C) Less than one (D) More than one

4-7 A moving bullet hits a solid target resting on a frictionless surface and gets embedded in it. What is conserved in this process ?
(A) Momentum and kinetic energy
(B) Kinetic energy alone
(C) Momentum alone
(D) Neither momentum nor kinetic energy

4-8 Two balls marked 1 and 2 of the same mass m and a third ball marked 3 of mass M are arranged over a smooth horizontal surface as shown in figure-4.93. Ball 1 moves with a velocity v_1 towards ball 2 and 3. All collisions are assumed to be elastic. If $M < m$, the number of collisions between the balls will be :

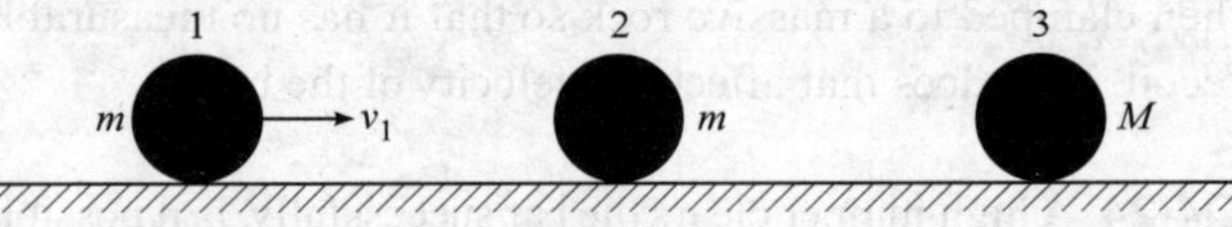

Figure 4.93

(A) One (B) Two
(C) Three (D) Four

4-9 In Q. No.4-8, if $M > m$, the number of collisions between the balls will be :
(A) One (B) Two
(C) Three (D) Four

4-10 Four particles, each of mass m, are placed at corners of a square of side a in the x-y plane. If the origin of the co-ordinate system is taken at the point of intersection of the diagonals of the square, the co-ordinates of the centre of mass of the system are :
(A) (a, a) (B) $(-a, a)$
(C) $(a, -a)$ (D) $(0, 0)$

4-11 Which one of the following statements is correct with reference to elastic collision between two bodies?
(A) Momentum and total energy are conserved but kinetic energy may be changed into some other form of energy
(B) Kinetic energy and total energy are both conserved but momentum is only if the two bodies have equal masses
(C) Momentum, kinetic energy and total energy are all conserved
(D) Neither momentum nor kinetic energy need be conserved but total energy must be conserved.

4-12 "The velocities in a head on elastic collision be interchanged" :
(A) If masses are equal only
(B) It may be possible if masses are not equal.
(C) It is always possible
(D) It is never possible

4-13 A body of mass m moves in a horizontal circle of radius r at contact speed v. Which pair of values correctly gives :

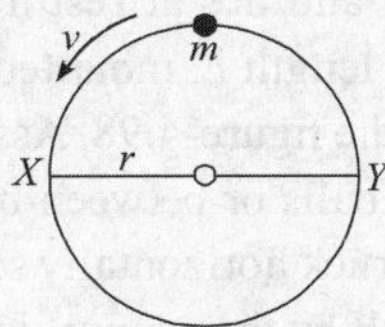

Figure 4.94

(i) the work done by the centripetal force,
(ii) the change in linear momentum of the body, when it moves from X to Y (where XY is a diameter) ?

	(i)	(ii)
(A)	$2mv^2$	$2mv$
(B)	πmv^2	$2mv$
(C)	0	0
(D)	0	$2mv$

4-14 For a particle moving in a horizontal circle with constant angular velocity :
(A) The linear momentum is constant but the energy varies
(B) The energy is constant but the linear momentum varies
(C) Both energy and linear momentum are constant
(D) Neither the linear momentum nor the energy is constant.

4-15 In a system of particles, internal forces can change :
(A) The linear momentum but not the kinetic energy
(B) The kinetic energy but not the linear momentum
(C) Linear momentum as well as kinetic energy
(D) Neither the linear momentum nor the kinetic energy

4-16 Three particles each of mass m are located at the vertices of an equilateral triangle ABC. They start moving with equal speeds v each along the medians of the triangle & collide at its centroid G. If after collision, A comes to rest and B retraces its path along GB, then C :
(A) Also comes to rest
(B) Moves with a speed v along CG
(C) Moves with a speed v along BG
(D) Moves with a speed along AG

4-17 A ball kept in a closed box moves in the box making collisions with the walls. The box is kept on a smooth surface. The velocity of the centre of mass :
(A) Of the box remains constant
(B) Of the box plus the ball system remains constant
(C) Of the ball remains constant
(D) Of the ball relative to the box remains constant.

4-18 A strip of wood of length l is placed on a smooth horizontal surface. An insect starts from one end of the strip, walks with constant velocity and reaches the other end in time t_1. It then flies off vertically. The strip moves a further distance l in time t_2:
(A) $t_2 = t_1$
(B) $t_2 < t_1$
(C) $t_2 > t_1$
(D) Either (B) or (C) depending on the masses of the insect and the strip

4-19 The centre of mass of a system of particle is at the origin. It follows that :
(A) The number of particle to the right of the origin is equal to the number of particle to the left
(B) The total mass of the particles to the right of the origin is same as the total mass to the left of the origin
(C) The number of particle on X-axis should be equal to the number of particles on Y-axis
(D) None of these

4-20 Six identical marbles are lined up in a straight groove made on a horizontal frictionless surface as shown in figure-4.95. Two similar marbles each moving with a velocity v collide with the row of 6 marbles from the left. What is observed ?

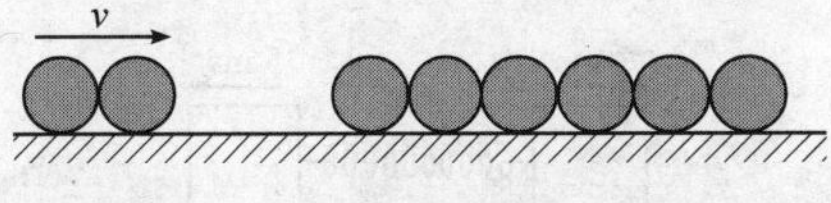

Figure 4.95

(A) One marble from the right rolls out with a speed $2v$, the remaining marbles do not move
(B) Two marbles from the right roll out with a speed v each, the remaining marbles do not move
(C) All six marbles in the row will roll out with a speed $v/6$ each, the two incident marbles will come to rest
(D) All eight marbles will start moving to the right, each with a speed of $v/8$

4-21 n small balls, each of mass m, impinge elastically each second on a surface with velocity u. The force experienced by the surface will be :
(A) mnu (B) $2\,mnu$
(C) $4\,mnu$ (D) $\frac{1}{2}\,mnu$

4-22 The bob A of a pendulum released from a height h hits head-on another bob B of the same mass of an identical pendulum initially at rest. What is the result of this collision ? Assume the collision to be elastic (see figure-4.96) :

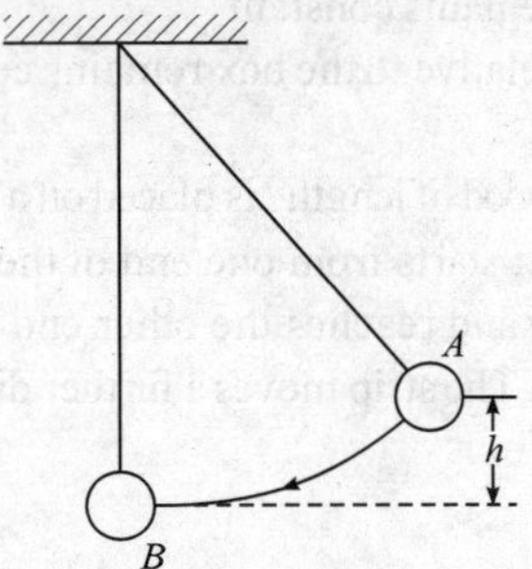

Figure 4.96

(A) Bob A comes to rest at B and bob B moves to the left attaining a maximum height h

(B) Bobs A and B both move to the left, each attaining a maximum height $\frac{h}{2}$

(C) Bob B moves to the left and bob A moves to the right, each attaining a maximum height $\frac{h}{2}$

(D) Both bobs come to rest

4-23 Two identical blocks each of mass 1 kg are joined together with a compressed spring. When the system is released from rest the two blocks appear to be moving with unequal speeds in the opposite direction as shown in figure-4.97. Choose the correct statements (s) :

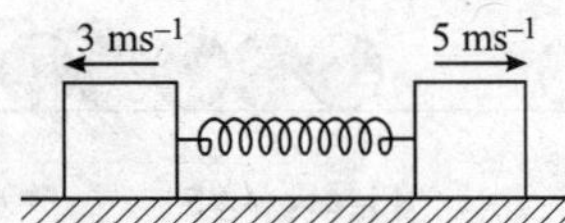

Figure 4.97

(A) It is not possible

(B) Whatever may be the speed of the blocks the centre of mass will remain stationary

(C) The centre of mass of the system is moving with a velocity of 2 ms^{-1}

(D) The centre of mass of the system is moving with a velocity of 1 ms^{-1}

4-24 A nucleus moving with a velocity $\vec{v}$ emits an α-particle. Let the velocity of the α-particle and the remaining nucleus be $\vec{v}_1$ and $\vec{v}_2$ and their masses be m_1 and m_2 :

(A) $\vec{v}$, $\vec{v}_1$ and $\vec{v}_2$ must be parallel to each other

(B) None of the two of $\vec{v}$, $\vec{v}_1$ and $\vec{v}_2$ should be parallel to each other.

(C) $\vec{v}_1 + \vec{v}_2$ must be parallel to $\vec{v}$

(D) $m_1\vec{v}_1 + m_2\vec{v}_2$ must be parallel to $\vec{v}$

4-25 A uniform sphere is placed on a smooth horizontal surface and a horizontal force F is applied on it at a distance h above the surface. The acceleration of the centre :

(A) Is maximum when $h = 0$

(B) Is maximum when $h = R$

(C) Is maximum when $h = 2R$

(D) Is independent of h

4-26 Five identical balls each of mass m and radius r are strung like beads at random and are at rest along a smooth, rigid horizontal thin rod of length L, mounted between immovable supports as shown in the figure-4.98. Assume $10r < L$ and that the collision between balls or between balls and supports are elastic. If one ball is struck horizontally so as to acquire a speed v, the average force felt by the support is:

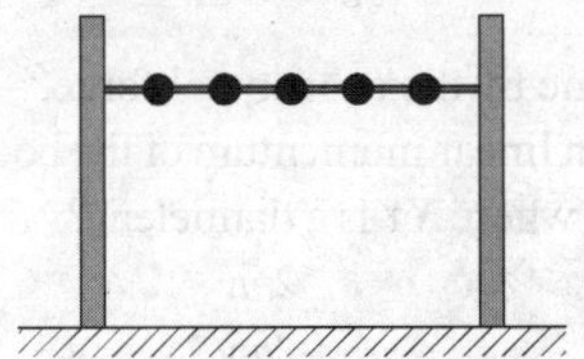

Figure 4.98

(A) $\frac{5mv^2}{L-5r}$ (B) $\frac{mv^2}{L-10r}$

(C) $\frac{5mv^2}{L-10r}$ (D) $\frac{mv^2}{L-5r}$

Paragraph for Question Nos. 27 to 28

A large heavy sphere and a small light sphere are dropped onto a flat surface from a height h. The radius of spheres is much smaller than height h. The large sphere collides with the surface with velocity v_0 and immediately thereafter with the small sphere. The spheres are dropped so that all motion is vertical before the second collision, and the small sphere hits the larger sphere at an angle α from its uppermost point, as shown in the diagram. All collisions are perfectly elastic and there is no surface friction between the spheres.

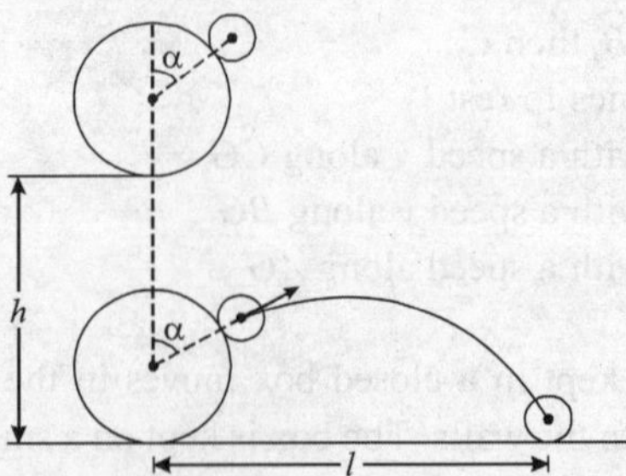

Figure 4.99

4-27 The angle made by velocity vector of small sphere with the vertical just after the second collision in the frame of large sphere :

(A) α (B) 2α

(C) $3\alpha/2$ (D) zero

4-28 Find the vertical velocity of smaller sphere just after the collision with respect to ground :

(A) $2v_0 \cos\alpha$ (B) $2v_0 \cos 2\alpha + v_0$

(C) $v_0 \cos\alpha + v_0$ (D) $v_0 \cos 2\alpha + v_0$

4-29 The end of a chain of length L and mass per unit length ρ, which is piled up on a horizontal platform is lifted vertically with a constant velocity u by a variable force F. Find F as a function of height x of the end above platform :

(A) $\rho(gx + 2u^2)$ (B) $\rho(2gx + \rho u^2)$

(C) $\rho(gx + u^2)$ (D) $\rho(u^2 - gx)$

4-30 Which of the following is correct about principle of conservation of momentum?

(A) Conservation of momentum can be applied only in absence of external forces

(B) Conservation of momentum can be applied only during collisions of bodies

(C) Conservation of momentum can be applied in a process even in the presence of external forces

(D) Conservation of momentum is not applicable in rocket propulsion

4-31 A car C of mass m is initially at rest on the boat A of mass M tied to the identical boat B of same, mass m through a massless inextensible string as shown in the figure-4.100. The car accelerates from rest to velocity v_0 with respect to boat A in time t_0 sec. At time $t = t_0$ the car applies brake and comes to rest relative to boat in negligible time. Neglect friction between boat and water find the velocity of boat A just after applying brake

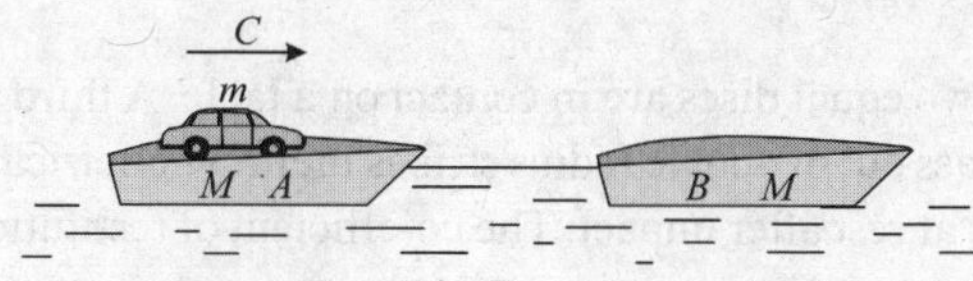

Figure 4.100

(A) $\dfrac{Mmv_0}{(2M+m)(M+m)}$ (B) $\dfrac{Mmv_0}{(M+2m)(M+m)}$

(C) $\dfrac{2Mmv_0}{(M+2m)(M+m)}$ (D) zero

4-32 A body is fired from point P and strikes at Q inside a smooth circular wall as shown in the figure-4.101. It rebounds to point S (diametrically opposite to P). The coefficient of restitution will be :

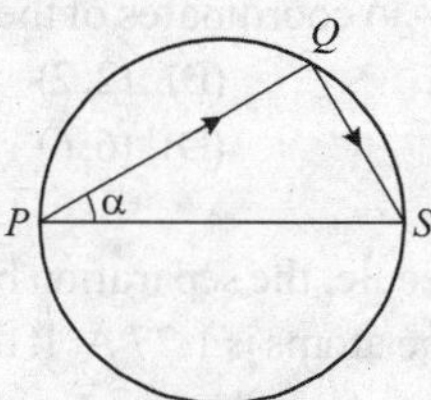

Figure 4.101

(A) $\cot\alpha$ (B) 1

(C) $\tan\alpha$ (D) $\tan^2\alpha$

4-33 A fixed U-shaped smooth wire has a semi-circular bending m between A and B as shown in the figure-4.102. A bead of mass 'm' moving with uniform speed v through the wire enters the semicircular bend at A and leaves at B. The magnitude of average B force exerted by the bead on the part AB of the wire is :

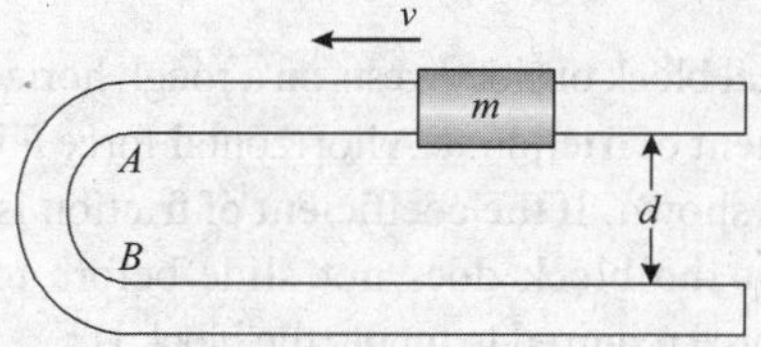

Figure 4.102

(A) 0 (B) $\dfrac{4mv^2}{\pi d}$

(C) $\dfrac{2mv^2}{\pi d}$ (D) None of these

4-34 A collision occurs between two identical balls each of mass m, moving with velocities $\vec{u}_1$ and $\vec{u}_2$, colliding head-on. The coefficient of restitution is 0.5. The energy lost in the collision is :

(A) $\dfrac{1}{4}m(\vec{u}_1 + \vec{u}_2)^2$ (B) $\dfrac{1}{4}m(\vec{u}_1 - \vec{u}_2)^2$

(C) $\dfrac{3}{16}m(\vec{u}_1 + \vec{u}_2)^2$ (D) $\dfrac{3}{16}m(\vec{u}_1 - \vec{u}_2)^2$

* * * * *

Numerical MCQs Single Options Correct

4-1 Three particles of the same mass lie in the $x-y$ plane. The (x, y) coordinates of their positions are (1, 1), (2, 2) and (3, 3) respectively. The $(x-y)$ coordinates of the centre of mass are :

(A) (1, 2) (B) (2, 2)
(C) (4, 2) (D) (6, 6)

4-2 In the HCl molecule, the separation between the nuclei of hydrogen and chlorine atoms is 1.27 Å. If the mass of a chlorine atom is 35.5 times that of a hydrogen atom, the centre of mass of the HCl molecule is at a distance of :

(A) $\frac{35.5\times1.27}{36.6}$ Å from the hydrogen atom

(B) $\frac{35.5\times1.27}{36.6}$ Å from the chlorine atom

(C) $\frac{1.27}{36.6}$ Å A from the hydrogen atom

(D) $\frac{1.27}{36.6}$ Å from the chlorine atom

4-3 A cubical block of side L rests on a rough horizontal surface with coefficient of friction μ. A horizontal force F is applied on the block as shown. If the coefficient of friction is sufficiently high so that the block does not slide before toppling, the minimum force required to topple the block is :

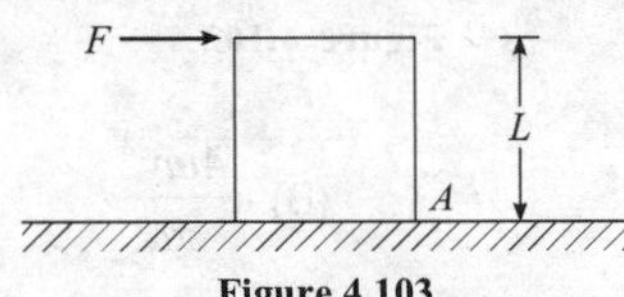

Figure 4.103

(A) Infinitesimal (B) $mg/4$
(C) $mg/2$ (D) $mg(1-\mu)$

4-4 A boy of mass m stands on one end of a wooden plank of length L and mass M. The plank is floating on water. If the boy walks from one end of the plank to the other end at a constant speed, the resulting displacement of the plank is given by :

(A) $\frac{mL}{M}$ (B) $\frac{ML}{m}$

(C) $\frac{mL}{(M-m)}$ (D) $\frac{mL}{(M+m)}$

4-5 A neutron moving at a speed v undergoes a head-on elastic collision with a nucleus of mass number A at rest. The ratio of the kinetic energies of the neutron after and before collision is :

(A) $\left(\frac{A-1}{A+1}\right)^2$ (B) $\left(\frac{A+1}{A-1}\right)^2$

(C) $\left(\frac{A}{A+1}\right)^2$ (D) $\left(\frac{A}{A-1}\right)^2$

4-6 A wooden block of mass 0.9 kg is suspended from the ceiling of a room by thin wires. A bullet of mass 0.1 kg moving horizontally with a speed of 10 ms^{-1} strikes the block and sticks to it. What is the height to which the block rises ? Take $g = 10\ ms^{-2}$:

(A) 2.5 m (B) 5.0 m
(C) 7.5 m (D) 10.0 m

4-7 In Q. No. 4-6, what is the loss in kinetic energy of the system due to impact ?

(A) 450 J (B) 400 J
(C) 350 J (D) 300 J

4-8 A shell of mass 2 m fired with a speed u at an angle θ to the horizontal explodes at the highest point of its trajectory into two fragments of mass m each. If one fragment falls vertically, the distance at which the other fragment falls from the gun is given by :

(A) $\frac{u^2 \sin 2\theta}{g}$ (B) $\frac{3u^2 \sin 2\theta}{2g}$

(C) $\frac{2u^2 \sin 2\theta}{g}$ (D) $\frac{3u^2 \sin 2\theta}{g}$

4-9 A rubber ball is dropped from a height of 5 m on a planet where the acceleration due to gravity is not known. On bouncing it rises to 1.8 m. The ball loses its velocity on bouncing by a factor of :

(A) $\frac{16}{25}$ (B) $\frac{2}{5}$

(C) $\frac{3}{5}$ (D) $\frac{9}{2}$

4-10. Two equal discs are in contact on a table. A third disc of same mass but of double radius strikes them symmetrically and remains at rest after impact. The co-efficient of restitution is :

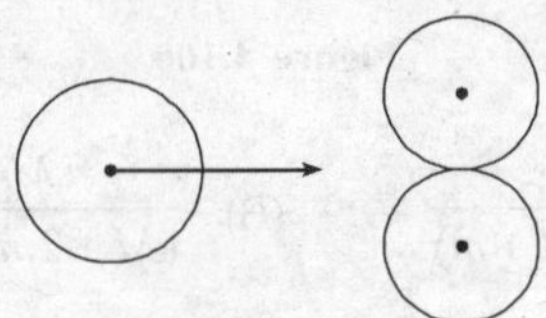

Figure 4.104

(A) $\frac{2}{3}$ (B) $\frac{1}{3}$

(C) $\frac{9}{16}$ (D) $\frac{\sqrt{3}}{2}$

4-11 A neutron mass 1.67×10^{-27} kg moving with a velocity 1.2×10^{7} ms^{-1} collides head-on with a deuteron of mass 3.34×10^{-27} kg initially at rest. If the collision is perfectly inelastic, the speed of the composite particle will be :

(A) 2×10^{6} ms^{-1} (B) 4×10^{6} ms^{-1}
(C) 6×10^{6} ms^{-1} (D) 8×10^{6} ms^{-1}

4-12 In Q. No. 4-11, if the collision were perfectly elastic, what would be the speed of deuteron after the collision ?

(A) 2×10^{6} ms^{-1} (B) 4×10^{6} ms^{-1}
(C) 6×10^{6} ms^{-1} (D) 8×10^{6} ms^{-1}

4-13 A loaded spring gun of mass M fires a 'shot' of mass m with a velocity v at an angle of elevation θ. The gun is initially at rest on a horizontal frictionless surface. After firing, the centre of mass of the gun-shot system :

(A) Moves with a velocity $v\, m/M$

(B) Moves with velocity $\frac{vm}{M}\cos\theta$ in the horizontal direction

(C) Remains at rest

(D) Moves with a velocity $\frac{vm\sin\theta}{M}$ in the vertical direction

4-14 A shell of mass m is at rest initially. It explodes into three fragments having masses in the ratio 2 : 2 : 1. The fragments having equal masses fly off along mutually perpendicular directions with speed v. What will be the speed of the third (lighter) fragment ?

(A) v (B) $\sqrt{2}v$
(C) $2\sqrt{2}v$ (D) $3\sqrt{2}v$

4-15 A ball P of mass 2 kg undergoes an elastic collision with another ball Q at rest. After collision, ball P continues to move in its original direction with a speed one-fourth of its original speed. What is the mass of ball Q ?

(A) 0.9 kg (B) 1.2 kg
(C) 1.5 kg (D) 1.8 kg

4-16 A rocket, set for vertical launching, has a mass of 50 kg and contains 450 kg of fuel. It can have a maximum exhaust speed of 2 km s^{-1}. If $g = 10$ ms^{-2}, what should be the minimum rate of fuel consumption to just lift it off the launching pad ?

(A) 2.5 kg s^{-1} (B) 5 kg s^{-1}
(C) 7.5 kg s^{-1} (D) 10 kg s^{-1}

4-17 In Q. No. 4-16, what should be the minimum rate of fuel consumption to give an initial acceleration of 20 ms^{-2} to the rocket ?

(A) 2.5 kg s^{-1} (B) 5 kg s^{-1}
(C) 7.5 kg s^{-1} (D) 10 kg s^{-1}

4-18 A bullet of mass 50 g is fired by a gun of mass 5 kg. If the muzzle speed of the bullet is 200 ms^{-1}, what is the recoil speed of the gun ?

(A) 1 ms^{-1} (B) 2 ms^{-1}
(C) 3 ms^{-1} (D) 4 ms^{-1}

4-19 A particle is projected with a velocity 200 m/s at an angle of 60º. At the highest point, it explodes into three particles of equal masses. One goes vertically upwards with a velocity 100 m/s, the second particle goes vertically downwards at same speed. What is the velocity of the third particle ?

(A) 120 m/s with 60º angle (B) 200 m/s with 30º angle
(C) 200 m/s horizontally (D) 300 m/s horizontally

4-20 A hockey player receives a corner shot at a speed of 15 m/s at an angle of 30º with the y-axis and then shoots the ball along the x-axis with a speed of 30 m/s. If the mass of the ball is 100 gm and it remains in contact with the hockey stick for 0.01 s, the force imparted to the ball in the x-direction is :

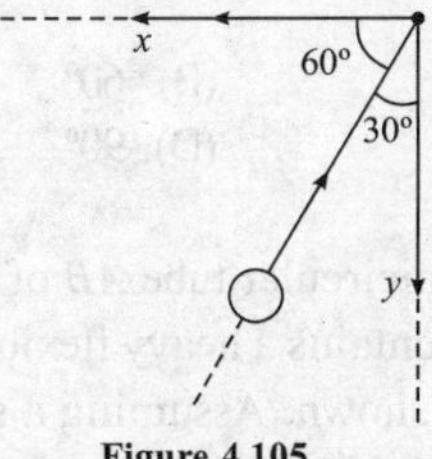

Figure 4.105

(A) 281.25 N (B) 187.5 N
(C) 562.5 N (D) 375 N

4-21 A shell is fired from a cannon with a speed of 100 ms^{-1} at an angle 60º with the horizontal (x-direction). At the highest point of its trajectory, the shell explodes into two equal fragments. One of the fragments moves along the negative x-direction with a speed of 50 ms^{-1}. What is the speed of the other fragment at the time of explosion ?

(A) 150 ms^{-1} (B) 50 ms^{-1}
(C) 100 ms^{-1} (D) 200 ms^{-1}

4-22 Four particles of masses 1 kg, 2 kg, 3 kg and 4 kg are placed at the corners of a square of side 2 m in the $x-y$ plane. If the origin of the co-ordinate system is taken at the mass of 1 kg, the (x, y) co-ordinates of the enter of mass, expressed in metre are :

(A) $\left(1, \frac{7}{5}\right)$ (B) $\left(2, \frac{7}{5}\right)$

(C) $\left(3, \frac{7}{5}\right)$ (D) $\left(4, \frac{7}{5}\right)$

4-23 A child is standing at one end of a long trolley moving with a speed v on a smooth horizontal track. If the child starts running towards the other end of the trolley with a speed u, the centre of mass of the system (trolley + child) will move with a speed :

(A) Zero (B) $(v+u)$
(C) $(v-u)$ (D) v

4-24 A blacksmith carries a hammer on his shoulder and holds it at the other end of its light handle in his hand. If he changes the point of support of the handle and x is the distance between the point of support and his hand, then the pressure on his hand varies with x as :

(A) x (B) x^2
(C) $\frac{1}{x}$ (D) $\frac{1}{x^2}$

4-25 A ball of mass m moving with a velocity v undergoes an oblique elastic collision with another ball of the same mass m but at rest. After the collision, if the two balls move with the same speeds, the angle between their directions of motion will be :

(A) 30º (B) 60º
(C) 120º (D) 90º

4-26 A smooth semicircular tube AB of radius r is fixed in a vertical plane and contains a heavy flexible chain of length πr and weight $W\pi r$ as shown. Assuming a slight disturbance to start the chain in motion, the velocity v with which it will emerge from the open end B of the tube is :

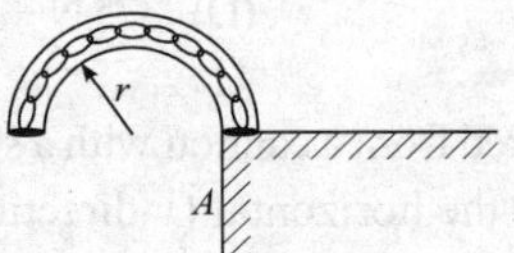

Figure 4.106

(A) $\frac{4gr}{\pi}$ (B) $\frac{2gr}{\pi}$
(C) $\sqrt{2gr\left(\frac{2}{\pi}+\pi\right)}$ (D) $\sqrt{2gr\left(\frac{2}{\pi}+\frac{\pi}{2}\right)}$

4-27 A ball of mass m moving horizontally at a speed v collides with the bob of a simple pendulum at rest. The mass of the bob is also m. If the collision is perfectly inelastic and both balls sticks, the height to which the two balls rise after the collision will be given by :

(A) $\frac{v^2}{g}$ (B) $\frac{v^2}{2g}$
(C) $\frac{v^2}{4g}$ (D) $\frac{v^2}{8g}$

4-28 In Q. No. 4-27, the ratio of the kinetic energy of the system immediately after the collision to that before the collision will be:

(A) 1 : 1 (B) 1 : 2
(C) 1 : 3 (D) 1 : 4

4-29 In Q. No. 4-27, if the collision is perfectly elastic, the bob of the pendulum will rise to a height of :

(A) $\frac{v^2}{g}$ (B) $\frac{v^2}{2g}$
(C) $\frac{v^2}{4g}$ (D) $\frac{v^2}{8g}$

4-30 If a man of mass M jumps to the ground from a height h and his centre of mass moves a distance x in the time taken by him to 'hit' the ground, the average force acting on him (assuming his retardation to be constant during his impact with the ground) is :

(A) $Mg\,h/x$ (B) $Mg\,x/h$
(C) $Mg\,(h/x)^2$ (D) $Mg\,(x/h)^2$

4-31 A radioactive nucleus of mass number A, initially at rest, emits an α-particle with a speed v. What will be the recoil speed of the daughter nucleus ?

(A) $\frac{2v}{A-4}$ (B) $\frac{2v}{A+4}$
(C) $\frac{4v}{A-4}$ (D) $\frac{4v}{A+4}$

4-32 A cart of mass M is tied at one end of a massless rope of length 10 m. The other end of the rope is in the hands of a man of mass M. The entire system is on a smooth horizontal surface. The man is at $x = 0$ and the cart at $x = 10$ m. If the man pulls the cart by the rope, the man and the cart will meet at a point :

(A) $x = 0$ (B) $x = 5$ m
(C) $x = 10$ m (D) They will never meet

4-33 A shell explodes into three fragments of equal masses. Two fragments fly off at right angles to each other with speed of 9 ms^{-1} and 12 ms^{-1}. What is the speed of the third fragment?

(A) 9 ms^{-1} (B) 12 ms^{-1}
(C) 15 ms^{-1} (D) 18 ms^{-1}

4-34 Four particles of masses m, m, 2 m and 2 m are placed at the four corners of a square of side a as shown in figure-4.107. The (x, y) coordinates of the centre of mass are :

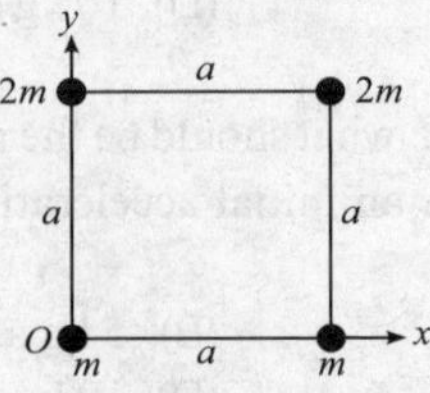

Figure 4.107

(A) $\left(\frac{a}{2}, 2a\right)$ (B) $\left(\frac{a}{2}, a\right)$

(C) $\left(\frac{a}{2}, \frac{2a}{3}\right)$ (D) $\left(a, \frac{a}{3}\right)$

4-35 A small coin is placed at a distance r from the centre of a gramophone record. The rotational speed of the record is gradually increased. If the coefficient of friction between the coin and the record is μ, the minimum angular frequency of the record for which the coin will fly off is given by :

(A) $\sqrt{\frac{2\mu g}{r}}$ (B) $\sqrt{\frac{\mu g}{2r}}$

(C) $\sqrt{\frac{\mu g}{r}}$ (D) $2\sqrt{\frac{\mu g}{r}}$

4-36 Sphere A of mass 'm' moving with a constant velocity u hits another stationary sphere B of the same mass. If e is the co-efficient of restitution, then ratio of velocities of the two spheres $v_A : v_B$ after collision will be :

(A) $\frac{1-e}{1+e}$ (B) $\frac{1+e}{1-e}$

(C) $\frac{e-1}{1-e}$ (D) $\frac{e-1}{1+e}$

4-37 A smooth sphere is moving on a horizontal surface with velocity vector $3\hat{i}+\hat{j}$ immediately before it hits a vertical wall. The wall is parallel to the vector $\hat{j}$ and the coefficient of restitution between the wall and the sphere is 1/3. The velocity vector of the sphere after it hits the wall is :

(A) $3\hat{i}-\frac{1}{3}\hat{j}$ (B) $-\hat{i}+\hat{j}$

(C) $\hat{i}-\hat{j}$ (D) $-\hat{i}-\frac{1}{3}\hat{j}$

4-38 From a point on smooth floor of a room a toy ball is shot to hit a wall. The ball then returns back to the point of projection. If the time taken by ball in returning is twice the time taken in reaching the wall, find the coefficient of restitution :

(A) $e=\frac{1}{2}$ (B) $e=\frac{1}{3}$

(C) $e=\frac{1}{4}$ (D) $e=0.2$

4-39 In the figure-4.108 shown, the heavy ball of mass $2m$ rests on the horizontal surface and the lighter balls of mass m is dropped from a height $h>2l$. At the instant the string gets taut, the upward velocity of the heavy ball will be :

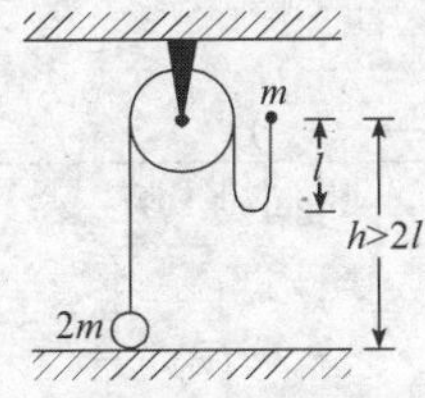

Figure 4.108

(A) $\frac{2}{3}\sqrt{gl}$ (B) $\frac{4}{3}\sqrt{gl}$

(C) $\frac{1}{3}\sqrt{gl}$ (D) $\frac{1}{2}\sqrt{gl}$

4-40 A shell is fired from a cannon with a velocity V at an angle θ with the horizontal direction. At the highest point in its path, it explodes into two pieces of equal masses. One of the pieces retraces its path to the cannon. The speed of the other piece immediately after the explosion is :

(A) $3V\cos\theta$ (B) $2V\cos\theta$

(C) $\frac{3}{2}V\cos\theta$ (D) $V\cos\theta$

4-41 A bullet moving with a velocity u passes through a plank which is free to move. The two are of equal mass. After passing through the plank, the velocity of the bullet becomes fu. Its velocity relative to the plank now is :

(A) fu (B) $(1-f)u$

(C) $(2f-1)u$ (D) $(2-f)u$

4-42 A particle of mass m_1 makes an elastic, one dimensional collision with a stationary particle of mass m_2. What fraction of the kinetic energy of m_1 is carried away by m_2 ?

(A) $\frac{m_1}{m_2}$ (B) $\frac{m_2}{m_1}$

(C) $\frac{2m_1m_2}{(m_1+m_2)^2}$ (D) $\frac{4m_1m_2}{(m_1+m_2)^2}$

4-43 Two balls with masses in the ratio of 1 : 2 moving in opposite direction have a head-on elastic collision. If their velocities before impact were in the ratio of 3 : 1, then velocities after impact will have the ratio :

(A) 5:3 (B) 7:5

(C) 4:5 (D) 2:3

4-44 Two identical balls of equal masses A and B, are lying on a smooth surface as shown in figure-4.109. Ball A hits the ball B (which is at rest) with a velocity $v = 16$ m/s. What should be the minimum value of coefficient of restitution e between A and B so that B just reaches the highest point of inclined plane : (Take $g = 10\ \text{m/s}^2$)

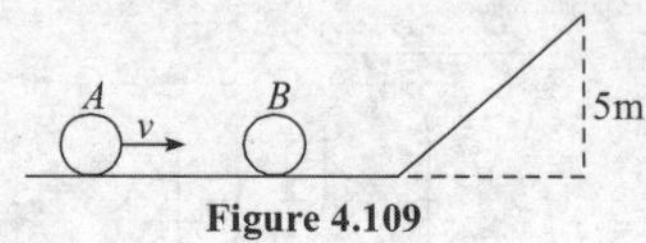

Figure 4.109

(A) $\frac{2}{3}$ (B) $\frac{1}{4}$

(C) $\frac{1}{2}$ (D) $\frac{1}{3}$

4-45 Two blocks of mass m_1 and m_2 are connected by light inextensible string passing over a smooth fixed pulley of negligible mass. The acceleration of the centre of mass of the system when blocks move under gravity is :

(A) $\left(\frac{m_2 - m_1}{m_1 + m_2}\right)g$ (B) $\left(\frac{m_1 + m_2}{m_1 - m_2}\right)g$

(C) $\left(\frac{m_1 + m_2}{m_1 - m_2}\right)g$ (D) $\left(\frac{m_1 - m_2}{m_1 + m_2}\right)^2 g$

4-46 A girl throws a ball with initial velocity v at an inclination of 45°. The ball strikes the smooth vertical wall at a horizontal distance d from girl and after rebounding returns to her hand. What is the co-efficient of restitution between wall and ball ?

(A) $v^2 - gd$ (B) $\frac{gd}{v^2 - gd}$

(C) $\frac{gd}{v^2}$ (D) $\frac{v^2}{gd}$

4-47 A small block of mass m is pushed towards a movable wedge of mass ηm and height h with initial velocity u. All surfaces are smooth. The minimum value of u for which the block will reach the top of the wedge :

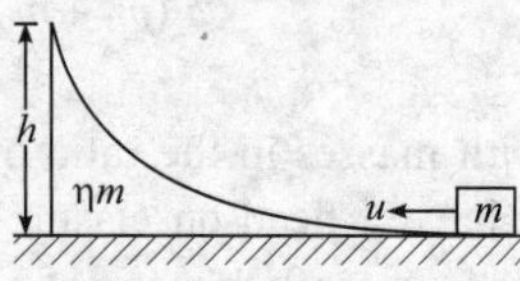

Figure 4.110

(A) $\sqrt{2gh}$ (B) $\eta\sqrt{2gh}$

(C) $\sqrt{2gh\left(1+\frac{1}{\eta}\right)}$ (D) $\sqrt{2gh\left(1-\frac{1}{\eta}\right)}$

4-48 A heavy ring of mass m is clamped on the periphery of a light circular disc. A small particle having equal mass is clamped at the centre of the disc. The system is rotated in such a way that the centre of mass moves in a circle of radius r with a uniform speed v. We conclude that an external force :

(A) $\frac{mv^2}{r}$ must be acting on the central particle

(B) $\frac{2mv^2}{r}$ must be acting on the central particle

(C) $\frac{2mv^2}{r}$ must be acting on the system

(D) $\frac{2mv^2}{r}$ must be acting on the ring.

4-49 A light particle moving horizontally with a speed of 12 m/s strikes a very heavy block moving in the same direction at 10 m/s. The collision is one-dimensional and elastic. After the collision, the particle will :

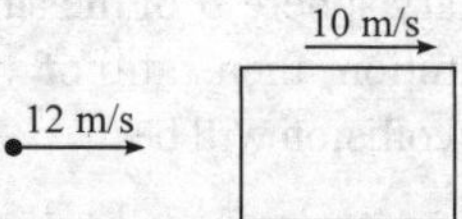

Figure 4.111

(A) Move at 2 m/s in its original direction
(B) Move at 8 m/s in its original direction
(C) Move at 8 m/s opposite to its original direction
(D) Move at 12 m/s opposite to its original direction

4-50 Two particles of masses m_1 and m_2 in projectile motion have velocities $\vec{v}_1$ and $\vec{v}_2$ respectively at time $t = 0$. They collide at time t_0. Their velocities become $\vec{v}_1'$ and $\vec{v}_2'$ at time $2t_0$ while still moving in air. The value of $[(m_1\vec{v}_1' + m_2\vec{v}_2') - (m_1\vec{v}_1 + m_2\vec{v}_2)]$ is :

(A) zero (B) $(m_1 + m_2)gt_0$

(C) $2(m_1 + m_2)gt_0$ (D) $\frac{1}{2}(m_1 + m_2)gt_0$

4-51 A chain of length ($l < 0.5\,\pi R$) placed on a smooth spherical surface of radius R with one of its ends fixed at the top the sphere. The value of tangential acceleration of each element of chain when its upper end is released :

(A) $\frac{Rg}{l}\left(1-\sin\frac{l}{R}\right)$ (B) $\frac{Rg}{l}\left(1-\cos\frac{l}{R}\right)$

(C) $\frac{Rg}{l}\left(1-\tan\frac{l}{R}\right)$ (D) $\frac{Rg}{l}\left(1-\cot\frac{l}{R}\right)$

4-52 A ball is released from a height h_0 above a horizontal surface rebound to a height h_1 after one bounce. The graph that relate h_0 to h_1 is shown below. If the ball (of the mass m)

was dropped from an initial height h and made three bounces, the kinetic energy of the ball immediately after the third impact with the surface was :

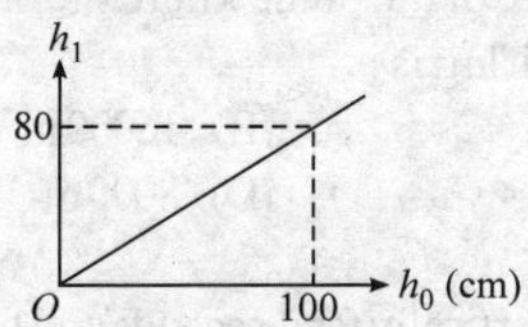

Figure 4.112

(A) $(0.8)^3$ mgh (B) $(0.8)^2$ mgh
(C) 0.8 mg $(h/3)$ (D) $[(1-(0.8)^3 \text{ mgh}]$

4-53 A ball of mass m is released from point A inside a smooth wedge of mass m as shown in figure-4.113. What is the speed of the wedge when the ball reaches point B ?

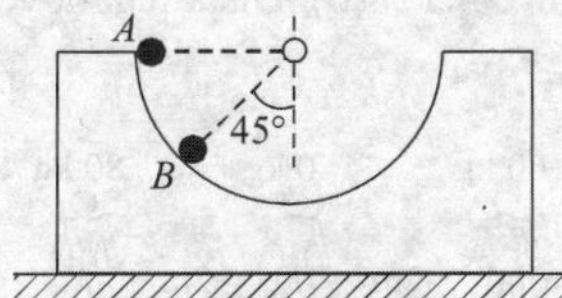

Figure 4.113

(A) $\left(\frac{gR}{3\sqrt{2}}\right)^{1/2}$ (B) $\sqrt{2gR}$

(C) $\left(\frac{5gR}{2\sqrt{3}}\right)^{1/2}$ (D) $\sqrt{\frac{3}{2}gR}$

4-54 Two blocks m_1 and m_2 are pulled on a smooth horizontal surface; and are joined together with a spring of stiffness k as shown in the figure-4.114. Suddenly, the block m_2 receives a horizontal velocity v_0, then the maximum extension x_{max} in the spring is :

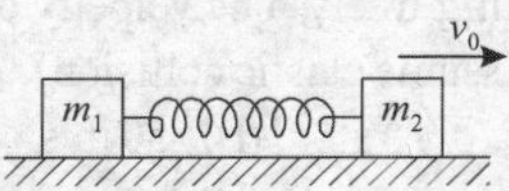

Figure 4.114

(A) $v_0\sqrt{\frac{m_1 m_2}{m_1+m_2}}$ (B) $v_0\sqrt{\frac{2m_1 m_2}{(m_1+m_2)k}}$

(C) $v_0\sqrt{\frac{m_1 m_2}{2(m_1+m_2)k}}$ (D) $v_0\sqrt{\frac{m_1 m_2}{(m_1+m_2)k}}$

4-55 The centre of mass of a non uniform rod of length L whose mass per unit length ρ varies as $\rho = \frac{k.x^2}{L}$ where k is a constant and x is the distance of any point from one end, is (from the same end) :

(A) $\frac{3}{4}L$ (B) $\frac{1}{4}L$

(C) $\frac{k}{L}$ (D) $\frac{3k}{L}$

4-56 Two objects move in the same direction in a straight line. One moves with a constant velocity V_1. The other starts at rest and has constant acceleration a. They collide when the second object has velocity $2V_1$. The distance between the two objects when the second one starts moving is :

(A) Zero (B) $\frac{V_1^2}{2a}$

(C) $\frac{V_1^2}{a}$ (D) $\frac{2V_1^2}{a}$

4-57 Figure-4.115 shows a boy on a horizontal platform A on a smooth horizontal surface, holding a rope attached to a box B. Boy pulls the rope with a constant force of 50 N. The combined mass of platform A and boy is 250 kg and that of box B is 500 kg. The velocity of A relative to the box B 5 s after the boy on A begins to pull the rope, will be :

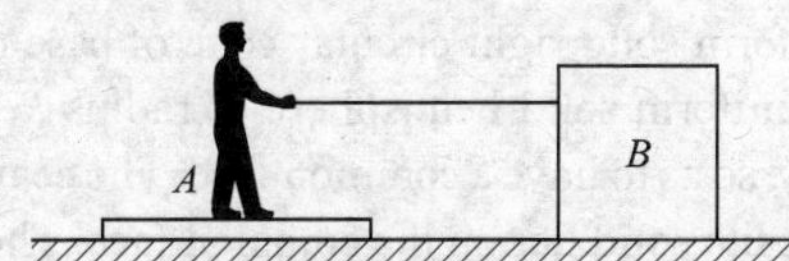

Figure 4.115

(A) 1 m/s (B) 1.5 m/s
(C) 2 m/s (D) 0.5 m/s

4-58 A wind-powered generator converts wind energy into electrical energy. Assume that the generator converts a fixed fraction of the wind energy intercepted by its blades into electrical energy. For wind speed v, the electrical power output will be proportional to :

(A) v (B) v^2
(C) v^3 (D) v^4

4-59 A ball falls vertically onto a floor, with momentum p, and then bounces repeatedly. The coefficient of restitution is e. The total momentum imparted by the ball to the floor is :

(A) $p(1+e)$ (B) $\frac{p}{1-e}$

(C) $p\left(1+\frac{1}{e}\right)$ (D) $p\left(\frac{1+e}{1-e}\right)$

4-60 A projectile of mass m is fired with velocity v from a point P, as shown below. Neglect air resistance, the magnitude of the change in momentum between the point P and arriving at Q is :

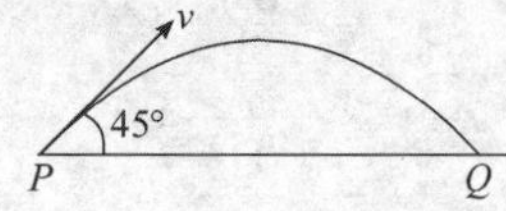

Figure 4.116

(A) Zero (B) $\frac{1}{2}mv$

(C) $mv\sqrt{2}$ (D) $2mv$

4-61 Two balls of equal mass moving in opposite direction have a head-on collision with speed 6 m/s. If the coefficient of restitution is 1/3, the velocity of each ball after impact will be :

(A) 18 m/s (B) 2 m/s

(C) 6 m/s (D) 4 m/s

4-62 An alpha particle collides elastically with a stationary nucleus and continues on at an angle of 60° with respect to the original direction of motion. The nucleus recoils at an angle of 30° with respect to this direction. Mass number of nucleus is

(A) 2 (B) 4

(C) 8 (D) 6

4-63 A uniform solid right circular cone of base radius R is joined to a uniform solid hemisphere of radius R and of the same density, so as to have a common face. The centre of mass of the composite solid lies on the common face. The height of the cone is :

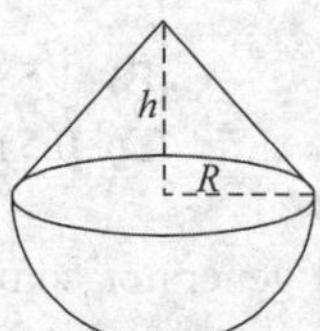

Figure 4.117

(A) $1.5R$ (B) $\sqrt{3}\,R$

(C) $3R$ (D) $2\sqrt{3}\,R$

4-64 A sphere moving with velocity v strikes a wall moving towards the sphere with a velocity u. If the mass of the wall is infinitely large the work done by the wall during collision will be:

(A) $m\,u\,(v+u)$ (B) $2\,m\,u\,(v+u)$

(C) $2\,m\,v\,(v+u)$ (D) $2\,m\,(v+u)$

4-65 A projectile of mass 20 kg is fired with a velocity of 400 m/s at an angle of 45° with the horizontal. At the highest point of the trajectory the projectile explodes into two fragments of equal mass, one of which falls vertically downward with zero initial speed. The distance of the point where the other fragment falls from the point of firing is :

(A) 24000 m (B) 16000 m

(C) 32000 m (D) 8000 m

4-66 A ball falls vertically for 2 seconds and hits a plane inclined at 30° to horizon. If the coefficient of restitution is $\frac{3}{4}$, find the time that elapses before it again hits the plane :

(A) 3 seconds (B) 2 seconds

(C) 5 seconds (D) 4 seconds

4-67 Three boys are standing on a horizontal platform of mass 170 kg as shown in figure-4.118(a). The exchange their position as shown in the figure-4.118(b). Distance moved by the platform is:

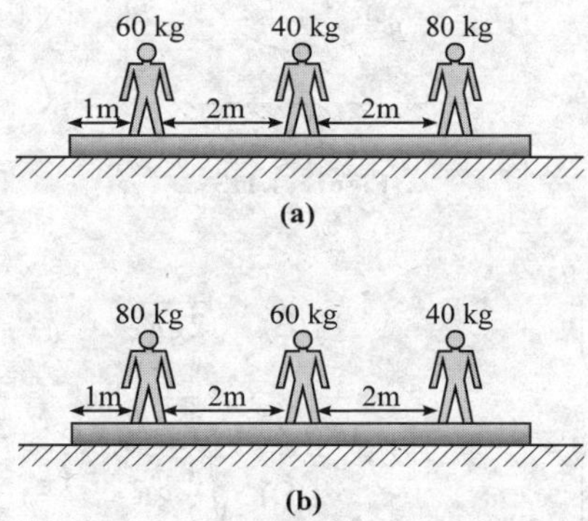

Figure 4.118

(A) 0.35 m (B) 0.55 m

(C) 0.45 m (D) 0.25 m

4-68 A platform of infinite mass is moving upward with velocity 5 m/s. At time $t = 0$, a ball which is at height 100 m above the platform starts falling freely. The velocity of ball just after the collision will be (Assume elastic collision) $(g = 10\text{ m/s}^2)$:

(A) 40 m/s (B) 50 m/s

(C) 20 m/s (D) None

4-69 A force exerts an impulse I on a particle changing its speed from U to $2U$. The applied force and the velocity are oppositely oriented along the same line. The work done by the force is :

(A) $\frac{3}{2}$IU (B) $\frac{1}{2}$IU

(C) IU (D) 2IU

4-70 What is the maximum offset that one can obtained by piling up three identical bricks of length l :

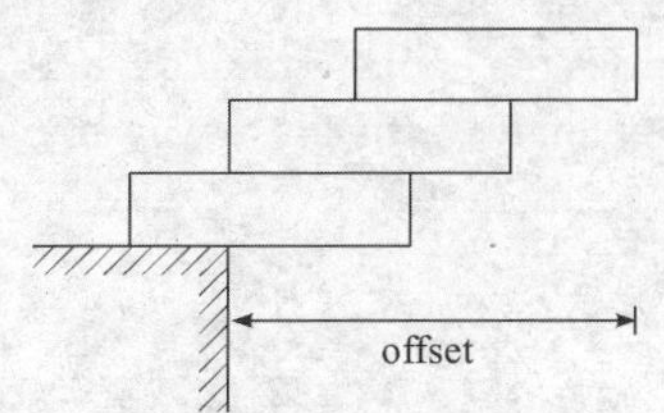

Figure 4.119

(A) $\frac{2}{3}l$ (B) $\frac{4}{3}l$

(C) $\frac{5}{6}l$ (D) $\frac{11}{12}l$

4-71 When the kinetic energy of the body is increased by 300 %, the momentum of the body is increased by :

(A) 20% (B) 50%

(C) 100% (D) 200%

4-72 Two astronauts, each of mass 75kg are floating next to each other in space, outside the space shuttle one of them pushes the other through a distance of 1m (an arms length) with a force of 300N. What is the final relative velocity of the two ?

(A) 2.0 m/s (B) 2.83 m/s

(C) 5.66 m/s (D) 4 m/s

4-73 A stream of water droplets, each of mass $m = 0.001$kg are fired horizontally at a velocity of 10 m/s towards a vertical steel plate where they collide. The droplets one spaced equidistant with a spacing of 1cm. What is approximate average force exerted on the plate by the water droplets. (Assuming that they do not rebound after collision.)

(A) 10 N (B) 100 N

(C) 1 N (D) 0.1 N

4-74 A bowler throws a ball horizontally along east direction with speed of 144 km/hr. The batsman hits the ball such that it deviates from its initial direction of motion by 74º north of east direction, without changing its speed. If mass of the ball is $\frac{1}{3}$ kg and time of contact between bat and ball is 0.02 s. Average force applied by batsman on ball is :

(A) 800 N, 53º East of North (B) 800 N, 53º North of East

(C) 800 N, 53º North of West (D) 800 N, 53º West of North

4-75 A small ball rolls off the top landing of a staircase. It strikes the mid point of the first step and then mid point of the second step. The steps are smooth & identical in height & width. The coefficient of restitution between the ball & the first step is :

(A) 1 (B) 3/4

(C) 1/2 (D) 1/4

4-76 *AB* and *CD* are two smooth parallel walls. A child rolls a ball along ground from *A* towards point *P* find *PD* so that ball reaches point *B* after striking the wall *CD*. Given coefficient of restitution $e = 0.5$:

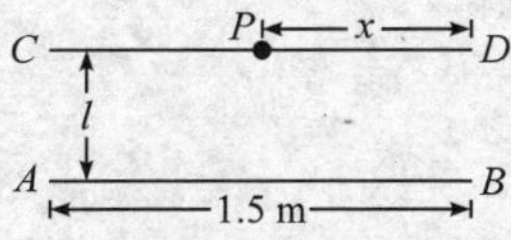

Figure 4.120

(A) 0.5m (B) 1.2m

(C) 1m (D) None of these

4-77 Body *A* of mass 4*m* moving with speed *u* collides with another body *B* of mass 2*m*, at rest. The collision is head on and elastic in nature. After the collision the fraction of energy lost by the colliding body *A* is :

(A) $\frac{1}{9}$ (B) $\frac{8}{9}$

(C) $\frac{4}{9}$ (D) $\frac{5}{9}$

4-78 On a frictionless surface a block of *M* moving at speed *v* collides elastically with another block of same mass *M* which is initially at rest. After collision the first block moves at an angle θ to its initial direction and has a speed $\frac{v}{3}$. The second block's speed after the collision is :

(A) $\frac{\sqrt{3}}{2}v$ (B) $\frac{2\sqrt{2}}{3}v$

(C) $\frac{3}{4}v$ (D) $\frac{3}{\sqrt{2}}v$

4-79 Which of the following statements are correct ?

(a) Centre of mass of a body always coincides with the centre of gravity of the body

(b) Centre of mass of a body is the point at which the total gravitational torque on the body is zero

(c) A couple on a body produce both translational and rotational motion in a body

(d) Mechanical advantage greater than one means that small effort can be used to lift a large load

(A) (b) and (d) (B) (a) and (b)

(C) (b) and (c) (D) (c) and (d)

4-80 Two persons of masses 55 kg and 65 kg respectively, are at the opposite ends of a boat. The length of the boat is 3.0 m and weighs 100 kg. The 55 kg man walks up to the 65 kg man and sits with him. If the boat is in still water the centre of mass of the system shifts by :

(A) 3.0m (B) 2.3m

(C) Zero (D) 0.75m

* * * * *

Advance MCQs with One or More Options Correct

4-1 In which of the following cases the centre of mass of a rod is certainly not at its centre ?
(A) The density continuously increases from left to right.
(B) The density continuously decreases from left to right.
(C) The density decreases from left to right upto the centre and then increase.
(D) The density increases from left to right upto the centre and then decrease.

4-2 When two blocks initially at rest connected by a compressed spring move towards each other under mutual interaction :
(A) Their velocities are equal and opposite.
(B) Their accelerations are equal and opposite.
(C) The force acting on them are equal and opposite.
(D) Their momentum are equal and opposite .

4-3 A body has its centre of mass at the origin. The x-coordinates of the particles :
(A) May be all positive
(B) May be all negative
(C) May be all non-negative
(D) May be positive for some case and negative in other cases

4-4 A body moving towards a finite body at rest collides with it. It is possible that :
(A) Both the bodies come to rest
(B) Both the bodies move after collision
(C) The moving body comes to rest and the stationary body starts moving
(D) The stationary body remains stationary, the moving body changes its velocity.

4-5 In an elastic collision between smooth balls :
(A) The kinetic energy remain constant
(B) The linear momentum remains constant
(C) The final kinetic energy is equal to the initial kinetic energy
(D) The final linear momentum is equal to the initial linear momentum

4-6 A nonzero external force acts on a system of particles. The velocity and the acceleration of the centre of mass are found to be v_0 and a_0 at an instant t. It is possible that :
(A) $v_0 = 0, a_0 = 0$ (B) $v_0 = 0, a_0 \neq 0$
(C) $v_0 \neq 0, a_0 = 0$ (D) $v_0 \neq 0, a_0 \neq 0$

4-7 In an elastic collision between spheres A and B of equal mass but unequal radii, A moves along the x-axis and B is stationary before impact. Which of the following is possible after impact ?
(A) A comes to rest
(B) The velocity of B relative to A remains the same in magnitude but reverses in direction
(C) A and B move with equal speeds, making an angle of 45° each with the x-axis
(D) A and B move with unequal speeds, making angles of 30° and 60° with the x-axis respectively.

4-8 A particle moving with kinetic energy = 3 J makes an elastic head-on collision with a stationary particle which has twice its mass. During the impact :
(A) The minimum kinetic energy of the system is 1 J
(B) The maximum elastic potential energy of the system is 2J
(C) Momentum and total energy are conserved at every instant
(D) The ratio of kinetic energy to potential energy of the system first decreases and then increases.

4-9 A long block A is at rest on a smooth horizontal surface. A small block B, whose mass is half of A, is placed on A at one end and projected along A with some velocity u. The coefficient of friction between the blocks is μ :

Figure 4.121

(A) The blocks will reach the final common velocity $\frac{u}{3}$.
(B) The work done against friction is two-thirds of the initial kinetic energy of B.
(C) Before the block reach a common velocity, the acceleration of A relative to B is $\frac{2}{3}\mu g$.
(D) Before the blocks reach a common velocity the acceleration of A relative to B is $\frac{3}{2}\mu g$.

4-10 A strip of wood of mass M and length l is placed on a smooth horizontal surface. An insect of mass m starts at one end of the strip and walks to the other end in time t, moving with a constant speed :
(A) The speed of the insect as seen from the ground is $< \frac{l}{t}$
(B) The speed of the strip as seen from the ground is $\frac{l}{t}\left(\frac{M}{M+m}\right)$
(C) The speed of the strip as seen from the ground is $\frac{l}{t}\left(\frac{m}{M+m}\right)$
(D) The total kinetic energy of the system is $\frac{1}{2}(m+M)\left(\frac{l}{t}\right)^2$

4-11 In one-dimensional collision between two identical particles A and B, B is stationary and A has momentum p before and after the impact, and $(p-J)$ during the impact :

(A) The total momentum of the 'A plus B' system is p before and after the impact, and $(P-J)$ during the impact.

(B) During the impact, A gives impulse J to B

(C) The coefficient of restitution is $\frac{2J}{P}-1$

(D) The coefficient of restitution is $\frac{J}{P}+1$

4-12 Two blocks A and B each of mass m are connected by a massless spring of natural length L and spring constant k. The blocks are initially resting on a smooth horizontal block C also of mass m moves on the floor with a speed v along the line joining A and B and collides elastically with A then :

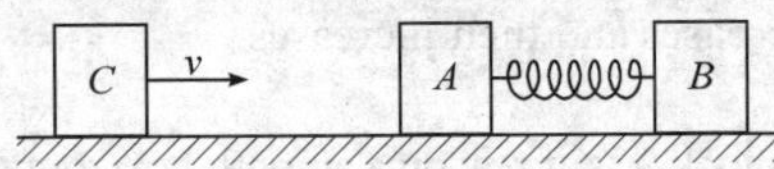

Figure 4.122

(A) The KE of the AB system at max. compression of the spring is zero

(B) The KE of AB system is at max compression is $(1/4)\,mv^2$

(C) The max compression of spring is $v\sqrt{(m/k)}$

(D) The maximum compression of spring is $v\sqrt{(m/2k)}$

4-13 The elastic collision between two bodies, A and B can be considered using the following model. A and B are free to move along a common line without friction. When separation between the surfaces is greater then $d=1$m, the interacting force is zero, when their distance less than d, a constant repulsive force $F=6$N is present. The mass of body A is $m_A=1$kg and it is initially at rest. The mass of body B is $m_B=3$kg and it is approaching towards A with a speed $v_0=2$ m/s. Then choose the correct option(s).

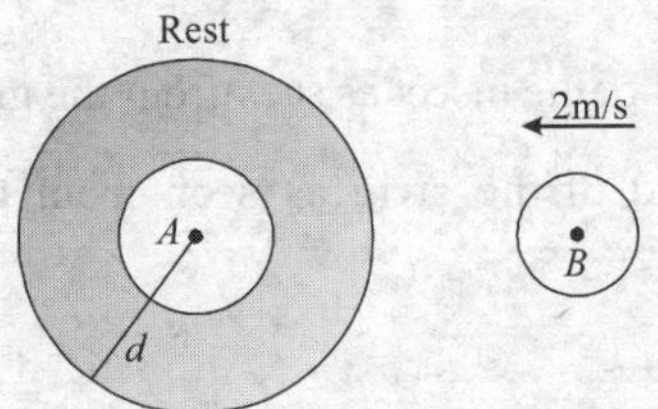

Figure 4.123

(A) The common velocity attained by the bodies are 1.5 m/s

(B) The minimum separation between the bodies is 0.25 m

(C) The minimum separation between the bodies is 0.75 m

(D) The common velocity attained by the bodies are 2.0 m/s

4-14 The sum of all the external forces on a system of particles is zero. Which of the following must be true for the system of particles ?

(A) The total mechanical energy is constant

(B) The total potential energy is constant

(C) The total kinetic energy is constant

(D) The total momentum is constant

4-15 Consider a particle at rest which may decay into two (daughter) particles or into three (daughter) particles. Which of the following is/are true? (There are no external forces):

(A) The velocity vectors of the daughter particles must lie in a plane.

(B) Given the total kinetic energy of system and the mass of each daughter particle, it is possible to determine the speed of each daughter particle.

(C) Given the speed (s) of all but one daughter particle it is possible to determine the speed of the remaining particle.

(D) The total momentum of the daughter particles is zero.

4-16 Three identical cylinders each of mass M and radius R are in contact and kept on a rough horizontal surface coefficient of friction between any cylinder and surface is μ. A force $F=\mu Mgt$ act on the first cylinder mark the correct statement.

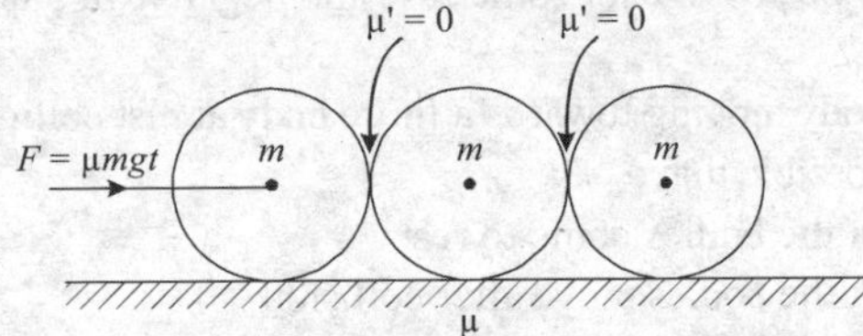

Figure 4.124

(A) The cylinder will start pure rolling and keep on rolling without sliding

(B) At $t=9$ second slipping will start

(C) Velocity of centre of mass of each sphere will keep on increasing

(D) After a certain value of F angular velocity of each sphere will become constant

4-17 A wooden block (mass M) is hung from a peg by a massless string. A speeding bullet (with mass m and initial speed v_0) collides with block at time $t=0$ and embeds in it. Let S be the system consisting of the block and bullet. Which quantities are NOT conserved between $t=-10$ sec to $t=+10$ sec ?

(A) The total linear momentum of S

(B) The horizontal component of the linear momentum of S

(C) The mechanical energy of S

(D) The angular momentum of S as measured about a perpendicular axis through the peg

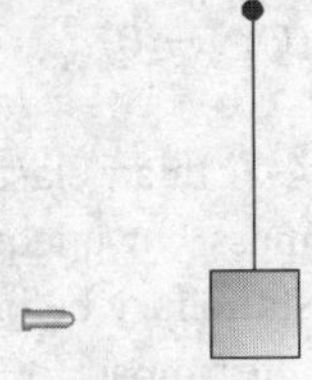

Figure 4.125

4-18 Velocity of a particle of mass 2kg changes from $\vec{v}_1 = 2\hat{i} - 2\hat{j}$ m/s to $\vec{v}_2 = (\hat{i} - \hat{j})$ m/s after colliding with a plane surface :

(A) the angle made by the plane surface with the positive x-axis is $90^\circ + \tan^{-1}\left(\frac{1}{3}\right)$

(B) the angle made by the plane surface with the positive x-axis is $\tan^{-1}\left(\frac{1}{3}\right)$.

(C) the direction of change in momentum makes an angle $\tan^{-1}\left(\frac{1}{3}\right)$ with the +ve x-axis

(D) the direction of change in momentum makes an angle $90^\circ + \tan^{-1}\left(\frac{1}{3}\right)$ with the plane surface

4-19 Two identical particles A and B of mass m each are connected together by a light and inextensible string of length l. The particle are held at rest in air in same horizontal level at a separation l. Both particles are released simultaneously and one of them (say A) is given speed v_0 vertically upward. Choose the correct options(s). Ignore air resistance.

(A) The maximum height attained by the centre of mass of the system of A and B is $\frac{v_0^2}{8g}$.

(B) The kinetic energy of the system of A and B when the centre of mass is at its highest point, is $\frac{mv_0^2}{2}$.

(C) The maximum height attained by the centre of mass of the system of A and B is $\frac{v_0^2}{4g}$

(D) The kinetic energy of the system of A and B when the centre of mass is its highest point, is $\frac{mv_0^2}{4}$

4-20 A disk moving on a frictionless horizontal table collides elastically with another identical disk as shown. The directions of motion of the two disks make angles θ and ϕ with the initial line of motion as shown. Then :

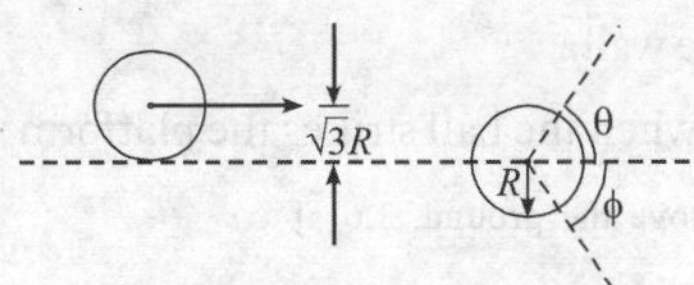

Figure 4.126

(A) $\theta = 30^\circ$ (B) $\theta = 60^\circ$

(C) $\phi = 30^\circ$ (D) $\phi = 60^\circ$

* * * * *

Unsolved Numerical Problems for Preparation of NSEP, INPhO & IPhO

For detailed preparation of INPhO and IPhO students can refer advance study material on www.physicsgalaxy.com

4-1 A projectile is fired from a gun at an angle of 45° with the horizontal and with a muzzle speed of 1500 ft/s. At the highest point in its flight the projectile explodes into two fragments of equal mass. One fragment, whose initial speed is zero, falls vertically. How far from this gun does the other fragment land, assuming a level terrain ?

Ans. [1.1×10^5 ft]

4-2 A ball is dropped at $t = 0$ from a height 12 m above the ground. At the instant of release a very massive platform is at a height 4 m above the ground and moving upward with velocity 3 m/s as shown in the figure. Find :

(a) The height reached by the ball after a perfectly elastic impact with the wall.

(b) The time when the ball strikes the platform second time.

Ans. [19.8 m above the ground, 3.6 s]

4-3 A block of mass 200 gm is suspended through a vertical spring. The spring is stretched by 1 cm when the block is in equilibrium. A particle of mass 120 gm is dropped on the block from a height of 45 cm. The particle sticks to the block after the impact. Find the maximum extension of the spring.

Ans. [6.1 cm]

4-4 A ball of mass m is projected with speed v into the barrel of a spring gun of mass M initially at rest on a frictionless surface. The mass m sticks in the barrel at the point of maximum compression of the spring. No energy is lost in friction. What fraction of the initial kinetic energy of the ball is stored in the spring ?

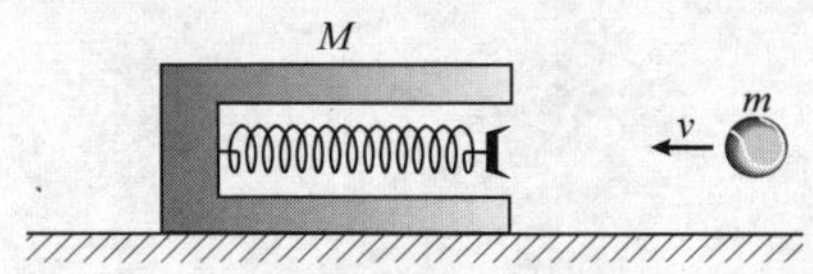

Figure 4.127

Ans. [$\frac{M}{m+M}$]

4-5 A wooden block of mass 10 g is dropped from the top of a cliff 100 m high. Simultaneously, a bullet of mass 10 g is fired from the foot of the cliff vertically upwards with a velocity of 100 m/s.

(i) Where and after what time will they meet ?

(ii) If the bullet, after striking the block, gets embedded in it, how high will it rise above the cliff before it starts falling ?

Ans. [4.9 m, 77.55 m]

4-6 The bob of a pendulum of length 980 cm is released from rest with its string making an angle 60° with the vertical. It collides with a ball of mass 20 gm resting on a smooth horizontal surface just at the position of rest of the pendulum. With what velocity will the bob move immediately after the collision ? What will be the maximum angular displacement of the bob after the collision ? The mass of the bob is 10 gm.

Ans. [980/3 cm/s]

4-7 A $m = 20$ gm bullet pierces through a plate of mass $M_1 = 1$ kg and then comes to rest inside a second plate of mass $M_2 = 2.98$ kg as shown in figure-4.128. It is found that the two plates, initially at rest, now move with equal velocities. Find the percentage loss in the initial velocity of the bullet when it is between M_1 and M_2. Neglect any loss of material of the plates, due to the action of the bullet.

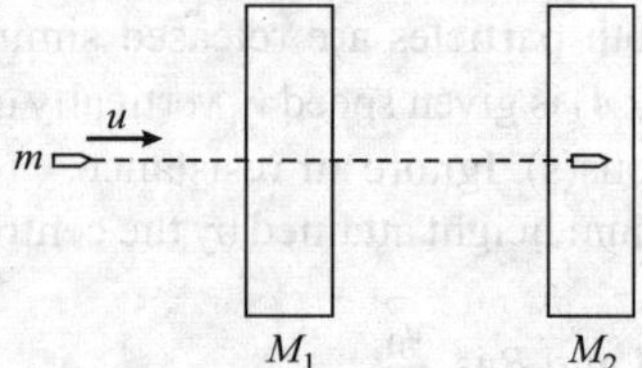

Figure 4.128

Ans. [25%]

4-8 A ball of mass m is shot with a velocity u at an angle θ with the horizontal which strikes the box of mass M resting at the edge of a smooth table as shown in figure-4.129. After striking the box ball falls down vertically. Find the value of u such that the box is raised to the point A shown in figure. Also find the horizontal distance l from which shot was fired.

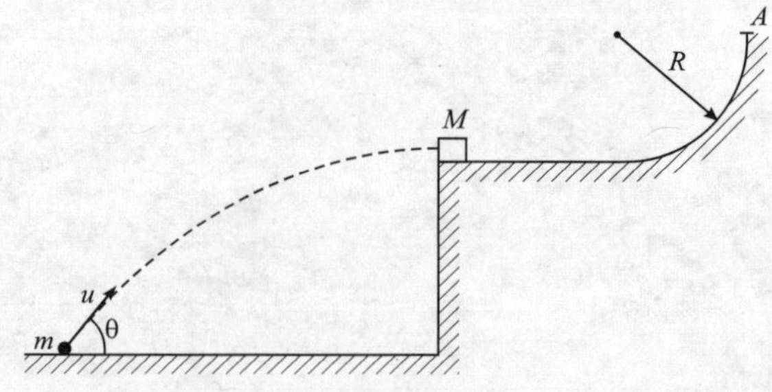

Figure 4.129

Ans. [$\frac{M\sqrt{2gR}}{m\cos\theta}$, $\frac{2M^2 R\tan\theta}{m^2}$]

4-9 A locomotive of mass m starts moving so that its velocity varies according to the law $v = a\sqrt{s}$, where a is a constant, and s is the distance covered. Find the total work done by all forces which are acting on the locomotive during the first t seconds after the beginning of the motion.

Ans. $[\frac{1}{8}ma^4t^2]$

4-10 A ball moving translationally collides elastically with another, stationary, ball of the same mass. At the moment of impact the angle between the straight line passing through the centres of the balls and the direction of the initial motion of the striking ball is equal to α. Assuming the balls to be smooth, find the fraction of the kinetic energy of the striking ball that returned into potential energy at the moment of the maximum deformation.

Ans. $[\frac{1}{2}\cos^2\alpha]$

4-11 A rod of length 1 m and mass 0.5 kg is fixed at one end is initially hanging vertical. The other end is now raised until it makes an angle 60° with the vertical. How much work is required ?

Ans. [1.225J]

4-12 A block of mass 2 kg is moving on a frictionless horizontal surface with a velocity of 1 m/s towards another block of equal mass kept at rest. The spring constant of the spring fixed at one end is 100 N/m. Find the maximum compression of the spring.

Figure 4.130

Ans. [10 cm]

4-13 A particle 1 moving with velocity $v = 10$ m/s experienced a head on collision with a stationary particle 2 of the same mass. As a result of collision, the kinetic energy of the system decreased by 50%. Find the magnitude and direction of the velocity of the particle 1 after collision.

Ans. [5m/s]

4-14 A 3 kg melon is balanced on a bald man's head. His friend shoots a 50 gm arrow at it with speed 25 m/s. The arrow passes through the melon and emerges at 10 m/s. Find the speed of the melon as it flies off the man's head.

Ans. [0.25 m/s]

4-15 A 42 kg girl walks along a stationary uniform beam of mass 21 kg. She walks with a speed of 0.75 m/s. What is the speed of the center of mass of the system of girl plus beam ?

Ans. [0.5m/s]

4-16 Two perfectly smooth elastic discs A and B, one k times as massive as the other, rest on a smooth horizontal table. The disc A is made to move towards B with velocity u and make a head on collision. Calculate the fraction of the kinetic energy transferred to B from A. Also show that the value of this fraction is the same whether B is k times as massive as A or vice versa.

Ans. $[\frac{4k}{(k+1)^2}]$

4-17 A ball of mass m moving at a speed v makes a head on collision with an identical ball at rest. The kinetic energy of the balls after the collision is three fourths of the original. Find the coefficient of restitution.

Ans. $[\frac{1}{\sqrt{2}}]$

4-18 Two vehicles A and B are traveling west and south, respectively, towards the same intersection where they collide and lock together. Before the collision A (9001 b) is moving with a speed of 40 mph, and B(12001 b) has a speed of 60 mph. Find the magnitude and direction of the velocity of the interlocked vehicles immediately after collision.

Ans. [38.33 mph]

4-19 An object of mass 5 kg is projected with a velocity of 20 m/s at an angle of 60° to the horizontal. At the highest point of its path the projectile explodes and breaks up into two fragments of masses 1 kg and 4 kg. The fragments separate horizontally after the explosion. The explosion releases internal energy such that the kinetic energy of the system at the highest point is doubled. Calculate the separation between the two fragments when they reach the ground.

Ans. [44.18 m]

4-20 A 120 gm ball moving at 18 m/s strikes a wall perpendicularly and rebounds straight back at 12 m/s. After the initial contact, the center of the ball moves 0.27 cm closer to the wall. Assuming uniform deceleration, show that the time of contact is 0.00075 seconds. How large an average force does the ball exert on the wall ?

Ans. [4800 N]

4-21 A horizontal plane supports a stationary vertical cylinder of radius R and a disc A attached to the cylinder by a horizontal thread AB of length l_0. An initial velocity v is imparted to the disc as shown in figure-4.131. How long will it move along the plane until it strikes against the cylinder ? The friction is assumed to be absent.

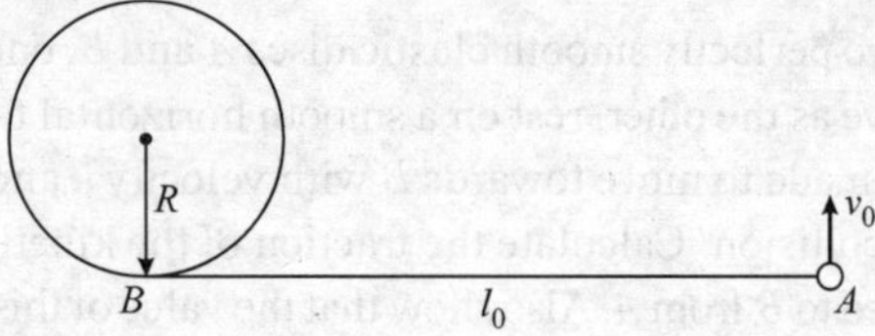

Figure 4.131

Ans. $[t = l_0^2/2v_0R]$

4-22 Two carts, initially at rest, are free to move on a horizontal plane. Cart *A* has mass 4.52 kg and cart *B* has a mass 2.37 kg. They are tied together, compressing a light spring in between them. When the string holding them together is burned, the cart *A* moves off with a speed of 2.11 m/s. (a) With what speed does cart *B* leave ? (b) How much energy was stored in the spring before the string was burned ?

Ans. [4.02 m/s, 29.3 J]

4-23 A light inextensible thread passes over a small frictionless pulley. Two blocks of masses $m = 1$ kg and $M = 3$ kg respectively are attached with the thread as shown in the figure-4.132. The heavier block rests on a horizontal surface. A shell of mass 1 kg moving upward with a velocity 10 ms^{-1} collides and sticks with the block of mass *m* as shown in the figure at $t = 0$. If the inclined plane is smooth. Calculate :

(a) maximum height ascended by *M*

(b) time '*t*' at that instant

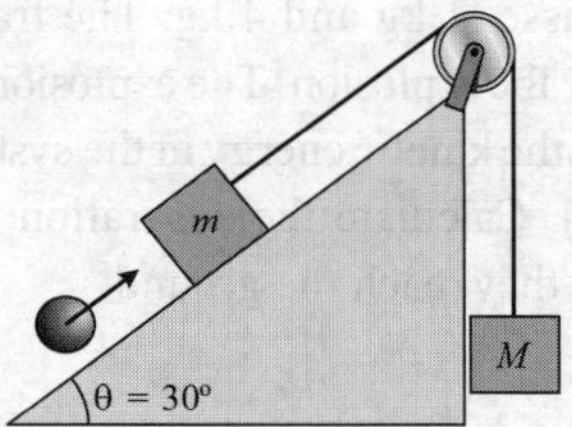

Figure 4.132

Ans. [(a) $\frac{1}{2}$ m, (b) 2.5 s]

4-24 A series of *N* identical balls are at rest on a smooth horizontal surface. The number 1 ball moves with velocity *u* towards the ball number 2 which in turn collides with the ball number 3 and so on. Find the speed of Nth ball if the coefficient of restitution for each impact is *e*.

Ans. $[\frac{u(1+e)^{N-1}}{2^{N-1}}]$

4-25 A steel ball of mass $m = 50$ gm falls from height $h = 1$ m on the horizontal surface of a massive slab. Find the cumulative momentum imparted to the slab by the ball after numerous bounces, if the coefficient of restitution between the ball and the slab is $e = 0.8$.

Ans. [2 N-s]

4-26 In the figure-4.133 shown *A* is a ball of mass 2 kg fixed at its position and S_1, S_2 are the walls facing *A*. Another ball *B* of mass 4 kg incident on the wall S_1 at an angle of incidence 60° and then successively it collides elastically with wall S_2 and S_3 as shown in figure-4.132. Trace the locus of centre of mass of the two balls during the motion of the ball *B*.

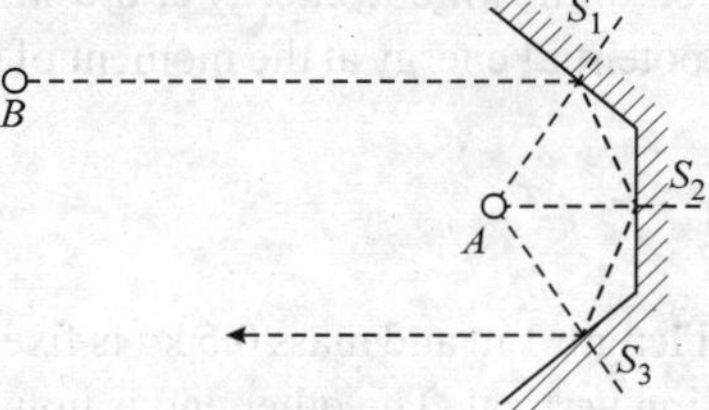

Figure 4.133

4-27 Two bars connected by a weightless spring of stiffness *k* and length l_0 rest on horizontal plane. A constant horizontal force *F* starts acting on one of the bars as shown in figure-4.134. Find the maximum and minimum distances between the bars during the subsequent motion of the system, if the masses of the bars are :

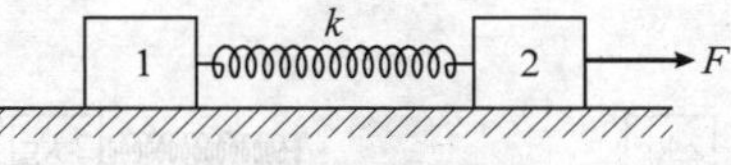

Figure 4.134

(a) Equal; (b) Equal to m_1 and m_2.

Ans. $[l_{max} = l_0 + F/k,\ l_{min} = l_0,\ l_{max} = l_0 + 2m_1 F/k(m_1 + m_2)]$

4-28 A raft of mass *M* with a man of mass *m* aboard stays motionless on the surface of a lake. The man moves a distance *l'* relative to the raft with velocity *v'* and then stops. Assuming the water resistance to be negligible, find : (a) the displacement of the raft *l* relative to the shore; (b) the horizontal component of the force with which the man acted on the raft during the motion.

Ans. $[-\frac{ml'}{M+m}, F = -\frac{mM}{M+m}\frac{dv'}{dt}]$

4-29 A shell flying with velocity $v = 500$ m/s bursts into three identical fragments so that kinetic energy of the system increases 1.5 times. What maximum velocity can one of the fragments obtain ?

Ans. [1 km/s]

4-30 Two identical buggies 1 and 2 with one man in each move without friction due to inertia along the parallel rails towards each other. When the buggies get opposite each other, the men exchange their places by jumping in the direction perpendicular to the motion direction. As a consequence, buggy 1 stops and buggy 2 keeps going in the same direction, with its velocity becoming equal to v. Find the initial velocities of each buggy, v_1 and v_2, if the mass of each buggy without a man equals M and the mass of each man is m.

Ans. $[\frac{Mv}{M-m}, \frac{mv}{M-m}]$

4-31 A 2 kg block rests over a small hole in a table. A woman beneath the table shoots a 15 gm bullet through the hole into the block, where it lodges. How fast was the bullet going if the block rises 75 cm above the table ?

Ans. [515 m/s]

4-32 A 1 kg block slides down an inclined plane of mass 3.2 kg having inclination 45°. If the inclined plane is fixed and the 1 kg block slides without friction, find the acceleration of the centre of mass of the system of the block and inclined plane.

Ans. [1.2 m/s^2]

4-33 A ball A of mass 10 kg and a ball B of unknown mass are placed on a horizontal frictionless table which rest against a rigid wall as shown in figure-4.135. The ball A moves towards the ball B with a velocity v. What should be the mass of B such that both A and B move with the same speed after A has undergone a collision with ball B and the wall ? All collisions are assumed to the elastic.

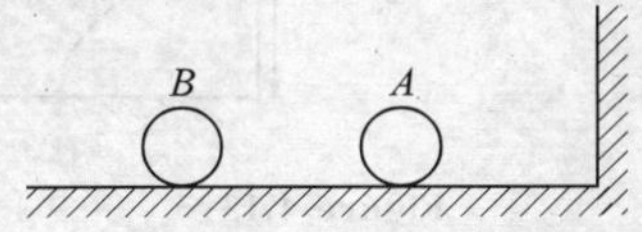

Figure 4.135

Ans. [30 kg]

4-34 A plastic ball is dropped from a height of one meter and rebounds several times from the floor. If 1.3 seconds elapse from the moment it is dropped to the second impact with the floor, what is the coefficient of restitution.

Ans. [0.04]

4-35 A chain is held on a frictionless table with one fifth of its length hanging over the edge. If the chain has a length l and a mass m, how much work is required to pull the hanging part back on the table ?

Ans. $[\frac{Mgl}{50}]$

4-36 The Atwood machine in figure-4.136 has a third mass attached to it by a limp string. After being released, the 2 m mass falls a distance x before the limp string becomes taut. Thereafter both the masses on the left rise at the same speed. What is this final speed ? Assume that pulley is ideal.

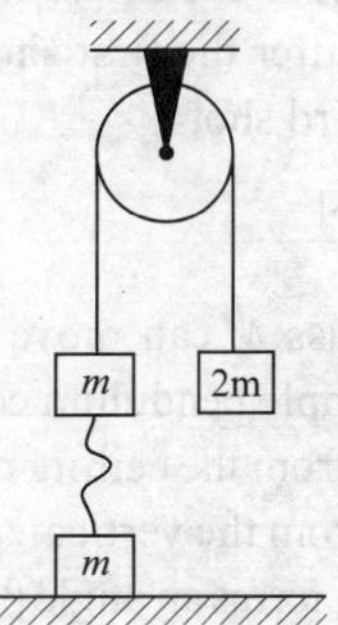

Figure 4.136

Ans. $[\sqrt{\frac{3gx}{8}}]$

4-37 A bullet of mass 20 gm travelling horizontally with a speed of 500 m/s passes through a wooden block of mass 10 kg initially at rest on a level surface as shown in figure-4.137. The bullet emerges with a speed of 100 m/s and the block slides 20 cm on the surface before coming to rest. Find the friction coefficient between the block and the surface.

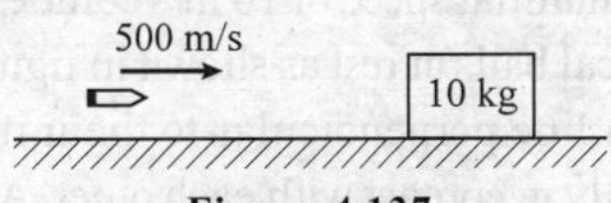

Figure 4.137

Ans. [0.16]

4-38 A particle A of mass m moving on a smooth horizontal surface collides with a stationary particle B of mass 2 m directly, situated at a distance d from a wall. The coefficient of restitution between A and B and between B and the wall is $e = 1/4$. Calculate the distance from the wall where they collide again. Assume that the entire motion takes place along a straight line perpendicular to the wall.

Ans. [$12d/13$]

4-39 An 80 kg caveman, standing on a branch of a tree 5 m high, swings on a vine and catches a 60 kg cavegirl at the bottom of the swing. How high will both of them rise ?

Ans. [1.632 m]

4-40 What is the thrust of a rocket that burns fuel at a rate of 1.3×10^4 kg/sec if the exhaust gases have a velocity 2.5×10^3 m/s with respect to the rocket.

Ans. [3.3×10^7 N]

4-41 A cannon is mounted on a railway wagon which stands on a straight section of the track. The mass of the wagon with the cannon, projectiles and man is 2000 kg and mass of each projectile is 25 kg. The cannon is fired in a horizontal direction along the track, the projectiles having an initial velocity of 1000 m/s with respect to the cannon (i) what should be the speed of the cannon after the first shot ? (ii) what should be the speed after the third shot ?

Ans. [12.5 m/s ,37.5 m/s]

4-42 A wagon of mass M can move without friction along horizontal rails. A simple pendulum consisting of a sphere of mass m is suspended from the ceiling of the wagon by a string of length l. Angle α from the vertical. Find the velocity of the wagon when the string forms an angle $\beta(\beta < \alpha)$ with the vertical and hence find the velocity of the wagon when the pendulum passes through its mean position.

Ans. [$2m\sin(\alpha/2)\sqrt{\dfrac{gl}{(M+m)M}}$]

4-43 A ball of mass $2m$ moving due east with a speed of $8u$ collides directly with a ball B of mass m and the velocity of B after collision is $5u$ due east. If the coefficient of restitution is 1/11, find the fraction of the total kinetic energy lost ?

Ans. [80/137]

4-44 A ball with initial speed of 10 m/s collides elastically with two other identical balls at rest as shown in figure-4.138, whose centres are on a line perpendicular to the initial velocity and which are initially in contact with each other. All the three balls are lying on a smooth horizontal table. The first ball is aimed directly at the contact point of the other two balls. All the balls are smooth. Find the velocities of the three balls after the collision.

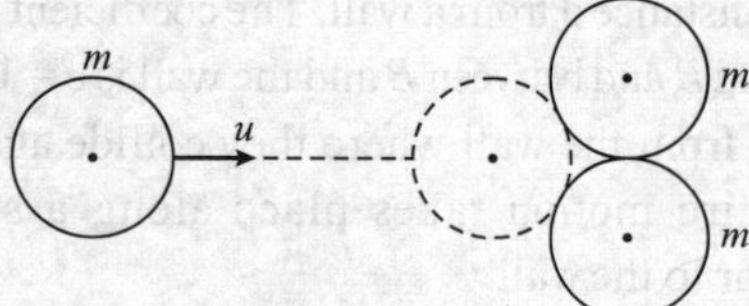

Figure 4.138

Ans. [2 m/s, 6.93 m/s at 30° with incident direction]

4-45 A rocket with initial mass 8000 kg is fired vertically. Its exhaust gases have a relative velocity of 2500 m/s and are ejected at a rate of 40 kg/s. (a) What is the initial acceleration of the rocket ? (b) What is its acceleration after 20 s have elapsed.

Ans. [2.7 m/s^2, 4.1 m/s^2]

4-46 A ball of mass m is moving with speed u to the left along the positive x-axis, toward the origin. It strikes another ball of mass $m/4$ at rest at the origin. After collision the incoming ball is reflected back to the right an angle of 37° to the positive x-axis with a speed of $u/5$. Find the speed and direction of motion of the other ball.

Ans. [4.66 u, 185.9°]

4-47 A shell of mass $3m$ is moving horizontally through air with velocity u when an internal explosion causes it to separates into two parts of masses m and $2m$, which continue to move horizontally in the same vertical plane. If the explosion generates additional energy of amount $12mu^2$, prove that the two fragments separate with relative speed $6u$.

4-48 A closed system consists of two particles of masses m_1 and m_2 which move at right angles to each other with velocities v_1 and v_2. Find :

(a) The momentum of each particle and

(b) The total kinetic energy of the two particles in the reference frame fixed to their center of mass.

Ans. [$\dfrac{m_1m_2}{m_1+m_2}\sqrt{v_1^2+v_2^2}$, $\dfrac{1}{2}\dfrac{m_1m_2}{m_1+m_2}(v_1^2+v_2^2)$]

4-49 A small disc A slides down with initial velocity equal to zero from the top of a smooth hill of height H having a horizontal portion as shown in figure-4.139. What must be the height of the horizontal portion h to ensure the maximum distance s covered by the disc ? What is it equal to ?

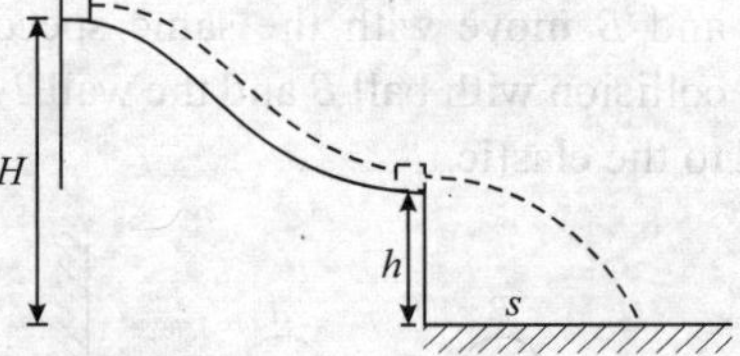

Figure 4.139

Ans. [$h/2$, H]

4-50 The inclined surfaces of two movable wedges of the same mass M are smoothly conjugated with the horizontal plane as shown in figure-4.140. A small block of mass m slides down the left wedge from a height h. To what maximum height will the block rises on the right wedge.

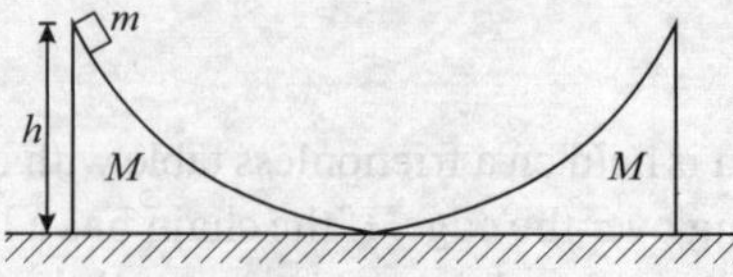

Figure 4.140

Ans. [$\dfrac{hM^2}{(M+m)^2}$]

4-51 A particle of mass m having collides with a stationary particle of mass M deviated by an angle $\pi/2$ whereas the particle M recoiled at an angle $\theta = 30°$ to the direction of the initial motion of the particle m. How much in percent and in what way has the kinetic energy of this system changed after the collision, if $M/m = 5$.

Ans. [– 40%]

4-52 A bullet of mass 0.25 kg is fired with velocity 302 m/s into a block of wood of mass 37.5 kg. It gets embedded into it. The block m_1 is resting on a long block m_2 and the horizontal surface on which it is placed. The coefficient of friction between m_1 and m_2 is 0.5. Find the displacement of m_1 on m_2 and the common velocity of m_1 and m_2. Mass $m_2 = 12.5$ kg.

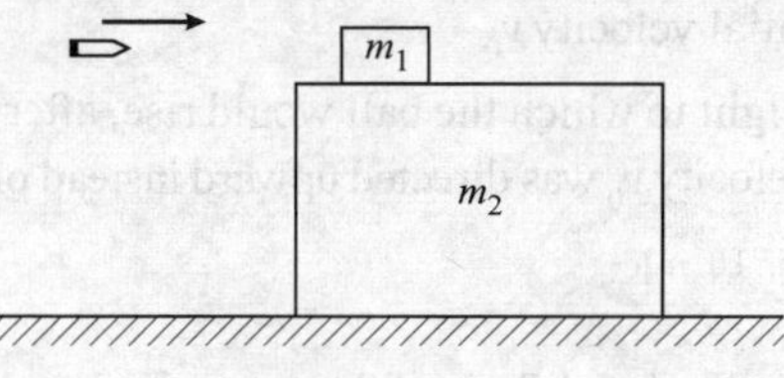

Figure 4.141

Ans. [0.1 m, 1.51 m/s]

4-53 A simple pendulum of length l and consisting of a ball of mass m is released from a position making an angle $\theta = \cos^{-1}(0.8)$ with the vertical and strikes at its lowest position a block of mass M resting on a rough horizontal plane. If the coefficient of kinetic friction between the plane and the block is 0.2 find

(a) How long the block will move along the plane, if the ball of the pendulum rebounds to an angle $\beta = \cos^{-1}(0.9)$A

(b) The coefficient of restitution, use $\dfrac{M}{m} = 10$ and $1 = 1$ m

Ans. [2.916 cm, 0.879]

4-54 A small disc of mass m slides down a smooth hill of height h without initial velocity and gets onto a plank of mass M lying on the horizontal plane at the base of the hill as shown in figure-4.142. Due to friction between the disc and the plank the disc slows down and, beginning with a certain moment, moves in one piece with the plank. Find the total work performed by the friction forces in this process.

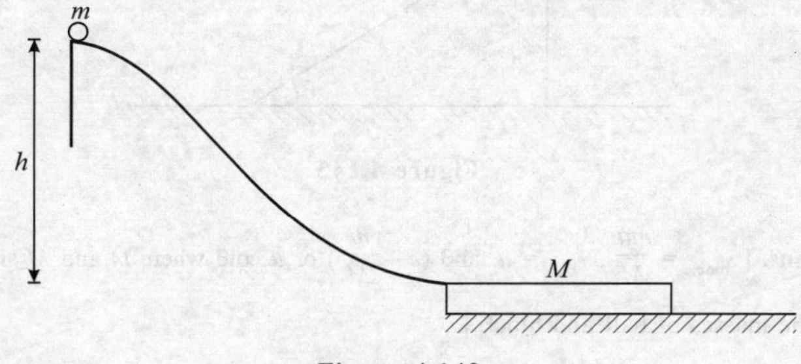

Figure 4.142

Ans. $[-\dfrac{mMgh}{m+M}]$

4-55 A steel ball of mass m falls from a height h on the horizontal surface of a massive slab. Find the cumulative momentum that the ball imparts to the slab after numerous bounces, if every impact decreases the velocity of the ball η times. ($\eta > 1$).

Ans. $[m\sqrt{2gh}\left(\dfrac{1+\eta}{1-\eta}\right)]$

4-56 An elastic body is projected from a given point with velocity u at angle with the horizontal and after hitting a vertical wall returns to the same point. Show that the distance of the point from the wall must be less than $\dfrac{eu^2}{(1+e)g}$, where e is the coefficient of restitution.

Ans. $[m\sqrt{2gh}\,\dfrac{\eta+1}{\eta-1}]$

4-57 A body of mass m moving with a velocity v in the x-direction collides with another body of mass M moving in the y-direction with a velocity u. They collapse into one body during the collision. Calculate.

(a) The direction and magnitude of the momentum of the final body.

(b) The fraction of the initial kinetic energy transformed into heat during the collision in terms of the masses.

Ans. $[\dfrac{mM(u^2+v^2)}{(M+m)(mv^2+Mv^2)}]$

4-58 A 10kg hammer strikes a nail at a velocity of 12.5 m/s and comes to rest in a time interval of 0.004 s. Find the impulse imparted to the nail and the average force imparted to the nail.

Ans. [125 N-s, 31300 N]

4-59 A wedge of mass M rests on an absolutely smooth, horizontal surface. A block of mass m is placed on the wedge, inclined at an angle α to the horizontal. All the surfaces are frictionless. Assuming that the system was at rest at the initial moment, find the velocity of the wedge when the block slides down the plane through a vertical height h.

Ans. $[\sqrt{\dfrac{2m^2gh\cos^2\alpha}{(M+m)(M+m\sin^2\alpha)}}]$

4-60 A mass of 2.9 kg is suspended from a string of length 50 cm and is at rest. Another body of mass 10 gm, which is moving horizontally with a velocity of 150 m/s strikes and sticks to it.

(i) What is the tension in the string when it makes an angle of 60° with the vertical.

(ii) Will it complete a vertical circle.

Ans. [135.3 N]

4-61 Three particles A, B and C of equal mass move with equal speed V along the medians of an equilateral triangle as shown in the figure-4.143. They collide at the centroid G of the triangle. After the collision., A comes to rest, B retraces its path with the speed V. What is the speed of C ?

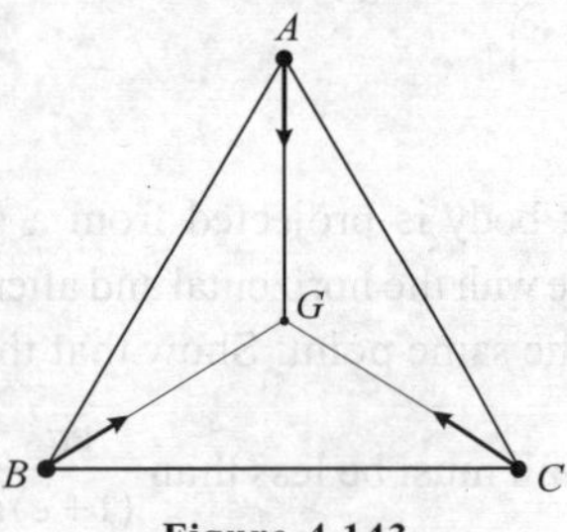

Figure 4.143

Ans. [V]

4-62 A block weighing 1 kg is released from rest at point A on a track which is one quadrant of a circle of radius 1.2 m as shown in figure-4.144. It slides down the track and reaches point B with a velocity of 3.6 m/s. From the point B it slides on a level surface a distance of 2.7 m to point C, where it comes to rest, (a) What was the coefficient of friction on the horizontal surface ? (b) How much work was done against friction as the body slid down the circular track from A to B ?

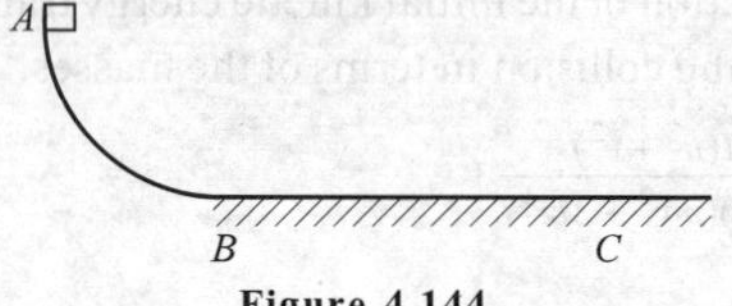

Figure 4.144

Ans. [.24, –5.28 J]

4-63 A cylindrical solid of mass 10^{-2} kg and cross sectional area 10^{-4} m^2 is moving parallel to its axis (the x-axis) with a uniform speed of 10^3 m/s in the positive direction. At $t = 0$, its front face passes the plane $x = 0$. The region to the right of this plane is filled with stationary dust particles of uniform density 10^{-3} kg/m^3. When a dust particle collides with the face of the cylinder, it sticks to its surface. Assuming that the dimensions of the cylinder remain practically unchanged, and that the dust sticks only to the front face of the cylinder, and the x coordinate of the front of the cylinder at $t = 150$ sec.

Ans. [10^5 m]

4-64 Two small identical discs, each of mass m, lie on a smooth horizontal plane. The discs are interconnected by a light non-deformed spring of length l_0 and stiffness k. At a certain moment one of the discs is set in motion in a horizontal direction perpendicular to the spring with velocity v_0. Find the maximum elongation of the spring in the process of motion, if it is known to be considerably less than unity.

Ans. [$\frac{mv_0^2}{kl_0}$]

4-65 A cart loaded with sand moves along a horizontal plane due to a constant force F coinciding in direction with the cart's velocity vector. In the process, sand spills through a hole in the bottom with a constant velocity r kg/s. Find the acceleration and velocity of the cart as a function of time. If at the initial, the cart with the loaded sand has the mass m_0 and its velocity was equal to zero. Neglect friction.

Ans. [$v = \frac{F}{r} \ln\left(\frac{m_0}{m_0 - rt}\right)$, $a = \frac{F}{(m_0 - rt)}$]

4-66 A ball falls under gravity from a height of 10 m, with an initial velocity v_0. It collides with the ground, loses 50% of its energy in collision and then rises to the same height. Find :

(a) The initial velocity v_0.

(b) The height to which the ball would rise, after collision, if the initial velocity v_0 was directed upward instead of downward.

Ans. [14 m/s, 10 m]

4-67 Two balls A and B are of the same size but the mass of A is double that of B. They move along the same line in opposite direction, A with velocity 2 u and B with velocity 3 u. If their total kinetic energy after collision is half their total kinetic energy before collision find the coefficient of restitution. Find also their velocities after collision.

Ans. [0.7, 5u/6, 8u/3]

4-68 Find the mass of the rocket as a function of time, it moves with a constant acceleration a, in absence of external forces. The gas escapes with a constant velocity u relative to the rocket and its mass initially was m_0.

Ans. [$m = m_0 e^{-(a/u)t}$]

4-69 A ball moves towards a smooth wedge with a velocity u as shown in figure-4.145. After collision the ball rebounds vertically upwards. The coefficient of restitution is e. Find the velocity of the wedge block and ball after collision. Do you need some other parameters to solve the given problems.

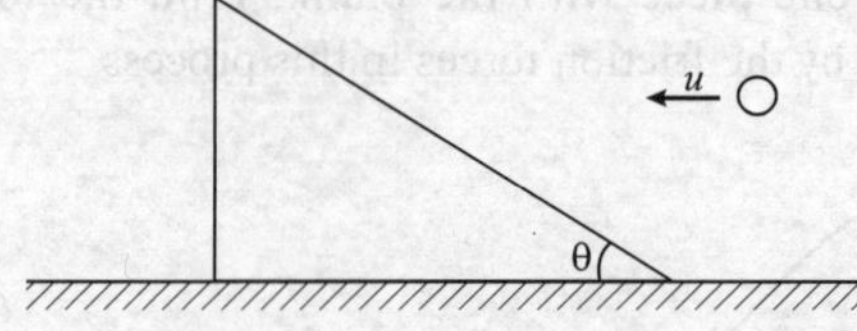

Figure 4.145

Ans. [$v_{block} = \frac{mu}{M}$, $v_{ball} = u \tan\theta \left(e - \frac{m}{M}\right)$ or $u \cot\theta$ where m and M are the masses of ball and block.]

4-70 Masses of the bodies A, B and C are 1 kg, 2 kg and 3 kg respectively. There is no friction between the ground and the bodies. Initially ball A is moving with a velocity 20 m/s collides inelastically ($e = 0.5$) with the ball B, which was initially at rest. The ball B further collides elastically to the block C (at rest), and then C collides elastically to the wall in front. Find the velocities of the three blocks after all collisions occurred.

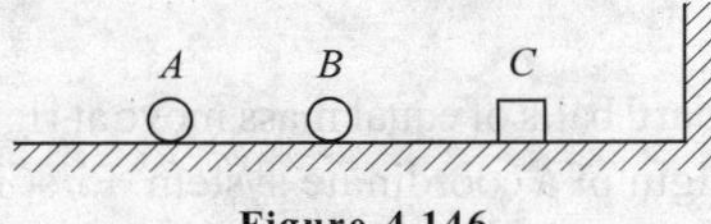

Figure 4.146

Ans. [$v_A = 9.4$ m/s, $v_B = 5.7$ m/s, $v_C = 2.4$ m/s]

4-71 Figure-4.147 shows a small block of mass m which is started with a speed v on the horizontal part of the bigger block of mass M placed on a horizontal floor. The curved part of the surface shown is semicircular. All the surfaces are frictionless. Find the speed of the bigger block when the smaller block reaches the point A of the surface.

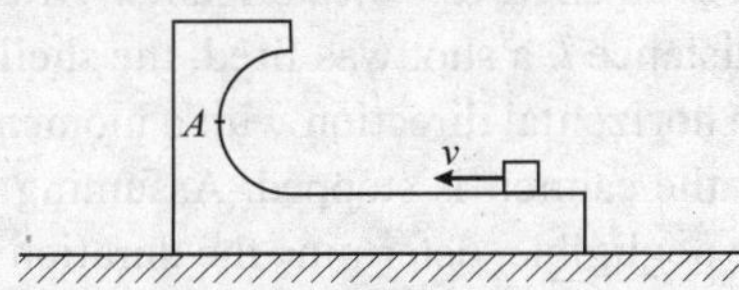

Figure 4.147

Ans. [$\frac{mv}{(M+m)}$]

4-72 From a uniform circular disc a circular hole is cut out touching the rim of the disc at the point A. Prove that the center of gravity G of the remainder is on the circumference of the hole if $AG^2 = AB.\ GB$ where B is the other end of the diameter through A of the disc.

4-73 A block of mass 2 kg moving at 2 m/s collides head on with another block of equal mass kept at rest. (a) Find the maximum possible loss in kinetic energy due to the collision. (b) If the actual loss in kinetic energy is half of this maximum, find the coefficient of restitution.

Ans. [2 J, $\frac{1}{\sqrt{2}}$]

4-74 A ball with a speed of 9 m/s strikes another identical ball such that after collision the direction of each ball makes an angle 30° with the original line of motion. Find the speeds of the two balls after the collision. Is the kinetic energy conserved in this collision process ?

Ans. [$3\sqrt{3}$, No]

4-75 N beads are resting on a smooth horizontal wire which is circular at the end with radius r as shown in figure. The masses of the beads are $m, m/2, m/4 ...., m/2^{n-1}$ respectively. Find the minimum velocity which should be imparted to the first bead of mass m such that the nth bead will fall in the tank shown in figure-4.148.

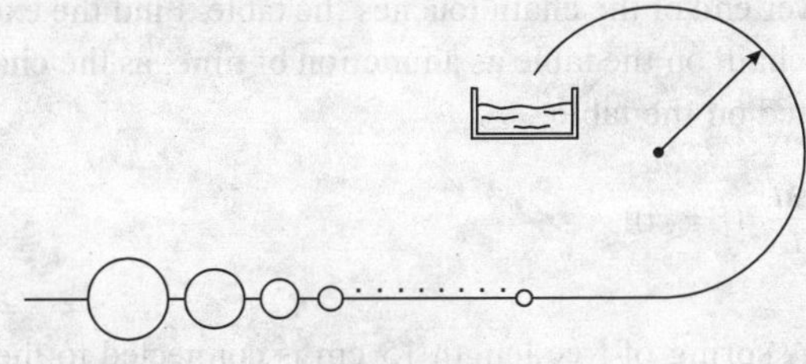

Figure 4.148

Ans. [$\left(\frac{3}{4}\right)^{n-1}\sqrt{4gr}$]

4-76 While moving in a wagon(5 kg) along a smooth road at 0.5 m/s, a 15 kg boy throws a 3 kg bag of sand in front of him with a speed 4 m/s relative to his original motion. How fast is he moving after he throws the bag of sand. What is his final direction of motion ?

Ans. [0.1 m/s backward]

4-77 Two men, each mass m, stand on the edge of a stationary buggy of mass m. Assuming the friction to be negligible, find the velocity of the buggy after both men jump off with the same horizontal velocity u relative to the buggy :

(a) Simultaneously;

(b) One after the other,

In what case will the velocity of the buggy be greater and how many times.

Ans. [$\frac{2mu}{M+2m}, \frac{mu}{M+m} + \frac{mu}{M+2m}$]

4-78 According to a FIR in police station, car A was sitting at rest waiting for a red light at a crossing when it was hit by an identical car B from rear side. Both cars had their hand brakes on, and from their skid marks it is surmised that they skidded together about 6m in the original direction of travel before coming to rest. Assuming a stopping force of about 0.7 times the combined weights of the cars (that is, $\mu = 0.7$), what must have been the approximate speed of car B just before the collision ?

Ans. [18.1 m/s]

4-79 A particle of mass M is at rest when it suddenly explodes into three pieces of equal masses. One piece flies out along the positive x-axis with a speed of 30 m/s, while another goes in the negative y direction with a speed of 20 m/s.

(a) Find the components of the velocity of the third piece.

(b) Repeat if the third piece has a mass $M/2$ and the other two each have mass $M/4$.

Ans. [–30 m/s, 20 m/s, –15 m/s, 10 m/s]

4-80 A vertical, uniform chain of total mass M and length L is being lowered onto a table at a constant speed V. At time $t = 0$, the lower end of the chain touches the table. Find the exerted by the chain on the table as a function of time, as the chain is deposited on the table.

Ans. [$\frac{VM}{L}(V + gt)$]

4-81 A spring of free length 15 cm is connected to the two masses as shown in the figure-4.149 and compressed 5 cm. The system is released on a smooth horizontal surface. Find the speed of each block when the spring is again at its free length. The force constant for spring is 2100 Nm^{-1}.

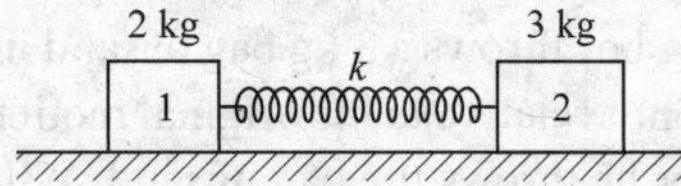

Figure 4.149

Ans. [1.575 m/s, 1.05 m/s]

4-82 A 44 gm bullet strikes and becomes embedded in a 1.54 kg block of wood placed on a horizontal surface just in front of the gun. If the coefficient of kinetic friction between the block and the surface is 0.28, and the impact drives the block a distance of 18 m before it comes to rest, what was the muzzle speed of the bullet ?

Ans. [360 m/s]

4-83 A 4200 kg rocket is traveling in outer space with a velocity of 150 m/s toward the sun. It wishes to alter its course by 30°, and can do this by shooting its rockets briefly in a direction perpendicular to its original motion. If the rocket gases are expelled at a speed of 2700 m/s, what mass of gas must be expelled ?

Ans. [131 kg]

4-84 The tennis ball may leave the racket of a top player on the serve with a speed of 65 m/s. If mass of the ball is 0.06 kg and is in contact with the racket for 0.03 sec, what is the average force n the ball ?

Ans. [130N]

4-85 A block of mass 2 kg slides down a 30° incline which is 3.6 m high. At the bottom, it strikes a block of mass 6 kg which is at rest on a horizontal surface. If the collision is elastic, and friction can be ignored, determine (a) the speeds of the two blocks after the collision and (b) how far back up the incline the smaller mass will go.

Ans. [4.2 m/s, 4.2 m/s, 1.8 m along incline]

4-86 A rocket ejects a steady jet whose velocity is equal to u relative to the rocket. The gas discharge rate equals r kg/s. Determine the acceleration of rocket in terms of the external force on rocket F and the speed u.

Ans. [$\frac{F + ru}{m}$]

4-87 Two billiard balls of equal mass move at right angles and meet at the origin of a coordinate system. First is moving up along the y-axis at 3 m/s and the other is moving to the right along the x-axis with speed 4.8 m/s. After the elastic collision, the second ball is moving along the positive y-axis. What is the final direction of the first ball, and what are their two speeds ?

Ans. [+ x direction, 4.8 m/s, 3 m/s]

4-88 A cannon of mass m starts sliding freely down a smooth inclined plane at an angle α to the horizontal. After the cannon covered the distance l, a shot was fired, the shell leaving the cannon in the horizontal direction with a momentum P. As a consequence, the cannon is stopped. Assuming the mass of the shell to be negligible, determine the duration of the shot.

Ans. [$t = \frac{P\cos\alpha - m\sqrt{2gl\sin\alpha}}{mg\sin\alpha}$]

4-89 Three identical particles A, B and C lie on a smooth horizontal table, Light inextensible strings which are just taut connect AB and BC and $\angle ABC$ is 135º. An impulse J is applied to the particle C in the direction BC. Find the initial speed of each particle. The mass of each particle is m :

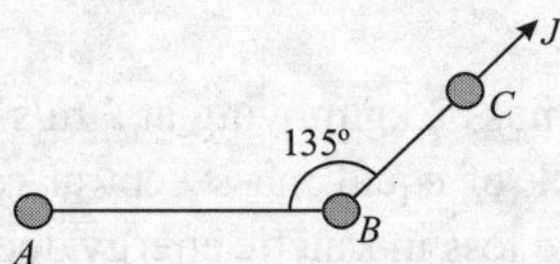

Figure 4.150

Ans. [$\frac{\sqrt{2}J}{7m}, \frac{\sqrt{10}J}{7m}, \frac{3J}{7m}$]

4-90 A flat car of mass M starts moving to the right due to a constant horizontal force F. Sand spills on the flat car from a stationary hopper. The velocity of loading is constant and equal to r kg/s. Find the time dependence of the velocity and the acceleration of the flat car in the process of loading. The friction is negligibly small.

Ans. [$\frac{Ft}{M\left(1+\frac{rt}{M}\right)}, \frac{F}{M\left(1+\frac{rt}{M}\right)^2}$]

4-91 A block of mass M with a semicircular track of radius R rests on a horizontal frictionless surfaces shown in figure-4.151.

A uniform cylinder of radius r and mass m is released from rest at the point A. The cylinder slips on the semicircular frictionless track. How far has the block moved when the cylinder reach the bottom of the track ? How fast is the block moving when the cylinder reaches the bottom of the track ?

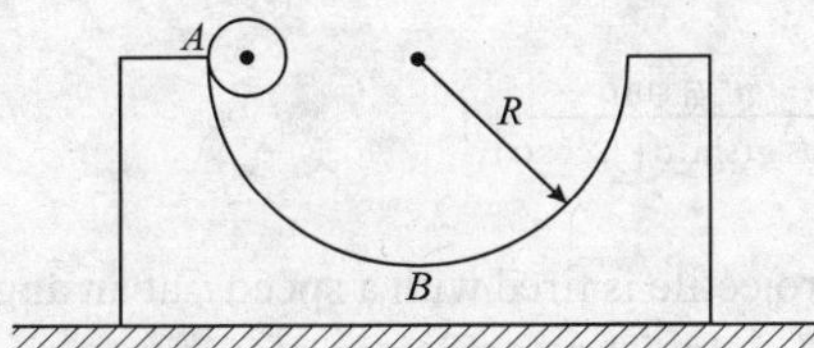

Figure 4.151

Ans. [$\frac{m(R-r)}{(M+m)}$, $m\sqrt{\frac{2g(R-r)}{M(M+m)}}$]

4-92 Two balls of masses m and $2m$ are suspended by two threads of same length l and from the same point of a ceiling. The ball m is pulled aside through an angle α and released from rest, after a tangential velocity v_0 towards the other stationary ball is imparted to it. To what height will the balls rise after collision if the collision is perfectly elastic ?

Ans. [$h_1 = \frac{1}{18g}[v_0^2 + 2gl(1-\cos\alpha)]$, $h_2 = \frac{4}{18g}[v_0^2 + 2g(1-\cos\alpha)]$]

4-93 Three identical discs A, B and C rest on a smooth horizontal plane as shown in figure-4.152. The disc A is set in motion with velocity v along the perpendicular bisector of the line BC joining the centres of the stationary discs. The distance BC between the centres of stationary discs B and C is n times the diameter of each disc. At what value of n will the disc A recoil, Stop, and move on after elastic collision. ?

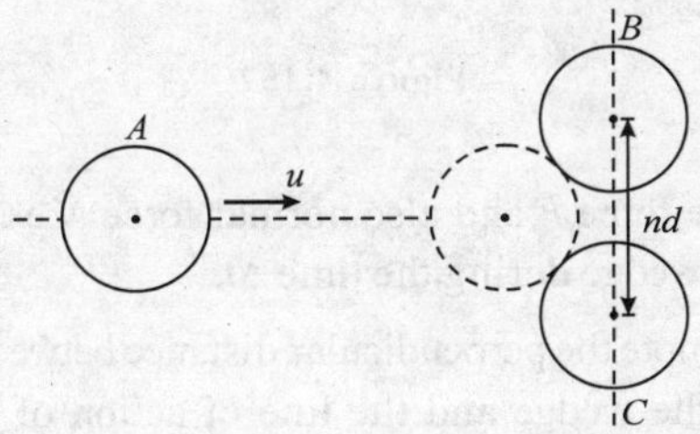

Figure 4.152

Ans. [$n < \sqrt{2}, n = \sqrt{2}, n > \sqrt{2}$]

4-94 A simple pendulum is suspended from a peg on a vertical wall. The pendulum is pulled away from the wall to a horizontal position and released as shown in figure-4.153. The ball hits the wall, the coefficient of restitution being $2/\sqrt{5}$. What is the minimum number of collisions after which the amplitude of oscillation becomes less than 60°.

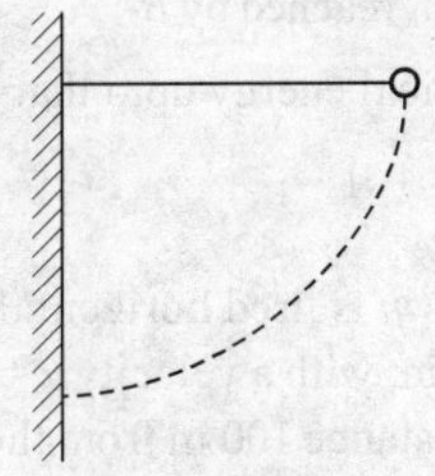

Figure 4.153

Ans. [4]

4-95 A block A of mass $2m$ is placed on another block B of mass 4 m which in turn is placed on ground. The two blocks have the same length $4d$ and they are placed as shown in figure-4.154. The coefficient of friction between the block B and the ground is μ. There is no friction between the two blocks. A small object of mass m moving horizontally along a line passing through the centre of mass of the block B and perpendicular to its face with a speed v collides elastically with the block B at a height d above the table.

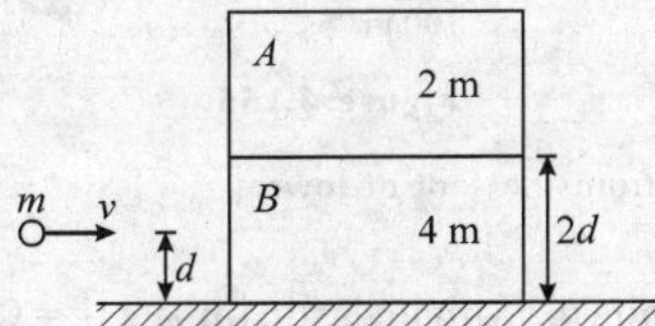

Figure 4.154

(a) What is the minimum value of v(say v_0) required to make the block A topple ?

(b) If $v = 2v_0$, find the distance at which the mass m falls on the table after collision from point P.

Ans. [$\frac{5}{2}\sqrt{6\mu gd}, -6d\sqrt{3\mu}$]

4-96 A hammer of mass M kg falls from a height h meter upon the top of an inelastic pile of mass m kg and drive it into the ground a distance x meter. Find the resistance of the ground when it is assumed to be constant. Find also the time during which the pile is in motion and the kinetic energy lost at the impact.

Ans. [$(M+m)g + \frac{M^2gh}{(M+m)x}$, $\frac{(M+m)x}{M} \cdot \sqrt{\frac{2}{gh}}$]

4-97 Two identical blocks A and B each of mass 2 kg hanging stationary by a light inextensible flexible string passing over a light and frictionless pulley. A shot C, of mass 1 kg moving vertically with velocity 9 m/s collides with block B and get stuck to it. Calculate :

(a) Time after which block B starts moving downward

(b) Maximum height reached by B

(c) Loss of mechanical energy upto that instant

Ans. [0.9 s, 0.81 m, 32.4 J]

4-98 A shot of mass m is fired horizontally from the top of a tower of height 100 m, with a velocity u = 50 m/s as shown in figure-4.155. At a distance 100 m from the foot of the tower a child throws a ball of same mass m in vertical direction with the same velocity u = 50 m/s. He throws the ball such that the ball will collides with the shot in its path and merged with it making an object of mass 2 m. Find the distance from the child, where this object lands on ground.

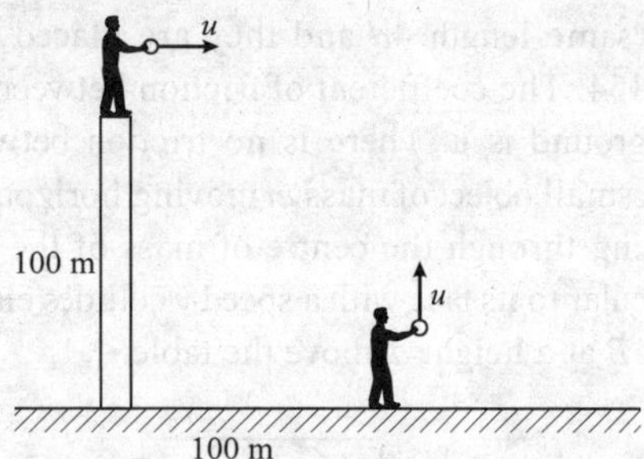

Figure 4.155

Ans. [213.27 m from the foot of tower]

4-99 Mass m_1 hits m_2 with inelastic impact (e = 0) while sliding horizontally with velocity v along the common line of centres of three equal mass as shown in figure-4.156. Initially, masses m_2 and m_3 are stationary and the spring is unstressed. Find :

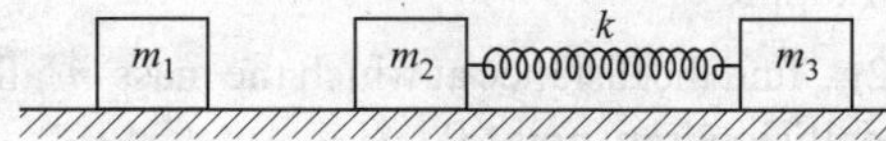

Figure 4.156

(a) The velocities of m_1, m_2 and m_3 immediately after impact.

(b) The maximum kinetic energy of m_3.

(c) The minimum kinetic energy of m_2.

(d) The maximum compression of the spring.

Ans. [$\frac{v}{2}$, 0, $\frac{2}{9}mv^2$, $\frac{mv^2}{72}$, $\frac{\sqrt{mv^2}}{6k}$]

4-100 A space ship of mass M moves in the absence of external forces with a constant velocity v_0. To change the motion direction, a jet engine is switched on. It starts ejecting a gas jet with velocity u, which is constant relative to the spaceship and directed at right angles to the spaceship motion. The engine is shut down when the mass of the spaceship decreases to m. Through what angle α did the motion direction of the spaceship deviate due to the jet engine operation ?

Ans. [$\alpha = \frac{u}{v} \ln \frac{M}{m}$]

4-101 A cannon of mass M located at the base of an inclined plane, shoots a shell of mass m in a horizontal direction with velocity v. To what vertical height does the cannon ascend the inclined plane as a result of recoil, if the angle of inclination of the plane is α and the coefficient of friction between the cannon and the plane is μ.

Ans. [$h = \frac{m^2 v_0^2 \sin\alpha}{2M^2 g(\sin\alpha + \mu\cos\alpha)}$]

4-102 A projectile is fired with a speed u at an angle θ above a horizontal field. The coefficient of restitution of collision between the projectile and the field is e. How far from the starting point, does the projectile makes its second collision with the field ?

Ans. [$\frac{(1+e)u^2 \sin 2\theta}{g}$]

4-103 A wedge of mass m and triangular cross section ($AB = BC = CA = 2R$) is moving with a constant velocity $-v\hat{i}$ towards sphere of radius R fixed on smooth horizontal table as shown in figure-4.157. The wedge makes an elastic collision with the fixed sphere and returns along the same path without any rotation. Neglect all friction and suppose that the wedge remains in contact with the spare for a very short time Δt, during which the sphere exerts a constant force F on the wedge.

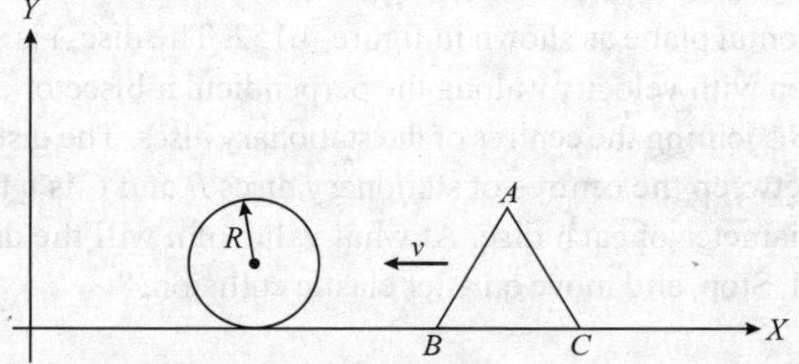

Figure 4.157

(a) Find the force F and also normal force N exerted by the table on the wedge during the time Δt.

(b) Let h denote the perpendicular distance between the centre of mass of the wedge and the line of action of F. Find the magnitude of the torque due to the normal force N about the centre of the wedge during the interval Δt.

Ans. [$\frac{2mv}{\Delta t}(i - \frac{1}{\sqrt{3}}k), -\left[\frac{2mv}{\sqrt{3}\Delta t} + mg\right]k, \tau N = \frac{4mvh}{\sqrt{3}\Delta t}$]

4-104 A cone of mass M, radius R and height H is hanging from its apex from the ceiling. Its height is vertical in this position. Now two small beads of masses m each are now stuck on the lateral surface of the cone. One at the rim of its base and other at the surface at its mid height on its opposite projector. In this situation find the angle made by the axis of the cone with the vertical.

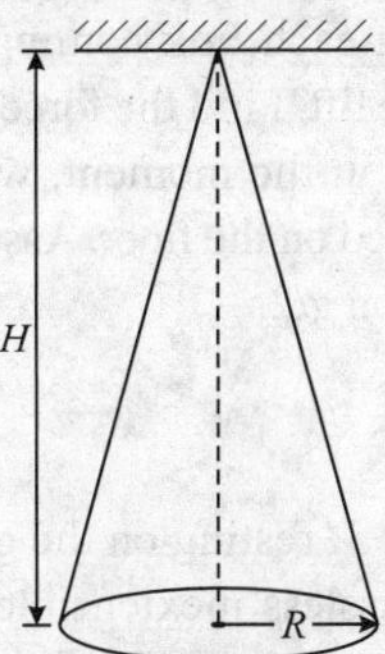

Figure 4.158

Ans. $[\theta = \tan^{-1}\dfrac{2mR}{3H(2m+M)}]$

4-105 A chain of mass m and length l rests on a rough surfaced table so that one of its ends hangs over the edge. The chain starts sliding off the table all by itself provided the overhanging part equals 1/3 of the chain length. What will be the total work performed by the friction forces acting on the chain by the moment it slides completely off the table ? Friction coefficient is μ.

Ans. $[-\dfrac{2\mu Mgl}{9}]$

4-106 A and B are two identical blocks of same mass $2m$ and same physical dimensions as shown in figure-4.159. A is placed over the block B which is attached to one end of the spring of natural length l and spring constant k. The other end of the spring is attached to a wall. The system is resting on a smooth horizontal surface with the spring in the relaxed state. A small object of mass m moving horizontally with speed v at a height d above the horizontal surface hits the block B along the line of their centre of mass in a perfectly elastic collision. There is no friction between A and B.

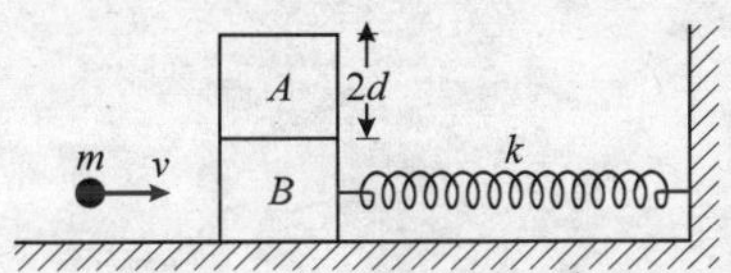

Figure 4.159

(a) Find the minimum value of v (say v_0) such that the block A will topple over block B.

(b) What is the energy stored in the spring when the blocks A and B returns to their initial position as before collision ?

Ans. [(a) $v_0 = 3d\sqrt{\left(\dfrac{k}{8m}\right)}$ (b) Zero]

4-107 The two masses on the right are slightly separated and initially at rest; the left mass is incident with speed v_0. Assuming head on elastic collisions, (a) if $M < m$, show that there are exactly two collisions and find all final velocities; (b) if $M > m$, show that there are three collisions and find all final velocities.

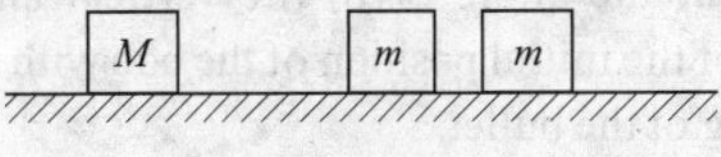

Figure 4.160

4-108 The block of mass M shown in figure-4.161, initially has a velocity v_0 to the right and its position is such that the spring exerts no force on it, i.e., the spring is not stretched or compressed. The block moves to the right a distance l before stopping in the dotted position shown. The spring constant is k and the coefficient of kinetic friction between block and table is μ. As the block moves the distance l, (a) what is the work done on it by the friction force ? (b) what is the work done on it by the spring force ? (c) are there other forces acting on the block, and if so, what work do they do ? (d) what is the total work done on the block ? (e) find the value of l.

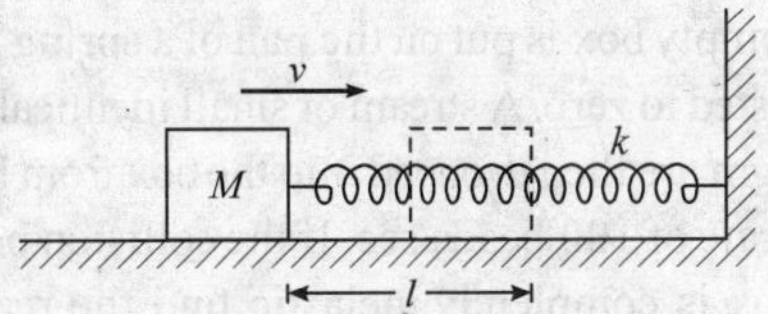

Figure 4.161

Ans. [μmgl, $-\dfrac{1}{2}kl^2$, No. 0, $-(\mu mgl + \dfrac{1}{2}kl^2)$,

$l = \dfrac{2mumg + \sqrt{4\mu^2 m^2 g^2 + 4kmv^2}}{2k}$]

4-109 A ball of mass m, moving with a velocity u along x-axis, strikes another ball of mass $2m$ kept at rest. The first ball comes to rest after collision and the other breaks into two equal pieces. One of the pieces starts moving along y-axis with a speed v. What will be the velocity of the other piece ?

Ans. [$\sqrt{u^2+v^2}$]

4-110 Two spheres of masses $2m$ and $3m$ move towards each other with speed u and v respectively. The centres of the sphere move in the same straight line. The coefficient of restitution is 1/2. Find :

(a) The condition for which motion of each sphere will be reversed on impact

(b) The condition for which each sphere will lose kinetic energy on impact.

Ans. [$\dfrac{2}{3} < \dfrac{u}{v} < 9, \dfrac{9}{11} < \dfrac{u}{v} < \dfrac{7}{3}$]

4-111 A bullet of mass M is fired with a velocity of 50 m/s, at an angle φ with the horizontal. At the highest point of its trajectory, it collides head on with a bob of mass 3 M suspended by a massless string of length 10/3 metres and gets embedded in the bob. After the collision, the string moves through an angle of 120°. Find (a) the angle φ (b) the vertical and horizontal coordinates of the initial position of the bob with respect of the point of firing of the bullet.

Ans. [120 m, 45 m]

4-112 An empty tin can of mass M is sliding with speed V_0 across a horizontal sheet of ice in a rain storm. The area of opening of the can is A. The rain is falling vertically at a rate of n drops per second per square metre. Each rain drop has a mass m and is falling with a terminal velocity V_n. (a) Neglecting friction, calculate the speed of the can as a function of time. (b) Calculate the normal force of reaction of ice on the can as a function of time.

Ans. [$v = M\dfrac{V_0}{M+mAnt}$, $Fn = Mg + nAm\ (Vn + gt)$ upwards]

4-113 An empty box is put on the pan of a spring balance and scale is adjusted to zero. A stream of small identical beads, each of mass 4.5 gm are then dropped into the box from height 7.6 m at constant rate of 100 beads/sec. If the collision between each bead and box is completely inelastic find the reading of the scale, 10 seconds after beads begin to hit the box.

Ans. [5 kg]

4-114 A very flexible uniform chain of mass M and length l is suspended vertically in a lift so that its lower end is just touching the surface of the floor. When the upper end of the chain is released, it falls with each link coming to rest the instant it strikes the floor of the lift. Find the force exerted by the floor of the lift on the chain at the moment, when one fourth of the chain has already rested on the floor. Assume that lift is moving up with an acceleration $g/2$.

Ans. [9Mg/8]

4-115 A heavy mass M resting on the ground is attached to a small mass m via massless inextensible string passing over a pulley. The string connected to M is loose. The smaller mass falls freely through a height h and the string becomes tight. Obtain the time from this instant when the heavier mass again makes contact with the ground. Also obtain the loss in K.E. when M is jerked into motion.

Ans. [$\dfrac{2m}{(M-m)g}\sqrt{\dfrac{2h}{g}}$, $\dfrac{Mmgh}{M+m}$]

4-116 A 54 kg girl on ice skates on a frozen lake pulls with a constant force on all light rope that is tied to a 41 kg sled. The sled is initially 22 m from the girl, and both the sled and the girl start from rest. Neglecting friction, determine the distance the girl travels to the point where she meets the sled.

Ans. [9.5 m]

* * * * *

Rigid Bodies and Rotational Motion

5

FEW WORDS FOR STUDENTS

In previous chapters, our study of mechanics has included the revolution of bodies around an axis. A slightly different kind of angular motions the spring of a leather ball when thrown. This latter type of motion is called rotational motion and is defined more precisely in this chapter. First we consider the motion of solid objects turning about a fixed axis, we will also discuss moving objects that combine translational and rotational motion, known as rolling motion.

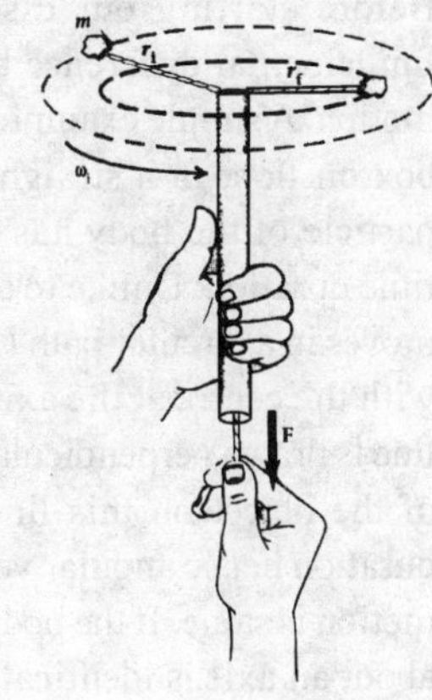

In this chapter, we'll describe several new concepts that are needed for rotatory motion, for making use of many principles that you already know.

CHAPTER CONTENTS

COVER APPLICATION

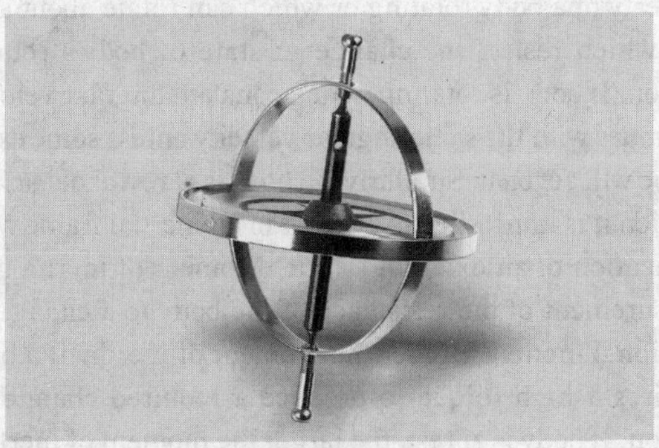

Figure-(a)

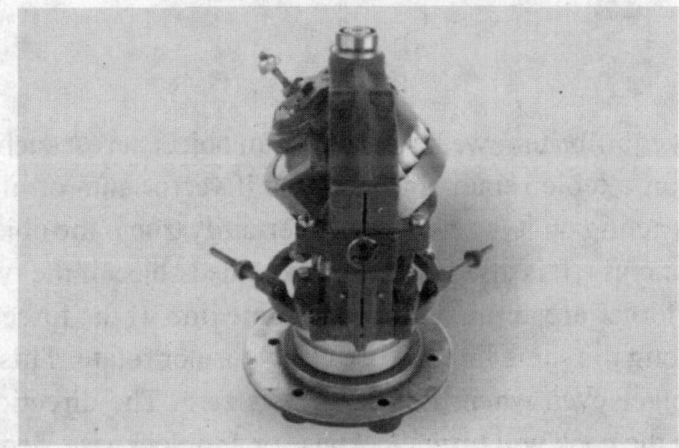

Figure-(b)

Figure-(a) shows a precision gyroscope which is a device used for measuring or maintaining orientation and angular velocity. It is a spinning wheel or disc in which the axis of rotation is free to assume any orientation by itself. Figure-(b) is the image of a vacuum powered aircraft gyroscope. Under light weight conditions of aircrafts for precision pneumatic powered devices are used including such gyroscopes.

In our everyday life, we often see the objects in our surrounding that rotate such as a door on its hinges, a pulley on its axle, or a *CD* on a *CD* player turntable. Our earth is involved in two simultaneous rotational motion. It spins on its axis once a day and it orbits the sun once a year. At atomic and nuclear level, all atoms and nucleons in nuclear spin and orbital motion play an important role in their properties.

Before starting our discussion, first we will discuss the fundamental difference between translational and rotational motion. A simple example of translational motion is dragging a box on floor in a straight line. In translational motion each particle of the body has the same displacement in the same time duration. Unlike to this in rotational motion each particle moves in a circular path (figure-5.1). All circles are concentric with the centre at the axis of rotation. In a rotating object if a line is drawn perpendicular to the axis of rotation then all points of the object on this line cover equal angles in equal time duration hence angular velocity of all the particles in rotational motion is same. If the body is a point mass its rotational motion about an axis is identical to circular motion and there is only one circle of rotation. Now first we discuss the fundamentals behind rotational motion and then we will explain every key concept related to rotational motion.

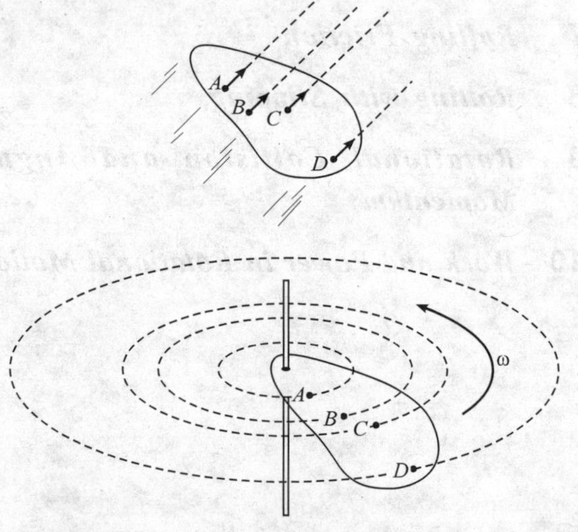

Figure 5.1

About equilibrium, we have studied an object at rest such as a book on a table remains motionless if vector sum of all the forces acting on it is zero. That is certainly true if the object is a point mass. It is also true for an extended object if the two or more forces are applied along the same line. If the forces are not along the same line the book may turn or rotate. This will take place even when the net force is zero. The direction in which the book will turn, clockwise or anticlockwise, depends on its size and shape as well as on its mass. In this chapter we will discuss the techniques necessary for describing rotational motion in general.

5.1 *Rotational Kinematics*

Rotational kinematics is the study of relations and analysis of angular displacement, angular velocity and angular acceleration in different situations, which we have already discussed in chapter-3, section-3.5. We can list up once again the rotational properties along with comparison with translational motion.

Table-5.1

Summary of the linear and rotational kinematic equations

Linear	**Rotational**
$v = \dfrac{dx}{dt}$	$\omega = \dfrac{d\theta}{dt}$
$a = \dfrac{dv}{dt} = v\dfrac{dv}{dx}$	$\alpha = \dfrac{d\omega}{dt} = \omega\dfrac{d\omega}{d\theta}$
$v = u + at$	$\omega = \omega_0 + \alpha t$
$s = ut + \dfrac{1}{2}at^2$	$\theta = \omega_0 + \dfrac{1}{2}dt^2$
$v^2 = u^2 + 2as$	$\omega^2 = \omega_0^2 + 2\alpha\theta$
$s_n = u + \dfrac{1}{2}a(2n-1)$	$\theta_n = \omega_0 + \dfrac{1}{2}\alpha(2n-1)$

5.2 *Moment of Inertia*

As we have studied Translational kinematics and dynamics in previous chapters, in rotational motion, we will also study the concepts of rotational dynamics. Before that one important thing required to be discussed in detail is the Moment of Inertia. As "*Inertia*" plays an important role in definition of Newton's first law which is also called as inertia law, moment of inertia is the key concept in defining the state of rotation. It is the property of a body rotating or which can rotate about an axis and which resists the change in state of body's rotational motion. If body is rotating with a constant angular velocity, it continues with the same angular velocity unless some external torque will act on it. Similarly if a body is at rest about an axis of rotation it is impossible to rotate it in an inertial frame without application of an external torque. Moment of inertia gives a measurement of the resistance of the body to a change in its rotational motion. Higher the moment of inertia of a body, it requires a high torque to produce a required change in its motion. If body is at rest, the larger the moment of inertia of a body, the more difficult it is to put that body into rotational motion. Similarly, the larger the moment of inertia of a body, the more difficult it is to stop its rotational motion.

In translation motion, the mass of a body m gives measure of the inertia of a body. But in rotational motion moment of inertia depends on mass of body as well as on its distribution about the axis of rotation.

For a very simple case of circular motion of a point mass, shown in figure-5.2, the moment of inertia is given as

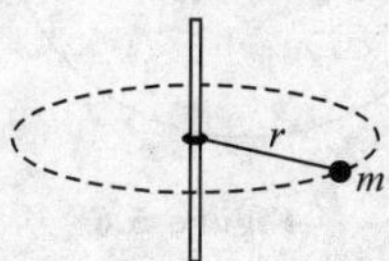

Figure 5.2

$$I = mr^2 \quad \ldots(5.1)$$

Here m is the mass of particle and r is its distance from axis of rotation. The above relation shows that the larger the distance of mass from axis of rotation, larger the moment of inertia is. But be careful that the relation in equation-(5.1) is strictly valid for point masses.

5.2.1 Moment of Inertia of a Rigid Body in Rotational Motion

Have a look at figure-5.3. A body of mass M is free to rotate about in axis of rotation passing through the body. We have already discussed that when a body is in rotational motion, its different particles are in circular motion of different radii. Consider an elemental mass dm in the body at a distance x from the axis of rotation. During rotation of body this dm will revolve about the same axis in a circle of radius x. The moment of inertia of the elemental mass dm is dI, it is given as

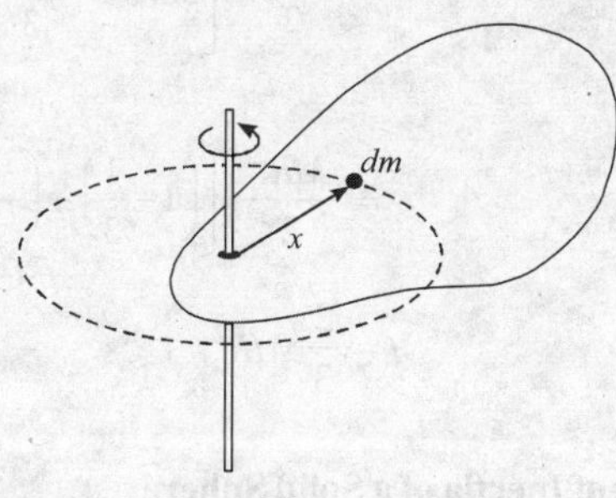

Figure 5.3

$$dI = dmx^2$$

Now the moment of inertia of the whole body can be evaluated by integrating the above expression for the whole body. Thus moment of inertia of the body is given by

$$I = \int dI = \int dmx^2 \quad \ldots(5.2)$$

This expression can be used to find the moment inertia of different object about the given axis of rotation. In next section we will evaluate some standard moment of inertias of some objects, which will be very helpful in study of further sections of rotational motion.

> Web Reference of Video Lectures at www.physicsgalaxy.com
>
> **Age Group -** High School Physics | Age 17-19 Years
> **Section -** MECHANICS
> **Topic -** Rigid Body Dynamics
> **Module Number -** 1 and 2

5.2.2 Moment of Inertia of Different Objects

Using equation-(5.2), we can evaluate moment of inertia of different shaped rigid bodies. We will solve this equation for some standard objects.

(i) Moment of Inertia of a Ring

Figure-5.4 shows a ring of mass M and radius R. To find its moment of inertia, we consider an elemental mass dm on it (see figure). When the ring rotates, the element dm will revolve in a circle of radius R, infect here radius of all the elements taken on ring will be same R. The moment of inertia of this elemental mass dm is given as

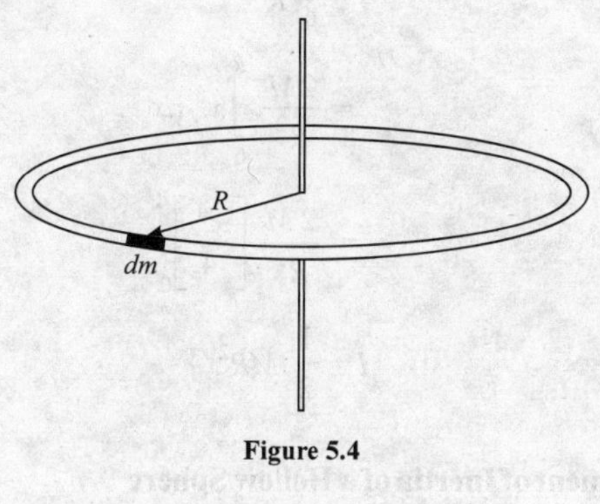

Figure 5.4

$$dI = dmR^2$$

Moment of inertia of the complete ring is

$$I = \int dI = \int dmR^2$$

$$I = R^2 \int dm$$

$$I = MR^2$$

(ii) Moment of Inertia of a Disc

Consider a disc of mass M and radius R, shown in figure-5.5. To find the moment of inertia of it, we consider an elemental ring of radius x and width dx. Its mass dm is given by

$$dm = \frac{M}{\pi R^2} \times 2\pi x\, dx$$

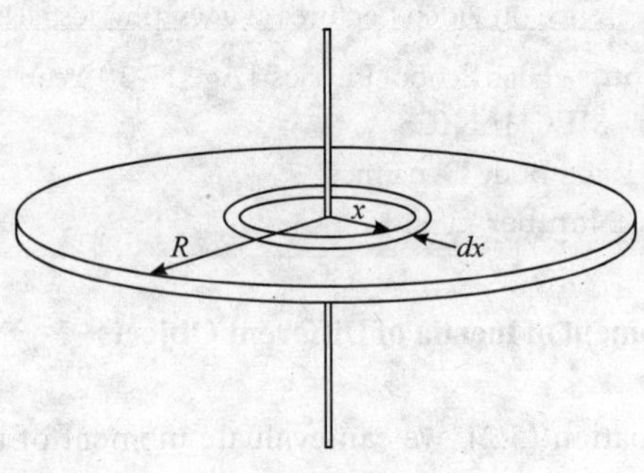

Figure 5.5

Now the moment of inertia of this elemental ring is given as

$$dI = dmx^2$$

or $$= \frac{2M}{R^2} x^3\, dx$$

Moment of inertia of whole disc is given by integration of above relation from 0 to R.

$$I = \int_0^R \frac{2M}{R^2} x^3\, dx$$

or $$= \frac{2M}{R^2} \int_0^R x^3\, dx$$

or $$= \frac{2M}{R^2} \left[\frac{x^4}{4}\right]_0^R$$

or $$I = \frac{1}{2} MR^2 \qquad \ldots (5.3)$$

(iii) Moment of Inertia of a Hollow Sphere

As we have already discussed that generally in case of hollow spherical section and circular arcs, we use polar form of integration, here to find the moment of inertia of the spherical shell shown in figure-5.6, we consider an elemental ring of width $Rd\theta$, at an angular distance θ from the reference line. If shell is of mass M and radius R, the mass of the elemental ring (strip) is given as

$$dm = \frac{M}{4\pi R^2} \times 2\pi R\cos\theta .\, Rd\theta$$

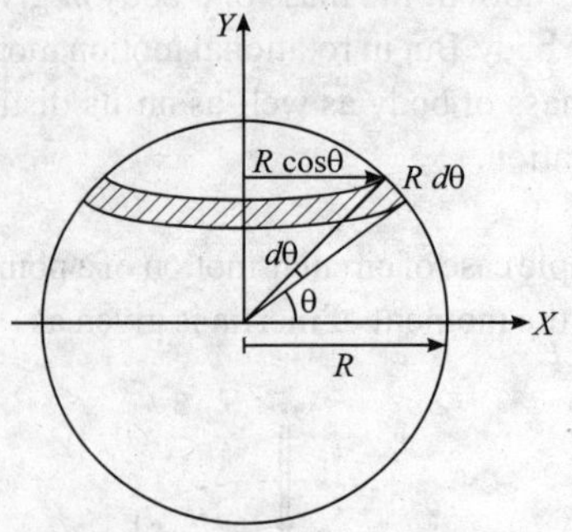

Figure 5.6

The moment of inertia of this elemental strip is given as

$$dI = dm\,(R\cos\theta)^2$$

or $$= \frac{MR^2}{2} \cos^3\theta\, d\theta$$

Now the moment of inertia of the shell is given by integrating this relation over its surface from bottom to top, given as

$$I = \frac{MR^2}{2} \int_{-\frac{\pi}{2}}^{+\frac{\pi}{2}} \cos^3\theta\, d\theta$$

or $$= \frac{MR^2}{2} \int_{-\frac{\pi}{2}}^{+\frac{\pi}{2}} (1 - \sin^2\theta)\cos\theta\, d\theta$$

or $$= \frac{MR^2}{2} \left[\sin\theta - \frac{\sin^2\theta}{3}\right]_{-\frac{\pi}{2}}^{+\frac{\pi}{2}}$$

or $$= \frac{MR^2}{2} \left[\left(1 - \frac{1}{3}\right) - \left(-1 + \frac{1}{3}\right)\right]$$

or $$I = \frac{2}{3} MR^2 \qquad \ldots (5.4)$$

(iv) Moment of Inertia of a Solid Sphere

Just by using the procedure above for hollow sphere, we can find the moment of inertia of a solid sphere. Here instead of using a ring or strip, we take an elemental disc at a distance x and of width dx from the centre of sphere, as shown in figure-5.7. The mass of this elemental disc is dm given as

$$dm = \frac{3M}{4\pi R^3} \times \pi\,(R^2 - x^2)\,.\, dx$$

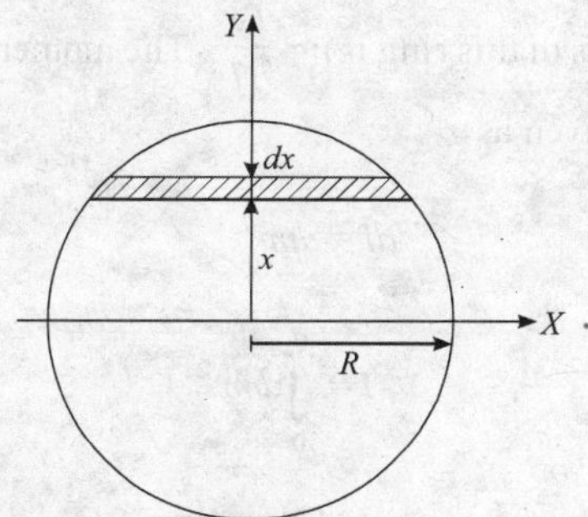

Figure 5.7

Moment of inertia of this disc is

$$dI = \frac{1}{2}\, dm\, (R^2 - x^2)$$

Moment of inertia of the whole sphere can be given by integrating the above dI within limits from $-R$ to $+R$. Thus

$$I = \int dI = \int \frac{1}{2} dm\, (R^2 - x^2)$$

or $$= \frac{1}{2} \int_{-R}^{+R} \frac{3M}{4R^3} (R^2 - x^2)^2 dx$$

or $$= \frac{3M}{8R^3} \int_{-R}^{+R} (R^4 + x^4 - 2R^2x^2) dx$$

or $$= \frac{3M}{8R^3} \left[\left(R^4 x + \frac{x^5}{5} - \frac{2R^2x^3}{3} \right) \right]_{-R}^{+R}$$

or $$= \frac{2}{5} MR^2 \qquad \ldots (5.5)$$

The above result can also be obtained by integrating thin elemental spherical shells in the solid sphere within limits 0 to R.

Alternative treatment

Instead of taking disc at a distance x from centre, we consider a thin elemental spherical shell of radius x and width dx, as shown in figure-5.8. Mass of this shell can be given as

$$dm = \frac{3M}{4\pi R^3} \times 4\pi x^2 . dx$$

Moment of inertia of this elemental shell is given as

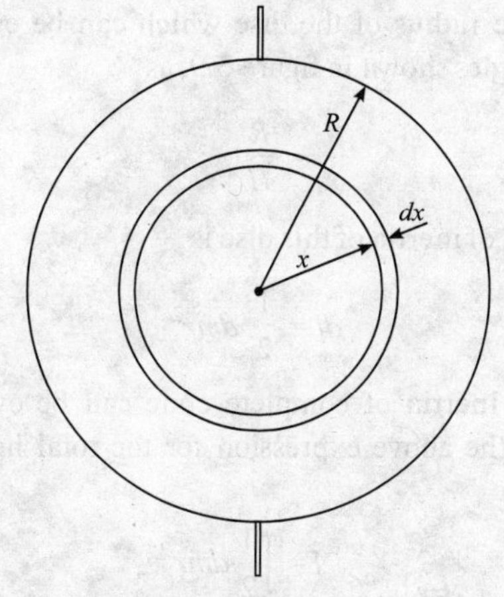

Figure 5.8

$$dI = \frac{2}{3}\, dm\, x^2$$

Substituting dm and integrating this within limits from 0 to R, gives

$$I = \int_0^R \frac{2}{3} . \frac{3M}{R^3} x^4\, dx$$

or $$= \frac{2M}{R^3} \left[\frac{x^5}{5} \right]_0^R$$

or $$= \frac{2}{5} MR^2$$

(v) Moment of Inertia of a Solid Cone

To find the moment of inertia of a solid cone of mass M, radius R and height H, we consider a disc at a distance x from the vertex of the cone. The mass of this disc is

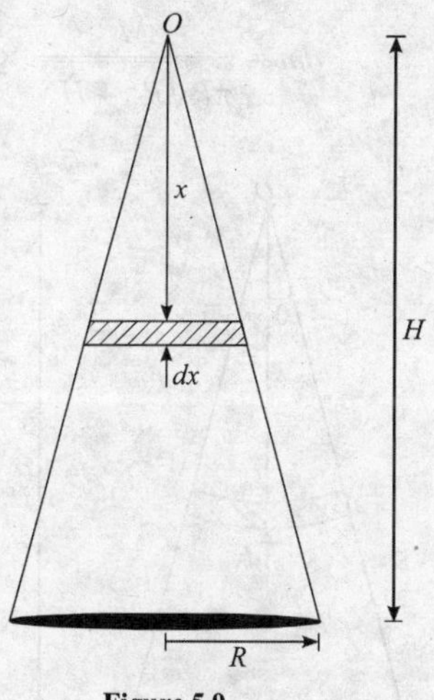

Figure 5.9

$$dm = \frac{3M}{\pi R^2 H} \times \pi r^2\, dx$$

Here r is the radius of the disc which can be evaluated by similar triangles shown in figure-5.9, as

$$\frac{r}{x} = \frac{R}{H}$$

and moment of inertia of this disc is

$$dI = \frac{1}{2}\, dmr^2$$

Moment of inertia of complete cone can be evaluated by integrating the above expression for the total height of the cone as

$$I = \int \frac{1}{2}\, dmr^2$$

or $$= \int_0^H \frac{1}{2}\frac{3M}{R^2}\left(\frac{Rx}{H}\right)^4 . dx$$

or $$= \frac{3}{2}\frac{MR^2}{H^4}\int_0^H x^4\, dx$$

or $$= \frac{3}{2}\frac{MR^2}{H^4}\left[\frac{x^5}{5}\right]_0^H$$

or $$= \frac{3}{10} MR^2 \qquad \ldots(5.6)$$

(vi) Moment of Inertia of a Hollow Cone

Here we consider elemental strips of vertical width dx at a distance x from the vertex of the cone. The actual width of this strip is dx secθ, where θ is the half angle of the cone. If cone mass is M, mass of the elemental strip ring is

$$dm = \frac{M}{\pi R\sqrt{R^2 + H^2}} \times 2\pi r\, .\, dx \sec\theta$$

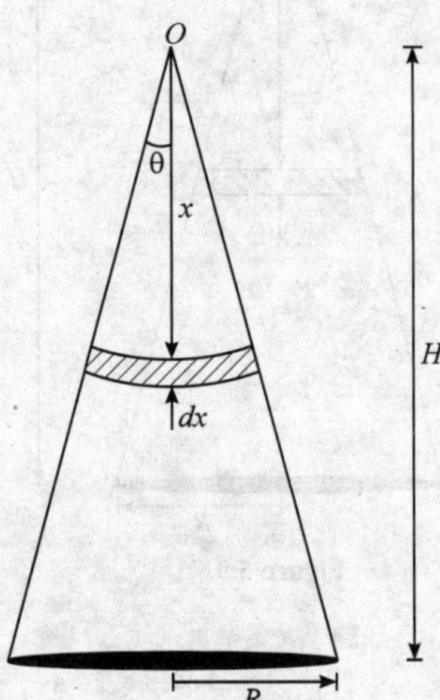

Figure 5.10

Where, radius of this ring is $r = \frac{Rx}{H}$. The moment of inertia of this ring is given as

$$dI = dmr^2$$

or $$I = \int_0^H dmr^2$$

or $$= \int_0^H \frac{2\,MR^2}{\sqrt{R^2 + H^2}} \times \frac{x^3}{H^3} dx \frac{\sqrt{R^2 + H^2}}{H}$$

or $$= \frac{2\,MR^2}{H^4}\int_0^H x^3 dx$$

or $$= \frac{2\,MR^2}{H^4}\left[\frac{x^4}{4}\right]_0^H$$

or $$= \frac{1}{2} MR^2 \qquad \ldots(5.7)$$

(vii) Moment of Inertia of Rod

Consider a rod of mass M and length L shown in figure-5.11. It is pivoted at its centre. We consider an element of width dx at a distance x from the axis of rotation. It will revolve in a circle of radius x when rod will rotate. Mass of this element is given as

$$dm = \frac{M}{L}\, dx$$

Moment of inertia of this element dm is

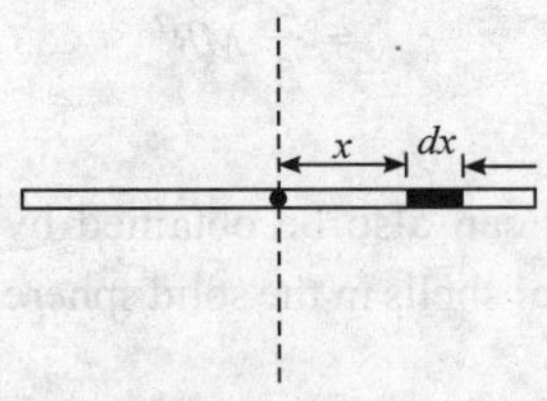

Figure 5.11

$$dI = dmx^2$$

Moment of inertia of the complete rod is given by integrating the above expression as

$$I = \int dmx^2$$

or $$= \int_{-L/2}^{+L/2} \frac{M}{L} x^2\, dx$$

or $$= \frac{M}{L}\left[\frac{x^3}{3}\right]_{-1/2}^{+1/2}$$

or $$= \frac{ML^2}{12} \qquad \ldots(5.8)$$

If rod is pivoted at one of its end, instead of centre, the limits of integration will become 0 to L and the moment of inertia will become

$$I = \int_0^L \frac{M}{L} x^2\, dx$$

or $$= \frac{M}{L}\left[\frac{x^3}{3}\right]_0^L$$

or $$= \frac{ML^2}{3} \qquad \ldots(5.9)$$

We can see that when rod is pivoted at an end, moment of inertia is higher than that obtained when it is pivoted at centre. This is due to the difference in mass distribution from the axis of rotation. As mass is distributed more away from the axis of rotation, increase in moment of inertia is more.

Web Reference of Video Lectures at www.physicsgalaxy.com

Age Group - High School Physics | Age 17-19 Years
Section - MECHANICS
Topic - Rigid Body Dynamics
Module Number - 3, 4, 5, 6, 7, 8 and 9

5.2.3 Moment of Inertia About a General Axis of Rotation

In previous sections, the moment of inertia of different objects, we have evaluated are about the axis of symmetry of the objects, generally passing through the centre of mass. For evaluation of moment of inertia about any randomly selected axis of rotation of body we use axes theorems. There are two axes theorems which are used frequently in problems.

1. Perpendicular Axes Theorem

This theorem is only valid for laminar objects that is only for two dimensional objects which are rotating about an axis passing through their centre of mass. Consider such a plate like object shown in figure-5.12. We rotate this body about an axis along x-axis, lying in the plane on body and passing through its centre of mass. Let the moment of inertia about this axis be I_1 and now if it is rotated about y-axis, which is also in its plane and passing through its centre of mass. Let moment of inertia about this axis be I_2. If the body is rotated about a third axis, which is perpendicular to both of the previous axes and also perpendicular to the plane of the body, its moment of inertia I_3 is given by the sum of I_1 and I_2.

$$I_3 = I_1 + I_2 \qquad \ldots(5.10)$$

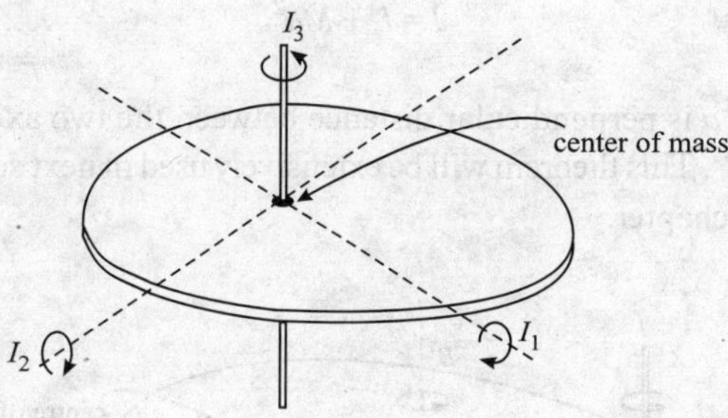

Figure 5.12

***Proof*:**

We consider an elemental mass dm in the body at a distance r from the main axis, which is perpendicular to the plane of body, as shown in figure-5.13. Let the distance of dm from x and y axes are a and b respectively. The moment of inertia of the whole body about main axis will be according definition of momentum of inertia

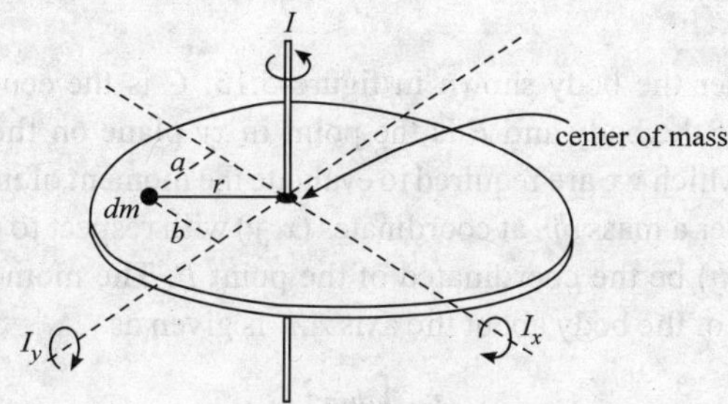

Figure 5.13

$$I = \int dm r^2$$

or $$I = \int dm(a^2 + b^2)$$

or $$= \int dm a^2 + \int dm b^2$$

or $$= I_x + I_y$$

2. Parallel Axes Theorem

It can be used for bodies of any shape rotating about any axis of rotation. Consider a body rotating about an axis AA' passing through it shown in figure-5.14. To find moment of inertia about this axis of rotation, first we find an imaginary axis BB' which is parallel to AA' and passing through centre of mass of the body. Now we evaluate the moment of inertia of the body if it were rotated about BB', let it be I_c. The moment of inertia of the body about the axis AA' is given as

$$I = I_c + Md^2 \qquad \dots(5.11)$$

Where d is perpendicular distance between the two axes AA' and BB'. This theorem will be extensively used in next sections of this chapter.

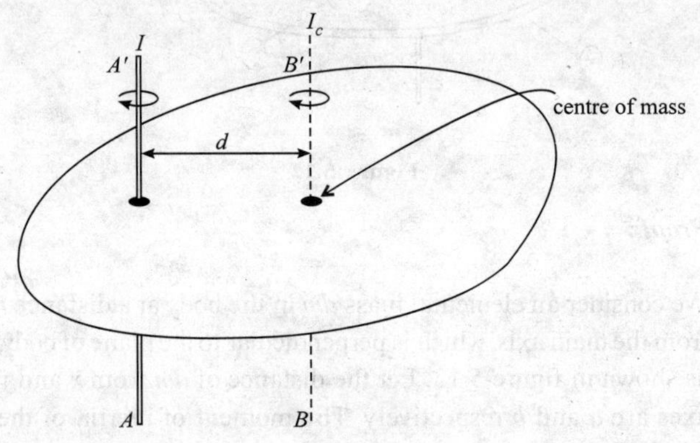

Figure 5.14

***Proof*:**

Consider the body shown in figure-5.15. C is the centre of mass of the body and P is the point in xy plane on the axis about which we are required to evaluate the moment of inertia. Consider a mass dm at coordinates (x, y) with respect to C and let (a, b) be the coordinated of the point P. The moment of inertia of the body about the axis AA' is given as

$$I = \int dm r^2$$

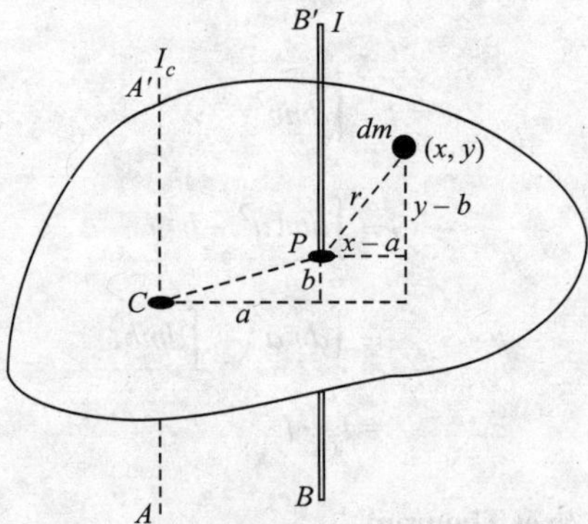

Figure 5.15

We have $r^2 = (x - a)^2 + (y - b)^2$, thus

$$I = \int dm[(x-a)^2 + (y-b)^2]$$

or $$= \int dm[(x^2 + y^2) + \int dm(a^2 + b^2) - 2a\int dmx - 2b\int dmy$$

or $$= \int dml^2 + \int dm\, d^2 - 2a\,(0) - 2b(0)$$

Here $\int dmy$ and $\int dmy$ are zero according to the definition of centre of mass, as the sum of mass moments of all the masses of system about centre of mass is equal to zero.

Here $\int dml^2$ is the moment of inertia of the body about the central axis BB', which is I_c and in the second term $\int dmd^2$, d is a constant distance between the two axes, thus it can be written as Md^2.

So we have $\qquad I = I_c + Md^2$

5.2.4 Application of Axes Theorems

Moment of Inertia of a Ring and Disk About Different Axes

When a ring rotates about the symmetry axis passing through its centre, as shown in figure-5.16(a), its moment of inertia is MR^2. Now consider an axis along the diameter (XX') of the ring shown in figure-5.16(b). If ring is rotated about this axis and if the moment of inertia be I and if we consider another diameter perpendicular to it (YY') and if ring rotates about this axis, again moment of inertia remains unchanged as both situations are identical. Now according to perpendicular axis theorem sum of these two equal moment of inertias must be equal to MR^2 (about axis ZZ'). Thus we have

$$I_z = MR^2 = I + I = 2I$$

or $$I = \frac{1}{2}MR^2 \qquad \dots(5.12)$$

Equation-(5.12) gives the moment of inertia of a ring when it rotates about a diametrical axis.

Now consider figure-5.16(c). In this situation the ring is rotating about a tangential axis which is perpendicular to the plane of ring. Moment of inertia of the ring about this axis can be evaluated by using parallel axis theorem as

$$I = I_c + MR^2$$

or $$= MR^2 + MR^2 = 2MR^2 \qquad \dots(5.13)$$

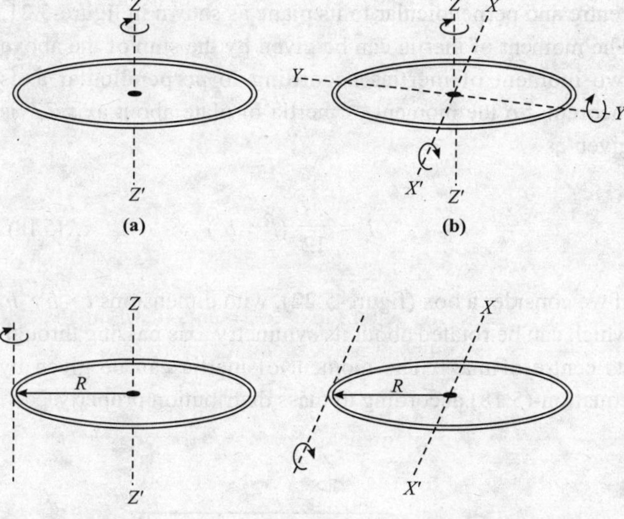

Figure 5.16

Similarly, figure-5.16(d), shows a ring which can rotate about an axis tangential to ring and lying in the plane of ring. Again using parallel axis theorem, moment of inertia of ring about this axis is

$$I = I_c + MR^2$$

or $$= \frac{1}{2} MR^2 + MR^2$$

$$= \frac{3}{2} MR^2 \quad \ldots(5.14)$$

In this situation I_c is the moment of inertia about the diametrical axis which is parallel to the given axis and passing through the centre of mass.

Similarly we can find these moment of inertia for a disc about diametrical and tangential axes. The results are given according to the situations shown in figure-5.17.

M.I. of disc about the central axis is [figure-5.17(a)]

$$I_c = \frac{1}{2} MR^2$$

M.I. of disc about the diametrical axis is [figure-5.17(b)]

$$I_z = \frac{1}{2} MR^2 = I + I = 2I$$

or $$= \frac{1}{4} MR^2 \quad \ldots(5.15)$$

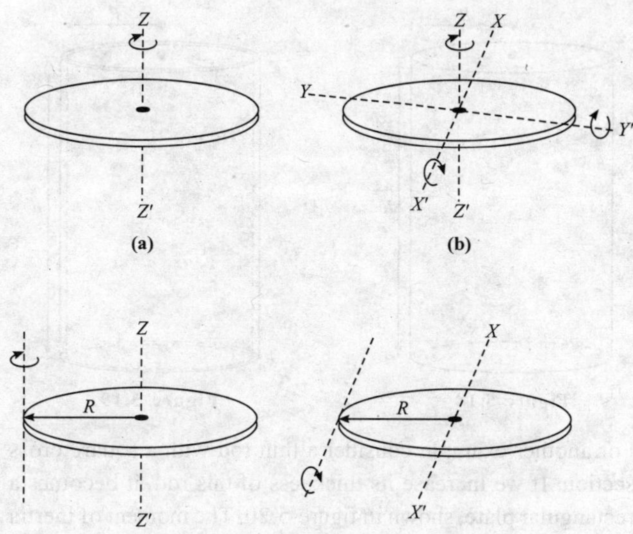

Figure 5.17

M.I. of disc about the tangential axis perpendicular to the plane of disc is [figure-5.17(c)]

$$I = I_c + MR^2$$

or $$= \frac{1}{2} MR^2 + MR^2$$

$$= \frac{3}{2} MR^2 \quad \ldots(5.16)$$

M.I. of disc about the tangential axis in the plane of disc is [figure-5.17(d)]

$$I = I_c + MR^2$$

or $$= \frac{1}{4} MR^2 + MR^2$$

$$= \frac{5}{4} MR^2 \quad \ldots(5.17)$$

Moment of inertia of different objects can be obtained by using axes theorems as we have obtained for ring and disc. Students are required to evaluate moment of inertias of different objects about any randomly selected axis of rotation for practice.

5.2.5 Mass Distribution and Moment of Inertia

We have read that moment of inertia of an object depends on its mass as well as its mass distribution about the axis of rotation. There are several objects which can be derived from the basic objects by changing their dimensions. For example if we increase the thickness of a disc it becomes a cylinder (figure-5.18). The expression for moment of inertia for the derived object will also remain same. Similarly if we think about a hollow cylinder shown in figure-5.19, it is derived from a ring. Its moment of inertia can be given directly as MR^2. On changing the dimensions, expression for moment of inertia will not change.

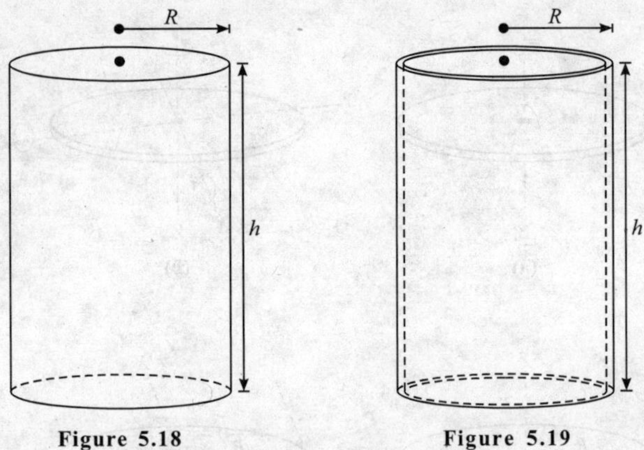

Figure 5.18 Figure 5.19

For another example consider a thin rod with a square cross section. If we increase its thickness of this rod, it becomes a rectangular plate, shown in figure-5.20. The moment of inertia of the rectangular plate can also be given by the expression used for rod as

$$I = \frac{Ml^2}{12}$$

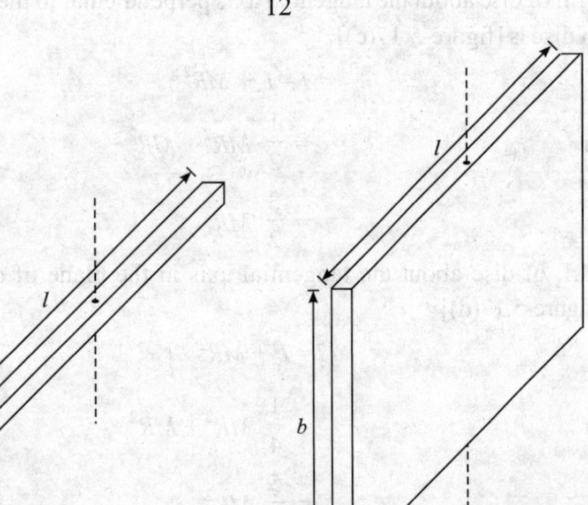

Figure 5.20

Now consider a rectangular plate shown in figure-5.21, with dimensions $l \times b$. If this plate is rotated about axis XX' and YY', the respective moment of inertias can be given as

$$I_{XX'} = \frac{Mb^2}{12} \quad \text{and} \quad I_{YY'} = \frac{Ml^2}{12}$$

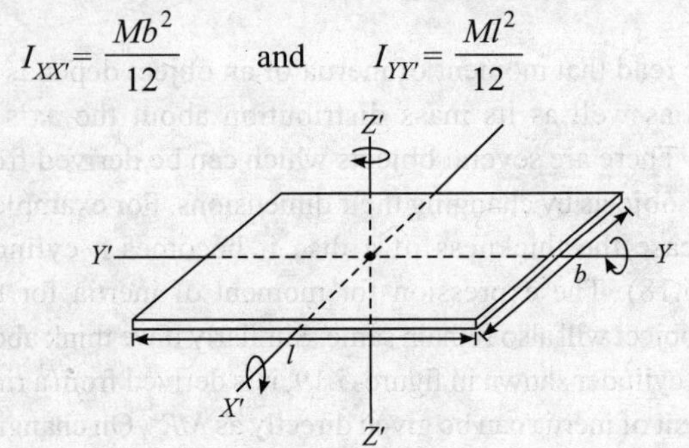

Figure 5.21

Now if this plate is rotated about the axis passing through its centre and perpendicular to its plane as shown in figure-5.21. The moment of inertia can be given by the sum of the above two moment of inertias according to perpendicular axes theorem. So the moment of inertia of plate about axis ZZ' is given as

$$I_c = \frac{M}{12}(l^2 + b^2) \qquad \ldots(5.18)$$

If we consider a box (figure-5.22), with dimensions $l \times b \times h$, which can be rotated about its symmetry axis passing through its centre of mass. The moment of inertia can be given by equation-(5.18) according to mass distribution property.

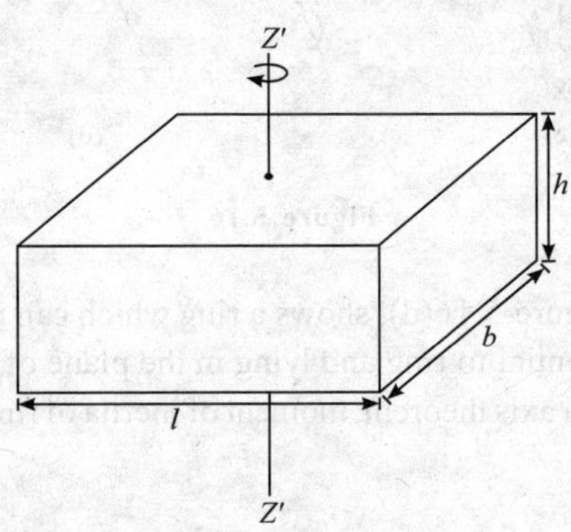

Figure 5.22

The Mass Distribution Property is stated as

"If size of a body in any or all dimensions is increased in such a way that its mass distribution about given axis of rotation remain same then expression of moment of inertia also remain same."

This mass distribution property can also be used for subtractive objects. If an object is removed from an object which is rotating about a given axis of rotation then for the remaining part expression of moment of inertia remain same as that of the original object if the object removed has same mass distribution as that of the original object. Let us understand this with the help of few examples. If a disc which is rotating about its central axis is cut into N identical sectors then each sector if alone rotates, it will have same expression of moment of inertia $\left(\frac{1}{2}\right)MR^2$ where M is the mass of sector alone. Similarly if a sphere of radius R is rotating about its diametrical axis and the sphere is cut into two identical halves then both the halves have same mass distribution about the given axis of rotation hence each hemisphere about the given axis of rotation will have moment of inertia given as $\left(\frac{2}{5}\right)MR^2$ where M is the mass of each hemisphere. Thus mass distribution property can also be stated as

"If a body is cut into N identical parts each of which has same mass distribution about the given axis of rotation then expression of moment of inertia of each part alone about the given axis of rotation will be same as that of the original body."

Illustrative Example 5.1

Find the moment of inertia of a spherical ball of mass m_1, radius r attached at the end of a thin straight rod of mass m_2 and length l, if this system is free to rotate about an axis passing through an end of the rod (end of rod opposite to sphere).

Solution

In this system shown in figure-5.23, the total moment of inertia can be given as the sum of moment of inertia of rod and that of the spherical ball.

Moment of inertia of the rod about the axis passing through an end is

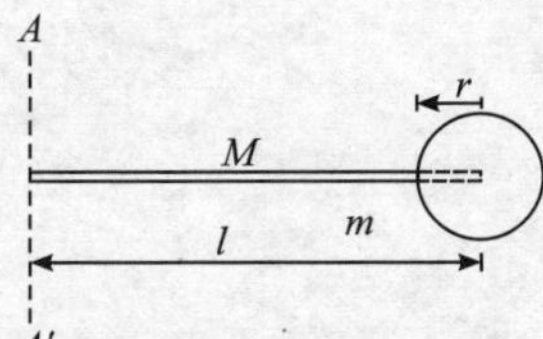

Figure 5.23

$$I_{rod} = \frac{Ml^2}{3}$$

Moment of inertia of the spherical ball about the axis passing through its geometrical centre is

$$I = \frac{2}{5}mr^2$$

Using parallel axes theorem we get its moment of inertia about the axis passing through the end of rod as

$$I_{AA'} = \frac{2}{5}mr^2 + ml^2$$

Thus total moment of inertia of the system can be given as

$$I_{Total} = I_{rod} + I_{AA'}$$

or $$= \frac{Ml^2}{3} + \left(\frac{2}{5}mr^2 + ml^2\right)$$

Illustrative Example 5.2

A rod of length l is pivoted about an end. Find the moment of inertia of the rod about this axis if the linear mass density of rod varies as $\rho = ax^2 + b$ kg/m.

Solution

As mass of the rod varies with its length, here we cannot use the expression $\frac{Ml^2}{3}$, which is only used for uniformly distributed mass along the length of rod pivoted at an end. In this case we consider an elemental length dx from the axis at a distance x. Let its mass be dm, where

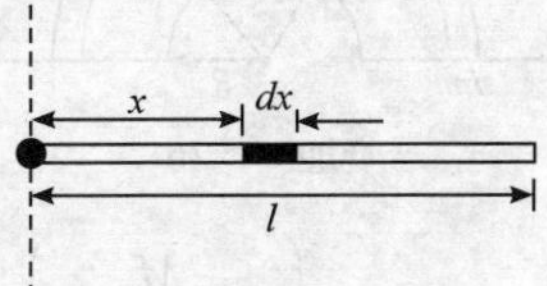

Figure 5.24

$$dm = \rho\, dx$$

or $$= (ax^2 + b)\, dx$$

During rotation of rod this dm revolves in a circle of radius x, hence its moment of inertia dI is given as

$$dI = dmx^2$$

or $$= (ax^2 + b)\, x^2\, dx$$

The moment of inertia of the whole rod is given by integrating the above expression within limits from 0 to l as

$$I = \int_0^l (ax^2 + b)x^2 dx$$

or $$= \left[\frac{ax^5}{5} + \frac{bx^3}{3}\right]_0^l$$

or $$= \frac{al^5}{5} + \frac{bl^3}{3}$$

Illustrative Example 5.3

Find the moment of inertia of half disc of radius R_2 and mass M about its centre, shown in figure-5.25. A smaller half disc of radius R_1 is cut from this disc.

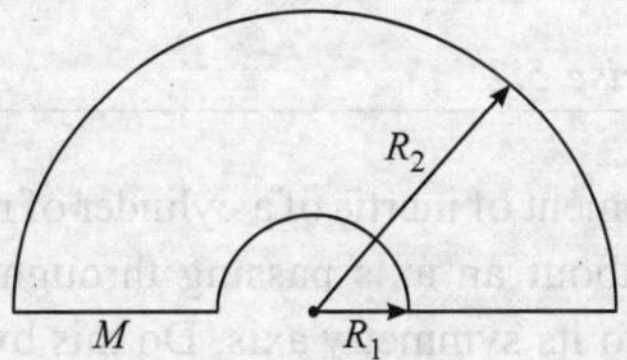

Figure 5.25

Solution

Moment of inertia of this object can be obtained as we have evaluated the moment of inertia of a disc by integrating elemental rings of radius x and width dx.

We consider an elemental half ring of radius x and width dx, as shown in figure-5.26. Let mass of this elemental disc be dm, which is given as

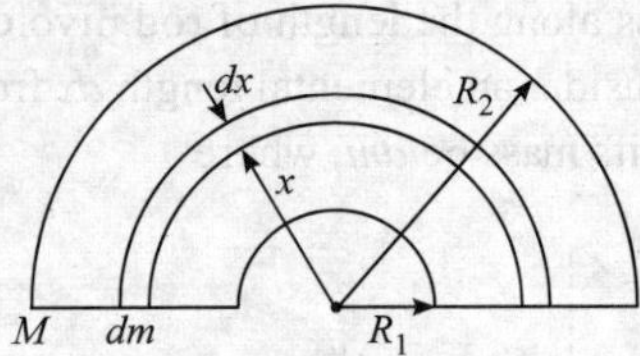

Figure 5.26

$$dm = \left(\frac{M}{\pi R_2^2 - \pi R_1^2}\right) \times \pi x\, dx$$

Moment of inertia of this elemental half ring can be given as

$$dI = dmx^2$$

$$= \left(\frac{M}{\pi R_2^2 - \pi R_1^2}\right) \times \pi x^3\, dx$$

Moment of inertia of the whole object can be given by integrating the above expression within limits from R_1 to R_2 as

$$I = \int_{R_1}^{R_2} \left(\frac{M}{R_2^2 - R_1^2}\right) \times x^3\, dx$$

or
$$= \left(\frac{M}{R_2^2 - R_1^2}\right) \times \left[\frac{x^4}{4}\right]_{R_1}^{R_2}$$

or
$$= \frac{1}{4} M(R_1^2 + R_2^2)$$

Web Reference of Video Lectures at www.physicsgalaxy.com
Age Group - High School Physics | Age 17-19 Years
Section - MECHANICS
Topic - Rigid Body Dynamics
Module Number - 10, 11, 13, 14, 15 and 16

Practice Exercise 5.1

(i) Find the moment of inertia of a cylinder of mass M radius R and length L about an axis passing through its centre and perpendicular to its symmetry axis. Do this by integrating an elemental disc along the length of the cylinder.

[$\frac{1}{4}MR^2 + \frac{1}{12}ML^2$]

(ii) Calculate the moment of inertia of a rod whose linear density changes from ρ to $\eta\rho$ from the thinner end to the thicker end. The mass of the rod is equal to M and length L. Consider the axis of rotation perpendicular to the rod and passing through the thinner end. Express your answer in terms of M, L and η.

[$\frac{1}{6}ML^2\frac{3\eta+1}{\eta+1}$]

(iii) Find MI of the triangular lamina of mass M about the axis of rotation AB shown in figure-5.27.

[$\left[\frac{Ml^2}{6}\right]$]

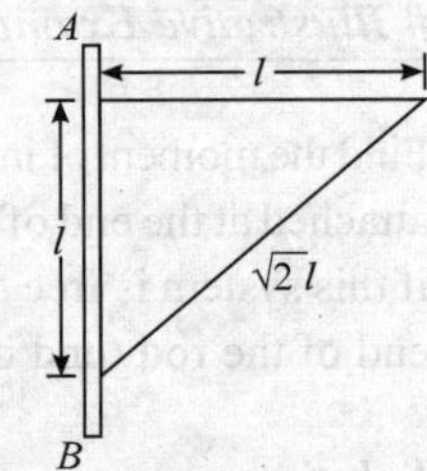

Figure 5.27

(iv) Find moment of inertia of a hemisphere of mass M shown in figure-5.28, about an axis AA' passing through its centre of mass.

[$\left[\frac{83}{320}MR^2\right]$]

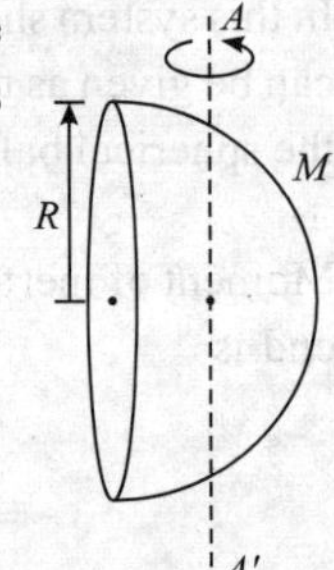

Figure 5.28

(v) Find moment of inertia of the half cylinder of mass M shown in figure-5.29, about the axis AA'.

[$\left[\left(\frac{9\pi-16}{6\pi}\right)MR^2\right]$]

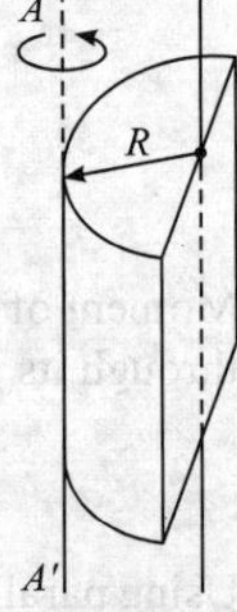

Figure 5.29

(vi) On the flat surface of a disc of radius a a small circular hole of radius b is made with its centre at a distance c from the centre of the disc. If mass of the whole uncut disc is M, calculate the moment of inertia of the holed disc about the axis of the circular hole.

[$\frac{1}{2}M\left[a^2 + 2c^2 - \frac{b^4}{a^2}\right]$]

(vii) One quarter section is cut from a uniform circular disc of radius R. This section has a mass M. It is made to rotate about a line perpendicular to its plane and passing through the centre of the original disc. Find its moment of inertia about the axis of rotation.

[$\frac{1}{2}MR^2$]

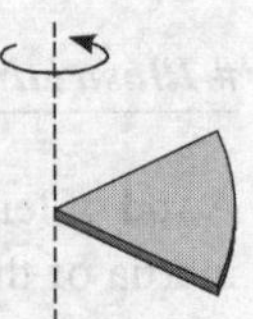

Figure 5.30

(viii) Calculate the moment of inertia of a wheel about its axis which is having rim of mass 24M and twenty four spokes each of mass M and length l.

[$32Ml^2$]

5.2.6 Radius of Gyration

We know that when a point object of mass m revolves in a circle of radius r, its moment of inertia is given as mr^2. Let an extended object of mass M rotate about a fixed axis of rotation and its moment of inertia be I, then radius of gyration of this object can be considered as the equivalent radius of the circular motion of this object, if treated as a point mass. The previous statement implies that if a point object of mass M (same as that of extended object) revolves in a circle of radius K, it will have moment of inertia MK^2. If this is equal to the previous moment of inertia I, K is termed as radius of gyration. Mathematically radius of gyration can be given as

"*It is the square of distance, when multiplied with the mass of the body, gives the moment of inertia of the body with respect to a given axis of rotation*"

For example, if a sphere of mass m and radius R is rotating about a tangential axis, its radius of gyration can be given as

$$MK^2 = \frac{7}{5}\, MR^2$$

or
$$K = \sqrt{\frac{7}{5}}\; R$$

Similarly, we can say that for a ring rotating about its central axis $K = R$, about diametrical axis $K = R/\sqrt{2}$, for a disc about central axis $K = R/\sqrt{2}$, about diametrical axis $K = R/2$ etc.

5.3 Torque and Newton's Second Law

In section 2.4, we have discussed about the turning effect of a force, torque. We know that for a body to be in rotational equilibrium, the sum of all the torque acting on it must be zero. Now what happens if net torque is not zero. The case is similar if net forces acting on a body is not zero, the body will accelerate according to Newton's second law. In rotational motion also the law holds good, but require some modification as when net torque on a body about a given axis of rotation is not zero, body will have angular acceleration. The magnitude of angular acceleration can be obtained by Newton's Second law in rotational motion.

In translational motion we use $F = ma$ ...(5.19)

In rotational motion we use $\tau = I\,\alpha$ ...(5.20)

Left hand side is the net torque acting on the body and on right hand side I is the moment of inertia of the body about the given axis and α is the angular acceleration of the body.

This corresponds to Newton's second law for translational motion, $a \propto F$, where torque has taken the place of force and correspondingly the angular acceleration α takes the place of the linear acceleration a. In the linear case, the acceleration is not only proportional to the net force but is also inversely proportional to the inertia of the body, which we call its mass m, thus we can write $a = F/m$. In case of rotational motion moment of inertia plays the role of mass.

As we have discussed that the rotational inertia of an object depends not only on its mass, but also on how that mass is distributed. For example, a large diameter cylinder will have greater rotational inertia than one of equal mass but smaller diameter (longer than previous). The former will be harder to start rotating, and harder to stop as its moment of inertia is larger. When the mass is concentrated farther from the axis of rotation, the rotational inertia is greater. This is the reason why in rotational motion the mass of a body can not be considered as concentrated at its centre of mass.

For understanding the application of Newton's second law in rotational motion, consider the rod shown in figure-5.31, pivoted at an end about which it can rotate. If two forces F_1 and F_2 are applied on it as shown, tend to rotate the rod. The respective torque of these forces are given as

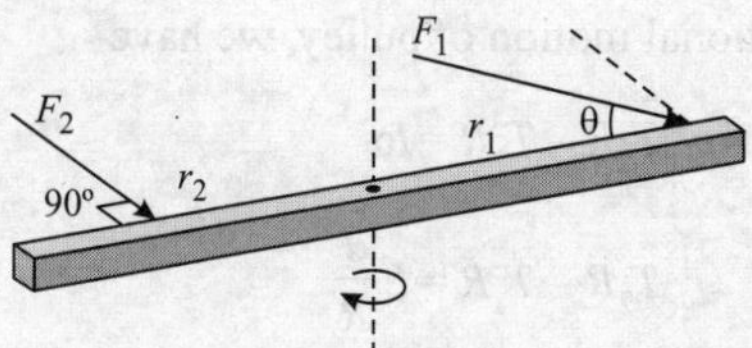

Figure 5.31

Clockwise torque due to force F_1 is $\tau_1 = F_1 \sin\theta \,.\, r_1$

Anticlockwise torque due to force F_2 is $\tau_2 = F_2 \,.\, r_2$

Let $\tau_1 > \tau_2$, the rod rotates in clockwise direction with an angular acceleration α, which can be shown from equation-(5.20), as ne torque is in clockwise direction, we have

$$F_1 r_1 \sin\theta - F_2 r_2 = \left(\frac{Ml^2}{3}\right)\alpha \qquad \text{...(5.21)}$$

As moment of inertia of the rod of mass M and pivoted at one of its end is given as $\frac{Ml^2}{3}$. Above equation-(5.21) will give initial angular acceleration of the rod.

Following examples will also explain the application of $\tau = I\alpha$ in different rotational problems.

Illustrative Example 5.4

Find the acceleration of m_1 and m_2 in an Atwood's Machine if there is friction present between surface of pulley and the thread and thread does not slip over the surface of pulley. Moment of inertia of pulley is I.

Solution

As there is friction between pulley and thread, tension in thread throughout will not remain same. Let on two sides of the pulley tension in thread be T_1 and T_2 and the masses are going with acceleration a. As thread does not slip of the surface of pulley, pulley will rotate and the linear acceleration of the particles on pulley at its rim will also be a, thus its angular acceleration can be given as

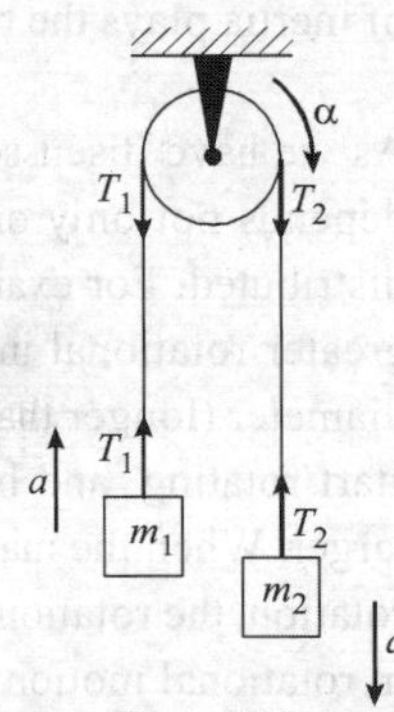

Figure 5.32

$$\alpha = \frac{a}{R}$$

Now we write motion equations for masses m_1 and m_2 as

$$T_1 - m_1 g = m_1 a \quad \dots(5.22)$$

or $$m_2 g - T_2 = m_2 a \quad \dots(5.23)$$

and for rotational motion of pulley, we have

$$T_2 R - T_1 R = I\alpha$$

or $$T_2 R - T_1 R = I\frac{a}{R}$$

or $$T_2 - T_1 = I\frac{a}{R^2} \quad \dots(5.24)$$

Adding equations-(5.22), (5.23) and (5.24), we get

$$(m_2 - m_1)g = \left(m_1 + m_2 + \frac{I}{R^2}\right)a$$

or $$a = \frac{(m_1 - m_2)g}{\left(m_1 + m_2 + \frac{I}{R^2}\right)} \quad \dots(5.25)$$

Illustrative Example 5.5

A uniform disc of radius R and mass M is mounted on an axis supported in fixed frictionless bearing. A light cord is wrapped around the rim of the wheel and suppose we hang a body of mass m from the cord.

(a) Find the angular acceleration of the disc and tangential acceleration of point on the rim.

(b) At a moment $t = 0$, the system is set in motion, find the time dependence of the angular velocity of the system and the kinetic energy of the whole system.

Solution

(a) The situation is shown in figure-5.33.

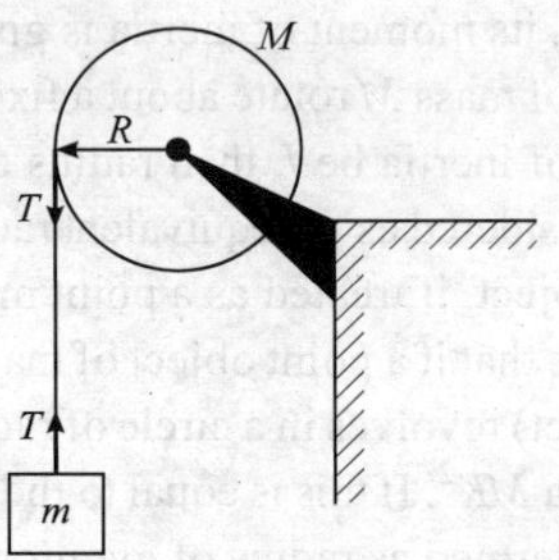

Figure 5.33

Let T be the tension in the cord for mass m going down, we have

$$mg - T = ma \quad \dots(5.26)$$

Where a is the tangential acceleration of a point on the rim of disc. If it rotates with angular acceleration α, we have

$$\alpha = \frac{a}{R}$$

For rotational motion of disc, we have

$$TR = \left(\frac{1}{2}MR^2\right)\alpha$$

or $$TR = \left(\frac{1}{2}MR^2\right)\frac{a}{R}$$

or $$T = \frac{1}{2}Ma \quad \dots(5.27)$$

From equations-(5.26) and (5.27), we have

$$mg - \frac{1}{2}Ma = ma$$

or $$a = \frac{2m}{M + 2m}g \quad \dots(5.28)$$

Angular acceleration of disc can now be written as

$$\alpha = \frac{a}{R} = \frac{2m}{M + 2m}\frac{g}{R} \quad \dots(5.29)$$

(b) The angular velocity of the system after time t can be given as

$$\omega = \alpha t$$

or $$= \frac{2mg}{R(M + 2m)} \cdot t$$

At this instant linear velocity of mass m is given as

$$v = \omega R = \frac{2mgt}{M+2m}$$

The kinetic energy of whole system is given as

$$(KE)_{whole} = \frac{1}{2}mv^2 + \frac{1}{2}I\omega^2$$

or $$= \frac{1}{2}m(\omega R)^2 + \frac{1}{2}\times\frac{1}{2}MR^2\omega^2$$

or $$= \frac{1}{4}\omega^2R^2(M+2m)$$

or $$= \frac{m^2g^2t^2}{M+2m}$$

Illustrative Example 5.6

A uniform cylinder of radius R and mass M can rotate freely about a stationary horizontal axis O. A thin cord of length l and mass m is wound on the cylinder in a single layer. Find the angular acceleration of the cylinder as a function of the length x of the hanging part of the cord. The wound part of the cord is supposed to have its centre of mass on the cylinder axis.

Solution

Let m' be the mass of hanging part of the cord as

$$m' = \frac{m}{l}x$$

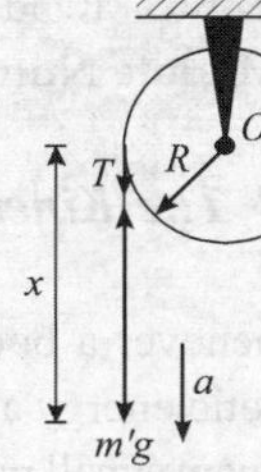

Figure 5.34

If the tension at the upper end of the cord, which is in contact with the cylinder is T and it is descending with an acceleration a, we have

$$\left(\frac{m}{l}x\right)g - T = \left(\frac{m}{l}x\right)a \qquad \ldots (5.30)$$

For cylinder which will be rotating with an angular acceleration

$\alpha = \frac{a}{R}$, we have

$$TR = I\alpha \qquad \ldots (5.31)$$

Here I is the moment of inertia of the cylinder plus the wound part of the cord, given as

$$I = \frac{1}{2}MR^2 + \frac{m}{l}(l-x)R^2 \qquad \ldots (5.32)$$

From equation-(5.31) and (5.32), we have

$$TR = \left[\frac{1}{2}MR^2 + \frac{m}{l}(l-x)R^2\right]\alpha$$

or $$T = \left[\frac{1}{2}MR + \frac{m}{l}(l-x)R\right]\alpha \qquad \ldots (5.33)$$

From equation-(5.30) and (5.33), we have

$$\left(\frac{m}{l}xg\right) - \left[\frac{1}{2}MR + \frac{m}{l}(l-x)R\right]\alpha = \left(\frac{m}{l}x\right)R\alpha$$

$$\left[\text{using } \alpha = \frac{a}{R}\right]$$

Solving, we get $$\alpha = \frac{2mgx}{(2m+M)Rl}$$

Illustrative Example 5.7

A cylinder of mass m suspended by two strings wrapped around the cylinder one near each end, the free ends of the string being attached to hooks on the ceiling, such that the length of the cylinder is horizontal. From the position of rest, the cylinder is allowed to roll down as suspension strings unwind, calculate

(a) The downward linear acceleration of the cylinder

(b) The tension in the strings

(c) The time dependence of the instantaneous power developed by gravity

Solution

(a) The situation is shown in figure-5.35. Let the downward linear acceleration of the cylinder be a, then we have for its linear motion

$$mg - 2T = ma \qquad \ldots (5.34)$$

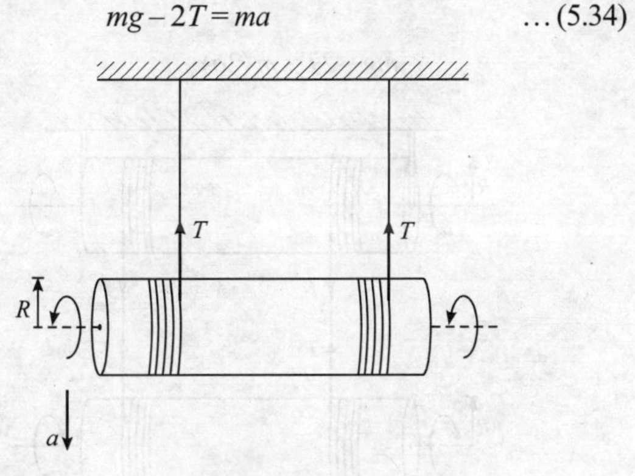

Figure 5.35

For its rotational motion, we have

$$2RT = I\alpha$$

or $$2RT = \left(\frac{1}{2}mR^2\right)\frac{a}{R}$$

or $$T = \frac{1}{4}ma \qquad \ldots(5.35)$$

From equations-(5.34) and (5.35), we get

$$\frac{1}{4}ma = \frac{1}{2}(mg - ma)$$

or $$a = \frac{2}{3}g$$

(b) Substituting the value of a in equation-(5.35), we get

$$T = \frac{1}{6}mg$$

(c) Velocity of the cylinder at time t is given as

$$v = at = \frac{2}{3}gt$$

Power developed due to gravity is

$$P = F \cdot v = mg \times \frac{2}{3}gt = \frac{2}{3}mg^2t$$

Illustrative Example 5.8

The arrangement shown in figure-5.36 consists of two identical uniform solid cylinders, each of mass m, on which two light threads are wound symmetrically. Find the tension of each thread in the process of motion. The friction in the axle of the upper cylinder is assumed to be absent.

Solution

For the situation shown in figure-5.36, all the forces acting on bodies are shown in figure-5.36. For translational motion of lower cylinder is

$$mg - 2T = m(2a) \qquad \ldots(5.36)$$

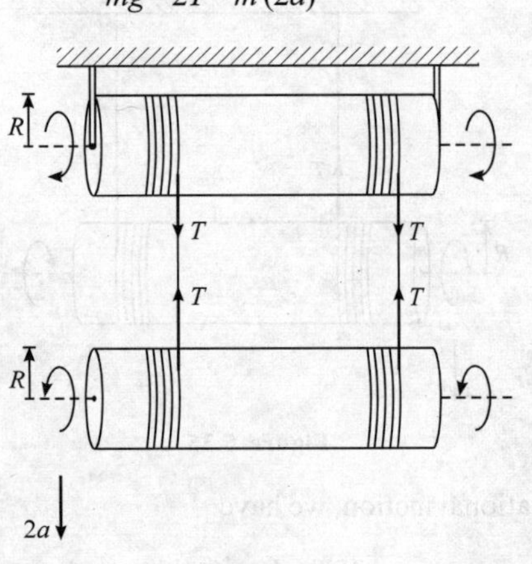

Figure 5.36

As tension on the two cylinders are equal, their angular acceleration will also be equal, thus if they are unwinding by angular acceleration $R\alpha$, the lower cylinder will go down with linear acceleration $2R\alpha$ i.e. $2a$.

For rotational motion of lower cylinder, we have

$$2TR = I\alpha$$

or $$2TR = \frac{1}{2}mR^2 \cdot \frac{a}{R}$$

or $$2T = \frac{1}{2}\text{ma} \qquad \ldots(5.37)$$

From equations-(5.36) and (5.37), we have

$$mg - \frac{1}{2}ma = 2\,\text{ma}$$

or $$a = \frac{2}{5}\text{g}$$

Substituting the value of a in equation-(5.37), we get

$$T = \frac{1}{10}\text{mg}$$

<u>Web Reference of Video Lectures at www.physicsgalaxy.com</u>
Age Group - High School Physics | Age 17-19 Years
Section - MECHANICS
Topic - Rigid Body Dynamics
Module Number - 12, 17, 18, 19, 20, 21 and 22

5.4 The Kinetic Energy of Rotation

Whenever a body rotates as shown in figure-5.37, there is a kinetic energy associated with the rotation. The body consists of many small particles, and the kinetic energy of a particle, say particle P, with mass dm has a kinetic energy dK. If at this instant body is rotating with angular velocity ω, particle P has velocity $r\omega$. Thus the kinetic energy dK is given as

$$dK = \frac{1}{2}dm(r\omega)^2$$

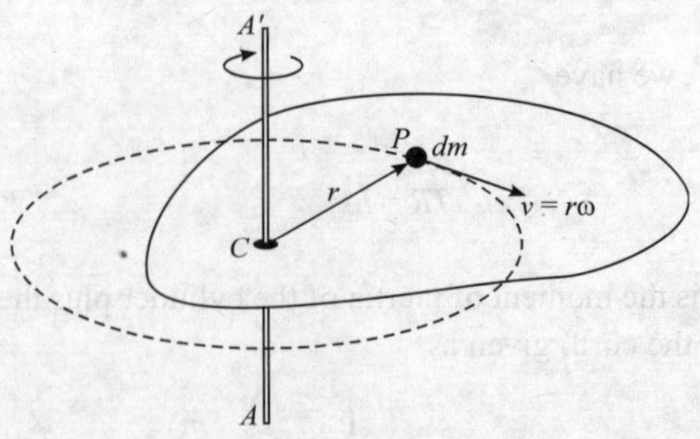

Figure 5.37

The total energy of the rotating body will be given by the integration of the above term for the whole mass of body, thus Total energy of rotation is

$$K = \int dK = \int \frac{1}{2} dm\, r^2 \omega^2$$

ω remains same for all the particles of the body (explained in section-(3.5)), so

$$K = \frac{1}{2} \omega^2 \int dm\, r^2$$

or

$$K = \frac{1}{2} I\omega^2 \qquad \ldots(5.38)$$

Equation-(5.38) gives the kinetic energy of a rotating body (sum of K.E. of body particles) rotating with angular velocity ω. If during rotation, centre of mass of the object undergoes translational motion it will have both translational and rotational kinetic energy. Then the total energy is written as

$$KE = \frac{1}{2} mv_{cm}^2 + \frac{1}{2} I_{cm}\omega^2 \qquad \ldots(5.39)$$

Where v_{cm} is the linear velocity of the centre of mass, I_{cm} is the moment of inertia about an axis through the centre of mass and ω is the angular velocity about this axis.

Illustrative Example 5.9

In an Atwood's machine the pulley mounted in horizontal frictionless bearings has a radius $R = 0.05$ m. The cord passing over the pulley carries a block of mass $m_1 = 0.75$ kg at one end and a block of mass $m_2 = 0.50$ kg on the other end. When set free from rest, the heavier block is observed to fall a distance 1 metre in 10 seconds. Find the moment of inertia of the pulley.

Solution

The situation is shown in figure-5.38 Let a be the linear acceleration. According to the given problem, the heavier block falls through a distance 1 m in 10 sec.

Figure 5.38

Now

$$s = ut + \frac{1}{2} at^2$$

or

$$1 = 0 + \frac{1}{2} a.(10)^2$$

$$\therefore \quad a = 1/50 = 0.02 \text{ m/sec}^2$$

Let v be the linear velocity at the end of 10 sec., then

$$v = u + at = 0 + 0.02 \times 10 = 0.2 \text{ m/s}$$

When the heavier mass falls through a distance 1 m, the loss of potential energy

$$= mgh = 0.75 \times 9.8 \times 1 = 7.35 \text{ joule}$$

The lighter mass ascends a distance 1 m and hence, the gain in its potential energy.

$$= 0.50 \times 9.8 \times 1 = 4.9 \text{ joule}$$

∴ Net loss of potential energy of the system

$$= 7.35 - 4.9 = 2.45 \text{ joule}$$

As there is no friction in the pulley, hence

Loss in potential energy = gain in kinetic energy of two blocks + rotational energy of pulley

$$\therefore \quad 2.45 = \frac{1}{2}(m_1 + m_2)v^2 + \frac{1}{2} I\omega^2$$

$$= \frac{1}{2}(m_1 + m_2)v^2 + \frac{1}{2} I\left(\frac{v}{R}\right)^2 \qquad (\because \omega = v/R)$$

$$= \frac{1}{2}(1.25)(0.2)^2 + \frac{1}{2} I\left(\frac{0.2}{0.05}\right)^2$$

$$= 0.0250 + 8I$$

$$\therefore \quad 8I = 2.45 - 0.0250 = 2.425$$

$$I = \frac{2.425}{8} = 0.3031 \text{ kg-m}^2$$

Illustrative Example 5.10

Find total energy of the inclined rod of mass m shown in figure-5.39, rotating with angular velocity ω, about a vertical axis XX', shown in figure.

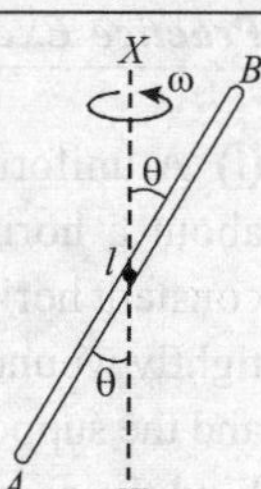

Figure 5.39

Solution

The mass of element dx shown in figure-5.40 is

$$dm = \frac{m}{l} dx$$

KE of this dm is

$$dE = \frac{1}{2}\left(\frac{m}{l} dx\right)(x \sin\theta .\, \omega)^2$$

Total energy of rod is

Figure 5.40

$$E = \int dE = \frac{1}{2}\frac{M}{l}\omega^2 \sin^2\theta . \int_{-l/2}^{+l/2} x^2 dx$$

$$E = \frac{1}{2}\frac{M}{l}\omega^2 \sin^2\theta \left[\frac{x^2}{3}\right]_{-l/2}^{+l/2}$$

$$= \frac{1}{6}\omega^2 \sin^2\theta \frac{l^3}{4}$$

$$= \frac{1}{24} m\omega^2 l \sin^2\theta$$

Alternative Solution

As shown in figure-5.39 moment of inertia of mass dm is

$$dI = dm\,(x \sin\theta)^2$$

Total MI of rod is $$I = \int dI = \int_{-l/2}^{+l/2} \frac{m}{l} dx \,.\, x^2 \sin^2\theta$$

$$I = \frac{1}{12} ml^2 \sin^2\theta$$

Web Reference of Video Lectures at www.physicsgalaxy.com

Age Group - High School Physics | Age 17-19 Years

Section - MECHANICS

Topic - Rigid Body Dynamics

Module Number - 30

Practice Exercise 5.2

(i) A uniform solid cylinder A of mass m_1 can freely rotate about a horizontal axis fixed to a mount B of mass m_2. A constant horizontal force F is applied to end P of a light thread tightly wound on the cylinder. The friction between the mount and the supporting horizontal surface is supposed to be absent. Find the acceleration of this point P and the kinetic energy of this system t seconds after beginning of motion.

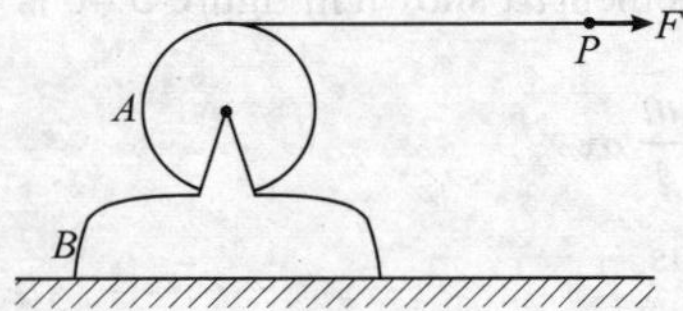

Figure 5.41

$[\frac{F(3m_1 + 2m_2)}{m_1(m_1 + m_2)}, \frac{F^2t^2(3m_1 + 2m_2)}{2m_1(m_1 + m_2)}]$

(ii) Two thin circular disc of mass 2 kg and radius 10 cm each are joined by a rigid massless rod of length 20 cm. The axis of the rod is along the perpendicular to the planes of the disc through their centres. This object is kept on a truck in such a way that the axis of the object is horizontal and perpendicular to the direction of motion of the truck. Its friction with the floor of the truck is large enough, so that the object can roll on the truck without slipping.

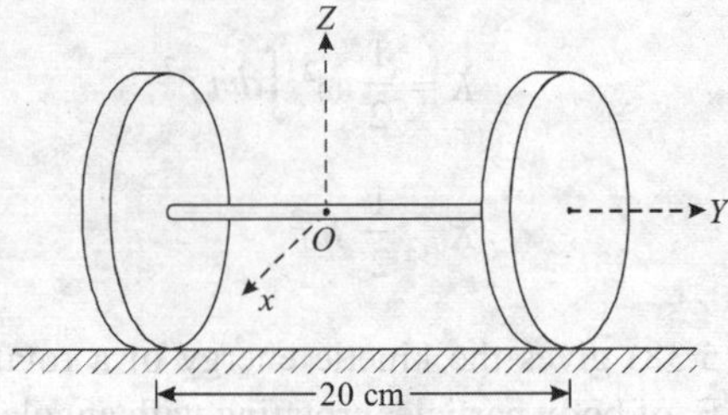

Figure 5.42

Take x-axis as the direction of motion of the truck and z-axis as the vertically upwards direction. If the truck has an acceleration 9 m/s^2, calculate :

(a) the friction force vector on each disc and

(b) the magnitude and direction of the frictional torque acting on each disc about the centre of mass O of the object. Express the torque in the vector form in terms of unit vector $\hat{i}$, $\hat{j}$ and $\hat{k}$ in x, y and z-directions.

[(a) $6\,\hat{i}$ N (b) $0.6\,(-\hat{j} \pm \hat{k})$, 0.85 Nm]

(iii) A uniform cylinder of radius R is spinned about its axis to the angular velocity ω_0 and then placed into a corner as shown in figure-5.43. The coefficient of friction between the corner wall, floor and the cylinder is equal to k. How many turns will the cylinder accomplish before it stops ?

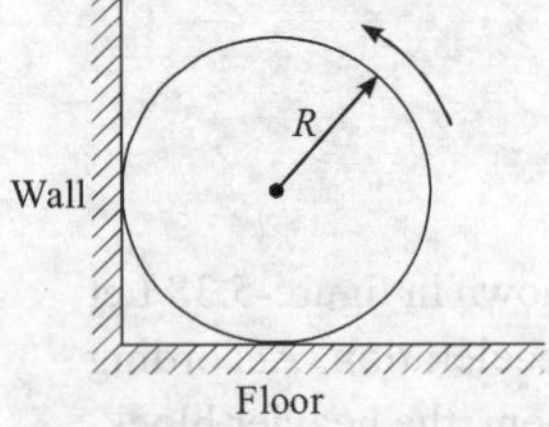

Figure 5.43

$[\frac{(1+k^2)\omega_0^2 R}{8\pi k(k+1)g}]$

(iv) A flywheel with the initial angular velocity ω_0 decelerates due to the forces whose moment relative to the axis is proportional to the square root of its angular velocity. Find the mean angular velocity of the flywheel averaged over the total deceleration time.

$[\frac{1}{3}\omega_0]$

(v) A uniform disc of radius R is first spinned about its axis to the angular velocity ω and then carefully placed with its flat face on a horizontal surface. How long will the disc be rotating on the surface if the friction coefficient is equal to μ ?

[$\frac{3\omega R}{4\mu g}$]

(vi) A uniform circular disc has radius R and mass m. A particle also mass m, is fixed at point A on the edge of the disc as shown in figure-5.44. The disc can rotate freely about a fixed horizontal cord PQ that is at a distance $R/4$ from the centre C at the disc. The line AC is perpendicular to PQ. Initially, the disc is held vertical with the point A at its highest position. It is then allowed to fall so that it starts rotating about PQ. Find the linear speed of the particle as it reaches the lowest position.

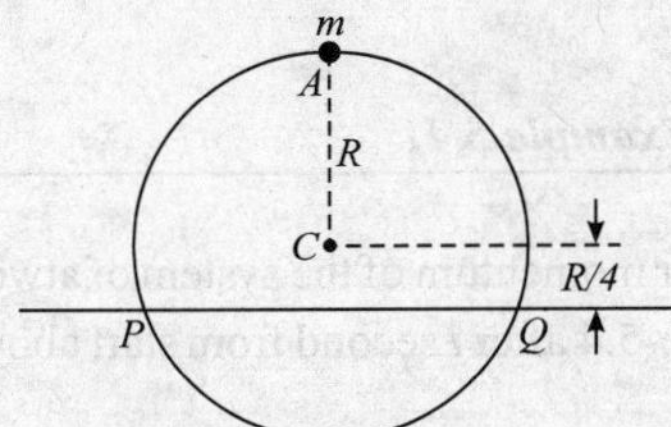

Figure 5.44

[$\sqrt{5gR}$]

(vii) A wheel of radius 6 cm is mounted so as to rotate about a horizontal axis through its centre. A string of negligible mass wrapped round its circumference carries a mass of 0.2 kg attached to its free end. When let fall, the mass descends through one meter in 5 seconds. Calculate the angular acceleration of the wheel, its moment of inertia and tension in the cord. Take $g = 10$ m/s^2.

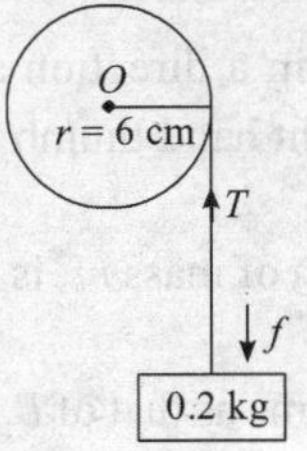

Figure 5.45

[4/3 rad/s^2, 0.0893 kg-m^2, 1.984 N]

5.5 Angular Momentum and its Conservation

Throughout this chapter we have seen that by using the appropriate angular variables, the kinematics and dynamic equations for rotational motion are analogous to those for ordinary translational motion. In same manner, the linear momentum, $p = mv$, also has a rotational analog, which is called angular momentum, and for a body rotating about a fixed axis it is defined in two ways.

5.5.1 Angular Momentum of Point Objects

The magnitude of angular momentum is the evaluated by moment of linear momentum. It is always evaluated with respect to a given point (or axis of rotation), so its value can be evaluated by multiplying the linear momentum with the shortest distance of the point from the line of momentum. For example, consider the situation shown in figure-5.46. A particle A of mass m is moving with a linear speed v along a straight line. If we find the angular momentum of this particle with respect to a point P shown in figure, it is given as

$$L_{AP} = mv \times d \quad \dots(5.40)$$

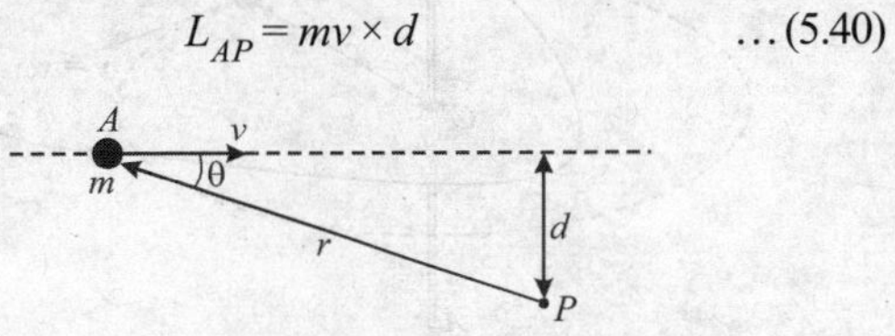

Figure 5.46

If the position vector of A from P is $\vec{r}$, then

$$L_{AP} = mv \times r\sin\theta$$

In vector form we can write as

$$\vec{L} = m(\vec{r} \times \vec{v}) \quad \dots(5.41)$$

It states that the direction of angular momentum is perpendicular to the plane containing vector $\vec{r}$ and vector $\vec{v}$, given by right hand thumb rule.

If a particle is revolving in a circular path, as shown in figure-5.47, here the shortest distance of linear momentum from the centre is its radius thus the angular momentum of particle about the centre of circle is mvr. Here the direction of angular momentum given by right hand thumb rule is in upward direction along the axis of circular motion in figure-5.48.

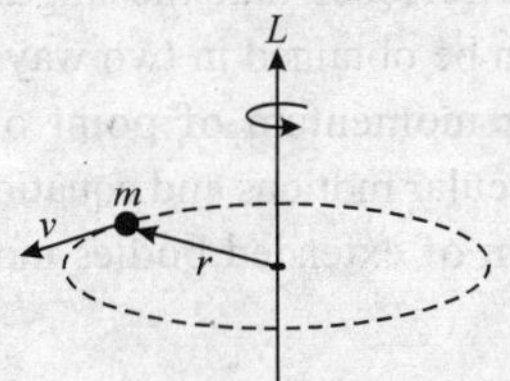

Figure 5.47

5.5.2 Angular Momentum of a Rigid Body in Rotation

Consider an extended body in rotational motion with an angular velocity ω. This body does not have any linear momentum, but different particles of the body have linear momentum. The particle which are far away from the axis of rotation have larger speed and the particles near to the axis have small speeds. Let us consider a small element of mass dm at a distance x from the axis of rotation shown in figure-5.48. During rotation of the body, this dm is in circular motion of radius x and it will have a linear $x\omega$, tangential to that circle. This dm has an angular momentum given as

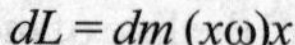

$$dL = dm\,(x\omega)x$$

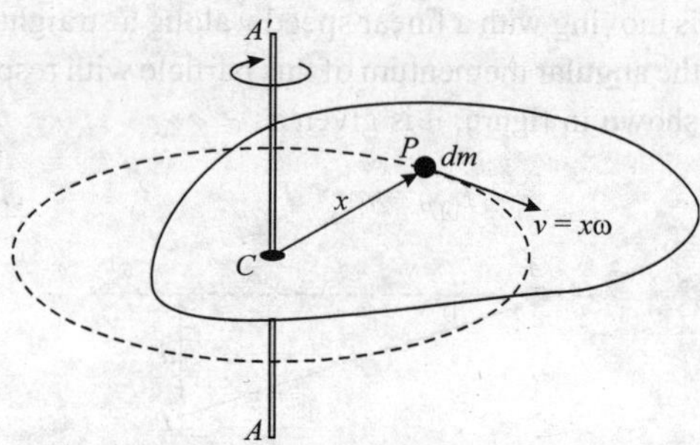

Figure 5.48

The angular momentum of the whole body can be given by integrating this expression for the whole mass of body as

$$L\int dL = \int dmx^2\omega$$

Angular velocity ω remains constant for all the particle of a body in rotation. Thus

$$L = \omega\int dmx^2$$

or $$L = I\omega \qquad \text{... (5.42)}$$

Here the term $\int dmx^2$ is the moment of inertia of an extended body (equation-(5.2)).

Above discussion releases that the angular momentum of moving bodies can be obtained in two ways. Equation-(5.41) gives the angular momentum of point objects moving in translational or circular motions and equation-(5.42) gives the angular momentum of extended bodies moving in rotational motion.

If a body has both translational and rotational motion, then its angular momentum is calculated by above equations but care must be taken in calculating the total angular momentum as right hand thumb rule gives the direction (signs) of respective angular momentums. For such cases explained above, which have both translational and rotational motion, we use the following relation to find the angular momentum of the body about a given point.

$$\boldsymbol{L} = \boldsymbol{L_c} + \boldsymbol{mvR} \qquad \text{... (5.43)}$$

Where $\boldsymbol{L}$ is the required angular momentum, $\boldsymbol{L_c}$ is the angular momentum of the body about its rotational axis in the reference frame of centre of mass and the last term in the equation mvR is the angular momentum of its translational motion about the point with respect to which the total angular momentum is required.

Now we consider few examples, which will make the concept of angular momentum clear to you and than we will discuss the conservative property of angular momentum like linear momentum.

 # Illustrative Example 5.11

Find the angular momentum of the system of atwood's machine used in example-5.4 after t second from start about point O, the axle of pulley.

Solution

We have already evaluated the acceleration of the masses in example-5.4. After time t, the velocity of the masses will be $v = at$. The angular velocity of the pulley will be $\omega = v/R$. Now for total angular momentum, we find the sum of angular moments of masses m_1, m_2 and the pulley about the point O.

The angular momentum of mass m_1 is

$$L_1 = m_1vR$$

The direction of L_1 is in a direction away from the plane of paper, according to right hand thumb rule.

The angular momentum of mass m_2 is $L_2 = m_2vR$

The direction of L_2 is same as that of L_1 as it is also in clockwise direction with respect to O.

The angular momentum of pulley is $L_3 = I\omega = I\left(\dfrac{v}{R}\right)$

As pulley is also rotating in clockwise direction, it is also in same direction as that of L_1 and L_2.

Thus the total angular momentum of the system at this instant is given as

$$L = m_1vR + m_2vR + I\frac{v}{R}$$

 # *Illustrative Example 5.12*

Consider the cylinder rolling on a horizontal plane. Its linear velocity is v and rotational angular velocity is ω. Find its angular momentum about point P on ground as shown in figure-5.49. What happens to this angular momentum if the cylinder is rotating in opposite direction but moving translationally in same direction.

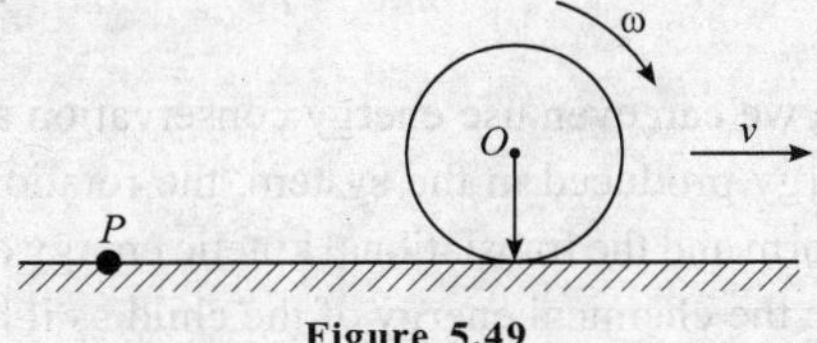

Figure 5.49

Solution

In the given situation, cylinder has both translational and rotational motion. We find its angular momentum about P by using the equation-(5.43).

The angular momentum of the cylinder about its axis of rotation passing through its centre of mass is given as

$$L_c = I\omega = \left(\frac{1}{2}mr^2\right)\omega$$

and the angular momentum of this cylinder's translational motion about P is

$$L_t = mvR$$

Total angular momentum of cylinder about point P is given as

$$L = \frac{1}{2}mr^2\omega + mvR$$

Here, two angular momenta are added as L_c is in the direction outward to the plane of paper due to clockwise rotation and mvR is also in outward direction as with respect to point P, cylinder is moving towards right (in clockwise direction).

If cylinder rotates in anticlockwise direction and moving in same direction, its total angular momentum will now be written as

$$L = \frac{1}{2}mr^2\omega - mvR$$

5.5.3 Conservation of Angular Momentum

In chapter-4, we have studied about the law of conservation of linear momentum. Similar law also exist for angular momentum. In previous case the restriction of the law depends on the net external force and in present case it is the net external torque which is governing the law.

For a general rotating body the angular momentum is given as

$$L = I\omega$$

Differentiating the above equation with respect to time

$$\frac{dL}{dt} = I\frac{d\omega}{dt}$$

or

$$\frac{dL}{dt} = I\alpha$$

Which is the relation of torque acting on a rotating body. Thus we can write the relation between torque acting on a body and its instantaneous angular momentum as

$$\tau = \frac{dL}{dt} \quad \ldots(5.44)$$

which is also verified by Newton's second law for rotational motion as "*The rate of change of angular momentum of a rotating body is equal to the net external torque acting on it*".

Now we can state the law of conservation of angular momentum as, if no external torque is acting on a body, that is $dL/dt = 0$, thus L value will not change or the angular momentum of the body remains constant. As in later part of previous chapter, we have explained the concept of linear momentum conservation in presence of external forces with the help of impulse imparted by an external force. Similar concept can also be defined for rotation.

According to equation-(5.44)

$$dL = \tau\, dt \quad \ldots(5.45)$$

Here the left side of the above equation is the change in angular momentum of a rotating body and the right side is known as angular impulse where τ is the external torque acting on the body. Here dL is the change in angular momentum due to the application of external torque for the duration dt. If external torque is acting in the same direction as that of angular momentum, it will increase and if it is acting in a direction opposite to that of angular momentum, it will decrease. The conservation equation can be written as

Initial angular momentum ± Angular Impulse = Final angular momentum

+ and – signs are used when the external torque will be acting in the direction of angular momentum or opposite to the direction of angular momentum.

Now we will take some examples for better understanding of the above concepts. First we take few examples of conservation of angular momentum in absence of external torque and then with external torque.

Illustrative Example 5.13

A disc with moment of inertia I_1, is rotating with an angular velocity ω_1 about a fixed axis. Another coaxial disc with moment of inertia I_2, which is at rest is gently placed on the first disc along the axis. Due to friction discs slips against each other and after some time both disc start rotating with a common angular velocity. Find this common angular velocity.

Solution

Due to the friction between their surfaces the already rotating disc gets retarded and the new disc gets accelerated. Friction between them exerts a torque on both of the discs, but as here it is the internal force of the system containing two discs and hence the torque on the two discs will also be an internal torque of the system and according the conservation law, internal torques can not alter the angular momentum of the system. Thus the final angular momentum of the two disc system must be equal to the initial angular momentum of the system. If the common angular velocity attained by the system is ω_2, when sliding stops, we have

$$I_1\omega_1 = (I_1 + I_2)\omega_2$$

or
$$\omega_2 = \frac{I_1}{I_1 + I_2}\,\omega_1$$

In this case, energy of the system will not remain conserved as the torque due friction between them will do work in slowing down first disc and speeding up the second disc and due to friction heat will also be generated.

Illustrative Example 5.14

A child of mass m is standing on the periphery of a circular platform of radius R, which can rotate about its central axis. The moment of inertia of platform is I. Child jumps off from the platform with a velocity u relative to platform. Find the angular speed of platform after child jumps off.

Solution

Initially the system was at rest, thus the initial angular momentum was zero. As child jumps of from the platform, it gains an angular momentum in the respective direction. This implies that the platform must also gain the same amount of angular momentum in opposite direction as the gun recoils when a bullet is fired from it.

When the child jumps off, the platform gains an angular velocity ω. Then the net velocity of child with respect to earth is $u - R\omega$. As no external torque is present, the net angular momentum of system must be finally zero, thus

$$m\,(u - R\omega)R = I\omega$$

or
$$\omega = \frac{muR}{mR^2 + I}$$

In this case we can even use energy conservation as the total kinetic energy produced in the system, the rotational energy of the platform and the translational kinetic energy of the child comes from the chemical energy of the child as it has pushed platform backward and itself forward. Be careful in using this as it is applicable if and only if during jump, the shoe of child does not slip on the platform. If slipping occurs, some energy will be lost in friction work. If no slipping occurs during jump we have reduction in chemical energy of child is

$$\Delta E = \frac{1}{2}\,mv^2 + \frac{1}{2}\,I\omega^2$$

Illustrative Example 5.15

Suppose in previous example, child stays at rest on the platform and one of his friend throws a ball of mass m_1 towards him from a direction tangential to the platform and the child on the platform catches the ball. Find the angular velocity of the platform after he catches the ball.

Solution

Again in this case no external torque is acting on the system so we can equate the angular momentum before catch and after catch. If after catching the ball platform start rotating with an angular speed ω, we have

Angular momentum of ball about centre of platform before catch =

Angular momentum of platform plus child plus ball after catch

$$muR = (I + mR^2 + m_1R^2)\omega$$

or
$$\omega = \frac{muR}{I + mR^2 + m_1R^2}$$

Here note that we are conserving angular momentum with respect to the centre pivot of the platform. This is because when child catches the ball, it has a linear momentum and due to it platform tend to gain a linear momentum, which develops a normal reaction on the pivot in opposite direction and it will not allow the platform to move translationally. If platform was resting on a smooth plane without pivot at the centre, after catching the ball platform will also move translationally with its rotational motion as in that case linear momentum of system will also remain conserved.

Illustrative Example 5.16

In previous problem, if initially the platform with the child is rotating with an angular speed ω_1. If child start walking along its periphery in opposite direction with speed u relative to platform, what will be the new angular speed of the platform.

Solution

As no external torque is present, we can conserve angular momentum before starting the walk and after starting the walk by child. As child walks in opposite direction to the rotation of platform, its angular momentum will be in opposite direction which will tend to decrease the total angular momentum, hence the angular speed of the platform must increase to maintain the angular momentum conservation we have

$$(I + mR^2)\omega_1 = I\omega_2 - m(u - R\omega_2)R$$

The term on left side of the above expression is the angular momentum of platform plus child system when child was at rest and the first term on right side of the expression is the angular momentum of the platform with increased angular speed (ω_2), when child starts walking. The second term on right side is the final angular momentum of the child. This term is negative due to his walking in opposite direction and we have taken the velocity of child as $(u - R\omega_2)$ because u is the relative speed of the child on platform which is rotating with angular speed ω_2 in opposite direction.

Again as we have used in the above example, be careful, that angular momentum conservation should always be used with respect to earth or some inertial reference frame.

Illustrative Example 5.17

A force F is applied tangential in the direction of rotation on a rotating wheel at an angular speed ω_1 about its central axis for a time t. Find the final angular speed of the wheel if its moment of inertia is I and radius is R.

Solution

In this case a torque is acting on the body in same direction as that of its rotation. It will increase its angular momentum and the increment can be given by the angular impulse as

Angular Impulse or change in angular momentum = FRt

If final angular speed becomes ω_2 we have

$$I\omega_1 + FRt = I\omega_2$$

or
$$\omega_2 = \omega_1 + \frac{FRt}{I}$$

The above result can also be obtained by use of angular speed equation $\omega_2 = \omega_1 + \alpha t$, where α is the angular acceleration of the wheel, which is given by $\alpha = \tau/I = FR/I$.

The concept of angular impulse is used very often when dealing with the concepts of rolling motion with slipping and some other examples of rolling motion. Now in next section, we will discuss rolling motion in detail.

Illustrative Example 5.18

A turn table of mass M and radius R is rotating with angular velocity ω_0 on frictionless bearing. A spider of mass m falls vertically onto the rim of the turn table and then walks in slowly towards the centre of the table. What is the angular velocity of the system when spider is at a distance r from the centre. Compute also the angular velocity of the turn table when the spider is at the rim and at the centre of the table. Is the energy of the system in this problem conserved ?

Solution

The angular momentum L_0 of the turn table is given by

$$L_0 = I_0\,\omega_0 \text{ (where } I_0 = \text{rotational inertia)}$$

If ω be the angular velocity of the turn table when the spider is at a distance r from the rim, then angular momentum of the system will be

$$L = (I_0 + m r^2)\,\omega$$

As no external torque acts on the system, the angular momentum is conserved, i.e.,

$$L = L_0$$

or
$$(I_0 + m r^2)\,\omega = I_0\,\omega_0$$

$$\Rightarrow \quad \omega = \frac{I_0\,\omega_0}{(I_0 + m r^2)} = \frac{\frac{1}{2}MR^2\omega_0}{\left(\frac{1}{2}MR^2 + m r^2\right)} \qquad [\because I_0 = \frac{1}{2}MR^2]$$

$$= \frac{\omega_0}{\left(1 + \frac{2m r^2}{MR^2}\right)} \qquad \ldots(5.46)$$

When spider is at the rim, $r = R$, hence

$$\omega_{rim} = \frac{\omega_0}{\left(1+\dfrac{2m R^2}{M R^2}\right)} = \frac{\omega_0}{\left(1+\dfrac{2m}{M}\right)} = \frac{\omega_0 M}{(M+2m)} \quad \dots(5.47)$$

When spider is at the centre of the turn table, $r = 0$

$$\omega_{centre} = \omega_0 \quad \dots(5.48)$$

This shows that the angular velocity of the turn table increases as spider moves from the rim towards the centre of the turn table.

The initial energy of the system is given by

$$E_0 = \frac{1}{2} I_0 \omega_0^2 + m r^2 \times 0 \frac{1}{4} M R^2 \omega_0^2 \quad \dots(5.49)$$

When the spider is at rim, the energy of the system is given by

$$E = \frac{1}{2}(I_0 + m R^2)\,\omega_{rim}^2$$

$$= \frac{1}{4} R^2 (M+2m)\left[\frac{M\omega_0}{M+2m}\right]^2$$

$$= \frac{1}{4} M R^2 \omega_0^2 \left[\frac{M}{M+2m}\right]$$

$$= \frac{E_0 M}{(M+2M)} \left[\because\ E_0 = \frac{1}{4} M R^2 \omega_0^2\right] \quad \dots(5.50)$$

From equations (5.49) and (5.50), we conclude that

$$E < E_0$$

i.e. energy is lost when the spider strikes the turn table.

Illustrative Example 5.19

A point mass is tied to one end of a cord whose other end passes through a vertical hollow tube, caught in one hand. The point mass is being rotated in a horizontal circle of radius 2 m with speed of 4 m/sec. The cord is then pulled down so that the radius of the circle reduces to 1 m. Compute the new linear and angular velocities of the point mass and compute the kinetic energies under the initial and final states.

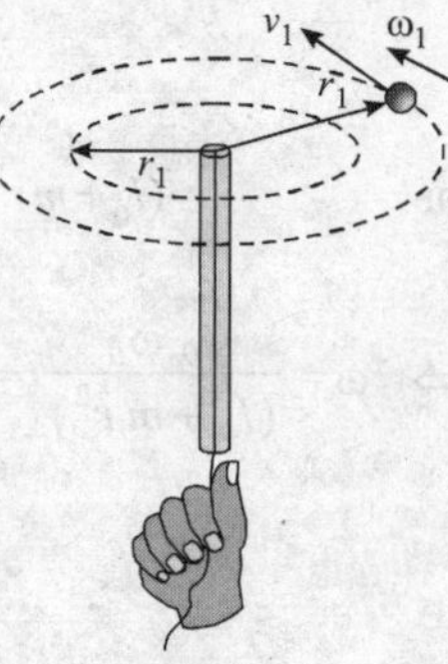

Figure 5.50

Solution

Here the force on the point mass due to cord is radial and hence the torque about the centre of rotation is zero. Therefore, the angular momentum must remain constant as the chord is shortened.

Let m, v_1 and ω_1 be the mass, linear velocity and angular velocity of the point mass respectively in the circle of radius r_1. Further let v_2 and ω_2 be the linear and angular velocities respectively of the point mass in a circle of radius r_2. Now

Initial angular momentum = Final angular momentum

$$I_1 \omega_1 = I_2 \omega_2$$

or $$m r_1^2 \frac{v_1}{r_1} = m r_2^2 \frac{v_2}{r_2}$$

or $$r_1 v_1 = r_2 v_2$$

$$\therefore \quad v_2 = \frac{r_1}{r_2} v_1 = \frac{2}{1} \times 4 = 8 \text{ m/s}$$

and $$\omega_2 = \frac{v_2}{r_2} = \frac{8}{1} = 8 \text{ rad/s}$$

$$\frac{\text{Final K.E.}}{\text{Initial K.E.}} = \frac{\frac{1}{2} I_2 \omega_2^2}{\frac{1}{2} I_1 \omega_1^2}$$

$$= \frac{m r_2^2 (v_2/r_2)^2}{m r_1^2 (v_1/r_1)^2} = \frac{v_2^2}{v_1^2} = \frac{(8)^2}{(4)^2} = 4$$

Illustrative Example 5.20

Two cylinders having radii R_1 and R_2 and rotational inertia I_1 and I_2 respectively, are supported by fixed axes perpendicular to the plane of figure-5.51. The large cylinder is initially rotating with angular velocity ω_0. The small cylinder is moved to the right until it touches the large cylinder and is caused to rotate by the frictional force between the two. Eventually, slipping ceases, and the two cylinders rotate at constant rates in opposite directions. (a) Find the final angular velocity ω_2 of the small cylinder in terms of I_1, I_2, R_1, R_2 and ω_0. (b) Is total angular momentum conserved in this case ?

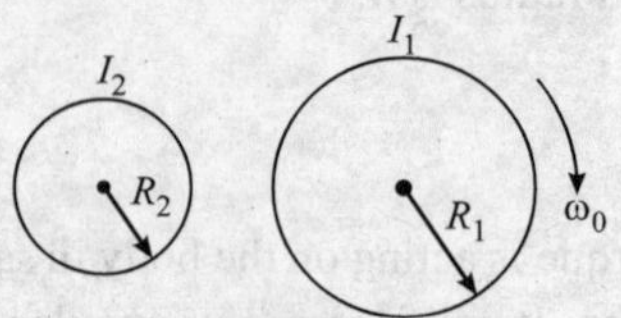

Figure 5.51

Solution

(a) When the two cylinders touch each other as shown in figure-5.52, a friction force acts between the two cylinders in opposite direction due to which first cylinder is retarded and second is accelerated, till their contact point move with same velocity so as to stop slipping between the two. If slipping stops after time t, then we have

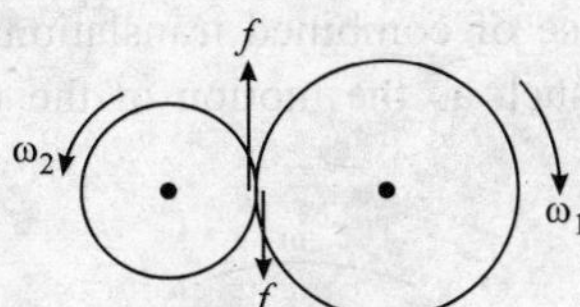

Figure 5.52

For first cylinder

$$I_1\omega_0 - fR_1 t = I_1\omega_{1f} \qquad \ldots (5.51)$$

and for second cylinder

$$fR_2 t = I_2\omega_{2f} \qquad \ldots (5.52)$$

Here ω_{1f} and ω_{2f} are the final angular velocities of the two cylinders such that linear speed of the two particles in contact on the two cylinders are equal, thus we have

$$R_1\omega_{1f} = R_2\omega_{2f} \qquad \ldots (5.53)$$

From equation (5.51), (5.52) & (5.53)

$$I_1\omega_0 - R_1\frac{I_2\omega_{2f}}{R_2} = I_1\omega_{2f}$$

or

$$I_1\omega_0 = I_1\left(\frac{R_2\omega_{2f}}{R_1}\right) + R_1\frac{I_2\omega_{2f}}{R_2}$$

or

$$\omega_{2f} = \left(\frac{I_1\omega_0 R_1 R_2}{I_1R_2^2 + I_2R_1^2}\right)$$

Alternative Solution

Let F be the frictional force and α_1, the angular acceleration, then the torque for the large cylinder is

$$\tau_1 = FR_1 = I_1\alpha_1 \qquad \ldots (5.54)$$

The final angular speed ω_1 of large cylinder is given by

$$\omega_1 = \omega_0 - \alpha_1 t$$

or

$$\alpha_1 = \frac{\omega_0 - \omega_1}{t} \qquad \ldots (5.55)$$

If α_2 be the angular acceleration of small cylinder, then the final angular speed ω_2 is given by

$$\omega_2 = 0 + \alpha_2 t$$

$$\Rightarrow \qquad \alpha_2 = \omega_2/t \qquad \ldots (5.56)$$

Further,

$$FR_2 = I_2\alpha_2 \qquad \ldots (5.57)$$

From equations (5.54) and (5.57) we have

$$\frac{I_1\alpha_1}{I_2\alpha_2} = \frac{FR_1}{FR_2} = \frac{R_1}{R_2} \qquad \ldots (5.58)$$

From equations (5.55) and (5.56)

$$\frac{\alpha_1}{\alpha_2} = \left(\frac{\omega_0 - \omega_1}{\omega_2}\right) \qquad \ldots (5.59)$$

Substituting this value of α_1/α_2 from equation (5.59) in equation (5.58), we get

$$\frac{I_1}{I_2}\left(\frac{\omega_0 - \omega_1}{\omega_2}\right) = \frac{R_1}{R_2} \qquad \ldots (5.60)$$

When the two cylinders move at constant rate, then

$$v = \omega_1 R_1 = \omega_2 R_2$$

$$\Rightarrow \qquad \frac{\omega_1}{\omega_2} = \frac{R_2}{R_1}$$

or

$$\omega_1 = (R_2/R_1)\,\omega_2 \qquad \ldots (5.61)$$

Substituting the value of ω_1 from equation (5.61) in equation (5.60), we get

$$\frac{I_1}{I_2}\left[\frac{\omega_0 - (R_2/R_1)\omega_2}{\omega_2}\right] = \frac{R_1}{R_2}$$

$$\omega_2 = \left[\frac{\omega_0}{R_2/R_1 + R_1I_2/R_2I_1}\right] \qquad \ldots (5.62)$$

Initial angular momentum $L_i = I\omega_0$, because the small cylinder is at rest.

Final angular momentum

$$L_f = L_1 + L_2 = I_1\omega_1 + I_2\omega_2$$

$$\therefore \qquad L_f = \frac{\omega_0}{\frac{R_2}{R_1} + \frac{R_1}{R_2}\left(\frac{I_2}{I_1}\right)}\left(I_1\frac{R_2}{R_1} + I_2\right)$$

Change in angular momentum,

$$\Delta L = L_f - L_i$$

$$\Rightarrow \qquad \Delta L = \omega_0\left[\frac{I_2(1 - R_1/R_2)}{R_2/R_1 + R_1 I_2/R_2 I_1}\right] \neq 0$$

Since $\qquad R_1 \neq R_2$

Thus angular momentum is not conserved. Thus if we observe, due to friction there is a net force on the two cylinders independently, but as the two are pivoted at centre, this pivots must apply an external force to keep the two cylinders at rest. Thus about any point we observe, there must be some torque due to the forces by or on pivots, thus in this case angular momentum is not conserved.

Web Reference of Video Lectures at www.physicsgalaxy.com

Age Group - High School Physics | Age 17-19 Years
Section - MECHANICS
Topic - Rigid Body Dynamics
Module Number - 23, 24, 25, 26, 27, 28 and 29

5.6 Rigid Body Rotation About a Moving Axis

In this section we will extend our analysis of the dynamics of rotational motion to some cases in which the axis of rotation moves. When that happens, the motion of the body is combined translation and rotation. In such situation we always consider that "*Every possible motion of a rigid body can be represented as a combination of translational motion of the centre of mass and rotation about an axis through the centre of mass*". This is true even when the centre of mass accelerates, so that it is not at rest in any inertial frame. For example when a bowler throws a ball with spin, in air ball follows a parabolic trajectory as it were a point mass and during this motion the ball is also rotating about its centre of mass. The translation of the centre of mass and the rotation about the centre of mass can be treated independently.

5.6.1 Energy of a Body in Simultaneous Translation and Rotational Motion

When a body has both translational and rotational motion, its total energy can be written as the sum of the two respective kinetic energies. For example, if a body of mass M is rotating about a given axis with an angular speed ω and its moment of inertia about that axis is I and simultaneously the axis moves with a linear velocity v, its total energy can be written as

$$K = KE_{tran} + KE_{rot} \qquad \dots(5.63)$$

$$K = \frac{1}{2}Mv^2 + \frac{1}{2}I\omega^2 \qquad \dots(5.64)$$

An important case of combined translation and rotation is rolling motion, such as the motion of the wheel shown in figure-5.53.

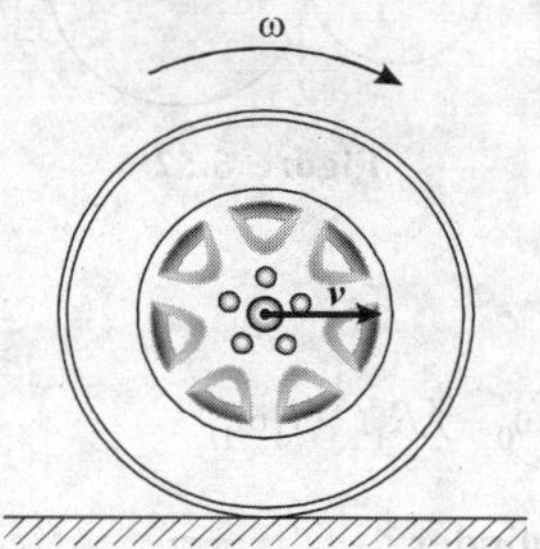

Figure 5.53

The wheel is symmetrical so its centre of mass is at its geometric centre. The rolling motion of this wheel can be analyzed by taking translational and rotational motion separately.

When centre of mass of a wheel moves translationally with a speed v_{cm}, all points on it are moving with speed v_{cm} along with the body in same direction and when it rotates with an angular speed ω about its centre, all points on it revolve in different circular paths with the same angular speed ω and the points will have linear tangential speed $r\omega$ if the point is at a distance r from the axis of rotation. If the angular speed of rotation is such that the linear tangential speed of the points on the periphery of the wheel is equal to the translational speed of wheel, then on combining the two motions, the resultant motion is known as pure rolling motion or rolling motion without slipping. This is shown in figure-5.54.

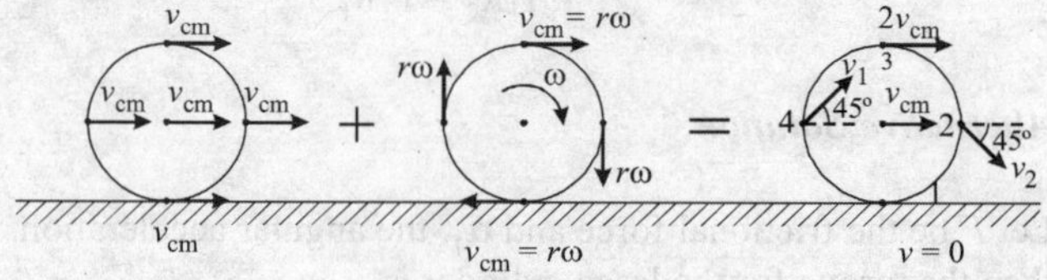

Figure 5.54

In this situation the point on the wheel that contacts the surface must be instantaneously at rest so that it does not slip. Hence the velocity $r\omega$ of the point of contact relative to the centre of mass must have same magnitude but opposite direction as the centre of mass velocity v_{cm}. Thus for pure rolling

$$v_{cm} = r\omega \qquad \dots(5.65)$$

The above relation is the condition of pure rolling. Figure 5.52 shows the velocity of a point on the wheel is the vector sum of the velocity of the centre of mass and the velocity of the point relative to the centre of mass. Thus while point 1, the point of contact, is instantaneously at rest, point 3 at the top of the wheel is moving forward twice as fast as the centre of mass, and point 2 and 4 at the sides have velocities at 45° to the horizontal moving at speed $\sqrt{2}$ times the centre of mass.

At any instant we can think of the wheel as rotating about an instantaneous axis of rotation that passes through the point of contact with the ground. The angular velocity ω is the same for this axis as for an axis through the centre of mass, an observer at the centre of mass sees the rim making the same number of revolutions per second as does an observer at the rim watching the centre of mass spin around him. If we think of the motion of the rolling wheel in this way, the kinetic energy of the wheel is $\frac{1}{2}I_0\omega^2$ where I_0 is the moment of inertia of the wheel about an axis through point 1. Using parallel axis theorem $I_0 = I_{cm} + MR^2$, where I_{cm} is the moment of inertia of the wheel with respect to an axis through the centre of mass. Thus the kinetic energy in this reference is

$$K = \frac{1}{2}I_0\omega^2 = \frac{1}{2}I_{cm}\omega^2 + \frac{1}{2}MR^2\omega^2$$

or $$= \frac{1}{2}I_{cm}\omega^2 + \frac{1}{2}Mv_{cm}^2 \qquad \ldots(5.66)$$

It is same as that given by equation-(5.64). It shows that while solving problems of rolling motion we can solve using both the methods i.e. one by considering the axis of rotation at the centre or in a reference frame attached to the centre of mass of the rolling body and the same problem can also be solved by taking reference frame attached to the instantaneous axis of rotation.

Illustrative Example 5.21

A primitive yo-yo is made by wrapping a string several times around a solid cylinder with mass M and radius R shown in figure-5.55. The end of the string stationary while releasing the cylinder with no initial motion. The string unwinds but does not slip or stretch as the cylinder drops and rotates. Use energy considerations to find the speed v of the centre of mass of the solid cylinder after it has dropped a distance h.

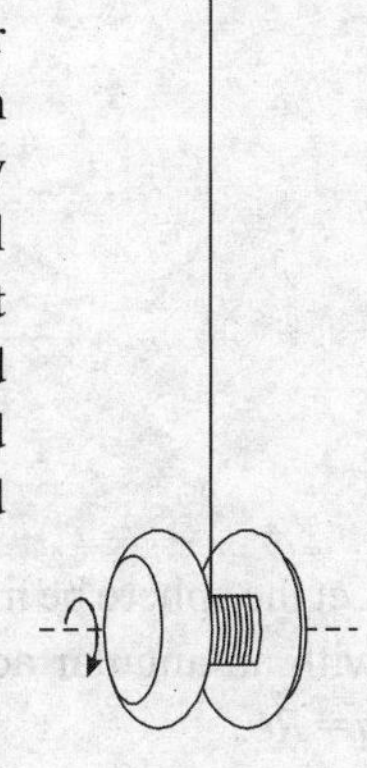

Figure 5.55

Solution

The upper end of the string is held fixed, not pulled upward, so the support in figure-5.53 does no work on the system of string and cylinder. There is friction between the string and cylinder, because the string never slips on the surface of cylinder, no energy is lost. Thus we can use conservation of mechanical energy. The initial kinetic energy of the cylinder was zero when it was released from rest and as it falls by a distance h, the work done by gravity is Mgh, thus we have

Final kinetic energy of the cylinder is

$$K = 0 + Mgh = \frac{1}{2}Mv^2 + \frac{1}{2}I\omega^2$$

or $$Mgh = \frac{1}{2}Mv^2 + \frac{1}{2}\left(\frac{1}{2}MR^2\right)\frac{v^2}{R^2}$$

or $$\frac{3}{4}Mv^2 = Mgh$$

or $$v = \sqrt{\frac{4}{3}gh}$$

Illustrative Example 5.22

A rolling body (it can be ring, sphere, ... etc) rolls down from the top of an inclined plane as shown in figure-5.56. Find how its velocity depends on its geometry.

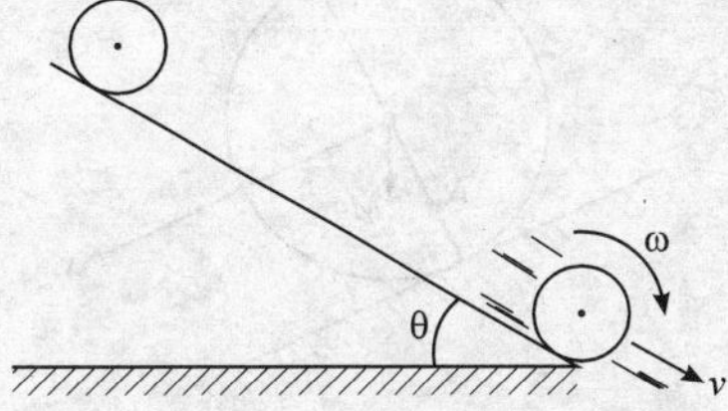

Figure 5.56

Solution

Different objects has different expression for moment of inertia. Here we consider that the moment of inertia is MK^2, where K is the radius of gyration of the body about the axis passing through centre of mass. Now applying energy conservation, when the body reaches the bottom of the plane the work done by gravity is equal to the gain in kinetic energy as no other work is done on it.

$$Mgh = \frac{1}{2}Mv^2 + \frac{1}{2}MK^2\left(\frac{v^2}{R^2}\right)$$

or $$v = \sqrt{\frac{2gh}{(1 + K^2/R^2)}} \qquad \ldots(5.67)$$

Equation-(5.67) shows that the bodies with same value of K when released from top, they'll reach simultaneously at the bottom and those with less value of K will reach earlier. If a solid sphere $\left(K=\sqrt{\frac{2}{5}}R\right)$ and a disc $\left(K=\frac{R}{\sqrt{2}}\right)$ of same radius and rolled from the top of an incline plane, sphere will reach the bottom earlier.

5.7 Rolling Friction

The rolling friction is the friction acting on the bottom most point of the rolling body, when it is in pure rolling motion. We have studied that during pure rolling the contact point of the body with the surface remains at rest, thus the friction acting on that point is either zero or it must be static friction. In both the cases no work is done by the friction and mechanical energy is conserved. In example-5.16, we have used energy conservation as work done by the friction is zero. This is the reason why we can ignore rolling friction in case of application of work-energy theorem or energy conservation. But there is a restriction for it that the rolling body and the surface over which it rolls are perfectly rigid. As shown in figure-5.57, the line of action of the normal force passes through the centre of the body, so its torque is zero, there is no sliding at the point of contact, so the friction force does no work.

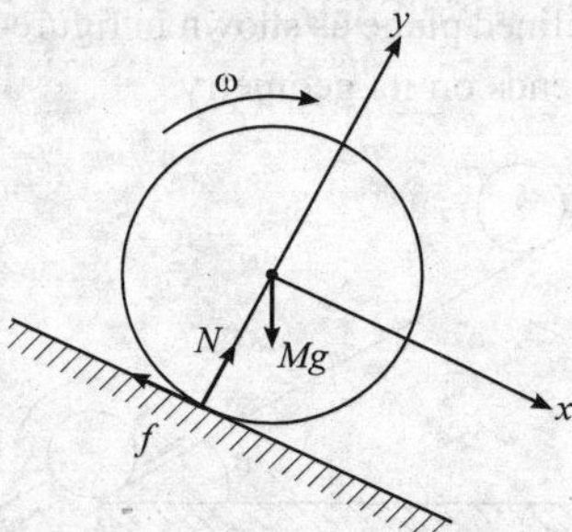

Figure 5.57

Figure-5.58 shows a more realistic situation in which the surface gets deformed in front of the sphere and due to these deformations, the contact forces on the sphere no longer act along a single point, but over an area the forces are concentrated on the front of the sphere as shown. As a result, the normal force now exerts a torque that opposes the rotation. In addition, there is some sliding of the sphere over the surface due to the deformation causing mechanical energy to be lost. The combination of these two effects is the phenomenon of rolling friction. Rolling friction also occurs if the rolling body is deformable, as an automobile tire. In general problems the rolling body and the surface are considered rigid enough that rolling friction can be ignored and we consider only the static friction acting on the bottom contact of the body as shown in figure-5.58 for dealing with the problems of dynamics only.

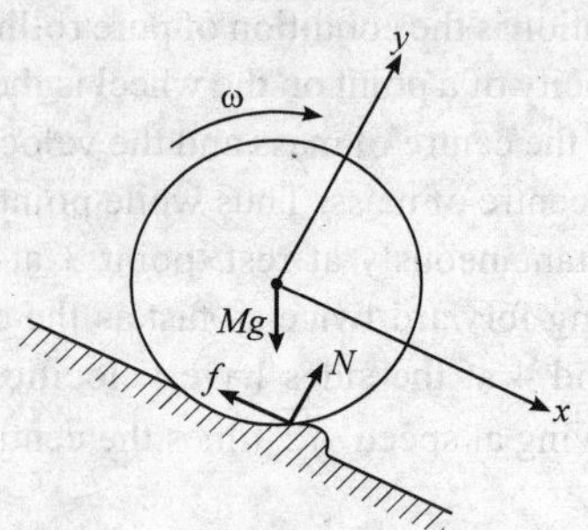

Figure 5.58

In problems of pure rolling motion, we consider friction at the bottom contact of the rolling body, but it does no work on the body as point of contact remains at rest and the friction which is acting at this point is the static friction which prevents this point to slide.

Further few examples make the concept clear for the case of static friction acting at the bottom contact of the body with the surface.

Illustration Example 5.23

A force F is applied tangential at the topmost point of a sphere of mass M and radius R. If the ground is rough enough to prevent sliding, find the linear acceleration of the sphere.

Solution

It is given that sphere does not slip on ground thus the friction between ground and sphere contact is the static friction, as point of contact P remains at rest.

For solving problem, we can choose the direction of friction either forward or backward and solution will give us the correct direction of it. We can solve the problem by both ways. First we consider the direction of friction on sphere in forward direction then on ground it is obviously in backward direction. Figure-5.59 shows the situation.

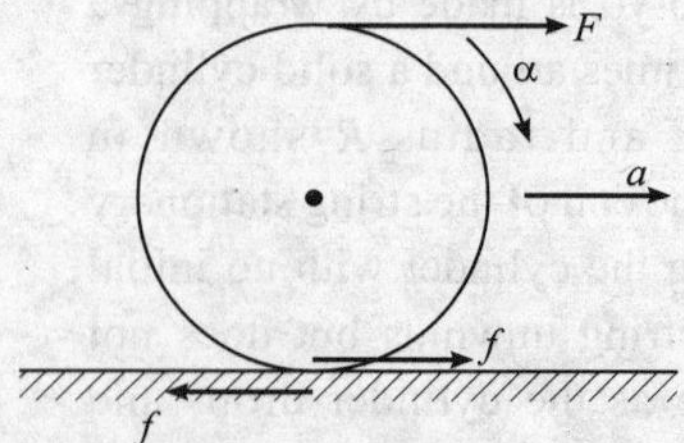

Figure 5.59

Let the sphere be moving with linear acceleration a and rotating with an angular acceleration α, which can be related to a as $a = R\alpha$.

For translational motion of the sphere, we have

$$F+f=Ma \quad \ldots(5.68)$$

For rotational motion of the sphere, we have

$$FR-fR=\left(\frac{2}{5}MR^2\right)\alpha \quad \ldots(5.69)$$

or
$$FR-fR=\left(\frac{2}{5}MR^2\right)\times\frac{a}{R}$$

or
$$F-f=\frac{2}{5}Ma \quad \ldots(5.70)$$

Adding equations-(5.68) and (5.70), we get

$$2F=\frac{7}{5}Ma$$

or
$$a=\frac{10F}{7M}$$

If we subtract equation-(5.70) from (5.68), we get

$$2f=\frac{3}{5}Ma$$

or
$$f=\frac{3}{10}Ma=\frac{3}{7}F \quad \ldots(5.71)$$

Equation-(5.71) gives the frictional force acting on the sphere which must be less then the limiting value of sliding friction as the sphere bottom point of contact is at rest. The friction value comes out positive implies that the direction of friction we've chosen correct i.e. in forward direction. In this case the bottom point of the surface of sphere have a tendency to move backward so friction acts on it in forward direction.

Alternative Solution :

Now we re-proceed the previous case by considering friction acting in backward direction as shown in figure-5.60. Here friction on ground is in forward direction.

Here for translational motion of sphere, we have

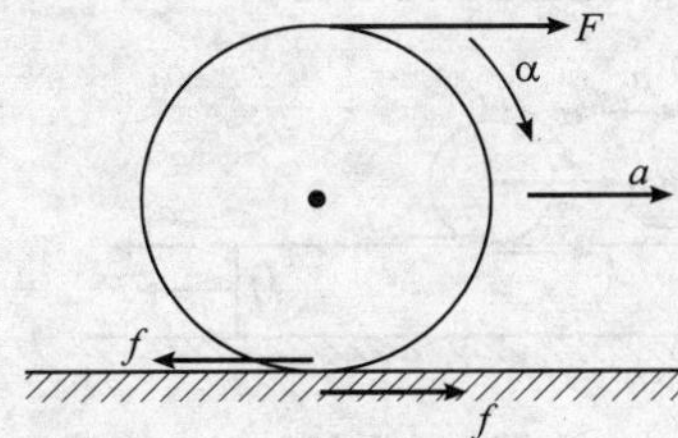

Figure 5.60

$$F-f=Ma \quad \ldots(5.72)$$

For its rotational motion, we have

$$FR+fR=\left(\frac{2}{5}MR^2\right)\alpha$$

As $a=R\alpha$, we have

$$FR+fR=\left(\frac{2}{5}MR^2\right)\times\frac{a}{R}$$

or
$$F+f=\frac{2}{5}Ma \quad \ldots(5.73)$$

Adding equations-(5.72) and (5.73)

$$2F=\frac{7}{5}Ma$$

or
$$a=\frac{10F}{7M}$$

Which is same as found in previous method, now substituting this value in equation-(5.73), we get

$$F+f=\frac{2}{5}M.\left(\frac{10F}{7M}\right)$$

or
$$f=-\frac{3F}{7} \quad \ldots(5.74)$$

Which is also same as that found in equation-(5.71) but with-ve sign, which shows that in this case the direction of friction, we have taken is opposite to that of the actual direction. Here we've considered that friction is acting on sphere in backward direction but equation-(5.74) shows that it is acting in forward direction.

NOTE : In problems of pure rolling you can consider friction in any direction and proceed the case with the dynamic and rotational equations. Solution will give you the correct direction of friction.

 # Illustration Example 5.24

A cylinder of mass M and radius R rolls without slipping down an inclined plane of length l. Find the linear acceleration of the cylinder. Also find the minimum friction coefficient required on the inclined plane for which the cylinder does not slip.

Solution

Situation is shown in figure-5.61. Let the friction on cylinder is acting in backward direction as shown in figure. Let cylinder rolls down with a linear acceleration a and along with it rotates with an angular acceleration α, which can be related to linear acceleration as $a = R\alpha$. Regarding cylinder we take friction is acting backward, solution will give us the actual direction of friction. We write the dynamic equation for its downward motion as

$$Mg\sin\theta - f = Ma \qquad \ldots(5.75)$$

Figure 5.61

For its rotational motion, only friction is there which will exert a clockwise torque on it as torque of Mg and N is zero. Thus we have

$$fR = I\alpha$$

or $$fR = \left(\frac{1}{2}MR^2\right)\left(\frac{a}{R}\right) \qquad [\text{As } \alpha = \frac{a}{R}]$$

or $$f = \frac{1}{2}\,\text{Ma} \qquad \ldots(5.76)$$

Using above value of f in equation-(5.75), we get

$$Mg\sin\theta = \frac{3}{2}\,\text{Ma}$$

or $$a = \frac{2}{3}\,g\sin\theta \qquad \ldots(5.77)$$

Substituting this value of a in equation-(5.76), we get the friction on cylinder is

$$f = \frac{1}{3}\,Mg\sin\theta$$

The above value of friction is positive so direction of friction on cylinder we have chosen was correct. It implies that the particles of cylinder at the bottom contact have tendency of moving forward, hence friction acts on them in forward direction. Here the cylinder is in pure rolling. Its bottommost point which is in contact with the inclined plain is at rest, thus the friction acting on it must be static friction which is always less than sliding friction. Hence for pure rolling we must have

$$f \le \mu Mg\cos\theta \qquad \ldots(5.78)$$

If μ is the coefficient of friction between the inclined plain and the cylinder. When equality holds, the cylinder is at the verge of slipping. Now if θ increases slightly or μ decreases, cylinder starts slipping and pure rolling no longer exist. Thus the value of μ for pure rolling should be such as that equation-(5.78) always holds true, thus

$$\frac{1}{3}\,Mg\sin\theta \le \mu Mg\cos\theta$$

or $$\mu \ge \frac{1}{3}\tan\theta$$

If on surface of incline plane value of μ becomes less than $\frac{1}{3}\tan\theta$, cylinder starts sliding. Like this problem, in every case there is a limiting value of friction coefficient below which no pure rolling can take place. Thus for pure rolling a minimum friction is required and there is no maximum limit for it if rolling friction is avoided.

 # Illustrative Example 5.25

A plank of mass M is placed on a smooth surface over which a cylinder of mass m and radius R is placed as shown in figure-5.62. Now the plank is pulled towards right with an external force F. If cylinder does not slip over the surface of plank find the linear acceleration of plank and cylinder and the angular acceleration of the cylinder.

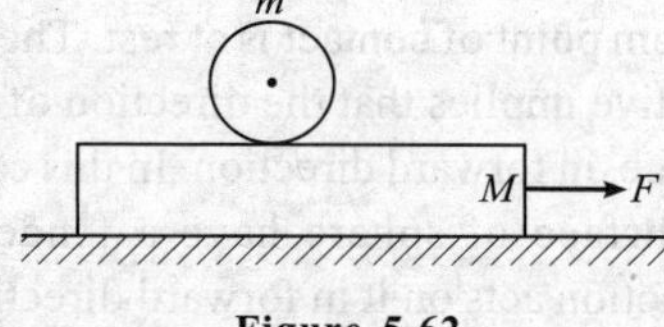

Figure 5.62

Solution

As it is given that cylinder does not slip over the plank surface, it is the case of pure rolling, we can use friction on cylinder in any direction. Here we choose toward right. As friction is acting on cylinder toward right, it must be toward left on plank as shown in force diagram in figure-5.63.

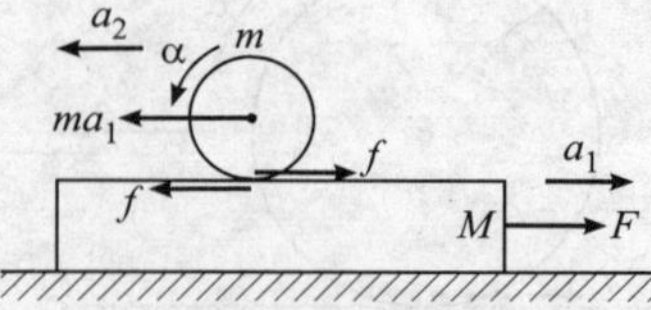

Figure 5.63

Let plank moves toward right with an acceleration a_1, cylinder will experience a Pseudo force in left direction ma_1, due to which it will roll toward left with respect to plank with an acceleration a_2. As we have used pseudo force, a_2 must be with respect to the plank. Let its angular acceleration during rolling be α, we have $a_2 = R\alpha$.

For translational motion of plank, we have

$$F - f = Ma_1 \quad \ldots(5.79)$$

For translational motion of cylinder with respect to plank we have

$$ma_1 - f = ma_2 \quad \ldots(5.80)$$

For rotational motion of cylinder with respect to plank, we have

$$fR = I\alpha$$

or $$fR = \left(\frac{1}{2}mR^2\right).\left(\frac{a_2}{R}\right)$$

or $$f = \frac{1}{2}\,ma_2 \quad \ldots(5.81)$$

From equation-(5.80) and (5.81), we get

$$ma_1 - \frac{1}{2}\,ma_2 = ma_2$$

or $$a_1 = \frac{3}{2}\,a_2 \quad \ldots(5.82)$$

Using equations-(5.79), (5.81) and (5.82), we get

$$F - \frac{1}{2}\,ma_2 = \frac{3}{2}\,Ma_2$$

or $$a_2 = \frac{2F}{3M + m}$$

From equation-(5.82) $$a_1 = \frac{3F}{3M + m}$$

As we have already discussed that the value of a_2 is relative to the plank. Thus net acceleration of the cylinder will be given as $a_1 - a_2$. Here one important point is to be noted that at the time of writing rotational dynamic equation of the cylinder, we have taken $a_2 = R\alpha$. Here a_2 was the relative acceleration of the cylinder with respect to plank. In such type of problems when a rolling motion takes place on an inertial or noninertial frames (bodies), the acceleration in the rotational equation must be relative as its rolling motion takes place on its reference.

Illustrative Example 5.26

Find the acceleration of the cylinder of mass m and radius R and that of plank of mass M placed on smooth surface if pulled with a force F shown in figure-5.64. Given that sufficient friction is present between cylinder and the plank surface to prevent sliding of cylinder.

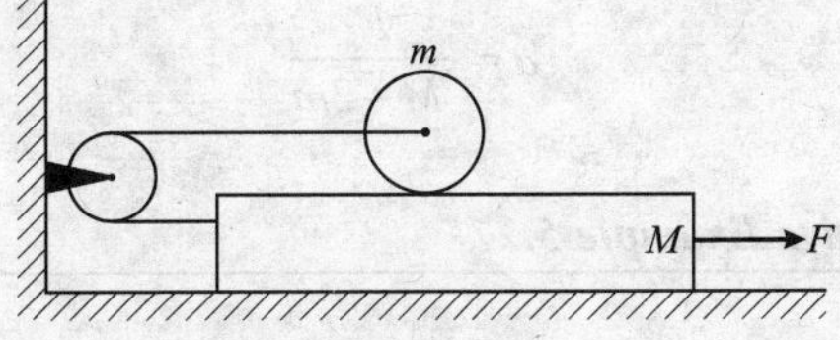

Figure 5.64

Solution

As cylinder does not slip over the plank surface, again we can use friction on cylinder in any direction. Here we consider toward right. As friction is acting on cylinder toward right, it must be toward left on plank as shown in figure-5.65. Here no pseudo force is shown in diagram as in this case the plank and cylinder are attached with a string, thus both will move with same acceleration. Plank toward right and cylinder toward left and as we know the acceleration of cylinder as such we need not to consider the cylinder in the non inertial frame.

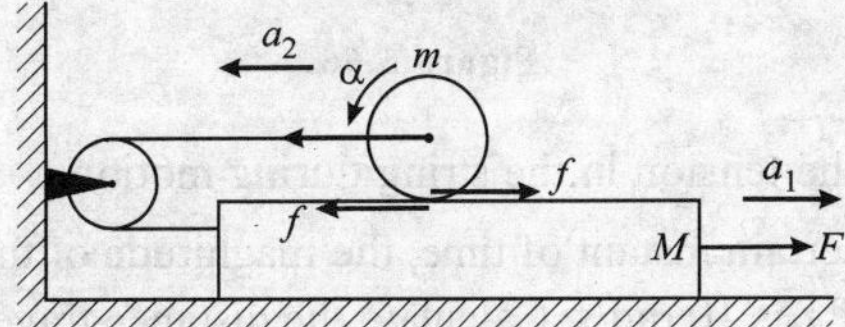

Figure 5.65

For plank the motion equation is

$$F - f - T = Ma_1 \quad \ldots(5.83)$$

For cylinder, translation motion equation is

$$T - f = ma_2 \quad [a_1 = a_2 = a] \quad \ldots(5.84)$$

For cylinder, rotational motion equation is

$$fR = I\alpha$$

As we've already discussed that in rotational motion equation, acceleration used must be relative to the surface on which rolling takes place, there the acceleration of cylinder with respect to the plank is 2 a. Thus we have

$$\alpha = \frac{2a}{R}$$

From torque equation $$fR = \left(\frac{1}{2}mR^2\right)\left(\frac{2a}{R}\right)$$

or $$f = ma \quad \ldots(5.85)$$

From equation-(5.84) and (5.85), we have

$$T = 2\,ma$$

Now using the above value of T in equation-(5.83), we get

$$F - ma - 2ma = Ma$$

or $$a = \frac{F}{M+3m}$$

Illustrative Example 5.27

A block X of mass 0.5 kg is held by a long massless string on a frictionless inclined plane of inclination 30° to the horizontal. The string is wound on a uniform solid cylindrical drum Y of mass 2 kg and of radius 0.2 m as shown in figure-5.66. The drum is given an initial angular velocity, such that the block X starts moving up

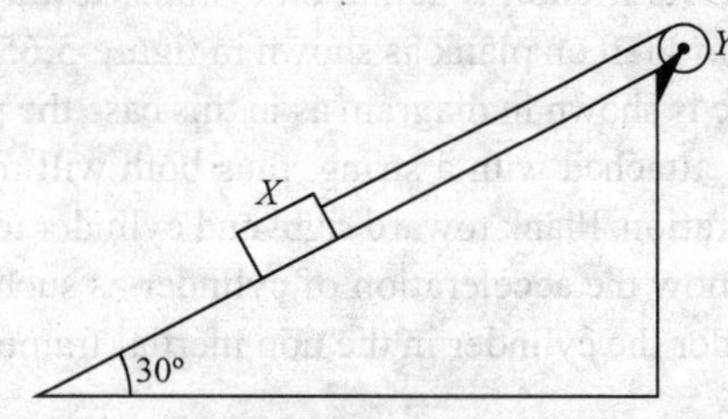

Figure 5.66

(a) Find the tension in the string during motion.

(b) At a certain instant of time, the magnitude of the angular velocity of Y is 10 rad/s. Calculate the distance travelled by X from that instant of time until it comes to rest.

Solution

(a) The forces acting on the mass X are shown in figure-5.67. When it rises upward its speed decreases as due to mg sinθ, the system (both mass and the drum) retards. If the retardation in mass X is a and the angular retardation in cylinder is α, we can relate the two as $a = R\alpha$.

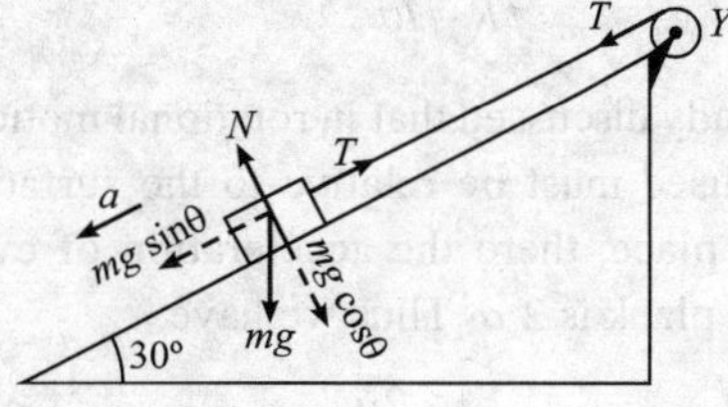

Figure 5.67

During motion the translational motion equation for mass X is

$$mg\sin\theta - T = ma \qquad \dots(5.86)$$

For rotational motion of cylinder the only force having torque on it is tension T, thus

$$TR = I\alpha$$

or $$TR = \left(\frac{1}{2}MR^2\right)\left(\frac{a}{R}\right)$$

or $$T = \frac{1}{2}Ma \qquad \dots(5.87)$$

From equation-(5.86) and (5.87), we have

$$mg\sin\theta - \frac{1}{2}Ma = ma$$

or $$a = \frac{2mg\sin\theta}{M+2m}$$

Using the above value of acceleration in equation-(5.87), we get

$$T = \frac{Mmg\sin\theta}{M+2m} = \frac{0.5\times 2\times 9.8\times 0.5}{2+2\times 0.5} = 1.633\text{ N.}$$

(b) Mass X will stop when the whole kinetic energy of drum and mass is converted into gravitational potential energy of the mass. If mass travels a distance L before coming to rest, its height ascended is L sinθ, thus we have

$$\frac{1}{2}I\omega^2 + \frac{1}{2}mv^2 = mgL\sin\theta$$

Initially, the block has speed $v = R\omega$. On solving the above equation, value of L obtained is

$$L = \frac{\frac{1}{2}\left(\frac{1}{2}MR^2\right) + \frac{1}{2}m(R\omega)^2}{mg\sin\theta}$$

or $$= \frac{(M+2m)R^2\omega^2}{4mg\sin\theta} = \frac{(2+2\times 0.5)(0.2)^2(10)^2}{4\times 0.5\times 9.8\times 0.5} = 1.224\text{ m}$$

Illustrative Example 5.28

A rough wedge of mass M is free to move on a smooth horizontal plane as shown in figure-5.68. The uniform cylinder of mass m is placed on the wedge and it begins to roll down without slipping. Show that the acceleration of cylinder on the surface of wedge is given as

$$a = \frac{2g\sin\theta(m+M)}{m+3M+2m\sin^2\theta}$$

Figure 5.68

Solution

As the cylinder is in pure rolling, we take friction on cylinder in upward direction and on the wedge in downward direction. Let us consider that the cylinder is rolling down the inline of wedge with an acceleration a and the wedge is accelerating toward right due to the normal reaction of cylinder on wedge with an acceleration a_1. All the forces acting on the two bodies are shown in figure-5.69.

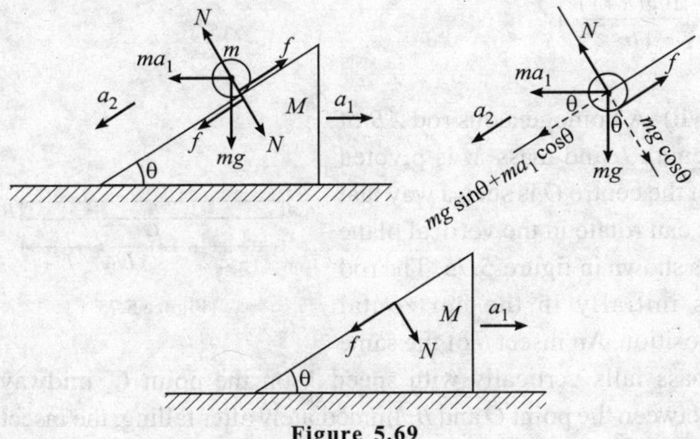

Figure 5.69

As wedge accelerates towards right with acceleration a_1, the cylinder rolling on its inclined surface experiences a pseudo force ma_1 toward left direction.

For translational motion of cylinder, we write its motion equation as

Along the incline

$$mg\sin\theta + ma_1\cos\theta - f = ma \quad \ldots(5.88)$$

Normal to incline

$$N + ma\sin\theta = mg\cos\theta \quad \ldots(5.89)$$

For rotational motion of cylinder, only friction will provide the anticlockwise torque for its rotation, we write its torque equation as

$$fR = I\alpha$$

or $$fR = \left(\frac{1}{2}mR^2\right)\left(\frac{a}{R}\right)$$

or $$f = \frac{1}{2}ma \quad \ldots(5.90)$$

For translation motion of wedge, we have

$$N\sin\theta - f\cos\theta = Ma_1 \quad \ldots(5.91)$$

Multiplying equation-(5.89) by $\sin\theta$, we get

$$N\sin\theta + ma_1\sin^2\theta = mg\sin\theta\cos\theta \quad \ldots(5.92)$$

From equations-(5.91) and (5.92), we have

$$ma_1\sin^2\theta + f\cos\theta = mg\sin\theta\cos\theta - ma_1$$

or $$a_1 = \frac{2mg\sin\theta\cos\theta - ma\cos\theta}{M + m\sin^2\theta}$$

[Using $f = \frac{1}{2}ma$]

Using this value of a_1 in equation-(5.88), we get

$$mg\sin\theta + m\cos\theta\left[\frac{2mg\sin\theta\cos\theta - ma\cos\theta}{M + m\sin^2\theta}\right] - \frac{1}{2}ma = ma$$

or $$a = \left[\frac{2g\sin\theta\,(m+M)}{m + 3M + 2m\sin^2\theta}\right]$$

Web Reference of Video Lectures at www.physicsgalaxy.com

Age Group - High School Physics | Age 17-19 Years
Section - MECHANICS
Topic - Rigid Body Dynamics
Module Number - 31, 32, 33, 34, 35 and 36

Practice Exercise 5.3

(i) A uniform solid cylinder of mass M and radius $2R$ rests on a horizontal table top. A string attached to it runs over a pulley (disc) of mass M and radius R that is mounted on a frictionless axle through its centre. A block of mass M is suspended from the free end of the string. The string doesn't slip over the pulley surface, and the cylinder rolls without slipping on the table top. Find the acceleration of the block.

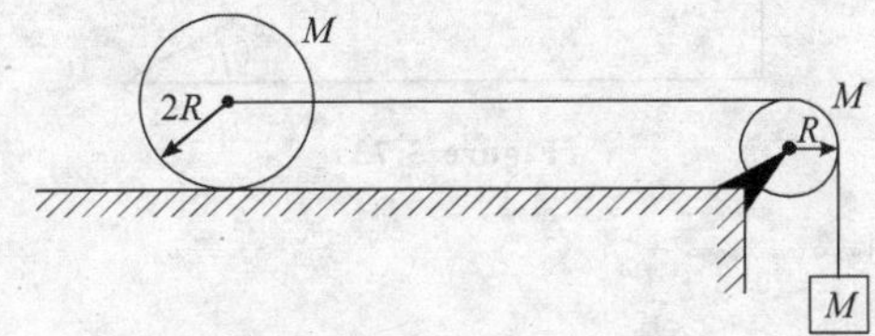

Figure 5.70

[$g/3$]

(ii) As shown in figure-5.71 the solid disc and pulley have the same radii and same mass distribution. The solid disc, pulley and the block have equal masses. The plane has a slope of 30°. The disc rolls on the incline without slipping or loss of energy. Find the acceleration of the hanging block. Consider there is no shipping of string over pulley surface. Take $g = 10\text{ m/s}^2$.

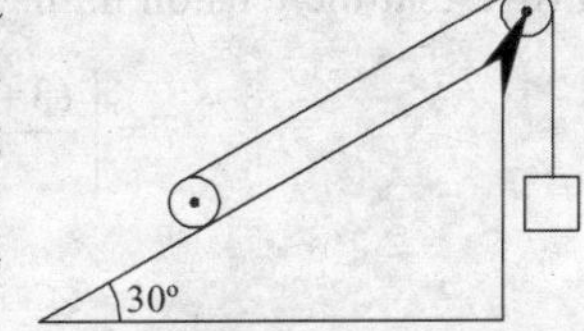

Figure 5.71

[2 m/s^2]

(iii) The axis of a cylinder of radius R and moment of inertia about its axis I is fixed at centre O as shown in figure-5.72. Its highest point A is in level with two plane horizontal surfaces. A block of mass M is initially moving to the right without friction with speed v_1. It passes over the cylinder to the dotted position. Calculate the speed v_2 in the dotted position and the angular velocity acquired by the cylinder if at the time of detaching from cylinder block stops slipping on it.

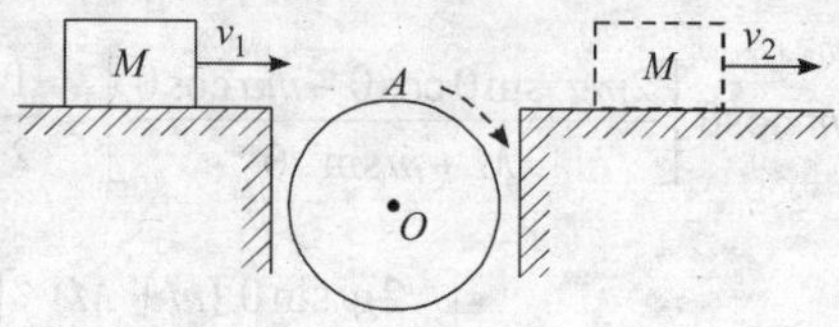

Figure 5.72

$$\left[\frac{v_1}{1+\frac{I}{MR^2}}, \frac{v_1}{R\left(1+\frac{I}{MR^2}\right)}\right]$$

(iv) A spool of thread of mass m is placed on an inclined smooth plane set at an angle θ to the horizontal. The free end of the thread is attached to the wall as shown in figure-5.73. Calculate the acceleration of the centre of mass of the spool, if its moment of inertia about its axis is I and the radius of the wound thread layer is r.

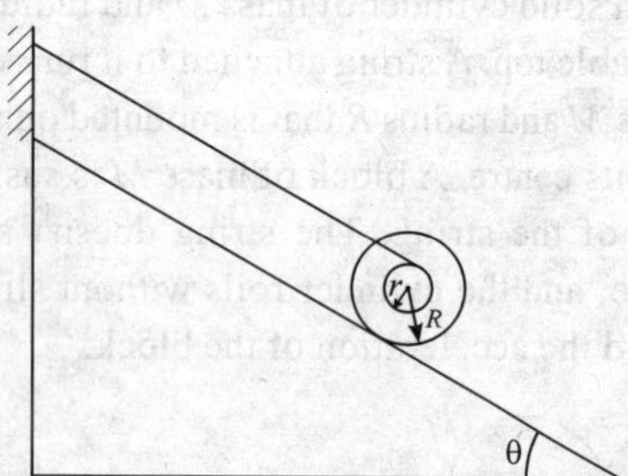

Figure 5.73

$$\left[\frac{g\sin\theta}{1+\frac{I}{mr^2}}\right]$$

(v) A uniform solid cylinder of mass M and radius R rolls on a rough inclined plane with its axis perpendicular to the line of greatest slope as shown in figure-5.74. As the cylinder rolls it winds up a light string which passes over a light and smooth pulley and attached to a mass m, the part of the string between pulley and cylinder being parallel to the line of greatest slope. Prove that the tension in the string is

$$T = \left[\frac{(3+4\sin\theta)\,Mmg}{3M+8m}\right]$$

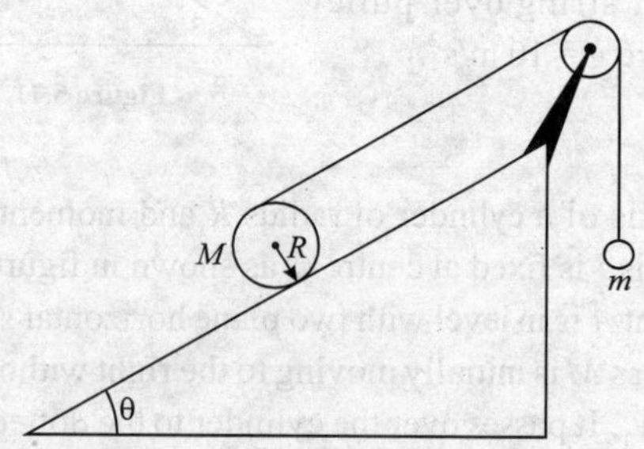

Figure 5.74

(vi) A small uniform ball of radius r rolls without slipping down from the top of a sphere of radius R. Find the angular velocity of the ball at the moment it breaks off the sphere. The initial velocity of the ball is negligible.

$$\left[\sqrt{\frac{10g(R+r)}{17r^2}}\right]$$

(vii) A homogeneous rod AB of length L and mass M is pivoted of the centre O is such a way that it can rotate in the vertical plane as shown in figure-5.75. The rod is initially in the horizontal position. An insect S of the same mass falls vertically with speed V on the point C, midway between the point O and B. Immediately after falling, the insect moves towards the end B such that the rod rotates with constant angular velocity ω.

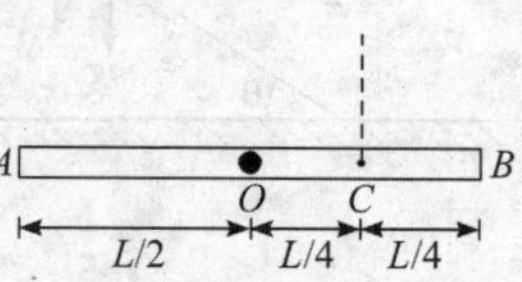

Figure 5.75

(a) Determine the angular velocity ω in terms of V and L.

(b) If the insect reaches the end B when the rod has turned through 90°, determine V.

$[12V/7L,\ 7\sqrt{2gL}/12]$

(viii) A cubical block of side 'a' moving with velocity v on a horizontal smooth plane as shown. It hits a ridge at point O. Find the angular speed of the block after it hits O.

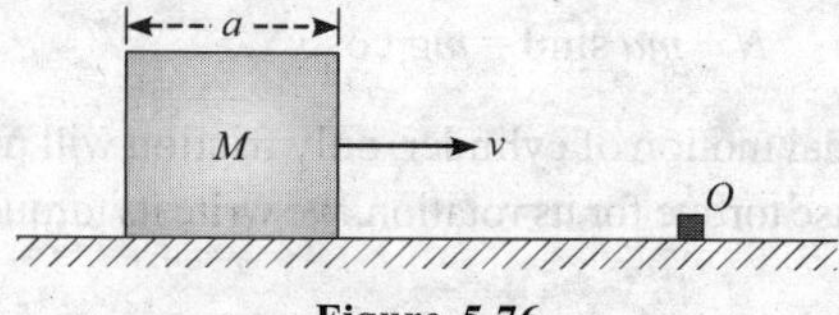

Figure 5.76

$$\left[\frac{3v}{4a}\right]$$

5.8 Rolling with Slipping

In previous section, we have discussed about pure rolling when body does not slip on ground. In pure rolling as no slipping takes place, no energy is lost against friction as friction is static at the bottom contact of the body, which will just oppose the tendency of motion of the particles of the body. We also know that for pure rolling, to take place, the friction on ground and the body particles in contact must be more then a certain value which is required for pure rolling. If friction goes below this value, it will not be able to stop the motion of the surface particles of the rolling body in contact with the ground and slipping of body starts and sliding friction will act on the body.

In case of slipping the bottom point of contact of the body with the ground will no longer be at rest. It slides either in backward direction or in forward direction depending on the initial rotating and translating condition of the body. As the bottom point of contact slides, the translational velocity of the rolling body will not be equal to $R\omega$ and we have two possible cases in rolling with sliding either $v > R\omega$ or $v < R\omega$, which now we will discuss in detail.

First we consider the case when translation velocity of a rolling body is more then $R\omega$, the tangential velocity of the points on surface of the body. Figure-5.77 shows such a situation.

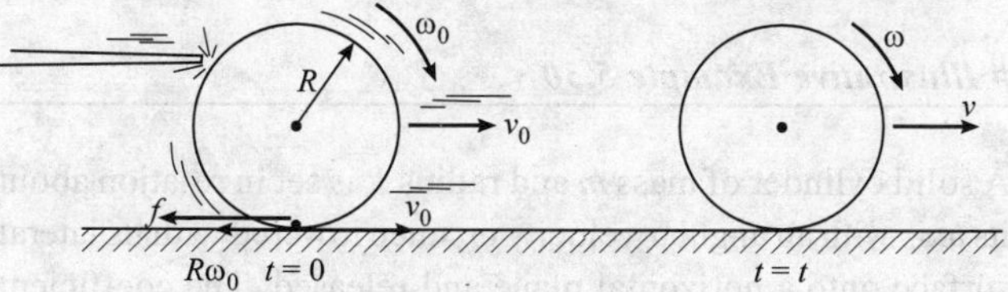

Figure 5.77

A billiard ball (sphere) is struck by a cue, which imparts a liner speed v_0 to it and due to angular impulse imparted by the cue the ball attains an initial angular velocity ω_0. The translational and angular speed imparted to the ball are such that $v_0 > R\omega_0$. As shown in figure, the bottom contact point has both the speeds, v_0 in forward direction and $R\omega_0$ in backward direction and here $v_0 > R\omega_0$, this point will skid on ground in forward direction and experiences sliding friction ($f = \mu N$) in backward direction.

In this case we can observe that sliding friction on ball is against the translational velocity hence it will reduce the translational velocity and simultaneously its torque on ball is in favour of angular velocity ω, thus it will increase ω. When, after some time translational speed (decreasing) becomes equal to tangential speed of the particles of ball's surface (increasing), sliding of the bottom cannot stop and pure rolling starts.

We will now deal the above situation analytically. Let us consider that the ball moves for a time t with sliding and after time t pure rolling starts and obviously after the t sliding friction stops acting and again a static friction appears which opposes the tendency of motion of the contact points.

For solving the cases of rolling with sliding, we generally use impulse equations (both linear and angular impulse). In above example if final translation velocity of body become v and angular velocity become ω, when the body start pure rolling, we have linear and angular impulse equations of frictional force.

During sliding, sliding friction acts for a time t, which imparts a linear impulse ft against the initial velocity of ball, thus we have

$$mv_0 - ft = mv \qquad \ldots(5.93)$$

For rotational motion of ball frictional force imparts an angular impulse fRt to the ball in favour of its angular velocity, thus we have

$$I\omega_0 + fRt = I\omega \qquad \ldots(5.94)$$

Solving the above equations, we can get the time t for which the sliding takes place if final v for ω is known, other can be obtained by using $v = R\omega$ as after this instant pure rolling starts.

During sliding, sliding friction is the only force acting on the ball, thus due to this the linear retardation of the ball can be given as

$$a = \frac{f}{m} = \frac{\mu N}{m}$$

This gives us the distance travelled by the ball before pure rolling starts as

$$s = v_0 t - \frac{1}{2} at^2$$

Due to friction ($f = \mu N$), here we can also find the angular acceleration of the ball as

$$\alpha = \frac{fR}{I} = \frac{\mu NR}{I}$$

It gives us the number of revolutions that the ball has made before pure rolling starts as

$$\theta = \omega_0 t + \frac{1}{2} \alpha t^2$$

All the speed equations (both linear and angular) can be used in these problems as the linear and angular accelerations are constant here. Now we discuss the second possibility of rolling with sliding when translational velocity of the body is less then the tangential velocity of the particles on the surface of the body.

Consider the situation shown in figure-5.78. A cylinder is first spinned on its axis at an angular speed ω_a and carefully placed on a rough surface having friction coefficient μ. As soon as it is placed on the ground as shown in figure, its bottom contact points skid in backward direction and experience sliding friction ($f = \mu N$) in forward direction, due to which the cylinder accelerates forward and gains translational speed and its torque will oppose the angular speed of cylinder due to which the angular speed decreases. Similar to the previous case after some time when v (translational speed) will become equal to $R\omega$ (tangential velocity of surface particles) and pure rolling starts.

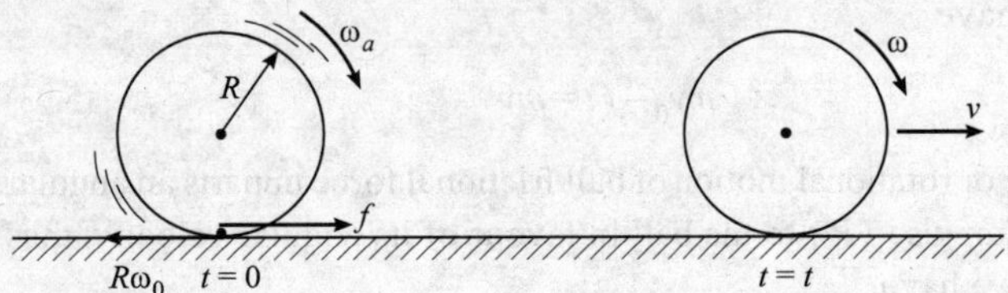

Figure 5.78

In this example, if sliding takes place for a time t our impulse equations will be written as

For translational motion, friction increases linear speed for time t, thus we have

$$0+ft=mv \qquad \ldots(5.95)$$

Initially cylinder does not have any linear velocity as it is lowered on ground slowly (carefully).

For rotational motion, friction decreases the angular velocity of the cylinder for the same time t, thus we have

$$I\omega - fRt = I\omega \qquad \ldots(5.96)$$

Note that here $v=R\omega$ as after time t pure rolling starts. Similar to the previous case we can write and solve the further speed equation for required quantities in the problems.

Now we take few examples for understanding the application of concept of rolling with sliding

Illustrative Example 5.29

A thin spherical shell of mass m and radius R lying on a rough horizontal surface is hit sharply and horizontally by a cue. Where should it be hit so that the shell does not slip on the surface ?

Solution

Figure 5.79 shows the situation. If cue hits the shell at a height h above the centre line, it shoots with an initial speed v (say) and it gains an initial angular speed ω(say) then according to the problem from start v should be equal to $R\omega$ as from start shell will start pure rolling. Let us take the impulse given by the cue to the ball as Fdt, then from impulse equations for the shell we have

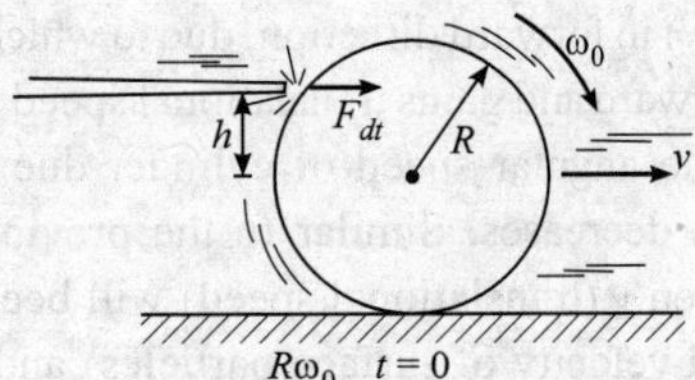

Figure 5.79

For translational motion

$$Fdt = mv \qquad \ldots(5.97)$$

For rotational motion

$$f\,hdt = I\omega$$

or
$$f\,hdt = \left(\frac{2}{3}mR^2\right)\left(\frac{v}{R}\right)$$

$$[\text{As } v + R\omega] \qquad \ldots(5.98)$$

Dividing equation-(5.97) and (5.98), we get

$$h = \frac{2}{3}R$$

Illustrative Example 5.30

A solid cylinder of mass m and radius R is set in rotation about its axis with an angular velocity ω_0, then lowered with its lateral surface onto a horizontal plane and released. The coefficient of friction between the cylinder and the plane is μ. Find

(a) How long the cylinder will move with sliding.

(b) Total work performed by friction.

Solution

(a) Figure-5.80 shows the corresponding situation. In this case sliding friction acts on cylinder in forward direction which increases its linear speed and decreases its angular speed. If after time t its pure rolling is started, we take its final velocity be v_f and final angular velocity be ω_f such that $v_f = R\omega_f$ as pure rolling starts.

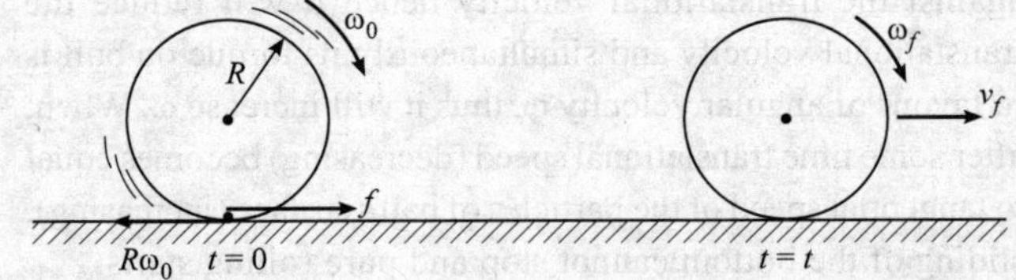

Figure 5.80

We have linear and angular impulse equations as

For translational motion

$$0+ft = mv_f$$

or
$$\mu mgt = mv_f \qquad \ldots(5.99)$$

Initial momentum of the cylinder is taken as zero as it does not have any translational speed.

For rotational motion, we have

$$I\omega_0 - fRt = I\omega_f$$

or $\left(\frac{1}{2}mR^2\right)\omega_0 - \mu mgRt = \left(\frac{1}{2}mR^2\right)\frac{v_f}{R}$ ... (5.100)

Dividing equations-(5.99) and (5.100), we get

$$\frac{\mu gt}{R\omega_0 - 2\mu gt} = 1$$

or $$\mu gt = R\omega_0 - 2\mu gt$$

or $$t = \frac{\omega_0 R}{3\mu g}$$

(b) During sliding, friction is the only force acting on the cylinder and we know that the work done by the friction is always negative or loss in kinetic energy of system. Here at $t = 0$ cylinder has kinetic energy

$$E_i = \frac{1}{2}I\omega_0^2$$

$$= \frac{1}{2}\left(\frac{1}{2}mR^2\right)\omega_0^2 = \frac{1}{4}mR^2\omega_0^2 \quad \text{... (5.101)}$$

Finally when pure rolling starts, kinetic energy of cylinder is

$$E_f = \frac{1}{2}mv_f^2 + \frac{1}{2}I\omega_f^2 \quad \text{... (5.102)}$$

During sliding the acceleration of cylinder due to friction ($f = \mu mg$) is $a = \frac{f}{m} = \mu g$, thus after time t it gains a velocity $v_f = \mu gt = \frac{1}{3}\omega_0 R$.

At this moment pure rolling starts, thus its angular velocity at this instant is $\omega_f = \frac{v_f}{R} = \frac{\mu gt}{R} = \frac{1}{3}\omega_0$

From equation-(5.102), final kinetic energy is

$$E_f = \frac{1}{2}m\left(\frac{1}{3}\omega_0 R\right)^2 + \frac{1}{2}\left(\frac{1}{2}mR^2\right)\left(\frac{1}{3}\omega_0\right)^2$$

$$= \frac{1}{12}m\omega_0^2R^2 \quad \text{... (5.103)}$$

According to Work Energy theorem, work done by friction can be given as

$$W_f = E_f - E_i$$

Substituting the value of E_i and E_f from equation-(5.101) and (5.103), we get

$$W_f = \frac{1}{12}m\omega_0^2R^2 - \frac{1}{4}m\omega_0^2R^2$$

$$= -\frac{1}{6}m\omega_0^2R^2$$

Illustrative Example 5.31

A billiard ball is struck by a cue. The line of action of the applied impulse is horizontal and passes through the centre of the ball. The initial velocity of the ball is v_0. If R is the radius, M is the mass of the ball and μ is the coefficient of friction between the ball and the floor, find how far the ball moves before it ceases to slip on the floor.

Solution

The situation is shown in figure-5.81. In the case as discussed before, the velocity of the bottom contact is in forward direction as due to striking the cue along the centre line, it can not impart any angular impulse to the ball and hence no initial angular velocity. Friction on ball acts in backward direction which will decrease its linear speed and increases the angular velocity until it starts pure rolling. If the ball moves a distance s in time t after which it starts pure rolling, we have the equations of linear and angular impulse for ball as

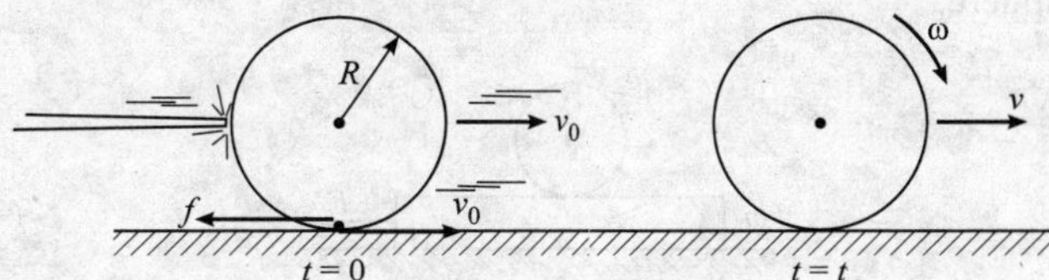

Figure 5.81

$$mv_0 - ft = mv \quad [v = \text{final velocity of ball}]$$

and $$0 + fR\,t = I\frac{v}{R}$$

$$[\frac{v}{R} = \text{final angular velocity of ball}]$$

Dividing the above equations we get

$$\frac{mv_0 - ft}{fRt} = \frac{mv}{\left(\frac{2}{5}mR^2\right)\frac{v}{R}}$$

or $$\frac{mv_0 - \mu mgt}{\mu mgt} = \frac{5}{2} \quad [\text{For sliding } f = \mu mg]$$

or $$t = \frac{2v_0}{7\mu g}$$

As friction is the only force on the ball in backward direction and v_0 its initial speed. After time t, ball starts pure rolling and during this time the ball covers a horizontal distance given as

$$s = v_0 t - \frac{1}{2}\mu gt^2 \quad [\text{As acceleration } a = \frac{f}{m} = \mu g]$$

or $$= v_0 \left(\frac{2v_0}{7ug}\right) - \frac{1}{2}\mu g \left(\frac{2v_0}{7ug}\right)^2$$

or $$= \frac{12v_0^2}{49\mu g}$$

Web Reference of Video Lectures at www.physicsgalaxy.com

Age Group - High School Physics | Age 17-19 Years
Section - MECHANICS
Topic - Rigid Body Dynamics
Module Number - 37, 38, 39, 40, 40, 41 and 42

Practice Exercise 5.4

(i) A plank of mass m_1 with a uniform sphere of mass m_2 placed on it rests on a smooth horizontal plane as shown in figure-5.82. A constant horizontal force F is applied to the plank. With what accelerations will the plank and the centre of the sphere move provided there is no sliding between the plank and the sphere.

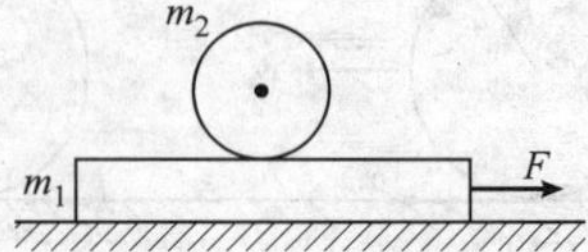

Figure 5.82

$[\frac{7F}{7m_1+2m_2}, \frac{2F}{7m_1+2m_2}]$

(ii) A cylinder of mass m and radius R is resting on a horizontal platform (which is parallel to the X-Y plane) with its axis fixed along the Y-axis and free to rotate about its axis as shown in figure-5.83. The platform is given a motion in the X-direction given by x = Acos (ωt). There is no slipping between the cylinder and platform. Find the maximum torque acting on the cylinder during its motion.

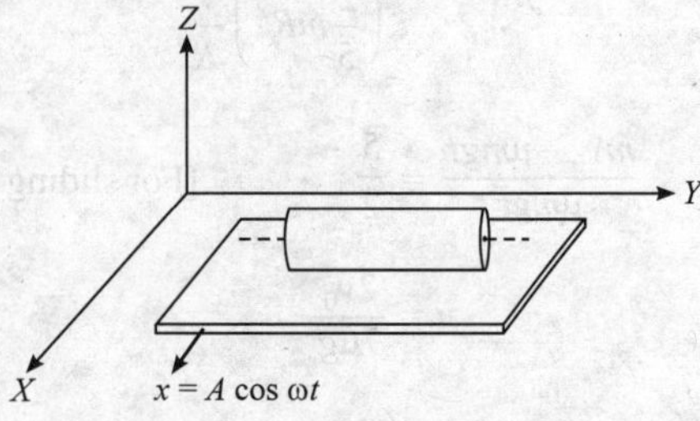

Figure 5.83

$[\frac{1}{3}mAR\omega^2]$

(iii) A hollow sphere of mass m and radius R is placed on a horizontal rough surface with friction coefficient μ. A horizontal force F is applied at the topmost point of shell to roll it. Find the maximum force which can be applied on to it so that shell remain in pure rolling.

[5μ mg]

(iv) A billiard ball of mass m and radius R initially at rest, is given a sharp horizontal impulse by a cue. The cue is held horizontally a distance h above the centre line as shown in figure-5.84.

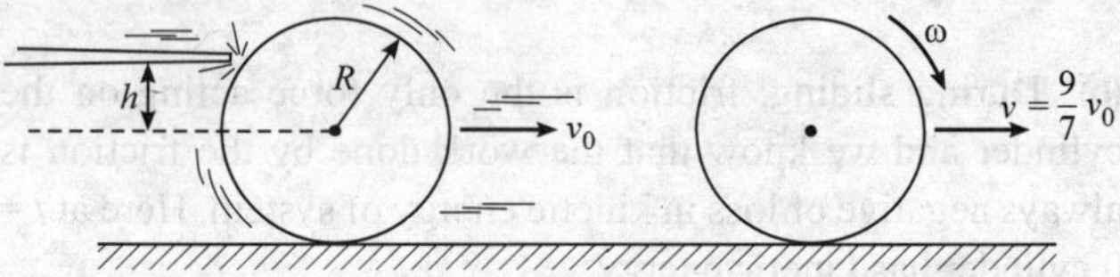

Figure 5.84

The ball leaves the cue with a speed v_0 and, because of its "*forward english*" eventually acquires a final speed of $9/7v_0$, find the value of h.

$[h = \frac{4R}{5}]$

(v) A hollow sphere is released from the top of an inclined plane of inclination θ. (a) What should be the minimum coefficient of friction between the sphere and the plane to prevent sliding ? (b) Find the kinetic energy of the ball as it moves down a length l on the incline if the friction coefficient is half the value calculated in part (a).

$[\frac{2}{5}\tan\theta, \frac{7}{8}mgl\sin\theta]$

5.9 Rotational Collision and Angular Momentum

In previous chapter, we have discussed head on and oblique collisions. In this section we will discuss the different cases of collision of two bodies in which during or after collision rotational motion of the body is also taken into account.

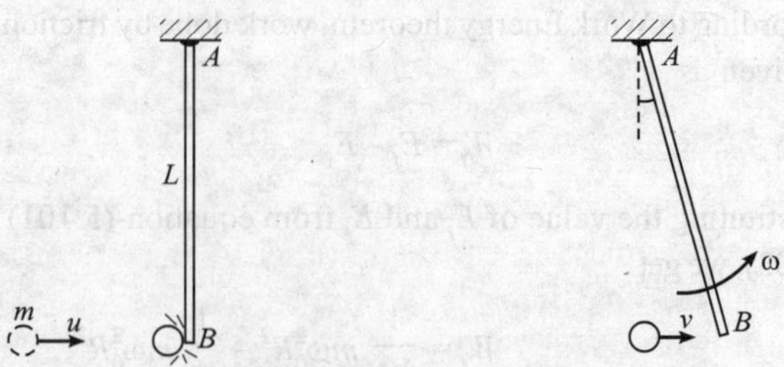

Figure 5.85

We first discuss the simplest case of a collision which is shown in figure-5.85. A rod AB of mass M and length L is hinged at the point A, is hanging vertically. A small ball of mass m moving with a speed u horizontally strike the end B of the rod elastically. Let us consider that after collision the rod will start rotating with angular speed ω and the ball continues to move forward with a less speed v. So the ball may rebound but we need not to consider this case, as if ball will rebound, the result will give the velocity v negative. The values of v and ω in this problem can be obtained in two ways using energy and angular momentum conservation or using impulse equations.

NOTE About Hinge at Point A : Students should note that when ball will strike the rod, and external impulse will be developed at the hinge which will prevent the rod to move forward, as rod can only rotate, can not translate. Due to this external impulse linear momentum of the system can not be conserved but angular momentum can be conserved about the hinge as here is no external torque or angular impulse about the hinge.

As stated in above paragraph, here we cannot use linear momentum conservation but as no external torque is present we use angular momentum conservation about the hinge as

$$muL = mvL + \left(\frac{ML^2}{3}\right)\omega \qquad \ldots(5.104)$$

Here mul is the angular momentum of the ball before striking the rod and it is the only angular momentum before collision as rod is at rest. After collision as ball will move with a speed v in same direction, its angular momentum is mul and that of rod is $I\omega$ as it starts rotation with initial angular velocity ω.

As collision is elastic we use kinetic energy conservation before and after collision as

$$\frac{1}{2}mu^2 = \frac{1}{2}mv^2 + \frac{1}{2}\left(\frac{ML^2}{3}\right)\omega^2 \qquad \ldots(5.105)$$

Now using the above two equations, we get the values of v and ω.

The other way of solving this problems is by breaking Equation-(5.104). It can be broken in two parts if required in some problems using impulse equations. Again consider the initial case when ball strikes the rod, a normal force is developed between the surface of ball and that of rod due to the push of ball against rod, the situation is shown in figure-5.86.

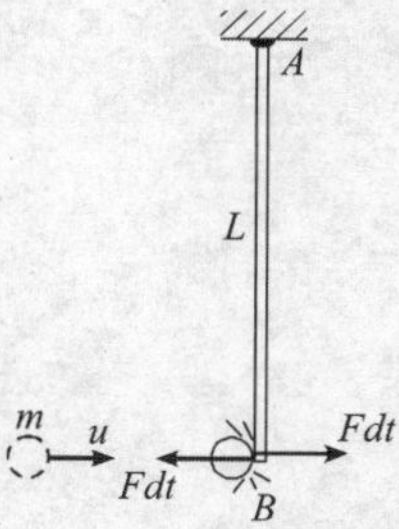

Figure 5.86

This interaction for F acts for a short duration (say dt) when the ball and rod are in contact. It retards the ball and its torque accelerates the rod in anticlockwise direction. We can use the impulse equations for ball (linear) and rod (angular).

For motion of ball, we have the linear impulse equation as

$$mu - Fdt = mv \qquad \ldots(5.106)$$

For motion of rod, we have the angular impulse equation as

$$0 + FLdt + I\omega$$

or
$$FLdt = \left(\frac{ML^2}{3}\right)\omega \qquad \ldots(5.107)$$

If we use the above two equations along with equation-(5.103), we can solve the problem. Here if equation-(5.106) and (5.107) are merged, it results equation-(5.104). This type of working might be of more utility in solving the problem instead of directly using energy conservations.

The previous case might also be of inelastic or partial elastic collision. If in previous problem with same initial conditions the collision is partial elastic and the coefficient of restitution is given as e, the angular momentum conservation equation-(5.104) remains same as no external torque is acting but now we cannot use energy conservation as collisions not perfectly elastic. Here we use the definition of coefficient of restitution that it is the ratio of velocity of separation after collision to the velocity of approach before collision. In this case it is used as

$$e = \frac{L\omega - v}{u}$$

or
$$L\omega - v = eu \qquad \ldots(5.108)$$

Solving the equation-(5.104) and (5.108), we get the results v and ω. If this collision were perfectly inelastic, we use $e = 0$, which comes from equation-(5.108), $v = L\omega$, as no separation occurs in perfectly inelastic collision. Here it is important to be noted that the ball and rod will be separate even if inelastic collision takes place because ball is in translational motion and rod is in rotational motion. Figure 5.87 explains the situation.

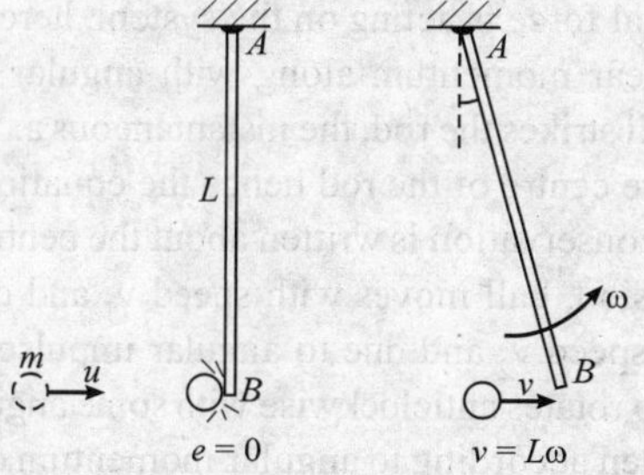

Figure 5.87

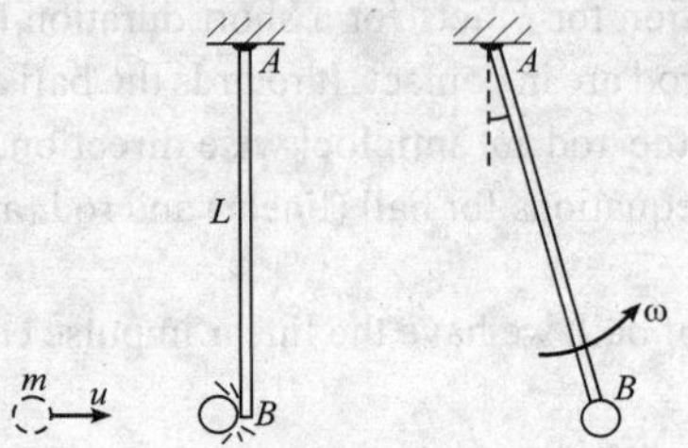

Figure 5.88

Now we consider one more case when ball sticks to the end of the rod and will rotate along with the rod. It is a specific type of inelastic collision as ball sticks to rod. Here again we can neither use energy conservation nor the coefficient of restitution equation. Only angular momentum conservation equation is sufficient for solving the problem as one of our previous variables reduces, the linear velocity of the ball. Consider figure-5.88. Ball and rod will start together in rotation with an initial angular velocity ω. Thus we write the angular momentum conservation equation as

$$muL = I\omega \qquad \text{[Here } I = \text{M.I. of rod plus ball]}$$

$$muL = \left(\frac{ML^2}{3} + mL^2\right)\omega \qquad \dots(5.109)$$

Here moment of inertia of the system is taken combined that of rod plus ball as both are in rotational motion with angular velocity ω after collision. Equation-(5.109) will give us the angular velocity ω of the system.

Now we discuss another case when rod is not hinged at an end. Consider the collision shown in figure-5.89. Here rod *AB* is placed on a smooth surface which is free to move on it and a ball moving with a velocity *u* strikes elastically at a point *P* of the rod at a distance *d* from the rod's centre as shown in figure.

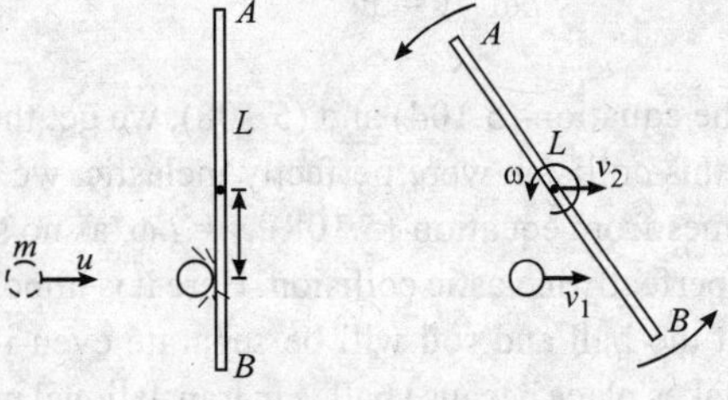

Figure 5.89

As no external force is acting on the system, here we can also conserve linear momentum along with angular momentum. When the ball strikes the rod, the instantaneous axis of rotation is taken at the centre of the rod hence the equation of angular momentum conservation is written about the centre of the rod. If after collision, ball moves with speed v_1 and centre of rod moves with speed v_2 and due to angular impulse of collision on rod, it also rotates anticlockwise with some angular velocity, let it be ω, then according to angular momentum conservation we have

$$mud = mv_1 d + I\omega$$

or $$mud = mv_1 d + \left(\frac{ML^2}{12}\right)\omega \qquad \dots(5.110)$$

From linear momentum conservation, we have

$$mu = mv_1 + Mv_2 \qquad \dots(5.111)$$

If collision is elastic, kinetic energy of system must remain conserved before and after collision. Thus we have

$$\frac{1}{2}mu^2 = \frac{1}{2}mv_1^2 + \frac{1}{2}mv_2^2 + \frac{1}{2}\left(\frac{ML^2}{12}\right)\omega^2 \qquad \dots(5.112)$$

Equations-(5.110), (5.111) and (5.112) gives the unknown parameters after collisions v_1, v_2 and ω. If this collision is not elastic, we use coefficient of restitution instead of energy conservation equation-(5.112), as

$$e = \frac{(v_2 + d\omega) - v_1}{u} \qquad \dots(5.113)$$

Here $v_2 + d\omega$ is the linear speed of point *P* after collision as rod moves translationally with velocity v_2 and rotates with angular velocity ω and v_1 is the final velocity of the ball after collision. For inelastic collision, *e* can be taken as zero.

 # Illustrative Example 5.32

A small disc and a thin uniform rod of length *L*, whose mass is η times greater than the mass of the disc, lie on a smooth horizontal plane. The disc is set in motion, in horizontal direction and perpendicular to the rod, with velocity *v*, after which it elastically collides with the end of the rod. Find the velocity of the disc and the angular velocity of the rod after the collision. At what value of η will the velocity of the disc after the collision be equal to zero ? Reverse the direction ?

Solution

The situation is shown in figure-5.90. If mass of disc is *m*, then mass of rod = η*m*, If v_1 and v_2 be the velocity of the disc and rod after collision, using linear momentum conservation, we have

$$mv = mv_1 + \eta mv_2$$

Figure 5.90

or $$v = v_1 + \eta v_2 \qquad \dots(5.114)$$

If after collision, rod starts rotating with angular speed ω, using conservation of angular momentum, we have

$$mv\frac{L}{2}=\left(\frac{\eta mL^2}{12}\right)\omega+mv_1\frac{L}{2}$$

or $$v=\frac{1}{6}\eta L\omega+v_1$$

or $$\omega=\frac{6(v-v_1)}{\eta L} \quad \dots(5.115)$$

As collision is elastic, using kinetic energy conservation, we get

$$\frac{1}{2}mv^2=\frac{1}{2}mv_1^2+\frac{1}{2}\eta mv_2^2+\frac{1}{2}I\omega^2$$

or $$v^2=v_1^2+\frac{3}{\eta}(v-v_1)^2+\eta\frac{(v-v_1)^2}{\eta^2}$$

Solving for v_1, we get

$$v_1=\frac{4-\eta}{4+\eta}v$$

Here we can see that v_1 is zero if $\eta = 4$ and v_1 will be negative when $\eta > 4$.

5.10 Work and Power in Rotational Motion

When someone pedal a bicycle, work is done in moving it. There are several examples in general life like this when energy is spent in rotating work. Such as a rotating motor drives water from a tank to the several floors of a building or a rotating car engine drives the car. This work can be explained using torque and angular displacement.

For example, suppose a force F is acting tangential at the rim of a pivoted wheel. Let the wheel rotate through an angle $d\theta$ in time dt, the work done by the force is given as $F\,.\,ds$, where ds is the displacement produced by the force F and it is given as $ds = R\,d\theta$, thus we have

$$dW=F\,Rd\theta$$

or $$dW=\tau\,d\theta$$

If the wheel rotates from an angle θ_1 to an angle θ_2, the total work done by the torque is

$$\int_{\theta_1}^{\theta_2}\tau\,d\theta \quad \dots(5.116)$$

If torque is constant during rotation than we can also use

$$W=\tau(\theta_2-\theta_1)=\tau\Delta\theta \quad \dots(5.117)$$

The equation-(5.116) is the rotational analog of the relation $W=\int Fds$, for the work done by a variable force in translational displacement.

If force applied is not tangential but at an angle to the radial direction it has an axial or radial component which would do no work because the displacement of the point of application has only a tangential component. An axial or radial component of force would also make no contribution to the torque about the axis of rotation, thus above equations-(5.116) and (5.117) are valid for any force no matter in which direction the force is acting.

When a torque does work on a rotating rigid body, the kinetic energy changes by an amount equal to the work done according to the work energy theorem. The agent who is doing work on the rotating body is giving energy to it, the amount of energy supplied or work done on it per second is known as the rotational power. If in time dt, work done is dW, we have

$$\frac{dW}{dt}=\tau\frac{d\theta}{dt}$$

Here dW/dt is the rate of doing work, or power P, and $d\theta/dt$ is the angular velocity ω of the rotating body, so

$$P=\tau\omega \quad \dots(5.118)$$

The above relation is the rotational analog of the relation $P = F\,.\,v$ for translational motion.

Practice Exercise 5.5

(i) A solid wooden door 1 m wide and 2 m high is hinged along one side and has a total mass of 50 kg. Initially open and at rest, the door is struck at its centre by a handful of sticky mud of mass 0.5 kg travelling at 12 m/s just before impact. Find the final angular velocity of the door.

[$\frac{72}{403}$ rad/s]

(ii) A thin uniform square plate with side l and mass M can rotate freely about a stationary vertical axis coinciding with one of its sides. A small ball of mass m flying with velocity v at right angles to the plate strikes elastically to the centre of it. Find the velocity of the ball v' after the impact and the horizontal component of the force which the axis will exert on the plate after the impact.

[$\frac{3m-4M}{3m+4M}v$, $\frac{72Mm^2v^2}{l(3m+4m)^2}$]

(iii) A uniform rod of mass 200 grams and length $L = 1$ m is initially at rest in vertical position. The rod is hinged at centre such that it can rotate freely without friction about a fixed horizontal axis passing through its centre. Two particles of mass $m = 100$ grams each having horizontal velocity of equal magnitude $u = 6$ m/s strike the rod at top and bottom simultaneously as shown and stick to the rod. Find the angular speed of rod when it becomes horizontal.

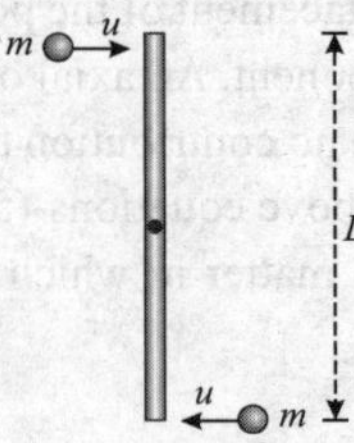

Figure 5.91

[9 rad/s]

(iv) A man of mass m_1 stands on the edge of a horizontal uniform disc of mass m_2 and radius R which is capable of rotating freely about a stationary vertical axis passing through its centre. The man walks along the edge of the disc through angle θ relative to the disc and then stops. Find the angle through which the disc turned the time the man stopped.

$[\dfrac{2m_1\theta}{2m_1 + m_2}]$

(v) A uniform rod AB of length $2l$ and mass $2m$ is suspended freely at A and hangs vertically at rest when a particle of mass m is fired horizontally with speed v to strike the rod at its mid point. If the particle is brought to rest by the impact, find : (a) the impulsive reaction at A, (b) the initial angular speed of the rod, and (c) the maximum angle the rod makes with the vertical in the subsequent motion.

$[mv/4,\ 3v/8l,\ \cos^{-1}\left(1 - \dfrac{3v^2}{32lg}\right)]$

(vi) A metre stick is held vertically with one end on the floor and is then allowed to fall. Find the speed of the other end when it hits the floor, assuming that the end of the floor does not slip. Take $g = 10\ \text{m/s}^2$.

$[\sqrt{30}\ \text{m/s}]$

Advance Illustrations Videos at www.physicsgalaxy.com

Age Group - Advance Illustrations
Section - Mechanics
Topic - Rigid Body Dynamics
Illustrations - 45 In-depth Illustration videos

* * * * *

Discussion Question

Q5-1 Can a single force applied to a body change both its translational and rotational motion ? Explain.

Q5-2 A meter stick, half of which is wood and the other half steel, is pivoted at the wooden end and a force is applied to the steel end. Next, it is pivoted at the steel end and the same force is applied at the wooden end. Does one get the same angular acceleration in each case ? Explain.

Q5-3 How a swimmer jumping form a height is able to increase the number of loops made in the air ?

Q5-4 The melting of the polar ice caps is supposed to be a possible cause of the variation of the earth's time period of rotation. Explain.

Q5-5 The angular velocity of the earth's rotation, it is 2π rad/day, in which reference frame we are thinking of ?

Q5-6 When an electrical motor is turned on, it takes longer to come up to final speed if there is a grinding wheel attached to the shaft. Why ?

Q5-7 Does a body rotating about a fixed axis have to be perfectly rigid for all points on the body to have the same angular velocity and the same angular acceleration ? Explain.

Q5-8 If you roll raw eggs on an incline plane, it is possible to tell which one is raw and which one is boiled. How ?

Q5-9 If you stop a spinning raw egg for the shortest instant you can and then release it, the egg will start spinning again. If you do the same to a hard boiled egg, it will remain stopped. Explain it.

Q5-10 A helicopter has a large main rotor that rotates in a horizontal plane and provides lift. There is also a small rotor on the tail that rotates in a vertical plane. What is the purpose of the tail rotor ?

Q5-11 A body is in pure rolling on a surface. Is it necessarily being acted upon by an external torque ?

Q5-12 Why it is more difficult to revolve a stone by tying it to a longer string than by tying it to a shorter string ?

Q5-13 A thin wheel can stay upright on its rim for a considerable velocity, while it falls from its upright position at the slightest disturbance, when stationary. Explain.

Q5-14 If there are two discs of equal masses but different thickness are made from different materials (different densities), which disc, will have the larger moment of inertia about the central axis.

Q5-15 A cylindrical container filled with cheese and another identical can filled with beer both roll down an incline plane. How different their linear and angular accelerations.

Q5-16 A person sits near the edge of a circular platform revolving with a uniform angular speed. What will be the change in the motion of the platform ? What will happen when the person starts moving from the edge towards the centre of the platform ?

Q5-17 The harder you hit the brakes while driving forward, the more the front end of your car will move down and the rear end move up. Why ? What happens when accelerating forward?

Q5-18 A car's speedometer read the speed of car. Will there be a correction in speedometer if tyres become old (snowed tyres).

Q5-19 When car is moving on a horizontal icy floor, if its brakes are locked, wheels stops rotating and start sliding. What happens to rotational kinetic energy ?

Q5-20 A rear wheel drive car accelerates quickly from rest, and the driver observes that the car noses up. Why does it do that ? Would a front wheel drive car do that ?

Q5-21 A disc rotates with constant angular velocity. Does a point on its rim have a tangential acceleration or a radial acceleration ? Are these accelerations constant ?

Q5-22 A disc is first spinned and then placed gently on a rough floor with its surface horizontal. Will centre of mass of disc advance in some direction ? Explain.

Q5-23 A cylinder of mass M and radius R can rotate about its axis of symmetry. Can mass inside the cylinder can be distributed such that the moment of inertia of it become more than MR^2.

Q5-24 A disc of metal is melted and recasted in the form of a solid sphere. What will happen to the moment of inertia about a vertical axis passing through the centre ? What will happen if it is recasted in the form of a thin ring.

Q5-25 A wheel is rolling without slipping on a horizontal surface. In an inertial frame of reference in which the surface is at rest, is there any point on the wheel that has a velocity that is purely vertical ? Is there any point that has a horizontal velocity component opposite to the velocity of the centre of mass ? Explain. What would be the results if wheel is slipping with rolling ?

Q5-26 If the atmosphere suddenly condensed into a solid mass and formed a thin layer on the surface of the earth, what effect would it have on the time of rotation of the earth about it axis ?

Q5-27 A point particle travels in a straight line at constant speed. The closest it comes to the origin of coordinates is a distance *l*. With respect to this origin, does the particle have nonzero angular momentum ? As the particle moves along its straight line path, does its angular momentum with respect to origin change.

Q5-28 An electric grinding wheel rotates for some time after the power is turned off, but an electric drilling machine stops after few seconds of turning off the power. Why ?

Q5-29 A cylindrical can rotates at constant angular velocity about a vertical axis. There is no friction and no external torque. At the bottom of can there a thick layer of ice, which rotates with the can. Suppose the ice melts, but none of the water escapes from the can. Is the angular velocity now greater than, the same as, or less than the original velocity ? Explain.

Q5-30 A student stands on a table rotating with an angular speed ω while holding two equal dumbbells at arm's length. Without moving anything else, the two dumbbells are dropped. What changes will be there in motion, if any ? What would be the changes if he bring the dumbbells to keep in touch with his chest by folding his arms ? Explain.

Q5-31 In previous question, if the student standing on a table (at rest) free to rotate about its central axis holding a rotating disc with smooth handles attached to its central axis of rotation. Initially he keep the axis of disc vertical such as the disc is rotating in a horizontal plane. What happens if he tilt the axis of rotating disc by 90° to make the disc to rotate in vertical plane. Explain the concept in the problems.

* * * * *

Conceptual MCQs Single Option Correct

5-1 A cylinder rolls up an inclined plane, reaches some height, and then rolls down (without slipping throughout these motions). The direction of the frictional force acting on the cylinder are :

(A) Up the incline while ascending and down the incline while descending.
(B) Up the incline while ascending as well as descending.
(C) Down the incline while ascending and up the incline while descending.
(D) Down the incline while ascending as well as descending.

5-2 Let I_1 and I_2 be the moments of inertia of two bodies of identical geometrical shape, the first made of aluminium and the second of iron then for a given axis of rotation :

(A) $I_1 < I_2$
(B) $I_1 = I_2$
(C) $I_1 > I_2$
(D) Relation between I_1 and I_2 depends on the actual shapes of the bodies.

5-3 A string of negligible thickness is wrapped several times around a cylinder kept on a rough horizontal surface. A man standing at a distance l from the cylinder holds one end of the string and pulls the cylinder towards him. There is no slipping anywhere. The length of the string passed through the hand of the man while the cylinder reaches his hands is :

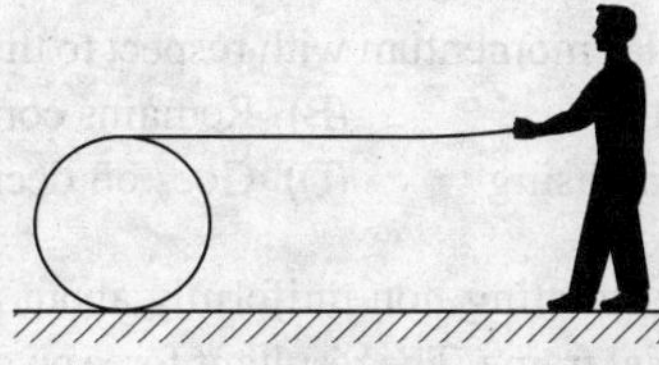

Figure 5.92

(A) l (B) $2l$
(C) $3l$ (D) $4l$

5-4 If there is no external force acting on a non rigid body, which of the following quantities must remain constant ?

(A) Angular momentum (B) Linear momentum
(C) Kinetic energy (D) Moment of inertia

5-5 A hollow sphere and a solid sphere having same mass and same radii are rolled down a rough inclined plane :

(A) The hollow sphere reaches the bottom first
(B) The solid sphere reaches the bottom with greater speed
(C) The solid sphere reaches the bottom with greater kinetic energy
(D) The two spheres will reach the bottom with same linear momentum

5-6 When a steady torque acts on a rotating rigid body, the body :

(A) Gets linear acceleration only
(B) Gets an angular acceleration
(C) Continues to rotate as a steady rate
(D) None of these

5-7 A wheel of radius 20 cm is pushed to move it on a rough horizontal surface. It is found to move through a distance of 60 cm on the road during the time it completes one revolution about the centre. Assume that the linear and the angular accelerations are uniform. The frictional force acting on the wheel by the surface is :

(A) Along the velocity of the wheel
(B) Opposite to the velocity of the wheel
(C) Perpendicular to the velocity of the wheel
(D) Zero

5-8 The density of a rod gradually decreases from one end to the other. It is pivoted at an end so that it can move about a vertical axis through the pivot. A horizontal force F is applied on the free end in the direction perpendicular to the rod. The quantities, that do not depend on which end of the rod is pivoted, are :

(A) Angular acceleration
(B) Angular velocity when the rod completes one rotation
(C) Angular momentum when the rod completes one rotation
(D) Torque of the applied force

5-9 A man stands in the middle of a rotating table which has an angular velocity ω. He is holding two equal masses at arms length in each hand. Without moving his arms he just drops the two masses. How will be the angular speed of table get changed?

(A) It will be greater than ω
(B) It will be less than ω
(C) It will not change
(D) The increase or decrease will be decided by the quantity of the masses dropped.

5-10 If two circular discs of the same weight and thickness are made from metals of different densities, which disc will have the larger moment of inertia about its central axis ?

(A) Cannot be predicted
(B) Disc with larger density
(C) Disc with smaller density
(D) Both have same moment of inertia

5-11 In the previous question, the smallest kinetic energy at the bottom of the incline will be achieved by :

(A) The solid sphere
(B) The hollow sphere
(C) The disc
(D) All will achieve same kinetic energy

5-12 A body is rotating uniformly about a vertical axis fixed in an inertial frame. The resultant force on a particle of the body not on the axis is :

(A) Vertical
(B) Horizontal and skew with the axis
(C) Horizontal and intersecting the axis
(D) None of these

5-13 A circular table rotates about a vertical axis with a constant angular speed ω. A circular pan rests on the rotating table and rotates along with the table. The bottom of the pan is covered with a uniform thick layer of ice which also rotates with the pan. The ice starts melting. The angular speed of the rotating table :

(A) Remains the same
(B) Decreases
(C) Increases
(D) May increases or decreases depending upon the thickness of ice layer

5-14 A uniform rod is kept vertically on a horizontal smooth surface at a point O. If it is rotated slightly and released, it falls down on the horizontal surface. The lower end will remain :

(A) At O
(B) At a distance less than $l/2$ from O
(C) At a distance $l/2$ from O
(D) At a distance larger than $l/2$ from O

5-15 A person sitting firmly over a rotating stool has his arms stretched. If he folds his arms, his angular momentum about the axis of rotation :

(A) Increases (B) Decreases
(C) Remains unchanged (D) Doubles

5-16 A solid sphere and a hollow sphere are identical in mass and radius. The ratio of their moment of inertia about a diameter is :

(A) 5 : 3 (B) 1 : 1
(C) 1 : 2 (D) 3 : 5

5-17 Consider four bodies-a ring, a cube, a disc and a sphere. All the bodies have the same diameter, equal to the length of the cube on each edge. All rotate about their axes through their respective centres of mass. Which one has the largest moment of inertia ?

(A) Ring (B) Cube
(C) Disc (D) Sphere

5-18 A circular disc A of radius r is made from an iron plate of thickness t and another circular disc B of radius $4r$ is made from another iron plate of thickness $t/4$. The relation between the moments of inertia I_A and I_B is :

(A) $I_A > I_B$
(B) $I_A = I_B$
(C) $I_A < I_B$
(D) Depends on the actual values of t and r

5-19 A plank P is placed on a solid cylinder S, which rolls on a horizontal surface. The two are of equal mass. There is no slipping at any of the surfaces in contact. The ratio of the kinetic energy of P to the kinetic energy of S is :

(A) 1 : 1
(B) 2 : 1
(C) 8 : 3
(D) 11 : 8

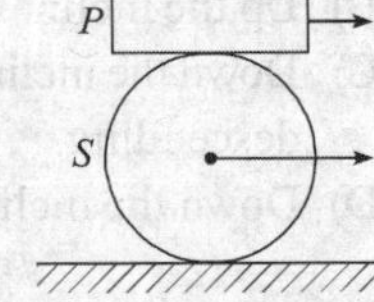

Figure 5.93

5-20 The locus of all the points on the X-Y plane, about which the moment of inertia of the rod along an axis parallel to z axis is same as that about O is [The rod is lying in XZ plane] :

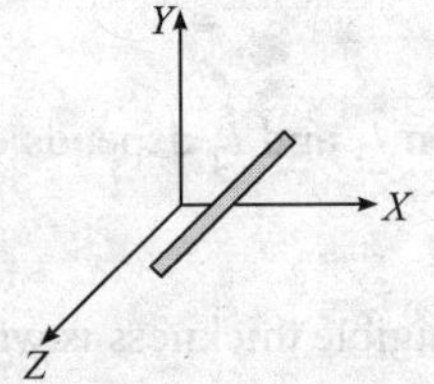

Figure 5.94

(A) Straight line (B) Circle
(C) Parabola (D) Ellipse

5-21 A particle moves with a constant velocity parallel to the X-axis. Its angular momentum with respect to the origin :

(A) Is constant (B) Remains constant
(C) Goes on increasing (D) Goes on decreasing

5-22 A body is rotating non uniformly about a vertical axis fixed in an inertial frame. The resultant force on a particle of the body not on the axis is :

(A) Vertical
(B) Horizontal and skew with the axis
(C) Horizontal and intersecting the axis
(D) None of these

5-23 Two uniform solid spheres having unequal masses and unequal radii are released from rest from the same height on a rough incline. If the spheres roll without slipping :

(A) The heavier sphere reaches the bottom first
(B) The bigger sphere reaches the bottom first
(C) The two spheres reach the bottom together
(D) The information given is not sufficient to tell which sphere will reach the bottom first

5-24 A sphere can roll without slipping on a surface inclined at an angle θ if the friction coefficient is more than $(2/7)g \sin \theta$. Suppose the friction coefficient is $(1/7)g \sin \theta$. If a sphere is released from rest on this incline then which of the following are possible situations :

(A) It will stay at rest
(B) It will make pure translational motion
(C) It will translate and rotate about the centre
(D) The angular momentum of the spheres about its centre will remain constant

5-25 Out of two eggs, both equal in weight and identical in shape and size, one is raw and the other is boiled. The ratio between the moments of inertia of raw to boiled one, about a central axis, will be :

(A) Equal to one (B) Greater than one
(C) Less than one (D) Less than half

5-26 The angular velocity of the engine (and hence of the wheel) of a scooter is proportional to the petrol input per second. The scooter is moving on a frictionless road with uniform velocity. If the petrol input in increased by 10% the linear velocity of the scooter is increased by :

(A) 50% (B) 10%
(C) 20% (D) 0%

5-27 Only under gravity and some initial impulse a sphere cannot roll without sliding on :

(A) A smooth horizontal surface
(B) A smooth inclined surface
(C) A rough horizontal surface
(D) A rough inclined surface

5-28 A closed cylindrical tube containing some water (not filling the entire tube) lies in a horizontal plane. If the tube is rotated about a perpendicular bisector, the moment of inertia of water about the axis :

(A) Increases
(B) Decreases
(C) Remains constant
(D) Increases if the rotation is clockwise and decreases if it is in anticlockwise

5-29 Let I_A and I_B be moments of inertia of a body about two axes A and B respectively. The axis A passes through the centre of mass of the body but B does not :

(A) $I_A < I_B$
(B) If $I_A < I_B$, the axes are parallel
(C) If the axes are parallel, $I_A < I_B$
(D) If the axes are not parallel, $I_A \geq I_B$

5-30 A circular platform is free to rotate in a horizontal plane about a vertical axis passing through its centre. A tortoise is sitting at the edge of the platform. Now, the platform is given an angular velocity ω_0. When the tortoise moves along a chord of the platform with a constant velocity (w.r.t. the platform), the angular velocity of the platform $\omega(t)$ will vary with time t as :

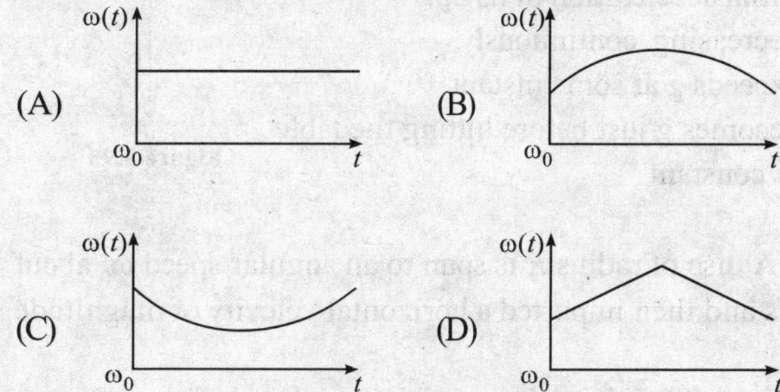

5-31 A triangle plate of uniform thickness and density is made to rotate about an axis perpendicular to the plane of the paper and (a) passing through A and (b) passing through B, by the application of the same force, F at C (midpoint of AB) as shown in the figure-5.95. The angular acceleration in both the cases are α_A and α_B respectively, then :

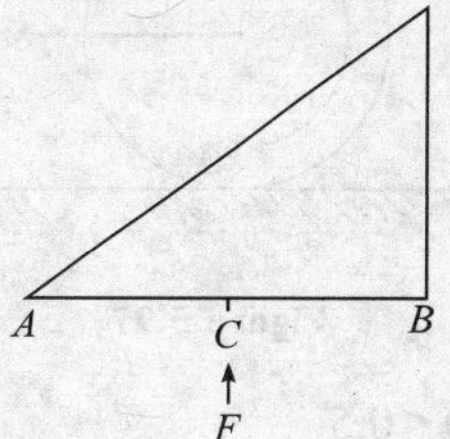

Figure 5.95

(A) $\alpha_A = \alpha_B$ (B) $\alpha_A < \alpha_B$
(C) $\alpha_A > \alpha_B$ (D) $\alpha_A = \alpha_B = 0$

5-32 A satellite is revolving round the earth. If the universal gravitational constant (G) was decreasing uniformly with time for the satellite, the quantity that still remains constant is :

(A) Weight (B) Radius
(C) Tangential speed (D) Angular momentum

5-33 A body is rolling without slipping on a horizontal plane. If the rotational energy of the body is 40% of the total kinetic energy, then the body might be :

(A) Cylinder (B) Hollow sphere
(C) Solid cylinder (D) Ring

5-34 A person is sitting near the edge of a rotating platform. When he walks towards the centre, then :

(A) Moment of inertia of system increases
(B) Angular velocity of platform decreases
(C) Angular velocity of platform increases
(D) Angular velocity of platform remains unchanged

5-35 A pencil is placed vertically on a table top with its point end up and its sticky eraser end down. As it falls over from this unstable position, its point of contact with the table remains stationary during its fall, the tangential acceleration of its tip.

(A) decreasing continuously

(B) exceeds g at some instant

(C) becomes g just before hitting the table

(D) is constant

Figure 5.96

5-36 A disc of radius R is spun to an angular speed ω_0 about its axis and then imparted a horizontal velocity of magnitude $\frac{\omega_0 R}{4}$ (at $t = 0$) with its plane remaining vertical. The coefficient of friction between the disc and the plane is μ. The sense of rotation and direction of its linear speed are shown in the figure-5.97. Choose the correct statement. The disc will return to its initial position :

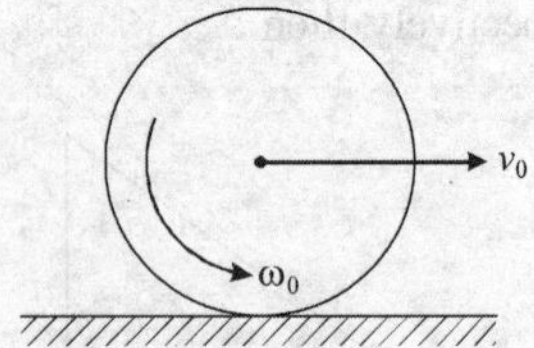

Figure 5.97

(A) if the value of $\mu < 0.5$

(B) irrespective of the value of μ ($\mu > 0$)

(C) if the value of $0.5 < \mu < 1$

(D) if $\mu > 1$

5-37 A rod of mass M and length L is placed on a smooth horizontal table and is hit by a ball moving horizontally and perpendicular to length of rod and sticks to it. Then conservation of angular momentum can be applied :

(A) About any point on the rod

(B) About a point at the centre of the rod

(C) About end point of the rod

(D) None

5-38 A block of mass m is held stationary against a rough wall by applying a force F as shown in figure-5.98. Which one of the following statements is incorrect ?

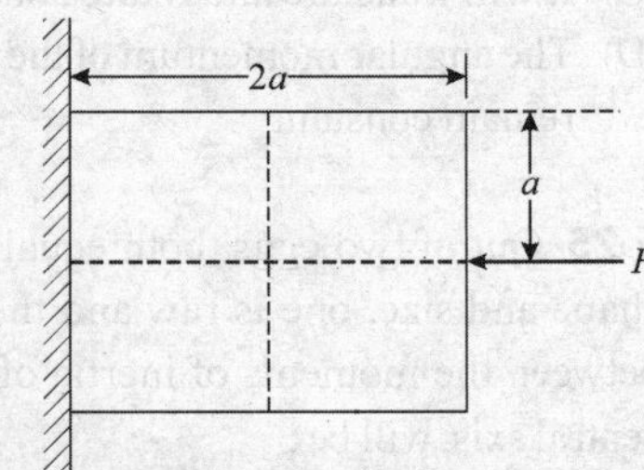

Figure 5.98

(A) frictional force $f = mg$

(B) normal reaction $N = F$

(C) F will not produce a torque

(D) N will not produce any torque

5-39 If net external torque, about a point, acting on the system is zero, then we can surely say :

(A) Kinetic energy of the system remains constant

(B) Mechanical energy of the system remains constant

(C) Torque of Internal forces is zero

(D) Momentum of system will remain constant

5-40 Figure-5.99 shows a smooth inclined plane fixed in a car accelerating on a horizontal road. The angle of incline θ is related to the acceleration a of the car as $a = g \tan \theta$. If the sphere is set in pure rolling on the incline :

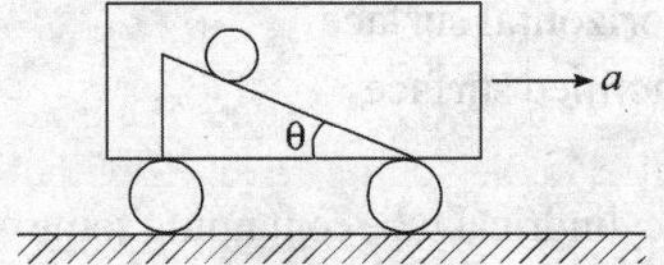

Figure 5.99

(A) It will continue pure rolling

(B) It will slip down the plane

(C) Its linear velocity will increase

(D) Its linear velocity will decrease

* * * * *

Numerical MCQs Single Options Correct

5-1 The moment of inertia of cylinder of radius a, mass M and height h about an axis parallel to the axis of the cylinder and distant b from its centre is :

(A) $\frac{1}{2}M(a^2+2b^2)$ (B) $\frac{1}{2}M(2a^2+b^2)$

(C) $\frac{1}{2}M(a^2+b^2)$ (D) $\frac{1}{2}M\left(\frac{a^2}{3}+\frac{b^2}{12}\right)$

5-2 AB and CD are two identical rods each of length L and mass M joined to form a cross. Find the M.I. of the system about a bisector of the angle between the rods (XY) :

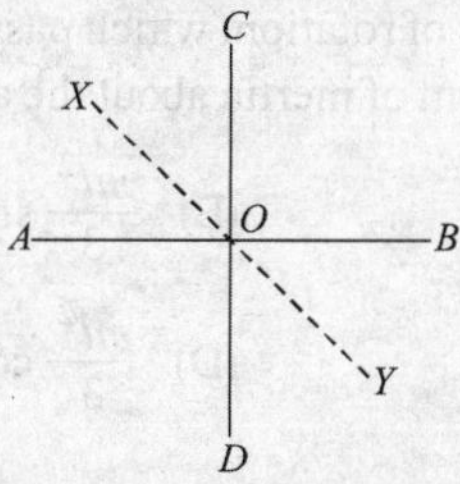

Figure 5.100

(A) $\frac{ML^2}{12}$ (B) $\frac{ML^2}{6}$

(C) $\frac{ML^2}{3}$ (D) $\frac{4ML^2}{3}$

5-3 A solid uniform disk of mass m rolls without slipping down an inclined plane with an acceleration a. The frictional force on the disk due to surface of the plane is :

(A) $2\,ma$ (B) $\frac{3}{2}\,ma$

(C) ma (D) $\frac{1}{2}\,ma$

5-4 A solid sphere of mass m and radius R is moving with velocity of centre of mass $v\,\hat{i}$ and angular velocity about centre of mass $\omega\,\hat{i}$. If the coefficient of friction between the sphere and ground is μ, the frictional force vector is (consider $v = \omega R$) :

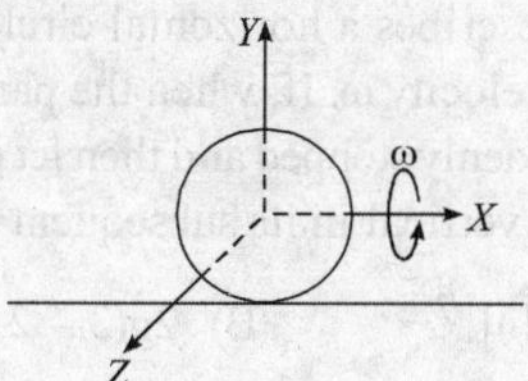

Figure 5.101

(A) $\mu mg(\hat{i}+\hat{k})$ (B) $\frac{\mu mg}{\sqrt{2}}(\hat{k}+\hat{i})$

(C) $\frac{\mu mg}{\sqrt{2}}(\hat{k}-\hat{i})$ (D) $\mu mg\,\hat{k}$

5-5 A disc of mass M and radius R is rolling with angular speed ω on a horizontal plane. The magnitude of angular momentum of the disc about a point on ground along the line of motion of disc is :

(A) $(1/2)\,MR^2\omega$ (B) $MR^2\omega$
(C) $(3/2)\,MR^2\omega$ (D) $2\,MR^2\omega$

5-6 Figure-5.102 shows a small wheel fixed coaxially on a bigger one of double the radius. The system rotates about the common axis. The strings supporting A and B do not slip on the wheels. If x and y be the distances travelled by A and B in the same time interval, then :

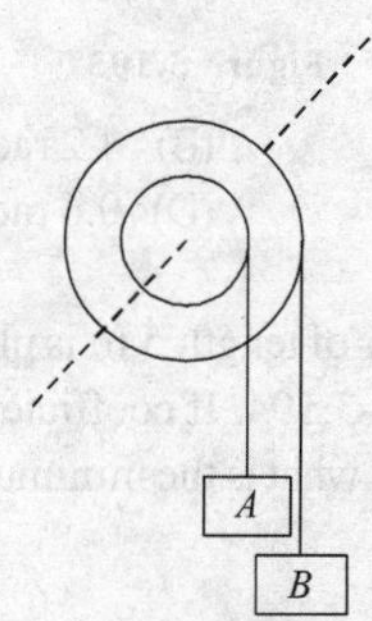

Figure 5.102

(A) $x = 2y$ (B) $x = y$
(C) $y = 2x$ (D) None of these

5-7 The centre of a wheel rolling on plane surface moves with a speed v_0. A particle on the rim of the wheel at the same level as the centre will be moving at speed :
(A) Zero (B) v_0
(C) $\sqrt{2}v_0$ (D) $2v_0$

5-8 A point A is located on the rim of a wheel of radius R which rolls without slipping along a horizontal surface with velocity v. The total distance travelled by the point A between successive moments at which it touches the surface is :
(A) $4R$ (B) $2R$
(C) $8R$ (D) $\sqrt{8}\,R$

5-9 A hollow straight tube of length $2l$ and mass m can turn freely about its centre on a smooth horizontal table. Another smooth uniform rod of same length and mass is fitted into the tube so that their centres coincide. The system is set in motion with an initial angular velocity ω_0. Find the angular velocity of the tube at the instant when the rod slips out of the tube :

(A) $\frac{\omega_0}{4}$ (B) $\frac{\omega_0}{5}$

(C) $\frac{\omega_0}{7}$ (D) $\frac{\omega_0}{2}$

5-10 The moment of inertia of the pulley system as shown in the figure-5.103 is 4 kgm^2. The radii of bigger and smaller pulleys 2 m and 1 m respectively. The angular acceleration of the pulley system is : (take $g = 10$ m/s^2)

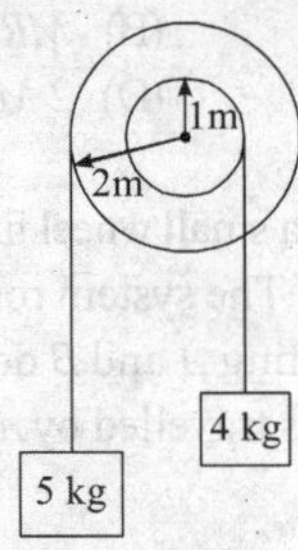

Figure 5.103

(A) 2.1 rad/s^2 (B) 4.2 rad/s^2
(C) 1.2 rad/s^2 (D) 0.6 rad/s^2

5-11 A uniform ladder of length 5 m is placed against the wall as shown in the figure-5.104. If coefficient of friction μ is the same for both the walls, what is the minimum value of μ for it not to slip ?

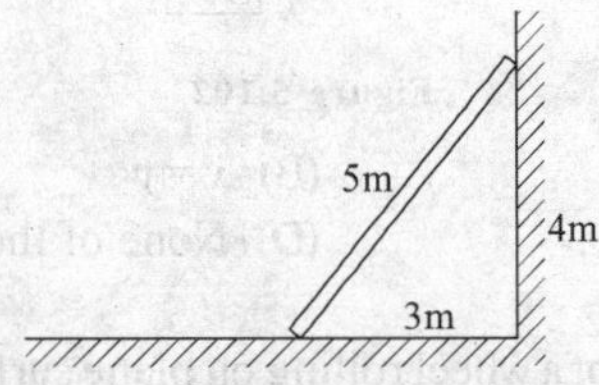

Figure 5.104

(A) $\mu = \frac{1}{2}$ (B) $\mu = \frac{1}{4}$

(C) $\mu = \frac{1}{3}$ (D) $\mu = \frac{1}{5}$

5-12 Two rings of the same radius and mass are placed such that their centres are at a common point and their planes are perpendicular to each other. The moment of inertia of the system about an axis passing through the centre and perpendicular to the plane of one of the rings is.
(mass of the ring = m, and radius = r) :

(A) $\frac{1}{2}mr^2$ (B) mr^2

(C) $\frac{3}{2}mr^2$ (D) $2\,mr^2$

5-13 A body is uniformly rotating about an axis fixed in an internal frame of reference. Let $\vec{A}$ be a unit vector along the axis of rotation and $\vec{B}$ be the unit vector along the resultant force on a particle P of the body away from the axis. The value of $\vec{A}.\vec{B}$ is :

(A) 1 (B) -1
(C) 0 (D) None of these

5-14 The moment of inertia of a uniform semicircular wire of mass M and radius r about a line perpendicular to the plane of the wire through the centre is :

(A) Mr^2 (B) $1/2(Mr^2)$
(C) $1/4(Mr^2)$ (D) $2/5(Mr^2)$

5-15 A uniform rod of mass m and length l makes a constant angle θ with an axis of rotation, which passes through one end of the rod. Its moment of inertia about the axis will be :

(A) $\frac{ml^2}{3}$ (B) $\frac{ml^2}{3}\sin\theta$

(C) $\frac{ml^2}{3}\sin^2\theta$ (D) $\frac{ml^2}{3}\cos^2\theta$

5-16 A particle of mass m and charge Q is attached to a string of length l. It is whirled in a vertical circle in the region of an electric field E as shown in the figure-5.105. What is the speed given to the particle at the point B, so that tension in the string when the particle is at A is ten times the weight of the particle ?

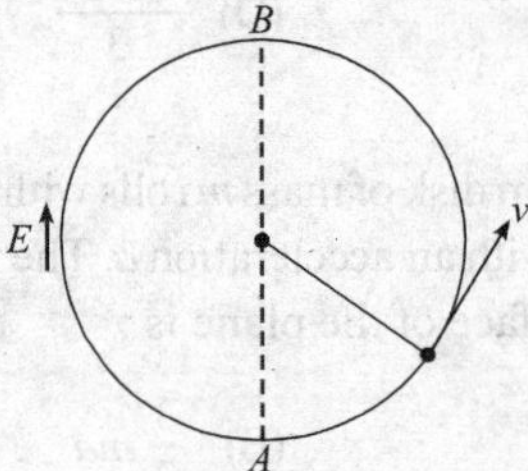

Figure 5.105

(A) $\sqrt{5gl}$ (B) $\sqrt{5\left(g - \frac{QE}{m}\right)l}$

(C) $\sqrt{\frac{QEl}{m}}$ (D) $\sqrt{5\left(g + \frac{QE}{m}\right)l}$

5-17 A particle is attached by a light string of length $3a$ to a fixed point and describes a horizontal circle of radius a with uniform angular velocity ω. If, when the particle is moving in this manner, is suddenly stopped and then let go, find its velocity when the string is vertical in its subsequent motion :

(A) $[2ga(3 - 2\sqrt{2})]^{1/2}$ (B) $2g(3 - 2\sqrt{2})$

(C) $ga(3 - 2\sqrt{2})$ (D) $\frac{2ga}{3 - 2\sqrt{2}}$

5-18 A uniform circular disc placed on a rough horizontal surface has initially a velocity V_0 and an angular velocity ω_0 as shown in the figure-5.106. The disc comes to rest after moving some distance in the direction of motion. Then $\frac{V_0}{r\omega_0}$ is :

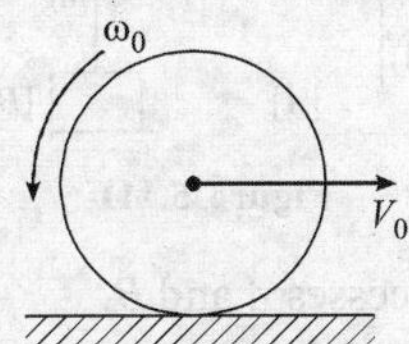

Figure 5.106

(A) $\frac{1}{2}$ (B) 1

(C) $\frac{3}{2}$ (D) 2

5-19 A cubical block of mass M and edge a slides down a rough inclined plane of inclination θ with a uniform velocity. The torque of the normal force on the block about its centre has a magnitude :

(A) Zero (B) Mga

(C) $Mga \sin\theta$ (D) $1/2(Mga \sin\theta)$

5-20 A hoop of radius r weights m kg. It rolls without sliding along a horizontal floor so that its centre of mass has a speed v m/s. How much work has to be done to stop it?

(A) $\frac{1}{2}mv^2$ (B) mv^2

(C) $2mv^2$ (D) $\frac{1}{3}mv^2$

5-21 A uniform rod AB of length l rotating with an angular velocity ω while its centre moves with a linear velocity $v = \frac{\omega l}{6}$. If the end A of the rod is suddenly fixed, the angular velocity of the rod will be :

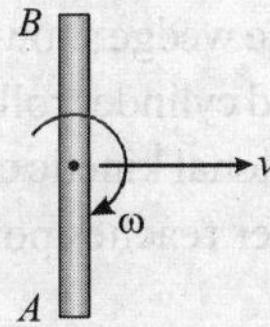

Figure 5.107

(A) $\frac{3}{4}\omega$ (B) $\frac{\omega}{3}$

(C) $\frac{\omega}{2}$ (D) $\frac{2}{3}\omega$

5-22 A homogeneous cylinder of mass M and radius r is pulled on a horizontal plane by a horizontal force F acting through its centre of mass. Assuming rolling without slipping, find the angular acceleration of the cylinder :

(A) $\frac{2F}{3Mr}$ (B) $\frac{3F}{2Mr}$

(C) $\frac{F}{3Mr}$ (D) $\frac{F}{2Mr}$

5-23 A disc of mass m_0 rotates freely about a fixed horizontal axis through its centre. A thin cotton pad is fixed to its rim, which can absorb water. The mass of water dripping onto the pad is μ per second. After what time will the angular velocity of the disc get reduced to half of its initial value ?

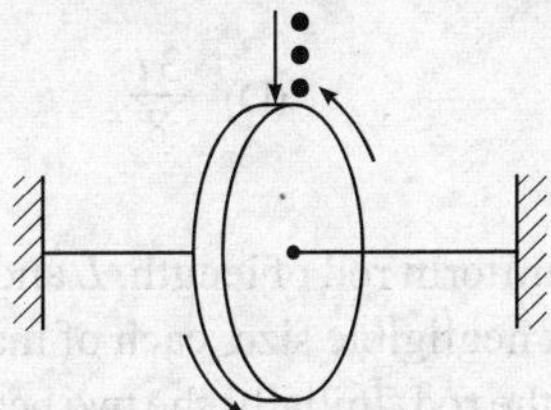

Figure 5.108

(A) $\frac{2m_0}{\mu}$ (B) $\frac{3m_0}{\mu}$

(C) $\frac{m_0}{\mu}$ (D) $\frac{m_0}{2\mu}$

5-24 A particle of mass m is projected with a velocity u at an angle of θ with horizontal. The angular momentum of the particle about the highest point of its trajectory is equal to :

(A) $\frac{mu^3 \sin^2\theta \cos\theta}{3g}$ (B) $\frac{3mu^3 \sin^2\theta \cos\theta}{3g}$

(C) $\frac{mu^3 \sin^2\theta \cos\theta}{2g}$ (D) $\frac{2mu^3 \sin\theta \cos^2\theta}{3g}$

5-25 A body is in pure rotation. The linear speed v of a particle, the distance r of the particle from the axis and the angular speed ω of the body are related as $\omega = v/r$. Thus :

(A) $\omega \propto \frac{1}{r}$ (B) $\omega \propto r$

(C) $\omega = 0$ (D) ω is independent of r.

5-26 One end of a uniform rod of mass m and length l is clamped. The rod lies on a smooth horizontal surface and rotates on it about the clamped end at a uniform angular velocity ω. The force exerted by the clamp on the rod has a horizontal component:

(A) $m\omega^2 l$ (B) Zero

(C) mg (D) $(1/2)m\omega^2 l$

5-27 A man pushes a cylindrical drum through a board of length l as shown in figure-5.109. The drum rolls forward on the ground a distance of $\frac{l}{2}$. There is no slipping at any instant. During the process of pushing the board the distance moved by the man on the ground is :

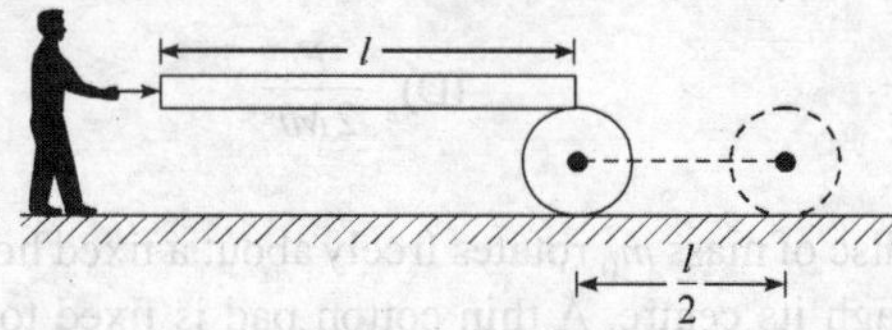

Figure 5.109

(A) $\frac{l}{2}$ (B) $\frac{3l}{4}$

(C) l (D) $\frac{3l}{8}$

5-28 A smooth uniform rod of length, L and mass M has two identical beads of negligible size, each of mass m, which can slide freely along the rod. Initially, the two beads A and B are at the centre of the rod and the system is rotating with an angular velocity ω_0 about an axis perpendicular to the rod and passing through the midpoint of the rod.

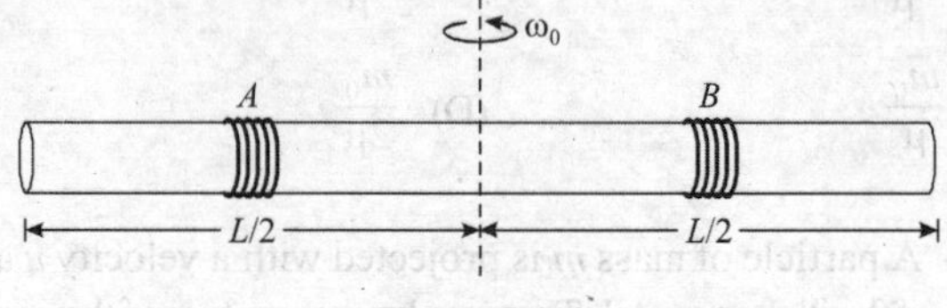

Figure 5.110

There is no external force when the beads reach the ends of the rod. The angular velocity of the system is :

(A) $\omega_0\sqrt{\frac{M}{M+6m}}$ (B) $\frac{M\omega_0}{M+6m}$

(C) ω_0 (D) Zero

5-29 A sphere and circular disc of same mass and radius are allowed to roll down an inclined plane from the same height without slipping. Find the ratio of times taken by these two to come to the bottom of incline :

(A) $\sqrt{14} : \sqrt{15}$ (B) 15:14

(D) $\sqrt{2} : 1$ (D) 7:9

5-30 A uniform disc of mass M= 2.50 kg and radius R= 0.20 m is mounted on an axle supported on fixed frictionless bearings. A light cord wrapped around the rim is pulled with a force 5 N. On the same system of pulley and string, instead of pulling it down, a body of weight 5 N is suspended. If the first process is termed A and the second B, the tangential acceleration of point P will be :

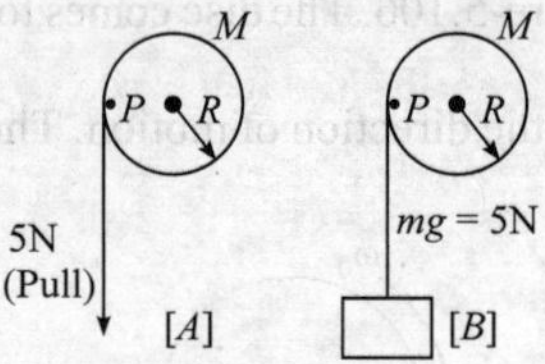

Figure 5.111

(A) Equal in the processes A and B.

(B) Greater in process A than in B.

(C) Greater in process B than in A.

(D) Independent of the two processes.

5-31 Two identical discs are moving with the same kinetic energy. One rolls and the other slides. The ratio of their speeds is :

(A) 1 : 1 (B) $\sqrt{2} : \sqrt{3}$

(C) 2 : 3 (D) 1 : 2

5-32 A bit of mud stuck to a bicycle's front wheel of radius r detaches and is flung horizontally forward when it is at the top of the wheel. The bicycle is moving forward at a speed v and it is rolling without slipping. The horizontal distance travelled by the mud after detaching from the wheel is :

(A) $\sqrt{2rv^2/g}$ (B) $\sqrt{8rv^2/g}$

(C) $\sqrt{4rv^2/g}$ (D) $\sqrt{16rv^2/g}$

5-33 A cylinder is released from rest from the top of an incline plane of inclination 60° where friction coefficient varies with distance x as $\mu = \frac{2-3x}{\sqrt{3}}$. Find the distance travelled by the cylinder on incline before it starts slipping :

(A) 1/3 m (B) $1/\sqrt{3}$ m

(C) 3m (D) $\sqrt{3}$ m

5-34 Portion of AB of the wedge shown in figure-5.112 is rough and BC is smooth. A solid cylinder rolls without slipping from A to B. The ratio of translational kinetic energy to rotational kinetic energy, when the cylinder reaches point C is :

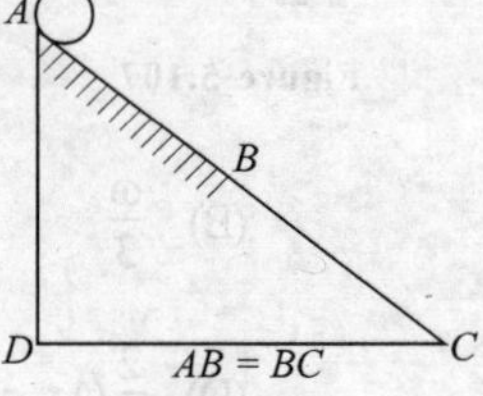

Figure 5.112

(A) 3/4 (B) 5
(C) 7/5 (D) 8/3

5-35 A ball is thrown down a lawn in such a way that it initially slides with a speed v_0 without rolling. It gradually picks up rotation motion. Find the speed of the ball at which there will be rolling without slipping :

(A) $\frac{2}{7}v_0$ (B) $\frac{2}{5}v_0$

(C) $\frac{5}{7}v_0$ (D) $\frac{3}{5}v_0$

5-36 A uniform sphere of mass m and radius r rolls without slipping down a inclined plane, inclined at an angle 45° to the horizontal. Find the magnitude of frictional coefficient at which slipping is absent :

(A) $\frac{1}{3}$ (B) $\frac{2}{7}$

(C) $\frac{1}{5}$ (D) $\frac{1}{7}$

5-37 The mass of earth is increasing at the rate of 1 part in 5×10^{19} per day due to the acceleration of meteors falling normally on the surface of earth evenly everywhere. Find the corresponding change of period of rotation of earth, taking the earth to be a sphere of uniform density:

(A) 8×10^{-19} hr/day (B) 5×10^{-19} hr/day
(C) 3×10^{-19} hr/day (D) 4×10^{-19} hr/day

5-38 A pendulum consists of a wooden bob of mass m and length l. A bullet of mass m_1 is fired towards the pendulum with a speed v_1. The bullet emerges out with a velocity $\frac{v_1}{3}$ and the bob just completes the motion along a vertical circle. Then v_1 is

(A) $\frac{3}{2}\left(\frac{m}{m_1}\right)\sqrt{5gl}$ (B) $\left(\frac{m}{m_1}\right)\sqrt{5gl}$

(C) $\frac{3}{2}\left(\frac{m}{m_1}\right)\sqrt{gl}$ (D) $\frac{3}{2}\left(\frac{m_1}{m}\right)\sqrt{5gl}$

5-39 A hollow sphere of outer radius R is allowed to roll down on an incline without slipping and it reaches a speed v_0 at the bottom of the incline. The incline is then made smooth by waxing and the sphere is allowed to slide without rolling and now the speed attained is $\frac{5}{4}v_0$. What is the radius of gyration of the sphere about an axis passing through its centre ?

(A) $\sqrt{\frac{2}{5}}R$ (B) $\frac{3R}{4}$

(C) $\frac{4R}{5}$ (D) $\sqrt{\frac{2}{3}}R$

5-40 A thin uniform heavy rod of length l hangs from a horizontal axis passing through one end. The initial angular velocity ω that must be imparted to it to rotate it through 90° is :

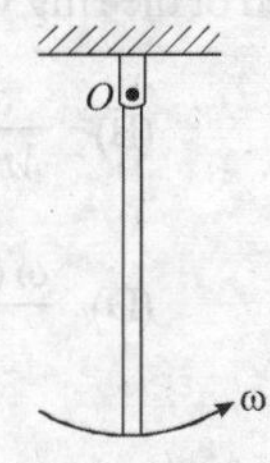

Figure 5.113

(A) $\sqrt{g/l}$ (B) $\sqrt{3g/l}$

(C) $\sqrt{2g/l}$ (D) $\sqrt{6g/l}$

5-41 A hollow sphere of radius R and mass m is fully filled with water of mass m. It is rolled down a horizontal plane such that its centre of mass moves with a velocity v. If it purely rolls :
(A) Kinetic energy of the sphere is 5/6 mv^2
(B) Kinetic energy of the sphere is 4/5 mv^2
(C) Angular momentum of the sphere about a fixed point on ground is 8/3 mvR
(D) Angular momentum of the sphere about a fixed point on ground is 14/5 mvR

5-42 Let $\vec{F}$ be a force acting on a particle having position vector $\vec{r}$. Let $\vec{\tau}$ be the torque of this force about the origin, then :

(A) $\vec{r}\cdot\vec{\tau}=0$ and $\vec{F}\cdot\vec{\tau}=0$ (B) $\vec{r}\cdot\vec{\tau}=0$ and $\vec{F}\cdot\vec{\tau}\neq 0$

(C) $\vec{r}\cdot\vec{\tau}\neq 0$ and $\vec{F}\cdot\vec{\tau}=0$ (D) $\vec{r}\cdot\vec{\tau}\neq 0$ and $\vec{F}\cdot\vec{\tau}\neq 0$

5-43 A body having its centre of mass at the origin has three of its particles $(a, 0, 0)$, $(0, a, 0)$, $(0, 0, a)$. The moments of inertia of the body about the X and Y axes are 0.20 kg-m^2 each. The moment of inertia about the Z-axis :
(A) Is 0.20 kg-m^2
(B) Is 0.40 kg-m^2
(C) Is $0.20\sqrt{2}$ kg-m^2
(D) Cannot be deduced with this information

5-44 Where must the cue hit a billiard ball so that it rolls without sliding from the start if R is the radius of the ball ?

(A) At a height $\frac{2}{5}$ R above centre.

(B) At a height equal to the radius from table
(C) At a height equal to 2R from the table
(D) At a height equal to $\frac{R}{2}$ from table.

5-45 A thin circular ring of mass M and radius r is rotating about its axis with an angular speed ω. Two particles having mass m each are now attached at diametrically opposite points of ring. The angular speed of the ring will become :

(A) $\frac{\omega M}{M+m}$ (B) $\frac{\omega M}{M+2m}$

(C) $\frac{\omega(M-2m)}{M+2m}$ (D) $\frac{\omega(M+2m)}{M}$

5-46 A sphere of mass m is given some angular velocity about a horizontal axis through its centre, and gently placed on a plank of mass m. The coefficient of friction between the two is μ. The plank rests on a smooth horizontal surface. The initial acceleration of the sphere relative to the plank will be :

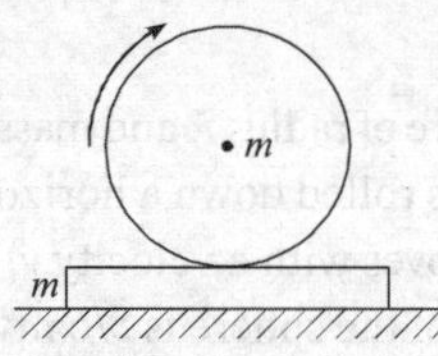

Figure 5.114

(A) Zero (B) μg
(C) $7/5\ \mu g$ (D) $2\ \mu g$

5-47 A particle of mass 10 kg is moving with a uniform speed of 6 m/sec, in $x-y$ plane along the line $3y = 4x + 10$ the magnitude of its angular momentum about the origin in $kg - m^2/s$ is :
(A) Zero (B) 80
(C) $30\sqrt{2}$ (D) 120

5-48 A fly wheel rotates about an axis. Due to friction at the axis, it experiences angular retardation proportional to its angular velocity. If its angular velocity falls to half the value while it makes n revolutions, how many more revolutions will it make before coming to rest ?
(A) $2n$ (B) n
(C) $n/2$ (D) $n/3$

5-49 If the distance of the moon from earth is r_m and the period of revolution is T_m, then the mass of the earth is :

(A) $\frac{4\pi^2 r_m^2}{GT_m}$ (B) $\frac{4\pi^2 r_m^3}{GT_m^2}$

(C) $\frac{4\pi^2 r_m}{GT_m}$ (D) $\frac{4\pi^2 r}{GT_m^2}$

5-50 A body of mass m slides down smooth incline and reaches the bottom with a velocity v. If the same mass were in the form of a ring which rolls down similar rough incline, the velocity of the ring at bottom would have been :

(A) v (B) $\sqrt{2}\ v$

(C) $v/\sqrt{2}$ (D) $\sqrt{2/5}\ .\ v$

5-51 A flywheel rotating about a fixed axis has a kinetic energy of 360 joules when its angular speed is 30 rad/sec. The moment of inertia of the wheel about the axis of rotation is :
(A) 0.6 kg × metre^2 (B) 0.15 kg × metre^2
(C) 0.8 kg × metre^2 (D) 0.75 kg × metre^2

5-52 A wheel initially at rest, is rotated with a uniform angular acceleration. The wheel rotates through an angle θ_1 in first one second and through an additional angle θ_2 in the next one second. The ratio θ_2/θ_1 is :
(A) 4 (B) 2
(C) 3 (D) 1

5-53 A thin uniform circular disc of mass M and radius R is rotating in a horizontal plane about an axis passing through its centre and perpendicular to the plane with angular velocity ω. Another disc of same mass but half the radius is gently placed over it coaxially. The angular speed of the composite disc will be :
(A) $5\omega/4$ (B) $4\omega/5$
(C) $2\omega/5$ (D) $5\omega/2$

5-54 A rod of mass M and length l is suspended freely from its end and it can oscillate in the vertical plane about the point of suspension. It is pulled to one side and then released. It passes through the equilibrium position with angular speed ω. What is the kinetic energy while passing through the mean position ?
(A) $Ml^2\omega^2$ (B) $Ml^2\omega^2/4$
(C) $Ml^2\omega^2/6$ (D) $Ml^2\omega^2/12$

5-55 A tube of length L is filled completely with an incompressible liquid of mass M and closed at both the ends. The tube is then rotated in a horizontal plane about one of its end with a uniform angular velocity ω. The force exerted by the liquid at the other end is :

(A) $\frac{M\omega^2 L}{2}$ (B) $M\omega^2 L$

(C) $\frac{M\omega^2 L}{4}$ (D) $\frac{M\omega^2 L^2}{2}$

5-56 We have two spheres, one of which is hollow and the other solid. They have identical masses and moment of inertia about their respectively diameters. The ratio of their radius is given by :
(A) 5 : 7 (B) 3 : 5
(C) $\sqrt{3} : \sqrt{5}$ (D) $\sqrt{3} : \sqrt{7}$

5-57 A stick of length L and mass M lies on a frictionless horizontal surface on which it is free to move in any way. A ball of mass m moving with speed v collides elastically with the stick as shown in figure-5.115. If after the collision ball comes to rest, then what should be the mass of the ball ?

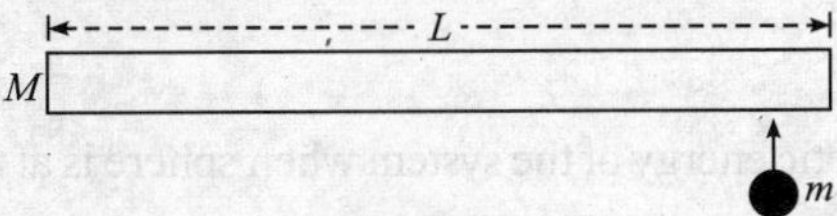

Figure 5.115

(A) $m = 2M$ (B) $m = M$

(C) $m = M/2$ (D) $m = M/4$

5-58 A uniform circular disc of mass 2m and radius R placed freely on a horizontal smooth surface as shown in the figure-5.116. A particle of mass m is connected to the circumference of the disc with a massless string. Now an impulse J is applied on the particle in the directions shown by dotted line. The acceleration of centre of mass of the disc just after application of impulse is (If $J = 10$ N-sec., $m = \sqrt{10}$kg and $R = 25$cm.):

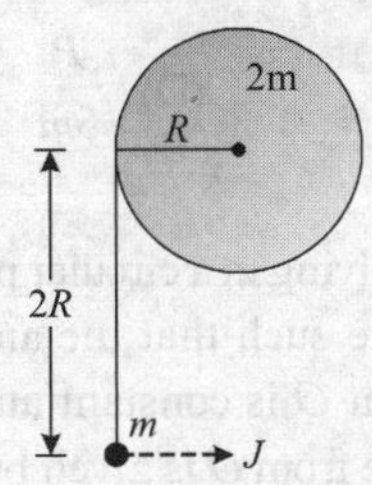

Figure 5.116

(A) 1 m/s^2 (B) 2 m/s^2

(C) 3 m/s^2 (D) 4 m/s^2

5-59 Moment of inertia of a uniform hexagonal plate about an axis LL' is 'I' as shown in the figure-5.117. The moment of inertia (about axis XX') of an equilateral uniform triangular plate of thickness double that of the hexagonal plate is (Ratio of specific gravity $\frac{\rho_t}{\rho_h} = 3$):

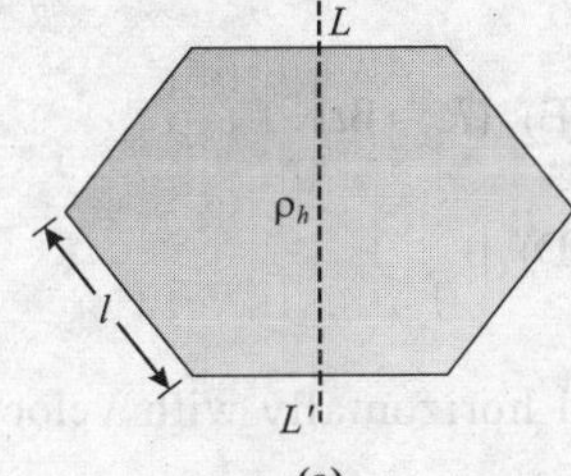

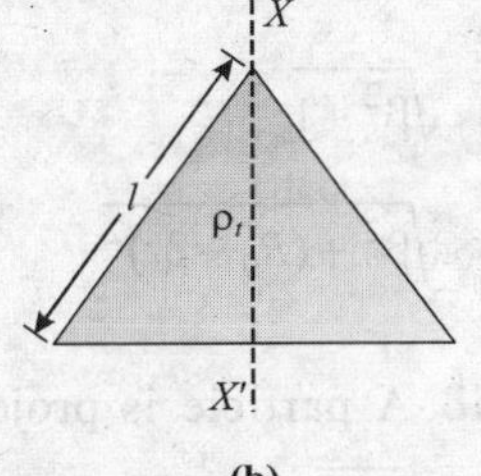

Figure 5.117

(A) $\frac{I}{5}$ (B) $\frac{I}{10}$

(C) I (D) Zero

Paragraph for Questions 60 & 61

A simplified model of a bicycle of mass M has two tires that each comes into contact with the ground at a point. The wheel base of this bicycle is W, and the centre of mass C of the bicycle is located midway between the tires and a height h above the ground. The bicycle is moving to the right, but slowing down at a constant acceleration a. Air resistance may be ignored. Assuming that the coefficient of sliding friction between each tyre and the ground is μ and that both tyres are skidding (sliding without rotating). Express your answer in terms of w, h, M and g.

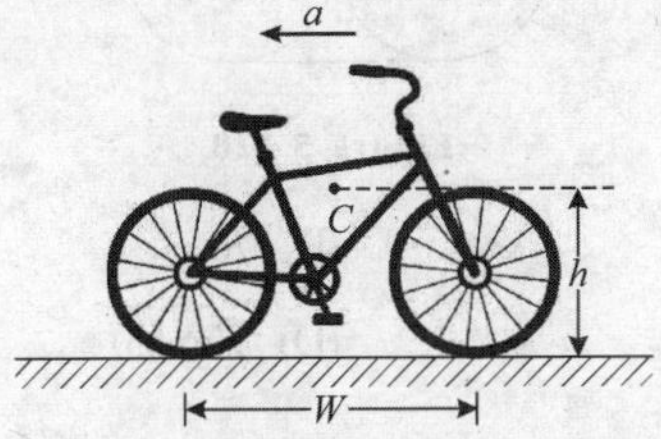

Figure 5.118

5-60 What is the maximum value of μ so that both tires remain in contact with the ground :

(A) $W/2h$ (B) $h/2W$

(C) $2h/W$ (D) W/h

5-61 What is the maximum value of a so that both tyres remain in contact with the ground ?

(A) $\frac{Wg}{h}$ (B) $\frac{Wg}{2h}$

(C) $\frac{hg}{2W}$ (D) $\frac{h}{2Wg}$

5-62 A rod of mass m and length $2R$ can rotate about an axis passing through O in vertical plane. A disc of mass m and radius $R/2$ is hinged to the other end P of the rod and can freely rotate about P. When disc is at lowest point both rod and disc has angular velocity ω. If rod rotates by maximum angle $\theta = 60°$ with downward vertical, then ω in terms of R and g will be (all hinges are smooth)

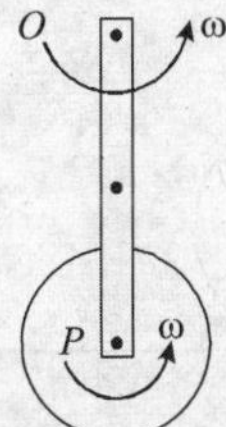

Figure 5.119

(A) $\sqrt{\frac{9g}{16R}}$ (B) $\sqrt{\frac{3g}{23R}}$

(C) $\frac{1}{3}\sqrt{\frac{g}{R}}$ (D) none of these

5-63 Three identical cylinders of radius R are in contact. Each cylinder is rotating with angular velocity ω. A thin belt is moving without sliding on the cylinders. Calculate the magnitude of velocity of point P with respect to Q. P and Q are two points of belt which are in contact with the cylinder.

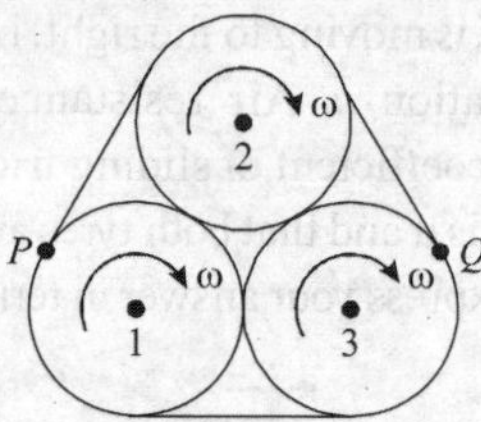

Figure 5.120

(A) $2R\omega$ (B) $R\omega$

(C) $R\omega/2$ (D) $R\omega\sqrt{3}$

Paragraph for Question Nos. 64 to 66

If no external force is acting on the system, net linear momentum of the system is conserved. If system is acted upon by some external force, the component of momentum of the system, along which no external force is present or their vector sum is zero, is conserved. If a sharp blow is given to a body its linear momentum changes immediately. Change in angular momentum not only depends on the magnitude of the blow but also on point of application. In the case of symmetrical body we take the axis of rotation through center of the body. A wedge of mass 4m is placed at rest on a smooth horizontal surface. A uniform solid sphere of mass m and radius r is placed at rest on the flat portion of the wedge at the point Q as shown in the figure. A sharp horizontal impulse P is given to the sphere at a point below $h = 0.4r$ from the center of the sphere. The radius of curvature of the curved portion of the wedge is R. Coefficient of friction to the left side of point Q is μ and to the right side of point Q is zero. For a body to roll on a surface without slipping, there should be no relative velocity between the points of contact.

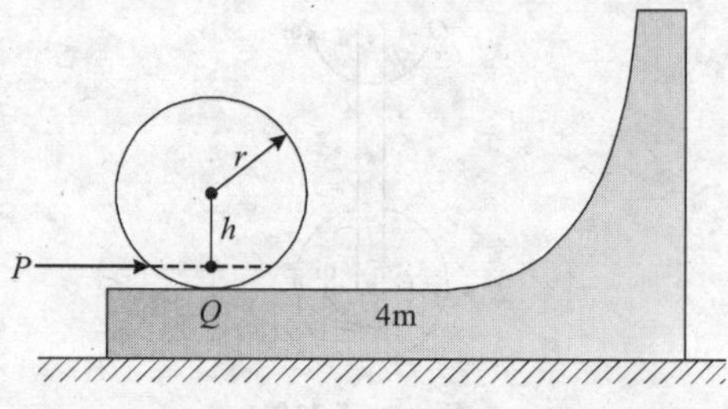

Figure 5.121

5-64 The maximum height to which the center of mass of the sphere will climb on the curved portion of the wedge is :

(A) $\dfrac{2P^2}{5m^2g}$ (B) $\dfrac{P^2}{5m^2g}$

(C) $\dfrac{P^2}{2m^2g}$ (D) none of these

5-65 Kinetic energy of the system when sphere is at the highest point is :

(A) $\dfrac{P^2}{10m}$ (B) $\dfrac{P^2}{5m}$

(C) $\dfrac{3P^2}{10m}$ (D) $\dfrac{3P^2}{5m}$

5-66 Speed of the wedge when sphere reaches the flat portion again :

(A) $\dfrac{2P}{5m}$ (B) $\dfrac{3P}{5m}$

(C) $\dfrac{8P}{5m}$ (D) $\dfrac{P}{5m}$

5-67 A particle is revolving in a circular path as shown in figure in the horizontal plane such that the angular velocity of the particle about the point O is constant and is equal to 1 rad/s. Distance of the particle from O is given by $R = R_0 - \beta t$ where R_0 and β are constant. The speed of the particle as a function of time is :

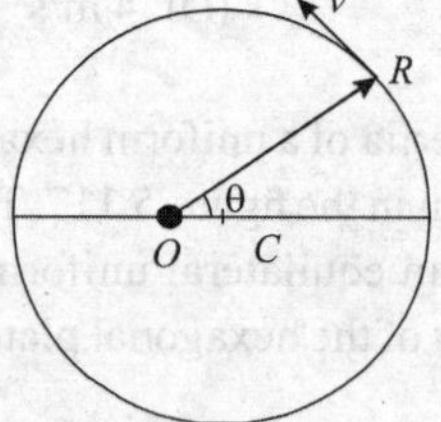

Figure 5.122

(A) $\sqrt{\beta^2+1}$ (B) $(R_0 - \beta t)$

(C) $\sqrt{\beta^2+(R_0-\beta t)^2}$ (D) β

5-68 A particle is projected horizontally with velocity $V_0 = \sqrt{2ga}$ along the smooth inside surface of a fixed hollow hemisphere of inner radius 'a' at the level of the centre 'O'. The subsequent motion of the particle is confined between the horizontal planes one through the centre and the other at a depth h. Find the value of h :

(A) $\frac{\sqrt{3}}{2}a$ (B) $\frac{\sqrt{3}-1}{3}a$

(C) $\frac{\sqrt{5}-1}{2}a$ (D) $\frac{\sqrt{5}}{2}a$

5-69 The wheel of radius R rolls without slipping on horizontal rough surface, and its centre O has an horizontal acceleration a_0 in forward direction. A point P on the wheel is a distance r from O and angular position θ from horizontal. For the given values of a_0, R and r, determine the angle θ for which point P has no acceleration in this position.

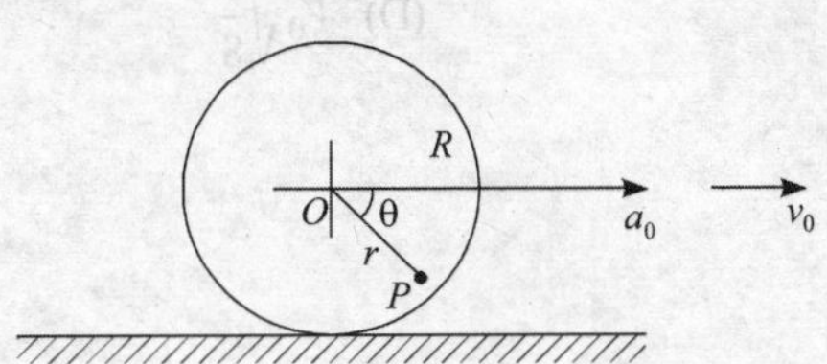

Figure 5.123

(A) $\cos^{-1}\frac{r}{R}$ (B) $\tan^{-1}\frac{r}{R}$

(C) $\sin^{-1}\frac{r}{R}$ (D) $\cos^{-1}\frac{r}{2R}$

5-70 A uniform ring of mass m and radius R is in uniform pure rolling motion on a horizontal surface. The velocity of the centre of ring is V_0. The kinetic energy of the segment ACB is :

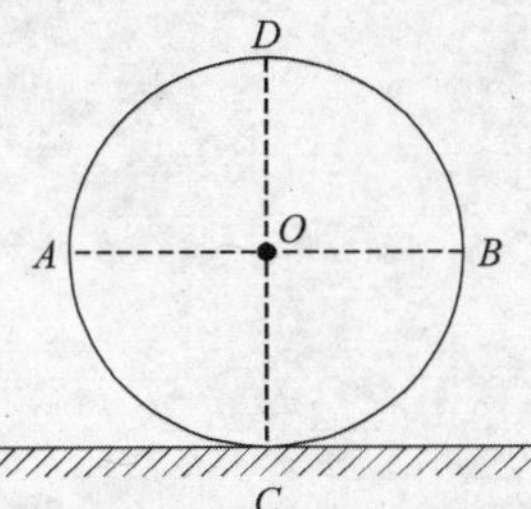

Figure 5.124

(A) $\frac{mV_0^2}{2}-\frac{mV_0^2}{\pi}$ (B) $\frac{mV_0^2}{2}+\frac{mV_0^2}{\pi}$

(C) $\frac{mV_0^2}{2}$ (D) mV_0^2

5-71 Let I be the moment of inertia of a uniform square plate about an axis AB that passes though its centre and is parallel to two of its sides. CD is a line in the plane of the plate that passes through the centre of the plate and makes an angle θ with AB. The moment of inertia of the plate about the axis CD is then equal to :

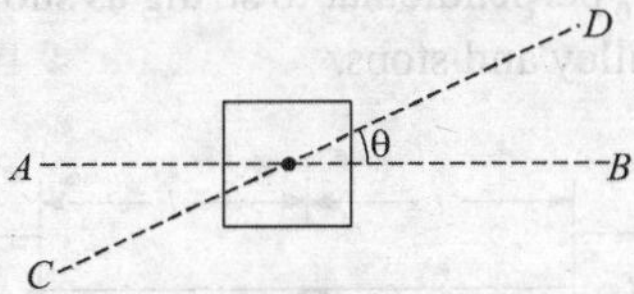

Figure 5.125

(A) I (B) $I\cos^2\theta$

(C) $I\sin^2\theta$ (D) $I\cos^2(\theta/2)$

5-72 A rectangular block has a square base measuring $a \times a$, and its height is h. It moves on a horizontal surface in a direction perpendicular to one of the edges of the base. The coefficient of friction is μ. It will topple if (choose the most appropriate option)

(A) $\mu > a/2h$ (B) $\mu > 2a/h$

(C) $\mu > a/h$ (D) $\mu > h/a$

5-73 A cubical block of mass $\frac{\sqrt{3}}{10}$ kg and edge 20 cm is placed on a rough horizontal surface as shown in the figure-5.126. A force of 1N is applied at one end of the block and the block remains stationary. The normal force exerted by the surface on the block acts ($g = 10$ m/s^2)

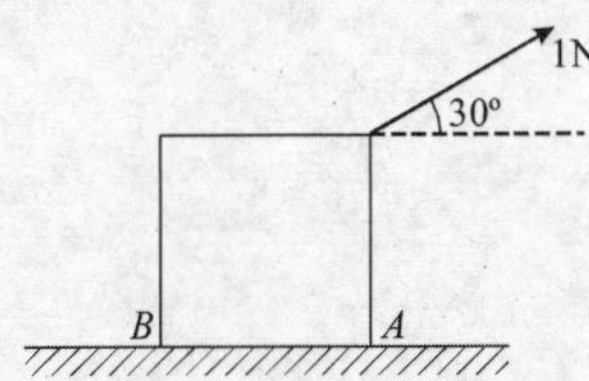

Figure 5.126

(A) through the centre of mass of the block

(B) through point A

(C) through point B

(D) through the point at a distance 5cm from A

5-74 A rope of mass 'm' is looped in a circle of radius R and rotated with a constant angular velocity about its axis in gravity free space. Find the tension in the rope ?

(A) $T = mR\omega_0^2$ (B) $2mR\pi\omega^2$

(C) $T = \frac{mR\pi\omega_0^2}{2\pi}$ (D) $4mR\pi\omega_0^2$

Paragraph for Question Nos. 75 to 76

Two identical blocks are placed on a smooth horizontal surface, connected by a light string of length $2l$. String touches a fixed smooth pulley at its mid-point initially. Which is attached to two smooth vertical walls as shown in figure-5.127. Block A is given a speed V_0 perpendicular to string as shown in diagram. B strikes the pulley and stops.

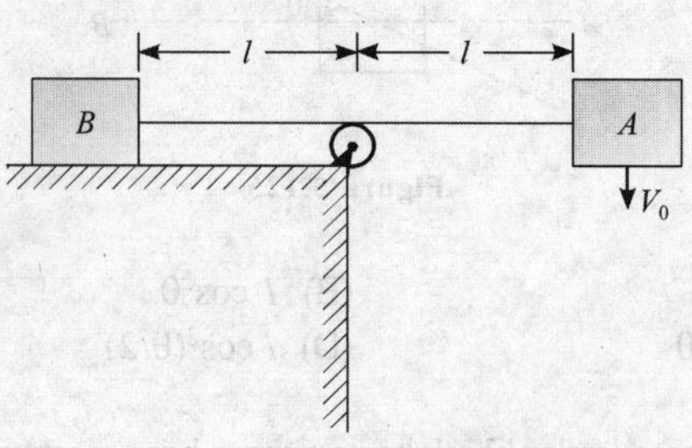

Figure 5.127

5-75 Speed of block B when it hits the pulley is :

(A) $\frac{V_0}{2}$ (B) $V_0\frac{\sqrt{3}}{2}$

(C) V_0 (D) $V_0\sqrt{\frac{3}{8}}$

5-76 Speed of A when it hits the wall is :

(A) $\frac{V_0}{2}$ (B) $V_0\frac{\sqrt{3}}{2}$

(C) V_0 (D) $V_0\sqrt{\frac{3}{8}}$

* * * * *

Advance MCQs with One or More Options Correct

5-1 A sphere, a disc and a ring of the same mass but of different density and radii are allowed to roll down on an inclined plane without slipping simultaneously, through the same height, then:
(A) The body of greater density will reach the bottom earliest
(B) The body of least density will reach the bottom earliest
(C) The sphere will reach the bottom earlier
(D) The ring will reach the bottom with the least linear momentum.

5-2 The axis of rotation of a purely rotating body :
(A) Must pass through the centre of mass
(B) May pass through the centre of mass
(C) Must pass through a particle of the body
(D) May pass through a particle of the body

5-3 In rear-wheel drive cars, the engine rotates the rear wheels and the front wheels rotate only because the cars moves. If such a car accelerates on a horizontal road, the friction :
(A) On the rear wheels is in the forward direction
(B) On the front wheels is in the backward direction
(C) On the rear wheels has larger magnitude than the friction on the front wheels
(D) On the car is in the backward direction

5-4 In the figure-5.128 are shown the lines of action and moment arms of two forces about the origin O. Imagining these forces to be acting on a rigid body pivoted at O, all vectors shown being in the plane of the figure, the magnitude and direction of the resultant torque will be :

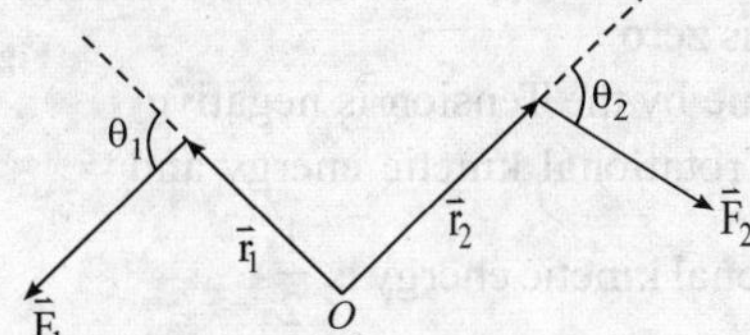

Figure 5.128

(A) $(F_2r_2 \sin \theta_2 - F_1r_1 \sin \theta_1)$ out of the plane of the page.
(B) $(F_1r_1 \sin \theta_1 - F_2r_2 \sin \theta_2)$ out of the plane of the page.
(C) $(F_2r_2 \sin \theta_2 - F_1r_1 \sin \theta_1)$ into the plane of the page.
(D) Zero.

5-5 Consider a wheel of a bicycle rolling on a level road at a linear speed v_0 :
(A) The speed of the particle A is zero
(B) The speed of B, C and D are equal to v_0
(C) The speed of C is $2v_0$
(D) The speed of B is greater than the speed of O.

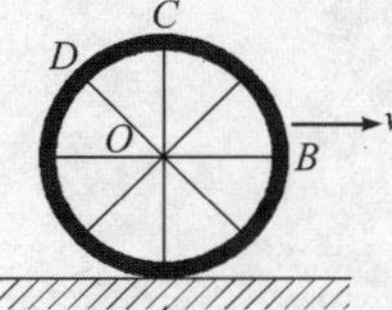

Figure 5.129

5-6 A sphere is rolled on a rough horizontal surface. It gradually slows down and stops. The force of friction tries to :
(A) Decrease the linear velocity
(B) Increase the linear velocity
(C) Increase the linear momentum
(D) Decrease the angular momentum

5-7 A sphere is rotating about a diameter at uniform angular speed then which of the following options is/are correct :
(A) The particles on the surface of the sphere do not have any linear acceleration
(B) The particles on the diameter mentioned above do not have any linear acceleration
(C) Different particles on the surface have different angular speeds
(D) All the particles on the surface have the same linear speed.

5-8 A smooth sphere A is moving on a frictionless horizontal plane with angular speed ω and centre of mass at velocity v. It collides elastically and head on with an identical sphere B at rest. Neglect friction everywhere. After the collision, their angular speeds are ω_A and ω_B, respectively. Then :
(A) $\omega_A < \omega_B$ (B) $\omega_A = \omega_B$
(C) $\omega_A = \omega$ (D) $\omega_B = 0$

5-9 A particle moves on a straight line with a uniform velocity. Its angular momentum :
(A) Is always zero
(B) Is zero about a point on the straight line
(C) Is not zero about a point away from the straight line
(D) About any given point remains constant

5-10 A thin uniform rod of mass m and length l is hanging freely from its topmost point and is free to rotate about its upper end. When it is at rest, it receives an impulse J at its lowest point normal to its length. Immediately after :
(A) The angular momentum of the rod is Jl
(B) Angular velocity of the rod is 3J/ml
(C) The K.E. of the rod is 3J²/2m
(D) The linear velocity of the midpoint of the rod is 3J/2m.

5-11 Two identical semicircular discs of mass 'm' each and radius 'R' are placed in the XY (horizontal) plane and the YZ (vertical) plane, respectively. They are so placed that they have their common diameter along the Y-axis. Then, the moment of inertia (I_n) of the system about the appropriate axis is given by (I_n refers to moment of inertia about axis n-where n is X, Y, Z)
(A) $I_X = \frac{1}{2}mR^2$ (B) $I_Y = \frac{1}{2}mR^2$
(C) $I_Z = \frac{3}{4}mR^2$ (D) $I_X = I_Y = I_Z$

5-12 A uniform ring placed on a rough horizontal surface is given a sharp impulse as shown in the figure-5.130. As a consequence, it acquires a linear velocity of 2 m/s. If coefficient of friction between the ring and the horizontal surface is 0.4 :

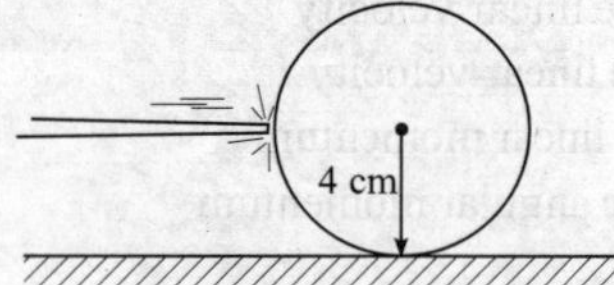

Figure 5.130

(A) Ring will start pure rolling after 0.25 s
(B) When ring will start pure rolling its velocity is 1 m/s
(C) After 0.5 s from impulse its velocity is 1 m/s.
(D) After 0.125 s from impulse its velocity is 1 m/s.

5-13 The density of rod gradually changes from one end to the other. It is pivoted at one of the end so that it can rotate about a vertical axis through the pivot. A horizontal force F is applied on the free end in a direction perpendicular to the rod. The quantities, that depend on axis of rotation (in this situation) are:
(A) Angular acceleration
(B) Total kinetic energy of the rod, when the rod completes one revolution
(C) Angular momentum when the rod completes one revolution
(D) Angular velocity of rod

5-14 A weightless rigid rod AB of length l connects two equal masses m one particle is fixed at the end B and the other at the middle of the rod as shown in the figure-5.131. The rod can rotate in the vertical plane freely around the hinge point A.

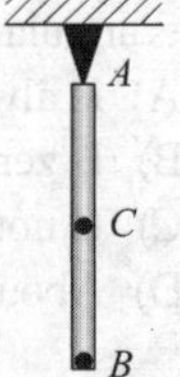

Figure 5.131

Choose the correct option(s).
(A) The minimum horizontal velocity required to be given to the particle B so as to make the rod go around in the complete vertical circle is $\sqrt{\frac{24gl}{5}}$
(B) The minimum horizontal velocity required to be given to the particle B so as to make the rod go around in the complete vertical circle is $\sqrt{\frac{24gl}{9}}$
(C) The ratio of compressive force in the rods AC and BC is 2 : 1 when the masses are at highest point.
(D) The ratio of compressive force in the rods AC and BC is 3 : 1 when the masses are at highest point.

5-15 Figure shows a horizontal rod AB which is free to rotate about two smooth bearing system. Two identical uniform rods each of mass m are attached to rod AB symmetrically about the centre of mass O of the rod AB. All the dimensions are given in the figure-5.132. The system is rotating with constant angular velocity ω in such a way that the upper rod is coming outward from the plane of the paper in the position shown. Gravity can be assumed to be absent in the experiment, then choose the correct option(s).

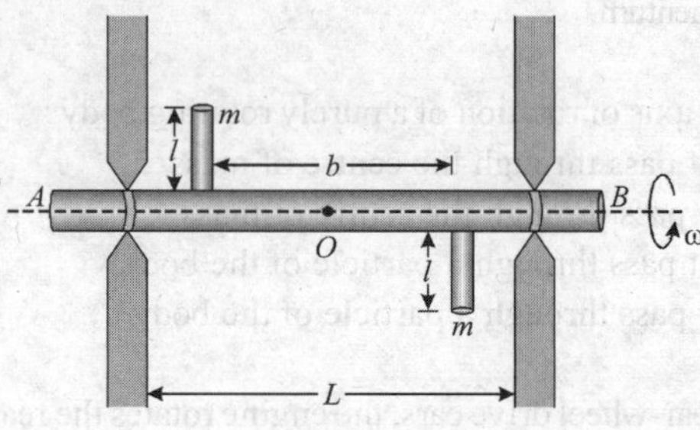

Figure 5.132

(A) The hinge reaction at A on the rod AB is downward
(B) The hinge reaction at B on the rod AB is upward
(C) The hinge reaction at B on the rod AB is downward
(D) The angular momentum of the system about point O is NOT along the rod AB.

5-16 A string is wrapped over a uniform cylinder, as shown in diagram (side view). When cylinder is released, string unwraps without any slipping and cylinder comes down. Which of the following is true ?

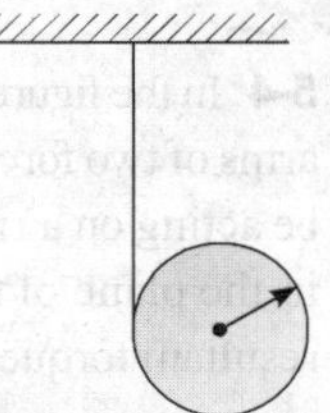

Figure 5.133

(A) Work done by Tension force on the cylinder is zero
(B) Work done by the Tension is negative
(C) Ratio of rotational kinetic energy and translational kinetic energy is $\frac{1}{2}$
(D) Ratio of rotational kinetic energy to translational kinetic energy is 2

* * * * *

Unsolved Numerical Problems for Preparation of NSEP, INPhO & IPhO

For detailed preparation of INPhO and IPhO students can refer advance study material on www.physicsgalaxy.com

5-1 Two masses M and m are connected by a light string going over a pulley of radius r. The pulley is free to rotate about its axis which is kept horizontal. The moment of inertia of the pulley about the axis is I. The system is released from rest. Find the angular momentum of the system when the mass m has descended through a height h. The string does not slip over the pulley.

Ans. [$\sqrt{2(M-m)\left\{M+m+\frac{I}{r^2}\right\}r^2gh}$]

5-2 A ball of radius $R = 10$ cm rolls without slipping down an inclined plane so that its centre moves with constant acceleration 2.5 cm/s^2. After a time of 2 sec from the beginning of its motion, its position is as shown in figure-5.134. Find

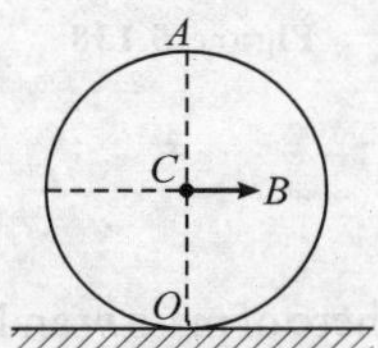

Figure 5.134

(a) the velocities of point A, B and O.

(b) the acceleration of these points.

Ans. [10 cm/s, 7.1 cm/s, 0, 5.6 cm/s^2, 2.5 cm/s^2, 2.5 cm/s^2]

5-3 A body of radius r and mass m is rolling horizontally without slipping with speed v. It then rolls up a hill to a maximum height h. If $h = 3v^2/4g$, what might the body be ? What is the body's moment of inertia.

Ans. [$R/\sqrt{2}$]

5-4 A conical pendulum is formed by a thin rod of length l and mass m, hinged at the upper end, rotates uniformly about a vertical axis passing through its upper end, with angular velocity ω. Find the angle θ between the rod and the vertical.

Ans. [$\theta = \cos^{-1}\left(\frac{3g}{2\omega^2 l}\right)$]

5-5 A wheel of radius R rolls without slipping along the x axis with constant speed v_0. Find the total distance covered by the point on the rim of the wheel during one complete revolution of the wheel.

Ans. [$8R$]

5-6 A spool (consider it as a double disc system joined by a short tube at their centre) is placed on horizontal surface as shown in figure-5.135. A light string wound several times over the short connecting tube leaves it tangentially and passes over light pulley. A weight of mass m is attached to the end of the string. The radius of the connecting tube is r and mass of the spool is M and radius is R. Find the acceleration of the falling mass m. Neglect the mass of the connecting tube and slipping of the spool.

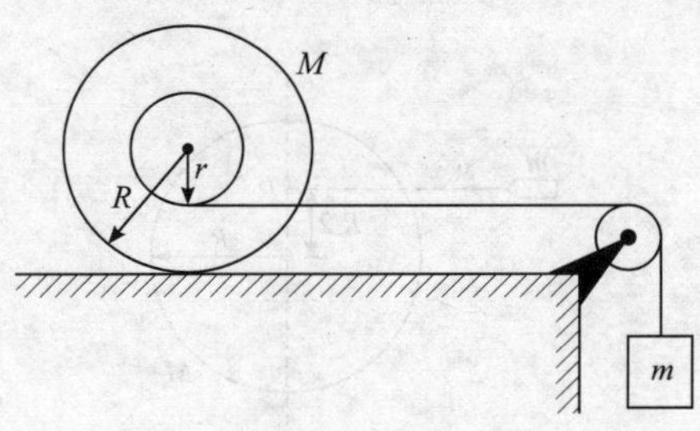

Figure 5.135

Ans. [$\frac{2mg}{2m+3M\left(\frac{R}{R-r}\right)^2}$]

5-7 A thin uniform rod AB of mass m and length l is rigidly attached at its midpoint to a rigid rotation axis OO' as shown in figure-5.136. The axis is set into rotation with constant angular velocity ω. Find the resultant moment of the centrifugal force about the point C where the rod is attached to the axis. The inclination of the rod AB to the axis of rotation OO' is θ.

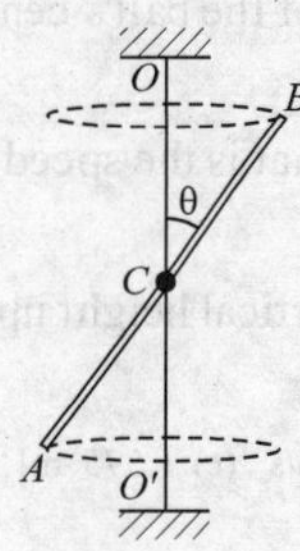

Figure 5.136

Ans. [$\frac{1}{24}m\omega^2 l^2 \sin 2\theta$]

5-8 A particle of mass m is projected at $t = 0$ from a point P on the ground with speed v_0 at an angle of 45° to the horizontal. Find the magnitude and direction of the angular momentum of the particle at time $t = v_0/g$.

Ans. [$\frac{mv_0^3}{2\sqrt{2}g}$]

5-9 What is the angular momentum of the seconds hand on a clock about an axis through the centre of the clockface if the clock hand has a length of 25 cm and a mass of 15 gm ?

Ans. [0.0314 J-s]

5-10 A solid uniform sphere, with radius $R = 0.2$ m and mass $M = 50$ kg, is at rest in an inertial reference frame in deep space. A bullet with mass $m = 20$ gm and a velocity $v = 400$ m/s strikes the sphere along the line shown in figure-5.137, and rapidly comes to rest within the sphere at point P. Determine the subsequent motion of the sphere and the embedded bullet.

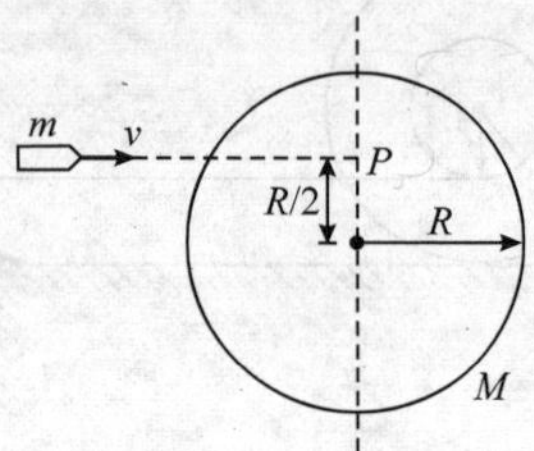

Figure 5.137

Ans. [v = 0.16 m/s, ω = 1.0 rad/sec]

5-11 In a spring gun, a spring of force constant 200 N/m is compressed 0.15 m. When fired, 80% of the elastic potential energy stored in the spring is eventually converted into kinetic energy of a 0.1 kg uniform ball that is rolling without slipping at the base of a ramp. The ball continues to roll without slipping up the ramp with 90% of the kinetic energy at the bottom converted into an increase in gravitational potential energy at the instant it stops.

(a) What is the speed of the ball's centre of mass at the base of the ramp ?

(b) At this position, what is the speed of a point at the top of the ball ?

(c) What maximum vertical height up the ramp does the ball move ?

Ans. [(a) 5 m/sec (b) 10 m/s (c) 1.575 m]

5-12 A diver makes 2.5 complete revolutions on the way from a 10 m high platform to the water below. Assuming zero initial vertical velocity, calculate the average angular velocity during a dive.

Ans. [11 rad/s]

5-13 (a) Compute the torque developed by an automotive engine whose output is 180 kW at an angular velocity of 4000 rev/min. (b) A drum of negligible mass, 0.5 m in diameter, is attached to the motor shaft, and the power output of the motor is used to raise a weight hanging from a rope wrapped around the drum. How large a weight can be lifted ? Assume constant speed (c) With what speed will the weight rise ?

Ans. [(a) 430 N-m (b) 172 kg (c) 104.65 m/s]

5-14 A stick of length l lies on horizontal table. It has a mass M and is free to move in any way on the table. A ball of mass m, moving perpendicularly to the stick at a distance d from its centre with speed v collides elastically with it as shown in figure-5.138. What quantities are conserved in the collision ? What must be the mass of the ball so that it remains at rest immediately after collision.

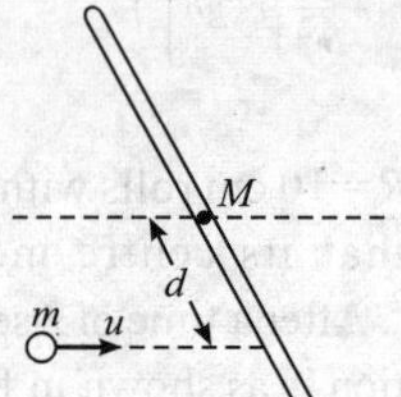

Figure 5.138

Ans. [$\frac{Ml^2}{12d^2 + l^2}$]

5-15 A small steel sphere of mass m and radius r rolls without slipping on the frictionless surface of a large hemisphere of radius $R (R >> r)$ whose axis of symmetry is vertical. It starts at the top from the rest. (a) What is the kinetic energy at the bottom ? (b) What fraction is the rotational kinetic energy of the total kinetic energy at the bottom ? (b) What fraction is the rotational kinetic energy of the total kinetic energy ? (c) What fraction is the translational kinetic energy of the total kinetic energy ? (d) Calculate the normal force that the small sphere will exert on the hemisphere at its bottom. How the results will be affected if r is not very small as compared to R.

Ans. [$mg(R - r)$, 2/7, 5/7, 17mg/7]

5-16 The carbide tips of the cutting teeth of a circular saw are 9.2 cm from the axis of rotation. (a) The no-load speed of the saw, when it is not cutting anything, is 5000 rev/min. Why is its no-load power output negligible ? (b) While cutting lumber, the angular speed of the saw slows to 2500 rev/min, and the power output is 2.1 hp. What is the tangential force that the wood exerts on the carbide tips.

Ans. [65 N]

5-17 A uniform rod of mass m and length l rests on a smooth horizontal surface. One of the ends of the rod is struck in a horizontal direction at right angles to the rod. As a result the rod obtains velocity v_0. Find the force with which one half of the rod will act on the other in the process of motion.

Ans. [$\frac{9}{2}\frac{mv_0^2}{l}$]

5-18 A smooth uniform rod *AB* of mass *M* and length *l* rotates freely with an angular velocity ω_0 in a horizontal plane about a stationary vertical axis passing through its end *A*. A small sleeve of mass *m* starts sliding along the rod from the point *A*. Find the velocity *V'* of the sleeve relative to the rod at the moment it reaches the other end *B*.

Ans. [$\dfrac{\omega_0 l}{\sqrt{1+\dfrac{3m}{M}}}$]

5-19 The flywheel of a large motor in a factory has mass 30 kg and moment of inertia 67.5 kg-m^2 about its rotation axis. The motor develops a constant torque of 600 N-m, and the flywheel starts from rest. (a) What is the angular acceleration of the flywheel ? (b) What is its angular velocity after making 4 revolutions ? (c) How much work is done by the motor during the first 4 revolutions ? (d) What is the average power output of the motor during the first 4 revolutions ?

Ans. [(a) 8.88 rad/s^2 (b) 21.2 rad/sec (c) 6.325 kW]

5-20 Figure-5.139 shows three identical kiting spools at rest on a rough horizontal ground initially. In each case the string is pulled in the direction shown in figure. In each case it is given that spool rolls without slipping. In what direction will each spool will move and with what acceleration. Moment of inertia of each spool is *I* and radius of inner tube is *r* and that of outer disc is *R*.

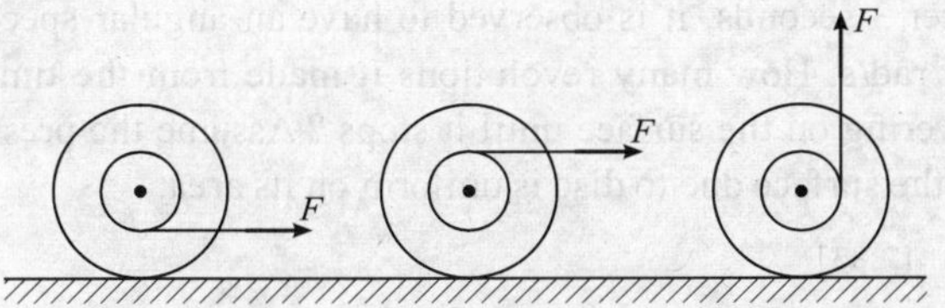

Figure 5.139

5-21 A 50 kg runner runs around the edge of a turntable mounted on frictionless bearings. With respect to earth the velocity of runner is 2 m/s. The turntable is rotating in opposite direction with an angular velocity of magnitude 0.2 rad/s with respect to earth. The radius of turntable is 4 m, and its moment of inertia is 1000 kg-m^2. Find the final angular velocity of the system if runner comes to rest relative to turntable.

Ans. [0.022 rad/s]

5-22 Two uniform thin rods *A* and *B* of length 0.6 m each and of masses 0.01 kg and 0.02 kg respectively are rigidly joined, end to end. The combination is pivoted at the lighter end *P* as shown in the figure-5.140 such that it can freely rotate about the point *P* in a vertical plane. A small object of mass 0.05 kg, moving horizontally this the lower end of the combination and sticks to it. What should be the velocity of the object so that the system could just be raised to the horizontal position ?

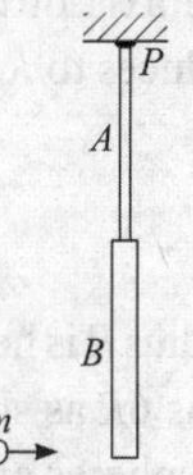

Figure 5.140

Ans. [6.3 m/s]

5-23 A insect of mass *m* stands on a horizontal disc platform of moment of inertia *I* which is at rest. What is the angular velocity of the disc platform when the insect goes along a circle of radius *r*, concentric with the disc, with velocity *v* relative to the disc.

Ans. [$\dfrac{mvr}{I+mr^2}$]

5-24 A uniform rod *AB* of mass *M* is placed in contact with a second rod *BC* of mass $m = M/2$ on a horizontal smooth table at right angles to each other as shown in figure-5.141. Find the initial velocity of *BC* and kinetic energy generated in it if an impulse *I* is imparted to *A*.

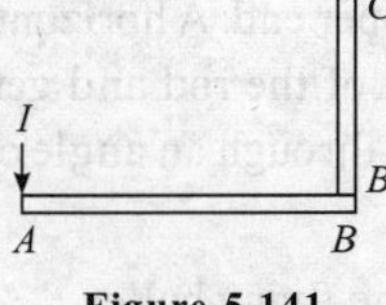

Figure 5.141

Ans. [$2I/3m$, $5I^2/3m$]

5-25 A uniform thin rigid rod of mass *M* and length *L* is standing vertically along y-axis on a smooth horizontal surface, with its lower end at the origin (0, 0). A slight disturbance at $t = 0$ causes the lower end to slip on the smooth surface along the positive *x*-axis, and the rod falling.

(i) What is the path followed by the centre of mass of the rod during its fall ?

(ii) Find the equation of the trajectory of a point on the rod located at a distance *r* from the lower end. What is the shape of the path of this point.

Ans. [Along y-axis, $\dfrac{x^2}{\left(\dfrac{L}{2}-r\right)^2}+\dfrac{y^2}{r^2}=1$]

5-26 A carpet of mass *M* made of inextensible material is rolled along its length in the form of a cylinder of radius *R* and is kept on a rough floor. The carpet starts unrolling without sliding on the floor when a negligible push is given to it. Calculate the horizontal velocity of the axis of the cylindrical part of the carpet when its radius reduces to $R/2$.

Ans. [$\sqrt{\frac{14gR}{3}}$]

5-27 A small sphere of radius R is held against the inner surface of a larger sphere of radius $6R$ as shown in figure-5.142. The masse of large and small spheres are $4M$ and M, respectively. This arrangement is placed on a horizontal table. There is no friction between any surfaces of contact. The small sphere is now released. Find the coordinates of the centre of the larger sphere when the smallest sphere reaches the other extreme position.

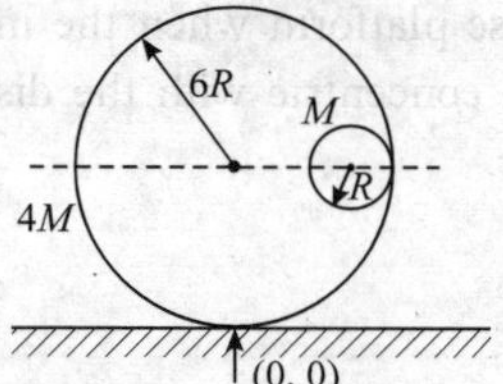

Figure 5.142

Ans. [$(L + 2R)$, 0]

5-28 A vertically oriented uniform rod of mass M and length l can rotate about its upper end. A horizontally flying of mass m strikes the lower end of the rod and gets stuck into it. As a result, the rod swings through an angle α. Assuming $m << M$. Find:

(a) The velocity of the flying bullet,

(b) The momentum increment in the system "*bullet + rod*" during impact; what causes the change of that momentum.

Ans. [$\frac{M}{m}\sqrt{\frac{2gl}{3}}\sin\frac{\alpha}{2}$, $M\sqrt{\frac{gl}{6}}\sin\frac{\alpha}{2}$]

5-29 A metre stick lies on a frictionless horizontal table. It has a mass M and is free to move in any way on the table. A small body of mass m moving with speed v, collides elastically with the stick. What must be the value of m if it is to remain at rest after the collision ?

Ans. [$\frac{Ml^2}{l^2 + 12d^2}$]

5-30 A uniform solid cylinder of radius R roll's over a horizontal plane passing into an inclined plane forming an angle α with the horizontal as shown in figure-5.143. Find the maximum value of the velocity v which still permits the cylinder to roll onto the inclined plane section without a jump. The sliding is assumed to be absent.

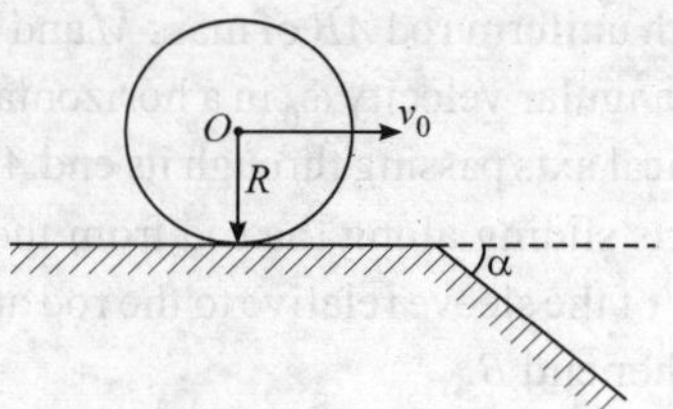

Figure 5.143

Ans. [$\sqrt{\frac{1}{3}gR\,(7\cos\alpha - 4)}$]

5-31 A small spherical marble of mass m and radius r is rolling without slipping on a rough track with speed v. The track further is in the shape of a vertical circle of radius R as shown in figure-5.144. With what minimum linear speed the marble is rolling so that it completely goes round the circle on the circular part of track.

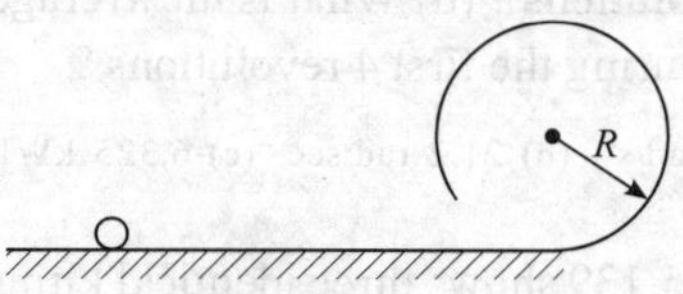

Figure 5.144

Ans. [$\sqrt{\frac{27}{7}g(R-r)}$]

5-32 A horizontal rotating disc placed on a rough surface has an angular speed of 8 rad/s when it is lowered on the surface. After 3 seconds, it is observed to have an angular speed of 2.6 rad/s. How many revolutions it made from the time of lowering on the surface until it stops ? Assume the pressure on the surface due to disc is uniform on its area.

Ans. [2.83]

5-33 A thin horizontal uniform rod AB of mass m and length l can rotate freely about a vertical axis passing through its end A. At a certain moment the end B starts experiencing a constant force F which is always perpendicular to the original position of the stationary rod and directed in the horizontal plane. Find the angular velocity of the rod as a function of its rotation angle φ counted relative to the initial position.

Ans. [$\omega = \sqrt{\frac{6F\sin\varphi}{ml}}$]

5-34 A disc of circumference S stands vertically on a horizontal surface as shown in figure-5.145. A horizontal force P acts on the centre of the disc. Half of the circumference (ABC) is rough and the friction is sufficient to prevent slipping when the disc rolls along XY. The other half of the circumference (ADC) is smooth. The disc starts from rest when P begins to act and the point C is at the bottom. Find the distance moved by the disc along xy when it completes one rotation.

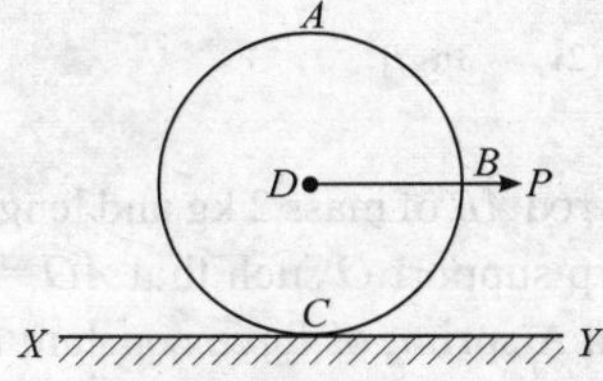

Figure 5.145

Ans. [19S/16]

5-35 A block of mass $m_1 = 2$ kg slides along a frictionless table with a speed of 10 m/s. Directly infront of it, and moving in the same direction is a block of mass $m_2 = 5$ kg moving at 3 m/s. A massless spring with a spring constant 11.2 N/cm is attached to m_2 as shown in figure-5.146. When the block collide, what is the maximum compression of the spring ? Assume that the spring does not bend.

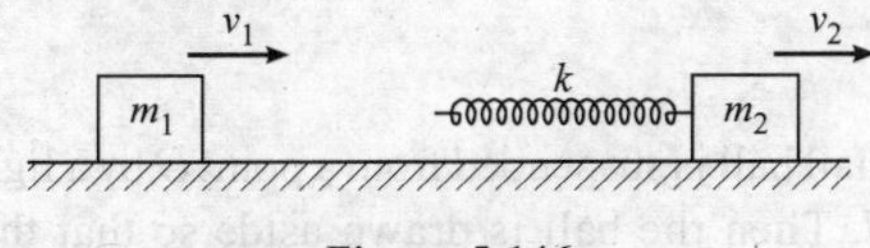

Figure 5.146

Ans. [0.25 m]

5-36 A uniform rod of length $2a$ is held with one end resting on a smooth horizontal table making an angle α with the vertical. Show that when the rod is released, its angular velocity when it makes an angle θ with the vertical is given by

$$\omega = \left[\frac{6g(\cos\alpha - \cos\theta)}{(1 + 3\sin^2\alpha)}\right]$$

5-37 A hollow sphere of radius r is rotating about a horizontal axis at some angular speed ω_0. It is gently lowered to ground and the coefficient of friction between sphere and the ground is μ. How far does the sphere move before it starts pure rolling ?

Ans. [$\frac{2}{25}\frac{\omega_0^2 r^2}{\mu g}$]

5-38 Discs A and B are mounted on a shaft XY and may be connected or disconnected by a coupling Z as shown in figure-5.147. The moment of inertia of disc A about the shaft is half that of disc B. The moments of inertia of the shaft and the coupling are negligible. Initially A is disconnected and rotated at an angular velocity ω. It is now coupled to disc B using couplings. It is found that 5000 J of thermal energy is developed in the coupling when the connection is made. What was the original kinetic energy of the disc A.

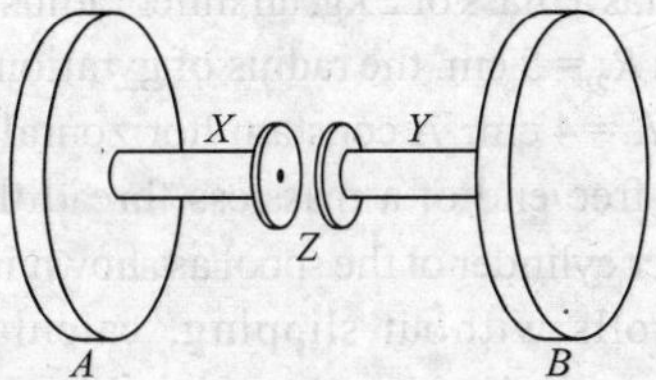

Figure 5.147

Ans. [7500 J]

5-39 A spool with thread wound on it, of mass m, rests on a rough horizontal surface as shown in figure-5.148. Its moment of inertia relative to its own axis is equal to $I = \gamma m R^2$, where γ is a numerical factor, and R is the outside radius of the spool. The radius of the wound thread layer is equal to r. The spool is pulled without sliding by the thread with a constant force F directed at an angle θ to the horizontal. Find : (a) The projection of the acceleration vector of the spool on the X-axis, and (b) the work performed by the force F during the first t seconds after the beginning of motion.

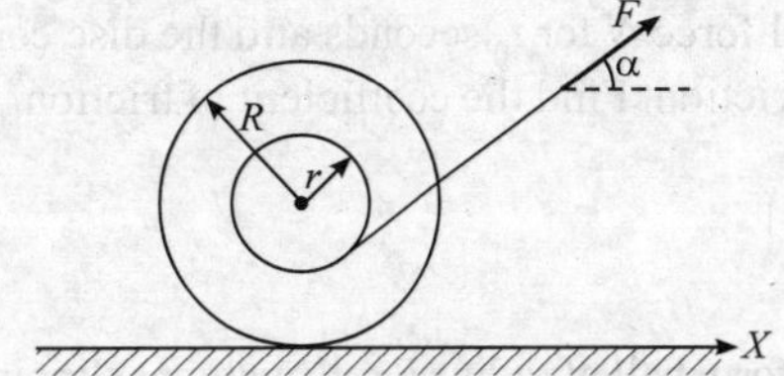

Figure 5.148

Ans. [$\frac{F\left(\cos\theta - \frac{r}{R}\right)}{m(1+\gamma)}$, $\frac{F^2 t^2\left(\cos\theta - \frac{r}{R}\right)^2}{2m(1+\gamma)}$]

5-40 A small body of mass m tied to an inextensible thread moves over a smooth horizontal plane. The other end of the thread is passed through a hole and drawn with a constant velocity v. Find the tension of the thread as the function of the distance r of m from the hole if at $r = r_0$, the angular velocity of the thread is equal to ω_0.

Ans. [$\frac{m\omega_0^2 r_0^4}{r^3}$]

5-41 A ball of mass m moving with velocity v_0 experiences a head on elastic collision with one of the spheres of a stationary rigid dumbbell as shown in figure-5.149. The mass of each sphere equals $m/2$, and the distance between them is l. Disregarding the size of the spheres, find the angular momentum of the dumbbell in the reference frame moving translationally and fixed to the centre of mass of the dumbbell.

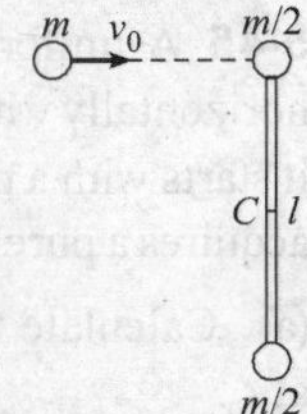

Figure 5.149

Ans. [$\frac{mlv_0}{3}$]

5-42 A spool has a mass of 2 kg, an inner radius $R_1 = 3$ cm, and an outer radius $R_2 = 5$ cm, the radius of gyration about the axis of the spool is $K = 4$ cm. A constant horizontal force of 5 N is applied to the free end of a massless thread that is wrapped around the inner cylinder of the spool as shown in figure-5.150. If the spool rolls without slipping, calculate the linear acceleration along the horizontal surface. What is the minimum coefficient of static friction required to prevent slipping ?

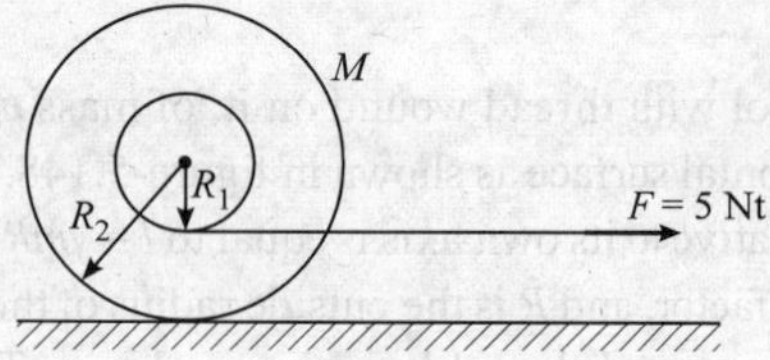

Figure 5.150

Ans. [$a = 2.439$ m/s^2, $\mu_{min} = 0.0062$]

5-43 A homogeneous disc of weight W and radius R rotates about the vertical axis OZ, the initial angular velocity being ω_0. During the motion, the brake block A is pressed to the disc, with a radial force N for t_0 seconds and the disc comes to rest because of friction. Find the coefficient of friction.

Ans. [$\frac{WR\omega_0}{2gNt_0}$]

5-44 A uniform ball of radius R rolls without slipping between two rails such that the horizontal distance is d between the two contact point of the rails to the ball. (a) Show that at any instant, velocity of centre of mass is given as

$$v_{cm} = \omega\sqrt{R^2 - \frac{d^2}{4}}$$

Discuss the above expression in the limits $d = 0$ and $d = 2$ R. (b) For a uniform ball starting from rest and descending a vertical distance h while rolling without slipping down a ramp, $v_{cm} = \sqrt{\frac{10gh}{7}}$, If the ramp is replaced with two rails, show that

$$v_{cm} = \sqrt{\frac{10gh}{5 + \frac{2}{1 - d^2/4R^2}}}$$

Neglect friction in above cases.

5-45 A uniform disc of mass m and radius R is projected horizontally with velocity v_0 on a rough horizontal floor so that it starts with a purely sliding motion at $t = 0$. After t_0 seconds it acquires a purely rolling motion.

(a) Calculate the velocity of the centre of mass of the disc at t_0.

(b) Assuming the coefficient of friction to be μ, calculate to. Also calculate the work done by the frictional force as a function of time and the total work done by it over a time t much longer than t_0.

Ans. [$v_0/3$, $\frac{1}{2}m\mu gt(2v_0 - 3\mu gt)$]

5-46 A uniform rod AB of mass 2 kg and length $l = 100$ cm is placed on a sharp support O such that $AO = a = 40$ cm and $OB = b = 60$ cm. A spring of force constant $k = 600$ N/m is attached to end B as shown in figure-5.151. To keep the rod horizontal, its end A is tied with a thread such that the spring is elongated by $y = 1$ cm. Calculate the reaction of support on the rod when the thread is burnt.

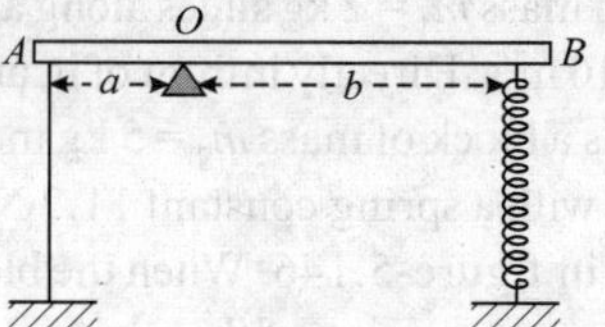

Figure 5.151

Ans. [20 N]

5-47 A small ball is suspended from a point O by a light thread of length l. Then the ball is drawn aside so that the thread deviates through an angle θ from the vertical and set in motion in a horizontal direction at right angles to the vertical plane in which the thread is located. What is the initial velocity that has to be imparted to the ball so that it could deviate through the maximum angle $\pi/2$ in the process of motion ?

Ans. [$\sqrt{2gl\sec\theta}$]

5-48 An object rotates about a fixed axis, such that a reference line on the object makes an angle $\theta = ae^{bt}$ with its starting position at time t. Find for a particle on object at a distance r from the axis of rotation, the tangential, the radial and the total acceleration of the point.

Ans. [$a_t = ab^2re^{bt}$, $a_r = a^2b^2re^{2bt}$, $a_T = ab^2re^{bt}\sqrt{1 + a^2e^{2bt}}$]

5-49 A rectangular rigid fixed block has a long horizontal edge. A solid homogeneous cylinder of radius R is placed horizontally at test with its length parallel to the edge such that the axis of the cylinder and the edge of the block are in the same vertical plane as shown in figure-5.152. There is sufficient friction present at the edge so that a very small displacement causes the cylinder to roll of the edge without slipping. Determine

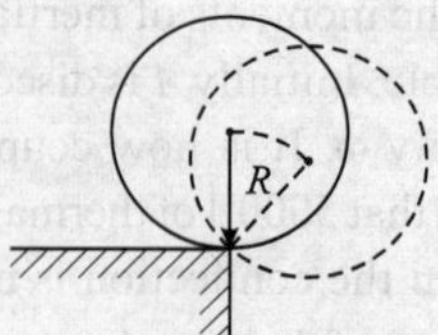

Figure 5.152

(a) The angle θ through which the cylinder rotates before it leaves contact with the edge.

(b) The speed of the centre of mass of the cylinder before leaving contact with the edge, and

(c) The ratio of the translational to rotational kinetic energies of the cylinder when its centre of mass is in horizontal line with the edge.

Ans. [$\cos^{-1}\left(\frac{4}{7}\right), \sqrt{\frac{4gR}{7}}$, 6]

5-50 A 392 N wheel comes off a moving truck and rolls without slipping along a highway. At the bottom of a hill it is rotating at 50 rad/s. The radius of the wheel is 0.6 m, and its moment of inertia about its rotation axis is 0.8 MR^2. Friction does 3000 J of work on the wheel as it rolls up the hill to a stop a height h above the bottom of the hill. Calculate h.

Ans. [29.1 m]

5-51 A grindstone in the form of a solid cylinder has a radius of 0.2 m and a mass of 30 kg. (a) What constant torque will bring it from rest to an angular velocity of 250 rev/min in 10 s? (b) Through what angle has it turned during that time? (c) Calculate the work done by the torque.

Ans. [1.57 N-m, 20.8 rev, 206 J]

5-52 A constant net torque equal to 20 N-m is exerted on a pivoted wheel for 8 sec, during which time the angular velocity of the wheel increases from zero to 100 re/min. The external torque is then removed and the wheel is brought to rest by friction in its bearings in 70 sec. Compute (a) the moment of inertia of the wheel about the rotation axis, (b) the friction torque (c) the total no. of revolutions made by the wheel in the 70 sec time interval.

Ans. [15.3 kg-m^2, 2.29 N-m, 58.3 rev]

5-53 In the arrangement shown in figure-5.153 a weight A possesses mass m, a pulley B possesses mass M. Also known are the moment of inertia I of the pulley relative to its axis and the radii of the pulley R and 2 R. The mass of the threads is negligible. Find the acceleration of the weight A after the system is set free.

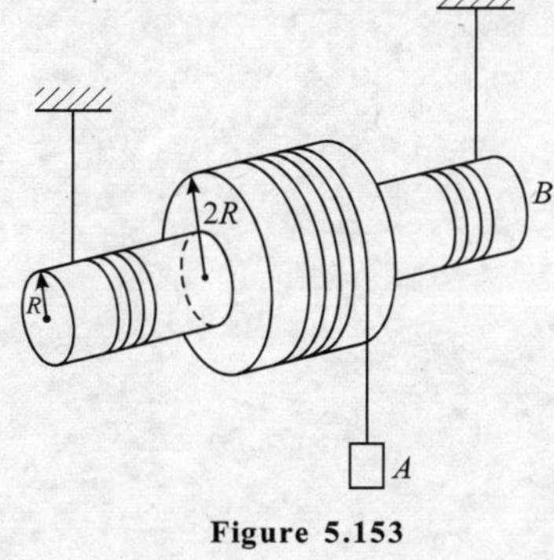

Figure 5.153

Ans. [$\dfrac{3(M+3m)g}{M+9m+\dfrac{I}{R^2}}$]

5-54 A solid spherical ball of radius 30 cm and mass M is connected to a point A on wall with a thread and freely rotate about its central axis with angular velocity 60 rad/sec. If the ball is resting on the vertical face of a wall, what time will elapse before it comes to rest ? The coefficient of friction between wall and ball is 0.25 and inclination of thread to vertical is 15°.

Ans. [10.13 sec]

5-55 A thin uniform rod of mass m and length l rotates with the constant angular velocity ω about the vertical axis passing through the rod's suspension point O. In doing so, the rod describes a conical surface with a half separated angle θ. Find the angle θ as well as the magnitude and direction of the reaction force at the point O.

Ans. [$\cos^{-1}\dfrac{3g}{2\omega^2 l}, \frac{1}{2}m\omega^2 l\sqrt{1+\dfrac{7g^2}{4\omega^4 l^2}}, \cos\varphi = \dfrac{4\cos\theta}{\sqrt{9+7\cos^2\theta}}$]

5-56 A rod of mass m and length l is held vertically on a smooth horizontal floor. Now it is released from this position, find the speed of its centre of mass when it makes an angle θ with the vertical.

Ans. [$\dfrac{\sqrt{6gl}\sin\dfrac{\theta}{2}\cos\theta}{\sqrt{1+3\sin^2\theta}}$]

5-57 Consider a cylinder of mass M and radius R lying on a rough horizontal plane. It has a plank lying on its top as shown in figure-5.154. A force F is applied on the plank such that the plank moves and causes the cylinder to roll. The plank always remains horizontal. There is no slipping at any point of contact. Calculate the acceleration of the cylinder and the frictional forces at the two contacts.

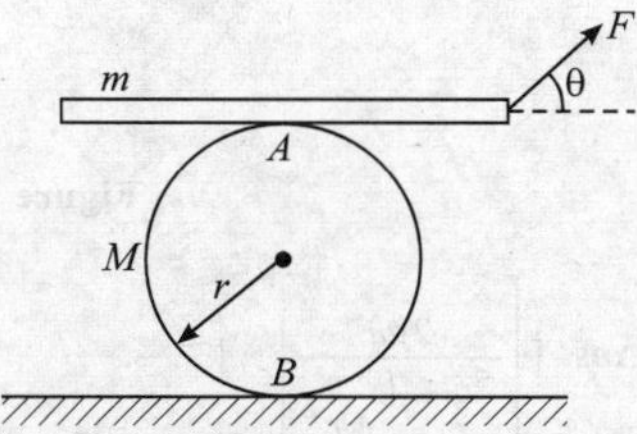

Figure 5.154

Ans. [$\dfrac{4F\cos\theta}{3M+8m}, \dfrac{3MF\cos\theta}{3M+8m}, \dfrac{MF\cos\theta}{3M+8m}$]

5-58 A uniform rod of length l and mass M is suspended on two vertical inextensible strings as shown in figure-5.155. Calculate tension T in the left string at the instant, when right string snaps.

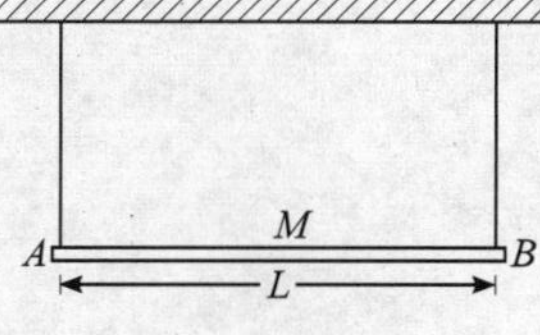

Figure 5.155

Ans. [$\dfrac{Mg}{4}$]

5-59 The mechanism shown in figure-5.156 is used to raise a wooden box of mass 50 kg. A string is wrapped around a cylinder that turns on an axle. The cylinder has radius 0.25 m and moment of inertia 0.92 kg-m^2 about the axle. What magnitude of the force F applied tangentially to the rotating crank handle is required to raise the box with an acceleration of 0.80 m/s^2. Here we can neglect the moment of inertia of the axle and the crank.

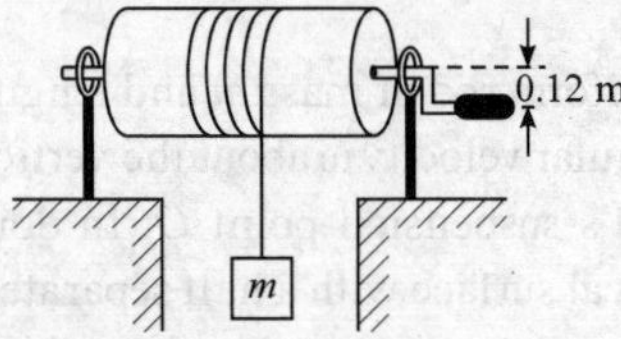

Figure 5.156

Ans. [1100 N]

5-60 A uniform spherical shell of mass M and radius R rotates about a vertical axis on frictionless bearings as shown in figure-5.157. A massless cord passes around the equator of the shell, over a pulley of rotational inertia I and radius r, and is attached to a small object of mass m falling under gravity. Neglect all frictions find the speed of the object after it has fallen a distance h from rest ?

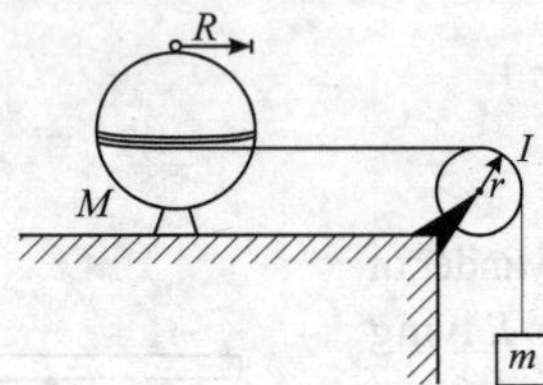

Figure 5.157

Ans. $\left[\left[\dfrac{2gh}{\frac{5}{3}+\frac{I}{Mr^2}}\right]^{1/2}\right]$

5-61 Show that if a rod held at an angle θ to the horizontal and released, its lower end will not slip the friction coefficient between rod and ground is

$$\mu = \frac{3\sin\theta\cos\theta}{1+3\sin^2\theta}$$

5-62 Two wooden disc, one with radius 2 cm and mass 1 kg and the other with radius 4 cm and mass 2 kg, are welded together coaxially and mounted on a frictionless axis through their common centre. A light string is wrapped around the edge of the smaller disc, and a 3 kg block is suspended from the free end of the string. What is the acceleration of the block after it is released ? Repeat the above process if the string is wrapped around the edge of the larger disc.

Ans. [4 m/s^2, 7.27 m/s^2]

5-63 A horizontal wooden disc of mass 8 kg and diameter 1m is pivoted on frictionless bearing about a vertical axis through its centre. We put a toy train track model in the disc. The track has a negligible mass and average diameter 0.95 m. The mass of model train is 1.2 kg which can run with a battery. When we switch on the engine the train moves anticlockwise, soon attaining a constant speed of 0.6 m/s with respect to the track. Find the magnitude and direction of the angular velocity of the disc relative to the earth.

Ans. [0.27 rad/s]

5-64 In the figure-5.158 shown, if the system is in equilibrium. Find the relation in μ_1 and μ_2 for the case (i) if the bar is just going to slide and (ii) if box is just going to slide.

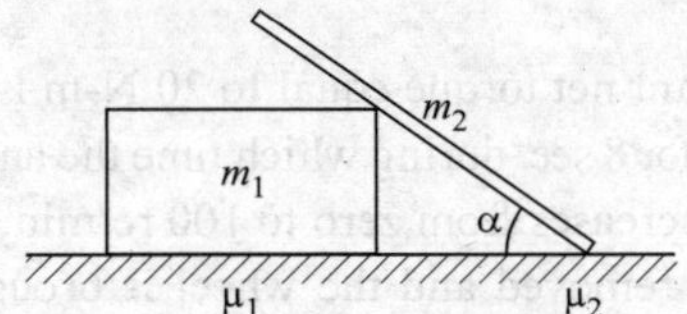

Figure 5.158

Ans. [(i) $\mu_1 m_1 g > \mu_2 m_2 g \dfrac{\sin\alpha - \mu_2\cos\alpha}{\sin\alpha + \mu_2\cos\alpha}$

(ii) $\mu_2 m_2 g > \mu_1 m_1 g \dfrac{\sin\alpha + \mu_1\cos\alpha}{\sin\alpha - \mu_1\cos\alpha}$]

* * * * *

Gravitation

6

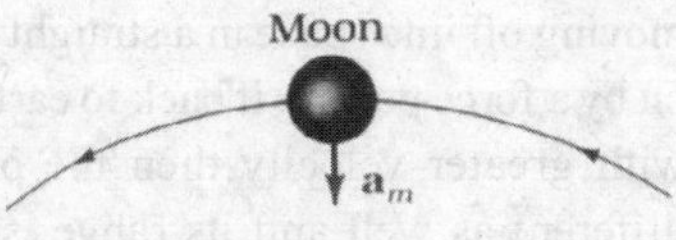

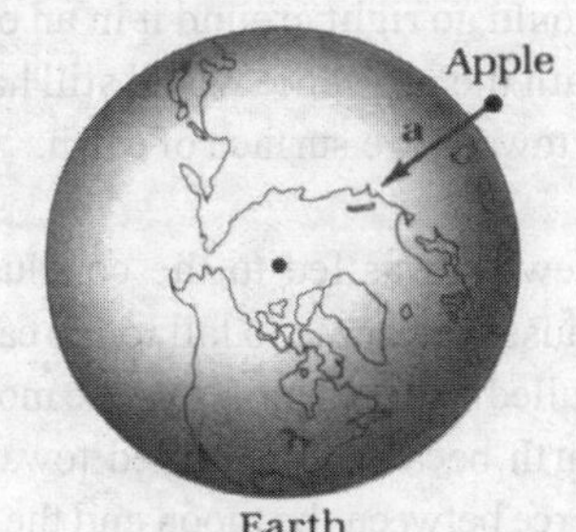

FEW WORDS FOR STUDENTS

In mechanics we have studied the interaction of physical bodies and the principles governing their motions and conservation laws. In this chapter we proceed to examine gravitational forces and the motion resulting from these forces which includes uniform circular motion. An in-depth understanding of gravitation allows us to explain the motion of the planets in universe and that of artificial satellites.

CHAPTER CONTENTS

COVER APPLICATION

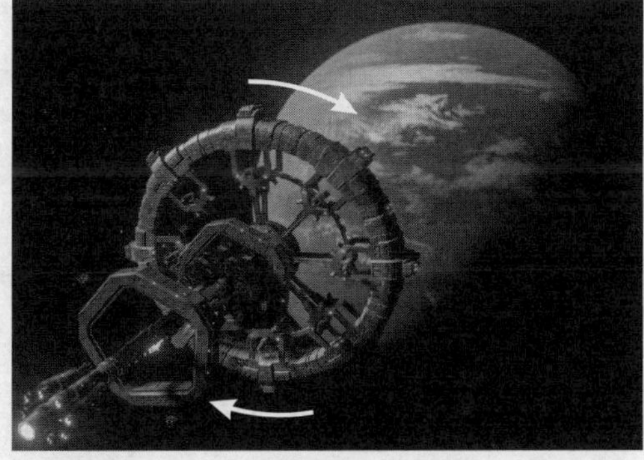

Figure-(a)

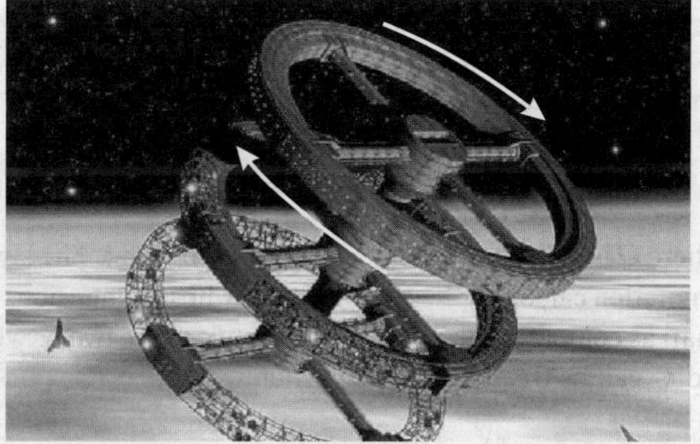

Figure-(b)

Figure-(a) and (b) shows the space station orbiting around the earth in a specific orbit. Inside spaceship due to weightlessness there is zero gravity but artificial gravity is developed by rotation of structure about its central axis so that in rotating frame centrifugal force on bodies inside will keep them in contact with the inside surface of the spaceship.

Newton observed that an object, an apple, when released near the earth surface is accelerated towards the earth. As acceleration is caused by an unbalanced force, there must be a force pulling objects towards the earth. If someone throws a projectile with some initial velocity, then instead of that object moving off into space in a straight line, it is continuously acted on by a force pulling it back to earth. If we throw the projectile with greater velocity then the path of projectile would be different as well and its range is also increased with initial velocity. If the projection velocity is further increased until at some initial velocity, the body would not hit the earth at all but would go right around it in an orbit. But at any point along its path the projectile would still have a force acting on it pulling it toward the surface of earth.

Newton was led to the conclusion that the same force that causes the apple to fall to the earth also causes the moon to be pulled to the earth. Thus the moon moves in its orbit about the earth because it is pulled toward the earth. But if there is a force between the moon and the earth, why not a force between the sun and the earth or why not a force between the sun and the other plants ? Newton proposed that the same force, named gravitational force which acts on objects near the earth surface also acts on all the heavenly bodies. He proposed that there was a force of gravitation between each and every mass in the universe.

6.1 Newton's Law of Universal Gravitation

All physical bodies are subject to the action of the forces of mutual gravitational attraction. The basic law describing the gravitational forces was stated by Sir Issac Newton and it is called Newton's Law of Universal gravitation.

The law is stated as : *"Between any two particles of masses* m_1 *and* m_2 *at separation r from each other there exist attractive forces* $\vec{F}_{AB}$ *and* $\vec{F}_{BA}$ *(as shown in figure-6.1) directed from one body to the other and equal in magnitude which is directly proportional to the product of the masses of the bodies and inversely proportional to the square of the distance between the two".* Thus we can write

$$F_{AB} = F_{BA} = G\frac{m_1 m_2}{r^2} \quad \ldots (6.1)$$

Where G is called universal gravitational constant. The law of gravitation can be applied to the bodies whose dimensions are small as compared to the separation between the two or when bodies can be treated as point particles.

Figure 6.1

If the bodies are not very small sized, we can not directly apply the expression in equation-(6.1) to find their natural gravitational attraction. In this case we use the following procedure to find the same. The bodies are initially split into small parts or a large number of point masses. Now using equation-(6.1) the force of attraction exerted on a particle of one body by a particle of another body can be obtained. Now we add all forces vectorially which are exerted by all independent particles of second body on the particle of first body. Finally the resultants of these forces is summed over all particles of the first body to obtain the net force experienced by the bodies. In general we use integration for basic summation of these forces.

Lets consider an example to understand the same. Figure-6.2(a) shows a uniform rod of mass M of length l and we wish to find the gravitational attraction on this rod due to a point particle of mass m placed at a distance r from one of its ends as shown.

To find this we consider a small element of width dx on the rod as shown in figure-6.2(b) at a distance x from the point mass m, the mass of this element can be given as

$$dm = \frac{M}{l}\,dx \quad \ldots (6.2)$$

(a)

(b)

Figure 6.2

Now we can find the gravitational attraction on dm due to the point mass m using Newton's law of universal gravitation. Thus we have the force on dm as

$$dF = \frac{Gm\,dm}{x^2}$$

or

$$dF = \frac{Gm\,M}{l\,x^2}\,dx$$

To find the net force on rod we integrate the above expression in proper limits as

$$F = \int dF = \int_r^{r+L} \frac{GMm}{l^0}\,\frac{1}{x^2}\,dx$$

or

$$F = \frac{GMm}{l}\left[\frac{1}{r} - \frac{1}{r+l}\right] \quad \ldots (6.3)$$

Here expression in equation-(6.3) gives net interaction force between the given point mass and the rod. In such a manner by using integration we can find interaction force between more extended bodies.

In ordinary laboratory experiments the attractive force between the bodies is very small in comparison to their weights and therefore it cannot be observed. Even through some more precise experiments allow us to demonstrate the presence of gravitational force. The first laboratory experiment for direct measurement of the force of gravitation was carried out by *H.* Cavendish in 1978 with the use of a torsional balance figure-6.3 shows the basic setup of Cavendish experiment. Two equal masses *m* are placed at the end of a relatively light rod *A*, the middle point of the rod is suspended from a sufficiently long thread. At the mid point of rod a small mirror *K* is fixed. The change in direction of the light ray reflected from the mirror as the rod turns can be directly observed and measured. The deflection of the ray makes it possible to determine the angle of twist of the string from which the rod is suspended and to compute the corresponding forces producing the twist. Two big lead balls of mass *M* are brought close to the suspended rod from different sides. The force of attraction exerted by big balls on the small one form a couple which rotates the rod until the moment of couple of gravitational forces is balanced by the torsional moment of the thread. The couple of torsional forces can be calculated by the known parameters such as torsional constant of the thread and the angle of turn of the reflected light ray. Varying the distances between the masses *m* and *M*, Cavendish determined the dependence of the force of gravitational attraction on the distance the results of this experiment confirmed the validity of Newton's Law of gravitation.

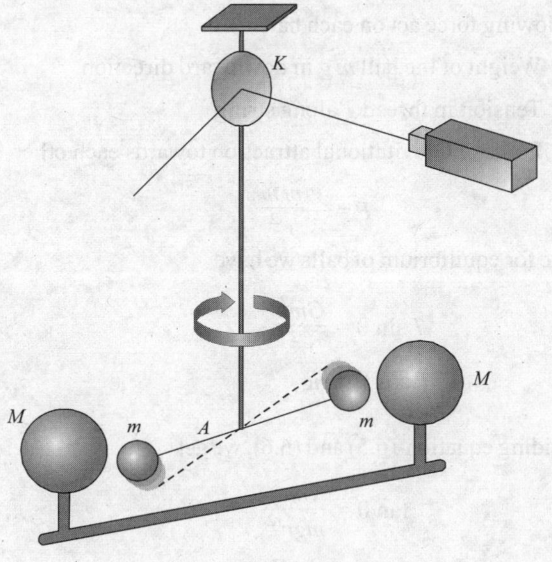

Figure 6.3

The results of Cavendish experiments were checked many times by several scientists by various modifications of the experiments. The results of precise measurements give the following value of gravitational constant.

$$G = 6.674 \times 10^{-11}\ \text{N-m}^2/\text{kg}^2$$

Let us take some example on Newton's Law of gravitation.

Illustrative Example 6.1

Three particles *A*, *B* and *C*, each of mass *m*, are placed in a line with $AB = BC = d$. Find the gravitational force on a fourth particle *P* of same mass, placed at a distance *d* from the particle *B* on the perpendicular bisector of the line *AC* as shown in figure-6.4

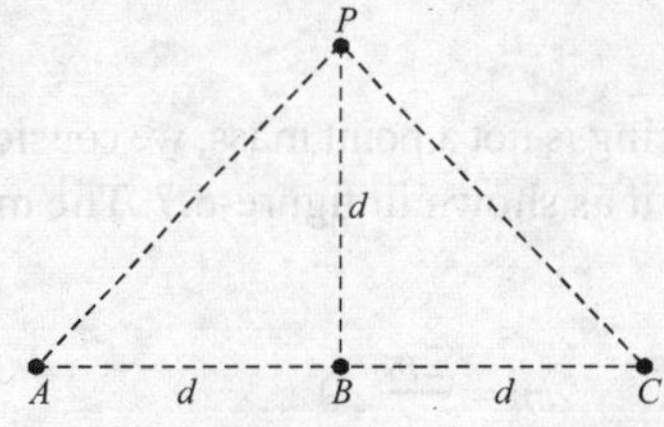

Figure 6.4

Solution

The forces acting on *P* are shown in figure-6.5.

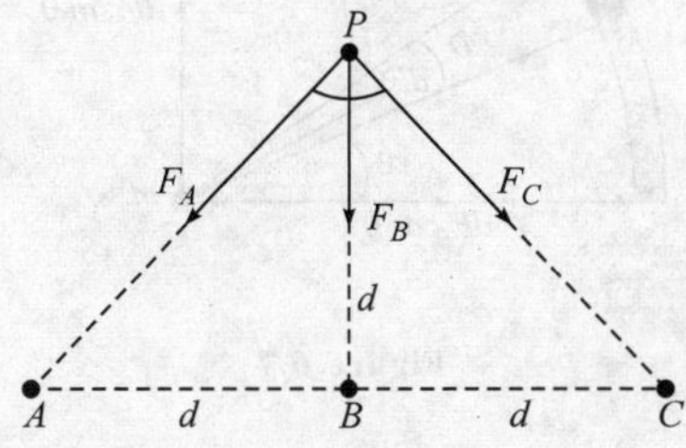

Figure 6.5

The force at *P* due to *A* along *PA* is

$$F_A = \frac{G m^2}{(AP)^2} = \frac{G m^2}{(\sqrt{2}d)^2} = \frac{G m^2}{2d^2}$$

The force at *P* due to *C* along *PC* is

$$F_C = \frac{G m^2}{(CP)^2} = \frac{G m^2}{(\sqrt{2}d)^2} = \frac{G m^2}{2d^2}$$

The force at *P* due to *B* is

$$F_B = \frac{G m^2}{d^2} \text{ along } PB$$

The resultant of F_A, F_B and F_C will be along PB, can be given as

$$F_P = F_B + F_A \cos 45° + F_C \cos 45°$$

$$= \frac{Gm^2}{d^2} + \frac{Gm^2}{2\sqrt{2}\, d^2} + \frac{Gm^2}{2\sqrt{2}\, d^2}$$

or $$\frac{Gm^2}{d^2}\left(\frac{1}{2\sqrt{2}} + \frac{1}{2\sqrt{2}} + 1\right) = \frac{Gm^2}{d^2}\left(1 + \frac{1}{\sqrt{2}}\right) \text{ along } PB$$

Illustrative Example 6.2

Find the force of attraction on a particle of mass m placed at the centre of a quarter ring of mass m and radius R as shown in figure-6.6.

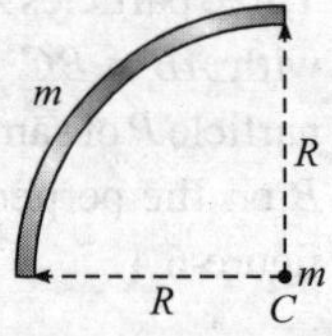

Figure 6.6

Solution

As the quarter ring is not a point mass, we consider an element of width $d\theta$ on it as shown in figure-6.7. The mass dm of this element is

$$dm = \frac{2m}{\pi}\, d\theta \qquad \ldots(6.4)$$

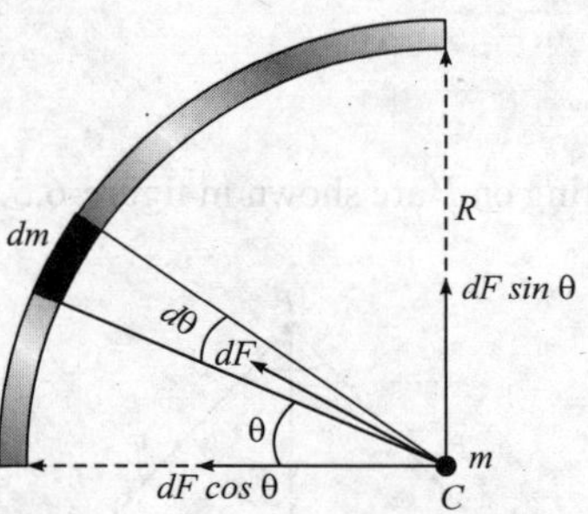

Figure 6.7

Now the force between m and dm is

$$dF = \frac{Gmdm}{R^2}$$

[Toward dm on mass m placed at C]

$$= \frac{2Gm^2}{\pi R^2}\, d\theta$$

This force has two components in X and Y directions; thus net force on m in X and Y direction are

$$F_X = \int dF_X = \int dF \cos\theta$$

$$= \int_0^{\pi/2} \frac{2Gm^2}{\pi R^2} \cos\theta \, d\theta = \frac{2Gm^2}{\pi R^2}$$

and $$F_Y = \int dF_Y = \int dF \sin\theta = \int_0^{\pi/2} \frac{2Gm^2}{\pi R^2} \sin\theta$$

$$d\theta = \frac{2Gm^2}{\pi R^2}$$

Thus net force on m is

$$F = \sqrt{F_X^2 + F_Y^2} = \frac{2\sqrt{2}Gm^2}{\pi R^2}$$

Illustrative Example 6.3

Two balls of mass m each are hung side by side by two long threads of equal length l. If the distance between upper ends is r, show that the distance r' between the centres of the ball is given by

$$g r'^2 (r - r') = 2l\, G m$$

Solution

The situation is shown in figure-6.8.

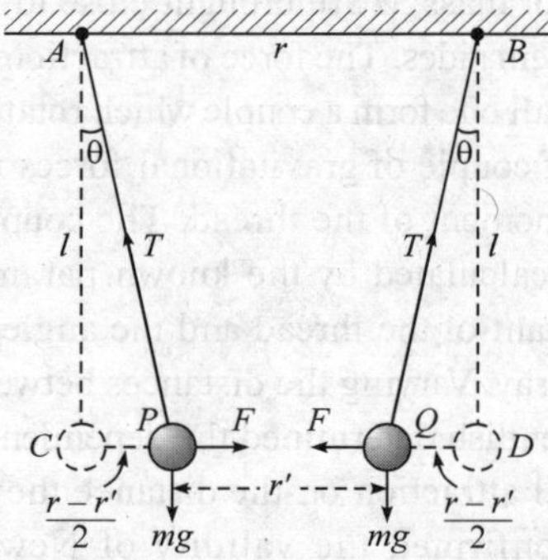

Figure 6.8

Following force act on each ball

(i) Weight of the ball mg in downward direction

(ii) Tension in thread T along string

(iii) Force of Gravitational attraction towards each other

$$F = G\frac{m\,m}{r'^2}$$

Here for equilibrium of balls we have

$$T \sin\theta = \frac{Gm^2}{r'^2} \qquad \ldots(6.5)$$

$$T \cos\theta = mg \qquad \ldots(6.6)$$

Dividing equation-(6.5) and (6.6), we get

or $$\tan\theta = \frac{Gm^2}{mgr'^2} \qquad \ldots(6.7)$$

In ΔACP $$\tan\theta = \frac{r - r'}{2l} \qquad \ldots(6.8)$$

From equation-(6.7) and (6.8)

$$\frac{r-r'}{l}=\frac{Gm^2}{mgr'^2}$$

or $\quad g\,r'^2\,(r-r')=2\,l\,G\,m$

<u>Web Reference of Video Lectures at www.physicsgalaxy.com</u>
Age Group - High School Physics | Age 17-19 Years
Section - GRAVITATION
Topic - Gravitation Theory
Module Number - 1 and 7

Practice Exercise 6.1

(i) Two spherical balls of mass 10 kg each are placed 10 cm apart. Find the gravitational force of attraction between them.

[6.674×10^{-7}N]

(ii) Two particles of equal mass go round a circle of radius R under the action of their mutual gravitational attraction. Find the speed of each particle.

[$v=\sqrt{\frac{Gm}{4R}}$]

(iii) Four particles of equal masses M move along a circle of radius R under the action of their mutual gravitational attraction. Find the speed of each particle.

[$\sqrt{\frac{GM}{R}\left(\frac{2\sqrt{2}+1}{4}\right)}$]

(iv) A mass M is split into two parts m and $(M-m)$, which are then separated by a certain distance. What ratio (m/M) maximises the gravitational force between the parts.

[$\frac{1}{2}$]

(v) In a double star, two stars (one of mass m and the other of 2 m) distance d apart rotate about their common centre of mass. Deduce an expression for the period of revolution. Show that the ratio of their angular momenta about the centre of mass is the same as the ratio of their kinetic energies.

[$2\pi\sqrt{\frac{d^3}{3Gm}}$]

6.2 Gravitational and Inertial Mass

In previous chapters of mechanics we've discussed and we know that the mass of an object is the proportionality factor between the net force exerted on the object and its acceleration or in other words it is Newton's second law of motion stated analytically as

$$\Sigma F=m\,a$$

We've also discussed that the mass of an object is that property (inertia) of object which causes it to resist a change in its velocity (state of motion). This is why we call the mass as inertial mass. For example a car is running on a flat highway and due to brake failure driver is not able to control it and on highway a child is playing in front of the uncontrolled car. Now you must stop the car externally before it crashes the child. In this case the force required to stop the car within the available distance depends on inertial mass of the car.

In previous section of the chapter we've discussed Newton's law of universal gravitation. The magnitude of gravitational force on an object of mass m due to another object of mass M is given as

$$F=\frac{GMm}{r^2}$$

In this expression the mass of the object is that property of the object which causes it to be attracted to another object by the gravitational force. Due to this reason the mass that appears in Newton's law of universal gravitation is often called the gravitational mass. When you are waiting for a train on a railway platform holding a bag of books, you exert a force on this bag. This force which you exert while holding the bag depends on the gravitational mass of the bag of books.

The difficulty you encounter in stopping the running car on highway has nothing to do with its gravitational mass. On the other hand the effort you expend in holding the bag of books has nothing to do with the inertial mass of the bag.

Thus on one hand mass of an object is a measure of an objects resistance to a change of velocity and on the other hand, it is a measure of gravitational attraction to other objects in its surroundings. In a simple language we can say that the mass used in Newton's second law of motion (in expression $F=ma$) is the inertial mass of object and the mass used in Newton's law of gravitation (in expression $F=\frac{Gm_1m_2}{r^2}$) is the gravitational mass of object.

Now the point of discussion is that why are two different properties of matter and both are called "mass". Several experiments are done which show that the two, gravitational and inertial mass of an object are proportional to each other. One such experiment is the measurement of acceleration of different objects during free fall. We have already discussed and we know that during free fall, all forces on an object are negligible except the force of gravity. The net force during free fall on an object is the gravitational force due to the earth. Let us consider a cricket ball in free fall near the earth's surface. If on releasing the ball falls with an acceleration a and m_I and m_G be its inertial and gravitational masses, we have

$$\frac{GM_e m_G}{R_e^2} = m_I a$$

Solving we get

$$a = \left(\frac{GM_e}{R_e^2}\right)\frac{m_G}{m_I} \quad \ldots(6.9)$$

Here the factor $\frac{GM_e}{R_e^2}$ is independent of the object whose motion we are describing, but m_G and m_I depend on the object. As we know for all freely falling objects the acceleration is same and equal to g thus we must have $a = g$. It implies that the ratio (m_G/m_I) must be independent of the object. In other words we can say that m_G must be proportional to m_I for each object. There we may choose the units in such a manner that they are made equal. The value of G evaluated in such a manner that from the results, using proper units, we get

$$g = \frac{GM_e}{R_e^2} \quad \ldots(6.10)$$

Thus $m_I = m_G$. We can also say that for an object numerical value of inertial mass is the same as the gravitational mass, is an experimental statement. The validity of statement depends on the accuracy of the experiments. The physical significance of this proportionality law for gravitational and inertial masses turns out to be of primary importance in the relativity theory. In relativity this is known as equivalence law for the gravitational and inertial mass of a body. This equivalence principle makes it possible to get the conclusion that for a very small region it is possible to choose such an accelerated reference frame in which there is gravitational field.

6.3 Gravitational Field

We can state by Newton's universal law of gravitation that every mass M produces, in the region around it, a physical situation in which, whenever any other mass is placed, force acts on it, is called gravitational field. This field is recognized by the force that the mass M exerts another mass, such as m, brought into the region.

6.3.1 Strength of Gravitational Field

We define gravitational field strength at any point in space to be the gravitational force per unit mass on a test mass (mass brought into the field for experimental observation). Thus for a point in space if a test mass m_0, experiences a force $\vec{F}$, then at that point in space gravitational field strength which is denoted by $\vec{g}$, is given as

$$\vec{g} = \frac{\vec{F}}{m_0} \quad \ldots(6.11)$$

Gravitational field strength $\vec{g}$ is a vector quantity and has same direction as that of the force on the test mass in field.

Generally magnitude of test mass is very small so that its gravitational field does not modify the field that is being measured. Student should also note that gravitational field strength is just the acceleration that a unit mass would experience at that point in space.

6.3.2 Gravitational Field Strength of a Point Mass

As per our previous discussion we can state that every point mass also produces a gravitational field in its surrounding. To find the gravitational field strength due to a point mass, we put a test mass m_0 at a point P at distance x from a point mass m then force on m_0 is given as

$$F_g = \frac{Gmm_0}{x^2} \quad \ldots(6.12)$$

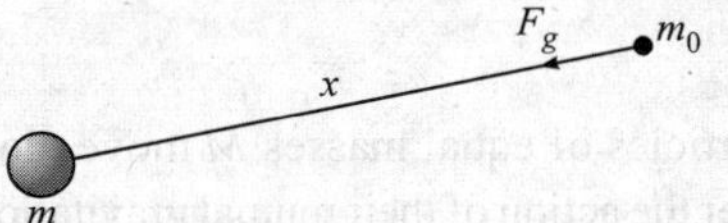

Figure 6.9

Now if at point P, gravitational field strength due to m is g_p, then it is given as

$$g_p = \frac{F_g}{m_0} = \frac{Gm}{x^2} \quad \ldots(6.13)$$

The expression in equation-(6.13) gives the gravitational field strength at a point due to a point mass.

Student should note that the expression in equation-(6.13) is only applicable for gravitational field strength due to point masses. It should not be used for extended bodies. However the expression can be integrated to get the gravitational field strength produced by the extended masses.

6.3.3 Gravitational Field Strength due to a Ring

Case-I : At the centre of ring

To find gravitational field strength at the centre of a ring of mass M and radius R, we consider an elemental mass dm on it as shown in figure-6.10. Let dg be the gravitational field at the centre of ring C due to the element dm.

Here we can simply state that another element of same mass exactly opposite to dm on other half of ring will produce an equal gravitational field at C in opposite direction. Thus due to all the elements on ring, the net gravitational field at centre C will be vectorially nullified and hence net gravitational field strength at C will be 0.

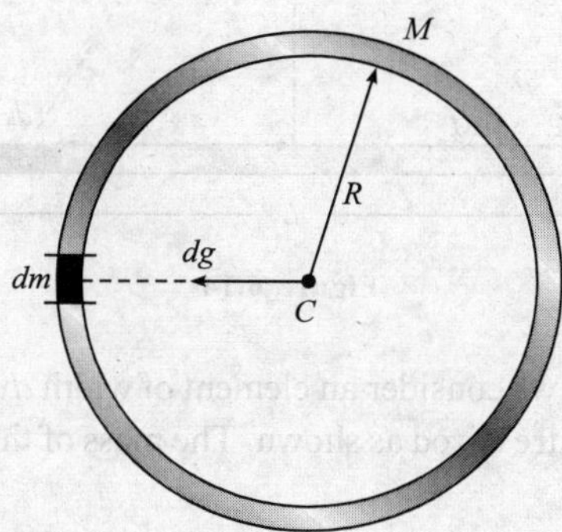

Figure 6.10

On the basis of above description, we can find gravitational field at the centre of ring, if a small part of ring is removed as shown in figure-6.11. Here we can state that at C net gravitational field strength is zero by symmetry if ring were complete. So if a small part is placed back at the gap the net field will again become zero in this case. Thus the gravitational field strength at centre due to this ring must be exactly equal to that produced by the removed part but in opposite direction so as to nullify it when placed in gap.

Here the mass of removed part can be given as

$$m = \frac{M}{2\pi R}x$$

[If x is very small and ring is uniform]

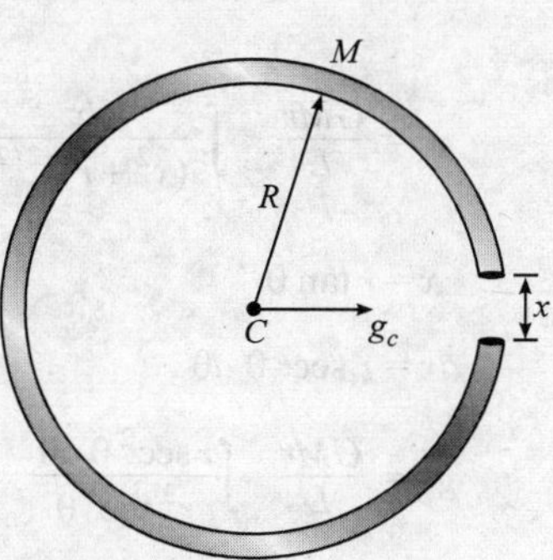

Figure 6.11

Thus gravitational field strength at centre g_c due to this ring is given as

$$g_c = \frac{Gm}{R^2} = \frac{GMx}{2\pi R^3}$$

Here direction of g_c at centre is toward the gap.

Case-II : At a point on the axis of ring

Figure-6.12 shows a ring of mass M and radius R placed in YZ plane with centre at origin. Here we wish to find the gravitational field strength at a point P on its axis at a distance x from its centre.

To find this we consider an element of length dl on ring as shown in figure-6.12. The mass dm of this element can be given as

$$dm = \frac{M}{2\pi R}\,dl \qquad \dots (6.14)$$

Let the gravitational field strength at point P due to the element dm is dg then it is given as

$$dg = \frac{Gdm}{(x^2+R^2)}$$

or

$$= \frac{GM\,dx}{2\pi R(x^2+R^2)}$$

This elemental gravitational field strength dg has two rectangular components, one along the axis of ring $dg\cos\theta$ and other perpendicular to the axis of ring, $dg\sin\theta$. Here when we integrate the result for the complete ring, $dg\sin\theta$ component will be cancelled out by symmetry and $dg\cos\theta$ will be summed up to give the net gravitational field strength at P.

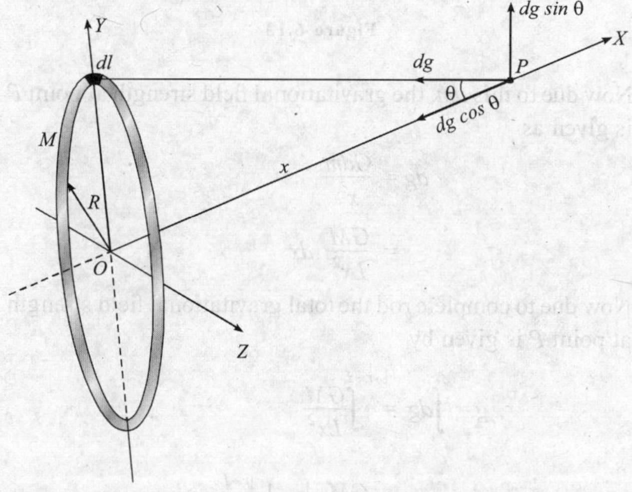

Figure 6.12

Thus here net gravitational field strength at P is given as

$$g = \int dg\cos\theta = \int_0^{2\pi R} \frac{GM\,dx}{2\pi R(x^2+R^2)} \times \frac{x}{\sqrt{x^2+R^2}}$$

or

$$= \frac{GMx}{2\pi R(x^2+R^2)^{3/2}} \int_0^{2\pi R} dl$$

$$= \frac{GMx}{2\pi R(x^2+R^2)^{3/2}}[2\pi R]$$

$$= \frac{GMx}{(x^2+R^2)^{3/2}} \quad ...(6.15)$$

6.3.4 Gravitational Field Strength due to a Rod

Case-I : At an axial point

Figure-6.13 shows a rod AB of mass M and length L. Here we wish to find the gravitational field strength due to rod at a point P situated at a distance r from one end of the rod. Figure-6.13(b) shows the analysis of the procedure for it. We consider an element of width dx on rod at a distance x from P. The mass of this element dm is given as

$$dm = \frac{M}{L}\,dx$$

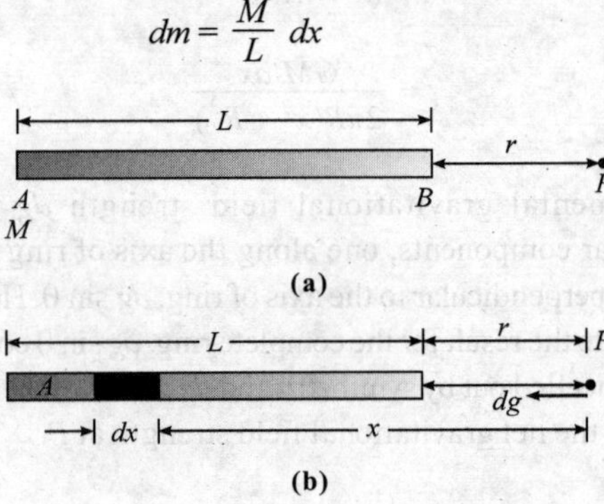

Figure 6.13

Now due to this dm, the gravitational field strength at point P is given as

$$dg = \frac{Gdm}{x^2}$$

$$= \frac{GM}{Lx^2}\,dx$$

Now due to complete rod the total gravitational field strength at point P is given by

$$g = \int dg = \int_r^{r+L} \frac{GM}{Lx^2}$$

or
$$g = \frac{GM}{L}\left[-\frac{1}{x}\right]_r^{r+L}$$

or
$$g = \frac{GM}{L}\left[\frac{1}{r} - \frac{1}{r+L}\right] \quad ...(6.16)$$

Case-II : At an equatorial point

Figure-6.14 shows a rod of mass M and length L and due to this rod we wish to find the net gravitational field at a point P on its equator (perpendicular bisector) as shown in figure-6.14.

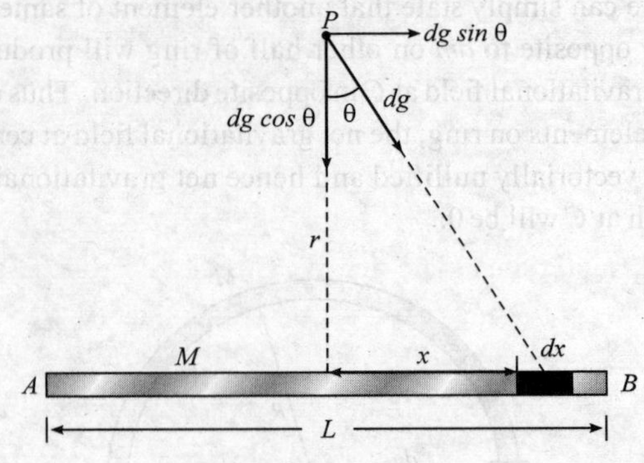

Figure 6.14

For this again we consider an element of width dx at a distance x from the centre of rod as shown. The mass of this element dx is given as

$$dm = \frac{M}{L}\,dx$$

Now let dg be the gravitational field strength at P due to the element of mass dm then dg is given as

$$dg = \frac{Gdm}{(x^2+r^2)}$$

or
$$= \frac{GM\,dx}{L(x^2+r^2)}$$

We resolve dg in two rectangular components $dg \sin\theta$ and $dg \cos\theta$, here on integration $dg \sin\theta$ gets cancelled out due to symmetry and $dg \cos\theta$ will be summed up. Thus the net gravitational field at point P is given as

$$g_p = \int dg\cos\theta = \int_{-1/2}^{+1/2} \frac{GMdx}{(x^2+r^2)} \cdot \frac{r}{\sqrt{x^2+r^2}}$$

or
$$= \frac{GMr}{L}\int_{-1/2}^{+1/2} \frac{dx}{(x^2+r^2)^{3/2}}$$

Here we put $x = r\tan\theta$

and $dx = r\sec^2\theta\,d\theta$

We get
$$g_p = \frac{GMr}{L}\int \frac{r\sec^2\theta\,d\theta}{r^3\sec^3\theta}$$

or
$$= \frac{GM}{Lr}\int \cos\theta\,d\theta$$

or
$$= \frac{GM}{Lr}[\sin\theta]$$

or
$$= \frac{GM}{Lr}\left[\frac{x}{\sqrt{x^2+r^2}}\right]_{-1/2}^{+1/2}$$

or $$= \frac{GM}{Lr}\left[\frac{L}{\sqrt{L^2+4r^2}}+\frac{L}{\sqrt{L^2+4r^2}}\right]$$

or $$= \frac{2GM}{r\sqrt{L^2+4r^2}} \quad \ldots(6.17)$$

6.3.5 Gravitational Field due to a Circular Arc

Figure-6.15 shows a circular arc AB of mass M, which subtend on angle ϕ at its centre O and we wish to find the gravitational field produced by the arc at its centre.

For this we consider on element on arc at an angular displacement θ from its angle bisector and of angular width $d\theta$ as shown in figure-6.15. The mass dm of this element of width $Rd\theta$ is given as

$$dm = \frac{M}{\phi}\,d\theta$$

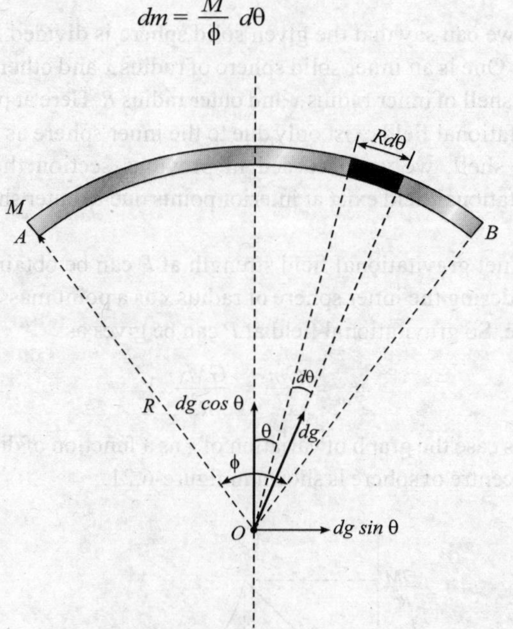

Figure 6.15

If dg be the gravitational field strength at O due to the element dm then we have

$$dg = \frac{Gdm}{R^2}$$

Now we resolve dg in two rectangular components, $dg\cos\theta$ along its angle bisector and another $dg\sin\theta$ perpendicular to its angle bisector. Here again we can state that on integration $dg\sin\theta$ will cancel out due to symmetry and $dg\cos\theta$ will be summed up. Thus net gravitational field strength at O due to complete arc will be given as

$$g_C = \int dg\cos\theta = \int_{-\phi/2}^{+\phi/2} \frac{Gdm}{R^2}\cos\theta$$

or $$= \int_{-\phi/2}^{+\phi/2} \frac{GM}{\phi R^2}\cos\theta\, d\theta$$

or $$= \frac{GM}{\phi R^2}\left[\sin\theta\right]_{-\phi/2}^{+\phi/2}$$

$$= \frac{2GM\sin\left(\frac{\phi}{2}\right)}{\phi R^2} \quad \ldots(6.18)$$

6.3.6 Gravitational Field Strength due to a Sphere

Care-I : Hollow sphere

Figure-6.16 shows a hollow sphere of mass M and radius R. If we think about the gravitational field in its surrounding, the direction must be along the arrows shown in its surrounding. Every mass placed in its surrounding must experience the gravitational force toward the centre of the shell. Thus we can state that it is because of its symmetrical geometrical shape and its uniform mass distribution.

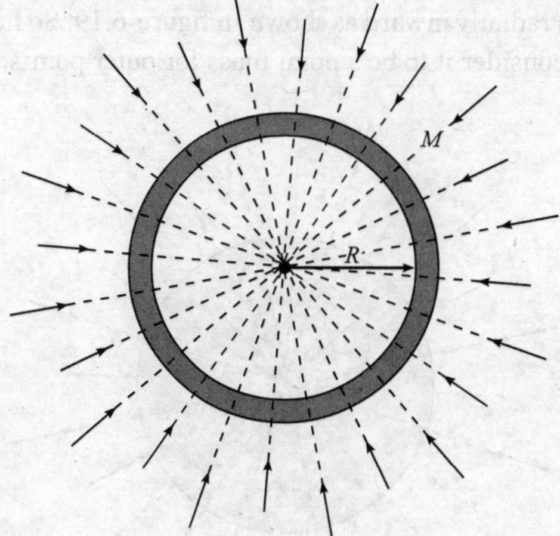

Figure 6.16

Thus we can state that for the case of a hollow spherical shell we consider its whole mass is concentrated at its centre and for outside points it behaves like a point mass.

Thus the gravitational field strength at different points due to a hollow spherical shell can be given as shown in figure-6.17.

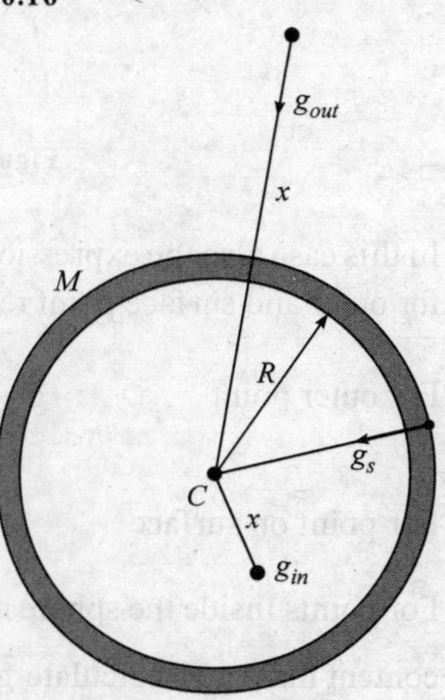

Figure 6.17

For outer points $g_{out} = \frac{GM}{x^2}$ [Behaving as a point mass]

For points on surface $g_s = \frac{GM}{R^2}$ [Behaving as a point mass]

For inner points $g_{in} = 0$ [As no mass is enclosed within it]

If we plot a variation graph for values of g with distance from centre, it is shown in figure-6.18.

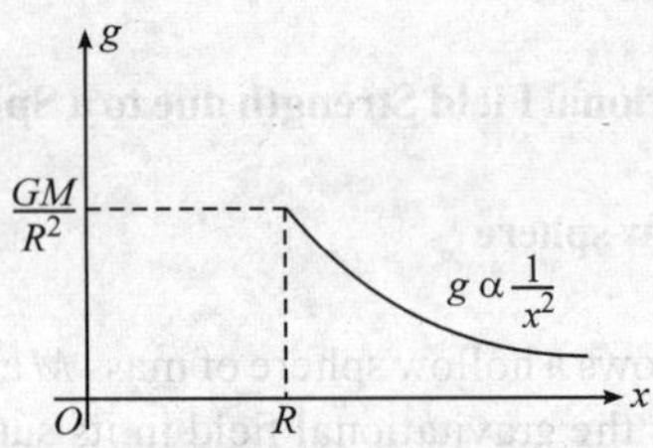

Figure 6.18

Case-II : Solid sphere

In case of a solid sphere also the direction of $\vec{g}$ at the nearby points is radially inward as shown in figure-6.19. So here also we can consider it to be a point mass for outer points.

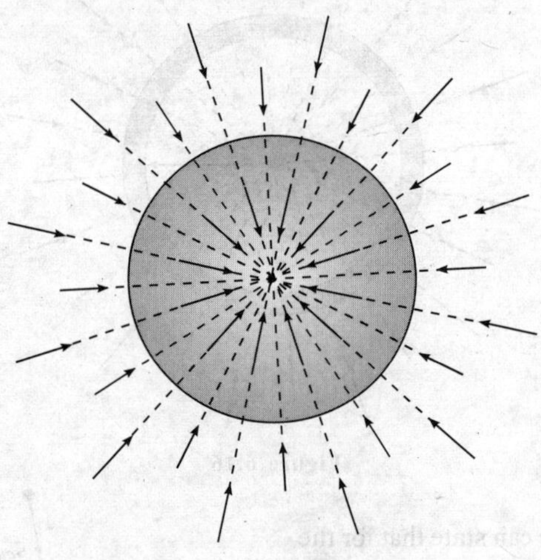

Figure 6.19

In this case also the expression for gravitational field strength for outer and surface point remains same. Thus we have

For outer point $g_{out} = \frac{GM}{x^2}$

For point on surface $g_s = \frac{GM}{R^2}$

For points inside the sphere now g is nonzero as there is mass content inside. To calculate $\vec{g}$ at interior points at a distance x from its centre, we consider an inner sphere of radius x as shown in figure-6.20. Say its mass is m, on the surface of which a point P exist where we wish to find the gravitational field, strength. The mass m is given as

$$m = \frac{M}{\frac{4}{3}\pi R^3} \times \frac{4}{3}\pi x^3 = \frac{M}{R^3} x^3 \quad \dots(6.19)$$

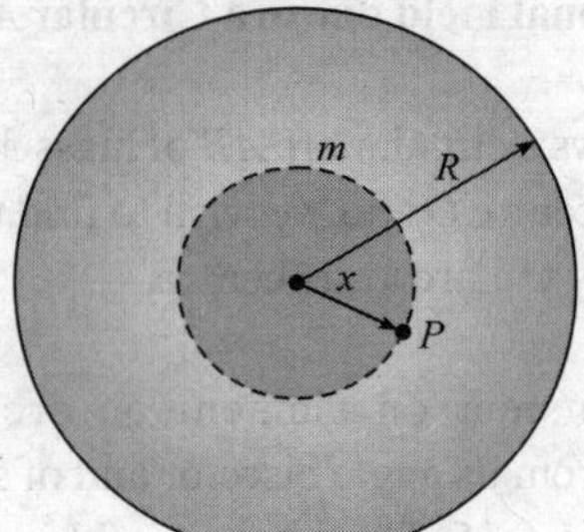

Figure 6.20

Now we can say that the given solid sphere is divided in two parts. One is an inner solid sphere of radius x and other is the outer shell of inner radius x and outer radius R. Here at point P gravitational field exist only due to the inner sphere as due to outer shell, we've discussed in previous section that, no gravitational field exist at interior points due to outer shell.

Thus net gravitational field strength at P can be obtained by considering the inner sphere of radius x as a point mass at the centre. So gravitational field at P can be gives as

$$g_{in} = \frac{Gm}{x^2} = \frac{GMx}{R^3} \quad \dots(6.20)$$

In this case the graph of variation of g as a function of distance from centre of sphere is shown in figure-6.21.

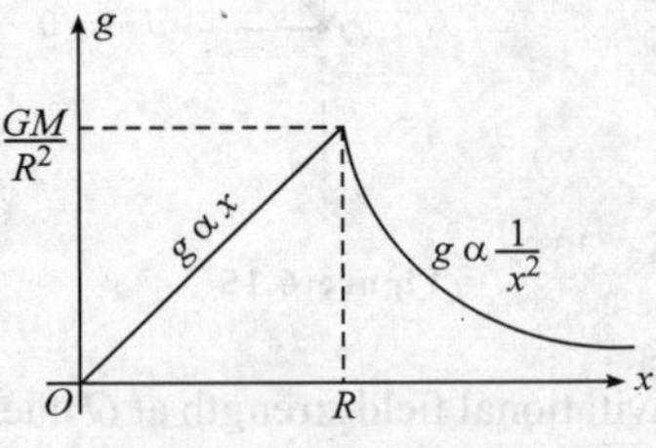

Figure 6.21

6.3.7 Gravitational Field Strength due to a Long Thread

Figure-6.22 shows a long thread of linear mass density λ kg/m and we wish to find the gravitational field strength at a point P situated at a distance r from the thread. Here we can state that the direction of gravitational field strength must be radially inward to the thread. For this as shown in figure we consider an element of width dx on thread at a distance x from point O. The mass dm of this element is given as

$$dm = \lambda\, dx \quad \dots(6.21)$$

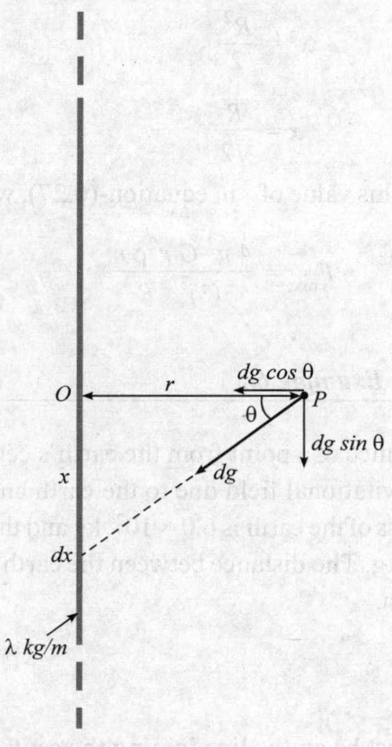

Figure 6.22

If dg be the gravitational field straight at point P due to the element dm, then dg can be given as

$$dg = \frac{Gdm}{(x^2 + r^2)} = \frac{G\lambda dx}{(x^2 + r^2)}$$

Here also from figure-6.22 we can see that dg can be resolved in rectangular components $dg \sin\theta$ and $dg \cos\theta$ where on integration $dg \sin\theta$ will be cancelled out and $dg \cos\theta$ will be summed up. Thus net gravitational field strength at P can be given as

$$g_P = \int dg \cos\theta$$

$$= \int_{-\infty}^{+\infty} \frac{G\lambda dx}{(x^2 + r^2)} \frac{r}{\sqrt{x^2 + r^2}}$$

$$= G\lambda r \int_{-\infty}^{+\infty} \frac{dx}{(x^2 + r^2)^{3/2}}$$

Here we substitute

$$x = r \tan\theta$$

and $\quad dx = r \sec^2\theta \, d\theta$

Changing the limits

$$x = -\infty \;\Rightarrow\; \theta = -\pi/2$$

and $\quad x = +\infty \;\Rightarrow\; \theta = +\pi/2$

Now we get $\quad g_P = G\lambda r \int_{-\pi/2}^{+\pi/2} \frac{r \sec^2\theta}{r^3 \sec^3\theta}$

$$= \frac{G\lambda}{r} \int_{-\pi/2}^{+\pi/2} \cos\theta \, d\theta$$

$$= \frac{G\lambda}{r} [\sin\theta]_{-\pi/2}^{+\pi/2}$$

$$= \frac{2G\lambda}{r} \quad \ldots (6.22)$$

6.3.8 Gravitational Field Strength Due to a Long Solid Cylinder

In case of a cylinder of uniform density we can qualitatively state that due to symmetry the direction of gravitational field strength must be again in radially inward direction directed to the axis of cylinder. If we wish to find the value of $\vec{g}$ at an outside point P_1, due to symmetry we can consider that whole mass of cylinder is concentrated uniformly on its axis and for outer points it will behave like a thread whose linear mass density can be given as

$$\lambda = \rho \,.\, 1 \,.\, \pi R^2 \quad \ldots (6.23)$$

[Mass of unit length]

Thus for an outer point P_1 the gravitational field strength can be given as

$$g = \frac{2G\lambda}{x}$$

$$g = \frac{2G\rho\pi R^2}{x} \quad \ldots (6.24)$$

Now for an interior point P_2 at a distance x from the axis of cylinder, we can consider an inner cylinder of radius x as shown in figure-6.23. The net gravitational field at point P_1 will only be due to this inner cylinder of radius x as due to the outer hollow cylinder, there will be no gravitational field at point P_1. Now if λ' be the linear mass density of the inner cylinder of radius x then λ' can be given as

$$\lambda' = \rho \,.\, 1 \,.\, \pi x^2 \quad \ldots (6.25)$$

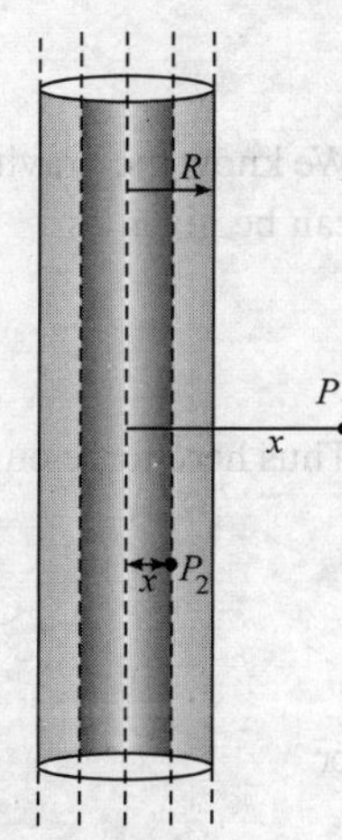

Figure 6.23

Now the gravitational field strength at point P_1 can be given as

$$g_{in} = \frac{2G\lambda'}{x}$$

$$= \frac{2G \,.\, \rho\pi x^2}{x}$$

$$= 2\,G\rho\pi x \quad \ldots (6.26)$$

Now we consider some examples to understand gravitational field strength in detail.

Illustrative Example 6.4

A ring of radius R is made from a thin wire of radius r. If ρ is the density of the material of wire then what will be the gravitational force exerted by the ring on the material particle of mass m placed on the axis of ring at a distance x from its centre. Show that the force will be maximum when $x = R/\sqrt{2}$ and the maximum value of force will be given as

$$F_{max} = \frac{4\pi^2 G r^2 \rho m}{(3)^{3/2} R^2}$$

Solution

The mass of ring can be given as

$$M = \rho \pi r^2 (2\pi R)$$

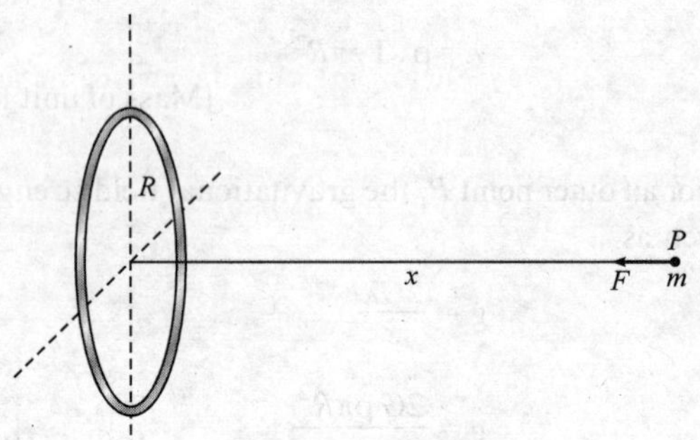

Figure 6.24

We know the gravitational field due to the ring at a distance x can be given as

$$g_P = \frac{GMx}{(x^2+R^2)^{3/2}}$$

Thus here force on mass m placed at point P can be given as

$$F = mg_P = \frac{GMmx}{(x^2+R^2)^{3/2}}$$

or $$F = \frac{2G\rho\pi^2 r^2 mx}{(x^2+R^2)^{3/2}} \quad \ldots(6.27)$$

If F is to be maximum, we have

$$\frac{dF}{dx} = 0$$

or $$\frac{dF}{dx} = 2\pi^2 G r^2 \rho m R \left[\frac{(R^2+x^2)^{3/2} - 3x^2(R^2+x^2)^{1/2}}{(R^2+x^2)^3}\right] = 0$$

or $$R^2 + x^2 - 3x^2 = 0$$

or $$x^2 = \frac{R^2}{2}$$

or $$x = \frac{R}{\sqrt{2}}$$

Substituting this value of x in equation-(6.27), we get

$$F_{max} = \frac{4\pi^2 G r^2 \rho m}{(3)^{3/2} R}$$

Illustrative Example 6.5

Find the distance of a point from the earth's centre where the resultant gravitational field due to the earth and the moon is zero. The mass of the earth is 6.0×10^{24} kg and that of the moon is 7.4×10^{22} kg. The distance between the earth and the moon is 4.0×10^5 km.

Solution

The point must be on the line joining the centres of the earth and the moon and in between them. Let the distance of this point from earth is x then gravitational field at this point due to earth is

$$g_e = \frac{GM_e}{x^2} = \frac{G \times 6 \times 10^{24}\text{ kg}}{x^2}$$

The gravitational field due to the moon at this point is

$$g_m = \frac{GM_m}{(4.0\times10^5 - x)^2} = \frac{G \times 7.4 \times 10^{22}}{(4.0\times10^5 - x)^2}$$

These fields are in opposite directions. For the resultant field to be zero

$$g_e = g_m$$

or $$\frac{6\times10^{24}}{x^2} = \frac{7.4\times10^{22}}{(4.0\times10^5 - x)^2}$$

or $$\frac{x}{4.0\times10^5 - x} = \sqrt{\frac{6\times10^{24}}{7.4\times10^{22}}} = 9$$

or $$x = 3.6 \times 10^5 \text{ km}$$

Illustrative Example 6.6

A uniform ring of mass m and radius a is placed directly above a uniform sphere of mass M and of equal radius. The centre of the ring is at a distance $\sqrt{3}a$ from the centre of the sphere. Find the gravitational force exerted by the sphere on the ring.

Solution

The gravitational field at any point on the ring due to the sphere is equal to the field due to a single particle of mass M

placed at the centre of the sphere. Thus, the force on the ring due to the sphere is also equal to the force on it by a particle of mass M placed at this point. By Newton's third law it is equal to the force on the particle by the ring. Now the gravitational field due to the ring at a distance $d = \sqrt{3}\,a$ on its axis is given as

$$g = \frac{Gmd}{(a^2 + d^2)^{3/2}} = \frac{\sqrt{3}\,Gm}{8\,a^2}$$

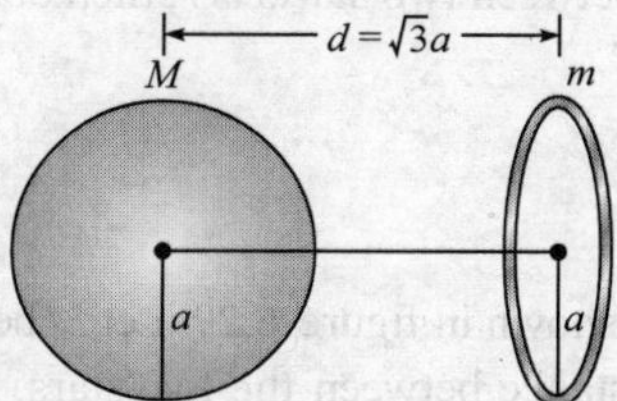

Figure 6.25

The force on sphere of mass M placed here is

$$F = Mg$$

$$= \frac{\sqrt{3}GMm}{8\,a^2}$$

Illustrative Example 6.7

The density inside a solid sphere of radius a is given by $\rho = \rho_0\, a/r$ where ρ_0 is the density at the surface and r denotes the distance from the centre. Find the gravitational field due to this sphere at a distance x from its centre.

Solution

To find the gravitational field at a point situated at a distance x from centre we consider elemental spherical shells of radius r and width dr as shown in figure-6.26. The mass of this shell is

$$dm = \rho \cdot 4\pi r^2\, dr$$

$$= \rho_0 \frac{a}{r} \times 4\pi r^2\, dr$$

$$= 4\pi\, \rho_0\, ar\, dr$$

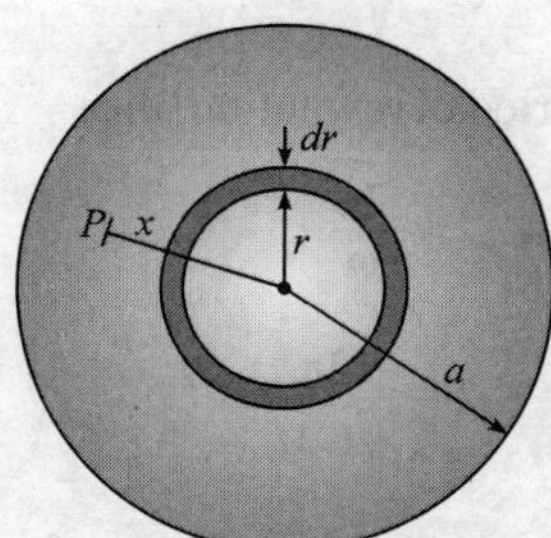

Figure 6.26

Now due to this shell gravitational field at point P is dg then dg is given as

$$dg = \frac{Gdm}{x^2}$$

$$= \frac{4\pi G\rho_0 ardr}{x^2}$$

Now net gravitational field at point P will be due to all the elemental shells within radius 0 to x, which is given as

$$g = \int dg = \int_0^x \frac{4\pi\rho_0 Gardr}{x^2}$$

$$= \frac{4\pi\rho_0 aG}{x^2}\int_0^x r\,dr$$

$$= \frac{4\pi\rho_0 aG}{x^2}\left[\frac{r^2}{2}\right]_0^x = 2\pi\rho_0 aG$$

Illustrative Example 6.8

A spherical hollow cavity is made in a lead sphere of radius R such that its surface touches the outside surface of the lead sphere and passes through its centre. The mass of the lead sphere before hollowing was M. What is the force of attraction that this sphere would exert on a particle of mass m which lies at a distance d from the centre of the lead sphere on the straight line joining the centres of the sphere and the hollow cavity (as shown in figure-6.27)

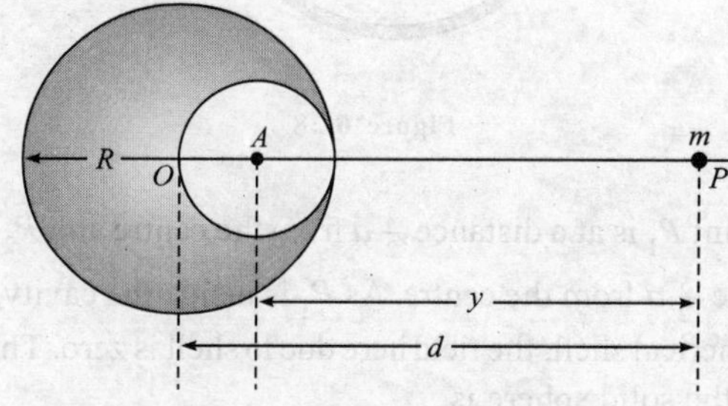

Figure 6.27

Solution

To calculate the force of attraction on the point mass m we should calculate the force due to the solid sphere and subtract from this the force which the mass of the hollowed cavity would have exerted on m, i.e.,

$$F = \frac{GmM}{d^2} - \frac{GmM'}{y^2}$$

From figure-6.27 $\quad y = [d - (R/2)]$

Here M and M' can be given as

$$M = \frac{4}{3}\pi R^3 \rho$$

and $$M' = \frac{4}{3}\pi\left(\frac{R}{2}\right)^3 \rho = \frac{M}{8}$$

So $$F = \frac{GmM}{d^2} - \frac{Gm(M/8)}{[d-(R/2)]^2}$$

$$= \frac{GMm}{d^2}\left[1 - \frac{1}{8[1-(R/2d)]^2}\right]$$

Illustrative Example 6.9

A uniform solid sphere of mass M and radius a is surrounded symmetrically by a uniform thin spherical shell of equal mass and radius $2a$. Find the gravitational field at a distance (a) $\frac{3}{2}a$ from the centre, (b) $\frac{5}{2}a$ from the centre.

Solution

The situation is shown in figure-6.28.

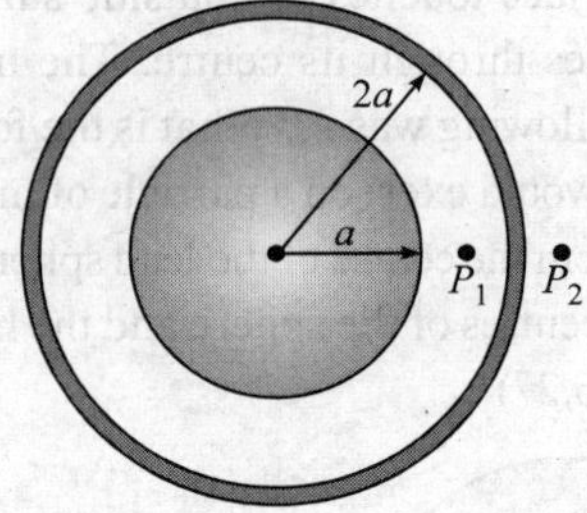

Figure 6.28

The point P_1 is at a distance $\frac{3}{2}a$ from the centre and P_2 is at a distance $\frac{5}{2}a$ from the centre. As P_1 is inside the cavity of the thin spherical shell, the field here due to shell is zero. The field due to the solid sphere is

$$g = \frac{GM}{\left(\frac{3}{2}a\right)^2} = \frac{4GM}{9a^2}$$

This is also the resultant field. The direction is towards the centre. The point P_2 is outside the sphere as well as the shell. Both may be replaced by single particles of the same mass at the centre. The field due to each of them is

$$g = \frac{GM}{\left(\frac{5}{2}a\right)^2} = \frac{4GM}{25a^2}$$

The resultant field is $g = 2g' = \dfrac{8GM}{25a^2}$ towards the centre.

Illustrative Example 6.10

Two small dense stars rotate about their common centre of mass, as a binary system with the period of 1 year for each. One star double of the mass of the other and the mass of the lighter one is of 1/3 the mass of the sun, given the distance between the earth and the sun is R.

If the distance between two starts is r, then obtain the relation between r and R.

Solution

The situation is shown in figure-6.29. Let M be the mass of sun and r be the distance between the two stars. The distance of two stars from the centre of the mass of the system r_1 and r_2 are given as

$$r_1 = r\frac{m_2}{m_1+m_2} = \frac{2}{3}r$$

and $$r_2 = r\frac{m_2}{m_1+m_2} = \frac{r}{3}$$

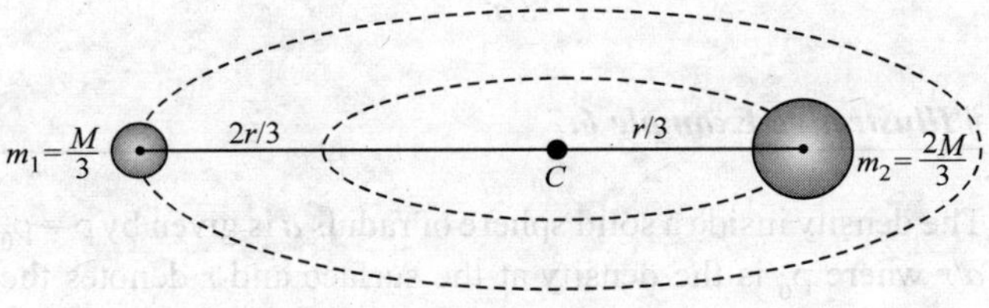

Figure 6.29

The gravitational force on m_2 is given by

$$F_g = \frac{Gm_1m_2}{r^2} = \frac{2}{9}\frac{GM^2}{r^2}$$

As for circular motion of m_2, we have

$$\frac{2}{9}\frac{GM^2}{r^2} = m_2r_2\omega^2 = \left(\frac{2}{3}M\right)\left(\frac{r}{3}\right)\omega^2$$

Where ω is the angular speed of the either star, solving we get

$$\omega = \sqrt{\frac{GM}{r^3}}$$

If T be the time period of revolution, then

$$T = \frac{2\pi}{\omega}$$

or $$T = \frac{2\pi}{\sqrt{GM}}r^{3/2} \qquad \ldots(6.28)$$

We know the time periods of revolution of earth around sun is given as

$$T^2 = \frac{4\pi^2 R^3}{GM} \quad ...(6.29)$$

According to the problem equating equation-(6.28) and (6.29), we get

$$r = R$$

Practice Exercise 6.2

(i) Two concentric spherical shells have masses M_1, M_2 and radii R_1, R_2 $(R_1 < R_2)$. What is the force exerted by this system on a particle of mass m_1 if it is placed at a distance $(R_1 + R_2)/2$ from the centre ?

$[\frac{4GM_1m}{(R_1+R_2)^2}]$

(ii) If the distance between the centres of Earth and Moon is D and mass of Earth is 81 times that of Moon. At what distance from the centre of Earth gravitational field will be zero ?

$[9D/10]$

(iii) A solid sphere of mass m and radius r is placed inside a hollow thin spherical shell of mass M and radius R as shown in figure-6.30. A particle of mass m' is placed on the line joining the two centres at a distance x from the point of contact of the sphere and the shell. Find the magnitude of the resultant gravitational force on this particle due to the sphere and the shell if (a) $r < x < 2r$, (b) $2r < x < 2R$ and (c) $x > 2R$.

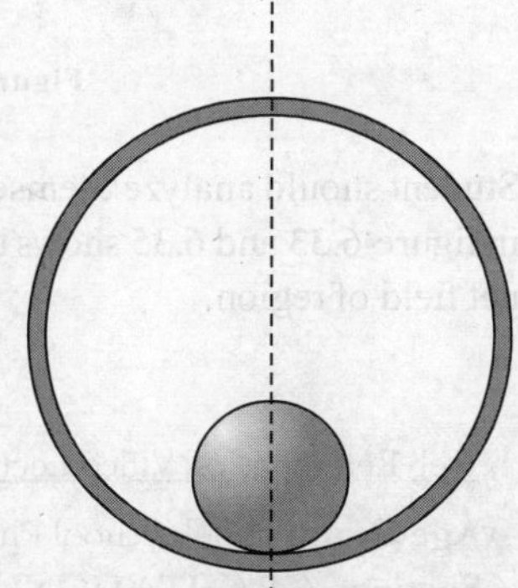

Figure 6.30

[(a) $\frac{Gmm'(x-r)}{r^3}$ (b) $\frac{Gmm'}{(x-r)^2}$ (c) $\frac{GMm'}{(x-R)^2} + \frac{Gmm'}{(x-r)^2}$]

(iv) The gravitational field in a region is given by $(2\hat{i} + 2\hat{j})$ N/kg. What is the work done by an external agent in slowly shifting a particle of mass 10 kg from origin to point (5, 4).

[– 180 J]

(v) Inside a uniform sphere of density ρ there is a spherical cavity whose centre is at a distance l from the centre of the sphere. Find the strength of the gravitational field inside the cavity.

Ans. $[\frac{4\pi}{3} G\rho l]$

(vi) A small point mass m is placed at the centre of curvature of a circular arc of radius R and mass $3m$ as shown in figure-6.31. Find the net gravitational force acting on the point mass.

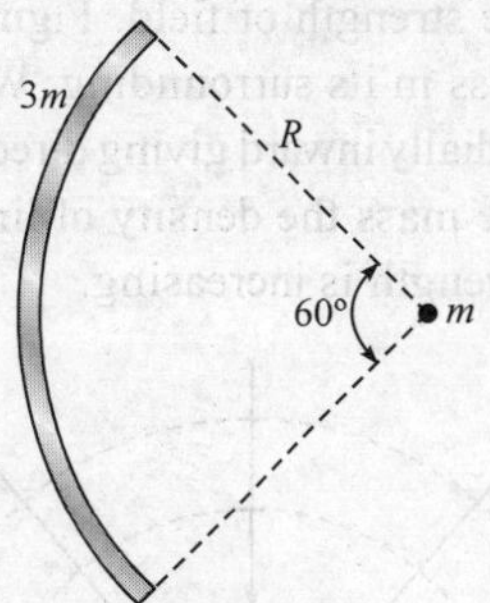

Figure 6.31

$[\frac{9Gm^2}{\pi R^2}]$

(vii) A small point mass m is to be thrown with such a speed at a distance x from the axis of a long cylinder of radius R and density ρ, so that m starts revolving around the cylinder in a circular orbit of radius x with centre on the axis of cylinder. Find the speed with which point mass is thrown.

$[R\sqrt{2G\rho\pi}]$

(viii) Figure-6.32 shows two uniform rods of mass M and length l placed on two perpendicular lines. A small point mass m is placed on the point of intersection of the two lines. Find the net gravitational force experienced by m.

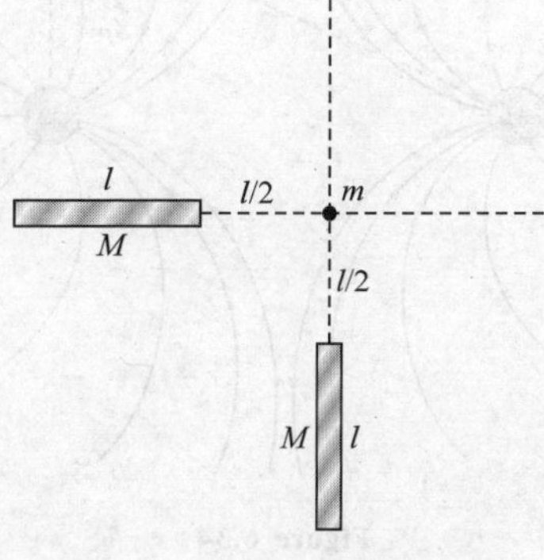

Figure 6.32

$[\frac{4\sqrt{2}\,GMm}{3l^2}]$

6.4 Gravitational Lines of Forces

Gravitational field can also be represented by lines of force. A line of force is drawn in such a way that at each point the direction of field is tangent to line that passes through the point. Thus tangent to any point on a line of force gives the direction of gravitational field at that point. By convention lines of force are drawn in such a way that their density is proportional to the strength of field. Figure-6.33 shows the field of a point mass in its surrounding. We can see that the lines of force are radially inward giving direction of field and as we go closer to the mass the density of lines is more which shows that field strength is increasing.

Figure 6.33

Figure-6.34 shows the configuration of field lines for a system of two equal masses separated by a given distance.

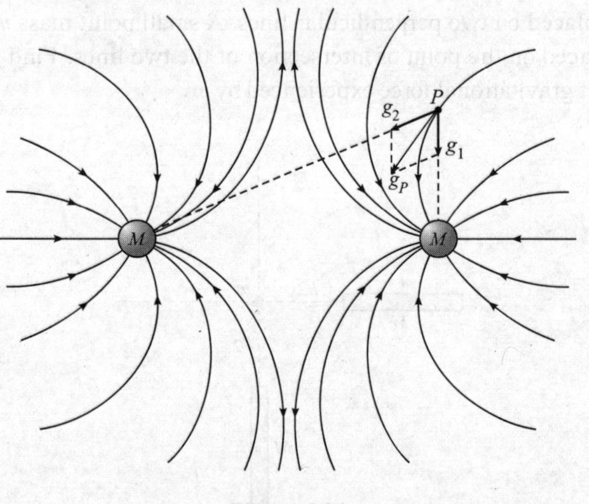

Figure 6.34

Here we can see that there is no point where any two lines of force intersects or meet. The reason is obvious that at one point in space there can never be two directions of gravitational fields. Students should note one more point that a line of force gives the direction of net gravitational field in the region. As shown in figure-6.35 if we consider a point P, there exist two gravitational field strengths $\vec{g}_1$ and $\vec{g}_2$ at P in different directions due to the two independent masses. Here we can see that the resultant gravitational field at P, $\vec{g}_P$ is along the tangent of the line of force passing through P. Thus in a system of two or more particles, gravitational lines of force are drawn in such a way that the net gravitational field strength direction at a point in space is along the tangent of the respective line of force. Figure-6.35 shows the configuration of gravitational field lines for the Earth and the Moon. Student should verify themselves about shape of these lines at different points in space

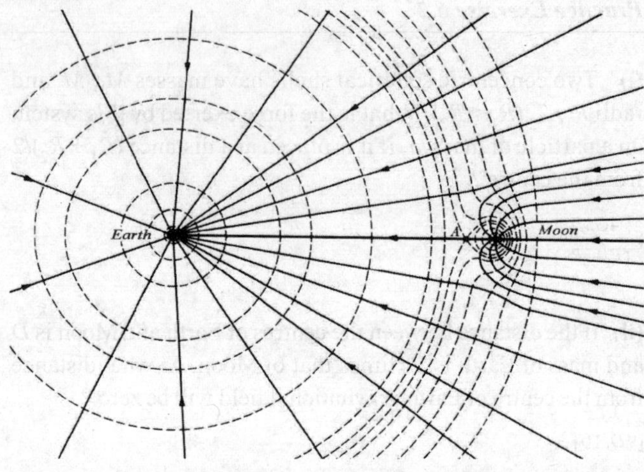

Figure 6.35

Student should analyze themselves that the dotted lines shown in figure-6.33 and 6.35 shows the equipotential surfaces for the net field of region.

> Web Reference of Video Lectures at www.physicsgalaxy.com
> **Age Group -** High School Physics | Age 17-19 Years
> **Section -** GRAVITATION
> **Topic -** Gravitation Theory
> **Module Number -** 8 and 20

6.5 Gravitational Field Strength of Earth

We can consider earth to be a very large sphere of mass M_e and radius R_e. Gravitational field strength due to earth is also regarded as acceleration due to gravity or gravitational acceleration. Now we find the values of g at different points due to earth.

6.5.1 Value of g on Earth's Surface

If g_s be the gravitational field strength at a point A on the surface of earth, then it can be easily obtained by using the result of a solid sphere. Thus for earth, value of g_s can be given as

$$g_s = \frac{GM_e}{R_e^2} \quad \ldots (6.30)$$

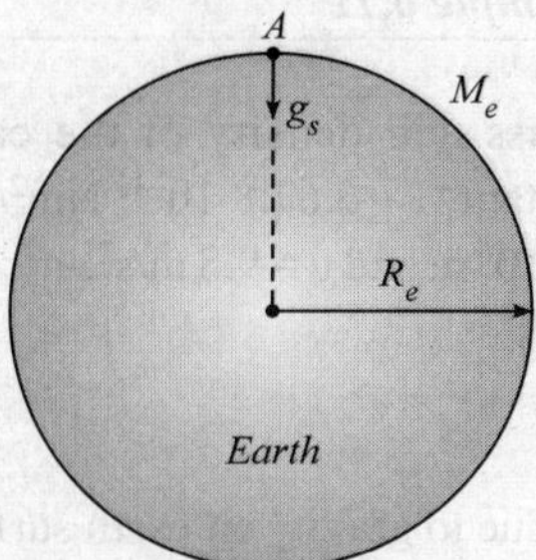

Figure 6.36

6.5.2 Value of *g* at a Height *h* Above the Earth's Surface

If we wish to find the value of *g* at a point *P* as shown in figure-6.37 at a height *h* above the Earth's surface. Then the value can be obtained as

$$g_h = \frac{GM_e}{(R_e+h)^2} \quad \ldots(6.31)$$

or
$$g_h = \frac{GM_e}{R_e^2\left(1+\frac{h}{R_e}\right)^2} = \frac{g_s}{\left(1+\frac{h}{R_e}\right)^2} \quad \ldots(6.32)$$

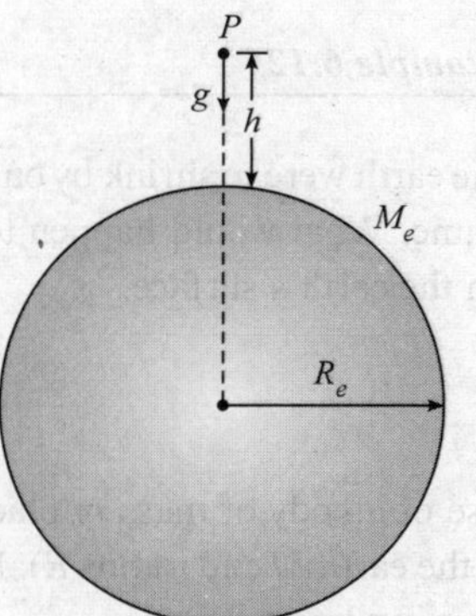

Figure 6.37

If point *P* is very close to Earth's surface then for $h << R_e$ we can rewrite the expression in equation-(6.32) as

$$g_h = g_s\left(1+\frac{h}{R_e}\right)^{-2}$$

$$\simeq g_s\left(1-\frac{2h}{R_e}\right) \quad \ldots(6.33)$$

[Using binomial approximation]

6.5.3 Value of *g* at a Depth *h* Below the Earth's Surface

If we find the value of *g* inside the volume of earth at a depth *h* below the earth's surface at point *P* as shown in figure-6.38, then we can use the result of *g* inside a solid sphere as

$$g_{in} = \frac{GM_e x}{R_e^3}$$

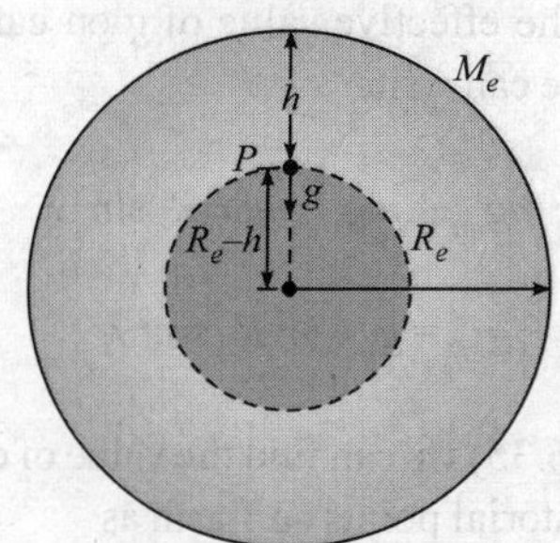

Figure 6.38

Here *x*, the distance of point from centre of earth is given as

$$x = R_e - h$$

Thus we have
$$g_h = \frac{GM_e(R_e-h)}{R_e^3} = g_s\left(1-\frac{h}{R_e}\right) \quad \ldots(6.34)$$

From equation-(6.30), (6.32) and (6.34) we can say that the value of *g* at earth's surface is maximum and as we move above the earth's surface or we go below the surface of earth, the value of *g* decreases.

6.5.4 Effect of Earth's Rotation on Value of *g*

Let us consider a body of mass *m* placed on Earth's surface at a latitude λ as shown in figure-6.39 This mass experiences a force mg_s towards the centre of earth and a centrifugal force $m\omega_e^2 R_e \sin\lambda$ relative to Earth's surface as shown in figure. If *N* is the normal contact force on mass then for equilibrium of body we have

$$N + m\omega^2 R_e \sin^2\lambda = mg_s$$

or
$$N = mg_s - m\omega^2 Re \sin^2\lambda$$

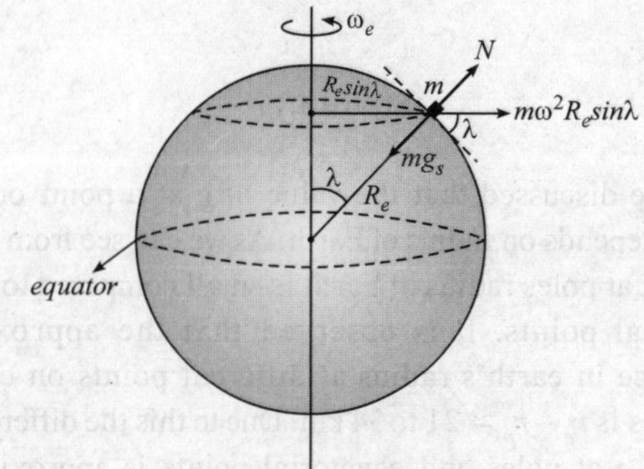

Figure 6.39

Here we can see that the normal contact force on body is less then mg_s on Earth's surface. At a point on Earth surface we don't feel this centrifugal force but actually it acts on us and due to this the effective weight of mass is decreased. If we consider g_{eff} as the effective value of g on earth surface at a latitude λ then we can write

$$mg_{eff} = mg_s - m\omega_e^2 R_e \sin^2\lambda$$

or
$$g_{eff} = g_s - \omega^2 R_e \sin^2\lambda \qquad \ldots(6.35)$$

From equation-(6.35) we can find the value of effective gravity at poles and equatorial points on Earth as

At poles $\lambda = 0 \Rightarrow g_{\text{poles}} = g_s = 9.83\text{ m/s}^2$

At equator $\lambda = \frac{\pi}{2} \Rightarrow g_{\text{equator}} = g_s - \omega^2 R_e = 9.78\text{ m/s}^2$

Thus we can see that the body if placed at poles of Earth, it will only have a spin, not circular motion so there is no reduction in value of g at poles due to rotation of earth. Thus at poles value of g on Earth surface is maximum and at equator it is minimum. But an average we take 9.8 m/s^2, the value of g everywhere on earth's surface.

6.5.5 Effect of Shape of Earth on Value of *g*

Till now we've considered that earth is spherical in its shape but this is not actually true. Due to some geological and astronomical reasons, the shape of earth is not exact spherical. It is ellipsoidal as shown in figure-6.40.

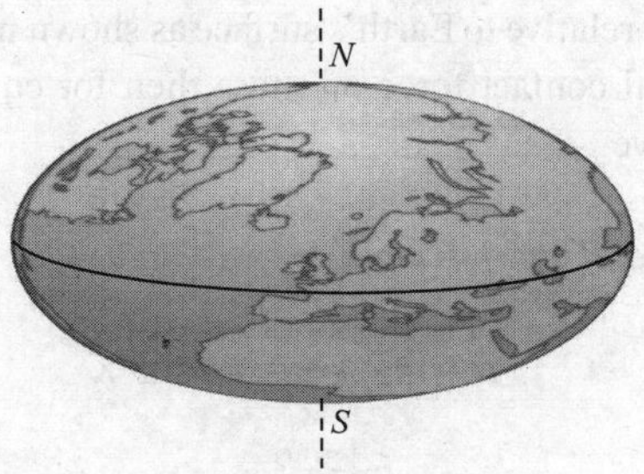

Figure 6.40

As we've discussed that the value of g at a point on earth surface depends on radius of Earth. As we can see from figure-6.40 that at poles radius of Earth is small compared to that at equatorial points. It is observed that the approximate difference in earth's radius at different points on equator and poles is $r_e - r_p \simeq 21$ to 34 km. Due to this the difference in value of g at poles and equatorial points is approximately $g_p - g_e \simeq 0.02$ to 0.04 m/s^2, which is very small. So for numerical calculations, generally, we ignore this factor while taking the value g and we assume Earth spherical in shape.

Illustrative Example 6.11

Calculate the mass and density of the earth. Given that gravitational constant $G = 6.67 \times 10^{-11}\text{ Nm}^2/\text{kg}^2$, the radius of the earth $= 6.37 \times 10^6$ m and $g = 9.8\text{ m/s}^2$.

Solution

The acceleration due to gravity on earth surface is given as

$$g_s = \frac{GM_e}{R_e^2}$$

or
$$M_e = \frac{g_s R_e^2}{G} = \frac{9.8\times(6.37\times10^6)^2}{6.67\times10^{-11}}$$
$$= 6 \times 10^{24}\text{ kg}$$

If ρ be the density of earth, then

$$M = \frac{4}{3}\pi R^3 \times \rho$$

or
$$\rho = \frac{3M}{4\pi R^3} = \frac{3\times(6\times10^{24})}{4\times3.14\times(6.37\times10^6)^3}$$
$$= 5.5 \times 10^3\text{ kg/m}^3$$

Illustrative Example 6.12

If the radius of the earth were to shrink by one percent, its mass remaining the same. What would happen to the acceleration due to gravity on the earth's surface.

Solution

Consider the case of a body of mass m placed on the earth's surface (mass of the earth M and radius R). If g is acceleration due to gravity, then we know that

$$g_s = \frac{GM_e}{R_e^2} \qquad \ldots(6.36)$$

Now, when the radius is reduced by 1%, i.e., radius becomes 0.99 R, let acceleration due to gravity be g', then

$$g' = \frac{GM}{(0.99R)^2} \qquad \ldots(6.37)$$

From equation-(6.36) and (6.37), we get

$$\frac{g'}{g} = \frac{R^2}{(0.99R)^2} = \frac{1}{(0.99)^2}$$

or
$$g' = g \times \left(\frac{1}{0.99}\right)^2$$

or
$$g' = 1.02\, g$$

Thus, the value of g is increased by 2%.

Illustrative Example 6.13

At what rate should the earth rotate so that the apparent g at the equator becomes zero ? What will be the length of the day in this situation ?

Solution

At earth's equator effective value of gravity is

$$g_{eq} = g_s - \omega^2 R_e$$

If g_{eff} at equator to be zero, we have

$$g_s - \omega^2 R_e = 0$$

or $$\omega = \sqrt{\frac{g_s}{R_e}}$$

Thus length of the day will be

$$T = \frac{2\pi}{\omega} = 2\pi\sqrt{\frac{R_e}{g_s}}$$

$$= 2 \times 3.14\sqrt{\frac{6.4\times10^6}{9.8}} = 5074.77 \text{ s}$$

$$\simeq 84.57 \text{ min.}$$

Illustrative Example 6.14

Calculate the acceleration due to gravity at the surface of Mars if its diameter is 6760 km and mass one-tenth that of earth. The diameter of earth is 12742 km and acceleration due to gravity on earth is 9.8 m/s^2.

Solution

We know that $$g = \left(\frac{GM}{R^2}\right)$$

So $$\frac{g_M}{g_E} = \left(\frac{M_M}{M_E}\right)\left(\frac{R_E}{R_M}\right)^2 = \left(\frac{1}{10}\right)\left(\frac{12742}{6760}\right)^2$$

$$\Rightarrow \quad \frac{g_M}{g_E} = 0.35 \quad \text{or} \quad g_M = 9.8 \times 0.35 = 3.48 \text{ m/s}^2$$

Illustrative Example 6.15

Two equal masses m and m are hung from a balance whose scale pans differ in vertical height by h. Calculate the error in weighing, if any, in terms of density of earth ρ.

Solution

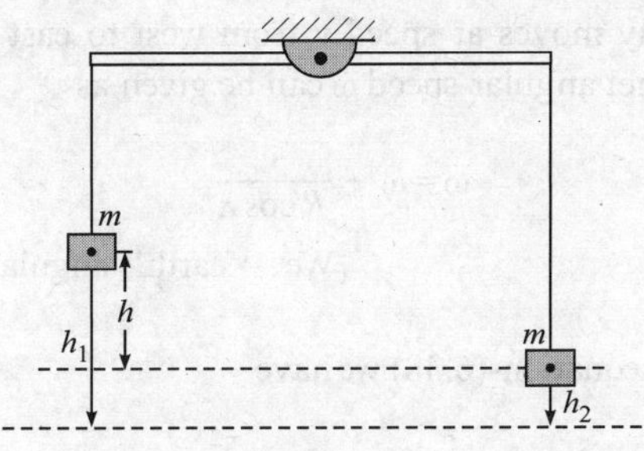

Figure 6.41

As with height 'g' varies as

$$g' = \frac{g}{[1+h/R]^2} = g\left[1 - \frac{2h}{R}\right]$$

And in accordance with figure-6.41, $h_1 > h_2$, so W_1 will be lesser than W_2 and

$$W_2 - W_1 = mg_2 - mg_1 = 2mg\left[\frac{h_1}{R} - \frac{h_2}{R}\right]$$

or $$W_2 - W_1 = 2m\frac{GM}{R^2}\frac{h}{R}$$

$$\left[\text{As } g = \frac{GM}{R^2} \text{ and } (h_1 - h_2) = h\right]$$

or $$W_2 - W_1 = \frac{2mhG}{R^3}\left(\frac{4}{3}\pi R^3\rho\right) = \frac{8}{3}\pi\rho Gmh$$

$$\left[\text{As } M = \frac{4}{3}\pi R^3\rho\right]$$

Illustrative Example 6.16

Calculate the apparent weight of a body of mass m at a latitude λ when it is moving with speed v on the surface of the earth from west to east at the same latitude.

Solution

If W be the apparent weight of body at latitude λ then from figure-6.42, we have

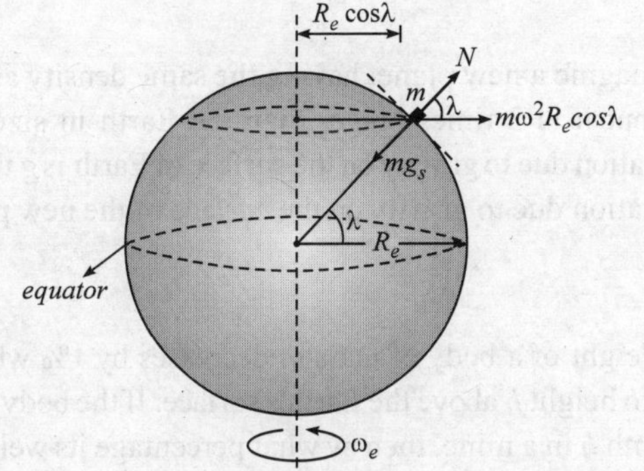

Figure 6.42

$$W = mg - m\omega^2 R \cos^2\lambda \qquad \dots(6.38)$$

When body moves at speed v from west to east relative to earth, its net angular speed ω can be given as

$$\omega=\omega_e+\frac{v}{R\cos\lambda}$$

[We $\rightarrow$ earth's angular velocity]

Now from equation-(6.38) we have

$$W=mg-m\left[\omega_e+\frac{v}{R\cos\lambda}\right]^2 R\cos^2\lambda$$

or
$$W=mg-m\left[\omega_e^2+\frac{v^2}{R^2\cos^2\lambda}+\frac{2\omega_e v}{R\cos\lambda}\right]R\cos^2\lambda$$

$$=mg-m\omega_e^2 R\cos^2\lambda-mv^2-2m\omega_e v\cos\lambda$$

$$=mg\left(1-\frac{\omega_e^2 R\cos^2\lambda}{g}-\frac{2\omega_e v\cos\lambda}{g}\right)$$

[Neglecting mv^2 as being very small]

Web Reference of Video Lectures at www.physicsgalaxy.com

Age Group - High School Physics | Age 17-19 Years
Section - GRAVITATION
Topic - Gravitation Theory
Module Number - 21 and 29

Practice Exercise 6.3

(i) Earth's mass is 80 times that of the moon and their diameters are 12800 and 3200 kms respectively. What is the value of g at the moon ? g on earth = 980 cm/s^2.

[196 cm/s^2]

(ii) The diameter of a planet is four times that of the earth. Find the time period of a pendulum on the planet, if it is a second pendulum on the earth. Take the mean density of the planet equal to that of the earth,

[1 s]

(iii) Imagine a new planet having the same density as that of Earth but it is 3 times bigger than the Earth in size. If the acceleration due to gravity on the surface of Earth is g then find acceleration due to gravity on the surface of the new planet.

[3g]

(iv) Weight of a body of mass m decreases by 1% when it is raised to height h above the Earth's surface. If the body is taken to a depth h in a mine, then by what percentage its weight will increase/decrease.

[decrease by 0.5%]

(v) A tunnel is dug along a chord of the earth at a perpendicular distance $R_e/2$ from the earth's centre. The wall of the tunnel may be assumed to be frictionless. Find the force exerted by the wall on a particle of mass m when it is at a distance x from the centre of the tunnel.

$[\frac{GM_e m}{2R_e^2}]$

(vi) Find the height over the earth's surface at which the weight of a body becomes half of its value at the surface.

[$(\sqrt{2}-1)$ times the radius of the earth]

(vii) A body is weighed by a spring balance to be 1.000 kg at the north pole. How much will it weight at the equator ? Account for the earth's rotation only. Take g_{pole} = 9.830 m/s^2. and R_e = 6400 km.

[0.9966 kg]

(viii) A body is suspended on a spring balance in a ship sailing along the equator with a speed v. Show that the scale reading will be very close to $W_0(1 \pm 2\,\omega v/g)$ where ω is the angular speed of the earth and W_0 is the scale reading when the ship is at rest. Explain also the significance of plus or minus sign.

6.6 Gravitational Potential Energy

We've already discussed that potential energy of a system is defined as work done in assembling a system. The gravitational potential energy of a system is defined, in two ways. These are

(i) Interaction Energy

(ii) Self Energy

6.6.1 Interaction Energy

This energy exist in a system of particles due to the interaction forces between the particles of system. Analytically this term is defined as the work done against the interaction of system forces in assembling the given configuration of particles. To understand this we take a simple example of interaction energy of two points masses.

Fiugre-6.43(a) shows a system of two point masses m_1 and m_2 placed at a distance r apart in space. Here if we wish to find the interaction potential energy of the two masses, this must be the work done in bringing the two masses from infinity (zero interaction state) to this configuration. For this we first fix m_1 at its position and bring m_2 slowly from infinity to its location.

If in the process m_2 is at a distance x from m_1 then force on it is

$$F = -\frac{Gm_1m_2}{x^2}\,\hat{i} \qquad \ldots(6.39)$$

(a)

(b)

Figure 6.43

This force is applied by the gravitational field of m_1 on m_2. If it is further displaced by a distance dx toward m_1 then work done by the field is

$$dW = \overline{\boldsymbol{F}} \cdot \overline{\boldsymbol{dx}}$$

$$= \frac{Gm_1m_2}{x^2}\,dx$$

Now in bringing m_2 from infinity to a position at a distance r from m_1 the total work done by the field is

$$W = \int dW - \int_{\infty}^{r} \frac{Gm_1m_2}{x^2}\,dx$$

$$= -Gm_1m_2\left[-\frac{1}{x}\right]_{\infty}^{r}$$

$$W = +\frac{Gm_1m_2}{r} \qquad \ldots(6.40)$$

Thus during the process field of system has done $\frac{Gm_1m_2}{r}$ amount of work. This work is positive because the displacement of body is in the direction of force.

Initially when the separation between m_1 and m_2 was very large (at infinity) there was no interaction between them. We conversely say that as a reference when there is no interaction the interaction energy of the system is zero and during the process system forces (gravitational forces) are doing work so system energy will decrease and becomes negative (as initial energy was zero). As a consequence we can state that in general if system forces are attractive, in assembling a system of particles work will be done by the system and it will spend energy in assembling itself. Thus finally the interaction energy of system will be negative. On the other hand if in a given system of particles, the system forces are repulsive, then in assembling a system some external forces have to do work against the system forces and in this case some work must be done by external forces on the system hence finally the interaction energy of the system of particles must be positive.

In above example as work is done by the gravitational forces of the system of two masses, the interaction energy of system must be negative and it can be given as

$$U_{12} = -\frac{Gm_1m_2}{r} \qquad \ldots(6.41)$$

As gravitational forces are always attractive, the gravitational potential energy is always taken negative.

6.6.2 Interaction Energy of a System of Particles

If in a system there are more then two particles then we can find the interaction energy of particles in pairs using equation-(6.41) and finally sum up all the results to get the total energy of the system. For example in a system of N particles with masses $m_1, m_2 \ldots m_n$ separated from each other by a distance $r_{12}, r_{13} \ldots$ where r_{12} is the separation between m_1 and m_2 and so on.

In the above case the total interaction energy of system is given as

$$U = -\frac{1}{2}\sum_{i=1}^{N}\sum_{j=1}^{N}\frac{Gm_im_j}{r_{ij}} \qquad \ldots(6.42)$$

In this expression the factor $\frac{1}{2}$ is taken because the interaction energy for each possible pair of system is taken twice during summation as for masses m_1 and m_3

$$U = -\frac{Gm_1m_3}{r_{13}} = -\frac{Gm_3m_1}{r_{31}}$$

Now to understand the applications of interaction energy we take few examples.

 # Illustrative Example 6.17

Three particles each of mass m are placed at the corners of an equilateral triangle of side d as shown in figure-6.44. Calculate (a) the potential energy of the system, (b) work done on this system if the side of the triangle is changed from d to $2d$.

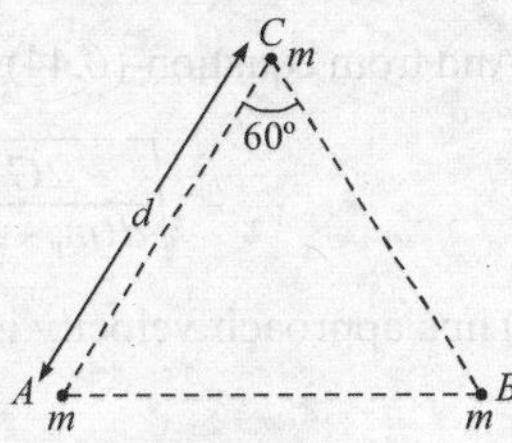

Figure 6.44

Solution

(a) As in case of two-particle system potential energy is given by $(-Gm_1m_2/r)$, so

$$U_i = U_{12} + U_{23} + U_{31}$$

or $$U_i = -3\,\frac{Gmm}{d} = -\frac{3Gm^2}{d}$$

(b) When d is changed to $2d$,

$$U_f = -\frac{3Gm^2}{2d}$$

Thus work done in changing in potential energy is given as

$$W = U_f - U_i = \frac{3Gm^2}{2d}$$

Illustrative Example 6.18

Two particles m_1 and m_2 are initially at rest at infinite distance. Find their relative velocity of approach due to gravitational attraction when their separation is d.

Solution

Initially when the separation was large there was no interaction energy and when they gets closer the system gravitational energy decreases and the kinetic energy increases.

When separation between the two particles is d, then according to energy conservation we have

$$\frac{1}{2}m_1v_1^2 + \frac{1}{2}m_2v_2^2 - \frac{Gm_1m_2}{d} = 0 \qquad \ldots(6.43)$$

As no other force is present we have according to momentum conservation

$$m_1v_1 = m_2v_2 \qquad \ldots(6.44)$$

From equation-(6.43) and (6.44)

$$\frac{1}{2}m_1v_1^2 + \frac{1}{2}\frac{m_1^2}{m_2}v_1^2 = \frac{Gm_1m_2}{d}$$

or $$v_1 = \sqrt{\frac{2Gm_2^2}{d(m_1+m_2)}} = \sqrt{\frac{2G}{d(m_1+m_2)}}\, m_2$$

And from equation-(6.44)

$$v_2 = \sqrt{\frac{2G}{d(m_1+m_2)}}\, m_1$$

Thus approach velocity is given as

$$v_{ap} = v_1 + v_2 = \sqrt{\frac{2G(m_1+m_2)}{d}}$$

Illustrative Example 6.19

Two particles A and B of mass 1 kg and 2 kg respectively are kept 1m apart and are released to move under mutual attraction. Find the speed of A when that of B is 3.6 cm/hour. What is the separation between the particles at this instant ?

Solution

Let the speed of A is v when the speed of B is 3.6 cm/hour $= 10^{-5}$ m/s. The particles move in opposite directions. Hence according to momentum conservation, we have

$$m_1v_1 = m_2v_2$$

$$(1) \times v = (2) \times (10^{-5})$$

or $$v = 2 \times 10^{-5}\ \text{m/s}$$

Potential energy of pair

$$= -\frac{Gm_1m_2}{d_0}$$

Initial potential energy

$$= -\frac{(6.67\times10^{-11})(1)(2)}{1}$$

$$= -13.34 \times 10^{-11}\ \text{J}$$

Let the separation at the given instant is d. Then

$$-13.34 \times 10^{-11} + 0 = -\frac{13.34\times10^{-11}}{d} + \frac{1}{2}(2)(10^{-5})^2$$

$$+ \frac{1}{2}(1)(2\times10^{-5})^2$$

By solving we get $d = 0.31$ m

6.6.3 Self Energy

It is the energy possessed by a body due to the interaction forces inside the body. This can be defined as the work done in assembling all the particles of a body in a definite shape and size or it is the work done in creating a body. Again we can say if the forces inside the body are attractive, work done in assembling is by the body itself and self energy of the body will be negative and if the forces inside the body are repulsive then some external work will be done in assembling the body and its self energy will be positive. As gravitational self energy of an object is concerned obviously it is always negative due to attractive forces. Lets take some basic and standard example to understand this concept.

We first find the gravitational self energy of a hollow sphere of mass M and radius R, as shown in figure-6.45. To assemble this we assume that we bring several mass elements dm step by

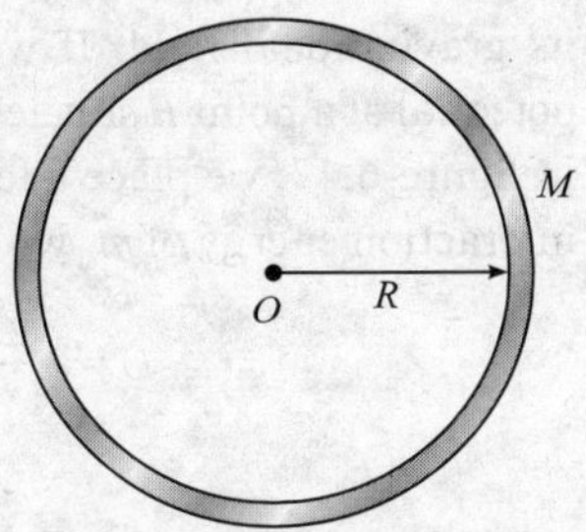

Figure 6.45

step from infinity to a spherical surface of radius R with centre O. Every dm is uniformly distributed on this surface. Now we consider an intermediate situation when mass of surface becomes m and a further dm is brought from infinity to the surface thus we can write the work done in bringing this elemental mass dm from infinity to a distance R from O as

$$dW = \frac{Gmdm}{R} \quad \ldots(6.45)$$

Here we can assume in a hollow sphere mass m is behaving as it is concentrated at O for outer points.

Now total work done in increasing the mass from 0 to M can be obtained by integrating the expression in equation-(6.45) within proper limits as

$$W = \int dW = \int_O^M \frac{Gmdm}{R}$$

$$= \frac{GM^2}{2R} \quad \ldots(6.46)$$

Here expression in equation-(6.46) is the work done in assembling the hollow sphere in space. As this work is done by the gravitational attractive forces of the body, this work is done by itself in assembling thus gravitational self energy of a hollow sphere of mass M and radius R is given as

$$U_{self} = -\frac{GM^2}{2R} \quad \ldots(6.47)$$

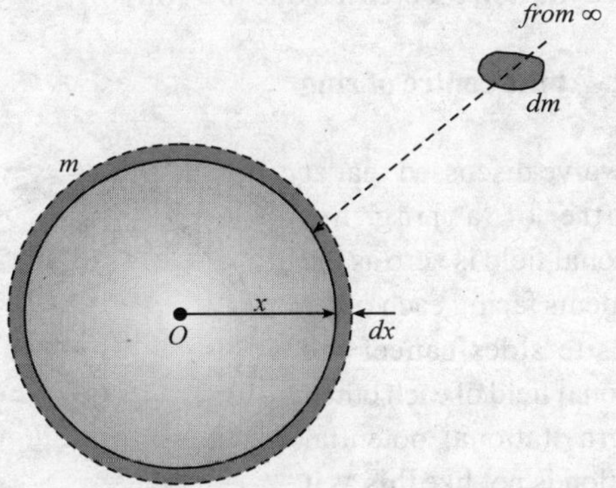

Figure 6.46

Students should keep the above result in mind as a standard result of gravitational self energy of a hollow sphere. The same amount of energy or work is required to split a hollow sphere of mass M and radius R into constituent particles and separating these particles to infinity (The process reverse of assembling).

We take one more similar standard example for gravitational self energy of a solid sphere of mass M and radius R. Again for it we'll create (assemble) a solid sphere in space. For this we bring several mass elements dm from infinity and start assembling at a point O in such way that the size of the assembled mass increases gradually layer by layer.

Now consider an intermediate situation when the radius of assembled matter increased to x and the mass becomes m if a further mass dm is brought from infinity to its surface which increases the radius of sphere by dx then work done in this process is

$$dW = \frac{Gmdm}{x} \quad \ldots(6.48)$$

If ρ be the density of sphere $\left[\rho = \frac{M}{\frac{4}{3}\pi R^3}\right]$ then we have

$$m = \rho \times \frac{4}{3}\pi x^3$$

and $$dm = \rho \times 4\pi x^2\, dx$$

Now from equation-(6.48)

$$dW = \frac{G(\rho \frac{4}{3}\pi x^3)(\rho\, 4\pi x^2 dx)}{x}$$

or $$dW = \frac{16}{3}\pi^2 G\rho^2 x^4\, dx$$

Now we can find the total work done in assembling this sphere to a radius R by integrating the above expression within proper limits as

$$W = \int dW \int_0^R \frac{16}{3}\pi^2 G\rho^2 x^4 dx$$

$$= \frac{16}{3}\pi^2 G\rho^2 \left[\frac{x^5}{5}\right]_0^R$$

$$= \frac{16}{15}\pi^2 G\rho^2 R^5$$

As we know the density of sphere is given as $\rho = \frac{M}{\frac{4}{3}\pi R^3}$, we have

$$W = \frac{16}{15}\pi^2 G\left[\frac{3M}{4\pi R^3}\right]^2 R^5 = \frac{3}{5}\frac{GM^2}{R} \quad \ldots(6.49)$$

Thus we get the above work is done by gravitational forces in assembling a solid sphere of mass M and radius R. Thus the self energy of the sphere is given as

$$U_{self} = -\frac{3}{5}\frac{GM^2}{R} \quad \ldots(6.50)$$

The above expression in equation-(6.50) is also a standard result which you can use directly in numerical problems. Similar to the previous case here also we can state that the magnitude of self energy is the amount of energy required to split a solid sphere into its constituent particles and separating them to infinity.

> Web Reference of Video Lectures at www.physicsgalaxy.com
> **Age Group** - High School Physics | Age 17-19 Years
> **Section** - GRAVITATION
> **Topic** - Gravitation Theory
> **Module Number** - 47, 48 & 49

6.7 Gravitational Potential

The gravitational potential at a point in gravitational field is the gravitational potential energy per unit mass placed at that point in gravitational field. Thus at a certain point in gravitational field, a mass m_0 has a potential energy U then the gravitational potential at that point is given as

$$V = \frac{U}{m_0} \qquad \dots(6.51)$$

or if at a point in gravitational field gravitational potential V is known then the interaction potential energy of a point mass m_0 at that point in the field is given as

$$U = m_0 V \qquad \dots(6.52)$$

Interaction energy of a point mass m_0 in a field is defined as work done in bringing that mass from infinity to that point. In the same fashion we can define gravitational potential at a point in field, alternatively as *"Work done in bringing a unit mass from infinity to that point against gravitational forces."*

When a unit mass is brought to a point in a gravitational field, force on the unit mass is $\vec{g}$ at a point in the field. Thus the work done in bringing this unit mass from infinity to a point P in gravitational field or gravitational potential at point P is given as

$$V_P = -\int_{\infty}^{P} \vec{g} \cdot \overrightarrow{dx} \qquad \dots(6.53)$$

Here negative sign shows that V_P is the negative of work done by gravitation field or it is the external required work for the purpose against gravitational forces.

6.7.1 Gravitational Potential due to a Point Mass

We know that in the surrounding of a point mass it produces its gravitational field. If we wish to find the gravitational potential at a point P situated at a distance r from it as shown in figure-6.47, we place a test mass m_0 at P and we find the interaction energy of m_0 with the field of m, which is given as

$$U = -\frac{Gmm_0}{x} \qquad \dots(6.54)$$

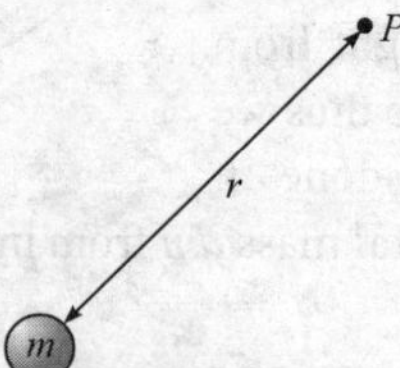

Figure 6.47

Now the gravitational potential at P due to m can be written as

$$V = \frac{U}{m_0} = -\frac{Gm}{r} \qquad \dots(6.55)$$

The expression of gravitational potential in equation-(6.55) is a standard result due to a point mass which can be used as an elemental form to find other complex results, we'll see later.

The same thing can also be obtained by using equation-(6.53) as

$$V_P = \int_{\infty}^{P} \vec{g} \cdot \overrightarrow{dx}$$

or

$$V_P = \int_{\infty}^{r} \frac{Gm}{x^2}\, dx$$

$$V_P = -\frac{Gm}{r} \qquad \dots(6.56)$$

6.7.2 Gravitational Potential due to a Ring

Case -I : At the centre of ring

Earlier we've discussed that at the centre of a ring net gravitational field is zero as the ring elements facing each other on opposite sides cancel the gravitational field of each other. But in gravitational potential the situation is not like this as it is a scaler quantity and here the distance of centre from each element dm on ring circumference is equal to R, thus every element dm produces an equal gravitational potential at C, given as

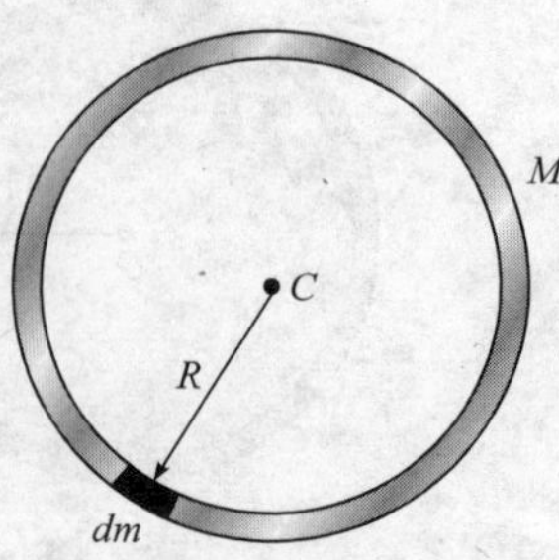

Figure 6.48

$$dV = -\frac{Gdm}{R}$$

Now due to the whole ring the gravitational potential at its centre C is given as

$$V_c = \int dV = -\int \frac{Gdm}{R} = -\frac{GM}{R} \quad \dots (6.57)$$

Case-II : At a point on the axis of ring

Figure-6.49 shows a ring of mass M and radius R placed in yz plane with its centre at origin. Here we wish to find the gravitational potential at a point P on the axis of the ring at a distance x from its centre.

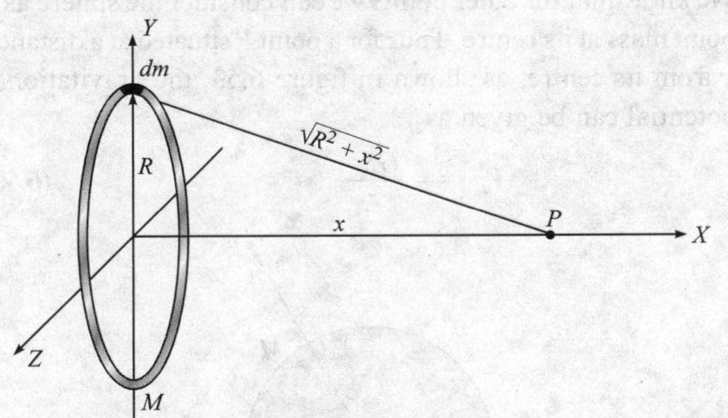

Figure 6.49

For this we consider an element of mass dm at a point on ring as shown in figure-6.49. Now due to this elemental mass dm if dV is the potential at point P then it is given as

$$dV = -\frac{Gdm}{\sqrt{x^2 + R^2}} \quad \dots (6.58)$$

Now as being a scaler, due to all the elements of ring, potential at point P will just be added up algebraically. Thus we can simply integrate the expression in equation-(6.58) for the complete ring as

$$V_P = \int dV = -\int \frac{Gdm}{\sqrt{x^2 + R^2}}$$

$$= -\frac{GM}{\sqrt{x^2 + R^2}} \quad \dots (6.59)$$

6.7.3 Work done in Displacement of a Body in Gravitational Field

When a body is displaced in a gravitational field, its interaction energy with the gravitational field changes and the work done is equal to the change in interaction energy of the body during its displacement.

If a body of mass m is displaced in a gravitational field from point A to B, then work done by external agent can be given as

$$W = U_B - U_A$$

$$= (mV_{gB}) - (mV_{gA})$$

$$= m(V_{gB} - V_{gA})$$

Figure 6.50

Thus work done in displacing a body in gravitational field can be given as

Work done = mass of body × gravitational potential difference of the terminal points.

Here as gravitational force is conservative the work done does not depend on the path along which body is being displaced in gravitational field.

Now we consider some examples to understand the concepts of gravitational energy and gravitational potential.

6.7.4 Relation in Gravitational field and Gravitational Potential

In region of gravitational field we can define field as gradient of potential in the same way we relate force and potential energy in conservative force fields.

$$\vec{g} = -\nabla V = -\text{grad } V$$

For one dimensional variation of field we use

$$\vec{g}_r = -\frac{dV}{dr}\hat{r}$$

When $\vec{g}_r$ is the gravitational field strength along the direction of $\hat{r}$.

For three dimensional variation in field we use

$$\vec{g} = -\left(\frac{\partial V}{\partial x}\hat{i} + \frac{\partial V}{\partial y}\hat{j} + \frac{\partial V}{\partial z}\hat{k}\right)$$

6.7.5 Gravitational Potential due to a Sphere

Case-I : Hollow sphere

We've already discussed that for outer points a sphere can be considered as a point mass at its centre C. Thus for an outer point P as shown in figure-6.51, situated at a distance x from its centre C, the gravitational potential can be written as

$$V_P = -\frac{GM}{x} \qquad \ldots (6.60)$$

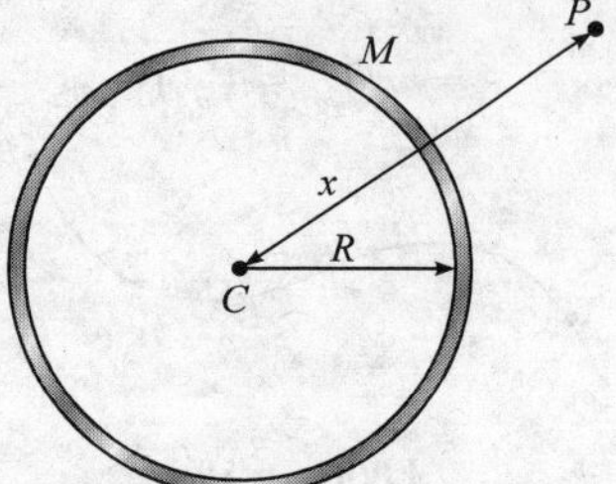

Figure 6.51

Similarly for a point on the outer surface of the sphere gravitational potential can be written as

$$V_s = -\frac{GM}{R} \qquad \ldots (6.61)$$

Here above expressions in equations-(6.60) and (6.61) are written directly from the standard results of gravitational potential due to a point mass. By definition of gravitational potential these are the magnitude of external work required to bring a unit mass from infinity to the given point in the gravitational field of the hollow sphere.

If we talk about the interior of the shell, we know that there exist no gravitational field inside the hollow sphere thus if we displace a mass inside it, no work is done in the process as no force will act on it. Thus if a unit mass is brought from infinity to the surface of the shell, work required is $-\frac{GM}{R}$. Now if we take this unit mass from its surface to any of its interior point, no work is required as there is no gravitational field inside. Thus at every internal point the gravitational potential remains same and equal to that of the surface of the shell, given as

$$V_{in} = -\frac{GM}{R} \qquad \ldots (6.62)$$

If we plot the variation of gravitational potential with distance from centre of a hollow sphere we get a graph shown in figure-6.52 as for different points in the surrounding of a hollow sphere, the gravitational potential is given as

$$V_{out} = -\frac{GM}{x} \qquad \ldots (6.63)$$

[For points $x > R$]

$$V_s = -\frac{GM}{R} \qquad \ldots (6.64)$$

[For points $x = R$ or on the surface]

$$V_{in} = -\frac{GM}{R} \qquad \ldots (6.65)$$

[For points $x < R$]

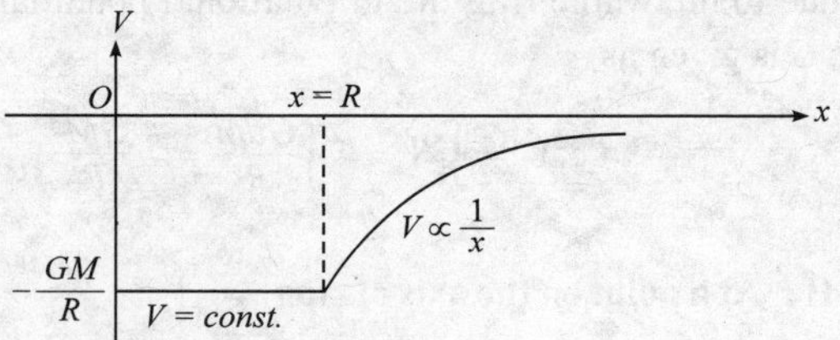

Figure 6.52

Case-II : Solid sphere

We know that for outer points we can consider the sphere as a point mass at its centre. Thus for a point P situated at a distance x from its centre, as shown in figure-6.53, the gravitational potential can be given as

$$V_{out} = -\frac{GM}{x} \qquad \ldots (6.66)$$

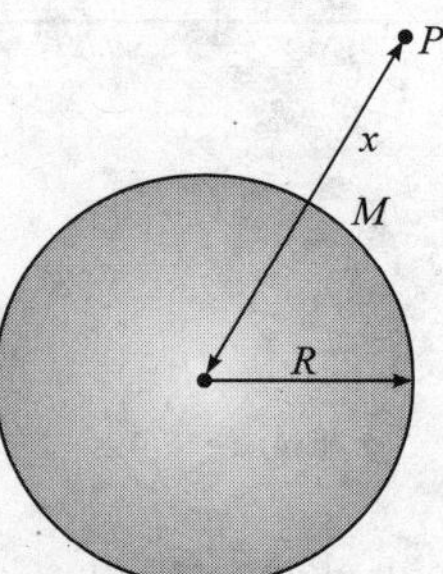

Figure 6.53

Similarly for points on the surface of this sphere, the gravitational potential is given as

$$V_s = -\frac{GM}{R} \qquad \ldots (6.67)$$

The above two results are same as that of a hollow sphere but the same is not true for an interior points as for a hollow sphere there is no gravitational field present inside, thus no work is done in displacing a mass inside it but for a solid sphere gravitational field strength at an interior point at a distance x from its centre is given as

$$g_{in} = \frac{GMx}{R^3} \qquad \ldots (6.68)$$

Thus according to definition of potential at an interior point the gravitational potential at a distance x from the centre of a solid sphere of radius R be given as

$$V_{in} = -\left[\int_{\infty}^{R} \vec{g}_{out} \cdot \vec{dx} + \int_{R}^{x} \vec{g}_{in} \cdot \vec{dx}\right]$$

$$V_{in} = \int_{\infty}^{R} \frac{GM}{x^2} dx + \int_{R}^{x} \frac{GMx}{R^3} dx$$

$$V_{in} = -\frac{GM}{R} + \frac{GM}{2R^3}(x^2 - R^2)$$

$$V_{in} = -\frac{GM}{2R^3}(3R^2 - x^2) \quad \ldots(6.69)$$

Now if we plot the variation of gravitational potential with the distance from centre of the sphere then we get the graph shown in figure-6.54, and the values of gravitational potential for different points in the surrounding of the solid sphere given as

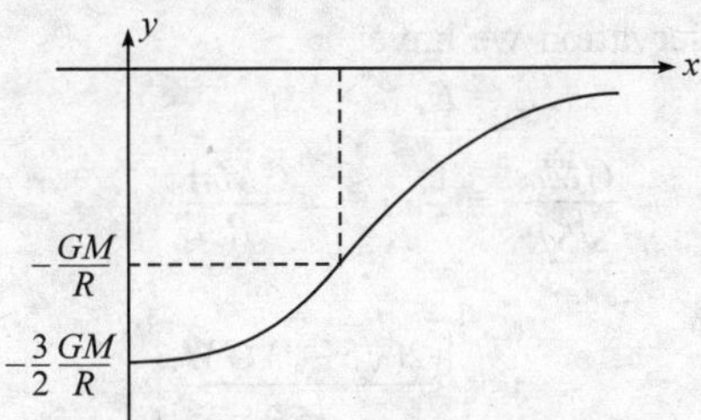

Figure 6.54

$$V_{out} = -\frac{GM}{x} \quad \ldots(6.70)$$

[For points $x > R$]

$$V_s = -\frac{GM}{R} \quad \ldots(6.71)$$

[For points on surface $x = R$]

$$V_{in} = -\frac{GM}{R}(3R^2 - x^2) \quad \ldots(6.72)$$

[For interior points $x < R$]

Gravitational potential at centre

$$V_C = -\frac{3}{2}\frac{GM}{R} \quad [\text{For } x = 0] \quad \ldots(6.73)$$

Web Reference of Video Lectures at www.physicsgalaxy.com

Age Group - High School Physics | Age 17-19 Years
Section - GRAVITATION
Topic - Gravitation Theory
Module Number - 34 to 40

6.8 Gravitational Potential Energy of a Body on Earth

6.8.1 On Earth's Surface

When a body of mass m is situated on earth surface, where gravitational potential due to earth is given as

$$V_{gs} = -\frac{GM_e}{R_e}$$

Assuming earth as a uniform sphere of radius R_e and mass M_e. Thus gravitational potential energy of the body of mass m due to its interaction with earth's field is given as

$$U_g = m\,V_{gs} = -\frac{GM_e m}{R_e} \quad \ldots(6.74)$$

$$= -m\,g_s R_e \ldots(6.75)$$

6.8.2 Above the Surface of Earth

If we find gravitational potential due to earth at a height h above the earth's surface, it is given as

$$V_{gh} = -\frac{GM_e}{(R_e + h)}$$

Thus the gravitational interaction energy of a small body of mass m at a height h above the earth's surface is

$$U_g = mV_{gh}$$

$$U_g = -\frac{GM_e m}{R_e + h}$$

$$U_g = -\frac{mg_s h}{(1 + h/R_e)} \quad [\text{As } g_s = \frac{GM_e}{R_e^2}] \quad \ldots(6.76)$$

6.8.3 Inside the Earth's Core

The gravitational potential inside the earth's core at a distance x from the centre is given as

$$V_{g\,in} = -\frac{GM_e}{2R_e^3}[3R_e^2 - x^2] \quad \ldots(6.77)$$

Thus gravitational interaction energy of a small body of mass m at a distance x from the centre of earth is given as

$$U_g = m\,V_{g\,in}$$

$$= -\frac{GM_e m}{2R_e^3}[3R_e^2 - x^2] \quad \ldots(6.78)$$

 # Illustrative Example 6.20

Find work done in shifting a body of mass m from a height h above the earth's surface to a height $2h$ above the earth's surface.

Solution

The gravitational potential at a height h and $2h$ above the earth surface is given as

$$V_h = -\frac{GM_e}{R_e + h}\; V_{2h} = \frac{GM_e}{R_e + 2h}$$

If a body of mass m is shifted from h to $2h$, work done in the process is

$$W = m(V_{2A} - V_h) = m\left[\frac{GM_e}{R_e + h} - \frac{GM_e}{R_e + 2h}\right]$$

Illustrative Example 6.21

A circular ring of mass M and radius R is placed in YZ plane with centre at origin. A particle of mass m is released from rest at a point $x = 2R$. Find the speed with which it will pass the centre of ring.

Solution

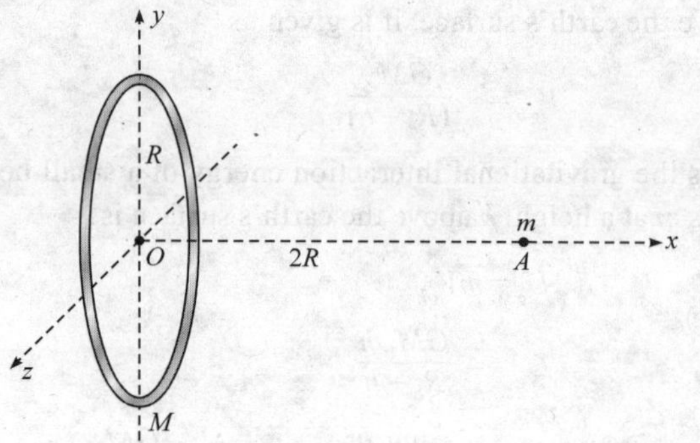

Figure 6.55

As shown in figure-6.55, first we find potential at A due to the ring, it is given as

$$V_A = -\frac{GM}{\sqrt{R^2+(2R)^2}} = -\frac{GM}{\sqrt{5}R}$$

Now potential at origin O due to ring is

$$V_0 = \frac{GM}{R}$$

When m moves from A to O, work done on it due to gravitational forces is

$$W = m(V_A - V_0) = m\left(-\frac{GM}{\sqrt{5}R} + \frac{GM}{R}\right)$$

$$= \frac{GMm}{R}\left(\frac{\sqrt{5}-1}{\sqrt{5}}\right)$$

This work done by gravitational forces on m must be equal to the increase in kinetic energy of the mass m, thus we have

$$\frac{1}{2}mv^2 = \left(\frac{\sqrt{5}-1}{\sqrt{5}}\right)\frac{GMm}{R}$$

or $$v = \left[\frac{2(\sqrt{5}-1)GM}{\sqrt{5}R}\right]^{1/2}$$

Alternative Method :

This problem can also be solved simply by using energy conservation. There initially when m was at rest at point A. The total energy of system is only gravitational potential energy given as

$$E_i = m\,.\,V_A = -\frac{GMm}{\sqrt{5}R}$$

Finally when m passes through O, the total energy of system is

$$E_f = \frac{1}{2}mv^2 + mV_0$$

$$= \frac{1}{2}mv^2 - \frac{GMm}{R}$$

As no external work is done on the system in this case, the total energy of system must be conserved, thus according to energy conservation we have

$$E_i = E_f$$

$$-\frac{GMm}{\sqrt{5}R} = \frac{1}{2}mv^2 - \frac{GMm}{R}$$

or $$v = \left[\frac{2(\sqrt{5}-1)GM}{\sqrt{5}R}\right]^{1/2}$$

Illustrative Example 6.22

Find the gravitational interaction energy of system consisting of a disc of mass M, radius R and a small mass m situated at a distance x from disc centre on its axis as shown in figure-6.56.

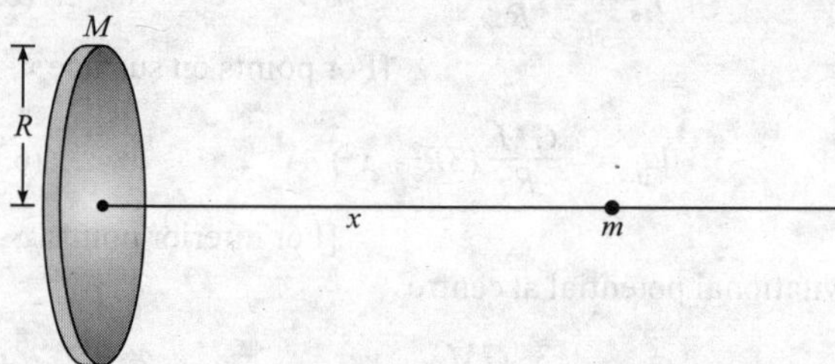

Figure 6.56

Solution

The gravitational potential energy of m with the disc can be given as

$$U = mV \qquad \ldots(6.79)$$

Where V is the gravitational potential due to disc at the point where m is situated. This can be obtained by integrating the elemental rings to form the disc as shown in figure-6.57.

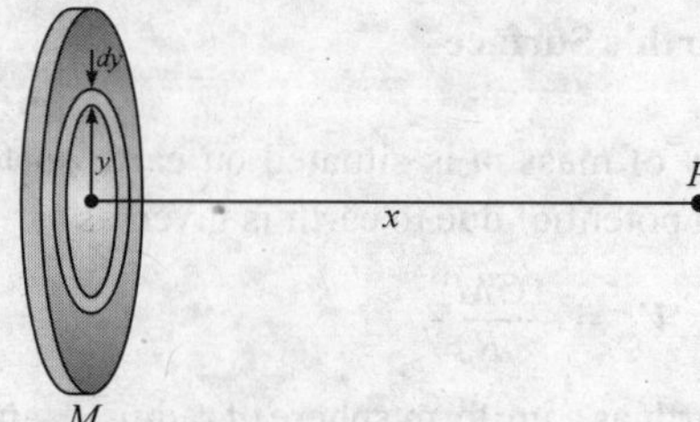

Figure 6.57

Let us consider an elemental ring of radius y and width dy in the disc as shown. Its mass dm can be given as

$$dm = \frac{M}{\pi R^2} \times 2\pi y\, dy = \frac{2My\, dy}{R^2}$$

Now due to this dm, gravitational potential at point P, a distance x away from disc centre is given as

$$dV = -\frac{Gdm}{\sqrt{x^2+y^2}} = -\frac{2G\, My\, dy}{R^2\sqrt{x^2+y^2}}$$

Net potential at P is

$$V = \int dV = -\int_0^R \frac{2G\, My\, dy}{R^2\sqrt{x^2+y^2}}$$

or

$$= -\frac{2GM}{R^2}\int_0^R \frac{y\, dy}{\sqrt{x^2+y^2}}$$

$$= -\frac{2GM}{R^2}\left[\sqrt{x^2+y^2}\right]_0^R$$

$$V = -\frac{2GM}{R^2}\left[\sqrt{x^2+y^2} - x\right]$$

Now from equation-(6.79) the gravitational potential energy of system is given as

$$U = mV = -\frac{2GMm}{R^2}\left[\sqrt{x^2+y^2} - x\right]$$

Illustrative Example 6.23

A small mass m is transferred from the centre of a hollow sphere of mass M to infinity. Find work done in the process. Compare this with the situation if instead of a hollow sphere, a solid sphere of same mass were there.

Solution

We know at infinity, gravitational potential is taken zero. Thus if V_C be the gravitational potential at centre of hollow sphere then external work required in the process is

$$W = m(0 - V_C)$$

or

$$= m\left(0 - \left(-\frac{GM}{R}\right)\right) = \frac{GMm}{R}$$

Here $V_C = -\frac{GM}{R}$, the potential at the centre of a hollow sphere of mass M and radius R.

If a solid sphere were there, we have at its centre

$$V_C = -\frac{3}{2}\frac{GM}{R}$$

Thus work required will be

$$W = m\left[0 - \left(-\frac{3}{2}\frac{GM}{R}\right)\right] = \frac{3}{2}\frac{GMm}{R}$$

We can see in second case more work is required for the process.

Illustrative Example 6.24

Given a thin homogeneous disc of radius a and mass m_1. A small sphere of mass m_2 is placed at a distance l from the disc on its axis of symmetry. Initially both are motionless in free space but they ultimately collide because of gravitational attraction. Assuming $a << l$, show that the relative velocity at the time of collision is given by

$$\left[2G(m_1+m_2)\left(\frac{2}{a} - \frac{1}{l}\right)\right]^{1/2}$$

Solution

The situation in shown in figure-6.58

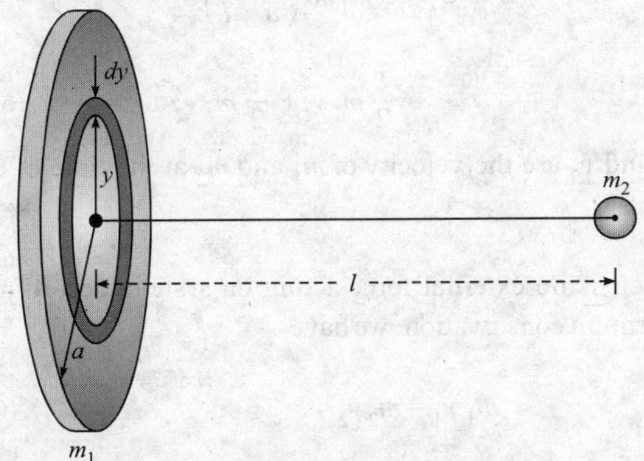

Figure 6.58

Here we first find the potential due to m_1 at the position of m_2. For this consider an elemental ring of radius y and width dy as shown in figure-6.58.

Let dm be the mass of the elemental ring considered here

$$dm = (2\pi y\, dy) \times \frac{m_1}{\pi a^2} = \frac{2m_1 y\, dy}{a^2}$$

We know that the potential due to a circular ring of radius t at a distance l is given by

$$dV = -\frac{G\, dm}{\sqrt{y^2+l^2}} = -\frac{2G\, m_1\, y\, dr}{a^2\sqrt{(y^2+l^2)}}$$

The total potential V at a distance l from the disc is given by

$$V = -\int_0^a \frac{2G\, m_1\, y\, dr}{a^2\sqrt{(y^2+l^2)}}$$

$$= -\frac{2G\, m_1}{a^2}\left[\sqrt{a^2+l^2} - l\right]$$

The potential energy of mass m_2 with the system is

$$U_i = m_2 V = -\frac{2G\,m_1\,m_2}{a^2}\left[\sqrt{a^2+l^2}-l\right]$$

When the two collide the final potential energy becomes

Now $$U_f = -\frac{2G\,m_1\,m_2}{a}\quad [\text{As}\quad l=0]$$

If $a << l$ then initial potential energy of system can be written as

$$U_i = -\frac{G\,m_1\,m_2}{l}\quad [\text{As}\quad a<<l]$$

Change in potential energy

$$= U_i - U_f$$

$$= G\,m_1\,m_2\left(\frac{2}{a}-\frac{1}{l}\right)$$

This change in potential energy of system must be equal to gain in kinetic energy of the two masses thus, we have

$$U_i - U_f = G\,m_1\,m_2\left(\frac{2}{a}-\frac{1}{l}\right)$$

$$= \frac{1}{2}m_1 v_1^2 + \frac{1}{2}m_2 v_2^2 \quad \ldots(6.80)$$

If v_1 and v_2 are the velocity of m_1 and m_2 at the time of their impact.

As their is no external force acting on system, according to momentum conservation, we have

$$m_1 v_1 = m_2 v_2 \quad \ldots(6.81)$$

Now from equation-(6.80) and (6.81) we get

$$v_1 = m_2\sqrt{\frac{2G}{m_1+m_2}\left(\frac{2}{a}-\frac{1}{l}\right)}$$

and $$v_2 = m_1\sqrt{\frac{2G}{m_1+m_2}\left(\frac{2}{a}-\frac{1}{l}\right)}$$

Relative velocity of m_1 and m_2 at the time of impact is

$$v_R = v_1 + v_2$$

$$= \sqrt{2G(m_1+m_2)\left(\frac{2}{a}-\frac{1}{l}\right)}$$

Illustrative Example 6.25

Figure-6.59 shows a ring of mass M_1 and a sphere of mass M_2 separated by a distance $\sqrt{3}\,R$. A small object of mass m is displaced from A to B. Find the work done by gravitational forces.

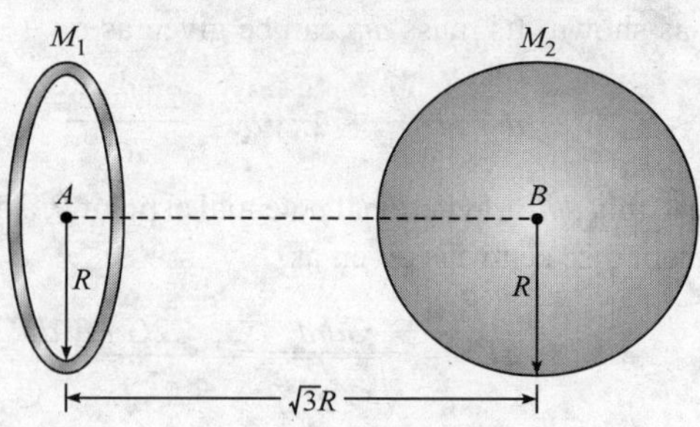

Figure 6.59

Solution

In this case as shifting is from A to B, work done by the gravitational forces is given as

$$W = m(V_A - V_B)$$

Where V_A and V_B are gravitational potentials at points A and B respectively, which can be given as

$$V_A = -\frac{GM_1}{R} - \frac{GM_2}{2R}$$

and $$V_B = -\frac{3GM_2}{2R} - \frac{GM_1}{R}$$

Thus work done by gravitational forces is

$$W = m\left[\left(-\frac{GM_1}{R}-\frac{GM_2}{2R}\right)-\left(\frac{3}{2}\frac{GM_2}{R}-\frac{GM_1}{2R}\right)\right]$$

$$= \left[\frac{GM_2}{R}-\frac{GM_1}{2R}\right]$$

$$= \frac{GM}{2R}(2M_2 - M_1)$$

Illustrative Example 6.26

A solid sphere of mass m and radius r is initially placed at a distance $5r$ from the centre of a point mass M as shown in figure-6.60. Now it is shifted to a position at a distance $3r$ from the point mass. During displacement, it is also uniformly expanded to a radius $2r$ so that its density decreases uniformly throughout its volume. Find the work required in this process.

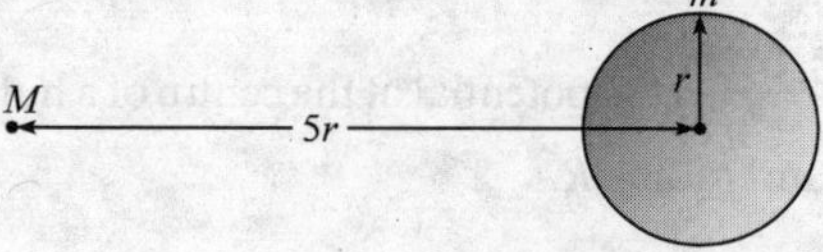

Figure 6.60

Solution

In this process during displacement the size of an object is also changing. This implies, we have to account for the self energy of object also. There initial total energy of system is

U_i = Self energy of M + Self energy of m + Interaction energy of m & M

$$= S_M + \left(-\frac{3}{5}\frac{Gm^2}{r}\right) + \left(-\frac{GMm}{5r}\right)$$

In final stage the radius of m becomes $2r$ and it is situated at a distance $3r$ from M as shown in figure-6.61.

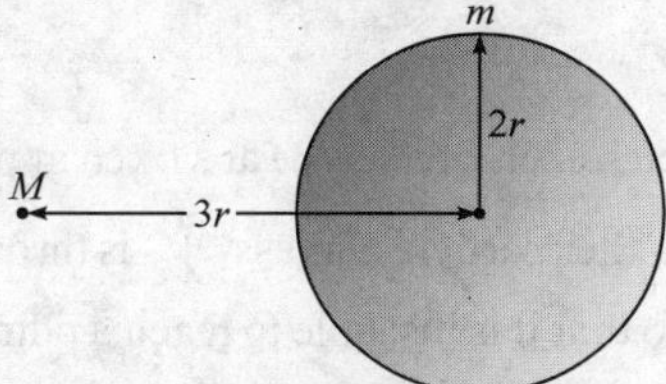

Figure 6.61

Now final total energy of system is given as

$$U_f = S_M + \left(-\frac{3}{5}\frac{Gm^2}{2r}\right) + \left(-\frac{GMm}{3r}\right)$$

Now external work required in the process is

$$W = U_f - U_i$$

$$= \left(S_M - \frac{3}{10}\frac{Gm^2}{r} - \frac{GMm}{3r}\right) - \left(S_M - \frac{3}{5}\frac{Gm^2}{r} - \frac{GMm}{5r}\right)$$

$$= \frac{3}{10}\frac{Gm^2}{r} - \frac{GMm}{r}\left(\frac{1}{3} - \frac{1}{5}\right)$$

$$= \frac{Gm}{30r}(9m - 4M)$$

Illustrative Example 6.27

A particle of mass m was transferred from the centre of the base of a uniform hemisphere of mass M and radius R to infinity. What work was performed in the process by the gravitational force exerted on the particle by the hemisphere ?

Solution

To find the initial energy of system first we find gravitational potential due to hemisphere at its centre. For this consider an elemental hemispherical shell of thickness dr at a distance r from the centre O of the hemisphere as shown in figure-6.62.

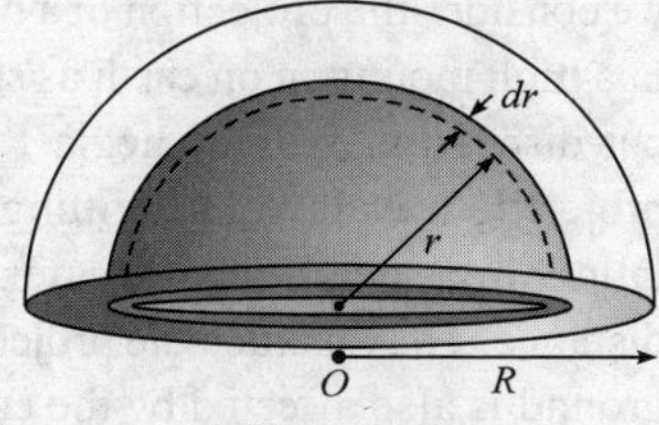

Figure 6.62

Let dm be the mass of the elementary strip. Then

$$dm = \frac{M}{\frac{1}{2}\left(\frac{4}{3}\pi R^3\right)} \times \left\{\frac{4\pi r^2}{2} \times dr\right\}$$

$$= \frac{3M}{R^3} r^2\, dr$$

The potential dV at point O due to this strip

$$dV = -\frac{G\,dm}{r}$$

$$= -\frac{G\left(\frac{3Mr^2 dr}{R^3}\right)}{r} = -\frac{3GM}{R^3} r\, dr$$

Thus potential at O due to hemisphere is given by integrating the above expression within proper limits as

$$V_0 = \int dV = -\frac{3GM}{R^3}\int_0^R r\, dr$$

$$= -\frac{3}{2}\frac{GM}{R}$$

Thus potential energy of mass m placed at point O is given as

$$U_i = mV_0$$

$$= -\frac{3}{2}\frac{GMm}{R}$$

We know potential energy of m at infinity $U_f = 0$

The work done in transferring m from centre of hemisphere to infinity is given as

$$W = U_f - U_i$$

$$= 0 - \left(-\frac{3}{2}\frac{GMm}{R}\right) = -\frac{3}{2}\frac{GMm}{R}$$

Illustrative Example 6.28

On the pole of earth a body is imparted velocity v_0 directed vertically up. Knowing the radius of the earth and the free-fall acceleration on its surface, find the height to which the body will ascend. The air drag is to be neglected.

Solution

Let m and M_e be the masses of the body and earth respectively.

Kinetic energy of the body at the pole

$$K_i = \frac{1}{2} mv_0^2$$

Potential energy of the body at the pole

$$U_i = -\frac{GMm}{R}$$

[Where R = radius of the earth]

P.E. of the body at height h is

$$U_f = -\frac{GMm}{(R+h)}$$

Using the conservation of energy, we have

$$K_i + U_i = U$$

or $$\frac{1}{2} mv_0^2 - \frac{GMm}{R} = -\frac{GMm}{(R+h)}$$

or $$v_0^2 = \frac{2GMh}{R(R+h)}$$

$$= \frac{2GMh}{R^2(1+h/R)}$$

or $$v_0^2 = \frac{2gh}{1+\frac{h}{R}} \qquad \left[\text{As } g = \frac{GM}{R^2}\right]$$

or $$v_0^2 = 2gh - \frac{v_0^2 h}{R} = h\left[\frac{2gR - v_0^2}{R}\right]$$

or $$h = \left[\frac{v_0^2 R}{2gR - v_0^2}\right]$$

Web Reference of Video Lectures at www.physicsgalaxy.com

Age Group - High School Physics | Age 17-19 Years

Section - GRAVITATION

Topic - Gravitation Theory

Module Number - 41 to 46

Practice Exercise 6.4

(i) Find the kinetic energy needed to project a body of mass m from the centre of a ring of mass M and radius R so that it will never come back.

$[\frac{GMm}{R}]$

(ii) How much work is done in circulating a small object of mass m around a sphere of mass m in a circle of radius R.

[0]

(iii) Distance between the centres of two stars is 10 a. The masses of these stars are M and 16 M and their radii a and $2a$, respectively. A body of mass m is fired straight from the surface of the larger star towards the smaller one. What should be its minimum initial speed to reach the surface of the smaller star ? Obtain the expression in terms of G, M and a.

$[\frac{3}{2}\sqrt{\frac{5Gm}{a}}]$

(iv) Find the gravitational potential due to a hemispherical cup of mass M and radius R, at its centre of curvature.

$[-\frac{GM}{R}]$

(v) Two particles each of mass M are fixed at positions $(0, a)$ and $(0, -a)$. Another particle of mass $M/2$ is thrown from origin along $+z$ axis so that it is just able to reach a point $(0, 0, 2\sqrt{3}a)$. Find the speed with which it was projected.

$[2\sqrt{\frac{GM}{a}\left(\frac{\sqrt{13}-1}{\sqrt{13}}\right)}]$

(vi) The gravitational field in a region is given by $\vec{g} = (2\hat{i} + 3\hat{j})$N/kg. Show that no work is done by the gravitational field when a particle is moved on the line $3y + 2x = 5$.

(vii) Find the gravitational potential energy of a system consisting of a uniform rod AB of mass M, length l and a point mass m as shown in figure-6.63.

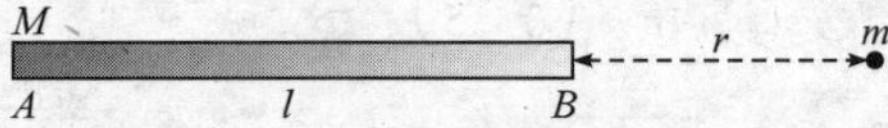

Figure 6.63

$[-\frac{GMm}{l} \ln\left(1+\frac{l}{r}\right)]$

6.9 Satellite and Planetary Motion

6.9.1 Motion of a Satellite in a Circular Orbit

To understand how a satellite continually moves in its orbit, we consider the projection of a body horizontally from the top of a high mountain on earth as shown in figure-6.64. Here till our discussion ends we neglect air friction. The distance the projectile travels before hitting the ground depends on the launching speed. The greater the speed, the greater the distance. The distance the projectile travels before hitting the ground is also affected by the curvature of earth as shown in figure-6.64. This figure was given by newton in his explanation of laws of gravitation. It shows different trajectories for different launching speeds. As the launching speed is made greater, a speed is reached where by the projectile's path follow the curvature of the earth. This is the launching speed which places the projectile in a circular orbit. Thus an object in circular orbit may be regarded as falling, but as it falls its path is concentric with the earth's spherical surface and the object maintains a fixed distance from the earth's centre. Since the motion may continue indefinitely, we may say that the orbit is stable.

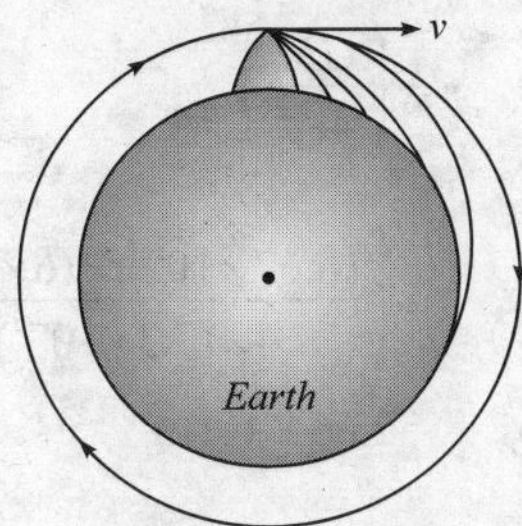

Figure 6.64

Let's find the speed of a satellite of mass m in a circular orbit around the earth. Consider a satellite revolving around the earth in a circular orbit of radius r as shown in figure-6.65.

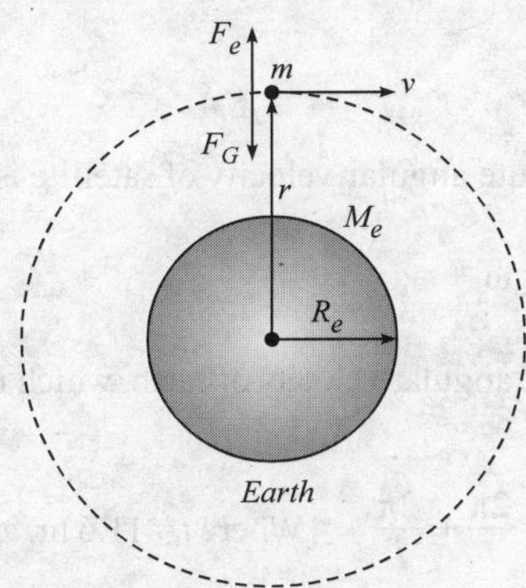

Figure 6.65

If its orbit is stable during its motion, the net gravitational force on it must be balanced by the centrifugal force on it relative to the rotating frame as

$$\frac{GM_e m}{r^2} = \frac{mv^2}{r}$$

or
$$v = \sqrt{\frac{GM_e}{r}} \qquad \ldots(6.82)$$

Expression in equation-(6.82) gives the speed of a satellite in a stable circular orbit of radius r.

6.9.2 Energies of a Satellite in a Circular Orbit

When there is a satellite revolving in a stable circular orbit of radius r around the earth, its speed is given by equation-(6.82). During its motion the kinetic energy of the satellite can be given as

$$K = \frac{1}{2}mv^2 = \frac{1}{2}\frac{GM_e m}{r} \qquad \ldots(6.83)$$

As gravitational force on satellite due to earth is the only force it experiences during motion, it has gravitational interaction energy in the field of earth, which is given as

$$U = -\frac{GM_e m}{r} \qquad \ldots(6.84)$$

Thus the total energy of a satellite in an orbit of radius r can be given as

Total energy E= Kinetic energy K + Potential Energy U

$$= \frac{1}{2}\frac{GM_e m}{r} - \frac{GM_e m}{r}$$

or
$$E = -\frac{1}{2}\frac{GM_e m}{r} \qquad \ldots(6.85)$$

From equation-(6.82), (6.83) and (6.84) we can see that

$$|TE| = |KE| = \frac{1}{2}|PE| \qquad \ldots(6.86)$$

The above relation in magnitudes of total, kinetic and potential energies of a satellite is very useful in numerical problem so students are advised to keep this relation in mind while handling satellite problems related to energy.

Now to understand satellite and planetary motion in detail, we take few example.

Illustrative Example 6.29

Estimate the mass of the sun, assuming the orbit of the earth round the sun to be a circle. The distance between the sun and earth is 1.49×10^{11} m and $G = 6.66 \times 10^{-11}$ Nm^2/kg^2.

Solution

Here the revolving speed of earth can be given as

$$v = \sqrt{\frac{GM}{r}} \qquad \text{[Orbital speed]}$$

Where M is the mass of sun and r is the orbit radius of earth.

We know time period of earth around sun is T = 365 days, thus we have

$$T = \frac{2\pi r}{v}$$

or $$T=2\pi r\sqrt{\frac{r}{GM}}$$

or $$M=\frac{4\pi^2 r^3}{GT^2}$$

$$=\frac{4\times(3.14)^2\times(1.49\times10^{11})^3}{(365\times24\times3600)^2\times(6.66\times10^{-11})}$$

$$=1.972\times10^{22}\text{ kg}$$

 # Illustrative Example 6.30

If the earth be one-half of its present distance from the sun, how many days will be in one year ?

Solution

If orbit of earth's radius is R, in previous example we've discussed that time period is given as

$$T=2\pi r\sqrt{\frac{r}{GM}}=\frac{2\pi}{\sqrt{GM}}r^{3/2} \quad \ldots(6.87)$$

If radius changes to $r'=\frac{r}{2}$, new time period becomes

$$T'=\frac{2\pi}{\sqrt{GM}}r'^{3/2} \quad \ldots(6.88)$$

From equation-(6.87) and (6.88) we have

$$\frac{T}{T'}=\left(\frac{r}{r'}\right)^{3/2}$$

or $$T'=T\left(\frac{r'}{r}\right)^{3/2}$$

$$=365\left(\frac{1}{2}\right)^{3/2}=\frac{365}{2\sqrt{2}}\text{ days}$$

 # Illustrative Example 6.31

An artificial satellite of the earth is to be established in the equatorial plane of the earth and to an observer at the equator it is required that the satellite will move eastward, completing one round trip per day. Determine the distance of the satellite from the centre of the earth. The mass of the earth is $M=6.00\times10^{24}$ kg and its angular velocity $\omega_0=7.30\times10^{-5}$ rad/s.

Solution

Velocity of satellite in orbit of radius r is

$$v=\sqrt{\frac{GM}{r}}$$

Its angular velocity is

$$\omega=\frac{v}{r}=\sqrt{\frac{GM}{r^{3/2}}}$$

According to problem

$$\omega=2\omega_0$$

Thus we have

$$2\omega_0=\sqrt{\frac{GM}{r^{3/2}}}$$

or $$r=\left(\frac{GM}{4\omega_0^2}\right)^{1/3}$$

$$=\left[\frac{(6.67\times10^{11})\times(6\times10^{24})}{4\times(7.3\times10^{-5})^2}\right]^{1/3}$$

$$=2.66\times10^7\text{ m}$$

 # Illustrative Example 6.32

A satellite revolving in a circular equatorial orbit of radius $r=2.00\times10^4$ km from west to east appear over a certain point at the equator every $t=11.6$ hours. Using this data, calculate the mass of the earth. The gravitational constant is supposed to be known.

Solution

Here, the absolute angular velocity of satellite is given by

$$\omega=\omega_s+\omega_E$$

Where ω_E is the angular velocity of earth, which is from west to east.

or $$\omega=\frac{2\pi}{t}+\frac{2\pi}{T} \quad \text{[Where } t=11.6\text{ hr. and } T=24\text{ hr.]}$$

From Kepler's III law, we have

$$\omega=\frac{\sqrt{GM}}{r^{3/2}}$$

Thus we have

$$\frac{\sqrt{GM}}{r^{3/2}}=\frac{2\pi}{t}+\frac{2\pi}{T}$$

or $$M=\frac{4\pi^2 r^3}{G}\left[\frac{1}{t}+\frac{1}{T}\right]^2$$

$$=\frac{4\pi^2(2\times10^7)^3}{(6.67\times10^{-11})}\left[\frac{1}{11.6\times3600}+\frac{1}{24\times3600}\right]^2$$

$$=6.0\times10^{24}\text{ kg}$$

Illustrative Example 6.33

An artificial satellite is describing an equatorial orbit at 1600 km above the surface of the earth. Calculate its orbital speed and the period of revolution. If the satellite is travelling in the same direction as the rotation of the earth (i.e., from west to east), calculate the interval between two successive times at which it will appear vertically overhead to an observer at a fixed point on the equator. Radius of earth = 6400 km.

Solution

We know that the period of the satellite is

$$T = \frac{2\pi}{\sqrt{GM}} r^{3/2} = \frac{2\pi}{\sqrt{gR^2}} r^{3/2}$$

Where $r = 6400 + 1600 = 800 \text{ km} = 8000 \times 10^3 \text{ m},$

$g = 9.8 \text{ m/sec}^2$ and $R = 6400 \times 10^3 \text{ m}$

Substituting values we get

$$T = 2 \times 3.14 \left[\frac{(8000\times10^3)^3}{9.8\times(6400\times10^3)^2}\right]^{1/2}$$

$$= 7096 \text{ s}$$

Further, orbital speed,

$$v = \sqrt{\frac{GM}{r}} = \sqrt{\frac{gR^2}{r}}$$

or
$$v = \sqrt{\left(\frac{9.8}{8000\times10^3}\right)} \times (6400 \times 10^3)$$

$$= 7083.5 \text{ m/s}$$

Let t be the time interval between two successive moments at which the satellite is overhead to an observer at a fixed position on the equator. As both satellite and earth are moving in same direction with angular speeds ω_S and ω_E respectively, we can write the time of separation as

$$t = \frac{2\pi}{\omega_S - \omega_E}$$

Here $\omega_S = \frac{2\pi}{7096}$ and $\omega_E = \frac{2\pi}{86400}$

Thus we have $t = \frac{86400\times7096}{86400-7096}$

$$= 7731 \text{ s}$$

Illustrative Example 6.34

A satellite of mass m is moving in a circular orbit of radius r. Calculate its angular momentum with respect to the centre of the orbit in terms of the mass of the earth.

Solution

The situation is shown in figure-6.66.

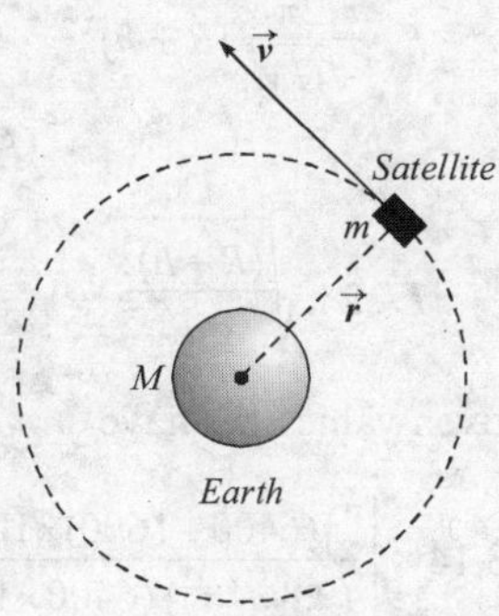

Figure 6.66

The angular momentum of the satellite with respect to the centre of orbit is given by

$$\vec{L} = \vec{r} \times m\vec{v}$$

Where $\vec{r}$ the position vector of satellite with respect to the centre of orbit and $\vec{v}$ is its velocity vector of satellite.

It case of circular orbit, the angle between $\vec{r}$ and $\vec{v}$ is 90º. Hence

$$L = m\,v\,r \sin 90^\circ = m\,v\,r \qquad \dots(6.89)$$

The direction is perpendicular to the plane of the orbit.

We know orbital speed of satellite is

$$v = \sqrt{\frac{GM}{r}} \qquad \dots(6.90)$$

From equation-(6.89) and (6.90), we get

$$L = m\sqrt{\frac{GM}{r}}\, r$$

or
$$L = (G\,M\,m^2\,r)^{1/2}$$

Illustrative Example 6.35

A satellite is launched into a circular orbit 1600 km above the surface of the earth. Find the period of revolution, if the radius of the earth $R = 6400$ km and the acceleration due to gravity is 9.8 m/s^2, At what height from the ground should it be launched so that it may appear stationary over a point on he earth's equator ?

Solution

We know that the orbital period of a satellite in an orbit of radius r is

$$T=\frac{2\pi}{\sqrt{GM}}r^{3/2}$$

$$T=\frac{2\pi}{\sqrt{GM}}(R+h)^{3/2} \quad \ldots(6.91)$$

[As here $r=R+h$]

or $$T=2\pi\sqrt{\frac{(R+h)^3}{gR^2}} \quad \left[\text{As } g=\frac{GM}{R^2}\right]$$

Substituting the given values, we have

$$T=2\times 3.14\times\left[\frac{[(6400+1600)\times 10^3 m]^3}{(9.8m/s^2)(6400\times 10^3 m)^2}\right]^{1/2}$$

$$=7090\text{ s}=6.97\text{ hour}$$

The satellite will appear stationary in the sky if its period of revolution round the earth is equal to period of revolution of the earth round its own axis (24 hours). Let us find the height of the satellite with this time period. Now from equation-(6.91), we have

$$h=\left[\frac{T^2gR^2}{4\pi^2}\right]^{1/3}-R$$

or, $$h=\left[\frac{(24\times 3600)^2\times(9.8)\times(6400\times 10^3)^2}{4\times(3.14)^2}\right]^{1/3}-(6400\times 10^3)$$

$$=4.23\times 10^7-0.64\times 10^7$$

$$=3.59\times 10^7=3.59\times 10^4\text{ km}$$

 # Illustrative Example 6.36

Two Earth's satellites move in a common plane along circular orbits. The orbital radius of one satellite $r = 7000$ km while that of the other satellite is $\Delta r = 70$ km less. What time interval separates the periodic approaches of the satellites to each other over the minimum distance?

Solution

Now for first satellite which is revolving about the earth (mass M and radius r) the orbital speed is

$$v=\sqrt{\frac{GM}{r}} \quad \ldots(6.92)$$

Let T_1 and T_2 be the time period for first and second satellites respectively. Then we know that

$$T_1=\frac{2\pi r}{v}=\frac{2\pi}{\sqrt{GM}}r^{3/2}$$

and $$T_2=\frac{2\pi}{\sqrt{GM}}(r-\Delta r)^{3/2}$$

As second satellite is revolving in a radius $(r-\Delta r)$. Know the period interval (T_1-T_2) is given by

$$T_1-T_2=\frac{2\pi}{\sqrt{GM}}[r^{3/2}-(r-\Delta r)^{3/2}]$$

$$=\frac{2\pi}{\sqrt{GM}}\left[r^{3/2}-r^{3/2}\left(1-\frac{\Delta r}{r}\right)^{3/2}\right]$$

$$=\frac{2\pi}{\sqrt{GM}}r^{3/2}\left[1-\left(1-\frac{3}{2}\frac{\Delta r}{r}\right)\right]$$

$$=\frac{2\pi}{\sqrt{GM}}r^{3/2}\left(\frac{3}{2}\frac{\Delta r}{r}\right).$$

Web Reference of Video Lectures at www.physicsgalaxy.com
Age Group - High School Physics | Age 17-19 Years
Section - GRAVITATION
Topic - Satellite Motion
Module Number - 1 to 5

Practice Exercise 6.5

(i) Two satellites A and B of the same mass are orbiting the earth at altitudes R and $3R$ respectively, where R is the radius of the earth. Taking their orbits to be circular, obtain the ratios of sun of their kinetic and magnitudes of potential energies.

[1 : 2]

(ii) A satellite of mass 1000 kg is supposed to orbit the earth at a height of 2000 km above the earth's surface. Find (a) Its speed in the orbit, (b) its kinetic energy, (c) the potential energy of the earth-satellite system and (d) its time period. Mass of the earth = 6×10^{24} kg.

[(a) 6.986 km/s; (b) 2.44×10^{10} J; (c) -4.88×10^{10} J; (d) 1.975 hrs]

(iii) A satellite is to revolve round the earth in a circle of radius 8000 km. With what speed should this satellite be projected into orbit? What will be the time period of its revolution? Take g at the surface = 9.8 m/s² and radius of the earth = 6400 km.

[7.08 km/s, 118.26 minutes]

(iv) Assuming the radius of the earth to be 6400 km, calculate the period of revolution of a satellite which is describing an equatorial orbit at 1400 km above the surface. If the satellite is travelling in the same direction as the rotation of the earth *i.e.* West to East, what is the interval between two successive times at which it will appear vertically overhead to an observer at a fixed point on the equator ? Take $g = 10\ m/s^2$.

[2.038 hr]

(v) A satellite of mass 2×10^3 kg has to be shifted from an orbit of radius $2R$ to another of radius $3R$, where R is the radius of the earth. Calculate the minimum energy required. Take mass of earth $= 6 \times 10^{24}$ kg, radius of earth $= 6.4 \times 10^6$ m.

[1.042×10^{10} J]

(vi) A double star is a system of two stars of different masses moving around the centre of inertia of the system due to gravitation. Find the distance between the components of the double star, if its total mass equals M and the period of revolution T.

[$\left[GM\left(\frac{T}{2\pi}\right)^2\right]^{1/3}$]

(vii) If a planet is suddenly stopped in its orbit supposed to be circular, show that it would fall into the sun in a time $(\sqrt{2}/8)$ times the period of the planet's revolution.

(viii) A particle would take a time t_1 to move down a straight tunnel from the surface of earth to its centre. If g is assumed to be constant, time would be t_2. Find t_1/t_2.

[$\frac{\pi}{2\sqrt{2}}$]

6.10 Motion of a Satellite in Elliptical Path

Wherever a satellite is in a circular or elliptical path, these orbits are called bounded orbits as satellite is moving in an orbit bounded to earth. The bound nature of orbit means that the kinetic energy of satellite is not enough at any point in the orbit to take the satellite to infinity. In equation-(6.85) negative total energy of a revolving satellite shows its boundness to earth. Even when a body is in elliptical path around the earth, its total energy must be negative. Lets first discuss how a satellite or a body can be in elliptical path.

Consider a body (satellite) of mass m in a circular path of radius r around the earth as shown in figure-6.67, we've discussed that in circular path the net gravitational frame on body is exactly balancing the centrifugal force on it in radial direction relative to a rotating frame with the body.

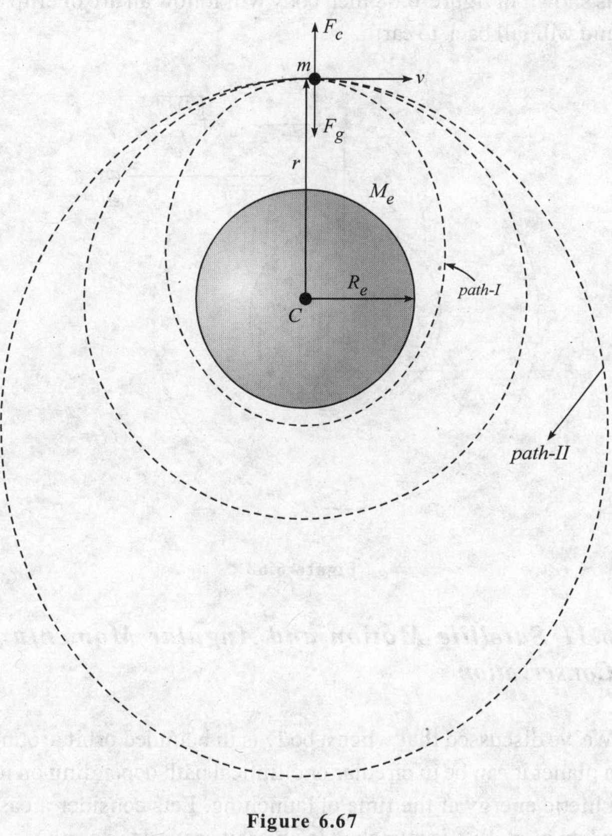

Figure 6.67

If suddenly the velocity of body decreases then the centrifugal force on it becomes less then the gravitational force acting on it and due to this it can not continue in the circular orbit and will come inward from the circular orbit due to unbalanced forces. Mathematical analysis shows that this path-I along which the body is now moving is an ellipse. The analytical calculations of the laws for this path is beyond the scope of this book. But students should keep in mind that if velocity of a body at a distance r from earth's centre tangential to the circular orbit is less than $\sqrt{\frac{GM_e}{r}}$ then its path will be elliptical with earth centre at one of the foci of the ellipse.

Similarly if the speed of body exceeds $\sqrt{\frac{GM_e}{r}}$ then it must move out of the circular path due to unbalancing of forces again but this time $F_c > F_g$. Due to this if speed of body is not increased by such a value that its kinetic energy can take the particle to infinity then it will follow in a bigger elliptical orbit as shown in figure-6.67 in path-II, with earth's centre at one of the foci of the orbit.

In above case when speed of body was decreased and its value is lesser then $\sqrt{\frac{GM_e}{r}}$ and the speed is decreased to such a value that the elliptical orbit will intersect the earth's surface as shown in figure-6.68 then body will follow an arc of ellipse and will fall back to earth.

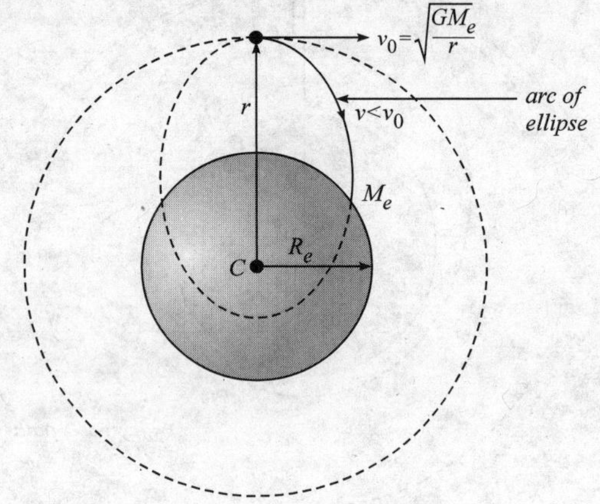

Figure 6.68

6.11 Satellite Motion and Angular Momentum Conservation

We've discussed that when a body is in bounded orbit around a planet it can be in circular or elliptical path depending on its kinetic energy at the time of launching. Lets consider a case when a satellite is launched in an orbit around the earth.

A satellite S is first fired away from earth surface in vertical direction to penetrate the earth's atmosphere. When it reaches point A, it is imparted a velocity in tangential direction to start its revolution around the earth in its orbit.

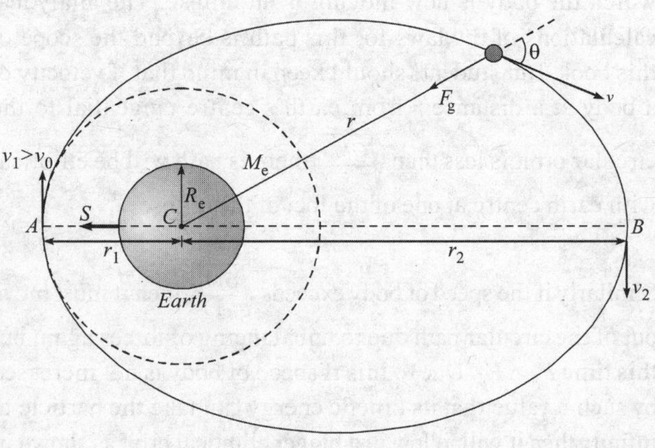

Figure 6.69

This velocity is termed as insertion velocity, if the velocity imparted to satellite is $v_0 = \sqrt{\frac{GM_e}{r_1}}$ then it starts following the circular path shown in figure-6.69. If velocity imparted is $v_1 > v_0$ then it will trace the elliptical path shown. During this motion the only force acting on satellite is the gravitational force due to earth which is acting along the line joining of satellite and centre of earth.

As the force on satellite always passes through centre of earth during motion, we can say that on satellite there is no torque acting about centre of earth this total angular momentum of satellite during its orbital motion remains constant about earth's centre.

As no external force is involved for earth-satellite system, no external work is being done here so we can also state that total mechanical energy of system also remains conserved.

In the elliptical path of satellite shown in figure if r_1 and r_2 are the shortest distance (perigee) and farthest distances (apogee) of satellite from earth and at the points, velocities of satellite are v_1 and v_2 then we have according to conservation of angular momentum, the angular momentum of satellite at a general point is given as

$$L = mv_1 r_1 = mv_2 r_2 = mvr \sin\theta \qquad \dots(6.93)$$

During motion the total mechanical energy of satellite (kinetic + potential) also remains conserved. Thus the total energy of satellite can be given as

$$E = \frac{1}{2} mv_1^2 - \frac{GM_e m}{r_1}$$

$$= \frac{1}{2} mv_2^2 - \frac{GM_e m}{r_2}$$

$$= \frac{1}{2} mv^2 - \frac{GM_e m}{r} \qquad \dots(6.94)$$

Using the above relations in equation-(6.93) and (6.94) we can find velocities v_1 and v_2 of satellite at nearest and farthest locations in terms of r_1 and r_2.

6.12 Kepler's Laws of Planetary Motion

The motions of planet in universe have always been a puzzle. In 17th century Johannes Kepler, after a life time of study worded out some empirical laws based on the analysis of astronomical measurements of Tycho Brahe. Kepler formulate his laws, which are kinematical description of planetary motion. Now we discuss these laws step by step.

6.12.1 Kepler's First Law [The Law of Orbits]

Kepler's first law is illustrated in the image shown in figure-6.70 It states that "*All the planets move around the sun in elliptical orbits with sun at one of the focus not at centre of orbit.*"

It is observed that the orbits of planets around sun are very less acentric or approximately circular.

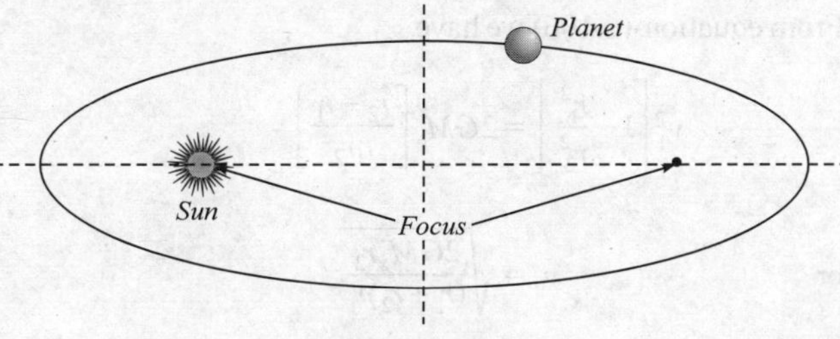

Figure 6.70

6.12.2 Kepler's Second Law [The Law of Areas]

Kepler's second Law is basically an alternative statement of law of conservation of momentum. It is illustrated in the image shown in figure-6.71(a). We know from angular momentum conservation, in elliptical orbit planet will move faster when it is nearer the sun. Thus when a planet executes elliptical orbit its angular speed changes continuously as it moves in the orbit. The point of nearest approach of the planet to the sun is termed perihelion. The point of greatest separation is termed aphelion. Hence by angular momentum conservation we can state that the planet moves with maximum speed when it is near perihelion and moves with slowest speed when it is near aphelion.

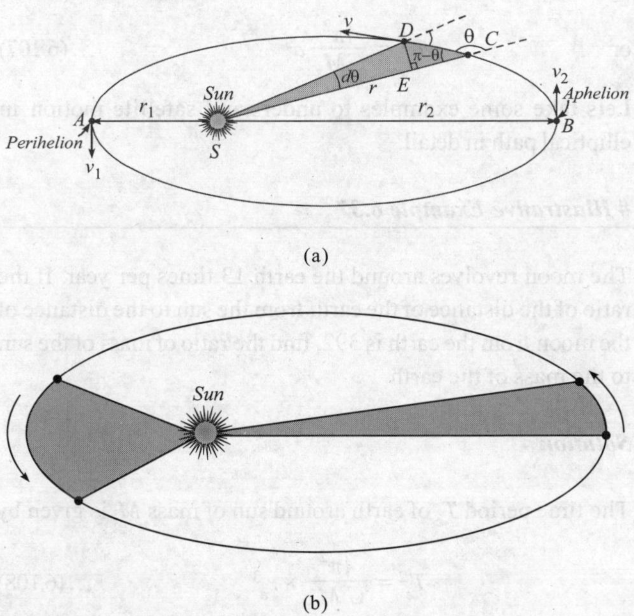

Figure 6.71

Kepler's second law states that *"The line joining the sun and planet sweeps out equal areas in equal time or the rate of sweeping area by the position vector of the planet with respect to sun remains constant."* This is shown in figure-6.71(b)

The above statement of Kepler's second law can be verified by the law of conservation of angular momentum. To verify this consider the moving planet around the sun at a general point C in the orbit at speed v. Let at this instant the distance of planet from sun is r. If θ be the angle between position vector $\vec{r}$ of planet and its velocity vector then the angular momentum of planet at this instant is

$$L = mvr\sin\theta \qquad \ldots(6.95)$$

In an elemental time the planet will cover a small distance $CD = dl$ and will travel to another adjacent point D as shown in figure-6.71(a), thus the distance $CD = vdt$. In this duration dt, the position vector $\vec{r}$ sweeps out an area equal to that of triangle SCD, which is calculated as

Area of triangle SCD is

$$dA = \frac{1}{2} \times r \times vdt\sin(\pi - \theta)$$

$$= \frac{1}{2} r\, v\sin\theta.\, dt$$

Thus the rate of sweeping area by the position vector $\vec{r}$ is

$$\frac{dA}{dt} = \frac{1}{2} rv\sin\theta \qquad \ldots(6.96)$$

Now from equation-(6.95)

$$\frac{dA}{dt} = \frac{L}{2m} = \text{constant} \qquad \ldots(6.97)$$

The expression in equation-(6.97) verifies the statement of Kepler' II law of planetary motion.

6.12.3 Kepler's Third Law [The Law of Periods]

Kepler's Third Laws is concerned with the time period of revolution of planets. It states that *"The time period of revolution of a planet in its orbit around the sun is directly proportional to the cube of semi-major axis of the elliptical path around the sun."*

If 'T' is the period of revolution and 'a' be the semi-major axis of the path of planet then according to Kepler's III Law, we have

$$T^2 \propto a^3 \qquad \ldots(6.98)$$

For circular orbits, it is a special case of ellipse when its major and minor axis are equal. If a planet is in a circular orbit of radius r around the sun then its revolution speed must be given as

$$v = \sqrt{\frac{GM_s}{r}} \qquad \ldots(6.99)$$

Where M_s is the mass of sun. There you can recall that this speed is independent from the mass of planet. Here the time period of revolution can be given as

$$T = \frac{2\pi r}{v}$$

or $$T = \frac{2\pi r}{\sqrt{\frac{GM_s}{r}}} \quad \ldots(6.100)$$

Squaring equation no.-(6.100), we get

$$T^2 = \frac{4\pi^2}{GM_s} r^3 \quad \ldots(6.101)$$

Equation-(6.101) verifies the statement of Kepler's third law for circular orbits. Similarly we can also verify it for elliptical orbits. For this we start from the relation we've derived earlier for rate of sweeping area by the position vector of planet with respect to sun which is given as

$$\frac{dA}{dt} = \frac{L}{2m} \quad \ldots(6.102)$$

Where L is the total angular momentum of planet during its motion consider the path of planet shown in figure-6.72 is an elliptical path with sun at one focus $(-ae, 0)$.

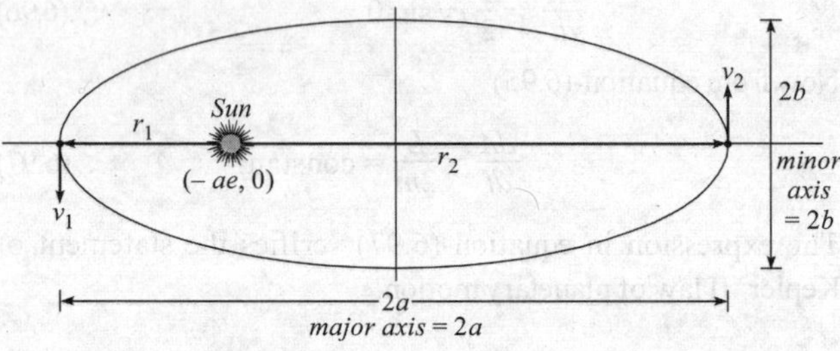

Figure 6.72

Here r_1 and r_2 are the shortest and farthest distance of planet from sun during its motion, which are given as

$$r_1 = a(1-e) \quad \ldots(6.103)$$

and $$r_2 = a(1+e) \quad \ldots(6.104)$$

Where e is the centricity. From geometry we know that the relation in semi major axis a and semiminor axis b is given as

$$b = a\sqrt{1-e^2} \quad \ldots(6.105)$$

If v_1 and v_2 are the planet speeds at perihelion and aphelion points then from conservation of momentum we have

$$L = mv_1 r_1 = mv_2 r_2 \quad \ldots(6.106)$$

From energy conservation we have

$$\frac{1}{2}mv_1^2 - \frac{GM_s m}{r_1} = \frac{1}{2}mv_2^2 - \frac{GM_s m}{r_2}$$

or $$v_1^2 - v_2^2 = 2GM_s\left[\frac{1}{r_1} - \frac{1}{r_2}\right]$$

From equation-(6.106) we have

$$v_1^2\left[1 - \frac{r_1^2}{r_2^2}\right] = 2GM_s\left[\frac{r_2 - r_1}{r_1 r_2}\right]$$

or $$v_1 = \sqrt{\frac{2GM_s r_2}{(r_1 + r_2)r_1}}$$

From equation-(6.103) and (6.104) we have

$$v_1 = \sqrt{\frac{GM_s}{a}\left(\frac{1+e}{1-e}\right)}$$

Now from equation-(6.102) we have the total area of ellipse traced by the planet is given as

$$A = \frac{L}{2m}T$$

or $$T = \frac{2m}{L}A = \frac{2m\pi ab}{L} = \frac{2m\pi ab}{mv_1 r_1}$$

or $$T = \frac{2m\pi a\left[a\sqrt{1-e^2}\right]}{m\left[\sqrt{\frac{GM_s}{a}\left(\frac{1+e}{1-e}\right)}\right][a(1-e)]}$$

or $$T^2 = \frac{4\pi^2}{GM_s}a^3 \quad \ldots(6.107)$$

Lets take some examples to understand satellite motion in elliptical path in detail.

Illustrative Example 6.37

The moon revolves around the earth 13 times per year. If the ratio of the distance of the earth from the sun to the distance of the moon from the earth is 392, find the ratio of mass of the sun to the mass of the earth.

Solution

The time period T_e of earth around sun of mass M_s is given by

$$T_e^2 = \frac{4\pi^2}{GM_s} \times r_e^3 \quad \ldots(6.108)$$

Where r_e is the radius of the earth.

Similarly, time period T_m of moon around earth is given by

$$T_m^2 = \frac{4\pi^2}{GM_e} \times r_m^3 \quad \ldots(6.109)$$

Dividing equation-(6.108) by equation-(6.109), we get

$$\left(\frac{T_e}{T_m}\right)^2 = \left(\frac{M_e}{M_s}\right)\left(\frac{r_e}{r_m}\right)^3$$

or
$$\left(\frac{M_s}{M_e}\right) = \left(\frac{T_m}{T_e}\right)^2 \times \left(\frac{r_e}{r_m}\right)^3 \quad \ldots(6.110)$$

Substituting the given values, we get

$$\left(\frac{M_s}{M_e}\right) = \left\{\frac{(1/3)}{1}\right\}^2 \times (392)^3 = 3.56 \times 10^5$$

Illustrative Example 6.38

A satellite revolves around a planet in an elliptical orbit. Its maximum and minimum distances from the planet are 1.5×10^7 m and 0.5×10^7 m respectively. If the speed of the satellite at the farthest point be 5×10^3 m/s, calculate the speed at the nearest point.

Solution

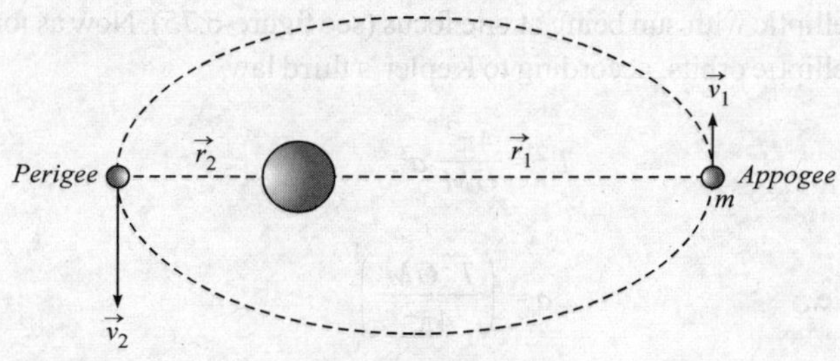

Figure 6.73

In case of elliptical orbit, the speed of satellite varies constantly as shown in figure-6.73. Thus according to the law of conservation of angular momentum, the satellite must move faster at a point of closest approach (Perigee) than at a farthest point (Apogee).

We know that

$$\vec{\mathbf{L}} = \vec{\mathbf{r}} \times m\,\vec{\mathbf{v}}$$

Hence, at the two points,

$$L = m\,v_1\,r_1 = m\,v_2\,r_2$$

or
$$\frac{v_1}{v_2} = \frac{r_2}{r_1}$$

Substituting the given values, we get

$$\frac{5\times10^3}{v_2} = \frac{0.5\times10^7}{1.5\times10^7}$$

$$v_2 = 1.5 \times 10^4 \text{ m/s}$$

Illustrative Example 6.39

Imagine a light planet revolving around a very massive star in a circular orbit of radius r with a period of revolution T. On what power of r, will the square of time period depend if the gravitational force of attraction between the planet and the star is proportional to $r^{-5/2}$.

Solution

As gravitation provides centripetal force

$$\frac{mv^2}{r} = \frac{K}{r^{5/2}},$$

i.e.,
$$v^2 = \frac{K}{mr^{3/2}}$$

So that
$$T = \frac{2\pi r}{v} = 2\pi r\sqrt{\frac{mr^{3/2}}{K}}$$

or
$$T^2 = \frac{4\pi^2 m}{K}\, r^{7/2}; \quad \text{so} \quad T^2 \propto r^{7/2}$$

Illustrative Example 6.40

A meteorite of mass m collides with a satellite which was orbiting around a planet in a circular path of radius R. Due to collision, the meteorite sticks to the satellite (mass $= 10\,m$) and the satellite is seen to have gone into an orbit whose minimum distance from the planet is $R/2$. Determine the velocity v of the meteorite before collision. Mass of the planet is M.

Solution

The situation before collision and after collision is shown in figure-6.74.

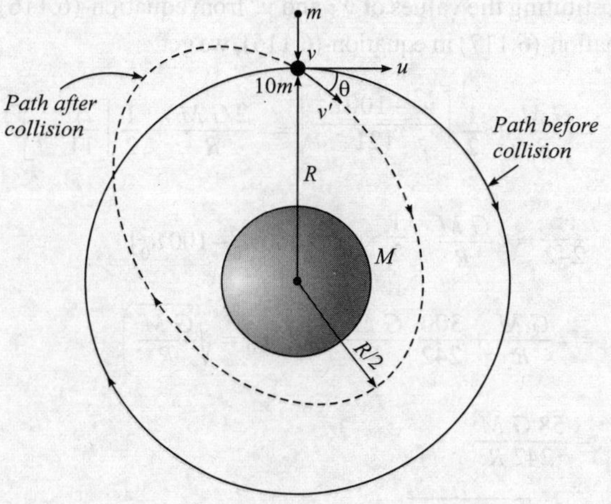

Figure 6.74

Before collision the speed of satellites is

$$u_0 = \sqrt{\frac{GM}{R}} \quad \ldots(6.111)$$

If after collision with meteorite the combined mass 11 m moves of an angle θ with the orbit as shown in figure-6.74. If finally 11 m moves at speed v' then applying the law of conservation of momentum along horizontal and vertical directions, we get

$$m v = 11\, m v' \sin\theta$$

or $$v' \sin\theta = (v/11) \quad \ldots(6.112)$$

$$10\, m u_0 = 11\, m v' \cos\theta$$

or $$v' \cos\theta = (10\, v_0/11) \quad \ldots(6.113)$$

After collision (Figure-6.74), applying the conservation of angular momentum, we have

$$11m\,(v'\cos\theta)\,R = 11\,m\,(v'')\,\frac{R}{2} \quad \ldots(6.114)$$

[If v'' is speed at perigee]

Applying the principle of conservation of energy, we have

$$-\frac{GM\,(11m)}{R} + \frac{1}{2}(11\,m)\,v'^2$$

$$= -\frac{GM\,(11\,m)}{(R/2)} + \frac{1}{2}(11\,m)\,v''^2$$

or $$-\frac{GM}{R} + \frac{v'^2}{2} = -\frac{2\,GM}{R} + \frac{v''^2}{2} \quad \ldots(6.115)$$

From equation-(6.112) and (6.113)

$$v'^2 = \left(\frac{v}{11}\right)^2 + \left(\frac{10\,u_0}{11}\right)^2 = \frac{v^2 + 100\,u_0^2}{121} \quad \ldots(6.116)$$

From equation-(6.114), $v'' = 2\,v'\cos\theta = (20/11)\,v_0$ ...(6.117)

Substituting the values of v'^2 and v'' from equation-(6.116) and equation-(6.117) in equation-(6.115), we get

$$-\frac{GM}{R} + \frac{1}{2}\left[\frac{v^2 + 100\,u_0^2}{121}\right] = -\frac{2\,GM}{R} + \frac{1}{2}\left[\frac{20}{11}u_0\right]^2$$

or $$\frac{v^2}{242} = -\frac{GM}{R} + \frac{1}{2} \times \frac{1}{121}\,[400\,u_0^2 - 100\,u_0^2]$$

$$= -\frac{GM}{R} + \frac{300}{242}\,\frac{GM}{R} \qquad \left(\text{As } u_0 = \sqrt{\frac{GM}{R}}\right)$$

$$= \frac{58\,GM}{242\,R}$$

or $$v = \sqrt{\left(\frac{58\,GM}{R}\right)}$$

Illustrative Example 6.41

Halley's comet has a period of 76 years and in the year 1986, had a distance of closest approach to the sun equal to 8.9×10^{10} m. What is the comet's farthest distance from the sun if the mass of sun is 2×10^{30} kg and $G = 6.67 \times 10^{-11}$ MKS units ?

Solution

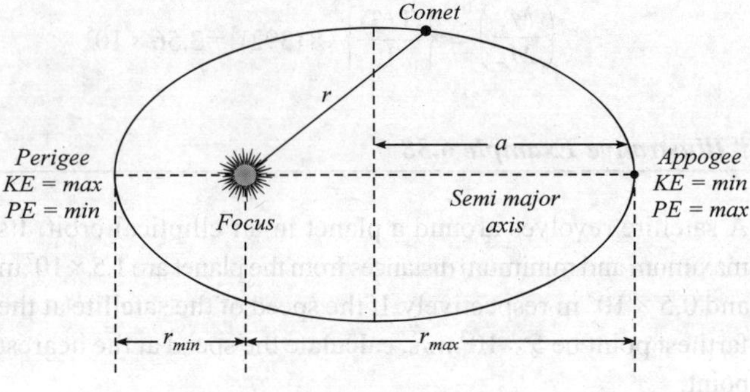

Figure 6.75

From the problem it is self-evident that the orbit of the comet is elliptic with sun being at one focus (see figure-6.75). Now as for elliptic orbits, according to Kepler's third law,

$$T^2 = \frac{4\pi^2}{GM}\,a^3,$$

i.e., $$a = \left(\frac{T^2 GM}{4\pi^2}\right)^{1/3}$$

or $$a = \left[\frac{(76 \times 3.15 \times 10^7)^2 \times 6.67 \times 10^{-11} \times 2 \times 10^{30}}{4\pi^2}\right]^{1/3}$$

$$\simeq 2.7 \times 10^{12}\,\text{m}$$

But in case of ellipse, we have

$$2a = r_{min} + r_{max},$$

or $$r_{max} = 2a - r_{min}$$

So $$r_{max} = 2 \times 2.7 \times 10^{12} - 8.9 \times 10^{10} \simeq 5.3 \times 10^{12}\,\text{m}$$

Illustrative Example 6.42

A satellite is revolving round the earth in a circular orbit of radius a with velocity v_0. A particle is projected from the satellite in forward direction with relative velocity $v = (\sqrt{5/4} - 1)\,v_0$. Calculate, during subsequent motion of the particle its minimum and maximum distances from earth's centre.

Solution

The corresponding situation is shown in figure-6.76

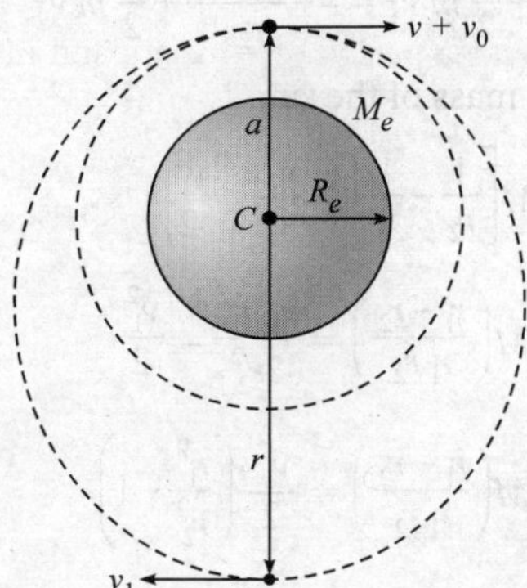

Figure 6.76

Initial velocity of satellite

$$v_0 = \sqrt{\left(\frac{GM}{a}\right)}$$

When particle is thrown with the velocity v relative to satellite, the resultant velocity of particle will become

$$v_R = v_0 + v$$

$$= \sqrt{\left(\frac{5}{4}\right)}\, v_0 = \sqrt{\left(\frac{5\,GM}{4\quad a}\right)}$$

As the particle velocity is greater than the velocity required for circular orbit, hence the particle path deviates from circular path to elliptical path. At positions of minimum and maximum distances velocity vectors are perpendicular to instantaneous radius vector. In this electrical path the minimum distance of particle from earth's centre is a and maximum speed in the path is v_R and let the maximum distance and minimum speed in the path is r and v_1 respectively.

Now as angular momentum and total energy remain conserved. Applying the law of conservation of angular momentum, we have

$$m\, v_1\, r = m\,(v_0 + v)\, a \qquad [m = \text{mass of particle}]$$

or $$v_1 = \frac{(v_0 + v)a}{r}$$

$$= \frac{a}{r}\left[\sqrt{\left(\frac{5\;GM}{4\quad a}\right)}\right]$$

$$= \frac{1}{r}\left[\sqrt{\left(\frac{5}{4} \times GMa\right)}\right]$$

Applying the law of conservation of energy

$$\frac{1}{2}\, m\, v_1^2 - \frac{G\,M\,m}{r} = \frac{1}{2}\, m\,(v_0 + v)^2 - \frac{G\,M\,m}{a}$$

or $$\frac{1}{2}\, m\left(\frac{5\,G\,M\,a}{4\quad r^2}\right) - \frac{G\,M\,m}{r} = \frac{1}{2}\, m\left(\frac{5\,G\,M}{4\quad a}\right) - \frac{G\,M\,m}{a}$$

$$\frac{5}{8} \times \frac{a}{r^2} - \frac{1}{r} = \frac{5}{8} \times \frac{1}{a} - \frac{1}{a} = -\frac{3}{8\,a}$$

or $$3r^2 - 8\,a\,r + 5\,a^2 = 0$$

or $$r = a \quad \text{or} \quad \frac{5a}{3}$$

Thus minimum distance of the particle $= a$

And maximum distance of the particle $= \dfrac{5a}{3}$

Illustrative Example 6.43

A sky lab of mass 2×10^3 kg is first launched from the surface of earth in a circular orbit of radius $2\,R$ (from the centre of earth) and then it is shifted from this circular orbit to another circular orbit of radius $3\,R$. Calculate the minimum energy required (a) to place the lab in the first orbit (b) to shift the lab from first orbit to the second orbit. Given, $R = 6400$ km and $g = 10$ m/s^2.

Solution

(a) The energy of the sky lab on the surface of earth

$$E_S = \text{KE} + \text{PE} = 0 + \left(-\frac{GMm}{R}\right) = -\frac{GMm}{R}$$

And the total energy of the sky lab in an orbit of radius $2R$ is

$$E_1 = -\frac{GMm}{4R}$$

So the energy required to place the lab from the surface of earth to the orbit of radius $2R$ is given as

$$E_1 - E_S = -\frac{GMm}{4R} - \left[-\frac{GMm}{R}\right] = \frac{3}{4}\frac{GMm}{R}$$

or $$\Delta E = \frac{3}{4}\frac{m}{R} \times gR^2 = \frac{3}{4}\, mgR \left[\text{As } g = \frac{GM}{R^2}\right]$$

or $$\Delta E = \frac{3}{4}(2 \times 10^3 \times 10 \times 6.4 \times 10^6)$$

$$= \frac{3}{4}(12.8 \times 10^{10}) = 9.6 \times 10^{10}\ \text{J}$$

(b) As for II orbit of radius $3R$ the total energy of sky lab is

$$E_2 = -\frac{GMm}{2(3R)} = -\frac{GMm}{6R}$$

or $$E_2 - E_1 = -\frac{GMm}{6R} - \left(-\frac{GMm}{4R}\right) = \frac{1}{12}\frac{GMm}{R}$$

or $$\Delta E = \frac{1}{12}\, mgR = \frac{1}{12}(12.8 \times 10^{10}) = 1.1 \times 10^{10}\ \text{J}$$

Illustrative Example 6.44

A satellite is revolving around a planet of mass M in an elliptic orbit of semimajor axis a. Show that the orbital speed of the satellite when it is at a distance r from the focus will be given by :

$$v^2 = GM\left[\frac{2}{r} - \frac{1}{a}\right]$$

Solution

As in case of elliptic orbit with semi major axes a, of a satellite total mechanical energy remains constant, at any position of satellite in the orbit, given as

$$E = -\frac{GMm}{2a}$$

or $$\text{KE} + \text{PE} = -\frac{GMm}{2a} \qquad \dots(6.118)$$

Now, if at position r, v is the orbital speed of satellite, we have

$$\text{KE} = \frac{1}{2}mv^2 \text{ and PE} = -\frac{GMm}{r} \qquad \dots(6.119)$$

So from equations-(6.118) and (6.119), we have

$$\frac{1}{2}mv^2 - \frac{GMm}{r} = -\frac{GMm}{2a}, \text{ i.e., } v^2 = GM\left[\frac{2}{r} - \frac{1}{a}\right]$$

Illustrative Example 6.45

A planet of mass m moves along an ellipse around the sun so that its maximum and minimum distances from the sun are equal to r_1 and r_2 respectively. Find the angular momentum of this plane relative to the centre of the sun.

Solution

If v_1 and v_2 are the velocities or planet at its apogee and perigee respectively then according to conservation of angular momentum, we have

$$m v_1 r_1 = m v_2 r_2$$

or $$v_1 r_1 = v_2 r_2$$

Figure 6.77

As the total energy of the planet is also constant, we have

$$-\frac{GMm}{r_1} + \frac{1}{2}mv_1^2 = -\frac{GMm}{r_2} + \frac{1}{2}mv_2^2$$

Where M is the mass of the sun.

or $$GM\left[\frac{1}{r_2} - \frac{1}{r_1}\right] = \frac{v_2^2}{2} - \frac{v_1^2}{2}$$

or $$GM\left(\frac{r_1 - r_2}{r_1 r_2}\right) = \frac{v_1^2 r_1^2}{2r_2^2} - \frac{v_1^2}{2}$$

or $$GM\left(\frac{r_1 - r_2}{r_1 r_2}\right) = \frac{v_1^2}{2}\left(\frac{r_1^2}{r_2^2} - 1\right)$$

$$= \frac{v_1^2}{2}\left(\frac{r_1^2 - r_2^2}{r_2^2}\right)$$

or $$v_1^2 = \frac{2GM(r_1 - r_2)r_2^2}{r_1 r_2(r_1^2 - r_2^2)} = \frac{2Gr_2}{r_1(r_1 + r_2)}$$

or $$v_1 = \sqrt{\left[\frac{2GMr_2}{r_1(r_1 + r_2)}\right]}$$

Now Angular momentum of planet is given as

$$L = m v_1 r_1$$

$$= m\sqrt{\left[\frac{2GM r_1 r_2}{(r_1 + r_2)}\right]}$$

Illustrative Example 6.46

A planet moves along an elliptical orbit around the sun. At the moment when it was at a distance r_0 from the sun its velocity was equal to v_0 and the angle between the radius vector r_0 and the velocity vector v_0 was equal to α. Find the maximum and minimum distances that will separate this planet from the sun during its orbital motion.

Solution

Planet revolving around the sun is shown in figure-6.78. Here we have assumed that the apogee and perigee of the planet are r_1 and r_2 respectively and the velocities of the planet at these point are v_1 and v_2 respectively.

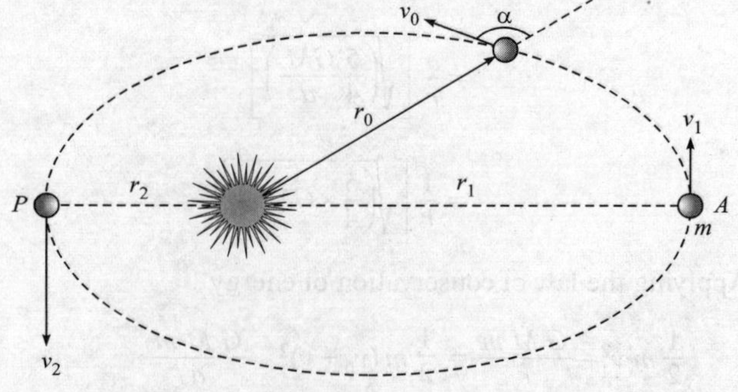

Figure 6.78

The angular momentum of planet at a position when it is at a distance r_0 from sun is given as

$$L = m\, v_0\, r_0 \sin\alpha$$

The angular momentum of planet at apogee is

$$L_A = m\, v_1\, r_1$$

According to law of conservation of Angular momentum, we have

$$m\, v_0\, r_0 \sin\alpha = m\, v_1\, r_1$$

or $$v_1 = \frac{v_0\, r_0 \sin\alpha}{r_1} \qquad \ldots(6.120)$$

Using the law of conservation of total energy of planet, we have

$$\frac{1}{2} m\, v_0^2 - \frac{G\, m\, M_s}{r_0} = \frac{1}{2} m\, v_1^2 - \frac{G\, m\, M_s}{r_1}$$

$$v_0^2 - \frac{2G\, M_s}{r_0} = v_1^2 - \frac{2G\, M_s}{r_1} \qquad \ldots(6.121)$$

Substituting the value of v_1 from equation-(6.120) in equation-(6.121), we get

$$v_0^2 - \frac{2G\, M_s}{r_0} = \frac{v_0^2\, r_0^2 \sin^2\alpha}{r_1^2} - \frac{2G\, M_s}{r_1}$$

or $$\left(v_0^2 - \frac{2G\, M_s}{r_0}\right) r_1^2 = v_0^2\, r_0^2 \sin^2\alpha - 2\, G\, M_s\, r_1$$

or $$\left(v_0^2 - \frac{2G\, M_s}{r_0}\right) r_1^2 + 2\, G\, M_s\, r_1 - v_0^2\, r_0^2 \sin^2\alpha = 0$$

or $$r_1 = \frac{-2G\, M_s \pm \sqrt{4G^2 M_s^2 + 4\left(v_0^2 - \frac{2G\, M_s}{r_0}\right)(v_0^2\, r_0^2 \sin^2\alpha)}}{2\left(v_0^2 - \frac{2G\, M_s}{r_0}\right)}$$

or $$= \frac{G\, M_s \pm \sqrt{G^2 M_s^2 - \left(\frac{2G\, M_s}{r_0} - v_0^2\right)(v_0^2\, r_0^2 \sin^2\alpha)}}{\left(\frac{2G\, M_s}{r_0} - v_0^2\right)}$$

or $$= \frac{1 \pm \sqrt{1 - \frac{v_0^2\, r_0^2 \sin^2\alpha}{G\, M_s}\left(\frac{2}{r_0} - v_0^2\right)}}{\left(\frac{2}{r_0} - \frac{v_0^2}{G\, M_s}\right)}$$

The above two values of r_1 corresponds to both perigee and apogee respectively.

Web Reference of Video Lectures at www.physicsgalaxy.com
Age Group - High School Physics | Age 17-19 Years
Section - GRAVITATION
Topic - Satellite Motion
Module Number - 10 to 14

Practice Exercise 6.6

(i) A planet of mass M moves around the sun along an ellipse so that its minimum distance from the sun is equal to r and the maximum distance to R. Making use of Kepler's laws, find its period of revolution around the sun.

[$\pi\sqrt{\frac{(r+R)^3}{2G\, M_s}}$]

(ii) Suppose we have made a model of the solar system scaled down in the ratio η but of materials of the same mean density as the actual material of the planet and the sun. How will the orbital periods of revolution of planetary models change in this case?

[*No Change*]

(iii) Two Earth's satellites move in a common plane along circular orbits. The orbital radius of one satellite r while that of the other satellite is Δr less. What time interval separates the periodic approaches of the satellites to each other over the minimum distance?

[$\frac{2\pi}{\sqrt{G\, M}}\, r^{3/2}\left(\frac{(r-\Delta r)^{3/2}}{r^{3/2} - (r-\Delta r)^{3/2}}\right)$]

(iv) A satellite is put in an orbit just above the earth's atmosphere with a velocity $\sqrt{1.5}$ times the velocity for a circular orbit at that height. The initial velocity imparted is horizontal. What would be the maximum distance of the satellite from the earth, when it is in the orbit.

[$2R_e$]

(v) A cosmic body A moves towards the sun S with velocity v_0 when far from the sun and aiming along a line whose perpendicular distance from the sun is d (figure-6.79). Find the minimum distance of this body from the sun. Take M as the mass of the sun.

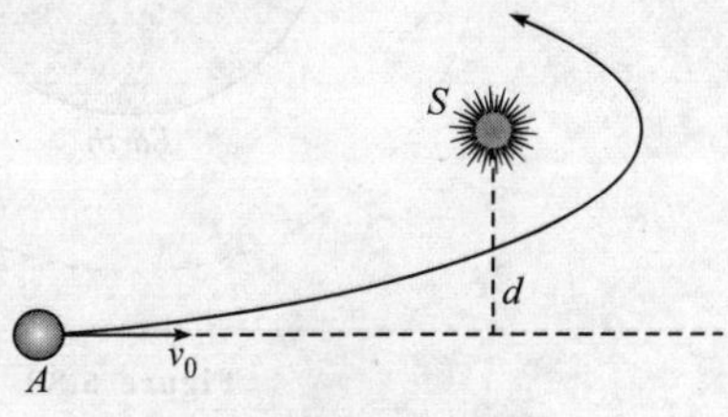

Figure 6.79

[$\frac{GM}{v_0^2}\left(\sqrt{\left(1 + \frac{d^2 v_0^4}{G^2 M^2}\right)} - 1\right)$]

(vi) Two satellites S_1 and S_2 revolve round a planet in coplanar circular orbits in the same sense. Their periods of revolutions are 1 hour and 8 hour respectively. The radius of the orbit of $S_1 = 10^4$ km. When S_2 is closest to S_1, find

(a) the speed of S_2 relative to S_1.

(b) the angular speed of S_2 as actually observed by an astronaut in S_1.

[(a) $\pi \times 10^4$ km/hr; (b) $\frac{\pi}{3}$ rad/hour]

(vii) If a planet revolve around the sun in an elliptical orbit such that its minimum distance from sun is r_1 and maximum distance is r_2. Find the distance of planet from sun when it is at a position where the line joining the planet and sun is perpendicular to the major axis of ellipse.

[$\frac{2r_1 r_2}{r_1 + r_2}$]

6.13 Projection of Satellites and Spaceships From Earth

To project a body into space, first it should be taken to a height where no atmosphere is present then it is projected with some initial speed. The path followed by the body also depends on the projection speed. Lets discuss the cases step by step.

Consider the situation shown in figure-6.80. A body of mass m is taken to a height h above the surface of earth to a point A and then projected with an insertion velocity v_p as shown in figure-6.80.

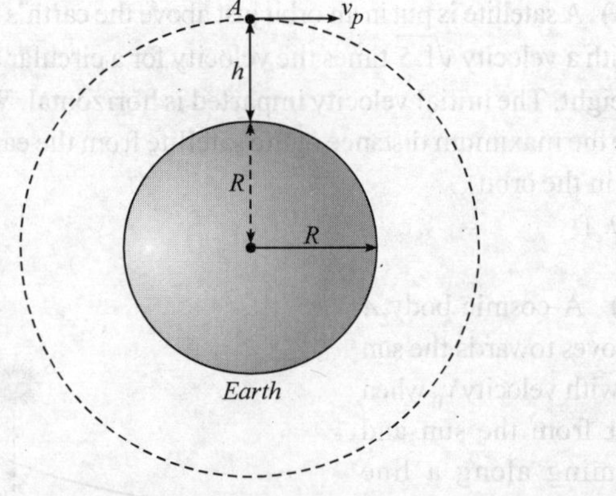

Figure 6.80

If we wish to launch the body as an earth's satellite in circular path the velocity of projection must be

$$v_p = \sqrt{\frac{GM_e}{R_e + h}} \qquad \ldots(6.122)$$

If h is small compared to radius of earth, we have

$$v_I = v_p = \sqrt{\frac{GM_e}{R_e}} = \sqrt{g_s R_e} = 7.93 \text{ km/s.} \qquad \ldots(6.123)$$

This velocity $v_I = 7.93$ km/s with which, when a body is thrown from earth's surface tangentially so that after projection it becomes a satellite of earth in a circular orbit around it, is called *"orbital speed"* or *"first cosmic velocity"*.

We've already discussed that if projection speed is lesser then the orbital speed, body will start following the inner ellipse and if velocity of projection is increased the body will follow the outer ellipse. If projection speed of body is increased, the outer ellipse will also become bigger and at a particular higher projection speed. It may also be possible that body will go to infinity and will never come back to earth again.

We have discussed that negative total energy of body shows its boundness. If we write the total energy of a body projected from point A as shown in figure is

$$E = \frac{1}{2} m v_p^2 - \frac{GM_e m}{R_e + h}$$

If after projection body becomes a satellite of earth then it implies it is bounded to earth and its total energy is negative. If at point A, that much of kinetic energy is imparted to the body so that total energy of body becomes zero then it implies that the body will reach to infinity and escape from gravitational field of earth. If v_{II} is such a velocity then we have

$$\frac{1}{2} m v_{II}^2 - \frac{GM_e m}{R_e + h} = 0$$

or

$$v_{II} = \sqrt{\frac{2GM_e}{R_e + h}} = \sqrt{2} v_I \qquad \ldots(6.124)$$

For $h << R_e$, we have

$$v_{II} = \sqrt{\frac{2GM_e}{R_e}} = \sqrt{2 g_s R_e} \qquad \ldots(6.125)$$

$$= 11.2 \text{ km/s}$$

Thus from earth's surface a body is thrown at a speed of 11.2 km/s, it will escape from earth's gravitation. If the projection speed of body is less then this value then total energy of body is negative and it will orbit the earth in elliptical orbit. This velocity is referred as the *"second cosmic velocity"* or *"escape velocity"*. When a body is thrown with this speed, it follows a parabolic trajectory and will become free from earth's gravitational attraction.

When body is thrown with speed more then v_{II} then it moves along a hyperbolic trajectory and also leaves the region where the earth's gravitational attraction acts. Also when it reaches infinity some kinetic energy will be left in it and it becomes a satellite of sun, that is a small artificial planet.

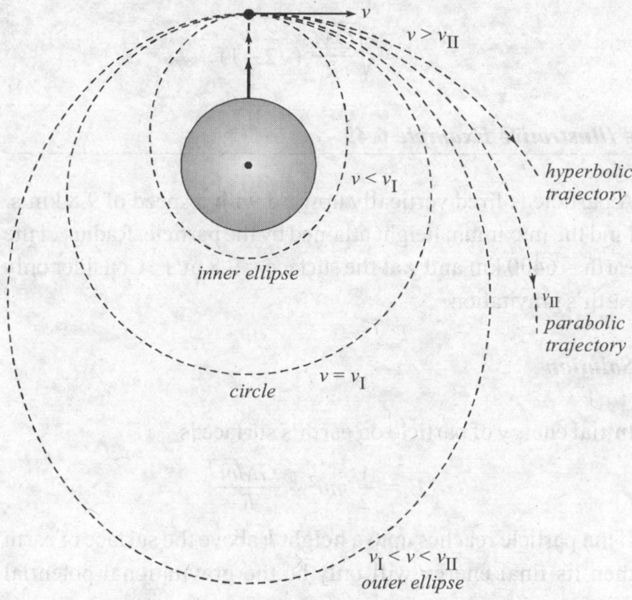

Figure 6.81

All the calculations we've performed till now do not take into account the influence of the sun and of the planets on the motion of the projected body. In other words we have assumed that the reference frame connected with the earth is an inertial frame and the body moves relative to it. But in reality the whole system body and the earth is in a non inertial from which is permanently accelerated relative to sun.

For a body projected into space, *a third cosmic velocity* is also defined and it is the velocity with which when a body is projected from earth, it may escape from our solar system. This velocity can be calculated approximately as follows. From equation-(6.124) we can see that the escape velocity of a body is $\sqrt{2}$ times its orbital speed when it is moving around earth. The same should be obviously true for earth or a body moving in earth's orbit around the sun. The velocity of earth relative to sun is measured and its value is $v_0 = 29.76$ km/sec. Thus when body is thrown from earth's surface at speed v_{II}, relative to earth it will escape from earth's gravitational attraction and will reach infinity and will have no kinetic energy left in it with respect to earth but as it is thrown from earths surface it must have a speed left in it equal to v_0 with which it can orbit around the sun. If the body is projected from earth's surface with such a speed so that it is able to overcome earth's attraction and at infinity it is left with an extra speed of $(\sqrt{2}-1)\,v_0$ then it will also be able to escape from the gravitational attraction of sun. If v_{III} be the third cosmic velocity from earth's surface than we have

$$\frac{1}{2}mv_{III}^2 = \frac{1}{2}mv_{II}^2 + \frac{1}{2}mv_0^2(\sqrt{2}-1)^2$$

On solving we get

$$v_{III} \cong 16.75 \text{ km/s} \qquad \ldots(6.126)$$

Lets take some examples to understand some basic concepts related to gravitational energy and projection.

6.14 Escaping From a Satellite

As we have seen that orbital speed of a body close to Earth's surface is $\sqrt{gR_e}$ and escape velocity is $\sqrt{2gR_e}$. This shows that the escape velocity is $\sqrt{2}$ times higher than orbital speed. Also we can state of the speed of a body orbitting around earth close to its surface is increased by 41.4% ($\simeq \sqrt{2}-1$) the body escape from earth's gravitational attraction. This can also be proven for a body orbitting around earth in an orbit of any radius. The orbital speed of a satellite of mass m around earth in orbit radius x is

$$v_0 = \sqrt{\frac{GM_e}{x}}$$

Potential energy of the orbitting satellite is

$$U = -\sqrt{\frac{GM_em}{x}}$$

If satellite speed is changed to v_e so that from orbit, it escapes from earth's gravitational attraction then we use

$$\frac{1}{2}mv_e^2 - \frac{GM_em}{x} \geq 0$$

$$\Rightarrow \qquad v_e = \sqrt{\frac{2GM_e}{x}} = \sqrt{2}\,v_0$$

Thus at any orbit of radius x for a satellite if its speed is increased by 41.4% the satellite will escape from earth's gravitational attraction.

Web Reference of Video Lectures at www.physicsgalaxy.com

Age Group - High School Physics | Age 17-19 Years
Section - GRAVITATION
Topic - Satellite Motion
Module Number - 15 to 19

 # Illustrative Example 6.47

A spaceship is launched into a circular orbit close to the earth's surface. What additional velocity has now to be imparted to the spaceship in the orbit to overcome the gravitational pull. (Radius of the earth = 6400 km and $g = 9.8$ m/sec).

Solution

In an orbit close to earth's surface velocity of space ship is

$$v = \sqrt{\frac{GM}{R}} = \sqrt{gR}$$

We know escape velocity is

$$v_{II} = \sqrt{2gR}$$

Hence additional velocity required to be imparted is

$$\Delta v = v_{II} - v$$

$$= (\sqrt{2}-1)\sqrt{gR}$$

$$= (\sqrt{2}-1)\sqrt{9.8 \times 6400 \times 10^3}$$

$$= 3.28 \times 10^3 \text{ m/s}$$

 # Illustrative Example 6.48

A spaceship approaches the moon (mass = M and radius = R) along a parabolic path which is almost tangential to its surface. At the moment of maximum approach, the brake rocket is fired to convert the spaceship into a satellite of the moon. Find the change in speed.

Solution

Figure-6.82 shows the corresponding situation

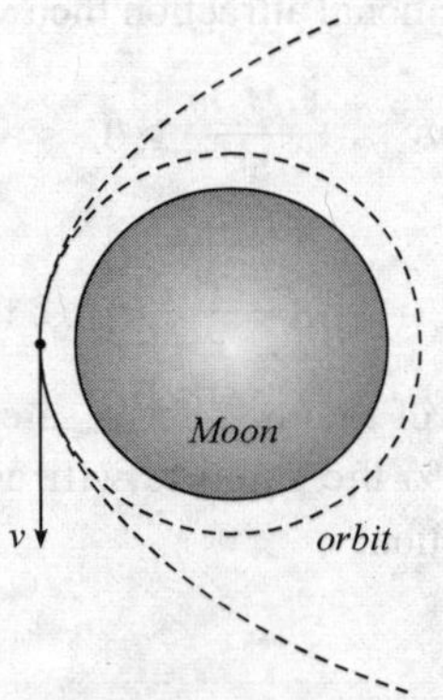

Figure 6.82

We know a particle follows a parabolic trajectory tangential to a planet when at the surface of planet it has escape velocity

$$v_{es} = \sqrt{\frac{2GM}{R}}$$

Now to transform it into a circular orbit its speed should be decreased to orbital speed

$$v_0 = \sqrt{\frac{GM}{R}}$$

Thus change in speed is

$$\Delta v = v_{es} - v_0$$

$$= \sqrt{\frac{GM}{R}}(\sqrt{2}-1)$$

 # Illustrative Example 6.49

A particle is fired vertically upward with a speed of 9.8 km/s. Find the maximum height attained by the particle. Radius of the earth = 6400 km and g at the surface = 9.8 m/s^2. Consider only earth's gravitation.

Solution

Initial energy of particle on earth's surface is

$$E_i = \frac{1}{2}mu^2 - \frac{GMm}{R}$$

If the particle reaches upto a height h above the surface of earth then its final energy will only be the gravitational potential energy.

$$E_f = -\frac{GMm}{R+h}$$

According to energy conservation, we have

$$E_i = E_f$$

or $$\frac{1}{2}mu^2 - \frac{GMm}{R} = -\frac{GMm}{R+h}$$

or $$\frac{1}{2}u^2 - gR = -\frac{gR^2}{R+h}$$

or $$h = \frac{2gR^2}{2gR - u^2} - R$$

$$= \frac{2 \times 9.8 \times (6400 \times 10^3)^2}{2 \times 9.8 \times 6400 \times 10^3 - (9.8)^2} - 6400 \times 10^3$$

$$= (27300 - 6400) \times 10^3$$

$$= 20900 \text{ km}$$

 # Illustrative Example 6.50

A satellite of mass m is orbiting the earth in a circular orbit of radius r. It starts losing energy slowly at a constant rate C due to friction. If M_e and R_e denote the mass and radius of the earth respectively, show that the satellite falls on the earth in a limit time t given by

$$t = \frac{G\,m\,M_e}{2\,C}\left(\frac{1}{R_e} - \frac{1}{r}\right)$$

Solution

Let velocity of satellite in its orbit of radius r be v then we have

$$v = \sqrt{\frac{GM_e}{r}}$$

When satellite approaches earth's surface, if its velocity becomes v', then it is given as

$$v' = \sqrt{\frac{GM_e}{R_e}}$$

The total initial energy of satellite at a distance r is

$$E_{T_i} = K_i + U_i$$

$$= \frac{1}{2}mv^2 - \frac{GM_e m}{r}$$

$$= -\frac{1}{2}\frac{GM_e m}{r} \quad \dots(6.127)$$

The total final energy of satellite at a distance R_e is

$$E_{T_f} = K_f + U_f$$

$$= \frac{1}{2}mv'^2 - \frac{GM_e m}{R_e}$$

$$= -\frac{1}{2}\frac{GM_e m}{R_e} \quad \dots(6.128)$$

As satellite is loosing energy at a rate C, if it takes a time t in reaching earth, we have

$$Ct = E_{T_i} - E_{T_f}$$

$$= \frac{1}{2}GM_e m\left[\frac{1}{R_e} - \frac{1}{r}\right]$$

or $$t = \frac{GM_e m}{2C}\left[\frac{1}{R_e} - \frac{1}{r}\right]$$

 # Illustrative Example 6.51

An artificial satellite is moving in a circular orbit around the earth with a speed equal to half the magnitude of escape velocity from the earth.

(i) Determine the height of the satellite above the earth's surface.

(ii) If the satellite is stopped suddenly in its orbit and allowed to fall freely onto the earth, find the speed with which it hits the surface of the earth.

Solution

(i) Let M and R be the mass and radius of the earth respectively. If m be the mass of satellite, then escape velocity from earth $v_e = \sqrt{2g\,R_e}$

Velocity of satellite $$= \sqrt{\frac{g\,R_e}{2}} \quad \dots(6.129)$$

Further we know orbital speed of satellite at a height h is

$$v_s = \sqrt{\left(\frac{G\,M_e}{r}\right)} = \sqrt{\left(\frac{R_e^2\,g}{R_e + h}\right)}$$

or $$v_s^2 = \frac{R^2\,g}{R + h} \quad \dots(6.130)$$

From equation-(6.129) and (6.130), we get

$$h = R = 6400\text{ km}$$

(ii) Now total energy at height h = total energy at earth's surface (principle of conservation of energy)

or $$0 - G\,M_e\frac{m}{R + h} = \frac{1}{2}\,m\,v^2 - G\,M_e\frac{m}{R_e}$$

or $$\frac{1}{2}\,m\,v^2 = \frac{G\,M_e\,m}{R_e} - \frac{G\,M_e\,m}{2\,R_e} \quad [\text{As } h = R]$$

Solving we get $$v = \sqrt{g\,R_e}$$

or $$v = \sqrt{9.8 \times 6400 \times 10^3} = 7.919\text{ km/s}$$

 # Illustrative Example 6.52

An artificial satellite of the moon revolves in a circular orbit whose radius exceeds the radius of the moon η times. In the process of motion, the satellite experiences a slight resistance due to cosmic dust. Assuming the resistance force to depend on the velocity of the satellite as $F = \alpha\,v^2$, where α is a constant, find how long the satellite will stay in orbit until it falls into the moon surface.

Solution

Let R be the radius of the moon. Then the satellite revolves in a circular orbit of radius ηR. If m be the mass of satellite and M, that of moon, then

$$\frac{m\,v_1^2}{\eta\,R} = \frac{G\,M\,m}{(\eta\,R)^2} \quad \text{or} \quad v_1 = \sqrt{\left(\frac{G\,M}{\eta\,R}\right)}$$

Let v_2 be the velocity of satellite when it falls at the moon's surface. Then

$$v^2 = \sqrt{\left(\frac{G\,M}{R}\right)}$$

Given that $$F = \alpha\,v^2$$

$$m\,\frac{dv}{dt} = \alpha\,v^2$$

or $$m\frac{dv}{v^2}=\alpha\, dt$$

Integrating this expression, we get

$$m\int_{\sqrt{GM/\eta R}}^{\sqrt{GM/R}}\frac{dv}{v^2}=\alpha\int_0^t dt$$

or $$-m\left[\frac{1}{\sqrt{\left(\frac{GM}{R}\right)}}-\frac{1}{\sqrt{\left(\frac{GM}{\eta R}\right)}}\right]=\alpha t$$

$$t=\frac{m}{\alpha}\sqrt{\left(\frac{R}{GM}\right)}\,[\sqrt{\eta}-1]$$

$$t=\frac{m}{\alpha}\frac{[\sqrt{\eta}-1]}{\sqrt{gR}}\quad\left[\text{As } \sqrt{\frac{GM}{R}}=\sqrt{gR}\right]$$

Alternative Method :

Let r be the orbital radius. Then

$$\frac{GMm}{r^2}=\frac{mv^2}{r}\quad\text{or}\quad v=\frac{GM}{r}$$

Where M and m are masses of moon and satellite respectively.

Total energy of satellite

$$E=\text{K.E.}+\text{P.E.}=\frac{1}{2}mv^2-\frac{GMm}{r}$$

or $$E=\frac{1}{2}m\left(\frac{GM}{r}\right)-\frac{GMm}{r}=-\frac{GMm}{2r}$$

Differentiating, we get

$$dE=\frac{GMm}{2r^2}\,dr \qquad \text{...(6.131)}$$

Further, $$\frac{dE}{dt}=-F.v=-(\alpha v^2)v=-\alpha v^3$$

$$=\alpha\left(\frac{GM}{r}\right)^{3/2}$$

or $$dE=-\alpha\left(\frac{GM}{r}\right)^{3/2}dt \qquad \text{...(6.132)}$$

From equation-(6.131) and (6.132), we get

$$\frac{GMm}{2r^2}\,dr=-\alpha\left(\frac{GM}{r}\right)^{3/2}dt$$

or $$dt=-\frac{m}{2\alpha\sqrt{GM}}\frac{1}{\sqrt{r}}\,dr$$

$$t=\frac{m}{\alpha\sqrt{GM}}\left[\sqrt{r}\right]_{\eta R}^{R}$$

$$=\frac{m}{\alpha\sqrt{GM}}\sqrt{R}\,[\sqrt{\eta}-1]$$

$$=\frac{m}{\alpha\sqrt{g}\,R}\times\sqrt{R}\,[\sqrt{\eta}-1]\,[\text{As } \sqrt{GM}=\sqrt{g}\,R.]$$

$$=\frac{m}{\alpha\sqrt{(gR)}}\,[\sqrt{\eta}-1]$$

6.15 Communication Satellites

Communication satellite around the earth are used by Information Technology for spreading information through out the globe.

Figure-6.83 shows as to how using satellites an information from an earth station, located at a point on earth's surface can be sent throughout the world.

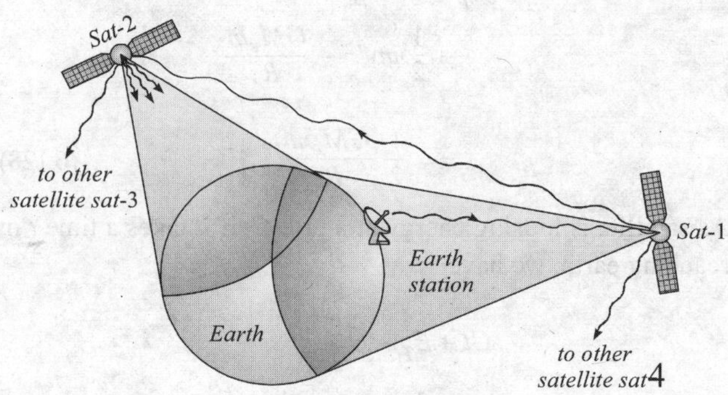

Figure 6.83

First the information is sent to the nearest satellite in the range of earth station by means of electromagnetic waves then that satellite broadcasts the signal to the region of earth exposed to this satellite and also send the same signal to other satellite for broadcasting in other parts of the globe.

6.15.1 Geostationary Satellite and Parking Orbit

There are so many types of communication satellites revolving around the earth in different orbits at different heights depending on their utility. Some of which are Geostationary satellites, which appears at rest relative to earth or which have same angular velocity as that of earth's rotation *i.e.*, with a time period of 24 hr. such satellite must be orbiting in an orbit of specific radius. This orbit is called parking orbit. If a Geostationary satellite is at a height h above the earth's surface then its orbiting speed is given as

$$v_{gs}=\sqrt{\frac{GM_e}{(R_e+h)}}$$

The time period of its revolution can be given by Kepler's third law as

$$T^2 = \frac{4\pi^2}{GM_e}(R_e + h)^3$$

or $$T^2 = \frac{4\pi^2}{g_s R_e^2}(R_e + h)^3$$

or $$h = \left(\frac{g_s R_e^2}{4\pi^2}T^2\right)^{1/3} - R_e$$

or $$h = \left[\frac{9.8\times[6.4\times10^6]\times[86400]^2}{4\times(3.14)^2}\right]^{1/3} - 6.4\times10^6$$

$$= 35954.6\,\text{km}$$

$$\simeq 36000\,\text{km}$$

Thus when a satellite is launched in an orbit at a height of about 36000 km above the equator then it will appear to be at rest with respect to a point on Earth's surface. A Geostationary satellite must have its orbit in equatorial plane due to the geographic limitation arose because of irregular geometry of earth (ellipsoidal shape).

6.15.2 Broadcasting Region of a Satellite

Now as we know the height of a geostationary satellite we can easily find the area of earth exposed to the satellite or area of the region in which the communication can be mode using this satellite.

Figure-6.84 shows earth and its exposed area to a geostationary satellite. Here the angle θ can be given as

$$\theta = \cos^{-1}\left(\frac{R_e}{R_e + h}\right)$$

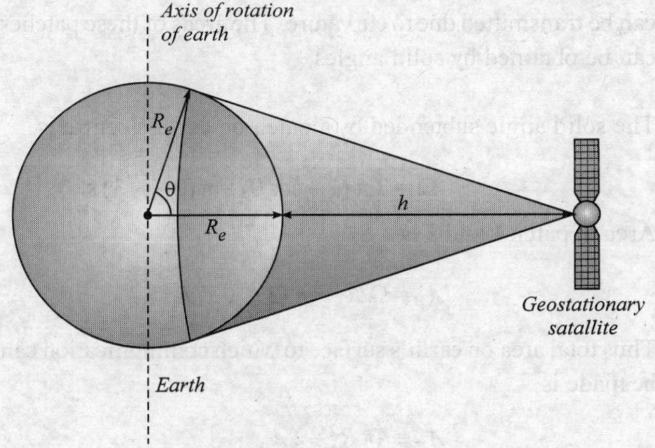

Figure 6.84

Now we can find the solid angle Ω which the exposed area subtend on earth's centre as

$$\Omega = 2\pi(1 - \cos\theta)$$

$$= 2\pi\left(1 - \frac{R_e}{R_e + h}\right) = \frac{2\pi h}{R_e + h}$$

Thus the area of earth's surface to geostationary satellite is

$$S = \Omega R_e^2 = \frac{2\pi h R_e^2}{R_e + h} \qquad \ldots(6.133)$$

Lets take some examples to understand the concept in detail.

 # Illustrative Example 6.53

A satellite is revolving around the earth in an orbit of radius double that of the parking orbit and revolving in same sense. Find the periodic time duration between two instants when this satellite is closest to a geostationary satellite.

Solution

We know that the time period of revolution of a satellite is given as

$$T^2 = \frac{4\pi^2}{GM_e} r^3 \qquad \text{[Kepler's III law]}$$

For satellite given in problem and for a geostationary satellite we have

$$\frac{T_1}{T_2} = \left(\frac{r_1}{r_2}\right)^3$$

or $$T_1 = \left(\frac{r_1}{r_2}\right)^3 \times T_2 = (2)^3 \times 24 = 192\,\text{hr}$$

If Δt be the time between two successive instants when the satellite are closed then we must have

$$\Delta t = \frac{\theta}{\omega_1} = \frac{2\pi + \theta}{\omega_2} = \frac{2\pi}{\omega_2 - \omega}$$

Where ω_1 and ω_2 are the angular speeds of the two planets

 # Illustrative Example 6.54

Find the minimum colatitude which can directly receive a signed from a geostationary satellite.

Solution

The farthest point on earth, which can receive signals from the parking orbit is the point where a length is drawn on earth surface from satellite as shown in figure-6.85.

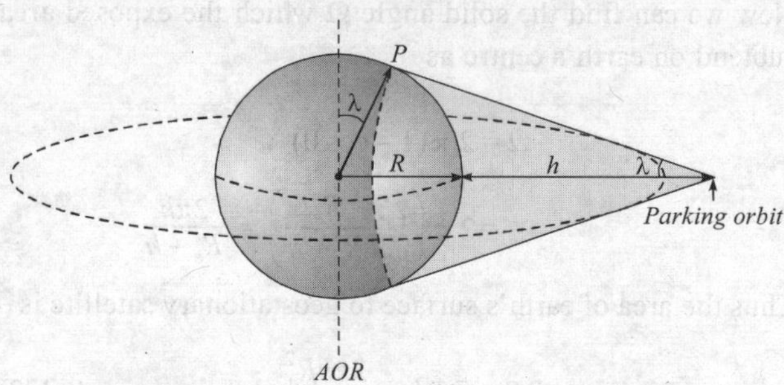

Figure 6.85

The colatitude λ of point P can be obtained from figure as

$$\sin\lambda = \frac{R_e}{R_e + h} \simeq \frac{1}{7}$$

We know for a parking orbit $h \simeq 6\,R_e$

Thus we have $\lambda = \sin^{-1}\left(\frac{1}{7}\right)$

Illustrative Example 6.55

If a satellite is revolving around the earth in a circular orbit in a plane containing earth's axis of rotation. If the angular speed of satellite is equal to that of earth, find the time it takes to move from a point above north pole to a point above the equator.

Solution

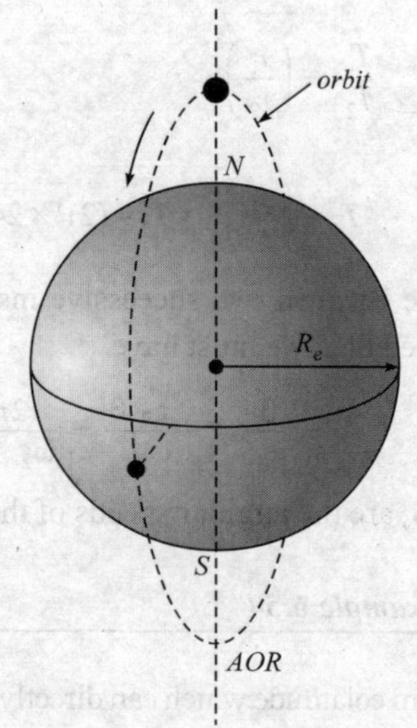

Figure 6.86

A satellite which rotates with angular speed equal to earth's rotation has an orbit radius 7 R_e and the angular speed of revolution is

$$\omega = \frac{2\pi}{T} = \frac{2\pi}{86400} = 7.27 \times 10^{-5}\ \text{rad/s}$$

When satellite moves from a point above north pole to a point above equator, it traverses an angle $\pi/2$, this time taken is

$$t = \frac{\pi/2}{\omega} = 21600\ \text{s} = 6\ \text{hrs.}$$

Illustrative Example 6.56

A satellite is orbiting around the earth in an orbit in equatorial plane of radius $2R_e$ where R_e is the radius of earth. Find the area on earth, this satellite covers for communication purpose in its complete revolution.

Solution

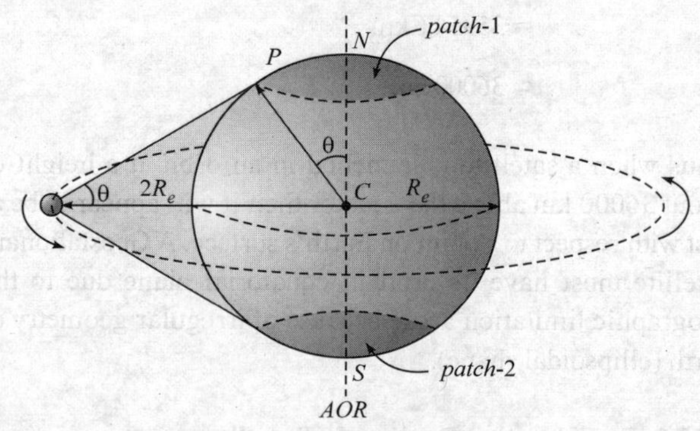

Figure 6.87

As shown in figure-6.87 when satellite S revolves, it covers a complete circular belt on earth's surface for communication. If the colatitude of the farthest point on surface upto which signals can be received (point P) is θ then we have

$$\sin\theta = \frac{R_e}{2R_e} = \frac{1}{2}$$

or $$\theta = \frac{\pi}{6}$$

During revolution satellite leaves two spherical patches 1 and 2 on earth surface at north and south poles where no signals can be transmitted due to curvature. The areas of these patches can be obtained by solid angles.

The solid angle subtended by a patch on earth's centre is

$$\Omega = 2\pi(1 - \cos\theta) = \pi(2 - \sqrt{3})\ \text{st.}$$

Area of patch 1 and 2 is

$$A_P = \Omega R_e^2 = \pi(2 - \sqrt{3})\,R_e^2$$

Thus total area on earth's surface to which communication can be made is

$$A_C = 4\pi R_e^2 - 2A_P$$
$$= 4\pi R_e^2 - 2\pi(2 - \sqrt{3})\,R_e^2$$

$$= 2\pi R_e^2 (2 - 2 + \sqrt{3})$$

$$= 2\sqrt{3} R_e^2$$

Web Reference of Video Lectures at www.physicsgalaxy.com

Age Group - High School Physics | Age 17-19 Years
Section - GRAVITATION
Topic - Satellite Motion
Module Number - 20 to 25

Practice Exercise 6.7

(i) For a low altitude orbit if $r \simeq r_P$, where r_P is planet radius, show that for a given average planetary density, the orbital period of satellite is independent of the size of the planet. Calculate its value if average density is ρ.

[$\sqrt{\frac{3\pi}{G\rho}}$]

(ii) What should be the orbit radius of a communication satellite so that it can cover 75% of the surface area of earth during its revolution.

[1.515 R_e]

(iii) The radius of a planet is R_1 and a satellite revolves around it in a circle of radius R_2. The time period of revolution is T. Find the acceleration due to the gravitational field of the planet at its surface.

[$\frac{4\pi^2 R_2^3}{T^2 R_1^2}$]

(iv) Two small dense stars rotate about their common centre of mass as a binary system with the period 1 year for each. One star is of double the mass of the other and the mass of the lighter one is $\frac{1}{3}$ of the mass of the Sun. Find the distance between the stars if distance between the Earth & the Sun is R.

[R]

(v) Two satellites are orbiting around earth in orbit radius $2R$ and $3R$ respectively. Find the time duration between two instants when the two planets are at closest separation when

(a) They are revolving in same direction.

(b) Opposite direction.

[(a) $\frac{2\pi}{\sqrt{GM}} \cdot \frac{8}{2\sqrt{2}-1} \cdot R^{3/2}$ (b) $\frac{2\pi}{\sqrt{GM}} \cdot \frac{8}{2\sqrt{2}+1} \cdot R^{3/2}$]

(vi) A particle is projected from point A, that is at a distance $4R$ from the centre of the Earth, with speed v_1 in a direction making 30° with the line joining the centre of the Earth and point A, as shown. Find the speed v_1 of particle if particle passes grazing the surface of the earth. Consider gravitational interaction only between these two.

(Use $\frac{GM}{R} = 6.4 \times 10^7$ m²/s²)

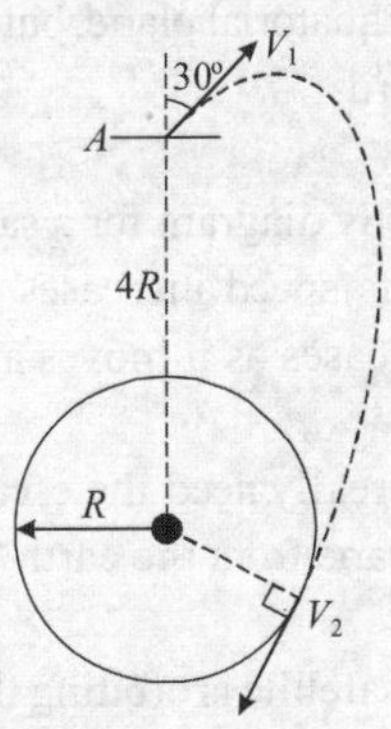

Figure 6.88

[$\frac{8000}{\sqrt{2}}$ m/s]

(vii) A mass of 6×10^{24} kg (equal to the mass of the earth) is to be compressed in a sphere in such a way that the escape velocity from its surface is 3×10^8 m/s. What should be the radius of the sphere ?

[8.893 mm]

Advance Illustrations Videos at www.physicsgalaxy.com

Age Group - Advance Illustrations
Section - Gravitation
Topic - Gravitation
Illustrations - 19 In-depth Illustration videos

* * * * *

Discussion Question

Q6-1 The sun's tide-raising power is only half as great as that of the moon. The direct pull of the sun on the earth, however, is about 175 times that of the moon. Why is then that the moon causes larger tides?

Q6-2 At noon the sun and the earth pull the objects on the earth's surface in opposite directions. At midnight the sun and the earth pull these objects in same direction. Is the weight of an object, as measured by a spring balance on the earth's surface, more at midnight as compared to its weight at noon ?

Q6-3 As measured by an observer on earth, would there be any difference in the periods of two satellites each in a circular orbit near the earth's equatorial plane, but one moving eastward and the other westward.

Q6-4 Draw a free body diagram for a satellite in an elliptical orbit showing why its speed increases as it approaches the parent body and decreases as it moves away.

Q6-5 Does a rocket really need the escape velocity from the very beginning to escape from the earth ?

Q6-6 If an artificial satellite is orbiting the earth, is it possible for the plane of the orbit to not pass through the center of the earth? On what property of the gravitational force is your answer based?

Q6-7 If a planet of given density were made larger, its force of attraction for an object on its surface would increase because of the planet's greater mass but would decrease because of the greater distance from the object to the centre of the planet. Which effect predominates?

Q6-8 An astronaut in a satellite releases a spoon out of the satellite into the space. Will the spoon fall to the earth ?

Q6-9 Can two particles be in equilibrium under the action of their mutual gravitational force ? Can three particles be ? Can one of the three particles be ?

Q6-10 Suppose an artificial satellite is in a circular orbit around the earth at a distance r_0 from the center of the earth. A short burst is fired from its rocket engine in a direction such that its speed quickly increases (but not enough to take it out of earth orbit). (a) What is the subsequent path of the satellite? (b) Will is perigee distance be greater than, less than, or equal to r_0? (c) Will its apogee distance be greater than, less than, or equal to r_0? (d) Will its period increase or decrease?

Q6-11 If the gravitational force on an object depends linearly on its mass, why is the acceleration of a freely falling object independent of its mass?

Q6-12 A satellite revolves around the earth in a circular orbit. What will happen to its orbit if universal gravitational constant start decreasing with time.

Q6-13 If the force of gravity acts on all bodies in proportion to their masses, why does a heavy body not fall faster than a rigid light body ?

Q6-14 The weight of an object is more at the poles than at the equator. Is it beneficial to purchase goods at equator and sell them at the pole ? Does it matter whether a spring balance is used or an equal-beam balance is used ?

Q6-15 Objects at rest on the earth's surface move in circular paths with a period of 24 hours. Are they in 'orbit' in the sense that an earth satellite is in orbit ? What would the length of the day have to be to put such objects in true orbit ?

Q6-16 A satellite is revolving around a planet in a circular orbit. What will happen if its speed is increased from v_0 to (a) $(\sqrt{5}v_0)$ (b) $2v_0$.

Q6-17 Because the earth bulges near the equator, the source of Mississippi River, although high above sea level, is nearer to the centre of the earth than its mouth. How can a river flow 'uphill' ?

Q6-18 The astronaut in a satellite orbiting the earth feels weightlessness. Does the weightlessness depends upon the distance of the satellite from the earth ? If so, how ? Explain your answer.

Q6-19 The total energy of the earth + sun system is negative. How do you interpret the negative energy of a system ?

Q6-20 Two air bubbles with radius r are present in water. Are these bubbles attracted or repelled?

Q6-21 Suppose an earth satellite, revolving in a circular orbit experiences resistance due to cosmic dust then what happens to the kinetic end potential energy of satellite.

Q6-22 Objects at rest on the earth's surface move in circular paths with a period of 24 hours. Are they in 'orbit' in the sense that an earth satellite is in orbit? Explain.

Q6-23 When a train moves from west to east at high speed, does its weight increase or decrease ?

Q6-24 A spacecraft spins about its axis. What would be the feeling of an astronaut inside it?

Q6-25 Can a satellite coast in a stable orbit in a planet not passing through the earth's centre ? Explain your answer.

Q6-26 If you are buying gold from a dealer who uses a spring scale to measure the amount of gold, and you wish to get the most gold for your money, do you want the measurement to be made at the equator or at the poles?

Q6-27 An apple falls from a tree. An insect in the apple finds that the earth is falling towards it with an acceleration g. Who exerts the force needed to accelerate the earth with this acceleration g ?

Q6-28 A spacecraft consumes more fuel in going from the earth to the moon than it takes for a return trip. Comment on this statement.

Q6-29 The planet Egabbac (in another solar system) has a radius twice that of the earth's, but an average mass density which is the same as the earth. Would the weight of an object on Egabbac's surface be the same as on the earth's, greater than on the earth's, or less than on the earth's? If greater or less than on the earth's, then by how much?

Q6-30 As measured by an observer on earth, would there be any difference in the periods of two satellites, each in a circular orbit near the earth in an equatorial plane, but one moving eastward and the other westward ?

Q6-31 When a toilet is flushed or a sink is drained, the water (and other stuff) begins to rotate about the drain on the way down. Assuming no initial rotation and a flow initially directly straight toward the drain, explain what causes the rotation and which direction it has in the northern hemisphere. (Note that this is a small effect and in most toilets the rotation is caused by directional water jets.) Would the direction of rotation reverse if water were forced up the drain?

Q6-32 The sun's speed relative to the earth (as measured with respect to background stars) is highest at around January 4 each year and lowest around July 4. When is the earth closest to the sun and when is it farthest from the sun? Does this effect tend to make summers and winters more severe or less severe in (a) the northern hemisphere, (b) the southern hemisphere?

Q6-33 Can a satellite move in a stable orbit in a plane not passing through the earth's centre ? Explain.

Q6-34 What will happen to an orbiting planet if all a sudden (a) it comes to stand still in the orbit (b) the gravitational force ceases to act on it?

Q6-35 Describe the way the mass of an astronaut and the gravitational force on the astronaut vary during a trip from the earth to the moon.

Q6-36 Would you expect the total energy of the solar system to be constant ? The total angular momentum ? Explain.

* * * * *

Conceptual MCQs Single Option Correct

6-1 If the gravitational force were proportional to $\frac{1}{r}$, then a particle in a circular orbit under such a force would have its original speed :

(A) Independent of r (B) $\propto \frac{1}{r}$

(C) $\propto \frac{1}{r^2}$ (D) $\propto r^2$

6-2 The ratio of acceleration due to gravity at a depth h below the surface of earth and at a height h above the surface of earth for $h << $ radius of earth :

(A) Is constant

(B) Changes linearly with h

(C) Changes parabolically with h

(D) Decreases

6-3 A uniform spherical shell gradually shrinks maintaining its shape and its wall thickness. The gravitational potential at the centre :

(A) Increases (B) Decreases

(C) Remains constant (D) Oscillates

6-4 If both the mass and radius of Earth decrease by 1%, the value of acceleration due to gravity will change by nearly :

(A) 1% decrease (B) 1.5% increase

(C) 1% increase (D) 2% decrease

6-5 In Q. No. 6-4, the escape velocity will :

(A) Be doubled (B) Be halved

(C) Be tripled (D) Not change

6-6 The magnitude of gravitational potential energy of the earth-satellite system is U with zero potential energy at infinite separation. The kinetic energy of satellite is K. If we consider mass of satellite << mass of earth. Then :

(A) $K = 2U$ (B) $K = \frac{U}{2}$

(C) $K = U$ (D) $K = 4U$

6-7 P is a point at a distance r from the centre of a solid sphere of radius R_0. The gravitational potential at P is V. If V is plotted as a function of r, then the curve representing the plot correctly is :

(A)
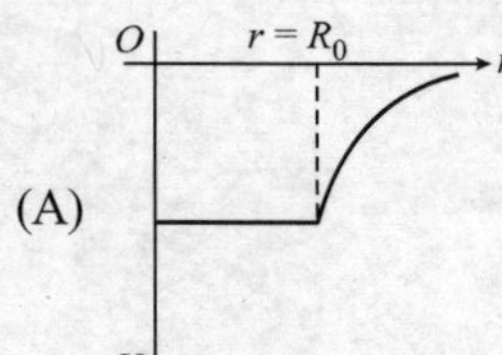

(B)
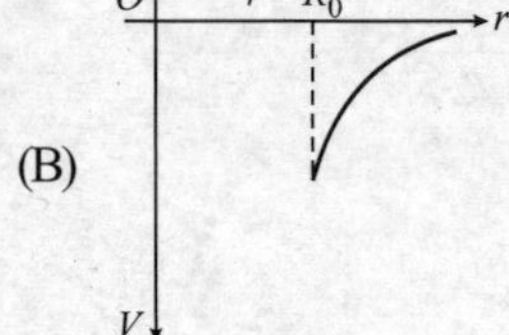

(C)
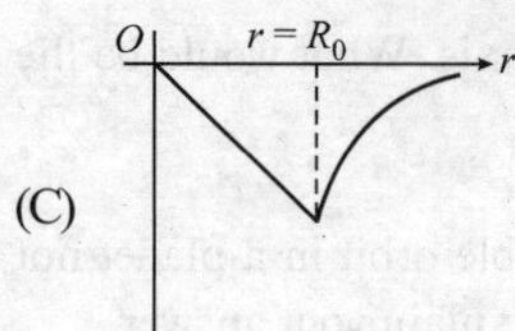

(D)
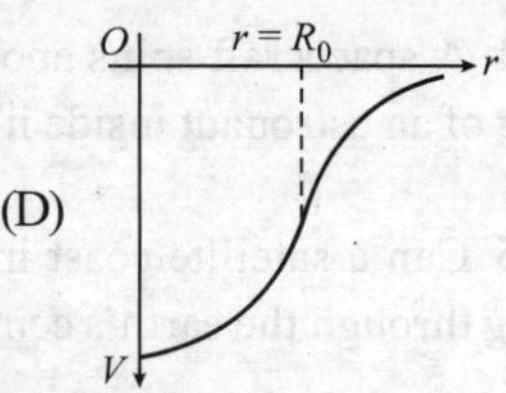

6-8 A system consists of n identical particles each of mass m. The total number of interactions between particles possible are :

(A) $n(n+1)$ (B) $\frac{1}{2}n(n+1)$

(C) $n(n-1)$ (D) $\frac{1}{2}n(n-1)$

6-9 A satellite revolving around the Earth loses some energy due to collision. What would be the effect on its velocity and distance from the centre of the Earth ?

(A) Velocity increases and distance decreases

(B) Both velocity and distance increase

(C) Both velocity and distance decrease

(D) Velocity decreases and distance increases

6-10 A particle on earth's surface is given a velocity equal to its escape velocity. Its total mechanical energy with zero potential energy reference at infinite separation will be :

(A) Negative (B) Positive

(C) Zero (D) Infinite

6-11 The gravitational potential energy magnitude of a body at a distance r from the centre of Earth is U. The weight of the body at that point is :

(A) Ur (B) $\frac{U}{r}$

(C) Ur^2 (D) Ur^3

6-12 A thin spherical shell of mass M and radius R has a small hole. A particle of mass m is released at the mouth of the hole. Then :

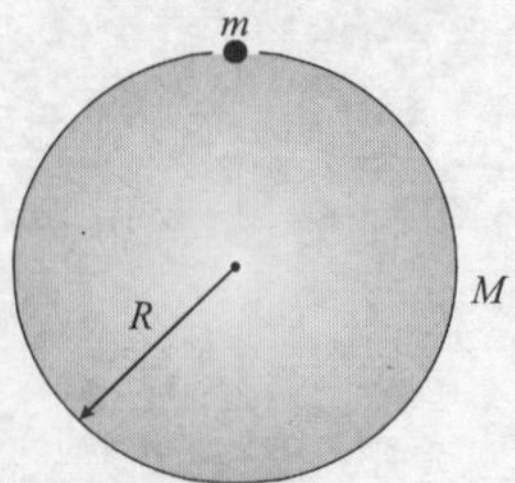

Figure 6.89

(A) The particle will execute simple harmonic motion inside the shell
(B) The particle will oscillate inside the shell, but the oscillations are not simple harmonic
(C) The particle will not oscillate, but the speed of the particle will go on increasing
(D) None of these

6-13 Two identical trains P and Q move with equal speeds on parallel tracks along the equator. P moves from east to west and Q from west to east.
(A) Train P exerts greater force on track
(B) Train Q exerts greater force on track
(C) Both exert equal force on track
(D) Data is insufficient to arrive at a conclusion

6-14 Two identical satellites are moving around the Earth in circular orbits at heights $3R$ and R respectively where R is the radius of the Earth. The ratio of their kinetic energies is :
(A) 2 : 1 (B) 1 : 2
(C) 3 : 1 (D) 2 : 3

6-15 A particle of mass m is projected vertically upwards. A uniform gravitational field $\vec{g}$ is acted vertically downwards. The most appropriate graph between magnitude of potential energy U and height h (<< radius of earth) is (assume U to be zero on surface of earth) :

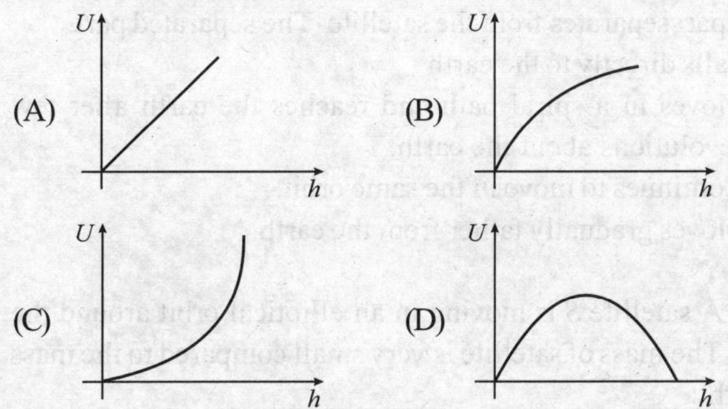

6-16 A satellite is to be stationed in an orbit such that it can be used for relay purposes (such a satellite is called a Geostationary satellite). The conditions such a satellite should fulfill is/are :
(A) Its orbit must lie in equatorial plane.
(B) Its sense of rotation must be from east to west.
(C) Its orbital radius must be 44900 km.
(D) Its orbit must be elliptical

6-17 Consider a planet in some solar system which has a mass double the mass of the Earth and density equal to the average density of the Earth. An object weighing W on the Earth will weigh :
(A) W (B) $2W$
(C) $W/2$ (D) $2^{1/3}W$

6-18 Figure-6.90 shows the variation of energy with the orbit radius r of a satellite in a circular motion. Mark the correct statement :

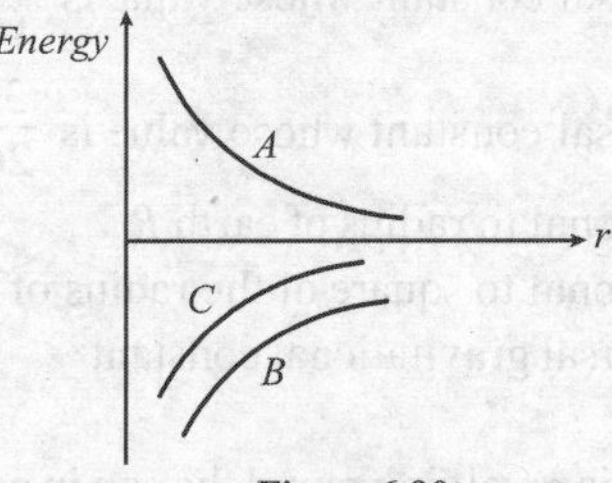

Figure 6.90

(A) C shows the total energy, B the kinetic energy and A the potential energy of the satellite
(B) A shows the kinetic energy, B the total energy and C the potential energy of the satellite
(C) A and B are the kinetic and potential energies and C the total energy of the satellite
(D) C and A are the kinetic and potential energies respectively and B the total energy of the satellite

6-19 If g_h and g_d be the accelerations due to gravity at height h and at depth d, above and below the surface of earth respectively. Assuming $h << R$ and $d << R$ and if $g_h = g_d$ then,
(A) $d = h$
(B) $d = 2h$
(C) $h = 2d$
(D) Data is insufficient to arrive at a conclusion.

6-20 A particle is placed in a field characterized by a value of gravitational potential given by $V = -kxy$, where k is a constant. If $\vec{E}_g$ is the gravitational field then,
(A) $\vec{E}_g = k(x\hat{i} + y\hat{j})$ and is conservative in nature
(B) $\vec{E}_g = k(y\hat{i} + x\hat{j})$ and is conservative in nature
(C) $\vec{E}_g = k(x\hat{i} + y\hat{j})$ and is non-conservative in nature
(D) $\vec{E}_g = k(y\hat{i} + x\hat{j})$ and is non-conservative in nature

6-21 Which of the following statements is wrong ?
(A) A ship moving from west to east, along the equator, shall have more less as compared to when it is at rest at the equator
(B) A ship moving from east to west, along the equator, shall have more weight as compared to when it is at rest
(C) Earth has retained its atmosphere because the value of $\sqrt{\frac{3kT}{m}}$ for air molecules is larger than escape velocity
(D) The time period of a simple pendulum of infinite length is the same as the time period of SHM of a ball in a tunnel along the diameter of earth

6-22 If the period of revolution of an artificial satellite just above the earth's surface is T and the density of earth is ρ, then ρT^2 :

(A) Is a universal constant whose value is $\dfrac{3\pi}{G}$

(B) Is a universal constant whose value is $\dfrac{3\pi}{2G}$

(C) Is proportional to radius of earth R

(D) Is proportional to square of the radius of earth R^2

Here G = universal gravitational constant

6-23 A planet is revolving round the sun in an elliptical orbit. Of the following, the property which is a constant during the motion of the planet is :

(A) The force of attraction between the planet and sun.

(B) The total energy of the "planet plus sun" system.

(C) The linear momentum of the planet.

(D) The kinetic energy of the planet about the sun.

6-24 Two air bubbles in water in a container in gravity free space:

(A) move toward each other

(B) move away from each other

(C) Do not move if system is left undisturbed.

(D) May move toward or away from each other depending upon the distance between them

6-25 A particle of mass m is located at a distance r from the centre of a shell of mass M and radius R. The force between the shell and mass is $F(r)$. The plot of $F(r)$ vs r is :

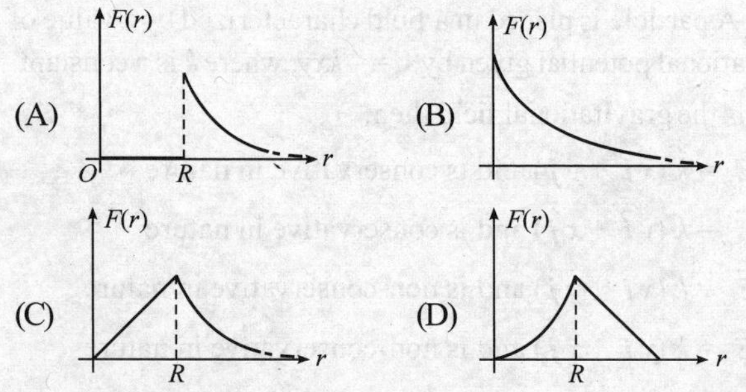

6-26 A sphere of mass M and radius R_2 has a concentric cavity of radius R_1 as shown in figure-6.91. The force F exerted by the sphere on a particle of mass m located at a distance r from the centre of sphere varies as $(0 \le r \le \infty)$:

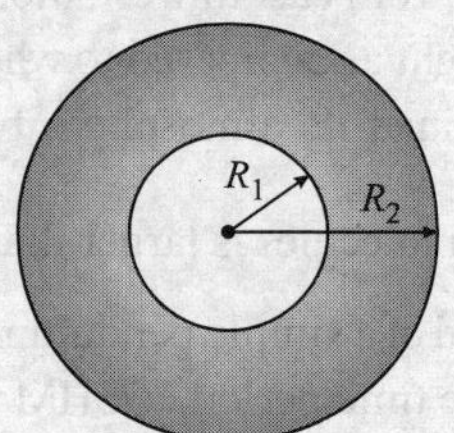

Figure 6.91

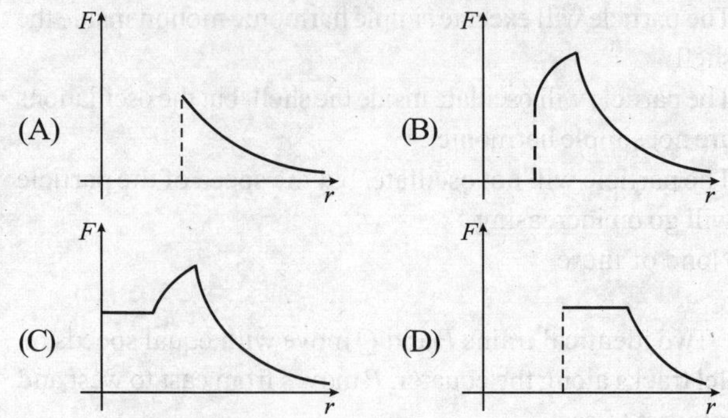

6-27 A shell of mass M and radius R has a point mass m placed at a distance r from its centre. The gravitational potential energy $U(r)$ vs r will be :

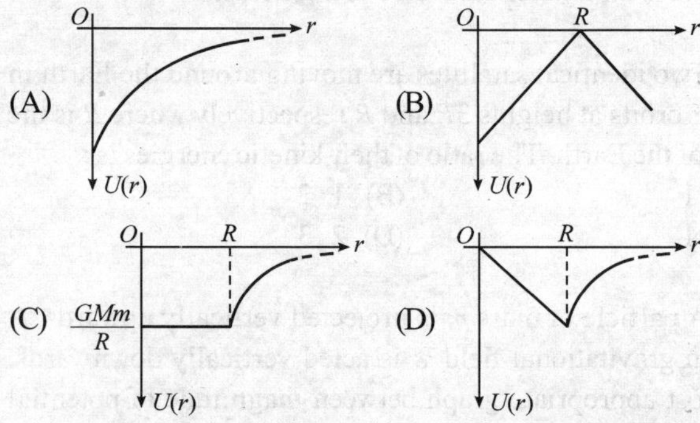

6-28 A satellite is orbiting round the earth. While in orbit a small part separates from the satellite. The separated part.

(A) Falls directly to the earth

(B) Moves in a spiral path and reaches the earth after few revolutions about the earth.

(C) Continues to move in the same orbit.

(D) Moves gradually father from the earth.

6-29 A satellite S is moving in an elliptical orbit around the earth. The mass of satellite is very small compared to the mass of earth :

(A) The acceleration of S is always directed towards the centre of the earth

(B) The angular momentum of S about the centre of the earth changes its direction but its magnitude remains constant

(C) The total mechanical energy of S varies periodically with time

(D) The linear momentum of S remains constant in magnitude

6-30 A planet of mass m is moving around the sun in an elliptical orbit of semi-major axis a :

(A) The total mechanical energy of the planet is varying periodically with time

(B) The total mechanical energy of the planet is constant and equals $-\dfrac{GmM_s}{2a}$, M_s is mass of sun

(C) Total mechanical energy of the planet is constant and equals $-\frac{GmM_s}{a}$, M_s is mass of sun

(D) Data is insufficient to arrive at a conclusion

6-31 Two stars of masses m_1 and m_2 distance r apart, revolve about their centre of mass. The period of revolution is :

(A) $2\pi\sqrt{\frac{r^3}{2G(m_1+m_2)}}$ (B) $2\pi\sqrt{\frac{r^3(m_1+m_2)}{2Gm_1m_2}}$

(C) $2\pi\sqrt{\frac{2r^3}{G(m_1+m_2)}}$ (D) $2\pi\sqrt{\frac{r^3}{G(m_1+m_2)}}$

6-32 A satellite in an equatorial orbit has a time period of 6 hrs. At a certain instant, it is directly overhead an observer on the equator of the earth. It is directly overhead the observer again after a time T. The possible value(s) of T is/are :

(A) 8 hr (B) 4.8 hr

(C) both (A) and (B) (D) none of these

6-33 A comet moves around the sun in an elliptical orbit. It is closest to the sun at a distance d_1 and its corresponding velocity is v_1, and if it is farthest from the sun at a distance d_2, then the corresponding velocity is :

(A) $\frac{v_1}{d_1}\cdot d_2$ (B) $v_1\cdot\frac{d_1}{d_2}$

(C) $v_1\cdot\sqrt{\frac{d_2}{d_1}}$ (D) $v_1\cdot\sqrt{\frac{d_1}{d_2}}$

6-34 A tunnel is made inside earth passing through center of earth. A particle is dropped from the surface of earth. Select the correct statement :

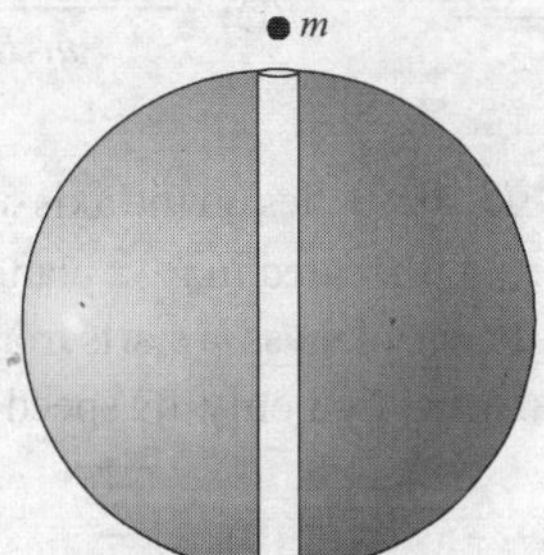

Figure 6.92

(A) Kinetic energy of particle is maximum at center and its potential energy is zero at center

(B) Velocity of particle is proportional to x [where x is distance of particle from center of earth

(C) Kinetic energy of particle is maximum when it reaches on the other side of tunnel

(D) Kinetic energy of particle is maximum at center

6-35 Two particles A and B (of masse m and $4m$) are released from rest in the two tunnels as shown in the figure-6.93. Which particle will cross the equatorial plane first ?

(A) A

(B) B

(C) Both simultaneously

(D) Data insufficient

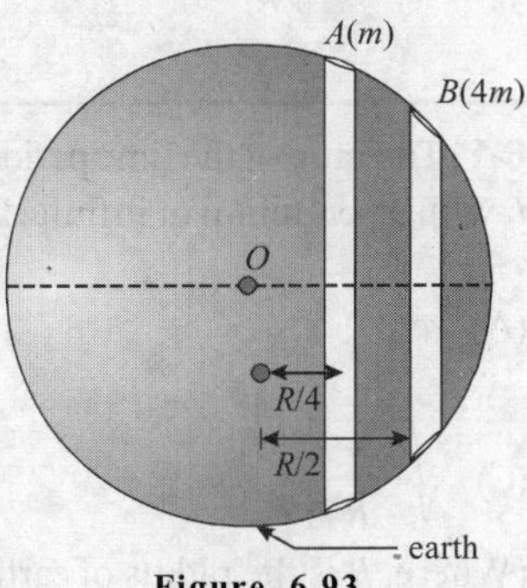

Figure 6.93

6-36 Identify the correct definition of gravitational potential at a point.

(A) it is defined in terms of the force required to displace a unit mass from infinity to that point

(B) it is defined in terms of the force required to move a unit mass from the surface of earth to that point

(C) it is defined in terms of the force required to displace a unit mass from that point to infinity

(D) none of these

6-37 The tidal waves in the sea are primarily due to :

(A) The gravitational effect of the moon on the earth

(B) The gravitational effect of the sun on the earth

(C) The gravitational effect of Venus on the earth

(D) The atmospheric effect of the earth itself

6-38 If the sun were suddenly replaced by a block hole of one solar mass, what would happen to the earth's orbit immediately after the replacement ?

(A) The earth would spiral into the black hole

(B) The radius of the earth's orbit would be unchanged, but the period of the earth's motion would increase

(C) The radius of the earth's orbit would be unchanged, but the period of the earth's motion would decrease

(D) Neither the radius of the orbit nor the period would change

6-39 A block of mass m is lying at a distance r from a spherical shell of mass m and radius r. Then :

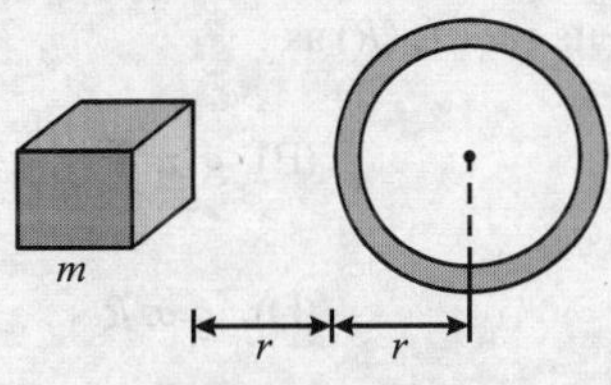

Figure 6.94

(A) Only gravitational field inside the shell is zero

(B) Gravitational field and gravitational potential both are zero inside the shell

(C) Gravitational potential as well as gravitational field inside the shell are not zero

(D) Can't be ascertained.

* * * * *

Numerical MCQs Single Options Correct

6-1 The ratio of the time period of a simple pendulum of length l_0 with a pendulum of infinite length is :

(A) zero (B) $\sqrt{\frac{l_0}{R}}$

(C) $\sqrt{\frac{l_0+R}{R}}$ (D) $\sqrt{\frac{R}{l_0+R}}$

(Where, R is the radius of earth)

6-2 The rotation of the earth having R radius about its axis speeds up to a value such that a man at latitude angle 60° feels weightlessness. The duration of the day in such a case is :

(A) $2\pi\sqrt{\frac{R}{g}}$ (B) $4\pi\sqrt{\frac{R}{g}}$

(C) $2\pi\sqrt{\frac{g}{R}}$ (D) $4\pi\sqrt{\frac{g}{R}}$

6-3 At what height the gravitational field reduces by 75% of the gravitational field at the surface of earth?

(A) R (B) $2R$

(C) $3R$ (D) $4R$

6-4 In a certain region of space gravitational field is given by $g=-\left(\frac{k}{r}\right)$. Taking the reference point to be at $r = r_0$ with potential $V = V_0$, the potential (V) at a general point r is given by :

(A) $V=K\ln\left(\frac{r}{r_0}\right)+v_0$ (B) $V=K\ln\left(\frac{r}{r_0}\right)-v_0$

(C) $V=K\ln\left(\frac{r_0}{r}\right)+v_0$ (D) $V=K\ln\left(\frac{r_0}{r}\right)-v_0$

6-5 Two different planets have same density but different radii. The acceleration due to gravity (g) on the surface of the planets is dependent on its radius (R) as :

(A) $g\propto\frac{1}{R^2}$ (B) $g\propto R^2$

(C) $g\propto\frac{1}{R}$ (D) $g\propto R$

6-6 A shell of mass M and radius R has another point mass m placed at a distance r from its centre ($r > R$). The force of attraction between the shell and point mass is :

(A) $F=\frac{GMm}{r}$ (B) $F=\frac{GMm}{r^2}$

(C) $F=$ zero (D) None of above

6-7 If g_h and g_d be the accelerations due to gravity at a height h and at depth d, above and below the surface of earth respectively. Assuming $h << R$ and $d << R$ and if $g_h = g_d$ then :

(A) $d = h$

(B) $d = 2h$

(C) $h = 2d$

(D) Data is insufficient to arrive at a conclusion.

6-8 A satellite is revolving round the earth in an orbit of radius r with time period T. If the satellite is revolving round the earth in an orbit of radius $r + \Delta r(\Delta r << r)$ with time period $T + \Delta T(\Delta T << T)$ then.

(A) $\frac{\Delta T}{T}=\frac{3}{2}\frac{\Delta r}{r}$ (B) $\frac{\Delta T}{T}=\frac{2}{3}\frac{\Delta r}{r}$

(C) $\frac{\Delta T}{T}=\frac{\Delta r}{r}$ (D) $\frac{\Delta T}{T}=-\frac{\Delta r}{r}$

6-9 Consider an infinite plane sheet of mass with surface mass density σ. The gravitational field intensity at a point P at perpendicular distance r from such a sheet is :

(A) Zero (B) $-\sigma G$

(C) $2\pi\sigma G$ (D) $-4\pi\sigma G$

6-10 Two identical thin rings each of radius R are coaxially placed at a distance R. If the rings have a uniform mass distribution and each has mass m_1 and m_2 respectively, then the work done in moving a mass m from centre of one ring to that of the other is :

(A) Zero (B) $\frac{Gm(m_1-m_2)(\sqrt{2}-1)}{\sqrt{2}R}$

(C) $\frac{Gm\sqrt{2}(m_1+m_2)}{R}$ (D) $\frac{Gmm_1(\sqrt{2}+1)}{m_2R}$

6-11 A point $P(R\sqrt{3}, 0, 0)$ lies on the axis of a ring of mass M and radius R. The ring is located in $y-z$ plane with its centre at origin O. A small particle of mass m starts from P and reaches O under gravitational attraction only. Its speed at O will be.

(A) $\sqrt{\frac{GM}{R}}$ (B) $\sqrt{\frac{Gm}{R}}$

(C) $\sqrt{\frac{GM}{\sqrt{2}R}}$ (D) $\sqrt{\frac{Gm}{\sqrt{2}R}}$

6-12 An artificial satellite moving in circular orbit around the earth has a total (kinetic + potential) energy E_0. Its potential energy and kinetic energy respectively are :

(A) $2E_0$ and $-2E_0$ (B) $-2E_0$ and $3E_0$

(C) $2E_0$ and $-E_0$ (D) $-2E_0$ and $-E_0$

6-13 The ratio of Earth's orbital angular momentum (about the Sun) to its mass is 4.4×10^{15} m^{2}s^{-1}. The area enclosed by the earth's orbit is approximately.

(A) $1 \times 10^{22}\, m^2$ (B) $3 \times 10^{22}\, m^2$

(C) $5 \times 10^{22}\, m^2$ (D) $7 \times 10^{22}\, m^2$

6-14 A particle is projected vertically upwards from the surface of earth (radius R_e) with a kinetic energy equal to half of the minimum value needed for it to escape. The height to which it rises above the surface of earth is :

(A) R_e (B) $2R_e$

(C) $3R_e$ (D) $4R_e$

Paragraph for Questions 15 & 20

A satellite of mass 5000kg is projected in space with an initial speed of 4000m/s making an angle of 30° with the radial direction from a distance 3.6×10^7m away from the center of the earth.

6-15 The angular momentum of satellite :

(A) 3.6×10^7 J-s (B) 4.9×10^7 J-s

(C) 9.2×10^7 J-s (D) 3.6×10^{14} J-s

6-16 The energy of satellite :

(A) 1.6×10^7 joule (B) 4.9×10^7 joule

(C) 0.2×10^7 joule (D) -1.5×10^{10} joule

6-17 The minimum distance of satellite from earth :

(A) 66.6×10^7 m (B) 14.9×10^7 m

(C) 1.29×10^7 m (D) 1.6×10^4 m

6-18 The maximum distance of satellite from earth.

(A) 6.6×10^7 m (B) 24.9×10^7 m

(C) 11.9×10^7 m (D) 1.6×10^4 m

6-19 The semi-major axis of the orbit of satellite :

(A) 6.6×10^7 m (B) 14.9×10^7 m

(C) 19.2×10^7 m (D) 1.6×10^4 m

6-20 Semi-minor axis of the orbit of satellite :

(A) 16.6×10^7 m (B) 3.92×10^7 m

(C) 10.2×10^{17} m (D) 2.6×10^4 m

6-21 Imagine a light planet revolving around a very massive star in a circular orbit of radius R with a period of revolution T. If the gravitational force of attraction between the planet and the star is proportional to $R^{-5/2}$, then :

(A) T^2 is proportional to R^2 (B) T^2 is proportional to $R^{7/2}$

(C) T^2 is proportional to $R^{3/2}$ (D) T^2 is proportional to $R^{3.75}$

6-22 A projectile is fired upwards from the surface of the earth with a velocity kv_e where v_e is the escape velocity and $k < 1$. If r is the maximum distance from the centre of the earth to which it rises and R is the radius of the earth, then r is :

(A) $\frac{R}{k^2}$ (B) $\frac{2R}{1-k^2}$

(C) $\frac{2R}{k^2}$ (D) $\frac{R}{1-k^2}$

6-23 Two satellites S_1 and S_2 revolve round a planet in coplanar circular orbits in the same sense. Their periods of revolution are 1 hour and 8 hour respectively. The radius of the orbit of S_1 is 10^4 km. The speed of S_2 relative to S_1 when they are closest (in kmh^{-1}) is :

(A) $10^4\pi$ (B) $2 \times 10^4\pi$

(C) $\frac{1}{2}10^4\pi$ (D) $4 \times 10^4\pi$

6-24 In previous problem what is the angular speed of S_2 as observed by an astronaut in S_1 when they are closest :

(A) $\frac{\pi}{2}$ (B) $\frac{\pi}{3}$

(C) $\frac{\pi}{4}$ (D) $\frac{\pi}{6}$

6-25 Two particles having masses m_1 and m_2 start moving towards each other from the state of rest from infinite separation. Their relative velocity of approach when they are interacting gravitationally and at a separation r will be :

(A) $\sqrt{\frac{G(m_1+m_2)}{r}}$ (B) $\sqrt{\frac{2G(m_1+m_2)}{r}}$

(C) $\sqrt{\frac{Gm_1m_2}{(m_1+m_2)r}}$ (D) $\sqrt{\frac{G(m_1+m_2)}{2r}}$

6-26 A body is imparted a velocity v from the surface of the earth. If v_0 is orbital velocity and v_e be the escape velocity then for :

(A) $v = v_0$, the body follows a circular track around the earth.

(B) $v > v_0$ but $< ve$, the body follows elliptical path around the earth.

(C) $v < v_0$, the body follows elliptical path and returns to surface of earth.

(D) $v > v_e$, the body follows hyperbolic path and escapes the gravitational pull of the earth.

(A) A, B (B) B, C

(C) A, B, C (D) A, B, C, D

6-27 A particle is launched from the surface of earth with speed v. For the particle to move as a satellite, which statement is correct ?

(A) $\frac{v_e}{2} < v < v_e$ (B) $\frac{v_e}{\sqrt{2}} < v < v_e$

(C) $v_e < v < \sqrt{2v_e}$ (D) $\frac{v_e}{\sqrt{2}} < v < \frac{v_e}{2}$

6-28 Two bodies of masses m and M are placed a distance d apart. The gravitational potential at the position where the gravitational field due to them is zero is V:

(A) $V=-\frac{G}{d}(m+M)$ (B) $V=-\frac{Gm}{d}$

(C) $V=\frac{GM}{d}$ (D) $V=-\frac{G}{d}\left(\sqrt{m}+\sqrt{M}\right)^2$

6-29 The orbital period of revolution of a planet round the Sun is T_0. Suppose we make a model of Solar system scaled down in the ratio η but of materials of the same mean density as the actual material of planet and the Sun has. The new orbital period is :

(A) ηT_0 (B) $\eta^2 T_0$
(C) $\eta^3 T_0$ (D) T_0

6-30 The time period of a spy satellite orbiting a few hundred kilometre above the earth's surface (R_{earth} = 6400 km) will approximately be :

(A) $\frac{1}{2}h$ (B) $1h$
(C) $2h$ (D) $4h$

6-31 Consider a thin uniform spherical layer of mass M and radius R. The potential energy of gravitational interaction of matter forming this shell is :

(A) $-\frac{GM^2}{R}$ (B) $-\frac{1}{2}\frac{GM^2}{R}$

(C) $-\frac{3}{5}\frac{GM^2}{R}$ (D) $-\frac{2}{3}\frac{GM^2}{R}$

6-32 If we consider a solid sphere of mass M and radius R, then the potential energy of gravitational interaction of matter forming this solid sphere is :

(A) $-\frac{GM^2}{R}$ (B) $-\frac{1}{2}\frac{GM^2}{R}$

(C) $-\frac{3}{5}\frac{GM^2}{R}$ (D) $-\frac{3}{2}\frac{GM^2}{R}$

6-33 What should be the period of rotation of earth so as to make any object on the equator weigh half of its present value?

(A) 2 hrs (B) 24 hrs
(C) 8 hrs (D) 12 hrs

6-34 An artificial satellite is describing an equatorial orbit at 3600 km above the earth's surface. Calculate its period of revolution ? Take earth radius 6400 km.

(A) 8.71 hrs (B) 9.71 hrs
(C) 10.71 hrs (D) 11.71 hrs

6-35 In previous question calculate orbital speed of satellite.

(A) 6.335 km/sec (B) 7.335 km/sec
(C) 8.335 km/sec (D) 9.335 km/sec

6-36 Three particles each having a mass of 100 gm are placed on the vertices of an equilateral triangle of side 20 cm. The work done in increasing the side of the triangle to 40 cm is $\left[G=6.67\times10^{-11}\frac{N-m^2}{kg^2}\right]$

(A) 5.0×10^{-12}J (B) 2.25×10^{-10}J
(C) 4.0×10^{-11}J (D) 6.0×10^{-15}J

6-37 If the time of revolution of a satellite is T, then Kinetic energy is proportional to :

(A) $1/T$ (B) $1/T^2$
(C) $1/T^3$ (D) $T^{-2/3}$

6-38 A Saturn year is 29.5 times the earth year. How far is the Saturn from the sun if the earth is 1.5×10^8 km away from the sun?

(A) 1.43×10^9 km (B) 2.43×10^9 km
(C) 3.43×10^9 km (D) 4.43×10^9 km

6-39 A spherical planet in space has a mass M_0 and diameter D_0. A particle of mass m falling freely near the surface of this planet will experience an acceleration due to gravity which is equal to :

(A) $\frac{GM_o}{D_o^2}$ (B) $\frac{4GmM_o}{D_o^2}$

(C) $\frac{4GM_o}{D_o^2}$ (D) $\frac{GmM}{D_o^2}$

6-40 A body falls freely towards the earth from a height $2R$, above the surface of the earth, where initially it was at rest. If R is the radius of the earth then its velocity on reaching the surface of the earth is :

(A) $\sqrt{\frac{4}{3}gR}$ (B) $\sqrt{\frac{2}{3}gR}$

(C) $\frac{4}{3}gR$ (D) $2gR$

6-41 Two satellite A and B are moving round a planet in circular orbit having radii R and $3R$ respectively, if the speed of satellite A is v the speed of satellite B will be :

(A) $v/3$ (B) $v/\sqrt{3}$
(C) $3v$ (D) data insufficient

6-42 The radius of a planet is R. A satellite revolves around it in a circle of radius r with angular speed ω. The acceleration due to gravity on planet's surface will be :

(A) $\frac{r^3\omega}{R}$ (B) $\frac{r^2\omega^3}{R}$

(C) $\frac{r^3\omega^2}{R^2}$ (D) $\frac{r^2\omega^2}{R}$

6-43 The gravitational field in a region is given by $\vec{g} = (4\hat{i} + \hat{j})$ N/kg. Work done by this field is zero when the particle is moved along the line :

(A) $y+4x=2$ (B) $4y+x=6$

(C) $x+y=5$ (D) all of the above

6-44 A particle of mass m is placed inside a spherical shell, away from its centre. The mass of the shell is M.

(A) The particle will move towards the centre.

(B) The particle will move away from the centre, towards the nearest wall.

(C) The particle will move towards the centre if $m < M$ and away from the centre if $m > M$

(D) The particle will remain stationary

Paragraph for Question Nos. 45 to 47

Supernova refers to the explosion of a massive star. The material in the central case of such a star continues to collapse under its own gravitational pull. If mass of the core is less than 1.4 times the mass of sun, its collapse finally results in a white dwarf star. However, if the core has a mass greater than this, it could end up soon as a neutron star and if its mass is more than about three solar masses, the collapse may still continue till the star becomes a very small object with an extremely high value of density called a 'Black hole'. Escape speed for a black hole is very large. The figure shows a block hole of radius R and another concentric sphere of radius R_S, called the 'Schwarzschild Radius'. It is the critical radius at which escape speed equals the speed of light c. Nothing even the light, can escape from within the sphere of Radius R_S. So light from a black hole cannot escape and hence the terminology 'black hole'. There has been astronomical evidence of a small and massive object at the centre of our galaxy the 'Milky way'. Suppose that there is a particle at a distance about 6 light years that orbits this massive object with an orbital speed of about 2×10^5 m/s. Use the given data wherever necessary and answer the questions that follow. $G = 6.67 \times 10^{-11}$ N – m^2/kg^2, Solar mass $M = 2 \times 10^{30}$ kg, $C = 3 \times 10^8$ m/s, 1 light year $= 9.5 \times 10^{15}$ m.

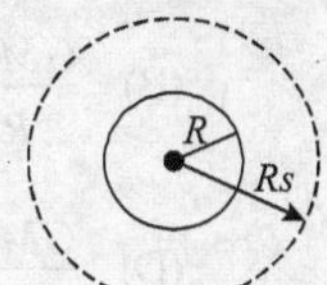

Figure 6.95

6-45 Mass (in kg) of the massive object at the centre of the milky way galaxy is of the order :

(A) 10^{32} (B) 10^{37}

(C) 10^{43} (D) 10^{29}

6-46 Theories suggest that it is not possible for a single star to have a mass of more than 50 solar masses. The massive object at the centre of milky way galaxy is most likely to be a :

(A) white dwarf (B) neutron star

(C) black hole (D) single ordinary star

6-47 If mass of earth $M_E \approx 6 \times 10^{24}$ kg and its radius $R_E = 6400$ km, to what fraction of its presents radius does the earth need to be compressed in order to become a black hole? (Give only the order of your answer)

(A) 10^{-4} (B) 10^{-9}

(C) 10^{-7} (D) 10^{-14}

6-48 A hole is drilled from the surface of earth to its centre. A particle is dropped from rest at the surface of earth. The speed of the particle when it reaches the centre of the earth in terms of its escape velocity on the surface of earth v_e is :

(A) $\frac{v_e}{2}$ (B) v_e

(C) $\sqrt{2}v_e$ (D) $\frac{v_e}{\sqrt{2}}$

6-49 Two small balls of mass m each are suspended side by side by two equal threads of length L. If the distance between the upper ends of the threads be a, the angle θ that the threads will make with the vertical due to attraction between the balls is :

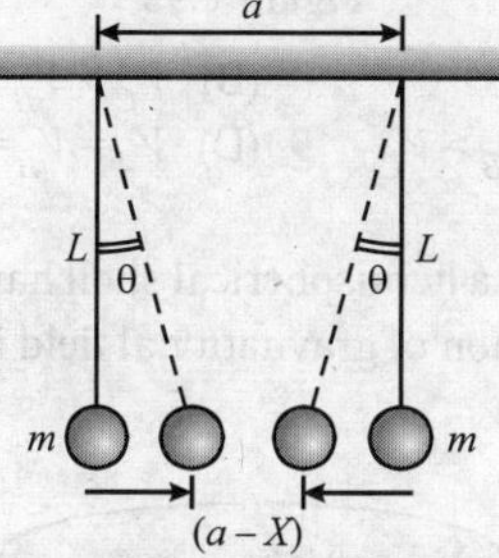

Figure 6.96

(A) $\tan^{-1}\frac{(a-X)g}{mG}$ (B) $\tan^{-1}\frac{mG}{(a-X)^2 g}$

(C) $\tan^{-1}\frac{(a-X)^2 g}{mG}$ (D) $\tan^{-1}\frac{(a^2-X^2)g}{mG}$

6-50 Two masses of mass m each are fixed at a separation distance of $2d$. A small mass m_s placed midway, when displaced slightly, starts oscillating. Then :

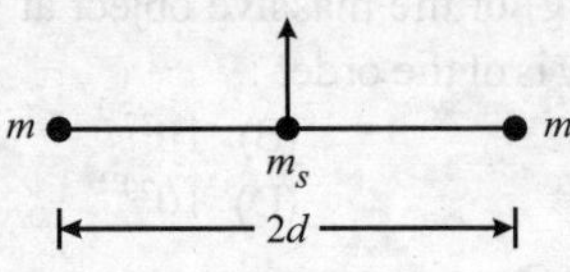

Figure 6.97

(A) Frequency of simple harmonic motion is given by $\frac{1}{2\pi}\sqrt{\frac{4Gm}{d^3}}$

(B) Frequency of simple harmonic motion is given by $\frac{1}{2\pi}\sqrt{\frac{2Gm}{d^3}}$

(C) Acceleration of the mass m_s is given by $\frac{Gm}{d^2}$

(D) Time period of vibration is $2\pi\sqrt{\frac{GM}{(2d)^3}}$

6-51 Mass M is uniformly distributed only on curved surface of a thin hemispherical shell. A, B and C are three points on the circular base of hemisphere, such that A is the centre. Let the gravitational potential at points A, B and C be V_A, V_B, V_C respectively. Then :

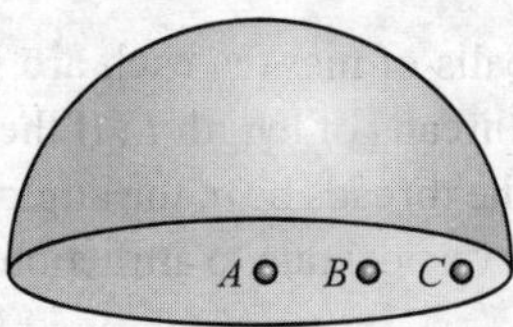

Figure 6.98

(A) $V_A > V_B > V_C$ (B) $V_C > V_B > V_A$

(C) $V_B > V_A$ and $V_B > V_C$ (D) $V_A = V_B = V_C$

6-52 Figure show a hemispherical shell having uniform mass density. The direction of gravitational field intensity at point P will be along :

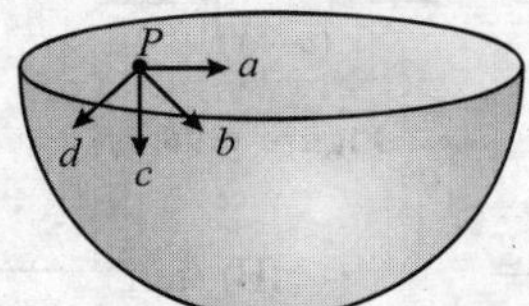

Figure 6.99

(A) a (B) b

(C) c (D) d

6-53 A straight rod of length l extends from $x = \alpha$ to $x = l + \alpha$. If the mass per unit length is $(a + bx^2)$. The gravitational force it exerts on a point mass m placed at $x = 0$ is given by :

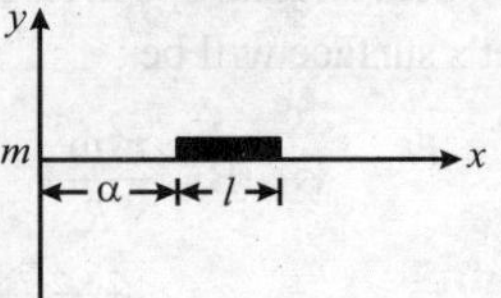

Figure 6.100

(A) $Gm\left(a\left(\frac{1}{\alpha}-\frac{1}{\alpha+l}\right)+bl\right)$ (B) $\frac{Gm(a+bx^2)}{l^2}$

(C) $Gm\left(\alpha\left(\frac{1}{a}-\frac{1}{a+l}\right)+bl\right)$ (D) $Gm\left(a\left(\frac{1}{\alpha+l}-\frac{1}{\alpha}\right)+bl\right)$

6-54 The planet with radii R_1, R_2 have densities ρ_1, ρ_2 respectively. Their atmospheric pressures are p_1, p_2 respectively. Therefore, the ratio of masses of their atmospheres, neglecting variation of g within the limits of atmosphere, is :

(A) $p_1 R_2 \rho_1 / p_2 R_1 \rho_2$ (B) $p_1 R_2 \rho_2 / p_2 R_1 \rho_1$

(C) $p_1 R_1 \rho_1 / p_2 R_2 \rho_2$ (D) $p_1 R_1 \rho_2 / p_2 R_2 \rho_1$

6-55 A satellite of mass m orbits the earth in an elliptical orbit having aphelion distance r_a and perihelion distance r_p. The period of the orbit is T. The semi-major and semi-minor axes of the ellipse are $\frac{r_a + r_p}{2}$ and $\sqrt{r_p r_a}$ respectively. The angular momentum of the satellite is :

(A) $\frac{m\pi(r_a + r_p)\sqrt{r_a r_p}}{T}$ (B) $\frac{2m\pi(r_a + r_p)\sqrt{r_a r_p}}{T}$

(C) $\frac{m\pi(r_a + r_p)\sqrt{r_a r_p}}{2T}$ (D) $\frac{m\pi(r_a + r_p)\sqrt{r_a r_p}}{4T}$

6-56 A uniform thin rod of mass m and length R is placed normally on surface of earth as shown. The mass of earth is M and its radius is R. Then the magnitude of gravitational force exerted by earth on the rod is :

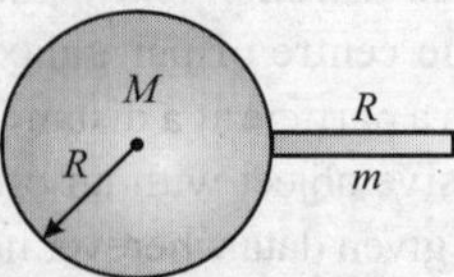

Figure 6.101

(A) $\frac{GMm}{4R^2}$ (B) $\frac{GMm}{2R^2}$

(C) $\frac{4GMm}{9R^2}$ (D) $\frac{GMm}{8R^2}$

6-57 A body of superdense material with mass twice the mass of earth but size very small compared to the size of earth starts from rest from $h << R$ above the earth's surface. It reaches earth in time t:

(A) $t = \sqrt{\frac{h}{g}}$ (B) $t = \sqrt{\frac{2h}{g}}$

(C) $t = \sqrt{\frac{2h}{3g}}$ (D) $t = \sqrt{\frac{4h}{3g}}$

6-58 Consider a mass m_0 enclosed by a closed imaginary surface S. Let $\vec{g}$ be the gravitational field intensity due to m_0 at the surface element $d\vec{S}$ directed as outward normal to it. The surface integral of the gravitational field over S is :

(A) $-m_0G$ (B) $-4\pi m_0G$

(C) $-\frac{m_0G}{4\pi}$ (D) None of above

6-59 A solid sphere of uniform density and radius R exerts a gravitational force of attraction F_1 on a particle placed at P. The distance of P from the centre of the sphere is $2R$. A spherical cavity of radius $\frac{R}{2}$ is now made in the sphere. The sphere (with cavity) exerts a gravitational force F_2 on the same particle at P. The ratio $\frac{F_1}{F_2}$ is :

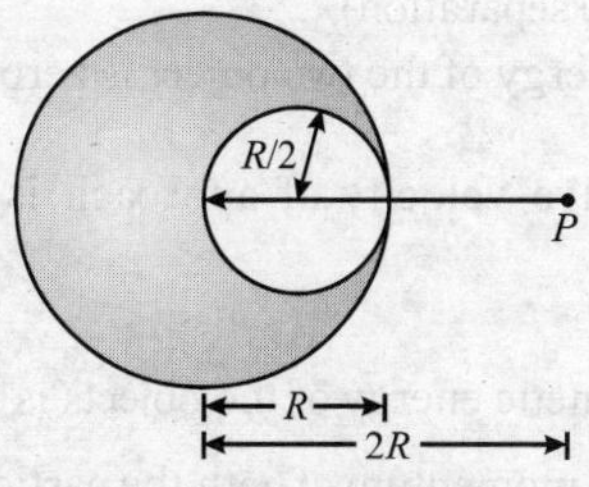

Figure 6.102

(A) $\frac{9}{7}$ (B) $\frac{7}{9}$

(C) $\frac{1}{2}$ (D) $\frac{4}{3}$

* * * * *

Advance MCQs with One or More Options Correct

6-1 Two objects of masses m and 4 m are at rest at an infinite separation. They move towards each other under mutual gravitational attraction. If G is the universal gravitational constant. Then at separation r: (Assume zero reference potential energy at infinite separation)

(A) The total energy of the two object is zero

(B) Their relative velocity of approach is $\left(\frac{10Gm}{r}\right)^{1/2}$ in magnitude

(C) The total kinetic energy of the objects is $\frac{4Gm^2}{r}$

(D) Net angular momentum of both the particles is zero about any point

6-2 A planet of mass m is revolving round the sun (of mass M_s) in an elliptical orbit. If $\vec{v}$ is the velocity of the planet when its position vector from the sun is $\vec{r}$, then areal velocity of the position vector of the planet is :

(A) $\vec{v} \times \vec{r}$ (B) $\vec{r} \times \vec{v}$

(C) $\frac{1}{2}(\vec{v} \times \vec{r})$ (D) $\frac{1}{2}(\vec{r} \times \vec{v})$

6-3 In Q. No. 6-2, if the planet rotates in counter clockwise direction, then areal velocity has a direction :

(A) Given by "Right Hand Thumb Rule"

(B) Given by "Left Hand Thumb Rule"

(C) Normal to the plane of orbit upwards

(D) Normal to the plane of orbit downwards

6-4 A particle of mass m lies at a distance r from the centre of earth. The force of attraction between the particle and earth as a function of distance is $F(r)$,

(A) $F(r) \propto \frac{1}{r^2}$ for $r < R$ (B) $F(r) \propto \frac{1}{r^2}$ for $r \geq R$

(C) $F(r) \propto r$ for $r < R$ (D) $F(r) \propto \frac{1}{r}$ for $r < R$

6-5 A planet is revolving round the sun in an elliptical orbit. The work done on the planet by the gravitational force of sun is zero :

(A) In some parts of the orbit

(B) In any part of the orbit

(C) In no part of the orbit

(D) In one complete revolution

6-6 A satellite is orbiting round the earth's surface in an orbit as close as possible to the surface of the earth.

(A) The time period of revolution of satellite is independent of its mass and is maximum.

(B) The orbital speed of satellite is maximum.

(C) The Kinetic energy of the satellite is minimum.

(D) The total energy of the "earth plus satellite" system is maximum.

6-7 Suppose universal gravitational constant starts to decrease, then :

(A) Length of the year will increase

(B) Earth will follow a spiral path of decreasing radius

(C) Kinetic energy of earth will decrease

(D) All of the above

6-8 A body is imparted a velocity v from the surface of the earth. If v_0 is orbital velocity and v_e be the escape velocity then for :

(A) $v = v_0$, the body follows a circular track around the earth

(B) $v > v_0$, but $< v_e$, the body follows elliptical path around the earth

(C) $v < v_0$, the body follows elliptical path and returns to surface of earth

(D) $v > v_e$, the body follows hyperbolic path and escapes the gravitational pull of the earth

6-9 Let V and E be the gravitational potential and gravitational field. Then select the correct alternative(s) :

(A) The plot of E against r (distance from centre) is discontinuous for a spherical shell

(B) The plot of V against r is continuous for a spherical shell

(C) The plot of E against r is discontinuous for a solid sphere

(D) The plot of V against r is continuous for a solid sphere

6-10 Inside a uniform sphere of mass M and radius R, a cavity of radius $R/3$ is made in the sphere as shown :

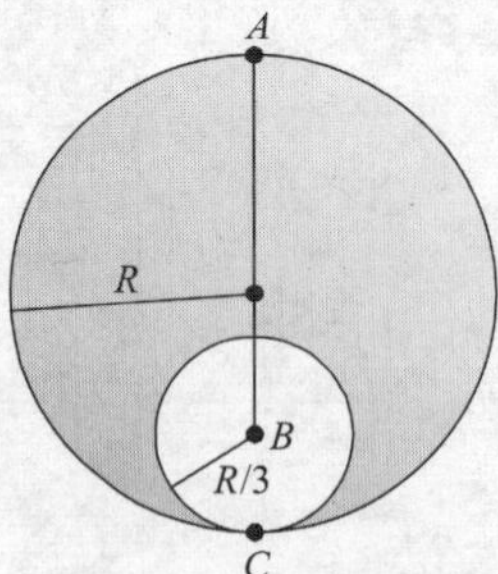

Figure 6.103

(A) Gravitational field inside the cavity is uniform

(B) Gravitational field inside the cavity is non-uniform

(C) The escape velocity of a particle projected from point A is $\sqrt{\frac{88GM}{15R}}$

(D) Escape velocity is defined for earth and particle system only

6-11 A solid sphere of uniform density and radius 4 units is located with its centre at the origin O. Two spheres of equal radii 1 unit with their centres at A (– 2, 0, 0) and B (2, 0, 0) respectively are taken out of the solid leaving behind cavities as shown in figure-6.104. Then :

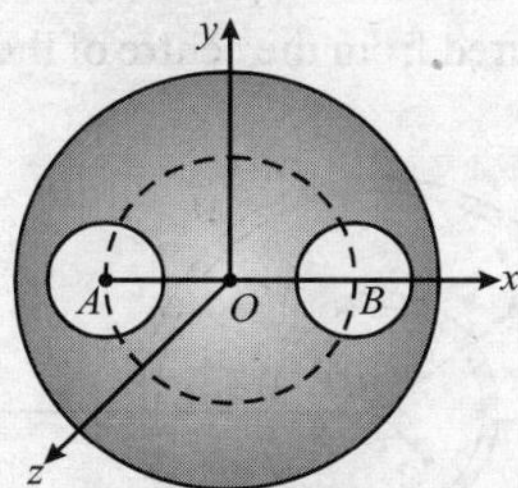

Figure 6.104

(A) The gravitational field due to this object at origin is zero
(B) The gravitational field at the point B (2, 0, 0) is zero
(C) The gravitational potential is the same at all points on the circle $y^2 + z^2 = 36$
(D) The gravitational potential is the same at all points on the circle $y^2 + z^2 = 4$

6-12 Two tunnels are dug from one side of the earth's surface to the other side, one along a diameter and the other along a chord. Now two particles are dropped from one end of each of the tunnels. Both the particles oscillate simple harmonically along the tunnels. Let T_1 and T_2 be the time periods and v_1 and v_2 be the maximum speed of the particles in the two tunnels. Then :

(A) $T_1 = T_2$ (B) $T_1 > T_2$
(C) $v_1 = v_2$ (D) $v_1 > v_2$

6-13 A satellite is revolving round the earth in an elliptical orbit :

(A) Gravitational force exerted by earth is equal to centripetal force at every point of trajectory.
(B) Power associated with gravitational force is zero at every point
(C) Work done by gravitational force is zero in some small parts of the orbit
(D) At some point, magnitude of gravitational force is greater than that of centripetal force

6-14 Two spherical planets have the same mass but densities in the ratio 1 : 8. For these planets, the :

(A) Acceleration due to gravity will be in the ratio 4 : 1
(B) Acceleration due to gravity will be is the ratio 1 : 4
(C) Escape velocities from their surfaces will be in the ratio $\sqrt{2}:1$
(D) Escape velocities from their surfaces will be in the ratio $1:\sqrt{2}$

6-15 An artificial satellite is in a circular orbit around the earth. The universal gravitational constant starts decreasing at time $t = 0$, at a constant rate with respect to time t. Then the satellite has its :

(A) Path gradually spiralling out, away from the centre of the earth
(B) Path gradually spiralling in, towards the centre of the earth
(C) Angular momentum about the centre of the earth remains constant
(D) Potential energy increases

6-16 Suppose an earth satellite, revolving in a circular orbit, experiences a resistance due to cosmic dust. Then :

(A) Its kinetic energy will increase
(B) Its potential energy will decrease
(C) It will spiral towards the earth and in the process its angular momentum will remain conserved
(D) It will get heated and burn off ultimately or fall somewhere on the surface of earth

6-17 A point P is lying at a distance r ($< a$) from the centre of shell of radius a. If g and V be the gravitational field and potential at the point P then :

(A) $g = 0$ (B) $g = -\frac{GM}{r^2}$
(C) $V = 0$ (D) $V = -\frac{GM}{a}$

* * * * *

Unsolved Numerical Problems for Preparation of NSEP, INPhO & IPhO

For detailed preparation of INPhO and IPhO students can refer advance study material on www.physicsgalaxy.com

6-1 At what distance from the center of the earth will a 1 kg object have a weight of 1 N? If released from rest at this distance, what will its initial acceleration be?

Ans. [2.023×10^7 m]

6-2 The radius of Mars is 3.4×10^6 m and the acceleration of a freely falling object on its surface is 3.7 m/s^2. Determine the mass of Mars.

Ans. [6.46×10^{23} kg]

6-3 Suppose we invent a unit of mass which we shall call the cavendish (C). One cavendish of mass is defined such that $G = 1.0000\,(AU)^3/(yr^2\,C)$. Our unit of length is the astronomical unit (AU), the earth-sun distance – $1\,AU = 1.496 \times 10^{11}$ m – and our unit of time is the year (yr). (a) Determine the conversion factor between C and kg. (b) Find the mass of the sun in C.

Ans. [(a) 1.984×10^{-29} C/kg; (b) 39.5 C]

6-4 Determine the fractional reduction of the acceleration of gravity due to an increase in elevation of 10 km near the earth's surface.

Ans. [0.003]

6-5 In figure-6.105, particle A has a mass of 1.4 kg and particle B has a mass of 3.1 kg. What is the gravitational field at point P?

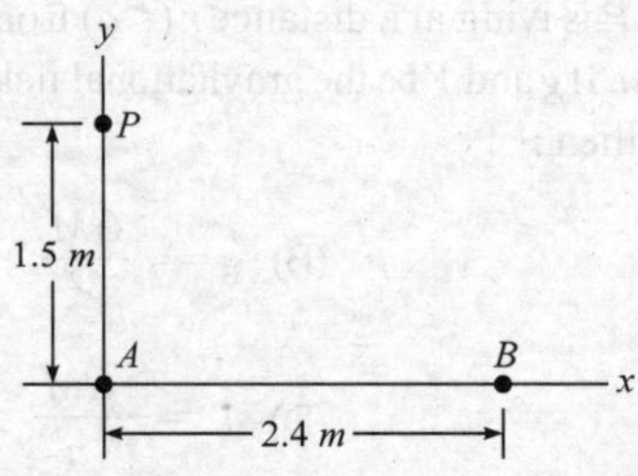

Figure 6.105

Ans. [$\vec{g} = (2.2 \times 10^{-11}$ N/kg$)\,\hat{i} - (5.5 \times 10^{-11}$ N/kg$)\,\hat{j}$]

6-6 While investigating the planet Norc in another solar system, we find that the radius of Norc is 9.54×10^6 m and that the period of a satellite put in circular orbit of radius 1.476×10^7 m is 8.09×10^3 s. Determine (a) the mass of Norc, (b) the average mass density of Norc, (c) the value of the gravitational field on the surface of Norc. (d) If the period of Norc's rotation about its axis is 1.04×10^4 s, what will be the reading on a spring scale (calibrated on earth) supporting a 1.0 kg object at Norc's equator ?

Ans. [(a) 2.908×10^{25} kg; (b) 8.00×10^3 kg/m^3; (c) 21.3 N/kg; (d) 17.8 N]

6-7 Two concentric shells of masses M_1 and M_2 are situated as shown in figure-6.106. Find the force on a particle of mass m when the particle is located at (a) $r = a$ (b) $r = b$ and (c) $r = c$. The distance r is measured from the centre of the shell.

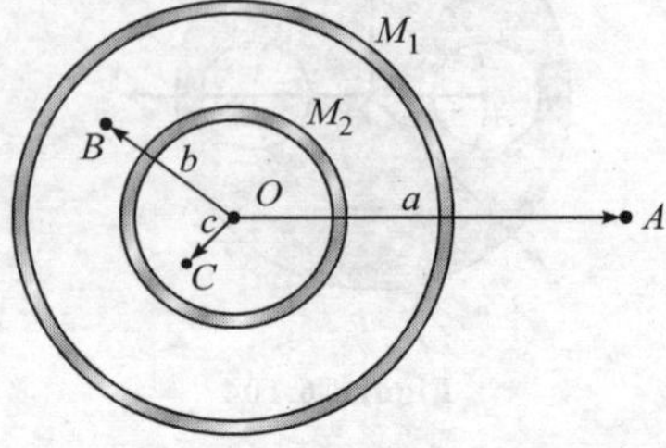

Figure 6.106

Ans. [(a) $Gm\,(M_1 + M_2)/a^2$; (b) (GMm/b^2); (c) 0]

6-8 Two point masses, each equal to M, are placed a distance $2a$ apart. Show that a small mass m placed midway between them on the line joining them will be in equilibrium and if it is slightly displaced from this position along the line perpendicular to the line joining the masses, it will execute simple harmonic oscillations. Calculate the frequency of these oscillations.

Ans. [$\dfrac{1}{2\pi}\sqrt{\dfrac{2GM}{a^3}}$]

6-9 Compute the mass and density of the moon if acceleration due to gravity on its surface is 1.62 m/s^2 and its radius is 1.74×10^6 m [$G = 6.67 \times 10^{-11}$ MKS units].

Ans. [7.35×10^{22} kg, 3.3×10^3 kg/m^3]

6-10 Two masses m_1 and m_2 are initially at rest at infinite distance apart. They approach each other due to gravitational interaction. Find the magnitude of the gravitational force on any sphere due to the other two.

Ans. [$\sqrt{[2G(m_1 + m_2)/d]}$]

6-11 Imagine a planet whose diameter and mass are both one half of those of earth. The day's temperature of this planet surface reaches upto 800 K. Make calculation and tell whether oxygen molecules are possible in the atmosphere of the planet. [Escape velocity from earth's surface = 11.2 km/s, $k = 1.38 \times 10^{-23}$ J/K, mass of oxygen molecule = 5.3×10^{-26} kg].

Ans. [Oxygen molecules cannot escape]

6-12 A thin rod of mass M and length L is bent in a semicircle as shown in Figure-6.107. (a) What is its gravitational force (both magnitude and direction) on a particle with mass m at O, the centre of curvature. (b) What would be the force on m if the rod is, in the form of a complete circle?

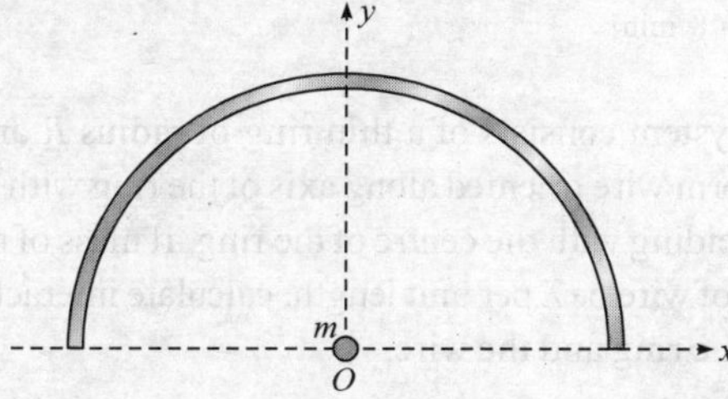

Figure 6.107

Ans. [(a) $\frac{2\pi GmM}{L^2}$, (b) 0]

6-13 Three identical bodies of mass M are located at the vertices of an equilateral triangle with side L. At what speed must they move if they all revolve under the influence of one another's gravitation in a circular orbit circumscribing the triangle while still preserving the equilateral triangle.

Ans. [$v = \sqrt{\frac{GM}{L}}$]

6-14 A smooth tunnel is dug along the radius of earth that ends at centre. A ball is released from the surface of earth along tunnel. Coefficient of restitution for collision between soil at centre and ball is 0.5. Calculate the distance travelled by ball just before second collision at centre. Given mass of the earth is M and radius of the earth is R.

Ans. [$d = 2R$]

6-15 A particle of mass m is subjected to an attractive central force of magnitude k/r^2, k being a constant. If at the instant when the particle is at an extreme position in its closed path, at a distance a from the centre of the force, its speed is $\sqrt{k/(2ma)}$, find the other extreme position.

Ans. [$\frac{a}{3}$]

6-16 If the radius of the earth shrinks by one percent, its mass remaining the same, by what per cent will the acceleration due to gravity on its surface change?

Ans. [Will increase by 2%]

6-17 In a certain region of space gravitational field is given by $I = -(K/r)$. Taking the reference point to be at $r = r_0$ with $V = V_0$, find the potential at position r.

Ans. [$K \ln \frac{r}{r_0} + V_0$]

6-18 A short, straight and frictionless tunnel is bored through the centre of the earth and a body is released from the surface into the tunnel. Show that the motion of the body in the tunnel will be simple harmonic and hence calculate the time taken by the body to travel from one end of the tunnel to the other. (Radius of the earth = 6.38×10^6 m and acceleration due to gravity at the surface = 9.81 ms^{-2}).

Ans. [42 min 14 s]

6-19 An iron ball of radius 1 m and density 8000 kg/m^3 is placed in water. A bubble of radius 1 cm is at a distance 1.5 m from the centre of the ball. Will there be a force of attraction or repulsion between them and what will be the magnitude of this force?

Ans. [3.7×10^{-9} N]

6-20 Two satellites A and B of equal mass move in the equatorial plane of the earth, close to the earth's surface. Satellite A moves in the same direction as that of the rotation of the earth while satellite B moves in the opposite direction. Calculate the ratio of the kinetic energy of B to that of A in the reference frame fixed to the earth. (g = 9.8 m/s^2 and radius of the earth = 6.37×10^6 m)

Ans. [1.27]

6-21 Three masses, 100 kg, 200 kg and 500 kg are placed at the vertices of an equilateral triangle with sides 10 m. They are rearranged by an agent on the vertices of a bigger triangle of sides 15 m and with the same in-centre. Calculate the work done by the agent.

Ans. [3.77×10^{-7} J]

6-22 A simple pendulum is a device in which a mass m (bob) is suspended from a support by means of a string (figure-6.108). If the string is pulled aside by a small angle from the vertical and released, the bob executes simple harmonic motion. For two pendula whose bob have the same gravitational mass, at one of which has an inertial mass 1% larger than the other, show that the one with the larger inertial mass has a time period approximately 0.5% greater than the other one.

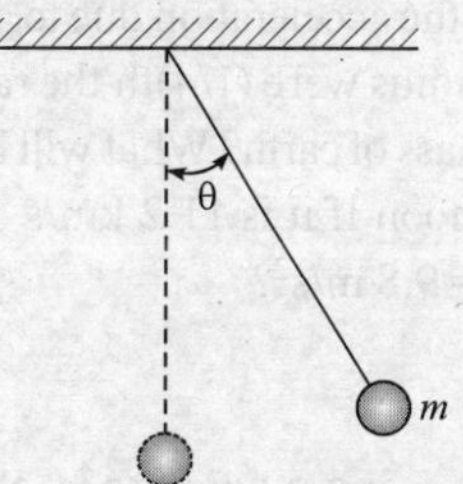

Figure 6.108

6-23 A satellite of Sun is in a circular orbit around the Sun, midway between the Sun and earth. Find the period of this satellite.

Ans. [129 days]

6-24 A spacecraft is in a circular orbit of radius $3R$ around the moon as shown in figure-6.109. At point A, the spacecraft fires a probe which is supposed to arrive at the surface of the moon at point B. Determine the necessary velocity v_r of the probe relative to the spacecraft just after ejection. Also calculate the angular displacement θ of the spacecraft when the probe arrives at point B. Assume velocity of spacecraft remains unchanged due to ejection of probe.

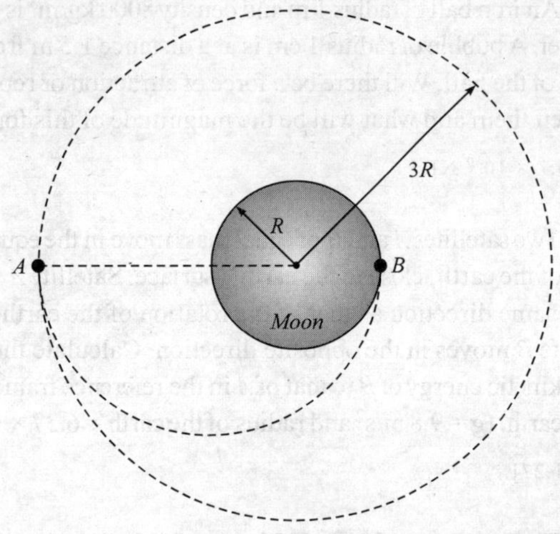

Figure 6.109

Ans. [v_r = 284 m/s; θ = 98°]

6-25 An object weighs 10 N at the north-pole of the earth. In a geostationary satellite distant $7R$ from the centre of earth (of radius R) what will be its (a) true weight, (b) apparent weight?

Ans. [(a) 0.2 N, (b) 0]

6-26 What is the energy required on earth surface to launch a m kg satellite from earth's surface to a circular orbit at an altitude $2R$.

Ans. [$\frac{5}{6}$ mgR]

6-27 What will be the acceleration due to gravity on the surface of the moon if its radius were (1/4)th the radius of earth and its mass (1/80)th the mass of earth? What will be the escape velocity on the surface of moon if it is 11.2 km/s on the surface of the earth given that $g = 9.8$ m/s^2?

Ans. [2.5 km/s]

6-28 In a gravitational field $\vec{g} = (2\hat{i} + 3\hat{j})$ N/kg. What is the work done in moving a particle from (1, 1) to (2, 1/3) along the line $2x + 3y = 5$.

Ans. [Zero]

6-29 A satellite is revolving in a circular equatorial orbit of radius $R = 2 \times 10^4$ km from east to west. Calculate the interval after which it will appear at the same equatorial town. Given that the radius of the earth = 6400 km and g (acceleration due to gravity) = 10 m/s^2.

Ans. [5 hr 48 min]

6-30 A system consists of a thin ring of radius R and a very long uniform wire oriented along axis of the ring with one of its ends coinciding with the centre of the ring. If mass of ring be M and mass of wire be λ per unit length, calculate interaction force between the ring and the wire.

Ans. [$\left[\frac{GM\lambda}{R}\right]$]

6-31 A pendulum beats seconds on the surface of the Earth. Calculate as to how much it loses or gains per day if it is taken to;

(a) a mine 8 km below,

(b) a point 8 km above, the surface. (Radius of the Earth $= 6.4 \times 10^6$ m)

Ans. [(a) 54 sec; (b) 107.9 sec]

6-32 Find the ratio of kinetic energy required to be given to a satellite to escape from earth to the kinetic energy required to be given to the satellite to revolve sound the earth in an orbit just above the earth surface.

Ans. [2 : 1]

6-33 If the time period of a satellite T_S is different from that of earth's rotation T_E and the satellite is moving in the direction of earth's rotation, show that the time interval between two successive appearances of the satellite overhead is given by

$$\frac{1}{T} = \frac{1}{T_S} \sim \frac{1}{T_E}$$

What will happen to this time interval if $T_S = T_E$

Ans. [$T = \infty$, *i.e.*, the satellite will appear stationary overhead]

6-34 Two identical solid spheres each of radius R are placed in contact with each other. It is observed that the gravitational attraction between the two is proportional to R^n. Find the value of n.

Ans. [n = 4]

6-35 The masses and radii of the earth and moon are M_1, R_1 and M_2, R_2 respectively. Their centres are at distance d apart. What is the minimum speed with which a particle of mass m should be projected from a point midway between the two centres so as to escape to infinity.

Ans. [$2\sqrt{\frac{G(M_1 + M_2)}{d}}$]

6-36 A 50 kg astronaut is floating at rest in space 35 m from her stationary 150,000 kg spaceship. About how long will it take her to float to the ship under the action of the force of gravity?

Ans. [About 10^5 s]

6-37 The eccentricity of earth's orbit is 0.017. What is the ratio of the maximum speed in its orbit to its minimum speed.

Ans. [1.034]

6-38 A satellite P is revolving around the Earth at a height h = radius of Earth (R) above equator. Another satellite Q is at a height $2h$ revolving in opposite direction. At an instant the two are at same vertical line passing through centre of sphere. Find the least time of after which again they are in this situation.

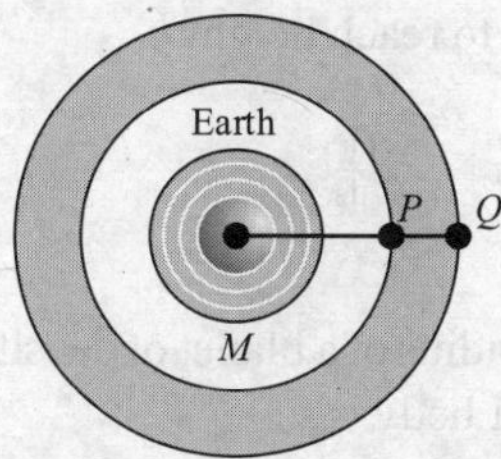

Figure 6.110

Ans. [$\dfrac{2\pi R^{3/2} 6\sqrt{6}}{\sqrt{GM}(2\sqrt{2}+3\sqrt{3})}$]

6-39 A man of mass m starts falling towards a planet of mass M and radius R. As he reaches near to the surface, he realizes that he will pass through a small hole in the planet. As he enters the hole, he sees that the planet is made of two pieces a spherical shell of negligible thickness of mass = $M/3$ and a point mass $M/3$ at centre. Find the change in force of gravity experienced by man.

Ans. [$\dfrac{2}{3}\dfrac{GMm}{R^2}$]

6-40 A pair of stars rotates about a common centre of mass. One of the stars has a mass M and the other m. Their centres are a distance d apart, d being large compared to the size of either star. Derive an expression for the period of revolution of the stars about their common centre of mass. Compare their angular momenta and kinetic energies.

Ans. [$\dfrac{m}{M}$]

6-41 A solid sphere of uniform density and radius R applies a gravitational force of attraction equal to F_1 on a particle placed at P, distance $2R$ from the centre of the sphere. A spherical cavity of radius $R/2$ is now made in the sphere as shown in figure. The sphere with cavity now applies a gravitational force F_2 on the same particle placed at P. Find the ratio of F_2/F_1.

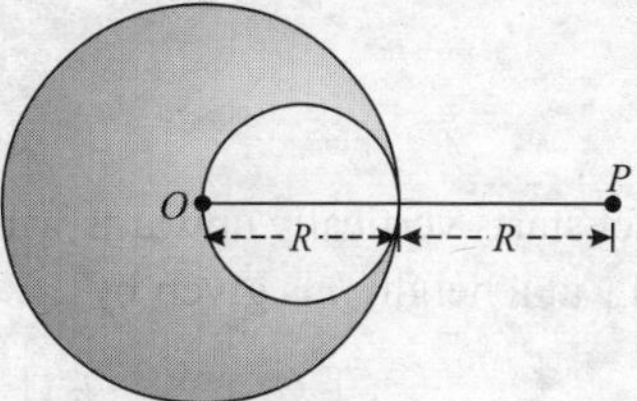

Figure 6.111

Ans. [7/9]

6-42 The optimal way of transferring a space vehicle from an inner circular orbit to an outer coplanar circular orbit is to fire its engines as it passes through A to increase its speed and place it in an elliptic transfer orbit. Another increase in speed as it passes through B will place it in the desired circular orbit. For a vehicle in a circular orbit about the earth at an altitude h_1 = 320 km, which is to be transferred to a circular orbit at an altitude h_2 = 800 km, determine:

(a) The required increases in speed at A and B.

(b) The total energy per unit mass required to execute the transfer. Radius of earth is 6370 km.

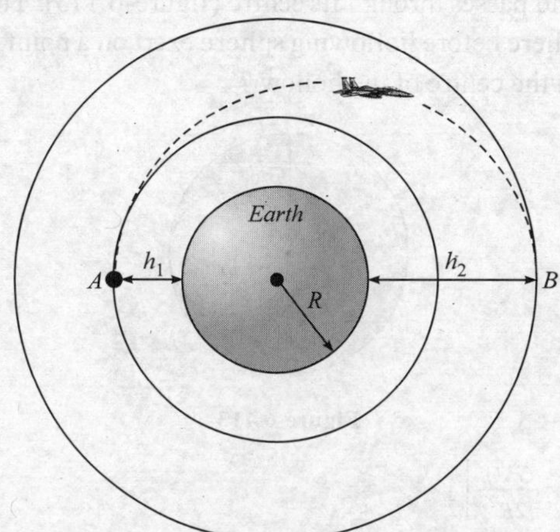

Figure 6.112

Ans. [(a) Δv_A = 147 m/s; Δv_B = 117 m/s (b) 201 MJ/kg]

6-43 A lunar probe is rocketed from earth directly toward the moon in such a way that it is always between the earth and the moon. The probe narrowly misses the moon and continues to travel beyond it on an extension of the line segment described above. At what distance from the center of the earth will the force due to the earth be equal to the force due to the moon?

Ans. [432 Mm]

6-44 A particle is projected from earth surface with a velocity

$\sqrt{\frac{4gR}{3}}$ in upward direction where R is the radius of earth. Find the velocity of particle when it is at half its maximum height.

Ans. [$\sqrt{\frac{gR}{3}}$]

6-45 A rocket starts vertically upwards with speed v_0. Show that its speed v at a height h is given by

$$v_0^2 - v^2 = \left[(2\,g\,h)\left(1+\frac{h}{r}\right)\right]$$

Where R is the radius of the earth. Hence deduce the maximum height reached by a rocket fired with speed equal to 90% of escape velocity.

6-46 A satellite is in a circular orbit very close to the surface of a planet. At some point it is given an impulse along its direction of motion, causing its velocity to increase η times. It now goes into an elliptical orbit. What is the maximum value of η can be used for this.

Ans. [$\sqrt{2}$]

6-47 A spherical hollow is made in lead sphere of radius R, such that its surface touches the outside surface of the lead sphere and passes through its centre (figure-6.113). The mass of the sphere before hollowing sphere exert on a point mass m placed at the centre of the hollow ?

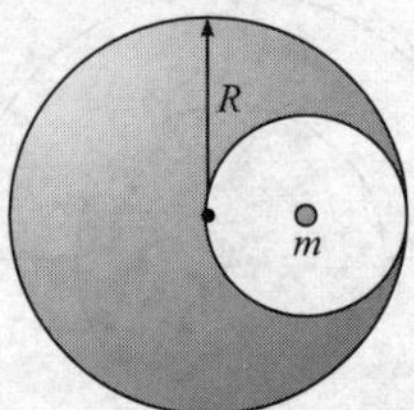

Figure 6.113

Ans. [$\left[F = \frac{GMm}{2R^2}\right]$]

6-48 If a satellite is revolving around a planet of density ρ with period T, show that the quantity ρT^2 is a universal constant.

6-49 Find the angular speed of earth so that a body lying at 30° latitude may become weightless.

Ans. [$\sqrt{\frac{4g}{3R}}$]

6-50 A projectile is fired vertically upward from the surface of earth with a velocity Kv_e where v_e is the escape velocity and $K < 1$. Neglecting air resistance, show that the maximum height to which it will rise measured from the centre of earth is $R/(1-K^2)$ where R is the radius of the earth.

6-51 A satellite is in a circular polar orbit of altitude 300 km. Determine the separation d at the equator between the ground tracks associated with two successive overhead passes of the satellite.

Ans. [d = 2520 km]

6-52 A satellite of mass 5 M orbits the earth in a circular orbit. At one point in its orbit, the satellite explodes into two pieces of masses M and 4 M. After the explosion, the mass M ends up travelling in the same circular orbit, but in opposite direction. Check finally 4 M will move in a bounded or unbounded orbit.

Ans. [Unbounded]

6-53 A body is projected vertically upwards from the surface of earth with a velocity sufficient to carry it to infinity. Calculate the time taken by it to reach height h.

Ans. [$\frac{1}{3}\sqrt{\frac{2R}{g}}\left[\left(1+\frac{h}{R}\right)^{3/2} - 1\right]$]

6-54 What is the radius of a planet of density ρ if at its surface escape velocity of a body is v.

Ans. [$v\sqrt{\frac{3}{8\pi G\rho}}$]

6-55 Consider two satellites A and B of equal mass, moving in the same circular orbit of radius r around the earth but in the opposite sense and therefore, on a collision course figure-6.114.
(a) Find the total mechanical energy $E_A + E_B$ of the two-satellite-plus-earth system before collision.
(b) If the collision is completely inelastic, find the total mechanical energy immediately after collision. Describe the subsequent motion of the combined satellite.

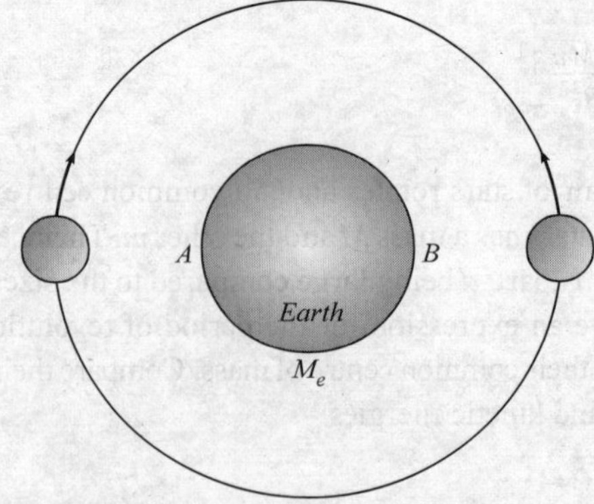

Figure 6.114

Ans. [$\frac{GM_e m}{r}, -\frac{2GM_e m}{r}$; the combined body falls directly down]

6-56 A satellite is circling around earth in an orbit of radius x.

If its radius is reduced by 1%, then by what percent its speed will increase.

Ans. [0.5%]

6-57 A body on the equator of a planet weighs half of its weight at the pole. The density of matter of the planet is 3 g/cm^3. Determine the period of rotation of the planet about its axis.

Ans. [3.16×10^{-4} rad/s]

6-58 Two satellites move in circular orbits around the earth at distances 9000 km and 9010 km from earth's centre. If the satellite which is moving faster has a period of revolution 90 minutes. Find the difference in their revolution periods.

Ans. [9 s]

6-59 A body is projected horizontally near the surface of the earth with $\sqrt{1.5}$ times the orbital velocity. Calculate the maximum height up to which it will rise above the surface of the earth.

Ans. [$2R$]

6-60 A satellite is orbiting around earth with its orbit radius 16 times as great as that of parking satellite. What is the period of this satellite.

Ans. [64 days]

6-61 What should be the radius of a planet with mass equal to that of earth and escape velocity on its surface is equal to the velocity of light. Given that mass of earth is $M = 6 \times 10^{24}$ kg.

Ans. [9 mm]

6-62 Treating the earth as a symmetrical sphere of radius R = 6400 km with field 9.8 N/kg at its surface, calculate the vertical speed with which a rocket should be fired so as to reach a height $4R$ from the surface.

Ans. [10 km/s]

6-63 A diametrical tunnel is dug across the earth and a ball is dropped into the tunnel from one side. Find the velocity of ball when it reaches the centre of earth.

Ans. [$\sqrt{gR}$]

6-64 Two satellites S_1 and S_2 revolve around a planet in coplanar circular orbits in the opposite sense. The periods of revolutions are T and ηT respectively. Find the angular speed of S_2 as observed by an astronaut in S_1, when they are closest to each other.

Ans. [$\left[\omega = \dfrac{2\pi(\eta^{2/3}+1)}{T(\eta^{2/3}-1)}\right]$]

6-65 A small body starts falling onto the sun from a distance equal to the radius of the Earth's orbit. The initial velocity of the body is equal to zero in the heliocentric reference frame. Making use of Kepler's laws, find how long the body will be falling.

Ans. [65 days]

6-66 The gravitational potential difference between the surface of planet and a point 20 m above the surface is 2 J/kg. If the gravitational field is uniform then find the work done in carrying a 5 kg body to a height of 4 m above the surface.

Ans. [2 J]

6-67 What would be the length of a day if angular speed of earth is increased such that bodies lying on he equator fly off?

Ans. [1.3 hr.]

6-68 A communication satellite is put in parking orbit. What is the time taken by a wave to go to satellite and come back to earth in its checking mode.

Ans. [0.25 s]

6-69 A cord of length 64 m is used to connect a 100 kg astronaut to a space-ship whose mass is much larger than that of the astronaut. Estimate the value of the tension in the cord. Assume that the space-ship is orbiting near earth surface. Also assume that the space-ship and the astronaut fall on a straight line from the earth's centre. The radius of the earth is 6400 km.

Ans. [3×10^{-2} N]

6-70 The escape velocity for a planet is 20 km/s. Find the potential energy of a particle of mass 1 mg on the surface of this planet.

Ans. [200 J]

6-71 A particle of mass 1 kg is placed at a distance of 4 m from the centre and on the axis of a uniform ring of mass 5 kg and radius 3 m. Find the work required to increase the distance of the particle from 4 m to $3\sqrt{3}$ m is.

Ans. [$\frac{G}{6}$ J]

6-72 A body of mass m rises to a height $h = R/5$ from the earth's surface where R is earth's radius. Find increase in potential energy.

Ans. [$\frac{5}{6}\,mgh$]

6-73 A missile which missed its target went into an orbit around the earth at a mean radius 4 times great as the parking orbit. Find the period of missile.

Ans. [8 days]

6-74 Compute the magnitude of the necessary launch velocity at B and angle α. If the projectile trajectory is to intersect the earth's surface so that the angle β equals 90°. The altitude at the highest point of the trajectory is 0.5 R.

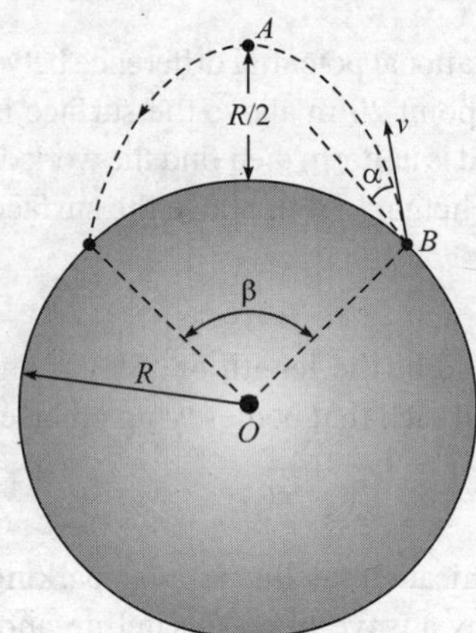

Figure 6.115

Ans. [v_B = 7560 m/s]

6-75 Suppose Moon's orbital motion around the earth is suddenly stopped. Making use of Kepler's third law find the time the moon shell take to fall on to the earth ?

Ans. [Approx 5 days]

6-76 Distance between the centres of two starts is 10 a. The masses of these starts are M and 16 M and their radii a and $2a$ respectively. A body of mass m is fired straight from the surface of the larger start towards the smaller star. What should be its minimum initial speed to reach the surface of the smaller star ? Obtain the expression in terms of G, M and a.

Ans. [$\frac{3}{2}\sqrt{\left(\frac{5GM}{a}\right)}$]

6-77 If a body is to be projected vertically upward from earth's surface to reach a height of 10 R, where R is the radius of earth. Find velocity required for this.

Ans. [$\sqrt{\frac{20}{11}gR}$]

6-78 A satellite of mass m is revolving round the earth at a height R above the surface of earth. If R is the radius of earth, what is the kinetic energy of satellite.

Ans. [$\frac{1}{4}mgR$]

6-79 A spaceship nears the Moon along a parabolic trajectory that almost touches the Moon's surface. In order to transfer into a circular orbit a retro engine fires at the instant of the closest approach. The engine ejects gas at a speed of u = 4 km/s relative to the spaceship in its direction of motion. If v_1 = velocity of spaceship in parabolic trajectory, when it almost touches the earth and v_2 = velocity of spaceship in circular orbit when it almost touches the earth. Then what fraction of total mass should the fuel burn to transfer space ship to circular orbit?

Ans. [$M = M_0 e^{\frac{v_1 - v_2}{u}}$; T = 3600 K]

6-80 If the earth be at one half its present distance from the sun, how many days will there be in a year?

Ans. [129 days]

6-81 At what height above the surface of earth the value of g is the same as that in a mine 10 km deep ?

Ans. [5 km]

6-82 A massive body moving radially from a planet of mass M, when at distance r from planet, explodes in such a way that two of its many fragments move in mutually perpendicular circular orbits around planet. Find the maximum distance between fragments before collision and their relative speed at the moment they collide.

Ans. [$d_{max} = \sqrt{2}r$; $v = \sqrt{\frac{GM}{r}}$]

6-83 Masses, assumed to be equal to m each, hang from strings of different lengths from the ends of a balance on the surface of the earth. If the strings have negligible mass and differ in length by h, show that the error in weighing, $W' - W$, is given by $W' - W = \frac{8\pi}{3} Gm\rho h$, where ρ is the density of the earth.

6-84 At what height above the earth's surface acceleration due to gravity becomes half its value on earth's surface.

Ans. [$(\sqrt{2} - 1)R$]

6-85 A ring of radius R = 4 m is made of a highly dense material. Mass of the ring is $m_1 = 5.4 \times 10^9$ kg distributed uniformly over its circumference. A highly dense particle of mass $m_2 = 6 \times 10^8$ kg is placed on the axis of the ring at a distance x_0 = 3 m from the centre. Neglecting all other forces, except mutual gravitational interaction of the two, calculate

(a) Displacement of the ring when particle is closest to it.

(b) Speed of the particle at that instant.

Ans. [(a) 0.3 m (b) 18 m/s]

6-86 Four particles each of mass M, move along a circle of radius R under the action of their mutual gravitational attractional. Find the speed of each particle.

Ans. [$\sqrt{\frac{GM}{R}\left(\frac{2\sqrt{2}+1}{4}\right)}$]

6-87 The density of the core of a planet is ρ_1 and that of the outer shell is ρ_2. The radii of the core and that of the planet are

R and $2R$ respectively. Gravitational acceleration at the surface of the planet is same as at a depth R. Find the ρ_1/ρ_2.

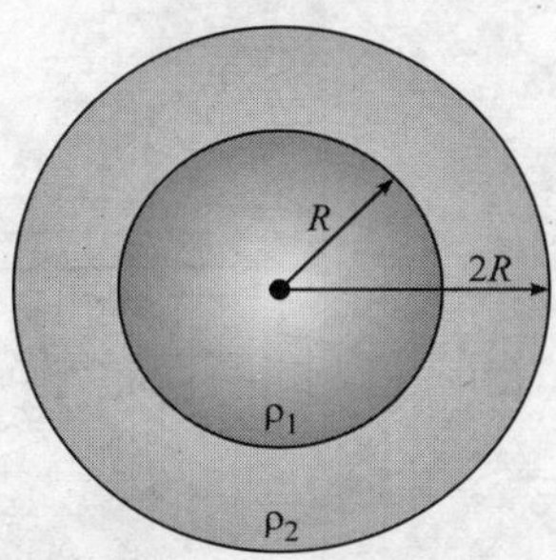

Figure 6.116

Ans. [$\left[\frac{\rho_1}{\rho_2}=\frac{7}{3}\right]$]

6-88 A planet moves along an elliptical orbit around the sun. At the moment when its distance from the sun is r_0, its velocity is v_0 at angle α to r_0. Find the maximum and minimum distance of this planet from the sun. Mass of the sun = M.

Ans. [$\frac{r_0}{2(n-1)}\left[1+\sqrt{1-4n(n-1)\sin^2\alpha}\right], \frac{r_0}{2(n-1)}\left[1-\sqrt{1-4n(n-1)\sin^2\alpha}\right]$]

6-89 If gravitational forces between a planet and a satellite is proportional to $R^{-5/2}$ if R is the orbit radius. Then the period of revolution of satellite is proportional to R^n. Find n.

Ans. [7/2]

6-90 A uniform sphere of radius a and density ρ is divided in two parts by a plane at a distance b from its centre. Calculate the mutual attraction between two parts.

Ans. [$\frac{1}{3}\pi^2\rho^2G(a^2-b^2)^2$]

6-91 A uniform sphere has a mass M and radius R. Find the pressure p inside the sphere, caused by gravitational compression, as a function of the distance r from its centre. Evaluate pressure at the centre of the Earth, assuming it to be a uniform sphere.

Ans. [$p = 3/8\ (1 - r^2/R^2)GM^2/\pi R^4$]

6-92 A meteorite approaching a planet of mass M (in the straight line passing through the centre of the planet) collides with an automatic space station orbiting the planet in the circular trajectory of radius R. The mass of the station is ten times as large as the mass the meteorites. As a result of collision, the meteorite sticks in the station which goes over to a new orbit with the minimum distance $R/2$ from the planet. Determine the velocity u of the meteorite before the collision.

Ans. [$\sqrt{58Gm/R}$]

6-93 Two satellites of the earth move in the same plane with radii a and b, b being slightly greater than a. What is the minimum interval between the instants when they are on the same line through the centre of the earth (i) when they move in the same direction, (ii) in opposite direction?

Ans. [$\frac{4\pi}{3\sqrt{GM}}\cdot\frac{a^{5/2}}{b-a}$; $\frac{4\pi}{3\sqrt{GM}}\cdot\frac{a^{5/2}}{b+a/3}$]

6-94 Two lead spheres of 20 cm and 2 cm diameter are placed with their centres 1.0 m apart. Calculate the force of attraction between the two spheres. The radius of the earth is 6.37×10^6 m, its density is 5.51×10^3 kg/m^2 and relative density of lead is 11.5.

Ans. [1.5×10^{-10} N]

6-95 A space vehicle is in circular orbit about the earth. The mass of the vehicle is 300 kg, and the radius of the orbit is $2R_e$. It is desired to transfer the vehicle to a circular orbit of radius $4R_e$

(a) What is the minimum energy required for the transfer ?

(b) If the transfer accomplished through an elliptical orbit, what initial and final velocity changes are required.

Take g = 10 m/s^2 at the earth's surfaces and R_e = 6400 km (radius of the earth).

Ans. [(a) 2.4×10^9 J, (b) 876 m/s, 734 m/s]

* * * * *

7

Fluid Mechanics

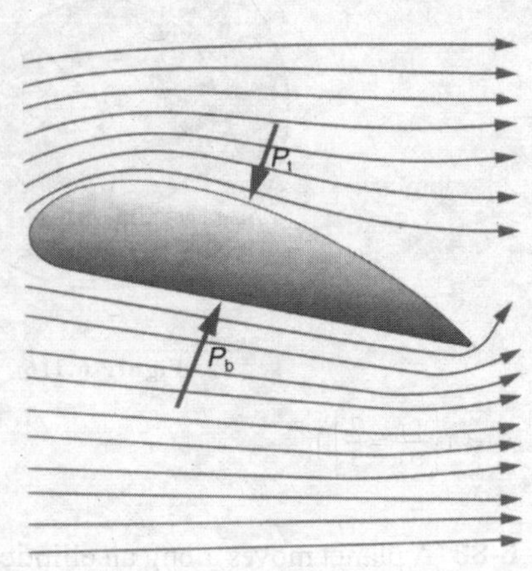

FEW WORDS FOR STUDENTS

After the detailed study of Newtonian mechanics, with applications to motions of different particles and rigid bodies, our next step is to discuss the behaviour of fluids, which are large collection of particles in a volume. In this chapter we will study the behaviour of fluids and develop relations of laws of mechanics, especially the law of conservation of energy with fluid bodies. These laws are strictly valid only for certain types of fluids and their flow in some ideal conditions.

CHAPTER CONTENTS

COVER APPLICATION

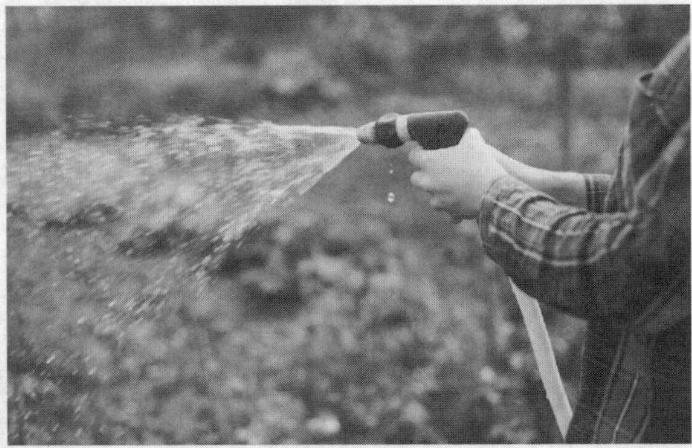

Figure-(a)

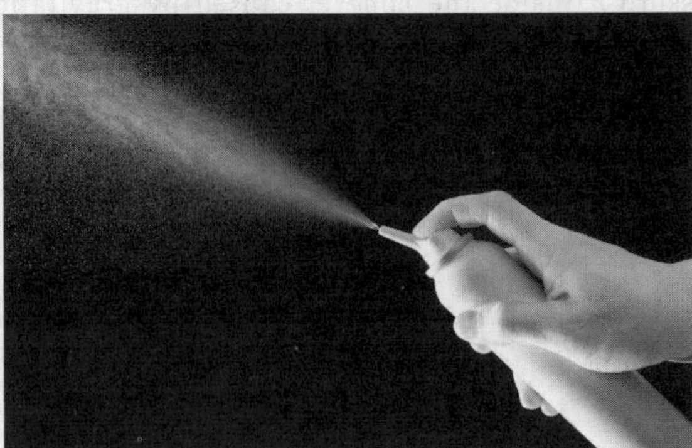

Figure-(b)

Figure-(a) shows the water jet through which a gardener is watering plants. The water jet splits into small droplets due to sudden decrease in pressure. The pressure is developed due to the pressure pump at the water source. Figure-(b) shows a deodorant in which perfume liquid is sealed at high pressure. When its nozzle is pressed the liquid is exposed to atmospheric pressure which is very very low compared to inside pressure which causes the liquid to eject in form of very small droplets.

All physical bodies are made of molecules which are in permanent motion. In solids the molecules oscillate about certain equilibrium position and the displacement of the molecules are so small that they do not affect the character of motion of solid bodies or its parts, as we've already covered in mechanics. The equilibrium positions of the molecules of a solid, that is their average position, are quite definite and fixed.

Every solid has a definite shape. To change this shape, that is to produce a deformation of the body, some forces must be applied to the body or to some of its parts. Solid bodies in contrast to fluid and gases, retain a definite geometrical form. Fluid and gases are physical bodies that have no definite shape and assume the shape of the vessel they fill.

The matter is that every body may behave as a solid, fluid or gas depending on the physical conditions and on the phenomenon in which it takes part. For example a rotating metal disc behaves as a rigid body while the same disc, when subject to heating, behaves as fluid. We first discuss a definite approach in which we distinguish between a solid, fluid or a gas.

In a gas the molecules are in a chaotic motion and collide with each other like small balls. The molecules are not connected with one another when they move. Because of permanent collisions they tend to move in all possible directions so that the gas fills uniformly the volume of vessel in which it is filled. That is why we define an amount of a gas is a physical body which does not possess its own definite shape and volume. Its volume is determined by the volume of the vessel which it fills. Thus the gas can be thought of as a continuous body which tend to expend and to fill the entire volume in which it is placed.

In a fluid or gas the molecules are not invariably connected with each other and the molecules can move quite arbitrarily relative to each other in their chaotic motion. In a fluid unlike to a gas, the average distance between the molecules remains almost constant. This means that an amount of a fluid is a physical body like a gas, which has no definite shape but unlike a gas posses an almost invariable volume. The volume of a fluid changes only when large external forces act on it. A given amount of a fluid is always separated by an interface from other solids or gases. In case of a gas medium adjoining a fluid we speak of a free surface of the fluid.

An amount of a gas is usually bounded either by a fluid surface or by a surface of some solids.

In mechanics we consider solids, fluids and gases as continuous bodies. A solid possesses a definite shape and a definite volume undergoing invariable conditions. An amount of fluid only possesses a definite volume and has no definite shape and an amount of gas has neither a definite shape nor volume.

7.1 The Concept of Pressure

A fluid or a gas placed in a closed volume can be subject to an external action. For example consider the situation shown in figure-7.1 A Fluid is filled in a container and its top is closed by a smooth light piston. A constant force F is applied to the piston and after that as piston and fluid are in equilibrium then obviously we can state that fluid also exert the same force F in upward direction on piston. Now consider a small cubical volume of fluid within its volume as shown in figure-7.1(a). As this is also in equilibrium net forces on it must also be zero. There must be some internal forces present on this volume as we know when some external forces are applied on a body, due to its elasticity some internal restoring forces develop with in the body. In solids we account for these forces in the form of stress in the solid body and the tangential components of these forces are accounted in sheer stress which produces sheer strain. But in fluids there is no tangential component. In static fluid internal forces are normal to the bounding surfaces.

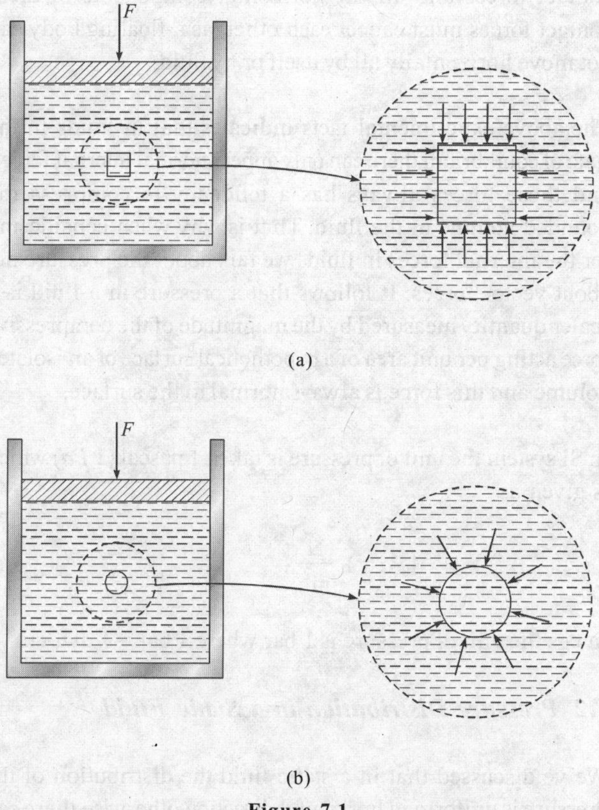

Figure 7.1

In figure-7.1(a) we can see that the forces exerted by the surrounding fluid on the small cubical volume are balanced and normal to its surface (hypothetical).

Similarly as shown in figure-7.1(b) we consider a small spherical volume and here also it is in equilibrium due to the radial (normal to bonding surface) inward forces on it by the surrounding fluid.

On the basis of similar concept we can explain the equilibrium of a floating body. For example consider the situation shown in figure-7.2.

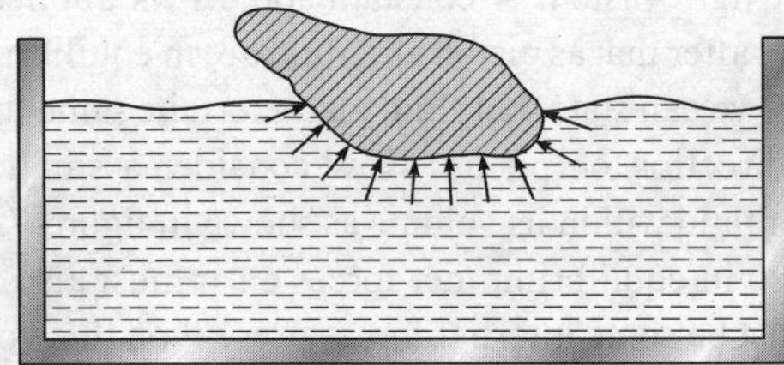

Figure 7.2

Here we can see that on the surface of submerged part of body which is in contact with the liquid molecules, the liquid molecules exerts normal forces at every local point of contact. For equilibrium of body we can state that the weight of body is balanced by the vertical upward components of all the normal contact forces and all the horizontal components of these contact forces must cancel each other, as a floating body can not move horizontally all by itself or by fluid.

The above experimental facts indicates that in fluids in the state of equilibrium there can only appear normal internal forces, and these forces always has a tendency to compress the bounded volume in the fluid. That is why when considering for the internal forces in fluids we talk about the pressure not about vector forces. It follows that a pressure in a fluid is a scaler quantity measured by the magnitude of the compressive force acting per unit area of a hypothetical surface of an isolated volume and this force is always normal to the surface.

In SI system the unit of pressure is taken 1 pascal (1 *Pa*) which is given as

$$1Pa = 1\ \frac{\text{N}}{\text{m}^2}$$

In cgs the unit of pressure is 1 bar where 1 bar = 1 dyn/cm^2

7.2 Pressure Distribution in a Static Fluid

We've discussed that in a static fluid the distribution of the pressure is uniform in horizontal direction otherwise there can be no equilibrium in the fluid. It follows that the free surface of an immovable fluid is always horizontal except near the walls of vessel where due to the surface tension it may be in curve shape, we'll discuss later about surface tension in detail.

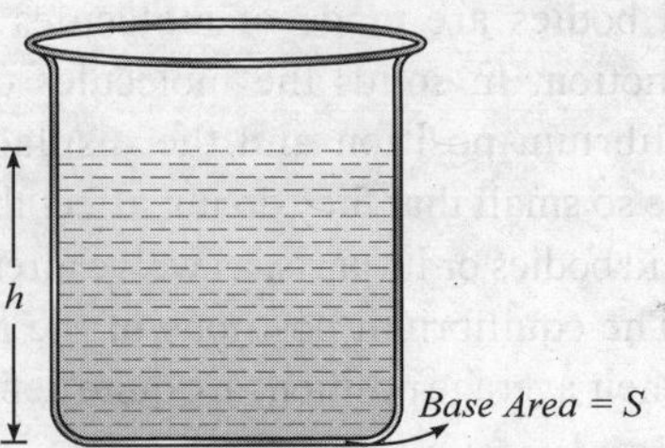

Figure 7.3

In this chapter we'll deal only with fluids that cannot be compressed, that is, with liquids. Consider the container shown in figure-7.3 filled with a liquid of density ρ, upto a height h. The weight of the liquid exerts a force on the bottom of the container. Where the pressure at the bottom can be defined as

$$P = \frac{mg}{S}$$

or $$P = \frac{(\rho hS)g}{S}$$

[Mass of liquid in container $m = \rho hS$]

or $$P = h\rho g \qquad \ldots(7.1)$$

Here from equation-(7.1) we can now see that pressure is directly proportional to both density and the depth of the liquid. Thus separate containers of different size, holding identical liquids of uniform density have equal pressure at equal depth. If two containers are filled to the same height, they have equal pressures at the bottom, even though the total force on the bottom surface due to the liquid is greater at the bottom of the large container. The pressure depends on the depth and not on the cross-section. A narrow long vertical tube of length 2m with water has the same pressure at its bottom as does a large lake that is 2m deep.

We've already discussed that a fluid exerts a force normal to all the bonding surfaces of the fluid thus a force must be exerted on the side walls of the container also and a corresponding pressure is present there. Moreover a pressure exist at any point within the body of the liquid. If the liquid is static, the pressure is independent of direction. As shown in figure, in a container filled with water, we consider three points A, B and C, pressure remains equal to $h\rho g$ at all these points. If we measure this pressure by a pressure measuring device in which the pressure exerted by water on rubber membrane is measured by the pressure gauge as shown in figure-7.4(b). The reading of the pressure meter at all three points is same even though the forces on the three membranes are in different directions. If the readings at the points along a horizontal surface (parallel to free surface) of liquid were not same then the pressure difference would cause fluid to flow which contradicts the practical situation that liquid is at rest. So the pressure in liquid must depend only on the height of the liquid above the point at which we are finding the pressure. Thus we can also state that in a static liquid, difference in pressure ΔP between two points that differ in depth by Δh is given as

$$\Delta P = \Delta h \rho g \quad \ldots (7.2)$$

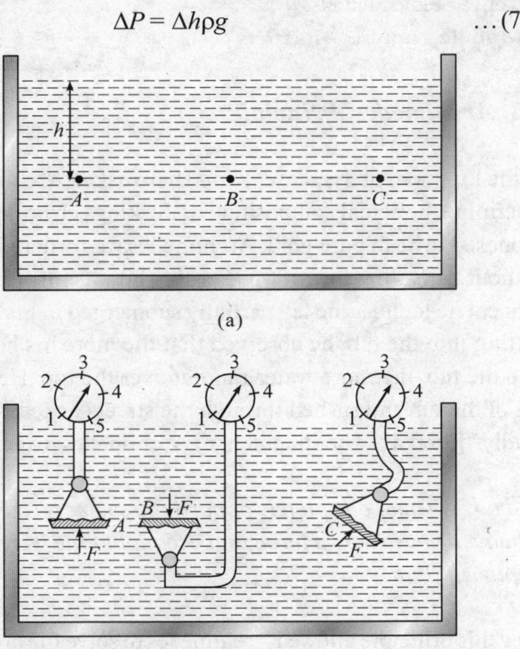

Figure 7.4

We have discussed that the pressure at any point in the body of liquid depends on the height of liquid column above that point. It does not depend on the shape of vessel.

To capture the concept in a better way, we take another example of a vessel filled with a liquid as shown in figure-7.5. The vessel is fitted with a long random stem pipe with a funnel. If we find the force at the bottom of vessel due to the liquid, then it is given as

$$F = \text{pressure at bottom} \times \text{surface area}$$

$$= h\rho g \times S$$

$$= h\rho g S$$

h
a
base area $S = ab$
where b = width of vessel

Figure 7.5

Here you can observe that in pressure we've taken the height h up to the free top surface of the liquid, no matter, whatever be the amount of liquid present and whatever be the shape of container, the force on bottom is same.

Now consider the situation shown in figure-7.6. Liquid is filled in an irregularly shaped container with four different openings.

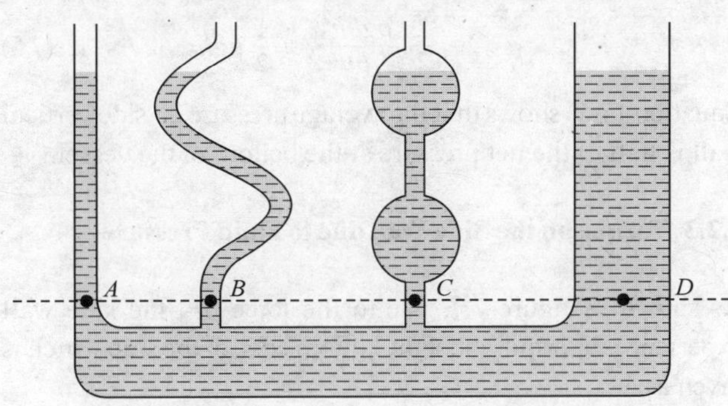

Figure 7.6

As we know in a static fluid the pressure at one horizontally level remains constant thus here also we can conclude that the pressure at the four points A, B, C and D remains constant.

7.2.1 Force on Side Wall of a Vessel

Force on the side wall of the vessel can not be directly determined as at different depths pressures are different. To find this we consider a strip of width dx at a depth x from the surface of the liquid as shown in figure-7.7, and on this strip the force due to the liquid is given as :

$$dF = x\rho g \times b\,dx \quad \ldots (7.3)$$

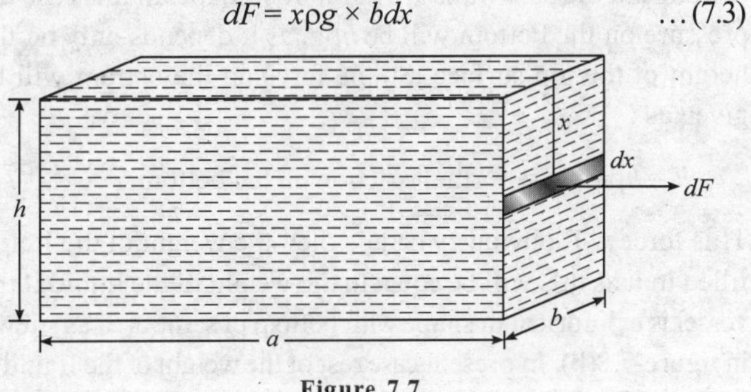

Figure 7.7

This force is acting in the direction normal to the side wall.

Net force can be evaluated by integrating equation-(7.3)

$$F = \int dF = \int_0^h x\rho g\, b\,dx$$

$$F = \frac{\rho g b h^2}{2} \quad \ldots (7.4)$$

7.2.2 Average Pressure on Side Wall

The absolute pressure on the side wall cannot be evaluated because at different depths on this wall pressure is different. The average pressure on the wall can be given as :

$$<p>_{av} = \frac{F}{bh}$$

$$= \frac{1}{2}\,\frac{\rho g b h^2}{bh} = \frac{1}{2}\,\rho g h \qquad \ldots(7.5)$$

Equation-(7.5) shows that the average pressure on side vertical wall is half of the net pressure at the bottom of the vessel.

7.2.3 Torque on the Side Wall due to Fluid Pressure

As shown in figure-7.7, due to the force dF, the side wall experiences a torque about the bottom edge of the side which is given as :

$$d\tau = dF \times (h - x)$$

$$= x\rho g b\, dx\, (h - x)$$

Thus net torque is $\tau = \int d\tau = \int_0^h \rho g b\,(hx - x^2)\,dx$

$$= \rho g b \left[\frac{h^3}{2} - \frac{h^3}{3}\right]$$

$$= \frac{1}{6}\,\rho g b h^3 \qquad \ldots(7.6)$$

7.2.4 Force on the Side Walls of a Random Shaped Vessel

If we consider a vessel shown in figure-7.8(a), which has a flat bottom and the side walls are random in shape. In this case the pressure on the bottom will be $h\rho g$, as it depends only on the height of the top surface. So the force on the bottom will be given as :

$$F = h\rho g \times S = \text{normal reaction on the bottom}$$

This force will obviously be less then the weight of the liquid filled in it as this will be equal to the weight of the liquid if the vessel is cylindrical in shape with bottom of same area as shown in figure-7.8(b). In present case rest of the weight of the liquid is balanced by the vertical component of the contact reaction F_c on the side walls as shown in figure-7.8(c).

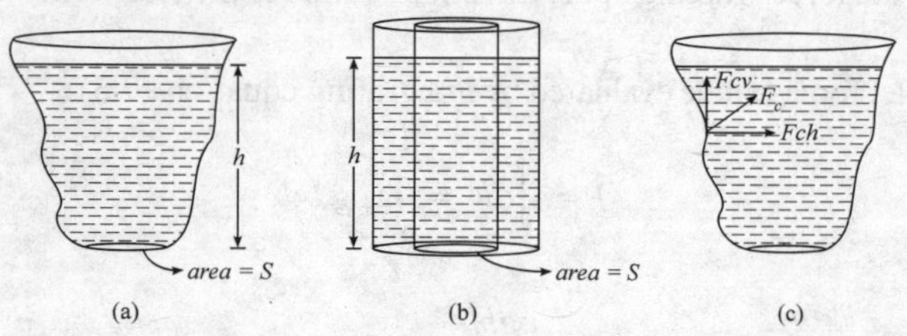

Figure 7.8

Web Reference of Video Lectures at www.physicsgalaxy.com
Age Group - High School Physics | Age 17-19 Years
Section - PROPERTIES OF MATTER
Topic - Fluid Statics
Module Number - 1 to 6

7.3 Archimedes Principle

In the kingdom of Syracuse, King Hiero asked Archimedes to determine the actual composition of the kings crown, which as supposed to be of pure gold. Archimedes was ordered to do so without damaging the crown. For this he was inspired by the concept he found as he lay partially submerged in his baths on getting into the tub, he observed that the more his body sank into the tub, the more water ran out over the top. He jumped out of the tub and rushed through the streets naked, shouting loudly "Eureka". The statement of Archimedes principle says

"A body whether completely or partially submerged in a fluid, is buoyed upward by a force that is equal to the weight of the displaced fluid".

How this principle allowed Archimedes to solve the problem of the king's crown, we'll see in examples later.

The above principle can be easily obtained by a simple mathematical analysis of finding forcc on a submerged body. For this let us consider a cylindrical block submerged in a container filled with a liquid as shown in figure-7.9. The top surface of the cylinder is at a depth l below the free surface of the liquid thus net force F_1 on the top surface of cylinder (in downward direction) can be given as

$$F_1 = \text{pressure of liquid} \times S$$

$$= l\rho g \times S \qquad [\rho = \text{density of liquid}] \qquad \ldots(7.7)$$

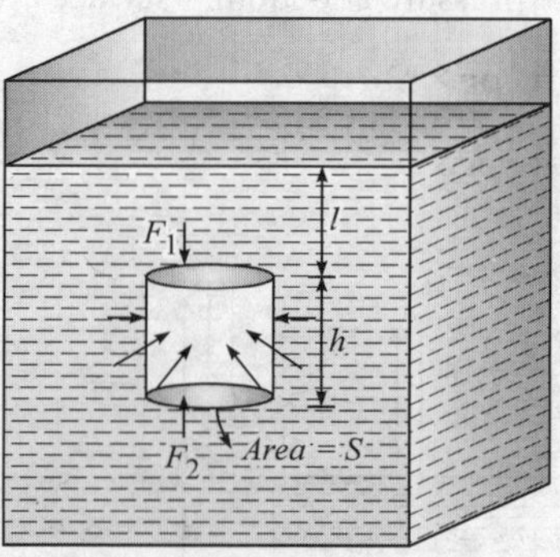

Figure 7.9

Similarly at the bottom surface the force F_2 on cylinder (in upward direction) can be given as

F_2 = pressure of liquid at point near bottom × S

$$= (l+h)\,\rho\, g \times S \qquad \ldots(7.8)$$

Here we can see that all the forces acting on cylindrical surface are horizontal and acting in radially inward direction all of which gets cancelled out. Thus net force on the cylindrical block is in upward direction and is given as

$$F_{up} = F_2 - F_1$$

$$= (l+h)\,\rho g S - l\rho g S$$

$$= h\rho g S \qquad \ldots(7.9)$$

= weight of the liquid displaced.

This upward force on cylinder due to the surrounding liquid is the buoyant force and is equal to the weight of the liquid in the volume displaced by the object. If we replace this cylinder by another cylinder of same size but of different material. The buoyant force remains the same. It depends only on the volume of the submerged object not on its mass or density. In above example if block is made of aluminium and liquid is water we can say that as aluminium is denser then water and the weight of cylinder is more then the buoyant force on it given by equation-(7.9) so it sinks to the bottom but if liquid used is mercury which has a greater density then that of aluminium then in this case the buoyant force on block is more then that of its weight and block will move up and will start floating. Hot air balloons, furnish another example of Archimedes principle. They float in air and because hot air density is less then the normal atmospheric air. A similar example can be seen for large ships, which float on water even through they are made of steel and carry dense objects, because the water is displaced by the submerged part of the ship.

 # Illustrative Example 7.1

A beaker of circular cross-section of radius 4 cm is filled with mercury upto a height of 10 cm. Find the force exerted by the mercury on the bottom of the beaker. The atmospheric pressure = 10^5 N/m^2. Density of mercury = 13600 kg/m^3. Take g = 10 m/s^2.

Solution

The pressure at the surface = atmospheric pressure = 10^5 N/m^2.

The pressure at the bottom

$$= 10^5\ \text{N/m}^2 + h\rho g$$

$$= 10^5\ \text{N/m}^2 + (0.1\ \text{m})\left(13600\frac{kg}{m^3}\right)\left(10\frac{m}{s^2}\right)$$

$$= 10^5\ \text{N/m}^2 + 13600\ \text{N/m}^2$$

$$= 1.136 \times 10^5\ \text{N/m}^2$$

The force exerted by the mercury on the bottom

$$= (1.136 \times 10^5\ \text{N/m}^2) \times (3.14 \times 0.04\ \text{m} \times 0.04\ \text{m})$$

$$= 571\ \text{N}$$

 # Illustrative Example 7.2

A cubical block of iron 5 cm on each side is floating on mercury in a vessel.

(i) What is the height of the block above mercury level ?

(ii) Water is poured in the vessel until it just covers the iron block. What is the height of water column.

Density of mercury = 13.6 gm/cm^3.,

Density of iron 7.2 gm/cm^3

Solution

Case-I : Suppose h be the height of cubical block of iron above mercury.

Volume of iron block = 5 × 5 × 5 = 125 cm^3

Mass of iron block = 125 × 7.2 = 900 gm

Volume of mercury displaced by the block

$$= 5 \times 5 \times (5-h)\ \text{cm}^3$$

Mass of mercury displaced

$$= 5 \times 5\,(5-h) \times 13.6\ \text{gm}$$

By the law floatation, weight of mercury displaced = weight of iron block

$$5 \times 5\,(5-h) \times 13.6 = 900$$

or $$(5-h) = \frac{900}{25 \times 13.6} = 2.65$$

$$h = 5 - 2.65 = 2.35\ \text{cm}$$

Case-II : Suppose in this case the height of iron block in water be x. The height of iron block in mercury will be $(5-x)$ cm.

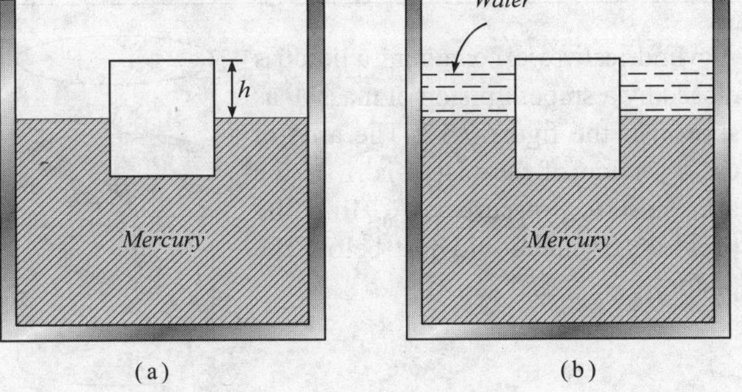

Figure 7.10

Mass of the water displaced

$$= 5 \times 5 \times (x) \times 1$$

Mass of mercury displaced

$$= 5 \times 5 \times (5 - x) \times 13.6$$

So, weight of water displaced + weight of mercury displaced = weight of iron block

or $\quad 5 \times 5 \times x \times 1 + 5 \times 5 \times 5 \times (5 - x) \times 13.6 = 900$

or $\quad x = (5 - x) \times 13.6 = 36$

Solving we get $x = 2.54$ cm

Illustrative Example 7.3

A tank containing water is placed on a spring balance. A stone of weight w is hung and lowered into the water without touching the sides and the bottom of the tank. Explain how the reading will change.

Solution

The situation is shown in figure-7.11. Make free-body diagrams of the bodies separately and consider their equilibrium. Like all other forces, buoyancy is also exerted equally on the two bodies in contact. Hence if the water exerts a buoyant force, say, B on the stone upward, the stone exerts the same force on the water downward. The forces acting on the 'water + container' system are : W, weight of the system downward, B, buoyant force of the stone downward; and the force R of the spring in the upward direction. For equilibrium

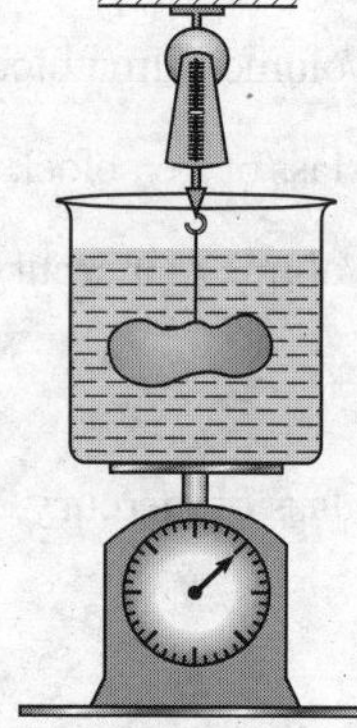

Figure 7.11

$$R = W + B$$

Thus the reading of the spring scale will increase by an amount equal to the weight of the liquid displaced, that is, by an amount equal to the buoyant force.

Illustrative Example 7.4

A cylindrical vessel containing a liquid is closed by a smooth piston of mass m as shown in the figure-7.12. The area of cross-section of the piston is A. If the atmospheric pressure is P_0, find the pressure of the liquid just below the piston.

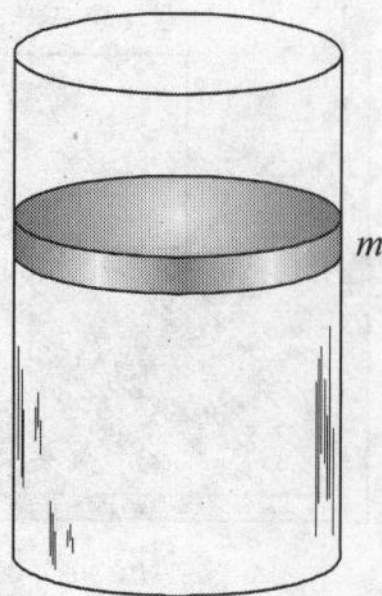

Figure 7.12

Solution

Let the pressure of the liquid just below the piston be P. The forces acting on the piston are

(a) its weight, mg (downward)

(b) force due to the air above it, $P_0 A$ (downward)

(c) force due to the liquid below it, PA (upward).

If the piston is in equilibrium,

$$PA = P_0 A + mg$$

or $$P = P_0 + \frac{mg}{A}$$

Illustrative Example 7.5

A rubber ball of mass m and radius r is submerged in water to a depth h and released. What height will the ball jump up to above the surface of the water ? Neglect the resistance of water and air. Take water density ρ.

Solution

Let the ball go up by x above the level of water. Let us now consider energy conservation between the initial and final positions. In both the positions kinetic energy of the body is zero. The potential energy in the first position with reference to the water level is $-mgh$ plus the work done by an external agent against the buoyant force which is $\left(\frac{4}{3}\pi r^3 \rho g\right)h$, where ρ is the density of the water.

or $$-mgh + \left(\frac{4}{3}\pi r^3 \rho g\right)h = mgx$$

$\Rightarrow$ $$x = \frac{\frac{4}{3}\pi r^3 \rho - m}{m} \times h$$

Illustrative Example 7.6

A cube of wood supporting a 200 g mass just floats in water. When the mass is removed, the cube rises by 2 cm. What is the size of the cube ?

Solution

If, l = side of cube, h = height of cube above water and ρ = density of wood.

Mass of the cube $= l^3 \rho$

Volume of cube in water $= l^2 (l - h)$

Volume of the displaced water $= l^2 (l - h) \times 1$

As the cube is floating

weight of cube + weight of wood = weight of liquid displaced or $$l^3 \rho + 200 = l^2 (l - h) \qquad \ldots(7.10)$$

After the removal of 200 gm mass, the cube rises 2 cm.

Volume of cube in water $= l^2 \times \{l - (h+2)\}$

or $$l^2 \times \{l - (h+2)\} = l^3 \rho \qquad \ldots(7.11)$$

Substituting the value of $l^3 \rho$ from equation-(7.11) in equation-(7.10), we get

$$l^2 \{l - (h+2)\} + 200 = l^2 (l - h)$$

or $$l^3 - l^2 h - 2 l^2 + 200 = l^3 - l^2 h$$

$$2 l^2 = 200$$

$$l = 10 \text{ cm}$$

Illustrative Example 7.7

A boat floating in a water tank is carrying a number of large stones. If the stones were unloaded into water, what will happen to water level ? Give the reason in brief.

Solution

Suppose W and w be the weights of the boat and stones respectively.

First, we consider that the boat is floating. It will displace $(W + w) \times 1$ cm^3 of water.

Thus displaced water $= (W + w)$ cm^3

[As density of water = 1 gm/cm^3]

Secondly, we consider that the stones are unloaded into water.

Now the boat displaces only $W \times 1$ cm^3 of water. If ρ be the density of stones, the volume of water displaced by stones

$= w/\rho$ cm^3

As $\rho > 1$, hence $w/\rho < w$, thus we have

Now $$(W + w/\rho) < (W + w)$$

This shows that the volume of water displaced in the second case is less than the volume of water displaced in the first case. Hence the level of water will come down.

Illustrative Example 7.8

Two solid uniform spheres each of radius 5 cm are connected by a light string and totally immersed in a tank of water. If the specific gravities of the sphere are 0.5 and 2, find the tension in the string and the contact force between the bottom of the tank and the heavier sphere.

Solution

The situation is shown in figure-7.13

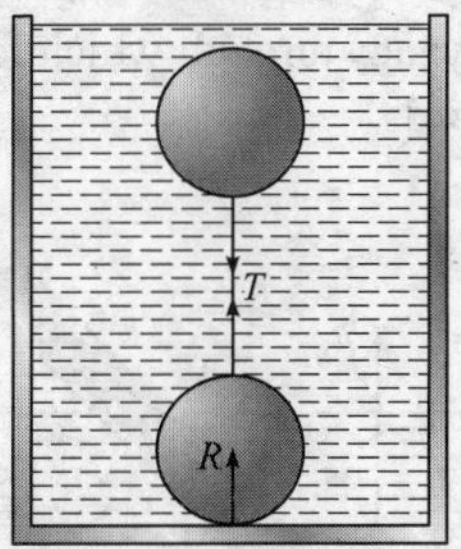

Figure 7.13

Let the volume of each sphere be V m^3 and density of water be ρ kg/m^3.

Upward thrust on heavier sphere $= V \rho g$

Weight of the heavier sphere $= V \times 2 \times \rho g$

For heavier sphere,

$$T + R + V \rho g = V \times 2 \times \rho g \qquad \ldots(7.12)$$

Where R is the reaction at the bottom.

Similarly for lighter sphere

$$T + V \times 0.5 \times \rho g = V \rho g \qquad \ldots(7.13)$$

Subtracting equation-(7.13) from equation-(7.12), we have

$$R + 0.5 \, V \rho g = V \rho g \qquad \ldots(7.14)$$

or $$R = 0.5 \, V \rho g \qquad \ldots(7.15)$$

From equation-(7.13)

$$T = 0.5 \, V \rho g$$

$$= 0.5 \times \left(\frac{4}{3} \times 3.14 \times 5^3 \times 10^6\right) \times 1000 \times 9.8$$

$$= 2.565 \text{ N}$$

Similarly $$R = 2.565 \text{ N}$$

Illustrative Example 7.9

A rod of length 6 m has a mass of 12 kg. If it is hinged at one end at a distance of 3 m below a water surface,

(i) What weight must be attached to other end of the rod so that 5 m of the rod is submerged ?

(ii) Find the magnitude and direction of the force exerted by the hinge on the rod. The specific gravity of the material of the rod is 0.5.

Solution

Let AC be the submerged part of the rod AB hinged at A as shown in figure-7.14. G is the centre of gravity of the rod and G' is the centre of buoyancy through which force of buoyancy F_B acts vertically upwards.

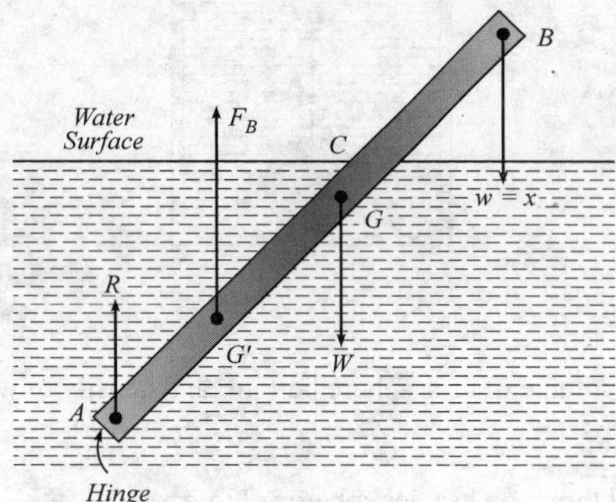

Figure 7.14

Since the rod is uniform,

The weight of part AC will be

$$\frac{5}{6} \times 12 = 10\,\text{kg}$$

[Because $AB = 6$ m and $AC = 5$ m]

The buoyancy force on rod at G' is

$$F_B = \frac{10}{0.5} = 20\,\text{kg weight}$$

(i) Let x be the weight attached at the end B. Balancing torques about A, we get

$$W \times AG + x \times AB = F_B \times AG'$$

$$12 \times 3 + x \times 6 = 20 \times (5/2) \qquad [\text{As} \quad AG' = 5/2\,\text{m}]$$

Solving we get $\qquad x = 2.33$ kg

(ii) Suppose R be the upward reaction acting on the hinge, then in equilibrium position, we have

$$W + x = F_B + R$$

or
$$R = W + x - F_B$$

$$= 12 + 2.33 - 20$$

$$= -5.67\text{ kg. wt.}$$

Negative sign shows that the reaction at the hinge is acting in the downward direction. The magnitude of the reaction is 5.67 kg wt.

 # Illustrative Example 7.10

A cylinder of area 300 cm^2 and length 10 cm made of material of specific gravity 0.8 is floated in water with its axis vertical. It is then pushed downward, so as to be just immersed. Calculate the work done by the agent who pushes the cylinder into the water.

Solution

Weight of the cylinder

$$= (300 \times 10^{-4}) \times (10 \times 10^{-2}) \times 800\,\text{kgf} = 2.4\,\text{kgf}$$

Let x be the length of the cylinder inside the water. Then by the law of flotation

$$2.4\,g = (300 \times 10^{-4} \times x) \times 1000\,g$$

or $\qquad x = 0.08$ m

When completely immersed,

$$F_b\,(\text{buoyant force}) = (300 \times 10^{-4} \times 0.1) \times 1000 \times g = 3\,g\,\text{N}$$

Thus to immerse the cylinder inside the water the external agent has to push it by 0.02 m against average upward thrust.

Increase in upward thrust $= 3\,g - 2.4\,g = 0.6\,g$ N

Since this increase in upthrust takes place gradually from 0 to $0.6\,g$, we may take the average upthrust against which work is done as $0.3\,g$ N.

or $\qquad$ work done $= 0.3\,g \times 0.02 = 0.0588$ J

 # Illustrative Example 7.11

A thin uniform rod of length $2l$ and specific gravity 3/4 is hinged at one end to a point height $l/2$ above the surface of water, with the other end immersed. Find the inclination of rod in equilibrium.

Solution

The situation is shown in figure-7.15.

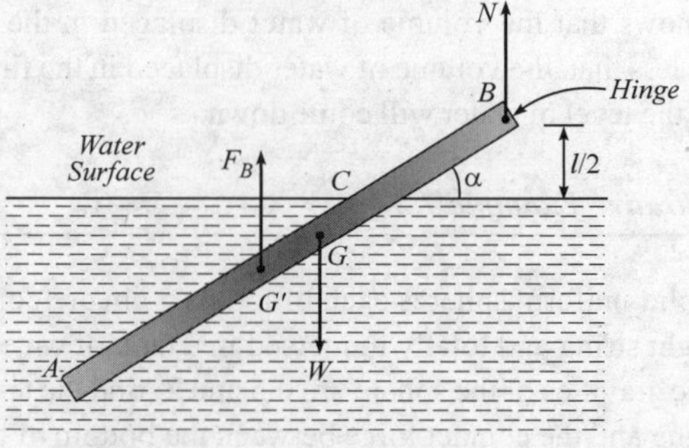

Figure 7.15

Let the length of rod outside water is x and its cross-sectional area is A. Here weight of rod is

$$W = 2lA \times \frac{3}{4}dg \quad \dots(7.16)$$

[d = density of water]

Buoyancy force on rod at the centre of gravity of submerged part is

$$F_B = (2l - x)A \times dg \quad \dots(7.17)$$

Let N be the upward force on rod by the hinge then for equilibrium of rod we have

$$N + F_B = W$$

or $$N = W - F_B$$

or $$= \frac{3}{2}lAdg - (2l - x)Adg$$

$$= Adg\left[\frac{3}{2}l - 2l + x\right]$$

$$= Adg\left(x - \frac{l}{2}\right) \quad \dots(7.18)$$

Now as rod is also in rotational equilibrium, taking net zero torque about point A, we have.

$$F_B \times \frac{2l - x}{2}\cos\alpha - W \times l\cos\alpha + N \times 2l\cos\alpha = 0 \quad \dots(7.19)$$

From equation-(7.16), (7.17) and (7.19), we have

or $$\frac{(2l - x)^2}{2}Adg - \frac{3}{2}l^2Adg + 2lAdg\left(x - \frac{l}{2}\right) = 0$$

or $$(2l - x)^2 - 3l^2 + 4l\left(x - \frac{l}{2}\right) = 0$$

or $$4l^2 + x^2 - 4lx - 3l^2 + 4lx - 2l^2 = 0$$

or $$x^2 - l^2 = 0$$

or $$x^2 = l^2$$

or $$x = l$$

Thus we have $\sin\alpha = \frac{l/2}{l} = \frac{1}{2}$ or $\alpha = 30^\circ$

Illustrative Example 7.12

A piece of an alloy of mass 96 gm is composed of two metals whose specific gravities are 11.4 and 7.4. If the weight of the alloy is 86 gm in water, find the mass of each metal in the alloy.

Solution

Suppose the mass of the metal of specific gravity 11.4 be m and the mass of the second metal of specific gravity 7.4 will be $(96 - m)$

Volume of first metal $= \frac{m}{11.4}\text{ cm}^3$

Volume of second metal $= \frac{96 - m}{7.4}\text{ cm}^3$

Total volume $= \frac{m}{11.4} + \frac{96 - m}{7.4}$

Buoyancy force in water $= \left(\frac{m}{11.4} + \frac{96 - m}{7.4}\right)$ gm weight

Apparent wt. in water $= 96 - \left[\left(\frac{m}{11.4}\right) + \frac{(96 - m)}{7.4}\right]$

According to the given problem,

$$96 - \left[\left(\frac{m}{11.4}\right) + \frac{(96 - m)}{7.4}\right] = 86$$

or $$\frac{m}{11.4} + \frac{(96 - m)}{7.4} = 10$$

Solving we get, $m = 62.7$ gm

Thus mass of second metal is $= 96 - 62.7$

$= 33.3$ gm

Web Reference of Video Lectures at www.physicsgalaxy.com
Age Group - High School Physics | Age 17-19 Years
Section - PROPERTIES OF MATTER
Topic - Fluid Statics
Module Number - 7 to 14

Practice Exercise 7.1

(i) To what height should a cylindrical vessel be filled with a homogeneous liquid to make the force with which the liquid presses on the side of the vessel equal to the force exerted by the liquid on the bottom of the vessel ?

[r]

(ii) A piece of copper having an internal cavity weighs 264 g in air and 221 g in water. Find the volume of the cavity. Density of copper is 8.8 g/cm^3

[13 cm^3]

(iii) A vessel full of water has a bottom of area 20 cm^2, top of area 20 cm^2, height 20 cm and volume half a litre as shown in figure-7.16.

(a) Find the force exerted by the water on the bottom.

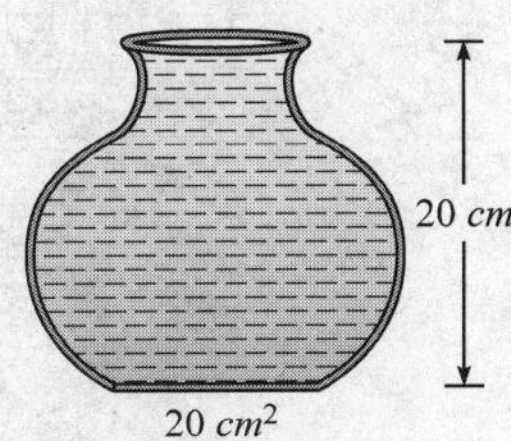

Figure 7.16

(b) Considering the equilibrium of the water, find the resultant force exerted by the sides of the glass vessel on the water. Atmospheric pressure = 1.0×10^5 N/m^2. Density of water = 1000 kg/m^3 and g = 10 m/s^2.

[(a) 204 N; (b) 1 N upward]

(iv) A hollow sphere of inner radius 9 cm and outer radius 10 cm floats half-submerged in a liquid of specific gravity 0.8. Calculate the density of the material of which the sphere is made. What would be the density of a liquid in which the hollow sphere would just float completely submerged ?

[1.476 gm/cm^3; 0.4 gm/cm^3]

(v) A piece of gold weighing 36 g in air, weighs only 34 g in water. If in this piece some copper is mixed with gold, find the amount of copper in it. Specific gravity of gold is 19.3 and that of copper is 8.9.

[2.225 g]

(vi) In previous problem if the piece is made of pure gold with some air cavities in it. Calculate the volume of the cavities left that will allow the weights given in that problem.

[0.135 cm^3]

(vii) A flat bottomed thin-walled glass tube has a diameter of 4 cm and it weighs 30 g. The centre of gravity of the empty tube is 10 cm above the bottom. Find the amount of water which must be poured into the tube so that when it is floating vertically in a tank of water, the centre of gravity of the tube and its contents is at the midpoint of the immersed length of the tube.

[110.53 g]

(viii) A uniform rod AB, 4 m long and weighing 12 kg, is supported at end A, with a 6 kg lead weight at B. The rod floats as shown in the figure-7.17 with one half to its length submerged. The buoyant force on the lead mass is negligible as it is of negligible volume. Find the tension in the cord and the total volume of the rod. Take g = 10 m/s^2.

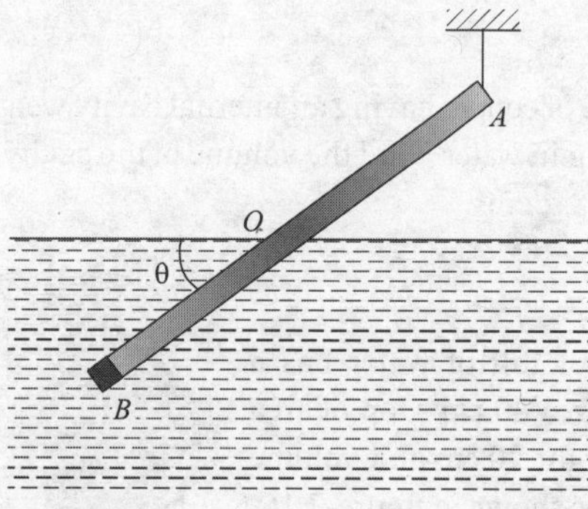

Figure 7.17

[20 N, 3.2×10^{-2} m^3]

(ix) Water stands at a depth H behind the vertical face of a dam and exerts a certain resultant horizontal force on the dam tending to slide it along its foundation and a certain torque tending to overturn the dam about the point O. If the total width of the dam is L, find (a) the total horizontal force (b) the total torque about O and (c) moment arm of the resultant horizontal force about the line through O.

[(a) $\frac{1}{2}\rho g L H^2$; (b) $\frac{1}{6}\rho g L H^3$; (c) $\frac{H}{3}$]

(x) The density of air in atmosphere decreases with height and can be expressed by the relation :

$$\rho = \rho_0 e^{-Ah}$$

where ρ_0 is the density at sea-level, A is a constant and h is the height. Calculate the atmospheric pressure at sea-level. Assume g to be constant.
(g = 9.8 m/s^2, ρ_0 = 1.3 kg/m^3 and $A = 1.2 \times 10^{-4}$ m^{-1})

[1.06×10^5 N/m^2]

7.4 *Pascal's Principle*

Some times while dealing with the problems of fluid it is desirable to know the pressure at one point if pressure at any other point in a fluid is known. For such types of calculations Pascal's Law is used extensively in dealing of static fluids. It is stated as

"The pressure applied at one point in an enclosed fluid is transmitted uniformly to every part of the fluid and to the walls of the container."

For example if we consider a closed vessel filled with a liquid as shown in figure-7.18. The pressure in the liquid at a point A at a depth x from the top of the vessel is

$$P_A = x\rho g$$

Now if we open the cork of the slight opening at the top surface then atmosphere pressure will act on the free surface of the liquid at the opening. Here according to Pascal's principle pressure at point A now be given as

$$P_A = P_0 + x\rho g \quad \text{...(7.20)}$$

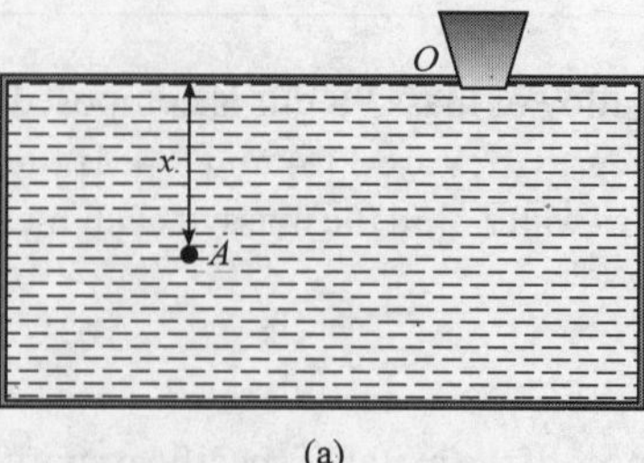

(a)

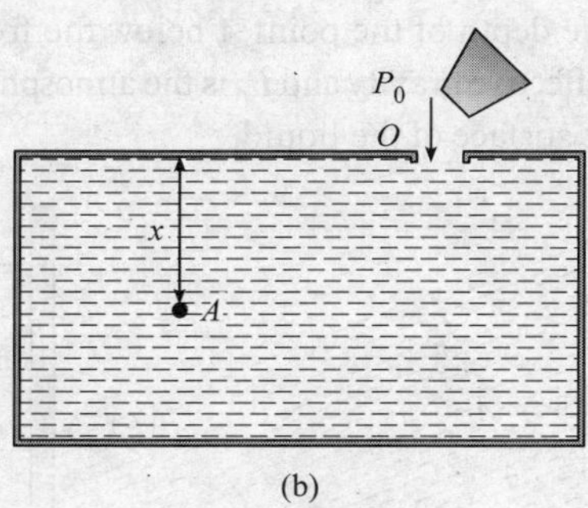

(b)

Figure 7.18

As at the opening O, pressure P_0 is acting, at each point throughout the volume of liquid the pressure is increased by the amount P_0

One more example can be considered better to explain the concept of Pascal's Principle. Consider the situation shown in figure-7.19, a tube having two different cross section S_1 and S_2, with pistons of same cross sections fitted at the two ends.

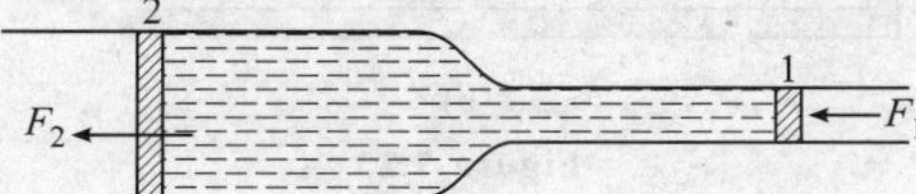

Figure 7.19

If an external force F_1 is applied to the piston 1, it creates a pressure $p_1 = F_1/S_1$ on the liquid enclosed. As the whole liquid is at the same level, everywhere the pressure in the liquid is increased by p_1. The force applied by the liquid on the piston 2 can be given as $F_2 = p_2 \times S_2$, and as the two pistons are at same level $p_2 = p_1$. Thus

$$F_2 = p_2 \times S_2$$

$$F_2 = \frac{F_1}{S_1} \times S_2 \qquad \ldots(7.21)$$

Equation-(7.21) shows that by using such a system the force can be amplified by an amount equal to the ratio of the cross sections of the two pistons. This is the principle of hydraulic press, we'll encounter in next few pages.

7.4.1 Pressure at the Different Levels of a Liquid

In different types of numerical problems, the major difficulty is due to the pressure determination at different points of the given situation of the problem. In this section, we'll discuss the same.

Consider the situation shown in figure-7.20(a), a U tube, filled with equal volumes of two different liquids 1 and 2. Psychologically the liquids should fill the tube in a way as shown in figure-7.20(a) but practically it is not, the real situation is shown in figure-7.20(b). Why does this happens ? The answer is simple if we calculate the pressures at the bottom of the U-tube in the two cases.

In case-1, the pressure at the left of the bottom is

$$P = P_0 + l\rho_1 g$$

At the right pressure is

$$P_2 = P_0 + l\rho_2 g$$

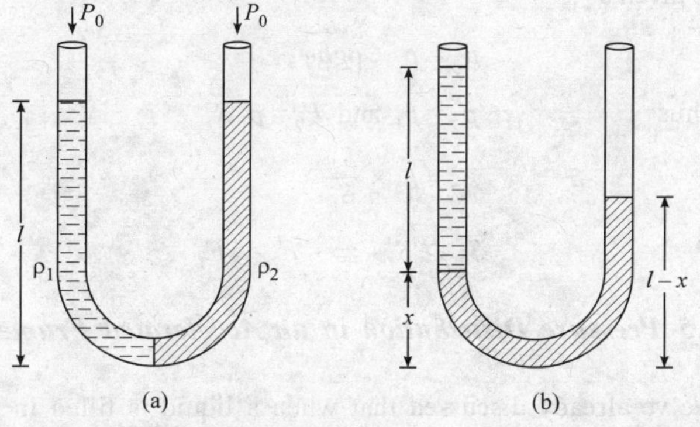

Figure 7.20

If $\rho_2 > \rho_1$ then $P_2 > P_1$ and the junction of the liquid can not remain in equilibrium, it will be displaced to the left as shown in figure-7.20(b). The displacement of the junction is such that the pressure on the two sides at every point must be same, then only the liquid remains in equilibrium.

In figure-7.20(b), if x be the displacement of the junction, the pressure at the bottom from the two sides must be same. Thus now $P_1 = P_2$, here P_1 and P_2 are given as

$$P_1 = P_0 + l\rho_1 g + x\rho_2 g$$

$$P_2 = P_0 + (l - x)\,\rho_2 g$$

On equating P_1 and P_2, we get the value of x.

7.4.2 The Hydraulic Lift

Figure-7.21 shows how Pascal's principle can be made the basis of a hydraulic lift. In operation, let an external force of magnitude F_1 be exerted downward on the left hand input piston, whose area is S_1. It results a force F_2 which will act on piston 2 by the incompressible liquid in the device.

Here $\quad F_2 = p_2 \times S_2$

And $\quad p_2 = p_B - \rho g h$

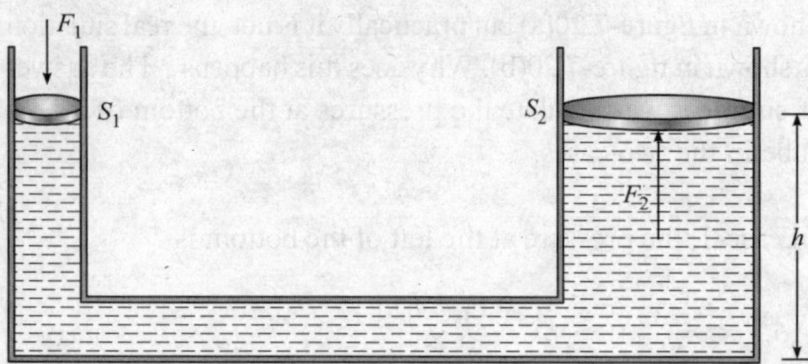

Figure 7.21

Where p_B is the pressure on the bottom of the device which can be given as :

$$p_B = p_1 + \rho g h$$

Thus $\quad p_2 = p_1$ and $F_2 = p_1 S_2$

or $\quad F_2 = F_1 \times \frac{S_2}{S_1}$

If $\quad S_2 >> S_1 \Rightarrow F_2 >> F_1$

7.5 Pressure Distribution in an Accelerated Frame

We've already discussed that when a liquid is filled in a container, generally its free surface remains horizontal as shown in figure-7.22(a) as for its equilibrium its free surface must be normal to gravity i.e. horizontal. Due to the same reason we said that pressure at every point of a liquid layer parallel to its free surface remains constant. Similar situation exist when liquid is in an accelerated frame as shown in figure-7.22(b). Due to acceleration of container, liquid filled in it experiences a pseudo force relative to container and due to this the free surface of liquid which remains normal to the gravity now is filled as shown in figure and normal to the direction of effective gravity. Thus we can get the inclination angle of free surface of liquid from horizontal as

$$\theta = \tan^{-1}\left(\frac{a}{g}\right) \qquad \ldots(7.22)$$

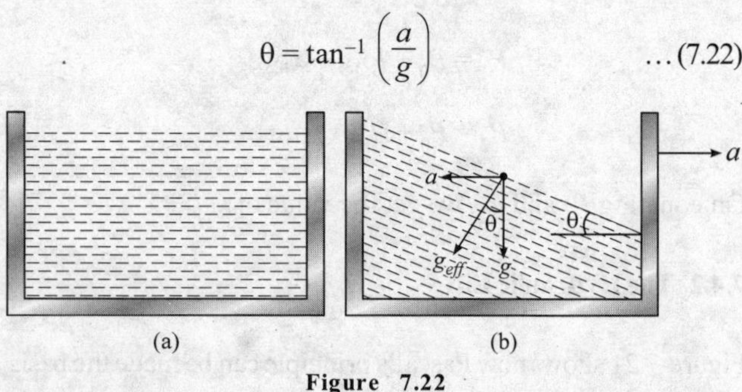

Figure 7.22

Now from equilibrium of liquid we can state that pressure at every point in a liquid layer parallel to the free surface (which is not horizontal), remains same for example if we find pressure at a point A in the accelerated container as shown in figure-7.23(a) is given as

$$P_A = P_0 + h\rho\sqrt{a^2 + g^2} \qquad \ldots(7.23)$$

Where h is the depth of the point A below the free surface of liquid along effective gravity and P_0 is the atmospheric pressure acting on free surface of the liquid.

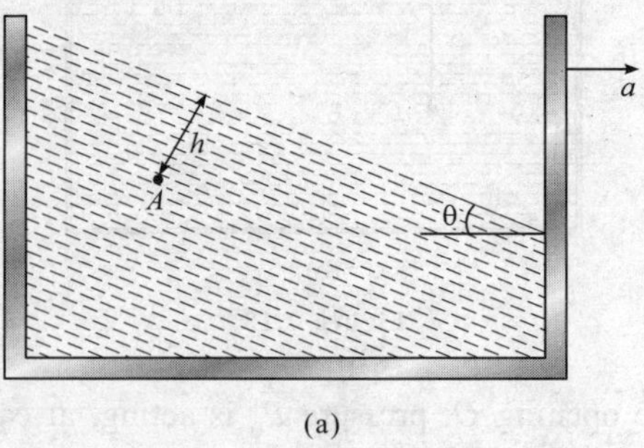

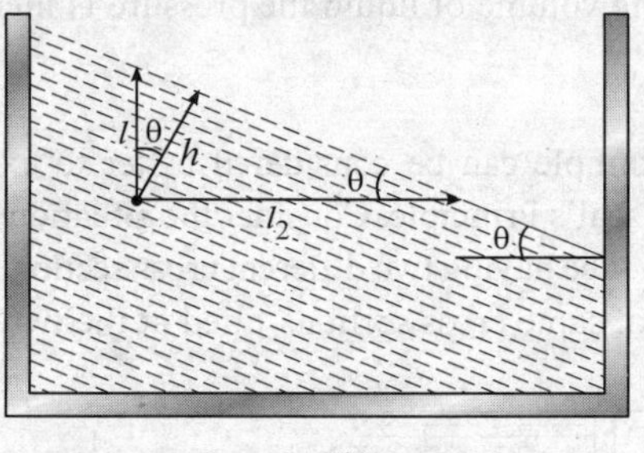

Figure 7.23

The pressure at point A can also be obtained in an another way as shown in figure-7.23(b). If l_1 and l_2 are the vertical and horizontal distances of point A from the free surface of liquid then pressure at point A can also be given as

$$P_A = P_0 + l_1\rho g = P_0 + l_2\rho a \qquad \ldots(7.24)$$

Here $l_1\rho g$ is the pressure at A due to the vertical height of liquid above A and according to Pascal's Law pressure at A is given as

$$P_A = P_0 + l_1\rho g \qquad \ldots(7.25)$$

Here we can write l_1 as

$$l_1 = h \sec\theta = \frac{h\sqrt{a^2 + g^2}}{g}$$

or from equation-(7.25)

$$P_A = P_0 + h\rho\sqrt{a^2 + g^2}$$

Similarly if we consider the horizontal distance of point A from free surface of liquid, which is l_2 then due to pseudo acceleration of container the pressure at point A is given as

$$P_A = P_0 + l_2\rho a \qquad \ldots(7.26)$$

Here l_2 is given as

$$l_2 = h \operatorname{cosec}\theta = \frac{h\sqrt{g^2 + a^2}}{a}$$

From equation-(7.24), we have

$$P_A = P_0 + h\rho\sqrt{g^2 + a^2}$$

Here students should note that while evaluating pressure at point A from vertical direction we haven't mentioned any thing about pseudo acceleration as along vertical length l_1, due to pseudo acceleration at every point pressure must be constant similarly in horizontal direction at every point due to gravity pressure remains constant.

Using the above concept we can write pressure equations for a static fluid. These pressure equations are very helpful in solving numerical examples.

To understand the concept of pressure equations, consider the example shown in figure-7.24. Two different liquids of densities ρ_1 and ρ_2 of column length l are poured in the two arms of the U-tube with base length $l/2$. Here we wish to find the difference in the free levels of the liquids h. Figure shows the equilibrium state of the two liquids in the U-tube. In this case h is given as

$$h = (l + x) - (\frac{l}{2} - x)$$

$$= \frac{l}{2} + 2x \qquad \ldots(7.27)$$

Now to find x, we start from point A where pressure is atmospheric pressure P_0, now the pressure at point B can be given as

$$P_0 + (\frac{l}{2} - x)\rho_2 g = P_B \qquad \ldots(7.28)$$

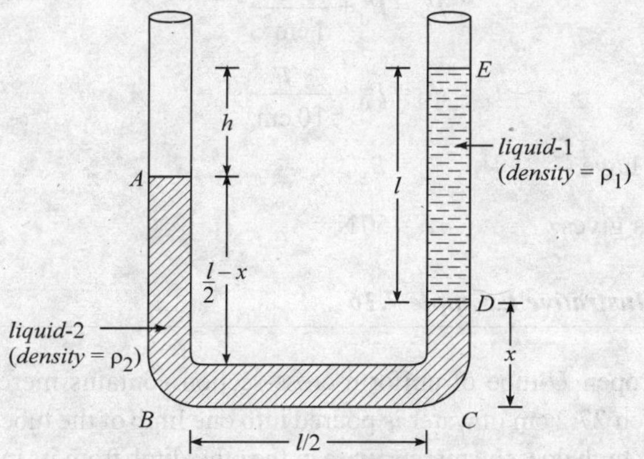

Figure 7.24

As points B and C are at same horizontal level pressure at point B and C must be same, thus

$$P_C = P_B = P_0 + (\frac{l}{2} - x)\rho_2 g \qquad \ldots(7.29)$$

Now pressure at point D is less then that at point C by $x\rho_2 g$, thus pressure at point D can be given as

$$P_0 + (\frac{l}{2} - x)\rho_2 g - x\rho_2 g = P_D \qquad \ldots(7.30)$$

Similarly we can write pressure at point E which is P_0 as

$$P_0 + (\frac{l}{2} - x)\rho_2 g - x\rho_2 g - l\rho_1 g = P_0 \qquad \ldots(7.31)$$

Here equation-(7.31) is called as pressure equation of the liquid in equilibrium from point A to E through the liquid columns thus on solving, we get

$$h = 2x = \frac{l(\rho_1 + \rho_2)}{\rho_1} \qquad \ldots(7.32)$$

7.5.1 Pressure Distribution in a Closed Accelerated Container

Consider the situation shown in figure-7.25. A closed tank car filled with water is accelerating on a horizontal track with an acceleration a. In this situation the constant pressure layers of liquid are inclined at an angle $\theta = \tan^{-1}(a/g)$ with horizontal. In the body of the whole liquid, the least pressure point is P (as we've discussed). If container is completely closed then P can be taken as a zero pressure point. If we wish to find pressure at a general point A at a depth h below the top surface of container and at a distance l from the right wall of container, then this can again be obtained directly by writing pressure equation for the liquid with respect to tank car from point P to A through point M. If can be written as

$$0 + h\rho g + l\rho a = P_A$$

or

$$P_A = h\rho g + l\rho a \qquad \ldots(7.33)$$

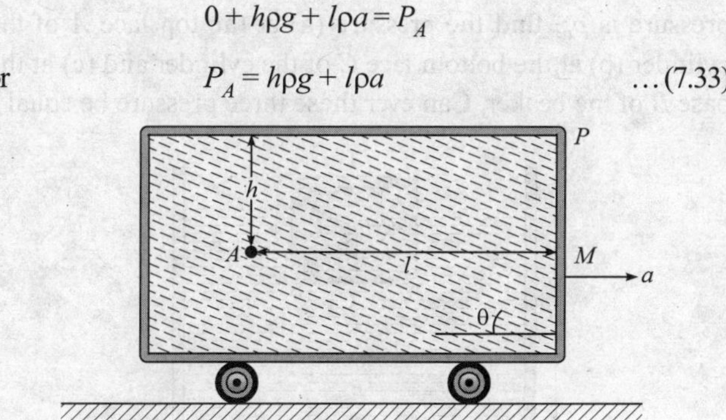

Figure 7.25

Thus we can simply get the pressure at point A as discussed by using pressure equation in a static fluid.

 # Illustrative Example 7.13

The liquids shown in figure-7.26 in the two arms are mercury (specific gravity = 13.6) and water. If the difference of heights of the mercury columns is 2 cm, find the height h of the water column.

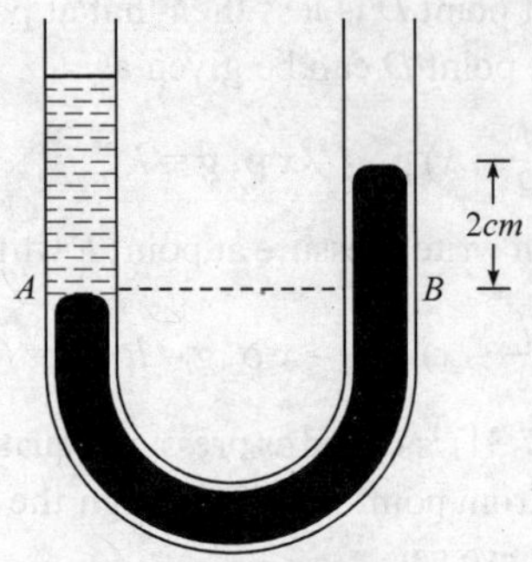

Figure 7.26

Solution

Suppose the atmospheric pressure = P_0

Pressure at $A = P_0 + h(1000)g$

Pressure at $B = P_0 + (0.02\text{ m})(13600)g$

These pressures are equal as A and B are at the same horizontal level. Thus,

$$h = (0.02\text{ m})\,13.6$$

$$= 0.27\text{ m} = 27\text{ cm}$$

 # Illustrative Example 7.14

A liquid of density ρ is filled in a beaker of cross-section S to a height H and then a cylinder of mass m and cross-section s is made to float in it as shown in figure-7.27. If the atmospheric pressure is p_0, find the pressure (a) at the top face A of the cylinder (b) at the bottom face C of the cylinder and (c) at the base B of the beaker. Can ever these three pressure be equal ?

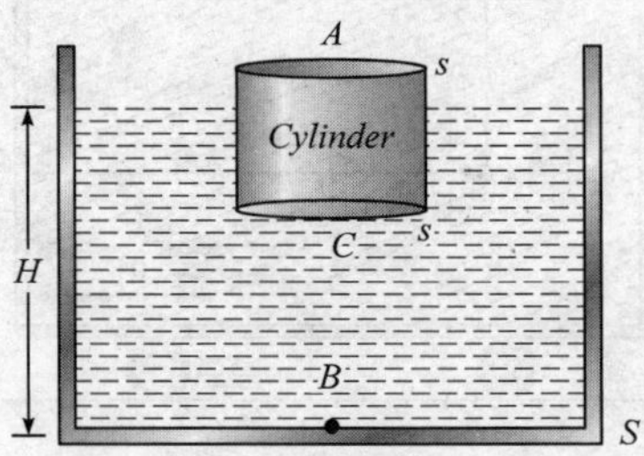

Figure 7.27

Solution

(a) Above the cross-section A there is external pressure due to atmosphere only.

So $\quad P_A = \text{Atmospheric pressure} = p_0$

(b) At the point C the pressure will be due to atmosphere and also due to the weight of the cylinder, i.e.,

$$p_C = p_0 + \frac{mg}{s}$$

If the system is in free fall (as in a satellite), $g \to 0$,

$$p_A = p_C = p_B = p_0 \qquad \text{[As weight = 0]}$$

 # Illustrative Example 7.15

The area of cross-section of the two arms of a hydraulic press are 1 cm² and 10 cm² respectively (Figure-7.28). A force of 5 N is applied on the water in the thinner arm. What force should be applied on the water in the thicker arm so that the water may remain in equilibrium ?

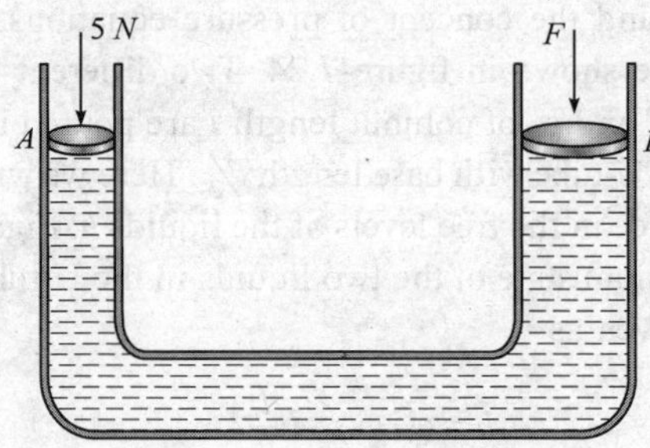

Figure 7.28

Solution

In equilibrium, the pressure at the two surfaces A and B should be equal as they lie in the same horizontal level. If the atmospheric pressure is P and a force F is applied to maintain the equilibrium, the pressures are

$$P_A = P_0 + \frac{5N}{1\text{ cm}^2}$$

$$P_B = P_0 + \frac{F}{10\text{ cm}^2}$$

We have $\quad P_A = P_B$

This gives $\quad F = 50\text{ N}$

 # Illustrative Example 7.16

An open U-tube of uniform cross-section contains mercury. When 27.2 cm of water is poured into one limb of the tube, (a) how high does the mercury rise in the other limb from its initial level ? (b) What is the difference in levels of liquids of the two sides ? ($\rho_w = 1$ and $\rho_{Hg} = 13.6$ units)

Solution

The situation is shown in figure-7.29.

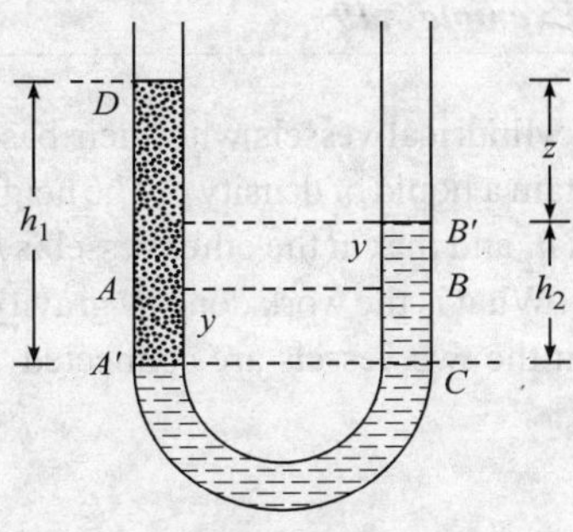

Figure 7.29

(a) If water depresses the mercury by y, the mercury in the other limb will rise by y above its initial level (as fluids are incompressible), so that from figure-7.29

$$h_2 = 2y$$

Now if h_1 is the height of water column above A', then as in a liquid, pressure is same at all points in the same level :

$$p_{A'} = p_C, \quad \text{or} \quad p_0 + h_1\rho_1 g = h_2\rho_2 g,$$

$$\text{or} \quad h_1\rho_1 = h_2\rho_2, \quad \text{or} \quad 27.2 \times 1 = 2y \times 13.6$$

Which on solution gives $y = 1$ cm, i.e., mercury rises by 1 cm from its initial level.

(b) The difference of level on two sides

$$z = h_1 - h_2 = 27.2 - 2 \times 1 = 25.2 \text{ cm},$$

i.e., the water level will stand 25.2 cm higher than the mercury level in the other limb.

Illustrative Example 7.17

Find the tension in the string holding a solid block of volume 1000 cm^3 and density 0.8 gm/cm^3 dipped in liquid and tied to the bottom of a container filled with liquid of density 1.2 gm/cm^3 as shown in figure-7.30.

(i) When container is moving upwards with an acceleration 4.9 m/s^2.

(ii) When container is stationary.

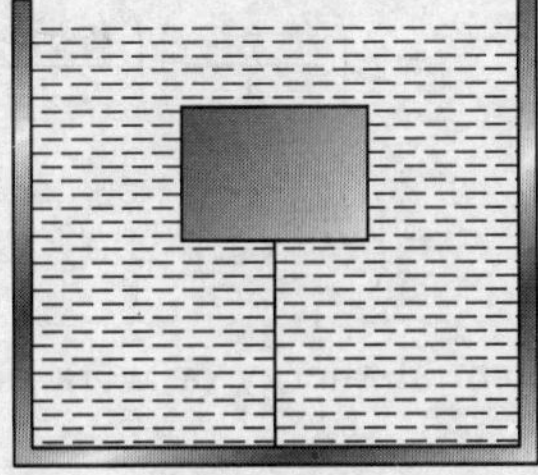
Figure 7.30

Solution

(i) In the container as accelerating upward, we can consider effective gravity g_{eff} as

$$g_{eff} = g + a \qquad \dots(7.34)$$

Figure-7.31 shows the free body diagram of block relative to container

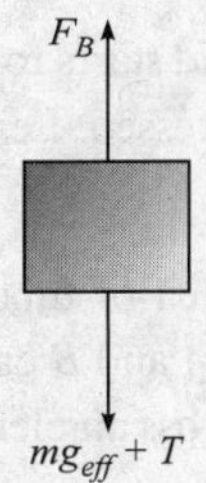

Figure-7.31

Here buoyant force on block can be given as

$$F_B = \frac{m}{\rho_s}\rho_l g_{eff} \qquad \dots(7.35)$$

Here ρ_s and ρ_l are the densities of solid and liquid respectively. Now for equilibrium of block relative to container, we have from equation-(7.34) and (7.35)

$$F_B = m(g + a) + T$$

$$\text{or} \quad \frac{m}{\rho_s}\rho_l (g + a) = m(g + a) + T \qquad \dots(7.36)$$

If v be the volume of container we have from equation-(7.36)

$$V\rho_l (g + a) = V\rho_s (g + a) + T$$

$$\text{or} \quad T = (\rho_l - \rho_s)\, V(g + a) \qquad \dots(7.37)$$

$$= (1.2 - 0.8) \times 1000 \times (980 + 490)$$

$$= 5.88 \times 10^5 \text{ dyne}$$

$$= 5.88 \text{ N}$$

(b) If container is at rest, from equation-(7.37) tension in string can be given as

$$T = (\rho_l - \rho_s)\, Vg$$

$$= (1.2 - 0.8) \times 100 \times 980 = 3.92 \times 10^5 \text{ dyne} = 3.92 \text{ N}$$

Illustrative Example 7.18

Length of a horizontal arm of a U-tube is L and ends of both the vertical arms are open to atmospheric pressure P_0. A liquid of density ρ is poured in the tube such that liquid just fills the horizontal part of the tube as shown in figure-7.32(a). Now one end of the opened ends is sealed and the tube is then rotated about a vertical axis passing through the other vertical arm with angular speed ω_0. If length of each vertical arm is a and in the sealed end liquid rises to a height y, find pressure in the sealed tube during rotation.

Solution

When tube is rotated, liquid starts to flow radially outward and air in sealed arm is compressed. Let the shift of liquid be y as shown in figure-7.32(b).

Let the cross sectional area of tube be S. Here the pressure difference between point A and B can be given by integrating the pressure difference across an element of width dx, which is given as

$$dP = dx\, \rho\, \omega^2 x$$

Now integrating from A to B, we get

$$P_B - P_A = \int_y^L \rho\omega^2 x\,dx$$

$$= \frac{\rho\omega^2}{2}\,(L^2 - y^2)$$

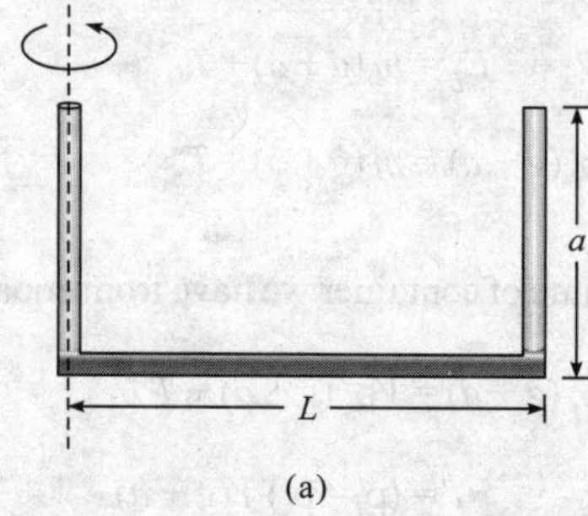

(a)

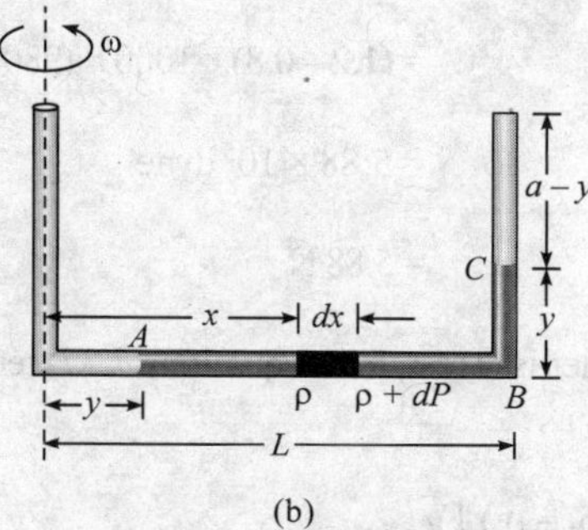

(b)

Figure 7.32

Thus pressure at point C can be given as

$$P_C = P_B - y\rho g$$

and at point A, pressure is atmospheric, thus we have

$$P_C = \frac{\rho\omega^2}{2}\,(L^2 - y^2) + \rho_0 - y\rho g$$

 # Illustrative Example 7.19

Two identical cylindrical vessels with their bases at the same level, each contain a liquid of density ρ. The height of the liquid in one vessel is h_1 and that in the other vessel is h_2. The area of either base is A. What is the work done by gravity in equalizing the levels when the two vessels are connected ?

Solution

The initial situation is shown in figure-7.33(a).

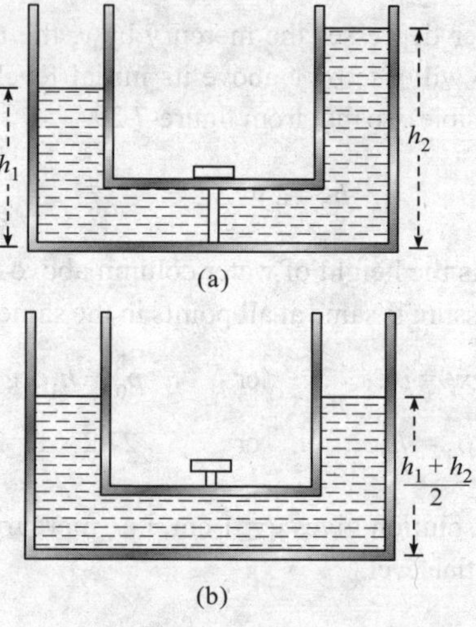

Figure 7.33

Initial potential energy of the system is given as

$$U_i = \frac{h_1}{2}\,(h_1 A\rho)\,g + \frac{h_2}{2}\,(h_2 A\,\rho)\,g = Ag\,\rho\left(\frac{h_1^2 + h_2^2}{2}\right)$$

Where $h_1/2$ and $h_2/2$ are the centre of gravity or columns of height h_1 and h_2 respectively.

The final potential energy of the system in the situation shown in figure-7.33(b) when the two level becomes equal is given as

$$U_f = \left(\frac{h_1 + h_2}{4}\right)\left[\left(\frac{h_1 + h_2}{2}\right)A\rho\right]g + \left(\frac{h_1 + h_2}{4}\right)\left[\left(\frac{h_1 + h_2}{2}\right)A\rho\right]g$$

Here final centre of gravity will be at a height $\left(\frac{h_1 + h_2}{4}\right)$

$$= 2\left(\frac{h_1 + h_2}{4}\right)\left(\frac{h_1 + h_2}{2}\right)A\,\rho\,g$$

$$= \left(\frac{h_1 + h_2}{2}\right)^2 A\,\rho\,g$$

The change in potential energy or work done by gravity is given as

$$W = U_f - U_i = \left(\frac{h_1 + h_2}{2}\right)^2 A\,\rho\,g - \left(\frac{h_1^2 + h_2^2}{2}\right) A\,\rho\,g$$

$$= \frac{A \rho g}{2}\left[-\frac{(h_2 - h_1)^2}{2}\right]$$

$$= -A \rho g \left(\frac{h_2 - h_1}{2}\right)^2$$

Negative sign shows that work is done by gravitational field on the liquid.

Web Reference of Video Lectures at www.physicsgalaxy.com
Age Group - High School Physics | Age 17-19 Years
Section - PROPERTIES OF MATTER
Topic - Fluid Statics
Module Number - 15 to 25

Practice Exercise 7.2

(i) A rubber ball of mass 10 gm and volume 15 cm^3 is dipped in water to a depth of 10m. Assuming density of water uniform throughout the depth if it is released from rest. Find (take $g = 9.8$ m/s^2)

(a) the acceleration of the ball, and

(b) the time taken by it to reach the surface.

[4.9m/s^2; 2.02s]

(ii) Figure-7.34 shows a *L*-shaped tube in which a liquid of density ρ is filled. Find with what acceleration the tube is accelerated toward right so that no liquid will fall out of the tube.

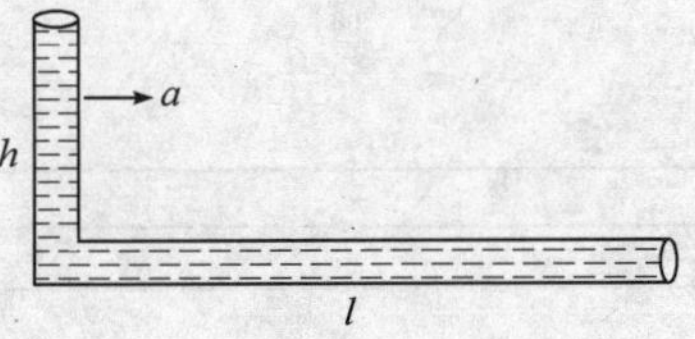

Figure 7.34

[$\frac{hg}{l}$]

(iii) A solid sphere of mass $m = 2$ kg and specific gravity $s = 0.5$ is held stationary relative to a tank filled with water as shown in figure-7.35. The tank is accelerating vertically upward with acceleration $a = 2$ m/s^2.

(a) Calculate tension in the thread connected between the sphere and the bottom of the tank.

(b) If the thread snaps, calculate acceleration of sphere with respect to the tank. Take density of water is $\rho = 1000$ kg/m^3 and $g = 10$ m/s^2.

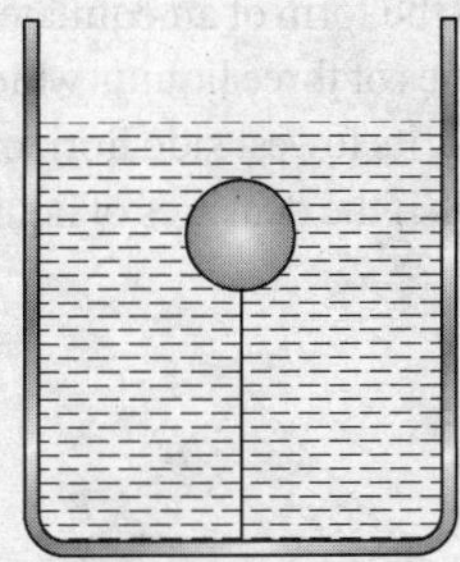

Figure 7.35

[(a) 24 N, (b) 12 m/s^2(upward)]

(iv) A closed tank filled with water is mounted on a cart. The cart moves with an acceleration 'a' on a plane road. What is the difference in pressure between points *B* & *A* shown in figure-7.36 ?

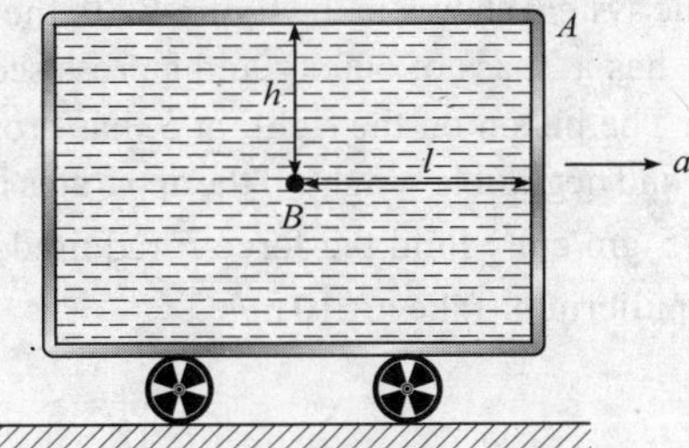

Figure 7.36

[($hg + al$)ρ]

(v) A rough surfaced metal cube of size 4 cm and mass 100 gm is placed in an empty vessel. Now water is filled in the vessel so that the cube is just immersed in the water. Find the average pressure on the bottom surface of vessel which is in contact with the cube. Take $g = 10$ m/s^2.

[1.00625 × 10^5 Pa]

(vi) A U-tube of length *L* contain liquid. It is mounted on a horizontal turn table rotating with an angular speed ω about one of its arms as shown in figure-7.37. Find the difference in heights between the liquid columns in two vertical arms.

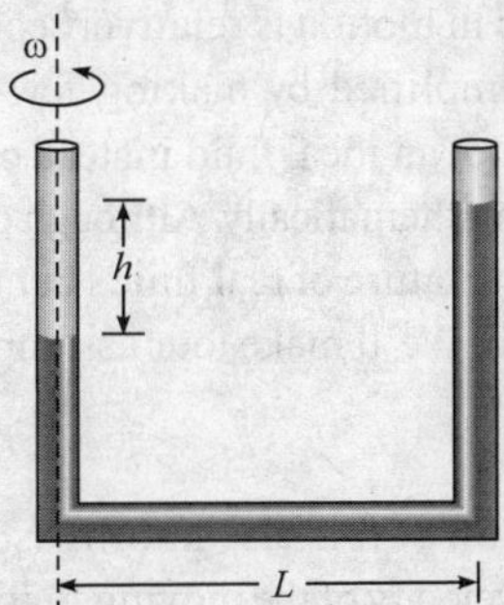

Figure 7.37

[$\frac{\omega^2 L^2}{2g}$]

(vii) A closed tube in the form of an equilateral triangle of side l contains equal volumes of three liquids which do not mix and is placed vertically with its lowest side horizontal. Find the value of x in the figure-7.38, if the densities of liquids are in arithmetic progression.

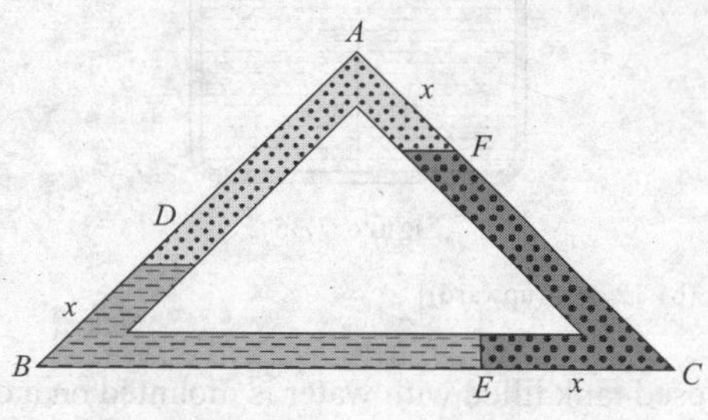

Figure 7.38

[$x = l/3$]

(viii) For the system shown in the figure-7.39, the cylinder on the left at L has a mass of 600 kg and a cross sectional area of 800 cm^2. The piston on the right, at S, has cross sectional area 25 cm^2 and negligible weight. If the apparatus is filled with oil ($\rho = 0.75$ gm/cm^3) Find the force F required to hold the system in equilibrium. Take $g = 10$ m/s^2.

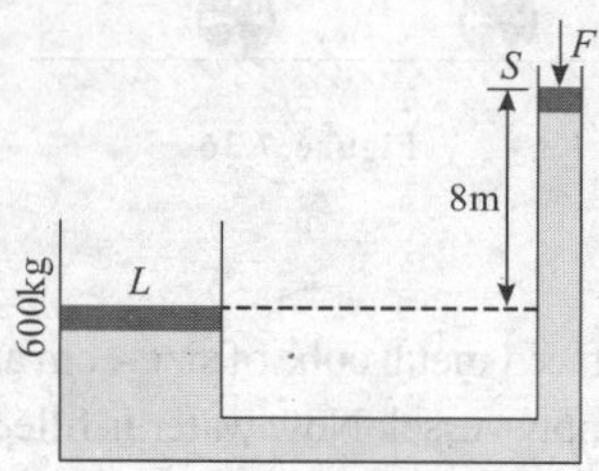

Figure 7.39

[37.5 N]

7.6 Fluid Dynamics

Up to now, we have studied only fluids at rest. Let us now study fluids in motion, the subject matter of hydrodynamics. The study of fluids in motion is relatively complicated, but the analysis can be simplified by making few assumptions. We discuss the motion of an ideal fluid instead of real fluid, as it is simpler to handle mathematically. Although our results may not fully agree with the nature of real fluids but these will be close enough to be useful. We'll make four assumptions for the ideal fluid, these are :

1. **Streamline flow :** It is also known as laminar or steady flow in which the velocity of the moving fluid at any fixed point does not change with time, either in magnitude or in direction. For example the smoke rising from a cigarette, is steady initially and as smoke rises, the speed of smoke particles increases and at a certain critical speed, the flow change its characteristics from steady to turbulent.

2. **Incompressible flow :** We assume in our analysis that the fluid is incompressible. That is, its density has a constant value.

3. **Nonviscous flow :** Viscosity of a fluid is a measure of how resistive the fluid is to flow. Basically it is a measurement of friction between the flowing layers of a fluid. For example, thick oil is more resistive to flow than water. As in absence of friction a block moves with a constant velocity, similarly in a nonviscous fluid, a moving object will not experience any drag force due to viscosity.

4. **Irrotational flow :** We assume that the flow is irrotational. Means that the particles of fluid will not provide any rotational motion to the uniform bodies moving along the fluid.

7.6.1 Representation of Streamlines

The density of streamlines in representative diagram is more where the velocity of the fluid is more. As shown in figure-7.40(a), when water flows in a pipe line, at the bottom the velocity of the layers is less as compared to the velocity of the particles of the layer above some layers. Thus the stream lines are denser at some height and rarer near the bottom. Unlike to this case, if we consider the flow of an ideal nonviscous fluid, as shown in figure-7.40(b). The density of streamlines will remain constant throughout the volume.

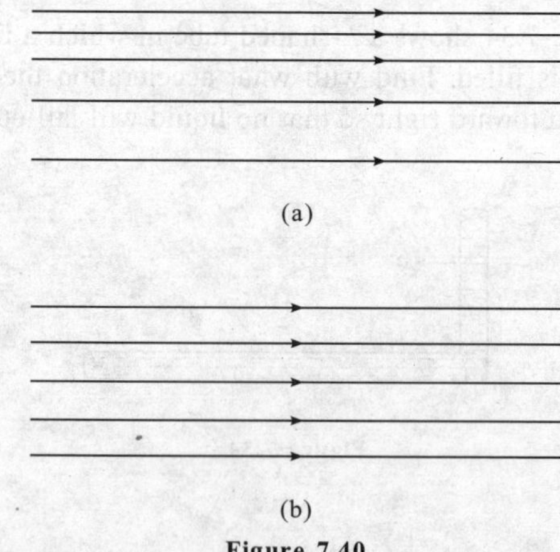

Figure 7.40

7.6.2 Laminar Versus Turbulent Flow

Let us examine how a fluid flows through a pipe. Friction forces exerted on the fluid by the pipe wall tend to restrain the flow, as do the viscous forces within the fluid. As a result, the fluid close to the walls flows more slowly than that near the center of the pipe. We show this effect in figure-7.41(a), where the lengths of the arrows indicate the magnitude of the velocity at various positions in the pipe.

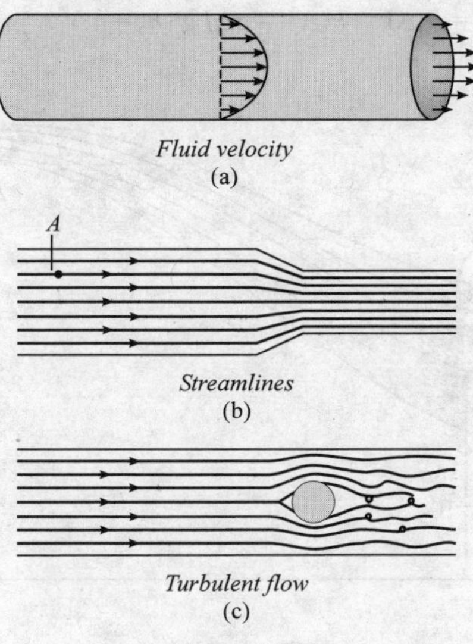

Figure 7.41

Another feature of flow through a pipe is shown in figure-7.41(b). Suppose a tiny speck of dust, like the one at point A, is flowing with the fluid. If the flow rate is low, the speck follows the line shown as it moves through the pipe. Other specks, and the fluid as well, follow similar smooth lines. We call these flow lines **streamlines,** and this is called **streamline,** or **laminar, flow.** In laminar flow, each element of the fluid follows a repeatable streamline.

If the speed of the fluid becomes high enough, the flow lines begin to behave erratically. At any instant, the flow lines may look like those in figure-7.41(c). An instant later, the lines will take another form. This situation, in which the flow lines are contorted and vary widely with time, is called **turbulent flow.**

As you might guess, friction (or viscous) energy losses are nearly always larger in turbulent flow than in laminar flow. Turbulence causes rapid, chaotic motion that in turn increases distances moved and friction losses. Because of this, turbulence is to be avoided if friction losses are to be minimized. Automakers wish to minimize turbulent air flow around their cars, for example (Figure-7.41). A means for predicting when turbulence occurs has obvious practical importance.

Although turbulence is very difficult to treat mathematically, there is a unifying concept that simplifies the situation. Experiment shows that flow changes from laminar to turbulent when a critical value is reached for what is called the **Reynolds number** N_R, a dimensionless constant given by

$$N_R = \frac{\rho v D}{\eta} \qquad \ldots(7.38)$$

for a fluid with density ρ, viscosity η, and speed v flowing through a pipe of diameter D. If N_R exceeds about 2000, the flow usually becomes turbulent. This is not a precise rule because careful design can postpone the onset of turbulence. Reynolds numbers of 40,000 have been achieved for special laminar flow systems. (Equation-7.38) is also applicable to a sphere of diameter D moving through a fluid. In that case, however, the critical value for N_R is about 10.)

Despite its lack of precision, the critical value of 2000 is very useful, as is the Reynolds number itself. For example, two systems, one of which is a scale model of another, give rise to similar flow if N_R is the same for both. Such systems are said to be *dynamically similar*. This concept forms the basis for small-scale wind tunnel tests of flow patterns around cars and planes. The flows are similar if v is increased by the same factor by which D is decreased because N_R remains unchanged.

7.6.3 Equation of Continuity

This equation defines the steady flow of a fluid in a tube. It states that if flow of a fluid is steady then the mass of fluid entering per second at one end is equal to the mass of fluid leaving per second at the other end.

Figure-7.42 shows a section of a tube in which at the ends, the cross sectional areas are A_1 and A_2 and the velocity of the fluid are v_1 and v_2 respectively.

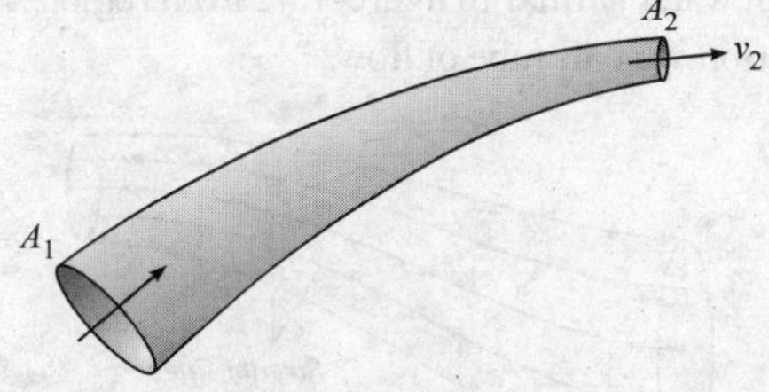

Figure 7.42

According to the equation of continuity, if flow is steady mass of fluid entering at end A_1 per second = mass of fluid leaving the end A_2 per second

In time dt the fluid enters a distance $v_1\, dt$ at end A_1 so the volume entered in time dt is $dV = A_1\, v_1\, dt$ and the volume entered per second is

$$\frac{dV}{dt} = A_1 v_1$$

Hence mass entering per second at A_1 is $= A_1 v_1 \rho$

Similarly mass leaving per second at A_2 is $= A_2 v_2 \rho$

According to the definition of steady flow

$$A_1 v_1 \rho = A_2 v_2 \rho$$

or

$$A_1 v_1 = A_2 v_2 \qquad \ldots(7.39)$$

Equation-(7.39) is known as equation of continuity, which gives that in steady flow the product of .

Web Reference of Video Lectures at www.physicsgalaxy.com
Age Group - High School Physics | Age 17-19 Years
Section - PROPERTIES OF MATTER
Topic - Fluid Dynamics
Module Number - 1 to 6

7.7 Bernoulli's Theorem

It is a basic consequence of energy conservations principle for a flowing fluid. It relates the variables describing the steady laminar flow of a fluid, assuming the fluid is incompressible and non viscous. The analytical result of the theorem is called Bernoulli's equation and it describes the relationship of fluid pressure, velocity and height as it moves along a pipe or in a tube of flow.

Figure-7.43 shows a fluid flowing smoothly from region A to region B. The situation shown in figure shows that a fluid is flowing in a pipe with cross sections at end A and B but it need not be constrained to a real pipe, let us consider an example of water flowing in a river. If we draw all of the streamlines within a portion of water similar to figure-7.42 from region A to region B this portion we call tube of flow.

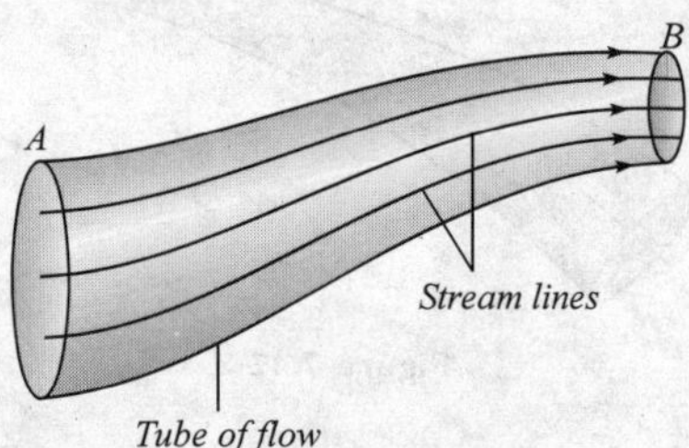

Figure 7.43

Now to establish a relation among the variables consider the tube of flow shown in figure-7.44. Here we apply work energy theorem for a small portion (volume ΔV) of fluid. Let fluid is flowing in a streamline manner with speed v_1 and v_2 at the ends A and B of the tube of flow. The pressure and areas of cross sections at ends A and B are P_1, A_1 and P_2, A_2 respectively. If ΔV volume of fluid enters into the tube at end A where pressure is P_1 then the work done in this displacement at A is $P_1\,\Delta V$. At the same time, the same amount of fluid (volume ΔV) moves out of the tube at end B. The work done in this case is $-P_2\,\Delta V$. Here negative sign indicates that the element of fluid at region B moves against the force due to the pressure of the fluid to its right. The work done by gravity in the net motion of fluid from region A to region B is $-mg\,(h_2 - h_1)$. Thus net work done is

$$W = P_1\Delta V - P_2\Delta V - \rho\Delta Vg\,(h_2 - h_1) \qquad \dots(7.40)$$

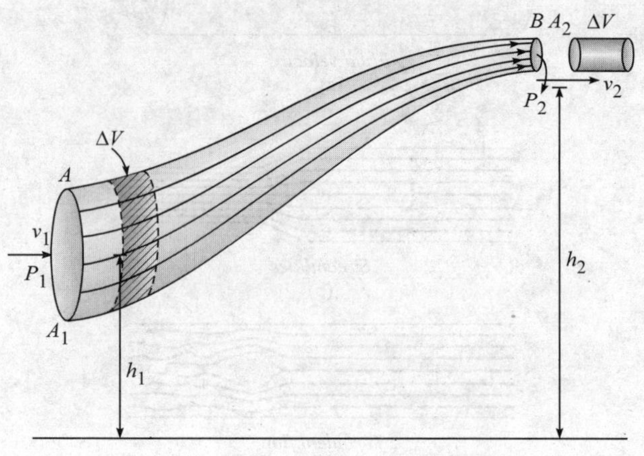

Figure 7.44

According to work energy theorem, we know this work must be equal to the change in kinetic energy of the flowing fluid from region A to region B. Thus we have

$$\frac{1}{2}\,(\rho\Delta V)\,v_2^2 - \frac{1}{2}\,(\rho\Delta V)\,v_1^2 = P_1\Delta V - P_2\Delta V - (\rho\Delta V)\,g\,(h_2 - h_1)$$

or

$$\frac{1}{2}\,\rho v_1^2 + \rho g h_1 + P_1 = \frac{1}{2}\,\rho v_2^2 + \rho g h_2 + P_2 \qquad \dots(7.41)$$

Here by observing equation-(7.41) we conclude that the sum of these three terms is constant for all cross-sections for a tube of flow in streamline flow of a fluid. The three terms are called kinetic energy per unit volume ($\frac{1}{2}\rho v^2$), gravitational potential energy per unit volume (ρgh) and pressure energy per unit volume (P) of the flowing fluid. Thus for any cross-section, sum of the three remains constant as

$$\frac{1}{2}\,\rho v^2 + \rho gh + P = \text{constant} \qquad \dots(7.42)$$

This equation-(7.42) is called Bernoulli's equation, for the steady, non viscous flow of an incompressible fluid. Under these conditions, Bernoulli's equation expresses conservation of energy in a flowing fluid.

If we consider a horizontal tube of flow then for two points in it we can write Bernoulli's equation as

$$P + \frac{1}{2}\,\rho v^2 = \text{constant} \qquad \dots(7.43)$$

Which implies that for such points there is a trade off between speed and pressure. If speed is high pressure will be low and vice versa.

There are several examples to this concept as follows :

The pressure in the air blown at high speed across the top of the vertical tube of a perfume atomizer (figure-7.45a) is less than the normal air pressure acting on the surface of the liquid in the bowl; thus perfume is pushed up the tube because of the reduced pressure at the top.

A ping pong ball can be made to float above a blowing jet of air (figure-7.45b), if the ball begins to leave the jet of air, the higher pressure outside the jet pushes the ball back in.

Airplane wings and other airfoils are designed to deflect the air so that although streamline flow is largely maintained, the streamlines are crowded together above the wing (figure-7.45c). Just as the flow lines are crowded together in a pipe constriction where the velocity is high, so the crowded streamlines above the wing indicate the air speed is greater than below and thee is thus a net upward force; this is called dynamic lift. Actually, Bernoulli's principle is only one aspect of the lift on a wing. Wings are usually tilted slightly upward so that air striking the bottom surface is deflected downward; the change in momentum of the rebounding air molecules results in an additional upward force on the wing. Turbulence also plays an important role; for example, if the wing is tilted upward too much, turbulence sets in behind the wing with a consequent loss of lift.

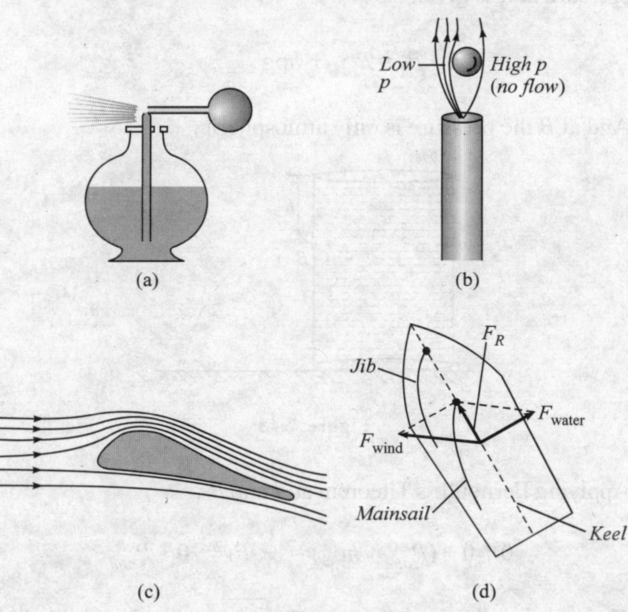

Figure 7.45

A sailboat can move against the wind, (figure-7.45d) and the Bernoulli effect aids in this considerably if the sails are arranged so the air velocity increases in the narrow constriction between the two sails. The normal behind the mainsail is larger than the reduced pressure in front of it and this pushes the boat forward. When going against the wind, the mainsail is set at an angle approximately midway between the wind direction and the boat's axis as shown. The force of the wind on the sail plus the Bernoulli's effect, acts nearly perpendicular to the sail. This would tend to make the boat move sideway but the keel beneath prevents this for the water exerts a force on the keel nearly perpendicular to it. The resultant of these two forces is almost directly forward shown.

Web Reference of Video Lectures at www.physicsgalaxy.com
Age Group - High School Physics | Age 17-19 Years
Section - PROPERTIES OF MATTER
Topic - Fluid Dynamics
Module Number - 7 to 12

7.8 Numerical Applications of Bernoulli's Theorem

There are several different cases in which Bernoulli's Equation can be applied but the major problem in the numerical problems is the selection of the points in the given situation where Equation is to be applied. We'll discuss several examples and applications concerned which will help you to select the points.

7.8.1 Pitot Tube

It is a device used to measure flow velocity of fluid. It is a U shaped tube which can be inserted in a tube or in the fluid flowing space as shown in figure-7.46. In the U tube a liquid which is immiscible with the fluid is filled upto a level C and the short opening M is placed in the fluid flowing space against the flow so that few of the fluid particles entered into the tube and exert a pressure on the liquid in limb A of U tube. Due to this the liquid level changes as shown in figure-7.45.

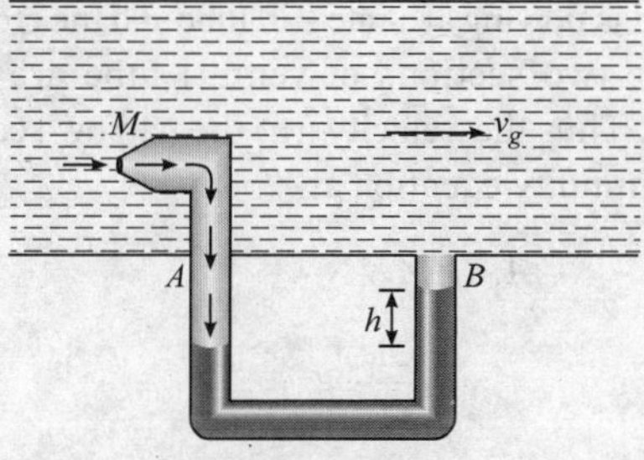

Figure 7.46

At end B fluid is freely flowing, which exert approximately negligible pressure on this liquid. The pressure difference at ends A and B can be given by measuring the liquid level difference h as

If it is a gas, then

$$P_A - P_B = h\rho g$$

If it is a liquid of density ρ, then

$$P_A - P_B = h(\rho - \rho_g)g$$

Now if we apply Bernoulli's equation at ends A and B we'l have

$$0 + 0 + P_A = \frac{1}{2}\rho v_g^2 + 0 + P_B$$

or $$\frac{1}{2}\rho v_g^2 = P_A - P_B = h\rho g \quad \ldots(7.44)$$

Now by using equations-(7.44), we can evaluate the velocity v, with which the fluid is flowing.

NOTE : Pitot tube is also used to measure velocity of aeroplanes with respect to wind. It can be mounted at the top surface of the plain and hence the velocity of wind can be measured with respect to plane.

In early 1920's such a device was also being used in ships to measure the velocity of ships with respect to sea water.

7.8.2 Venturimeter

It is a device used to measure velocity of fluids (liquids only), in pipe lines. This is a hollow tube with slightly narrow cross section at the middle, as shown in figure-7.47, it can be inserted in series with a flowing line.

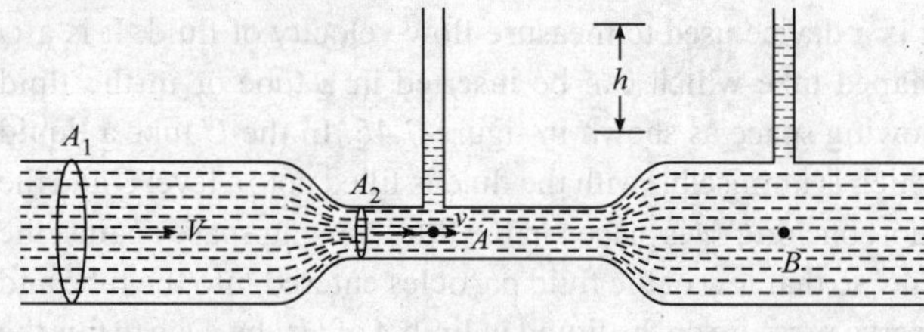

Figure 7.47

Let the liquid is flowing at a rate V in tube and the cross-sectional areas of the two sections of venturi tube are A_1 and A_2 respectively. Thus the velocity v at the narrow section can be given by continuity equation as

$$A_1 V = A_2 v$$

or $$v = \frac{A_1}{A_2} V$$

Here we choose points A and B for Bernoulli's Application, just below the two small pipes open in atmosphere. Due to less cross section at A velocity of liquid is high and hence low pressure of liquid here. Thus liquid rises upto a less height in this pipe as compared to that at B.

According to Bernoulli's Theorem at A and B

$$\frac{1}{2}\rho\left(\frac{A_1}{A_2}V\right)^2 + P_A = \frac{1}{2}\rho(V)^2 + P_B \quad \ldots(7.45)$$

Here pressure difference between points A and B can be evaluated by measuring the height difference between the two pipes as

$$P_B - P_A = h\rho g$$

or from equation-(7.45) $$\frac{1}{2}\rho\left(\frac{A_1^2}{A_2^2} - 1\right)V^2 = P_B - P_A = h\rho g$$

or $$V = \sqrt{\frac{2gh}{\frac{A_1^2}{A_2^2} - 1}}$$

7.8.3 Torecelli's Theorem

This concept is used to evaluate the velocity of liquid flowing out from a hole in a container.

The example can be taken as shown in figure-7.48. If from the surface of the liquid at a depth h, a hole is made of small cross section. The liquid will come out from this hole with some speed, say v. To evaluate this speed, we apply Bernoulli's theorem at two points A and B, just inside and outside the hole.

At point A as the cross-section of the vessel is large, we can consider the velocity of liquid particles close to zero and the pressure at A is given as

$$P_A = P_{atm} + h\rho g$$

And at B the pressure is only atmospheric.

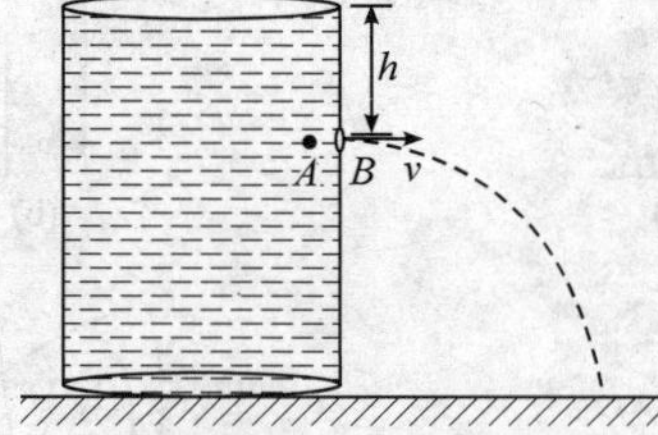

Figure 7.48

Applying Bernoulli's Theorem at A and B

$$0 + 0 + (P_{atm} + h\rho g) = \frac{1}{2}P v^2 + 0 + P_{atm}$$

or $$v = \sqrt{2gh} \quad \ldots(7.46)$$

Equation-(7.46) is known as Torecelli's Theorem and the velocity with which liquid comes out, is called efflux velocity.

This equation is used in problems concerned with liquid draining out from a vessel and in cases of conservation of momentum (cases of variable mass).

7.8.4 Freely Falling Liquid

When liquid falls freely under gravity, the area of cross section of the stream continuously decreases, as the velocity increases.

For example, we consider water coming out from a tap, as shown in figure-7.49. Let its speed near the mouth of tap is v_0 and at a depth h it is v, then we have

$$v^2 = v_0^2 + 2gh$$

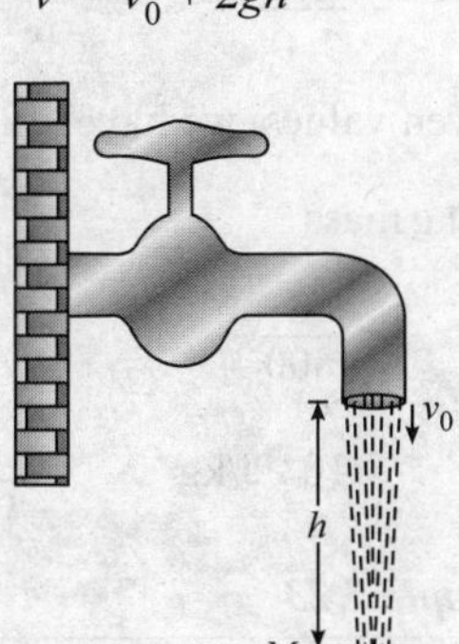

Figure 7.49

If cross section of tap is A then according to the equation of continuity, the cross section at point M (say a) can be given as

$$v_0 A = a\sqrt{v_0^2 + 2gh}$$

or $$a = \frac{v_0 A}{\sqrt{v_0^2 + 2gh}}$$

7.8.5 Force of Reaction due to Ejection of Water

Consider an example shown in figure-7.50. As the water comes out from the vessel with some speed (generally $\sqrt{2gh}$), it has some momentum, which was initially almost zero, when it is in the container. This change in momentum is due to a force on water ejecting in forward direction and the reaction of this force must be experienced by the container and the liquid inside. If the hole has a cross section s and liquid is coming with a speed given by the equation-(7.46), the rate at which liquid comes out is

$$\mu = Av\rho \text{ kg/s}$$

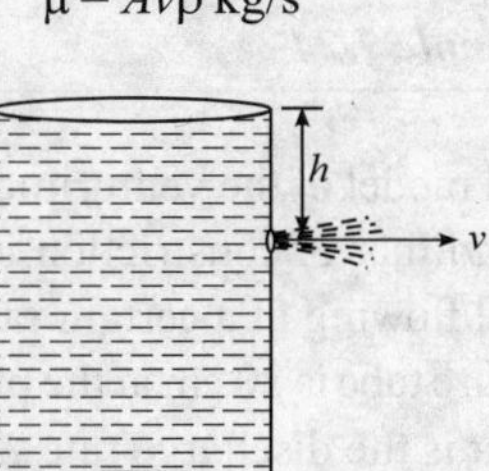

Figure 7.50

The change in momentum per second i.e. the force is

$$F = (Av\rho)\, v$$

$$= Av^2\rho \text{ N}$$

 # *Illustrative Example 7.20*

A water pipe with internal diameter of 1 inch carries water at ground floor of a house with velocity 3 ft/sec and at pressure 25 lb/inch^2. Another pipe of internal diameter 1/2 inch is connected to it and takes water to the first floor 25 feet above ground. What is the velocity and water pressure at first floor ?

Solution

According to Bernoulli's theorem

$$P_G + \rho g h_G + \frac{1}{2}\rho v_G^2 = P_F + \rho g h + \frac{1}{2}\rho v_F^2$$

G is used for ground and F for first floor. Here $h_G = 0$ (reference height), we get

$$P_G + \frac{1}{2}\rho v_G^2 = P_F + \rho g h + \frac{1}{2}\rho v_F^2 \qquad \ldots(7.47)$$

According to continuity equation

$$A_F v_F = A_G v_G \qquad \ldots(7.48)$$

From equation-(7.48),

$$v_F = \frac{A_G v_G}{A_F} = \frac{\pi(0.5)^2 \times 3}{\pi(0.25)^2}$$

$$= 12 \text{ ft/s}$$

From equation-(7.47)

$$P_F = P_G - \frac{1}{2}\rho(v_F^2 - v_G^2) - \rho g h$$

$$= 25 \times 144 - 1.94\left[\frac{1}{2}(144 - 9) + 32 \times 25\right]$$

$$= 1917 \text{ lb/ft}^2 = 13.3 \text{ lb/inch}^2$$

 # *Illustrative Example 7.21*

Water stands up to a height H in a tank, whose side walls are vertical. A hole is made on one of the walls at a depth h below the water surface. Find at what distance from the foot of the wall does the emerging stream of water strike the floor and for what value of h this range is maximum ?

Solution

The situation is shown in figure-7.51.

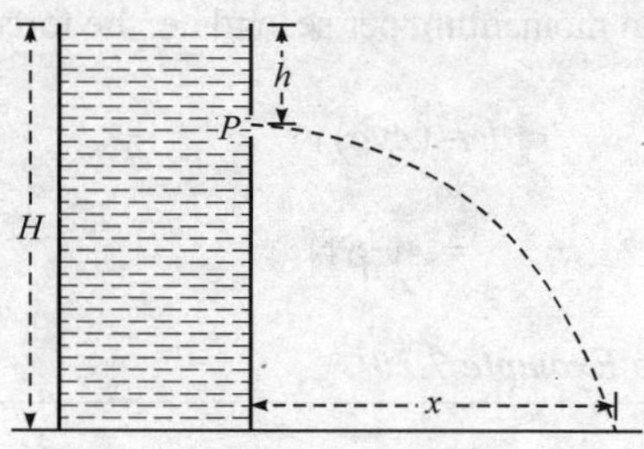

Figure 7.51

Here, we have $v_A = \sqrt{(2gh)}$, ... (7.49)

and $(H-h) = \frac{1}{2} g t^2$ ... (7.50)

The distance x is given by

$$x = v_A \times t \quad \text{... (7.51)}$$

From equation-(7.50),

$$t = \sqrt{\left(\frac{2(H-h)}{g}\right)} \quad \text{... (7.52)}$$

Substituting the value of v_A from equation-(7.49) and the value of t from equation-(7.52) in equation-(7.51), we get

$$x = \sqrt{(2gh)} \times \sqrt{[2(H-h)/g]}$$

$$= 2\sqrt{[h(H-h)]} \quad \text{... (7.53)}$$

The range x will be maximum when $\frac{dx}{dh} = 0$

or $\frac{dx}{dh} = 2\,\frac{1}{2}\,h^{-1/2}(H-h)^{-1/2} - 2h^{1/2}\,\frac{1}{2}\,(H-h)^{1/2} = 0$

Solving we get $h = H/2$

From equation-(7.53), substituting the value of h we get

$$x = 2\sqrt{\frac{H}{2} \times \left(H - \frac{H}{2}\right)} = H$$

Illustrative Example 7.22

In a horizontal pipe line of uniform area of cross section, the pressure falls by 8 N/m² between two points separated by a distance of 1 km. What is the change in kinetic energy per kg of the oil flowing at these points ? Density of oil is 800 kg/m³.

Solution

According to Bernoulli's theorem,

$$P_1 + \frac{1}{2}\rho v_1^2 = P_2 + \frac{1}{2}\rho v_2^2 \text{ (pipe is horizontal)}$$

or $P_1 - P_2 = \frac{1}{2}\rho (v_2^2 - v_1^2)$

or $\frac{P_1 - P_2}{\rho} = \frac{1}{2}(v_2^2 - v_1^2)$

= change in K.E. per kg mass.

or change in K.E. per kg mass of oil

$$= \frac{P_1 - P_2}{\rho}$$

Substituting the given values, we have

Change in K.E. per kg mass

$$= \frac{8}{800}$$

$$= 10^{-2} \text{ J/kg}$$

Illustrative Example 7.23

Air is streaming past a horizontal aeroplane wing such that its speed is 120 m/s over the upper surface and 90 m/s at the lower surface. If the density of air is 1.3 kg/m³, find the difference in pressure between the top and bottom of the wing. If the wing is 10 m long and has an average width 2 m, calculate the gross lift of the wing.

Solution

According to Bernoulli's equation for a horizontal plane, we have

$$p_1 + \frac{1}{2}\rho v_1^2 = p_2 + \frac{1}{2}\rho v_2^2,$$

i.e., $p_1 - p_2 = \frac{1}{2}\rho (v_2^2 - v_1^2)$

So $p_1 - p_2 = \frac{1}{2} \times 1.3 \times (120^2 - 90^2)$

$= 4.1 \times 10^3 \text{ N/m}^2$

Now as Gross lift $= \Delta p \times A$

So Gross lift $= 4.1 \times 10^3 \times (10 \times 2) = 8.2 \times 10^4$ N

Illustrative Example 7.24

In an experimental model of the venturimeter, the diameter of the pipe is 4 cm and that of constriction is 3 cm. With water filling the pipe and flowing at a certain rate the height of the liquids in the pressure tube is 20 cm at the pipe and 15 cm at the constrictions. What is the discharge rate ?

Solution

According to continuity equation

$$A_1 v_1 = A_2 v_2$$

$$(\pi \times 4) v_1 = \pi (3/2)^2 v_2 \quad \text{or} \quad v_2 = \frac{16 v_1}{9}$$

The pressure at the cross-sections are

$$P_1 = 20 \times 1 \times 980 = 19600 \text{ dynes/cm}^2$$

and $$P_2 = 15 \times 1 \times 980 = 14700 \text{ dynes/cm}^2$$

Using Bernoulli's theorem, we have

$$v_2^2 - v_1^2 = \frac{2}{d}(P_1 - P_2)$$

$$\left(\frac{16 v_1}{9}\right)^2 - v_1^2 = \frac{2}{1}(19600 - 14700)$$

Solving we get $\quad v_1 = 112.249$ cm/s

Now discharge rate $= Q = A_1 v_1 = 4\pi \times 67.4$

$= 1411.13 \text{ cm}^3/\text{s}$

Illustrative Example 7.25

A nonviscous liquid of constant density 1000 kg/m^3 flows in a streamline motion along a tube of variable cross section. The tube is kept inclined in the vertical plane as shown in figure-7.52.

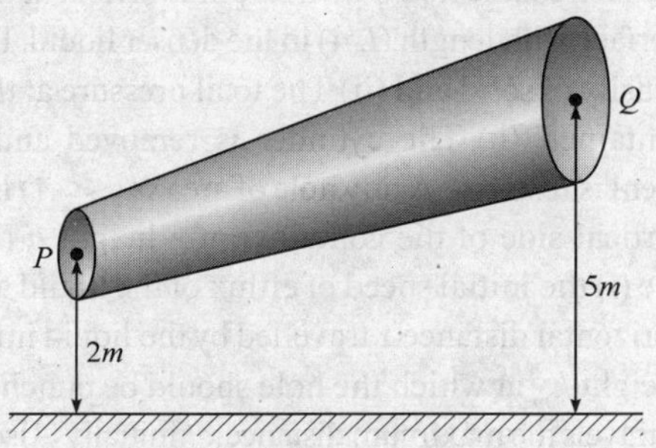

Figure 7.52

The area of cross-section of the tube at two points P and Q at heights of 2 meters and 5 metres are respectively 4×10^{-3} m^2 and 8×10^{-3} m^2. The velocity of the liquid at point P is 1 m/s. Find the work done per unit volume by the pressure and the gravity forces as the liquid flows from point P to Q.

Solution

As fluid is going up work done per unit volume is negative as

So $$\left(\frac{dW}{dV}\right)_g = -\frac{dU}{dV}$$

$$= -\frac{mg(h_2 - h_1)}{V} = -\rho g (h_2 - h_1)$$

$$= -2.94 \times 10^4 \text{ J/m}^3 \qquad \dots (7.54)$$

For ideal fluid from equation of continuity, we have

or $$A_1 v_1 = A_2 v_2$$

So $$v_2 = \frac{A_1 v_1}{A_2} = \frac{4 \times 10^{-3} \times 1}{8 \times 10^{-3}} = 0.5 \text{ m/s} \qquad \dots (7.55)$$

Now as work done per unit volume by pressure,

$$\left(\frac{dW}{dV}\right)_p = \frac{PdV}{dV} = P = (p_1 - p_2)$$

But by Bernoulli's theorem,

$$p_1 + \rho g h_1 + \frac{1}{2}\rho v_1^2 = p_2 + \rho g h_2 + \frac{1}{2}\rho v_2^2$$

So $$\left(\frac{dW}{dV}\right)_p = (p_1 - p_2) = \rho g (h_2 - h_1) + \frac{1}{2}\rho (v_2^2 - v_1^2)$$

Which in the light of equation-(7.53) and (7.54) yields

$$\left(\frac{dW}{dV}\right)_p = 2.94 \times 10^4 + \frac{1}{2} \times 10^3 [(0.5)^2 - 1^2] = 29025 \text{ J/m}^3$$

Illustrative Example 7.26

A Pitot tube figure-7.53 is mounted along the axis of a gas pipeline whose cross-sectional area is equal to S.

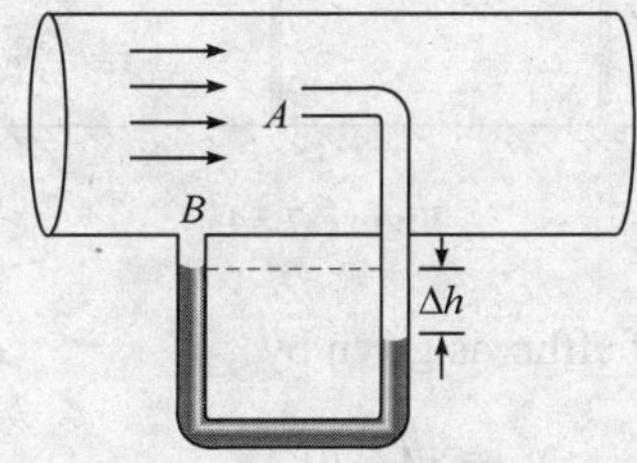

Figure 7.53

Assuming the viscosity to be negligible, find the volume of the gas flowing across the section of the pipe per unit time, if the difference in the liquid columns is equal to Δh, and the densities of the liquid and the gas are ρ_0 and ρ respectively.

Solution

Applying Bernoulli's theorem at points A and B, we have

$$P_A + \frac{1}{2}\rho v_A^2 = P_B + 0 \qquad [\text{As } v_B = 0]$$

or $$\frac{1}{2}\rho v_A^2 = P_B - P_A = \Delta h \rho_0 g$$

$$v_A = \sqrt{\left(\frac{2\Delta h\,\rho_0\,g}{\rho}\right)}$$

Volume of the gas flowing

$$Q = S\,v_A$$

or
$$Q = S\sqrt{\left(\frac{2\Delta h\,\rho_0\,g}{\rho}\right)}$$

Illustrative Example 7.27

A cylindrical tank 1 m in radius rests on a platform 5 m high. Initially the tank is filled with water up to a height of 5 m. A plug whose area is $10^{-4}\,m^2$ is removed from an orifice on the side of the tank at the bottom. Calculate (a) initial speed with which the water flows from the orifice (b) initial speed with which the water strikes the ground and (c) time taken to empty the tank to half its original volume (d) Does the time to be emptied the tank depend upon the height of stand.

Solution

The situation is shown in figure-7.54.

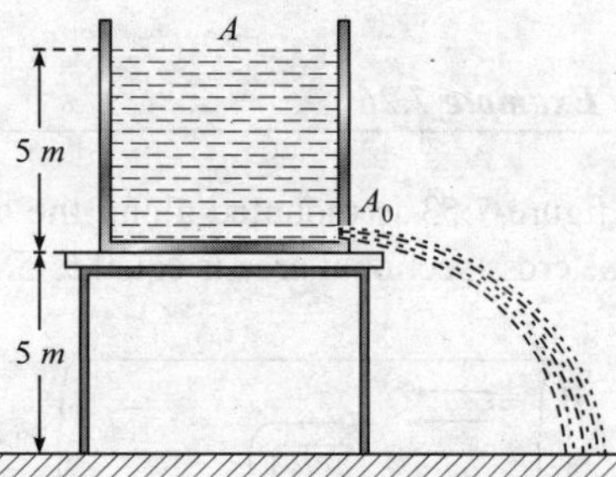

Figure 7.54

(a) As speed of efflux is given by

$$v_H = \sqrt{(2gh)}$$

or
$$= \sqrt{2\times10\times5} \simeq 10\,\text{m/s}$$

(b) As initial vertical velocity of water is zero, so its vertical velocity when it hits the ground

$$v_V = \sqrt{2gh}$$

$$= \sqrt{2\times10\times5} \simeq 10\,\text{m/s}$$

So the initial speed with which water strikes the ground.

$$v = \sqrt{v_H^2 + v_V^2}$$

$$= 10\sqrt{2} = 14.1\,\text{m/s}$$

(c) When the height of water level above the hole is y, velocity of flow will be $v = \sqrt{2gy}$ and so rate of flow

$$\frac{dV}{dt} = A_0 v = A_0\sqrt{2gy}$$

or
$$-A\,dy = (\sqrt{2gy})\,A_0\,dt \qquad [\text{As} \quad dV = -A\,dy]$$

Which on integration improper limits gives

$$\int_H^0 \frac{A\,dy}{\sqrt{2gy}} = \int_0^t A_0\,dt$$

$$t = \frac{A}{A_0}\sqrt{\frac{2}{g}}\,[\sqrt{H} - \sqrt{H'}]$$

So
$$t = \frac{\pi\times1^2}{10^{-4}}\sqrt{\frac{2}{10}}\,[\sqrt{5} - \sqrt{(5/2)}]$$

$$= 9.2\times10^3\,\text{s} \simeq 2.5\,\text{h}$$

(d) No, as expression of t is independent of height of stand.

Illustrative Example 7.28

A container of large uniform cross-section area A resting on a horizontal surface, holds two immiscible, non-viscous and incompressible liquids of densities d and $2d$ each of height $(H/2)$ as shown in figure-7.55. The lower density liquid is open to the atmosphere having pressure p_0. (a) A homogeneous solid cylinder of length L $(L < H/2)$, cross-sectional area $(A/5)$ is immersed such that it floats with its axis vertical at the liquid-liquid interface with length $(L/4)$ in the denser liquid. Determine (i) The density of solid and (ii) The total pressure at the bottom of the container. (b) The cylinder is removed and original arrangement is restored. A tiny hole of area s $(s << A)$ is punched on the vertical side of the container at a height h $(h < H/2)$. Determine (i) the initial speed of efflux of the liquid at the hole (ii) the horizontal distance x travelled by the liquid initially and (iii) the height h_m at which the hole should be punched so that the liquid travels the maximum distance x_m initially. Also calculate x_m.

Solution

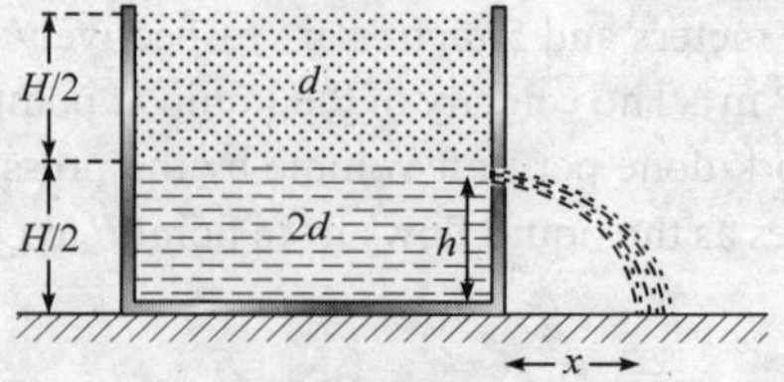

Figure 7.55

(a) (i) As for floating, $W = Th$

$$V\rho g = V_1 d_1 g + V_2 d_2 g$$

or $$L\left(\frac{A}{5}\right)\rho = \left(\frac{3}{4}L\right)\left(\frac{A}{5}\right)d + \left(\frac{1}{4}L\right)\left(\frac{A}{5}\right)2d$$

or $$\rho = \frac{3}{4}d + \frac{2}{4}d = \frac{5}{4}d$$

(ii) Total pressure = p_0 (weight of liquid + weight of solid)/A

Thus $$p = p_0 + \frac{H}{2}dg + \frac{H}{2}2dg + \frac{5}{4}d\times\left(\frac{A}{5}\times L\right)\times g\times\frac{1}{A}$$

or $$p = p_0 + \frac{3}{2}H\,dg + \frac{1}{4}L\,dg + p_0 + \frac{1}{4}(6H+L)\,dg$$

(b) (i) By Bernoulli's theorem for a point just inside and outside the hole

$$p_1 + \frac{1}{2}\rho v_1^2 = p_2 = \frac{1}{2}\rho v_2^2$$

or $$p_0 + \frac{H}{2}dg + \left(\frac{H}{2} - h\right)2dg = p_0 + \frac{1}{2}(2d)v^2$$

or $$g(3H - 4h) = 2v^2$$

or $$v = \sqrt{(g/2)(3H-4h)}$$

(ii) As at the hole vertical velocity of liquid is zero so time taken by it to reach the ground,

$$t = \sqrt{(2h/g)}$$

Here we have $$x = vt = \sqrt{\frac{g}{2}(3H-4h)}\times\sqrt{\frac{2h}{g}}$$

$$= \sqrt{h(3H-4h)} \quad \ldots(7.56)$$

(iii) For x to be maximum x^2 must be maximum, thus we have

$$\frac{d}{dh}(x^2) = 0$$

or $$\frac{d}{dh}(3Hh - 4h^2) = 0$$

or $$3H - 8h = 0,$$

or $$h = (3/8)H$$

Substituting the value of h in equation-(7.56), we get

$$x_{max} = \sqrt{\frac{3H}{8}\left(3H - \frac{3}{2}H\right)} = \frac{3}{4}H$$

Illustrative Example 7.29

The side wall of a wide vertical cylindrical vessel of height h = 75 cm has a narrow vertical slit running all the way down to the bottom of the vessel. The length of the slit is l = 50 cm and the width b = 1.0 mm. With the slit closed, the vessel is filled with water. Find the resultant force of reaction of water flowing out the vessel immediately after the slit is opened.

Solution

Consider an element of length dx of the slit as shown in figure-7.56.

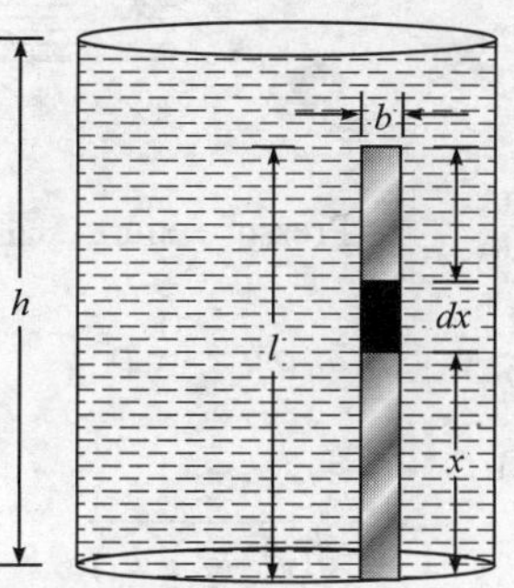

Figure 7.56

Area of the slit = $b\,dx$

Discharge per sec. through this area = $\rho\,(b\,dx)\,v$

Force of reaction due to element dx

$$dF = -\rho\,(b\,dx)\,v^2 \quad \ldots(7.57)$$

Negative sign is used because this is opposite to v.

Applying Bernoulli's theorem at point A, we have

$$P_a = P_a + \rho g(h-x) + \frac{1}{2}\rho v^2$$

or $$v^2 = -2\rho g(h-x) \quad \ldots(7.58)$$

Substituting the value of v^2 from equation-(7.58) in equation-(7.57), we get

$$dF = \rho\,(b\,dx)\,2\rho g(h-x)$$

$$F = 2\rho g b\int_0^l (h-x)\,dx$$

or $$F = 2\rho g b\left[hl - \frac{l^2}{2}\right] = \rho g b l\,[2h - l]$$

Substituting the given values, we get

$$F = (1000)(9.8)(1\times10^{-3})(0.5)[2\times0.75 - 0.5]$$

$$= 5\text{ N}$$

Illustrative Example 7.30

A bent tube is lowered into a water stream as shown in figure-7.57. The velocity of the stream relative to the tube is equal to $v = 2.5$ m/s. The closed upper end of the tube located at the height $h_0 = 12$ cm has a small orifice. To what height h will the water jet spurt ?

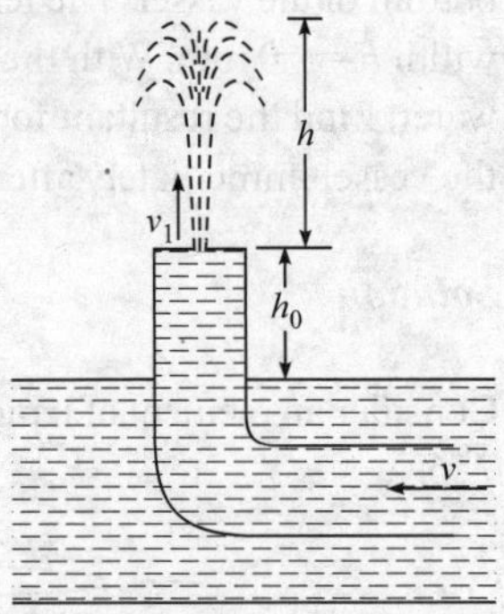

Figure 7.57

Solution

$$(\text{K.E.})_{\text{lower end}} = \text{Pressure energy} + \text{K.E.}$$

or
$$\frac{1}{2}\rho v^2 = h_0 \rho g + \frac{1}{2}\rho v_1^2$$

Solving it, we get

$$v_1 = \sqrt{(v^2 - 2gh_0)} \qquad \ldots(7.59)$$

The kinetic energy at the opening is converted into potential energy. Thus

$$\frac{1}{2}\rho v_1^2 = \rho g h \quad \text{or} \quad v_1^2 = 2gh \qquad \ldots(7.60)$$

From equation-(7.59) and (7.60), we get

$$v^2 - 2gh_0 = 2gh$$

$$h = \frac{v^2}{2g} - h_0 \qquad \ldots(7.61)$$

Now
$$h = \frac{(2.5)^2}{2\times 9.8} - 0.12 = 0.20\text{ m}$$

Illustrative Example 7.31

What work should be done in order to squeeze all water from a horizontally located cylinder figure-7.58 during the time t by means of a constant force acting on the piston ? The volume of water in the cylinder is equal to V, the cross-sectional area of the orifice is s, with s being considerably less than the piston area. The friction and viscosity are negligibly small.

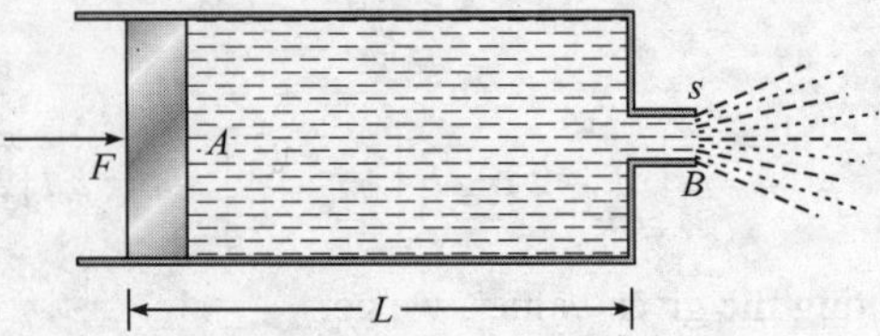

Figure 7.58

Solution

Work done $\qquad = F\cdot L \qquad \ldots(7.62)$

If v be the velocity at point B, then applying Bernoulli's theorem at points A and B, we have

$$P_A + P_0 = \frac{1}{2}\rho v^2 + P_0$$

Force on piston
$$F = PS = \frac{1}{2}\rho v^2 S \qquad \ldots(7.63)$$

Discharge through orifice $= s\,v$ per unit time

Discharge during time $t = s\,v\,t$

This discharge is equal to V. Thus

$$V = s\,v\,t$$

or
$$v = (V/s\,t) \qquad \ldots(7.64)$$

From equation-(7.63) and (7.64)

$$F = \frac{1}{2}\rho\left(\frac{V}{st}\right)^2 S$$

Thus work done is

$$W = FL = \frac{1}{2}\rho\left(\frac{V}{st}\right)^2 SL$$

or
$$= \frac{1}{2}\rho\left(\frac{V}{st}\right)^2 V$$

or
$$= \frac{1}{2}\rho\frac{V^3}{s^2t^2} \qquad \ldots(7.65)$$

Illustrative Example 7.32

The horizontal bottom of a wide vessel with an ideal fluid has a round orifice of radius R_1 over which a round closed cylinder is mounted, whose radius $R_2 > R_1$ figure-7.59. The clearance between the cylinder and the bottom of the vessel is very small, the fluid density is ρ. Find the static pressure of the fluid in the clearance as a function of the distance r from the axis of the orifice (and the cylinder), if the height of the fluid is equal to h.

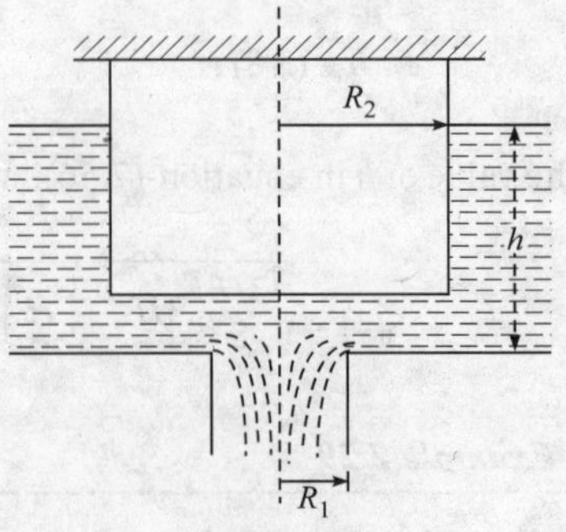

Figure 7.59

Solution

In the figure-7.60 shown, we consider the three section 1, 2 and 3 at radius R_1, r and R_2 respectively. Let D be the width of the gap. Applying continuity equation, we have

$$2\pi R_1 D v_1 = 2\pi R_2 D v_2 = 2\pi r D v$$

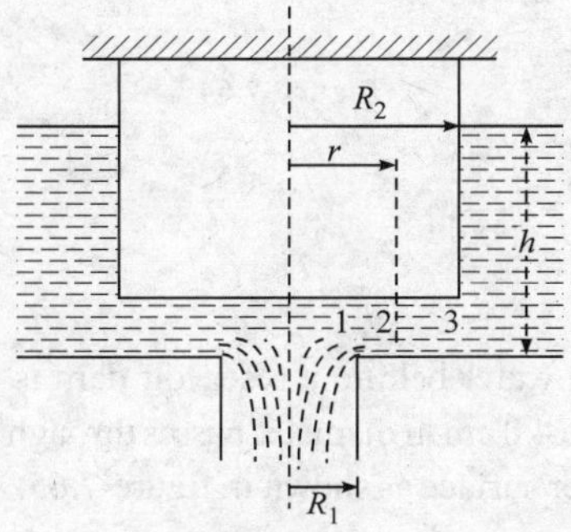

Figure 7.60

Where v is the water flow velocity at a distance r from axis. Here, we get

$$v_1 R_1 = v_2 R_2 = v r \quad \dots(7.66)$$

Applying Bernoulli's equation between these points, we have

$$P + \frac{1}{2}\rho v^2 = P_a + \frac{1}{2}\rho v_1^2 = P_2 + \frac{1}{2}\rho v_2^2$$

Where P_a = atmospheric pressure

Now $$P + \frac{1}{2}\rho v^2 = P_a + \frac{1}{2}\rho v_1^2$$

or $$P = P_a + \frac{1}{2}\rho v_1^2 - \frac{1}{2}\rho v^2$$

or $$P = P_a + \frac{1}{2}\rho v_1^2\left[1 - \left(\frac{v}{v_1}\right)^2\right]$$

or $$P = P_a + \frac{1}{2}\rho v_1^2\left[1 - \left(\frac{R_1}{r}\right)^2\right] \quad \left[\text{As } \frac{v}{v_1} = \frac{R_1}{r}\right] \dots(7.67)$$

$$P = P_a + \rho g h\left[1 - \frac{R_1^2}{r^2}\right] \quad [\text{As } v_1 = \sqrt{2gh}\,] \dots(7.68)$$

Web Reference of Video Lectures at www.physicsgalaxy.com
Age Group - High School Physics | Age 17-19 Years
Section - PROPERTIES OF MATTER
Topic - Fluid Dynamics
Module Number - 13 to 23

Practice Exercise 7.3

(i) A river of width 12 m flowing at 20 kph mixes with another river of width 8 m flowing at 16 kph and spreads in another stream of width 16 m. Find the flow velocity of water after mixing assuming the depth of river are same.

[23 kph]

(ii) A siphon has a uniform circular base of diameter $\frac{8}{\sqrt{\pi}}$ cm with its crest A 1.8 m above water level as in figure-7.61. Find (a) velocity of flow (b) discharge rate of the flow in m³/s (c) absolute pressure at the crest level A. [Use $P_0 = 10^5$ N/m² & $g = 10$ m/s²]

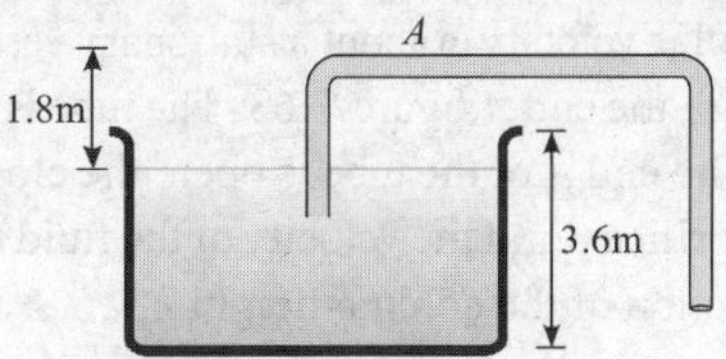

Figure 7.61

[(a) $6\sqrt{2}$ m/s, (b) $9.6\sqrt{2} \times 10^{-3}$ m³/s (c) 4.6×10^4 N/m²]

(iii) On the opposite sides of a wide vertical vessel filled with water two identical holes are opened, each having cross-sectional area S. The height difference between them is equal to Δh. Find the resultant force of reaction of the water flowing out of the vessel.

[$F = (2\,\Delta h\,\rho\,g\,S)$]

(iv) Water flows through a horizontal tube as shown in figure-7.62. If the difference of heights of water column in the vertical tubes is 2 cm, and the areas of cross-section at A and B are 4 cm² and 2 cm² respectively, find the rate of flow of water across any section. Take $g = 10$ m/s².

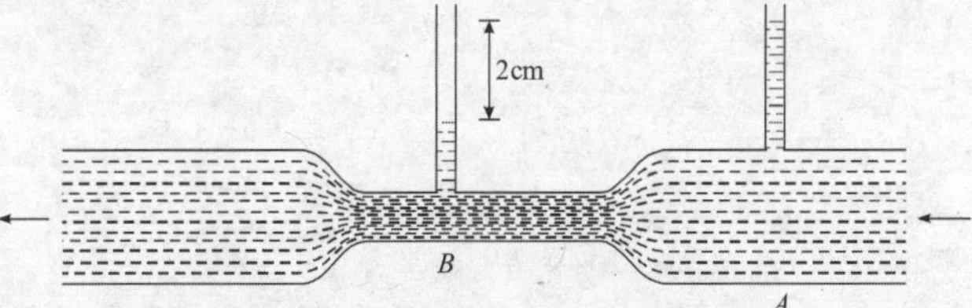

Figure 7.62

[146.05 cm³/s]

(v) A cylindrical vessel filled with water upto a height of 2 m stands on a horizontal plane. The side wall of the vessel has a plugged circular hole touching the bottom. Find the minimum diameter of the hole so that the vessel begins to move on the floor if the plug is removed. The coefficient of friction between the bottom of the vessel and the plane is 0.4, and total mass of water plus vessel is 100 kg.

[0.1128 m]

(vi) Water is flowing through two horizontal pipes of different diameters which are connected together. In the first pipe the speed of water is 4 m/s and the pressure is 2.0×10^4 N/m^2. Calculate the speed and pressure of water in the second pipe. The diameters of the pipes are 3 cm and 6 cm respectively.

[2.75×10^4 N/m^2]

(vii) A horizontal oriented tube *AB* of length *l* rotates with a constant angular velocity ω about a stationary vertical axis *OO'* passing though the end *A* figure-7.63. The tube is filled with an ideal fluid. The end *A* of the tube is open, the closed end *B* has a very small orifice. Find the velocity of the fluid relative to the tube as a function of the column height *h*.

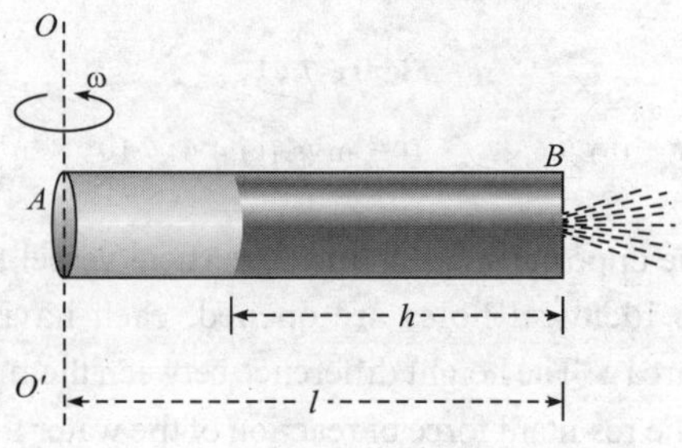

Figure 7.63

[$\omega h \sqrt{\left(\frac{2l}{h} - 1\right)}$]

(viii) For the arrangement shown is figure-7.64, find the time interval after which the water jet ceases to cross the wall. Area of the tank is *A* and area of orifice is *a*.

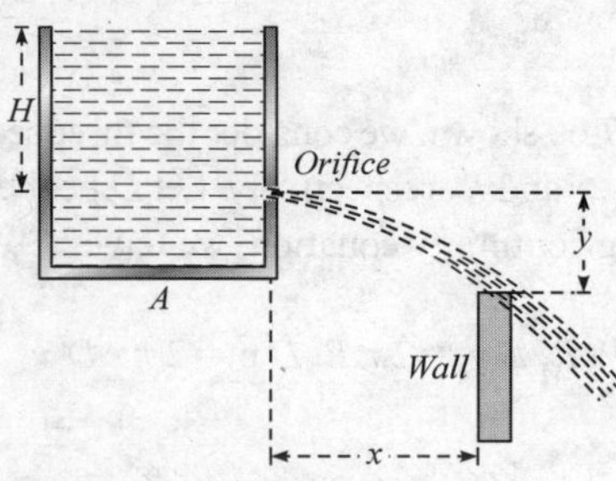

Figure 7.64

[$\frac{A}{a}\sqrt{\left(\frac{2}{g}\right)}\left[\sqrt{H} - \sqrt{\frac{x^2}{4y}}\right]$]

(ix) The fresh water behind a reservoir dam is 15 m deep. A horizontal pipe 4.0 cm in diameter passes through the dam 6.0 m below the water surface as shown in figure-7.65. A plug secures the pipe opening. (a) Find the minimum friction force between the plug and pipe wall to that plug does not eject out. (b) The plug is removed. What volume of water flows out of the pipe in 3.0 hour ? Take $g = 10$ m/s^2.

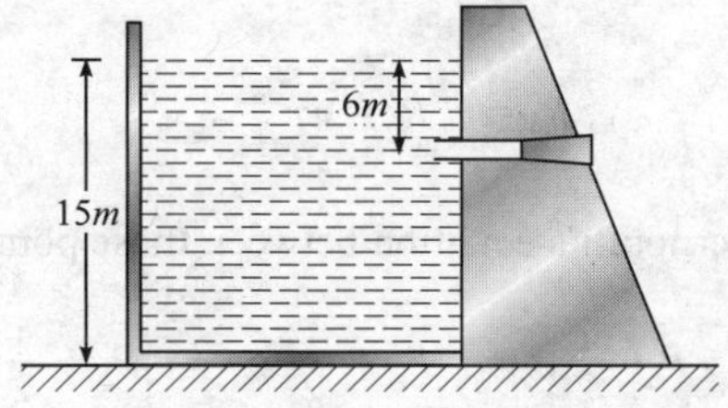

Figure 7.65

[(a) 75.36 N; (b) 148.59 m^3]

* * * * *

Discussion Question

Q7-1 Why does a uniform wooden stick or log float horizontally ? If enough iron is added to one end, it will float vertically; explain this also.

Q7-2 A block of wood is floating on water at 0° C with a certain volume V outside the water-level. The temperature of water is slowly raised from 0°C to 20°C. How will the volume V change with rise in temperature?

Q7-3 Explain why a soft plastic bag weighs the same when empty or when filled with air at atmospheric pressure? Would the weights be the same if measured in vacuum?

Q7-4 Explain why an air bubble in water rises from bottom to top and grows in size ?

Q7-5 A beaker containing water is placed on the pan of a balance which shows a reading of M.g. A lump of sugar of mass mg and volume v is now suspended by a thread (from an independent support) in such a way that it is completely immersed in water without touching the beaker and without any overflow of water. How will the reading change as time passes on ?

Q7-6 A smooth air-tight piston connected to a spring of force constant k and unstretched length l separates two regions of a tube as shown in figure. Region A is evacuated and region B is open to the atmosphere. How will you use this set up to determine the atmospheric pressure ?

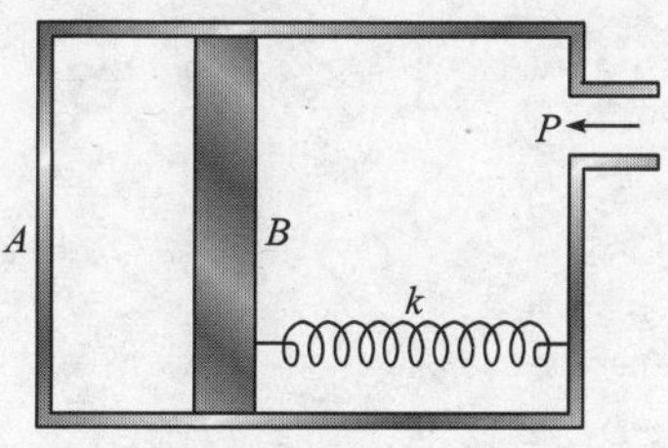

Figure 7.66

Q7-7 A ball floats on the surface of water in a container exposed to atmosphere. Will the ball remain immersed at its initial depth or will it sink or rise somewhat if the container is shifted to moon.

Q7-8 A bucket of water is suspended from a spring balance. Does the reading of balance change (a) when a piece of stone suspended from a string is immersed in the water without touching the bucket ? (b) when a piece of iron or cork is put in the water in the bucket ?

Q7-9 A boy is carrying a fish in one hand and a bucket full of water in the other hand. He then places the fish in the bucket thinking that in accordance with Archimedes' principle he is now carrying less weight as the weight of the fish will reduce due to upthrust. Is he right ?

Q7-10 A piece of ice is floating in water. What will happen to the level of water when all ice melts ? What will happen if the beaker is filled not with water but with liquid (a) denser than water (b) lighter than water ?

Q7-11 A man is sitting in a boat which is floating in a pond. If the man drinks some water from the pond, what will happen to the level of water in the pond ?

Q7-12 A bucket of water is suspended from a spring balance. Does the reading of balance change (a) when a piece of stone suspended from a string is immersed in the water without touching the bucket? (b) when a piece of iron or cork is put in the water in the bucket?

Q7-13 A vessel containing water is given a constant acceleration towards the right, along a straight horizontal path. Which of the diagrams (Figure-7.67) represents the surface of the liquid ?

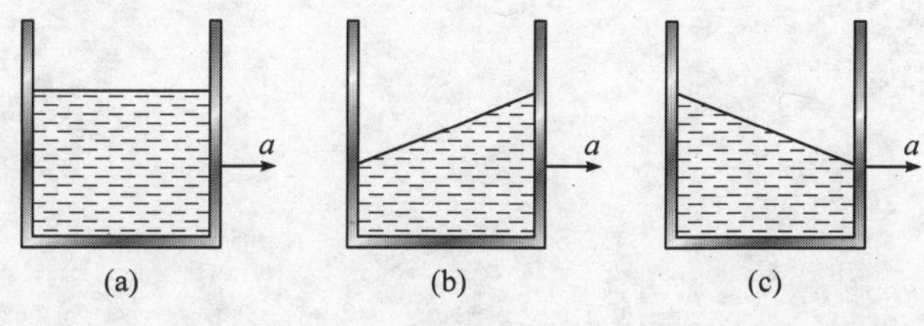

Figure 7.67

Q7-14 A beaker exactly full of water has an ice piece floating in it. As the cube melts what happens to the water level if (a) the cube contains on air bubble (b) the cube contains (i) a lead piece and (ii) a cork piece.

Q7-15 Two vessels have the same base area but different shapes. The first vessel takes twice the volume of water that the second vessel requires to fill up to a particular common height. Is the force exerted by water on the base of the vessel the same in the two cases ? If so, why do the vessels filled with water to that same height give different readings on a weighing scale ?

Q7-16 A boat containing some piece of material is floating in a pond. What will happen to the level of water in the pond if on unloading the pieces in the pond, the piece (a) floats (b) sinks ?

Q7-17 A weightless balloon is filled in water. What will be its apparent weight when weighed in water.

Q7-18 Explain why a small iron needle sinks in water while a large iron ship floats.

Q7-19 A block of wood floats in a bucket of water in a lift. Will the block sink more or less if the lift starts accelerating up.

Q7-20 A bottle full of a liquid is fitted with a tight cork. Explain why a slight blow on the cork may be sufficient to break the bottle ?

Q7-21 A metal cube is floating in mercury in a bottle. The bottle is connected to a vacuum pump so that all the air in it is evacuated. Find whether the submerged part of metal cube will increase or decrease. Explain why ?

* * * * *

Conceptual MCQs Single Option Correct

7-1 A body of density ρ is dropped from rest from a height h into a lake of density σ ($\sigma > \rho$). Neglecting all dissipative effect, the acceleration of body while it is in the lake is :

(A) $g\left(\frac{\sigma}{\rho}-1\right)$ upwards (B) $g\left(\frac{\sigma}{\rho}-1\right)$ downwards

(C) $g\left(\frac{\sigma}{\rho}\right)$ upwards (D) $g\left(\frac{\sigma}{\rho}\right)$ downwards

7-2 A piece of ice, with a stone frozen inside it, is floating in water contained in a beaker. When the ice melts, the level of water in the beaker :

(A) Rises
(B) Falls
(C) Remains unchanged
(D) Falls at first and then rises to the same height as before

7-3 Bernoulli's Theorem is based on :

(A) Law of Conservation of Energy
(B) Law of Conservation of Mass
(C) Law of Conservation of Momentum
(D) Law of Conservation of Angular Momentum

7-4 A wooden block, with a coin placed on its top, floats in water as shown in figure-7.68. The distance l and h are shown there. After some time the coin falls into the water. Then :

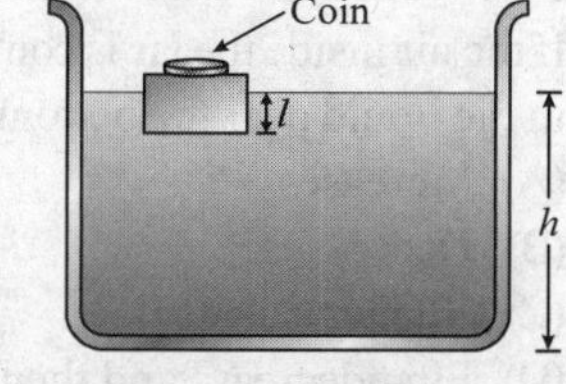

Figure 7.68

(A) l decreases and h increases
(B) l increases and h decreases
(C) Both l and h increase
(D) Both l and h decreases

7-5 A block of wood floats in a liquid in a beaker with 3/4ths of the its volume submerged under the liquid. If the beaker is placed in an enclosure that is falling freely under gravity, the block will :

(A) Float with 3/4ths of its volume submerged
(B) Float completely submerged
(C) Float with any fraction of its volume submerged
(D) Sink to the bottom

7-6 Which one of the following statements is correct ? When a fluid passes through the narrow part of non-uniform pipe :

(A) Its velocity and pressure both increase
(B) Its velocity and pressure both decrease
(C) Its velocity decreases but its pressure increase
(D) Its velocity increases but its pressure decreases

7-7 A solid iron ball and a solid aluminium ball of the same diameter are released together on a deep lake. Which ball will reach the bottom first ?

(A) Aluminium ball
(B) Iron ball
(C) Both balls will reach the bottom at the same time
(D) The aluminium ball will never reach the bottom and will remain suspended in the lake

7-8 A cube of ice is floating in a liquid of relative density 1.25 contained in a beaker. When the ice melts, the level of the liquid in the beaker ?

(A) Rises
(B) Falls
(C) Remains unchanged
(D) Falls at first and then rises to the same height as before

7-9 A boat carrying a number of large stones is floating in a water tank. What will happen to the water level if the stones are unloaded into the water ? The water level :

(A) Remains unchanged
(B) Rises
(C) Falls
(D) Rises till half the number of stones are unloaded and then begins to fall

7-10 A body floats in a liquid contained in a vessel. The vessel falls vertically with an acceleration a ($< g$). If V_i and V_f be the initial and final volume of the body immersed in the liquid then :

(A) $V_i > V_f$ (B) $V_i < V_f$
(C) $V_i = V_f$ (D) Data Insufficient

7-11 A medical suspension bottle is shaken well to disperse the sediment uniformly and immediate, the bottle is placed on a digital weighing machine gently. If W be the actual combined weight of the bottle and the medicine, then the weight recorded by the weighing machine immediately after placing the bottle will be :

(A) More than W (B) Less than W
(C) Equal to W (D) Nothing can be said

7-12 Two vessels A and B of cross-sections as shown contain a liquid up to the same height. As the temperature rises, the liquid pressure at the bottom (neglecting expansion of the vessels) will :

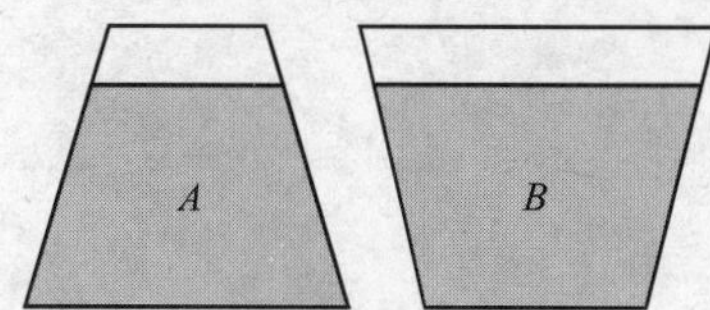

Figure 7.69

(A) Increase in A, decrease in B
(B) Increase in B, decrease in A
(C) Increase in both A and B but more in A
(D) Increase in both A and B equally

7-13 It is found that the measured weight ($\neq$ zero) of an empty thin polythene bag has not changed when the bag is filled with air. Two students were asked reason for this :

Saara: Air is so light that weighing machine need to have large precision to measure weight of filled air.

Vasu: Force of buoyance increases by the same amount as the weight of added air.

(A) Saara is correct, Vasu is wrong
(B) Vasu is correct, Saara is wrong
(C) Both are correct
(D) Both are wrong

7-14 A container contains liquid upto height H and kept on a horizontal frictionless surface as shown in the figure-7.70. At $t = 0$, the container is given a constant acceleration a_0 along positive x-axis. The pressure at point P depends upon :

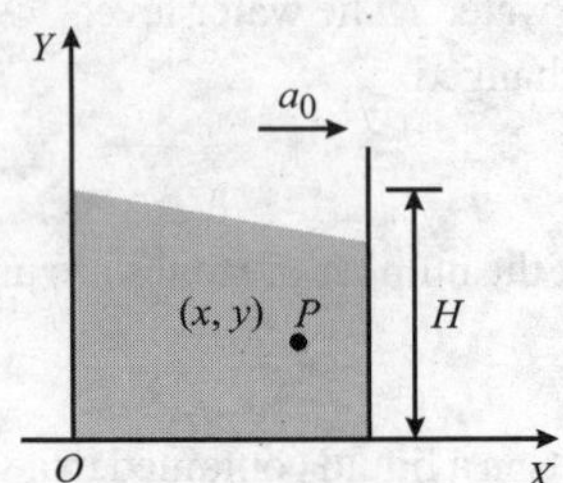

Figure 7.70

(A) Only on the x-co-ordinate of the point P
(B) Only on the y-co-ordinate of the point P
(C) On both x and y co-ordinates of the point P
(D) None

7-15 The weight of an aeroplane flying in air is balanced by :
(A) Upthrust of the air which will be equal to the weight of the air having the same volume as the plane
(B) Force due to the pressure difference between the upper and lower surfaces of the wings, created by different air speed on the surface
(C) Vertical component of the thrust created by air currents striking the lower surface of the wings
(D) Force due to the reaction of gases ejected by the revolving propeller

7-16 A closed rectangular tank is completely filled with water and is accelerated horizontally with an acceleration a towards right. Pressure is (i) maximum at, and (ii) minimum at :

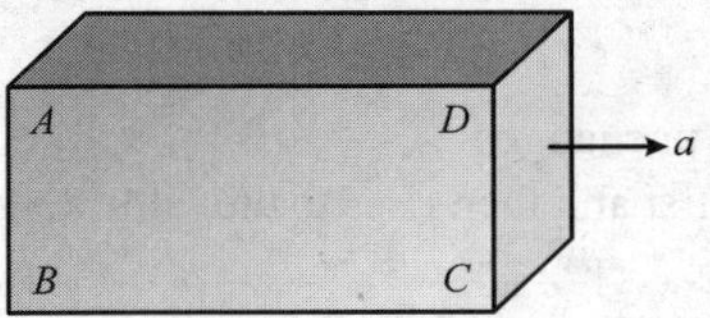

Figure 7.71

(A) (i) B (ii) D
(B) (i) C (ii) D
(C) (i) B (ii) C
(D) (i) B (ii) A

7-17 A beaker containing a liquid is kept inside a big closed jar. If the air inside the jar is continuously pumped out, the pressure in the liquid near the bottom of the liquid will :
(A) Increases
(B) Decreases
(C) Remain constant
(D) First decrease and then increase

* * * * *

Numerical MCQs Single Options Correct

7-1 A large open tank has two small holes in its vertical wall as shown in figure-7.72. One is a square hole of side 'L' at a depth '$4y$' from the top and the other is a circular hole of radius 'R' at a depth 'y' from the top. When the tank is completely filled with water, the quantities of water flowing out per second from both holes are the same. Then, 'R' is equal to :

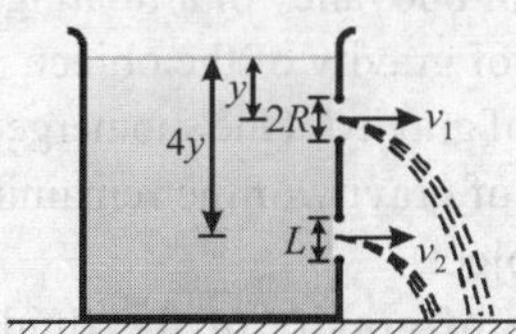

Figure 7.72

(A) $\frac{L}{\sqrt{2\pi}}$ (B) $2\pi L$

(C) $\sqrt{\frac{2}{\pi}}.L$ (D) $\frac{L}{2\pi}$

7-2 A cubical block of copper of side 10 cm is floating in a vessel containing mercury. Water is poured into the vessel so that the copper block just gets submerged. The height of water column is : ($\rho_{Hg} = 13.6$ g/cc, $\rho_{Cu} = 7.3$ g/cc, $\rho_{water} = 1$ gm/cc)

(A) 1.25 cm (B) 2.5 cm

(C) 5 cm (D) 7.5 cm

7-3 A block of silver of mass 4 kg hanging from a string is immersed in a liquid of relative density 0.72. If relative density of silver is 10, then tension in the string will be : (Take $g = 10$ m/s^2)

(A) 37.12 N (B) 42.34 N

(C) 73 N (D) 21.15 N

7-4 A tube in vertical plane is shown in figure-7.73. It is filled with a liquid of density ρ and its end B is closed. Then the force exerted by the fluid on the tube at end B will be.
[Neglect atmospheric pressure and assume the radius of the tube to be negligible in comparison to l] :

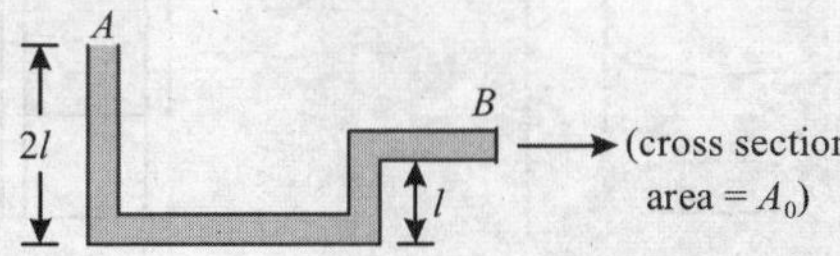

Figure 7.73

(A) $P_{atm} A_0$ (B) $(P_{atm} + \rho g l) A_0$

(C) $(P_{atm} + 2\rho g l) A_0$ (D) $(P_{atm} + 4\rho g l) A_0$

7-5 In the figure shown-7.74 water is filled in a symmetrical container. Four pistons of equal area A are used at the four opening to keep the water in equilibrium. Now an additional force each of magnitude F is applied at each piston. The increase in the pressure at the centre of the container due to this addition is :

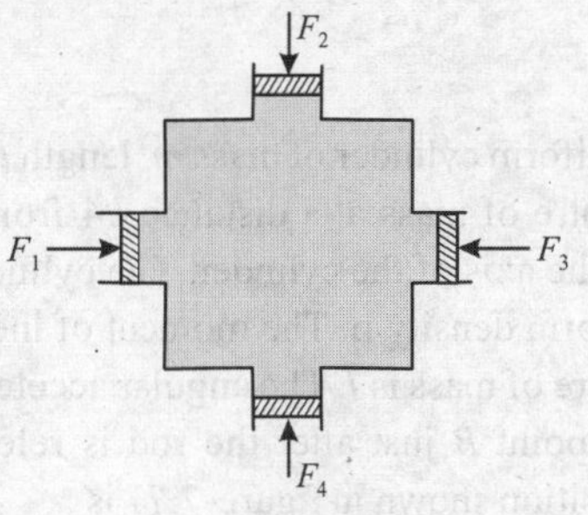

Figure 7.74

(A) $\frac{F}{A}$ (B) $\frac{2F}{A}$

(C) $\frac{4F}{A}$ (D) 0

7-6 A block of iron is kept at the bottom of a bucket full of water at 2°C. The water exerts bouyant force on the block. If the temperature of water is increased by 1°C the temperature of iron block also increases by 1°C. The bouyant force on the block by water :

(A) will increase

(B) will decrease

(C) will not change

(D) may decrease or increase depending on the values of their coefficient of expansion

7-7 A U-tube of base length "l" filled with same volume of two liquids of densities ρ and 2ρ is moving with an acceleration "a" on the horizontal plane. If the height difference between the two surfaces (open to atmosphere) becomes zero, then the height h is given by :

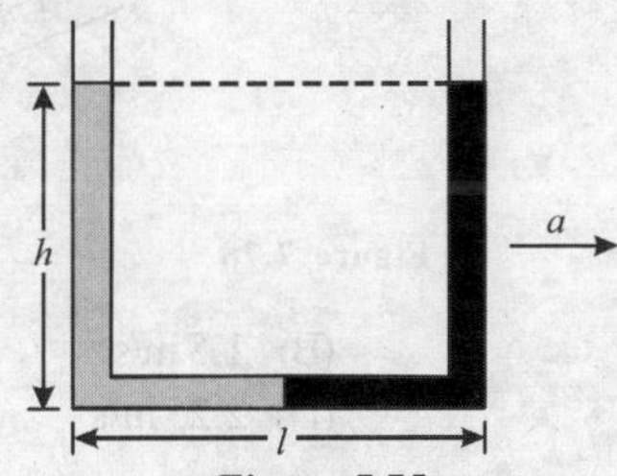

Figure 7.75

(A) $\frac{a}{2g}l$ (B) $\frac{3a}{2g}l$

(C) $\frac{a}{g}l$ (D) $\frac{2a}{3g}l$

7-8 The velocity of the liquid coming out of a small hole of a large vessel containing two different liquids of densities 2ρ and ρ as shown in figure-7.76 is :

(A) $\sqrt{6gh}$

(B) $2\sqrt{gh}$

(C) $2\sqrt{2gh}$

(D) $\sqrt{gh}$

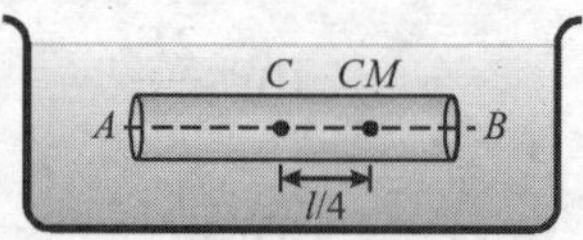

Figure-7.76

7-9 A non uniform cylinder of mass m, length l and radius r is having its centre of mass at a distance $l/4$ from the centre C and lying on the axis of the cylinder. The cylinder is kept in a liquid of uniform density ρ. The moment of inertia of the rod about the centre of mass is I. The angular acceleration of point A relative to point B just after the rod is released from the horizontal position shown in figure-7.77 is :

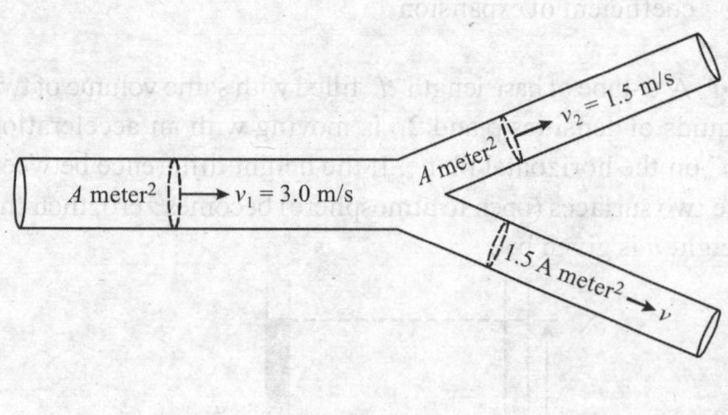

Figure 7.77

(A) $\frac{\pi\rho g l^2 r^2}{I}$ (B) $\frac{\pi\rho g l^2 r^2}{4I}$

(C) $\frac{\pi\rho g l^2 r^2}{2I}$ (D) $\frac{3\pi\rho g l^2 r^2}{4I}$

7-10 An incompressible liquid flows through a horizontal tube as shown in the figure-7.78. Then the velocity 'v' of the fluid is :

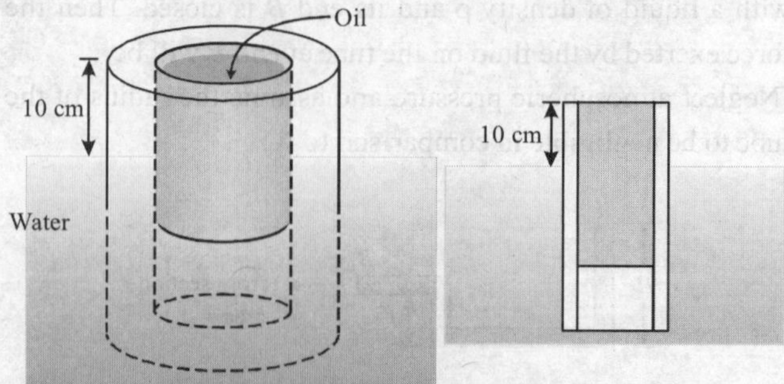

Figure 7.78

(A) 3.0 m/s (B) 1.5 m/s

(C) 1.0 m/s (D) 2.25 m/s

7-11 An unsymmetrical sprinkler shown in the top view of the setup has frictionless shaft and equal fluid flows through each nozzle with a velocity of 10 m/sec relative to nozzle. If the shaft is rotating at constant angular speed then its angular speed of rotation is :

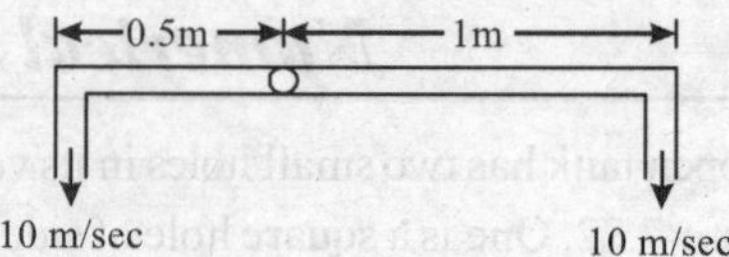

Figure 7.79

(A) 3 rad/s (B) 4 rad/s

(C) 2 rad/s (D) 10 rad/s

7-12 The centre of buoyancy of a floating object is :

(A) At the centre of gravity of the object.

(B) At the centre of gravity of the submerged part of the object.

(C) At the centre of gravity of the remaining part outside the fluid of the object.

(D) At the centre of gravity of the fluid displaced by the submerged part of the object.

7-13 A uniform rod OB of length $1m$, cross-sectional area $0.012m^2$ and relative density 2.0 is free to rotate about O in vertical plane. The rod is held with a horizontal string AB which can withstand a maximum tension of $45N$. The rod and string system is kept in water as shown in figure-7.80. The maximum value of angle α which the rod can make with vertical without breaking the string is : (Take $g = 10$ m/s^2)

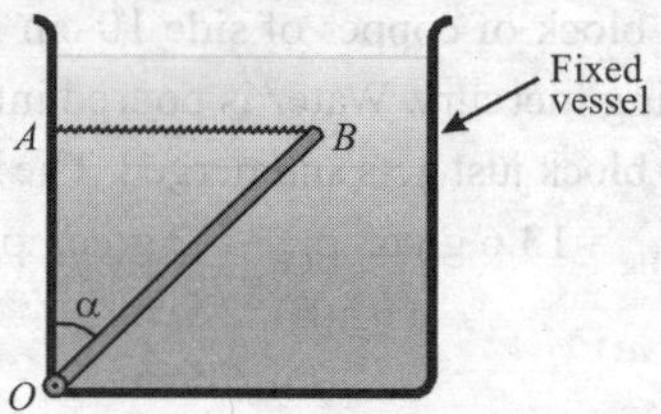

Figure 7.80

(A) 45° (B) 37°

(C) 53° (D) 60°

7-14 A tube with both ends open floats vertically in water. Oil with a density 800 kg/m^3 is poured into the tube. The tube is filled with oil upto the top end in equilibrium state. The portion out of the water is of length 10 cm. Find the length of oil column :

Figure 7.81

(A) 50 cm (B) 60 cm

(C) 90 cm (D) 100 cm

7-15 Following are some statements about buoyant force: (Liquid is of uniform density)

(i) Buoyant force depends upon orientation of the concerned body inside the liquid.

(ii) Buoyant force depends upon the density of the body immersed.

(iii) Buoyant force depends on the fact whether the system is on moon or on the earth.

(iv) Buoyant force depends upon the depth at which the body (fully immersed in the liquid) is placed inside the liquid.

Of these statements :

(A) Only (i), (ii) and (iv) are correct.
(B) Only (ii) is correct.
(C) Only (iii) and (iv) are correct.
(D) (i), (ii) and (iv) are incorrect.

7-16 An ideal fluid is flowing through the given tubes which is placed on a horizontal surface. If the liquid has velocities V_A and V_B, and pressures P_A and P_B at points A and B respectively, then the correct relation is (A and B are at same height from ground level, the figure shown-7.82 is as if the system is seen from the top) :

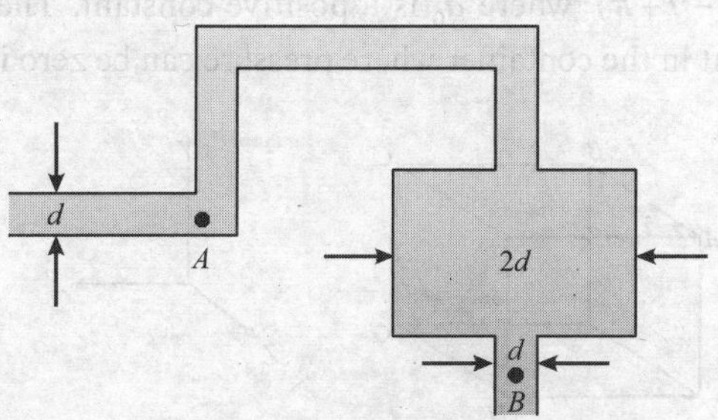

Figure 7.82

(A) $V_A > V_B, P_A < P_B$ (B) $V_A < V_B, P_A > P_B$
(C) $V_A = V_B, P_A = P_B$ (D) $V_A > V_B, P_A = P_B$

7-17 There is a small hole in the bottom of a fixed container containing a liquid upto height 'h'. The top of the liquid as well as the hole at the bottom are exposed to atmosphere. As the liquid comes out of the hole. (Area of the hole is 'a' and that of the top surface is 'A') :

(A) The top surface of the liquid accelerates with acceleration = g

(B) The top surface of the liquid accelerates with acceleration = $g\dfrac{a^2}{A^2}$

(C) The top surface of the liquid retards with retardation = $g\dfrac{a}{A}$

(D) The top surface of the liquid retards with retardation = $\dfrac{ga^2}{A^2}$

7-18 A fixed container of height 'H' with large cross-sectional area 'A' is completely filled with water. Two small orifice of cross-sectional area 'a' are made, one at the bottom and the other on the vertical side of the container at a distance $H/2$ from the top of the container. Find the time taken by the water level to reach a height of $H/2$ from the bottom of the container.

(A) $\dfrac{2A}{3a}\sqrt{\dfrac{2H}{g}}$ (B) $\dfrac{2A}{3a}(\sqrt{2}-1)\sqrt{\dfrac{H}{g}}$

(C) $\dfrac{3A}{2a}(\sqrt{2}-1)\sqrt{\dfrac{H}{g}}$ (D) $\dfrac{3A}{2a}\sqrt{\dfrac{2H}{g}}$

7-19 The manometer shown below is used to measure the difference in water level between the two tanks. Calculate this difference for the conditions indicated.

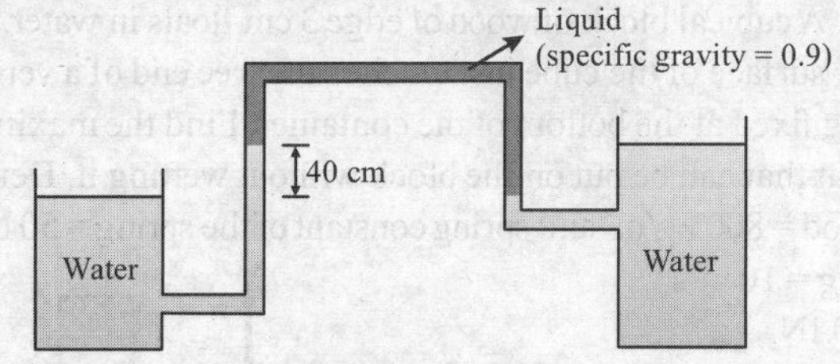

Figure 7.83

(A) 2 cm (B) 4 cm
(C) 6 cm (D) 8 cm

7-20 A cylindrical vessel filled with water is released on a fixed inclined surface of angle θ as shown in figure-7.84. The friction coefficient of surface with vessel is μ (< tan θ). Then the constant angle made by the surface of water with the incline will be: (Neglect the viscosity of liquid)

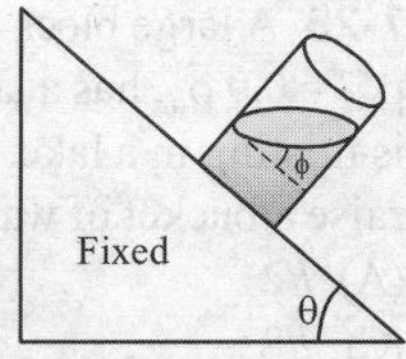

Figure 7.84

(A) $\tan^{-1}\mu$ (B) $\theta - \tan^{-1}\mu$
(C) $\theta + \tan^{-1}\mu$ (D) $\cot^{-1}\mu$

7-21 A copper piece of mass 10 g is suspended by a vertical spring. The spring elongates 1 cm over its natural length to keep the piece in equilibrium. A beaker containing water is now placed below the piece so as to immerse the piece completely in water. Find the approximate elongation of the spring. Density of copper = 9000 kg/m^3. Take g = 10 m/s^2.

(A) 0.45cm (B) 0.89cm
(C) 1.02cm (D) 1.86cm

7-22 A vessel contains oil (density = 0.8 gm/cm^3) over mercury (density = 13.6 gm/cm^3). A uniform sphere floats with half its volume immersed in mercury and the other half in oil. The density of the material of sphere in gm/cm^3 is:

(A) 3.3 (B) 6.4
(C) 7.2 (D) 12.8

7-23 A block is partially immersed in a liquid and the vessel is accelerating upwards with an acceleration "a". The block is observed by two observers O_1 and O_2, one at rest and the other accelerating with an acceleration "a" upward. The total buoyant force on the block is :

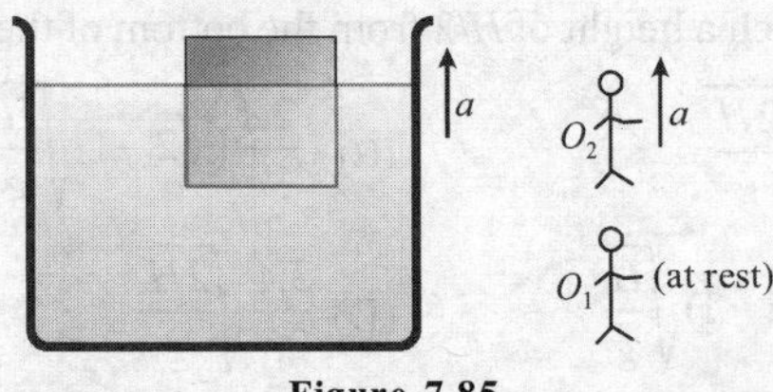

Figure 7.85

(A) same for O_1 and O_2 (B) greater for O_1 than O_2
(C) greater for O_2 than O_1 (D) data is not sufficient

7-24 A cubical block of wood of edge 3 cm floats in water. The lower surface of the cube just touches the free end of a vertical spring fixed at the bottom of the container. Find the maximum weight that can be put on the block without wetting it. Density of wood = 800 kg/m^3 and spring constant of the spring = 50 N/m. Take g = 10 m/s^2.

(A) 0.1N
(B) 0.35N
(C) 0.5N
(D) 0.7N

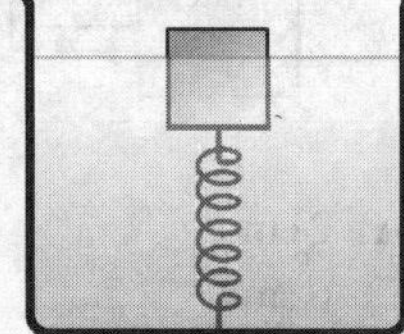

Figure 7.86

7-25 A large block of ice cuboid of edge length 'l' and density $\rho_{ice} = 0.9\,\rho_w$, has a large vertical hole along its axis. This block is floating in a lake. Find out the length of the rope required to raise a bucket of water through the hole :

(A) $l/2$ (B) $l/4$
(C) $l/8$ (D) $l/10$

7-26 For a fluid which is flowing steadily, the level in the vertical tubes is best represented by :

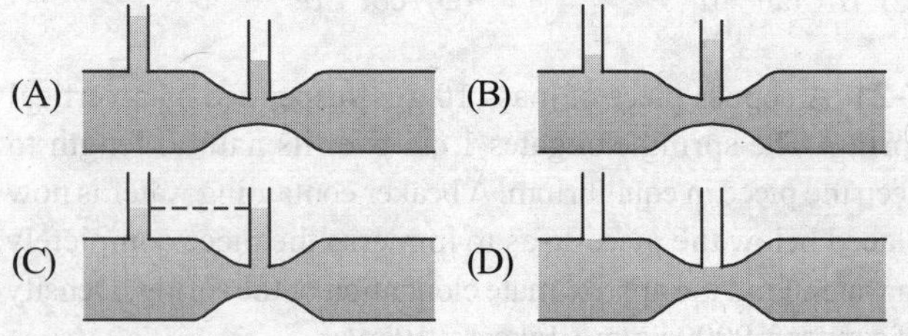

7-27 A cylindrical wooden float whose base area S and the height H drifts on the water surface. Density of wood d and density of water is ρ. What minimum work must be performed to take the float out of the water?

(A) $\dfrac{S^2 gd}{2\rho}$ (B) $\dfrac{Sgd^2H^2}{\rho}$

(C) $\dfrac{Sgd^2H^2}{2\rho}$ (D) $\dfrac{2S^3gd^2}{\rho H^2}$

7-28 A circular cylinder of height h_0 = 10 cm and radius r_0 = 2 cm is opened at the top and filled with liquid. It is rotated about its vertical axis. Determine the speed of rotation so that half the area of the bottom gets exposed. (g = 10 m/sec^2) :

(A) 25 rad/s (B) 50 rad/s
(C) 100 rad/s (D) 200 rad/s

7-29 Water flows in a horizontal tube as shown in figure-7.87. The pressure of water changes by 600 N/m^2 between A and B where the areas of cross-section are 30 cm^2 and 15 cm^2 respectively. Find the rate of flow of water through the tube :

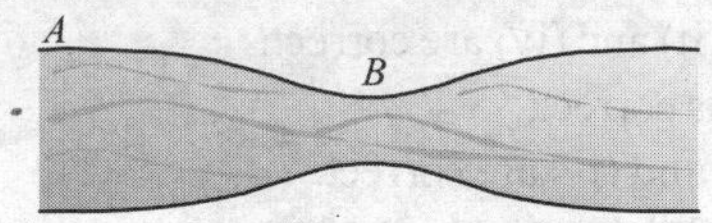

Figure 7.87

(A) 600 cm^3/s (B) 1200 cm^3/s
(C) 1800 cm^3/s (D) 2400 cm^3/s

7-30 The cubical container $ABCDEFGH$ which is completely filled with an ideal (nonviscous and incompressible) fluid, moves in a gravity free space with a acceleration of $a = a_0(\hat{i} - \hat{j} + \hat{k})$ where a_0 is a positive constant. Then the only point in the container where pressure can be zero is :

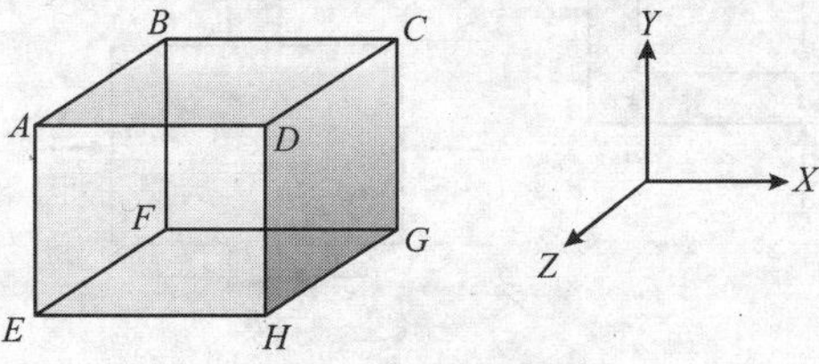

Figure 7.88

(A) B (B) C
(C) E (D) H

7-31 To measure the atmospheric pressure, four different tubes of length 1m, 2m, 3m and 4m are used. If the height of the mercury column in the tubes is h_1, h_2, h_3, h_4 respectively in the four cases, then h_1:h_2:h_3:h_4 is :

(A) 1 : 2 : 3 : 4 (B) 4 : 3 : 2 : 1
(C) 1 : 2 : 2 : 1 (D) 1 : 1 : 1 : 1

7-32 An open tank 10m long and 2m deep is filled up to 1.5 m height of oil of specific gravity 0.82. The tank is uniformly accelerated along its length from rest to a speed of 20 m/s horizontally. The shortest time in which the speed may be attained without spilling any oil is : [g = 10 m/s^2]

(A) 20 s (B) 18 s
(C) 10 s (D) 5 s

7-33 Water (density ρ) is flowing through the uniform horizontal tube of cross-sectional area A with a constant speed v as shown in the figure-7.89. The magnitude of force exerted by the water on the curved corner of the tube is (neglect viscous forces)

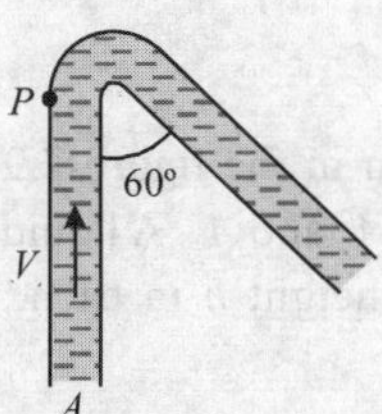

Figure 7.89

(A) $\sqrt{3}\rho Av^2$ (B) $2\rho Av^2$

(C) $\sqrt{2}\rho Av^2$ (D) $\frac{\rho Av^2}{\sqrt{2}}$

7-34 An open rectangular tank 1.5 m wide 2m deep and 2m long is half filled with water. It is accelerated horizontally at 3.27 m/sec² in the direction of its length. Determine the depth of water at rear end of tank. [$g = 9.81$ m/sec²]

(A) 0.9m (B) 1.2m

(C) 1.5m (D) 1.7m

7-35 In a given U-tube (open at one-end and closed at other end as shown) find out the correct relation between p and p_{atm} :
Given $d_2 = 2 \times 13.6$ gm/cm³ $d_1 = 13.6$ gm/cm³

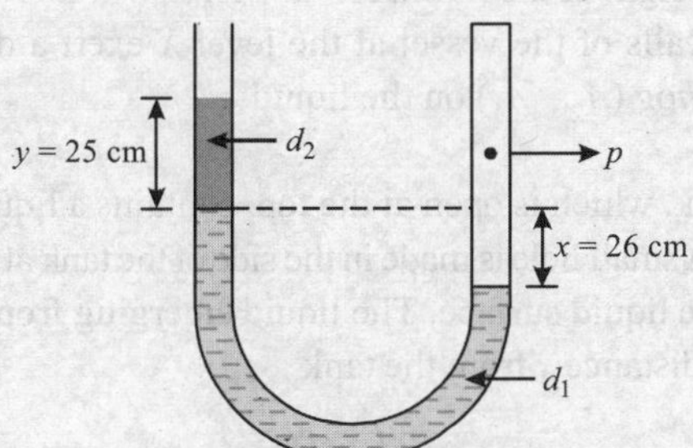

Figure 7.90

(A) $p_{atm} = p$ (B) $p_{atm} = 2p$

(C) $p_{atm} = p/2$ (D) $p_{atm} = p/4$

7-36 One end of a long iron chain of linear mass density λ is fixed to a sphere of mass m and specific density 1/3 while the other end is free. The sphere along with the chain is immersed in a deep lake. If specific density of iron is 7, the height h above the bed of the lake at which the sphere will float in equilibrium is (Assume that the part of the chain lying on the bottom of the lake exerts negligible force on the upper part of the chain.) :

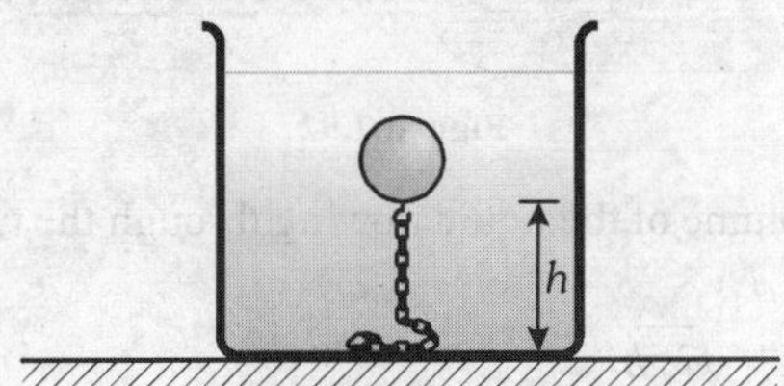

Figure 7.91

(A) $\frac{16}{7}\frac{m}{\lambda}$ (B) $\frac{7m}{3\lambda}$

(C) $\frac{5m}{2\lambda}$ (D) $\frac{8m}{3\lambda}$

* * * * *

Advance MCQs with One or More Options Correct

7-1 An ideal liquid flows through a horizontal tube. The velocities of the liquid in the two sections, which have areas of cross-section A_1 and A_2, are v_1 and v_2 respectively. The difference in the levels of the liquid in the two vertical tubes is h :

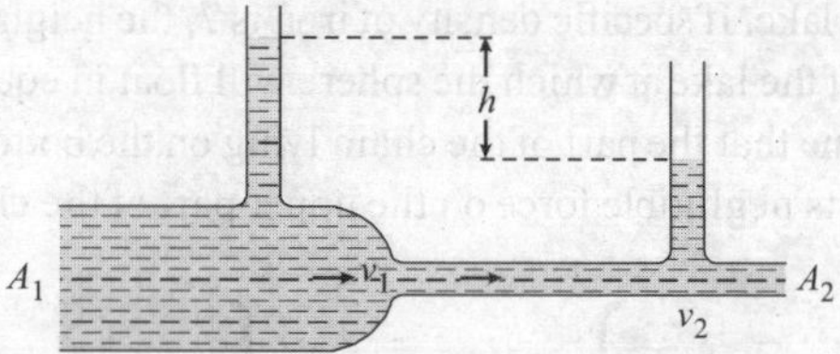

Figure 7.92

(A) The volume of the liquid flowing through the tube in unit time is A_1v_1
(B) $v_2 - v_1 = \sqrt{2gh}$
(C) $v_2^2 - v_1^2 = 2gh$
(D) The energy per unit mass of the liquid is the same in both sections of the tube

7-2 An object is weighted at the North Pole by a beam balance and a spring balance, giving readings of W_B and W_S respectively. It is again weighed in the same manner at the equator, giving reading of W_B' and W_S' respectively. Assume that the acceleration due to gravity is the same everywhere and that the balances are quite sensitive :

(A) $W_B = W_S$ (B) $W_B' = W_S'$
(C) $W_B = W_B'$ (D) $W_S' < W_S$

7-3 A spring balance reads W_1 when a ball is suspended from it. A weighing machine reads W_2 when ball is placed on it. Now ball is submerged in a tank of liquid and also suspended with a spring balance, if the spring balance reads W_3 and the weighing machine reads W_4 then which of the following is correct :

(A) $W_1 > W_3$ (B) $W_1 < W_3$
(C) $W_2 < W_4$ (D) $W_2 > W_4$

7-4 In the previous Q. No. 7-3 :

(A) $W_1 + W_2 = W_3 + W_4$ (B) $W_1 + W_3 = W_2 + W_4$
(C) $W_1 + W_4 = W_2 + W_3$ (D) None of these

7-5 A massless conical flask filled with a liquid is kept on a table in vacuum. The force exerted by the liquid on the base of the flask is W_1. The force exerted by the flask on the table is W_2 :

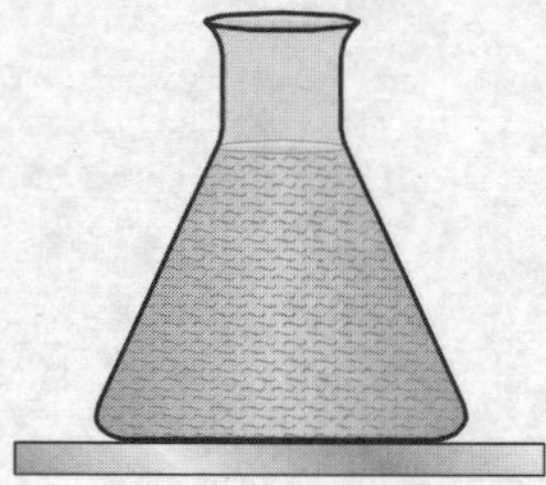

Figure 7.93

(A) $W_1 = W_2$ (B) $W_1 > W_2$
(C) $W_1 < W_2$
(D) The force exerted by the liquid on the walls of the flask is $(W_1 - W_2)$

7-6 The vessel shown in the figure-7.94 has two sections of areas of cross-section A_1 and A_2. A liquid of density ρ fills both the sections, up to a height h in each. Neglect atmospheric pressure :

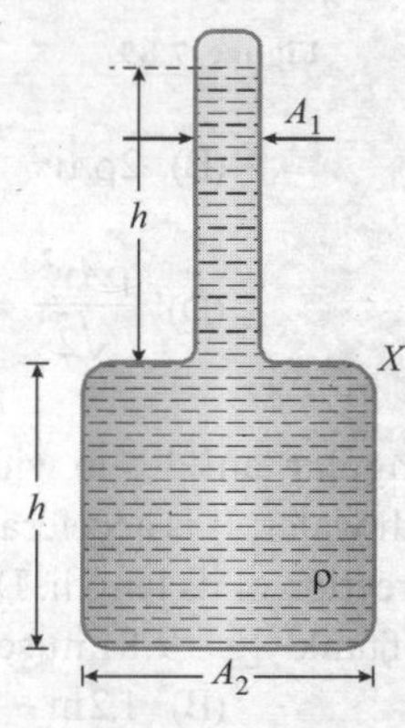

Figure 7.94

(A) The pressure at the base of the vessel is $2h\rho g$
(B) The force exerted by the liquid on the base of the vessel is $2h\rho gA_2$
(C) The weight of the liquid is $< 2h\rho gA_2$
(D) The walls of the vessel at the level X exert a downward force $h\rho g\,(A_2 - A_1)$ on the liquid

7-7 A tank, which is open at the top, contains a liquid up to a height H. A small hole is made in the side of the tank at a distance y below the liquid surface. The liquid emerging from the hole lands at a distance x from the tank :

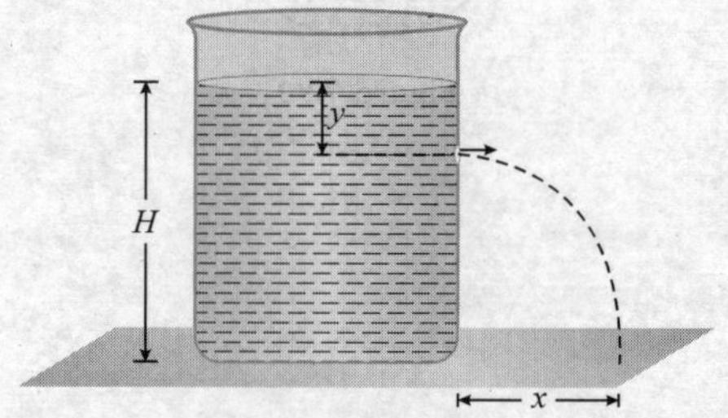

Figure 7.95

(A) If y is increased from zero to H, x will first increase and then decrease
(B) x is maximum for $y = H/2$
(C) The maximum value of x is H
(D) The maximum value of x will depend on the density of the liquid

7-8 In the figure-7.96, an ideal liquid flows through the tube, which is of uniform cross-section. The liquid has velocities v_A and v_B and pressures p_A and p_B at points A and B respectively :

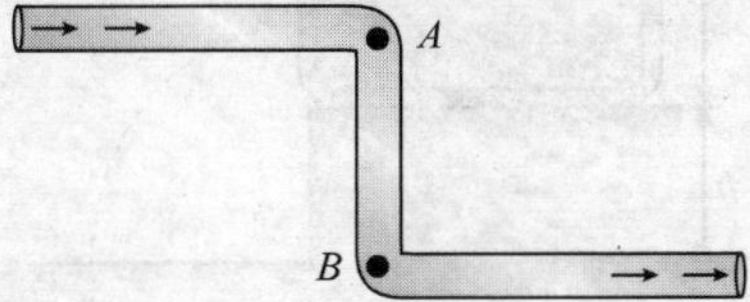

Figure 7.96

(A) $v_A = v_B$ (B) $v_B > v_A$
(C) $p_A = p_B$ (D) $p_B > p_A$

7-9 A liquid of density ρ comes out with a velocity v from a horizontal tube of area of cross-section A. The reaction force exerted by the liquid on the tube is F :
(A) $F \propto v$ (B) $F \propto v^2$
(C) $F \propto A$ (D) $F \propto \rho$

7-10 A piece of ice is floating in a liquid. What happens to the level of liquid when all ice melts ?
(A) level remains same if liquid is water
(B) level falls if liquid is water
(C) level will rise if liquid is denser than water
(D) level will rise if liquid is lighter than water

7-11 A beaker exactly full of water has an ice piece floating in it. As the cube melts, what happens to water level ?
(A) it remains unchanged if the cube contains an air bubble
(B) the level falls if the cube contains some lead pieces inside it
(C) the level will rise if the cube contains some cork pieces inside
(D) the level remains the same if the cube contains some cork pieces inside it

7-12 An iron casting weighs 27 kg in air and 18 kg in water. Density of iron is 7800 kg/m^3 :
(A) outer volume of casting is 6000 cm^3
(B) outer volume of casting is 9000 cm^3
(C) volume of cavity inside the casting is 780 cm^3
(D) volume of cavity inside the casting is 5538 cm^3

7-13 A ball of density ρ is dropped onto a horizontal solid surface. It bounces elastically from the surface and returns to its original position in time t_1. Next, the ball is released from the same height, but this time it strikes the surface of a liquid of density ρ_L (> ρ but less than 2ρ), and takes t_2 second to come back to its original height :
(A) $t_2 > t_1$ (B) $t_2 > t_1$
(C) the motion of the ball is not simple harmonic
(D) If $\rho = \rho_L$, then the speed of the ball inside the liquid will be independent of its depth

7-14 Siphon is a device to transfer liquid from a higher level to a lower level. The condition of working of a siphon is :

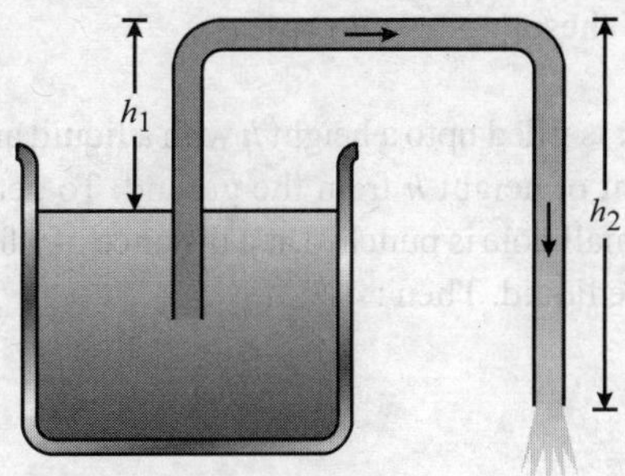

Figure 7.97

(A) $h_2 > h_1$
(B) $h_2 = 2\,h_1$
(C) h_1 should be less than the height of corresponding liquid barometer
(D) h_1 should be greater than the height of corresponding liquid barometer

7-15 Equal volumes of liquid are poured in the three vessels A, B and C. All the vessels have same base area. Select the correct alternative(s) :

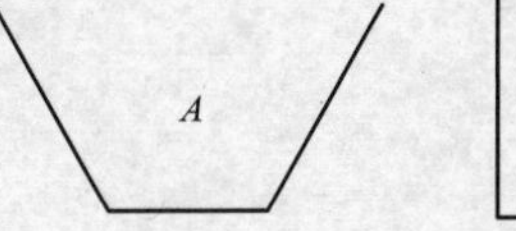

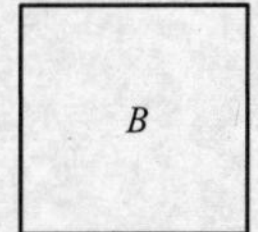

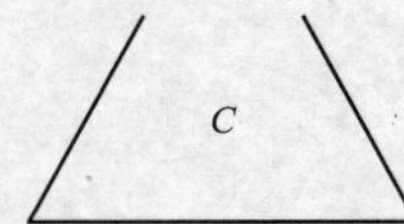

Figure 7.98

(A) The force on the base will be maximum in vessel A
(B) The force on the base will be maximum in vessel C
(C) Net force exerted by liquid in all the three vessels is equal
(D) Net force exerted by liquid in vessel A is maximum

7-16 Water is flowing in streamline motion through a tube with its axis horizontal. Consider two points A and B in the tube at the same horizontal level :
(A) the pressure at A and B are equal for any shape of the tube
(B) the pressure can never be equal
(C) the pressures are equal if the tube has a uniform cross-section
(D) the pressure may be equal even if the tube has a non-uniform cross-section

7-17 A vessel is filled with mercury to a height of 0.9 m. Barometric height is 0.7 m. mercury :

(A) the vessel can be completely emptied with the aid of a siphon
(B) the vessel cannot be emptied completely with the aid of a siphon
(C) the vessel can be emptied with at least 0.7 m height of mercury remaining in the vessel
(D) none of these

7-18 A tank is filled upto a height h with a liquid and is placed on a platform of height h from the ground. To get maximum range x_m a small hole is punched at a distance of y from the free surface of the liquid. Then :

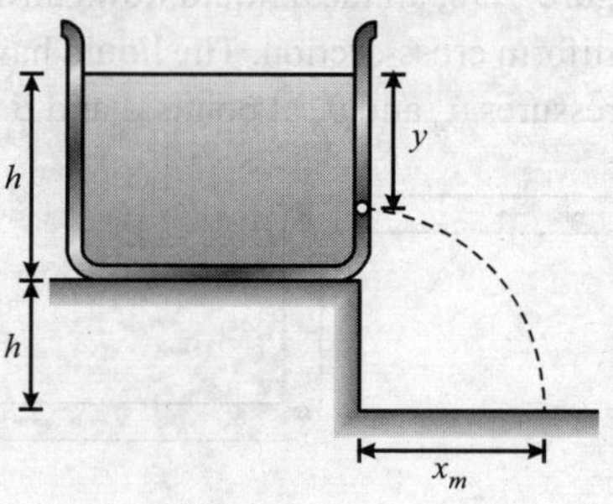

Figure 7.99

(A) $x_m = 2h$ (B) $x_m = 1.5h$
(C) $y = h$ (D) $y = 0.75h$

* * * * *

Unsolved Numerical Problems for Preparation of NSEP, INPhO & IPhO

For detailed preparation of INPhO and IPhO students can refer advance study material on www.physicsgalaxy.com

7-1 A block of wood floats in water with two-thirds of its volume submerged. In oil the block of floats with 0.90 of its volume submerged. Find the density of (a) wood and (b) oil, if density of water is 10^3 kg/m^3.

Ans. [(a) 667 $\frac{kg}{m^3}$, (b) 740 $\frac{kg}{m^3}$]

7-2 A balloon filled with hydrogen has a volume of 1 m^3 and its mass is 1 kg. What would be the volume of the block of a very light material which it can just lift ?

Ans. [$\frac{1}{300}$ m^3]

7-3 A horizontal pipe line carries water in a streamline flow. At a point along the pipe where the cross-sectional area is 10 cm^2, the water velocity is 1 m/s and the pressure is 2000 *Pa*. What is the pressure of water at another point where the cross-sectional area is 5 cm^2 ?

Ans. [500 Pa]

7-4 A glass tube of radius 0.8 cm floats vertical in water, as shown in figure-7.100. What mass of lead pellets would cause the tube to sink a further 3 cm ?

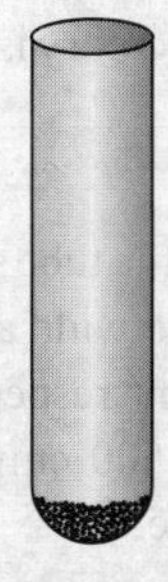

Figure 7.100

Ans. [6.03 g]

7-5 When equal volumes of two substances are mixed together, the specific gravity of the mixture is 4. But when equal weights of the same substance are mixed together, the specific gravity of the two is 3. Find the specific gravity of two substances.

Ans. [6 and 2]

7-6 Water from a tap emerges vertically downwards with an initial speed of 1 m/s. The cross-sectional area of the tap is 10^{-4}m^2. Assume that the pressure is constant throughout the stream of water and that the flow is steady. Find the cross-sectional area of the stream 0.15 m below the tap.

Ans. [5×10^{-5} m^2]

7-7 A jet of water issues vertically at a speed of 30 feet per second from a nozzle of 0.1 square inch cross-section. A ball weighing one pound is balanced in the air by impact of water on its underside. Find the height of the ball above the level of jet. Take $g = 3$ft/s^2.

[4.6 feet]

7-8 A large open tank has two holes in the wall. One is a square hole of side L at a depth y from the top and the other is a circular hole of radius R at a depth $4y$ from the top. When the tank is completely filled with water, the quantities of water flowing out per second from both holes are the same. Find the value of R.

Ans. [$\frac{L}{\sqrt{2\pi}}$]

7-9 A tank 5 m high is half filled with water and then is filled to the top with oil of density 0.85 g/cm^3. What is the pressure at the bottom of the tank due to these liquids?

Ans. [4.53×10^4 N/m^2]

7-10 A stone of density 2.5 g/cm^3 completely immersed in sea water is allowed to sink from rest. Calculate the depth to which the stone would sink in two seconds. Neglect the effect of friction. Specific gravity of sea water is 1.025 and acceleration due to gravity is 9.8 m/s^2.

Ans. [23.128 m]

7-11 A ping-pong ball has a volume V and density $(1/10)^{th}$ of water. What force would be required to hold it completely submerged under water?

Ans. [(9/10) $V\sigma_{wg}$ downwards]

7-12 Water is flowing continuously from a tap having a bore of internal diameter 8×10^{-3} m. Calculate the diameter of the water stream at a distance 2×10^{-1} m below the tap. Assume that the water velocity as it leaves the tap is 0.4 m/s

Ans. [3.6×10^{-3} m]

7-13 A certain block weighs 15 N in air. It weighs 12 N when immersed in water. When immersed in another liquid, it weighs 13 N? Calculate the relative density of (a) the block (b) the other liquid.

Ans. [(a) 5, (b) 2/3]

7-14 A cylindrical tank 1 m in radius rest on a platform 5 m high. Initially the tank is filled with water to a height of 5 m. A plug, whose area is 10^{-4} m^2, is removed from an orifice on the side of the tank at the bottom. Calculate the following :

(i) initial speed with which the water flows from the orifice,

(ii) initial speed with which the water strikes the ground.

(iii) time taken to empty the tank to half its original value.

Ans. [(i) 10 m/s, (ii) 14.1 m/s, (iii) $-3140\ \frac{\sqrt{2}}{\sqrt{10}}\left[\left(\frac{5}{2}\right)^{1/2}-(5)^{1/2}\right]$]

7-15 A vertical uniform U tube open at both ends contains mercury. Water is poured in one limb until the level of mercury is depressed 2 cm in that limb. What is the length of water column when this happens.

Ans. [54.4 cm]

7-16 A piece of copper having an internal cavity weigh 264 gm in air and 221 gm in water. Find the volume of cavity. Density of copper is 8.8 gm/cm^3

Ans. [13 cm^3]

7-17 A beaker of mass 1 kg contains 2 kg of water and rests on a scale. A 2 kg block of aluminum (specific gravity 2.70) suspended from a spring scale is submerged in water, as shown in figure-7.101. Find the readings of both scales.

Ans. [Reading of lower scale = 36.66 N,
Reading of upper scale = 12.34 N,]

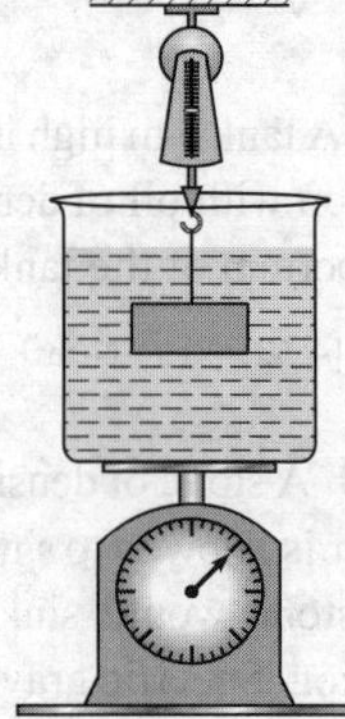

Figure 7.101

7-18 A piece of brass (alloy of copper and zinc) weighs 12.9 g in air. When completely immersed in water it weighs 11.3 g. What is the mass of copper contained in the alloy ? Specific gravities of copper and zinc are 8.9 and 7.1 contained in the alloy? Specific gravities of copper and zinc are 8.9 and 7.1 respectively.

Ans. [7.61 g]

7-19 Figure-7.102 shows a hydraulic press with the larger piston of diameter 35 cm at a height of 1.5 m relative to the smaller piston of diameter 10 cm. The mass on the smaller piston is 20 kg. What is the force exerted on the load by the larger piston. The density of oil in the press is 750 kg/m^3. Takes $g = 9.8$ m/s^2.

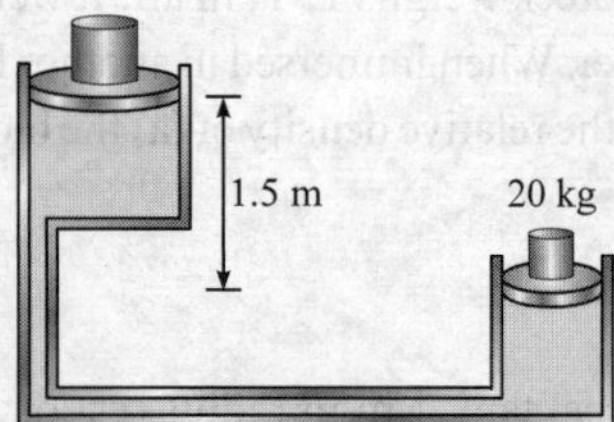

Figure 7.102

Ans. [1.3×10^3 N]

7-20 Two identical cylindrical vessels (area of cross-section 3.5×10^{-3} m^2) with their bases at the same level contain liquid of density 800 kg/m^3. The height of liquid in one vessel is 0.3 m and in the other it is 0.1 m. Assuming $g = 10$ m/s^2, find the workdone by gravity in equalising levels when the vessels are interconnected at bottom.

Ans. [0.28 J]

7-21 An open cubical tank completely filled with water is kept on a horizontal surface. Its acceleration is then slowly increased to 2 m/s^2 as shown in the figure-7.103. The side of the tank is 1 m. Find the mass of water that would spill out of the tank.

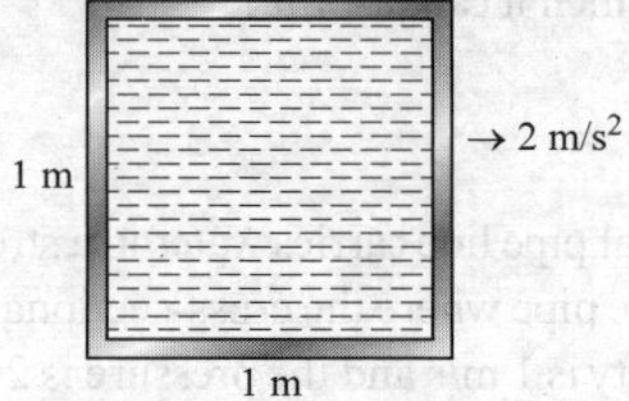

Figure 7.103

Ans. [100 kg]

7-22 A vertical *U*-tube of uniform inner cross-section contains mercury in both its arms. Glycerine (density 1.3 g/cm^3) column of length 10 cm is introduced into one of the arms. Oil of density 0.8 g/cm^3 is poured into the other arm until the upper surface of oil and glycerine are in the same horizontal level. Find the length of oil column. (density of mercury is 13.6 g/cm^3)

Ans. [9.61 cm]

7-23 Water flows through the tube shown in figure-7.104. The areas of cross-section of the wide and the narrow portions of the tube are 5 cm^2 and 2 cm^2 respectively. The rate of flow of water through the tube is 500 cm^3/s. Find the difference of mercury levels in the *U*-tube.

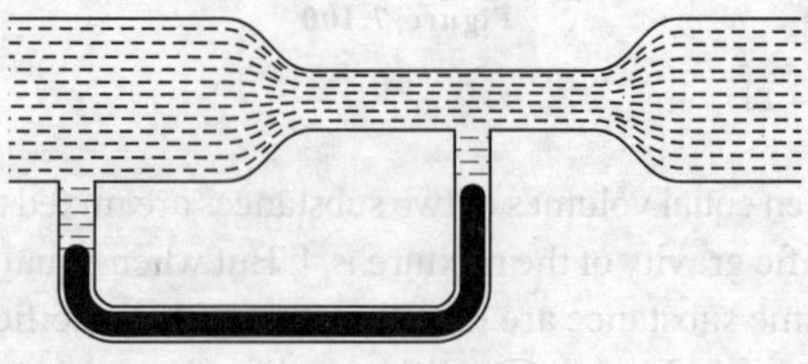

Figure 7.104

Ans. [1.97 cm]

7-24 A person can change the volume of his body by taking air into his lungs. The amount of change can be determined by weighing the person under water. Suppose that under water a person weighs 20.0 N with partially full lungs and 40.0 N with empty lungs. Find the change in body volume.

Ans. [2.04×10^{-3} m^3]

7-25 A vessel contains oil over mercury. A homogeneous sphere floats with half volume immersed in mercury and the other half in oil. If density of oil. If density of oil is 0.8 gm/cm^3 and that of mercury is 13.6 gm/cm^3 what is the density of material of sphere.

Ans. [7.2 gm/cm^3]

7-26 The tension in a string holding a solid block below the surface of a liquid (of density greater than that of solid) as shown in figure-7.105 is T_0 when the system is at rest. What will be the tension in the string if the system has upward acceleration a?

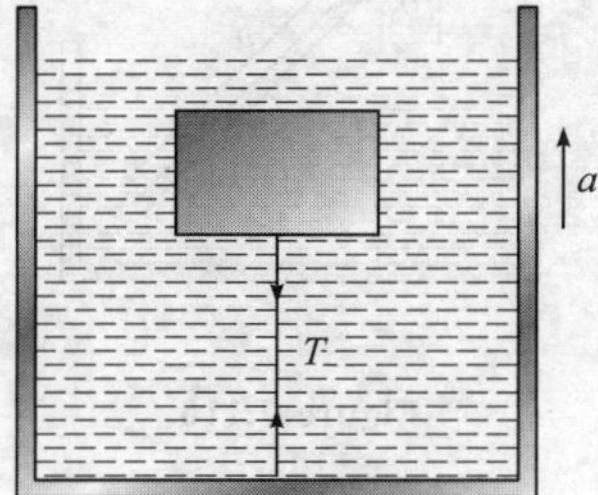

Figure 7.105

Ans. [$T = T_0 \, [1 + (a/g)]$]

7-27 A J-tube, shown in figure-7.106, contains a volume V of dry air trapped in arm A of the tube. The atmospheric pressure is H cm of mercury. When more mercury is poured in arm B, the volume of the enclosed air and its pressure changes. What should be the difference in mercury levels in the two arms so as to reduce the volume of air to 1/2.

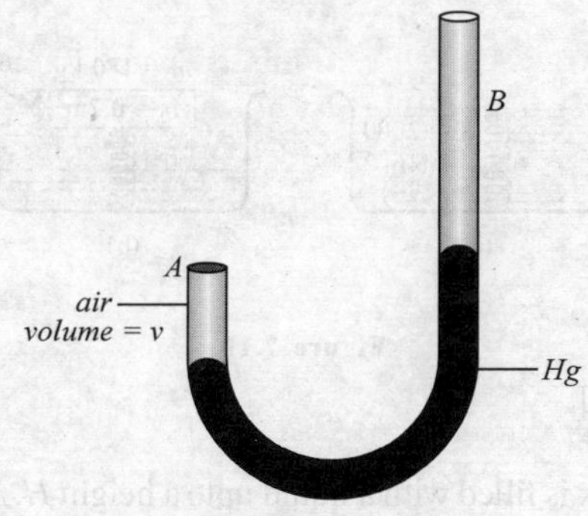

Figure 7.106

Ans. [H cm]

7-28 A block of ice with an area A and a height h floats in water of density ρ_0. What work should be performed to submerge the ice block completely into water if density of ice is ρ_1?

Ans. [$W = \dfrac{Agh^2(\rho_0 - \rho_1)^2}{2\rho_0}$]

7-29 A solid ball of density half that of water falls freely under gravity from a height of 19.6 m and then enters water. Upto what depth will the ball go? How much time will it take to come again to the water surface? Neglect air resistance and viscosity effects in water. (g = 9.8 m/s^2).

Ans. [19.6 m and 4 s]

7-30 (a) Consider a stream of fluid of density ρ with speed v_1 passing abruptly from cylindrical pipe of cross-sectional area a_1 into a wider cylindrical pipe of cross-sectional area a_2 (see figure-7.107). The jet will mix with the surrounding fluid and, after the mixing, will flow on almost uniformly with an average speed v_2. Without referring to the details of the mixing, use momentum ideas to show that the increase in pressure due to the mixing is approximately

$$P_2 - P_1 = \rho \, v_2 \, (v_1 - v_2)$$

(b) Show from Bernoulli's principle that in a gradually widening pipe we would get

$$P_2 - P_1 = \tfrac{1}{2} \, \rho \, (v_1^2 - v_2^2)$$

and explain the loss of pressure [the difference is $\frac{1}{2} \rho (v_1 - v_2)^2$] due to the abrupt enlargement of the pipe. Can you draw an analogy with elastic and inelastic collisions in particle mechanics ?

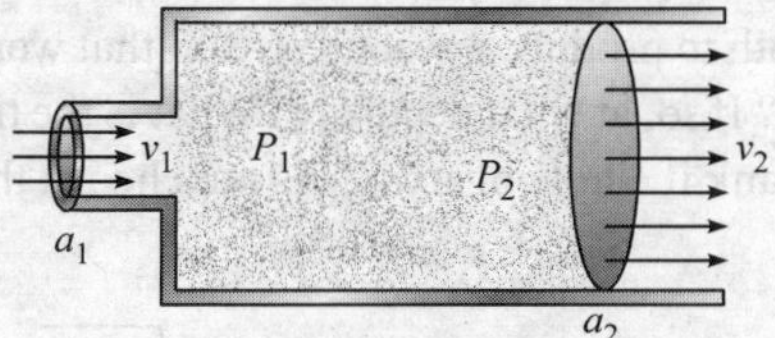

Figure 7.107

7-31 A U-tube containing a liquid is accelerated horizontally with a constant acceleration a_0. If the separation between the vertical limbs is l, find the difference in the heights of the liquid in the two arms.

Ans. [$a_0 \, l/g$]

7-32 The tank in figure-7.108 discharges water at constant rate for all water levels above the air inlet R. Find the height above datum to which water would rise in the manometer tubes M and N.

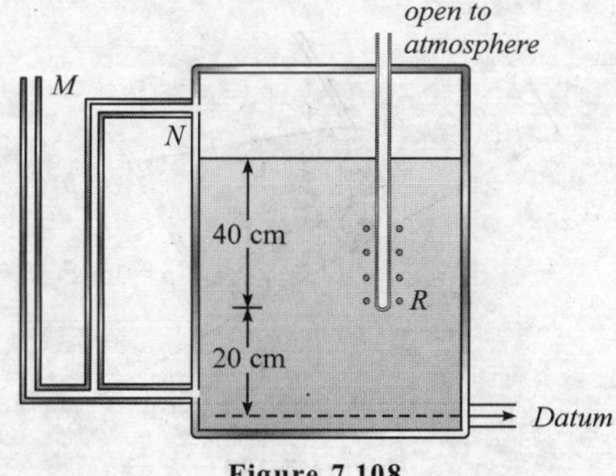

Figure 7.108

Ans. [20 cm, 60 cm]

7-33 The time period of a simple pendulum is T. Now the bob is immersed in a liquid of density σ. If density of material of bob is ρ, what will be the new time period of the pendulum.

Ans. $[T\sqrt{\frac{\rho}{\rho-\sigma}}]$

7-34 A rubber ball with a mass M and radius R is submerged into a liquid of density ρ to a depth h and released. What height will the ball jump up above the surface of water? (Neglect resistance of water and air.)

Ans. $[\frac{(4/3\,\pi R^3\rho - M)\,h}{M}]$

7-35 A cubical vessel of height 1 m is full of water. Find the work done in pumping out whole water.

Ans. [4900 J]

7-36 A tank of cross-sectional area A is filled with water to a height H. A hole is punched in one of the walls at a depth h below the water surface. (a) Show that the distance x from the foot of the wall at which the resulting stream strikes the floor is given by $x = 2\sqrt{h(H-h)}$. (b) Could a hole be punched at another depth to produce a second stream that would have the same range? If so, at what depth? (c) What is the time taken to empty the tank if a hole of area A_0 is punched at the bottom of the tank?

Ans. [(b) yes, at depth $(H-h)$ (c) $t = (A/A_0)\sqrt{(2H/g)}$]

7-37 A large block of ice 5 m thick has a vertical hole drilled through and is floating in the middle of a lake. What is the minimum length of a rope required to scoop up a bucket full of water through the hole ?

Ans. [0.5 m]

7-38 A rectangular container of water undergoes constant acceleration down an incline as shown in figure-7.109. Determine the slope tan θ of the free surface using the coordinate system shown. Take $g = 10\ \text{m/s}^2$.

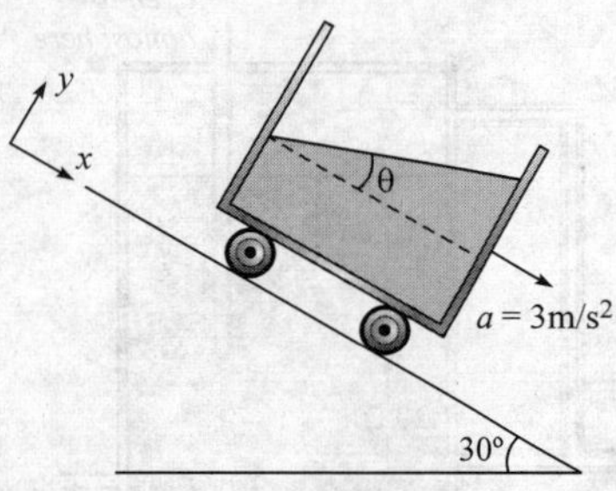

Figure 7.109

Ans. [0.23]

7-39 An iron casting containing a number of cavities weights 6000 N in air and 4000 N in water. What is the volume of the cavities in the casting? Density of iron is 7.87 g/cm^3.

Ans. [0.12 m^3]

7-40 A uniform rod of length b capable of tuning about its end which is out of water, rests inclined to the vertical. If its specific gravity is 5/9, find the length immersed in water.

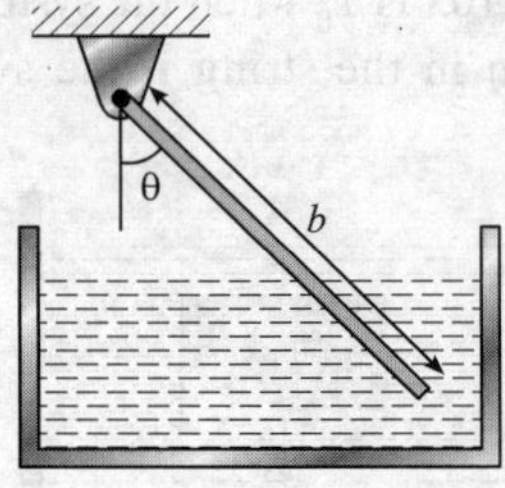

Figure 7.110

Ans. [b/3]

7-41 In a tank of horizontal cross-sectional area 1 m^2, a spring with force constant 2000 Nm^{-1} is fixed in vertical position upto the height of the water as shown in figure-7.111 (a). A block of mass 180 kg is gently placed over the spring and it attains the equilibrium position as shown in figure-7.111 (b). If base area of the block is 0.2 m^2 and height 60 cm, then find compression in the spring at equilibrium position.
(Take $g = 10\ \text{m/s}^2$; $\rho_w = 1000\ \text{kg/m}^3$):

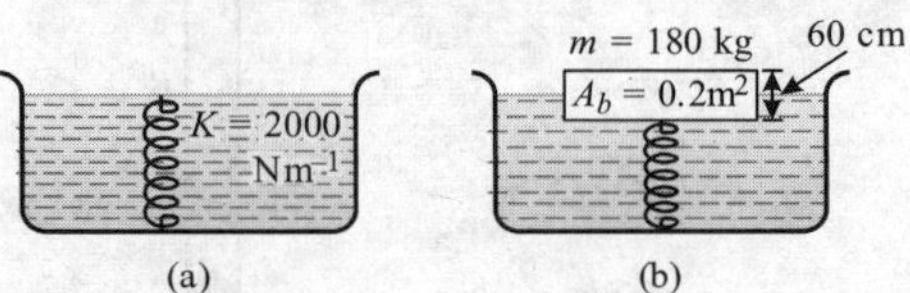

Figure 7.111

Ans. [40 cm]

7-42 A tank is filled with a liquid upto a height H. A small hole is made at the bottom of this tank. Let t_1 be the time taken to empty first half of the tank and t_2 the time taken to empty rest half of the tank. Then find $\frac{t_1}{t_2}$.

Ans. [0.414]

7-43 A ball of density ρ_0 falls from rest from a point P onto the surface of a liquid of density ρ in time T. It enters the liquid, stops, moves up, and returns to P in a total time $3T$. Neglect viscosity, surface tension and splashing. Find the ratio of $\frac{\rho}{\rho_0}$.

Ans. [3]

7-44 In the arrangement shown in figure-7.112 a viscous liquid whose density is 1 gm/cm^3 flows along a tube out of a wide tank *A*. Find the velocity of the liquid flow if h_1 = 10 cm, h_2 = 20 cm, h_3 = 35 cm. All the distances *l* are equal.

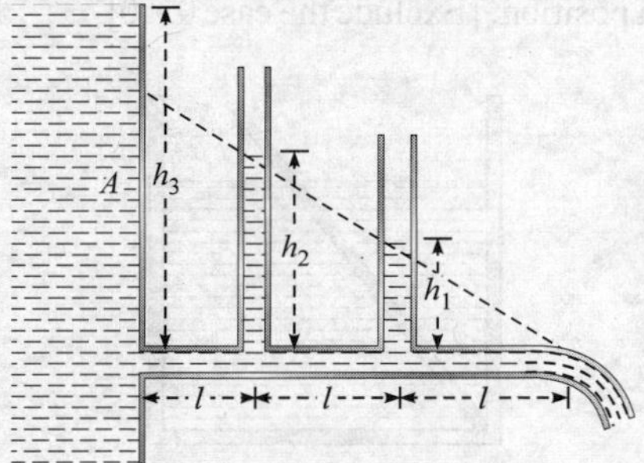

Figure 7.112

Ans. [1 m/s]

2-45 A block of wood weighs 12 kg and has a relative density 0.6. It is to be in water with 0.9 of its volume immersed. What weight of a metal is needed (a) if the metal is on the top of wood, (b) if the metal is attached below the wood? [*RD* of metal = 14].

Ans. [(a) 6 kg, (b) 6.5 kg]

7-46 A level controller is shown in the figure-7.113 it consists of a thin circular plug of diameter 10 cm and a cylindrical plug of diameter 20 cm tied together with a light rigid rod of length 10 cm. The plug fits in smoothly in a drain hole at the bottom of the tank which opens into atmosphere. As water fills up and the level reaches height *h*, the plug opens. Find *h*. Determine the level of water in the tank when the plug closes again. The float has a mass 3 kg and the plug may be assumed as massless.

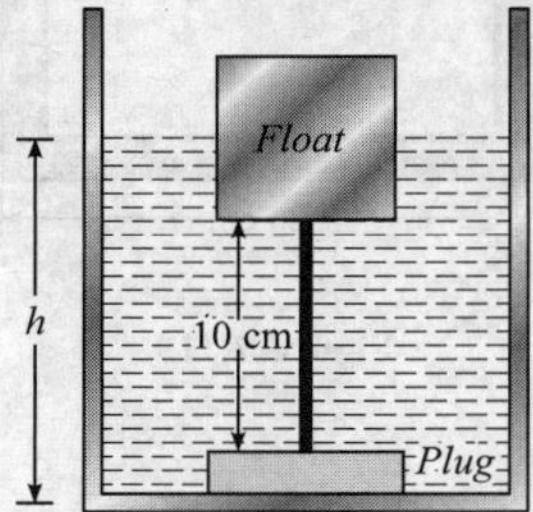

Figure 7.113

Ans. [$h_1 = \frac{2(3+\pi)}{15\pi}$, $h_2 = \frac{3+\pi}{10\pi}$]

7-47 Two communicating cylindrical tubes contain mercury. The diameter of one vessel is three times larger than the diameter of one vessel is three times larger than the diameter of the other. A column of height 68 cm is poured into the narrow vessel. How much will the mercury level rise in the other vessel and how much will it sink in the narrow one ? How much will the mercury level rise in the narrow vessel if the column of water of the same height is poured into the broad vessel.

Ans. [0.5 cm, 4.5 cm, result will be same]

7-48 The *U*-tube acts as a water siphon. The bend in the tube is 1 m above the water surface. The tube outlet is 7 m below the water surface. The water issues from the bottom of the siphon as a free jet at atmospheric pressure. Determine the speed of the free jet and the minimum absolute pressure of the water in the bend. Given atmospheric pressure = 1.01 × 10^5 N/m^2, *g* = 9.8 m/s^2 and density of water = 10^3 kg/m^3.

Ans. [11.7 m/s, 2.27 × 10^4 N/m^2]

7-49 The interface of two liquids of densities ρ and 2ρ respectively lies at the point *A* in a U tube at rest. The height of liquid column above *A* is 8*a*/3 where *AB* = *a*. The cross sectional area of the tube is *S*. With what angular velocity the tube must be whirled about a vertical axis at a distance '*a*' such that the interface of the liquids shifts towards *B* by 2*a*/3.

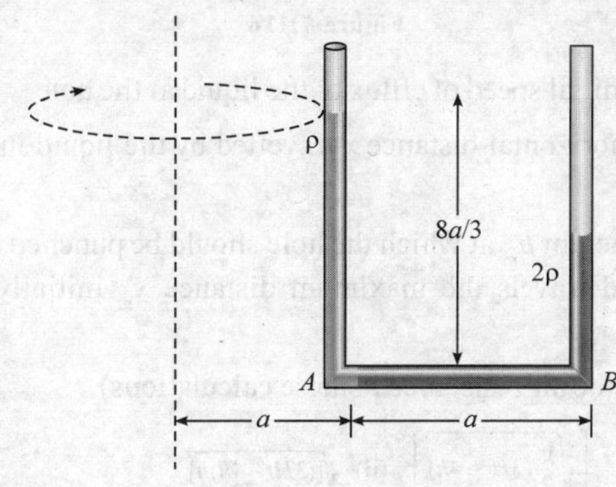

Figure 7.114

Ans. [$\sqrt{\frac{18g}{19a}}$]

7-50 Figure-7.115 shows the top view of a cylindrical can mounted on a turntable. The can is filled with water. At a depth *h* below the water surface are two horizontal tubes of length *l* and cross-sectional area *a*, with right-angle bends at their ends. Show that, as the water jets emerge from the tubes, there is a torque τ exerted on the system given by the expression *t* = 4ρ*gh* (*r* + *l*) *a*, where ρ is the density of the water.

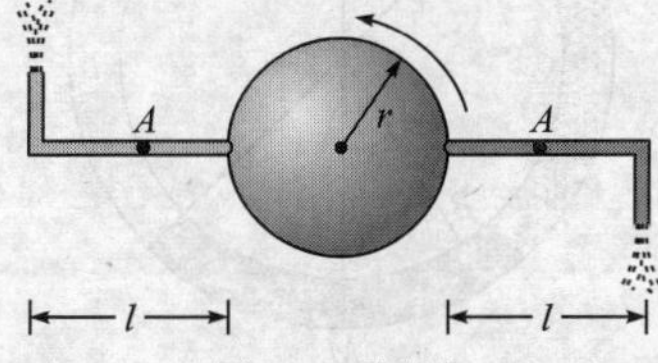

Figure 7.115

7-51 A wooden stick of length *L*, radius *R* and density ρ has a small metal piece of mass *m* (of negligible volume) attached to its one end. Find the minimum value for the mass *m* (in terms of given parameters) that would make the stick float vertically in equilibrium in a liquid of density σ.

Ans. [$\pi R^2 L\rho\left[\sqrt{\frac{\sigma}{\rho}}-1\right]$]

7-52 A container of large uniform cross-sectional area A resting on a horizontal surface holds two immiscible, non-viscous and incompressible liquids of densities d and $2d$, each of height $H/2$ as shown in figure-7.116. The lower density liquid is open to the atmosphere having pressure P_0. A tiny hole of area s ($s << A$) is punched on the vertical side of the container at a height h ($h < H/2$). Determine :

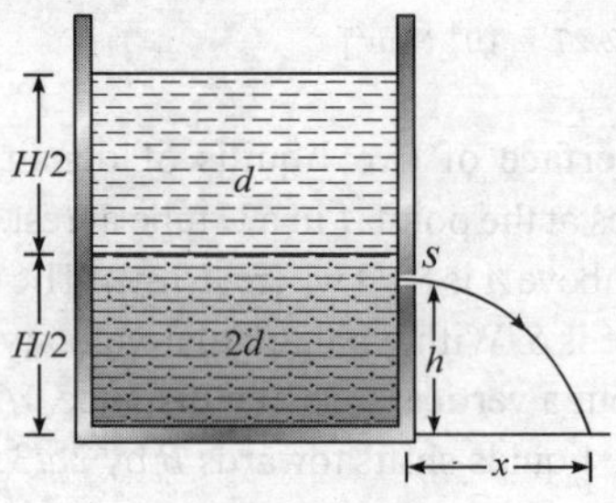

Figure 7.116

(i) the initial speed of efflux of the liquid at the hole.

(ii) the horizontal distance x travelled by the liquid initially, and

(iii) the height h_m at which the hole should be punched so that the liquid travels the maximum distance x_m initially. Also calculate x_m.

(Neglect the air resistance in these calculations)

Ans. [(i) $v = \left[\sqrt{\frac{g}{2}(3H-4h)}\right]$, (ii) $\sqrt{[(3H-4h)h]}$,

(iii) $\sqrt{\left[\left(3H - \frac{4\times 3}{8}H\right)\frac{3}{8}H\right]} = \frac{3H}{4}$]

7-53 A small tube is bent in the form of a circle whose plane is vertical. Equal quantities by volume of two fluids of densities ρ and σ fill half the tube. Find the angle ϕ that the radius passing through the common surface makes with the vertical.

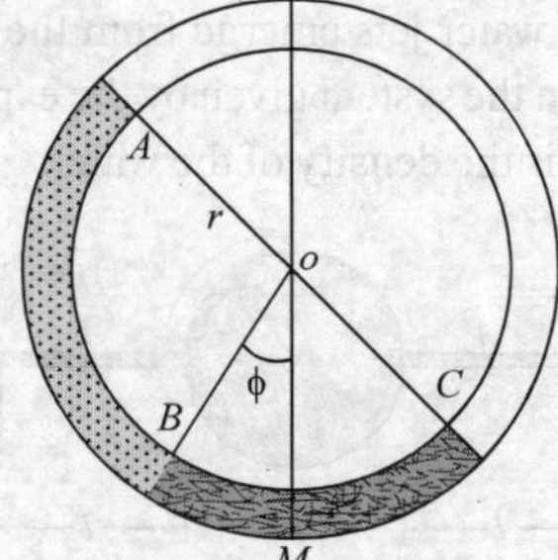

Figure 7.117

Ans. [$\tan\phi = \frac{\rho - \sigma}{\rho + \sigma}(\rho > \sigma)$]

7-54 A rectangular air mattress has a length 2.0 m, a width 0.50 m and thickness 0.08 m. What is the maximum mass of a man who lying on the mattress can float on water if the mass of the mattress is 2.0 kg. What is the density of the mattress?

Ans. [78 kg and 25 kg/m^3]

7-55 A wooden plank of length 1m and uniform cross-section is hinged at one end to the bottom of tank as shown in figure-7.118. The tank is filled with water upto a height of 0.5 m. Find the angle θ that the plank makes with the vertical in the equilibrium position. [Exclude the case $\theta = 0$].

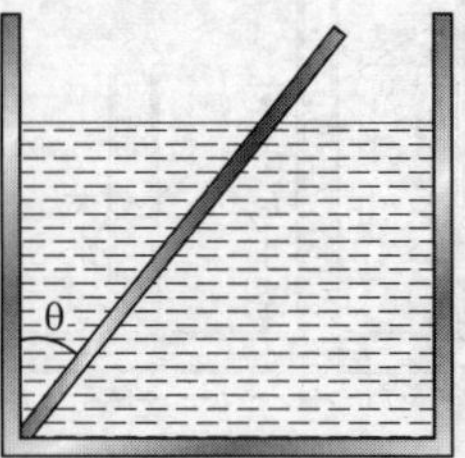

Figure 7.118

Ans. [θ = 45°]

7-56 The cross-sectional area of the U-tube shown in the figure-7.119 is everywhere uniform and of value 1.25×10^{-3} m^2. The horizontal section of the tube is of length 20 cm. When at rest, the limbs of the tube contain a liquid of density 2.5 up to equal heights. If the tube is rotated with angular velocity of 8.4 rad/s about one limb, calculate the volume of liquid that flows from one limb to the other.

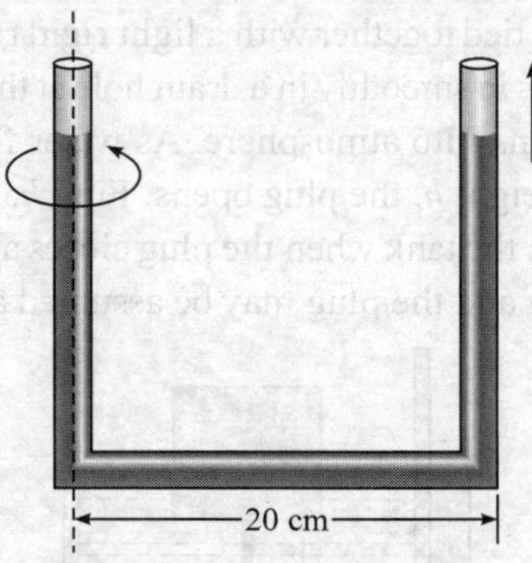

Figure 7.119

Ans. [88.2 cm^3]

7-57 Calculate the rate of flow of glycerine of density 1.25×10^3 kg/m^3 through the conical section of a pipe if the radii of its ends are 0.1 m and 0.04 m and the pressure drop across its length is 10 N/m^2.

Ans. [6.44×10^{-4} m^3/s]

7-58 A cube of ice of edge 4 cm is placed in an empty cylindrical glass of inner diameter 6 cm. Assume that the ice melts uniformly form each side so that it always retains its cubical shape. Remembering that ice is lighter than water, find the length of the edge of the ice cube at the instant it just leaves contact with the bottom of the glass.

Ans. [2.26 cm]

7-59 A cylindrical tank having cross-sectional area $A = 0.5\ m^2$ is filled with two liquids of densities $\rho_1 = 900\ kg/m^3$ and $\rho_2 = 600\ kg/m^3$ to a height $h = 60$ cm each as shown in figure-7.120. A small hole having area $a = 5\ cm^2$ is made in right vertical wall at a height $y = 20$ cm from the bottom. Calculate
(a) velocity of efflux
(b) horizontal force F to keep the cylinder in static equilibrium, if it is placed on a smooth horizontal plane and
(c) minimum and maximum values of F to keep the cylinder in static equilibrium, if the coefficient of friction between the cylinder and the plane is $\mu = 0.01$. $g = 10\ m/s^2$.

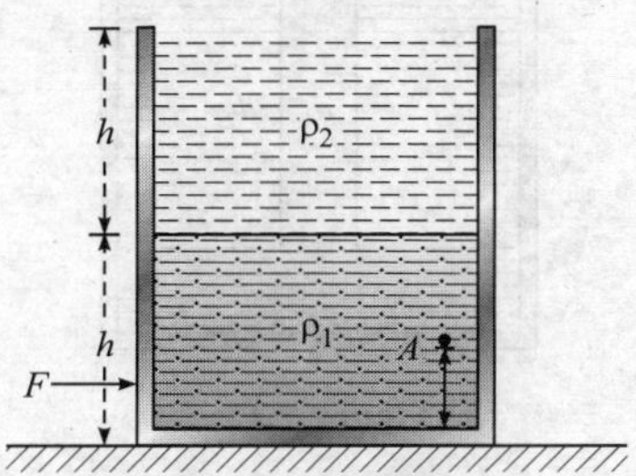

Figure 7.120

Ans. [(a) 4 m/s, (b) 7.2 N, (c) Zero, 52.2 N]

7-60 A conical vessel without a bottom stands on a table. A liquid is poured with the vessel & as soon as the level reaches h, the pressure of the liquid raises the vessel. The radius of the base of the vessel is R and half angle of the cone is α and the weight of the vessel is W. What is the density of the liquid ?

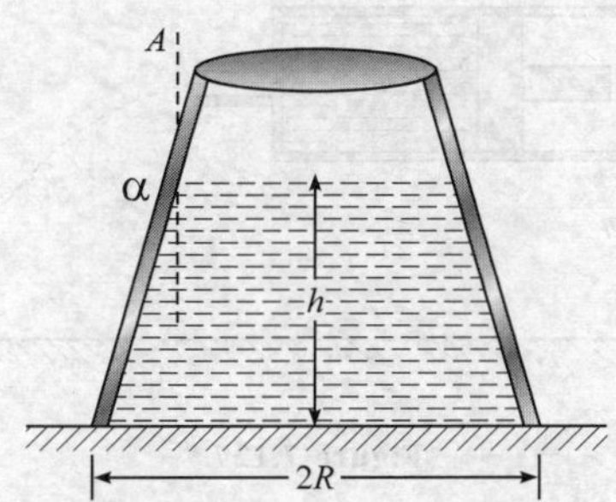

Figure 7.121

Ans. [$\rho = \dfrac{W}{\pi h^2 \rho g \tan\alpha\left(R - \frac{1}{3} h \tan\alpha\right)}$]

7-61 Water flows in a horizontal pipe whose one end is closed with a value and the pressure gauge falls to $1 \times 10^5\ N/m^2$ when the valve is opened. Calculate the speed of water flowing in the pipe.

Ans. [20 m/s]

7-62 A liquid is kept in a cylindrical vessel which is rotated along its axis. The liquid rises at the sides. If the radius of the vessel is 0.05 m and the speed of rotation is 2 rev. per sec., find the difference in the height of the liquid at the centre of the vessel and at its sides.

Ans. [0.02 m]

7-63 A cylindrical tank of base area A has a small hole of area 'a' at the bottom. At time $t = 0$, a tap starts to supply water into the tank at a constant rate $\alpha\ m^3/s$.
(a) What is the maximum level of water h_{max} in the tank?
(b) Find the time when level of water becomes h ($< h_{max}$).

Ans. [(a) $\dfrac{\alpha^2}{2ga^2}$, (b) $\dfrac{A}{ag}\left[\dfrac{\alpha}{a}\ln\left\{\dfrac{\alpha - a\sqrt{2gh}}{\alpha}\right\} - \sqrt{2gh}\right]$]

7-64 The figure-7.122 shows a siphon in action. The liquid flowing through the siphon has a density of $1.5\ gm/cm^3$. Calculate the pressure difference between
(a) Points A and D,
(b) Pints B and C

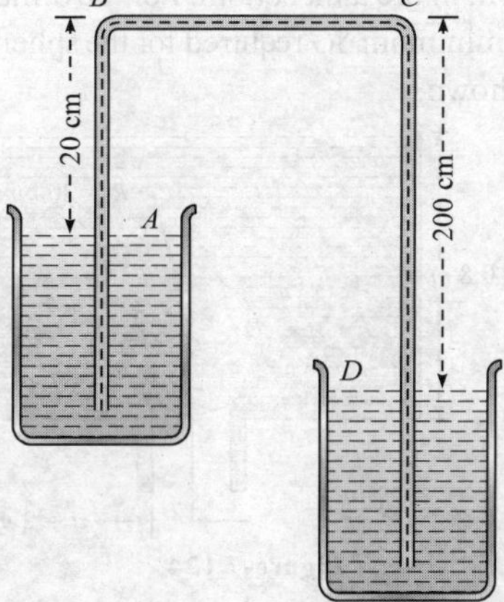

Figure 7.122

Ans. [(a) 0, (b) $26460\ N/m^2$]

7-65 A ball of density d is dropped onto a horizontal solid surface. It bounces elastically from the surface and returns to its original position in a time t_1. Next, the ball is released and it falls through the same height before striking the surface of a liquid of density d_L.
(a) if $d < d_L$, obtain an expression (in terms of d, t_1 and d_L) for the time t_2 the ball takes to come back to the position from which it was released.
(b) is the motion of the ball simple harmonic ?
(c) if $d = d_L$, how does the speed f the ball depend on its depth inside the liquid ? Neglect all frictional and other dissipative forces. Assume the depth of the liquid to be large.

Ans. [(a) $t_1\left(\dfrac{d_L}{d_L - d}\right)$, (b) No]

7-66 A water clock used in ancient Greek is designed as a closed vessel with a small orifice O. The time is determined according to the level of the water in the vessel. What should be the shape of the vessel be for the time scale to be uniform. Find mathematical equation governing curve AOB.

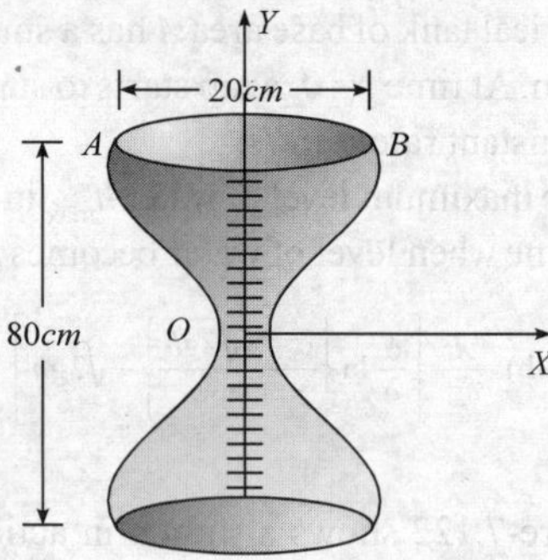

Figure 7.123

Ans. [$y = 4 \times 10^{-3}\, x^4$]

7-67 A sphere of radius R, made from material of specific gravity SG, is submerged in a tank of water. The sphere is placed over a hole, of radius a, in the tank bottom. For the dimensions given, determine the minimum SG required for the sphere to remain in the position shown.

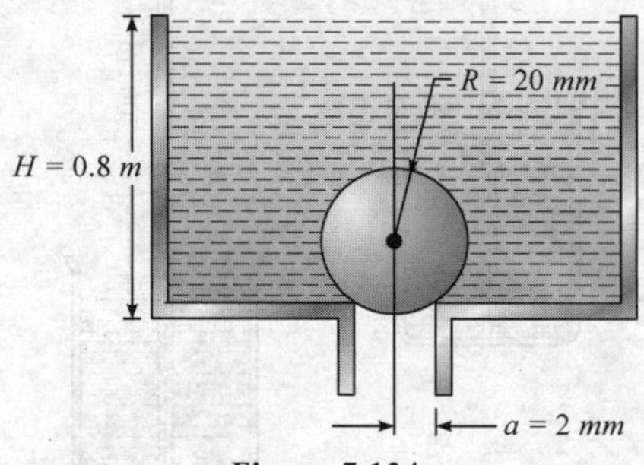

Figure-7.124

Ans. [$SG > 0.70$]

7-68 Two identical containers are open at the top and are connected at the bottom via a tube of negligible volume and a valve which is closed. Both containers are filled initially to the same height of 1.00 m, one with water, the other with mercury, as the drawing indicates. The valve is then opened. Water and mercury are immiscible. Determine the fluid level in the left container when equilibrium is re-established.

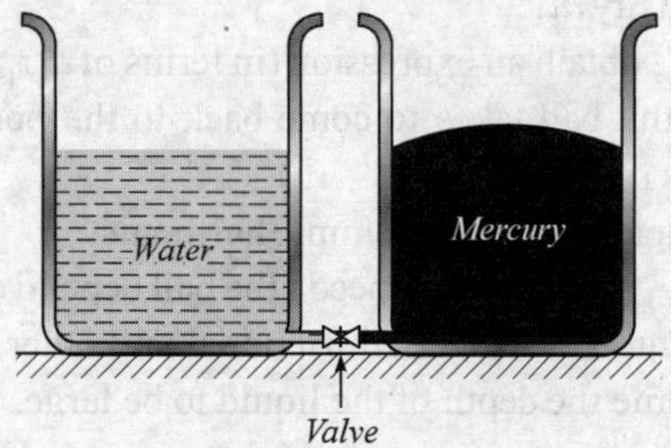

Figure 7.125

Ans. [1.46 m]

7-69 A thin rod of length L & area of cross-section S is pivoted at its lowest point P inside a stationary, homogeneous & non-viscous liquid (Figure-7.126). The rod is free to rotate in a vertical plane about a horizontal axis passing through P. The density d_1 of the material of the rod is smaller than the density d_2 of the liquid. The rod is displaced by a small angle θ from its equilibrium position and then released. Show that the motion of the rod is simple harmonic and determine its angular frequency in terms of the given parameters.

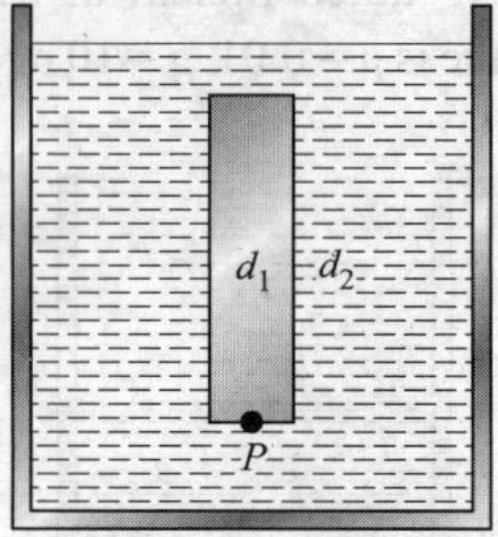

Figure 7.126

Ans. [$\omega = \left[\dfrac{3(d_2 - d_1)g}{2d_1L}\right]^{1/2}$]

7-70 A syringe of diameter $D = 8$ mm and having a nozzle of diameter $d = 2$ mm is placed horizontally at a height of 1.25 m as shown in the figure-7.127. An incompressible and non-viscous liquid is filled in syringe and the piston is moved at speed of $v = 0.25$ m/s. Find the range of liquid jet on the ground.

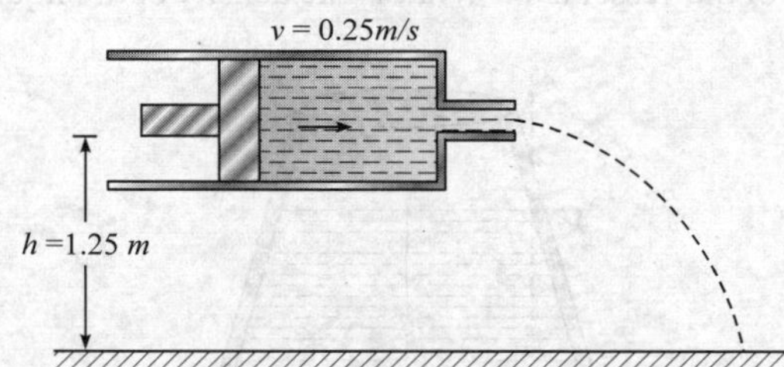

Figure 7.127

Ans. [2 m]

7-71 A water pipe with internal diameter of 2 cm carries water at the floor of a house with velocity 2 m/s and at pressure 2×10^5 N/m^2. Another pipe of internal diameter 1 cm is connected to it and takes water to 1st floor, 5 m above ground. What is the velocity and water pressure at 1st floor? (Take $g = 10$ m/s^2).

Ans. [8 m/s, 1.2×10^5 N/m^2]

7-72 Water and oil are poured into the two limbs of a U-tube containing mercury (figure-7.128). The interfaces of the mercury and the liquids are at the same height in both limbs. Determine the height of the water column h_1 if that of the oil $h_2 = 20$ cm. The density of the oil is 0.9.

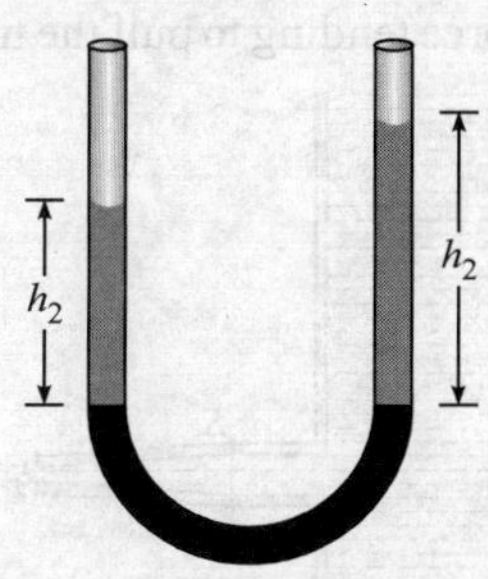

Figure 7.128

Ans. [18 cm]

7-73 Pure water is added drop by drop to a vessel of volume V filled with a salt solution of specific gravity γ which is allowed to overflow. Find the specific gravity of the solution when a volume U of water has been poured.

Ans. [$\rho = 1 + (\gamma - 1)\, e^{U/V}$]

7-74 Water flows out of a big tank along a tube at right angles. The inside radius of the tube is equal to r as shown in figure-7.129. The length of the horizontal section of the tube is equal to l. The water flow rate is Q litres/second. Find the moment of reaction forces of flowing water, acting on the tube's walls, relative to the point O.

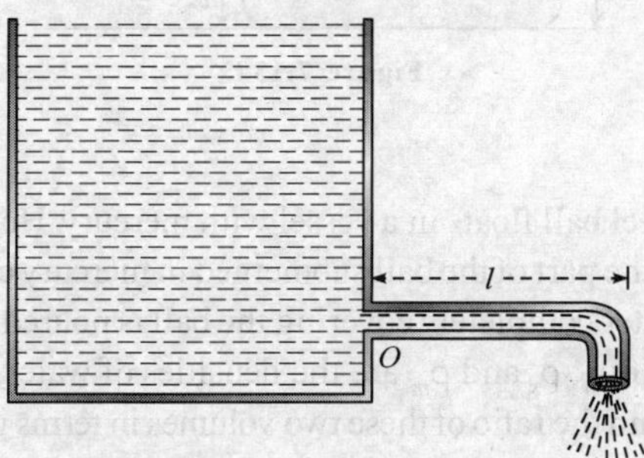

Figure 7.129

Ans. [$\left(\frac{Q^2\rho}{\pi r^2}\right) l$]

7-75 A cylindrical tank with a height $h = 1$ m is filled with water up to its brim. (a) what time is required to empty the tank through an orifice at its bottom it the cross-sectional area of the orifice is $\frac{1}{400}$ that of tank? (b) Compare this time with that required for the same volume of water to flow out of the tank if the water level in the tank is maintained constant at a height $h = 1$ m from the orifice.

Ans. [(a) 3 min. (b) 1.5 min.]

7-76 An open rectangular tank with dimensions 5 m × 4 m × 3 m contains water upto a height of 2 m is accelerated horizontally along the longer side.

(a) Determine the maximum acceleration that can be given without spilling the water.

(b) If this acceleration is increased by 20%. Calculate the percentage of water spilt over.

(c) If initially, the tank is closed at the top and is accelerated horizontally by 9 m/s^2, find the gauge pressure at the bottom of the front and rear walls of the tank. ($g = 10$ m/s^2)

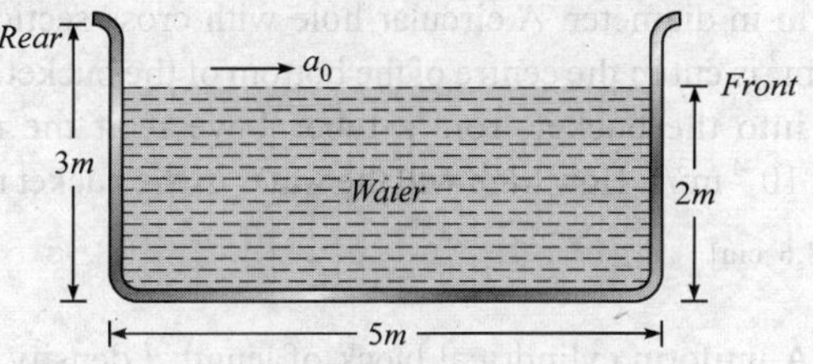

Figure 7.130

Ans. [(a) 4 m/s^2 (b) 10% (c) Zero, 4.5 × 10^5 pa]

7-77 Two holes, each of area $A = 0.2$ cm^2 are drilled in the wall of a vessel filled with water. The distances of the holes from the level of water are h and $h + H$. Find the point where the streams flowing out of the holes intersect. The level of water is maintained in the vessel by regulated supply.

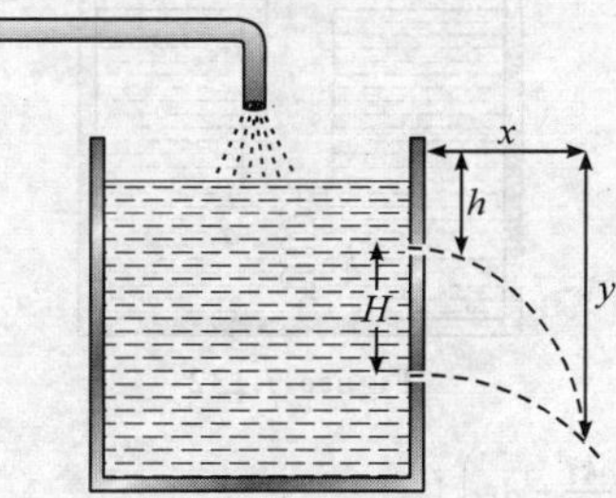

Figure 7.131

Ans. [$x = 2\sqrt{h(h+H)}$, $y = H + 2h$]

7-78 A vertical tube has diameter 0.016 m at its bottom end from which water flows out at the rate of 1.2 kg per minute. The pressure at the end is atmospheric pressure 0.7 m of mercury. If the diameter of the tube is 0.004 m at a height of 0.3 m from the bottom end, find the pressure there.

Ans. [0.7303 m of mercury]

7-79 A cylinder tank of height 0.4 m is open at the top and has a diameter 0.16 m. Water is filled in it upto a height of 0.16 m. Calculate how long will it take to empty the tank through a hole of radius 5 × 10^{-3} m in its bottom.

Ans. [46.265 s]

7-80 A large open top container of negligible mass and uniform cross-sectional area A has a small hole of cross-sectional area $A/100$ in its side wall near the bottom. The container is kept on a smooth horizontal floor and contains a liquid of density ρ and mass m_0. Assuming that the liquid starts flowing out horizontally

through the hole at $t = 0$, Calculate
(i) the acceleration of the container, and
(ii) its velocity when 75% of the liquid has drained out

Ans. [(i) 0.2 m/sec^2, (ii) $10\sqrt{\left(\frac{2m_0}{A\rho g}\right)}$]

7-81 A cylindrical bucket, open at the top, is 0.200 m high and 0.100 m in diameter. A circular hole with cross-section area 1.00 cm^2 is cut in the centre of the bottom of the bucket. Water flows into the bucket from a tube above it at the rate of 1.30×10^{-4} m^3/s. How high will the water in the bucket rise?

Ans. [8.6 cm]

7-82 A uniform cylindrical block of length l density d_1 and area of cross section A floats in a liquid of density d_2 contained in a vessel ($d_2 > d_1$). The bottom of the cylinder just rests on a spring of constant k. The other end of the spring is fixed to the bottom of the vessel. A weight that may be placed on top of the cylinder such that the cylinder is just submerged in the liquid. Find the weight.

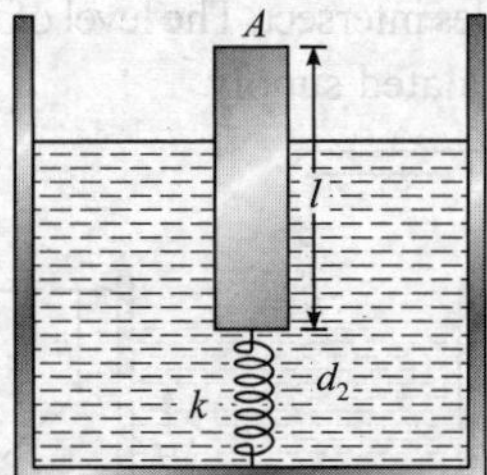

Figure 7.132

Ans. [$l(d_2 - d_1)\left(\frac{k}{d_2} + Ag\right)$]

7-83 Water leaks out from an open tank through a hole of area 2 mm^2 in the bottom. Suppose water is filled up to height of 80 cm and the area of cross-section of the tank is 0.4 m^2. the pressure at the open surface and at the hole are equal to the atmospheric pressure. Neglect the small velocity of the water near the open surface in the tank. (a) Find the initial speed of water coming out of the hole. (b) Find the speed of water coming out when half of water has laked out. (c) Find the volume of water leaked out during a time interval dt after the height remained is h. Thus find the decrease in height dh in terms of h and dt. (d) From the result of part (c) find the time required for half of the water to leak out.

Ans. [(a) 4 m/s, (b) $\sqrt{8}$ m/s,
(c) (2 mm^2) $\sqrt{2gh}\ dt$, $\sqrt{2gh} \times 5 \times 10^{-6}$ dt, (d) 6.5 hours]

7-84 A side wall of a wide open tank is provided with a narrowing tube through which water flows out. The cross-sectional area of the tube decreases from $S = 3.0$ cm^2 to $s = 1.0$ cm^2. The water level in the tank is $h = 4.6$ m higher than in the tube. Neglecting the viscosity of water, find the horizontal component of the force tending to pull the tube out of the tank.

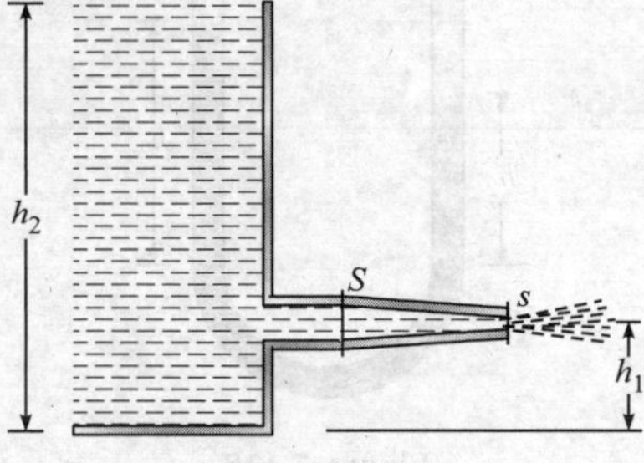

Figure 7.133

Ans. [6 N]

7-85 A fixed cylindrical tank having large cross-section area is filled with two liquids of densities ρ and 2ρ and in equal volumes as shown in the figure-7.134. A small hole of area of cross-section $a = \sqrt{6}$ cm^2 is made at height $h/2$ from the bottom. Find the area of cross-section of stream of liquid in cm^2 just before it hits the ground.

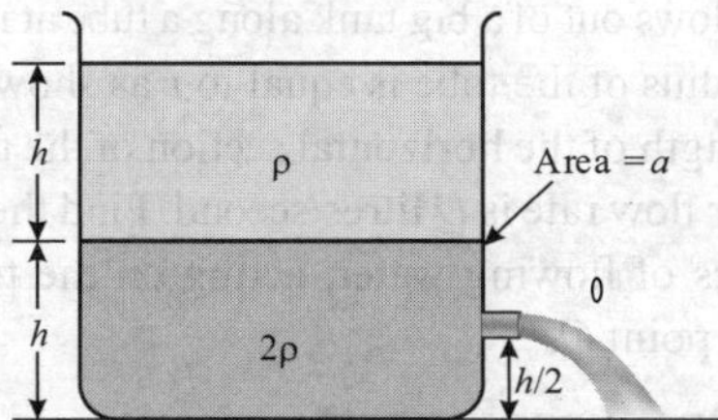

Figure 7.134

Ans. [2]

7-86 A steel ball floats in a vessel with mercury. How will the volume of the part of the ball submerged in mercury change if a layer of water completely covering the ball is poured above the mercury? If ρ_w, ρ_s and ρ_m are the densities of water, steel and mercury, find the ratio of these two volumes in terms in of ρ_w, ρ_s and ρ_m.

Ans. [$\left[\frac{V_0}{V_1} = \frac{1-\rho_w/\rho_m}{1-\rho_w/\rho_s}\right]$]

7-87 Water flows through a tube shown in figure-7.135. The areas of cross-section at A and B are 1 cm^2 and 0.5 cm^2 respectively. The height difference between A and B is 5 cm. If the speed of water at A is 10 cm/s find (a) the speed at B and (b) the difference in pressures at A and B.

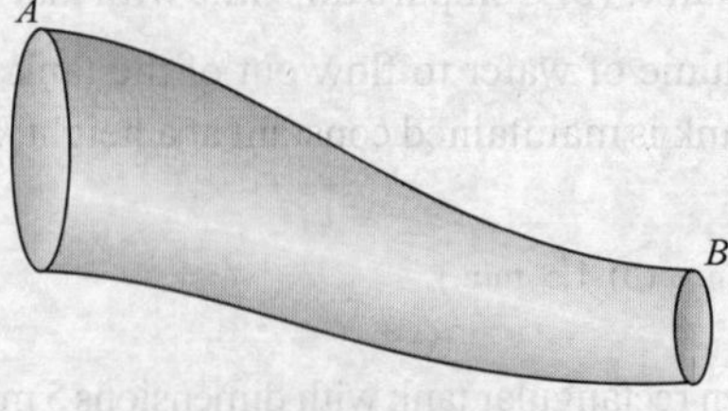

Figure 7.135

Ans. [(a) 20 cm/s, (b) 485 N/m^2]

* * * * *

ANSWERS & SOLUTIONS

CONCEPTUAL MCQS Single Option Correct

1	(B)	**2**	(A)	**3**	(C)
4	(C)	**5**	(C)	**6**	(A)
7	(C)	**8**	(B)	**9**	(A)
10	(D)	**11**	(B)	**12**	(A)
13	(D)	**14**	(A)	**15**	(A)
16	(C)	**17**	(A)	**18**	(D)
19	(B)	**20**	(A)	**21**	(A)
22	(A)	**23**	(A)	**24**	(A)
25	(C)	**26**	(B)	**27**	(D)
28	(B)	**29**	(C)	**30**	(B)
31	(C)	**32**	(B)	**33**	(B)
34	(B)	**35**	(A)		

NUMERICAL MCQS Single Option Correct

1	(D)	**2**	(D)	**3**	(A)
4	(C)	**5**	(B)	**6**	(C)
7	(D)	**8**	(B)	**9**	(C)
10	(D)	**11**	(D)	**12**	(B)
13	(C)	**14**	(A)	**15**	(D)
16	(C)	**17**	(D)	**18**	(A)
19	(A)	**20**	(D)	**21**	(B)
22	(D)	**23**	(C)	**24**	(D)
25	(D)	**26**	(B)	**27**	(C)
28	(D)	**29**	(B)	**30**	(D)
31	(B)	**32**	(B)	**33**	(B)
34	(C)	**35**	(B)	**36**	(C)
37	(C)	**38**	(B)	**39**	(A)
40	(C)	**41**	(A)	**42**	(B)
43	(B)	**44**	(D)	**45**	(C)
46	(B)	**47**	(C)	**48**	(B)
49	(B)	**50**	(C)	**51**	(B)
52	(A)	**53**	(C)	**54**	(C)
55	(B)	**56**	(D)	**57**	(C)
58	(B)	**59**	(D)	**60**	(A)
61	(A)	**62**	(C)	**63**	(D)
64	(D)	**65**	(D)	**66**	(B)
67	(D)	**68**	(A)	**69**	(D)
70	(B)	**71**	(C)	**72**	(B)
73	(D)	**74**	(C)	**75**	(A)
76	(B)	**77**	(B)	**78**	(A)
79	(C)	**80**	(D)	**81**	(A)
82	(A)	**83**	(A)	**84**	(A)
85	(A)	**86**	(B)	**87**	(D)
88	(C)	**89**	(B)	**90**	(C)
91	(C)	**92**	(D)	**93**	(A)
94	(C)	**95**	(B)	**96**	(B)
97	(C)	**98**	(A)	**99**	(D)
100	(C)	**101**	(B)	**102**	(D)
103	(B)	**104**	(A)	**105**	(A)
106	(B)	**107**	(B)	**108**	(D)
109	(B)	**110**	(A)	**111**	(A)
112	(C)	**113**	(A)	**114**	(A)
115	(D)				

ADVANCE MCQs One or More Option Correct

1	(A)	**2**	(A, B, C)	**3**	(B, D)
4	(A, C, D)	**5**	(B, C)	**6**	(B, D)
7	(A, C)	**8**	(A, B, C)	**9**	(B, C, D)
10	(B, C)	**11**	(A, B, C)	**12**	(A, C, D)
13	(A, C)	**14**	(A, D)	**15**	(B, C, D)
16	(C, D)				

Solutions of PRACTICE EXERCISE 1.1

(i) For A $\quad v_A = \dfrac{30}{t}$

$\Rightarrow \quad 20 = \dfrac{30}{t}$

$\Rightarrow \quad t = \dfrac{3}{2}\,hr = 90$ min

For B actual riding time is

$$70\text{ min} = \frac{7}{6}\,hr$$

$$v_B = \frac{30}{7} \times 6 = \frac{180}{7} = 25.75 \text{ kph}$$

(ii) Time for sound to travel 1 km

$$t = \frac{100}{340} = 2.94 \text{ sec}$$

Thus $\quad N = 3$ for $t = 0$, 1 and 2 seconds

(iii) Time to overtake $\quad t = \dfrac{10}{5} = 2$s

Road distance covered $\quad = 25 \times 2 + 5 = 55$ m

(iv) $\dfrac{l(t_1)}{v_0}$ ——— l ——— $\dfrac{t_2/2}{v_1}$ $\dfrac{t_2/2}{v_2}$

$$\text{Mean velocity} = \frac{2l}{t_1 + t_2};$$

We use $\quad l = v_0 t_1$

$\Rightarrow \quad t_1 = l/v_0$

and $\quad l = \dfrac{v_1 t_2}{2} + \dfrac{v_2 t_2}{2}$

$\Rightarrow \quad t_2 = \dfrac{2l}{v_1 + v_2}$

$$= \frac{2l}{\dfrac{l}{v_0} + \dfrac{2l}{v_1 + v_2}} = \frac{2v_0(v_1 + v_2)}{v_1 + v_2 + 2v_0}$$

(v) If car turn off the highway at a distance x from point $D\,(CD=x)$

time to reach point B by car is

$$t=\frac{L-x}{v}+\frac{\sqrt{L^2+x^2}}{\frac{b}{\eta}}$$

t is min when $\frac{dt}{dx}=0$

Which results $x=\frac{l}{\sqrt{\eta^2-1}}$

(vi) If v_1 and v_2 are velocity of sound and wind we use

$$t_1=\frac{l}{v_1+v_2};$$

$$t_2=\frac{l}{v_1-v_2}$$

$$v_1+v_2=\frac{l}{t_1}$$

$$v_1-v_2=\frac{l}{t_2}$$

Solving we get $v_1=\frac{l}{2}\left(\frac{1}{t_1}+\frac{1}{t_2}\right)$

and $v_2=\frac{l}{2}\left(\frac{1}{t_1}-\frac{1}{t_2}\right)$

(vii) If sides are x and $x+1$, we use

$$\frac{x+(x+1)}{4}-\frac{\sqrt{x^2+(x+1)^2}}{4}=0.5$$

on solving we get $x=3$ & $x+1=4$

(viii) Time taken by car to reach wall

$$t=\frac{20}{40}=0.5\text{ hr}$$

Total distance travelled by fly in 0.5 hr is

$$s=100\times 0.5=50\text{ km}$$

Each trip distance will be in converging GP so number of trips will be ∞

Solutions of PRACTICE EXERCISE 1.2

(i) During acceleration $v=at=4\times 5=20$ m/s

$$s_1=\frac{1}{2}at^2=\frac{1}{2}\times 4\times (5)^2=50\text{ m}$$

During uniform motion $s_2=vt=20\times 25=500$ m

During retardation $t=\frac{1}{a}=\frac{20}{2}-10$ sec

$$s_3=vt-\frac{1}{2}at^2$$

$$=20\times 10-\frac{1}{2}\times 2\times (10)^2=100\text{ m}$$

Total distance $=50+500+100=650$ m

(ii) (a) $a=\frac{48\times\frac{5}{18}}{3.6}=3.7\text{m/s}^2$

(b) $a=\frac{48\times\frac{5}{18}}{10.2-3.6}=2.01\text{m/s}^2$

(c) $a=\frac{v^2}{2s}=\frac{\left(140\times\frac{5}{18}\right)^2}{2\times 400}=1.89\text{ m/s}^2$

(iii) As time are equal $t=\sqrt{\frac{2\sqrt{2}L}{a}}=\frac{2L}{v}$

$$\frac{2\sqrt{2}L}{a}=\frac{4L^2}{v^2}$$

$$\Rightarrow\quad a=\frac{v^2}{\sqrt{2}L}$$

(iv) Overtaking time $=\frac{600}{20}=30$ s

If car's initial speed is u,

$$600=4(30)+\frac{1}{2}(1)(30)^2$$

$$\Rightarrow\quad u=5\text{ m/s}$$

After 30 sec car's speed $v=5+(1)(30)=35$ m/s

in next 20 sec separation between car & truck $=(35-20)\times 20=300$ m

Note: This problem can also be sloved easily using graphs.

(v) Time to which motorcycle accelerates

$$t_1=\frac{v_1}{a_1}=\frac{10}{1}=105$$

and $s_1=\frac{1}{2}(1)(10)^2=50$ m

Time to which car accelerates

$$t_2 = \frac{v_2}{a_2} = \frac{15}{0.5} = 30s$$

and $$s_2 = \frac{1}{2}(0.5)(30)^2 = 225\,\text{m}$$

If overtaking occurs at time t, we use

$$50 + 10(t-10) = 225 + 15(t-30)$$

$$10t - 50 = 15t - 225$$

$$5t = 175$$

$$t = \frac{175}{5} = 35\text{ s}$$

at $$t = 35\text{ s}$$

Distance is $$s = 50 + 10(35-10) = 300\,\text{m}$$

Note: This problem

(vi) $$30 = 20t_R + \frac{(20)^2}{2a}$$

$$10 = 10t_R + \frac{(10)^2}{2a}$$

Solving (1) and (2) we get

$$a = 10\text{ m/s}^2$$

$$t_R = 0.5\text{ s}$$

Thus at 15 m/s $$s = 15t_R + \frac{(15)^2}{2a}$$

$$= 15 \times 0.5 + \frac{225}{20}$$

$$= 7.5 + 11.25 = 18.75\,\text{m}$$

(vii) A —u— l, $2t$ — C —v_c— l, t — B —v→

For unform acceleration $v^2 = v_c^2 + 2al$

$$v_c^2 = u^2 + 2al$$

Solving $$v_c = \sqrt{\frac{v^2 + u^2}{2}}$$

Also $$v_c = u + 2at$$

and $$v = v_c + at$$

Substituting v_c and elaminating at we get

$$v = 7u$$

(viii) If t is normal runing time then

$$t = \frac{l}{80}$$

Delhi — 80 kph — 100 kph — Pune; segments x_1 (t_1), x_2 (t_2), $l - x_1 - x_2$ (t_3)

Here $$t_1 = \frac{x_1}{80} + 2$$

$$t_2 = \frac{100-80}{20} = 1\text{ hr}$$

$$t_3 = \frac{l - x_1 - x_2}{100}$$

Here $$x_2 = 80(1) + \frac{1}{2}(20)(1)^2 = 90\text{ km}$$

Thus total time $$t = t_1 + t_2 + t_3 = \frac{l}{80}$$

$$\left(\frac{x_1}{80} + 2\right) + 1 + \left(\frac{l - x_1 - 90}{100}\right) = \frac{l}{80}$$

Soving it gives $$l - x_1 = 840\,\text{km}$$

(ix) Distance of event-1 is

$$s_1 = 350 + \frac{1}{2} \times 0.03 \times (30)^2 = 363.5\,\text{m}$$

Distance of event-2 is $$s_2 = \frac{1}{2} \times 0.03 \times (90)^2 = 121.5\,\text{m}$$

Distance between event-1 and 2 frame of train

$$= 350\,\text{m}$$

Distance between event-1 and 2 frame of ground

$$= s_1 - s_2 = 242\,\text{m}$$

Speed of frome in which both event occur at same place

$$v = \frac{242}{60} = 4.03\text{ m/s}$$

(x) Stopping distance of car-1

$$= \frac{(10)^2}{2 \times 2} = 25\,\text{m}$$

Stopping distance of car-2

$$= \frac{(12)^2}{2 \times 2} = 36\,\text{m}$$

Separation between cars

$$= 150 - 25 - 36 = 89\,\text{m}$$

(xi) After time t

$$40t = \frac{1}{2} \times 4 \times t^2$$

$$t = 20 \text{ s}$$

Distance between then at time t

$$x = 40t - 2t^2$$

x is max when $\frac{dx}{dt} = 40 - 4t = 0 \Rightarrow t = 10 \text{ s}$

$$x_{max} = 40(10) - 2(10)^2 = 200 \text{ m}$$

Solutions of PRACTICE EXERCISE 1.3

(i) Given that $1.6 = \frac{1}{2} a (4)^2$ which gives

$$a = 0.2 \text{ m/s}^2$$

First mark is at $s_1 = \frac{1}{2} a (2)^2 = \frac{1}{2}\, 0.2 \times (2)^2 = 0.4 \text{ m}$

Fourth mark is at $s_4 = \frac{1}{2} a (8)^2 = \frac{1}{2} \times 0.2 \times (8)^2 = 6.4 \text{ m}$

(ii) Total time of fall is $t = \sqrt{\frac{2 \times 176.4}{9.8}} = 6\text{s}$

Time internal between drops = 2s

Location of second drop $= \frac{1}{2} \times 9.8 \times (4)^2 = 78.4 \text{ m}$

Location of third drop $= \frac{1}{2} \times 9.8 \times (2)^2 = 19.6 \text{ m}$

(iii) $h = uT - gT^2$ gives

$$u = \frac{h + \frac{1}{2} gT^2}{T}$$

Max hight in $H = \frac{u^2}{2g} = \frac{(2h + gT^2)^2}{8gT^2}$

(iv) Projection speed $u = \sqrt{2gh} = 10\text{m/s}$

Total time of motion $t = \frac{2u}{g} = 2\text{s}$

Internal between balls $= 0.5\text{s}$

Height of 2nd ball $h_2 = 10(1.5) - \frac{1}{2}(10)(1.5)^2 = 3.75 \text{ m}$

Height of 3rd ball $h_3 = 10(1) - \frac{1}{2}(10)(1)^2 = 5 \text{ m}$

Height of 4th ball $h_4 = 10(0.5) - \frac{1}{2}(10)(0.5)^2 = 3.75 \text{ m}$

(v) If at the bottom & of window speed of potential is u and v

$$v = u - 32 \times 0.5$$

and $v^2 = u^2 - 2 \times 32 \times 5$

Solving we get $u = 16 \text{ } f/s;\ v = 4f/\text{sec}$

Height above window the potential rises is

$$h = \frac{v^2}{2g} = \frac{(u)^2}{2 \times 32} = \frac{1}{16} ft$$

(vi) Given that $-h = ut_1 - \frac{1}{2} gt_1^2$ ...(1)

$$h = ut_2 + \frac{1}{2} gt_2^2 \quad ...(2)$$

$$h = \frac{1}{2} gt_3^2 \quad ...(3)$$

Solving (1), (2) and (3) we get

$$t_3 = \sqrt{t_1 t_2}$$

(vii) We use

$$3 = \sqrt{\frac{2h}{g}} + \frac{h}{340}$$

Solving we get $h = 40.7 \text{ m}$

(viii) If time to fall is t, we use

$$60 = 5t + \frac{1}{2}(10)t^2$$

$$t^2 + t - 12 = 0$$

$$t = 3 \text{ sec}$$

Distance of teacher from building

$$= 2 \times 3 = 6 \text{ m}$$

(ix) Fall in $3s$ is $h = \frac{1}{2}(10)(3)^2 = 45 \text{ m}$

Total time of fall for boy $= \sqrt{\frac{2 \times 100}{10}} = \sqrt{20}s$

Time available for batman $= (\sqrt{20} - 3)s = 1.472s$

We use $100 = u(\sqrt{20} - 3) + \frac{1}{2}(10)(\sqrt{20} - 3)^2$

Solving we get $u = 60.5 \text{ m/s}$

(x) Given that $-27.3 = u(16) - \frac{1}{2}(9.8)(16)^2$

Solving we get $u = 76.8\text{ m/s}$

Max height by apple $H = \frac{(76.8)^2}{2\times 9.8} + 27.3 = 327.45\text{ m}$

(xi) Height ascend in 1 min is

$$h = \frac{1}{2}\times 30\times (60)^2 = 54000\text{ m}$$

Further height reached $= \frac{(1800)^2}{2\times 10} = \frac{324\times 10^4}{20} = 162000\text{ m}$

maximum height attained $= 54000 + 162000\text{ m}$

$= 216000\text{ m} = 216\text{ km}$

Total time taken $t = 60 + \frac{1800}{10} + \sqrt{\frac{2\times 216000}{10}}$

$= 447.84\text{ s}$

Solutions of PRACTICE EXERCISE 1.4

(i) Total distance travelled can be calculated by area under *v-t* curve shown in figure

$$s = \frac{1}{2}\times 30\times 50 = 750\text{ m}$$

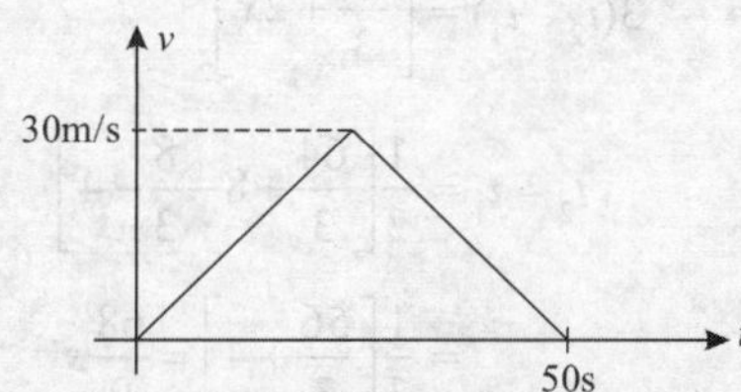

(ii) Average velocity is zero at $t = 15$s when displacement is zero. This can be shown by dotted line in graph mentioned below

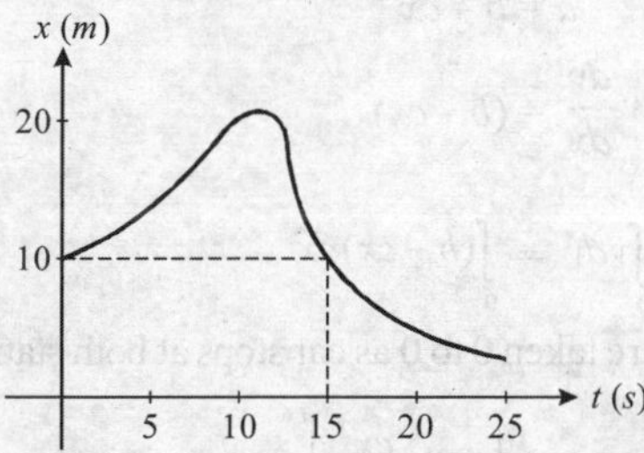

(iii) Given that $t_1 + t_2 = 4$ min. ...(1)

Total distance is $s = \frac{1}{2}v_m(t_1 + t_2) = 4km$

$v_m = 2\text{ km/min}$

Here we also have $a_1 = \frac{v_m}{t_1}$ and $a_2 = \frac{v_m}{t_2}$

From equation (1) $\frac{2}{a_1} + \frac{2}{a_2} = 4$

$$\frac{1}{a_1} + \frac{1}{a_2} = 2$$

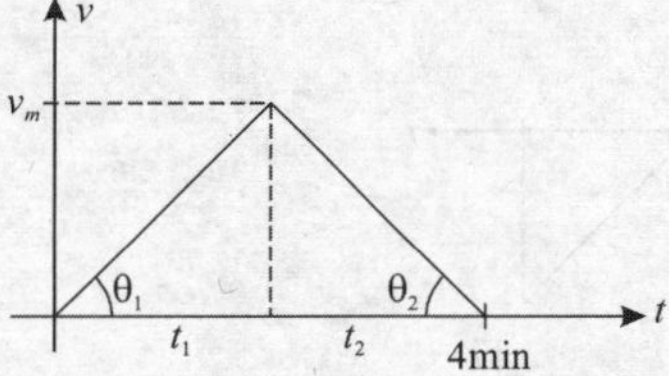

(iv) Below given *v-t* graph shows the motion

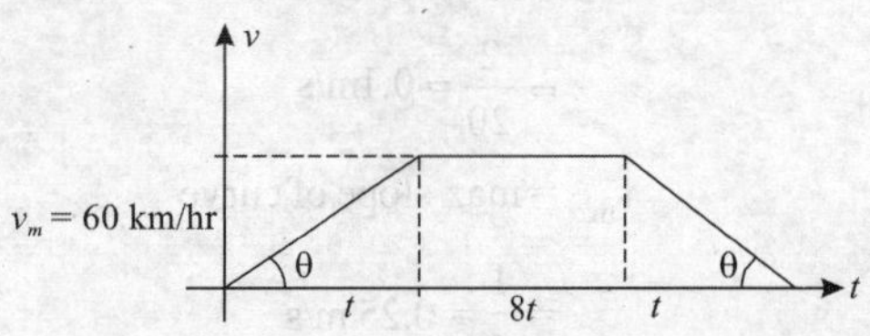

Average speed $= \frac{\text{Area under } v\text{ - }t \text{ curve}}{10t}$

$$= \frac{\frac{1}{2}\times 60\times 18t}{10t} = 54\text{ kph}$$

(v) Motion v-t graph is sown below

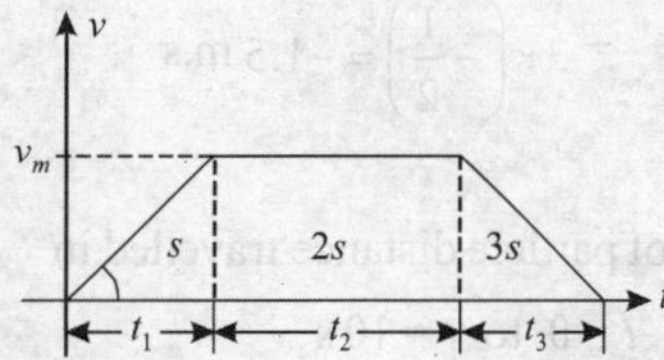

Total distance = 6*s*

Total time $= t_1 + t_2 + t_3$

Angular speed $= \frac{6s}{t_1 + t_2 + t_3}$

Max speed we use $v_m = \frac{2s}{t_1} = \frac{6s}{t_3} = \frac{2s}{t_2}$

Ratis of average speed to max speed

$$= \frac{6s}{\frac{2s}{v_m} + \frac{2s}{v_m} + \frac{6s}{v_m}} \Big/ v_m$$

$$= \frac{6}{10} = \frac{3}{5}$$

(vi)

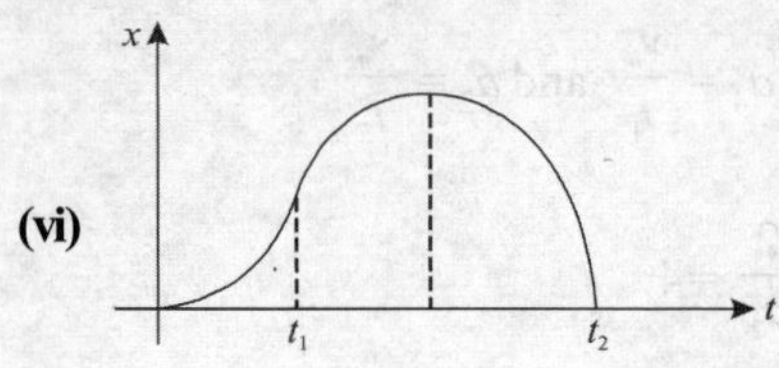

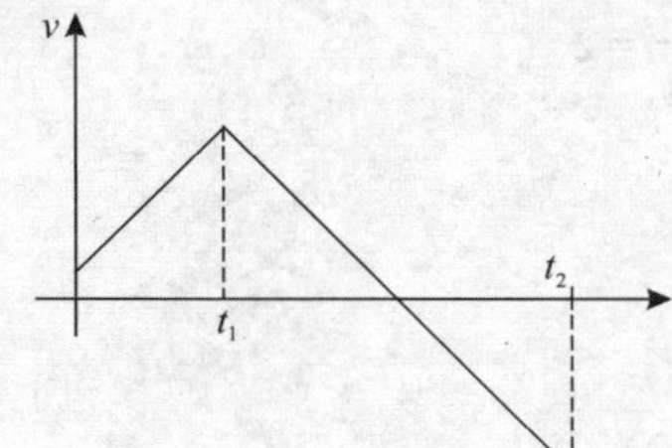

(vii) (a) $v_{avg} = \dfrac{\text{Total displacement}}{\text{Total time}}$

$= \dfrac{2}{20} = 0.1\text{m/s}$

(b) $v_{\max} = \text{max slope of curve}$

$= \dfrac{1}{4} = 0.25 \text{ m/s}$

(c) Instant velocity and mean velocity equal at the point where tangent to cuve passing through origin touches i.e

at $t = 16 \text{ s}$

(viii) acceleration $a = v.\dfrac{dv}{dx}$

$= 3\times\left(-\dfrac{1}{2}\right) = -1.5 \text{ m.s}$

(ix) Position time curve of particle distance travelled in

$t = 0$ to $t = 10$ s

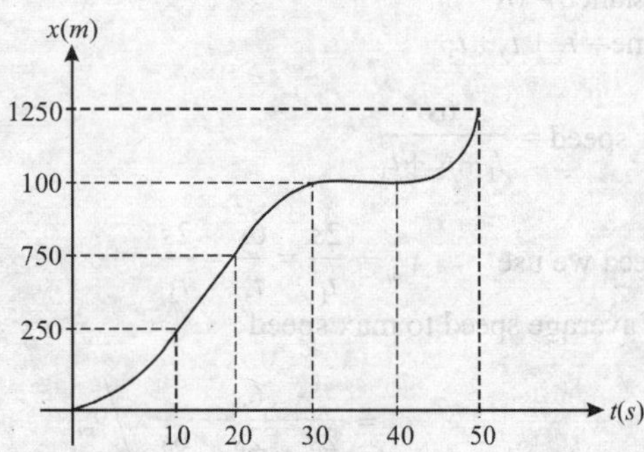

$s_1 = \dfrac{1}{2}\times 5\times(10)^2 = 250 \text{ m}$

$t = 10$ to $t = 20$

$s_2 = vt = 50\times 10 = 500 \text{ m}$

$t = 20$ to $t = 30$

$s_3 = s_1 = 250 \text{ m}$

$t = 30$ to $t = 40$

$s_4 = 0$

$t = 40$ to $t = 50$

$s_5 = s_1 = 350 \text{ m}$

Solutions of PRACTICE EXERCISE 1.5

(i) Given that $t = \sqrt{x} + 3$

$x = (t-3)^2 = t^2 - 6t + 9$

$v = \dfrac{dx}{dt} = 2t - 6 = 0$

at $t = 3\text{s}$ $x = 0 \text{ m}$

(ii) Given that $v = \dfrac{3}{x^2+2}$

$$\frac{dx}{dt} = \frac{3}{x^2+2}$$

$$\int_2^4 (x^2+2)dx = \int_{t_1}^{t_2} 3dt$$

$$3(t_2 - t_1) = \left[\frac{x^3}{3} + 2x\right]_2^4$$

$$t_2 - t_1 = \frac{1}{3}\left[\frac{64}{3} + 8 - \frac{8}{3} - 4\right]$$

$$= \frac{1}{3}\left[\frac{56}{3} + 4\right] = \frac{68}{9} s$$

Average velocity $v_{\text{avg}} = \dfrac{4-2}{t_2 - t_1} = \dfrac{2\times 9}{68} = 0.264 \text{ m/s}$

(iii) Given that $a = b - cx$

$$v\frac{dv}{dx} = (b - cx)$$

$$\int_0^0 vdv = \int_0^l (b - cx)dx$$

[limits for v are taken 0 to 0 as car stops at both stations]

$$0 = \left[bx - \frac{cx^2}{2}\right]_0^l$$

$$bl - \frac{cl^2}{2} = 0$$

$$l = \frac{2b}{c}$$

(iv) $x = t^3 - 6t^2 + 3t + 4$

$$v = \frac{dx}{dt} = 3t^2 - 12t + 3$$

$$a = \frac{dv}{dt} = 6t - 12 = 0$$

at $t = 2$ sec

$$v = 3(2)^2 - 12(2) + 3$$
$$= -9 \text{ m/s}$$

(v) $\vec{r} = \vec{b}t(1-\alpha t)$

(a) $$\vec{v} = \frac{\overrightarrow{dr}}{dt} = \vec{b} - 2\vec{b}\alpha t = \vec{b}(1-2\alpha t)$$

$$\vec{a} = \frac{d\vec{v}}{dt} = -2\vec{b}\alpha$$

(b) At which position $\vec{r} = 0$

$\Rightarrow$ $t = 1/\alpha$

For uniform acceleration distance covered in accelerated and retarded motion are equal in equal time interval so total distance is

$$s = b\left(\frac{1}{2\alpha}\right)\left[1-\alpha\left(\frac{1}{2\alpha}\right)\right] \times 2$$

$$= \frac{b}{2\alpha}$$

(vi) $a = -kv$

$$\frac{vdv}{dx} = kv$$

$$\int_{v_0}^{v_t} dv = -\int_0^l kdx$$

$$v_f - v_0 = -kl$$

$$v_f = v_0 - kl$$

When box is at a distance x from starting potential ts speed is

$$v = v_0 - kx$$

$$\frac{dx}{dt} = v_0 - kx$$

$$\int_0^l \frac{dx}{v_0 - kx} = \int_0^t dt$$

$$t = -\frac{1}{k}[\ln(v_0 - kx)]_0^l$$

$$= \frac{1}{k}\ln\left(\frac{v_0}{v_0 - kl}\right)$$

(vii) $a = Cv^2$

$$\frac{vdv}{dx} = -Cv^2$$

$$\int_u^{v_f} \frac{vdv}{v} = -\int_0^{2\pi R} Cdx$$

$$[\ln v]_u^{v_f} = -2\pi RC$$

$$\ln\left(\frac{v_f}{u}\right) = e^{-2\pi RC}$$

$$v_f = ue^{-2\pi RC}$$

Solutions of PRACTICE EXERCISE 1.6

(i)

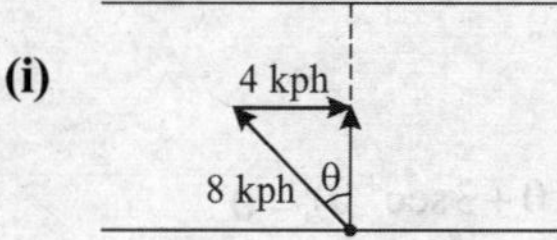

here $\theta = \sin^{-1}\frac{1}{2} = 30°$

Time to cross the river

$$t = \frac{0.5}{\sqrt{8^2 - 4^2}} = \frac{0.5}{\sqrt{48}}$$

$$t = \frac{1}{8\sqrt{3}} hr$$

$$= 4.33 \text{ min}$$

(ii)

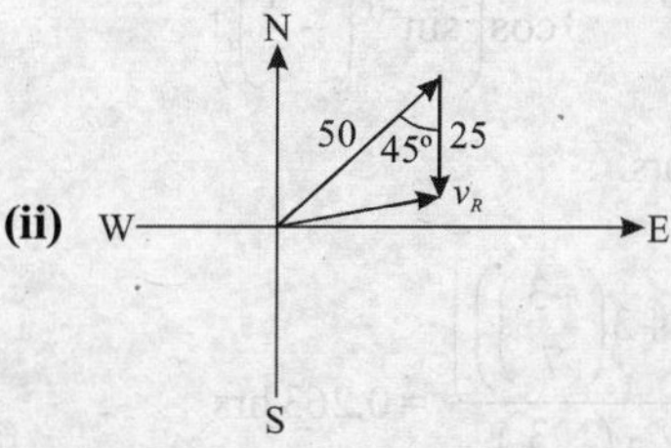

resultant speed of plane is

$$v_R = \sqrt{(50)^2 + (25)^2 - 2(50)(25)\cos 45°}$$

$$= 36.837 \text{ kph}$$

Displacement of plane in 2hrs

$$= 36.837 \times 2 = 73.67 \text{ km}$$

(iii)

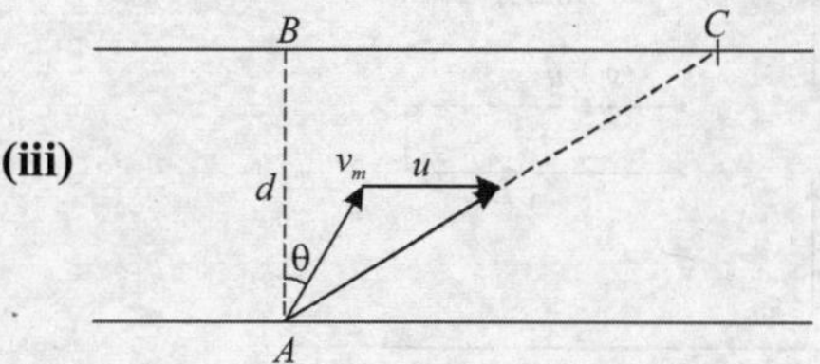

Time to cross the river

$$t_1 = \frac{d}{v_m \cos\theta}$$

Total drift $\quad BC = (u + v_m \sin\theta)\cdot \dfrac{d}{v_m \cos\theta}$

Time to return form C to B

$$t_2 = \frac{BC}{v_{mg}}$$

Total time $\quad T = t_1 + t_2$

$$T = \frac{0.5}{3\cos\theta} + \frac{0.5}{3\cos\theta}\frac{(2+3\sin\theta)}{5}$$

T will be least when $\quad \dfrac{dT}{d\theta} = 0$

$$\frac{0.5}{3}\sec\theta\tan\theta + \frac{0.1}{3}(2\sec\theta\tan\theta + 3\sec^2\theta) = 0$$

$$5\tan\theta + 2\tan\theta + 3\sec\theta = 0$$

$$7\tan\theta = -3\sec\theta$$

$$\sin\theta = -\frac{3}{7} \simeq 25^\circ 22'$$

$$\Rightarrow \quad \cos\theta = \sqrt{\frac{40}{7}}$$

Here θ could be negative to reduce distance BC

Time to cross is $t_1 = \dfrac{d}{v_m \cos\theta} = \dfrac{0.5}{3\cos\left(\sin^{-1}\left(-\dfrac{3}{7}\right)\right)}$

$$= 0.1845 \text{ hrs}$$

Time of walk is $\quad t_2 = \dfrac{0.5\left[\left(2+3\left(\dfrac{-3}{7}\right)\right)\right]}{15\sin^{-1}\left(-\dfrac{3}{7}\right)} = 0.263 \text{ hrs}$

(iv) Total time $\quad T = 0.1845 + 0.0263 = 0.2108$ hrs $= 12.65$ min

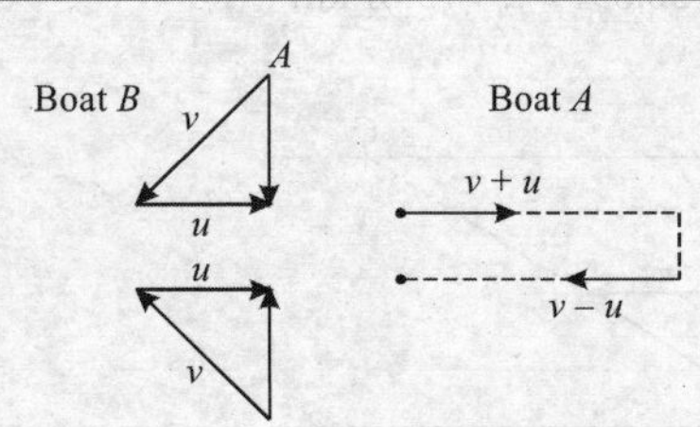

Time of motion of boat A

$$t_A = \frac{l}{v+u} + \frac{l}{v-u}$$

Time of motion of boat B

$$t_B = \frac{2l}{\sqrt{v^3 - u^2}}$$

$$\frac{t_A}{t_B} = 1.8 \qquad [\text{given that } v = 1.2u]$$

(v)

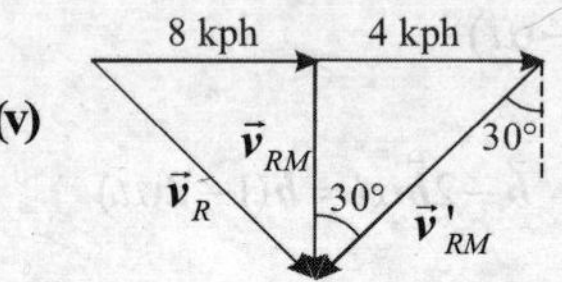

$$\vec{v}_R - \vec{v}_M = \vec{v}_{RM}$$

$$\vec{v}_R = \vec{v}_M + \vec{v}_{RM}$$

Here $\quad v_{RM} = 4\sqrt{3}kph$

Thus $\quad v_R = \sqrt{8^2 + (4\sqrt{3})^2}$

$$= 4\sqrt{7}\text{kph}$$

(vi)

$$a_{AB} = (a + 0.3t) \text{ m/s}^2$$

$$v_{AB} = 40 \text{ m/s}$$

$$s = 225 \text{ m}$$

If in time t_1, if A and B are just about to collide then

$$\int_{40}^{0} dv_{AB} = -\int_{0}^{t_1}(a+0.3t)dt$$

$$\Rightarrow \quad 40 = at_1 + \frac{0.3t_1^2}{2} \qquad \ldots(1)$$

Also $\quad \displaystyle\int_{40}^{v_{AB}} dv_{AB} = \int_{0}^{t}(a+0.3t)dt$

$$\Rightarrow \quad v_{AB} - 40 = -at - \frac{0.3t^2}{2}$$

and $\quad \displaystyle\int_{0}^{225} ds = \int_{0}^{t_1} 40 - at - \frac{0.3t^2}{2}\, dt$

$$\Rightarrow \quad 225 = 40t_1 - \frac{at_1^2}{2} - \frac{0.3t_1^3}{6} \qquad \ldots(2)$$

From (1) and (2) we get $\quad a = 2.5 \text{ m/s}^2$

$$t_1 = 10 \text{ s}$$

(vii) ② ① A $v_2 = v$ $1/2aT^2$ B $v_1 = aT$

$$v_{21} = v - aT$$

$$a_{21} = -a$$

$$s = \frac{1}{2}aT^2$$

Using $$s = v_{21}t + \frac{1}{2}a_{21}t^2$$

We get $$\frac{1}{2}aT^2 = (v - aT)t - \frac{1}{2}at^2$$

$$t^2 - \frac{2}{a}(v - aT)t + T^2 = 0$$

Difference of roots $$t_2 - t_1 = \sqrt{\frac{4}{a^2}(v - aT)^2 - 4T^2}$$

$$= \frac{2}{a}\sqrt{v(v - 2aT)}$$

Here t_1 and t_2 are times when displacements of both bodies are equal.

(viii)

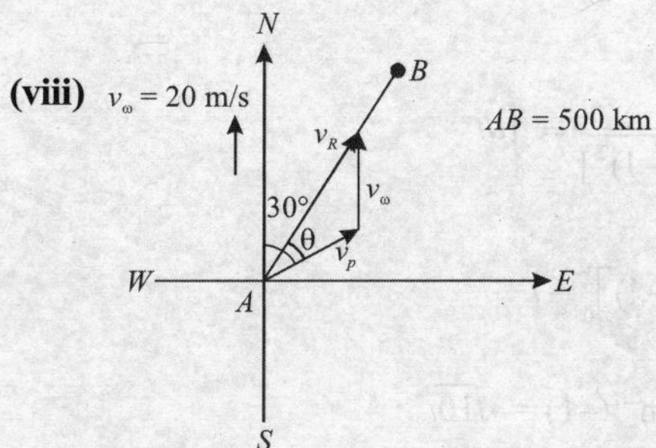

In the vector triangle we use

$$\frac{v_p}{\sin 30°} = \frac{v_\omega}{\sin\theta}$$

$$\sin\theta = \frac{v_\omega}{v_p}\sin 30°$$

$$= \frac{20}{150} \times \frac{1}{2} = \frac{1}{15}$$

$$\theta = \sin^{-1}\frac{1}{15}$$

Time taken to go from A to B is

$$t = \frac{AB\cos 30°}{v_\omega + v_p\cos(\theta + 30°)} = 50\,\text{min}$$

(ix) (a)

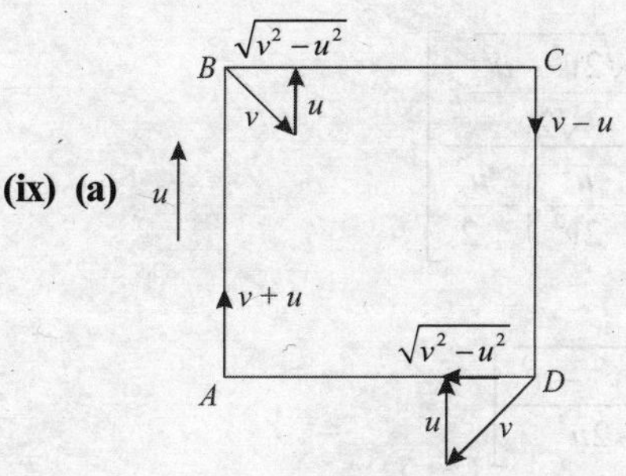

time to complete the square is

$$t = \frac{a}{v + u} + \frac{a}{\sqrt{v^2 - u^2}} + \frac{a}{v - u} + \frac{a}{\sqrt{v^2 - u^2}}$$

$$t = \frac{2av}{v^2 - u^2} + \frac{2a}{\sqrt{v^2 - u^2}}$$

$$t = 2a\left(\frac{v + \sqrt{v^2 - u^2}}{v^2 - u^2}\right)$$

(b)

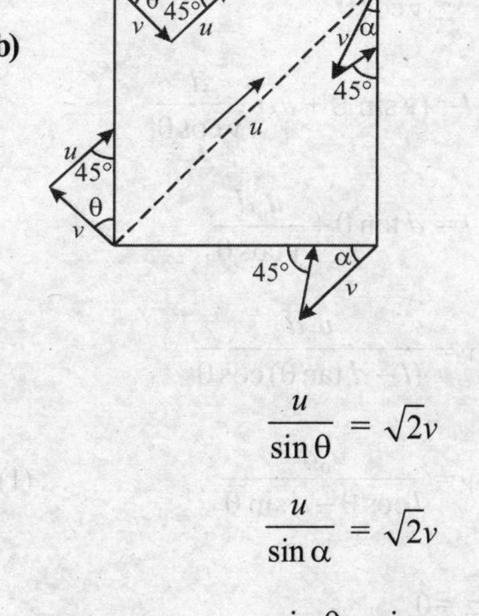

$$\frac{u}{\sin\theta} = \sqrt{2}v$$

$$\frac{u}{\sin\alpha} = \sqrt{2}v$$

$$\sin\theta = \sin\alpha = \frac{u}{\sqrt{2}v}$$

Time to complete the square is

$$t = \frac{2a}{v\cos\alpha + \frac{u}{\sqrt{2}}} + \frac{2a}{v\cos\alpha - \frac{u}{\sqrt{2}}}$$

$$t = 2a\left[\frac{2v\cos\theta}{v^2\cos^2\theta - \frac{u^2}{2}}\right]$$

$$\cos\theta = \sqrt{1 - \frac{u^2}{2v^2}}$$

$$t = 2a\left[\frac{\dfrac{2\sqrt{2}}{4v}\dfrac{\sqrt{2v^2-u^2}}{\sqrt{2v}}}{2v^2\left(1-\dfrac{u^2}{2v^2}\right)-\dfrac{u^2}{2}}\right]$$

$$t = 2a\left[\frac{2\sqrt{2}\sqrt{2v^2-u^2}}{2v^2-2u^2}\right]$$

$$= \frac{2\sqrt{2}a\sqrt{2v^2-u^2}}{v^2-u^2}$$

(x)

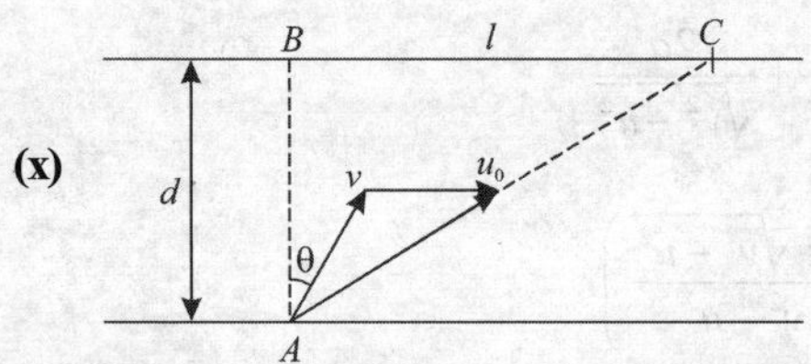

Time to cross $\quad t = \dfrac{d}{v\cos\theta}$

Total drift $\quad l = (v\sin\theta + u_0)\dfrac{d}{v\cos\theta}$

$$\Rightarrow \quad l = d\tan\theta + \frac{u_0 d}{v\cos\theta}$$

$$\Rightarrow \quad v = \frac{u_0 d}{(l - d\tan\theta)\cos\theta}$$

$$v = \frac{u_0 d}{l\cos\theta - d\sin\theta} \quad \ldots(1)$$

v is minimum when $\dfrac{dv}{d\theta} = 0$

$$-l\sin\theta - d\cos\theta = 0$$

$$\tan\theta = -\frac{d}{l}$$

$$\sin\theta = -\frac{d}{\sqrt{l^2+d^2}}$$

and $\quad \cos\theta = \dfrac{l}{\sqrt{l^2+d^2}}$

From (1) we have $\quad v_{\min} = \dfrac{u_0 d}{\sqrt{l^2+d^2}}$

Solutions of PRACTICE EXERCISE 1.7

(i) $x = 2 - \alpha t \quad ; \quad y = \beta t^2$

$v_x = -\alpha \quad ; \quad v_y = 2\beta t$

$a_x = 0 \quad ; \quad a_y = 2\beta$

$$v = \sqrt{\alpha^2 + 4\beta^2 t^2}$$

$$= \sqrt{12.96 + 12.96t^2}$$

$$a = 2\beta = 3.6\text{ m/s}^2$$

$$v_{t=3} = \sqrt{12.96(10)} = 11.38\text{ m/s}$$

$$a_{t=3} = 3.6\text{ m/s}^2$$

(ii) $a_x = 5\text{m/s}^2$

$$x = \frac{1}{2}at^2 = \frac{5}{2}t^2 \quad \ldots(1)$$

$$a_y = 10 - 10y\text{ m/s}^2$$

$$\int_0^{v_y} v\,dv = \int_0^y (10 - 10y)dy$$

$$\frac{v_y^2}{2} = 10y - 5y^2$$

$$\frac{dy}{dt} = v_y = \sqrt{20y - 10y^2}$$

$$\int_0^y \frac{dy}{\sqrt{10[1-(y-1)^2]}} = \int_0^t dt$$

$$\frac{1}{\sqrt{10}}\left[\sin^{-1}(y-1)\right]_0^y = t$$

$$\sin^{-1}(y-1) - \sin^{-1}(-1) = \sqrt{10}t$$

From equation (1)

$$\sin^{-1}(y-1) - \frac{3\pi}{2} = \sqrt{10}\sqrt{\frac{2x}{5}}$$

$$2\sqrt{x} = \sin^{-1}(y-1)\ \frac{3\pi}{2}$$

(iii) $a_x = ay^2$

$a_y = -g$

as $\quad y_t = ut - \dfrac{1}{2}gt^2 \quad \ldots(1)$

$$a_x = a\left(ut - \frac{1}{2}gt^2\right)^2$$

$$\frac{dv_x}{dt} = a_x = au^2t^2 + \frac{ag^2t^4}{4} - augt^3$$

$$\int_0^{v_x} dv_x = \int_0^t \left(au^2t^2 + \frac{ag^2t^4}{4} - augt^3 \right) dt$$

$$\frac{dx}{dt} = v_x = \frac{au^2t^3}{3} + \frac{ag^2t^5}{20} - \frac{augt^4}{4}$$

$$\int_0^x dx = \int_0^t \left(\frac{au^2t^3}{3} + \frac{ag^2t^5}{20} - \frac{augt^4}{4} \right) dt$$

$$x_t = \frac{au^2t^4}{12} + \frac{ag^2t^6}{120} - \frac{augt^5}{20} \quad \dots(2)$$

Diplacement $\quad r = \sqrt{x_t^2 + y_t^2}$

(iv) $\quad a_x = bt^2$

$$\int_0^{v_x} dv_x = \int_0^t bt^2 dt$$

$$\Rightarrow \quad \frac{dx}{dt} = v_x = \frac{bt^3}{3}$$

$$\Rightarrow \quad \int_0^x dx = \int_0^t \frac{bt^3}{3} dt$$

$$x = \frac{bt^4}{12}$$

Substituting time of flight in (1) we get

$$x = \frac{bR^2}{48g_0^2} \left[\ln \left(\frac{R + \sqrt{2RH - H^2}}{R - H} \right) \right]^4$$

$$a_y = -g\left(1 - \frac{2y}{R}\right)$$

$$\int_0^{v_y} v_y dv_y = -\int_H^y g_0 \left(1 - \frac{2y}{R}\right) dy$$

$$\frac{v_y^2}{2} = \left[-\frac{g_0 y^2}{R} + g_0 y \right]_H^y$$

$$\frac{dy}{dt} = v_y = \sqrt{2\left[\left(\frac{g_0 y^2}{R} - g_0 y\right) + \left(\frac{g_0 H^2}{R} - g_0 H\right)\right]}$$

$$dy = \sqrt{\frac{2g_0}{R}[(R-y)^2 - (R-H)^2]}\, dt$$

$$\int_H^0 \frac{dy}{\sqrt{(R-y)^2 - (R-H)^2}} = \int_0^t \sqrt{\frac{2g_0}{R}} dt$$

$$\ln \left[\frac{(R-y) + \sqrt{(R-y)^2 - (R-H)^2}}{R-H} \right]_H^0 = \sqrt{\frac{2g_0}{R}} t$$

$$\ln \left[\frac{R + \sqrt{2RH - H^2}}{R-H} \right] = \sqrt{\frac{2g_0}{R}} t$$

(v) Given that $\quad \vec{r} = \vec{b} \sin \omega t + \vec{c} \cos \omega t$

Here $\quad \vec{b} = b\hat{i}$

$\vec{c} = c\hat{j}$

$\Rightarrow \quad x = b \sin \omega t \quad \dots(1)$

$y = \cos \omega t \quad \dots(2)$

Squaring and adding (1) and (2), we get

$$\frac{x^2}{b^2} + \frac{y^2}{c^2} = 1$$

(vi) Given that $\quad x = 2 \cos \pi t \quad \dots(1)$

$y = 1 - 4 \cos 2\pi t$

$y = 1 - (2 \cos^2 \pi t - 1)$

$y = 5 - 8 \cos^2 \pi t \quad \dots(2)$

From (1) and (2) $\quad y = 5 - 2x^2$

$$v_x = \frac{dx}{dt} = -2\pi \sin \pi t$$

$$v_y = 8\pi \sin 2\pi t$$

$$a_x = \frac{dv}{dt} = -2\pi^2 \cos \pi t$$

$$a_y = 16\pi^2 \cos 2\pi t$$

at $t = 0$

$v_x = 0 \qquad a_x = -2\pi^2$

$v_y = 0 \qquad a_y = 16\pi^2$

$\Rightarrow \quad v = 0 \quad a = \sqrt{a_x^2 + a_y^2} = 158.98 \text{m/s}^2$

at $t = 1.5$ s

$v_x = 2\pi \qquad a_x = 0$

$v_y = -8\pi \qquad a_y = 16\pi^2$

$v = \sqrt{v_x^2 + v_y^2} = 28.89$ m/s

$= 6.28$ m/s

$a = \sqrt{a_x^2 + a_y^2} = 16\pi^2$

$= 157.75 \text{ m/s}^2$

Solutions of PRACTICE EXERCISE 1.8

(i) (a)

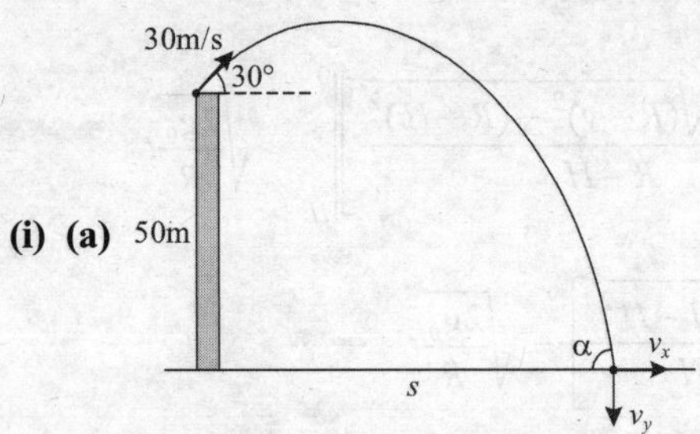

$$u_x = 30 \cos 30° = 15\sqrt{3} \text{ m/s}$$

$$u_y = 30 \sin 30° = 15 \text{ m/s}$$

If t is the time of flight, we use

$$-50 = 15t - 5t^2$$

$$t^2 - 3t - 10 = 0$$

$$t^2 - 3t - 10 = 0$$

$$(t-5)(t+2) = 0$$

$$t = 5 \text{ s}$$

(b) Distance $\quad s = 15\sqrt{3} \times 5 = 75\sqrt{3}$ m

(c) At the time of hit $\quad v_x = 15\sqrt{3}$ m/s

And $\quad v_y = u_y - gt = 15 - 10 \times 5 = -35$ m/s

$$v = \sqrt{v_x^2 + v_y^2} = 43.58 \text{ m/s}$$

(d) $\alpha = \tan^{-1}\left(\dfrac{v_y}{v_x}\right) = \tan^{-1}\left(\dfrac{35}{15\sqrt{3}}\right) = \tan^{-1}\left(\dfrac{7}{3\sqrt{3}}\right)$

(ii)

$$u_x = 24 \cos 30° = 12\sqrt{3} \text{ m/s}$$

$$u_y = 24 \sin 30° = 12 \text{ m/s}$$

If t is time of flight, we use

$$-20 = 12t - 5t^2$$

$$5t^2 - 12t - 20 = 0$$

$$t = \frac{12 \pm \sqrt{144 + 400}}{10}$$

$$= 1.2 \pm 2.33$$

$$t = 3.53 \text{ s}$$

Distence on ground where stone will hit

$$s = u_x t$$

$$= 12\sqrt{3} \times 3.53$$

$$= 73.37 \text{ m}$$

(iii)

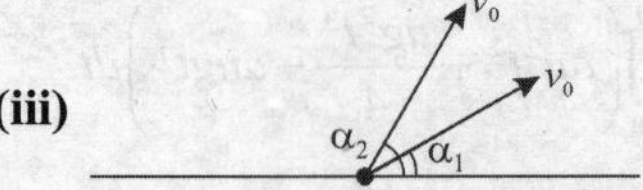

Velocity of bodies 1 and 2 after time t

$$\vec{v}_1 = v_0 \cos\alpha_1 \hat{i} + (v_0 \sin\alpha_1 - gt)\hat{j}$$

$$\vec{v}_2 = v_0 \cos\alpha_2 \hat{i} + (v_0 \sin\alpha_2 - gt)\hat{j}$$

$$\vec{v}_R = \vec{v}_2 - \vec{v}_1$$

$$= [(\cos\alpha_2 - \cos\alpha_1)\hat{i} + (\sin\alpha_2 - \sin\alpha_1)\hat{j}]$$

$$|\vec{v}_R| = v_0[(\cos\alpha_2 - \cos\alpha_1)^2 + (\sin\alpha_2 - \sin\alpha_1)^2]^{1/2}$$

$$= v_0[2 - \cos(\alpha_2 - \alpha_1)]^{1/2}$$

$$= 2v_0 \sin\left(\frac{\alpha_2 - \alpha_1}{2}\right)$$

Distance between bodies after time t is

$$s = v_R t = 2v_0 t \sin\left(\frac{\alpha_2 - \alpha_1}{2}\right)$$

(iv) If ball hits the edge of nth step, its coordinets are

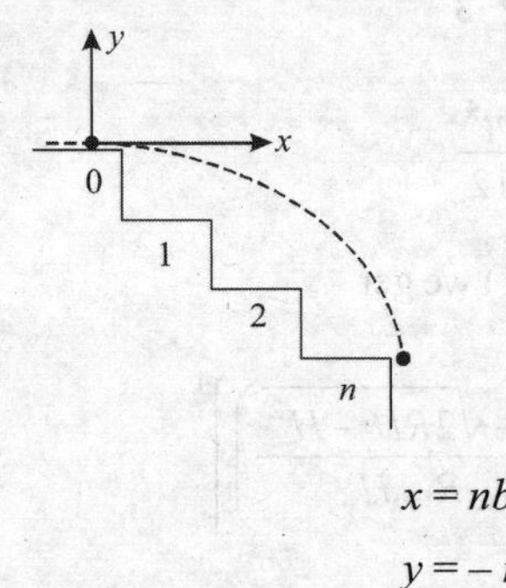

$$x = nb$$

$$y = -nh$$

Equation of trajectory $\quad y = -\dfrac{gx^2}{2u^2}$

Subsituting values of x & y

$$nh = \frac{gn^2b^2}{2u^2}$$

$$n = \frac{2hu^2}{gb^2}$$

(v) Time of flight of shot

$$t = \frac{2v_2 \sin\alpha}{g}$$

Velocity of shot relative to boat in horizontal direction is

$$v_2 \cos\alpha - v_1$$

Time of flight of shot $= \dfrac{2v_2 \sin\alpha}{g}$

Range of shot with respect to boat is

$$= \frac{2v_2 \sin\alpha}{g}(v_2 \cos\alpha - v_1)$$

(vi) $\vec{v}_1 = (25-10t)\hat{j}$

$$\vec{v}_2 = \frac{25}{2}\hat{i} + \left(\frac{25\sqrt{3}}{2} - 10t\right)\hat{j}$$

Velocity of 2 w.r. to 1 is

$$\vec{v}_{21} = \vec{v}_2 - \vec{v}$$

$$= \frac{25}{2}\hat{i} + \left(\frac{25\sqrt{3}}{2} - 25\right)\hat{j}$$

Separation after $t = 1.7$ sec is

$$s = v_{21} \times t$$

$$= \sqrt{\left(\frac{25}{2}\right)^2 + \left(\frac{25\sqrt{3}}{2} - 25\right)^2} \times 1.7$$

$$= 22.0 \text{ m}$$

(vii)

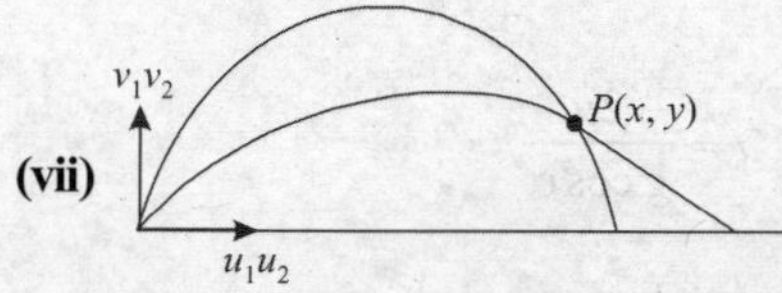

if t_1 and t_2 are time of crossing point P then

$$x = u_1 t_1 = u_2 t_2$$

$$y = v_1 t_1 - \frac{1}{2}gt_1^2 = v_2 t_2 - \frac{1}{2}gt_2^2$$

$$v_1 t_1 - \frac{1}{2}gt_1^2 = v_2\left(\frac{u_1 t_1}{u_2}\right) - \frac{1}{2}g\left(\frac{u_1 t_1}{u_2}\right)^2$$

$$\frac{1}{2}gt_1^2\left(\frac{u_1^2}{u_2^2} - 1\right) + t_1\left(v_1 - \frac{v_2 u_1}{u_2}\right) = 0$$

$$t_1 = \frac{2(v_2 u_1 - v_1 u_2)u_2}{g(u_1^2 - u_2^2)}$$

and

$$t_2 = \frac{u_1 t_1}{u_2} = \frac{2(v_2 u_1 - v_1 u_2)u_1}{g(u_1^2 - u_2^2)}$$

$$\Delta t = t_2 - t_1 = \frac{2(v_2 u_1 - v_1 u_2)}{g(u_1 + u_2)}$$

(viii)

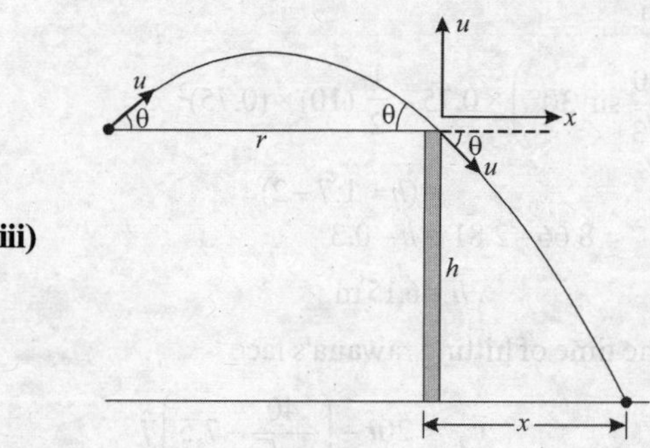

For ball to graze top of tower

$$r = \frac{u^2 \sin 2\theta}{g}$$

$$\Rightarrow \quad rg = u^2 \sin 2\theta$$

After grazing, equation of trajectory

$$-h = x\tan(-\theta) - \frac{gx^2}{2u^2\cos^2\theta}$$

$$x^2\left(\frac{g}{2u^2}\sec^2\theta\right) + x(\tan\theta) - h = 0$$

$$g^{x^2} + x\left(\frac{\sin\theta}{\cos\theta}2u^2\cos\theta\right) - 2u^2 h\cos^2\theta = 0$$

$$x = \frac{-u^2\sin 2\theta \pm \sqrt{u^4\sin^2 2\theta + 8u^2 gh\cos^2\theta}}{2g}$$

$$x = \frac{-u^2\sin 2\theta}{2g} + 4\sqrt{u^2\sin^2 2\theta + 8gh\cos^2\theta}$$

[discarding – ve sing]

$$= -\frac{u^2\sin\theta\cos\theta}{g} + \frac{2u\cos\theta\sqrt{u^2\sin^2\theta + 2gh}}{2g}$$

$$x = \frac{u\cos\theta}{g}\left[\sqrt{u^2\sin^2\theta + 2gh} - u\sin\theta\right]$$

(ix)

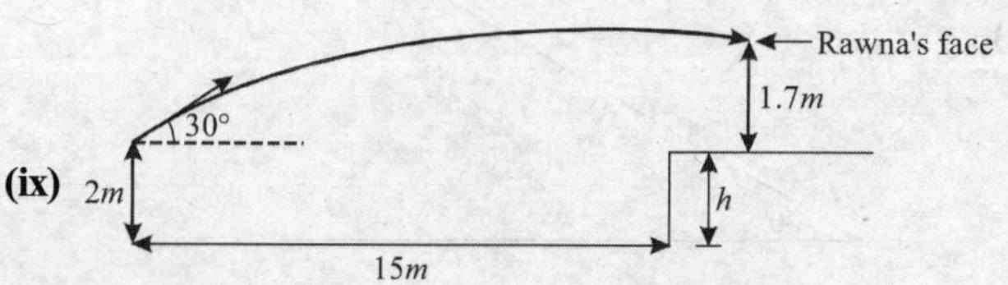

If projection speed is u

In x direction

$$15 = u\cos\theta \times 0.75$$

$$u = \frac{20\times 2}{\sqrt{3}} = \frac{40}{\sqrt{3}} \text{ m/s}$$

In y direction

$$\left(\frac{40}{\sqrt{3}}\sin 30°\right)\times 0.75-\frac{1}{2}(10)\times(0.75)^2$$

$$=(h+1.7-2)$$

$$8.66-2.81=h-0.3$$

$$h=6.15\text{ m}$$

Velocity at the time of hitting rawana's face

$$\vec{v}_f=20\hat{i}+\left(\frac{40}{2\sqrt{3}}-7.5\right)\hat{j}$$

$$=20\hat{i}+4.04\hat{j}$$

$$v_f=20.40\text{ m/s}$$

(x)

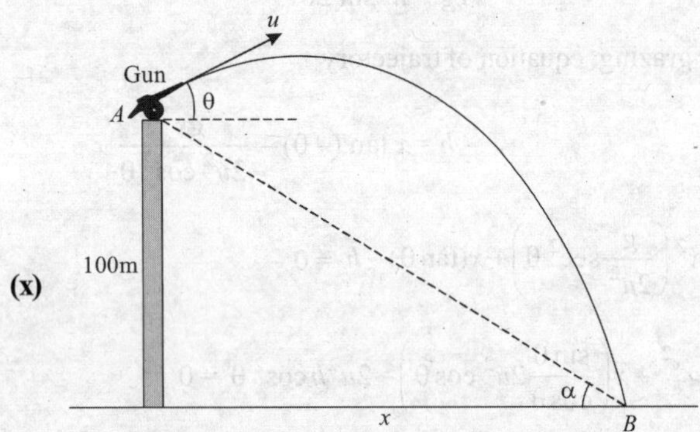

By equation of trajectory we use

$$-100=x\tan\theta-\frac{5x^2}{(150)^2\cos^2\theta}$$

For max range $\frac{dx}{d\theta}=0$

Solving we get $\theta=46.3°$

Solutions of PRACTICE EXERCISE 1.9

(i)

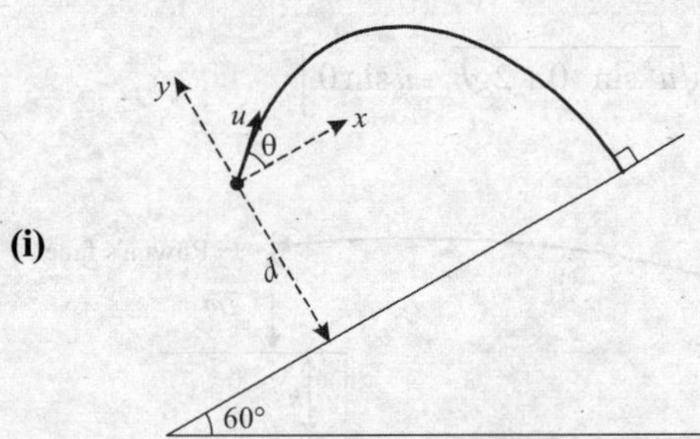

In y direction $-d=u\sin\theta\, t-\frac{1}{2}(g\cos 60°)t^2$ ...(1)

In x direction $0=u\cos\theta-(g\sin 60°)t$ ...(2)

$\Rightarrow$ $t=\frac{2u\cos\theta}{g\sqrt{3}}$

From (1)

$$-d=u\sin\theta\left(\frac{2u\cos\theta}{g\sqrt{3}}\right)-\frac{g}{4}\left(\frac{4u^2\cos^2\theta}{3g^2}\right)$$

$$-d=\frac{u^2\sin 2\theta}{\sqrt{3}g}-\frac{u^2\cos^2\theta}{3g}$$

$$u^2=3gd\times\left(\frac{1}{\cos^2\theta-\sqrt{3}\sin 2\theta}\right) \quad ...(1)$$

For u to be maximum we use

$$\frac{d}{d\theta}(\cos^2\theta-\sqrt{3}\sin 2\theta)=0$$

$$-2\cos\theta\sin\theta-2\sqrt{3}\cos 2\theta=0$$

$$-\sin 2\theta-2\sqrt{3}\cos 2\theta=0$$

$$\tan 2\theta=-2\sqrt{3}$$

$$\sin 2\theta=-\frac{2\sqrt{3}}{\sqrt{13}}$$

$$\cos 2\theta=\sqrt{\frac{1}{13}}$$

From (1) $u_{max}=\sqrt{\frac{1}{2}gd(\sqrt{13}-1)}$

(ii) Time of flight $t=\frac{2u}{g\cos\alpha}$

$$R_1=\frac{1}{2}g\sin\alpha t^2$$

$$R_1+R_2=\frac{1}{2}g\sin\alpha(2t)^2$$

$$R_1+R_2+R_3=\frac{1}{2}g\sin\alpha(3t)^2$$

$$R_2=3R_1$$

$$R_3=5R_1$$

$\Rightarrow$ $R_1:R_2:R_3=1:3:5$

(iii)

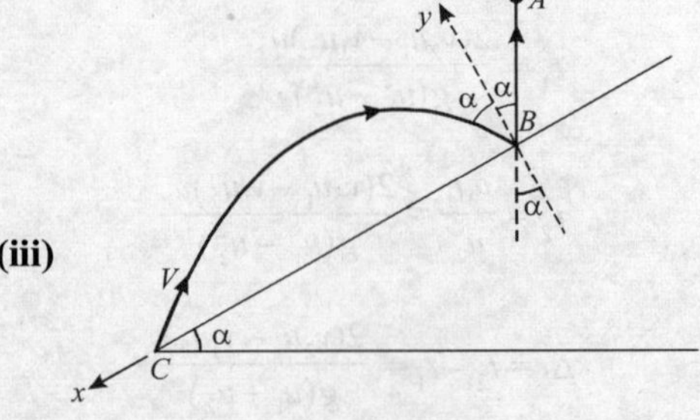

We solve the problem by considering motion starts from A
If particle starting from potential A then its speed at B

$$v = \sqrt{2gh}$$

$$t_{AB} = \sqrt{\frac{2h}{g}}$$

Velocity at point C is $V_x = V_B \sin\alpha + g\sin\alpha\,(t_{AB})$

$$V_x = \sqrt{2gh}\sin\alpha + g\sin\alpha\left(\frac{2\sqrt{2gh}}{g}\right)$$

$$V_x = 3\sqrt{2gh}\sin\alpha$$

and $V_y = \sqrt{2gh}\cos\alpha$

$$V = \sqrt{2gh}(9\sin^2\alpha + \cos^2\alpha)^{1/2}$$

$$V = \sqrt{2gh}(1 + 8\sin^2\alpha)^{1/2}$$

Total time of flight

$$T = \left(\sqrt{\frac{2h}{g}} + 2\sqrt{\frac{2h}{g}}\right)\times 2$$

$$= 6\sqrt{\frac{2h}{g}} = 6\left(\frac{V}{g\sqrt{1+8\sin^2\alpha}}\right)$$

$$= \frac{6V}{g\sqrt{1+8\sin^2\alpha}}$$

(iv)

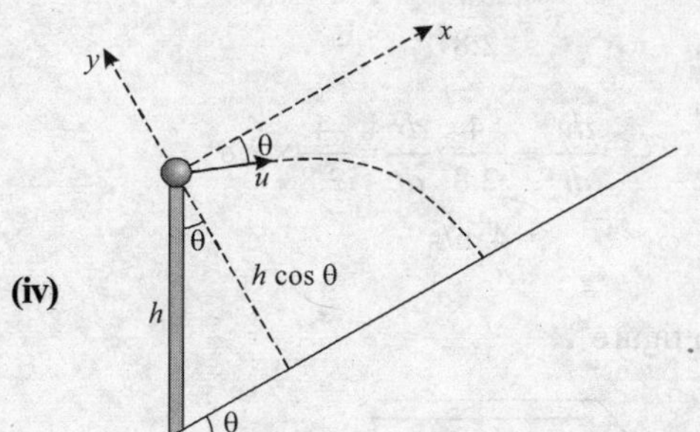

If time of flight is t we have

$\Rightarrow$ $$0 = u\cos\theta - g\sin\theta\, t$$

$\Rightarrow$ $$t = \frac{u\cos\theta}{g\sin\theta}$$

Along y direction

$$h\cos\theta = u\sin\theta\left(\frac{u\cos\theta}{g\sin\theta}\right) + \frac{1}{2}g\cos\theta\left(\frac{u\cos\theta}{g\sin\theta}\right)^2$$

$$h = \frac{u^2}{g} + \frac{u^2}{2g}\cot^2\theta$$

$$u = \sqrt{\frac{2gh}{2+\cot^2\theta}}$$

Distance along plane $l = h\sin\theta + \dfrac{(u\cos\theta)^2}{2g\sin\theta}$

$$l = h\sin\theta + \frac{h}{(2\cot^2\theta)}\cdot\frac{\cos^2\theta}{\sin\theta}$$

$$l = h\frac{\sin^2\theta(2+\cot^2\theta) + \cos^2\theta}{\sin\theta\cdot(2+\cot^2\theta)}$$

$$l = \frac{2h}{\sin\theta(2+\cot^2\theta)}$$

Solutions of PRACTICE EXERCISE 1.10

(i) For mid point M $\quad v_{Mx} = \dfrac{d}{dt}\left(\dfrac{x}{2}\right) = \dfrac{1}{2}\dfrac{dx}{dt} = \dfrac{v}{2}$

$$v_{My} = \frac{d}{dt} = \left(\frac{y}{2}\right) = -\frac{1}{2}\frac{dy}{dt}$$

$$= \frac{v_B}{2} = \frac{1}{2}v\cot\theta$$

$$v_M = \sqrt{v_x^2 + v_y^2} = \frac{v}{2}\sqrt{1+\cot^2\theta}$$

$$= \frac{v}{2}\text{cosec}\theta$$

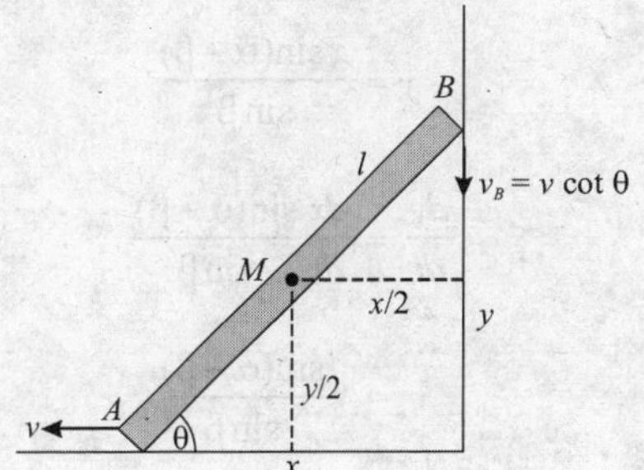

(ii)

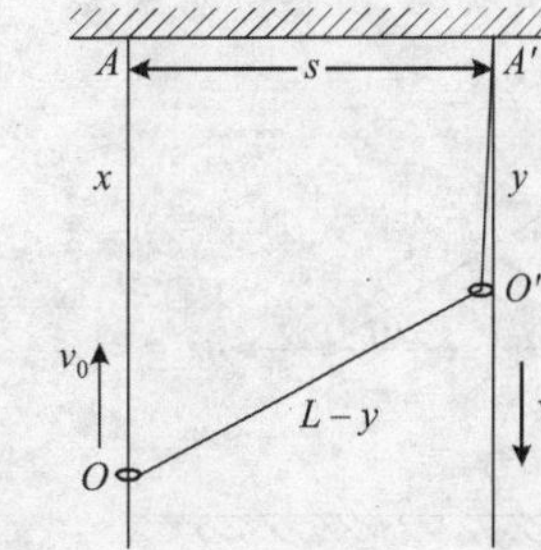

We use $$v = \frac{dy}{dt}$$

$$v_0 = -\frac{dx}{dt}$$

Also $s^2 + (x-y)^2 = (L-y)^2$

Differentiating w.r.t to t

$$2(x-y)\left(\frac{dx}{dt} - \frac{dy}{dt}\right) = 2(L-y)\left(-\frac{dy}{dt}\right)$$

$$(-v_0 - v)\cos\alpha = -v$$

$$v_0 = \frac{v(1-\cos\alpha)}{\cos\alpha}$$

(iii) We use in figure shown

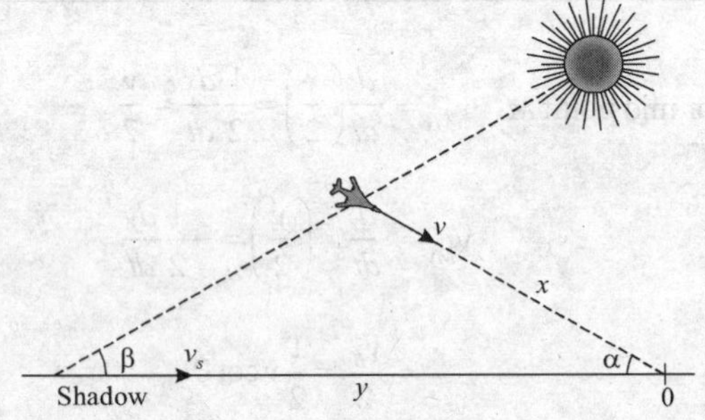

we use $v = \frac{dx}{dt}$ and $v_s = -\frac{dy}{dt}$

$$\frac{x}{\sin\beta} = \frac{y}{\sin(\alpha+\beta)}$$

$$y = \frac{x\sin(\alpha+\beta)}{\sin\beta}$$

$$\frac{dy}{dt} = \frac{dx}{dt}\frac{\sin(\alpha+\beta)}{\sin\beta}$$

$$v_s = v\frac{\sin(\alpha+\beta)}{\sin\beta}$$

(iv) We use from figure

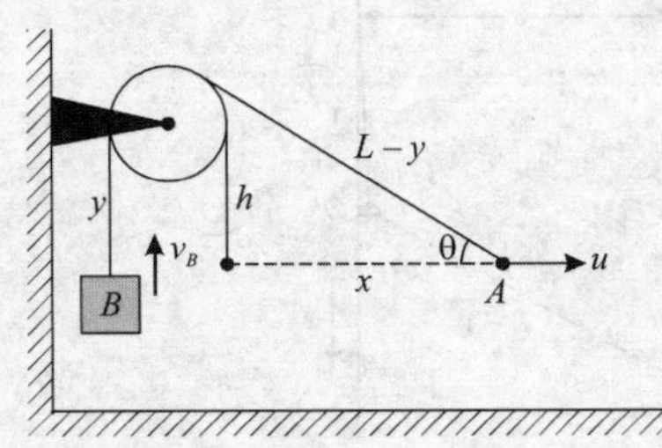

we use $v_B = -\frac{dy}{dt}$ and $u = \frac{dx}{dt}$

$$h^2 + x^2 = (L-y)^2$$

$$2x\frac{dx}{dt} = 2(L-y)\left(-\frac{dy}{dt}\right)$$

$$u\cos\theta = v_B$$

(v) We use from figure

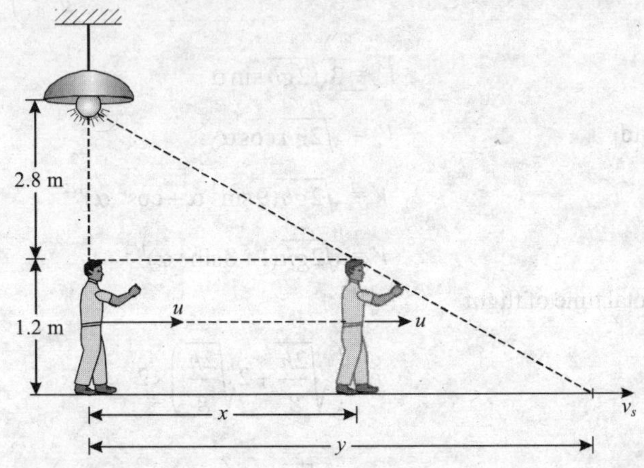

we use $\frac{dx}{dt} = u$ and $\frac{dy}{dt} = v_s$

$$\frac{x}{2.8} = \frac{y}{4}$$

$$y = \frac{4x}{2.8}$$

$$\frac{dy}{dt} = \frac{4}{2.8}\cdot\frac{dx}{dt} = \frac{4}{2.8}\times 2.8$$

$$= 4 \text{ m/s}$$

(vi) We use from figure

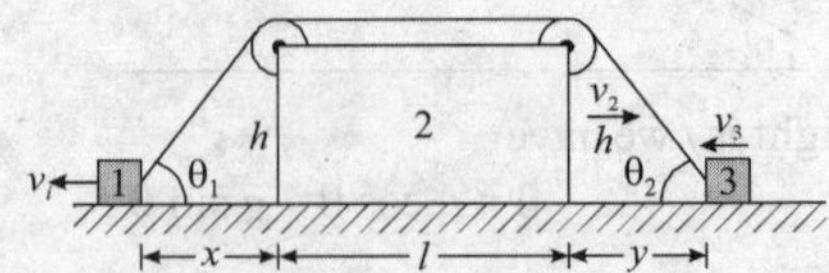

we use $\frac{dx}{dt} = v_1 + v_2$ and $-\frac{dy}{dt} = v_2 + v_3$

$$\sqrt{h^2 + x^2} + \sqrt{h^2 + y^2} = L - l$$

Different w.r. to t

$$\frac{x}{\sqrt{h^2+x^2}}\cdot\frac{dx}{dt} + \frac{y}{\sqrt{h^2+y^2}}\cdot\frac{dy}{dt} = 0$$

$$(v_1 + v_2)\cos\theta_1 - (v_2 + v_3)\cos\theta_2 = 0$$

$$v_3 = \frac{(v_1 + v_2)\cos\theta_1}{\cos\theta_2} - v_2$$

(vii) If A is moving at v_A, we can use velocity components along string for both masses to be equal

$$v_A \cos\theta = v$$

$$v_A = v \sec\theta$$

Solutions of PRACTICE EXERCISE 1.11

(i) We use $V_A \uparrow$ then

(a) $V_A = 2V_P - V_B = 2\times 5 - 10 = 0$ m/s

(b) $V_A = 2V_P - V_B = 2\times 5 + 20 = 30$ m/s

(ii) (a) $x_A + 2x_B + 2x_C = 0$

$\Rightarrow$ $a_A + 2a_B + 2a_C = 0$ taking all in downward motion

(b) $2x_A + x_B + 2x_C = 0$

$\Rightarrow$ $2a_A + a_B + 2a_C = 0$ taking all in downward motion

(iii) (a) If B moves toward right by x and A move toward right by y and l is length wound on motor we use

$$2x + y = l$$

$$2v_B + v_A = v$$

(b) If A goes up by x and B goes up by y & l is length wond on motor we use

$$4y + x = l$$

$$4v_B + v_A = v$$

(iv) (a) If B moves down by x and A goes up by y we use

$$y = 2x$$

$$v_A = 2v_B$$

(b) If A goes up by x and B moves down by y we use

$$y = 3x$$

$$v_B = 3v_A$$

(v) If B moves down by x and A moves up by y and C moves toward right by z we have constrained relation

$$3y - 4x = z$$

$$3v_A - 4v_B = v_C \quad \ldots(1)$$

$$3a_A - 4a_B = a_C \quad \ldots(2)$$

From (1) $\quad v_C = 3\times 3 - 4\times 20 = -71$ cm/s (left ward)

$$s = ut + \frac{1}{2}at^2$$

$$27 = -71\times 3 + \frac{1}{2}\times a\times 9$$

$$a_C = \frac{(27 + 243)\times 2}{9} = 60 \text{ cm/s}^2 \quad \text{(right ward)}$$

From (2) $\quad a_A = \frac{a_C}{3} = 20 \text{ cm/s}^2$ (upward)

(vi) If A goes down by x, B goes up by y and C goes down by z, constrined relation is

$$z = \frac{y}{2} \Rightarrow v_C = \frac{v_B}{2} \Rightarrow a_C = \frac{a_B}{2}$$

$$x = \frac{3y}{2} \Rightarrow v_A = \frac{3}{2}v_B \Rightarrow a_A = \frac{3}{2}a_B$$

After 12 s, velocity of A will be

$$v_A = a_A(12)$$

$$7.2 = a_A(12)$$

$$a_A = \frac{7.2}{12} \text{ m/s}^2 = 6 \text{ m/s}^2 \downarrow$$

$$a_B = \frac{2}{3}a_A = 4 \text{ m/s}^2 \uparrow$$

$$a_C = \frac{a_B}{2} = 2 \text{ m/s}^2 \downarrow$$

v_B at $t = 8$ is $\quad v_B = a_B(8) = 4\times 8 = 32$ m/s $\uparrow$

Displacement of block B after 8 sec is

$$s = \frac{1}{2}at^2$$

$$s = \frac{1}{2}\times 4\times (8)^2 = 128 \text{ m} \uparrow$$

(vii) If A goes up by x, B goes down by y, C goes up z and D goes down by w, we use

$$w = \frac{y - x}{2} \Rightarrow 2v_D = v_B - v_A \Rightarrow 2a_D = a_B + a_A \quad \ldots(1)$$

$$z = z(y - x) \Rightarrow v_C = 2v_B - 2v_A \Rightarrow a_C = 2a_B - 2a_A \quad \ldots(2)$$

Given that $\quad a_C + a_B = 6 \quad \ldots(3)$

$$a_D + a_A = 11 \quad \ldots(4)$$

From (1) $\quad 2(11 - a_A) = a_B - a_A$

$$a_A + a_B = 22 \quad \ldots(3)$$

From (2) $\quad 6 - a_B = 2a_B - 2a_A$

$$3a_B - 2a_A = 6 \quad \ldots(4)$$

From (3) and (4) $\quad 5a_B = 50$

$$a_B = 25 \text{ m/s}^2$$

From (3) $\quad a_C = 6 - a_B = 6 - 25 = -19 \text{ m/s}^2$

Velocity of block C after 3s from start is

$$v_C = a_C(3) = 19 \times 3 = 57 \text{ m/s} \downarrow$$

Solutions of PRACTICE EXERCISE 1.12

(i) If B moves down by x, A moves up by y we have

$$y = 2x$$
$$a_A = 2a_B$$

(ii) If A move toward left by x, B moves along A by y we use

$$y = 2x$$
$$a_{BA} = 2a_A = 6 \text{m/s}^2$$
$$a_{Bx} = 6 \cos 30° - 3 = 3\sqrt{3} - 3 \text{ m/s}^2$$
$$a_{By} = 6 \sin 30° = 3 \text{ m/s}^2$$
$$a_B = \sqrt{a_{Bx}^2 + a_{By}^2} = \sqrt{(3\sqrt{3}-3)^2 + (3)^2}$$
$$= \sqrt{27 + 9 - 18\sqrt{3} + 9}$$
$$= \sqrt{45 - 18\sqrt{3}}$$
$$= 3\sqrt{5 - 2\sqrt{3}} \text{ m/s}^2$$

(iii) Here from figure we use

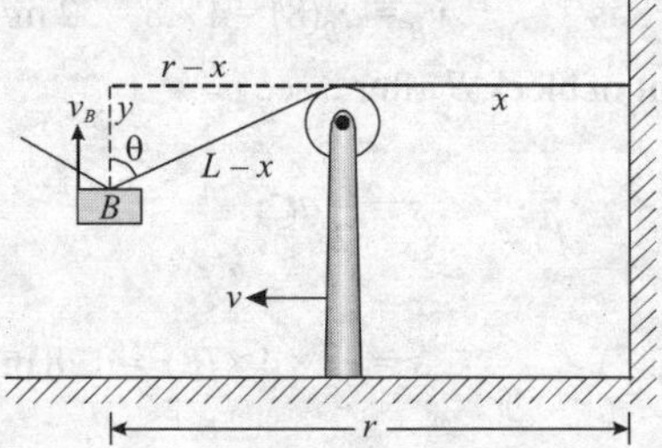

we use $v = \dfrac{dx}{dt}$ and $v_B = -\dfrac{dy}{dt}$

We have $y^2 + (r - x)^2 = (L - x)^2$

Differentiating w.r. to t

$$2y\frac{dy}{dt} - 2(r - x)\frac{dx}{dt} = -2(L - x)\frac{dx}{dt}$$
$$-v_B \cos\theta - v \sin\theta = -v$$
$$v_B = \frac{v(1 - \sin\theta)}{\cos\theta}$$

(iv) (a) If A goes toward left by x and B moves toward right on A by y we use

$$y = 2x$$
$$a_{BA} = 2a_A$$

and
$$a_{BG} = 2a_A - a_A = a_A$$
$$= a$$

(b) If A moves toward left by x, B slides down by y on A, we use

$$y = 3x$$
$$a_{BA} = 3a_A = 3a$$
$$a_{BG} = \sqrt{a_{Bx}^2 + a_{By}^2}$$
$$= \sqrt{(3a\cos\theta + a)^2 + (3a\sin\theta)^2}$$
$$= a\sqrt{10 + 6\cos\theta}$$

(v) If pulley goes up by x block will move up by $2x$. If point P on string goes down by y pulley will go up by $y/2$. Thus we have

$$\frac{y}{2} = x$$

or
$$y = 2x$$
$$v_{\text{block}} = v_P = v$$

(vi) If block B goes down by x and block A goes up by y and C moves toward left by z, we use

$$2(2x - y) = z$$
$$4x - 2y = z$$

Reltation in velocities of A, B and C is

$$4v_B - 2v_A = v_C$$

$\Rightarrow$
$$4a_B = 2a_A + a_C$$

Solutions of CONCEPTUAL MCQS Single Option Correct

Sol. 1 (B) Initial velocity is time derivative of displacement with $t = 0$ which is equal to C and initial acceleration is time derivative of velocity with $t = 0$ which is equal to $2B$ so the ratio is $C/2B$.

Sol. 2 (A) As throughout motion the slope of graph is constant, speed is not changing.

Sol. 3 (C) As both are accelerated by same acceleration and project at same initial velocity magnitude then at same displacement their final velocities must be same in rectilinear motion.

Sol. 4 (C) As both cars are moving at same velocities, they will be at rest with respect to each other.

Sol. 5 (C) As throughout motion acceleration is constant and positive taken in downward direction, speed increases initially and changes direction at every impact.

Sol. 6 (A) In portion OA slope of graph is increasing which is indicating accelerated motion.

Sol. 7 (C) In portion *AB* slope of curve is constant hence uniform motion.

Sol. 8 (B) In portion *OA* slope of graph is decreasing which is indicating retarded motion.

Sol. 9 (A) As particles are equally accelerated with same initial speed then always they will be at rest with respect to each other.

Sol. 10 (D) As shown in graph speed first increases at a constant rate then decreases at the same rate so possible option among the given cases only (D) is correct.

Sol. 11 (B) Acceleration of particle is given as

$$a = v\frac{dv}{dx}$$

$$\Rightarrow \qquad \frac{dv}{dx} = \frac{a}{v}$$

In the given graph as displacement increases, acceleration is decreasing but due to acceleration, v is increasing so from above equation we can see that $\frac{dv}{dx}$ will be decreasing.

Sol. 12 (A) The area between speed time graph and time axis gives the distance travelled.

Sol. 13 (D) Sum of positive and negative displacements with signs of particle gives the total increase in displacement but if we add the areas as asked in question, it gives the total distance travelled.

Sol. 14 (A) Sum of the vectors along the three sides of a triangle will be zero and the remaining *CA* will be the resultant of all the forces.

Sol. 15 (A) With uniform acceleration the velocity of particle increases at constant rate till 2 seconds then due to negative acceleration it decreases at same rate and drop to zero at 4 seconds.

Sol. 16 (C) At point *B* the velocity of particle is decreasing which indicates that particle is retarding hence the force is in the direction opposite to the motion.

Sol. 17 (A) As vertical motion of both bullet and stone is free fall under gravity, both will reach simultaneously.

Sol. 18 (D) As throughout motion the ball has acceleration g in downward dirction so slope of v-t graph must be constant. Only possible option here is (D).

Sol. 19 (B) Maximum acceleration will have maximum slope of v-t curve which is the portion *BC* in the given curve.

Sol. 20 (A) The relative velocity of rain drops with respect to car will be inclined to the direction opposite to motion of car so drops will hit the front screen only.

Sol. 21 (A) To cross the river in shortest time swimmer has to head in direction perpendicular to the bank of river so that his crossing velocity will be maximum.

Sol. 22 (A) As slope of A is more than that of B hence option (A) is correct.

Sol. 23 (A) If motion is not defined we can only state that average speed will always be greater than or equal to average velocity magnitude and no other inference can be deduced but for instantaneous motion option (A) is always correct.

Sol. 24 (A) For first half time velocity increases at a constant rate so slope of v-t curve increases upto half time then acceleration decreases so slope of v-t curve decreases for last half time and finally acceleration becomes zero so v-t curve will become horizontal

Sol. 25 (C) Relation in velocity and displacement of a free fall motin is $v^2 = 2gs$ which is a parabolic curve symmetric about s axis hence option (C) is correct.

Sol. 26 (B) A balloon is rising up with an acceleration a and stone is falling down at acceleration g so the acceleration of stone with respect to balloon is (g)-$(-a)$ downward $= g + a$ downward.

Sol. 27 (D) First and second part of journey is symmetric hence only possible option is (D).

Sol. 28 (B) As both particles have same acceleration, their relative acceleration is zero hence the path of motion of one with respect to other will be a straight line and the line is vertical because their relative velocity along horizontal is zero.

Sol. 29 (C) The square of speed of ball projected vertically up varies with height h of the ball in a linear manner hence the graph of KE verses height will be a straight line between $h = 0$ to h. Hence option (C) is correct.

Sol. 30 (B) As initial velocity is positive and decreasing that indicates initial acceleration is negative then after time t it becomes positiv hence option (B) is correct.

Sol. 31 (C) Speed of ball decreases as it reaches maximum height and then again increases in a non linear manner hence among the options given only possible option is (C).

Sol. 32 (B) Concept accelerates so the speed increases linearly with time. But the distance fallen increases as t^2. So the average speed occurs at half of time taken to pass the window, which is before it has covered half of the height of the window.

Sol. 33 (B) Particle comes to rest when sum of area under *a-t* curve is zero which happens at $t = 0, 2, 4$.

Sol. 34 (B) For the motion from *A* to *B*

applying $s = vt$

$$2 = 0.25\, t_{AB}$$

$$t_{AB} = 8$$

For the motion from *B* to *C*

$$-\frac{dv}{dl} = \frac{0.125}{\frac{\pi}{2}} = \frac{1}{4\pi} = -\frac{dv}{dl} \times \frac{dt}{dt}$$

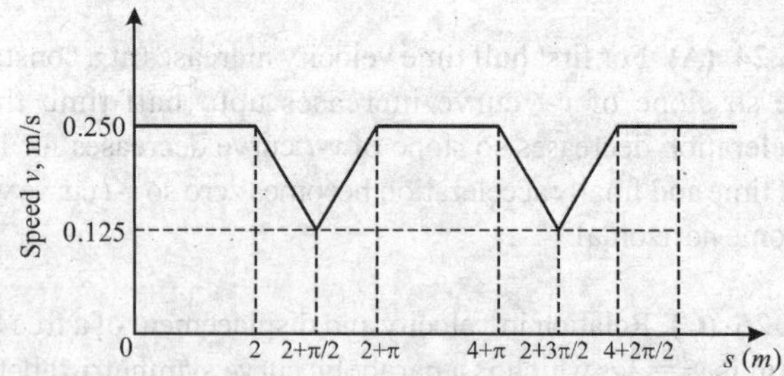

$$\int_0^{t_{BC}} \frac{dt}{4\pi} = \int_{0.25}^{0.125} -\frac{dv}{v}$$

$\Rightarrow$ $$t_{BC} = 4\pi \ln 2$$

$$t_{BC} = t_{CD} = t_{EF} = t_{FG}$$

$$t_{AB} = t_{DE}$$

Total time will be sum of all times $= 16\,(1 + \pi \ln 2)$

Sol. 35 (A) Vector sum of four vectors can be zero if they form a closed polygon so that net displacement will be zero, that is possible only with option (A).

Solutions of NUMERICAL MCQS Single Options Correct

Sol. 1 (D) Since the direction of acceleration is opposite of initial velocity, first let us check if body comes to rest at some time before 12 seconds. Let this time is t_1.

Using $v = u + at$

$$0 = 10 - 2t_1$$

$$t_1 = 5 \text{ s}$$

Distance travelled by particle in 5*s*,

$$s_1 = 10(5) - \frac{1}{2}(2)(5)^2$$

$$s_1 = 25 \text{ m}$$

Now, body starts to move in negative *x*-direction and accelerates for

$$(12 - 5) = 7 \text{ seconds}$$

$$s_2 = 0 + \frac{1}{2}(2)(7)^2$$

$$s_2 = 49 \text{ m}$$

Total distance traversed by the particle in 12 seconds,

$$s = s_1 + s_2$$

$$s = 25 \text{ m} + 49 \text{ m}$$

$$s = 74 \text{ m}$$

Sol. 2 (D) Area covered under velocity-time graph gives distance covered by body

Thus, area covered from 1 s to 7 s

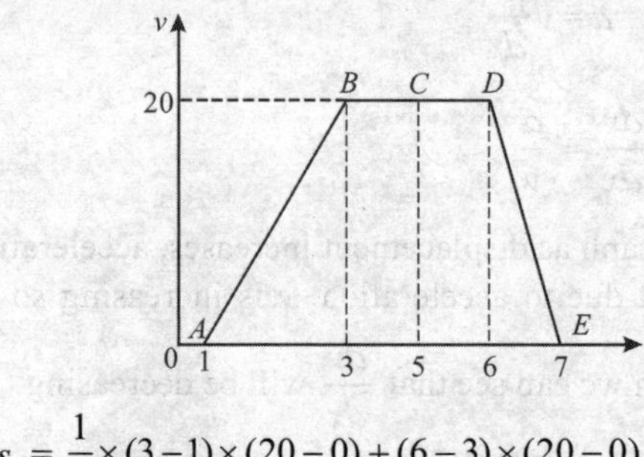

$$s_1 = \frac{1}{2} \times (3-1) \times (20-0) + (6-3) \times (20-0) + \frac{1}{2}(7-6)(20-0)$$

$$s_1 = \frac{1}{2} \times 2 \times 20 + 3 \times 20 + \frac{1}{2} \times 20$$

$$s_1 = 20 + 60 + 10 = 90 \text{m}$$

Distance covered by particle from 5*s* to 7*s*,

$$s_2 = (6-5) \times (20-0) + \frac{1}{2} \times (7-6) \times (20-0)$$

$$s_2 = 20 + \frac{1}{2} \times 20$$

$$s_2 = 30 \text{m}$$

Required fraction, $$f = \frac{s_2}{s_1} = \frac{30}{90} = \frac{1}{3}$$

Sol. 3 (A) The velocity of particle becomes zero after,

$$t_1 = \frac{0-6}{-2} = 3 \text{ s}$$

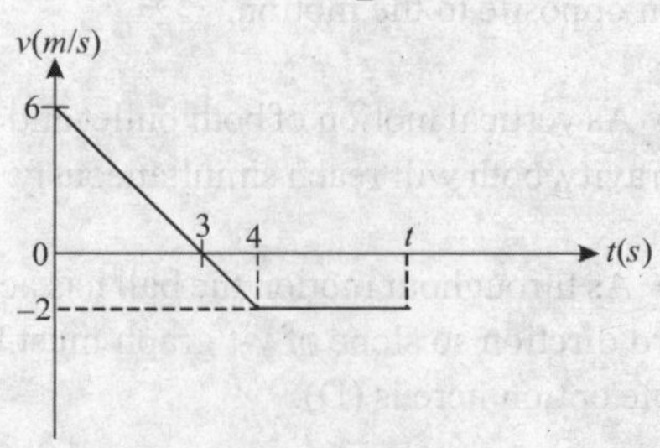

Velocity of particle after 4*s*,

$$v = 6 - 2 \times 4 = -2 \text{ m/s}$$

When particle reaches *O*, its displacement becomes zero. Thus, are of velocity - time graph must be zero

$$\Rightarrow \left[\frac{1}{2} \times (3-0) \times (6-0)\right]$$

$$-\left[\frac{1}{2} \times (4-3) \times (2-0) + (t-4)(2-0)\right] = 0$$

$$\left[\frac{1}{2} \times 3 \times 6\right] - \left[\frac{1}{2} \times 2 + 2(t-4)\right] = 0$$

$$9 - 1 - 2(t-4) = 0$$

$$2(t-4) = 8$$

$$t - 4 = 4$$

$$t = 8s$$

Sol. 4 (C) Velocity of car is

$$v = 6 + 8t - t^2$$

$$a = \frac{dv}{dt} = \frac{d}{dt}(6 + 8t - t^2)$$

$$a = 8 - 2t$$

Instantaneous acceleration at

$$t = 4.5s,$$

$$\left.\frac{dv}{dt}\right|_{t=4.5s} = 8 - 2(4.5)$$

$$a = -1 \text{m/s}^2$$

Sol. 5 (B)

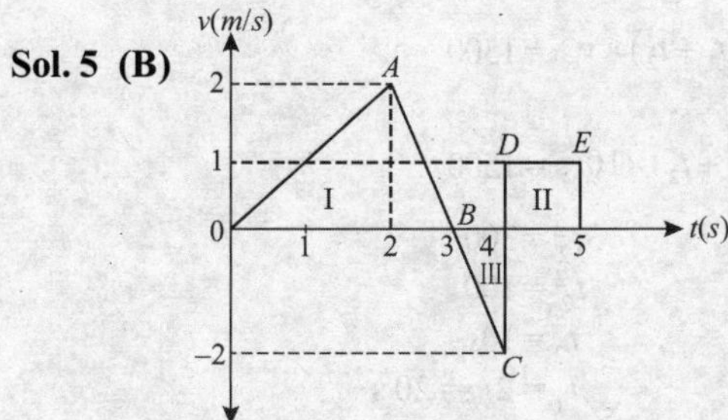

Displacement = (areas of I + II) – (area of III)

$$= \left[\frac{1}{2} \times (3-0) \times (2-0) + (5-4) \times (1-0)\right]$$

$$-\left[\frac{1}{2} \times (4-3)(2-0)\right]$$

$$= 4 - 1$$

$$= 3\text{m}$$

Sol. 6 (C) Slope of velocity-time graph gives acceleration,

$$a_{OA} = \frac{2-0}{2-0} = 1 \text{ m/s}^2$$

Sol. 7 (D) Slope of portion *DE* is zero. Hence, *DE* will have zero acceleration.

Sol. 8 (B) Initial velocity,

$$u = 17 \text{ m/s}$$

Acceleration, $a = -2 \text{ m/s}^2$

Since the particle is continuously experiencing retardations, let the time at which its velocity becomes zero is '*t*'

Using $v = u + at$

$$0 = 17 - 2t$$

$$t = 8.5s$$

0 → A 8s → B 8.5s (v = 0)
0s 9s ← C

Distance covered by particle in 9th second

$$= AB + BC$$

Velocity of particle at *A*,

$$v_A = 17 - 2(8)$$

$$v_A = 1 \text{ m/s}$$

Distance *AB*, $s_{AB} = \frac{v_B^2 - v_A^2}{2a} = \frac{0-(1)^2}{2(-2)} = \frac{1}{4} = 0.25 \text{ m}$

Distance *BC*, $s_{BC} = \frac{v_C^2 - v_B^2}{2a} = \frac{(1)^2 - 0}{2(2)} = \frac{1}{2} = 0.25\text{m}$

Thus, distance covered in 9th second of its motion

$$= 0.25 \text{ m} + 0.25 \text{ m}$$

$$= 0.5 \text{ m}$$

Sol. 9 (C) Time taken by ball to go from *A* to *B*

$$= \frac{4}{2} = 2 \text{ s}$$

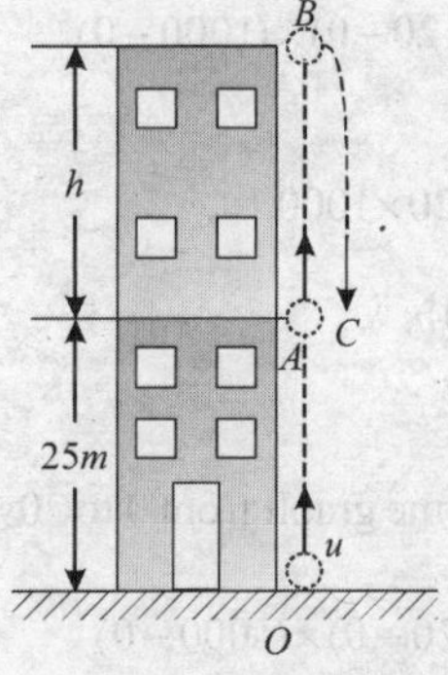

Let velocity of ball at *A* is v_A

Using $v = u + at$

$$0 = v_A - (10)(2)$$

$$v_A = 20 \text{ m/s}$$

Using $v^2 = u^2 + 2as$

$$0 = v_A^2 - 2gh$$

$$0 = (20)^2 - 2 \times 10 \times h$$

$$h = 20\,m$$

Thus, maximum height reached by the ball,

$$s = 25m + 20m = 45m$$

Using $v^2 = u^2 + 2as$

$$0 = u^2 - 2 \times 10 \times 45$$

$$u^2 = 900$$

$$u = 30 \text{ m/s}$$

Sol. 10 (D) Velocity of particle is

$$v = x^2 + x$$

$$a = \frac{dv}{dt} = v\frac{dv}{dx}$$

$$a = (x^2 + x)\cdot\frac{d}{dx}(x^2 + x)$$

$$a = (x^2 + x)(2x + 1)$$

$$a|_{x=2m} = [(2)^2 + 2][2(2) + 1]$$

$$a = 6 \times 5$$

$$a = 30 \text{ m/s}^2$$

Sol. 11 (D) After 120*s* from start of its journey, the direction of rocket is reversed. So, the rocket has reached its maximum height at 120*s*

Area under velocity-time graph from 0 to 120*s* is the maximum height reached by rocket

$\Rightarrow$ Area under curve $A = \frac{1}{2} \times (120 - 0) \times (1000 - 0)$

$$= \frac{1}{2} \times 120 \times 1000$$

$$= 60000\,m$$

$$= 60\,km$$

Sol. 12 (B) Area under velocity-time graph from 0 to 20*s*,

$$A_2 = \frac{1}{2} \times (20 - 0) \times (1000 - 0)$$

$$= \frac{1}{2} \times 20 \times 1000$$

$$= 10000 \text{ m}$$

$$= 10 \text{ km}$$

Sol. 13 (C) Mean velocity $= \frac{\text{Total height reached}}{\text{Total time taken}}$

$$v_m = \frac{60000m}{120s}$$

$$= 500 \text{ m/s}$$

Sol. 14 (A) The rocket accelerates from 0*s* to 20*s*, acceleration = slope of $v - t$ graph

$$a = \frac{1000}{20} = 50 \text{ m/s}^2$$

Sol. 15 (D) Distance covered = 1.5 km

$$= 1500 \text{ m}$$

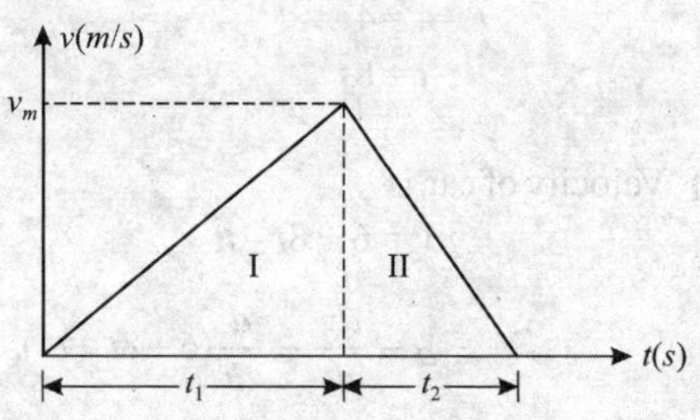

$$\frac{v_m}{t_1} = 5 \quad \ldots(1)$$

and

$$\frac{v_m}{t_2} = 10 \quad \ldots(2)$$

From (1) and (2), $5t_1 = 10t_2$

$$t_1 = 2t_2 \quad \ldots(3)$$

Area under $v - t$ graph = distance covered

$$\frac{1}{2}(t_1 + t_2) \times v_m = 1500$$

$$\frac{1}{2}(2t_2 + t_2) \times 10t_2 = 1500$$

$$3t_2^2 = 300$$

$$t_2^2 = 100$$

$$t_2 = 10s$$

$\Rightarrow$ $t_1 = 2t_2 = 20 \text{ s}$

Total time to cover 1.5 km

$$= t_1 + t_2$$

$$= 20 \text{ s} + 10 \text{ s}$$

$$= 30 \text{ s}$$

Sol. 16 (C) Distance covered by first ball (*A*) in 3 s,

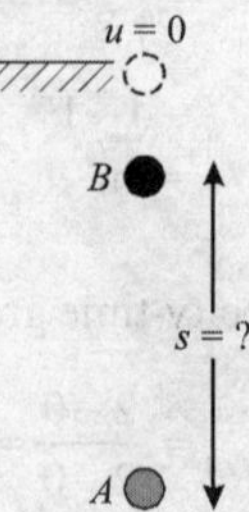

$$s_A = 0 + \frac{1}{2} \times 10 \times (3)^2 = 45\text{ m}$$

Distance covered by second ball (B) in 2 s,

$$s_B = \frac{1}{2} \times 10 \times (2)^2 = 20\text{ m}$$

Separation between A and B,

$$s = s_A - s_B = (45 - 20)\text{ m}$$
$$= 25\text{ m}$$

Sol. 17 (D) Area under $F - t$ graph = change in momentum

$$\Delta P = \left[\frac{1}{2} \times 2 \times 10\right] + [2 \times 10] + \left[\frac{1}{2} \times 2 \times 10\right]$$
$$= 10 + 20 + 10$$
$$= 40\text{ N-s}$$

Sol. 18 (A) After 1s, the ball has reached its maximum height

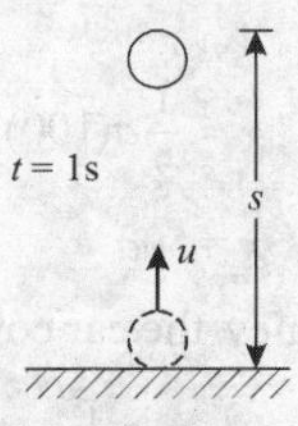

Using $v = u + at$

$$0 = u - 10\,(1)$$
$$u = 10\text{ m/s}$$

Now, $v^2 = u^2 + 2as$

$$0 = (10)^2 - 2 \times 10 \times s$$

$$s = \frac{100}{20} = 5\text{m}$$

Sol. 19 (A) Using $v = u + at$

$$v = 0 + an$$
$$v = an$$

$$\Rightarrow \quad a = \frac{v}{n} \qquad \ldots(1)$$

Distance travelled in n seconds,

$$s_n = un + \frac{1}{2}an^2$$

$$s_n = 0 + \frac{1}{2}\left(\frac{v}{n}\right)n^2$$

$$s_n = \frac{1}{2}vn \qquad \ldots(2)$$

Distance travelled in $(n-3)$ seconds,

$$s_{n-3} = u\,(n-3) + \frac{1}{2}a\,(n-3)^2$$

$$s_{n-3} = 0 + \frac{1}{2}\left(\frac{v}{n}\right)(n^2 + 9 - 6n)$$

$$s_{n-3} = \frac{v}{2n}(n^2 - 6n + 9)$$

Displacement of body in last 3 seconds = $s_n - s_{n-3}$

$$s = \frac{1}{2}vn - \frac{v}{2n}(n^2 - 6n + 9)$$

$$s = \frac{vn}{2} - \frac{vn}{2} + \frac{6v}{2} - \frac{9v}{2n}$$

$$s = \frac{v}{2n}(6n - 9)$$

Sol. 20 (D) Slope of displacement-time graph gives velocity,

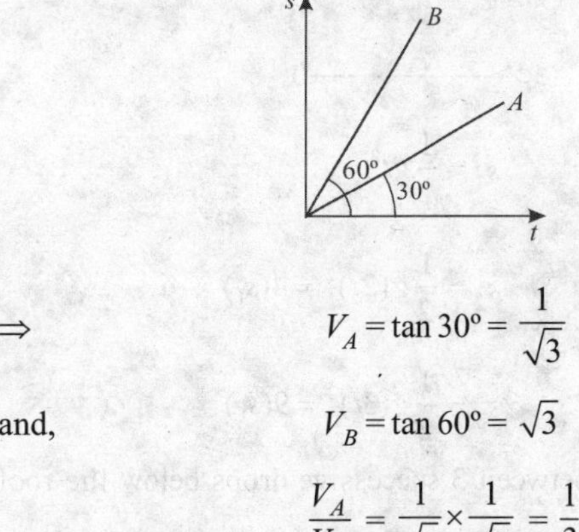

$$\Rightarrow \quad V_A = \tan 30^\circ = \frac{1}{\sqrt{3}}$$

and, $V_B = \tan 60^\circ = \sqrt{3}$

$$\frac{V_A}{V_B} = \frac{1}{\sqrt{3}} \times \frac{1}{\sqrt{3}} = \frac{1}{3}$$

Sol. 21 (B) Initial velocity, $u = 9$ m/s

Acceleration, $a = -2\text{ m/s}^2$

Let body comes to rest at time 't'

$\Rightarrow \quad 0 = 9 - 2t$

$t = 4.5$ s

$9m/s$ → O ——— A 4s → 4.5s B ($v = 0$); 5s ←

Velocity of body at A,

$$v_A = 9 - (2)(4)$$
$$= 1\text{ m/s}$$

Using $v^2 = u^2 + 2as$

$$0 = v_A^2 + 2a(s_{AB})$$
$$0 = (1)^2 - 2(2)(s_{AB})$$
$$s_{AB} = 0.25\text{m}$$

Similarly, $s_{BA} = 0.25\text{m}$

$\therefore$ Distance covered by particle in fifth second of its motion,

$$s = s_{AB} + s_{BA} = 0.25\text{m} + 0.25\text{ m}$$
$$= 0.5\text{m}$$

Sol. 22 (D) Area under $v-t$ graph gives displacement

Displacement = (area of upper trapezium) – (area of lower trapezium)

$$= \left\{\left[\frac{(4-0)+(3-1)}{2}\right](4-0)\right\} - \left\{\left[\frac{(8-4)+(7-5)}{2}\right](2-0)\right\}$$

$$= 12 - 6$$

$$= 6\text{ m}$$

This displacement is the distance of particle from origin.

Sol. 23 (C) Let the drops fall at an internal of t seconds

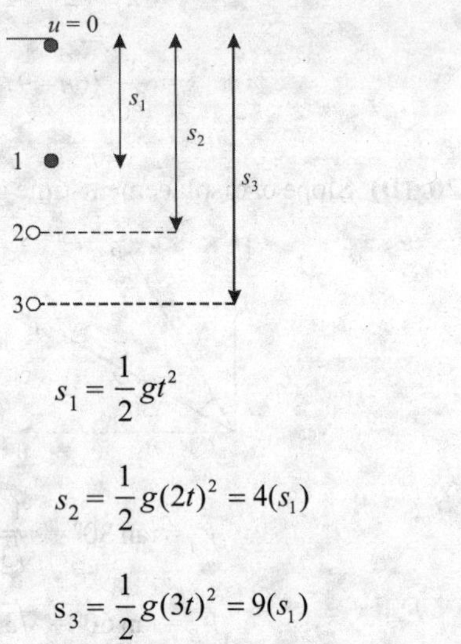

$$s_1 = \frac{1}{2}gt^2$$

$$s_2 = \frac{1}{2}g(2t)^2 = 4(s_1)$$

$$s_3 = \frac{1}{2}g(3t)^2 = 9(s_1)$$

Thus, separation between 3 successive drops below the roof are in ratio

$$s_1 : s_2 - s_1 : s_3 - s_2$$

$$s_1 : 3s_1 : 5s_1 := 1 : 3 : 5$$

Sol. 24 (D) We have $\quad a = 32 - 4v$

$$\frac{dv}{dt} = 32 - 4v$$

$$\frac{dv}{32-4v} = dt$$

Integrating both sides, we get

$$\int_4^v \frac{dv}{32-4v} = \int_0^{\ln 2} dt$$

$$-\frac{1}{4}[\ln(32-4v)]_4^v = \ln 2 - 0$$

$$\ln\left(\frac{32-4v}{16}\right) = \ln\left(\frac{1}{16}\right)$$

$$32 - 4v = 1$$

$$4v = 31$$

$$v = \frac{31}{4}$$

Sol. 25 (D) Change in velocity is given as

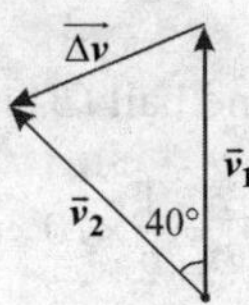

from figure shown as $|\vec{v}_1| = |\vec{v}_2| = v$ we use

$$|\overrightarrow{\Delta v}| = 2v\sin 20^\circ$$

Sol. 26 (B) Initial velocity, $u = 0$

Let acceleration of car is 'a'

Using $\qquad s = ut + \frac{1}{2}at^2$

$$x = 0 + \frac{1}{2}a(10)^2$$

$$x = \frac{1}{2}a(100)$$

$$x = 50a \qquad \ldots(1)$$

In $20s$ from start of journey, the car covers a distance $(x+y)$

$$\Rightarrow \qquad x + y = 0 + \frac{1}{2}a(20)^2$$

$$x + y = 200\,a \qquad \ldots(2)$$

Dividing (1) by (2), we get

$$\frac{x}{x+y} = \frac{50a}{200a}$$

$$\frac{x}{x+y} = \frac{1}{4}$$

$$4x = x + y$$

$$y = 3x$$

Sol. 27 (C) Initial velocity, $u = 0$

acceleration $\qquad a = kt$

$$\Rightarrow \qquad \frac{dv}{dt} = kt$$

$$\Rightarrow \qquad \int_0^v dv = \int_0^t kt$$

Integrating both sides, we get

$$v = \frac{kt^2}{2}$$

$$\Rightarrow \qquad \frac{dx}{dt} = \frac{kt^2}{2}$$

$$\Rightarrow \qquad \int_0^x dx = \int_0^t \frac{k}{2} t^2 dt$$

Again integrating both sides, we get

$$x = \frac{k}{6}t^3 = \frac{1}{6}kt \cdot t^2$$

$$x = \frac{1}{6}at^2$$

Sol. 28 (D) Slope of $v - t$ graph gives acceleration

$$a_{max} = \text{slope of } BC$$

$$a_{max} = \frac{60-20}{40-30} = \frac{40}{10} = 4 \text{ m/s}^2$$

Sol. 29 (B) Retardation = slope of CD

$$m = \frac{0-60}{70-40} = \frac{-60}{30} = -2 \text{ m/s}^2$$

Magnitude of retardation = 2 m/s^2

Sol. 30 (D) Velocity required by rocket at the end of 1 min (60 s),

$$v = 0 + 10 \times 60$$

$$v = 600 \text{ m/s}$$

Now, after the fuel is exhausted, it continues to move up under the action of gravity, i.e. its motion will be retarded. let it's velocity becomes zero after t seconds,

$$0 = 600 - 10t$$

$$t = 60 \text{ s}$$

Sol. 31 (B)

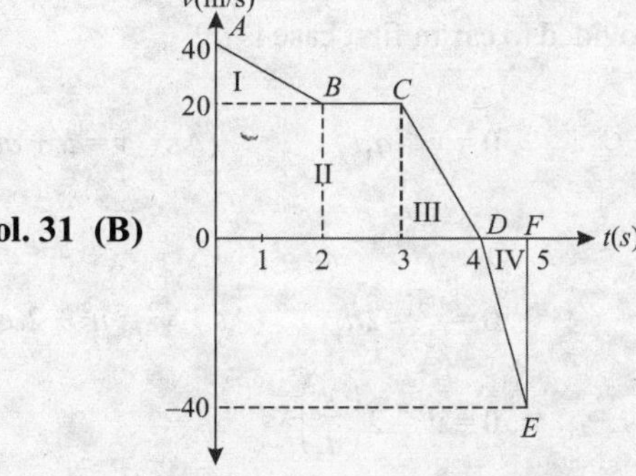

Area under $v - t$ graph

I: $\frac{1}{2} \times 2 \times 20 = 20$

II: $3 \times 20 = 60$

III: $\frac{1}{2} \times 1 \times 20 = 10$

IV: $\frac{1}{2} \times 1 \times 40 = 20$

Distance covered by body

$$= 20 + 60 + 10 + 20$$

$$= 110 \text{ m}$$

Displacement of body $= (20 + 60 + 10) - 20$

$$= 70 \text{ m}$$

Sol. 32 (B) Displacement of particle is

$$x = -\frac{2}{3}t^2 + 16t + 2$$

Differentiating w.r.t. t, we get

$$v = \frac{dx}{dt} = -\frac{2}{3}(2t) + 16$$

$$v = -\frac{4t}{3} + 16$$

For $v = 0$,

$$\frac{4t}{3} = 16$$

$$t = 12 \text{ s}$$

Sol. 33 (B) Displacement of particle is

$$x = 2 - 5t + 6t^2$$

Differentiating w.r.t. time, we get

$$v = \frac{dx}{dt} = -5 + 12t$$

at $t = 0$,

$$v = -5 \text{ m/s}$$

Sol. 34 (C) Distance covered by parachutist in 10 s before parachute opens out,

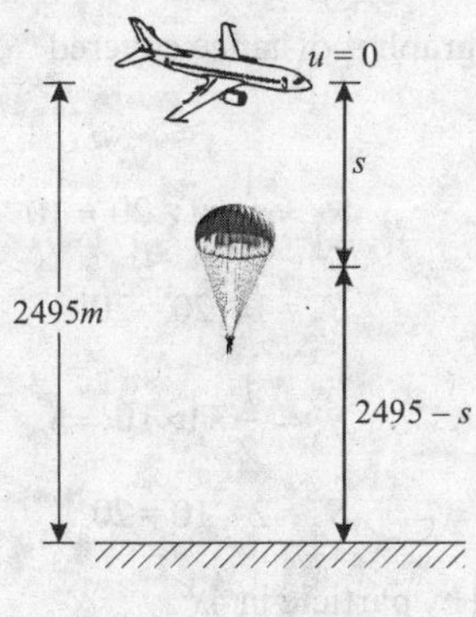

$$s = 0 + \frac{1}{2} \times 10 \times (10)^2$$

$$s = 500 \text{ m}$$

Velocity acquired by parachutist before opening parachute,

$$v = 0 + 10 \times 10$$

$$v = 100 \text{ m/s}$$

Now, after opening parachute,

his initial velocity, $u = 100$ m/s

Distance it has to reach further,

$$s_2 = 2495 - 500$$

$$s_2 = 1995 \text{ m}$$

Retardation, $a = 2.5$ m/s^2

$$\Rightarrow \quad v^2 = (100)^2 - 2 \times 2.5 \times 1995$$

$$v^2 = 10000 - 9975$$

$$v^2 = 25$$

$$v = 5 \text{ m/s}$$

Sol. 35 (B) Acceleration of particle is

$$a = kt + c$$

$$\frac{dv}{dt} = kt + c$$

$$dv = (kt + c)dt$$

Integrating both sides, we get

$$v = \frac{kt^2}{2} + ct$$

Sol. 36 (C)

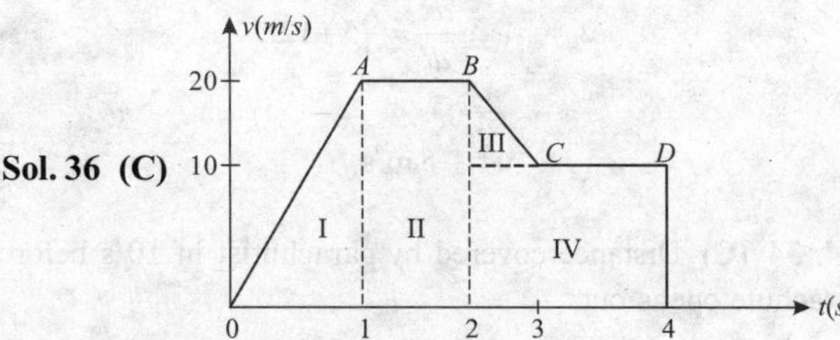

Area under $v - t$ graph = distance covered

Area :

I $\quad S_1 = \frac{1}{2} \times 1 \times 20 = 10$

II $\quad S_2 = 1 \times 20 = 20$

III $\quad S_3 = \frac{1}{2} \times 1 \times 10 = 5$

IV $\quad S_4 = 2 \times 10 = 20$

Distance covered by particle in 4s

$$= 10 + 20 + 5 + 20$$

$$= 55 \text{ m}$$

Sol. 37 (C) The two situations described in the question are shown below

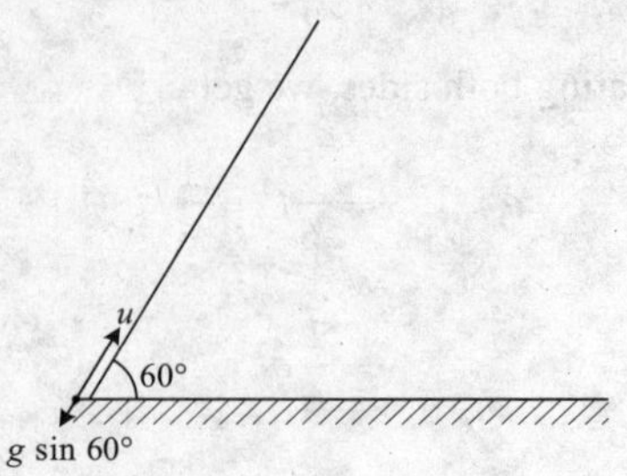

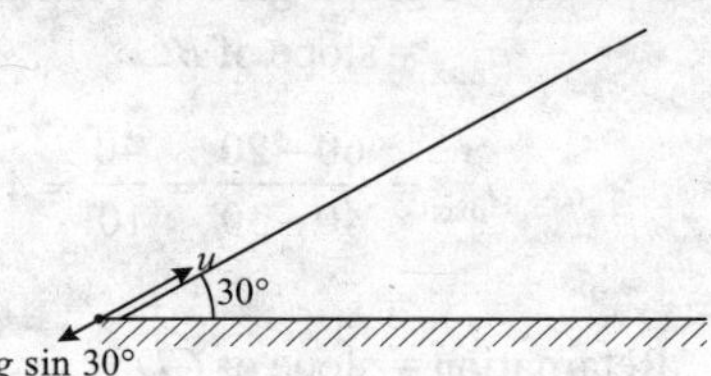

For motion of object in both cases, we use

Along the incline acceleration is given as

$$v^2 - u^2 = 2as$$

$$= 0 - u^2 = 2(-g \sin \theta) \cdot x_1$$

Taking $v = 0$ we get

$$\Rightarrow \quad \text{(Stopping distance)} \quad x_1 = \frac{u^2}{2g \sin 60°}$$

$$\Rightarrow \quad \text{(Stopping distance)} \quad x_2 = \frac{u^2}{2g \sin 30°}$$

$$\Rightarrow \quad \frac{x_1}{x_2} = \frac{\sin 30°}{\sin 60°} = \frac{1 \times 2}{2 \times \sqrt{3}} = 1 : \sqrt{3}$$

Sol. 38 (B) Let the time taken to stop the car is 't'.
If retardation provided to car in first case is a_1,

Then,

$$0 = v - a_1 t \qquad (\text{As} \quad v = u + at)$$

$$\Rightarrow \quad a_1 = \frac{v}{t}$$

Also, $\quad 0 = v^2 - 2a_1 x \qquad (\text{As} \quad v^2 = u^2 + 2as)$

$$0 = v^2 - 2\left(\frac{v}{t}\right)x$$

$$v = \frac{2x}{t} \qquad \ldots(1)$$

If speed becomes 'nv' and retardation is a_2(say)

Then, $\quad 0 = nv - a_2 t \qquad (\text{As} \quad v = u + at)$

$$a_2 = \frac{nv}{t}$$

Again, $0 = (nv)^2 - 2a_2x'$

where x' is the new distance over which the car can be stopped

$$0 = n^2v^2 - 2\left(\frac{nv}{t}\right)x'$$

$$\frac{2x'}{t} = nv \quad \ldots(2)$$

From (1) and (2), we get

$$\frac{2x'}{t} = n\left(\frac{2x}{t}\right)$$

$$x' = nx$$

Sol. 39 (A)

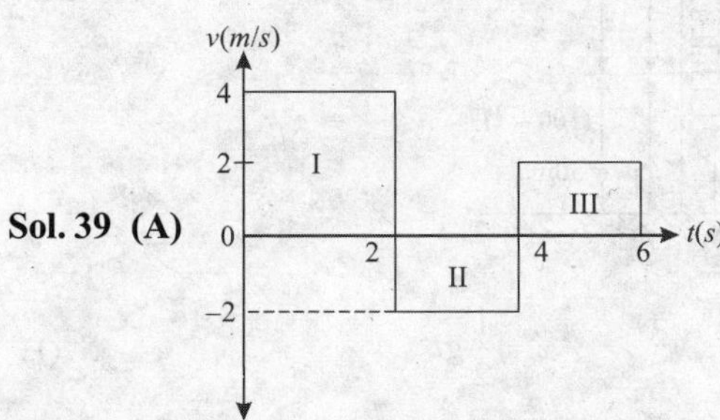

Area of rectangle $\text{I} = (2 \times 4) = 8$

Area of rectangle $\text{II} = (2 \times 2) = 4$

Area of rectangle $\text{III} = (2 \times 2) = 4$

distance covered by body $= 8 + 4 + 4 = 16m$

Displacement of body $= 8 - 4 + 4 = 8m$

Sol. 40 (C) Distance travelled in t^{th} second,

$$s_1 = u + \frac{f}{2}(2t-1)$$

Distance travelled in $(t+1)^{\text{th}}$ second,

$$s_2 = u + \frac{f}{2}[2(t+1)-1]$$

$$s_2 = u + \frac{f}{2}[2t+1]$$

Given that $s_1 + s_2 = 100\text{ cm}$

$$u + \frac{f}{2}(2t-1) + u + \frac{f}{2}(2t+1) = 100$$

$$2u + \frac{f}{2}[2t - 1 + 2t + 1] = 100$$

$$2u + \frac{f}{2}(4t) = 100$$

$$2u + 2ft = 100$$

$$u + ft = 50$$

From I equation, $v = u + ft = 50\text{ cm/s}$

Sol. 41 (A) Area under $v-t$ graph gives distance travelled by train

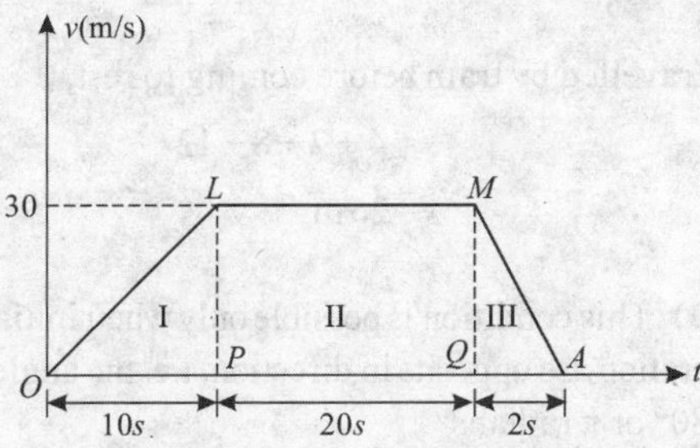

$$\text{Area I} = \frac{1}{2} \times 10 \times 30 = 150\text{ m}$$

$$\text{Area II} = 20 \times 30 = 600\text{ m}$$

$$\text{Area III} = \frac{1}{2} \times 2 \times 30 = 30\text{ m}$$

Distance travelled $= 150 + 600 + 30\text{ m}$

$= 780\text{ m}$

Sol. 42 (B) Let stone remains in air for n second

Distance covered by it in n^{th} second,

$$s_1 = 0 + \frac{g}{2}(2n-1)$$

Distance covered in first 3 seconds,

$$s_2 = 0 + \frac{1}{2}g(3)^2 = \frac{9g}{2}$$

As $s_1 = s_2$

$$\frac{g}{2}(2n-1) = \frac{9g}{2}$$

$$2n - 1 = 9$$

$$n = 5\text{ s}$$

Sol. 43 (B) Here we draw the corresponding velocity-time graph from the given $a-t$ graph

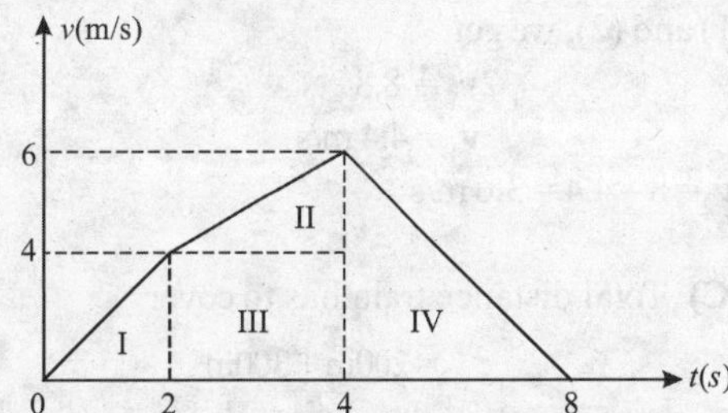

Area of $\text{I} = \frac{1}{2} \times 2 \times 4 = 4$

Area of $\text{II} = \frac{1}{2} \times 2 \times 2 = 2$

Area of $\text{III} = 2\times 4 = 8$

Area of $\text{IV} = \frac{1}{2}\times 4\times 6 = 12$

Distance travelled by train before coming to rest,

$$s = 4+2+8+12$$

$$s = 26\text{m}$$

Sol. 44 (D) This condition is possible only when initial velocity and acceleration are opposite in direction, i.e. the angle between these is 180° or π radians

Sol. 45 (C) Velocity of B relative to A,

$$v_{BA} = 5\text{m/s}$$

and, velocity of C relative to A,

$$v_{CA} = 15\text{ m/s}$$

Let both cover the distance l in time t

For car B, $\quad l = 5t + \frac{1}{2}at^2 \quad \ldots(1)$

For car C, $\quad l = 15t \quad \ldots(2)$

As it is moving with constant speed

$$\Rightarrow \quad t = \frac{l}{15} = \frac{1500}{15} = 100\text{ s}$$

Substituting values of l and t in equation (1), we get

$$1500 = 5(100) + \frac{1}{2}a(100)^2$$

$$1000 = \frac{a}{2}(10000)$$

$$a = \frac{2}{10} = 0.2\text{ m/s}^2$$

Sol. 46 (B) Let speed of cars be v_1 and v_2

$$v_1 + v_2 = 8 \quad \ldots(1)$$

and $\quad v_1 - v_2 = 0.8 \quad \ldots(2)$

Solving (1) and (2), we get

$$2v_1 = 8.8$$

$$v_1 = 4.4\text{ m/s}$$

and $\quad v_2 = 8 - 4.4 = 3.6\text{ m/s}$

Sol. 47 (C) Total distance train has to cover

$$= 200\text{m} + 300\text{m}$$

$$= 500\text{m}$$

Initial velocity, $\quad u = 3\text{m/s}$

Final velocity, $\quad v = 5\text{m/s}$

Let time taken to cross the bridge is 't' and acceleration is 'a'

we use $\quad v^2 = u^2 + 2as$

$$\Rightarrow \quad (5)^2 = (3)^2 + 2a(500)$$

$$25 = 9 + 1000a$$

$$a = \frac{2}{125}\text{ m/s}^2$$

Using $v = u + at$

$$5 = 3 + \frac{2}{125}\times t$$

$$t = 125s$$

Sol. 48 (B) Let they cross each other at 't'

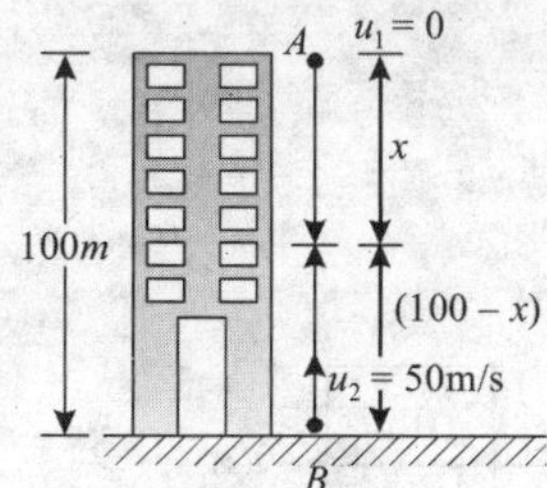

For ball A, $\quad x = \frac{1}{2}gt^2 \quad \ldots(1)$

For ball B, $\quad 100 - x = 50t - \frac{1}{2}gt^2 \quad \ldots(2)$

From (1) and (2), we get

$$100 - \frac{1}{2}gt^2 = 50t - \frac{1}{2}gt^2$$

$$t = 2\text{ s}$$

Alternatively: Solve using relative speed of one ball with respect to other

$$\Rightarrow \quad t = \frac{100}{50} = 2s$$

Sol. 49 (B) Initial velocity, $\vec{v}_i = (20\hat{j})$ m/s

Final velocity, $\quad \vec{v}_f = (20\hat{i})$ m/s

$$\overrightarrow{\Delta v} = \vec{v}_f - \vec{v}_i = 20\hat{i} - 20\hat{j}$$

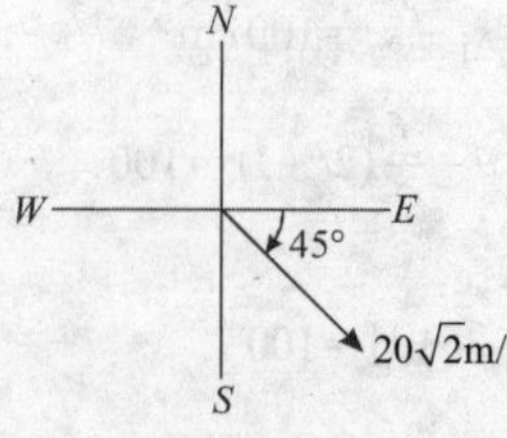

$$|\overrightarrow{\Delta v}| = \sqrt{(20)^2 + (-20)^2} = 20\sqrt{2}\text{ m/s}$$

$$\tan\theta = \frac{-20}{20} = -1$$

$$\theta = -45° \text{ (south – East)}$$

Sol. 50 (C) From graph we use

$$v = -\frac{1}{2}s + 50$$

Differentiating both sides, with respect to t, we have

$$v = -2\frac{dv}{dt}$$

$$2\frac{dv}{v} = -dt$$

Now, integrating both sides

$$2\int_{50}^{0}\frac{dv}{v} = -\int_{0}^{t}dt$$

$$t = 2[\ln v]_{50}^{0}$$

$$\Rightarrow \quad t \to \infty$$

Sol. 51 (B) Initial and final velocities of particle are

$$\vec{v}_i = 5\hat{i} \text{ m/s}$$

$$\vec{v}_f = 5\hat{j} \text{ m/s}$$

$$t = 10s$$

$$\vec{a} = \frac{\vec{v}_f - \vec{v}_i}{t} = \frac{5\hat{j} - 5\hat{i}}{10}$$

$$\vec{a} = -\frac{1}{2}\hat{i} + \frac{1}{2}\hat{j} \quad \text{[North-West]}$$

$$|\vec{a}| = \sqrt{\left(\frac{-1}{2}\right)^2 + \left(\frac{1}{2}\right)^2}$$

$$= \frac{1}{\sqrt{2}} \text{ m/s}^2$$

Sol. 52 (A) $m = 2kg$

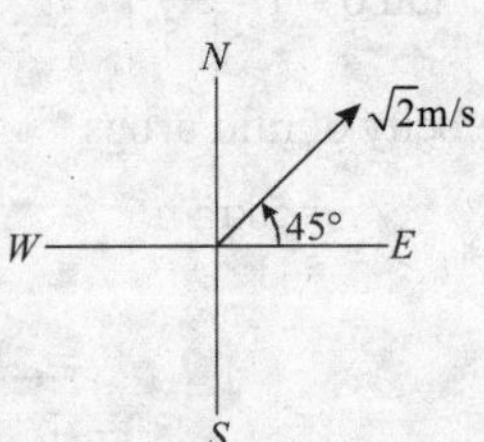

Initial velocity, $\vec{u} = \sqrt{2}\cos 45°\hat{i} + \sqrt{2}\sin 45°\hat{j}$

$$= (\hat{i} + \hat{j}) \text{ m/s}$$

Force, $\vec{F} = -0.2\hat{i}N$

$\Rightarrow$ Acceleration, $\vec{a} = \frac{\vec{F}}{m} = \frac{-0.2\hat{i}}{2} = -0.1\,\hat{i} \text{ m/s}^2$

At $t = 10$ s

$$\vec{v} = \vec{u} + \vec{a}t$$

$$\vec{v} = (\hat{i} + \hat{j}) + 10(-0.1\hat{i})$$

$$\vec{v} = \hat{i} + \hat{j} - \hat{i}$$

$$\vec{v} = +\hat{j}$$

Thus, velocity after 10 s is 1m/s due North

Sol. 53 (C) $\vec{x}_1 = 30\hat{j}m$

$$\vec{x}_2 = 20\hat{i}m$$

$$\vec{x}_3 = -30\sqrt{2}\cos 45°\hat{i} - 30\sqrt{2}\sin 45°\hat{j}$$

$$\vec{x}_3 = -30\hat{i} - 30\hat{j}$$

Displacement, $\vec{x} = \vec{x}_1 + \vec{x}_2 + \vec{x}_3$

$$= 30\hat{j} + 20\hat{i} - 30\hat{i} - 30\hat{j}$$

$$= -10\hat{i}$$

Thus, its position is 10 m due west

Sol. 54 (C)

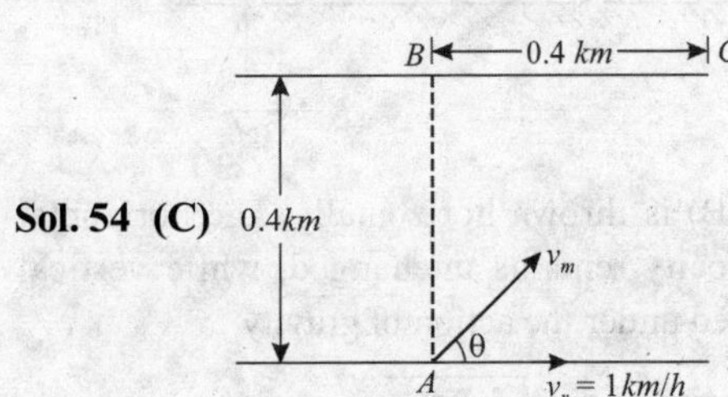

$$v_m \sin\theta = \frac{0.4}{t} \quad \ldots(1)$$

$$v_m \cos\theta + v_r = \frac{0.4}{t} \quad \ldots(2)$$

From (1) and (2),

$$v_m \sin\theta = v_m\cos\theta + v_r$$

$$5\sin\theta = 5\cos\theta + 1$$

$$5\sqrt{1-\cos^2\theta} = 5\cos\theta + 1$$

$$25(1 - \cos^2\theta) = 25\cos^2\theta + 1 + 10\cos\theta$$

$$50\cos^2\theta + 10\cos\theta - 24$$

$$\cos\theta = \frac{3}{5}, -\frac{4}{5}$$

$$\theta = 53°$$

Sol. 55 (B)

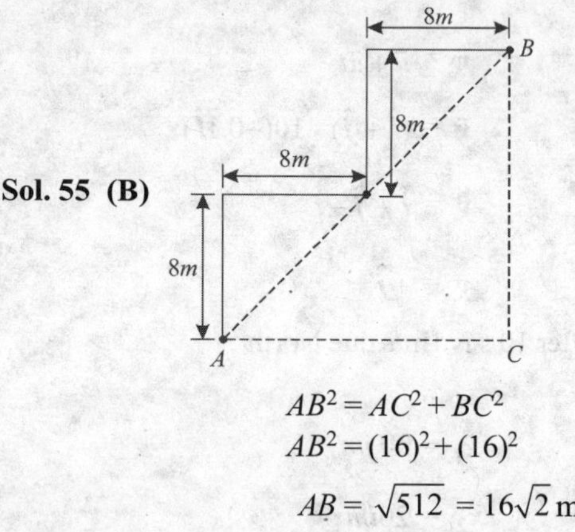

$$AB^2 = AC^2 + BC^2$$
$$AB^2 = (16)^2 + (16)^2$$
$$AB = \sqrt{512} = 16\sqrt{2}\text{ m}$$

Sol. 56 (D) When particle is thrown in vertical downward direction with velocity u, then final velocity when it reaches ground,

$$v = \sqrt{u^2 + 2gh}$$

Another particle (B) is thrown horizontally. The horizontal component of velocity remains unchanged, while vertical component is gained under the action of gravity

$\Rightarrow$ Resultant velocity $= \sqrt{u^2 + 2gh}$

Ratio of velocities $= 1:1$

Sol. 57 (C) Area made by $v - t$ graph = distance covered

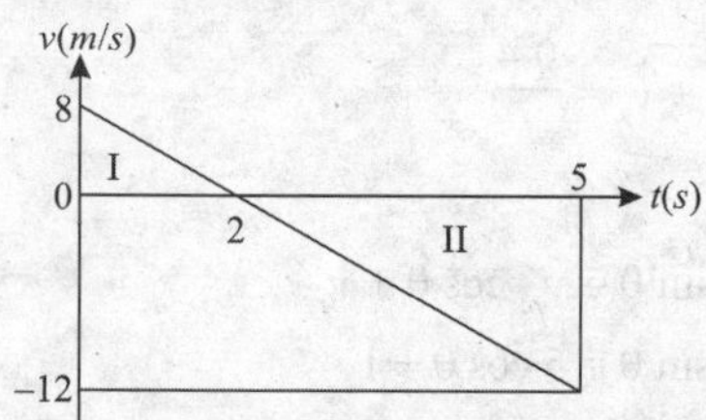

$$\text{Area of I} = \frac{1}{2} \times 2 \times 8 = 8$$

$$\text{Area of II} = \frac{1}{2} \times 3 \times 12 = 18$$

Distance moved by particle

$$= 8 + 18$$
$$= 26\text{m}$$

Sol. 58 (B) Velocity of car w.r.t. ground,

$$\vec{v}_{cg} = 8\hat{i} \text{ m/s}$$

Velocity of train w.r.t. car,

$$\vec{v}_{tc} = 15\hat{j} \text{ m/s}$$

Velocity of train w.r.t. ground,

$$\vec{v}_{tg} = \vec{v}_{tc} + \vec{v}_{cg}$$

$$\vec{v}_{tg} = 15\hat{j} + 8\hat{i}$$

$$|\vec{v}_{tg}| = \sqrt{(15)^2 + (8)^2}$$
$$= \sqrt{289}$$
$$= 17 \text{ m/s}$$

Sol. 59 (D) Velocity of rain w.r.t. ground,

$$\vec{v}_{rg} = -3\hat{j} \text{ km/h}$$

Velocity of man w.r.t. ground,

$$\vec{v}_{mg} = 4\hat{i} \text{ km/h}$$

Velocity of rain w.r.t. man,

$$\vec{v}_{rm} = \vec{v}_{rg} - \vec{v}_{mg}$$

$$\vec{v}_{rm} = (-3\hat{j} - 4\hat{i}) \text{ km/h}$$

$$|\vec{v}_{rm}| = \sqrt{(-3)^2 + (-4)^2}$$
$$= \sqrt{25} = 5 \text{ km/h}$$

Sol. 60 (A) Velocity of man w.r.t. ground,

$$\vec{v}_{mg} = 5\hat{i} \text{ km/h}$$

Velocity of rain w.r.t. man,

$$\vec{v}_{rm} = \vec{v}_{rg} - \vec{v}_{mg}$$

$$= \vec{v}_{rg}\hat{j} - 5\hat{i}$$

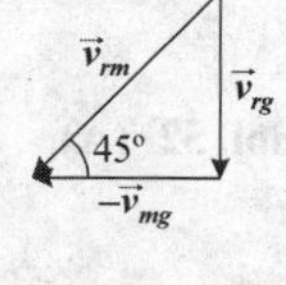

$$\tan\theta = 1 = \left|\frac{\vec{v}_{rg}}{5}\right|$$

Thus, downward velocity of rain drops

$$= 5 \text{ km/h}$$

Sol. 61 (A)

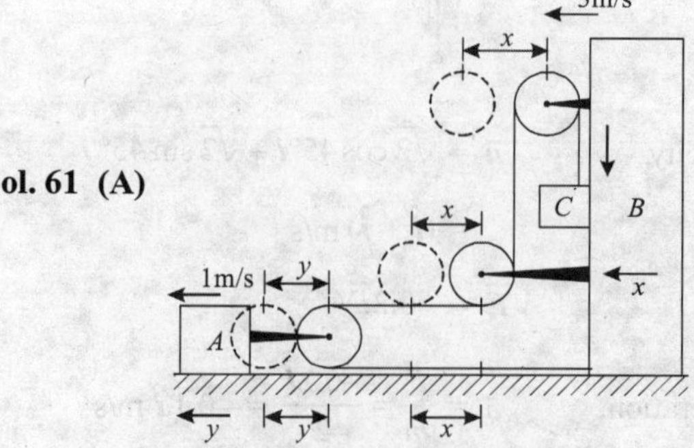

C comes down by $(3x - 2y)$

$$v_c = 3x - 2y = (3 \times 3) - (2 \times 2)$$
$$v_c = 9 - 4$$
$$v_c = 5 \text{ m/s}$$

Sol. 62 (C) At highest point of projectile, the particle has only horizontal component of velocity

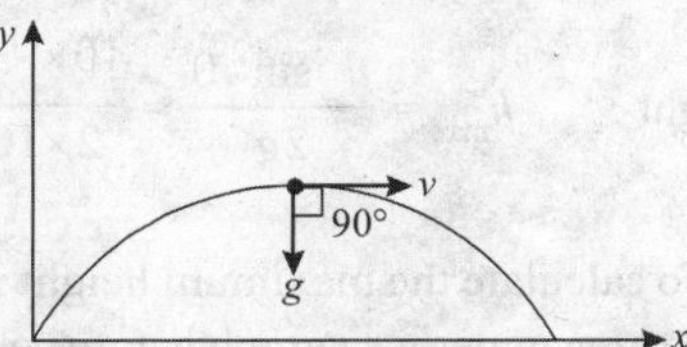

Thus, angle between velocity & acceleration = 90°

Sol. 63 (D) Horizontal range = Maximum height

$$\frac{u^2 \sin 2\theta}{g} = \frac{u^2 \sin^2 \theta}{2g}$$

$$2 \sin \theta \cos \theta = \frac{\sin^2 \theta}{2}$$

$$4 \cos \theta = \sin \theta$$

$$\tan \theta = 4$$

Sol. 64 (D)

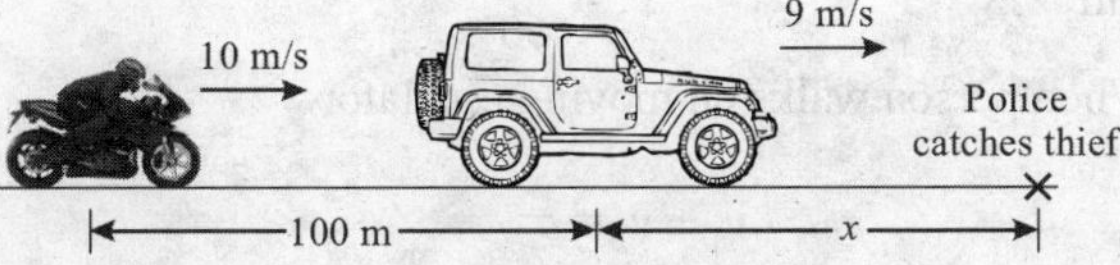

Let police man takes t second to catch the thief

$$10 = \frac{100 + x}{t} \quad \ldots(1)$$

For thief, $$9 = \frac{x}{t} \quad \ldots(2)$$

$\Rightarrow$ $$x = 9t \quad \ldots(3)$$

From (1) and (3), we get

$$10t = 100 + 9t$$
$$t = 100 \text{ s}$$

Sol. 65 (D) Using relative speed of third car, we have

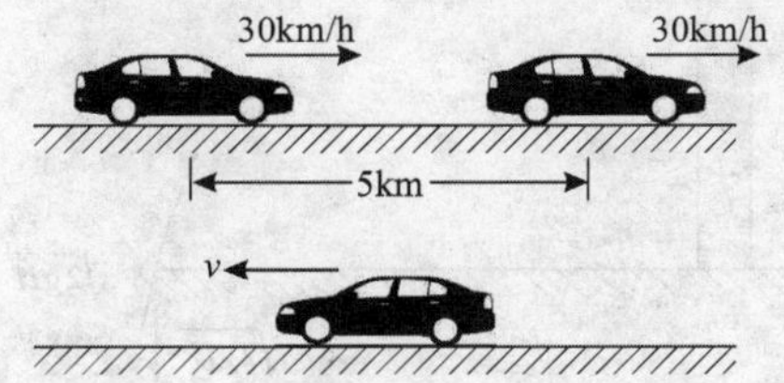

$$v + 30 = \frac{5}{\left(\frac{4}{60}\right)}$$

$\Rightarrow$ $$v + 30 = \frac{5 \times 60}{4} = 75$$

$\Rightarrow$ $$v = 75 - 30 = 45 \text{ km/h}$$

Sol. 66 (B) Angle made by projectile with horizontal,

$$\theta = 30°$$

when projectile is making 90° with the initial, then, the projectile makes an angle 60° with the horizontal. Since there is no acceleration in horizontal, horizontal component of velocity remains same

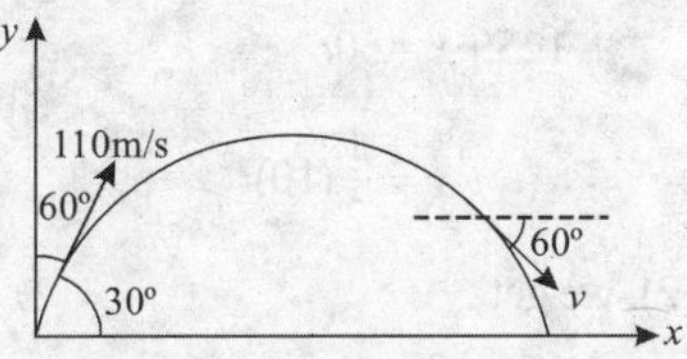

$$u \cos 30° = v \cos 60°$$

$$110 \frac{\sqrt{3}}{2} = \frac{v}{2}$$

$$v = 110\sqrt{3} \text{ m/s}$$

In vertical direction,

$$-v \sin 60° = u \sin 30° - 10t$$

$$-110\sqrt{3} \times \frac{\sqrt{3}}{2} = 110 \times \frac{1}{2} - 10t$$

$$\frac{-330}{2} = \frac{110}{2} - 10t$$

$$t = \frac{11}{2} + \frac{33}{2}$$

$$t = \frac{44}{2}$$

$$t = 22 \text{ s}$$

Sol. 67 (D) Range, $$R = \frac{u^2 \sin 2\theta}{g}$$

Maximum height reached,

$$H = \frac{u^2 \sin^2 \theta}{2g}$$

Time of flight, $$T = \frac{2u \sin \theta}{g}$$

New range, $$R' = u_x T + \frac{1}{2} a_x T^2$$

$$R' = u\cos\theta \cdot \frac{2u\sin\theta}{g} + \frac{1}{2}\cdot\frac{g}{2}\left[\frac{2u\sin\theta}{g}\right]^2$$

$$R' = R + 2H$$

Sol. 68 (A) Let the separation between them is 125m after time 't' and B has covered a distance 'x' in this time

A
$u_1 = 50\text{m/s}$
B
$u_2 = 0$
125m
x

For A, $$125 + x = 50t \quad \ldots(1)$$

For B, $$x = \frac{1}{2}(10)t^2 \quad \ldots(2)$$

From (1) and (2), we get

$$125 + 5t^2 = 50t$$

$$t^2 - 10t + 25 = 0$$

$$t = 5 \text{ s}$$

Sol. 69 (D) Acceleration of stone relative to aeroplane,

$$\vec{a}_{sa} = \vec{a}_{sg} - \vec{a}_{ag}$$

$$= -10\hat{j} - 5\hat{j}$$

(Considering downward as negative)

$$= -15\hat{j}$$

Thus, $\vec{a}_{sa}$ is 15 m/s^2 downward

Sol. 70 (B) The acceleration will remain equal to 9.8 m/s^2 as at highest point speed is zero and no air resistance acts on it

Sol. 71 (C) $$y = x - x^2$$

Comparing it with equation of trajectory,

$$y = x\tan\theta - \frac{gx^2}{2u^2\cos^2\theta}$$

$$= x\tan\theta - \frac{x^2\tan\theta}{R}$$

$$\tan\theta = 1$$

$$\Rightarrow \quad \theta = 45° \quad \text{(angle of projection)}$$

$$\frac{\tan 45°}{R} = 1$$

$$R = 1m \quad \text{(Range)}$$

Also, we use $$\frac{g}{2u^2\cos^2\theta} = 1$$

$$\frac{10}{2u^2\cos^2 45°} = 1$$

$$u^2 = 10$$

$$u = \sqrt{10} \text{ m/s}$$

Time of flight, $$T = \frac{2\sqrt{10}\sin 45°}{10}$$

$$T = 0.45s$$

Maximum height $$h_{max} = \frac{u^2\sin^2\theta}{2g} = \frac{10\times \frac{1}{2}}{2\times 10} = 0.25\text{m}$$

Sol. 72 (B) To calculate the maximum height reached by the rocket, lets find area under $v - t$ graph before velocity becomes zero,

i.e. in I quadrant

$$\text{Area} = \frac{1}{2}\times 132\times 1200$$

$$H = 79200\text{m}$$

$$H = 79.2\text{ km}$$

Sol. 73 (D) Let speed of stalled escalator is v_1 and that of person is v_2. If length of escalator is x

Then,

$$v_1 = \frac{x}{90} \quad \ldots(1)$$

and $$v_2 = \frac{x}{60} \quad \ldots(2)$$

When person walks on moving escalator

$$v_1 + v_2 = \frac{x}{t} \quad \ldots(3)$$

$$\frac{x}{90} + \frac{x}{60} = \frac{x}{t}$$

$$t = \frac{(90)(60)}{(90)+(60)} = 36 \text{ s}$$

Sol. 74 (C) The horizontal component of velocity always remains unchanged

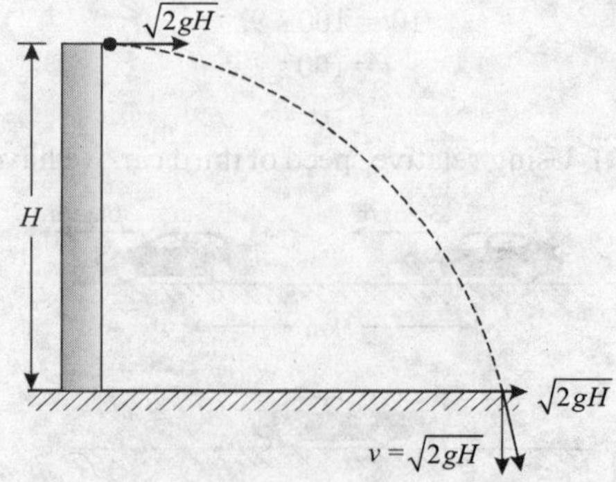

The initial velocity in vertical is zero

The vertical component of velocity as it reaches ground,

$$v^2 = 0^2 + 2gH$$
$$v = \sqrt{2gH}$$

Resultant velocity $= \sqrt{(\sqrt{2gH})^2 + (\sqrt{2gH})^2} = 2\sqrt{gH}$

Sol. 75 (A) A —— 40 km/h → —— B ; ← 60 km/h

Let distance between A and B is x

$\Rightarrow$ Average speed is $v_{avg} = \dfrac{2x}{\dfrac{x}{40} + \dfrac{x}{60}}$

$$= \frac{2x}{\dfrac{3x+2x}{120}}$$
$$= \frac{2x \times 120}{5x}$$
$$= 48 \text{ km/h}$$

Since the train returns to its initial position,

Total displacement $= 0$

Average velocity $= 0$

Sol. 76 (B) Initial velocity, $\vec{u} = 50\hat{j}$ km/h (North)

final velocity, $\vec{v} = -50\hat{i}$ km/h (West)

Change in velocity, $\overrightarrow{\Delta v} = \vec{v} - \vec{u}$

$$= (-50\hat{i} - 50\hat{j}) \text{ km/h}$$
$$|\overrightarrow{\Delta v}| = \sqrt{(-50)^2 + (-50)^2}$$
$$= \sqrt{5000}$$
$$= 50\sqrt{2} \text{ km/h towards south-west}$$

Sol. 77 (B) Velocity of bird

$$v = |t-2| \text{ m/s}$$
$$\frac{dx}{dt} = t - 2$$
$$dx = (t-2)dt$$

Integrating both sides,

$$\int_0^x dx = \int_0^4 (t-2)dt$$
$$x = \left[\frac{t^2}{2} - 2t\right]_0^4$$
$$x = 8 - 8 = 0$$

The displacement of bird is zero

Let time after which bird changes its direction of motion is t_1

$$v = 0$$

i.e. $t = 2$ s

Distance, $D = \left|\int_0^2 (t-2)dt\right| + \left|\int_2^4 (t-2)dt\right|$

$$D = 2 + 2$$
$$D = 4 \text{ m}$$

Sol. 78 (A) Let us make some assumptions first

Initial velocity $= u$

Height of tower $= H$

For particle A,

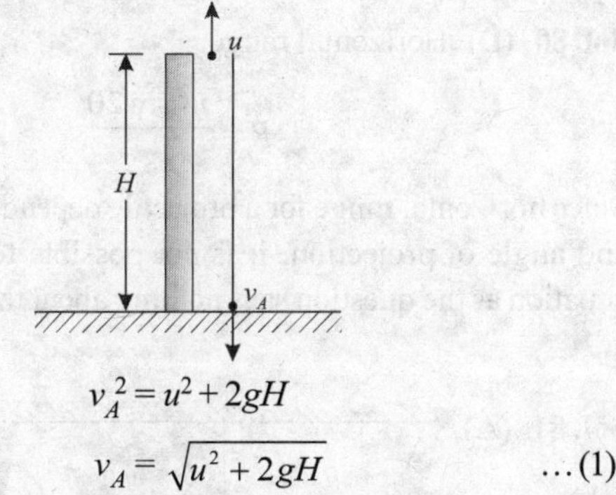

$$v_A^2 = u^2 + 2gH$$
$$v_A = \sqrt{u^2 + 2gH} \quad \ldots(1)$$

For particle B,

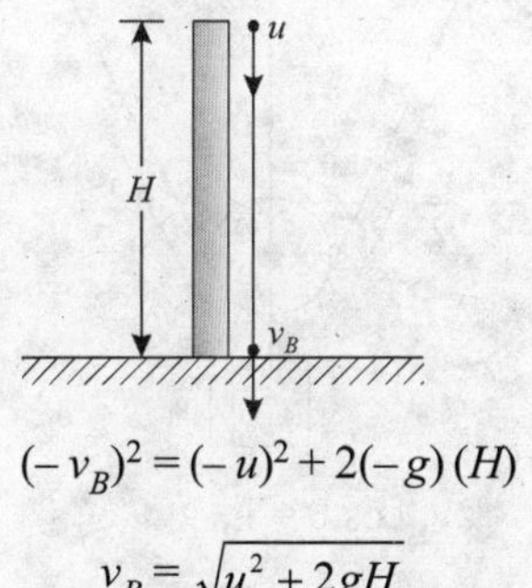

$$(-v_B)^2 = (-u)^2 + 2(-g)(H)$$
$$v_B = \sqrt{u^2 + 2gH}$$

For particle C,

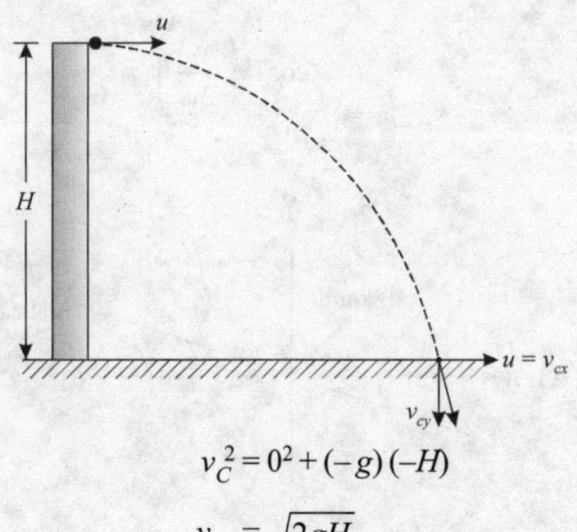

$$v_C^2 = 0^2 + (-g)(-H)$$
$$v_{Cy} = \sqrt{2gH}$$

The horizontal component of velocity remains unchanged

$\Rightarrow$ Resultant velocity

$$v_C = \sqrt{u^2 + 2gH}$$

$$\Rightarrow \quad v_A = v_B = v_C$$

Sol. 79 (C) Horizontal component of velocity remains same

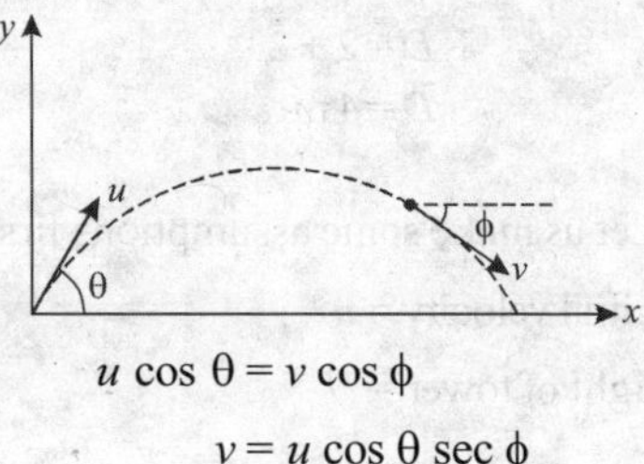

$$u \cos \theta = v \cos \phi$$

$$v = u \cos \theta \sec \phi$$

Sol. 80 (D) Horizontal range,

$$R = \frac{u^2 \sin 2\theta}{g}$$

Since horizontal range for a projectile depend on initial velocity and angle of projection, it is not possible to predict in these situation as the question says nothing about their initial velocity

Sol. 81 (A)

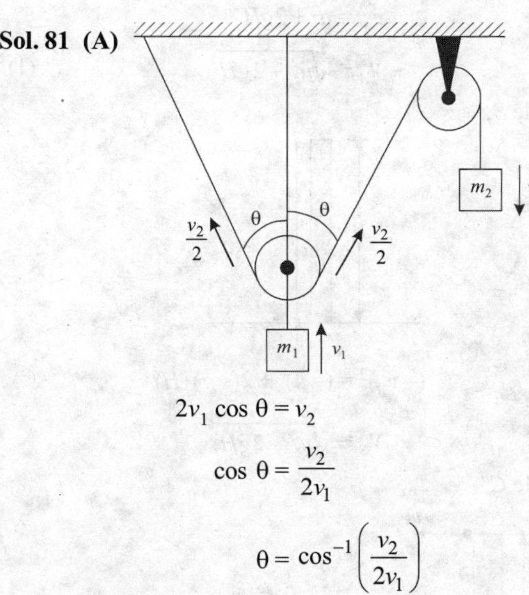

$$2v_1 \cos \theta = v_2$$

$$\cos \theta = \frac{v_2}{2v_1}$$

$$\theta = \cos^{-1}\left(\frac{v_2}{2v_1}\right)$$

Sol. 82 (A)

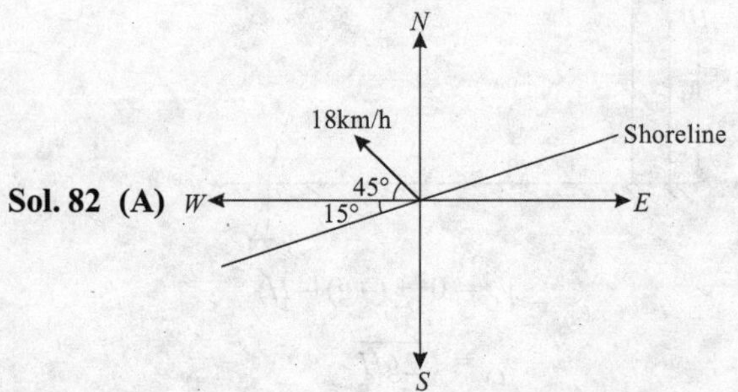

Component of velocity of boat along the shoreline,

$$v = 18 \cos (45° + 15°)$$

$$v = 18 \cos 60°$$

$$v = 9 \text{ km/h}$$

Sol. 83 (A) $\quad R_{max} = \frac{u^2}{g}$

Range of gun, $\quad R = \frac{u^2 \sin 2\theta}{g}$

$$R = \frac{R_{max}}{2}$$

$$\frac{u^2 \sin 2\theta}{g} = \frac{u^2}{2g}$$

$$\Rightarrow \quad \sin 2\theta = \frac{1}{2}$$

$$\Rightarrow \quad 2\theta = 30°$$

$$\Rightarrow \quad \theta = 15°$$

Sol. 84 (A) Let boy catches bus after time 't' seconds then we use

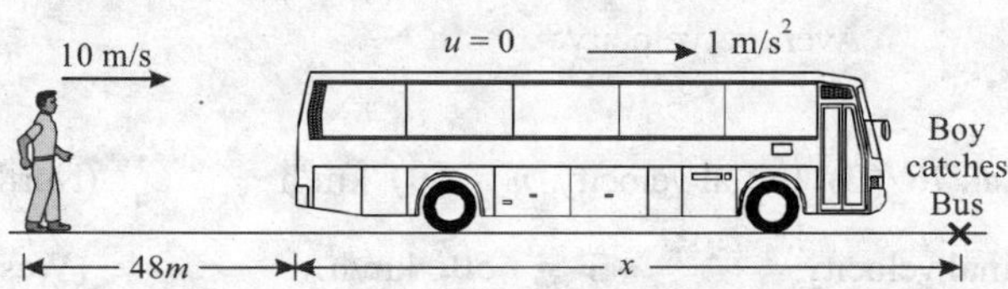

For Bus, $\quad x = \frac{1}{2}(1)t^2 \quad \ldots(1)$

For Boy $\quad 48 + x = 10t \quad \ldots(2)$

From (1) and (2), we get

$$48 + \frac{t^2}{2} = 10t$$

$$96 + t^2 = 20t$$

$$\Rightarrow \quad t^2 - 20t + 96 = 0$$

$$\Rightarrow \quad t = 12s, 8s$$

So, the boy catches the bus at 8 seconds

Sol. 85 (A) Writing equation for straight line from 0 to 6s

$$a(t) = \frac{5}{6}t$$

$$\Rightarrow \quad \frac{dv}{dt} = \frac{5}{6}t$$

Integrating both sides, we get

$$v = \frac{dx}{dt} = \frac{5}{12}t^2$$

Thus, velocity at end of 6 seconds

$$v_6 = \frac{5}{12}(6)^2 = 15\text{ m/s}$$

Distance covered till 6 seconds,

$$s_6 = \frac{5}{36}t^3 = \frac{5}{36}(6)^3 = 30\text{m}$$

From 6*s* to 12*s*, the aeroplane has constant acceleration,

$$\Rightarrow \quad s_{6-12} = 15(6) + \frac{1}{2}(5)(6)^2$$

$$= 90 + 90$$

$$= 180\text{m}$$

Total distance covered

$$= 30\text{m} + 180\text{m}$$

$$= 210\text{m}$$

Sol. 86 (B) The cyclist should drive along the direction of rain with wind speed, so that horizontal relative speed of wind becomes zero w.r. to man

$$\Rightarrow \quad v_m = 2\text{m/s North}$$

Sol. 87 (D) The information given in the question is not sufficient as without numerical values x_A and x_B cannot be compared

Sol. 88 (C) Acceleration of particle during motion

$$a = \frac{W \pm F}{m}$$

for upward motion if acceleration is a_1 for downward motion it is a_2, we use $a_1 > a_2$ hence $t_1 < t_2$

Sol. 89 (B) From figure

$$\tan\theta = \frac{6t}{2t} = 3$$

$$x = \frac{vt}{3\sqrt{2}}$$

and $$y = 2t$$

$$x + y = \frac{vt}{\sqrt{2}}$$

$$\frac{vt}{3\sqrt{2}} + 2t = \frac{vt}{\sqrt{2}}$$

$$v\left(\frac{1}{\sqrt{2}} - \frac{1}{3\sqrt{2}}\right) = 2$$

$$v\left(\frac{2}{3\sqrt{2}}\right) = 2$$

$$v = 3\sqrt{2}\text{ m/s}$$

Sol. 90 (C) Let speed of bullet is v

Velocity of bullet relative to car along x-axis

$$= (v\cos\theta - 13)$$

and along y-axis $$= v\sin\theta$$

$$(v\cos\theta - 13) = \frac{2}{t} \quad \ldots(1)$$

$$\Rightarrow \quad v\sin\theta = \frac{3}{t} \quad \ldots(2)$$

From (1) and (2), $$t = \frac{1}{13}\left[\frac{3}{\tan\theta} - 2\right]$$

$$\Rightarrow \quad t = \frac{1}{13}(2) = 0.15s$$

Sol. 91 (C) In order to hold umbrella exactly vertical, the cylist has to travel in the direction of horizontal component of rain

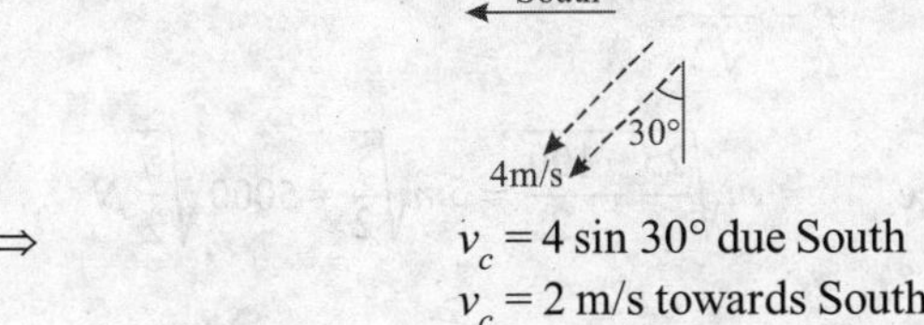

$$\Rightarrow \quad v_c = 4\sin 30° \text{ due South}$$

$$v_c = 2\text{ m/s towards South}$$

Sol. 92 (D) $$\frac{v}{t} = a$$

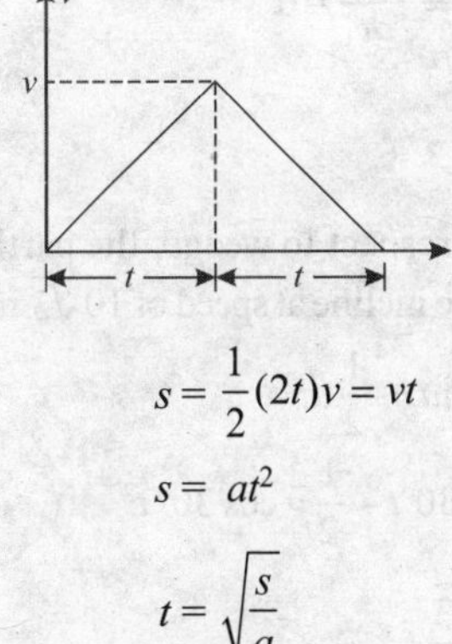

$$s = \frac{1}{2}(2t)v = vt$$

$$s = at^2$$

$$t = \sqrt{\frac{s}{a}}$$

Thus, time to go to another station,

$$2t = 2\sqrt{\frac{s}{a}}$$

Sol. 93 (A) Taking origin at O and OC as y-axis equation of bridge is

$$y = \frac{x^2}{20}$$

So, slope at $$F = \frac{dy}{dx} = \frac{2x}{20} = \frac{2\times 10}{20} = 1$$

At point F, $mg\frac{1}{\sqrt{2}} - N = \frac{mv^2}{R}$

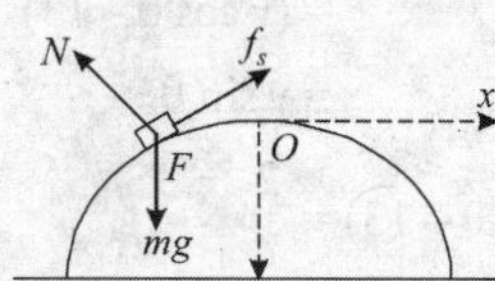

$$N = \frac{mg}{\sqrt{2}} - \frac{mv^2}{R} \quad \text{and} \quad f_s = \frac{mg}{\sqrt{2}}$$

At F, $R = \frac{(1+1)^{3/2}}{\frac{1}{10}} = 20\sqrt{2}$ (metre)

$$N = \frac{10m}{\sqrt{2}} - \frac{100m}{20\sqrt{2}} = \frac{5m}{\sqrt{2}}$$

$$f_s = \frac{10m}{\sqrt{2}}$$

$\Rightarrow$ Net force $= m\sqrt{\frac{25}{2} + \frac{100}{2}} = 5m\sqrt{\frac{5}{2}} = 5000\sqrt{\frac{5}{2}}\,N$

Sol. 94 (C) At the instant shown,

$$3x_B + \sqrt{x_D^2 + 16} = L$$

So $3v_B + \frac{x_D}{\sqrt{16 + x_D^2}}\frac{dx_D}{dt} = 0$

So, $v_B = 0.6$ m/s

Sol. 95 (B) With respect to wedge, the particle moves at 30º from the plane of the incline at speed of $10\sqrt{3}$ m/s. Along normal to the inclines $S = ut + \frac{1}{2}at^2$

$$0 = 10\sqrt{3}\sin 30^\circ t - \frac{1}{2}g\cos 30^\circ t^2$$

$$\Rightarrow 0 = 5\sqrt{3} - \frac{5\sqrt{3}}{2}t$$

$$\Rightarrow t = 2\text{s}$$

Sol. 96 (B) $T_w = \frac{d}{v+v_w} + \frac{d}{v-v_w}$ $\quad T_0 = \frac{2d}{v}$

$$T_w = \frac{d}{v}\left(\frac{1}{1+x} + \frac{1}{1-x}\right) x = \frac{v_w}{v} \quad \& \ x < 1$$

$$\Rightarrow T_w = \frac{2d}{v}\left(\frac{1}{1-x^2}\right)$$

Hence $T_w > T_0$

Sol. 97 (C) $v_{p_x} = 5, v_{p_y} = 5$

$5\sqrt{2} = 7.1$ m/s approx

Sol. 98 (A) $\frac{l}{\sin 30^\circ} = \frac{l'}{\sin 60^\circ}$

$\Rightarrow l' = \sqrt{3}l$

$l'\omega'\cos 30^\circ = v\cos 30^\circ$

$l\omega = \cos 60^\circ(v + l'\omega') = \cos 60^\circ(2v) = v$

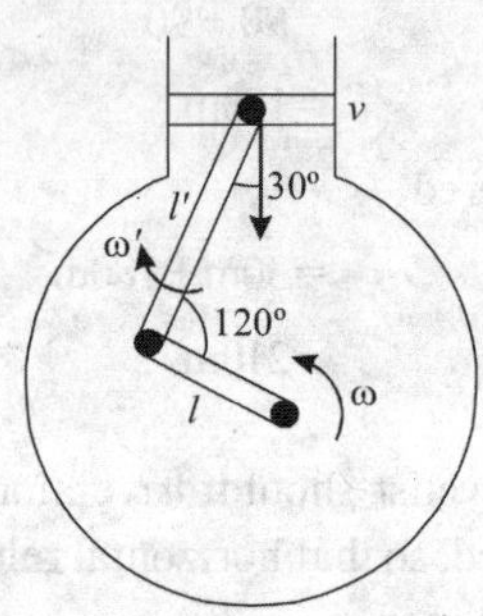

$$\omega = v/l = \frac{40\sqrt{3}}{0.1\sqrt{3}} = 400 \text{ rad/s}$$

Sol. 99 (D) Area under acceleration-time graph gives change in velocity

Hence $A_{\text{total}} = \frac{4\times 4}{2} - 4\times 1$

$= 8 - 4$

$V_f - V_i = 4$

$V_f - 3 = 4$

$V_f = 7$ m/s

Sol. 100 (C) If particle travels from A to B in time t we use $\theta = \omega t$ and

$$AN = R\sin\frac{\theta}{2}$$

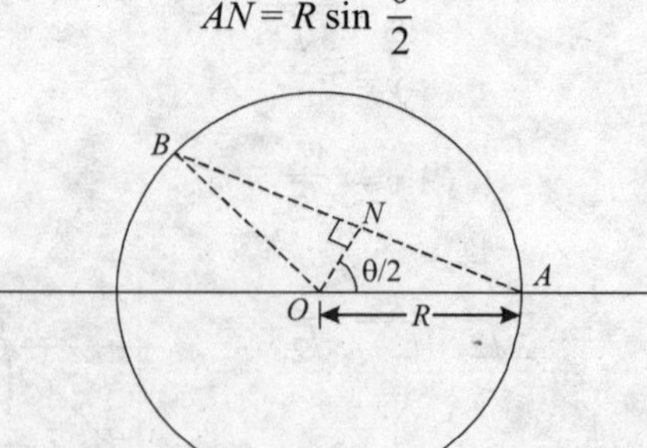

$$\Rightarrow AN = R\sin\frac{\omega t}{2}$$

$$\Rightarrow AB = 2R\sin\frac{\omega t}{2}$$

$\Rightarrow$ average velocity $= \dfrac{AB}{t} = \dfrac{2R}{2\pi} 3\omega \sin\dfrac{\omega}{2} = \left(\dfrac{2\pi}{3\omega}\right) = \dfrac{3\sqrt{3}\omega R}{2\pi}$

Sol. 101 (B) $v_y = v \sin 30° - g \cos 30°\ t$

$$t = \frac{v \sin 30°}{g \cos 30°} = \frac{v}{g}\frac{1}{\sqrt{3}} = \frac{1}{\sqrt{3}} \text{ sec}$$

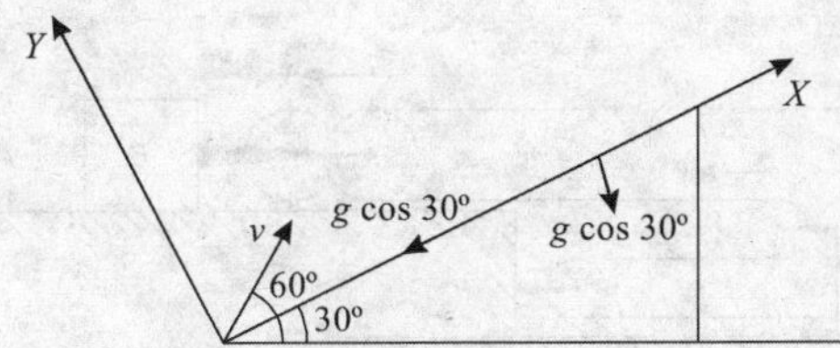

Sol. 102 (D) $y = y = \dfrac{C}{6}t^6$

$\Rightarrow$ $v = \dfrac{dy}{dt} = Ct^5$

$a = \dfrac{dv}{dt} = 5Ct^4$

$\dfrac{a}{v} = \dfrac{5}{t}$

So, at $t = 5$ sec, $\dfrac{a}{v} = 1$

$\Rightarrow$ $a = v$

Sol. 103 (B) $R = \dfrac{u_2^2}{g(1+\sin\alpha)}$ ...(i)

$\Rightarrow$ $u_2^2 = Rg(1 + \sin\alpha)$ ...(ii)

$2R\cos\alpha = \dfrac{u_3^2}{g}$

$\Rightarrow$ $u_3^2 = 2\,Rg\cos\alpha$ ...(iii)

Now, $u_1 u_2 = Rg\sqrt{1-\sin^2\alpha} = Rg\cos\alpha = \dfrac{u_3^2}{2}$

$\Rightarrow$ $u_3^2 = 2u_1u_2$

Sol. 104 (A) $a = -\dfrac{dv}{dt}$

$kv^2 = \dfrac{dv}{dt}, \int_0^t k dt = \int_{v_0}^{v} -\dfrac{dv}{v^2}$

$kt + \dfrac{1}{v_0} = \dfrac{1}{v}$

$v = \dfrac{v_0}{1 + kv_0 t}$

Sol. 105 (A) For first particle, $ut - \dfrac{1}{2}gt^2 = -H$

$$\Rightarrow \quad t_1 = \frac{u \pm \sqrt{u^2 + 2gH}}{g} = \frac{u + \sqrt{u^2+2gH}}{g}$$

For second particle,

$$ut + \frac{1}{2}gt^2 = +H$$

$$\Rightarrow \quad t_2 = \frac{-u \pm \sqrt{u^2+2gH}}{g} = \frac{-u+\sqrt{u^2+2gH}}{g}$$

$$\Rightarrow \quad \Delta t = 2u/g$$

Sol. 106 (B) The velocity triangle is drawn in the adjacent figure: $\overrightarrow{AP}$ = velocity of river water, $\overrightarrow{PQ}$ = velocity of swimmer with respect to water, and $\overrightarrow{AQ}$ the resultant. For maximum θ (i.e., for minimum drift) AQ will be tangent to the circle of all possible choices for $\overrightarrow{PQ}$

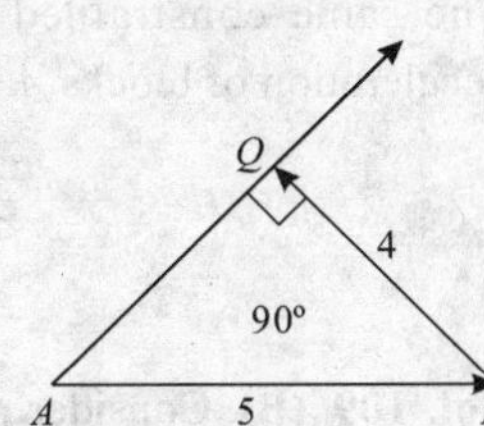

$\sin\theta = \dfrac{4}{5}$

$\tan\theta = \dfrac{4}{3}$

$x = 3$ km

Sol. 107 (B) From 0 to 2 seconds, the block B will move up. At 2 seconds, it will be at rest and there after starts to move down

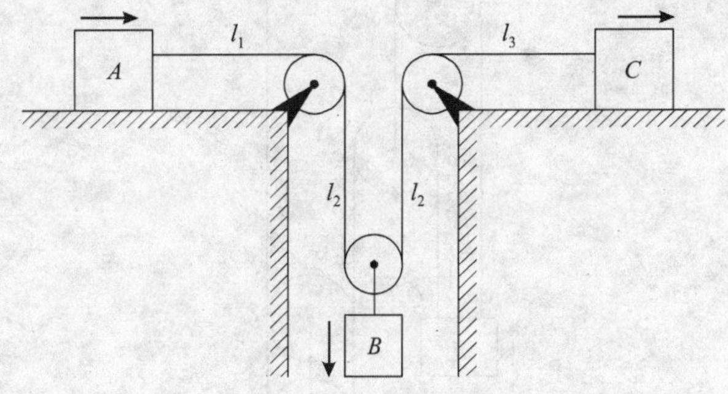

$$l_1 + 2l_2 + l_3 = \text{constant}$$

Differentiating w.r.t. t, we get

$$-v_1 + 2v_2 + v_3 = 0$$

$$-(2\times 5) + 2v_2 + 4 = 0$$

$$2v_2 = 6$$

$$v_2 = 3 \text{ m/s}$$

Sol. 108 (D) If block A goes down by a distance x, string 2 will go up by same distance x and due to this, string 3 will go down by $\frac{3x}{4}$

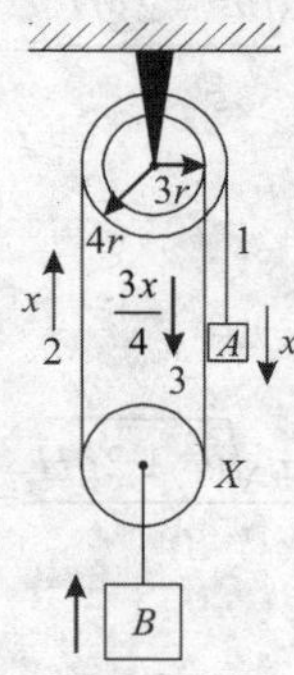

So, pulley X has to go up by distance

$$\frac{\frac{x}{4}}{2} = \frac{x}{8}$$

The same constrained relation exists for velocities and acceleration of blocks A and B so we use

$$a_B = \frac{a_A}{8} = \frac{2}{8} = \frac{1}{4} = 0.25 \text{ m/s}^2$$

Sol. 109 (B) Consider pulleys as X, Y and Z as shown. The block A is tied to two strings which pass over two pulleys X and Y and B is connected to Z

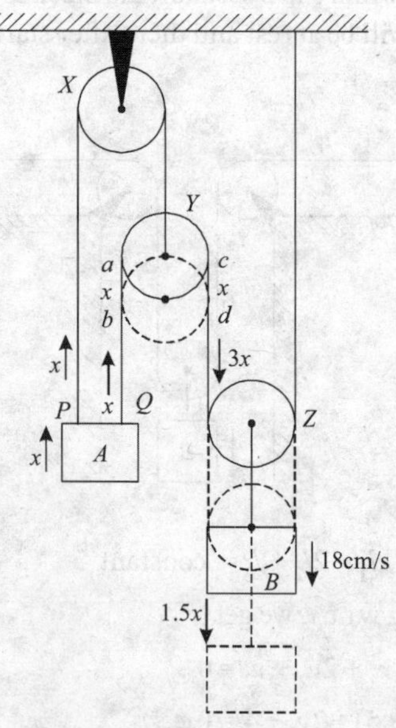

If mass A goes up by a distance x, point P and Q also go up by distance x and pulley Y go down by distance x

Thus, the length ab and cd and the distane x by upward movement of Q is $3x$. So, B goes down by $1.5\,x$

The same constraint relation applies to velocity

$$\Rightarrow \quad 1.5\,v_A = 18$$

$$v_A = \frac{18}{1.5} = 12 \text{ cm/s}$$

Sol. 110 (A)

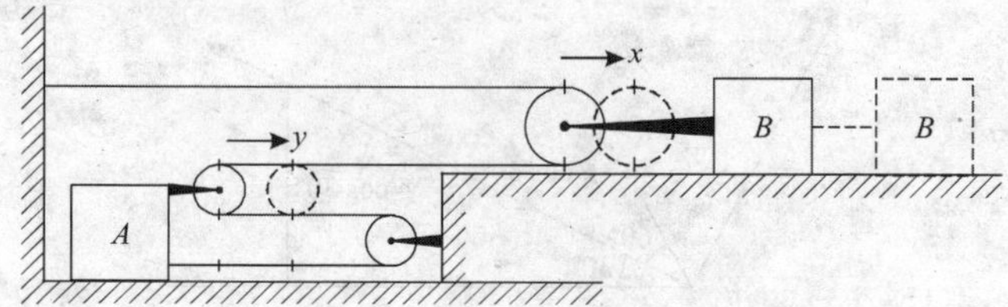

If B goes towards right by x, then A goes towards right by y. This can seen from figure above

Same constraint apply to displacement and velocities of blocks

$$2x = 3y$$

$$\Rightarrow \quad 2v_B = 3v_A$$

$$v_A = \frac{2v_B}{3} = \frac{2 \times 300 \text{ mm/s}}{3}$$

$$v_A = 200 \text{ mm/s}$$

Sol. 111 (A) $u_x = 0$, $a_x = g \sin\alpha$
$u_y = 20$ m/s, $a_y = g\cos\alpha$

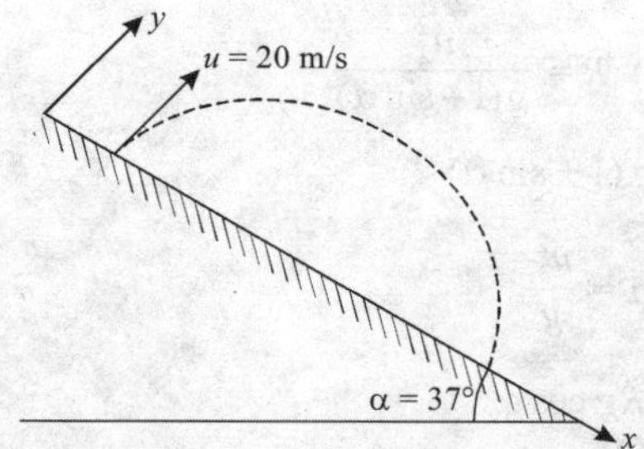

Let time of flight is T

$$s_y = u_yT - \frac{1}{2}a_yT^2$$

$$0 = 20T - \frac{1}{2}(10\sin 37°)T^2$$

$$4T^2 = 20T$$

$$T = 5s$$

Range, $$R = s_x = u_xT + \frac{1}{2}a_xT^2$$

$$s_x = 0 + \frac{1}{2}\left(10 \times \frac{3}{5}\right)(5)^2$$

$$s_x = 75 \text{ m}$$

Sol. 112 (C) The position coordinates of particle, velocity and acceleration at any time are given as

$$x = 5t - 2t^2 \qquad y = 10t$$

$$\Rightarrow \quad v_x = \frac{dx}{dt} = 5 - 4t \qquad \frac{dy}{dt} = 10$$

$$\Rightarrow \quad v_x = 5 - 4t \qquad v_y = 10$$

$$a_x = \frac{dv}{dt} = -4 \qquad a = \frac{dv}{dt} = 10$$

$$\Rightarrow \quad a_x = -4 \qquad a_y = 0$$

Thus acceleration of particle at $t = 2$ s is $= -4$ m/s^2.

Sol. 113 (A) Velocity of swimmer with respect to river is given as

$$V_{SR} = 20 \text{ m/s}$$

Flow velocity of river with respect to ground is given as

$$V_{RG} = 10 \text{ m/s}$$

Velocity of swimmer with respect to ground can be calculated as

$$\vec{V}_{SG} = \vec{V}_{SR} + \vec{V}_{RG}$$

The angle of resulting motion of swimmer with the bank as shown in figure is given as

$$\sin\theta = \left|\frac{\vec{V}_{RG}}{\vec{V}_{SR}}\right|$$

$$\Rightarrow \quad \sin\theta = \frac{10}{20}$$

$$\Rightarrow \quad \sin\theta = \frac{1}{2}$$

$$\Rightarrow \quad \theta = 30° \text{ west}$$

Sol. 114 (A) Equation of trajectory is of a projectile motion is given as

$$y = x\tan\theta - \frac{gx^2}{2u^2\cos^2\theta}$$

For identical trajectories for same angle of projection, we should have

$$\frac{g}{u^2} = \text{constant for both planets}$$

$$\Rightarrow \quad \frac{9.8}{5^2} = \frac{g'}{3^2}$$

$$\Rightarrow \quad g' = \frac{9.8 \times 9}{25} = 3.528 \text{ m/s}^2$$

$$\Rightarrow \quad g' = 3.5 \text{ m/s}^2$$

Sol. 115 (D) Average velocity of any particle's motion can be given as

$$\vec{V}_{avg} = \frac{\text{Total displacement}}{\text{Time taken}}$$

$$\Rightarrow \quad \vec{V}_{avg} = \frac{(x_2 - x_1)\hat{i} + (y_2 - y_1)\hat{j}}{t_2 - t_1}$$

$$\Rightarrow \quad \vec{V}_{avg} = \frac{(13-2)\hat{i} + (14-3)\hat{j}}{5-0}$$

$$\Rightarrow \quad \vec{V}_{avg} = \frac{11\hat{i} + 11\hat{j}}{5} = \frac{11}{5}(\hat{i} + \hat{j})$$

ADVANCE MCQs One or More Option Correct

Sol. 1 (A) As after a time the slope of graph is becoming zero which indicates that particle is coming to rest.

Sol. 2 (A, B, C) As starting point and final point is same, displacement and average velocity is zerio and as it is moving with uniform acceleration in upward and downward journey with start or final speed *0* or *u*, its average speed is *u/2*.

Sol. 3 (B, D) An object moving moving at uniform speed if changes direction possible option is (B) and (D) as velocity is changing due to change in direction and this is an accelerated motion.

Sol. 4 (A, C, D) In case of motion of a particle on closed path displacement is zero in complete motion but average speed will be non sero hence option (A) is correct. Option (B) is valid only for uniform acceleration which is not specified so it is not always correct. (C) is correct by definition of average velocity. Option (D) is correct as if particle is moving in negative direction its velocity is negative and if it is decreasing than it indicates that acceleration is opposite to velocity so it is positive.

Sol. 5 (B, C) Acceleration of a particle changes either the magnitude of velocity or its direction or both hence option (B) is correct. If a particle is moving in positive direction then its velocity is positive and if speed is decreasing that means it is retarding hence acceleration direction is negative hence option (C) is correct.

Sol. 6 (B, D) Option (A) is not possible as at one time instant two speeds are shown and Option (C) is also not possible as it containes vertical straight lines.

Sol. 7 (A, C) $\vec{V}_B = \vec{V}_{BA} + \vec{V}_A$

$$\left|\vec{V}_B\right| = \left|\vec{V}_{BA} + \vec{V}_A\right|$$

$$= \sqrt{V_{BA}^2 + V_A^2} = \sqrt{5^2 + 15^2} = 5\sqrt{10} \text{ m/s}$$

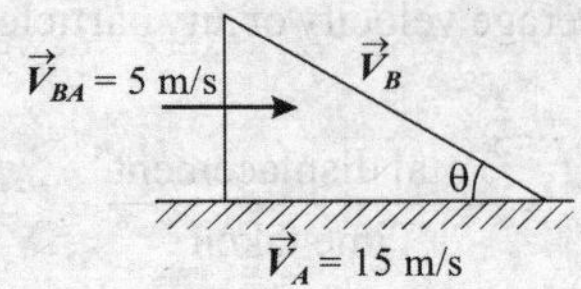

$$\tan\theta = \tan^{-1}\left(\frac{1}{3}\right)$$

$$\theta = \tan^{-1}\left(\frac{1}{3}\right)$$

Sol. 8 (A, B, C)

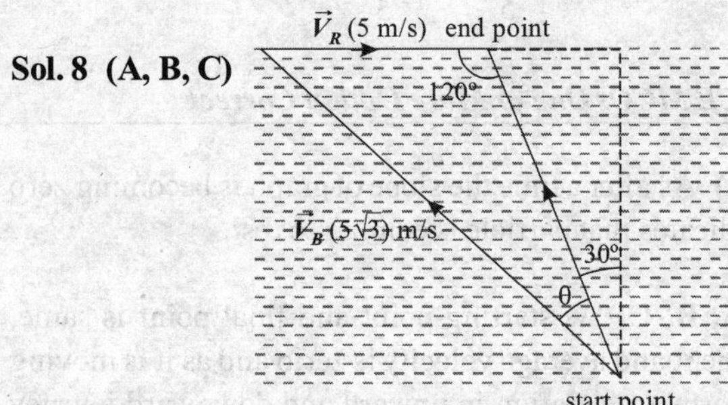

The velocity of motor boat is given as $\vec{v}_m = \vec{v}_{mw} + \vec{v}_w$

$$\Rightarrow \frac{5}{\sin\theta} = \frac{5\sqrt{3}}{\sin 120°}$$

$$\Rightarrow \sin\theta = \frac{1}{2}$$

$$\Rightarrow \theta = 30°$$

Sol. 9 (B, C, D) Displacement is given as

$$x = 3t^3 - 18t^2 + 36t \quad \ldots\text{(i)}$$

$$\Rightarrow v = 9(t-2)^2 \quad \ldots\text{(ii)}$$

$$a = 18(t-2) \quad \ldots\text{(iii)}$$

Sol. 10 (B, C) Time of flight is

$$T = \frac{2u\sin\theta}{g} = \frac{2\times 10\times\frac{1}{2}}{10} = 1\text{ s}$$

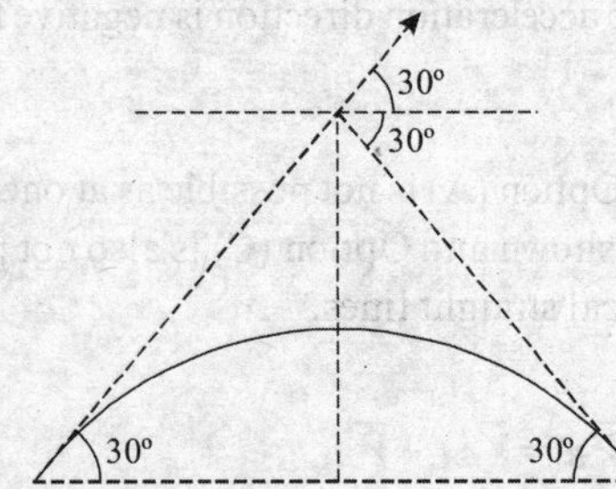

Sol. 11 (A, B, C) By constrained relation we use

$$-2T\times 6 + 3Ta_A = 0$$

$$\Rightarrow a_A = 4\text{m/s}^2$$

$$-2T\times 3 + 3Tv_A = 0$$

$$\Rightarrow v_A = 2\text{m/s}^2$$

$$T\times 2 - 2T\times 3 + Tv_C = 0$$

$$\Rightarrow v_C = 4\text{m/s}$$

Sol. 12 (A, C, D) From A to B, $v_{AB} = \frac{x}{t}$ ...(1)

From A to C,

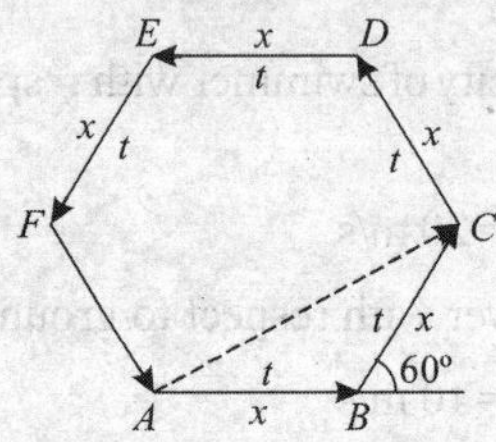

Displacement, $AC = \sqrt{(AB)^2 + (BC)^2 + 2(AB)(BC)\cos 60°}$

$$AC = \sqrt{x^2 + x^2 + 2x^2\times\frac{1}{2}} = x\sqrt{3}$$

$$\Rightarrow v_{AC} = \frac{x\sqrt{3}}{t+t} = \frac{\sqrt{3}}{2}v \quad \ldots(2)$$

Displacement, $AF = x$

$$v_{AF} = \frac{x}{5t} = \frac{v}{5} \quad \ldots(3)$$

Sol. 13 (A, C) Initial velocity, $u = 10$ m/s

Acceleration, $a = -5\text{m/s}^2$

Let displacement of particle before coming to rest is s, then

$$0 = (10)^2 - 2(5)s \quad (\text{As } v^2 = u^2 + 2as)$$

$$s = \frac{100}{10} = 10\text{m}$$

If particle reverses its direction of motion after t seconds,

$$0 = 10 - 5t \quad (\text{As } v = u + at)$$

$$t = 2s$$

Distance travelled in first 3 seconds = Distance travelled in first 2 seconds + Distance travelled from $2s$ to $3s$

$$= 10\text{ m} + \left[0 + \frac{1}{2}(5)(1)^2\right]\text{m}$$

$$= 10 + 2.5$$

$$= 12.5\text{ m}$$

Sol. 14 (A, D) Area under $a-t$ graph gives change in velocity, from this, it can be inferred that the velocity changes by more than 7 m/s, so it has to be zero once before the particle changes direction of motion.

However, the displacement of body can never be zero as the particle continues to move further.

Sol. 15 (B, C, D) Velocity of particle at B

$$v_B = \sqrt{\frac{v_A^2 + v_C^2}{2}} = \sqrt{\frac{7^2 + 17^2}{2}} = \sqrt{169}$$

$$v_B = 13 \text{ m/s}$$

Average velocity from A to B

$$= \frac{v_A + v_B}{2}$$

$$= \frac{7+13}{2} = 10 \text{ m/s}$$

Average velocity from B to C

$$= \frac{v_B + v_C}{2}$$

$$= \frac{13+17}{2} = 15 \text{ m/s}$$

Time to go from A to B, $t_1 = \dfrac{13-7}{a} = \dfrac{6}{a}$

Time to go from B to C, $t_2 = \dfrac{17-13}{a} = \dfrac{4}{a}$

$$\frac{t_1}{t_2} = \frac{3}{2}$$

Sol. 16 (C, D)

$h = 4$ m, y, θ, A, $h = 3$ m, B

$$(y-h) + \sqrt{x^2+h^2} = l$$

$$\frac{dy}{dt} + \frac{x}{\sqrt{x^2+h^2}}\frac{dx}{dt} = 0$$

$$\frac{dy}{dt} = -\frac{x}{\sqrt{x^2+h^2}}\frac{dx}{dt}$$

$$\frac{dy}{dt} = -\frac{3}{5}v_A$$

$$|U_B| = \frac{3}{5}v_A$$

$$\frac{d^2y}{dt^2} = v_A^2\frac{h^2}{(x^2+h^2)^{3/2}}$$

$$a_B = v_A^2\frac{16}{(5)^3}$$

$$a_B = \frac{16}{125}v_A^2$$

* * * * *

ANSWERS & SOLUTIONS

CONCEPTUAL MCQS Single Option Correct

1	(B)	**2**	(B)	**3**	(D)
4	(A)	**5**	(D)	**6**	(D)
7	(A)	**8**	(B)	**9**	(C)
10	(A)	**11**	(B)	**12**	(B)
13	(B)	**14**	(B)	**15**	(D)
16	(C)	**17**	(B)	**18**	(B)
19	(A)	**20**	(D)	**21**	(B)
22	(D)	**23**	(B)		

NUMERICAL MCQS Single Option Correct

1	(A)	**2**	(B)	**3**	(A)
4	(B)	**5**	(C)	**6**	(B)
7	(C)	**8**	(D)	**9**	(B)
10	(A)	**11**	(B)	**12**	(B)
13	(C)	**14**	(D)	**15**	(D)
16	(A)	**17**	(B)	**18**	(B)
19	(C)	**20**	(B)	**21**	(D)
22	(B)	**23**	(B)	**24**	(A)
25	(D)	**26**	(B)	**27**	(C)
28	(C)	**29**	(A)	**30**	(C)
31	(C)	**32**	(C)	**33**	(B)
34	(A)	**35**	(A)	**36**	(C)
37	(C)	**38**	(C)	**39**	(C)
40	(B)	**41**	(A)	**42**	(B)
43	(C)	**44**	(C)	**45**	(A)
46	(B)	**47**	(D)	**48**	(C)
49	(B)	**50**	(A)	**51**	(C)
52	(A)	**53**	(D)	**54**	(C)
55	(C)	**56**	(D)	**57**	(B)
58	(B)	**59**	(C)	**60**	(C)
61	(B)	**62**	(D)	**63**	(A)
64	(B)	**65**	(D)	**66**	(D)
67	(B)	**68**	(A)	**69**	(C)
70	(A)	**71**	(B)	**72**	(C)
73	(C)	**74**	(B)	**75**	(B)
76	(A)	**77**	(C)	**78**	(A)
79	(D)	**80**	(B)	**81**	(A)
82	(A)	**83**	(C)	**84**	(D)
85	(A)	**86**	(B)	**87**	(A)
88	(A)	**89**	(B)	**90**	(C)

ADVANCE MCQs One or More Option Correct

1	(C, D)	**2**	(B, D)	**3**	(A, C)
4	(A, B, C, D)	**5**	(A, B, C, D)	**6**	(B, C)
7	(B, D)	**8**	(B, C)	**9**	(A, D)
10	(A, B, C)	**11**	(B, C)	**12**	(A, C)
13	(A, D)	**14**	(A, B, D)	**15**	(A, B, C)
16	(A, C)	**17**	(A, C)		

Solutions of PRACTICE EXERCISE 2.1

(i) By constrained relation we use

$$a_2 = a_3 = \frac{a_1}{2} = a$$

and equation of motion we can write

$$m_3 g - T_1 = m_3 a \quad \ldots(1)$$

$$T_1 - 2T_2 = m_2 a \quad \ldots(2)$$

$$T_2 = m_1(2a) \quad \ldots(3)$$

$$(1) + (2) + 2 \times (3) \Rightarrow m_3 g = (m_3 + m_2 + 4m_1)a$$

$$a = \frac{m_3}{m_3 + m_2 + 4m_1} g$$

$$= \frac{400}{1700} g = \frac{4g}{17} = 2.35 \text{ m/s}^2$$

$$a_2 = a_3 = 2.35 \text{ m/s}^2$$

$$a_1 = 2 \times 2.35 = 4.7 \text{ m/s}^2$$

Here $T_1 = m_3 g - m_3 a = 0.4\,(10 - 2.35) = 3.06 \text{ N}$

$$T_2 = m_1\,(2a)$$

$$= 0.2 \times 2 \times 2.35 = 0.94 \text{ N}$$

(ii) (a) As the two blocks move together their acceleration is

$$a = \frac{F}{m_1 + m_2} = \frac{5}{7}$$

$$= 0.714 \text{ m/s}^2$$

(b) If N is the normal content four between the two blocks, equation of motion for m_2 is

$$N = m_2 a = 4 \times \frac{5}{7} = \frac{20}{7}$$

$$= 2.85 \text{ N}$$

(iii) (a) String tension

$$T = \frac{F}{2} = \frac{124}{2} = 62\text{N},$$

As weight of blocks is higher than T, no block will start so

$$a_A = a_B = 0$$

(b) String tension $\quad T = \dfrac{F}{2} = \dfrac{294}{2} = 147\text{N}$

as $T < m_A g \quad a_A = 0$

and for block $B \quad T - m_B g = m_B a_B$

$$a_B = \frac{T - m_B g}{m_B} = \frac{147 - 100}{10}$$

$$= 4.7 \text{ m/s}^2$$

(c) String tension $T = \frac{F}{2} = \frac{424}{2} = 212\text{ N}$

as $T > m_A g$ and $T > m_B g$ we use

$$a_A = \frac{T - m_A g}{m_A} = \frac{212-200}{20} = 0.6\text{ m/s}^2$$

$$a_B = \frac{T - m_B g}{m_B} = \frac{212-100}{10} = 11.2\text{ m/s}^2$$

(iv) If T, and T_2 be the tensions in left and right strings equation of motion we use

$$T_1 - mg = ma \quad \ldots(1)$$

$$T_2 - T_1 - f = 2ma \quad \ldots(2)$$

$$12mg - T_2 = 12ma \quad \ldots(3)$$

Adding above equations

$$11mg - f = 15ma$$

$$f = 11\,mg - 15\,ma$$

$$f = 11 \times 4 \times 10 - 15 \times 4 \times 5$$

$$f = 440 - 380$$

$$f = 140\text{ N}$$

(v) **(a)** If 5 kg block move down with acceleration a, 2kg will move toward right with $2a$ and equation of motion will be

$$T = 2(2a) \quad \ldots(1)$$

$$5g - 2T = 5a \quad \ldots(2)$$

$(1) \times 2 + (2)$ gives $\quad 5g = 13a$

$$a = \frac{5g}{13}$$

Thus $\quad a_{5\text{kg}} = \frac{5g}{13}$ downward and

$a_{2\text{kg}} = \frac{10g}{13}$ toward right

(b) We can write equation of motion as

$$0.5g - T_1 = 0.5a \quad \ldots(1)$$

$$T_1 - T_2 - 0.1g(\sin 30°) = 0.1a \quad \ldots(2)$$

$$T_2 - 0.05g = 0.05a \quad \ldots(3)$$

Adding (1), (2) and (3) we get

$$0.4g = 0.65a$$

$a = \frac{8g}{13}$ downward for B and upward for A

(vi) Acceleration of block and rope is

$$a = \frac{F}{M+m}$$

(a) Force which the rope exerts on block is

$$T_1 = Ma = \frac{MF}{M+m}$$

(b) Tension at the mid point of rope is

$$T_2 = \left(M + \frac{m}{2}\right)a = \frac{\left(M + \frac{m}{2}\right)F}{M+m}$$

(vii) Acceleration of masses

$$a = \frac{2m - m}{2m + m} - g$$

$$g = \frac{g}{3} = 3.27\text{ m/s}^2$$

Speed of masses after travelling a distance of 6.54 m is

$$v = \sqrt{2 \times 3.27 \times 6.54} = 6.54\text{ m/s}$$

Now string is cut and both masses will be in free fall so if t_1 and t_2 are time taken by masses to reach ground, we use

For mass m $\quad -19.62 = 6.54\,t_1 - 4.9\,t_1^2$

$$-4 = \frac{4t_1}{3} - t_1^2$$

$$-4t_1 - 12 = 0$$

$$t_1 = \frac{4 \pm \sqrt{16+144}}{6} = 2.78\text{ s}$$

For mass $2m$ $\quad 6.54 = 6.54\,t_2 + 4.9\,t_2^2$

$$4 = 4t_2 + 3t_2^2$$

$$3t_2^2 + 4t_2 - 4 = 0$$

$$t_2 = \frac{-4 \pm \sqrt{16+48}}{6}$$

$$= \frac{4}{6} = \frac{2}{3}\text{ s}$$

(viii) If A sides down at acceleration a B will move up relative to A with same acceleration. We draw FBD of A and B as

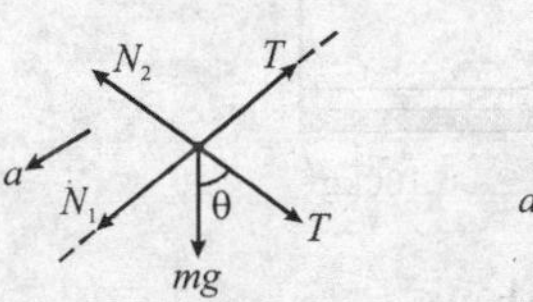

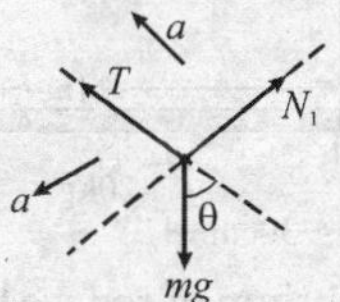

Equations of motion, we use

$$N_1 + Mg\sin\theta - T = Ma \quad \ldots(1)$$

$$mg\sin\theta - N_1 = ma \quad \ldots(2)$$

$$T - mg\cos\theta = ma \quad \ldots(3)$$

From (1), (2) and (3)

$$(mg\sin\theta - ma) + Mg\sin\theta - (Ma + mg + \cos\theta) = Ma$$

$$a(M+2m) = g((M+m)\sin\theta - m\cos\theta)$$

$$a = \left[\frac{(M+m)\sin\theta - m\cos\theta}{M+2m}\right]g$$

Thus $a_M = a$

and $a_m = \sqrt{2}a$

Solutions of PRACTICE EXERCISE 2.2

(i) For equilibrium of weight w_2 we use

$$w_1 \cos 53° + w_3 \cos 37° = w_2 \quad \ldots(1)$$

and $w_1 \sin 53° = w_3 \sin 37° \quad \ldots(2)$

$$4w_1 = 3w_3$$

from (1) and (2) we have

$$\frac{3w_1}{5} + \frac{4w_3}{5} = 400$$

$$3w_1 + 4w_3 = 2000$$

$$3\left(\frac{3w_3}{4}\right) + 4w_3 = 2000$$

$$25w_3 = 8000$$

$$w_3 = \frac{8000}{25} = 320\text{ N}$$

and $w_1 = \dfrac{3w_3}{4} = 240\text{ N}$

(ii) For equilibrium of the two string joints we write

$$F_1 = F_2 = \frac{60}{\sqrt{2}} = 42.42\text{ N}$$

also $w = \dfrac{60}{\sqrt{2}} = 42.42\text{ N}$

(iii)

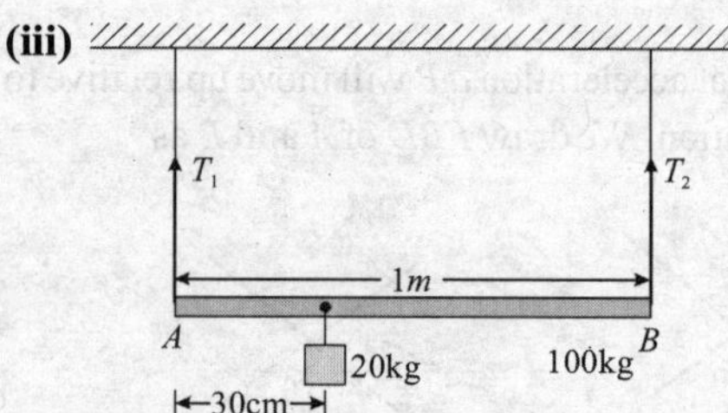

For equilibrium of rod we have

$$T_1 + T_2 = 120g \quad \ldots(1)$$

Torque about point A is

$$\tau_A = 20g \times 30 + 100g \times 50 - T_2 \times 100 = 0$$

$$60 + 500 - T_2 = 0$$

$$T_2 = 560\text{ N}$$

From (1) $T_1 = 1200 - 560 = 640\text{ N}$

(iv) (a) For equilibrium of weight, we use

$$T_1 \sin 30° + T_2 \sin 45° = w$$

$$\frac{T_1}{2} + \frac{T_2}{\sqrt{2}} = w$$

$$T_1 + \sqrt{2}T_2 = 2w \quad \ldots(1)$$

and $T_1 \cos 30° = T_2 \cos 45°$

$$\sqrt{3}T_1 = \sqrt{2}T_2 \quad \ldots(2)$$

From (1) and (2) $T_1 + \sqrt{3}T_1 = 2w$

$$T_1 = \frac{2w}{1+\sqrt{3}}$$

and from (2) $T_2 = \dfrac{\sqrt{6}w}{(1+\sqrt{3})}$

(b) For equilibrium of weight, we use

$$T_1 \cos 60° + w = T_2 \sin 45°$$

$$T_1 + 2w = \sqrt{2}T_2 \quad \ldots(1)$$

and $T_1 \sin 60° = T_2 \cos 45°$

$$\sqrt{3}T_1 = \sqrt{2}T_2 \quad \ldots(2)$$

from (1) and (2) $\sqrt{3}T_1 - T_1 = 2w$

$$T_1 = \frac{2w}{\sqrt{3}-1}$$

and from (2) $T_2 = \dfrac{\sqrt{6}w}{\sqrt{3}-1}$

(v)

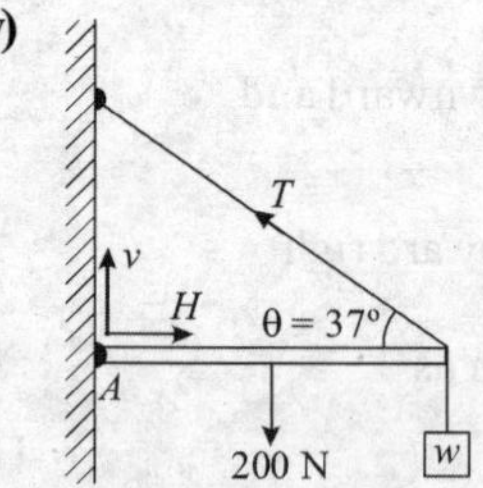

For equilibrium of boom, we use

$$V + T\sin\theta = 1200 \quad \ldots(1)$$

and $H = T\cos\theta \quad \ldots(2)$

Taking torque about hinge A, we have

$$200 \times 2.5 + 1000 \times 5 - T\sin\theta \times 5 = 0$$

$$T\sin\theta = \frac{5500}{5} = 1100$$

$$T = \frac{1100}{3/5} = 1833.33\text{N}$$

From (1) $V = 1200 - 1100 = 100\,\text{N}$

From (2) $H = \dfrac{5500}{3} \times \dfrac{4}{5} = 1466.67\,\text{N}$

(vi) For equilibrium of masses if tension in strings are T_1, T_2 and T_3, we use

$$T_1 \cdot r_4 = T_2 \cdot r_3$$

and $T_2 \cdot r_2 = T_3 r_1$

$$4Mg = 3T_2 \quad \ldots(1)$$

$$2T_2 = mg \sin\theta \quad \ldots(2)$$

From (1) and (2) $4Mg = \dfrac{3}{2} mg \sin\theta$

$$\frac{M}{m} = \frac{3}{8}\sin\theta$$

(vii) If F_R is the force required to crack the nut using nut cracker we can use

$$F_R \times 25 = F \times 2$$

$$F_R = \frac{30 \times 2}{25} = 2.4\,\text{N}$$

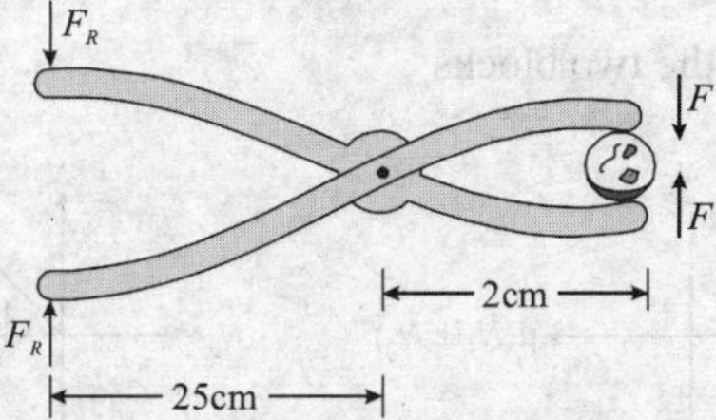

Solutions of PRACTICE EXERCISE 2.3

(i) If m and M move together acceleration of system will be

$$a = \frac{M_1 g}{M_1 + m + M} \quad \ldots(1)$$

FBD of m relative to wedge is

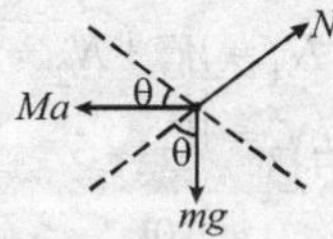

for m not to slip on M, we use

$$mg \sin\theta = ma \cos\theta$$

or $a = g \tan\theta$

From (1) $\dfrac{M_1 g}{M_1 + m + M} = g \tan\theta$

$$M_1 = \frac{m + M}{(\cot\theta - 1)}$$

(ii) FBD of m_1 and m_2 relative to the wedge are

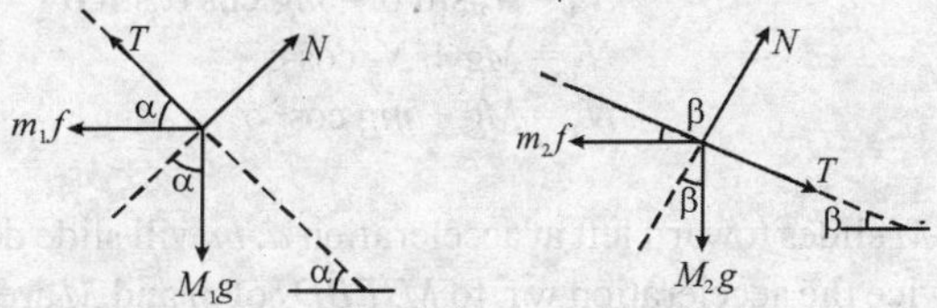

For equilibrium of m_1 and m_2, we use

$$m_1 g \sin\alpha = m_1 f \cos\alpha + T \quad \ldots(1)$$

$$T + m_2 g \sin\beta = m_2 f \cos\beta \quad \ldots(2)$$

$(1) + (2) \Rightarrow$

$$g(m_1 \sin\alpha + m_2 \sin\beta) = f(m_1 \cos\alpha + m_2 \cos\beta)$$

$$f = g\left(\frac{m_1 \sin\alpha + m_2 \sin\beta}{m_1 \cos\alpha + m_2 \cos\beta}\right)$$

from (1) substituting f, we get

$$T = \frac{m_1 m_2 g \sin(\alpha - \beta)}{m_1 \cos\alpha - m_2 \cos\beta}$$

(iii) If M moves toward right with acceleration a, m will move down with same acceleration relative to M

FBD of m and M are

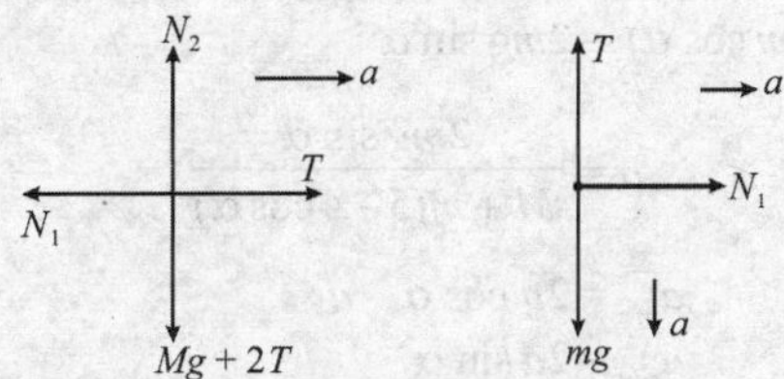

Equations of motion of blocks

$$T - N_1 = Ma \quad \ldots(1)$$

$$mg - T = ma \quad \ldots(2)$$

$$N_1 = ma \quad \ldots(3)$$

Adding (1), (2) and (3) we get

$$mg = (M + 2m)a$$

$$a = \frac{m}{M + 2m} g$$

Acceleration of m w.r. to ground is

$$a_m = \sqrt{2}a = \frac{\sqrt{2}mg}{M + 2m}$$

(iv) Here *FBD* of M is

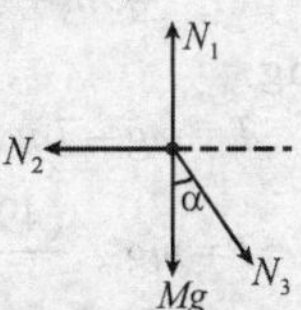

Here $N_3 = mg \cos\alpha$

For equilibrium of prism, we use

$$N_2 = N_3 \sin\alpha = mg\cos\alpha\sin\alpha$$

and $$N_1 = Mg + N_3\cos\alpha$$

$$N_1 = Mg + mg\cos^2\alpha$$

(v) If M slides toward left at acceleration a, m will slide down with twice the acceleration w.r. to M. *FBDs* of m and M are

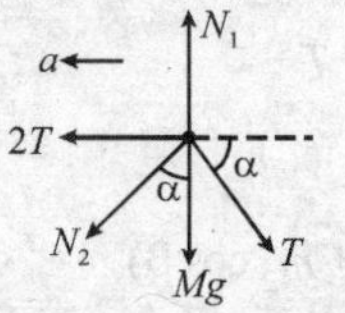

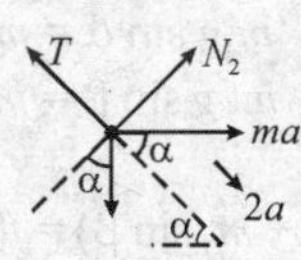

FBD of M *FBD* of m w.r.t M

Equations of motion

$$2T + N_2\sin\alpha - T\cos\alpha = Ma \quad \ldots(1)$$

$$N_2 + ma\sin\alpha = mg\cos\alpha \quad \ldots(2)$$

$$ma\cos\alpha + mg\sin\alpha - T = 2ma \quad \ldots(3)$$

From (1), (2) and (3)

$$(ma\cos\alpha + mg\sin\alpha - 2ma)(2-\cos\alpha)$$
$$+ (mg\cos\alpha - ma\sin\alpha)\sin\alpha = Ma$$
$$2ma\cos\alpha + 2mg\sin\alpha - 4ma$$
$$- ma\cos^2\alpha - mg\sin\alpha\cos\alpha + 2\,ma\cos\alpha$$
$$+ mg\cos\alpha\sin\alpha - ma\sin^2\alpha = Ma$$
$$a(M + 5m - 4m\cos\alpha) = 2mg\sin\alpha$$

$$a = \frac{2mg\sin\alpha}{M + m(5-4\cos\alpha)}$$

$$a_{mx} = 2a\cos\alpha - a$$
$$a_{my} = 2a\sin\alpha$$

$$a_m = \sqrt{a_{mx}^2 + a_{my}^2}$$
$$= \sqrt{5-4\cos\alpha}$$

$$a = \frac{2mg\sin\alpha\sqrt{5-4\cos\alpha}}{M + m(5-4\cos\alpha)}$$

(vi) If man and platform has an acceleration a upward, m will have an acceleration $7a$, we use

$$mg - T = 7ma \quad \ldots(1)$$
$$7T - Mg = Ma \quad \ldots(2)$$

$(1)\times 7 + (2) \Rightarrow$

$$(7m - M)g = (49m + M)a$$

$$a = \left(\frac{7m - M}{49m + M}\right)g$$

From (1) tension in string

$$T = mg - 7ma$$

$$T = mg - \frac{(49m^2 - 7mM)g}{49m + M}$$

$$T = \frac{8mMg}{49m + M}$$

Solutions of PRACTICE EXERCISE 2.4

(i) (a) To start the block sliding in upward direction

$$F\cos\alpha > mg\sin\alpha + \mu_s N \quad \ldots(1)$$

$$N = mg\cos\alpha + F\sin\alpha \quad \ldots(2)$$

From (1) & (2) $$F\cos\alpha > mg\sin\alpha + \mu_s(mg\cos\alpha + F\sin\alpha)$$

or $$F > mg\,\frac{(\sin\alpha + \mu_s\cos\alpha)}{(\cos\alpha - \mu_s\sin\alpha)}$$

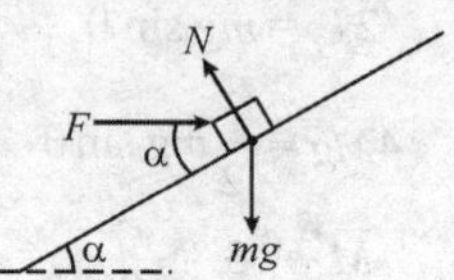

If $F \to \infty \Rightarrow$ $\cos\alpha = \mu_s\sin\alpha$

or $\mu_s = \cot\alpha$

(b) If $\mu_s < \cot\alpha$ and block slides then to maintain its uniform speed, force must be equal to

$$F = \frac{mg(\sin\alpha + \mu_k\cos\alpha)}{(\cos\alpha - \mu_k\sin\alpha)}$$

(ii) *FBD* of the two blocks

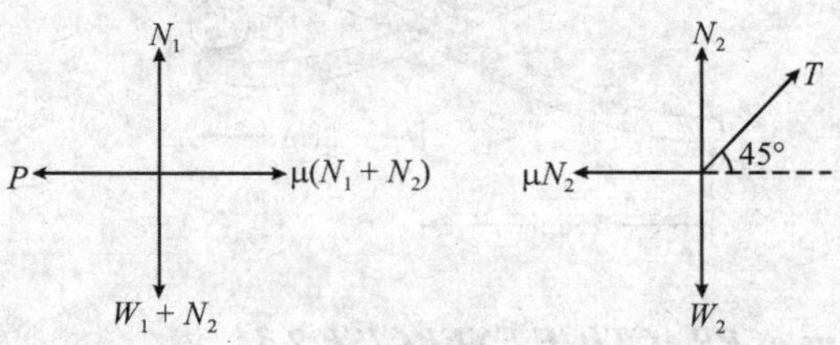

To start sliding $$P = \mu(N_1 + N_2) \quad \ldots(1)$$

$$\frac{T}{\sqrt{2}} = \mu N_2 \quad \ldots(2)$$

$$N_2 + \frac{T}{\sqrt{2}} = W_2 \quad \ldots(3)$$

$$N_1 = W_1 + N_2 \quad \ldots(4)$$

From (2) and (3) $N_2 + \mu N_2 = W_2$

$$N_2 = \frac{100}{1.25} = 80\text{N}$$

From (4) $N_1 = 280\text{ N}$

From (1) $P = 0.25\,(280 + 80)$

$$= \frac{360}{4} = 90\text{N}$$

$$T = 0.25 \times 80\sqrt{2} = 20\sqrt{2}\text{N}$$

(iii) *FBD* man + plank

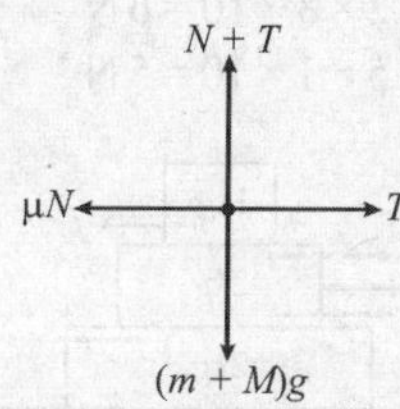

To start sliding $T = \mu N$ ...(1)

$N + T = (m + M)g$ ...(2)

From (1) and (2) $T = \mu[(m + M)g - T]$

or $T = \dfrac{\mu(M+m)g}{1+\mu}$

(iv) For limiting equilibrium of ladder

$N_1 + 0.5\,N_2 = 200$ ...(1)

$N_2 = 0.5\,N_1$ ...(2)

From (1) and (2),

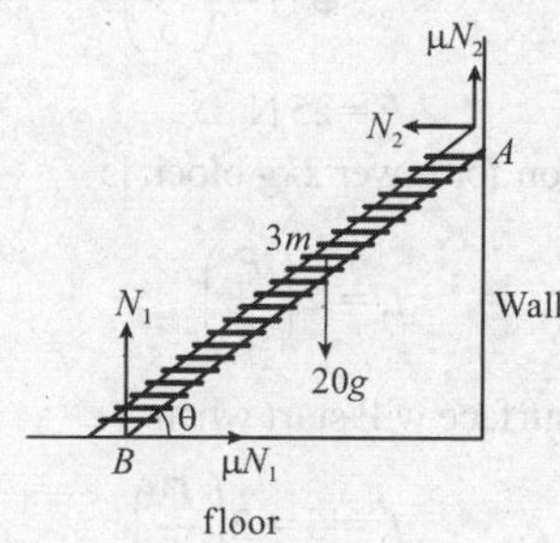

$$N_1 = \frac{200}{1.25} = 160N$$

$$N_2 = 80\,N$$

Taking torque about point B

$$\tau_B = 200 \times 1.5 \cos\theta - 80 \times 3 \sin\theta - 40 \times 3 \cos\theta = 0$$

$$180 \cos\theta = 240 \sin\theta$$

$$\tan\theta = \frac{180}{240} = \frac{3}{4}$$

or $\theta = 37°$

(v) For block B, not to slide

$mg = \mu N$ ...(1)

Here acceleration of system is

$$a = \left(\frac{F}{m+M}\right)$$

and $N = Ma = \dfrac{MF}{m+M}$ ...(2)

From (1) and (2) $mg = \dfrac{\mu MF}{m+M}$

$$F = \frac{mg}{\mu}\left(1 + \frac{m}{M}\right)$$

(vi) Equation of motion for A and C are

$M_3g - T = M_3a$ ...(1)

$T - \mu(M_1 + M_2)\,g - \mu\,M_2g = M_1a$ ...(2)

(1) + (2) $\Rightarrow$

$$M_3g - \mu(m_1 + 2M_2)g = (M_1 + M_3)a$$

$$a = \frac{M_3g - \mu(M_1 + 2M_2)g}{M_1 + M_3}$$

(vii) We consider M move toward right at acceleration a, m goes down w.r to M with same acceleration

FBDs of M and m are

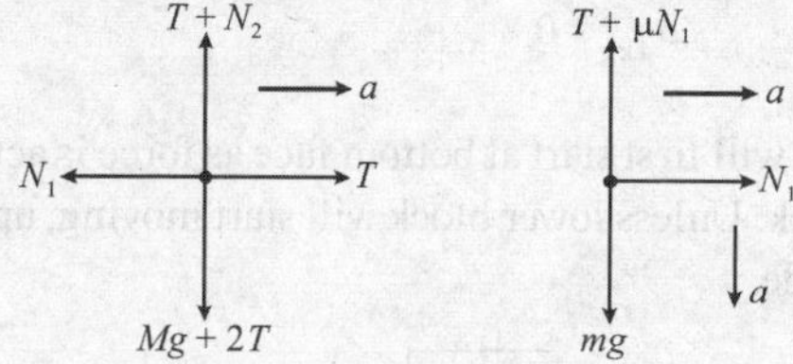

Equations of motion

$T - N_1 = Ma$ ...(1)

$N_1 = ma$ ...(2)

$mg - T - \mu N_1 = ma$ ...(3)

From (1), (2) and (3)

$$mg - (M + m)\,a - \mu ma = ma$$

$$a = \frac{mg}{M + 2m + 4m}$$

Acceleration of m is $a_m = \sqrt{2}a = \dfrac{\sqrt{2}g}{\left(2 + \mu + \dfrac{M}{m}\right)}$

Solutions of PRACTICE EXERCISE 2.5

(i) If we consider both blocks move together then acceleration would be

$$a = \frac{15-5}{5} = 2\text{ m/s}^2 \qquad [f_{bottom} = \mu_1(5g)]$$

Considering friction at $2kg$ block to be f its equation of motion

$$5 - f = 2a$$

$$f = 5 - 2 \times 2 = 1\text{N}$$

As limiting friction between the blocks is 4N hence this is static friction so both blocks will move together

$$a_{2kg} = a_{3kg} = 2\text{m/s}^2$$

(ii) (a) Limiting friction at top & bottom surfaces are

$$f_T = 0.2 \times 2 \times 10 = 4N$$

$$f_B = 0.1 \times 6 \times 10 = 6N$$

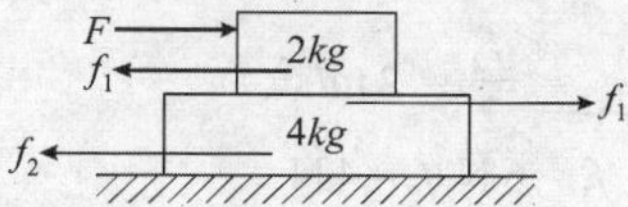

Sliding will start at top surface when

$$F = f_T = 4\text{ N}$$

(b) At $F > 4$ N, 2 kg will move with acceleration

$$a = \frac{F-4}{2}\text{ m/s}^2$$

and 4 kg will remain at rest as f_1 can never exceed f_B

Thus for $F = 2$ N,

Both blocks will be at rest

and for $F = 6$ N,

$$a_{2\text{kg}} = \frac{6-4}{2} = 1\text{ m/s}^2$$

and $a_{4\text{kg}} = 0$

(iii) (a) Sliding will first start at bottom face as force is acting on the lower block. Unless lower block will start moving, upper block cannot slide.

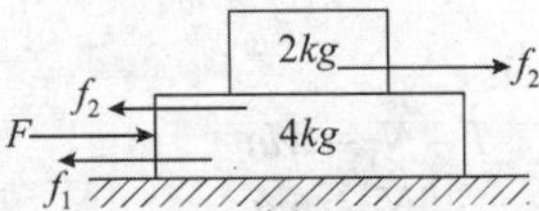

(b) Lower block will start sliding when $F > f_B$

i.e. $f > 6$ N

(c) At $F > 6$ N

Both blocks will move together with acceleration

$$a = \frac{F-6}{6}\text{ m/s}^2$$

Equation of motion for 2 kg block

$$f_2 = 2a = 2\left(\frac{F-6}{6}\right)$$

At upper surface sliding will start when

$$f_2 = f_T = 4\text{ N}$$

$$\Rightarrow \quad 4 = 2\left(\frac{F-6}{6}\right)$$

$$F - 6 = 12$$

$$F = 18\text{ N}$$

(d) At $F = 3$ N

$$a_{2\text{kg}} = 0;\ a_{4\text{kg}} = 0;\ f_1 = f_2 = 3\text{ N}$$

at $F = 12$ N

$$a_{2\text{kg}} = a_{4\text{kg}} = \frac{F-6}{6} = 1\text{ m/s}^2;$$

and $f_1 = 6\text{ N};\ f_2 = 2a = 2\text{ N}$

at $F = 24$ N

$$a_{4\text{kg}} = \frac{F-6-4}{4} = \frac{14}{4} = 3.5\text{m/s}^2;$$

and $a_{2\text{kg}} = \dfrac{f_2}{2} = 2\text{ m/s}^2;$

and $f_1 = 6\text{ N}, f_2 = 4\text{ N}$

(iv) Limiting frictions at the two surfaces are

$$f_{1L} = 0.2 \times 3 \times 10 = 6\text{ N}$$

$$f_{2L} = 0.5 \times 1 \times 10 = 5\text{ N}$$

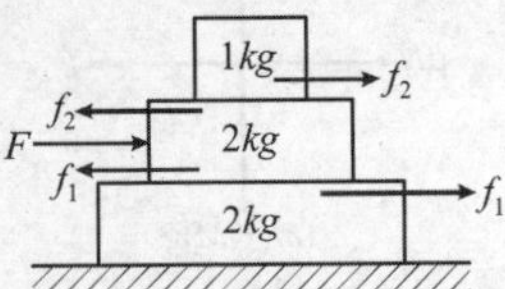

(a) If all blocks move together, acceleration is

$$a = \frac{F}{5}\text{ m/s}^2$$

Equation of motion for 1 kg block is

$$f_2 = 1\left(\frac{F}{5}\right)$$

1 kg will start sliding when

$$f_2 = 5\text{ N} = \left(\frac{F}{5}\right)$$

$$\Rightarrow \quad F = 25\text{ N}$$

Equation of motion for lower $2kg$ block is

$$f_1 = 2\left(\frac{F}{5}\right)$$

Sliding at lower surface will start when

$$f_1 = 6 = 2\left(\frac{F}{5}\right)$$

$$F = 15\text{ N}$$

Thus sliding will start between lower and middle blocks at

$$F = 15\text{ N}$$

(b) At $F > 15$ N,

Upper two blocks will move together with acceleration

$$a = \frac{F-6}{3}\text{ m/s}^2$$

1 kg block will slide when

$$f_2 = 1\left(\frac{F-6}{3}\right) = 5$$

$$F = 15 + 6 = 21\text{ N}$$

(c) For $F = 10$ N,

All blocks will move together at

$$a = \frac{F}{5} = 2\text{ m/s}^2;$$

$$f_1 = 2a = 4\text{ N};$$

$$f_2 = 1a = 2\text{ N}$$

For $F = 18$ N, $\quad a_{\text{lower 2kg}} = \dfrac{F_{2L}}{2} = \dfrac{6}{2} = 3\text{m/s}^2;$

$$a_{1\text{kg}} = a_{2\text{kg}} = \frac{F-6}{3} = 4\text{m/s}^2;$$

$$f_1 = 6N;\ f_2 = 1a = 4\text{ N}$$

For $F = 25$N,

$$a_{\text{lower 2kg}} = \frac{f_{2L}}{2} = \frac{6}{2} = 3 \text{ m/s}^2;$$

$$a_{\text{middle 2kg}} = \frac{F-H}{2} = 7 \text{ m/s}^2;$$

$$a_{1\text{kg}} = \frac{f_{2L}}{1} = 5 \text{ m/s}^2;$$

$$f_1 = 5\text{ N};\ f_2 = 6\text{ N}$$

Solutions of PRACTICE EXERCISE 2.6

(i) Tension in string $\quad T = m_A g = 2 \times 9.8 = 19.6$N

For block B $\quad T = \mu m_B g$

$$m_B = \frac{T}{\mu g} = \frac{19.6}{0.2 \times 9.8} = 10 \text{ kg}$$

For spring $T = kx$

$$x = \frac{T}{k} = \frac{19.6}{1960} = 0.01\text{m} = 1\text{cm}$$

(ii) Spring force $\quad F_s = k\left(\frac{R}{4}\right) = \frac{mg}{4}$

FBD of ring is shown in figure

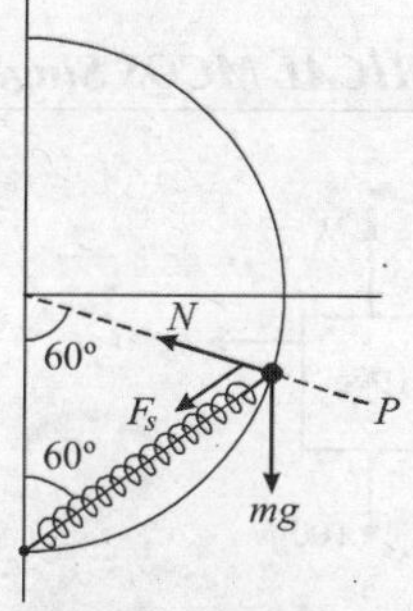

Equation of motion in tangential direction is

$$mg\cos 30° + \frac{mg}{4}\cos 30° = ma$$

$$mg\left(\frac{\sqrt{3}}{2} + \frac{\sqrt{3}}{8}\right) = ma$$

$$a = \frac{5\sqrt{3}g}{8} = \frac{25\sqrt{3}}{4} \text{ m/s}^2$$

Along radial direction

$$N + \frac{mg}{4}\sin 30° = mg\sin 30°$$

$$N = \frac{mg}{2} - \frac{mg}{8}$$

$$= \frac{3mg}{8} - \frac{30}{8} = 3.75\text{N}$$

(iii) Initial tension in spring

$$F_s = m_1 g$$

When the string in cut spring tension does not change instantly so acceleration of m_1 will be zero

For block m_2, we use

$$m_2 g + F_s = m_2 a$$

$$a = \frac{m_2 g + m_1 g}{m_2} = \left(1 + \frac{m_1}{m_2}\right)g$$

After string in cut m_3 is in free fall so its acceleration will be g

(iv) Friction on 2 kg block is

$$f_1 = 0.2 \times 2 \times 10 = 4\text{ N}$$

Friction on 4 kg block is

$$f_2 = 0.1 \times 4 \times 10 = 4\text{ N}$$

Equation of motion for 2 kg blocks is

$$20 - kx - 4 = 2 \times 2$$

$$kx = 12\text{ N}$$

$$\Rightarrow \qquad x = \frac{12}{1000} = 0.012\text{ m}$$

Equation of motion for 4kg block is

$$kx - 4 = 4a$$

$$4a = 8$$

$$a = 2 \text{ m/s}^2$$

Solutions of CONCEPTUAL MCQS Single Option Correct

Sol. 1 (B) Total displacement of wedge A with respect to B must be equal to the increase in length of string on the slant surfaces of the two wedges.

Sol. 2 (B) Smaller steps ensure less horizontal force by man on ground due to which friction will be less and maintained below the limiting friction so that walking will be without sliding.

Sol. 3 (D) In the given system as pulley A is massless, string tension will be zero for its equilibrium and C is in free fall at acceleration g. So by constrained relations A will move up by twice the distance as that of C hence option (D) is correct.

Sol. 4 (A) Initially as height decreases velocity in downward direction (negative) will increase and after bounce it changes to positive and becomes zero at $h = d/2$.

Sol. 5 (D) As acceleration of bicycle is positive, forward friction on rear wheel must be more than backward friction on front wheel.

Sol. 6 (D) As A is in equilibrium friction on it must act in upward direction but in that case friction on B must be in opposite (downward) direction and in that case it cannot be in equilibrium, if B falls then A will also fall so option (D) is correct.

Sol. 7 (A) If θ is the angle of repose then it is independent of the mass of the body placed on the inclined plane.

Sol. 8 (B) If mass of A is higher then its acceleration due to gravity is g and due to air friction is f/m so net acceleration of A in upward motion is $-(g+f/m)$ which is less compared to that of B as its mass is higher so it will ascend more height than B.

Sol. 9 (C) When the two blocks move together the acceleration of blocks are equal and when they start sliding then the lower block will have a constant acceleration and upper one will have increasing acceleration so only option (C) can be correct.

Sol. 10 (A) The box can slide only when the force on it is more than the limiting friction between box and the floor. For this the certain case will be when $\mu M < \mu' M'$ which is always there in case of option (A).

Sol. 11 (B) As angle increases the static friction which is balancing the weight component of the block along the incline also increases so static friction will be $Mg \sin\theta$ and when the block starts sliding then it experiences kinetic friction given as $\mu Mg \cos\theta$.

Sol. 12 (B) On the left side the force on arm of beam balance is less than $3mg$ as the system is sliding so the balance will rotate toward right side.

Sol. 13 (B) Contact force is the resultant of normal reaction and the friction acting on the body. If the angle between the contact force and vertical is decreases then its horizontal component which is friction will decrease.

Sol. 14 (B) In first case the acceleration of block is g, in second case it is $g/3$ and in third case it is $g/2$ hence option (B) is correct.

Sol. 15 (D) As angle of repose is different for the two blocks that means the friction coefficient is different in the two cases and angle of repose is independent of the mass of body placed on incline so all cases of masses are possible.

Sol. 16 (C) Normal force never changes the speed of particle hence its KE must remain constant.

Sol. 17 (B) In equilibrium of a body, vector sum of all the forces acting on bodies is zero so at equilibrium acceleration of body must always be zero.

Sol. 18 (B) If the spring is cut in two parts (half length) then the force constant of each part of spring become doubled so the slope of line will also get doubled as $F = kx$.

Sol. 19 (A) If there is no acceleration in the elevator then coin will fall with acceleration g relative to floor and will take equal time in all cases.

Sol. 20 (D) Net content force between seat and man is the vector sum of normal reaction and friction so in case of acceleration it is more than weight and for uniform motion it is equal to weight.

Sol. 21 (B) If $\theta \to 0$ $T \to \infty$

and $\theta \to \frac{\pi}{2}, T \to \frac{mg}{2}$

Sol. 22 (D) Static friction starts acting when some external force acts on body. In this case $T = mg \sin\theta$.

Sol. 23 (B) Because in downward journey F and mg Both will act downward, while in upward journey only mg will act downward.

Solutions of NUMERICAL MCQS Single Options Correct

Sol. 1 (A)

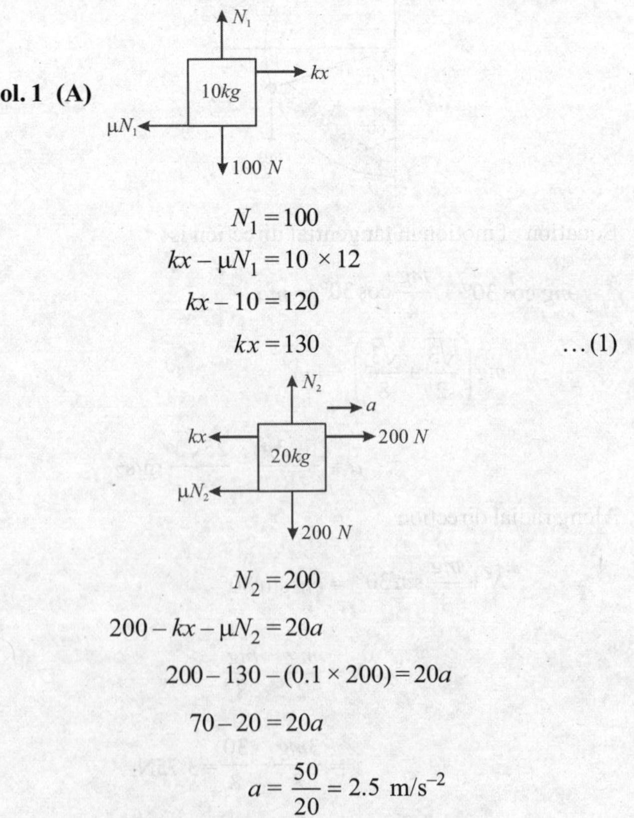

$$N_1 = 100$$

$$kx - \mu N_1 = 10 \times 12$$

$$kx - 10 = 120$$

$$kx = 130 \quad \ldots(1)$$

$$N_2 = 200$$

$$200 - kx - \mu N_2 = 20a$$

$$200 - 130 - (0.1 \times 200) = 20a$$

$$70 - 20 = 20a$$

$$a = \frac{50}{20} = 2.5 \text{ m/s}^{-2}$$

Sol. 2 (B) $N = ma$

To prevent block m from falling,

$$\mu N > mg$$

$$\mu ma > mg$$

$$a > \frac{g}{\mu}$$

Sol. 3 (A)

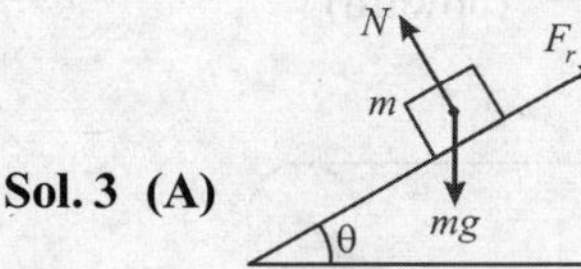

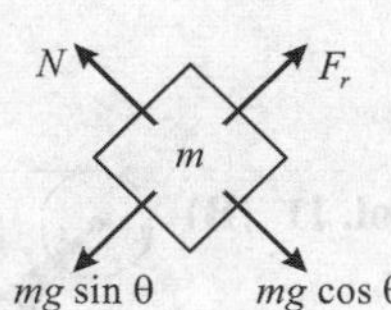

Since the body is at rest,

$$N = mg\cos\theta$$

$$F_r = mg\sin\theta$$

Magnitude of force acting on block by inclined surface,

$$F = \sqrt{N^2 + F_r^2}$$

$$= \sqrt{(mg\cos\theta)^2 + (mg\sin\theta)^2}$$

$$F = mg\sqrt{\cos^2\theta + \sin^2\theta}$$

$$F = mg$$

Sol. 4 (B) Let coefficient of friction is μ

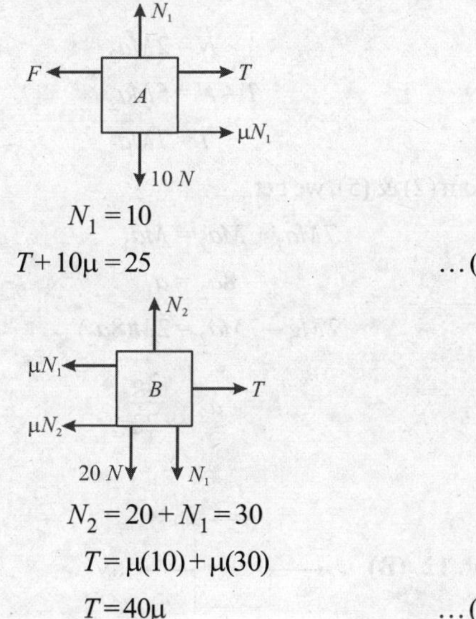

$$N_1 = 10$$

$$T + 10\mu = 25 \qquad \ldots(1)$$

$$N_2 = 20 + N_1 = 30$$

$$T = \mu(10) + \mu(30)$$

$$T = 40\mu \qquad \ldots(2)$$

From (1) and (2), we get

$$50\mu = 25$$

$$\mu = 0.5$$

Sol. 5 (C)

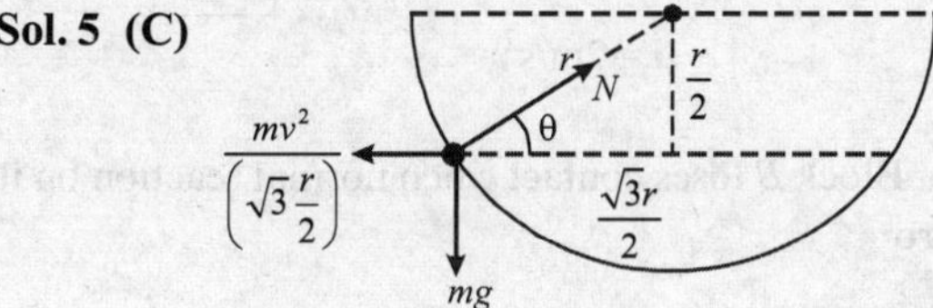

$$N\cos\theta = \frac{mv^2}{\frac{\sqrt{3}r}{2}} \qquad \ldots(1)$$

$$N\sin\theta = mg \qquad \ldots(2)$$

Dividing (1) by (2) $\quad \tan\theta = \frac{mg}{\frac{2mv^2}{\sqrt{3}r}} = \frac{\sqrt{3}rg}{2v^2}$

$$v^2 = \frac{\sqrt{3}rg}{2\tan\theta}$$

From figure, $\quad \tan\theta = \frac{\frac{r}{2}}{\sqrt{3}\frac{r}{2}} = \frac{1}{\sqrt{3}}$

$$\Rightarrow \quad v^2 = \frac{\sqrt{3}rg}{2\left(\frac{1}{\sqrt{3}}\right)} = \frac{3rg}{2}$$

$$\Rightarrow \quad v = \sqrt{\frac{3rg}{2}}$$

Sol. 6 (B) Since 100g is at rest,

$$T = 1\text{N}$$

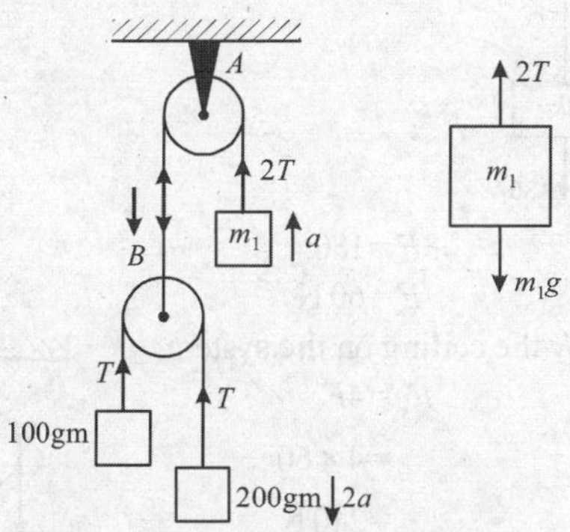

If m_1 is going up at acceleration a, we use

$$2T - m_1g = m_1a \qquad \ldots(1)$$

For 100g to be at rest, acceleration of 200 gm mass is $2a$ if m_1 is going up at a

T
200g
2N

$$2 - T = 0.2\,(2a)$$

$$2 - 1 = 0.4a$$

$$a = \frac{10}{4} = \frac{5}{2}\ \text{m/s}^2$$

From (1), we have

$$2(1) - 10m_1 = m_1\left(\frac{5}{2}\right)$$

$$2 = 10m_1 + \frac{5m_1}{2}$$

$$4 = 25m_1$$

$$m_1 = \frac{4}{25} = 0.16\ \text{kg} = 160\ \text{g}$$

Sol. 7 (C)

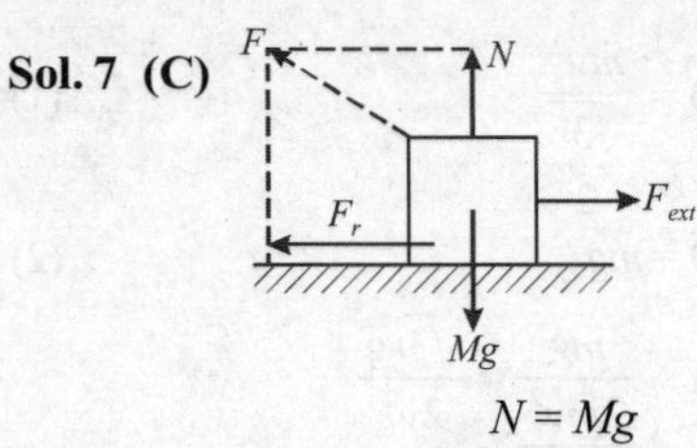

$$N = Mg$$

Force by surface on body,

$$F = \sqrt{N^2 + F_r^2}$$

$$F = \sqrt{M^2g^2 + \mu^2M^2g^2}$$

$$F = Mg\sqrt{1+\mu^2}$$

This is the maximum value of F

If applied force (F_{ext}) is zero, then friction force acting on body is also zero. Hence force by surface on body,

$$F = Mg$$

Thus, $$Mg \le F \le Mg\sqrt{1+\mu^2}$$

Sol. 8 (D)

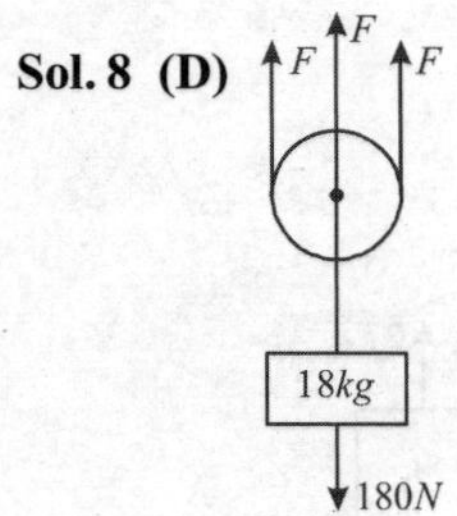

$$3F = 180$$

$$F = 60\text{ N}$$

Force exerted by the ceiling on the system,

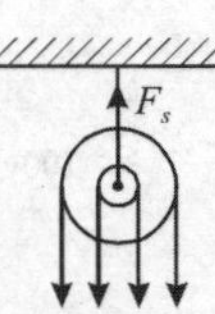

$$F_s = 4F$$

$$= 4 \times 60$$

$$= 240\text{ N}$$

Sol. 9 (B) $$F = \frac{m|(\vec{v} - \vec{u})|}{t}$$

$$F = \frac{(10 \times 10^{-3}\,kg)[5-(-5)]}{0.01}$$

$$F = \frac{10^{-2} \times 10}{10^{-2}} = 10\text{N}$$

Sol. 10 (A)

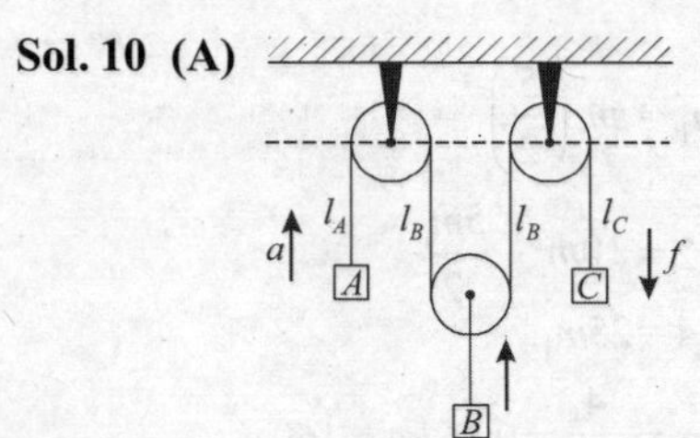

In figure $$l_A + 2l_B + l_C = \text{constant}$$

Double differentiating above equation

$$-a_A - 2a_B + a_C = 0$$

(Assuming increase in length as positive)

$$a_B = \frac{a_C - a_A}{2}$$

$$a_B = \frac{f-a}{2} \quad \text{(upward)}$$

Sol. 11 (B)

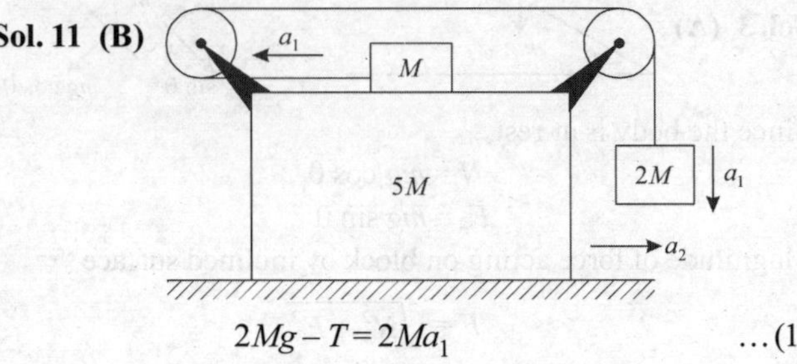

$$2Mg - T = 2Ma_1 \quad \dots(1)$$

$$T + Ma_2 = Ma_1 \quad \dots(2)$$

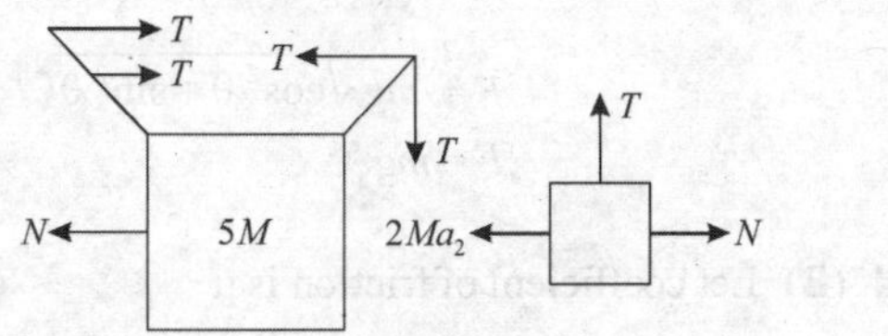

$$N = 2Ma_2 \quad \dots(3)$$

$$T - N = 5Ma_2 \quad \dots(4)$$

$$T = 7Ma_2 \quad \dots5)$$

From (2) & (5), we get

$$7Ma_2 + Ma_2 = Ma_1$$

$$8a_2 = a_1 \quad \dots(6)$$

$$2Mg - 7Ma_2 = 2M(8a_2)$$

$$a_2 = \frac{2g}{23}$$

Sol. 12 (B)

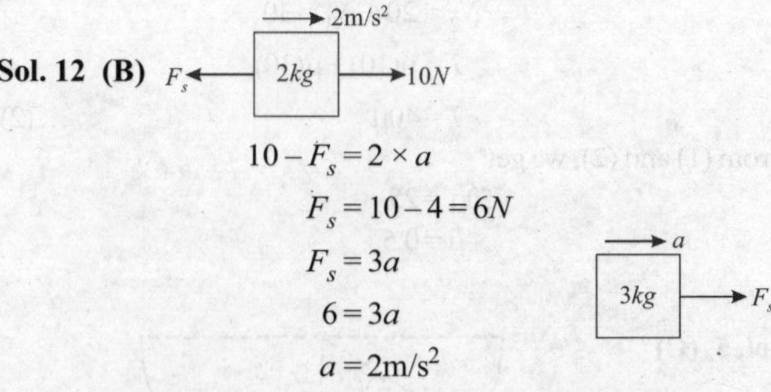

$$10 - F_s = 2 \times a$$

$$F_s = 10 - 4 = 6N$$

$$F_s = 3a$$

$$6 = 3a$$

$$a = 2\text{m/s}^2$$

Sol. 13 (C) Block B loses contact when normal reaction on it becomes zero

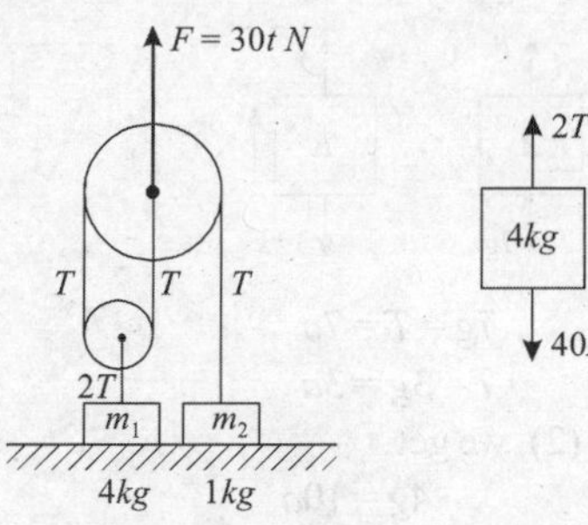

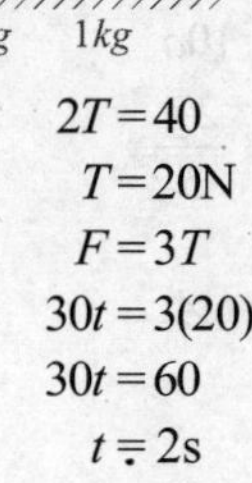

i.e.

$$2T = 40$$
$$T = 20\text{N}$$
$$F = 3T$$
$$30t = 3(20)$$
$$30t = 60$$
$$t = 2\text{s}$$

Sol. 14 (D) Situation is given as

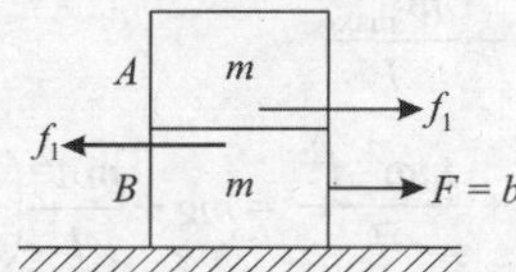

FBDs of *A* and *B* as

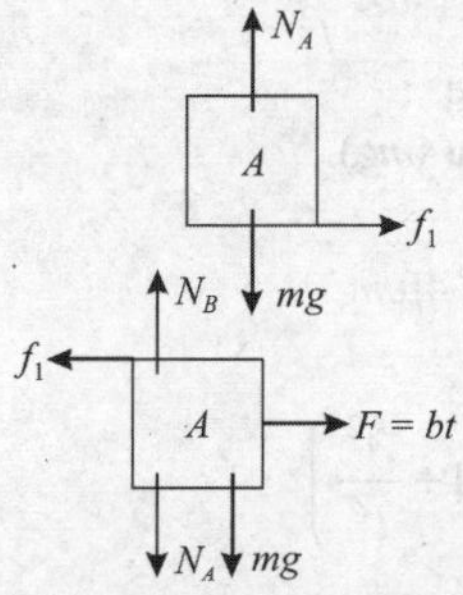

equations of motion of *A* and *B* when they move together are

$$f_1 = ma$$
$$F - f_1 = ma$$

sliding starts when $f_1 = \mu mg$

$$F - \mu mg = \mu mg$$
$$F = 2\mu mg = bt$$
$$t = \frac{2\mu mg}{b}$$

Sol. 15 (D) *FBD* of blocks are

N', m_1, T_2, $\mu N'$, $40N$; $30°$, T_1, T_2, $60°$, $120°$, $8N$

$$N' = 40\text{N}$$
$$T_2 = 40\mu$$

$$\frac{8}{\sin(90° + 60°)} = \frac{T_1}{\sin 90°} = \frac{T_2}{\sin 120°}$$

$$16 = T_1 = \frac{2T_2}{\sqrt{3}}$$

$$\frac{2T_2}{\sqrt{3}} = 16$$

$$40\mu = \frac{\sqrt{3} \times 16}{2}$$

$$\mu = \frac{\sqrt{3}}{5} = 0.35$$

Sol. 16 (A) Downward acceleration of body is

$$a = g \text{ sing } \theta - \mu g \cos\theta$$
$$a = g [\sin\theta - 0.1 x \cos\theta]$$

Acceleration will remain +ve upto $x = 10 \tan\theta$

$\Rightarrow$ at $x > 10 \tan\theta$ body starts retarding and speed decreases

Sol. 17 (B) Angle of Repose is $\theta = \tan^{-1}(\mu_s)$

$$= \tan^{-1}(0.75) = 37°$$

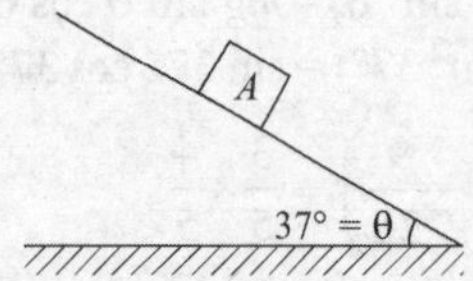

when θ exceeds slightly above 37°, we use

$$a = g \sin\theta - \mu_k g \cos\theta$$

$$a = 10 \times \frac{3}{5} - 0.5 \times 10 \times \frac{4}{5}$$

$$a = 6 - 4$$
$$a = 2\text{m/s}^2$$

Sol. 18 (B) Maximum tension at bottom most point is given by

$$T_1 = mg + \frac{mv^2}{2} \quad ...(1)$$

Minimum tension at top most point is given by

$$T_2 = \frac{mv^2}{2} - mg \quad ...(2)$$

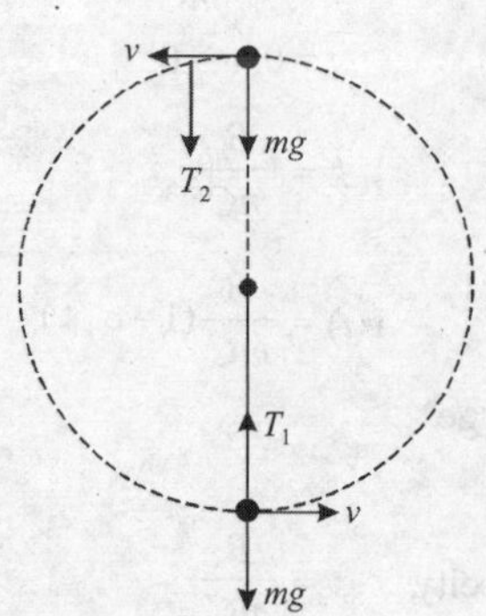

$$\frac{T_1}{T_2} = \frac{5}{3}$$

$$\frac{2mg + mv^2}{mv^2 - 2mg} = \frac{5}{3}$$

$$6g + 3v^2 = 5v^2 - 10g$$

$$16g = 2v^2$$

$$v^2 = 80$$

$$v = \sqrt{80} = 4\sqrt{5} \text{ m/s}$$

Sol. 19 (C) The acceleration of the blocks down the incline will be $g \sin\theta$ so *FBD* of m wr to M in limiting state is

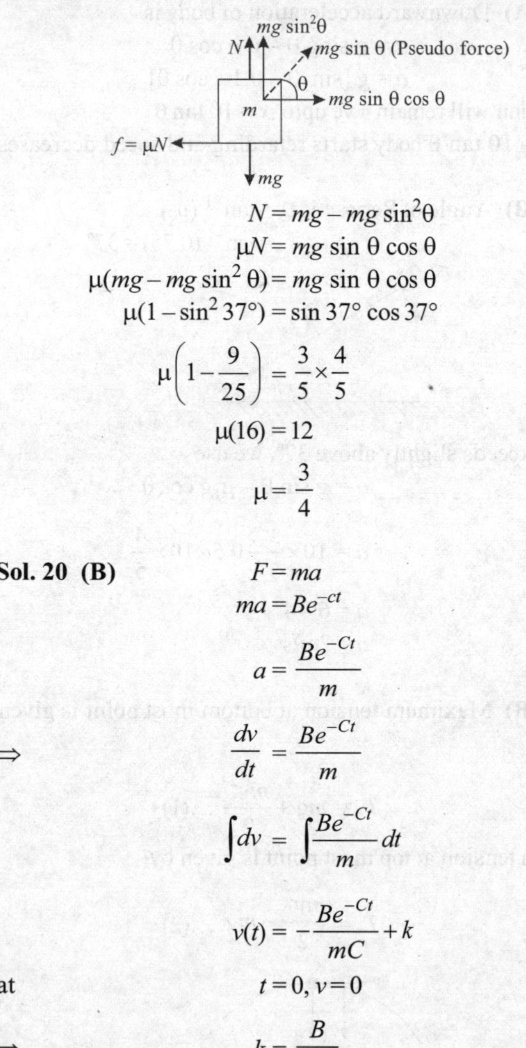

$$N = mg - mg\sin^2\theta$$

$$\mu N = mg \sin\theta \cos\theta$$

$$\mu(mg - mg\sin^2\theta) = mg\sin\theta\cos\theta$$

$$\mu(1 - \sin^2 37°) = \sin 37° \cos 37°$$

$$\mu\left(1 - \frac{9}{25}\right) = \frac{3}{5} \times \frac{4}{5}$$

$$\mu(16) = 12$$

$$\mu = \frac{3}{4}$$

Sol. 20 (B)

$$F = ma$$

$$ma = Be^{-ct}$$

$$a = \frac{Be^{-Ct}}{m}$$

$$\Rightarrow \quad \frac{dv}{dt} = \frac{Be^{-Ct}}{m}$$

$$\int dv = \int \frac{Be^{-Ct}}{m} dt$$

$$v(t) = -\frac{Be^{-Ct}}{mC} + k$$

at $\quad t = 0, v = 0$

$$\Rightarrow \quad k = \frac{B}{mC}$$

$$\Rightarrow \quad v(t) = \frac{B}{mC}(1 - e^{-ct})$$

When t is very large

$e^{-ct} \to 0$

$\Rightarrow$ Terminal velocity, $\quad v = \dfrac{B}{mC}$

Sol. 21 (D)

$$7g - T = 7a \quad \ldots(1)$$

$$T - 3g = 3a \quad \ldots(2)$$

Adding (1) and (2), we get

$$4g = 10a$$

$$a = \frac{2g}{5}$$

Sol. 22 (B) $\quad v = \omega A$

Let tension in string is T

maximum tension in string is

$$T = mg + \frac{mv_{\max}^2}{l}$$

$$T = mg + \frac{m\omega^2 A^2}{l} = mg + \frac{mA^2}{l}\left(\frac{g}{l}\right) \quad \left[\text{as } \omega = \sqrt{\frac{g}{l}}\,\right]$$

$$T = mg + mg\frac{A^2}{l^2}$$

for block not to slide

$$T = f < \mu(4mg)$$

$$mg\left(1 + \frac{A^2}{l^2}\right) < 4\mu mg$$

$$\mu > \frac{1}{4}\left(1 + \frac{A^2}{l^2}\right)$$

Sol. 23 (B)

$$k \propto \frac{1}{l}$$

$$\frac{k}{k'} = \frac{l'}{l} = \frac{2\frac{l}{3}}{l}$$

$$k' = \frac{3k}{2}$$

Sol. 24 (A) For equilibrium of man and frame

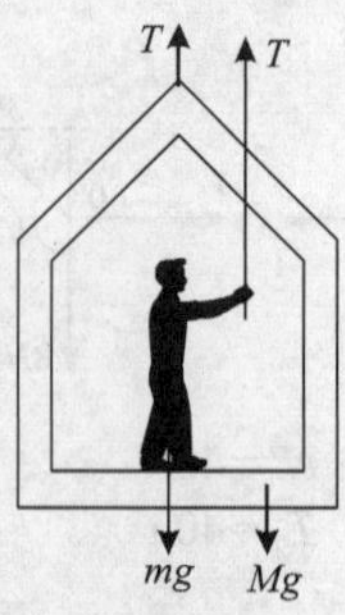

$$2T = (M+m)g$$

$$T = \frac{(M+m)g}{2}$$

Sol. 25 (D) $s = \frac{1}{2}at^2$

maximum acceleration of car is

$$a = \mu g$$

$$s = \frac{1}{2}\mu g t^2$$

$$t^2 = \frac{2s}{\mu g} \Rightarrow t = \sqrt{\frac{2s}{\mu g}}$$

$$t \propto \frac{1}{\sqrt{\mu}}$$

Sol. 26 (B)

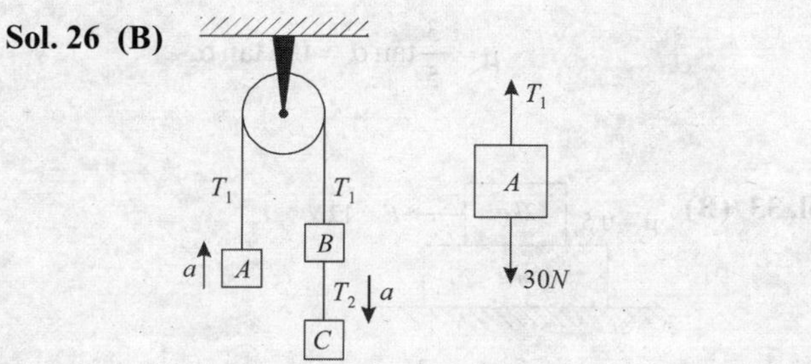

For A, $T_1 - 30 = 3a$ ...(1)

$\Rightarrow$ $T_1 = 30 + 3a$

For B, $30 + T_2 - T_1 = 3a$ ...(2)

For C, $30 - T_2 = 3a$ ...(3)

$$T_2 = 30 - 3a$$

From (1), (2) and (3),

$$30 + 30 - 3a - 30 - 3a = 3a$$

$$9a = 30$$

$$a = \frac{10}{3} \text{ m/s}^2$$

$$T_2 = 30 - 3\left(\frac{10}{3}\right)$$

$$T_2 = 20 \text{ N} = 2 \text{ kgwt}$$

Sol. 27 (C) m_1 comes to rest w.r.t. plank when relative slipping between them stops.

Applying conservation of linear momentum to find final velocity of system w.r.t. surface.

$$1 \times 10 = (1+2)v$$

$\Rightarrow$ $v = \frac{10}{3}$ m/s

So, for block, $u = 10$ m/s,

and $v = \frac{10}{3}$ m/s

$$a = -\mu g = -5 \text{ m/s}^2$$

we use $v = u - at$

$\Rightarrow$ $\frac{10}{3} = 10 - 5t$

$$5t = 10 - \frac{10}{3} = \frac{20}{3}$$

$$t = \frac{4}{3} \text{ s}$$

Sol. 28 (C)

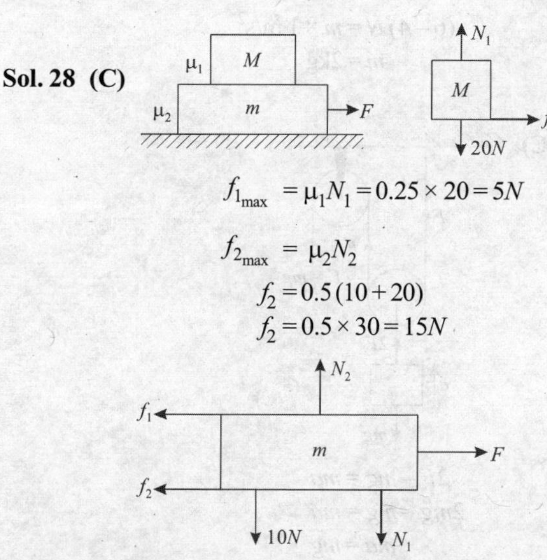

$$f_{1_{max}} = \mu_1 N_1 = 0.25 \times 20 = 5N$$

$$f_{2_{max}} = \mu_2 N_2$$

$$f_2 = 0.5(10+20)$$

$$f_2 = 0.5 \times 30 = 15N$$

when both board and block start sliding at $F > 15$ N their acceleration will be

$$a = \frac{F-15}{3}$$

to start sliding between board and block we use

$$f_{1max} = Ma$$

$$5 = 2\left(\frac{F-15}{3}\right)$$

$\Rightarrow$ $F = 22.5$ N

Sol. 29 (A) When lift goes upwards with constant acceleration a,

$$W_1 = m(g+a) \quad ...(1)$$

When lift goes downwards with constant acceleration a,

$$W_2 = m(g-a) \quad ...(2)$$

$$\frac{W_1}{W_2} = \frac{m(g+a)}{m(g-a)} = \frac{2}{1}$$

$$g + a = 2g - 2a$$

$$3a = g$$

$$a = \frac{g}{3} = \frac{10}{3} = 3.33 \text{ m/s}^2$$

Sol. 30 (C) Since the block does not move till the applied force reaches $4N$, there is a friction force with its limiting value to be $4N$

Now, when applied force is $6N$, body accelerates at 1 m/s^2

From Newton's second law,

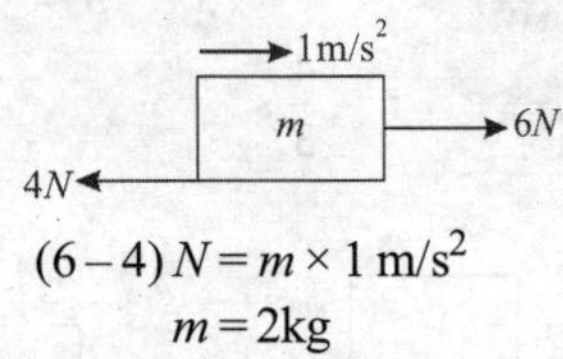

$$(6 - 4)\,N = m \times 1 \text{ m/s}^2$$

$$m = 2\text{kg}$$

Sol. 31 (C)

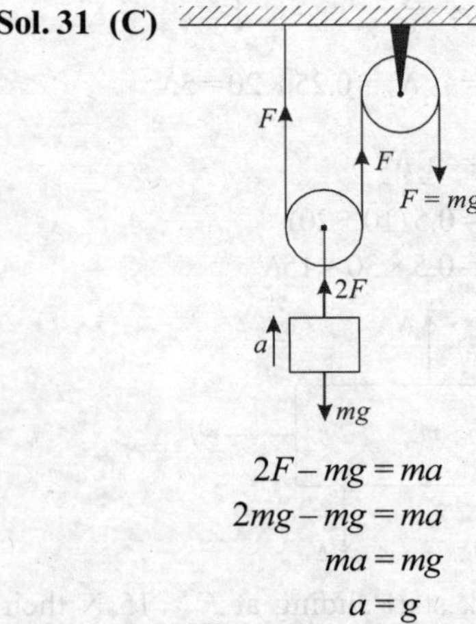

$$2F - mg = ma$$

$$2mg - mg = ma$$

$$ma = mg$$

$$a = g$$

Sol. 32 (C) Way up

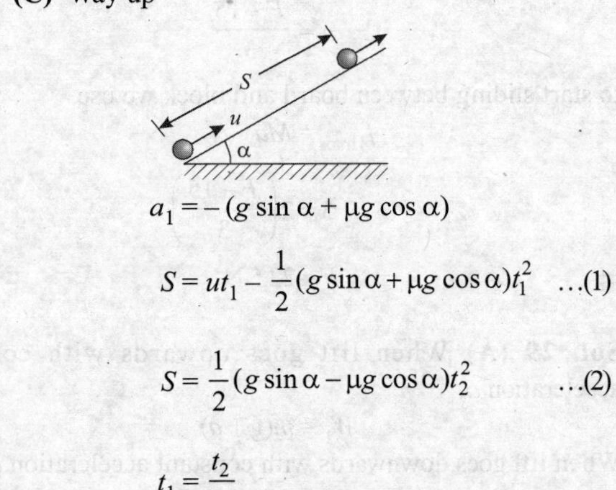

$$a_1 = -(g \sin \alpha + \mu g \cos \alpha)$$

$$S = ut_1 - \frac{1}{2}(g \sin \alpha + \mu g \cos \alpha)t_1^2 \quad \ldots(1)$$

$$S = \frac{1}{2}(g \sin \alpha - \mu g \cos \alpha)t_2^2 \quad \ldots(2)$$

Given $\quad t_1 = \dfrac{t_2}{2}$

From I equation while way up,

$$0 = u - (g \sin \alpha + \mu g \cos \alpha)t_1$$

$$u = (g \sin \alpha + \mu g \cos \alpha)t_1 \quad \ldots(3)$$

From (1) and (3), we get

$$S = \frac{1}{2}(g \sin \alpha + \mu g \cos \alpha)t_1^2$$

$$t_1 = \sqrt{\frac{2S}{g \sin \alpha + \mu g \cos \alpha}}$$

$$t_2 = \sqrt{\frac{2S}{g \sin \alpha - \mu g \cos \alpha}}$$

$$\Rightarrow \quad \frac{2S}{g \sin \alpha + \mu g \cos \alpha} = \frac{1}{4}\frac{2S}{g \sin \alpha - \mu g \cos \alpha}$$

$$4g \sin \alpha - 4\mu g \cos \alpha = g \sin \alpha + \mu g \cos \alpha$$

$$3g \sin \alpha = 5\,\mu g \cos \alpha$$

$$\mu = \frac{3}{5} \tan \alpha = 0.6 \tan \alpha$$

Sol. 33 (B) $\mu = 0.5$ [2kg block on 4kg block, $F = 12N$]

$$f_{\max} = \mu N_1$$

$$= 0.5 \times 20$$

$$= 10\text{ N}$$

to start sliding between blocks we use

$$f_{\max} = 4a$$

and $\quad F - f_{\max} = 2a$

$$\Rightarrow \quad F = \frac{3f_{\max}}{2} = 15\text{N}$$

$\Rightarrow$ at $F = 12$N, $f < 10$N and both blocks move together

$$\Rightarrow \quad a = \frac{12}{6} = 2 \text{ m/s}^2$$

Sol. 34 (A) 100 N ← (block) 10kg on 40kg (slab), $\mu_s = 0.6$, $\mu_k = 0.4$

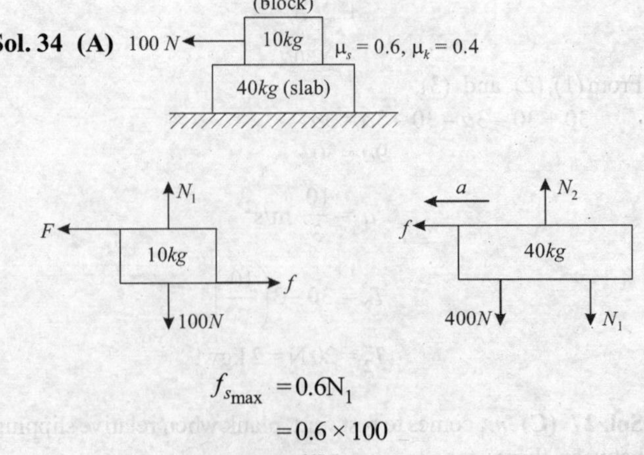

$$f_{s\max} = 0.6\text{N}_1$$

$$= 0.6 \times 100$$

$$= 60\text{N}$$

to start sliding between slab and block

$$F - f = 10\,a$$

and $$f = 40\,a$$

$$\Rightarrow \quad F = \frac{5f}{4} = 75\text{N}$$

as $F > 75$N, acceleration of slab will be

$$a = \frac{f_k}{40} = \frac{0.4 \times 100}{40} = 1 \text{ m/s}^2$$

Sol. 35 (A)

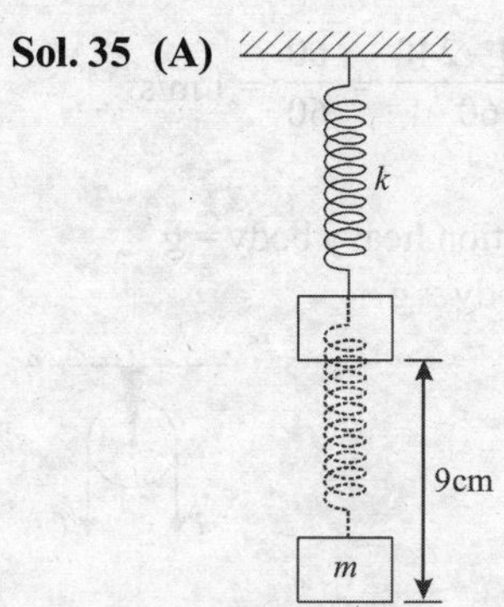

Let spring constant of the spring is k

Under equilibrium conditions,

$$mg = k(9\text{cm}) \quad \ldots(1)$$

When spring is cut into 3 equal parts, the spring constant of each becomes

$$k' = 3k$$

If elongation in spring is 'x'

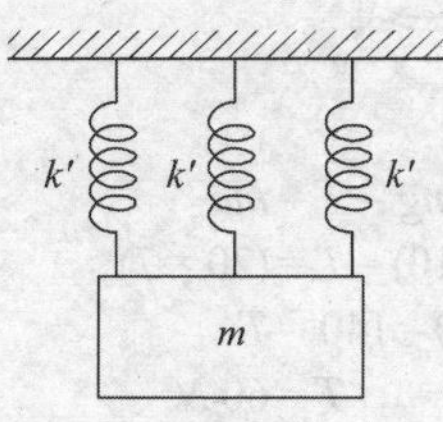

$$3k'x = mg$$

$$3(3k)x = mg \quad \ldots(2)$$

From (1) and (2), we get

$$9k = 9kx$$

$$x = 1 \text{ cm}$$

Sol. 36 (C)

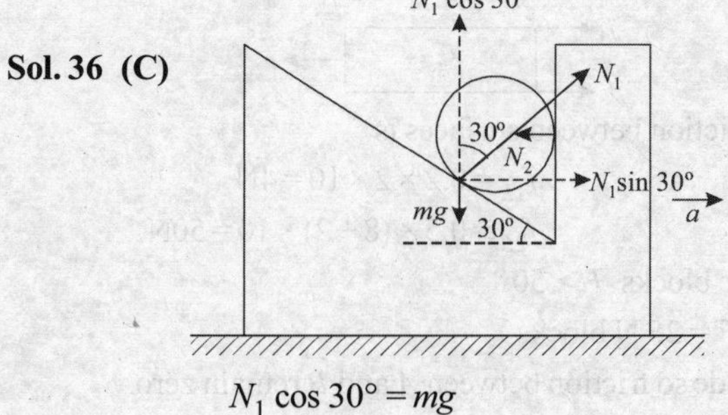

$$N_1 \cos 30° = mg$$

The ball leaves the frame when

$$N_2 = 0$$

$$\Rightarrow \quad N_1 \sin 30° = ma$$

$$\tan 30° = \frac{a}{g}$$

$$a = \frac{g}{\sqrt{3}}$$

Sol. 37 (C)

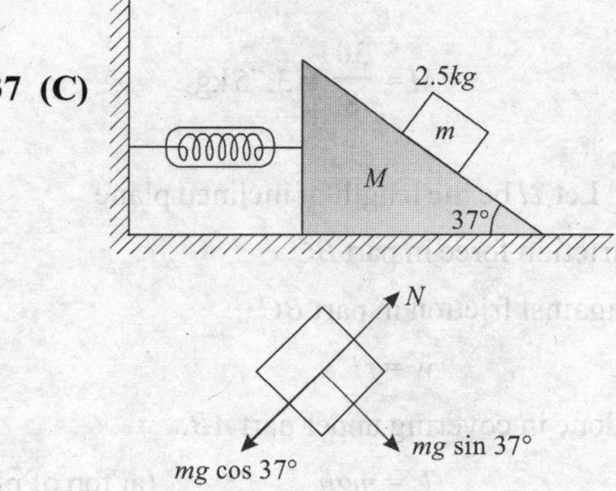

$$N = \text{mg} \cos 37°$$

$$N = 2.5 \times 10 \times \frac{4}{5}$$

$$N = 20\,\text{N}$$

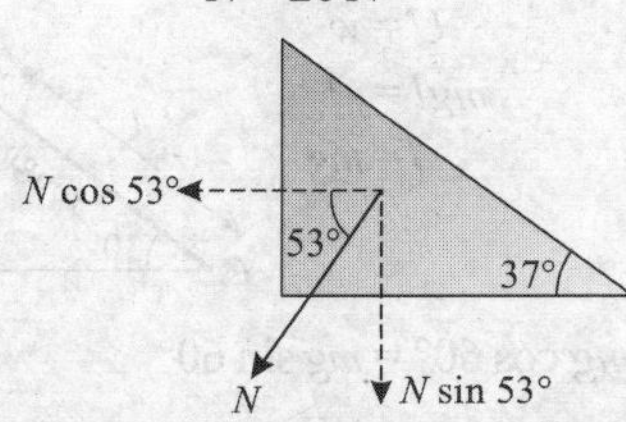

Reading of spring balance,

$$R = \text{N} \cos 53°$$

$$R = 20 \times \frac{3}{5}$$

$$R = 12\text{N}$$

Sol. 38 (C)

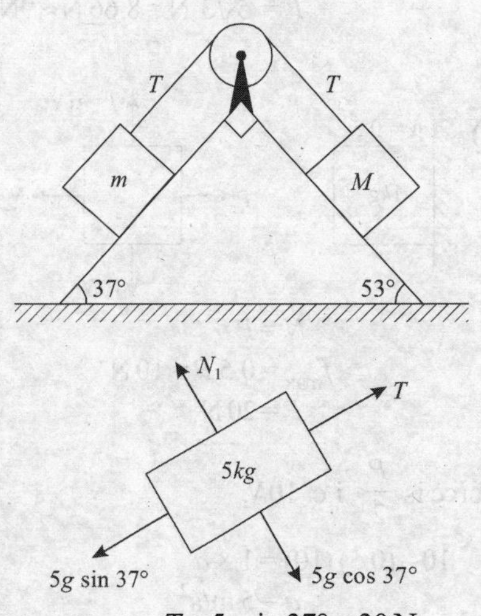

$$T = 5g \sin 37° = 30\,\text{N}$$

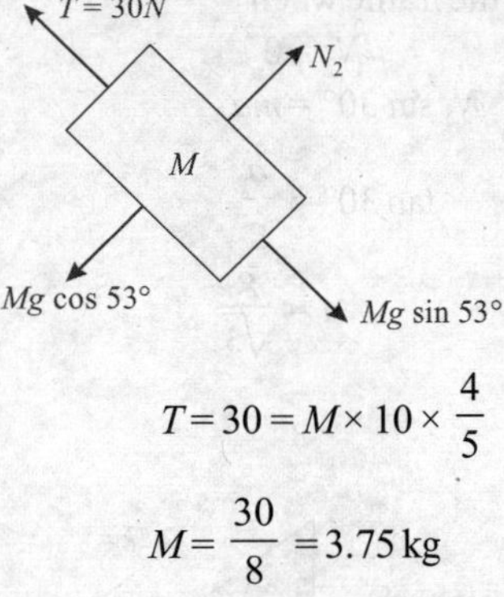

$$T = 30 = M \times 10 \times \frac{4}{5}$$

$$M = \frac{30}{8} = 3.75 \text{ kg}$$

Sol. 39 (C) Let $2l$ be the length of inclined plane

Let f be the friction force in part BC

Work done against friction in part BC

$$w = fl$$

No work is done in covering upper part AB.

$$U = mgh \quad \text{(at top of plane)}$$

$$\sin 30° = \frac{h}{2l}$$

$$\Rightarrow \quad h = 2l \sin 30° = l$$

$$U = w$$

$$mgl = fl$$

$$f = mg$$

Sol. 40 (B) $\mu\, mg \cos 60° = mg \sin 60°$

$$\mu = \sqrt{3}$$

Now, if force F is applied to pull it along the incline,

$$F = \text{mg} \sin 60° + \mu mg \cos 60°$$

$$F = \frac{5\sqrt{3}}{2} + \frac{5\sqrt{3}}{2}$$

$$F = 5\sqrt{3}\ \text{N} = 8.66\ \text{N} \approx 9\text{N}$$

Sol. 41 (A)

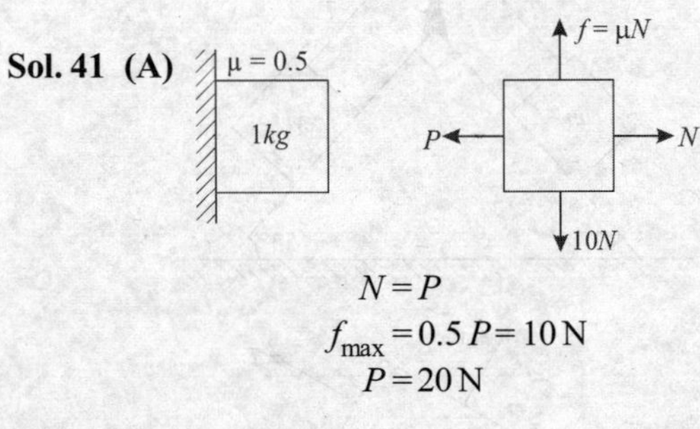

$$N = P$$

$$f_{\max} = 0.5\,P = 10\ \text{N}$$

$$P = 20\ \text{N}$$

If applied force is $\frac{P}{2}$, i.e. $10N$,

$$10 - (0.5)(10) = 1 \times a$$

$$a = 5 \text{ m/s}^2$$

Sol. 42 (B)

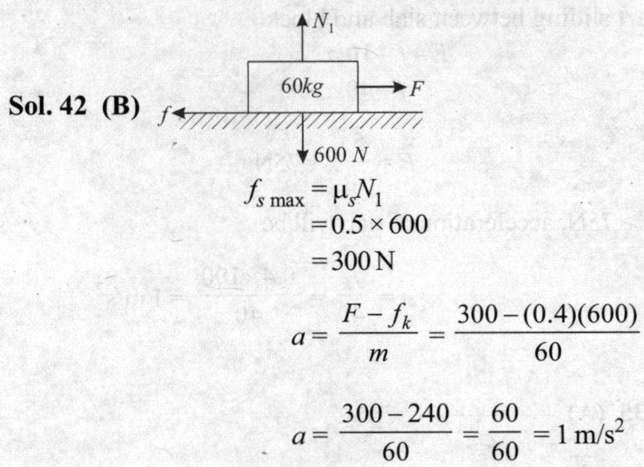

$$f_{s\max} = \mu_s N_1$$

$$= 0.5 \times 600$$

$$= 300\ \text{N}$$

$$a = \frac{F - f_k}{m} = \frac{300 - (0.4)(600)}{60}$$

$$a = \frac{300 - 240}{60} = \frac{60}{60} = 1 \text{ m/s}^2$$

Sol. 43 (C) Downward acceleration heavy body $= g$

Upward acceleration of lighter body $= g$

If T is tension in the string

$$T - mg = ma$$

$$T - mg = mg$$

$$T = 2mg$$

Downwards force on pulley,

$$2T = 4mg$$

Sol. 44 (C)

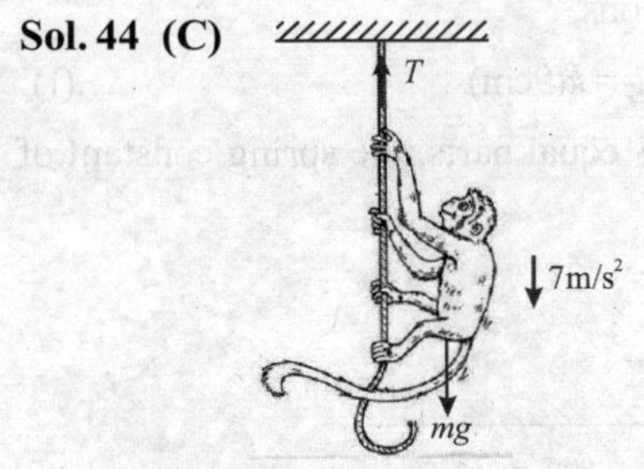

$$mg - T = ma$$

$$(20 \times 10) - T = (20 \times 7)$$

$$200 - 140 = T$$

$$T = 60\ N$$

Sol. 45 (A)

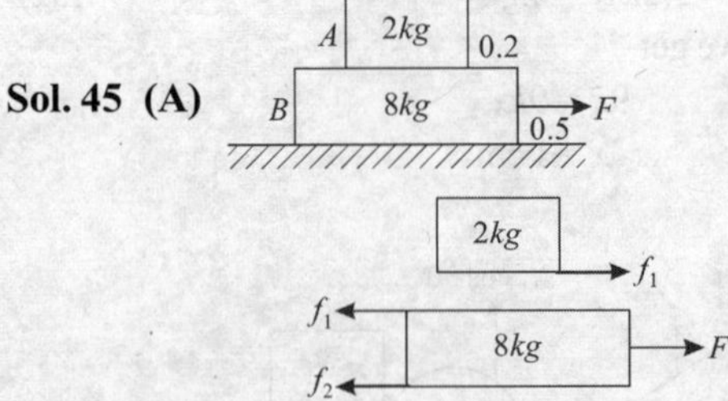

limiting friction between surfaces is

$$f_{1L} = 0.2 \times 2 \times 10 = 4\text{N}$$

$$f_{2L} = 0.5 \times (8 + 2) \times 10 = 50\text{N}$$

to slide the blocks $F > 50$

hence at $F = 25$ N blocks

will not slide so friction between A and B remain zero.

Sol. 46 (B) When man is sliding down we use

$$mg - \eta\, mg = ma$$

$$a = g(1-\eta)$$

Sol. 47 (D)

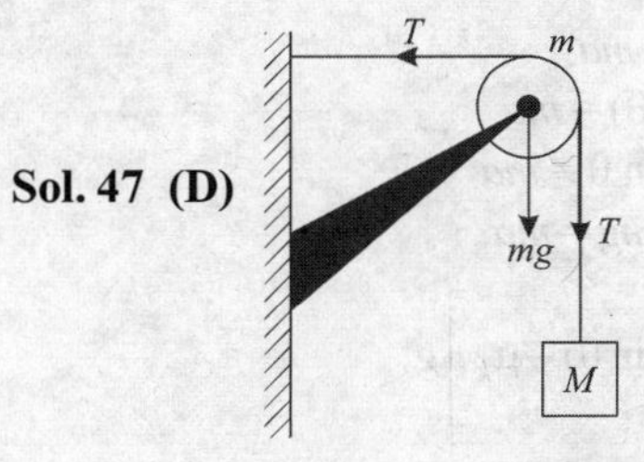

$$T = Mg$$

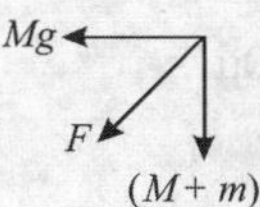

$$F = \sqrt{M^2g^2 + (M+m)^2g^2}$$

$$F = \left[\sqrt{M^2 + (M+m)^2}\right]g$$

Sol. 48 (C)

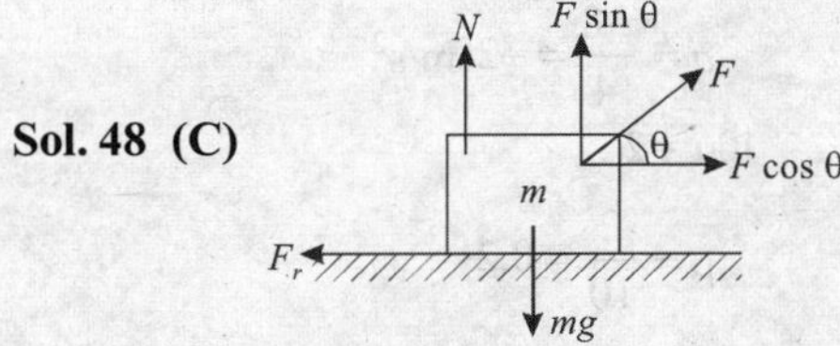

Force of friction $= F\cos 30°$ (since the block is at rest)

$$= \frac{\sqrt{3}F}{2}$$

Sol. 49 (B)

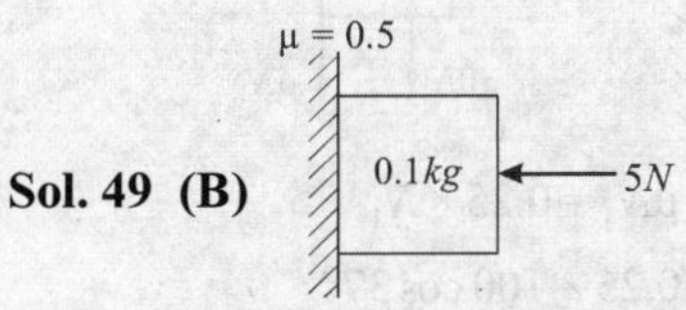

$$f_{max} = 0.5 \times 5 = 2.5\text{N}$$

$$W = 0.1 \times 9.8 = 0.98\text{N}$$

As block is held at rest, friction is given as

$$f = W = 0.98\text{N}$$

Sol. 50 (A) Let initial acceleration of system is '*a*'

$$f = ma$$

$$\mu mg = ma$$

$$a = 2\text{m/s}^2$$

$$kx - f = Ma$$

$$1000x - 2 = 4 \times 2$$

$$1000x = 10$$

$$x = \frac{1}{100}\text{m} = 1\text{cm}$$

Sol. 51 (C)

$$F = \frac{Gm_1m_2}{r^2}$$

$$1N = \frac{G(1kg)(1kg)}{1m^2}$$

$$G = 1\,\text{Nm}^2\text{kg}^{-2}$$

Sol. 52 (A)

$$T - W_1 = \frac{W_1}{g}(a+g) \quad \ldots(1)$$

$$W_2 - T = \frac{W_2}{g}(a-g) \quad \ldots(2)$$

Adding (1) and (2), we get

$$W_2 - W_1 = \frac{W_1a}{g} + W_1 + \frac{W_2a}{g} - W_2$$

$$2W_2 - 2W_1 = \frac{a}{g}(W_1 + W_2)$$

$$a = \frac{2(W_2 - W_1)}{W_2 + W_1}g$$

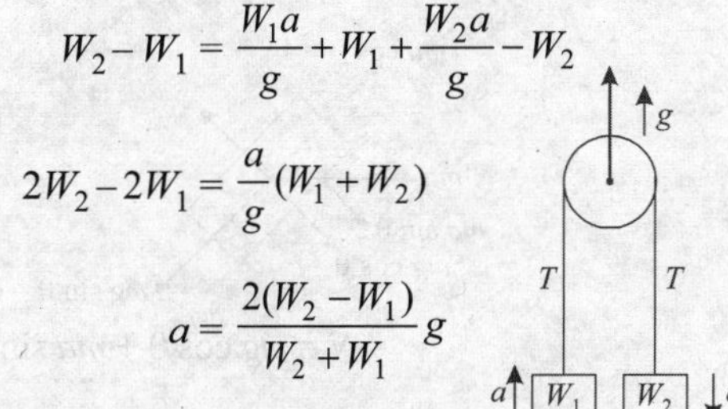

Substituting value of '*a*' in (1), we get

$$T = \frac{W_1a}{g} + 2W_1$$

$$T = 2W_1\left[\frac{W_2 - W_1}{W_1 + W_2}\right] + 2W_1$$

$$T = \frac{2W_1W_2 - 2W_1^2 + 2W_1^2 + 2W_1W_2}{W_1 + W_2}$$

$$T = \frac{4W_1W_2}{W_1 + W_2}$$

Sol. 53 (D)

acceleration of blocks is $a = \frac{5g - 4g}{9} = \frac{g}{9}$

For 1kg block we use $T_2 - g = \dfrac{g}{9}$

$\Rightarrow \qquad T_2 = \dfrac{10g}{9}$

Sol. 54 (C)

F_1 → ← F_2, F_r ←

$$F_1 = F_2 + F_r$$
$$10 = 2 + F_r$$
$$F_r = 8\text{N (left)}$$

If F_1 is removed, the frictional force is acting opposite to applied force of $2N$ and this will be balanced so block will remain at rest and net force on it will be zero.

Sol. 55 (C)

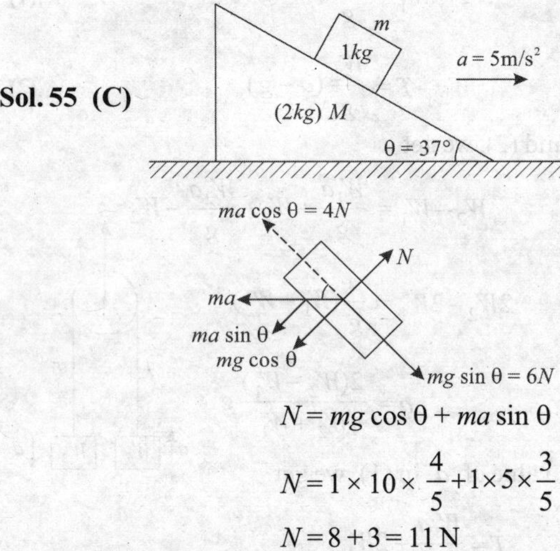

$$N = mg\cos\theta + ma\sin\theta$$
$$N = 1\times 10\times\frac{4}{5} + 1\times 5\times\frac{3}{5}$$
$$N = 8 + 3 = 11\text{ N}$$

As we have $\qquad mg\sin\theta > \text{ma}\cos\theta,$

The block cannot remain stationary w.r.t. wedge.

Acceleration of block w.r.t. wedge,

$$a = \frac{mg\sin\theta - ma\cos\theta}{m}$$
$$a = \frac{6-4}{1} = 2\text{ m/s}^2$$

Sol. 56 (D)

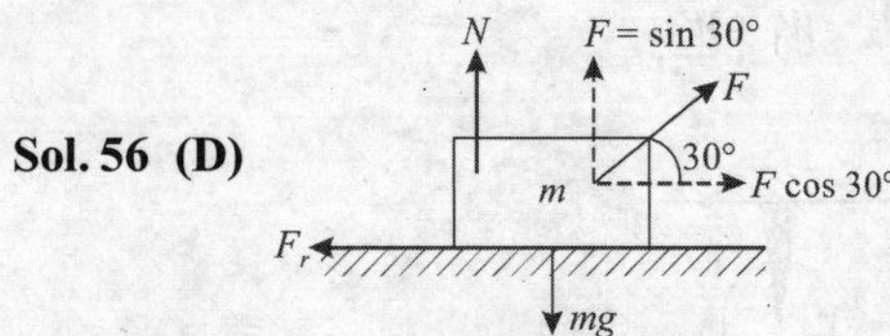

Let tension in string is F

$$F_r = \mu_s N$$
$$N + F\sin\theta = mg$$

$\Rightarrow \qquad N = mg - F\sin\theta \qquad \ldots(1)$

to start sliding $\qquad F\cos\theta = F_r = \mu_s N$

$$F\cos\theta = \mu_s(mg - F\sin\theta)$$

$\Rightarrow \qquad F\cos\theta = \mu_s mg - \mu_s F\sin\theta$

$\Rightarrow \qquad F(\cos\theta + \mu_s\sin\theta) = \mu_s mg$

$\Rightarrow \qquad F = \dfrac{\mu_s mg}{\cos\theta + \mu_s\sin\theta}$

Sol. 57 (B) $F\cos\theta - \mu_k N = ma$

$F\cos\theta - \mu_k(mg - F\sin\theta) = ma$

$\Rightarrow F\cos\theta - \mu_k mg + \mu_k F\sin\theta = ma$

$\Rightarrow F(\cos\theta + \mu_k\sin\theta) - \mu_k mg = ma$

$\Rightarrow a = \left[\left(\dfrac{F}{mg}\right)(\cos\theta + \mu_k\sin\theta) - \mu_k\right]g$

Sol. 58 (B) $\qquad a = \dfrac{f}{m} = \dfrac{\mu(20)}{2} = 10\mu$

From $v - t$ graph,

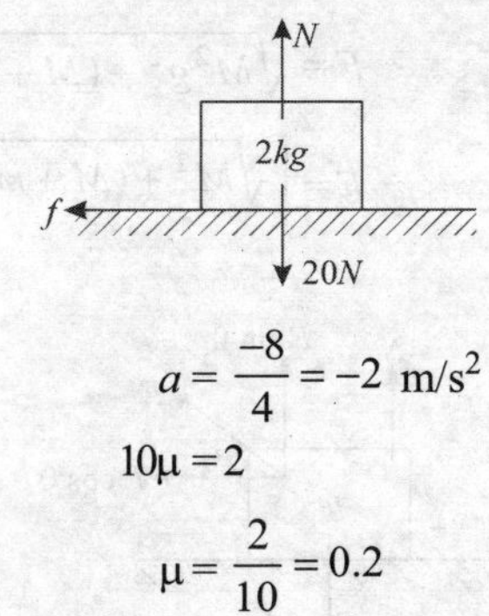

$$a = \frac{-8}{4} = -2\text{ m/s}^2$$
$$10\mu = 2$$
$$\mu = \frac{2}{10} = 0.2$$

Sol. 59 (C)

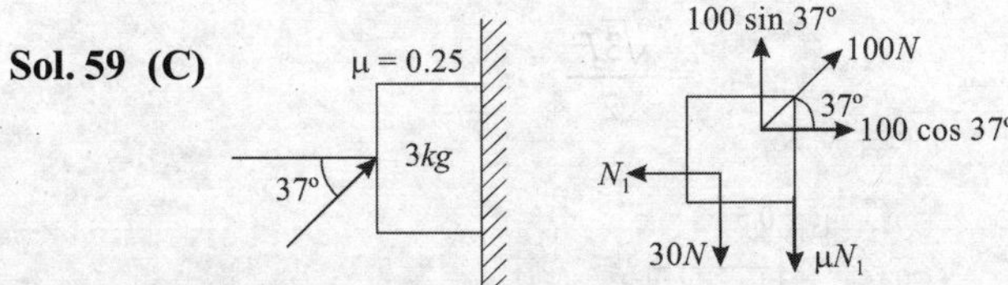

Limiting friction force $\qquad = \mu N_1 = 0.25\times N_1$

$\qquad = 0.25\times 100\cos 37°$

$\qquad = 25\times\dfrac{4}{5} = 20\text{N}$

upward sliding force $\qquad = 100\sin 37° = 100\times\dfrac{3}{5} = 60\text{N}$

net upward force $\qquad = 60 - 30 = 30\text{N}$

This is more than 20N so block will slide up and friction will be 20N downward.

Sol. 60 (C)

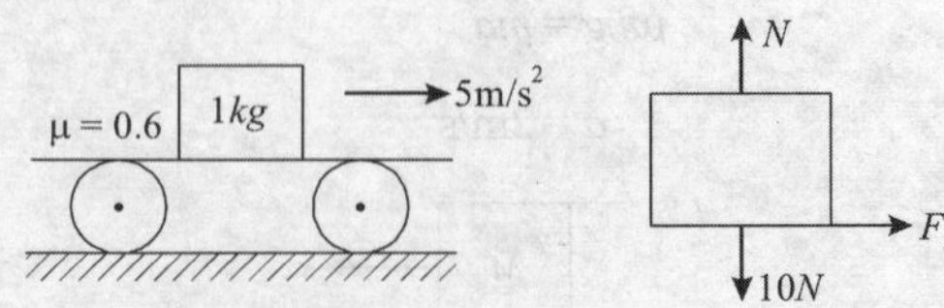

Since there is no slipping,

Frictional force, $F_r = ma$

$= 1 \times 5 = 5\text{N}$

Sol. 61 (B)

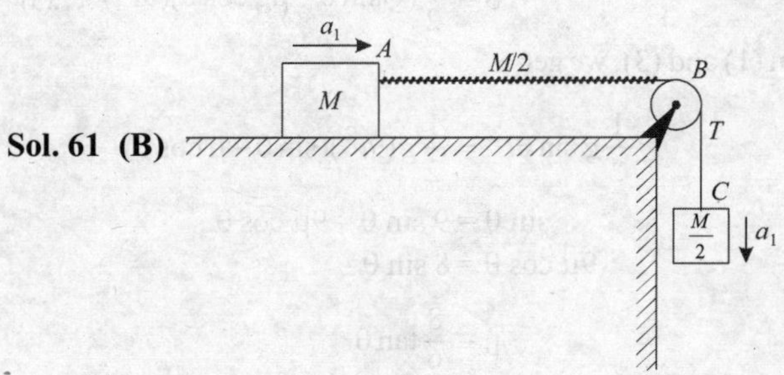

Initial acceleration is $a_1 = \dfrac{\left(\dfrac{Mg}{2}\right)}{M + \dfrac{M}{2} + \dfrac{M}{2}} = \dfrac{g}{4}$

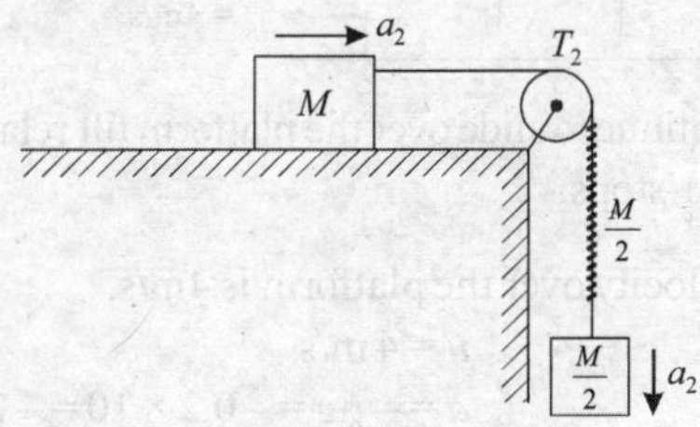

Final acceleration is $a_f = \dfrac{Mg}{M + \dfrac{M}{2} + \dfrac{M}{2}} = \dfrac{g}{2}$

Sol. 62 (D)

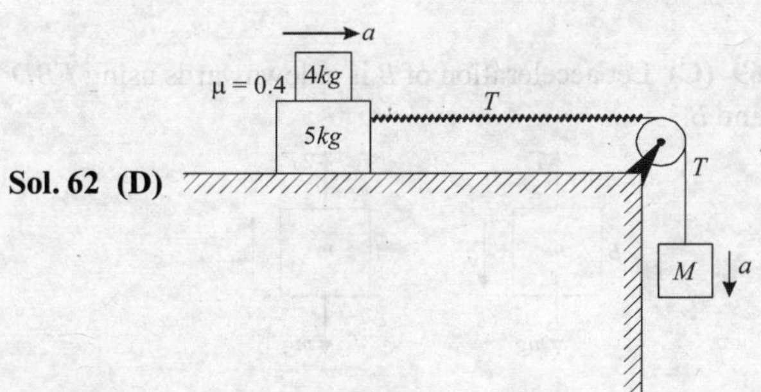

Common acceleration of system is

$$a = \frac{Mg}{M+9}$$

for 4kg block we use $f = 4a = \dfrac{4Mg}{M+9}$

to slide $f = 0.4 \times 4 \times 10$

$= 16\text{N}$

$\Rightarrow \dfrac{4Mg}{M+9} = 16$

$\Rightarrow 40M = 16M + 144$

$\Rightarrow M = 6 \text{ kg}$

Sol. 63 (A)

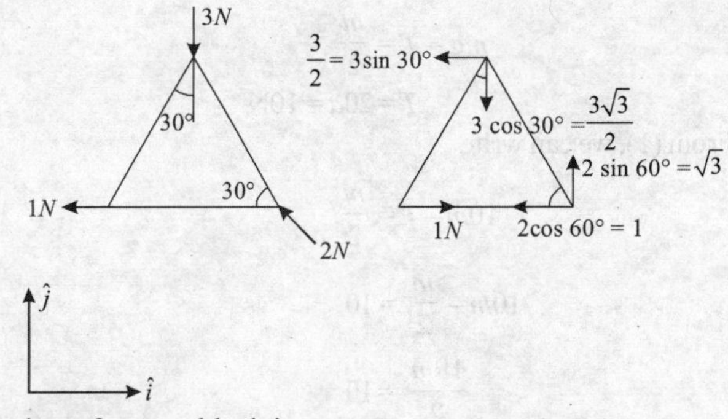

Resultant force on block is,

$$\vec{F} = 1\hat{i} - 1\hat{j} - \frac{3}{2}\hat{i} + \sqrt{3}\hat{j} - \frac{3\sqrt{3}}{2}\hat{j}$$

$$\vec{F} = \frac{-3}{2}\hat{i} - \frac{\sqrt{3}}{2}\hat{j}$$

$$|\vec{F}| = \sqrt{\frac{9}{4} + \frac{3}{4}} = \sqrt{\frac{12}{4}} = \sqrt{3}\text{ N}$$

Sol. 64 (B) Let length of beam is 'l', and the two pans are at a distance of 'x' and '$l - x$' from the hinged point. If true weight of body is A, then

$$Ax = 6(l - x) \quad \ldots(1)$$

$$A(1 - x) = 24x \quad \ldots(2)$$

Dividing (1) by (2), we get

$$\frac{6}{A} = \frac{A}{24}$$

$$A^2 = 144$$

$$A = 12\text{gm}$$

Sol. 65 (D) The block strikes the floor after 2s

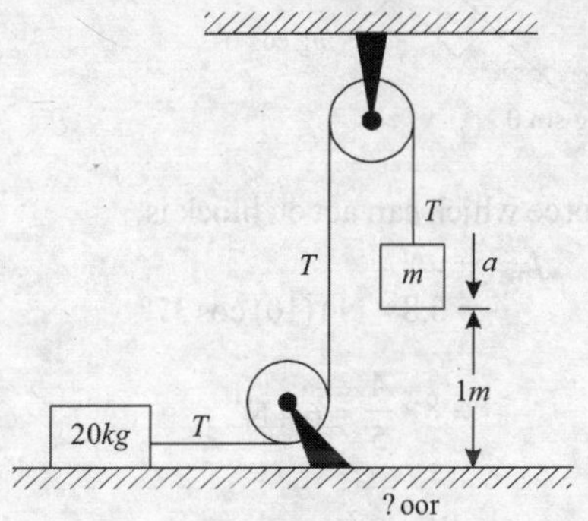

Using $s = ut + \dfrac{1}{2}at^2$

$$1 = \frac{1}{2} \times a(2)^2$$

$$1 = \frac{1}{2} \times a \times 4$$

$$a = \frac{1}{2} \text{ m/s}^2$$

$$mg - T = ma$$

$$mg - T = \frac{m}{2} \quad \text{...(1)}$$

$$T = 20a = 10\text{N}$$

From (1), we can write

$$10m - T = \frac{m}{2}$$

$$10m - \frac{m}{2} = 10$$

$$\frac{19m}{2} = 10$$

$$m = \frac{20}{19}\text{ kg}$$

Weight of hanging block,

$$w = mg$$

$$w = \frac{200}{19}\text{ N}$$

$$w = 10.53\text{N}$$

Sol. 66 (D)

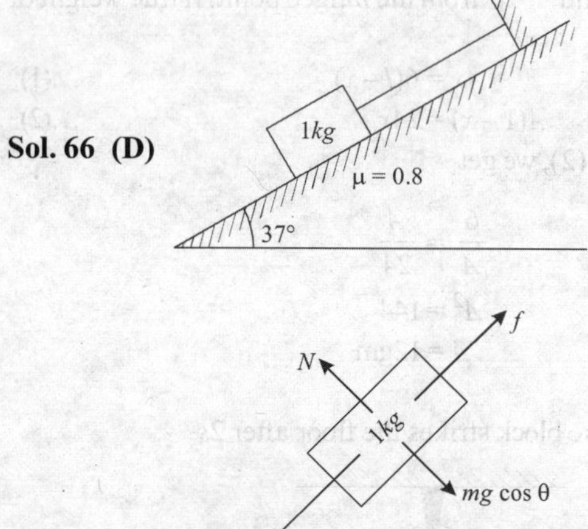

Maximum friction force which can act on block is,

$$f_{max} = \mu N$$

$$= 0.8 \times (1)(10)\cos 37°$$

$$= 8 \times \frac{4}{5} = 6.4\text{N}$$

$$mg \sin\theta = 10 \times \frac{3}{5} = 6\text{N}$$

$\Rightarrow$ $mg \sin\theta < f_{max}$, the block will not slide at also no tension is required in string to hold it at rest.

Sol. 67 (B) Let time taken to slide down smooth inclined plane is 't'. If length of plane is S

$$S = \frac{1}{2}(g \sin\theta)t^2 \quad \text{...(1)}$$

When it slides on rough inclined plane,

$$S = \frac{1}{2}(g \sin\theta - \mu g \cos\theta)(3t)^2 \quad \text{...(2)}$$

$$S = \frac{1}{2}(g \sin\theta - \mu g \cos\theta)(9t^2) \quad \text{...(3)}$$

From (1) and (3), we get

$$\frac{1}{2} g \sin\theta t^2 = \frac{1}{2} g(9t^2)(\sin\theta - \mu\cos\theta)$$

$$\sin\theta = 9\sin\theta - 9\mu\cos\theta$$

$$9\mu\cos\theta = 8\sin\theta$$

$$\mu = \frac{8}{9}\tan\theta$$

$$\mu = \frac{8}{9}\tan 45° = \frac{8}{9}$$

Sol. 68 (A)

μ = 0.2, m, M, v_0 = 4m/s

Block will continue to slide over the platform till relative slipping between them stops.

The initial velocity over the platform is 4m/s,

$$u = 4\text{ m/s}$$

$$a = -\mu g = -0.2 \times 10 = -2\text{m/s}^2$$

$$v = 0$$

$$s = ?$$

Using

$$v^2 = u^2 + 2as$$

$$0 = 16 - 2 \times 2 \times s$$

$$s = 4\text{m}$$

Sol. 69 (C) Let acceleration of B is a downwards using FBD of A and B

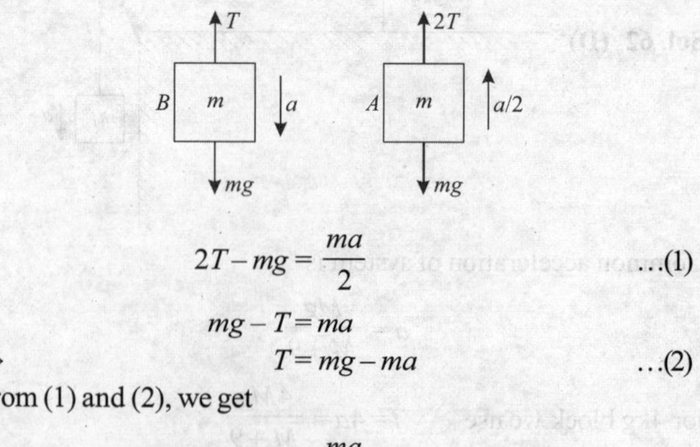

$$2T - mg = \frac{ma}{2} \quad \text{...(1)}$$

$$mg - T = ma$$

$\Rightarrow$

$$T = mg - ma \quad \text{...(2)}$$

From (1) and (2), we get

$$2mg - 2ma - mg = \frac{ma}{2}$$

$$mg = \frac{5ma}{2}$$

$$a = \frac{2g}{5}$$

Sol. 70 (A)

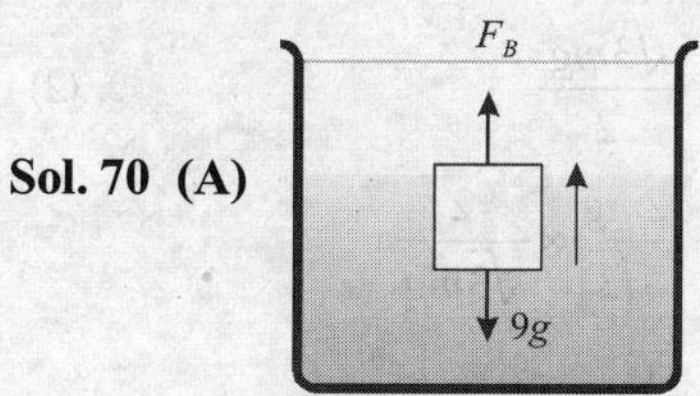

If F_B is upward buoyant force on block we use

$$F_B - 9g = \frac{9g}{3}$$
$$F_B = 9g + 3g$$
$$F_B = 12g \quad \ldots(1)$$

When sand of mass 'm' is put inside box

$$(9+m)g - F_B = (9+m)\frac{g}{4}$$
$$(9+m)g - 12g = (9+m)\frac{g}{4}$$
$$9+m-12 = \frac{9+m}{4}$$
$$4(m-3) = 9+m$$
$$4m - 12 = 9+m$$
$$3m = 21$$
$$m = 7 \text{ kg}$$

Sol. 71 (B)

$$N = ma$$
$$f_{max} = \mu N = mg$$
$$\mu ma = mg$$
$$a = \frac{g}{\mu}$$

Sol. 72 (C)

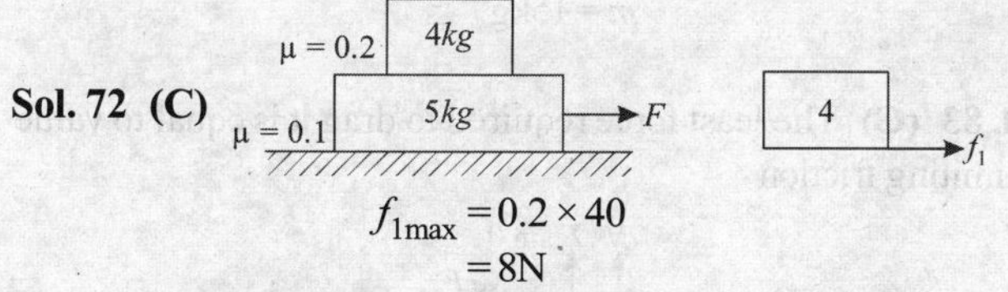

$$f_{1max} = 0.2 \times 40$$
$$= 8\text{N}$$

Maximum acceleration of 4kg block

$$= \frac{f_{1max}}{4kg}$$
$$= 2\text{m/s}^2$$

Sol. 73 (C)

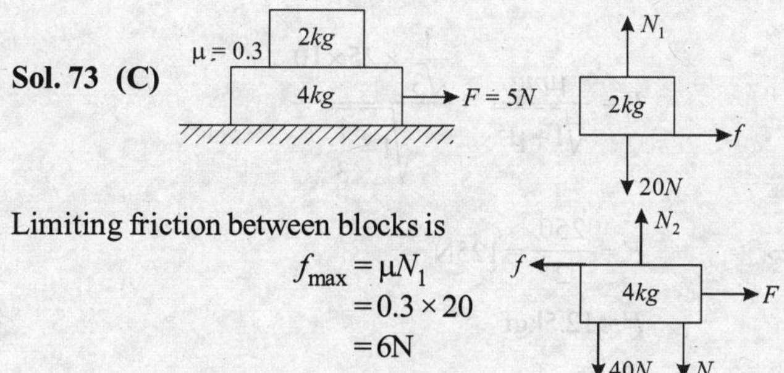

Limiting friction between blocks is

$$f_{max} = \mu N_1$$
$$= 0.3 \times 20$$
$$= 6\text{N}$$

To start sliding between blocks we use

$$f_{max} = 2\left(\frac{F}{6}\right) = 6 \Rightarrow F = 18\text{N}$$

$\Rightarrow$ at $F = 15$ N both blocks move together at $a = \frac{F}{6} = \frac{5}{2}$ m/s²

$$\Rightarrow f = 2a = 2 \times \frac{5}{2} = 5\text{N}$$

Sol. 74 (B) Initially, mass on the right,

$$M_1 = m_1 + m_2$$

On removing the clamp, total mass on right side should be equal to $\frac{2T}{g}$, where T = tension in the string

$$M_2 = \frac{2T}{g} = \frac{4m_1m_2}{m_1+m_2}$$

Change in mass, $\Delta M = M_2 - M_1$

$$= \frac{4m_1m_2}{m_1+m_2} - (m_1+m_2)$$
$$= \frac{4m_1m_2 - m_1^2 - m_2^2 - 2m_1m_2}{(m_1+m_2)}$$
$$= \frac{-(m_1-m_2)^2}{m_1+m_2}$$

Negative sign shows that this mass has to be removed from right side

Sol. 75 (B) Acceleration of system,

$$a = \frac{P}{m_A + m_B}$$

$$a = \frac{10}{2+3} = \frac{10}{5} = 2\text{m/s}^2$$
$$P - F_{AB} = m_A a$$
$$10 - F_{AB} = 2 \times 2$$
$$F_{AB} = 6\text{N}$$

Sol. 76 (A) The force of friction between the blocks can be in vertical direction only. Since there is no net force or acceleration in this direction, force of interaction between the blocks is zero in all the cases.

Sol. 77 (C)

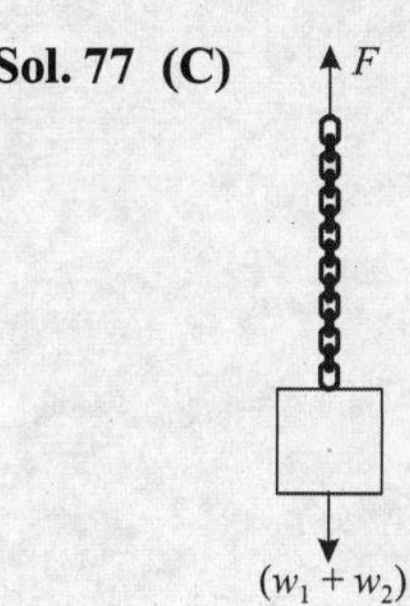

As chain is in equilibrium

$$F = w_1 + w_2$$

Sol. 78 (A)

Let mass of rope is M

Acceleration of system, $a = \dfrac{F}{m}$

Tension at a distance x from the end,

$$T = \frac{(y-x)Ma}{y}$$

$$T = \frac{(y-x)}{y} M \cdot \frac{F}{M} = \frac{(y-x)F}{y}$$

Sol. 79 (D) Friction force acting on block

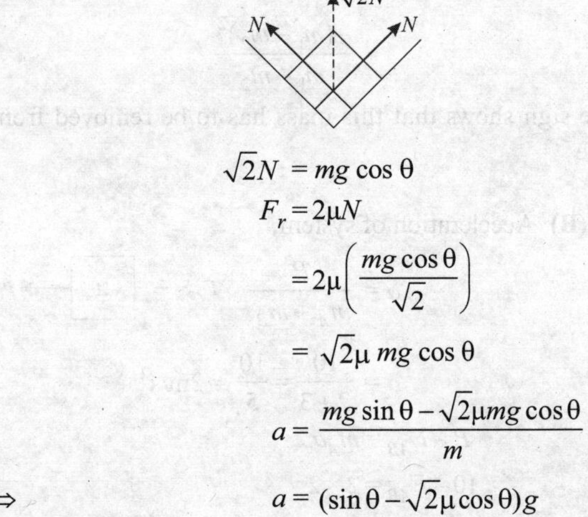

$$\sqrt{2}N = mg\cos\theta$$

$$F_r = 2\mu N$$

$$= 2\mu\left(\frac{mg\cos\theta}{\sqrt{2}}\right)$$

$$= \sqrt{2}\mu\, mg\cos\theta$$

$$a = \frac{mg\sin\theta - \sqrt{2}\mu mg\cos\theta}{m}$$

$$\Rightarrow \quad a = (\sin\theta - \sqrt{2}\mu\cos\theta)g$$

Sol. 80 (B) In initial position

$$\frac{T_1}{\sin 90^\circ} = \frac{mg}{\sin 120^\circ}$$

$$\Rightarrow \quad T_1 = \frac{2mg}{\sqrt{3}} \quad \ldots(1)$$

After string is cut, at position B

$$T_2 = mg\cos 30^\circ$$

$$T_2 = \frac{\sqrt{3}mg}{2} \quad \ldots(2)$$

$$\Rightarrow \quad \frac{T_1}{T_2} = \frac{2mg}{\sqrt{3}} \times \frac{2}{\sqrt{3}mg}$$

$$\Rightarrow \quad \frac{T_1}{T_2} = \frac{4}{3}$$

$$\Rightarrow \quad \frac{T_2}{T_1} = \frac{3}{4}$$

Sol. 81 (A) $W = mg = 400\text{ N}$

$$\Rightarrow \quad m = 40\text{ kg}$$

$$mg + ma = 600\text{ N}$$

(when he jumps up with acceleration 'a')

$$40a = 200$$

$$\Rightarrow \quad a = 5\text{ ms}^{-2}$$

Sol. 82 (A)

$$T = 60\text{ N} \quad \ldots(1)$$

$T = \mu N$ (To prevent A from moving)

$$T = \mu(50 + 10m)$$

$$\Rightarrow \quad \mu(50 + 10m) = 60$$

$$\Rightarrow \quad 50 + 10m = \frac{60}{0.3} = 200$$

$$\Rightarrow \quad m = 15\text{kg}$$

Sol. 83 (C) The least force required to drag it is equal to value of limiting friction

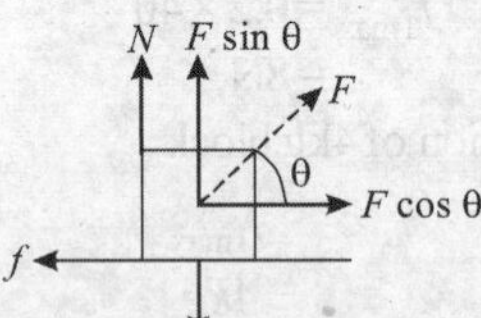

Minimum force is applied at an angle θ, such that $\theta = \tan^{-1}\mu$ and the minimum value of force is

$$F = \frac{\mu mg}{\sqrt{1+\mu^2}} = \frac{\frac{1}{\sqrt{3}} \times 25 \times 10}{\sqrt{1+\frac{1}{3}}}$$

$$\Rightarrow \quad F = \frac{250}{2} = 125\text{N}$$

$$F = 12.5\text{kgf}$$

Sol. 84 (D)

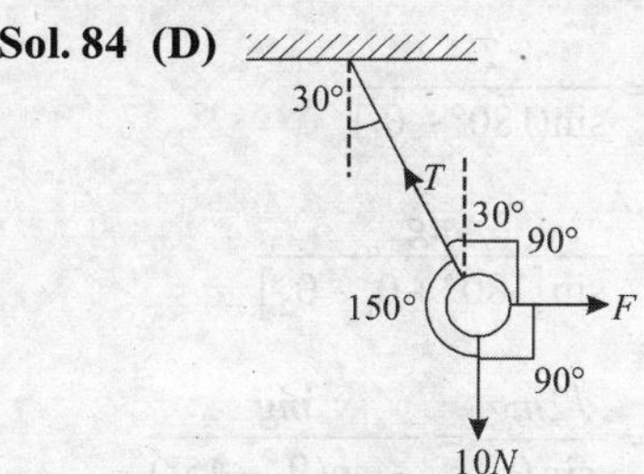

For equilibrium of particle

$$\frac{mg}{\sin 120°} = \frac{F}{\sin 150°}$$

$$\Rightarrow \quad F = \frac{0.5\times 10}{\frac{\sqrt{3}}{2}} = \frac{10}{\sqrt{3}}\,\text{N}$$

Sol. 85 (A) Speed of plane = 720 km/h = 200 m/s

$$a = \frac{v^2}{r}$$

$$r = \frac{v^2}{a} = \frac{(200)^2}{9g-g} = \frac{40000}{8\times 10}$$

$$r = 500\,\text{m}$$

Sol. 86 (B)

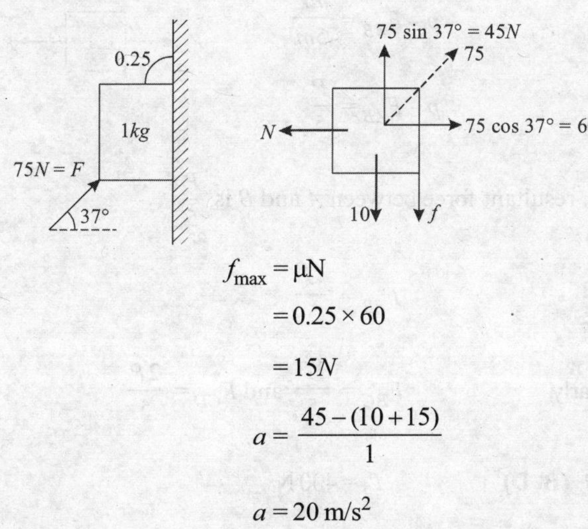

$$f_{max} = \mu N$$

$$= 0.25\times 60$$

$$= 15N$$

$$a = \frac{45-(10+15)}{1}$$

$$a = 20\,\text{m/s}^2$$

Sol. 87 (A) Both the scales will read 10 kg as tension in ideal balances connected in series remain same.

Sol. 88 (A) Since the rods are rigid and particles are attached to vertices, resultant force on A is zero.

Sol. 89 (B)

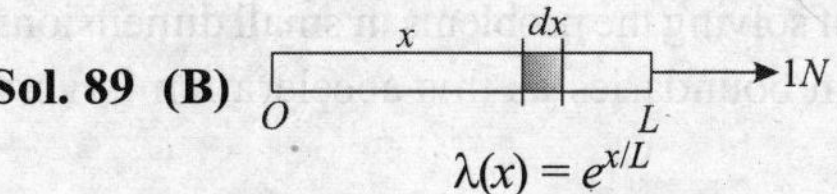

$$\lambda(x) = e^{x/L}$$

Total mass of rope, $M = \int_0^L \lambda(x)dx$

$$M = \int_0^L e^{x/L}dx$$

$$M = L\left[e^{x/L}\right]_0^L = L(e-1)$$

Acceleration of rope, $a = \frac{F}{M} = \frac{1}{L(e-1)}$

Mass of rope from 0 to $L/2$ is

$$m = L\left[e^{x/L}\right]_0^{L/2}$$

$$m = L(e^{1/2}-1)$$

$$T = ma$$

$$T = L(e^{1/2}-1)\times\frac{1}{L(e-1)}$$

$$\Rightarrow \quad T = \frac{\sqrt{2.7}-1}{2.7-1} = 0.38\,\text{N}$$

Sol. 90 (C)

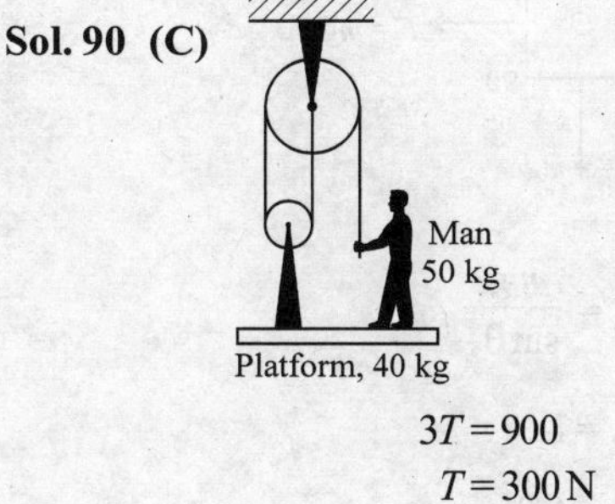

$$3T = 900$$

$$T = 300\,\text{N}$$

ADVANCE MCQs One or More Option Correct

Sol. 1 (C, D) Perpendicular force never changes the magnitude of velocity so its kinetic energy will remain constant and if at uniform speed force is acting in normal direction, motion of particle must be in circular path.

Sol. 2 (B, D) As Earth is rotating about its own axis as well as revolving around Sun, its motion has two accelerations so it is not an inertial reference frame.

Important : Actually Earth is a non inertial reference frame but on Earth due to its low acceleration we can apply Newton's

Laws for simplicity of solving the problems in small dimensions of bodies and system boundaries as this acceleration is very small.

Sol. 3 (A, C) When bicycle is accelerating then due to the external paddling force the rear wheel rotates in such a way that friction acts on it in forward direction which is the driving force on bicycle. Front wheel is pushed due to the frame of bicycle which is attached at the axle of the front wheel so friction on it is in backward direction to oppose the motion. When no paddling is done then friction on both wheels will act in backward direction. So options (A) and (C) are correct for these two cases.

Sol. 4 (A, B, C, D) As friction on car is acting in forward direction and that on plank is acting in backward direction it will tend to impart acceleration to both bodies which will be inversely proportional to their masses and string will maintain their acceleration equal by tension if acceleration of car is less than that of plank in absence of string otherwise string will become slack.

Sol. 5 (A, B, C, D) $\dfrac{mg}{\sin(90°+\theta_2)} = \dfrac{T_2}{\sin 90°} = \dfrac{mg}{\sin(180°-\theta_2)}$

Comparing I and III terms, we get

$$\frac{mg}{\cos\theta_2} = \frac{mg}{\sin\theta_2}$$

$$\tan\theta_2 = 1$$

$$\Rightarrow \quad \theta_2 = 45°$$

Comparing I and II terms,

$$\frac{mg}{\cos 45°} = T_2$$

$$T_2 = \sqrt{2}mg$$

$$\frac{T_1}{\sin\theta_2} = \frac{T_2}{\sin(180°-\theta_1)}$$

$$= \frac{mg}{\sin[180°+\theta_1-\theta_2]}$$

$$\sqrt{2}T_1 = \frac{\sqrt{2}mg}{\sin\theta_1} = \frac{mg}{-\sin(\theta_1-45°)}$$

Comparing II and III terms,

$$\frac{-\sqrt{2}}{\sin\theta_1} = \frac{1}{\dfrac{\sin\theta_1}{\sqrt{2}} - \dfrac{\cos\theta_1}{\sqrt{2}}}$$

$$-\sin\theta_1 + \cos\theta_1 = \sin\theta_1$$

$$2\sin\theta_1 = \cos\theta_1$$

$$\tan\theta_1 = \frac{1}{2}$$

$$\Rightarrow \quad \sin\theta_1 = \frac{1}{\sqrt{5}}$$

$$T_1 = \frac{mg}{\dfrac{1}{\sqrt{5}}} = \sqrt{5}\,mg$$

$$T_1 = \sqrt{5}\,mg$$

Sol. 6 (B, C) Acceleration of system $= \dfrac{P}{5m}$

$$p - F_{AB} = \frac{mP}{5m}$$

$$p - F_{AB} = \frac{P}{5}$$

Thus, resultant force between A and B is $\dfrac{P}{5}$

$$F_{AB} = \frac{4P}{5}$$

Similarly, $\quad F_{BC} = \dfrac{3P}{5}$ and $F_{CD} = \dfrac{2P}{5}$

Sol. 7 (B, D) $\quad T_2 = 400\text{ N}$

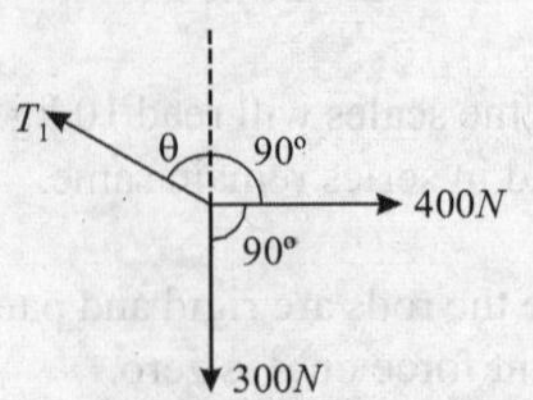

$$\frac{300}{\sin(90+\theta)} = \frac{T_1}{\sin 90^\circ} = \frac{400}{\sin(180-\theta)}$$

$$\frac{300}{\cos\theta} = T_1 = \frac{400}{\sin\theta}$$

$$\tan\theta = \frac{4}{3}$$

$\Rightarrow$ $\theta = 53^\circ$

$$T_1 = \frac{400}{\sin 53^\circ} = 500\text{ N}$$

Sol. 8 (B, C)

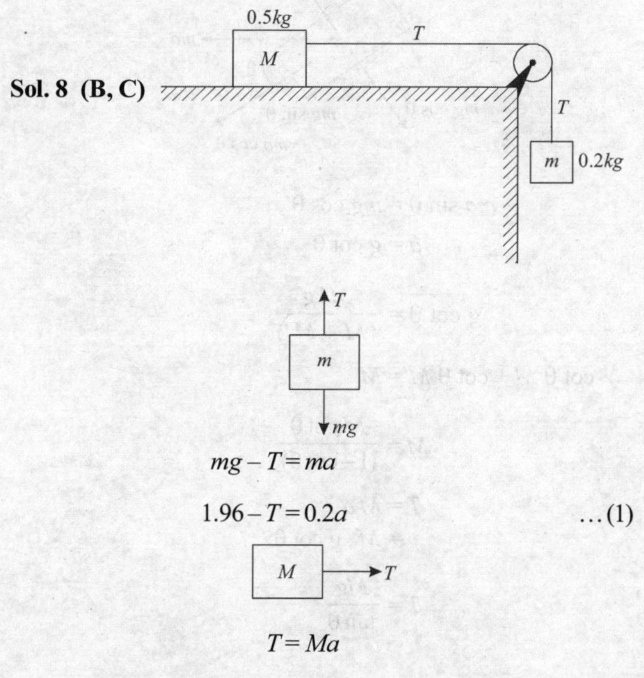

$$mg - T = ma$$

$$1.96 - T = 0.2a \qquad \ldots(1)$$

$$T = Ma$$

$$T = 0.5a \qquad \ldots(2)$$

From (1) and (2),

$$1.96 - 0.5a = 0.2a$$

$$a = 2.8\text{ m/s}^2$$

For block of mass m,

Let block comes to rest in t seconds,

$$0 = 7 - 2.8t$$

$$t = 2.5\text{ s}$$

Distance covered during this time,

$$s = 7(2.5) - \frac{1}{2}(2.8)(2.5)^2$$

$$s = 17.5 - 8.75$$

$$s = 8.75\text{ m}$$

Thus, in 5 seconds, it will be in its same position and distance covered by it

$$D = s + s = 17.5\text{ m}$$

Sol. 9 (A, D)

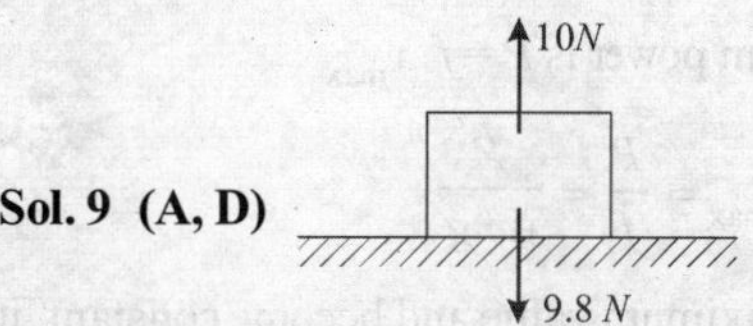

By Newton's III law,

The block exerts a force of 10N on the table and the reaction of which is also 10N

The block has upward acceleration.

Sol. 10 (A, B, C)

$$f_{1\max} = 0.2 \times 10 \times 10$$

$$= 20\text{N}$$

As $f_{1\max} < P$, friction force

$f_1 = 15$N and block do not move

When both P and Q acts, resultant applied force,

$$R = \sqrt{P^2 + Q^2} = \sqrt{15^2 + 20^2}$$

$$= \sqrt{625} = 25\text{ N}$$

$R > f_{1\max}$, thus block moves when both P and Q acts

$$a = \frac{R - f_{1\max}}{m}$$

$$= \frac{25 - 20}{10} = \frac{5}{10} = 0.5\text{ m/s}^2$$

Direction of $\vec{R}$, $\tan\theta = \frac{15}{20} = \frac{3}{4}$

$$\theta = \tan^{-1}\frac{3}{4} \qquad \text{(east of north)}$$

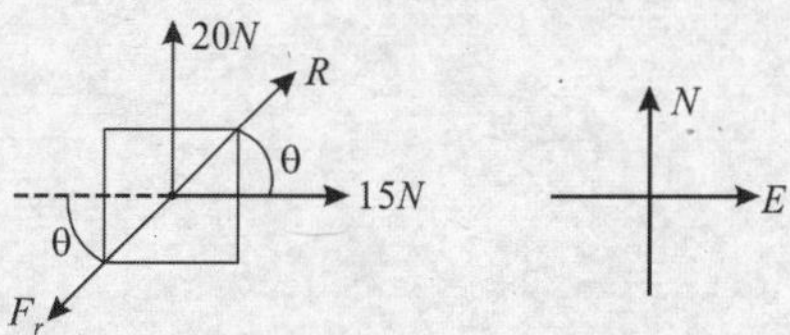

Thus, direction of force of friction (F_r) will be opposite to R, i.e. west of south.

Sol. 11 (B, C) As the system is in free fall centre of mass of system will fall at g and on upper block net downward force is $2mg$ (own weight + spring force) hence its initial acceleration is $2g$.

Sol. 12 (A, C) Maximum power is $P = f \cdot v_{max}$

$$\Rightarrow \quad v_{max} = \frac{P}{f} = \frac{P}{\mu mg}$$

As speed increases to maximum value and become constant, it does not change as long as constant power is being supplied by force.

Sol. 13 (A, D) $T\cos\theta_0 = mg$ ...(i)

$T\sin\theta_0 = mg_0$ ...(ii)

(ii)/(i) $\tan\theta_0 = \dfrac{a}{g}$

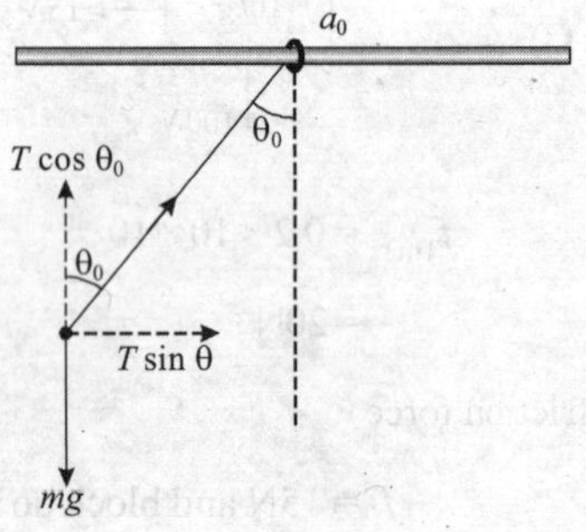

$\theta_0 = 30°$

$$T = \frac{mg}{\cos 30°} = \frac{2mg}{\sqrt{3}}$$

Sol. 14 (A, B, D) The particle experiences two forces in the ground frame

(i) mg (vertically down)

(ii) N (which is perpendicular to the groove)

If it falls vertically in ground frame

$N = 0$ and $a_{PG} = g$

Sol. 15 (A, B, C) As $m_1 g \sin 30° = m_2 g = T$, no friction will act on m_1 so $T = 20$ N and net contact force on m_1 is the normal reaction by ground which is $m_1 g \cos 30° = 20\sqrt{3}\ N$

Sol. 16 (A, C) $M'g - T = M'a$

$T = Ma$

$M'g = a(M + M')$

$$a = \frac{M'g}{(M+M')}$$

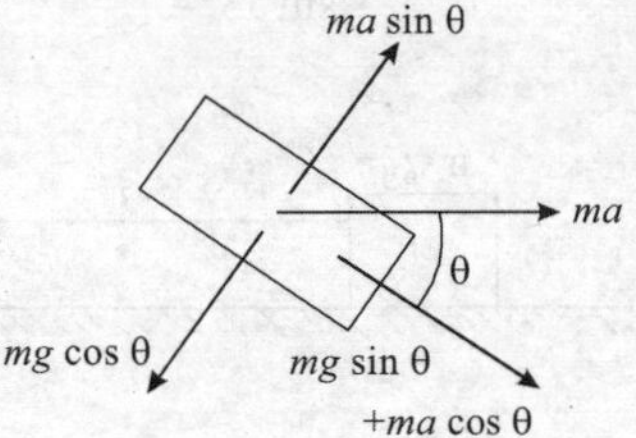

$$ma\sin\theta = mg\cos\theta$$

$$a = g\cot\theta$$

$$g\cot\theta = \frac{M'g}{(M+M')}$$

$$\cot\theta\, M + \cot\theta\, M' = M'$$

$$M = \frac{M\cot\theta}{(1-\cot\theta)}$$

$$T = Ma$$

$$= M \cdot g\cot\theta$$

$$T = \frac{Mg}{\tan\theta}$$

Sol. 17 (A, C) $Mg - T = Ma$ ...(i)

$T = ma$ ...(ii)

Solving (i) and (ii) $\quad a = \dfrac{Mg}{(M+m)}$

FBD of man $\quad Mg - N = Ma$

$$N = \frac{Mmg}{(M+m)}$$

N

a

Mg

* * * * *

ANSWERS & SOLUTIONS

CONCEPTUAL MCQS Single Option Correct

1	(B)	**2**	(A)	**3**	(A)
4	(D)	**5**	(C)	**6**	(B)
7	(C)	**8**	(A)	**9**	(C)
10	(D)	**11**	(C)	**12**	(C)
13	(A)	**14**	(D)	**15**	(A)
16	(A)	**17**	(A)	**18**	(A)
19	(C)	**20**	(A)	**21**	(B)
22	(C)	**23**	(D)	**24**	(A)
25	(A)	**26**	(B)	**27**	(C)
28	(A)	**29**	(C)	**30**	(C)
31	(C)	**32**	(D)	**33**	(B)
34	(B)	**35**	(A)	**36**	(A)
37	(A)				

NUMERICAL MCQS Single Option Correct

1	(B)	**2**	(C)	**3**	(A)
4	(A)	**5**	(A)	**6**	(A)
7	(D)	**8**	(A)	**9**	(C)
10	(B)	**11**	(D)	**12**	(C)
13	(D)	**14**	(C)	**15**	(C)
16	(D)	**17**	(C)	**18**	(B)
19	(D)	**20**	(D)	**21**	(A)
22	(B)	**23**	(B)	**24**	(C)
25	(A)	**26**	(C)	**27**	(D)
28	(A)	**29**	(B)	**30**	(B)
31	(A)	**32**	(A)	**33**	(D)
34	(D)	**35**	(A)	**36**	(D)
37	(B)	**38**	(D)	**39**	(B)
40	(D)	**41**	(A)	**42**	(A)
43	(A)	**44**	(C)	**45**	(A)
46	(D)	**47**	(B)	**48**	(B)
49	(C)	**50**	(D)	**51**	(C)
52	(C)	**53**	(C)	**54**	(C)
55	(C)	**56**	(B)	**57**	(C)
58	(A)	**59**	(A)	**60**	(C)
61	(D)	**62**	(A)	**63**	(B)
64	(B)	**65**	(C)	**66**	(A)
67	(D)	**68**	(B)	**69**	(B)
70	(C)	**71**	(A)	**72**	(A)
73	(B)	**74**	(B)	**75**	(B)
76	(A)	**77**	(C)	**78**	(C)
79	(B)	**80**	(B)	**81**	(D)
82	(D)	**83**	(A)	**84**	(C)
85	(C)	**86**	(A)	**87**	(B)
88	(D)	**89**	(B)	**90**	(C)
91	(A)	**92**	(A)	**93**	(B)
94	(A)	**95**	(D)	**96**	(D)
97	(A)	**98**	(A)	**99**	(B)
100	(A)	**101**	(A)		

ADVANCE MCQs One or More Option Correct

1	(B, C, D)	**2**	(B, C, D)	**3**	(A, B)
4	(B, D)	**5**	(B, C, D)	**6**	(A, D)
7	(B, C)	**8**	(B, C)	**9**	(B, D)
10	(A, C)	**11**	(A, B, D)	**12**	(B, C)
13	(A, B, C)	**14**	(C, D)	**15**	(A, D)
16	(A, D)	**17**	(A, C)	**18**	(A, C)
19	(B, C)	**20**	(A, C)	**21**	(B, C)

Solutions of PRACTICE EXERCISE 3.1

(i) (a) To slide the block,

$$F\cos 30° > \mu(mg + F\sin 30°)$$

$$F > \frac{\mu mg}{\cos 30° - \mu \sin 30°}$$

$$= \frac{0.3\times 25\times 10}{\frac{\sqrt{3}}{2} - 0.3\times\frac{1}{3}} = 104.74\text{N}$$

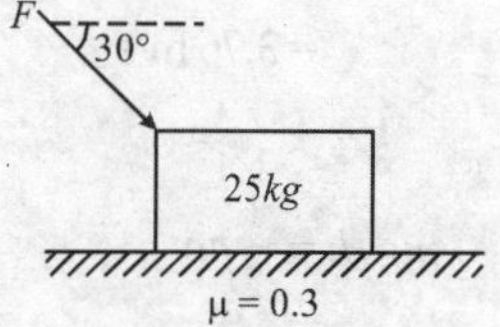

(b) Work done $= F\cos 30° \times 6$

$= 544.27J$

(c) Work done by friction is

$$w_f = -\text{work done by worker} = -544.27\text{J}$$

(d) As no displacement of block in vertical direction

$$w_N = w_{Mg} = 0$$

(e) As no gain in *KE* because of balanced forces acting on crate

$$w_{\text{total}} = 0$$

(ii) $w = mgh = 55 \times 10 \times 3 = 1650J$

(iii) $w = \Delta U = \frac{1}{2}kx^2 = \frac{1}{2}(kx)(x) = \frac{1}{2}Fx = \frac{1}{2}\times 20\times 0.05$

$= 0.5J$

(iv) Given that

$$46 = \frac{1}{2}k_1(0.12)^2$$

$$\Rightarrow \quad k_1 = \frac{2\times 46}{0.144} = 638.89\text{ N/m}$$

and

$$270 = \frac{1}{2}k_2(0.27)^2$$

$$\Rightarrow \quad k_2 = \frac{2\times 270}{(0.27)^2} = 7407.4\text{ N/m}$$

Here $$\frac{k_1}{k_2} \neq \frac{x_1}{x_2}$$

$\Rightarrow$ k does not very linearly with x

(v) $$w = \int F dx = \int_0^{0.1} 10x^2 dx$$

$$= \frac{10}{3}\left[x^3\right]_0^{0.1} = \frac{0.1}{3} = 3.33 \times 10^{-3} J$$

Solutions of PRACTICE EXERCISE 3.2

(i) We use $k_A + mgh = k_B$

$$0 + m(10)\left(\frac{1}{\sqrt{2}}\right) = \frac{1}{2}mv_B^2$$

$$v_B = \sqrt{10\sqrt{2}}$$

$$= 3.76 \text{ m/s}$$

(ii) Here we use $mg_P h = \frac{1}{2}mv^2$

Where $g_P \rightarrow$ gravity on planet

$$g_P = \frac{v^2}{2h} = \frac{(4.1)^2}{2 \times (1.47 - 0.32)}$$

$$= 7.3 \text{ m/s}^2$$

Planet is not earth

(iii) If initially spring is compressed by a distance x, initial energy stored in it would be $\frac{1}{2}kx^2$. From its initial position to the maximum height we use

$$K_i + \frac{1}{2}kx^2 - mg(h) = K_f$$

$$0 + \frac{1}{2} \times 350 \times x^2 - 1.8 \times 10 \times 3.6 = 0$$

$$x^2 = 0.37$$

$$x = 0.608 \text{ m}$$

(iv) Using w-E theorem for motion of block till it stops is

$$\frac{1}{2}mv_0^2 - mgh - \mu mgd = 0$$

$$d = \frac{v_0^2 - 2gh}{2\mu g}$$

$$= \frac{36 - 2 \times 10 \times 1.1}{2 \times 0.6 \times 10} = 1.167 \text{ m}$$

(v) While sliding on curved parts block does not loose any energy, it looses energy againt friction only on flat part. If block looses its whole energy in sliding a distance x on flat part, we use

$$K_i + mgh - \mu mgx = K_f$$

$$0 + 10 \times 1.5 - 0.2 \times 10 \times x = 0$$

$$x = 7.5 \text{ m}$$

Length of flat part is $3m$ so

$$7.5 = 3 + 3 + 1.5$$

Thus block will finally come to rest at the mid point of that part.

Solutions of PRACTICE EXERCISE 3.3

(i) If friction on person at horizontal belt is f we can use power expanded

$$P = f.v$$

$$f = \frac{400}{2} = 200 \text{ N}$$

If belt is inclined at an angle θ then we use

$$P = (f\cos\theta + mg\sin\theta).v$$

$$600 = (200\cos\theta + 800\sin\theta) \times 2$$

$$2\cos\theta + 8\sin\theta = 3$$

$$2\sqrt{1\sin^2\theta} = 3 - 8\sin\theta$$

$$4 - 4\sin^2\theta = 9 + 64\sin^2\theta - 48\sin\theta$$

$$68\sin^2\theta - 48\sin\theta + 5 = 0$$

$$\sin\theta = \frac{48 \pm \sqrt{2304 - 1360}}{136}$$

$$= \frac{48 \pm 30.72}{136} = 0.579 \text{ or } 0.127$$

$\Rightarrow$ $\theta = 35.45° \text{ or } 7.31°$.

(ii) Driving force on bus at maximum speed will balance the total opposing force on it so we use

$$f_D = 1000 N$$

$$P = f_D \cdot v_{max}$$

$$v_{max} = \frac{P}{f_D} = \frac{50000}{1000} = 50 \text{ m/s}$$

When speed is 25 m/s, driving force will be

$$f_D = \frac{P}{v} = \frac{50000}{25} = 2000 \text{ N}$$

We use $$a = \frac{f_D - 1000}{m} = 1 \text{ m/s}^2$$

(iii) At constant speed driving for a is equal to all opposition forces on automobiles and we use

$$P = f_D . v$$

$$f_D = \frac{P}{v} = \frac{30 \times 746}{50 \times 4/9} = 1007.1 \text{ N}$$

(iv) Power required to pull the tape is

$$P = fv = 0.98 \times 0.025$$

$$= 0.0245 \ W$$

Percentage of input power used in pulling tape is

$$= \frac{0.0245}{1.8} \times 100$$

$$= 1.36\%$$

(v) For a circular area of diameter D, volume flow rate of wind at speed v is

$$r = \text{Area} \times \text{Speed}$$

$$= \frac{\pi D^2}{4} \times v$$

Kinetic energy of wind flowing per second through blades is

$$k = \frac{1}{2}(\rho r)v^2$$

$$k = \frac{\pi \rho D^2}{8} v^3$$

If 100% transfer of energy take place then power delivered by wind mill is:

$$P = k = \frac{\pi}{8} \rho D^2 v^3$$

(vi) Total resistance force will be

$$f_r = 10 \times 10^3 \text{ N}$$

Total opposition on train is

$$f_{op} = f_r + mg \sin \theta$$

$$= 10 \times 10^3 + 10^6 \times 9.8 \times \frac{1}{49}$$

$$= 10^4 + 20 \times 10^4 = 21 \times 10^4$$

Engine power $\quad P = f_{op} . v$

$$= 21 \times 10^5$$

$$= 2.1 \times 10^6 W$$

If engine is shut down, retardation of train is

$$a = \frac{f_{op}}{m} = \frac{21 \times 10^4}{10^6} = 0.21 \text{ m/s}^2$$

Distancing travelled before it comes to rest is

$$s = \frac{v^2}{2a} = \frac{100}{0.42} = 238.095 \text{ m.}$$

Solutions of PRACTICE EXERCISE 3.4

(i) Given that tangential acceleration

$$a_t = 2 \text{m/s}^2$$

Its normal acceleration is

$$a_N = \frac{v^2}{R} = \frac{(30)^2}{500} = \frac{9}{5}$$

$$= 1.8 \text{ m/s}^2$$

Total acceleration of particle

$$a_T = \sqrt{a_t^2 + a_N^2}$$

$$= \sqrt{(2)^2 + (1.8)^2} = 2.69 \text{ m/s}^2$$

(ii) Tangential acceleration of a print at a distance r from axis is

$$a_t = r\beta = rat$$

Angular acceleration after time t is be given as

$$\frac{d\omega}{dt} = \beta = at$$

$$\int_0^\omega d\omega = \int_0^t at \, dt$$

$$\omega = \frac{at^2}{2}$$

Normal acceleration of the point is

$$a_N = \omega^2 r$$

$$= \frac{a^2 t^4}{4} r$$

If after time t, α is the angle between its velocity and total acceleration vector, we use

$$\tan \alpha = \frac{a_N}{a_t} = \frac{\left(\frac{1}{4} a^2 t^4 r\right)}{rat} = \frac{1}{4} at^3$$

or $\quad t = \left(\frac{4 \tan \alpha}{a}\right)^{1/3}$

(iii) We use $\quad \frac{d\omega}{dt} = -k\sqrt{\omega}$

$$\int_{\omega_0}^{0}\frac{d\omega}{\sqrt{\omega}} = -\int_0^{t_f} k\,dt \quad [t_f \rightarrow \text{total rotation time}]$$

$$2\sqrt{\omega_0} = kt_f$$

$$t_f = \frac{2\sqrt{\omega_0}}{k}$$

At a general time t angular speed is

$$\frac{d\theta}{dt} = \omega = \frac{1}{4}k^2t^2$$

$$\int_0^{\theta_0} d\theta = \int_0^{t_f}\frac{1}{4}k^2t^2\,dt$$

$$\theta_0 = \frac{1}{12}k^2t_f^3$$

$$\omega_{avg} = \frac{\theta_0}{t_f} = \frac{1}{12}k^2t_f^2$$

$$= \frac{1}{12}k^2\cdot\frac{4\omega_0}{k^2} = \frac{\omega_0}{3}$$

(iv) Angular acceleration

$$\alpha = \frac{\omega d\omega}{d\theta} = \alpha_0\cos\theta$$

$$\Rightarrow \quad \int_0^{\omega}\omega\,d\omega = \int_0^{\theta}\alpha_0\cos\theta\,d\theta$$

$$\frac{\omega^2}{2} = \alpha_0\sin\theta$$

$$\omega = \sqrt{2\alpha_0\sin\theta}$$

Solutions of PRACTICE EXERCISE 3.5

(i) (a) We use $\quad mgL = \frac{1}{2}mv^2$

$$v = \sqrt{2gL}$$

(b) At the top of circular track if speed of ball is v_1, we use

$$\frac{1}{2}mv^2 - mg[2(L-h)] = \frac{1}{2}mv_1^2$$

$$mgL - mg[0.5L] = \frac{1}{2}mv_1^2$$

$$v_1 = \sqrt{gL}$$

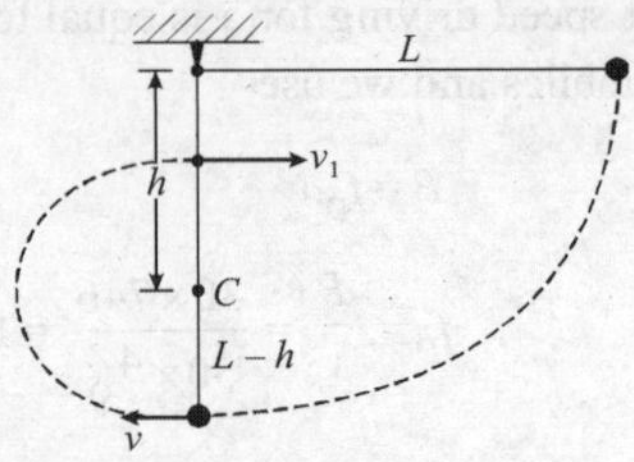

(ii) At the position where cloths falls off we use $N = 0$

$$\Rightarrow \quad mg\cos 60° = m\omega^2 r$$

$$\omega = \sqrt{\frac{g}{2r}} = \sqrt{\frac{10\times 2}{2\times 0.65}} = 3.92 \text{ rad/s}$$

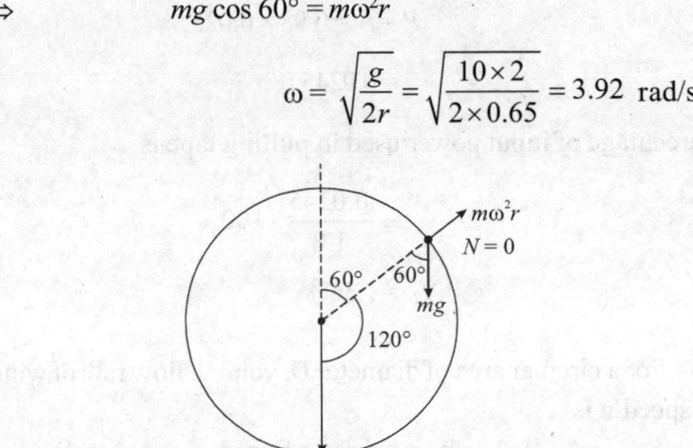

(iii) After displacement by angle θ if speed of ball is v, we use

$$mgr(1-\cos\theta) = \frac{1}{2}mv^2$$

$$v = \sqrt{2gr(1-\cos\theta)}$$

Along radial direction

$$mg\cos\theta = N + \frac{mv^2}{r}$$

$$N = mg\cos\theta - \frac{mv^2}{r}$$

$$N = mg\cos\theta - 2mg(1-\cos\theta)$$

$$N = mg(3\cos\theta - 2)$$

At angle $\theta = \beta$, if $N = 0$ we have

$$3\cos\beta = 2$$

$$\Rightarrow \quad \beta = \cos^{-1}\left(\frac{2}{3}\right)$$

After angle β ball leaves contact with inner wall and get in touch with outer wall.

(iv) As $T = 0$ at point B at $\theta = 127°$ we use

$$\cos 127° = \frac{2gR - u^2}{3gR}$$

$$-\frac{3}{5} \times 3gR = 2gR - u^2$$

$$u^2 = \left(2 + \frac{9}{5}\right) gR = \frac{19}{5} gR$$

$$u = \sqrt{\frac{19}{5} gR}$$

Then $$v = \sqrt{u^2 - 2gR(1 - \cos\theta)}$$

$$= \sqrt{\frac{19}{5} gR - 2gR\left(1 + \frac{3}{5}\right)}$$

$$= \sqrt{\left(\frac{19}{5} - \frac{16}{5}\right) gR}$$

$$= \sqrt{\frac{3}{5} gR} = \sqrt{30} \text{ m/s}$$

Max height particle can rise further is

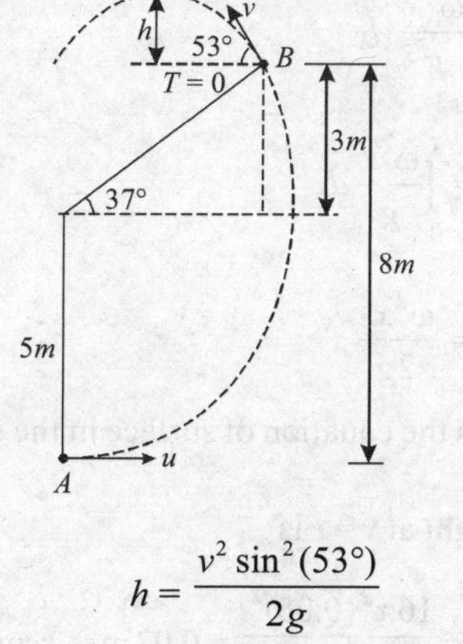

$$h = \frac{v^2 \sin^2(53°)}{2g}$$

$$= \frac{30\left(\frac{16}{25}\right)}{2g} = \frac{48}{50} = 0.96 \text{ m}$$

(v) Plane speed 220 kph in a circle of radius 180 m

At the bottom effective weight of pilot is

$$N = mg + \frac{mv^2}{R}$$

$$= mg + m\left(\frac{\left[220 \times \frac{5}{18}\right]^2}{180}\right)$$

$$\cong mg + m(20) \cong 3mg$$

(a) Only due to motion increase in weight is $2mg$ thus increase in g's will be 2

(b) Total effective weight is $3mg$.

(vi) Particle breaks off the hemispherical surface at angle ϕ such that

$$\cos\phi = \frac{2}{3} \quad \left[\text{Thus } \sin\phi = \sqrt{1 - \frac{4}{9}} = \frac{\sqrt{5}}{3}\right]$$

and speed of particle at point B is

$$v = \sqrt{2gR(1 - \cos\phi)} = \sqrt{\frac{2}{3} gR}$$

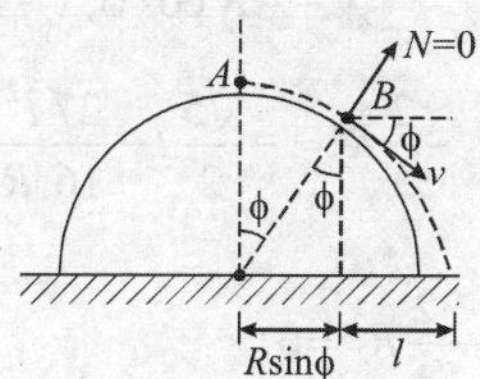

Distance l is such that

$$l = v\cos\phi . t$$

Where t is time of flight given by

$$R\cos\phi = v\sin\phi\, t + \frac{1}{2} gt^2$$

$$t^2 + \frac{2v}{g}\sin\phi t - \frac{2R\cos\phi}{g} = 0$$

$$t = -\frac{\sqrt{5}}{3}\sqrt{\frac{2}{3}}\sqrt{\frac{R}{g}} + \sqrt{\frac{10}{9 \times 3} \cdot \frac{R}{g} + \frac{4}{3}\frac{R}{g}}$$

$$t = -\frac{\sqrt{10}}{3\sqrt{3}}\sqrt{\frac{R}{g}} + \sqrt{\frac{46}{27}\frac{R}{g}} = \sqrt{\frac{R}{27g}}\ (\sqrt{46} - \sqrt{10})$$

Thus distance s is given as

$$s = R\sin\phi + l = R\sin\phi + v\cos\phi t$$

$$= \frac{\sqrt{5}}{3} R + \frac{2}{3}\sqrt{\frac{2}{3} gR}\sqrt{\frac{R}{27g}}\ (\sqrt{46} - \sqrt{10})$$

$$s = \frac{R}{3}[\sqrt{5} + \frac{4}{9}(\sqrt{23} - \sqrt{5})]$$

$$= \frac{R}{27}[4\sqrt{23} + 5\sqrt{5}]$$

Alternative Solutions:

We have $$\cos\phi = \frac{2}{3}$$

and $$\sin\phi = \frac{\sqrt{5}}{3}$$

Speed of particle at point B is

$$v = \sqrt{\frac{2}{3}gR}$$

$$y = -x\tan\phi - \frac{gx^2}{2u^2\cos^2\phi}$$

$$y = -\frac{\sqrt{5}}{2}x - \frac{gx^2}{2\left(\frac{2}{3}gR\right)\left(\frac{4}{9}\right)}$$

$$y = -\frac{\sqrt{5}}{2}x - \frac{27}{16}\frac{x^2}{R}$$

at $\quad y = -R\cos\phi,\ x = l$

$$-\frac{2}{3}R = -\frac{\sqrt{5}}{2}l - \frac{27}{16}\frac{l^2}{R}$$

$$l^2 + \frac{8\sqrt{5}}{27}lR - \frac{32}{81}R^2 = 0$$

$$l = -\frac{4\sqrt{5}}{27}R + \frac{R}{2}\sqrt{\frac{64\times 5}{27\times 27} + \frac{4\times 32}{27\times 3}\times\frac{9}{9}}$$

$$l = -\frac{4\sqrt{5}R}{27} + \frac{4R}{27}\sqrt{5+18}$$

$$l = \frac{4R}{27}(\sqrt{23} - \sqrt{5})$$

Distance s will be $\quad s = R\sin\phi + l$

$$= \frac{\sqrt{5}}{3}R + \frac{4R}{27}(\sqrt{23} - \sqrt{5})$$

$$= \frac{R}{27}(5\sqrt{5} + 4\sqrt{23})$$

Solutions of PRACTICE EXERCISE 3.6

(i) (a) At outer edge $\quad \omega^2 r = 1.5\,g$

$$\Rightarrow \quad \omega = \sqrt{\frac{1.5\times 10}{480}} = 0.1768 \text{ rad/s}$$

Rotation frequancy is $\quad f = \dfrac{\omega}{2\pi} = 0.0281 \text{ sec}^{-1}$

(b) Rotation Period $\quad T = \dfrac{1}{f} = 35.52 \text{ sec}$

(c) At *a* distance r_1 we use $\omega^2 r_1 = 0.75\,g$

$$\Rightarrow \quad \frac{1.5g}{r}\times r_1 = 0.75\,g$$

$$\Rightarrow \quad r_1 = \frac{r}{2} = \frac{480}{2} = 240 \text{ m}$$

(ii) For no skipping tendency banking angle is

$$\theta = \tan^{-1}\frac{v^2}{rg} = \tan^{-1}\left[\frac{(80\times {}^5\!/\!_{18})^2}{200\times 10}\right]$$

$$\Rightarrow \quad \theta = \tan^{-1}(0.247) = 13.87°$$

(iii) Figure shows the rotating liquid at angular speed ω. *A* point *P* on liquid surface in Evolving in *a* circle of radius x. For its equilibrium in rotating surface frame, we use

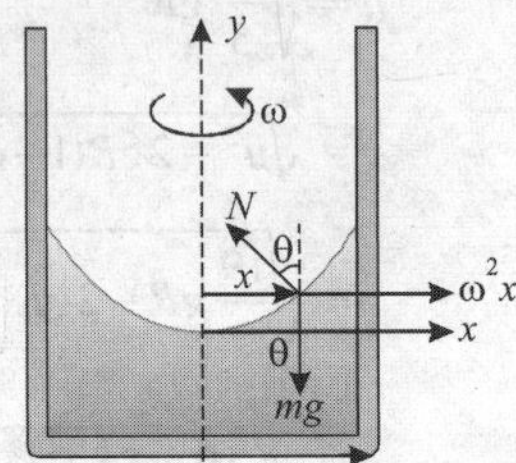

$$N\sin\theta = m\omega^2 x \qquad \ldots(1)$$

$$N\cos\theta = mg \qquad \ldots(2)$$

$$\Rightarrow \quad \tan\theta = \frac{dy}{dx} = \frac{\omega^2 x}{g}$$

$$\Rightarrow \quad dy = \frac{\omega^2 x}{g}dx$$

$$\int_0^y dy = \int_0^x \frac{\omega^2 x}{g}dx$$

$$y = \frac{\omega^2 x^2}{2g} \qquad \ldots(3)$$

Equation-(3) is the equation of surface in the given coordinate system

$\Rightarrow$ liquid height at $x = r$ is

$$y = \frac{\omega^2 r^2}{2g} = \frac{16\pi^2(0.05)^2}{2\times 10} = 0.02 \text{ m} = 2 \text{ cm}$$

(iv) For equilibrium of bead at angle θ, we use

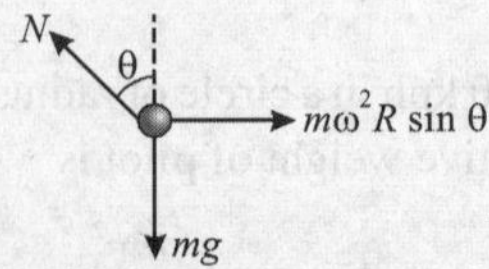

$$N\sin\theta = m\omega^2 R\sin\theta \Rightarrow N = m\omega^2 R, \qquad \ldots(1)$$

$$N\cos\theta = mg \qquad \ldots(2)$$

For steady position case *I* is when $\theta = 0$
and case II is at $\theta < 90°$ & $\theta \neq 0$ from equation (1) & (2)

$$\theta = \cos^{-1}\left(\frac{g}{\omega^2 R}\right)$$

(v) (a) For equilibrium of particle P in frame of bowl, we use

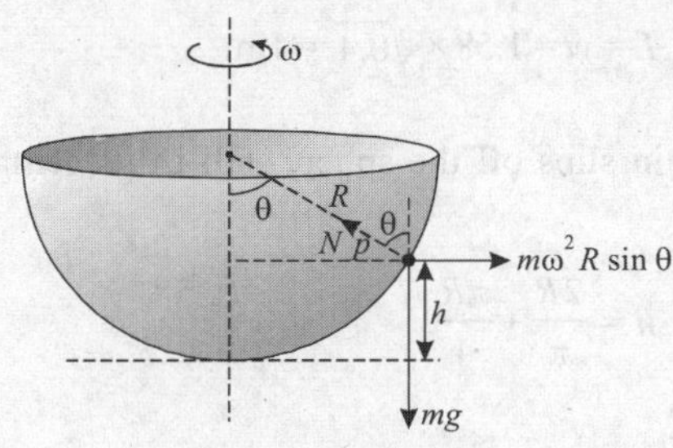

$$N \sin\theta = m\omega^2 R \sin\theta \quad \ldots(1)$$

$$N \cos\theta = mg \quad \ldots(2)$$

and we have $$h = R(1-\cos\theta) \quad \ldots(3)$$

From (1) & (2) we have

$$\cos\theta = \frac{g}{\omega^2 R}$$

From (3) $$h = R - \frac{g}{\omega^2} \quad \ldots(4)$$

(b) For non-zero value of h

$$R > \frac{g}{\omega^2}$$

$$\Rightarrow \quad \omega > \sqrt{g/R} = \sqrt{\frac{9.8}{0.1}} = \sqrt{98} = 7\sqrt{2} \text{ rad/sec}$$

(c) From equation-(4) we use $\Delta h = -\dfrac{\Delta g}{\omega^2}$

$$\Delta g = \omega^2 \Delta h = 98 \times 10^{-4} = 9.8 \times 10^{-3} \text{ m/s}^2$$

(vi) In frame of rod for equilibrium of sleeve

$$m\omega^2 (l_0 + x) = kx$$

$$\Rightarrow \quad x = \frac{m\omega^2 l_0}{(k - m\omega^2)}$$

Total energy of system in final state is obtained by work done on system which is given as

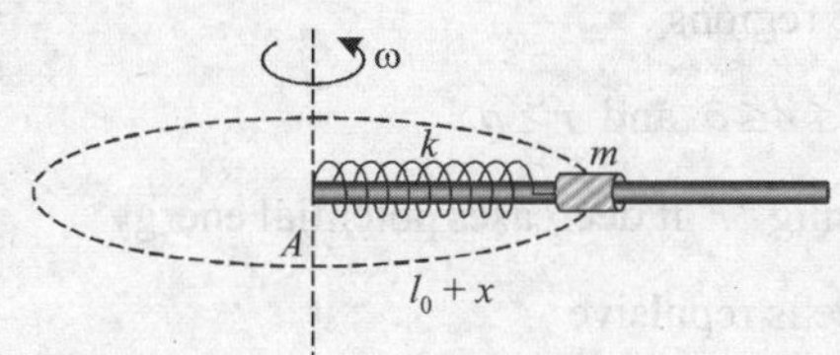

$$\omega = \frac{1}{2}mv^2 + \frac{1}{2}kx^2$$

$$\omega = \frac{1}{2}m(l_0+x)^2\omega^2 + \frac{1}{2}k\left(\frac{m\omega^2 l_0}{k - m\omega^2}\right)^2$$

$$\omega = \frac{1}{2}m\omega^2\left(\frac{kx}{m\omega^2}\right)^2 + \frac{1}{2}k\left(\frac{m\omega^2 l_0}{k - m\omega^2}\right)^2$$

$$= \frac{1}{2}m\omega^2\left(\frac{kl_0}{k - m\omega^2}\right)^2 + \frac{1}{2}k\left(\frac{m\omega^2 l_0}{k - m\omega^2}\right)^2$$

$$= \frac{1}{2}m\omega^2 l_0^2 k\left(\frac{k + m\omega^2}{(k - m\omega^2)^2}\right)$$

Solutions of PRACTICE EXERCISE 3.7

(i) (a) For the spring S $\quad F = kx$

at $F = 100$ N, $x = 1$ m $\Rightarrow k = 100$ N/m

If spring compresses by x by mass, using work energy theorem we have

$$mg \sin\theta\,(l + x) - \tfrac{1}{2}kx^2 = 0$$

$$\Rightarrow \quad 10 \times 10 \times 0.5\,(l+2) - 0.5 \times 100 \times 2^2 = 0$$

$$\Rightarrow \quad l + 2 - 4 = 0$$

$$\Rightarrow \quad l = 2\text{m}$$

Thus total distance the mass slides before comming to rest is $l + x = 2 + 2 = 4$m

(b) When mass reaches the spring its speed v is given as

$$v = \sqrt{2gl\sin\theta}$$

$$\Rightarrow \quad v = \sqrt{20} \text{ m/s}$$

(ii) $m = 0.5$ kg, $v = ax^{3/2}$, $a = 5\text{ m}^{-1/2}\text{ s}^{-1}$, $W = ?$

Initial velocity at $x = 0$, $v_0 = a \times 0 = 0$

Final velocity at $x = 2$, $v_2 = a \times 2^{3/2} = 5 \times 2^{3/2}$

Work done = Increase in kinetic energy = $\frac{1}{2}\text{m}\,(v_2^2 - v_0^2)$

$$= \frac{1}{2} \times 0.5\,[(5 \times 2^{3/2})^2 - 0] = 50 \text{ J}$$

(iii) When block starts sliding spring force on it is given as

$$kx = \text{mg}\sin\theta + \mu_s \text{mg}\cos\theta$$

$$\Rightarrow \quad x = \frac{mg}{k}(\sin\theta + \mu_s\cos\theta)$$

At this state potential energy of spring is $U = \frac{1}{2}kx^2$

$$\Rightarrow \quad U = \frac{1}{2}k\left(\frac{mg(\sin\theta + \mu_s \cos\theta)}{k}\right)^2$$

$$\Rightarrow \quad U = \frac{[mg(\sin\theta + \mu_s \cos\theta)]^2}{2k}$$

(iv) Using equation $F = -\frac{dU}{dr}$, we obtain the expression for the force

$$F = \frac{6U_0}{a}\left\{2\left(\frac{a}{r}\right)^{13} - \left(\frac{a}{r}\right)^7\right\}$$

At equilibrium the force must be zero. Therefore the equilibrium separation r_0 is given as

$$r_0 = 2^{1/6}a$$

(v) At angular displacement θ, speed of bob is

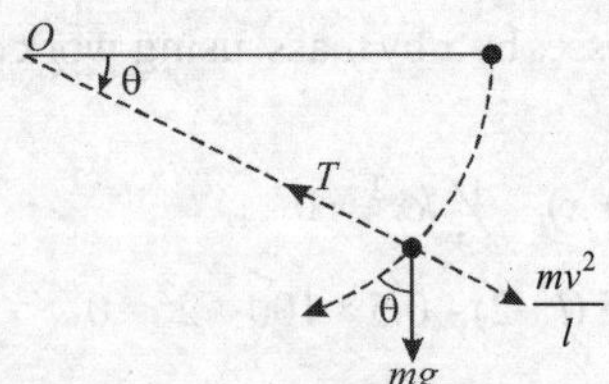

$$v = \sqrt{2gl\sin\theta}$$

For equilibrium of bob in rotating frame, we use

$$T = \text{mg} \sin\theta + \frac{mv^2}{l} = 3\text{mg} \sin\theta$$

at $T = 2\text{mg}$, we use

$$2\text{mg} = 3\text{mg} \sin\theta$$

$$\theta = \sin^{-1}\left(\frac{2}{3}\right)$$

(vi) (a) Energy stored in spring is $\frac{1}{2}kx^2$ which is transformed to kinetic energy of ball as

$$\frac{1}{2}kx^2 = \frac{1}{2}mv^2$$

$$v = \sqrt{\frac{k}{m}}x = \sqrt{\frac{100}{0.1}} \times 0.05 = 1.58 \text{ m/s}$$

(b) Time taken by ball to reach ground is

$$t = \sqrt{\frac{2h}{g}} = \sqrt{\frac{2\times 2}{10}} = \sqrt{0.4} \text{ sec}$$

Thus horizontal distance travelled by ball before hitting the ground is

$$L = vt = 1.58 \times \sqrt{0.4} = 1\text{m}$$

(vii) As chain slips off the sphere, fall in its centre of mass height is

$$h = \frac{2R}{\pi} + \frac{\pi R}{4}$$

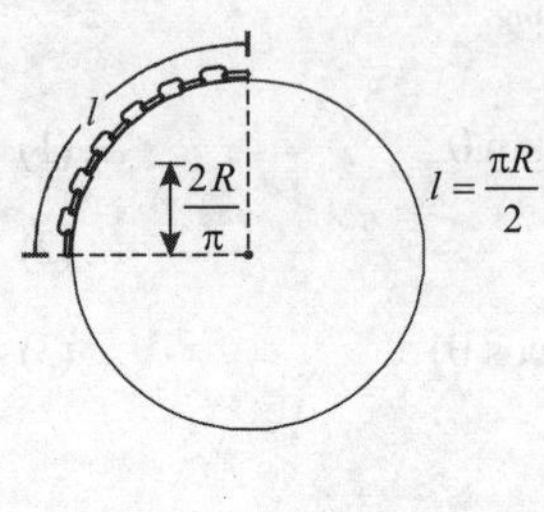

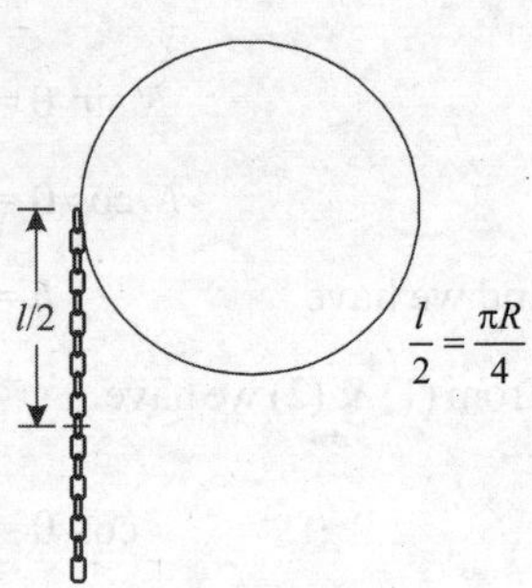

By work energy theorem, we use

$$mgh = \tfrac{1}{2}mv^2$$

or $$v = \sqrt{2gh} = \sqrt{2g\left(\frac{2R}{\pi} + \frac{\pi R}{4}\right)}$$

$$\Rightarrow \quad v = \sqrt{gR\left(\frac{4}{\pi} + \frac{\pi}{2}\right)}$$

(viii) $U = \frac{K}{2a^3}(3a^2 - r^2);\ 0 \le r \le a$

$$U = \frac{K}{r};\ r \ge a$$

$$\vec{F} = -\frac{dU}{dr}\hat{r}$$

$$\Rightarrow \quad F = -\frac{Kr}{a^3};\quad 0 \le r \le a$$

$$F = \frac{k}{r^2};\ r \ge a$$

In both the regions

$$0 \le r \le a \text{ and } r \ge a$$

On increasing 'r' it decreases potential energy

Hence force is repulsive

(b) $\overset{V}{\leftarrow}$ $r = 0$ —— ● $\overset{F}{\rightarrow}$ —— $\overset{V_0}{\leftarrow}$ $r = \infty$

In $0 \le r \le \infty; F > 0$

So particle reaches origin;

If $v > 0$

$$K_i + U_i = K_f + U_f$$

$$\Rightarrow \frac{1}{2}mV_0^2 + 0 = \frac{1}{2}mV^2 + \frac{3K}{2a}$$

$$\Rightarrow \frac{1}{2}mV^2 + 0 = \frac{1}{2}mV_0^2 + \frac{3K}{2a} > 0$$

$$\Rightarrow V_0 > \sqrt{\frac{3K}{ma}} \quad \therefore V_{0\min} = \sqrt{\frac{3K}{ma}}$$

(c) If $V_0 = \sqrt{\frac{2K}{am}}$

Particle stops at $r = r_0$ ($r_0 > 0$) & then starts travelling towards infinity.

(ix) As rate of work by the applied force is constant we use

$$F.v = \text{constant} = k \text{ (say)}$$

$$\Rightarrow \quad a = \frac{k}{mv} \quad \ldots(1)$$

$$\frac{vdv}{dx} = \frac{k}{mv}$$

$$\int_u^v v^2 dv = \int_0^x \frac{k}{m} dx$$

$$v^3 - u^3 = \frac{3kx}{m} \quad \ldots(2)$$

also from equations-(1)

$$\frac{dv}{dt} = \frac{k}{mv}$$

$$\int_x^v v dv = \int_0^t \frac{k}{m} dt$$

$$v^2 - u^2 = \frac{2kt}{m} \quad \ldots(3)$$

$\frac{(2)}{(3)}$ gives

$$\frac{v^3 - u^3}{v^2 - u^2} = \frac{3x}{2t}$$

$$\Rightarrow \quad t = \frac{3}{2}\frac{(u+v)x}{(u^2 + v^2 + 4v)}$$

(x) We use $\vec{F} = -\nabla U$

$$\vec{F} = -[2y\,\hat{i} + (2x+z)\,\hat{j} + y\,\hat{k}]$$

Solutions of CONCEPTUAL MCQS Single Option Correct

Sol. 1 (B) At position x_1 the force on the right of this point is positive that is toward right and on the left of this point is negative which is toward left hence the body will be in unstable equilibrium at point x_1. Similarly with the same logic we can see that at point x_2 the body is in stable equilibirum.

Sol. 2 (A) Centripetal force is the resultant of all real forces acting on the particle directed along the radial direction inward which does not act sparately on the particle. In this case there are only two forces on particle mg and string tension.

Sol. 3 (A) Normal reaction at the highest point of the track will be given by centrifugal force minus the weight of the block so it will be maximum when centrifugal force is maximum which is the case when radius of curvature is minimum hence option (A) is correct.

Sol. 4 (D) Due to Earth's rotation at points on earth which are revolving in circular motion effective value of g decreases due to outward centrifugal force acting on bodies on surface so at these points effective value of g increases but at poles which are always at rest value of g ramain the same.

Sol. 5 (C) If power is constant then by using the relation $P = F.v$ we can state that $a.v$ = constant then using $dv/dt = k/v$ we get $v = (2kt)^{1/2}$ then using $dx/dt = (2kt)^{1/2}$ on integrating we get displace ment is directly proportional to $t^{3/2}$.

Sol. 6 (B) Normal reaction at surface will be equal to weight of body minus the centrifugal force on body. So in this case normal force is higher where radius is less hence option (B) is correct.

Sol. 7 (C) When the ball is released, we know that after an anglular displacement $\theta = \cos^{-1}(-2/3)$ ball leaves contact with the inner wall of the tube and get in contact with the outer wall of the tube hence option (C) is correct.

Sol. 8 (A) The normal force between the train and track will be equal to its weight minus the centrifugal force on the train. The force will be higher in case where the centrifugal force is less so the lower speed train will press the track with more force. As relative to earth speed of both trains are equal so the train which is running west to east will move fast will press the track with less force hence option (A) is correct.

Sol. 9 (C) Using work energy theorem from starting point from where the ball is released to the point where the spring will have maximum elongation we can calculate the mass of the ball. It can be written as

$$0 + mgh - (1/2)kh^2 = 0 \quad \ldots(1)$$

and to lift the block

$$kh = Mg \quad \ldots(2)$$

Sol. 10 (D) For a planetary motion of body being a bounded motion its total energy and potential energy must be negative with respect to zero energy at infinite separation from the center of force. So among the given option (D) is correct.

Sol. 11 (C) The only forces acting on the aircraft are is weight and the upthrust due to air pressure on its wings in direction normal to the wings surface hence option (C) is correct.

Sol. 12 (C) As K.E. of both are same negative work done by the force to stop both must be same so displacements are also equal.

Sol. 13 (A) Tensions in the rod will be providing the centripetal force on the outer sections of the rod at any point tension in the rod is given by $T = m\omega^2 r$ where at a distance x from pivoted end of rod we use $m = M(l - x)/l$ and $r = (l + x)/2$ so substituting values we get $T = M(l^2 - x^2)/2l$ which implies that at inner point tension is more than the outer point.

Sol. 14 (D) In vertical circular motion as the motion is accelerated, body cannot be in equilibrium.

Sol. 15 (A) Here the force on particle is given as $F = -dU/dx = -2x + 4$ which is zero at $x = 2$ and at this point d^2U/dx^2 is positive which corresponds to minimum energy so this is the point of stable equilibrium.

Sol. 16 (A) For a body driven by a constant force, power $P = F.v$ and we can use $v = at$ so $P = Fat$ which is a linear function.

Sol. 17 (A) As motor cycle is ascending on the overbridge, the component of weight along radial dirction increases so the normal force also increases.

Sol. 18 (A) The power of the body is $P = mav = 4v$.

Sol. 19 (C) Work done by the weight of body is $W = mg.(1/2)g\,(2n - 1)$ for n^{th} second of motion hence option (C) is correct.

Sol. 20 (A) For uniformly accelerated motion particles momentum is given as $p = mat$ and its kinetic energy is given as $K = (1/2)ma^2t^2$ and the ratio of the two is $p/K = 2/at$.

Sol. 21 (B) As a particle falls its gravitational potential energy decreases and kinetic energy increases with speed given as $v = gt$ so the possible option is (B).

Sol. 22 (C) The kinetic energy of wind per unit time is $(1/2)(\rho Av)v^2$ where ρ is the density of wind, A is the area of cross section of the blades and v is wind speed. The electrical power output is proportional to this value so option (C) is correct.

Sol. 23 (D) With the given function we can find the potential energy function as $U(x) = (1/2)kx^2 - (1/3)ax^3$ by considering zero potential energy at $x = 0$ then out of given options only option (D) is possible.

Sol. 24 (A) As throughout motion acceleration is positive, speed continuously increases so KE also increases continuously with positive slope. The slope of KE is $= d(KE)/dt = mva$ hence only possible option is (A).

Sol. 25 (A) We use

$$\vec{F} = \nabla U = -\cos(x+y)\,\hat{i} - \cos(x+y)\,\hat{j}$$

$$\vec{F}\Big|_{\left(0,\frac{\pi}{4}\right)} = -\frac{1}{\sqrt{2}}\hat{i} - \frac{1}{\sqrt{2}}\hat{j}$$

$$\left|\vec{F}\right|_{\left(0,\frac{\pi}{4}\right)} = 1$$

Sol. 26 (B) $U = 40(xy) + C$

As the mid point of rod the particle would be at equilibrium so from conservation of mechanical energy between A and the mid point of the rod

$$\frac{1}{2}mv_0^2 = 40\left(\frac{a}{2}\right)\left(\frac{a}{2}\right)$$

Where $a = 1\text{ m}$

$\Rightarrow$ $$v_0 = a\sqrt{\frac{40}{2m}}$$

So, $v_0 = 2\text{ m/s}$

Sol. 27 (C) From work energy theorem

$$W_{mg} + W_F = \frac{1}{2}m(v_f^2 - v^2)$$

$$-2Fh = \frac{1}{2}m(v_f^2 - v^2)$$

Where $$h = \frac{v^2}{2\left(g + \frac{F}{m}\right)}$$

$$v_f = v\sqrt{\frac{mg - F}{mg + F}}$$

Sol. 28 (A) $\tan\theta = \frac{v^2}{Rg}$

and $\frac{h}{d} = \tan\theta$

Sol. 29 (C) $F = kt$

$$m\int_0^v dv = k\int_0^t tdt$$

$$mv = kt^2$$

$$v = \frac{k}{m}t^2$$

$$KE = \frac{1}{2}mv^2 = \frac{1}{2}m\frac{k^2}{m^2}t^4 = \left(\frac{k^2}{2m}\right)t^4$$

$$KE \propto t^4$$

Sol. 30 (C) From work energy theorem in the frame which is attached to point A, we have

$$max_m - \frac{1}{2}kx_m^2 = 0$$

$$\Rightarrow \quad x_{max} = \frac{2ma}{k}$$

Sol. 31 (C) W.D. from ground frame = 6.4 × 50 = 320 J

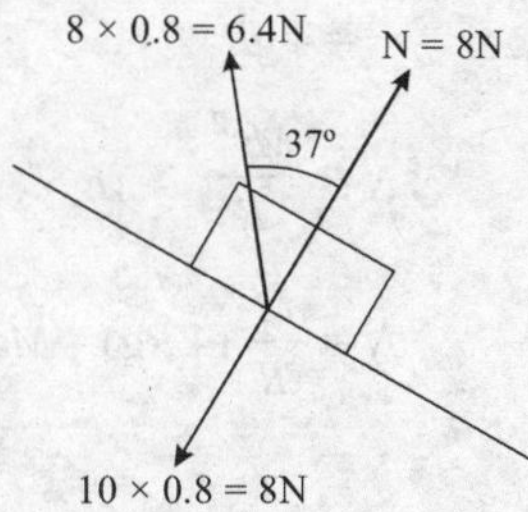

From elevator frame, displacement = 0.

Sol. 32 (D) The radius of curvature $\rho = \frac{v^2}{a_N}$. As projection point $a_N = g\cos\theta$ and $v = u$ and at topmost point $a_N = g$ and $v = u\cos\theta$.

Sol. 33 (B) We draw the *FBD* of the coin

f_T = tangential component of frictional force on coin

f_R = radial component of frictional force on coins

$f_T = m_\alpha r$

$$f_r = m\omega_f^2 r$$

$$\sqrt{f_R^2 + f_T^2} \le \mu_g mg$$

$$2\pi N = \frac{\omega_f^2}{2\alpha}$$

Solving the equations, we get

$$N = \frac{\left(\left(\frac{\mu_g g}{r} - \alpha^2\right)\right)^{1/2}}{4\pi\alpha}$$

Sol. 34 (B) $W = \oint \vec{F}.d\vec{r}$

$$= \oint \frac{bd\vec{r}}{|d\vec{r}|R}.d\vec{r}$$

$$= \frac{b}{R}\oint |d\vec{r}| = \frac{2\pi Rb}{R} = 2\pi bJ$$

Sol. 35 (A) Average speed in x-direction is

$$<v_x> = \frac{\Delta x}{T/2}, \text{ where } T = \frac{2\pi R}{v}$$

$$\Rightarrow <v_x> = -\frac{2R\cos 60^\circ}{\frac{T}{2}} = \frac{2R}{\frac{2\pi R}{v}} = -\frac{v}{\pi}$$

Sol. 36 (A) $W_{agent} = W_{F_0} = \int_0^{\pi/2} \vec{F}_0 \cdot d\vec{r}$

$$W_{F_0} = \frac{\pi F_0 l}{2}$$

By conservation of mechanical energy

$$\frac{\pi F_0 l}{2} = \frac{1}{2}mv_1^2 + mgl$$

$$v_1 = \sqrt{\frac{l}{m}(\pi F_0 - 2mg)}$$

Sol. 37 (A) $\frac{1}{2}KA^2 = \frac{1}{2}mv^2 + \frac{1}{2}2mv^2$

$$\Rightarrow \quad mv^2 = \frac{1}{3}KA^2$$

Work done by friction on $Q = \frac{1}{2}2mv^2$

$$= \frac{1}{3}KA^2$$

Solutions of NUMERICAL MCQS Single Options Correct

Sol. 1 (B) $w = mg\,\dfrac{h}{2} + Mgh$

$$w = \left(M + \frac{m}{2}\right) gh$$

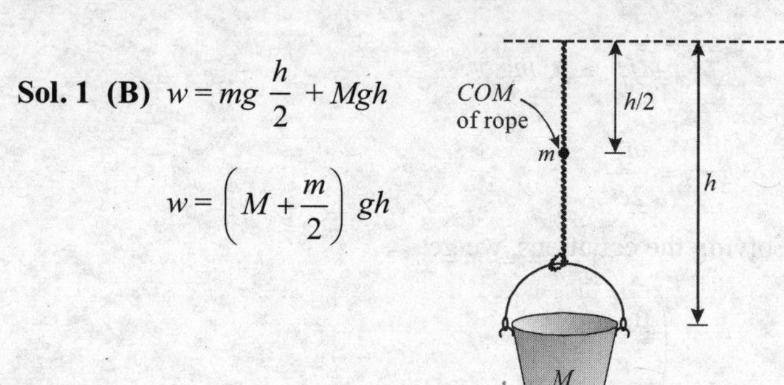

Sol. 2 (C) $x = \dfrac{t^3}{3}$

$$dw = F\,.\,dx$$

$$w = \int F.dx = \int m\frac{dv}{dt}\;.\,dx$$

$$w = \int m(2t)\;.\;t^2\,dt$$

$$w = 4\int_0^2 t^3\,dt$$

$$w = 4\left[\frac{t^4}{4}\right]_0^2 = 16\text{ J}$$

Sol. 3 (A) Block M has to be at rest

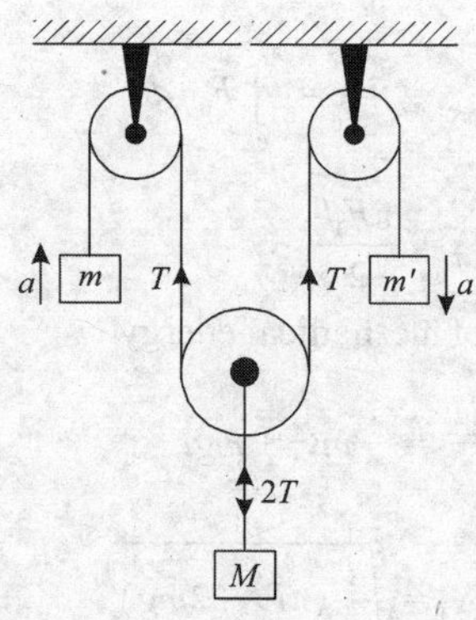

For equilibrium $\quad 2T = Mg$

$$T = \frac{Mg}{2} \qquad \ldots(1)$$

Let acceleration of m' is 'a' downwards and that of m is 'a' upwards.

$$m'g - T = m'a \qquad \ldots(2)$$

$$T - mg = ma \qquad \ldots(3)$$

Subtracting (2) from (3), we get

$$T = \frac{2mm'g}{m+m'} \qquad \ldots(4)$$

From (1) and (4), we can write

$$\frac{Mg}{2} = \frac{2mm'g}{m+m'}$$

$$\frac{4}{M} = \frac{1}{m} + \frac{1}{m'}$$

Sol. 4 (A) The angular velocity and angular acceleration remains constant :

$$\Rightarrow \quad \frac{v}{r} = \frac{v'}{r'} \qquad (v = \omega r)$$

$$\frac{20}{r} = \frac{v'}{r/2}$$

$$v' = 10\ cm/s$$

Similarly, $\quad \dfrac{a}{r} = \dfrac{a'}{r'}$

$$\frac{20}{r} = \frac{a'}{r/2}$$

$$a' = 10\ cm/s^2$$

Sol. 5 (A) Potential energy of cube at postion 1,

$$U_1 = Mg\,(4R) = 4\,MgR$$

At position 2,

$$U_1 = U_2 + K_2$$

$$4\,MgR = 2\,MgR + \frac{1}{2}\,Mv^2$$

$$4\,MgR = Mv^2$$

$$v^2 = 4\,gR$$

$$N = \frac{Mv^2}{R} - Mg$$

$$N = \frac{M}{R}(4\,Rg) - Mg = 3\,Mg$$

Sol. 6 (A) [figure: $\frac{13l_0}{12}$, l_0, m, m, $\frac{5l_0}{12}$]

Elongation in spring,

$$x = \frac{13l_0}{12} - l_0 = \frac{l_0}{12}$$

work done by lifting force,

$$w = mg\left(\frac{5l_0}{12}\right) + \frac{1}{2}k\left(\frac{l_0}{12}\right)^2$$

$$w = \frac{5mgl_0}{12} + \frac{kl_0^{\,2}}{288}$$

Sol. 7 (D) The z-component of the force and the x-component of displacement are not used in work done so total work done is given as

$$dW = F_y dy = 3xydy$$

$$\Rightarrow \quad dW = 6x^4 dx$$

$$\Rightarrow \quad W = \int dW = \int_0^2 6x^4 dx = \frac{6}{5}\left[x^5\right]_0^2 = \frac{192}{5}$$

Sol. 8 (A) $\cos\theta = \dfrac{BC}{l}$

$$BC = l\cos\theta$$

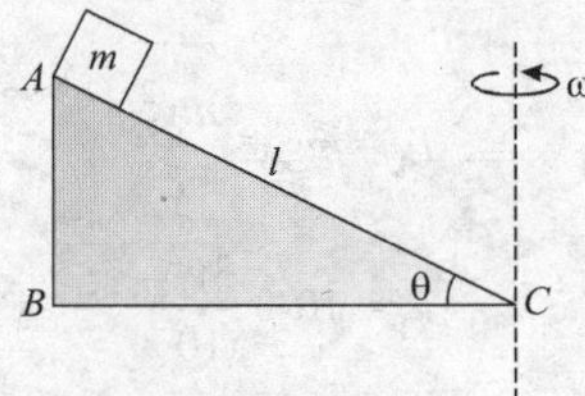

$$N\sin\theta = m\omega^2 R \qquad \ldots(1)$$

$$N\cos\theta = mg \qquad \ldots(2)$$

Dividing (1) by (2),

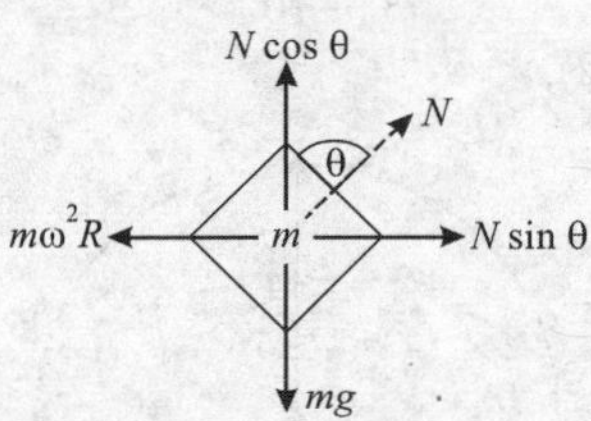

$$\frac{\sin\theta}{\cos\theta} = \frac{\omega^2 R}{g}$$

$$\Rightarrow \quad R = BC = l\cos\theta$$

$$\omega^2 = \frac{g\sin\theta}{l\cos^2\theta}$$

$$\omega = \sec\theta\sqrt{\frac{g\sin\theta}{l}}$$

Sol. 9 (D) $U = \lambda(x+y)$

$$\vec{F} = -\left[\frac{\partial U}{\partial x}\hat{i} + \frac{\partial U}{\partial y}\hat{j}\right]$$

$$\vec{F} = -\lambda\hat{i} - \lambda\hat{j}$$

$$w = \vec{F}.\vec{x}$$

$$w = (-\lambda\hat{i} - \lambda\hat{j}) \qquad [(2-1)\hat{i} + (3-1)\hat{j}]$$

$$w = (-\lambda\hat{i} - \lambda\hat{j}).(\hat{i} + 2\hat{j})$$

$$w = -\lambda - 2\lambda$$

$$w = -3\lambda$$

Sol. 10 (B) Let increase in lengh of spring is x

$kx \leftarrow$ m $\rightarrow m\omega^2 x$, $\rightarrow m\omega^2 l$

At equilibrium,

$$kx = m\omega^2 x + m\omega^2 l$$

$$kx - m\omega^2 x = m\omega^2 l$$

$$x = \frac{m\omega^2 l}{k - m\omega^2}$$

Sol. 11 (D) The car is in *a* state of free fall. so tension in the string is zero.

Sol. 12 (C) Work done to stretch *a* length x of spring ,

$$W_1 = \frac{1}{2}kx^2$$

work done to stretch the spring to length $2x$,

$$W = \frac{1}{2}k(2x)^2 = 4W_1$$

work done to stretch further length x,

$$W_2 = W - W_1 = 3W_1$$

$$\Rightarrow \quad W_2 = 3W_1$$

Sol. 13 (D) Power, $P = F.v$

$$P = F.(2a) \qquad (\text{As } v = u + at)$$

$$\Rightarrow \quad P = F.\frac{2F}{m}$$

$$\Rightarrow \quad P = \frac{2F^2}{m}$$

Sol. 14 (C) $P = \dfrac{mgh}{t} = \dfrac{30\times10\times6}{10} = 180W$

Sol. 15 (C) From, $x = 2\text{m}$ to $x = 3.5\text{m}$,

From, $y = mx + c$

$$U_1 = -4x + 10$$

$$F_1 = -\frac{dU_1}{dx} = +4\text{N}$$

$$W_1 = +4\times(3.5-2)$$

$$= +6J$$

From, $x = 3.5\text{m}$ to $x = 4.5\text{m}$

$$U_2 = +2x + 2$$

$$F_2 = -\frac{dU_2}{dx} = -2\text{N}$$

$$W_2 = -2\times(4.5-3.5)$$

$$W_2 = -2J$$

work done from 4.5 m to 5m = 0

$$\frac{1}{2}mv^2 = W_1 + W_2$$

$$\frac{1}{2} \times 2 \times v^2 = 6 - 2 = 4$$

$$\Rightarrow \quad v = 2\text{m/s}$$

Sol. 16 (D) Area under $F - x$ graph,

$$A = \frac{1}{2}(4)(10) + (4 \times 10) + \frac{1}{2} \times 4 \times 10$$

$$W = 20 + 40 + 20$$

From work-energy theorem,

$$W = \frac{1}{2}mv^2$$

(as body starts from rest)

$$80 = \frac{1}{2} \times 0.1 \times v^2$$

$$v^2 = 1600$$

$$v = 40\text{m/s}$$

Sol. 17 (C) $P_{\text{out}} = \frac{mgh}{t} = \frac{2 \times 10 \times 10}{1} = 200W$

$$\eta = \frac{P_{out}}{P_{in}}$$

$$\frac{40}{100} = \frac{200}{P_{in}}$$

$$P_{in} = 500\ W$$

As $\quad 1\text{Hp} = 746\ W$

$$\Rightarrow \quad 500\ W = \frac{500}{746}\text{Hp} = 0.67\text{Hp}$$

Sol. 18 (B) From conservation of energy,

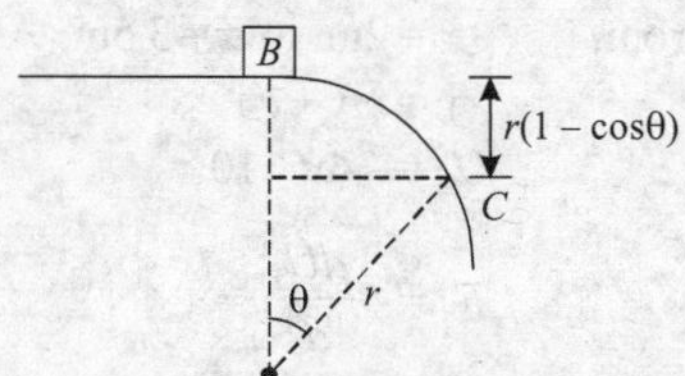

Let velocity of block at C is v

$$\frac{1}{2}mv_0^2 + mgr(1 - \cos\theta) = \frac{1}{2}mv^2$$

$$v = \sqrt{v_0^2 + 2gr(1 - \cos\theta)}$$

when block leaves the surface,

$$N = 0$$

$$mg\cos\theta = \frac{mv^2}{r}$$

$$rg\cos\theta = v_0^2 + 2gr(1 - \cos\theta)$$

$$3rg\cos\theta = \frac{rg}{4} + 2rg$$

$$3\cos\theta = \frac{9}{4}$$

$$\cos\theta = \frac{3}{4}$$

$$\theta = \cos^{-1}\left(\frac{3}{4}\right)$$

Sol. 19 (D) $T_1 = mg + \frac{mv_1^2}{L}$

$$T_1 = 10 + \frac{3v_1^2}{10} \quad \ldots(1)$$

$$T_2 = \frac{mv_2^2}{L} - mg$$

$$T_2 = \frac{3v_2^2}{10} - 10 \quad \ldots(2)$$

Dividing (1) by (2),

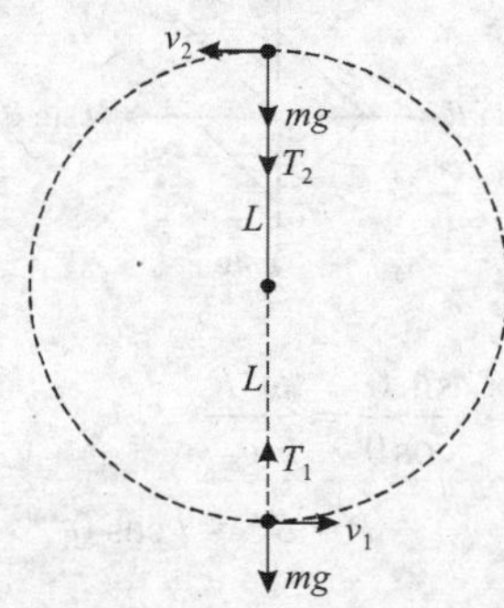

$$\frac{T_1}{T_2} = 4 = \frac{100 + 3v_1^2}{3v_2^2 - 100}$$

$$12v_2^2 - 400 = 100 + 3v_1^2$$

$$12v_2^2 = 500 + 3v_1^2 \quad \ldots(3)$$

From conservation of energy,

$$\frac{1}{2}mv_2^2 + mg(2L) = \frac{1}{2}mv_1^2$$

$$v_2^2 + 4 \times 10 \times \frac{10}{3} = v_1^2$$

$$v_1^2 = v_2^2 + \frac{400}{3} \quad \ldots(4)$$

From (3) & (4), we get

$$12 v_2^2 - 400 = 100 + 3 v_2^2 + 400$$

$\Rightarrow$ $$9 v_2^2 = 900$$

$\Rightarrow$ $$v_2^2 = 100$$

$\Rightarrow$ $$v_2 = 10 \text{m/s}$$

Sol. 20 (D) $T \cos\theta = mg$ ...(1)

$T \sin\theta = m\omega^2 (l \sin\theta)$ ...(2)

Dividing (1) by (2),

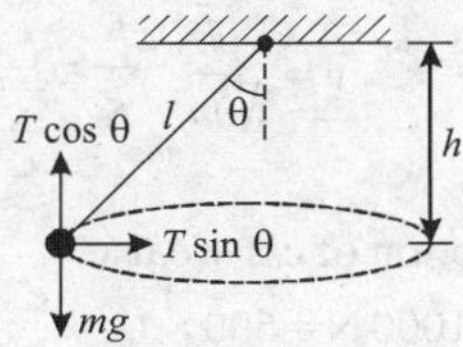

$$\cos\theta = \frac{g}{\omega^2 l}$$

$$\frac{h}{l} = \frac{g}{(2\pi P)^2 l}$$

$$4\pi^2 P^2 = \frac{g}{h}$$

$$P = \frac{1}{2\pi}\sqrt{\frac{g}{h}}$$

Sol. 21 (A) For block describing circle on the table.

$T = m\omega_1^2 l_1$ ...(1)

For block describing conical pendulum,

$T \cos\theta = mg$

$T \sin\theta = m\omega_2^2 (l_2 \sin\theta)$

$\Rightarrow$ $T = m\omega_2^2 l_2$ ...(2)

From (1) and (2), $\omega_1^2 l_1 = \omega_2^2 l_2$

$$\frac{l_1}{l_2} = \frac{\omega_2^2}{\omega_1^2}$$

Sol. 22 (B) Since the same force is applied on both springs,

$$k_A x_A = k_B x_B$$

$$2k_B x_A = k_B x_B$$

$2x_A = x_B$ ...(1)

$E_A = E = \frac{1}{2} k_A x_A^2$ ...(2)

$E_B = \frac{1}{2} k_B x_B^2$ ...(3)

Dividing (2) by (3), we get

$$\frac{E}{E_B} = \frac{k_A x_A^2}{k_B x_B^2} = \frac{2k_B}{k_B} \times \frac{x_A^2}{4x_A^2} = \frac{1}{2}$$

$$E_B = 2E$$

Sol. 23 (B) Let mass of man is M and that of boy is $\frac{M}{2}$

Let velocity of man is v_m and that of boy is v_B

$$\frac{1}{2} M v_m^2 = \frac{1}{2}\left[\frac{1}{2}\left(\frac{M}{2}\right) v_B^2\right]$$

$$v_m^2 = \frac{v_B^2}{4}$$

$v_m = \frac{v_B}{2}$ ...(1)

when man speeds up by 1m/s,

$$(KE)_{\text{man}} = (KE)_{\text{boy}}$$

$$\frac{1}{2} M (v_m + 1)^2 = \frac{v_B^2}{2}$$

$v_m + 1 = \frac{v_B}{\sqrt{2}}$ ...(2)

From (1) & (2), we get

$$\frac{v_B}{2} + 1 = \frac{v_B}{\sqrt{2}}$$

$$v_B\left(\frac{1}{\sqrt{2}} - \frac{1}{2}\right) = 1$$

$$v_B\left(\frac{\sqrt{2}-1}{2}\right) = 1$$

$$v_B = \frac{2}{\sqrt{2}-1} \times \frac{\sqrt{2}+1}{\sqrt{2}+1}$$

$$= 2(\sqrt{2}+1) \text{ m/s}$$

Sol. 24 (C) $Mg - F = \frac{Mg}{4}$

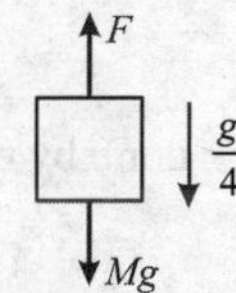

$$F = \frac{3Mg}{4}$$

work done by cord on the block

$$= F.d.\cos 180°$$

$$= -\frac{3Mgd}{4}$$

Sol. 25 (A) As $T_0 = M\omega^2 l$

$\Rightarrow$ $T_0 = M4\pi^2 f^2 l$

$$\Rightarrow \quad f = \frac{1}{2\pi}\sqrt{\frac{T_0}{Ml}}$$

$$\Rightarrow \quad f = \frac{1}{2\pi}\left[\frac{T_0}{Ml}\right]^{1/2}$$

Sol. 26 (C) We use work energy theorem as

$$mg\frac{l}{2} = \frac{1}{2}mv^2$$

$$\Rightarrow \quad v^2 = gl$$

$$\Rightarrow \quad v = \sqrt{gl}$$

Sol. 27 (D)

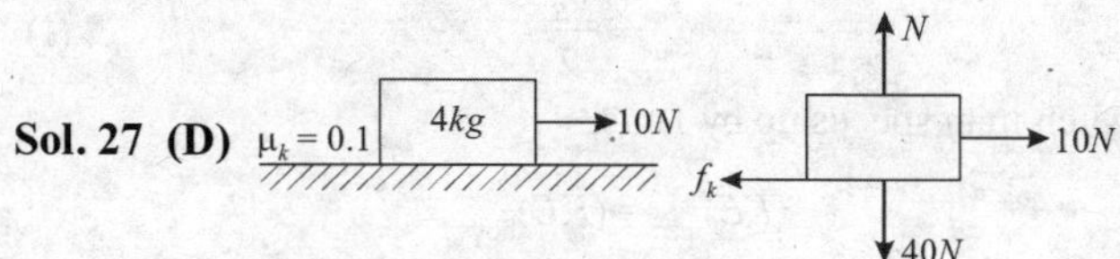

$$f_k = \mu_k N = 0.1 \times 40 = 4\text{N}$$

Net force acting on block,

$$F = 10 - 4 = 6\text{N}$$

Acceleration of block,

$$a = \frac{F}{m} = \frac{6}{4} = \frac{3}{2}\text{ m/s}^2$$

Distance covered by block in $\sqrt{20}$ seconds,

$$S = \frac{1}{2}at^2$$

$$S = \frac{1}{2} \times \frac{3}{2} \times (\sqrt{20})^2$$

$$S = 15\text{m}$$

work done by applied force,

$$w_a = F_a \times s = 10 \times 15 = 150\,J$$

work done by frictional force,

$$w_f = f \times s = 4 \times 15 = 60\,J$$

work done by net force,

$$w_{\text{net}} = F \times s = 6 \times 15 = 90\,J$$

Sol. 28 (A) Speed will be maximum when,

$$F = kx$$

$$x = \frac{F}{k}$$

From conservation of energy,

$$0 - \frac{1}{2}kx^2 + Fx = \frac{1}{2}mv^2$$

$$-\frac{1}{2}kx^2 + kx^2 = \frac{1}{2}mv^2$$

$$\frac{kx^2}{2} = \frac{1}{2}mv^2$$

$$v = \sqrt{\frac{k}{m}}\,.\,x$$

$$v = \sqrt{\frac{k}{m}}\,.\,\frac{F}{k} = \frac{F}{\sqrt{mk}}$$

Sol. 29 (B) For motion of car we use

$$F - 1000\text{ N} = 500 \times 1$$

$$F = 1500\text{ N}$$

Power,

$$P = F\,.\,v = 1500 \times 5 = 7500\text{ W} = 7.5\text{ kW}$$

Sol. 30 (B) Centripetal acceleration,

$$a_c = \frac{v^2}{r} = \frac{4}{r^2}$$

$$v = \frac{2}{\sqrt{r}}$$

Momentum of particle,

$$P = mv$$

$$\Rightarrow \quad P = \frac{2m}{\sqrt{r}}$$

Sol. 31 (A)

$$T\sin\theta = m\omega^2(l\sin\theta)$$

$$T = m\omega^2 l \quad \ldots(1)$$

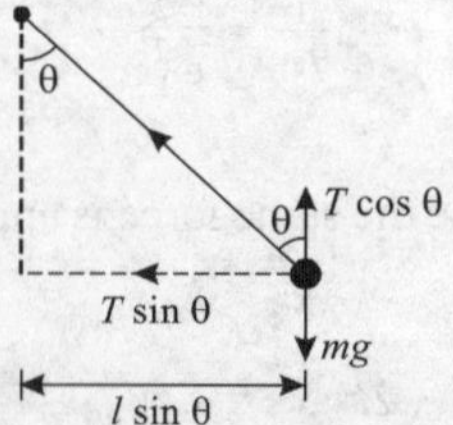

For M to be in equilibrium in vertical direction

$$T = Mg \quad \ldots(2)$$

From (1) & (2), we get

$$m\omega^2 l = Mg$$

$$\Rightarrow \quad m(2\pi f)^2 l = Mg$$

$$\Rightarrow \quad 4\pi^2 f^2 ml = Mg$$

$$\Rightarrow \quad f^2 = \frac{Mg}{4\pi^2 ml}$$

$$\Rightarrow \quad f = \frac{1}{2\pi}\sqrt{\frac{Mg}{ml}}$$

Sol. 32 (A) For stable circular motion of centre of mass of rope, we use

$$T = m\omega^2\left(\frac{l}{2}\right)$$

for breaking $\quad 40 = 0.2\,\omega^2(1)$

$$\Rightarrow \quad \omega^2 = \frac{400}{2}$$

$$\Rightarrow \quad \omega^2 = 200$$

$$\Rightarrow \quad \omega = 10\sqrt{2}\ \text{rad/s}$$

Sol. 33 (D) Work done by tension = zero as string is massless and frictionless which can never do work.

Sol. 34 (D)

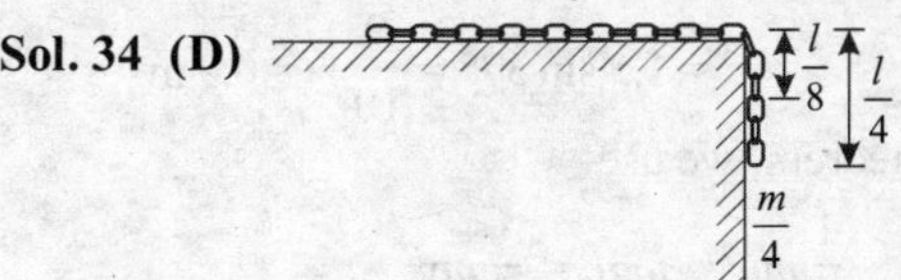

$$w = \frac{mg}{4}\left(\frac{l}{8}\right) = \frac{1}{32}mgl$$

Sol. 35 (A) By work energy theorem, we use

$$W_F = mgL(1 - \cos\theta)$$

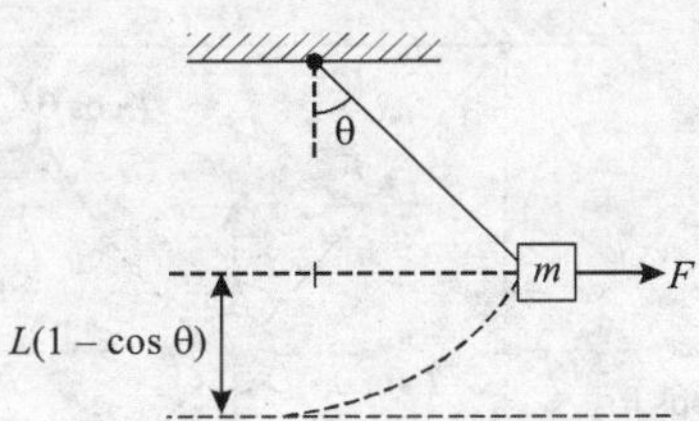

Sol. 36 (D) $\quad w = F.S = ma.s$

$$w = ma.\frac{1}{2}at^2$$

As $\quad a = \frac{v}{t_1}$

$$\Rightarrow \quad w = \frac{1}{2}m\frac{v^2}{t_1^2}t^2$$

Sol. 37 (B) When chain has left the vertex,

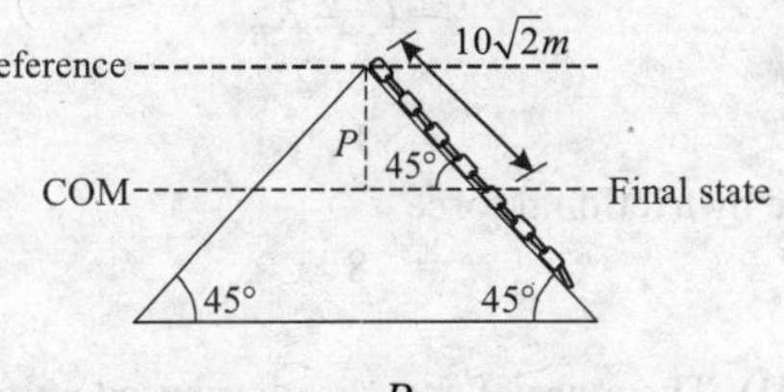

$$\sin 45° = \frac{P}{10\sqrt{2}}$$

$$P = 10m$$

$P.E$ is decreased by the same factor by which $K.E$ is increased,

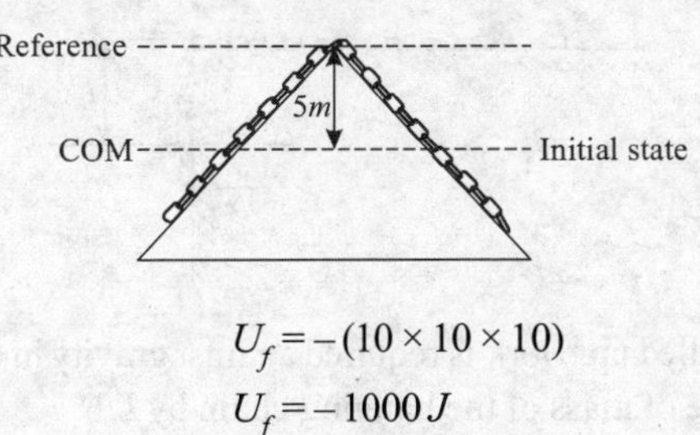

$$U_f = -(10 \times 10 \times 10)$$

$$U_f = -1000\,J$$

$$U_i = -(10 \times 10 \times 5)$$

$$U_i = -500\,J$$

$$\Delta k + \Delta U = 0$$

$$\frac{1}{2} \times 10 \times v^2 - 500 = 0$$

$$v^2 = 100$$

$$v = 10\text{m/s}$$

Sol. 38 (D) The minimum velocity that should be imparted to the bob so that it completes vertical circle is

$$v = \sqrt{5gl}$$

At lowest position, $\quad T = mg + \frac{mv^2}{l}$

$$T = mg + \frac{m(5gl)}{l}$$

$$T = 6\text{mg}$$

Sol. 39 (B) Potential energy of block at A,

$$U_A = 1 \times 10 \times 1 = 10\text{ J}$$

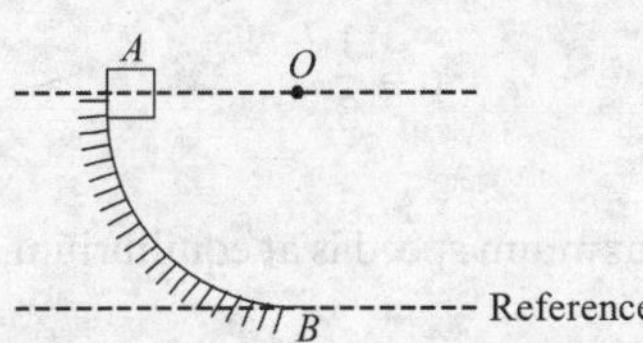

kinetic energy of block at B,

$$K_B = \frac{1}{2} \times 1 \times (2)^2 = 2\text{ J}$$

Loss in energy,

$$L = U_A - K_B$$
$$= 10 - 2$$
$$= 8\text{ J}$$

work done by frictional force

$$= -8\text{ J}$$

Sol. 40 (D) The mass of chain is distributed uniformly along the length of the chain and as the surface is smooth, we can assume that mass of the hanging part is at its centre of mass.

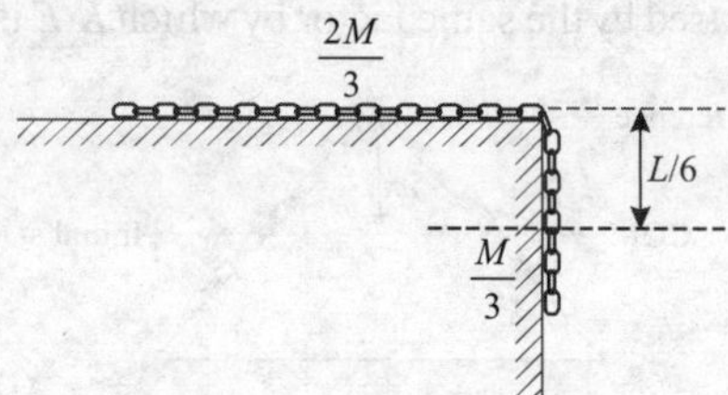

When pulled up, work is required against gravity in displacing the centre of mass of the hanging chain by $L/6$.

$$w = \frac{M}{3} \times g \times \frac{L}{6} = \frac{MgL}{18}$$

Sol. 41 (A)

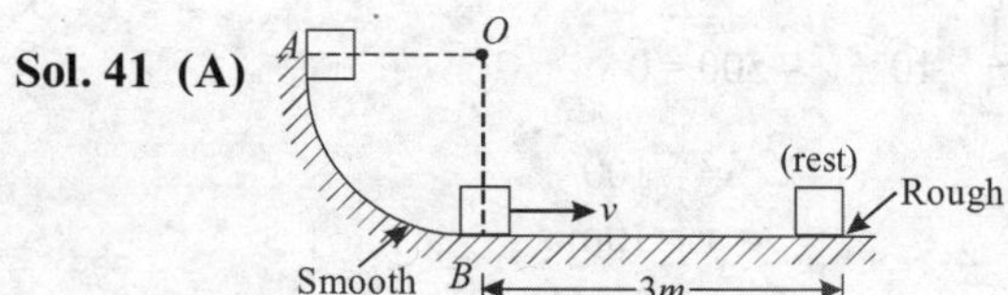

Kinetic energy at B = Potential energy at A

$$K_B = mg\,(1)$$

$$\frac{1}{2}mv^2 = mg$$

$$v^2 = 20$$

$$v = \sqrt{20}\text{ m/s}$$

By conservation of energy,

$$\frac{1}{2}mv^2 - \mu\, mgx = 0$$

$$\frac{1}{2}(20) - \mu(10)(3) = 0$$

$$\mu = \frac{1}{3}$$

Sol. 42 (A) Maximum speed is at equilibrium, when block is descended by x

$$2kx = mg$$

$$x = \frac{mg}{2k}$$

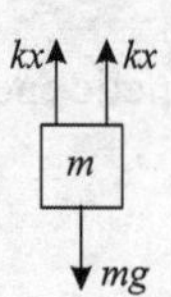

Sol. 43 (A) Let angle when tension in the string becomes zero is ϕ

We use $\cos\phi = \dfrac{2gl - u^2}{3gl}$

$$\cos\phi = \frac{(2 \times 10 \times 1.5) - 57}{3 \times 10 \times 1.5}$$

$$\cos\phi = \frac{30 - 57}{45} = -\frac{27}{45} = -\frac{3}{5}$$

$$\theta = 127°$$

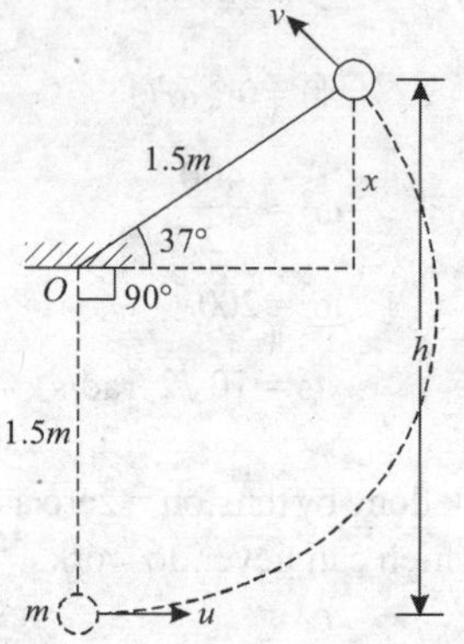

In figure we use $x = 1.5 \sin 37° = \dfrac{9}{10}\,m = 0.9\text{ m}$

by work energy theorem, we use

$$\frac{1}{2}mu^2 - mgh = \frac{1}{2}mv^2$$

$$\frac{57}{2} = (10)(2.4) + \frac{v^2}{2}$$

$$v^2 = 9$$

$$v = 3\text{m/s}$$

Sol. 44 (C) Let speed of bob at B is v

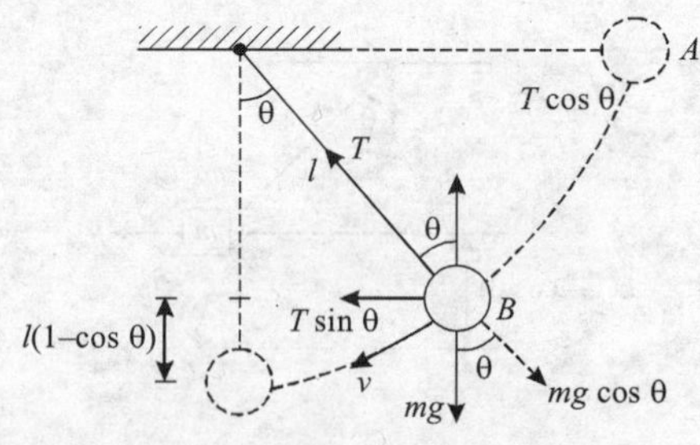

Tension at θ angle is $T = mg\cos\theta + \dfrac{mv^2}{l}$

$$\left[\text{here } v = \sqrt{2gl\cos\theta}\,\right]$$

$$2mg = mg\cos\theta + \frac{mv^2}{l}$$

$$mv^2 = 2\,mgl - mgl\cos\theta$$

$$3\cos\theta = 2$$

$$\theta = \cos^{-1}\left(\frac{2}{3}\right)$$

Sol. 45 (A) The light rod cannot slack during revolution and particle is able to move to topmost point of circle, when it reaches the topmost point, its velocity becomes zero but due to its inertia, it will fall in forward direction and completes the circle.

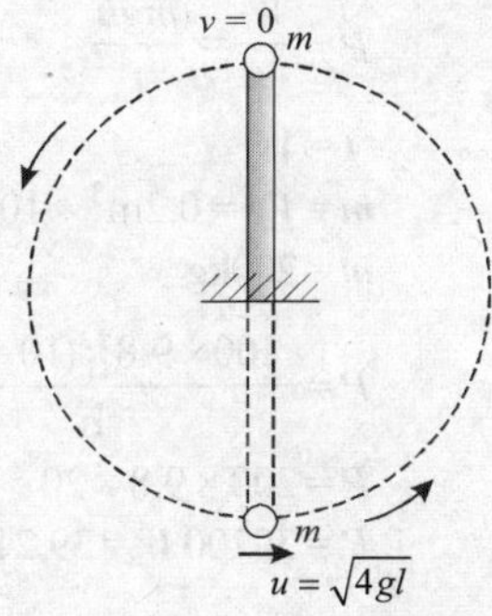

Sol. 46 (D) Given mass and initial velocity

$$m = 0.01\ kg$$

$$\vec{u} = 4\hat{i} + 16\hat{k}\ \text{m/s}$$

$$|\vec{u}| = \sqrt{(4)^2 + (16)^2}$$

$$|\vec{u}| = \sqrt{272}\ \text{m/s}$$

$$\vec{v} = 8\hat{i} + 20\hat{j}$$

$$|\vec{v}| = \sqrt{(8)^2 + (20)^2}$$

$$|\vec{v}| = \sqrt{464}\ \text{m/s}$$

$$W = \vec{F}\cdot\vec{S}$$

$$W = m\vec{a}\cdot\vec{s}$$

$$W = m\left(\frac{v^2 - u^2}{2}\right)$$

$$W = 0.01 \times \left[\frac{464 - 272}{2}\right]$$

$$W = 0.01 \times 96$$

$$W = 0.96\ \text{J}$$

Sol. 47 (B) Resulting force on ball is

$$F = \sqrt{(mg)^2 + (m\omega^2 r)^2}$$

$$F = \sqrt{10000 + \left[10 \times \frac{4\pi^2}{\pi^2}(4) \times (0.5)\right]^2}$$

$$F = \sqrt{10000 + 6400}$$

$$F = \sqrt{16400}$$

$$F = 128\ \text{N}$$

Sol. 48 (B) Centripetal acceleration is

$$a_c = k^2 r t^2$$

$$\frac{v^2}{r} = k^2 r t^2$$

$$v^2 = k^2 r^2 t^2$$

$$\Rightarrow \quad v = k\,r\,t$$

Tangential acceleration is

$$a_t = \frac{dv}{dt} = kr$$

$$F_t = ma_t$$

$$= mkr$$

work is done by tangential forces, as radial forces are perpendicular to v

$$P = F_t v$$

$$= (mkr)(krt)$$

$$= mk^2 r^2 t$$

Sol. 49 (C) Let speed of ball at B is v

Kinetic energy at A,

$$k_A = \frac{1}{2}(1)(5)^2 = 12.5\,J$$

$$k_A = U_B + k_B$$

$$12.5 = (1)(10)(1) + \frac{1}{2}(1)v^2$$

$$v^2 = 5$$

Force acting on particle at B,

$$F = \sqrt{(mg)^2 + \left(\frac{mv^2}{r}\right)^2}$$

$$F = \sqrt{(10)^2 + \left(\frac{1\times 5}{1}\right)^2}$$

$$F = \sqrt{125}$$

$$F = 5\sqrt{5}\ \text{N}$$

Sol. 50 (D) Let each mass is stretched by $\frac{x}{2}$, work done by spring on each mass is

$$W = -\frac{1}{2}(2k)\left(\frac{x}{2}\right)^2$$

As we consider spring constant of half spring is $2k$

$$\Rightarrow \quad W = -\frac{1}{4}kx^2$$

Sol. 51 (C)

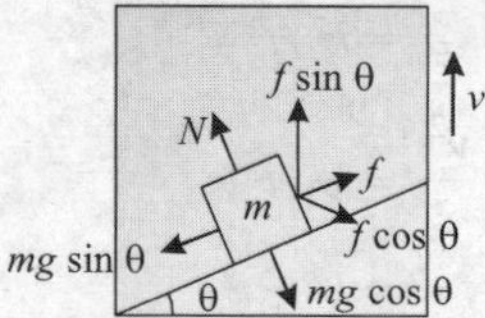

As block does not slide over the wedge, friction on block

$$f = mg \sin\theta$$

$$= \sin\theta \qquad \ldots(1)$$

work done by force of friction,

$$w = f \sin\theta \times vt$$

$$w = mg \sin^2\theta vt$$

Sol. 52 (C)

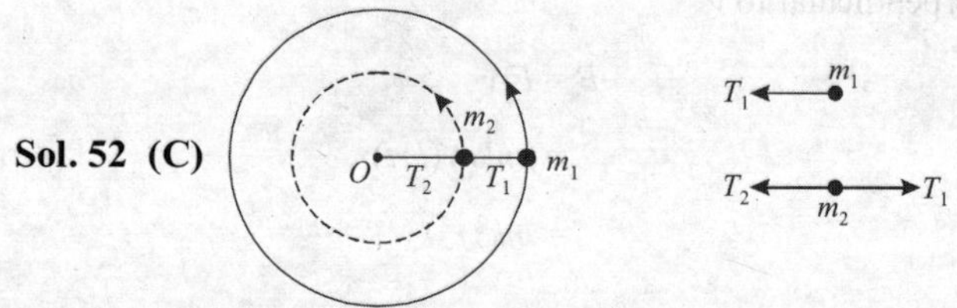

Tensions in strings are calculated by equilibrium of masses in rotating from as shown above are

$$T_1 = m_1\omega^2 r$$

$$T_2 = T_1 + m_2\omega^2 \frac{r}{2}$$

$$T_2 = m_1\omega^2 r + m_2\omega^2 \frac{r}{2}$$

$$T_2 = \left(\frac{2m_1 + m_2}{2}\right)\omega^2 r$$

$$\frac{T_2}{T_1} = \frac{2m_1 + m_2}{2m_1}$$

Sol. 53 (C)

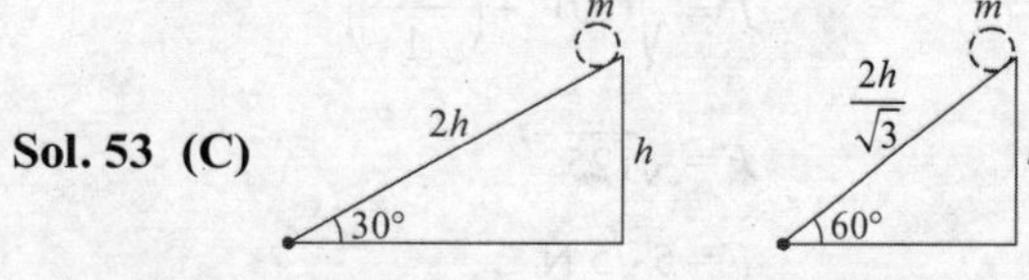

$$K_1 = 0 + [mg \sin 30° - \mu\, mg \cos 30°]\, 2h$$

$$K_2 = 0 + [mg \sin 60° - \mu\, mg \cos 60°]\frac{2h}{\sqrt{3}}$$

$$K_2 > K_1$$

Sol. 54 (C) $\frac{1}{2}kx^2 = \frac{1}{2}mv^2$

$$600 \times (0.05)^2 = (15 \times 10^{-3})\, v^2$$

$$v^2 = 100$$

$$v = 10 \text{ m/s}$$

Maximum range, $R = \frac{v^2}{g} = \frac{(10)^2}{10} = 10\,\text{m}$

Sol. 55 (C) $P = \frac{W}{t} = \frac{mgh}{t}$

$$t = 1s$$

$$m = V\rho = 0.2\text{m}^3 \times 1000\,\text{kg/m}^3$$

$$m = 200\text{kg}$$

$$P = \frac{200 \times 9.8 \times (10+10)}{1}$$

$$P = 200 \times 9.8 \times 20$$

$$P = 39200\, W = 39.2\,\text{kW}$$

Sol. 56 (B) Let x be the extension in spring when 2kg block leaves the contact with surface

$$T = 20\text{N}$$

$$kx = 20$$

$$x = \frac{1}{2}\text{m}$$

Using work energy theorem, we have

$$mgx = -\frac{1}{2}kx^2 = \frac{1}{2}mv^2$$

$$v = \sqrt{2gx - \frac{kx^2}{m}} = \sqrt{2\times 10\frac{1}{2} - \frac{40\times 1}{4(5)}}$$

$$v = 2\sqrt{2}\text{ m/s}$$

Sol. 57 (C) Work done by gravity = change in $K.E.$

Let velocity of particle at point B is v

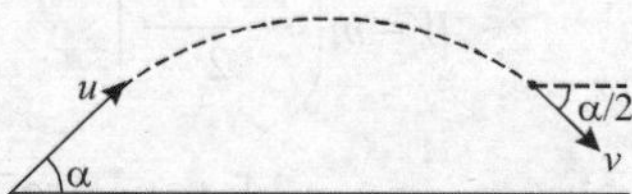

The horizontal component of velocity remains constant

$$u\cos\alpha = v\cos\frac{\alpha}{2}$$

$$v = \frac{u\cos\alpha}{\cos\alpha/2}$$

$$w = \frac{1}{2}mv^2 - \frac{1}{2}m(u\cos\alpha)^2$$

$$= \frac{1}{2}m\left[\frac{u^2\cos^2\alpha}{\cos^2\alpha/2} - u^2\cos^2\alpha\right]$$

$$= \frac{1}{2}mu^2\cos^2\alpha\left[\sec^2\frac{x}{2} - 1\right]$$

$$= \frac{1}{2}mu^2\cos^2\alpha\tan^2\frac{\alpha}{2}$$

Sol. 58 **(A)** The equation of the given line is

$$3y + kx = 5$$

$$y = -\frac{kx}{3} + \frac{5}{3}$$

Slope of line is $m_1 = -\frac{k}{3}$

Slope of line of action of force is

$$m_2 = \frac{3}{2}$$

work done will be zero, when m_1 and m_2 are perpendicular to each other.

$$m_1 m_2 = -1$$

$$-\frac{k}{3} \times \frac{3}{2} = -1$$

$$k = 2$$

Sol. 59 **(A)** Since the particle is given just enough speed to complete the vertical circle,

$$u^2 = 5gR = 5g$$

$$v^2 = u^2 - 2gR$$

$$v^2 = 5g - 2g$$

$$v^2 = 3g$$

Centripetal acceleration,

$$a_c = \frac{v^2}{R} = 3g$$

Tangential acceleration,

$$a_T = g$$

$$a_{\text{total}} = \sqrt{a_T^2 + a_c^2}$$

$$= \sqrt{g^2 + 9g^2}$$

$$= g\sqrt{10}$$

Sol. 60 **(C)** Power supplied is

$$P = \frac{3t^2}{2} \text{ watt}$$

$$\frac{dw}{dt} = \frac{3t^2}{2}$$

$$dw = \frac{3t^2}{2} dt$$

$$\int_0^k dw = \int_0^2 \frac{3}{2} t^2 dt$$

$$k = \frac{3}{2}\left[\frac{t^3}{3}\right]_0^2$$

$$\frac{1}{2} mv^2 = \frac{3}{2} \times \frac{8}{3}$$

$$\frac{1}{2} \times 2 \times v^2 = 4$$

$$v^2 = 4$$

$$v = 2\text{m/s}$$

Sol. 61 **(D)** Relative density of ice,

$$R_i = 0.9$$

Hense, 90% of volume of ice is immersed in water.

When ice melts completely, the level of water remains same.

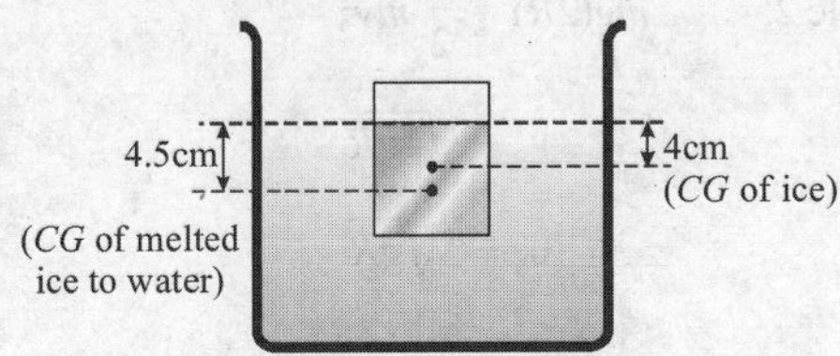

$$900 = \frac{m}{(0.1)^3}$$

$$\Rightarrow \quad m = 0.9\text{kg}$$

$$\Delta u = mg(0.04) - mg(0.045)$$

$$\Delta u = 0.9 \times 10 \times (-5 \times 10^{-3})$$

$$\Delta u = -0.045 \text{ J}$$

Sol. 62 **(A)** Let final velocity of particle is v

$$\frac{1}{2} mv_0^2 - \frac{3}{4} \cdot \frac{1}{2} mv_0^2 = \frac{1}{2} mv^2$$

$$\frac{v_0^2}{4} = v^2$$

$$\Rightarrow \quad v = \frac{v_0}{2}$$

From first equation of motion,

$$\frac{v_0}{2} = v_0 - \mu g t_0$$

$$\frac{v_0}{2} = \mu g t_0$$

$$\mu = \frac{v_0}{2gt_0}$$

Sol. 63 **(B)** For particle 1,

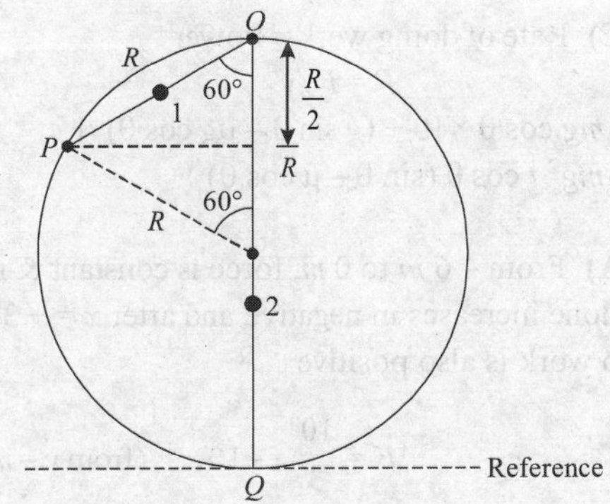

$$mg(2R) - mg\left(\frac{3R}{2}\right) = \frac{1}{2}mv_1^2$$

$$\frac{gR}{2} = \frac{v_1^2}{2}$$

$$v_1^2 = gR$$

$$v_1 = \sqrt{gR} \quad \ldots(1)$$

For particle 2, $mg(2R) = \frac{1}{2}mv_2^2$

$$v_2 = \sqrt{4gR}$$

$$v_2 = 2\sqrt{gR} \quad \ldots(2)$$

$$\frac{v_1}{v_2} = \frac{1}{2}$$

Sol. 64 (B) The particle has travelled some distance on the horizontal path

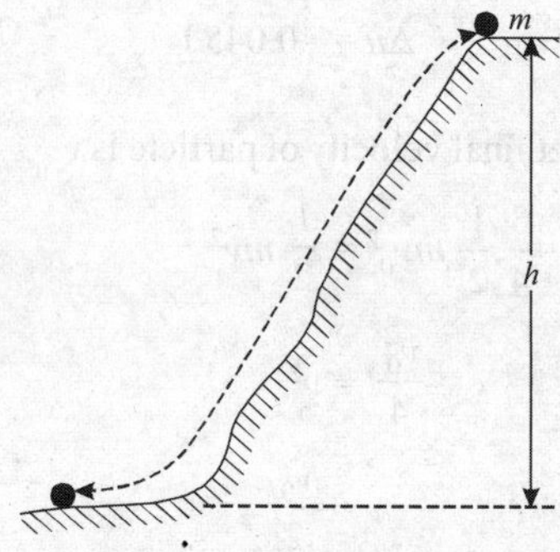

The work done to return the object ot its initial position along the same path will be preater than mgh

On the way down,

Loss in $P.E$ = work done against friction

$$mgh = w_f$$

On the way up,

Net work is done to increase the $P.E$ as well as against friction.

$\Rightarrow$ $w = w_f + mgh$

$$w = 2mgh$$

Sol. 65 (C) Rate of doing work = Power

$$P = F \,.\, v$$

$$P = \mu\, mg \cos\theta \times [0 + (g \sin\theta - \mu g \cos\theta)\, t]$$

$$P = \mu\, mg^2\, t \cos\theta\, (\sin\theta - \mu \cos\theta)$$

Sol. 66 (A) From – 6 m to 0 m, force is constant & negative. So, work done increases in negative and after $x = +3$, force is positive so work is also positive

$$F = \frac{10}{3}x - 10 \quad \text{(from } y = mx + c\text{)}$$

$$w = \int dw = \int f\,.dx$$

$$w = \int\left(\frac{10}{3}x - 10\right)dx$$

$$w = \frac{10}{3}\frac{x^2}{2} - 10x$$

$$w = \frac{5x^2}{3} - 10x$$

The graph will be parabola upwards as shown in option (A).

Sol. 67 (D) $F \propto S^{-1/3}$

$$a \propto S^{-1/3}$$

$$v\frac{dv}{dS} \propto S^{-1/3}$$

$$\int v\,dv = k\int S^{-1/3}\,dS$$

$$\frac{v^2}{2} = \frac{3kS^{2/3}}{2}$$

$$v = k\sqrt{3}\,S^{1/3}$$

$$v \propto S^{1/3}$$

$$P = F \,.\, v$$

$$P \propto S^{-1/3} \,.\, S^{1/3}$$

$$P \propto S^0$$

Sol. 68 (B) As particle has descended through distance 'h'

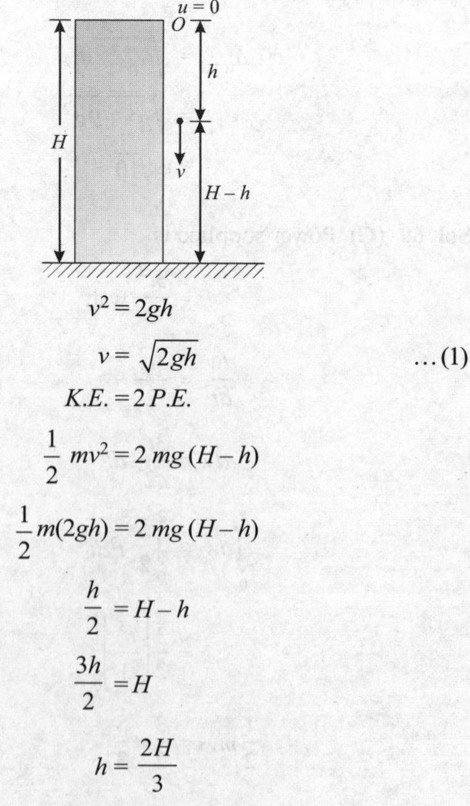

$$v^2 = 2gh$$

$$v = \sqrt{2gh} \quad \ldots(1)$$

$$K.E. = 2\,P.E.$$

$$\frac{1}{2}mv^2 = 2\,mg\,(H - h)$$

$$\frac{1}{2}m(2gh) = 2\,mg\,(H - h)$$

$$\frac{h}{2} = H - h$$

$$\frac{3h}{2} = H$$

$$h = \frac{2H}{3}$$

Height of particle from ground,

$$H - h = H - \frac{2H}{3} = \frac{H}{3}$$

Speed of particle at that instant,

$$v = \sqrt{2g\left(\frac{2H}{3}\right)}$$

$$v = 2\sqrt{\frac{gH}{3}}$$

Sol. 69 (B)

$$w = F.S$$
$$w = ma.S$$
$$a = -\frac{20}{2} = -10\text{m/s}^2$$
$$S = \frac{1}{2} \times 2 \times 20 = 20\text{m}$$
$$w = 2 \times (-10)(20)$$
$$w = -400\text{ J}$$

Sol. 70 (C) Case-I.

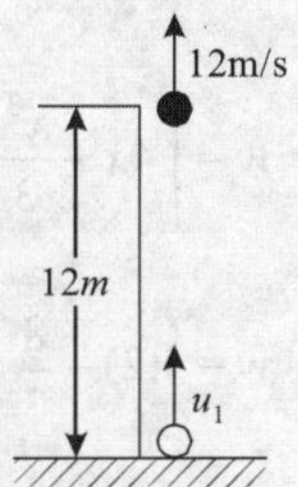

Let speed with which the ball is thrown up is u_1

$$(12)^2 = u_1^2 - 2 \times 9.8 \times 12$$
$$u_1^2 = 379.2$$
$$KE_1 = \frac{1}{2} mu_1^2 = \frac{1}{2} m(379.2)$$

Case-II.

v = 0

12m

u_2

$$(0)^2 = u_2^2 - 2 \times 9.8 \times 12$$
$$u_2^2 = 235.2$$
$$KE_2 = \frac{1}{2} mu_2^2 = \frac{1}{2} \text{m}(235.2)$$

$$\%\text{ energy charge} = \frac{KE_2 - KE_1}{KE_1} \times 100$$
$$= -38\%$$

Negative sign shows that energy is saved.

Sol. 71 (A) Potential energy at A,

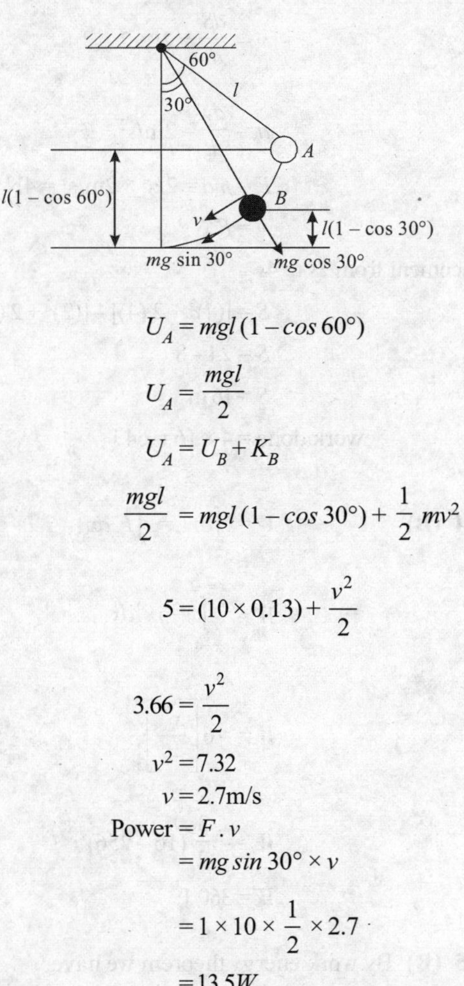

$$U_A = mgl(1 - cos\,60°)$$
$$U_A = \frac{mgl}{2}$$
$$U_A = U_B + K_B$$
$$\frac{mgl}{2} = mgl(1 - cos\,30°) + \frac{1}{2}mv^2$$
$$5 = (10 \times 0.13) + \frac{v^2}{2}$$
$$3.66 = \frac{v^2}{2}$$
$$v^2 = 7.32$$
$$v = 2.7\text{m/s}$$
$$\text{Power} = F.v$$
$$= mg\,sin\,30° \times v$$
$$= 1 \times 10 \times \frac{1}{2} \times 2.7$$
$$= 13.5W$$

Sol. 72 (A) Let the length of spring at the situation shown in figure is l

$$\cos 37° = \frac{h}{l}$$
$$l = \frac{h}{\cos 37°} = \frac{5h}{4}$$

Extension in spring,

$$x = l - h = \frac{5h}{4} - h = \frac{h}{4}$$

$$\frac{1}{2}kx^2 + \frac{1}{2}kx^2 = \frac{1}{2}mv^2$$
$$2 \times \frac{1}{2} \times 1000 \times \frac{h^2}{16} = \frac{1}{2}(5)v^2$$
$$v^2 = 25h^2$$
$$v = 5h\text{m/s}$$

Sol. 73 (B) $S = t^2 + 2t$

$$v = \frac{dS}{dt} = 2t + 2$$

$$a = \frac{dv}{dt} = 2\text{m/s}^2$$

$$F = ma = 2kg \times 2\text{m/s}^2 = 4\text{N}$$

As $w = F.S$

Displacement from $2s$ to $4s$

$$S = [(4)^2 + 2(4)] - [(2)^2 + 2(2)]$$

$$S = 24 - 8$$

$$S = 16\text{m}$$

work done $= 4 \times 16 = 64$ J

Sol. 74 (B) $W = \int dw = \int F\, dx$

$$W = \int_{x=4}^{x=-2} -6x^3 dx$$

$$W = -6\left[\frac{x^4}{4}\right]_4^{-2}$$

$$W = -\frac{3}{2}(16 - 256)$$

$$W = 360 \text{ J}$$

Sol. 75 (B) By work energy theorem we have

$$mgs \sin\theta = \frac{1}{2}mv^2$$

$$v^2 - 2gs\sin\theta = \text{constant}$$

Sol. 76 (A) Work by all forces is

$$w = KE = \frac{1}{2}mv^2$$

$$w = \frac{1}{2}\left(\frac{4}{3}\pi r^3 \cdot \rho\right).(r^2)^2$$

As $v \propto r^2$ for terminal speed as $F = mg$

$\Rightarrow$ $w \propto r^7$

Sol. 77 (C) Power to particle is

$$P = F.v$$

$$P = ma.v$$

$$P = m.v\frac{dv}{ds}v$$

$$P = \frac{mv^2 dv}{ds}$$

$$v^2 dv = \frac{P}{m}ds$$

$$\int_{v_1}^{v_2} v^2 dv = \frac{P}{m}\int_0^S ds$$

$$\frac{P}{m}S = \frac{v_2^3}{3} - \frac{v_1^3}{3}$$

$$S = \frac{m}{3P}(v_2^3 - v_1^3)$$

Sol. 78 (C) Work done by the force is

$$w = \int dw = \int |\vec{F}|.dx$$

$$w = \int_0^2 (4 - x^2)\,dx$$

$$w = \left[4x - \frac{x^3}{3}\right]_0^2$$

$$w = 4(2) - \frac{8}{3}$$

$$w = 8 - \frac{8}{3} = \frac{16}{3} = 5.33\,J$$

maximum kinetic energy $= 5.33$J which we can check by $\frac{dK}{dx} = 0$ which is at $x = 2$m

Sol. 79 (B) $a_t = \alpha t$

$\Rightarrow$ $v = \frac{\alpha t^2}{2}$

$$a_{\text{total}} = \sqrt{a_r^2 + a_t^2}$$

$$\tan 45° = \frac{a_t}{a_r} = 1$$

$$\frac{\alpha t \times 4 \times 2}{\alpha^2 t^4} = 1$$

at $t = 2s$

$$\frac{\alpha(2) \times 4 \times 2}{\alpha^2 (2)^4} = 1$$

$$\alpha = 1 \text{ m/s}^3$$

Sol. 80 **(B)** By energy conservation if block goes to a distance x_1 on other side then we use

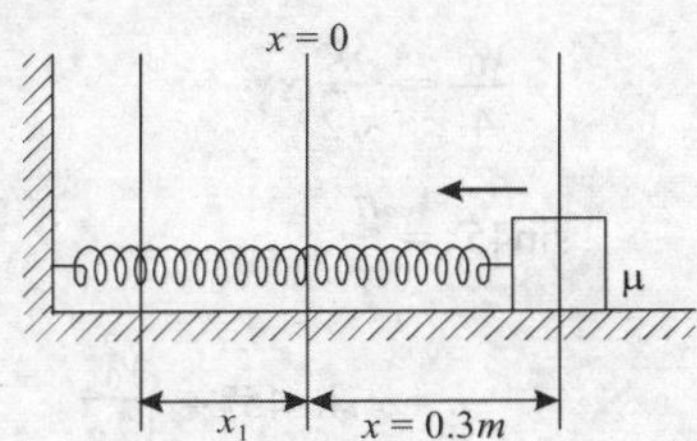

$$0+\frac{1}{2}kx^2-\frac{1}{2}kx_1{}^2-\mu mg(x+x_1)=0$$

$$\frac{1}{2}(20)(0.09)-\frac{1}{2}(20)x_1{}^2-(0.04)(1)(10)(0.3+x_1)=0$$

$$0.9-10x_1{}^2-0.12-0.4x_1=0$$

$$10x_1{}^2+0.4x_1-0.78=0$$

$$\Rightarrow x_1=0.26\text{ m}$$

Again if block covers a distance x_2 to the right of mean position,

$$0+\frac{1}{2}kx_1^2-\frac{1}{2}kx_2^2-\mu mg(x_1+x_2)=0$$

$$0+\frac{1}{2}(20)(0.26)^2-\frac{1}{2}(20)x_2^2-(0.04)(1)(10)(0.26+x_2)=0$$

$$0.676-10x_2^2-0.104-0.4x_2=0$$

$$10x_2^2+0.4x_2-0.572=0$$

$$\Rightarrow x_2=0.22\text{ m}$$

The distance covered by block from mean position decreases each time by 0.04 *m*.

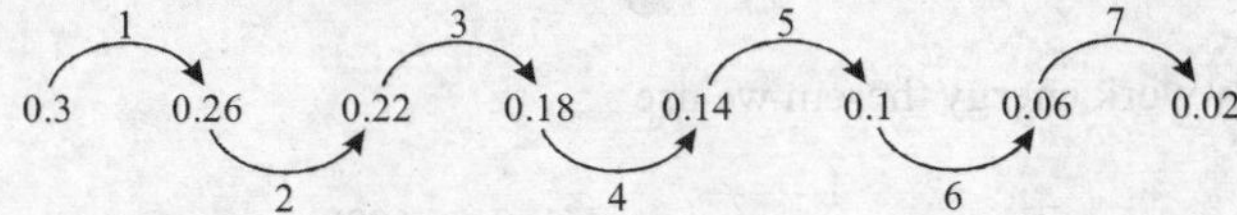

Thus, block passes the mean position seven times before coming to rest when $kx < \mu mg$.

Sol. 81 **(D)** Using work energy theorem

$$mgh+\frac{1}{2}mv^2=mg(2R)$$

$$gh+\frac{v^2}{2}=2gR$$

$$\frac{v^2}{2}=2gR-gh$$

$$v^2=2g(2R-h)$$

$$v=\sqrt{2g(2R-h)}$$

Sol. 82 **(D)** Power supplied to block is

$$P=F.v$$

$$P=\mu mg.v$$

$$v=\frac{P}{\mu mg}$$

Sol. 83 **(A)**

$$f_{1\,max}=(0.4)(1)(10)=4\text{ N}$$

$$f_{2\,max}=(0.4)(2)(10)=8\text{ N}$$

Let m_1 is shifted to right by x_0

$$kx_0=\mu m_2 g$$

$$Fx_0=\mu m_1 gk_0+\frac{1}{2}kx_0^2$$

$$F=\mu m_1 g+\frac{\mu m_2 g}{2}=8\text{N}$$

Sol. 84 **(C)** Work done by the force on particle is

$$w=\int dw=\int F\,dx$$

$$w=\int\frac{K}{v}\,dx$$

$$w=\int\frac{K}{dx}\,dt\,dx$$

$$w=\int Kdt$$

$$w=Kt$$

Sol. 85 **(C)** Net acceleration of block is

$$a=\frac{F_B-W}{m}$$

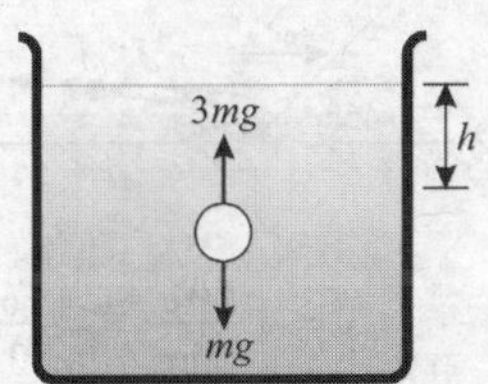

$$a=\frac{3mg-mg}{m}=2g$$

$$a=20\text{ m/s}^2 \qquad \text{(upwards)}$$

If velocity acquired by block as it reaches surface is *v*,

$$v^2=2ah$$

$$v^2=2\times 20\times h$$

$$v^2=40h \qquad \ldots(1)$$

Now, after block has left the surface & is in air, it is under action of acceleration due to gravity,

$$0 = v^2 - 2gx$$

where x is maximum height the ball will reach

$$0 = 40h - 20x$$

$$x = 2h$$

Sol. 86 (A) Let spring is elongated by distance x.

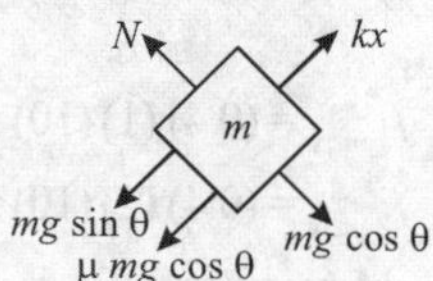

$$kx = \mu\, mg \cos\theta + mg \sin\theta \quad \ldots(1)$$

As M is descended by x.

$$Mgx = \frac{1}{2}kx^2$$

$$Mg = \frac{kx}{2} \quad \ldots(2)$$

From (1) & (2), we get $Mg = \dfrac{\mu mg\cos\theta + mg\sin\theta}{2}$

$$(10)M = \frac{\frac{3}{4}\times m\times 10\times\frac{4}{5} + m\times 10\times\frac{3}{5}}{2}$$

$$M = \frac{\frac{3m}{5}+\frac{3m}{5}}{2} = \frac{3m}{5}$$

Sol. 87 (B) By conservation of momentum,

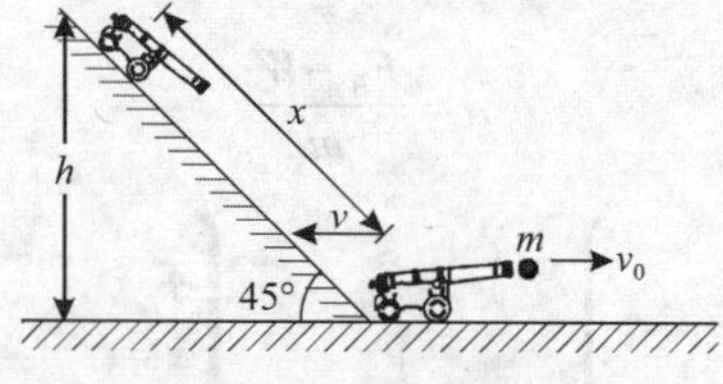

$$v = -\frac{mv_0}{2m} = -\frac{v_0}{2}$$

So, the direction of velocity of cannon will be opposite to the shell

By energy conservation work energy theorem, we use

$$\frac{1}{2}mv^2 - \mu\, mg\cos\theta\, x - mg\sin\theta\, x = 0$$

$$\frac{1}{2}m\frac{v_0^2}{4} = \left(\frac{mg}{\sqrt{2}} + \frac{1}{2}\frac{mg}{\sqrt{2}}\right)x$$

$$\frac{v_0^2}{8} = \left(\frac{g}{\sqrt{2}} + \frac{g}{2\sqrt{2}}\right)x$$

$$\frac{v_0^2}{4} = \frac{3g}{\sqrt{2}}x$$

$$\sin 45° = \frac{h}{x}$$

$$h = x\sin 45° = \frac{v_0^2}{12g}$$

Sol. 88 (D) In the refrence frame of the sphere, there are two forces :

(i) mg (downward gravity)

(ii) ma (horizontal inertial force)

By work energy theorem

$$0 + maR\sin\theta + mgR(1-\cos\theta) = \frac{1}{2}mv^2$$

$$\Rightarrow\; mgR\sin\theta + mgR - mgR\cos\theta = \frac{1}{2}mv^2$$

$$\Rightarrow\; v^2 = 2gR(1+\sin\theta-\cos\theta)$$

$$v = \sqrt{2Rg(1+\sin\theta-\cos\theta)}$$

Sol. 89 (B)

By work energy therem we use

$$\frac{1}{2}mv_0^2 = mgl(1-\cos 60°)$$

$$\frac{v_0^2}{2} = (9.8)(5)\left(1-\frac{1}{2}\right)$$

$$v_0^2 = 9.8\times 5$$

$$v_0^2 = 49$$

$$v_0 = 7\text{m/s}$$

Sol. 90 (C)

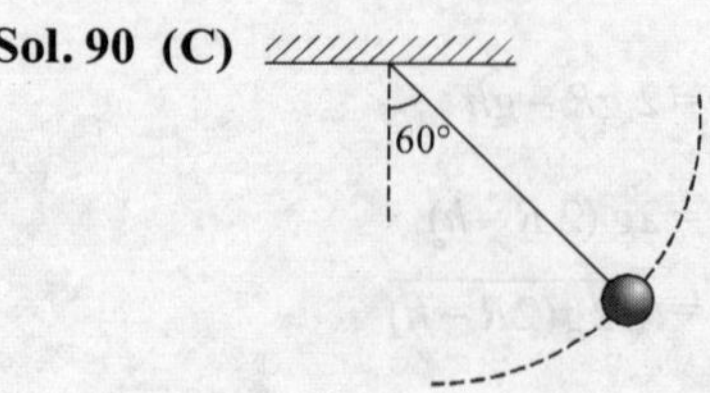

$$T\cos\theta = mg \qquad \ldots(1)$$

$$T\sin\theta = \frac{mv^2}{r} \qquad \ldots(2)$$

From (1) & (2), we get

$$\tan\theta = \frac{v^2}{rg} = \frac{(10)^2}{(10)(10)} = 1$$

$$\theta = 45°$$

Sol. 91 (A)

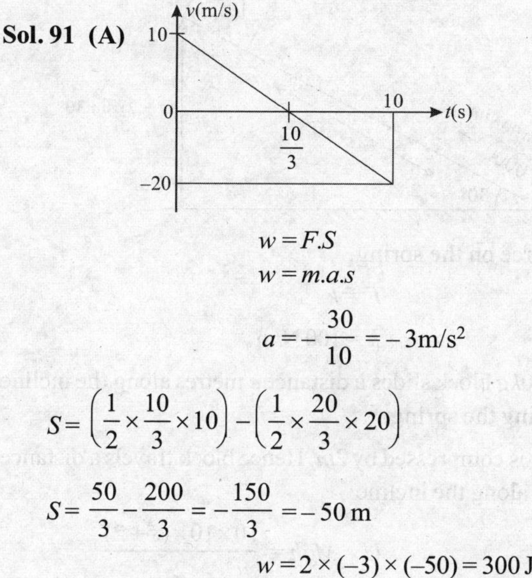

$$w = F.S$$
$$w = m.a.s$$
$$a = -\frac{30}{10} = -3\text{m/s}^2$$
$$S = \left(\frac{1}{2}\times\frac{10}{3}\times 10\right) - \left(\frac{1}{2}\times\frac{20}{3}\times 20\right)$$
$$S = \frac{50}{3} - \frac{200}{3} = -\frac{150}{3} = -50\text{ m}$$
$$w = 2\times(-3)\times(-50) = 300\text{ J}$$

Sol. 92 (A)

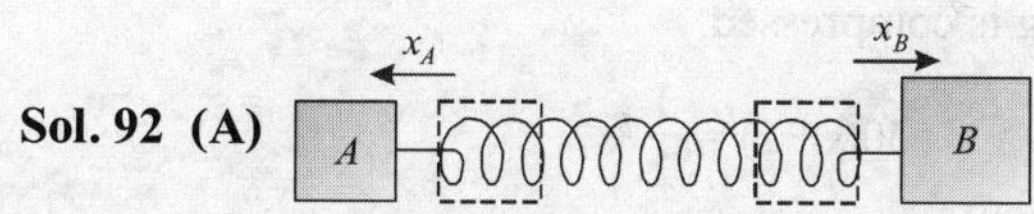

$$x_A + x_B = x_0$$
$$m(-x_A) + 2m(x_B) = 0$$
$$\frac{x_A}{x_B} = \frac{2}{1}$$
$$x_A = 2x_B \Rightarrow v_A = 2v_B$$

using energy conservation

$$\frac{1}{2}kx^2 = \frac{1}{2}mv_A{}^2 + \frac{1}{2}(2m)v_B^2$$
$$kx^2 = m(4v_B{}^2) + (2m)v_B^2$$
$$6mv_B^2 = kx^2$$
$$v_B{}^2 = \frac{kx^2}{6m}$$
$$v_B = \sqrt{\frac{k}{6m}}\,x$$
$$\Rightarrow \qquad v_A = 2\sqrt{\frac{k}{6m}}\,x$$

Relative velocity of blocks,

$$v = v_A - (-v_B)$$
$$v = v_A + v_B$$
$$v = 3\sqrt{\frac{k}{6m}}\,x = \sqrt{\frac{9k}{6m}}\,x$$
$$v = \sqrt{\frac{3k}{2m}}\,x$$

Sol. 93 (B)

$$U = \frac{1}{2}kx^2, x < 0$$
$$U = 0, x \geq 0$$
$$K + U = E$$
$$\frac{1}{2}mv^2 = E - U$$

For $x \geq 0$, $\qquad U = 0 \qquad \left[\text{As } x = \sqrt{\frac{2E}{K}}\right]$

$$\Rightarrow \qquad \frac{1}{2}mv^2 = E$$
$$v = \sqrt{\frac{2E}{m}}$$

Sol. 94 (A)

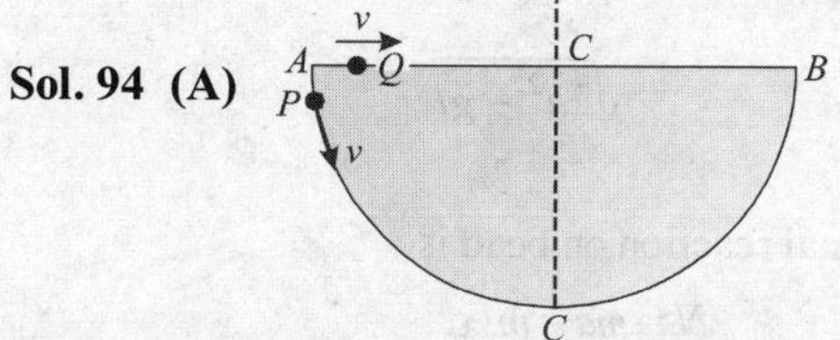

Particle P reaches point C quickly compared to Q as always horizontal component of P is more and so the time taken by Q is more compared to P $t_P < t_Q$.

Sol. 95 (D) (i) Using work energy theorem we have

$$0 + mg(4R) = \frac{1}{2}mv^2$$
$$4gR = \frac{v^2}{2}$$
$$N = \frac{mv^2}{R} = \frac{m8gR}{R} = 8mg$$
$$F_Q = \sqrt{N^2 + (mg)^2}$$
$$F_Q = \sqrt{64m^2g^2 + m^2g^2} = \sqrt{65}\,mg$$

(ii) For block to exert force on track equal to weight, we use at topmost point

$$\frac{mv^2}{R} = 2mg \Rightarrow v^2 = 2Rg$$

Using work-energy theorem we have

$$mg(h) = \frac{1}{2}m(2Rg) + mg(2R)$$

$$h = 3R$$

Sol. 96 (D)

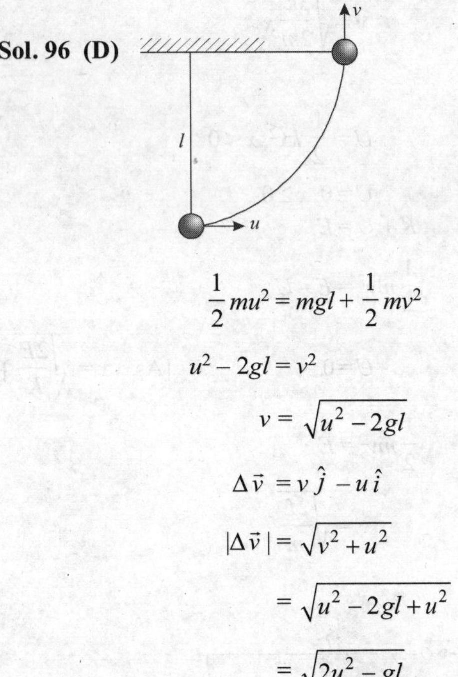

$$\frac{1}{2}mu^2 = mgl + \frac{1}{2}mv^2$$

$$u^2 - 2gl = v^2$$

$$v = \sqrt{u^2 - 2gl}$$

$$\Delta\vec{v} = v\hat{j} - u\hat{i}$$

$$|\Delta\vec{v}| = \sqrt{v^2 + u^2}$$

$$= \sqrt{u^2 - 2gl + u^2}$$

$$= \sqrt{2u^2 - gl}$$

Sol. 97 (A) Normal reaction on bead is

$$N = ma = mL\alpha$$

$$f = \mu N = m\omega^2 L$$

$$\mu mL\alpha = m(\alpha t)^2 L$$

$$t = \sqrt{\frac{\mu}{\alpha}}$$

Sol. 98 (A)

f N α $mg \cos\alpha$ α mg $mg \sin\alpha$

For equilibrium of insect we use

$$mg \sin\alpha = f$$

$$mg \sin\alpha = \mu N = \mu\, mg \cos\alpha$$

$$\tan\alpha = \mu = \frac{1}{3}$$

$$\cot\alpha = 3$$

Sol. 99 (B) By work energy theorem we have

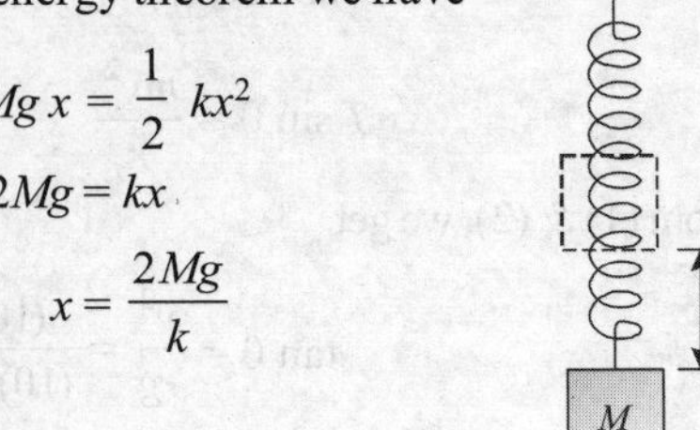

$$Mg\,x = \frac{1}{2}kx^2$$

$$2Mg = kx$$

$$x = \frac{2Mg}{k}$$

Sol. 100 (A)

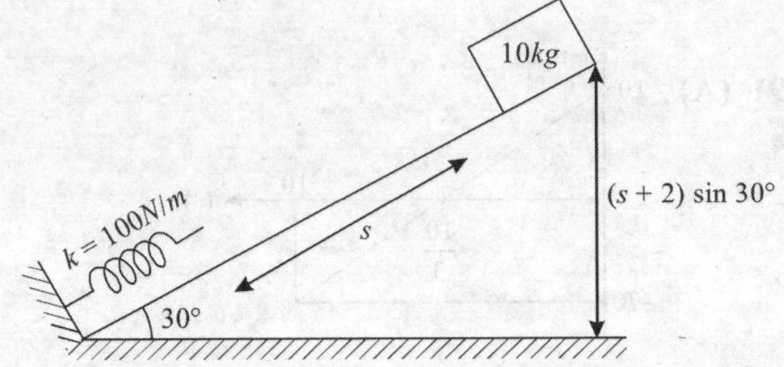

Applied force on the spring,

$$F = kx$$

$$k = 100 \text{ N/m}$$

Let mass $10kg$ block slides a distance s metres along the incline before hitting the spring.

The spring is compressed by $2m$. Hence block travels a distance of $(s+2)m$ along the incline.

Initial P.E., $U = Mgh = \dfrac{10 \times 10 \times (s+2)}{2}$

$$= 50(s+2)$$

When spring is compressed,

$$50(s+2) = \frac{1}{2}kx^2$$

$$50(s+2) = \frac{1}{2} \times 100 \times (2)^2$$

$$s + 2 = 4$$

$$s = 2m$$

$$v^2 = 0^2 + 2(g \sin 30°)\, 2$$

$$v^2 = 2 \times 10 \times \frac{1}{2} \times 2 = 20$$

$$v = \sqrt{20} \text{ m/s}$$

Sol. 101 (A) Area under $F - x$ graph = work done

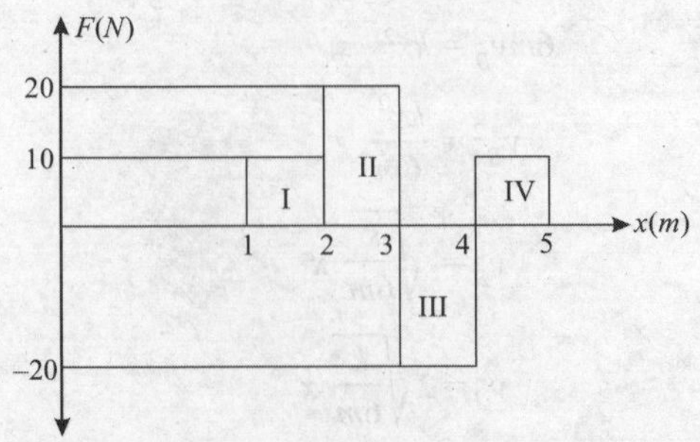

Area of I = 10
Area of II = 20
Area of III = 20
Area of IV = 10
work done = 10 + 20 – 20 + 10 = 20J

Solutions of ADVANCE MCQs One or More Option Correct

Sol. 1 (B, C, D) When ball is released it accelerates due to gravity and its acceleration becomes zero when spring force balances its weight and then it retards and comes to rest after covering equal distance where spring force will be twice the weight of ball in upward direction hence options (B), (C) and (D) are correct.

Sol. 2 (B, C, D) The minimum speed requierd to complete the circular motion is $(5gl)^{1/2}$ = 5.42m/s which is more than the imparted speed so particle will not be able to attain the maximum height due to the initial speed which is $v^2/2g$ = 90m. The string will slack before it reaches the 90 height above the initial point.

Sol. 3 (A, B) Inside a system of particles the conservative forces causes decrease in potential energy of the system when work done by these forces is positive which imparts kinetic energy in particles of the system.

Sol. 4 (B, D) When the direction of friction (static or kinetic) on a body is in the direction of motion of the point where friction is acting then work done by the friction will be positive in a given frame of reference. In a conservative force field internal forces of system can increase the kinetic energy of system by doing work and by accounting of work done by pseudo force on a particles of a system we can use work energy theorem for analysis of dynamics of body in non-inertial reference frames.

Sol. 5 (B, C, D) The work done by a force on an object in any reference frame is zero only if the displacement of point of application of force in the direction of force is zero.

Sol. 6 (A, D) Power developed by a force acting on a body is $P = mav$. If a = constant we can use $v = at$ so we get $P = ma^2t$ and we can use displacement of body as $x = (1/2)at^2$.

Sol. 7 (B, C) As KE is proportional to time we can use speed of body is proportional to $\sqrt{t}$ then as acceleration $a = dv/dt$ we get acceleration is inversely proportional to $\sqrt{t}$ hence options (B) and (C) are correct.

Sol. 8 (B, C) As the projectile goes up power of gravitational force is negative as displacement is opposite to the force and when it comes down it becomes positive and at the topmost point as velocity is normal to weight it is zero. Magnitude of power can be given as $P = mg \cdot v_y = mg\,(u_y - gt)$ hence options (B) and (C) are correct.

Sol. 9 (B, D) The resultant of all forces may provide a constant magnitude of acceleration mv^2/r towards the centre.

Sol. 10 (A, C) As work is done by the spring that means spring energy is being released so initially spring would be in either compressed or elongated state and finally it comes to its natural length.

Sol. 11 (A, B, D) Tension in a string on which a force is directly applied is equal to the applied force. Here weight of block is = 20N and for displacement of block by x the kinetic enregy gain is = $40x - 20x = 20x$ = 40J which gives x = 2m. If we calculate the power developed by this force on block then it is $P = F.v$ where $v = at$ as motion is uniformly accelerated and displacement of block is proportional to t^2. Thus here power developed will be varying linearly with t and parabolically with displacement.

Sol. 12 (B, C) Work done by spring on block,

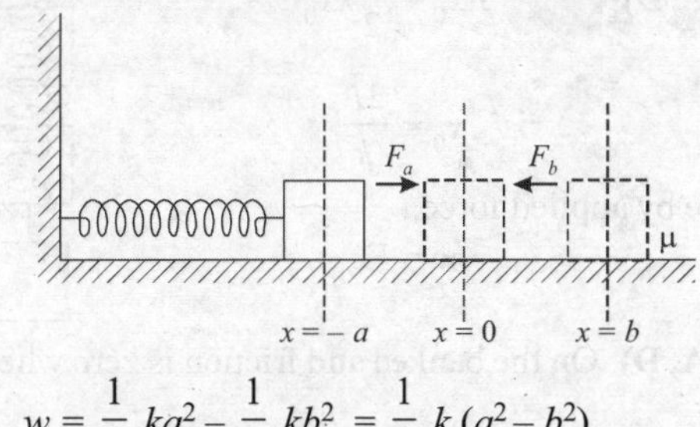

$$w_s = \frac{1}{2}ka^2 - \frac{1}{2}kb^2 = \frac{1}{2}k(a^2 - b^2)$$

By work energy theorem,

$$K_i + w = K_f$$

$$0 + \frac{1}{2}ka^2 - \mu mg(a+b) - \frac{1}{2}kb^2 = 0$$

$$\mu mg(a+b) = \frac{1}{2}k(a^2 - b^2)$$

$$\mu = \frac{k(a-b)}{2mg}$$

Sol. 13 (A, B, C) $U = 3x + 4y$

$$\vec{F} = -\frac{dU}{dx}$$

$$\vec{F} = -\frac{\partial U}{\partial x}\hat{i} - \frac{\partial U}{\partial y}\hat{j}$$

$$\vec{F} = (-3\hat{i} - 4\hat{j})\text{ N}$$

$$\vec{a} = \frac{\vec{F}}{m} = (-3\hat{i} - 4\hat{j})\text{ m/s}^2$$

$$|\vec{a}| = \sqrt{(-3)^2 + (-4)^2} = 5\text{m/s}^2$$

when particle crosses y-axis ($x = 0$)

$$S_x = u_x t + \frac{1}{2} a_x t^2$$

$$0 - 6 = 0 + \frac{1}{2}(-3)t^2$$

At $t = 2$s $$S_y = u_y t + \frac{1}{2} a_y t^2$$

$$y - 4 = 0 - \frac{1}{2}(4)\, t^2$$

$$y - 4 = -2(2)^2 = -8$$

$$y = -4 \text{ m}$$

the particle crosses y-axis at $y = -4$

$$v_x = u_x + a_x t$$

$$\bar{v}_x = 0 - (3)(2)\,\hat{i} = -6\,\hat{i}$$

$$\bar{v}_y = 0 - (4)(2)\,\hat{j} = -8\,\hat{i}$$

$$|\bar{v}| = \sqrt{(-6)^2 + (-8)^2} = 10 \text{ m/s}$$

Sol. 14 (C, D) $$Fx_0 = \frac{1}{2} k x_0^2$$

$$x_0 = \frac{2F}{k}$$

work done by applied force,

$$w = Fx_0$$

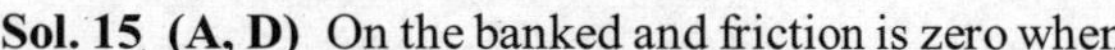

Sol. 15 (A, D) On the banked and friction is zero when

$$mg \sin\theta = \frac{mv^2}{R} \cos\theta$$

$\Rightarrow$ $$v = \sqrt{Rg \tan\theta}$$

And for a vehicle at rest on incline it does not slide if $\theta <$ angle of repose.

Sol. 16 (A, D) $$U = 15 + (x - 3)^2$$

$$U(5) = 19 \;\;\&\;\; KE(5) = 50$$

Total mechanical energy $= 50 + 19 = 69$ J

$$U_{\min} \equiv U(x - 3) = 15 \text{ J}$$

$$KE_{\max} = 69 - U_{\min} = 69 - 15 = 54 \text{ J}$$

Sol. 17 (A, C) Force on the particle will be given as

$$\vec{F} = -\nabla U$$

$$= \frac{\partial U}{\partial x}\hat{i} - \frac{\partial U}{\partial y}\hat{j} = -(6xy^2 + 6)\hat{i} - (6x^2 y)\hat{j}$$

Now, for acceleration at ($t = 0$) and $x = 1$, $y = 1$

$$\vec{a} = \frac{\vec{F}}{M} = 12\hat{i} - 6\hat{j}$$

$$|\vec{a}| = 6\sqrt{5} \text{ m/s}^2$$

Particle is at rest at $x = 1$, $y = 1$. Then

$$\text{P.E.} + \text{K.E.} = \text{M.E.}$$

$$U(1, 1) + \text{K.E.}(1, 1) = \text{M.E.}$$

$$\Rightarrow \text{M.E} = 9\text{J}$$

$$\Delta U + \Delta K = \Delta W$$

$$\Delta W = \Delta U = U(0, 0) - U(1, 1)$$

$$\Delta W = -9 \text{ J}$$

Sol. 18 (A, C) Apply $\tau = I\alpha$ about O

$$mgx = \left(\frac{mL^2}{12} + mx^2\right)\alpha$$

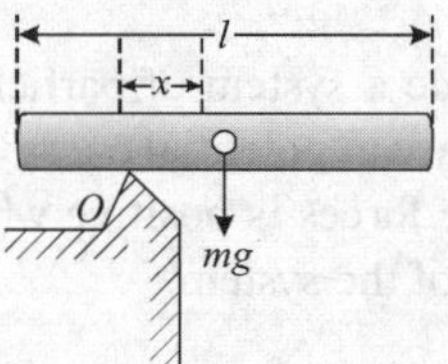

For α to be maximum $d\alpha/dx = 0$ which gives $x = \dfrac{L}{2\sqrt{3}}$ and $\alpha = \dfrac{\sqrt{3}g}{L}$

Sol. 19 (B, C) In the region AB the speed of particle is uniform hence no work is being done on the particle. In region BC particle is retarding so work done by external forces on the particle is negative.

Sol. 20 (A, C) As soon as the block hits the wall, the suspension point B comes to a stop, while the particle C keeps moving with a velocity v_0 towards left. In order that it complete a full circle, it must have enough kinetic energy so as to make it to the top of the circle.

$$\frac{1}{2} m v_0^2 = mg.\, 2l$$

i.e., $v_0 = \sqrt{4gl}$,

Since velocity at the highest point being zero.

Sol. 21 (B, C) As both man and plank gains speed due to friction, work done by friction is positive for both.

* * * * *

ANSWERS & SOLUTIONS

CONCEPTUAL MCQS Single Option Correct

1	(C)	2	(C)	3	(B)
4	(B)	5	(A)	6	(C)
7	(C)	8	(B)	9	(C)
10	(D)	11	(A)	12	(A)
13	(D)	14	(B)	15	(B)
16	(C)	17	(B)	18	(C)
19	(D)	20	(B)	21	(B)
22	(A)	23	(D)	24	(D)
25	(D)	26	(B)	27	(B)
28	(B)	29	(C)	30	(C)
31	(A)	32	(D)	33	(B)
34	(C)				

NUMERICAL MCQS Single Option Correct

1	(B)	2	(A)	3	(C)
4	(D)	5	(A)	6	(B)
7	(A)	8	(B)	9	(B)
10	(C)	11	(B)	12	(D)
13	(D)	14	(C)	15	(B)
16	(A)	17	(C)	18	(B)
19	(D)	20	(D)	21	(A)
22	(A)	23	(D)	24	(C)
25	(D)	26	(D)	27	(D)
28	(B)	29	(B)	30	(A)
31	(C)	32	(B)	33	(C)
34	(C)	35	(C)	36	(A)
37	(B)	38	(A)	39	(A)
40	(A)	41	(C)	42	(D)
43	(B)	44	(B)	45	(D)
46	(B)	47	(C)	48	(C)
49	(B)	50	(C)	51	(B)
52	(A)	53	(A)	54	(D)
55	(A)	56	(A)	57	(B)
58	(C)	59	(D)	60	(C)
61	(B)	62	(B)	63	(B)
64	(B)	65	(A)	66	(A)
67	(A)	68	(B)	69	(B)
70	(D)	71	(C)	72	(D)
73	(A)	74	(D)	75	(B)
76	(C)	77	(B)	78	(B)
79	(A)	80	(C)		

ADVANCE MCQs One or More Option Correct

1	(A, B)	2	(C, D)	3	(C, D)
4	(B, C)	5	(B, C, D)	6	(B, D)
7	(All)	8	(All)	9	(A, B, D)
10	(A, C)	11	(A, C)	12	(B, D)
13	(A, C)	14	(A, D)	15	(A, D)
16	(B, C, D)	17	(All)	18	(A, C)
19	(A, D)	20	(A)		

Solutions of PRACTICE EXERCISE 4.1

(i) For the uniform disc its mass is proportional to area thus mass of given object is

$$m_1 = k\left(\pi R^2 - \frac{R^2}{2}\right) = \left(\frac{2\pi - 1}{2}\right)kR^2$$

The mass of square when it is cut from disc is

$$m_2 = \frac{kR^2}{2}$$

As common centre of mass of m_1 and m_2 must be at disc centre and if centre of mass of given object is at *a* distance *x* from *C*, we use

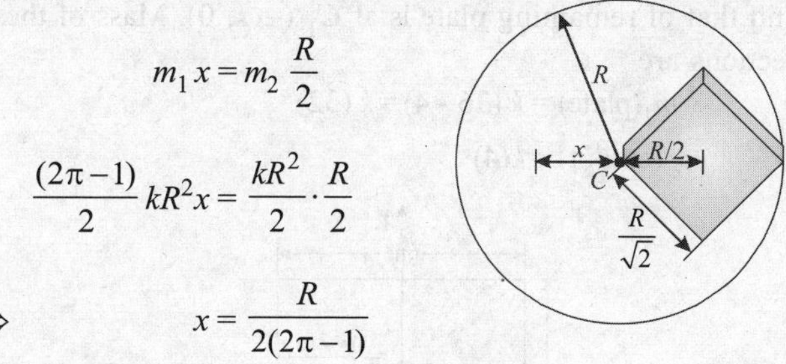

$$m_1 x = m_2 \frac{R}{2}$$

$$\frac{(2\pi-1)}{2}kR^2 x = \frac{kR^2}{2}\cdot\frac{R}{2}$$

$$\Rightarrow \qquad x = \frac{R}{2(2\pi - 1)}$$

(ii) In the given situation *x* and *y* components of velocity of centre of mass are

$$v_{cx} = \frac{2\times 3 + 5\times 5\times\left(\frac{1}{2}\right)}{4+5+2} = \frac{37}{22}$$

and $$v_{cy} = \frac{4\times 2 + 5\times 5\times \sqrt{3}/2}{4+5+2} = \frac{16 + 25\sqrt{3}}{22}$$

Thus angle θ is given as

$$\theta = \tan^{-1}\frac{v_{cy}}{v_{cx}} = \tan^{-1}\left(\frac{16+25\sqrt{3}}{37}\right)$$

(iii) Coordinates of linear bodies centre of mass are

Square	Triangle	Disc
$\left(\frac{l}{2}, \frac{l}{2}\right)$	$\left(\frac{l}{2}, l + \frac{l}{2\sqrt{3}}\right)$	$\left(\frac{3l}{2}, \frac{l}{2}\right)$

Thus coordinates of centre of mass of system is

$$x_c = \frac{l^2 \times l/2 + \frac{\sqrt{3}l^2}{4}\times l/2 + \frac{\pi l^2}{4}\times\frac{3l}{2}}{l^2 + \frac{\sqrt{3}l^2}{4} + \frac{\pi l^2}{4}}$$

$$= \frac{l(3\pi + \sqrt{3} + 4)}{2(4 + \pi + \sqrt{3})}$$

$$y_c = \frac{l^2 \times \frac{l}{2} + \frac{\sqrt{3}l^2}{4}\left(1+\frac{1}{2\sqrt{3}}\right)l + \frac{\pi l^2}{4} \times \frac{l}{2}}{l^2 + \frac{\sqrt{3}l^2}{4} + \frac{\pi l^2}{4}}$$

$$= \frac{l(\pi + 2\sqrt{3} + 5)}{2(4 + \pi + \sqrt{3})}$$

(iv) In the given situation $m_2 \neq m_3$ so centre of mass cannot be located at C no matter whatever be the value of m_4.

(v) In figure for the plate centre of mass is directly proportional to the area. Here centre of mass of square cutout is at C_2 (2, 0) and that of remaining plate is at C_1 ($-x_C$, 0). Mass of these sections are

$$m_1(\text{plate}) = k(36-4) = k(32)$$

$$m_2\ (\text{cutout}) = k(4)$$

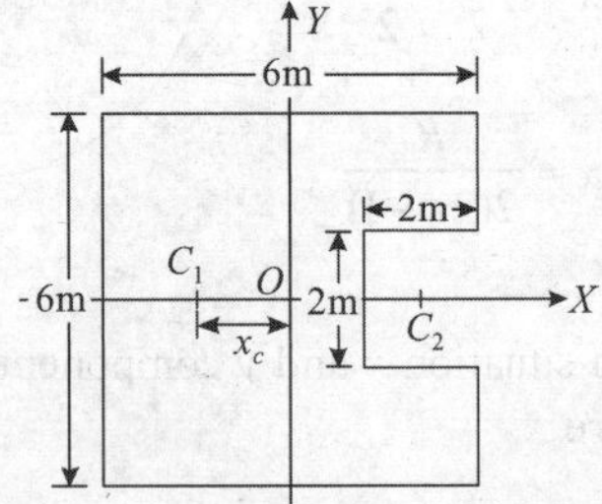

Common centre of mass must be at origin so, we use

$$m_1 x_C = m_2 (2)$$

$$k(32) x_C = k(4)(2)$$

$$\Rightarrow \quad x_C = \frac{1}{4} = 0.25 \text{ m}$$

Solutions of PRACTICE EXERCISE 4.2

(i) Considering element of angular width $d\theta$ as shown in figure, its x coordinate is $R\cos\theta$ and its mass is

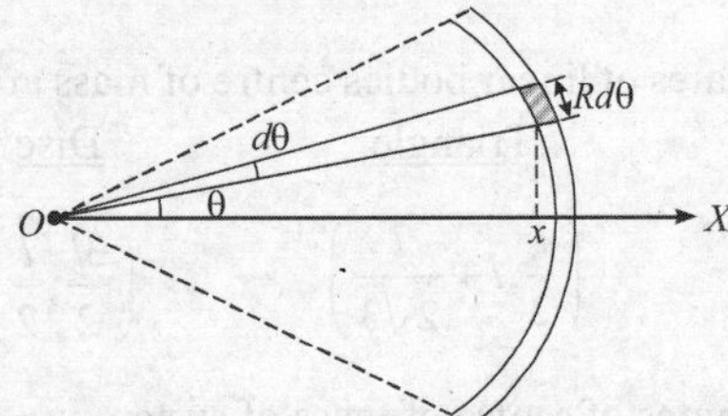

$$dm = \frac{m}{\phi}.d\theta$$

Thus centre of mass of arc is given as

$$x_c = \frac{1}{m}\int dmx = \frac{1}{m}\int_{-\phi/2}^{+\phi/2} \frac{m}{\phi}\, d\theta.R\cos\theta$$

$$= \frac{R}{\phi}.(2\sin\phi/2) = \frac{2R\sin\frac{\phi}{2}}{\phi}$$

(ii) Consider an elemental arc AB of radius r and width dr as shown in figure

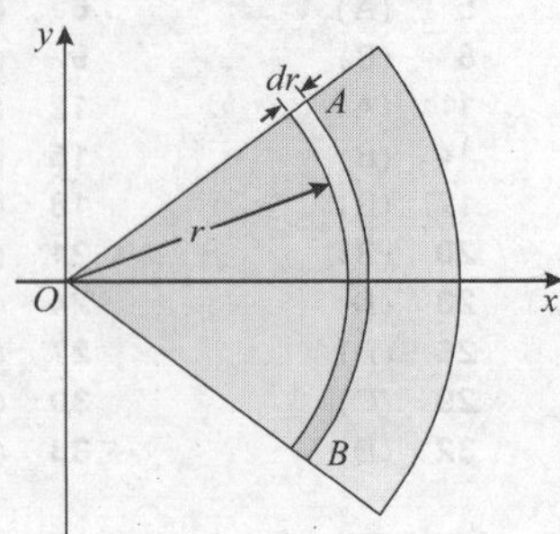

If we consider σ as the surface mass density of the disc then the mass dm of the arc AB is given as

$$dm = \sigma(2r\,\theta dr) = 2\sigma r\theta dr$$

Due to symmetry of mass center of mass of this arc must be on the angle bisector i.e. on x-axis at distance $x = \frac{r\sin\theta}{\theta}$. (This is result of previous problem we are using here)

Now center of mass of the sector is given as

$$x_c = \frac{\int xdm}{M}$$

$$x_c = \frac{\int_0^R \left(\frac{r\sin\theta}{\theta}\right)(2\sigma r\theta dr)}{\sigma(\text{Area of the sector})}$$

$$= \frac{\int_0^R \left(\frac{r\sin\theta}{\theta}\right)(2\sigma r\theta dr)}{\sigma(r^2 2\theta)}$$

$$= \frac{R\sin\theta}{3\theta}$$

(iii) Centre of mass of quarter disc cut is at point $C_1\left(\frac{4a}{3\pi}, \frac{4a}{3\pi}\right)$ & let that of remaining part is at C_2 (r_1 r) such that common centre of mass must be located at centre of square $\left(\frac{a}{2}, \frac{a}{2}\right)$

Thus we use

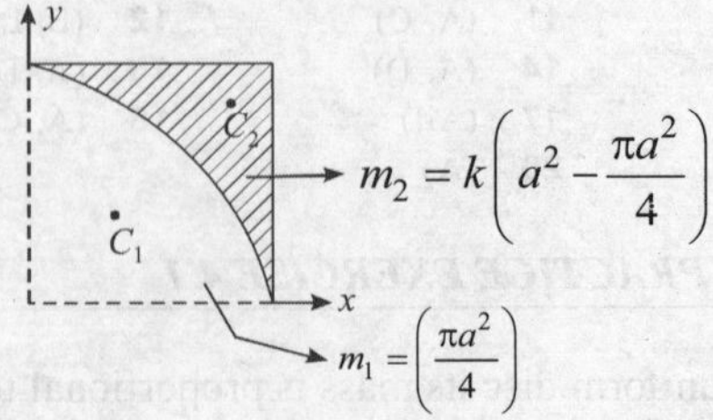

$$\frac{a}{2} = \frac{k.\frac{\pi a^2}{4} \times \frac{4a}{3\pi} + ka^2\left(\frac{4-\pi}{4}\right) \times r}{ka^2}$$

$$\Rightarrow \quad \frac{a}{2} = \frac{a}{3} + \frac{4-\pi}{4} r$$

$$\Rightarrow \quad r = \frac{2a}{3(4-\pi)}$$

(iv) Mass of they cone cut is

$$m_1 = k\left(\frac{1}{3}\pi\left(\frac{R}{2}\right)^2 R\right) = k\left(\frac{\pi R^3}{12}\right)$$

[its centre of mass is a height $R/4$]

Mass of remaining hemisphere is

$$m_2 = \frac{2}{3}\pi R^3 - \frac{\pi R^3}{12} = k\left(\frac{7}{12}\pi R^3\right)$$

[let its centre of mass is at a height y]

As common centre of mass of $m_1 + m_2$ is at a height $\frac{3R}{8}$, we use

$$\frac{3R}{8} = \frac{k\left(\frac{\pi R^3}{12}\right).\frac{R}{4} + k\left(\frac{7}{12}\pi R^3\right)y}{k\left(\frac{2}{3}\pi R^3\right)}$$

$$\Rightarrow \quad \frac{2}{3} \times \frac{3R}{8} = \frac{R}{48} + \frac{7y}{12}$$

$$\Rightarrow \quad \frac{7y}{12} = \frac{R}{4} - \frac{R}{48} = \frac{11R}{48}$$

$$\Rightarrow \quad y = \frac{11R}{28}$$

(v) Considering an elemental disc of radius y and width dx at a distance x from origin, its mass dm is taken as

$$dm = \rho.\pi y^2\, dx = \frac{\pi\rho x\, dx}{k}$$

Location of centre of mass is

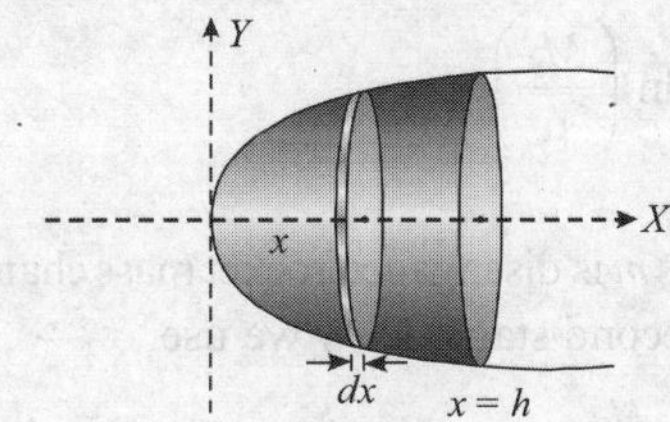

$$x_c = \frac{1}{m}\int dmx = \frac{\int_0^h \pi\rho x dx.x}{\int_0^h \pi\rho x dx} = \frac{h^3/3}{h^2/2} = \frac{2h}{3}$$

Solutions of PRACTICE EXERCISE 4.3

(i) If boat travels a distance x toward right, the displacement of centre of mass of system must be zero, Thus we use

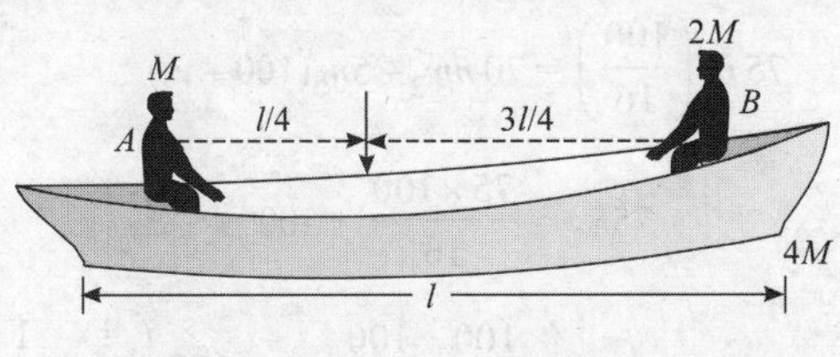

$$0 = \frac{M(1/4 + x) - 2M(3l/4 - x) + 4Mx}{7M}$$

$$\Rightarrow \quad \frac{Ml}{4} + 5Mx = \frac{3Ml}{2} - 2Mx$$

$$\Rightarrow \quad 7x = \frac{5l}{4}$$

$$\Rightarrow \quad x = \frac{5l}{28}$$

(ii) If shall is fired at muzzle at speed v_1, we use

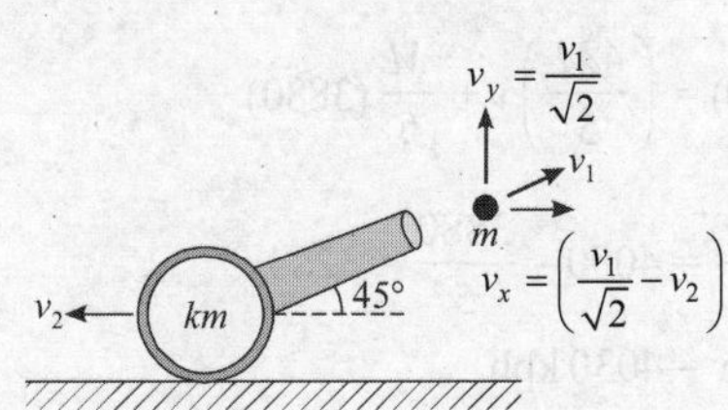

$$m\left(\frac{v_1}{\sqrt{2}} - v_2\right) = kmv_2$$

$$\Rightarrow \quad v_2 = \frac{v_1}{\sqrt{2}(k+1)}$$

Thus ratio of kinetic energies is

$$\frac{K_{shell}}{K_{gun}} = \frac{\frac{1}{2}m\left[\frac{v_1^2}{2} + \left(\frac{v_1}{\sqrt{2}} - v_2\right)^2\right]}{\frac{1}{2}kmv_2^2}$$

$$= \frac{\frac{v_1^2}{2} + \frac{k^2 v_1^2}{2(k+1)^2}}{\left(k\frac{v_1^2}{2(k+1)^2}\right)}$$

$$= \frac{2k^2 + 2k + 1}{k}$$

(iii) After first shot if speed of car is v_1, we use

$$75\, mv = 5m(100 - v)$$

$$\Rightarrow \quad v_1 = \frac{500}{80} = \frac{100}{16} \text{ m/s}$$

If after second shot speed of car is v_2, we use

$$75\, m\left(\frac{100}{16}\right) = 70\, mv_2 - 5m\,(100 - v_2)$$

$$75\, v_2 = \frac{75 \times 100}{16} + 500$$

$$v_2 = \frac{100}{16} + \frac{100}{15} \text{ m/s} = 100\left(\frac{1}{16} + \frac{1}{15}\right) \text{m/s}$$

(iv) When block reaches ground and if B is displaced toward right by x, the displacement of centre of mass of system in horizontal direction must be zero hence we use

$$4M\,(l - x) = 20\, Mx$$

$$x = \frac{l}{6}$$

(v) If final velocity of shuttle is v, we use by momentum conservation

$$M(4000) = \left(\frac{4M}{5}\right)v + \frac{M}{5}\,(3880)$$

$$\Rightarrow \quad \frac{4v}{5} = 4000 - \frac{3880}{5} = 3224$$

$$\Rightarrow \quad v = 4030 \text{ kph}$$

(vi) As at slow speed position of centre of mass will not change suddenly, we use

$$\frac{m}{4} \times 15 = \frac{3m}{4}\,(-y)$$

$$\Rightarrow \quad y = -5 \text{ cm}$$

(vii) As total momentum at explosion in x and y direction remain zero and we consider m kg mass moves at an angle θ to x direction, we use

Along x dir. $1 \times 12 = m \times 40 \cos\theta$ ...(1)

Along y dir. $2 \times 8 = m \times 40 \sin\theta$ ...(2)

Squaring and adding equations (1) & (2) we get

$$\sqrt{144 + 256} = 40\,\text{m}$$

$$\Rightarrow \quad m = 0.5 \text{ kg}$$

Thus total mass of shell is $= 1 + 2 + 0.5 = 3.5$ kg

(viii) When m starts from rest it breaks off at an angular displacement $\cos^{-1}\left(\frac{2}{3}\right)$. At this point centre of mass of block and hemisphere is located at a point $P\,(x, y)$ with origin at C, then we use

$$x = \frac{m\left(\frac{\sqrt{5}R}{3}\right) + 4m(0)}{5m} = \frac{R}{3\sqrt{5}}$$

$$y = \frac{m\left(\frac{2R}{3}\right) + 4m\left(\frac{R}{2}\right)}{5m} = \frac{8}{15}R$$

Distance CP is

$$\sqrt{x^2 + y^2} = R\sqrt{\frac{1}{45} + \frac{64}{225}} = \sqrt{\frac{69}{225}} = \sqrt{\frac{23}{75}}R$$

Solutions of PRACTICE EXERCISE 4.4

(i) Equations of motion we use for mass and container as-

For mass $m_1 g - T = m_1\, a$ ...(1)

For container $T + bv_0 - (m_0 - bt)\, g = (m_0 - bt)\, a$ ...(2)

Adding above two equations, we get

$$m_1 g + bv_0 - m_0 g + btg = (m_0 + m_1 - bt)\, a$$

$$\Rightarrow \quad a = \frac{(m_1 - m_0 + bt)g + bv_0}{m_0 + m_1 - bt}$$

(ii) Rocket will lift up when upthrust on rocket will balance its height

$$kv_0 = (M - kt)\, g$$

$$\Rightarrow \quad t = \frac{Mg - kv_0}{kg} = \frac{M}{k} - \frac{v_0}{g}$$

(iii) (a) If rocket has constant exhaust velocity $\left(\frac{dm}{dt} = -C\right)$ during its motion we use

$$mv = m\,(v + dv) - dm\,(u - v - dv)$$

$$mdv = u\, dm$$

$$\Rightarrow \quad \int_0^{v_1} dv = -u \int_{M_i}^{\mu} \frac{dm}{m}$$

[In integration we use –ve sign as mass is decreasing]

$$v_1 = u \ln\left(\frac{M_i}{\mu}\right)$$

(b) After a mass m is disengaged rocket mass changes to $(\mu - m)$ at the start of second stage. Now we use

$$\int_{v_1}^{v_2} dv = -u \int_{\mu - m}^{M_f} \frac{dm}{m}$$

$$\Rightarrow \quad v_2 - v_1 = u \ln\left(\frac{\mu - m}{M_f}\right)$$

$$v_2 = u\left[\ln\left(\frac{M_i}{\mu}\right) + \ln\left(\frac{\mu - m}{M_f}\right)\right]$$

$$v_2 = u\ln\left[\frac{M_i(\mu - m)}{\mu M_f}\right]$$

(c) If there is only one stage of mass M_1 the final mass after exhaust of fuel will be $(M_f + m)$. Thus we use

$$\int_0^{v_f} dv = -u\int_{M_i}^{M_f+m}\frac{dm}{m}$$

$$v_f = u\ln\left(\frac{M_1}{M_f + m}\right)$$

Here we can clearly see that $v_2 > v_f$.

(iv) Using impulse momentum equation for the particle we have

$$mv + Fdt - \rho dt\, v_0 = (m + dm)(v + dv)$$

$$(F - \rho v_0)\, dt = \rho\, vdt + (M + \rho t)\, dv$$

$$(F - \rho v_0 - \rho v)\, dt = (M + \rho t)\, dv$$

$$\int_0^v \frac{dv}{F - \rho v_0 - \rho v} = \int_0^t \frac{dt}{M + \rho t}$$

$$\frac{F - \rho v_0 - \rho v}{F - \rho v_0} = \frac{\text{M}}{M + \rho t}$$

$$F - \rho v_0 - \rho v = \frac{(F - \rho v_0)M}{m}$$

$$v = \frac{F - \rho v_0}{\rho}\left(1 - \frac{M}{m}\right)$$

$$v = \frac{dx}{dt} = \frac{dx\rho}{dm} = \frac{F - \rho v_0}{\rho}\left(1 - \frac{M}{m}\right)$$

$$\int_0^s dx = \int_M^m \frac{F - \rho v}{\rho^2}\left(1 - \frac{M}{m}\right) dm$$

$$S = \left[\frac{F - \rho v}{\rho^2}(m - M) - M\, ln\left(\frac{m}{M}\right)\right]$$

$$= \frac{F - \rho v}{\rho^2}\left[m - M\left(1 + \ln\left(\frac{m}{M}\right)\right)\right]$$

(v) As gases are ejected out during motion we use

$$\int_0^v m dv = \int_{m_0}^{m_0/2} u\, dm$$

$$v = u\ln 2 = 2\ln(2)\text{ m/s}$$

(vi) (a) At an instant equation of conservation of momentum for car is

$$m_0 v_0 = (m_0 + qt)\, v$$

$$\Rightarrow \quad v = \frac{m_0 v_0}{m_0 + qt}$$

$$\text{using } \int_0^L dx = \int_0^t \frac{m_0 v_0}{m_0 + qt} dt$$

$$L = \frac{m_0 v_0}{q}\ln\left(\frac{m_0 + qt}{m_0}\right)$$

$$m_0 + qt = m_0\, e^{\frac{qL}{m_0 v_0}}$$

$$t = \frac{m_0}{q}\left(e^{\frac{qL}{m_0 v_0}} - 1\right)$$

Thus mass after time t is

$$m = m_0 + qt = m_0\, e^{\left(\frac{qL}{m_0 v_0}\right)}$$

(b) Speed of car after time t is

$$v = \frac{m_0 v_0}{m_0 + qt} = v_0 e^{-\left(\frac{qL}{m_0 v_0}\right)}$$

Solutions of PRACTICE EXERCISE 4.5

(i) Time of collision is $t = \frac{100}{100} = 1$ sec & it occurs at *a* depth $\frac{1}{2}gt^2 = 5$ m below the top of building

Speed of masses at the time of collision are

For 0.03 kg $\quad v_1 = gt = 10$ m/s

For 0.02 kg $\quad v_2 = u - gt = 100 - gt = 90$ m/s

If common velocity after collision is v_c, we use

$$0.02 \times 90 - 0.03 \times 10 = 0.05\, v_c$$

$$v_c = \frac{1.5}{0.05} = 30\text{ m/s upward}$$

Thus max height attained by common mass is

$$h = \frac{v_c^2}{2g} = \frac{900}{20} = 45\text{ m}$$

$\Rightarrow$ height above the building combination rises

$$= 45 - 5 = 40\text{ m}$$

(ii) By conservation of momentum in x & y direction we use along x direction

$$m_B v = m_A v_A \cos\theta \qquad \ldots(1)$$

If A moves at an angle θ to initial direction of B which is taken as x axis

Along y direction

$$m_B \frac{v}{2} = m_A v_A \sin\theta \quad \ldots(2)$$

$$\frac{(2)}{(1)} \Rightarrow \tan\theta = \frac{1}{2}$$

$$\theta = \tan^{-1}\frac{1}{2}$$

As collision is elastic we use

$$\frac{1}{2}m_B v^2 = \frac{1}{2}m_B\frac{v^2}{4} + \frac{1}{2}m_A v_A^2$$

$$\Rightarrow m_A v_A \cos\theta \,.\, v = m_A v_A \cos\theta . \frac{v}{4} + m_A v_A^2$$

$$\Rightarrow v\cos\theta = \frac{1}{4}v\cos\theta + V_A$$

$$\Rightarrow V_A = \frac{3}{4}v\cos\theta \quad [\text{As } \tan\theta = \frac{1}{2} \Rightarrow \cos\theta = \frac{2}{\sqrt{5}}]$$

$$\Rightarrow V_A = \frac{3}{4} \times \frac{2}{\sqrt{5}}v = \frac{3v}{2\sqrt{5}}$$

(iii) Let v = velocity of the ball after collision along the normal and v' = velocity of the ball after collision along incline

J = impulse on ball

$= v - (-2\cos 30°) = v + \sqrt{3}$

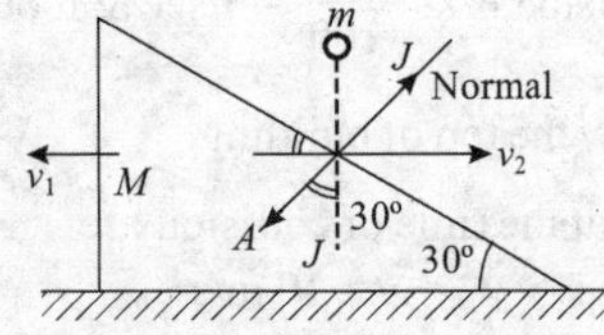

Impulse on wedge

$J\sin 30° = Mv_1 = 2v_1$

$$\Rightarrow v = 4v_1 - \sqrt{3} \quad \ldots(1)$$

Coefficient of restitution

$$e = -\left(\frac{v_2 - v_1}{u_2 - u_1}\right)$$

$$\Rightarrow \frac{1}{2} = \frac{\left(v + \frac{v_1}{2}\right)}{2\cos 30°}$$

$$\Rightarrow v = \frac{\sqrt{3}}{2} - \frac{v_1}{2} \quad \ldots(2)$$

Solving (1) & (2), we get $v_1 = \frac{1}{\sqrt{3}}$ m/s & $v = \frac{1}{\sqrt{3}}$ m/s

For the ball velocity along incline remains constant.

$\Rightarrow v' = 2\sin 30° = 1$ m/s

$$\Rightarrow \text{Final velocity of ball } v_2 = \sqrt{1^2 + \left(\frac{1}{\sqrt{3}}\right)^2} = \frac{2}{\sqrt{3}} \text{ m/s.}$$

(iv) When m leaves M, both would be moving at same speed horizontally so we use

$mu = (m + M)v$

$$\Rightarrow v = \frac{mu}{m+M}$$

The mass m will also have *a* vertical speed v_y due to which it rises to a maximum height H

Using work energy theorem we have

$$\frac{1}{2}mu^2 - mgH = \frac{1}{2}(m+M)\left(\frac{mu}{m+M}\right)^2$$

$$u^2 - 2gH = \frac{mu^2}{m+M}$$

$$\Rightarrow H = \frac{Mu^2}{2g(M+m)}$$

(v) Initial state at $t = 0$

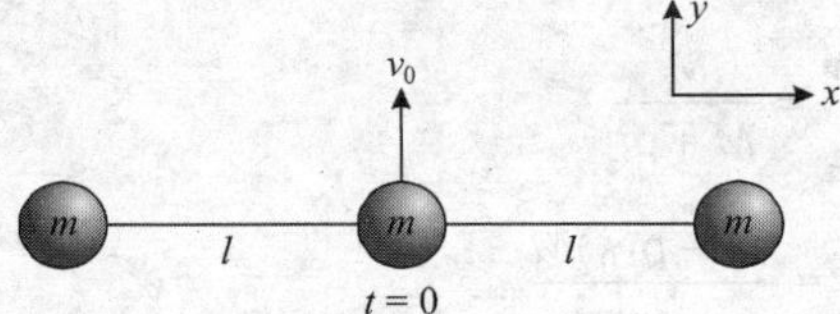

Final state at time t

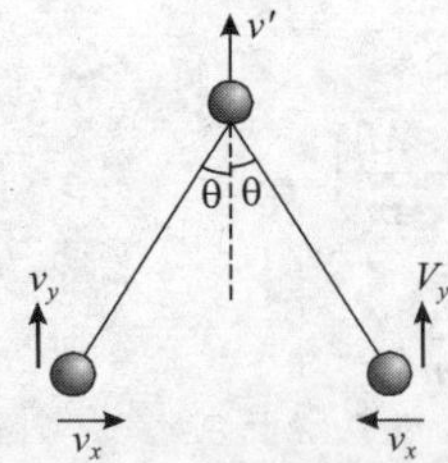

At any instant t by momentum conservation we use

$$mv_0 = mv' + 2mv_y$$

$$v_0 = v' + 2v_y \quad \ldots(1)$$

At the time of collision $\theta = 0$

$$\Rightarrow v' = v_y = \frac{v_0}{3}$$

Using conservation of energy we have

$$\frac{1}{2}mv_0^2 = \frac{1}{2}mv'^2 + \frac{1}{2}m(v_x^2 + v_y^2) \times 2$$

$$\Rightarrow v_0^2 = \frac{v_0^2}{9} + 2\left[v_x^2 + \frac{v_0^2}{9}\right]$$

$$\Rightarrow \quad v_0^2\left[1-\frac{1}{9}-\frac{2}{9}\right] = 2v_x^2$$

$$v_6^2\left(\frac{9-3}{9}\right) = 2v_x^2$$

$$\Rightarrow \quad v_x = \frac{v_0}{\sqrt{3}}$$

$\Rightarrow$ Net velocity of A at the time of collision is $= \sqrt{v_x^2 + v_y^2}$

$$V_A = \sqrt{\frac{v_0^2}{3}+\frac{v_0^2}{9}} = v_0\sqrt{\frac{4}{9}}$$

$$= \frac{2v_0}{3} = \frac{2}{3}\times 9 = 6\text{ ms}^{-1}$$

(vi) We solve the problem for a general case when direction of u is at an angle θ to line AB as shown in figure

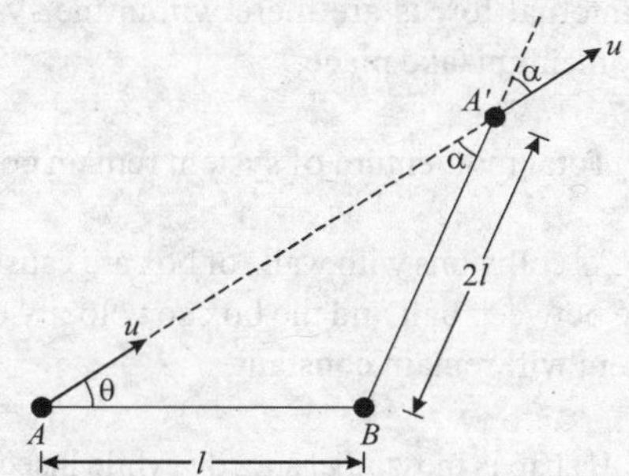

If at position A' string gets tight we use

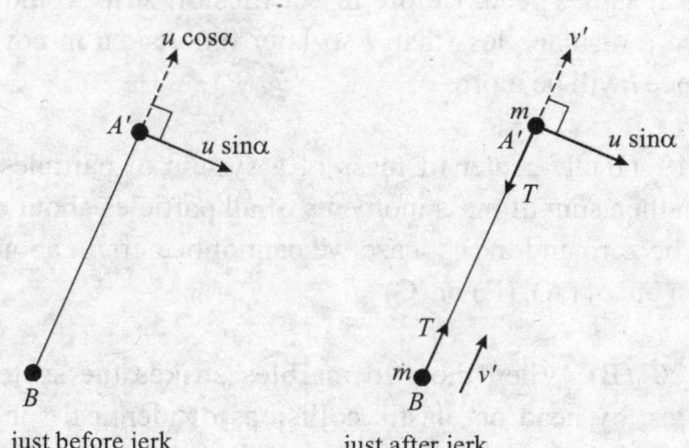

In $\Delta AA'B$ we use

$$\frac{\sin\theta}{2l} = \frac{\sin\alpha}{l}$$

$$\sin\alpha = \frac{1}{2}\sin\theta \qquad \dots(1)$$

Velocity of A normal to string remains constant during jerk.
Using impulse momentum theorem we have

$$\int T dt = mv' - 0 \text{ (for } B) \qquad \dots(2)$$

$$\int -T dt = mv' - mu\cos\alpha \text{ (for } A) \qquad \dots(3)$$

adding equation-(2) & (3) we get

$$0 = mv' + mv' - mu\cos\alpha$$

$$2v' + v = u\cos\alpha \qquad \dots(4)$$

$$\Rightarrow \quad v' = \frac{u\cos\alpha}{2} \qquad \dots(5)$$

$$\text{Impulse} = \int T dt = mv' = \frac{mu\cos\alpha}{2} \qquad \dots(6)$$

Now we can analyse cases mentioned in parts (a), (b) and (c) as given in table below.

		θ	α	$\lvert v'\rvert$	$\int T\,dt$
(a)	u along BA	π	0	$u/2$	$\frac{mu}{2}$
(b)	u at 120° with AB	2π/3	$\cos^{-1}\left(\frac{\sqrt{13}}{4}\right)$	$u\frac{\sqrt{13}}{8}$	$\frac{mu\sqrt{13}}{8}$
(c)	u normal to AB	π/2	π/6	$\frac{u\sqrt{3}}{4}$	$\frac{mu\sqrt{3}}{4}$

(vii) $m_1 \rightarrow v_0$ m_2 at rest (initially) … $m_1\,m_2 \rightarrow v_f$ (finally)

Using momentum conservation:

$$m_1v_0 = (m_1+m_2)\,v_f \qquad \dots(1)$$

$$\Rightarrow \quad v_f = m_1v_0\,(m_1+m_2)$$

$$\text{Given that } \frac{1}{2}(m_1+m_2)\,v_f^2 = \frac{2}{3}\left(\frac{1}{2}m_1v_0^2\right) \qquad \dots(2)$$

$$\Rightarrow \quad \frac{1}{2}(m_1+m_2)\left(\frac{m_1v_0}{m_1+m_2}\right)^2 = \frac{2}{3}\left(\frac{1}{2}m_1v_0^2\right)$$

$$\Rightarrow \quad \frac{m_1^2}{(m_1+m_2)^2}+\frac{m_2m_1}{(m_1+m_2)^2} = \frac{2}{3}$$

$$\Rightarrow \quad 3m_1^2+3m_1m_2 = 2\,(m_1+m_2)^2$$

$$\Rightarrow \quad 3m_1^2+3m_1m_2 = 2m_1^2+2m_2^2+4m_1m_2$$

$$\Rightarrow \quad m_1^2-2m_2^2-m_1m_2 = 0$$

$$\Rightarrow \quad \frac{m_1^2}{m_1m_2}-\frac{2m_2^2}{m_1m_2}-1 = 0$$

$$\Rightarrow \quad \left(\frac{m_1}{m_2}\right)-2\left(\frac{m_2}{m_1}\right)-1 = 0$$

$$\text{Let } \frac{m_1}{m_2} = x$$

$$\Rightarrow \quad x-\frac{2}{x}-1 = 0$$

$$\Rightarrow \quad x^2-x-2 = 0$$

$$x = \frac{1+\sqrt{1+8}}{2}$$

$$x = \frac{1+3}{2}$$

$$x = 2, -1 \text{ (rejected)}$$

$\Rightarrow \quad x = 2$

$\Rightarrow \quad \frac{m_1}{m_2} = 2$

Solutions of CONCEPTUAL MCQS Single Option Correct

Sol. 1 (C) As gases are ejected and to conserve momentum rocket is propelled forward, it gains energy.

Sol. 2 (C) When a body is moving in circle tied to a string, say in presence of gravity in a conical pendulum and if string is cut then due to gravity or any other external force its angular momentum will change.

Sol. 3 (B) When 1 will hit 2, under elastic collision 1 will come to rest and 2 will gain speed v as balls are identical then same collision occur between 2 and three and finally 1 and 2 will come to rest and 3 will move at speed v.

Sol. 4 (B) According to law of conservation of energy total energy always remain conserved but due to dissipation of energy kinetic energy will not be conserved in inelastic collision. As no external force is there momentum will remain conserved.

Sol. 5 (A) As the collision is inelastic, kinetic energy will not be conserved but for ball and earth as a system total momentum will remain conserved.

Sol. 6 (C) As always we consider the mass of bullet to be less than mass of rifle and in the process of firing total momentum will be conserved so the higher mass body will have lower kinetic energy.

Sol. 7 (C) As the collision is inelastic, kinetic energy will not be conserved but for bullet and target as a system total momentum will remain conserved.

Sol. 8 (B) After first collision ball 1 come to rest and ball 2 moves forward and as $M < m$ after second collision the velocity of second ball will remain in same direction so no more collision will occur.

Sol. 9 (C) If $M > m$ then after second collision ball 2 will return and collide again with ball 1 after which it will come to rest and ball 1 will move with this velocity so one more collision take place between ball 2 and 1.

Sol. 10 (D) By symmetry center of mass is at the geometric center of the system.

Sol. 11 (A) During elastic collision between two bodies at the point of maximum deformation in bodies potential energy stored in bodies deformation is maximum so kinetic energy of system is minimum. Thus during collision kinetic energy of system is not conserved.

Sol. 12 (A) Only when masses of bodies are equal in elastic head on collision then the velocities are swapped.

Sol. 13 (D) In uniform circular motion as speed is constant there is no change in kinetic energy so work done is always zero and vectorially direction of velocity is reversed so change in momentum is $2mv$.

Sol. 14 (B) Due to constant speed, kinetic energy remain constant and due to change in direction of velocity momentum changes.

Sol. 15 (B) Due to the work done by internal forces kinetic energy of system of particles can change but both action and reaction of internal forces are there within the system so no change in momentum take place.

Sol. 16 (C) Total momentum of system remain conserved.

Sol. 17 (B) As collisions with walls of box are causing internal contact force between ball and the box so velocity of center of mass of system will remain constant.

Sol. 18 (C) If strip is moving at speed v while insect is moving over the strip then after it flies off vertically, strip continue to move at same speed. Before insect flies off strip would have moved a distance less than l so later time taken in covering distance l will be more.

Sol. 19 (D) If center of mass of a system of particles is at origin then sum of mass moments of all particles about origin must be zero and in that case we cannot be certain about any option out of (A), (B) or (C).

Sol. 20 (B) When the two marbles strikes the system of marbles, by head on elastic collisions of identical spherical bodies we can say that these two marbles will come to rest and next two will be set in motion and same phenomenon happens for next set of marbles hence (B) is correct.

Sol. 21 (B) The force on surface will be the total momentum imparted to surface per unit time. In this case the momentum change in one ball is $2mu$ and per unit time total change in momentum is $2mun$.

Sol. 22 (A) For elastic head on collision of two identical bodies velocities are interchanged hence option (A) is correct.

Sol. 23 (D) As the initial momentum of the system is zero, always total momentum must be zero as no external force is acting on the system so both blocks having same mass must move in opposite direction always with equal velocities so this case is not possible.

Sol. 24 (D) Final vector momentum of the system must be in the direction of initial momentum which is in the direction of initial velocity vector of the moving particle.

Sol. 25 (D) As net external force on sphere is F, no matter wherever it is applied, the acceleration in center of mass will be F/m.

Sol. 26 (B) Average force $= \dfrac{\text{change in momentum at support}}{\text{time between two collisions at support}}$

$$\langle F \rangle = \frac{2mv}{\left(\dfrac{L-10r}{v}\times 2\right)} = \frac{mv^2}{L-10r}$$

Sol. 27 (B) As collision is elastic angle of reflection is same as that of incidence angle in frame of big sphere small sphere will rebound at an angle 2α with vertical as shown in figure.

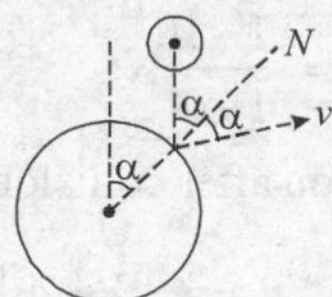

Sol. 28 (B) In frame of larger sphere, the smaller sphere is travelling with $2v_0$ before second collision. Since larger sphere is massive in comparison. Since larger sphere is massive in comparison to smaller sphere, the smaller sphere will rebound with same velocity $2v_0$ as collision is elastic and surface frictionless, the small sphere will reflect back at same angle.

Sol. 29 (C) Force is rate of change of momentum in chain plus the weight of chain at x

$$F = \rho xg + Pu^2$$

Sol. 30 (C) When total impulse of external force is zero we can use conservation of momentum.

Sol. 31 (A) When the car C accelerates to a velocity v_0 relative to the double-boat system, the two boats accelerate to the left

V_C(to right) + v_A(to left) $= v_0$

$mv_C = 2Mv_A$

Solving, we find $v_A = \dfrac{mv_0}{m+2M}, v_C = \dfrac{2Mv_0}{m+2M}$

After the car brakes to a stop, the tension in the string connecting A, B becomes zero. Applying conservation of momentum to A and C

$$mv_C - Mv_A = (m+M)\,v_A'$$

We find the velocity of A(to right)

$$\Rightarrow \quad v_A' = \frac{mMv_0}{(m+M)(m+2M)}$$

Sol. 32 (D) Let υ_1 and υ_2 be the speed of the bodies before and after striking.

$\upsilon_1 \sin\alpha = \upsilon_2 \cos\alpha$ (as there is no friction)

$$e\,\upsilon_1 \cos\alpha = \upsilon_2 \cos\left(\frac{\pi}{2}-\alpha\right)$$

$$\Rightarrow \quad e = \frac{\upsilon_2 \sin\alpha}{\upsilon_1 \cos\alpha} = \tan^2\alpha$$

Sol. 33 (B) Choosing the positive X-Y axis as shown in the figure, the momentum of the bead at A is $\vec{p}_i = +\,m\vec{v}$. The momentum of the bead at B is $= \vec{p}_f = -m\vec{v}$.

Therefore, the magnitude of the change in momentum between A and B is

$$\Delta\vec{p} = \vec{p}_f - \vec{p}_i = -2m\vec{v}$$

The time interval taken by the bead to reach from A to B is

$$\Delta t = \frac{\pi \cdot d/2}{v} = \frac{\pi d}{2v}$$

Therefore, the average force

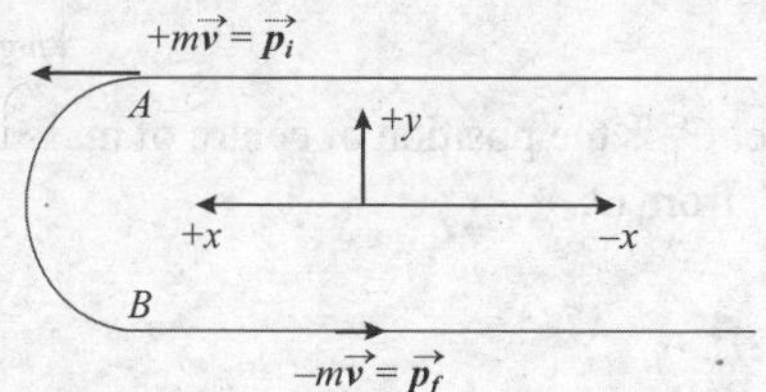

$$F_{av} = \frac{\Delta p}{\Delta t}$$

$$= \left(2mv / \frac{\pi d}{2v}\right) = \frac{4mv^2}{\pi d}$$

Sol. 34 (C) Energy lost in the collisions $= \dfrac{1}{4} mU_{rel}^2 (1-e^2)$.

Solutions of NUMERICAL MCQS Single Option Correct

Sol. 1 (B) Let mass of each particle is m

$$x_{CM} = \frac{m_1x_1 + m_2x_2 + m_3x_3}{m_1 + m_2 + m_3}$$

$$x_{CM} = \frac{m(1)+m(2)+m(3)}{m+m+m} = \frac{6m}{3m} = 2$$

Similarly,

$$y_{CM} = \frac{m_1y_1 + m_2y_2 + m_3y_3}{m_1+m_2+m_3} = \frac{6m}{3m} = 2$$

$\Rightarrow$ The coordinates of centre of mass are (2,2)

Sol. 2 (A) Distance of *CM* from m_1,

$$x = \frac{m_2 l}{m_1 + m_2}$$

As the centre of mass of HCl molecule is at *a* distance of *x* from *H*

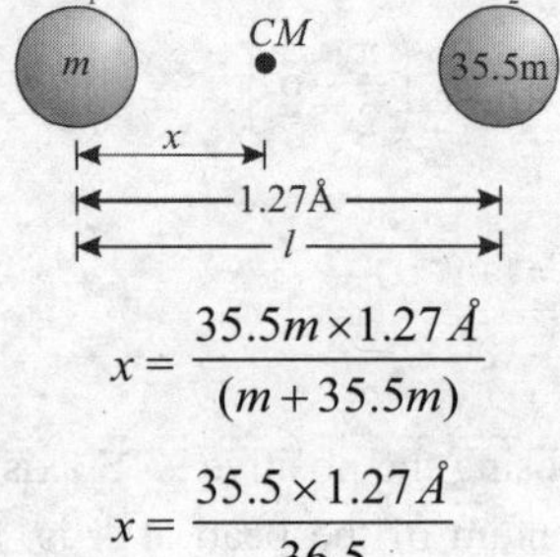

We use $$x = \frac{35.5m \times 1.27\,\text{Å}}{(m + 35.5m)}$$

$$\Rightarrow \quad x = \frac{35.5 \times 1.27\,\text{Å}}{36.5}$$

Sol. 3 (C) Here frictional force acting on block is passing through *A* and will not produce any torque about *A*

Thus to topple the block

$$FL > \frac{mgL}{2}$$

$$F > \frac{mg}{2}$$

Sol. 4 (D) Let C_1 is the position of centre of mass initially. Distance of C_1 from *O*,

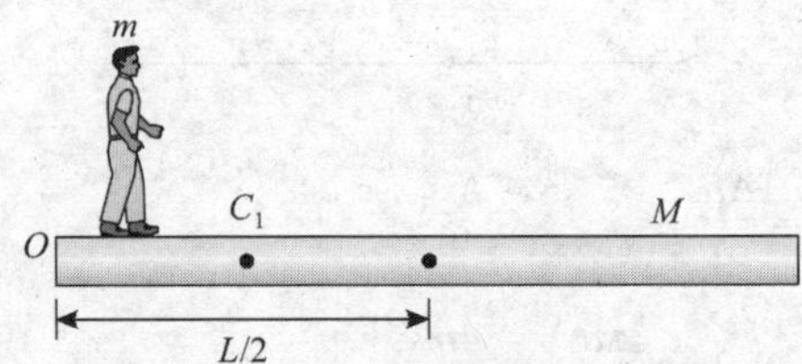

$$OC_1 = \frac{m \times o + \frac{ML}{2}}{m + M} = \frac{ML}{2(m+M)}$$

Now, when boy moves to other end of plank,

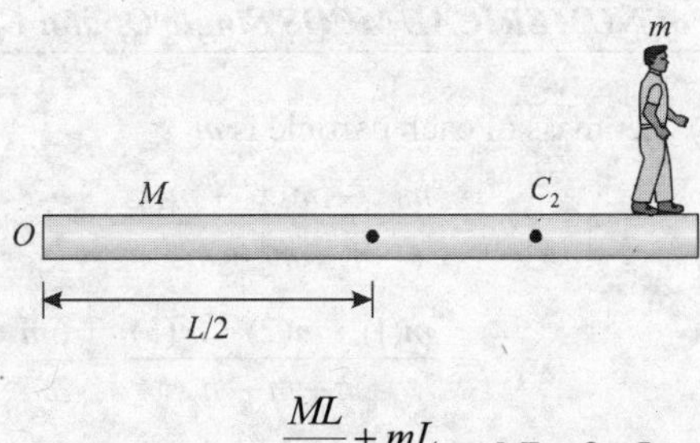

$$OC_2 = \frac{\frac{ML}{2} + mL}{m + M} = \frac{ML + 2mL}{2(m+M)}$$

Since no external force is present on the system, the centre of mass remains fixed and the plank is displaced by $OC_2 - OC_1$

$$\Delta x = OC_2 - OC_1$$

$$= \frac{ML + 2mL}{2(m+M)} - \frac{ML}{2(m+M)}$$

$$= \frac{2mL}{2(m+M)}$$

$$= \frac{mL}{(m+M)}$$

Sol. 5 (A) Mass of neutron, $m_1 = 1$ unit

Mass of nucleus, $m_2 = A$ units

Here, $u_1 = v$ and $u_2 = 0$

Therefore, velocity of neutron after collision,

$$v = \frac{m_1 - m_2}{m_1 + m_2} u_1 + \frac{2m_2}{m_1 + m_2} u_2$$

$$\therefore \quad v_1 = \frac{1 - A}{1 + A} v$$

Kinetic energy of neutron after collision,

$$k_2 = \frac{1}{2}(1)\left[\frac{1-A}{1+A}\right]^2 v^2 \quad \ldots(1)$$

Kinetic energy of neutron before collision,

$$k_2 = \frac{1}{2}(1)v^2 \quad \ldots(2)$$

$$\frac{k_2}{k_1} = \left(\frac{1-A}{1+A}\right)^2 = \left(\frac{A-1}{A+1}\right)^2$$

Sol. 6 (B) Mass of bullet, $m = 0.1$ kg

Mass of block, $M = 0.9$ kg

Initial velocity of bullet, $v = 100$ m/s

Let velocity of system (block + bullet) after bullet gets embedded in block is v'.

Applying conservation of linear momentum,

$$mv = (m + M)\, v'$$

$$v' = \frac{mv}{m + M} = \frac{0.1 \times 100}{0.1 + 0.9} = 10 \text{ m/s}$$

$$\frac{1}{2}(M + m)\, v'^2 = (M + m)gH$$

$$\frac{100}{2} = 10 \times H$$

$$H = 5 \text{ m}$$

Sol. 7 (A) Initial *K. E.* of system, $K_1 - \frac{1}{2} mv^2$

$$= \frac{1}{2}(0.1)(100)^2$$

$$= 500 \text{ J}$$

Final *K. E.* of system, $K_2 = \frac{1}{2}(m + M) v'^2$

$$= \frac{1}{2}(1)(10)^2$$

$$= 50 \text{ J}$$

Loss in *K. E.*, $\Delta K = K_1 - K_2$

$$= (500 - 50) \text{ J}$$

$$= 450 \text{ J}$$

Sol. 8 (B) At highest point of trajectory, the shell has only horizontal component of velocity, $u \cos \theta$

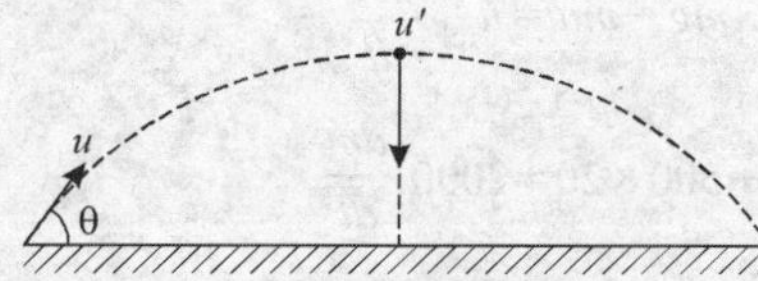

Let u' is the horizontal velocity of other fragment.
By conservation of momentum,

$$(2m) u \cos \theta = m \times 0 + mu$$

$$u' = 2u \cos \theta$$

Time taken by this fragment to reach ground.

$$t = \frac{u \sin \theta}{g}$$

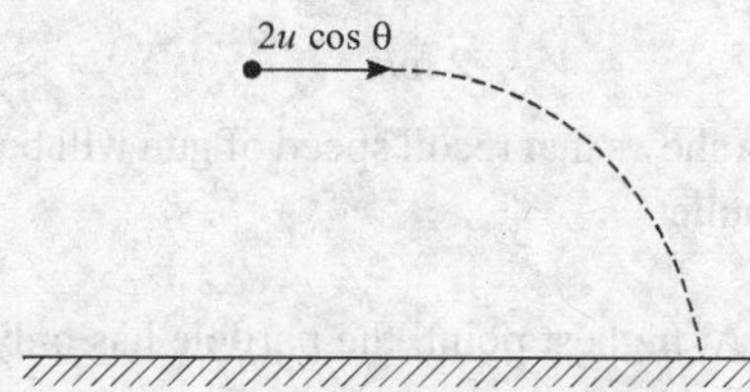

Horizontal distance travelled by this fragment,

$$x = 2u \cos \theta \times \frac{u \sin \theta}{g}$$

$$x = \frac{2u^2 \sin \theta \cos \theta}{g}$$

$$x = \frac{u^2 \sin 2\theta}{g}$$

Distance from gun, $D = \frac{R}{2} + x$

$$= \frac{u^2 \sin 2\theta}{2g} + \frac{u^2 \sin 2\theta}{g}$$

$$= \frac{3u^2 \sin 2\theta}{2g}$$

Sol. 9 (B) Let acceleration due to gravity of planet is '*a*'

$$v_1^2 = 0 + 2a(5) \quad \ldots(1)$$

$$0 = v_2^2 - 2a(1.8) \quad \ldots(2)$$

From (1) & (2),

$$\frac{v_1^2}{v_2^2} = \frac{2a(5)}{2a(1.8)} = \frac{25}{9}$$

$$\frac{v_1}{v_2} = \frac{5}{3}$$

$$v_2 = \frac{3v_1}{5}$$

Ball loses its velocity by *a* factor of

$$\frac{v_1 - v_2}{v_1}$$

$$f = \frac{v_1 - \frac{3v_1}{5}}{v_1} = \frac{2v_1}{5}$$

Sol. 10 (C) $\cos \theta = \frac{2\sqrt{2}R}{(2R + R)} = \frac{2\sqrt{2}}{3}$

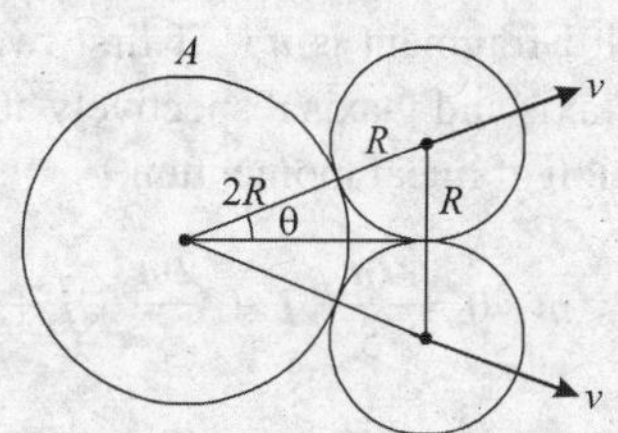

Let initial velocity of *A* is *u*
Final velocity of small balls = *v*
Applying conservation of linear momentum.

$$mu = 2mv \cos \theta$$

$$e = \frac{\text{separation velocity along line of impact}}{\text{approach velocity along line of impact}}$$

$$\Rightarrow \quad e = \frac{v}{u \cos \theta}$$

$$\Rightarrow \quad e = \frac{1}{2\cos^2 \theta} = \frac{1}{2 \times \frac{8}{9}} = \frac{9}{16}$$

Sol. 11 (B) Since the collision is perfectly inelastic, both bodies will stick together and move as *a* single system. Applying conservation of linear momentum,

$$(1.6 \times 10^{-27} \times 1.2 \times 10^{7}) + 0 = (1.67 + 3.34) \times 10^{-27} \times v$$

$$v = \frac{1.92 \times 10^{-20}}{5.01 \times 10^{-27}} = 0.38 \times 10^{+7}$$

$$\approx 4 \times 10^{6} \text{ m/s}$$

Sol. 12 (D) $v_2 = \frac{m_2 - m_1}{m_2 + m_1} u_2 + \frac{2m_1}{m_1 + m_2} u_1$

Here, $u_1 = 1.2 \times 10^{7}$ m/s, $u_2 = 0$

$$m_1 = 1.67 \times 10^{-27} \text{ kg},$$

$$m_2 = 3.34 \times 10^{-27} \text{ kg}$$

$$v_2 = \frac{3.34 \times 10^{-27}}{5.01 \times 10^{-27}} \times 1.2 \times 10^{7}$$

$$\Rightarrow \quad v_2 = 0.8 \times 10^{7} = 8 \times 10^{6} \text{ m/s}$$

Sol. 13 (D) Since the system is at rest initially and no horizontal external force is present, the *COM* remains at rest in horizontal direction but in vertical direction velocity of *COM* is

$$v_{CM} = \frac{mv \sin\theta}{M}$$

Sol. 14 (C) Let masses of fragments are $\frac{2m}{5}$, $\frac{2m}{5}$ and $\frac{m}{5}$.

Let speed of third fragment is $u\hat{r}$ if first two fragments fly along positive *x*-axis and *y*-axis respectively at speed *v*. Using conservation of linear momentum,

$$m \times 0 = \frac{2m}{5} v\hat{i} + \frac{2m}{5} v\hat{j} + \frac{m}{5} u\hat{r}$$

$$u\hat{r} = -(2v)\hat{i} - (2v)\hat{j}$$

$$|\vec{u}| = \sqrt{(-2v)^2 + (-2v)^2}$$

$$= \sqrt{4v^2 + 4v^2}$$

$$= 2\sqrt{2}\, v$$

Sol. 15 (B) Let mass of *Q* is *m* and initially *P* was moving with speed *v* and as direction of *P* is not changing this collision must be head on

After collisions, we use

$$v_1 = \frac{m_1 - m_2}{m_1 + m_2} u_1 + \frac{2m_2}{m_1 + m_2} u_2$$

$$\Rightarrow \quad \frac{v}{4} = \frac{2 - m}{2 + m} v + 0$$

$$2 + m = 8 - 4m$$

$$5m = 6$$

$$m = 1.2 \text{ kg}$$

Sol. 16 (A) To lift off the rocket

$$mg = u_{\text{rel}} \frac{dm}{dt}$$

$$500 \times 10 = 2000 \times \frac{dm}{dt}$$

$$\frac{dm}{dt} = 2.5 \text{ kg/s}$$

Sol. 17 (C) If initial acceleration of rocket is *a*, we use

$$mg + ma = u_{\text{rel}} \frac{dm}{dt}$$

$$500 \times 10 + 500 \times 20 = 2000 \frac{dm}{dt}$$

$$\frac{dm}{dt} = \frac{15000}{2000} = \frac{15}{2}$$

$$\frac{dm}{dt} = 7.5 \text{ kg/s}$$

Sol. 18 (B) By conservation of momentum, we use

$$V = -\frac{mv}{M}$$

$$V = \frac{-(50 \times 10^{-3})(200)}{5}$$

$$V = -2 \text{ m/s}$$

Negative sign shows that recoil speed of gun will be in opposite direction to bullet.

Sol. 19 (D) At highest point, the particle has only horizontal component of velocity,

$$v_x = 200 \cos 60° = 100 \text{ m/s}$$

If mass of particle is taken as '*m*', then after explosion, mass of each fragment is $\frac{m}{3}$

Applying conservation of linear momentum,

$$m(100\hat{i}) = \frac{m}{3}(100\hat{i}) + \frac{m}{3}(100)(-\hat{j}) + \frac{m}{3}\vec{v}$$

$$\vec{v} = 300\,\hat{i}$$

$$|\vec{v}| = 300 \text{ m/s}$$

Sol. 20 (D) Initial velocity of ball is

$$\vec{u} = 15\cos 60°\,\hat{i} + 15\sin 60\,\hat{j}$$

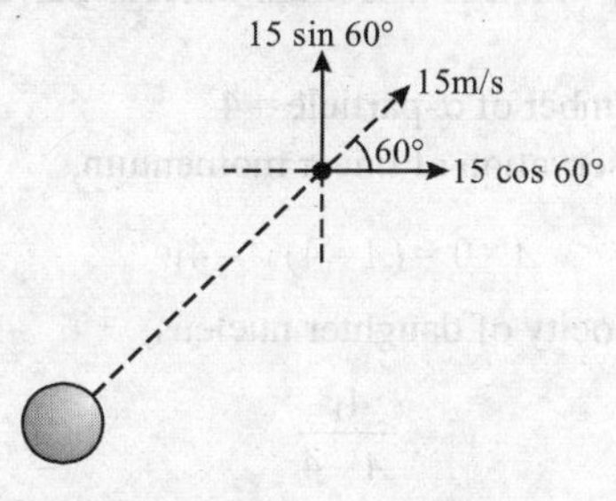

$$\vec{u} = \frac{15}{2}\hat{i} + \frac{15\sqrt{3}}{2}\hat{j}$$

after hit $\quad \vec{v}_x = -30\hat{i}$

$$|\vec{F}_x| = \frac{m(|\vec{v}_x| - |\vec{u}_x|)}{t} = \frac{0.1\left[-30 - \frac{15}{2}\right]}{0.01}$$

$$|\vec{F}_x| = 10\,(37.5)$$

$$F_x = 375\text{N}$$

Sol. 21 (A) At highest point of trajectory, the shell has only horizontal component of velocity,

$\Rightarrow \quad u_x = 100\cos 60° = 50\text{m/s}$

Applying conservation of linear momentum,

$$m(50\hat{i}) = \frac{m}{2}(-50\hat{i}) + \frac{m}{2}\vec{v}$$

$\Rightarrow \quad \vec{v} = 150\hat{i}$ m/s

Sol. 22 (A) $\quad x_{CM} = \dfrac{m_1x_1 + m_2x_2 + m_3x_3 + m_4x_4}{m_1 + m_2 + m_3 + m_4}$

Y, X; 4kg (0, 2); 3kg (2, 2); 1kg (0, 0); 2kg (2, 0)

$$x_{CM} = \frac{(1\times 0) + (2\times 2) + (3\times 2) + (4\times 0)}{1+2+3+4}$$

$$x_{CM} = \frac{10}{10} = 1$$

$$y_{CM} = \frac{m_1y_1 + m_2y_2 + m_3y_3 + m_4y_4}{m_1 + m_2 + m_3 + m_4}$$

$$y_{CM} = \frac{(1\times 0) + (2\times 0) + (3\times 2) + (4\times 2)}{1+2+3+4} = \frac{14}{10} = \frac{7}{5}$$

Thus coordinates of CM are $\left(1, \frac{7}{5}\right)$

Sol. 23 (D) Since the system is isolated and no external force is present, the motion of centre of mass will not be affected. The centre of mass will continue to move with same speed.

Sol. 24 (C) Let length of hammer is l

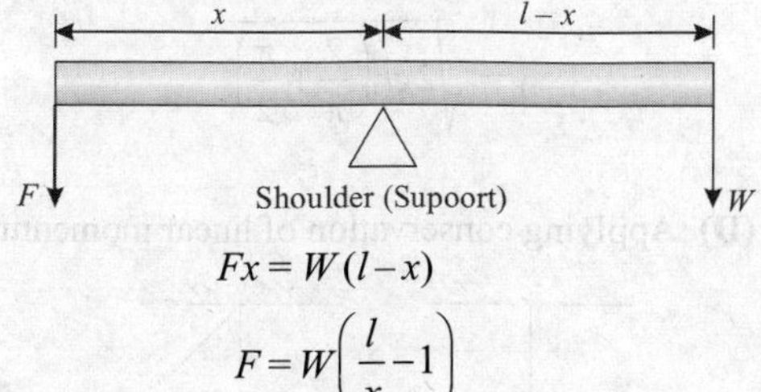

$$Fx = W(l - x)$$

$$F = W\left(\frac{l}{x} - 1\right)$$

The force and hence pressure on his hand is proportional to $1/x$.

Sol. 25 (D)

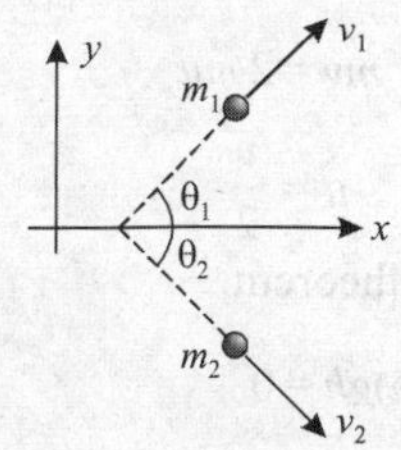

$$m_1u_1 = m_1v_1\cos\theta_1 + m_2v_2\cos\theta_2$$

$$m_1v_1\sin\theta_1 = m_2v_2\sin\theta_2$$

$$\frac{1}{2}m_1u_1^2 = \frac{1}{2}m_1v_1^2 + \frac{1}{2}m_2v_2^2$$

If $\quad m_1 = m_2$ and m_2 is at rest,

$$\theta_1 + \theta_2 = 90°$$

Sol. 26 (D) Applying energy conservation, Potential energy in 'A' is converted to kinetic energy in B

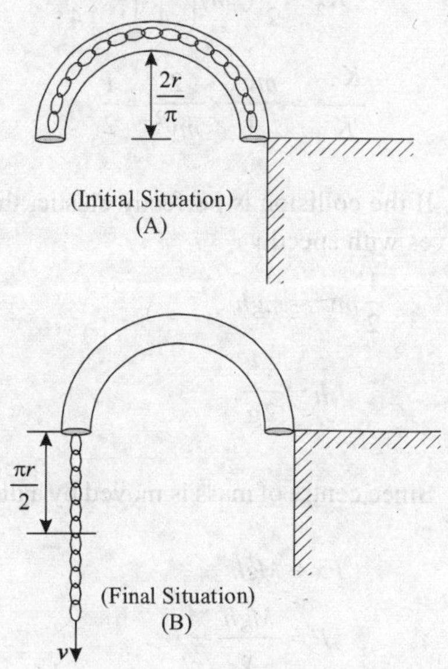

(Initial Situation) (A)

(Final Situation) (B)

$$W\pi r\left(\frac{2r}{\pi}+\frac{\pi r}{2}\right)=\frac{1}{2}\left(\frac{W\pi r}{g}\right)v^2$$

$$\Rightarrow \quad v^2 = 2gr\left(\frac{2}{\pi}+\frac{\pi}{2}\right)$$

$$\Rightarrow \quad v = \sqrt{2gr\left(\frac{2}{\pi}+\frac{\pi}{2}\right)}$$

Sol. 27 (D) Applying conservation of linear momentum,

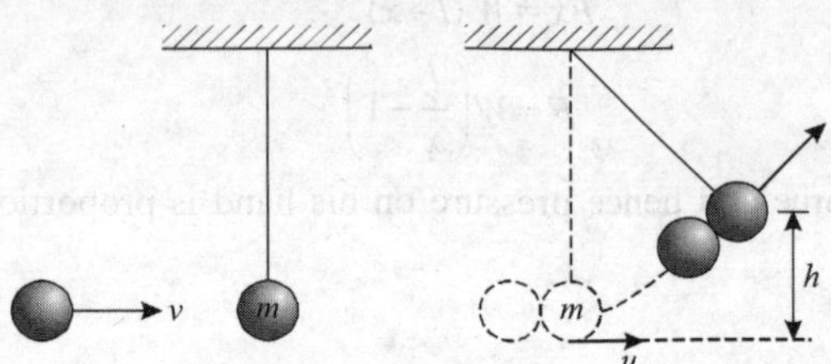

$$mv = 2\,mu$$

$$\Rightarrow \quad u = \frac{v}{2}$$

using work-energy theorem

$$\frac{1}{2}(2\,m)u^2 - (2m)gh = 0$$

$$\Rightarrow \quad h = \frac{u^2}{2g} = \frac{v^2}{8g}$$

Sol. 28 (B) Initial kinetic energy of system,

$$K = \frac{1}{2}\,mv^2 + 0 = \frac{1}{2}\,mv^2$$

Final kinetic energy of system,

$$K_2 = \frac{1}{2}\,(2m)\,u^2$$

$$\Rightarrow \quad K_2 = \frac{1}{2}\,(2m)\left(\frac{v^2}{4}\right) = \frac{mv^2}{4}$$

$$\frac{K_2}{K} = \frac{mv^2}{4}\times\frac{2}{mv^2} = \frac{1}{2}$$

Sol. 29 (B) If the collision is perfectly elastic, the ball stops and bob moves with speed v

$$\Rightarrow \quad \frac{1}{2}\,mv^2 = mgh$$

$$\Rightarrow \quad h = \frac{v^2}{2g}$$

Sol. 30 (A) Since centre of mass is moved by a distance x, we use

$$Fx = Mgh$$

$$\Rightarrow \quad F = \frac{Mgh}{x}$$

Sol. 31 (C) Mass number = Mass of protons + Mass of neutrons.

An α-particle, which is *a* Helium nucleus has 2 protons & 2 neutrons.

Thus, mass number of α-particle = 4

Applying conservation of linear momentum,

$$A \times 0 = (A-4)\,v' - 4v$$

where v' = velocity of daughter nucleus,

$$v' = \frac{4v}{A-4}$$

Sol. 32 (B) Since the cart and man are of same mass, the centre of mass of system lies at $x = 5$ m. So, they will meet at COM of system.

Sol. 33 (C) Let speed of third fragment is $(v\hat{i} + v\hat{j})$m/s.

$$0 = m(9\hat{i}) + m(12\hat{j}) + m(v\hat{i} + v\hat{j})$$

$$v_x = -9\text{m/s}$$

$$v_y = -12\text{m/s}$$

$$v = \sqrt{v_x^2 + v_y^2} = \sqrt{9^2 + 12^2} = \sqrt{225}$$

$$v = 15\text{ m/s}$$

Sol. 34 (C) $x_{CM} = \dfrac{(m\times 0)+(m\times a)+(2m\times a)+(2m\times 0)}{m+m+2m+2m}$

$$x_{CM} = \frac{ma+2ma}{6m} = \frac{3ma}{6m} = \frac{a}{2}$$

$$y_{CM} = \frac{(m\times 0)+(m\times 0)+(2m\times a)+(2m\times a)}{m+m+2m+2m}$$

$$y_{CM} = \frac{4ma}{6m} = \frac{2a}{3}$$

Thus, coordinates of CM is $\left(\dfrac{a}{2}, \dfrac{2a}{3}\right)$

Sol. 35 (C) For coil to just fly – off,

$$\mu mg = m\omega^2 r$$

$$\omega^2 = \frac{\mu g}{r}$$

$$\omega = \sqrt{\frac{\mu g}{r}}$$

Sol. 36 (A) $\quad m_1 = m,\ m_2 = m$

$$u_1 = u,\ u_2 = 0$$

After collision velocity of first sphere

$$v_1 = \left(\frac{m_1 - em_2}{m_1 + m_2}\right) u_1 + \frac{m_2}{m_1 + m_2} (1+e) u_2$$

$$v_1 = \frac{m - em}{m + m} u + 0$$

$$v_1 = \frac{m}{2m} (1-e) u = \frac{1-e}{2} u$$

velocity of second sphere after collision is

$$v_2 = \left(\frac{m_2 - em_1}{m_1 + m_2}\right) u_2 + \frac{m_1}{m_1 + m_2} (1+e) u_1$$

$$v_2 = 0 + \frac{m}{2m} (1+e) u$$

$$v_2 = \frac{(1+e)u}{2}$$

$$\frac{v_1}{v_2} = \frac{v_A}{v_B} = \frac{1-e}{2} \times \frac{2}{1+e} = \frac{1-e}{1+e}$$

Sol. 37 (B) The component of velocity parallel to wall remains unchanged, while $\hat{i}$ component will become $\left(-\frac{1}{3}\right)(3\hat{i}) = -\hat{i}$

Thus, velocity of sphere after hitting wall,

$$\vec{v} = -\hat{i} + \hat{j}$$

Sol. 38 (A) Time $= \dfrac{\text{Distance}}{\text{Speed}}$

If ball takes twice the time in returning, it implies its speed is halved.

$$e = \frac{v/2}{v} = \frac{1}{2}$$

Sol. 39 (A) Velocity of mass m just before string becomes tight,

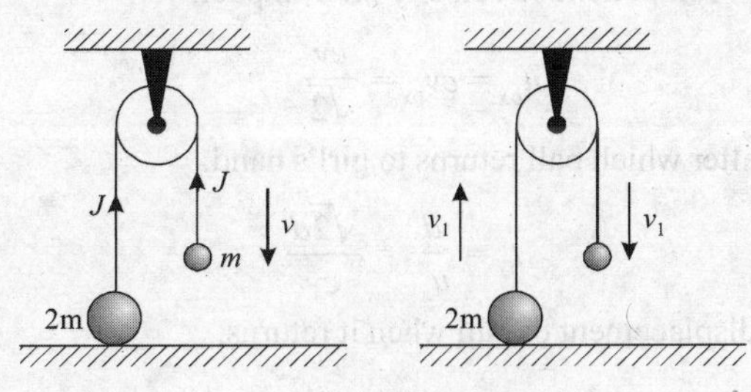

$$v = \sqrt{2gh} = \sqrt{4gl} = 2\sqrt{gl}$$

Impulse = change in momentum

For mass $2m$, $\quad J = 2m \cdot v_1$

For mass m, $\quad J = mv - mv_1$

$$mv - J = mv_1$$

$$\Rightarrow \quad mv - 2mv_1 = mv_1$$

$$3mv_1 = mv$$

$$v_1 = \frac{v}{3} = \frac{2}{3}\sqrt{gl}$$

Sol. 40 (A) Let speed of other piece is u after explosion, At highest point, the shell has only horizontal component of velocity, *i.e.* $V\cos\theta$.

Since one piece retraces its path, it implies it has same velocity $V\cos\theta$ but in opposite direction. Applying conservation of linear momentum,

$$mV\cos\theta = -\frac{mV\cos\theta}{2} + \frac{mu}{2}$$

$$\frac{3mV\cos\theta}{2} = \frac{mu}{2}$$

$$u = 3V\cos\theta$$

Sol. 41 (C) Let speed of plank after bullet leaves plank is v. Applying conservation of linear momentum,

$$mu = mfu + mv$$

$$v = u - fu = u(1-f)$$

Velocity of bullet relative to plank, $fu - v$

$$v_r = fu - u + uf = u(2f - 1)$$

Sol. 42 (D) Let initial velocity of m_1 is u and after collision, velocities of m_1 & m_2 are v_1 & v_2 respectively.

$$v_1 = \frac{m_1 - m_2}{m_1 + m_2} u$$

$$v_2 = \frac{2m_1}{m_1 + m_2} u$$

Kinetic energy of m_2 after collision,

$$k_2 = \frac{1}{2} m_2 \cdot \left(\frac{2m_1}{m_1 + m_2} u\right)^2$$

$$\Rightarrow \quad k_2 = \frac{1}{2} \frac{m_2 \cdot (4m_1^2 u^2)}{(m_1 + m_2)^2}$$

Kinetic energy of m_1 before collision,

$$k_i = \frac{1}{2} m_1 u^2$$

$$f = \frac{k_2}{k_i} = \frac{4m_1^2 m_2 u^2}{2(m_1 + m_2)^2} \times \frac{2}{m_1 u^2}$$

$$\Rightarrow \quad f = \frac{4m_1 m_2}{(m_1 + m_2)^2}$$

Sol. 43 (B) $\frac{m_1}{m_2} = \frac{1}{2}, \frac{u_1}{u_2} = \frac{3}{1}$

$m_2 = 2m_1, u_1 = -3u_2$

(since velocities are opposite in direction)

$$v_1 = \frac{m_1 - m_2}{m_1 + m_2} u_1 + \frac{2m_2}{m_1 + m_2} u_2$$

$$v_1 = \frac{m_1 - 2m_1}{m_1 + 2m_1}(-3u_2) + \frac{2(2m_1)}{m_1 + 2m_1} u_2$$

$$v_1 = \frac{+3m_1u_2}{3m_1} + \frac{+4m_1u_2}{3m_1}$$

$$v_1 = +u_2 + \frac{4u_2}{3} = \frac{7u_2}{3}$$

$$v_2 = \frac{m_2 - m_1}{m_2 + m_1} u_2 + \frac{2m_1}{m_2 + m_1} u_1$$

$$v_2 = \frac{2m_1 - m_1}{2m_1 + m_1} u_2 + \frac{2m_1}{2m_1 + m_1}(-3u_2)$$

$$v_2 = \frac{m_1u_2}{3m_1} - \frac{6m_1u_2}{3m_1} = \frac{-5u_2}{3}$$

$$|v_1| = \frac{7u_2}{3}, |v_2| = \frac{5u_2}{3}$$

$$\frac{|v_1|}{|v_2|} = \frac{7}{5}$$

Sol. 44 (B) For B to just reach highest point of inclined plane

$$\frac{1}{2}mv^2 = mg(5)$$

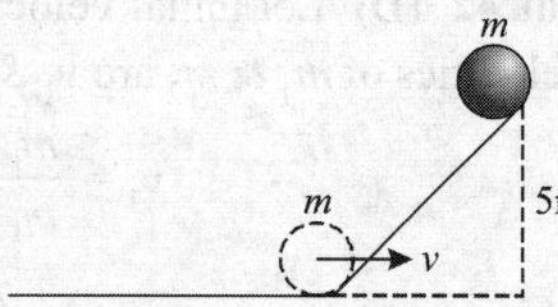

$$\frac{v^2}{2} = 50$$

$$v^2 = 100$$

$$v = 10 \text{ m/s}$$

Where v is velocity of B after collision,

$$10 = \frac{(1+e)m}{2m}(16) + 0$$

$$10 = (1+e)8$$

$$\Rightarrow \quad 1 + e = \frac{5}{4}$$

$$\Rightarrow \quad e = \frac{5}{4} - 1 = \frac{1}{4}$$

Sol. 45 (D) The acceleration of blocks,

$$a = \left(\frac{m_1 - m_2}{m_1 + m_2}\right)g$$

$$a_{CM} = \frac{m_1a - m_2a}{m_1 + m_2}$$

(Since acceleration of both are opposite in direction)

$$a_{CM} = \frac{m_1 - m_2}{m_1 + m_2} \times a$$

$$\Rightarrow \quad a_{CM} = \left(\frac{m_1 - m_2}{m_1 + m_2}\right)^2 g$$

Sol. 46 (B) Initial x – component of velocity,

$$v_{ox} = \frac{v}{\sqrt{2}}$$

Initial y – component of velocity,

$$v_{oy} = \frac{v}{\sqrt{2}}$$

Time before impact is

$$t_1 = \frac{d}{v_{ox}} = \frac{\sqrt{2}d}{v}$$

$$v_y = v_{oy} - gt_1$$

$$v_y = \frac{v}{\sqrt{2}} - g\frac{\sqrt{2}d}{v} = \frac{v^2 - 2gd}{\sqrt{2}v}$$

Height of ball immediately before impact,

$$h_1 = v_{oy}t_1 - \frac{1}{2}gt_1^2$$

$$h_1 = \frac{v}{\sqrt{2}} \cdot \frac{\sqrt{2}d}{v} - \frac{g\left(\frac{\sqrt{2}d}{v}\right)^2}{2}$$

$$\Rightarrow \quad h_1 = d - g\frac{d^2}{v^2}$$

The y – component of velocity does not change after impact,

$$u_{oy} = v_y = \frac{v^2 - 2gd}{\sqrt{2}v}$$

The x – component of velocity after impact,

$$u_{ox} = ev_{ox} = \frac{ev}{\sqrt{2}}$$

Time after which ball returns to girl's hand,

$$t_2 = \frac{d}{u_x} = \frac{\sqrt{2}d}{ev}$$

Now, displacement of ball when it returns,

$$-h_1 = u_{oy}t_2 - \frac{gt_2^2}{2}$$

$$\left(d - g\frac{d^2}{v^2}\right) + \frac{v^2 - 2gd}{v\sqrt{2}} \cdot \frac{\sqrt{2}d}{ev} - \frac{g}{2}\left(\frac{\sqrt{2}d}{ev}\right)^2 = 0$$

The quadratic equation on 'e' can be rewritten as,

$$\left(d - g\frac{d^2}{v^2}\right)e^2 + \frac{d}{v^2}(v^2 - 2gd)e - \frac{gd^2}{v^2} = 0$$

$$\Rightarrow \qquad e_1 = \frac{gd}{v^2 - gd} \qquad (\text{As } \; 0 \le e \le 1)$$

Sol. 47 (C) Let common velocity of system when A reaches the topmost point is v

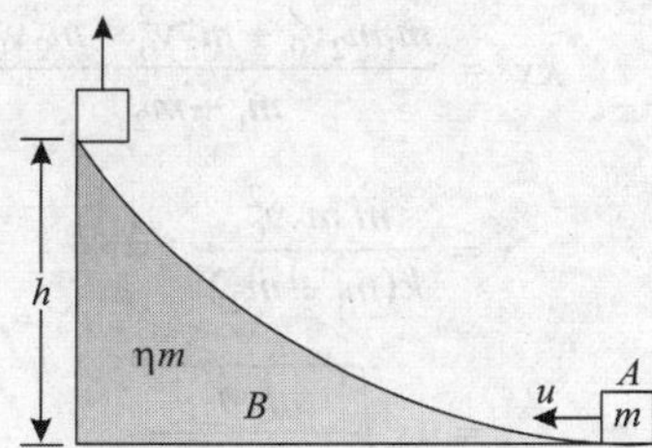

From conservation of linear momentum,

$$mu = (m + \eta\, m)\, v$$

$$v = \frac{u}{1+\eta}$$

Applying conservation of energy,

$$\frac{1}{2}mu^2 = \frac{1}{2}(m + \eta m)v^2 + mgh$$

$$u^2 = (1+\eta)\, v^2 + 2\, gh$$

$$u^2 = (1+\eta)\frac{u^2}{(1+\eta)^2} + 2gh$$

$$u^2 = \left(1 - \frac{1}{(1+\eta)}\right) = 2gh$$

$$u^2(1 + \eta - 1) = 2gh\,(1+\eta)$$

$$u^2 = \left(\frac{1+\eta}{\eta}\right)(2\, gh)$$

$$u^2 = 2\, gh\left(1 + \frac{1}{\eta}\right)$$

$$u = \sqrt{2gh\left(1 + \frac{1}{\eta}\right)}$$

Sol. 48 (C) External force on system,

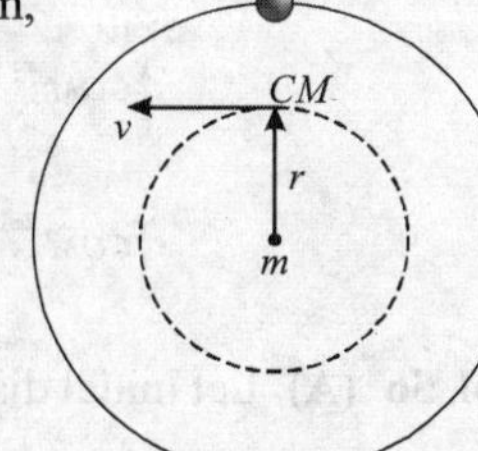

$$F_c = \frac{(m+m)v^2}{r}$$

$$F_c = \frac{2mv^2}{r}$$

Sol. 49 (B) After collision we use

$$v_1 = \frac{m_1 - m_2}{m_1 + m_2}u_1 + \frac{2m_2}{m_1 + m_2}u_2$$

Since particle is light, its mass is negligible and mass of block, $m_2 = m$ (let)

u_1 12m/s → m_1 $\qquad$ [m_2] → u_2 12m/s

$$\Rightarrow \qquad v_1 = -\frac{m}{m}(12) + \frac{2m}{m}(10)$$

$$v_1 = -12 + 20 = 8\text{m/s}$$

Sol. 50 (C) Change in momentum $= F\,(2t_0)$

$$= (m_1 + m_2)\, g\,(2\, t_0)$$

Since the external force present here is gravity only.

Sol. 51 (B) We consider an element of width $d\theta$ as shown in figure

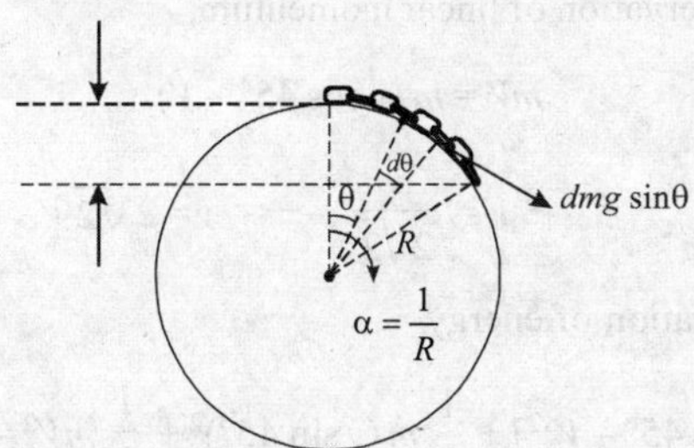

Total tangential force on chain is

$$\int dmg \sin\theta$$

$$= \int_0^{l/R} \frac{m}{l} Rg \sin\theta\, d\theta$$

$$= \frac{mRg}{l}\left[1 - \cos\left(\frac{l}{R}\right)\right]$$

tangential acceleration is

$$a_t = \frac{F_{\text{tangential}}}{M}$$

$$= \frac{Rg}{l}\left[1 - \cos\left(\frac{l}{R}\right)\right]$$

Sol. 52 (A) Initially, potential energy of ball $= mgh$

h_0 is the highest point before release and

h_1 is the highest point after one bounce

Since graph is a straight line, the ratio of

$$\frac{h_1}{h_0} = 0.8 \text{ (gradient)}$$

So, after one bounce, the potential energy becomes 0.8 of initial

P.E. The kinetic energy of the ball immediately after impact with the surface is the same as the *P.E.* at maximum height.

After first bounce, $K_1 = 0.8\ mgh$

After second bounce, $K_2 = (0.8)^2\ mgh$

After third bounce, $K_3 = (0.8)^3\ mgh$

Sol. 53 (A) Let v = velocity of ball *w.r.t.* wedge

V = velocity of wedge

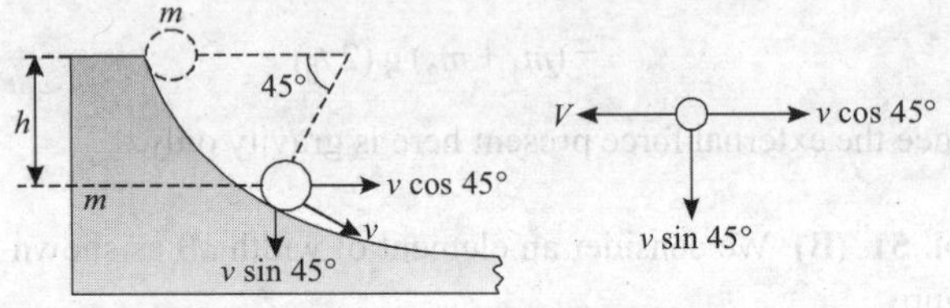

Using conservation of linear momentum,

$$mV = m\,(v\cos 45° - V)$$

$$V = \frac{v}{2\sqrt{2}} \Rightarrow v = 2\sqrt{2}\,V$$

By conservation of energy,

$$\frac{1}{2}m\,[(v\cos 45° - V)^2] + \frac{1}{2}m\,(v\sin 45°)^2 + \frac{1}{2}mV^2 = mgh$$

$$\left(\frac{v}{\sqrt{2}} - V\right)^2 + \left(\frac{v}{\sqrt{2}}\right)^2 + V^2 = 2gh$$

$$\left(\frac{2\sqrt{2}V}{\sqrt{2}} - V\right)^2 + \left(\frac{2\sqrt{2}V}{\sqrt{2}}\right)^2 + V^2 = 2g\left(\frac{g}{\sqrt{2}}\right)$$

$$V^2 + 4V^2 + V^2 = gR\sqrt{2}$$

$$6V^2 = g\,R\sqrt{2}$$

$$V = \sqrt{\frac{gR}{6}\sqrt{2}}$$

$$V = \sqrt{\frac{gR}{3\sqrt{2}}}$$

Sol. 54 (D) Let common velocity of both blocks after spring is completely extended is v then using conservation of linear momentum,

m_1 —k— m_2 → v_0

$$m_2 v_0 = (m_1 + m_2)\,v$$

$$v = \frac{m_2 v_0}{m_1 + m_2}$$

From conservation of energy,

$$\frac{1}{2}m_2 {v_0}^2 - \frac{1}{2}kx^2 = \frac{1}{2}(m_1 + m_2)\,v^2$$

$$\frac{1}{2}m_2 {v_0}^2 - \frac{1}{2}kx^2 = \frac{1}{2}(m_1 + m_2)\frac{m_2^2 v_0^2}{(m_1 + m_2)^2}$$

$$kx^2 = m_2 {v_0}^2 - \frac{m_2^2 v_0^2}{m_1 + m_2}$$

$$kx^2 = \frac{m_1 m_2 v_0^2 + m_2^2 v_0^2 - m_2^2 v_0^2}{m_1 + m_2}$$

$$x = \frac{m_1 m_2 v_0^2}{k(m_1 + m_2)}$$

$$x = v_0\sqrt{\frac{m_1 m_2}{(m_1 + m_2)k}}$$

Sol. 55 (A) Consider an element of mass dm and length dx at a distance x from end of rod. Here mass dm is

$$dm = \frac{K}{L}x^2 dx$$

L; x; x = 0; dx; x = L

Mass of rod, $M = \int dm$

$$\Rightarrow \quad M = \int_{x=0}^{x=L} \frac{k}{L}\,x^2\,dx$$

$$\Rightarrow \quad M = \frac{k}{L}.\frac{L^3}{3} = \frac{kL^2}{3}$$

Centre of mass of rod is located at

$$x_{COM} = \frac{1}{M}\int dm\,x$$

$$x_{COM} = \frac{3}{KL^2}\int_0^L \frac{kx^2}{L}dx\,.\,x$$

$$x_{COM} = \frac{3}{kL^2}\,.\,\frac{k}{L}\,.\,\frac{L^4}{4}$$

$$x_{COM} = \frac{3L}{4}$$

Sol. 56 (A) Let initial distance between A and B is x

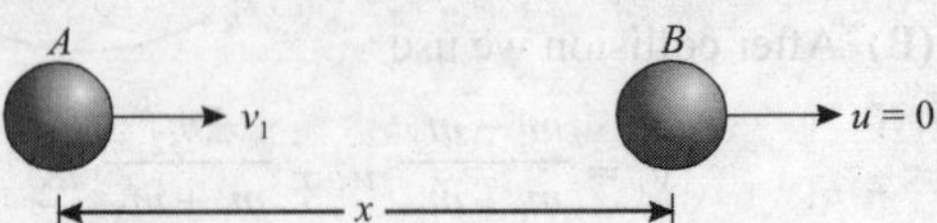

Distance covered by B when its velocity becomes $2V_1$

$$(2V_1)^2 = 0 + 2\,aS$$

$$S = \frac{4V_1^2}{2a} = \frac{2V_1^2}{a}$$

for A, $$V_1 = \frac{x+s}{t}$$

$$t = \frac{x+s}{V_1} = \frac{x + \frac{2V_1^2}{a}}{t_1} \qquad \ldots(1)$$

for B, $$S = \frac{2V_1^2}{a} = \frac{1}{2}at^2$$

$$t = \frac{2V_1}{a} \qquad \ldots(2)$$

From (1) and (2), we get

$$\frac{x + \frac{2V_1^2}{a}}{V_1} = \frac{2V_1}{a}$$

$$\Rightarrow \quad \frac{ax + 2V_1^2}{aV_1} = \frac{2V_1}{a}$$

$$\Rightarrow \quad ax = 0$$

$$\Rightarrow \quad x = 0$$

Sol. 57 (B) Acceleration of boy,

$$a_b = \frac{50}{250} = \frac{1}{5}\text{ m/s}^2$$

$$v_b = 0 + \frac{1}{5} \times 5 = 1\text{ m/s}$$

Acceleration of box,

$$a_{\text{box}} = \frac{50}{500} = \frac{1}{10}\text{ m/s}^2$$

$$v_{\text{box}} = 0 + \frac{1}{10} \times 5 = 0.5\text{ m/s}$$

$$v_{b,\,\text{box}} = 1 - (-0.5) = 1.5\text{ m/s}$$

Sol. 58 (C) Kinetic energy of wind intercepting the blades per second is sectional

$$K = \frac{1}{2}(\rho A v)(v^2)$$

[Here $A \to$ area of blades through which wind flows]

A fraction of this kinetic energy per second will be converted to electrical output hence $P \propto v^3$.

Sol. 59 (D) Let the speed of particle before and after impact be u and v respectively. Then,

$$e = -\frac{v}{u} \quad \Rightarrow \quad v = -eu$$

Change in momentum for the first impact

$$= emu - (-mu) = ep + p = p\,(1+e)$$

For second impact, change in momentum

$$= e^2p - (-ep) = ep\,(1+e)$$

The total change in momentum is

$$= p\,(1+e) + ep\,(1+e) + e^2p\,(1+e) + \ldots$$

$$= p\,(1+e)\,(1 + e + e^2 + \ldots)$$

$$= p\,(1+e)\left(\frac{1}{1-e}\right)$$

$$= \frac{p(1+e)}{(1-e)}$$

Sol. 60 (C) Change in momentum vector between P & Q is

$$\overrightarrow{\Delta P} = (mv\cos 45° + mv\cos 45°)\,\hat{i}$$

$$|\vec{P}| = \frac{mv}{\sqrt{2}} + \frac{mv}{\sqrt{2}} = \frac{2mv}{\sqrt{2}}$$

$$|\vec{P}| = \sqrt{2}\,mv$$

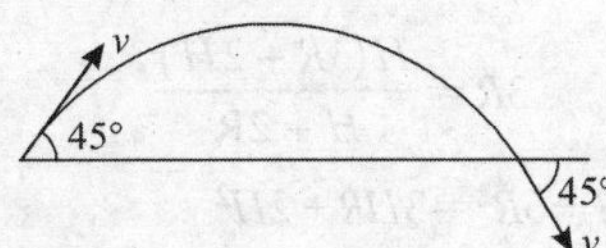

Sol. 61 (B) If v is velocity of each ball after impact we use

$$e = \frac{v - (-v)}{6 - (-6)} = \frac{1}{3}$$

$$\frac{2v}{12} = \frac{1}{3}$$

$$v = 2\text{ m/s}$$

(As initial speeds are equal final speed of the two balls will also be equal)

Sol. 62 (B) As $\theta + \phi = 90°$

This is possible only when two bodies have equal mass

Thus, mass of nucleus = mass of α – particle

$\Rightarrow$ Mass no. of nucleus = 4

Sol. 63 (B) Mass of cone,

$$m_2 = \rho.\,\frac{1}{3}\,\pi R^2 H$$

Mass of hemisphere,

$$m_1 = \rho\,.\,\frac{4}{3}\,\pi R^3$$

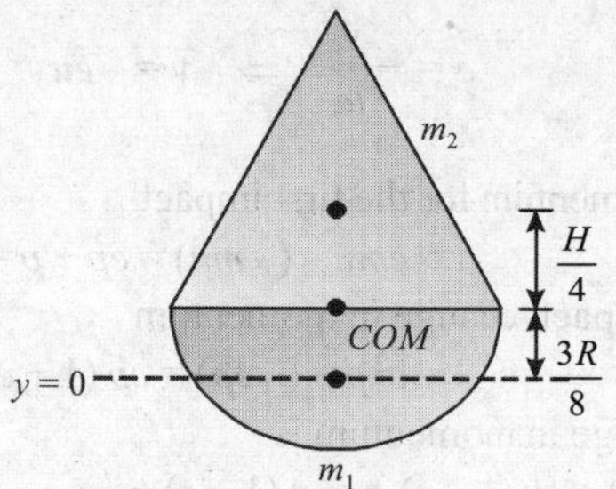

Centre of mass of system is

$$y_{COM} = \frac{m_1 y_1 + m_2 y_2}{m_1 + m_2}$$

$$\frac{3R}{8} = \frac{0 + \rho.\frac{1}{3}\pi R^2 H.\left(\frac{3R}{8} + \frac{H}{4}\right)}{\rho\left(\frac{1}{3}\pi R^2 H + \frac{4}{3}\pi R^3\right)}$$

$$\frac{3R}{8} = \frac{\pi R^2 H\left(\frac{3R}{8} + \frac{H}{4}\right)}{\pi R^2 H + 2\pi R^3}$$

$$\frac{3R}{8} = \frac{\pi H\left(\frac{3R + 2H}{8}\right)}{\pi H + 2\pi R}$$

$$3R = \frac{H(3R + 2H)}{H + 2R}$$

$$3RH + 6R^2 = 3HR + 2H^2$$

$$H^2 = 3R^2 \Rightarrow H = \sqrt{3}\,R$$

Alternatively: use $m_1\left(\frac{3R}{8}\right) = m_2\left(\frac{H}{4}\right)$

Sol. 64 (B) Work done $= F\,.\,S$

$$w = \frac{m[v - (-u)]}{t}\,.\,(u + u)\,t$$

$$w = 2\,mu\,(v + u)$$

Sol. 65 (A) At highest point of trajectory, the projectile has only horizontal component of velocity,

i.e., $(400 \cos 45°)$m/s

At highest point, after explosion,

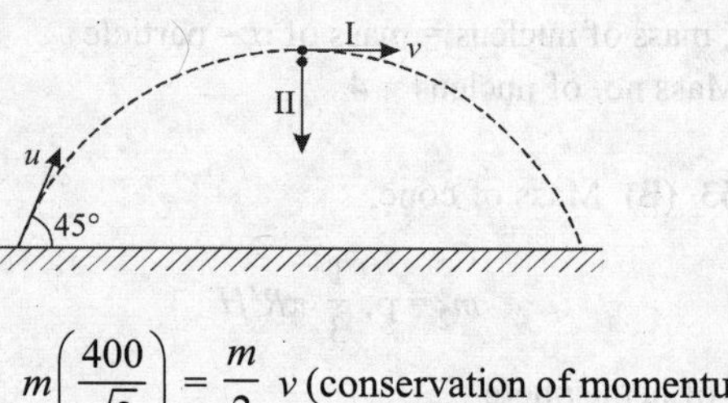

$$m\left(\frac{400}{\sqrt{2}}\right) = \frac{m}{2}\,v \text{ (conservation of momentum)}$$

$$v = 400\sqrt{2}\text{ m/s}$$

First part moves horizontally with speed $400\sqrt{2}$ m/s and second part falls down.

For first part, its vertical component of velocity is zero

Maximum height reached,

$$H = \frac{u^2 \sin^2\theta}{2g} = \frac{(400)^2 \sin^2 45°}{20}$$

$$H = 4000\text{ m}$$

$$H = \frac{1}{2}gt^2$$

$$4000 = \frac{1}{2} \times 10 \times t^2$$

$$t = 20\sqrt{2}\text{ s}$$

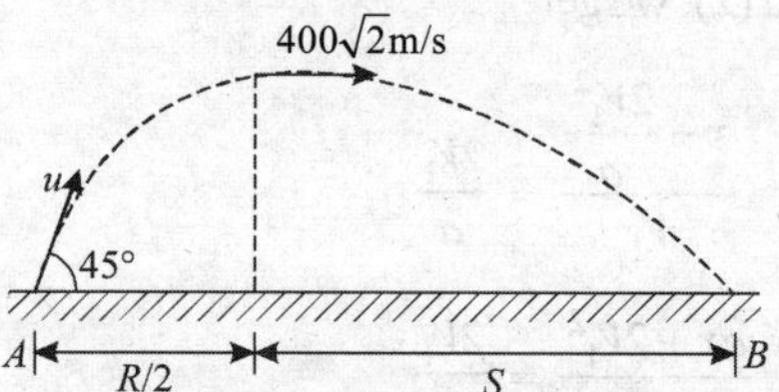

Distance covered horizontally during this time,

$$s = 400\sqrt{2} \times 20\sqrt{2}$$

$$s = 8000 \times 2 = 16000\text{ m}$$

Distance between A and $B = \frac{R}{2} + S$

$$= \frac{u^2}{2g} + S$$

$$= \frac{(400)^2}{2 \times 10} + 16000$$

$$= 8000 + 16000$$

$$= 24000\text{ m}$$

Sol. 66 (A) The ball strikes the inclined plane with velocity,

$$v = gt = 10\,(2) = 20\text{ m/s}$$

After impact, component of velocity parallel to plane remains unaffected.

$$v_P = v \sin\theta$$

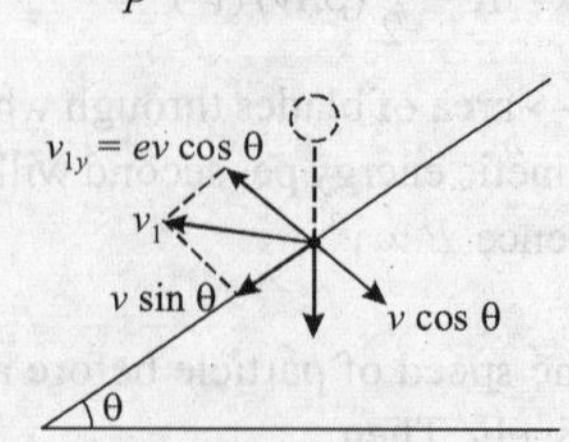

and the component perpendicular to plane becomes

$$v_{1y} = ev\cos\theta$$

For next impact after time T we use

$$0 = (ev\cos\theta)\,T - \frac{1}{2}(g\cos\theta)\,T^2$$

$$T = \frac{2ev}{g} = \frac{2\left(\frac{3}{4}\right)(20)}{10} = 3\text{s}$$

Sol. 67 (A) Initially, centre of mass of system,

$$x_i = \frac{(60\times 1)+(40\times 3)+(80\times 5)\times(170\times 3)}{60+40+80+170}$$

$$x_i = \frac{1090}{350} = \frac{109}{35}\,m \text{ (from left side)}$$

After persons exchange their positions,

$$x_f = \frac{(80\times 1)+(60\times 3)+(40\times 5)+(170\times 3)}{80+60+40+170}$$

$$x_f = \frac{970}{350} = \frac{97}{35}\text{ m}$$

Since no external force is present, the position of centre of mass remains fixed and platform is moved by,

$$x_i - x_f = \frac{109-97}{35} \approx 0.35\text{m}$$

Sol. 68 (B)

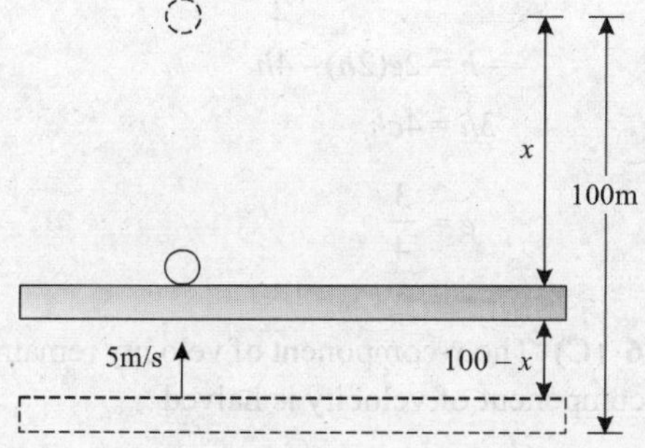

$$x = \frac{1}{2}gt^2 \qquad \dots(1)\text{ (for ball)}$$

$$100 - x = 5t \qquad \dots(2)\text{ (for platform)}$$

From (1) & (2), we get

$$100 - \frac{1}{2}gt^2 = 5t$$

$$100 - 5t^2 = 5t$$

$$t^2 + t - 20 = 0$$

$$(t-4)(t+5) = 0$$

$$t = 4s$$

Velocity of ball after 4s,

$$v = 0 + 10\times 4 = 40\text{ m/s}$$

Velocity of ball just after collision,

$$v' = (40-(-5)) + 5$$

$$v' = 50\text{ m/s}$$

Sol. 69 (B) Change in momentum $= I = m\,(3U)$

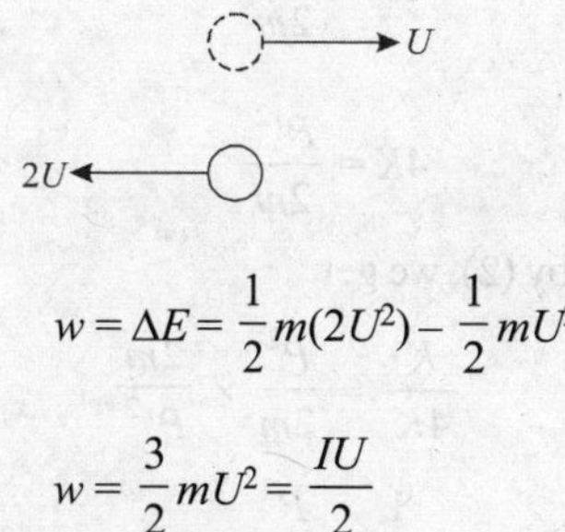

$$w = \Delta E = \frac{1}{2}m(2U^2) - \frac{1}{2}mU^2$$

$$w = \frac{3}{2}mU^2 = \frac{IU}{2}$$

Sol. 70 (D) To obtain maximum overhang of one brick on the table, the centre of gravity should be over the table's edge

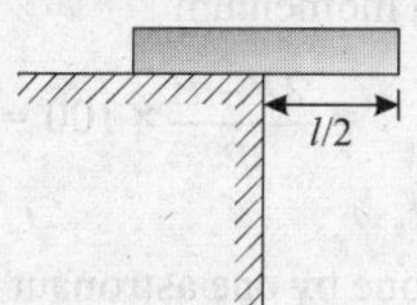

For two bricks,

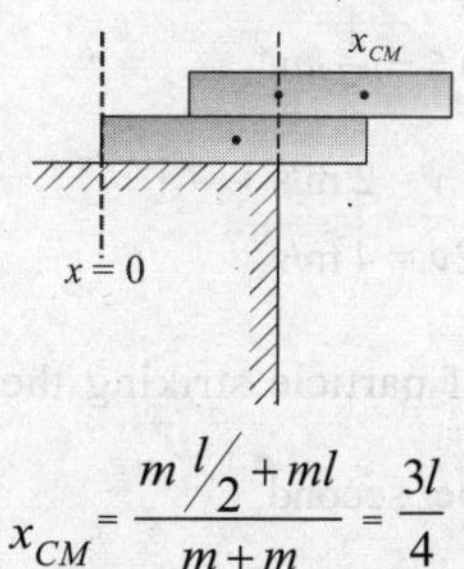

$$x_{CM} = \frac{m\,{}^{l}\!/_{2} + ml}{m+m} = \frac{3l}{4}$$

The centre of gravity of two bricks is midpoint of brick's overlap,

i.e.,
$$\frac{l+\frac{l}{2}}{2} = \frac{3l}{4}$$

The overhang is related to harmonic numbers,

$$H_n = 1 + \frac{1}{2} + \frac{1}{3} + \dots \frac{1}{n}$$

and maximum overhang possible $= \dfrac{Hn}{2}$

Thus, for three bricks,

$$H_3 = \left(\frac{1+\frac{1}{2}+\frac{1}{3}}{2}\right) l = \left(\frac{6+3+2}{12}\right) = \frac{11l}{12}$$

Sol. 71 (C) $\qquad K = \dfrac{P^2}{2m} \qquad \dots(1)$

New kinetic energy, $K' = K + 300\,\%$ of K

$$K' = K + 3K$$

$$K' = 4K$$

$$K' = \frac{P'^2}{2m}$$

$$4K = \frac{P'^2}{2m} \quad \ldots(2)$$

Dividing (1) by (2), we get

$$\frac{K}{4K} = \frac{P^2}{2m} \times \frac{2m}{P'^2}$$

$$\frac{1}{4} = \frac{P^2}{P'^2}$$

$$\Rightarrow \quad P' = 2P$$

Percentage change in momentum

$$= \frac{2P - P}{P} \times 100 = 100\%$$

Sol. 72 (D) Work done by one astronaut on another astronaut is

$$300 \times 0.5 = \frac{1}{2}mv^2$$

$$v = 2 \text{ m/s}$$

Relative velocity is $2v = 4$ m/s

Sol. 73 (A) No. of particle striking the plats per second

$$n = \frac{10\text{m/s}}{0.01\text{m}} = 1000 \text{ per second}$$

force exerted by the water droplets,

$$F = mnv$$

$$= 1000 \times 0.001 \times 10$$

$$= 10\,\text{N}$$

Sol. 74 (D) $144 \text{ Km/h} = 144 \times \frac{5}{18} = 40$ m/s

$$\frac{|\vec{V}_2 - \vec{V}_1|}{\sin 74^\circ} = \frac{40}{\sin(90 - 37^\circ)}$$

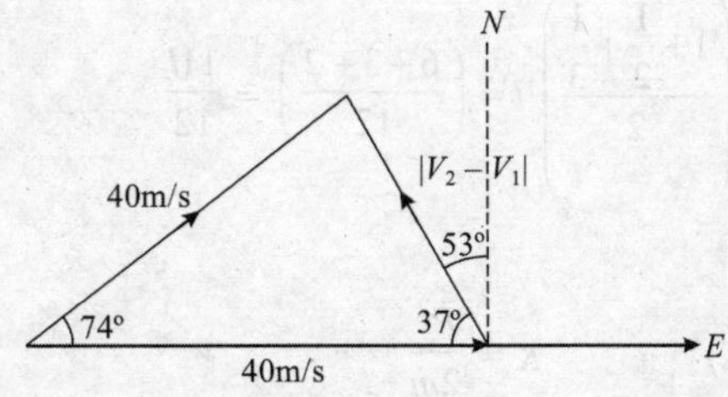

$$\Rightarrow \quad |V_2 - V_1| = \frac{40 \times 2\sin 37^\circ \cos 37^\circ}{\cos 37^\circ}$$

$$= 48 \text{ m/s}$$

$$\text{Change in momentum} = \frac{1}{3} \times 48 = 16 \text{ kpm/s}$$

$$f_{\text{ang}} = \frac{16}{0.02} = 800\,\text{N}$$

From figure we can see that direction is 53° west of north.

Sol. 75 (B) The horizontal velocity of the ball during the motion remains constant

Thus, the journey from C to F takes twice the time as taken from A to C

Time of flight from A to C,

$$t = \sqrt{\frac{2h}{g}}$$

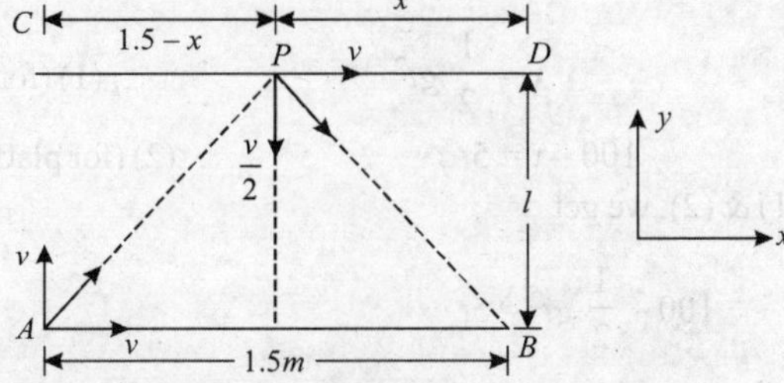

and velocity with which ball strikes at C,

$$v^2 = 0^2 + 2gh$$

$$v = \sqrt{2gh}$$

The velocity with which ball rebounds,

$$v_1 = ev$$

$$-h = ev(2t) - \frac{1}{2}g(2t)^2$$

$$-h = 2e(2h) - 4h$$

$$3h = 4eh$$

$$e = \frac{3}{4}$$

Sol. 76 (C) The x-component of velocity remains same while the y-component of velocity is halved

So, the ball will cover twice the distance in x-direction compared to before collision

As we use

$$x = 2(1.5 - x)$$

$$x = 3 - 2x$$

$$3x = 3$$

$$x = 1 \text{ m}$$

Sol. 77 (B) As collision is head-on elastic the velocity of body B is given as

$$v_B = \left(\frac{m_2 - m_1}{m_1 + m_2}\right)u_2 + \left(\frac{2m_1}{m_1 + m_2}\right)u_1$$

$$\Rightarrow \quad v_B = \frac{2(4m)u}{6m} = \frac{4}{3}u$$

Fraction of energy lost by body A in the collision is given as

$$f = \frac{KE_f}{KE_i}$$

$$\Rightarrow \quad f = \frac{\frac{1}{2}m_2 v_B^2}{\frac{1}{2}m_1 u_1^2} = \frac{\frac{1}{2}\times 2m \times \left(\frac{4}{3}u\right)^2}{\frac{1}{2}\times 4m \times u^2} = \frac{8}{9}$$

Sol. 78 (B) Figure below shows the process of collision as described in question

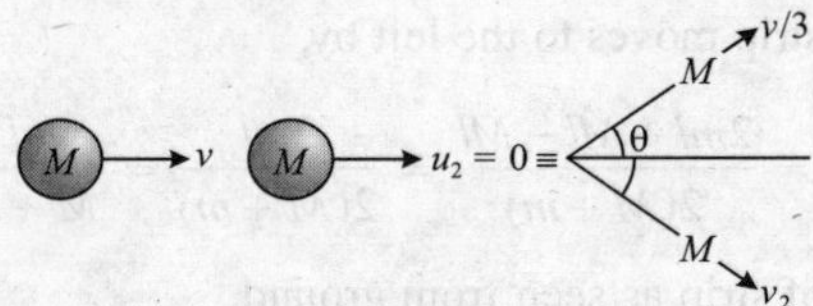

For elastic collision, kineric energy before and after collision remain conserved, so we use

$$\frac{1}{2}Mv^2 + 0 = \frac{1}{2}M\left(\frac{v}{3}\right)^2 + \frac{1}{2}Mv_2^2$$

$$\Rightarrow \quad v^2 = \frac{v^2}{9} + v_2^2$$

$$\Rightarrow \quad v_2^2 = \frac{8v^2}{9}$$

$$\Rightarrow \quad v_2 = \frac{2\sqrt{2}v}{3}$$

Sol. 79 (A) Centre of mass may or may not coincide with centre of gravity. Only for small sized objects on earth surface it is true. Hence option (a) is not correct.

Centre of mass of a body is the point at which the total mass is concentrated. If external force is applied on COM, torque will be zero. Thus option (b) is correct.

Torque due to couple forces only produces rotational motion in body not the translational motion because net force is zero due to equal and opposite forces acting on body. Hence option (c) is not correct.

If a small if front lift the heavy object the efficiency of machine is high

$$\text{Mechanical Advantage} = \frac{\text{output force}}{\text{input force}}$$

Mechanical advantage > 1 ⇒ Output force > Input force. Hence option (d) is correct.

Sol. 80 (C) Figure below shows the situation described in the question.

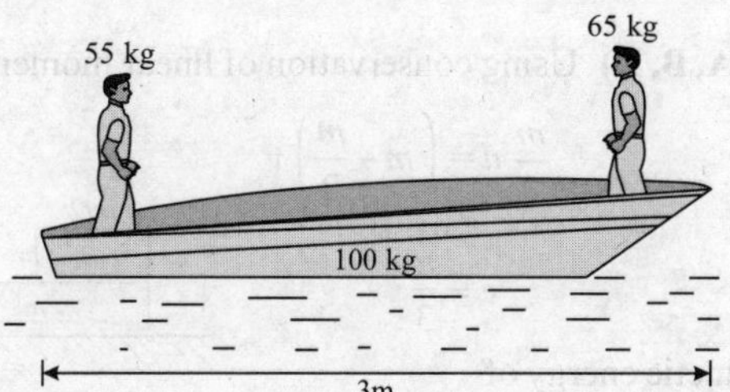

As there is no external force acting on system so centre of mass will not shift.

Solutions of ADVANCE MCQs One or More Option Correct

Sol. 1 (A, B) If density of rod is continuously increase or decrease from one end to another center of mass of rod will shift to either end from center.

Sol. 2 (C, D) Spring always exert equal force on the two ends of spring and in absence of external force the total momentum of system must be conserved.

Sol. 3 (C, D) If center of mass is located at origin then either masses are distributed on both negative and positive directions or all are at origin only.

Sol. 4 (B, C) Option (C) can be true in cases of elastic head on collision between same mass bodies and option (D) can be true when a moving body strikes a fixed body.

Sol. 5 (B, C, D) Even for smooth balls as collision is elastic total kinetic energy will not remain constant but initial and final kinetic energy will be same as during collision it transforms to potential energy and recover again and as no external force is there momentum will remain conserved.

Sol. 6 (B, D) If an external force is present on a system of particles then acceleration of its center of mass must be non zero and no other inference can be obtained hence (B) and (D) both can be correct.

Sol. 7 (All) For elastic collisions all the given options can be correct depending upon the impact parameter and masses of the spheres.

Sol. 8 (All) When the two particles will be moving at equal speeds during collision, the kinetic energy of the system will be minimum which can be obtained by momentum conservation and total energy conservation as no energy dissipation is there. On solving we get options (A), (B) and (C) are correct. As during collision first kinetic energy of system transforms to potential energy and then it recovers back, option (D) is also correct.

Sol. 9 (A, B, D) Using conservation of linear momentum,

$$\frac{m}{2}u = \left(m + \frac{m}{2}\right)v$$

$$v = \frac{u}{3}$$

Initial kinetic energy of

$$B = \frac{1}{2}\left(\frac{m}{2}\right)u^2$$

$$k_B = \frac{1}{4}mu^2$$

$$\frac{1}{2}\frac{mu^2}{2} - w_f = \frac{1}{2}\left(\frac{3m}{2}\right)\frac{u^2}{9}$$

$$\frac{1}{4}mu^2 - \frac{1}{12}mu^2 = w_f$$

$$w_f = \frac{3mu^2 - mu^2}{12} = \frac{mu^2}{6}$$

$$= \frac{2}{3} \times \frac{1}{4}mu^2$$

$$w_f = \frac{2}{3}k_B$$

Force of friction between blocks,

$$f = \mu\left(\frac{m}{2}\right)g$$

Acceleration of A to right,

$$a_A = \frac{\mu mg}{2(m)} = \frac{\mu g}{2}$$

Acceleration of B to left,

$$a_B = \frac{\mu mg}{2\left(\frac{m}{2}\right)} = \mu g$$

Acceleration of A relative to B,

$$a_{AB} = a_A - (-a_B)$$

$$a_{AB} = \frac{\mu g}{2} + \mu g$$

$$a_{AB} = \frac{3\mu g}{2}$$

Sol. 10 (A, C) Since the strip is not fixed, it is free to move on a horizontal surface

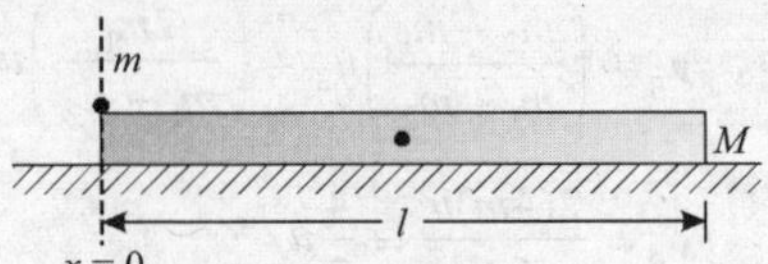

Also, no external forces are present. So, the position of centre of mass remains fixed

Initially, centre of mass of system is given by,

$$x_i = \frac{m \times 0 + \frac{Ml}{2}}{m + M} = \frac{Ml}{2(M+m)}$$

when insect reaches other end,

$$x_f = \frac{ml + \frac{Ml}{2}}{m + M} = \frac{(2m+M)l}{2(M+m)}$$

Thus, the strip moves to the left by,

$$x_i - x_f = \frac{2ml + Ml - Ml}{2(M+m)} = \frac{2ml}{2(M+m)} = \frac{ml}{M+m}$$

As speed of strip as seen from ground,

$$v_{sg} = \frac{ml}{(M+m)t} = \frac{l}{t}\left(\frac{m}{(M+m)}\right)$$

and speed of insect seen from ground,

$$v_{ig} < \frac{l}{t}$$

Sol. 11 (A, C) Linear momentum remains conserved as no external force is present

Relative velocity of approach $= \frac{P}{m}$

Relative velocity of separation

$$= \frac{J}{m} - \frac{(P-J)}{m} = \frac{2J-P}{m}$$

$$e = \frac{2J-P}{P} = \frac{2J}{P} - 1$$

Sol. 12 (B, D) Since the collision between A and C is perfectly elastic, velocity of A after collision is v and C comes to rest

Applying conservation of linear momentum,

$$mv = 2\,mv'$$

$$v' = \frac{v}{2}$$

Where v' is common velocity of system after maximum compression in spring

Kinetic energy of system at maximum compression,

$$k_{AB} = \frac{1}{2}(2\,m)v'^2 = \frac{1}{2}(2m)\,\frac{v^2}{4} = \frac{mv^2}{4}$$

Applying energy conservation,

$$\frac{1}{2}mv^2 - \frac{1}{2}kx^2 = \frac{1}{2}(2m)\left(\frac{v}{2}\right)^2$$

$$\Rightarrow \quad \frac{mv^2}{2} = kx^2$$

$$\Rightarrow \quad x = \sqrt{\frac{mv^2}{2k}} = v\sqrt{\frac{m}{2k}}$$

Sol. 13 (A, C) Velocity of COM which will be common in both bodies at minimum separation is

$$v_0 = \frac{3\times 2}{1+3} = 1.5 \text{ m/s}$$

As time t we use

$$\Rightarrow \quad 6t = 2 - 2t$$

$$\Rightarrow \quad t = 0.25 \text{ s}$$

$$\Delta E = \frac{1}{2}(3)(2)^2 - \frac{1}{2}(1+3)(1.3)^2 = 1.5 \text{ J}$$

$$\Rightarrow \quad \Delta s = \frac{1.5}{6} = 0.25 \text{ m}$$

Minimum distance $= 1 - 0.25 = 0.75$ m

Sol. 14 (A, D) As no external force is present on system total momentum will remain conserved & as no external work is done, total mechanical energy of system coil remain constant.

Sol. 15 (A, D) As no external force is present on system, total momentum remain conserved (zero) hence final momentum of all particles must be in a plane so that their vector sum remain zero.

Sol. 16 (B, C, D) $F_{max} = \mu Mg$

$$\Rightarrow \quad \alpha_{max} = \frac{f_{max}.R}{I_{CM}} = \frac{2\mu g}{R}$$

At the time of slipping

$$\alpha_{max}.R = a = \frac{F - 3f_{max}}{3M}$$

Sol. 17 (All) Net force on system and net torque about peg is not zero over the given time interval.

Sol. 18 (A, C) Impulse = change in momentum

$$= 2(\vec{v}_2 - \vec{v}_1)$$

$$= 2(3\hat{i} - \hat{j})$$

As impulse is in the normal direction of colliding surface

$$\tan\theta = \frac{1}{3}$$

$$\theta = \tan^{-1}\left(\frac{1}{3}\right)$$

$$\alpha = 90^\circ + \tan^{-1}\left(\frac{1}{3}\right)$$

Sol. 19 (A, D) As the string becomes tight speed of balls is

$$\frac{mv_0}{2m} = \frac{v_0}{2}$$

If COM is v_b raised up by height h we use

$$2mgh = \frac{1}{2}(2m)\left(\frac{v_0}{2}\right)^2$$

$$\Rightarrow \quad h = \frac{v_0^2}{8g}$$

$$\Rightarrow \quad K = \frac{mv_0^2}{2} - 2mgh = \frac{mv_0^2}{2} - \frac{mv_0^2}{4} = \frac{mv_0^2}{4}$$

Sol. 20 (A, D)

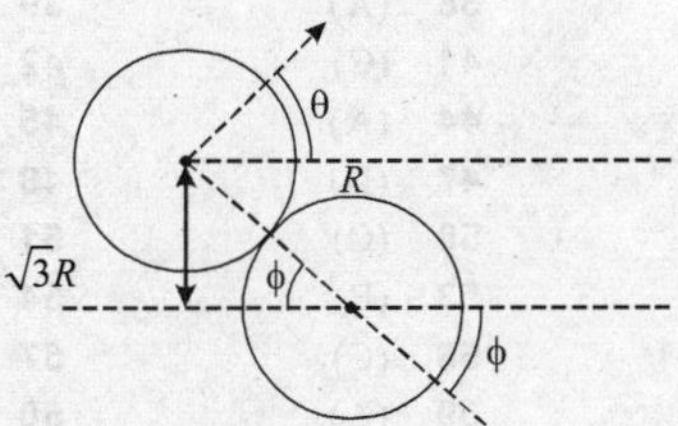

For elastic collision $\theta + \phi = 90^\circ$ and from figure we use

$$\sin\theta = \frac{\sqrt{3}}{2} \quad \Rightarrow \quad \theta = 60^\circ \text{ hence } \phi = 30^\circ$$

* * * * *

ANSWERS & SOLUTIONS

CONCEPTUAL MCQS Single Option Correct

1	(B)	2	(A)	3	(B)
4	(B)	5	(B)	6	(B)
7	(A)	8	(D)	9	(C)
10	(C)	11	(D)	12	(C)
13	(B)	14	(C)	15	(C)
16	(D)	17	(A)	18	(C)
19	(C)	20	(B)	21	(B)
22	(B)	23	(C)	24	(C)
25	(C)	26	(D)	27	(B)
28	(A)	29	(C)	30	(B)
31	(B)	32	(D)	33	(B)
34	(C)	35	(B)	36	(B)
37	(D)	38	(D)	39	(C)
40	(A)	41	(A)		

NUMERICAL MCQS Single Option Correct

1	(A)	2	(A)	3	(D)
4	(C)	5	(C)	6	(C)
7	(C)	8	(C)	9	(C)
10	(A)	11	(C)	12	(C)
13	(C)	14	(A)	15	(C)
16	(D)	17	(A)	18	(A)
19	(D)	20	(B)	21	(C)
22	(A)	23	(D)	24	(C)
25	(D)	26	(D)	27	(C)
28	(B)	29	(A)	30	(B)
31	(B)	32	(D)	33	(A)
34	(B)	35	(C)	36	(B)
37	(A)	38	(A)	39	(B)
40	(B)	41	(C)	42	(A)
43	(D)	44	(A)	45	(B)
46	(D)	47	(D)	48	(B)
49	(B)	50	(C)	51	(C)
52	(C)	53	(B)	54	(C)
55	(A)	56	(C)	57	(D)
58	(D)	59	(A)	60	(A)
61	(B)	62	(A)	63	(D)
64	(A)	65	(C)	66	(A)
67	(C)	68	(C)	69	(C)
70	(A)	71	(A)	72	(A)
73	(B)	74	(C)	75	(D)
76	(A)				

ADVANCE MCQs One or More Option Correct

1	(C, D)	2	(B, D)	3	(A, B, C)
4	(B, C)	5	(A, C, D)	6	(A)
7	(B)	8	(C, D)	9	(B, C, D)
10	(All)	11	(B, C)	12	(A, B C)
13	(A, C, D)	14	(A, C)	15	(A, B, D)
16	(A, C)				

Solutions of PRACTICE EXERCISE 5.1

(i) Mass of elemental disc as shown in figure is

$$dm = \frac{M}{L}dx$$

Moment of inertia of the elemental disc about the given axis of rotation is-

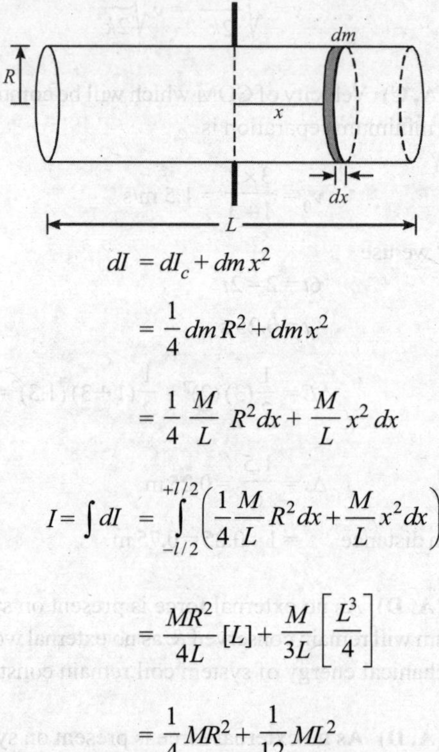

$$dI = dI_c + dm\,x^2$$

$$= \frac{1}{4}dm\,R^2 + dm\,x^2$$

$$= \frac{1}{4}\frac{M}{L}R^2 dx + \frac{M}{L}x^2\,dx$$

$$I = \int dI = \int_{-l/2}^{+l/2}\left(\frac{1}{4}\frac{M}{L}R^2 dx + \frac{M}{L}x^2 dx\right)$$

$$= \frac{MR^2}{4L}[L] + \frac{M}{3L}\left[\frac{L^3}{4}\right]$$

$$= \frac{1}{4}MR^2 + \frac{1}{12}ML^2$$

(ii) Consider an element at a distance x from thinner end of width dx, we use its mass dm as

$$dm = \left[\frac{\rho(\eta-1)}{L}x + \rho\right]dx$$

Total mass of rod is

$$M = \int dm\left(\frac{\rho(\eta-1)}{L}x + \rho\right)dx$$

$$= \frac{\rho(\eta-1)}{L}\left(\frac{L^2}{2}\right) + \rho L$$

$$= \frac{\rho(\eta-1)L}{2} + \rho L$$

$$= \frac{1}{2}\rho(\eta+1)L \qquad \ldots(1)$$

Moment of inertia of element is

$$dI = dm\,x^2$$

Moment of inertia of rod is

$$I=\int dI=\int_0^L\left[\rho+\frac{\rho(\eta-1)}{L}x\right]x^2dx$$

$$\Rightarrow\qquad I=\frac{\rho L^3}{3}+\frac{\rho(\eta-1)}{L}\cdot\frac{L^4}{4}$$

$$\Rightarrow\qquad I=\frac{1}{12}\rho L^3(3\eta+1)\qquad\ldots(2)$$

From (1) and (2) we get

$$I=\frac{1}{6}ML^2\left(\frac{3\eta+1}{\eta+1}\right)$$

(iii) Mass of elemental strip is as shown in figure is

$$dm=\frac{2M}{l^2}\times(l-x)\,dx$$

Moment of inertia of strip about given axis is-

$$dI=dm\,x^2$$

$$I=\int dI=\int_0^l\frac{2M}{l^2}(l-x)dx\cdot x^2$$

$$\Rightarrow\qquad I=\frac{2M}{l^2}\left[\frac{lx^3}{3}-\frac{x^4}{4}\right]_0^l$$

$$\Rightarrow\qquad I=\frac{2Ml^2}{3}-\frac{Ml^2}{2}=\frac{1}{6}Ml^2$$

NOTE: You can also try solving this problem without using integration by mass distribution property.

(iv) For figure shown using parallel axes theorem

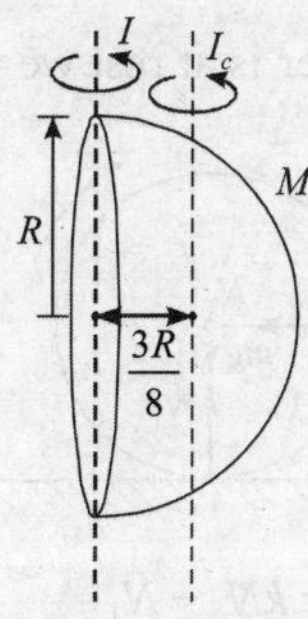

Figure 5.28

$$I=I_c+M\left(\frac{3R}{8}\right)^2$$

$$\Rightarrow\qquad I_c=\frac{2}{5}MR^2-\frac{9MR^2}{64}\qquad\left[\text{As } I=\frac{2}{5}MR^2\right]$$

$$\Rightarrow\qquad I_c=\frac{83}{320}MR^2$$

(v) Moment of inertia of the half cylinder about the axis through its centre of mass is given as

$$I_c=I-M\left(\frac{4R}{3\pi}\right)^2$$

$$=\frac{1}{2}MR^2-\frac{16}{9\pi^2}MR^2$$

Now moment of inertia about axis AA' is

$$I_{AA'}=I_c+M\left(R-\frac{4R}{3\pi}\right)^2$$

$$I_{AA'}=\frac{1}{2}MR^2-\frac{16MR^2}{9\pi^2}+MR^2+\frac{16MR^2}{9\pi^2}-\frac{8MR^2}{3\pi}$$

$$=\left(\frac{3}{2}-\frac{8}{3\pi}\right)MR^2$$

$$=\left(\frac{9\pi-16}{6\pi}\right)MR^2$$

(vi) Mass of section cut is

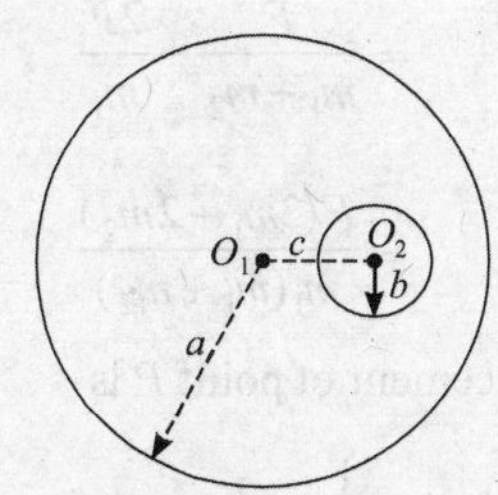

$$m=\frac{M}{\pi a^2}\cdot\pi b^2=\frac{Mb^2}{a^2}$$

Moment of inertia of remaining disc about O_2 is

$$I=I_{\text{disc}}-I_{\text{hole cut}}$$

$$=\left(\frac{1}{2}Ma^2+Mc^2\right)-\frac{1}{2}\left(\frac{Mb^2}{a^2}\right)\times b^2$$

$$=\frac{1}{2}M\left[a^2+2c^2-\frac{b^4}{a^2}\right]$$

(vii) As the section is cut from a uniform circular disc, such uniform sections have mass distribution like a disc only so using the property of mass distribution for moment of inertia the expression for moment of inertia of such a section is same as that of a uniform disc.

(viii) Length of each spoke is 'l'. So the radius of wheel is 'l'

mass $24M$ and also having 24 spokes of mass 'M' of each. moment of inertia of a wheel about axis is

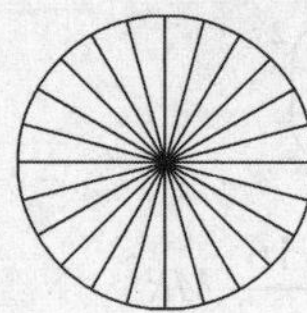

$$24Ml^2 + \frac{Ml^2}{3} \times 24 = 32\,Ml^2$$

Solutions of PRACTICE EXERCISE 5.2

(i) Equation of motion of cylinder + mount system is

$$F = (m_1 + m_1)a \;\Rightarrow\; a = \frac{F}{m_1 + m_2}$$

for relation of cylinder

$$FR = \frac{1}{2}m_1R^2 \cdot \alpha \;\Rightarrow\; \alpha = \frac{2F}{m_1R}$$

Acceleration of point P is

$$a_P = a + R\alpha$$

$$= \frac{F}{m_1 + m_2} + \frac{2F}{m_1}$$

$$= \frac{F(3m_1 + 2m_2)}{m_1(m_1 + m_2)}$$

In t seconds, displacement of point P is

$$s = \frac{1}{2}a_Pt^2$$

The kinetic energy of system = work done by external force

$$= F.s$$

$$= F \cdot \frac{1}{2}\left(\frac{F(3m_1 + 2m_2)}{m_1(m_1 + m_2)}\right)t^2$$

$$= \frac{F^2t^2(3m_1 + 2m_2)}{2m_1(m_1 + m_2)}$$

(ii) (a) Given mass of disc $m = 2$kg and radius $R = 0.1$ m. Frictional force on the disc should be in forward direction. Let a_0 be the linear acceleration of COM of disc and α the angular acceleration about its COM. Then,

$$a_0 = \frac{f}{m} = \frac{f}{2} \qquad \ldots(i)$$

$$\alpha = \frac{\tau}{I} = \frac{f\,R}{\frac{1}{2}mR^2} = \frac{2f}{mR} = \frac{2f}{2 \times 0.1} = 10f \qquad \ldots(ii)$$

Since, there is no slipping between disc and truck, therefore

Acceleration of point P = Acceleration of point Q

$$\Rightarrow \quad a_0 + R\,\alpha = a$$

$$\Rightarrow \quad \left(\frac{f}{2}\right) + (0.1)(10f) = a$$

$$\Rightarrow \quad \frac{3}{2}f = a \;\Rightarrow\; f = \frac{2a}{3} = \frac{2 \times 9.0}{3}\text{ N} \;\Rightarrow\; f = 6\text{ N}$$

Since, this force is acting in positive x-direction, we use in vector form

$$\vec{f} = (6\hat{i})N$$

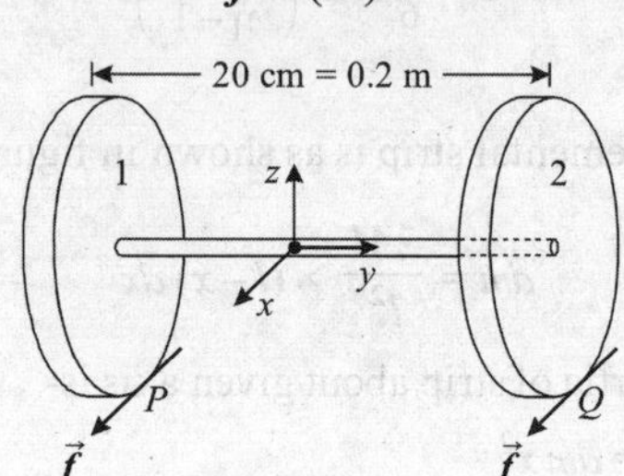

(b) $\vec{\tau} = \vec{r} \times \vec{f}$ here, $\vec{f} = (6\hat{i})N$ (for both the discs)

$$\vec{r}_P = \vec{r} = -0.1\hat{j} - 0.1\hat{k} \text{ and } \vec{r}_Q = \vec{r}_2 = 0.1\hat{j} - 0.1\hat{k}$$

Therefore, frictional torque on disk 1 about point O (centre of mass).

$$\vec{\tau}_1 = \vec{r}_1 \times \vec{f} = (-0.1\hat{j} - 0.1\hat{k}) \times (6\hat{i})\text{N-m}$$

$$= (0.6\hat{k} - 0.6\hat{j}) \Rightarrow \vec{\tau}_1 = 0.6(\hat{k} - \hat{j})\text{N-m}$$

and $|\vec{\tau}_1| = \sqrt{(0.6)^2 + (0.6)^2} = 0.85$ N-m

Similarly, $\vec{\tau}_2 = \vec{r}_2 \times \vec{f} = 0.6(-\hat{j} - \hat{k})$

and $|\vec{\tau}_1| = |\vec{\tau}_2| = 0.85$ N-m

(iii) As center of cylinder is at rest we use

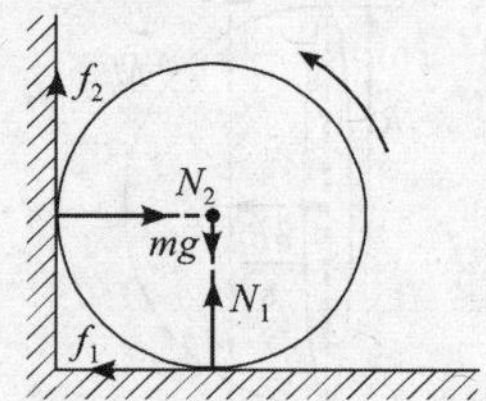

$$mg = kN_2 + N_1 \qquad \ldots(1)$$

$$N_2 = kN_1 \qquad \ldots(2)$$

Solving equation (1) & (2) we get

$$N_1 = \frac{mg}{k^2 + 1}$$

$$N_2 = \frac{\mu mg}{k^2 + 1}$$

Torque due to friction on cylinder is

$$\tau = (f_1 + f_2)R = \mu(N_1 + N_2)R$$

$$\Rightarrow \qquad = \frac{k(1+k)}{k^2+1} MgR$$

angular retardation of cylinder is

$$\alpha = \frac{\tau}{I} = \frac{k(1+k)MgR}{(k^2+1)} \cdot \frac{1}{\frac{1}{2}MR^2} = \frac{2k(1+k)g}{(k^2+1)R}$$

Total angle rotated by cylinder before it stops is given as-

$$\theta = \frac{\omega_0^2}{2\alpha} = \frac{\omega_0^2(k^2+1)R}{4k(1+k)g}$$

turns completed by cylinder

$$N = \frac{\theta}{2\pi} = \frac{\omega_0^2(k^2+1)R}{8\pi k(1+k)g}$$

(iv) Given that $\tau \, \alpha \sqrt{\omega}$

Thus angular acceleration of wheel α is also proportional to $\sqrt{\omega}$

$$\Rightarrow \qquad \alpha = -k\sqrt{\omega} \text{ [}-ve\text{ sign indicates deceleration]}$$

$$\Rightarrow \qquad \int_{\omega_0}^{\omega} \frac{d\omega}{\sqrt{\omega}} = \int_0^t -kdt$$

$$\Rightarrow \qquad 2(\sqrt{\omega_0} - \sqrt{\omega}) = kt$$

here $\omega = 0$ at $t_0 = \dfrac{2\sqrt{\omega_0}}{k}$

$$\Rightarrow \qquad \omega = \left(\sqrt{\omega_0} - \frac{1}{2}kt\right)^2$$

Mean angular velocity of fly wheel is given as

$$\omega_{avg} = \frac{\Delta\theta}{t_0} = \frac{1}{t_0}\int_0^{t_0} \omega dt = \frac{1}{t_0}\int_0^{t_0}\left(\omega_0 + \frac{1}{4}k^2t^2 - \sqrt{\omega_0}\,kt\right)dt$$

$$= \frac{\omega_0 t_0 + \frac{1}{12}k^2t_0^3 - \frac{\sqrt{\omega_0}}{2}kt_0^2}{t_0}$$

$$= \omega_0 + \frac{1}{12}k^2\left(\frac{2\sqrt{\omega_0}}{k}\right)^2 - \frac{\sqrt{\omega_0}}{2}k\left(\frac{2\sqrt{\omega_0}}{k}\right)$$

$$= \omega_0 + \frac{\omega_0}{3} - \omega_0 = \frac{\omega_0}{3}$$

(v) Considering an elemental ring of radius x and width dx in the disc, tangental friction acting on this element is-

$$df = \mu\left(\frac{M}{\pi R^2} \times 2\pi x dx\right)g$$

Torque on the disc due to this friction is

$$d\tau = df \cdot x = \frac{2\mu M x^2 g dx}{R^2}$$

Total retarding torque on disc is

$$\tau = \int d\tau = \frac{2\mu Mg}{R^2}\int_0^R x^2 dx$$

$$\Rightarrow \qquad = \frac{2}{3}\mu MgR$$

angular retardation of disc due to this torque is

$$\alpha = \frac{\tau}{I} = \frac{\frac{2}{3}\mu MgR}{\frac{1}{2}MR^2} = \frac{4}{3}\frac{\mu g}{R}$$

time of motion $\qquad t = \dfrac{\omega}{\alpha} = \dfrac{3\omega R}{4\mu g}$

(vi) When disc rotates by 180° by work energy theorem we use

$$mg\left(\frac{R}{2}\right) + mg\left(\frac{5R}{2}\right) = \frac{1}{2}\left(\frac{1}{4}mR^2 + \frac{mR^2}{16} + m\frac{25R^2}{16}\right)\omega^2$$

$$\Rightarrow \qquad 3gR = \frac{15}{16}R^2\omega^2$$

$$\Rightarrow \qquad \omega = \sqrt{\frac{16}{5}\frac{g}{R}}$$

Velocity of particle $\quad v_p = \dfrac{5R}{4}\omega = \dfrac{5}{4}R\sqrt{\dfrac{16}{5}\dfrac{g}{R}} = \sqrt{5gR}$

(vii) As mass falls one meter in 5sec we use

$$s = \frac{1}{2}at^2$$

$$\Rightarrow \qquad 1 = \frac{1}{2} \times a \times 5^2$$

$$\Rightarrow \qquad a = \frac{2}{25} = 0.08 \text{ m/s}^2$$

angular acceleration of wheel is

$$\alpha = \frac{a}{R} = \frac{0.08}{0.06} = \frac{4}{3} \text{ rad/s}^2$$

equation of motion of bodies are

for block $\qquad 0.2g - T = 0.2a$

$$\Rightarrow \qquad T = 0.2 \times 10 - 0.2 \times 0.08$$

$$= 2 - 0.016 = 1.984 \text{ N}$$

for wheel we use

$$TR = I\alpha$$

$$\Rightarrow \qquad I = \frac{TR}{\alpha} = \frac{1.984 \times 0.06}{(4/3)}$$

$$= 0.0893 \text{ kg-m}^2$$

Solutions of PRACTICE EXERCISE 5.3

(i)

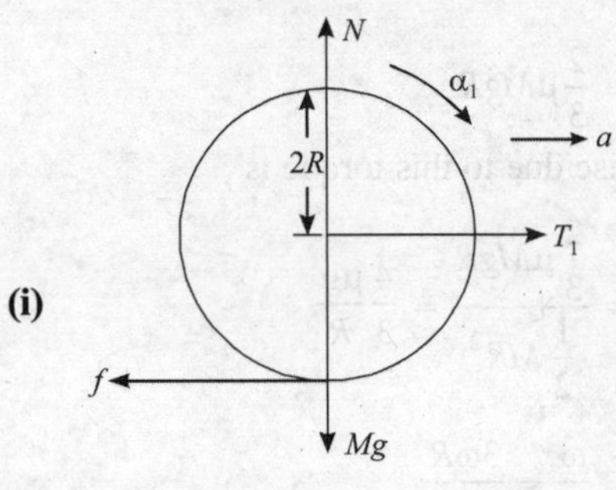

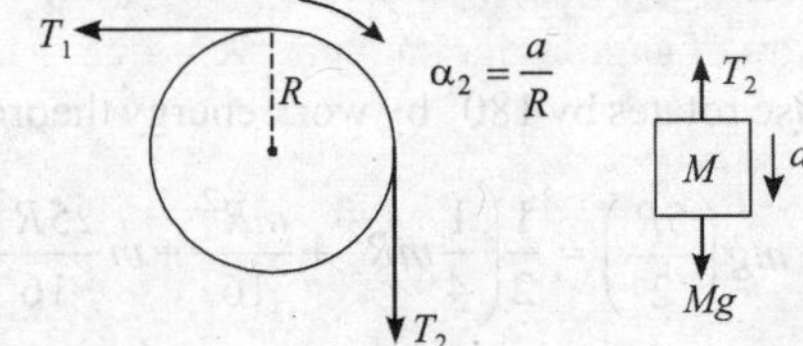

$$T_1 - f = Ma \qquad \dots(1)$$

$$f(2R) = \frac{M(2R)^2}{2}\alpha_1$$

$$\Rightarrow \qquad f = MR\alpha_1 \qquad \dots(2)$$

$$(T_2 - T_1)R = \frac{MR^2}{2}\alpha_2$$

for no slipping, we use

$$T_2 - T_1 = \frac{MR}{2}\alpha_2 \qquad \dots(3)$$

$$Mg - T_2 = Ma \qquad \dots(4)$$

$$a = 2R\alpha_1 \text{ and } a = R\alpha_2$$

Adding equation-(1), (2), (3) & (4); we have

$$Mg = Ma + MR\alpha_1 + \frac{MR}{2}\alpha_2 + Ma$$

$$\Rightarrow \quad g = a + \frac{a}{2} + \frac{a}{2} + a$$

$$g = 3a$$

$$a = \frac{g}{3}$$

(ii) If disc moves up in pure rolling at acceleration a then block will go down at acceleratin $2a$. Equation of motion of bodies are

$$mg - T_2 = m(2a) \qquad \dots(1)$$

$$T_2R - T_1R = \frac{1}{2}MR^2\left(\frac{2a}{R}\right) \qquad \dots(2)$$

$$T_1 - \frac{mg}{2} - f = ma \qquad \dots(3)$$

$$T_1R + fR = \frac{1}{2}mR^2\left(\frac{a}{R}\right) \qquad \dots(4)$$

Adding equations (3) and (4) we get

$$2T_1 - \frac{mg}{2} = \frac{3}{2}ma$$

$$\Rightarrow \qquad T_1 = \frac{mg}{4} + \frac{3ma}{4}$$

from equations (1) & (2) we use-

$$mg - \left(\frac{mg}{4} + \frac{3ma}{4}\right) = 3ma$$

$$\frac{3mg}{4} = \frac{15}{4}ma$$

$$a = \frac{g}{5} = 2\text{m/s}^2$$

(iii) By conservation of angular momentum we use-

$$Mv_1R = I\left(\frac{v_2}{R}\right) + Mv_2R$$

$$\Rightarrow \qquad v_2 = \frac{v_1}{1 + \dfrac{I}{MR^2}}$$

Thus $\qquad \omega = \dfrac{v_2}{R} = \dfrac{v_1}{R\left(1 + \dfrac{I}{MR^2}\right)}$

(iv) If spool acceleration is a and angular acceleration is

$$\alpha = \frac{a}{r}, \text{ we use}$$

$$mg\sin\theta - T = ma \qquad \dots(1)$$

$$Tr = I\left(\frac{a}{r}\right) \qquad \dots(2)$$

from (1) and (2) we get

$$a = \frac{g\sin\theta}{1 + \dfrac{I}{mr^2}}$$

(v) If cylinder rolls down at acceleration a, mass m goes up at acceleration $2a$ so we use

$$T - mg = m(2a) \qquad \dots(1)$$

$$Mg\sin\theta - T - f = Ma \qquad \dots(2)$$

$$fR - TR = \frac{1}{2}MR^2\left(\frac{a}{R}\right) \quad \ldots(3)$$

Adding equations (2) & (3) we get

$$Mg\sin\theta - 2T = \frac{3}{2}Ma$$

$$\Rightarrow \quad a = \frac{2}{3}g\sin\theta - \frac{4}{3}\frac{T}{M}$$

from equtaion (1) we use

$$T - mg = 2m\left(\frac{2}{3}g\sin\theta - \frac{4}{3}\frac{T}{M}\right)$$

$$\Rightarrow \quad T - mg = \frac{4}{3}mg\sin\theta - \frac{8m}{3M}T$$

$$\Rightarrow \quad T\left(1 + \frac{8m}{3M}\right) = mg\left(\frac{4}{3}\sin\theta + 1\right)$$

$$\Rightarrow \quad T = \frac{Mmg(4\sin\theta + 3)}{3M + 8m}$$

(vi) By conservation of energy we use

$$\frac{1}{2}mv_{cm}^2 + \frac{1}{2}I_{cm}\omega^2 = mg(R+r)(1-\cos\theta)$$

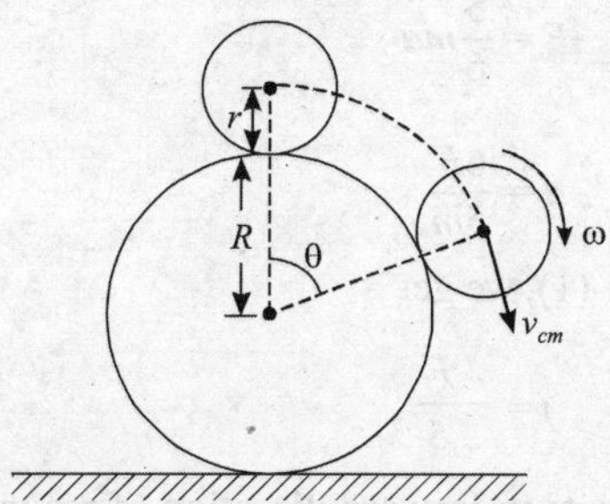

$$\frac{1}{2}mv_{cm}^2 + \frac{1}{2}\cdot\frac{2}{5}Mr^2\frac{v_{cm}^2}{r^2} = mg(R+r)(1-\cos\theta)$$

$$\Rightarrow \quad \frac{7}{10}mv_{cm}^2 = mg(R+r)(1-\cos\theta) \quad \ldots(1)$$

$$\Rightarrow \quad \frac{mv_{cm}^2}{R+r} = \frac{10}{7}mg(1-\cos\theta)$$

If N is the normal reaction acting on the ball then for circular motion of its centre of mass, we use

$$\Rightarrow \quad mg\cos\theta - N = \frac{10}{7}mg(1-\cos\theta)$$

At the moment ball breaks off from the surface of sphere $N = 0$, so we use

$$\Rightarrow \quad mg\cos\theta = \frac{10}{7}mg(1-\cos\theta)$$

$$\Rightarrow \quad \frac{7}{10}\cos\theta + \cos\theta = 1$$

$$\Rightarrow \quad \cos\theta = \frac{10}{17}$$

$$\theta = \cos^{-1}\left(\frac{10}{17}\right)$$

From Equation (1) we use

$$\Rightarrow \quad v_{cm}^2 = \frac{10}{7}mg(R+r)\left(1 - \frac{10}{17}\right)$$

$$\Rightarrow \quad v_{cm} = \sqrt{\frac{10g(R+r)}{17}}$$

$$\Rightarrow \quad \omega_{cm} = \frac{v_{cm}}{r} = \sqrt{\frac{10g(R+r)}{17r^2}}$$

(vii) (a) Just after insect falls on rod if its angular velocity is ω, by conservation of angular momentum we use

$$MV\frac{L}{4} = \left(\frac{ML^2}{12} + \frac{ML^2}{16}\right)\omega$$

$$\omega = \frac{12V}{7L}$$

(b) When insect is at a distance x from O angular momentum of rod (with insect) is

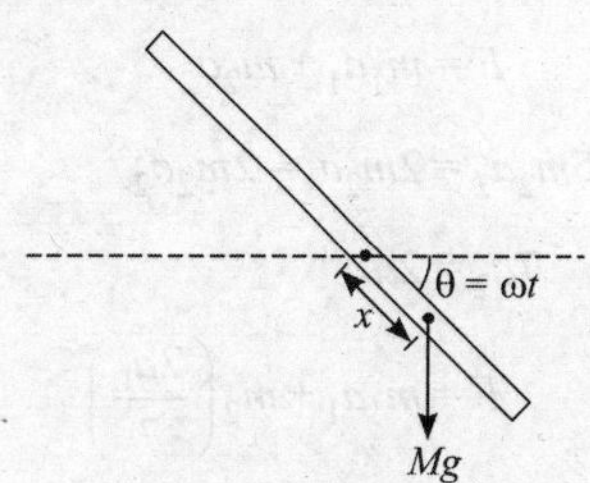

$$J = I\omega = \left(Mx^2 + \frac{ML^2}{12}\right)\omega$$

torque on rod at this instant is

$$\tau = Mg.\,x\cos\omega t = \frac{dJ}{dt} = 2Mx\omega\frac{dx}{dt}$$

$$\int_{L/4}^{L/2} dx = \frac{1}{2}\frac{g}{\omega}\int_0^{t=\pi/2\omega}\cos\omega t\,dt$$

$$\Rightarrow \quad \frac{L}{4} = \frac{g}{2\omega^2}[\sin\omega t]_0^{\pi/2} = \frac{g}{2\omega^2}$$

$$\Rightarrow \quad \frac{L}{4} = \frac{g}{2\left(\frac{12V}{7L}\right)^2}$$

$$\Rightarrow \quad V = \frac{7\sqrt{2gL}}{12}$$

(viii) When the block hits the ridge at point O, it starts rotating about O with angular speed ω which can be obtained by conservation of angular momentum about point O as no external torque will be present about point O on block at the point of collision. Thus we use

$$Mv\left(\frac{a}{2}\right) = \frac{2Ma^2}{3}\omega$$

$$\Rightarrow \quad \omega = \frac{3v}{4a}$$

Solutions of PRACTICE EXERCISE 5.4

(i) For the two bodies, equation of motion of bodies for accelerations a_1 and a_2 are

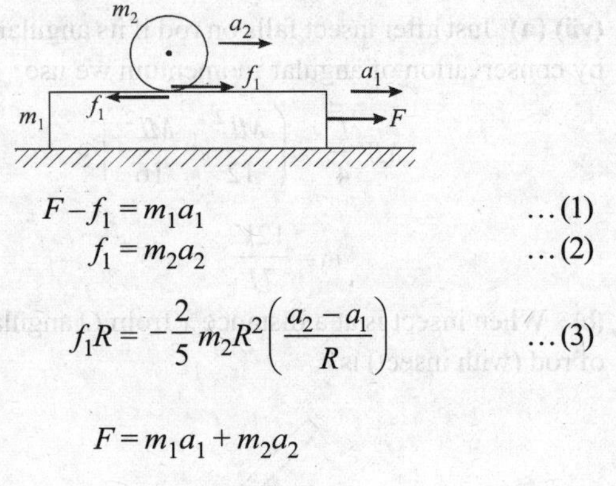

$$F - f_1 = m_1a_1 \quad \ldots(1)$$

$$f_1 = m_2a_2 \quad \ldots(2)$$

$$f_1R = -\frac{2}{5}m_2R^2\left(\frac{a_2 - a_1}{R}\right) \quad \ldots(3)$$

from (1) & (2) $\quad F = m_1a_1 + m_2a_2$

from (2) & (3) $\quad 5m_2a_2 = 2m_2a_1 - 2m_2a_2$

$$\Rightarrow \quad 7a_2 = 2a_1$$

$$\Rightarrow \quad F = m_1a_1 + m_2\left(\frac{2a_1}{7}\right)$$

$$\Rightarrow \quad a_1 = \frac{7F}{7m_1 + 2m_2}$$

$$\Rightarrow \quad a_2 = \frac{2F}{7m_1 + 2m_2}$$

(ii) Maximum torque will act on cylinder at its extreme positions of oscillatory motion. The cylinder will move in influence of pseudo force with respect to platform as shown in figure. Thus equation of motion of cylinder is

$$mA\omega^2 - f = ma_{max} \quad \ldots(1)$$

and $$fR = \frac{1}{2}mR^2\left(\frac{a_{max}}{R}\right) \quad \ldots(2)$$

adding (1) and (2) $A\omega^2 = \frac{3}{2}a_{max}$

$$\Rightarrow \quad a_{max} = \frac{2}{3}A\omega^2$$

$\Rightarrow$ Maximum angular acceleration is

$$\alpha_{max} = \frac{a_{max}}{R} = \frac{2}{3}\frac{A\omega^2}{R}$$

Maximum torque on cylinder is

$$\tau_{max} = I\alpha_{max}$$

$$= \frac{1}{2}MR^2\left(\frac{2}{3}\frac{A\omega^2}{R}\right)$$

$$= \frac{1}{3}mAR\omega^2$$

(iii) If friction is considered at the point of contact in backward direction and shell rolls with acceleration a then the equations of motion of shell, we have

$$F - f = ma \quad \ldots(1)$$

$$F(2R) = \left(\frac{5}{3}mR^2\right)\alpha = \left(\frac{5}{3}mR^2\right)\left(\frac{a}{R}\right)$$

$$\Rightarrow \quad F = \frac{5}{6}ma$$

$$\Rightarrow \quad a = \frac{6F}{5m}$$

From equation-(1), we get

$$f = -\frac{F}{5}$$

Thus friction acts in forward direction of magnitude $F/5$ and the shell will be in pure rolling until $f < \mu mg$, so

$$\frac{F}{5} < \mu mg$$

$$\Rightarrow \quad F < 5\,\mu mg$$

(iv) if cue imparts an impulse J to ball and initial angular speed of ball is ω_0, we use

$$J = mv_0 \quad \ldots(1)$$

and $$Jh = \frac{2}{5}mR^2\omega_0 \quad \ldots(2)$$

from (1) and (2)

$$\omega_0 = \frac{5}{2}\frac{v_0h}{R^2}$$

Conserving angular momentum about a point O on ground, we use

$$mv_0R + \frac{2}{5}mR^2\left(\frac{5}{2}v_0\frac{h}{R^2}\right) = m\left(\frac{9}{7}v_0\right)R + \frac{2}{5}mR^2\left(\frac{9v_0}{7R}\right)$$

$$\left(1+\frac{h}{R}\right) = \left(\frac{9}{7}+\frac{18}{35}\right)$$

$$h = \left(\frac{63}{35}-1\right)R = \frac{4}{5}R$$

(v) **(a)** For pure rolling of shell, we use

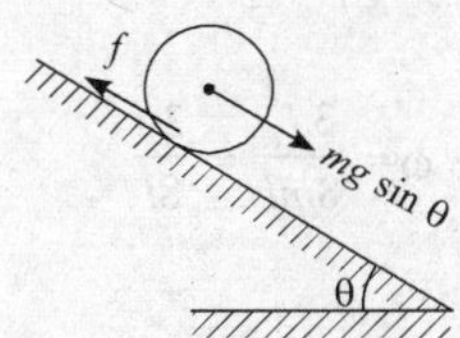

$$mg\sin\theta - f = m\left(\frac{g\sin\theta}{1+\frac{2}{3}}\right) \qquad \left[\text{for hollow sphere } \frac{k^2}{R^2} = \frac{2}{3}\right]$$

$$\Rightarrow \qquad f = \frac{2}{5}mg\sin\theta$$

to prevent sliding $f < \mu\, mg\cos\theta$

$$\Rightarrow \qquad \frac{2}{5}mg\sin\theta < \mu mg\cos\theta$$

$$\Rightarrow \qquad \mu > \frac{2}{5}\tan\theta$$

(b) If $\mu = \frac{1}{5}\tan\theta$ then friction on shell will be

$$f = \mu mg\cos\theta = \frac{1}{5}mg\sin\theta$$

acceleration of shell is $a = g\sin\theta - \mu g\cos\theta = \frac{4}{5}g\sin\theta$

angular acceleration of shell is

$$\alpha = \frac{fR}{I} = \frac{\frac{1}{5}mgR\sin\theta}{\frac{2}{3}mR^2} = \frac{3}{10}\frac{g\sin\theta}{R}$$

time of sliding $\qquad t = \sqrt{\frac{2l}{a}} = \sqrt{\frac{5l}{2g\sin\theta}}$

speed attained by shell as it travells a distance l of inclined is

$$v = at$$

$$\Rightarrow \qquad = \sqrt{\frac{8}{5}gl\sin\theta}$$

angular speed attained by shall as it travels a distance l

$$\omega = \alpha t$$

$$\Rightarrow \qquad = \frac{3}{10}\frac{g\sin\theta}{R}\cdot\sqrt{\frac{5l}{2g\sin\theta}}$$

$$\Rightarrow \qquad = \sqrt{\frac{6gl\sin\theta}{40R^2}}$$

Final kinetic energy of ball is

$$K = \frac{1}{2}mv^2 + \frac{1}{2}I\omega^2$$

$$= \frac{1}{2}m\left(\frac{8}{5}gl\sin\theta\right) + \frac{1}{2}\left(\frac{2}{3}mR^2\right)\left(\frac{9}{40}\frac{gl\sin\theta}{R^2}\right)$$

$$\Rightarrow \qquad = \left(\frac{4}{5}+\frac{3}{40}\right)gl\sin\theta$$

$$\Rightarrow \qquad = \frac{7}{8}mgl\sin\theta$$

Solutions of PRACTICE EXERCISE 5.5

(i) By conservation of angular momentum use

$$m(mud).u.(l/2) = \left[\frac{Ml^2}{3} + m(mud)\cdot\left(\frac{l}{2}\right)^2\right]\omega$$

$$0.5\times 12\times 0.5 = \left[\frac{(50)(1)^2}{3} + 0.5\times(0.5)^2\right]\omega$$

$$\Rightarrow \qquad 3 = \left(\frac{50}{3}+\frac{1}{8}\right)\omega$$

$$\Rightarrow \qquad \omega = \frac{72}{403}\text{ rad/s}$$

(ii) By angular momentum conservation. we use

$$mv\left(\frac{l}{2}\right) = mv'\left(\frac{l}{2}\right) + \frac{Ml^2}{3}\omega$$

$$mv = mv' + \frac{2}{3}Ml\omega \qquad \ldots(1)$$

as collision is elastic, we use

$$v = \frac{\omega l}{2} - v' \quad \ldots(2)$$

From exerted (1) & (2)

$$mv = mv' + \frac{2}{3}M(v+v')\times 2$$

$$mv - \frac{4}{3}Mv = \left(m + \frac{4}{3}M\right)v'$$

$$v' = \left(\frac{3m-4M}{3m+4M}\right)v$$

and
$$\omega = \frac{2}{l}(v+v') = \frac{2v}{l}\left(1+\frac{3m-4M}{3m+4M}\right)$$

$$= \frac{12mv}{l(3m+4M)}$$

Force by axis on plate is

$$F = M\omega^2\frac{l}{2} = \frac{72Mm^2v^2}{l(3m+4M)^2}$$

(iii) Before collision of particles angular momentum of the system about the centre of rod is given as

$$L_i = mu\frac{l}{2} + mu\frac{l}{2} = mul$$

After collision the two particles stick to the rod and if rod now rotates at angular speed ω then by conservation of angular momentum, we have

$$L_i = L_f$$

$$mul = \left(\frac{1}{12}Ml^2 + 2m\left(\frac{l}{2}\right)^2\right)\omega$$

$$\omega = \frac{12mu}{(M+6m)l} = \frac{12\times 0.1\times 6}{(0.2+6\times 0.1)\times 1} = 9 \text{ rad/s}$$

As centre of mass of rod is located at centre, during rotation work done by gravity is zero so there will be no change in kinetic energy of the rod. When rod becomes horizontal than also it would be rotating at angular speed 9 rad/s.

(iv) Using angular momentum conservation we have

$$m_1R^2\omega_1 = \frac{1}{2}m_2R^2\omega_2$$

$$\Rightarrow \quad m_1\left(\frac{\theta-\theta_{disc}}{\Delta t}\right) = \frac{1}{2}m_2\left(\frac{\theta_{disc}}{\Delta t}\right)$$

$$\Rightarrow \quad \theta_{disc} = \frac{2m_1\theta}{m_2+2m_1}$$

(v) If at the time of collision inpulsive reaction at A is J and J_1 is the impulse between particle and rod, we use

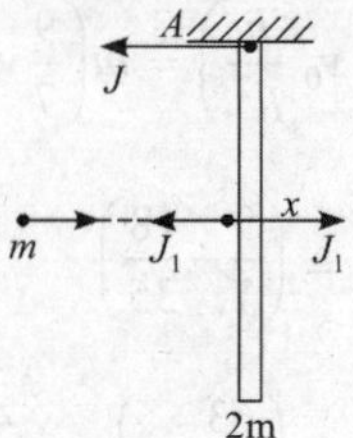

$$J_1 = mv$$

and
$$J_1 l = \frac{2m(2l)^2}{3}\omega$$

$$\Rightarrow \quad \omega = \frac{3J_1}{8ml} = \frac{3v}{8l}$$

for rod we use

$$J_1 - J = 2m(l\omega)$$

$$\Rightarrow \quad J = J_1 - 2ml\left(\frac{3v}{8l}\right) = \frac{mv}{4}$$

If rod gets displaced by an angle and before coming to rest, we use

$$\frac{1}{2}\left(\frac{2m(2l)}{3}\right)^2\left(\frac{3v}{8l}\right)^2 = 2mgl(1-\cos\phi)$$

$$\Rightarrow \quad \cos\phi = 1 - \frac{3v^2}{32gl}$$

$$\Rightarrow \quad \phi = \cos^{-1}\left(1-\frac{3v^2}{32gl}\right)$$

(vi) When meter stick hits the floor, if its angular speed is ω, we use

$$mg\frac{l}{2} = \frac{1}{2}\left(\frac{ml^2}{3}\right)\omega^2$$

$$\Rightarrow \quad \omega = \sqrt{\frac{3g}{l}}$$

Speed of tip of rod is $v = \omega l = \sqrt{3gl}$

$$= \sqrt{3\times 10\times 1} = \sqrt{30} \text{ m/s}$$

Solutions of CONCEPTUAL MCQS Single Option Correct

Sol. 1 (B) As the external force on cyclinder is the weight component of cyclinder acting along the dirction of incline which is acting in downward direction all the time due to which its acceleration is always in downward direction so friction will act in diretion upward along the incline all the time while ascending as well as descending so as to maintain the direction of angular acceleration.

Sol. 2 (A) For identical geometrical shape the mass of iron body will be more than that of aluminimum body hence moment of inertia of iron body will be more as expression for moment of inertia for both bodies will be same for same axis of rotation.

Sol. 3 (B) When the cylinder moves a distance l, the topmost point on the cylinder will travel a distance $2l$ for the case of pure rolling hence option (B) is correct.

Sol. 4 (B) In absence of external force only linear momentum will remain conserved. As the body is non rigid, it can store potential energy and its moment of inertia is also variable.

Sol. 5 (B) For pure rolling on inclined plane the acceleration of body is given as $a = g \sin \theta/(1 + K^2/R^2)$ hence solid sphere will have higher acceleration and will reach the bottom with greater speed.

Sol. 6 (B) For a rigid body, an external torque produces angular acceleration.

Sol. 7 (A) As body is not in pure rolling and given that the distance covered is less than circumference of the wheel so this is the case of $v < R\omega$ and in this case friction will act in forward direction.

Sol. 8 (D) For this rod as linear density varies from one end to another its moment of inertia also changes if its pivoted end is changes so all physical quantities that depend upon moment of inertia will change. Hence only option (D) is correct.

Sol. 9 (C) As masses are just dropped, these will have same speed when these are in hands after dropping so no effect will be there on the angular speed of the table.

Sol. 10 (C) The moment of inertia of a disc about its central axis is $(1/2)MR^2$ and if mass of two discs are same then moment of inertia will be more if radius is large which will be of smaller density disc.

Sol. 11 (D) As the bodies are in pure rolling (without sliding) so no energy dissipation take place and all will reach the bottom with same kinetic energy (Rotational + Translational).

Sol. 12 (C) For a uniformly rotating body the acceleration of any particle will be only normal acceleration which will pass through the axis of rotation hence option (C) is correct.

Sol. 13 (B) As ice melts, due to centrifugal force in frame of pan, water moves outward and total moment of inertia incerases and to conserve angular momentum angular speed decreases.

Sol. 14 (C) As no external horizontal force is there on rod, its center of mass falls vertically so the lower end will be at a distance $l/2$ from O after it falls on ground.

Sol. 15 (C) Man folds his arms only by the internal forces so no change in angular momentum will be there.

Sol. 16 (D) Moment of inertial of a solid sphere is $(2/5)MR^2$ and that of a hollow sphere is $(2/3)MR^2$.

Sol. 17 (A) Compare the standard moment of inertias of the bodies.

Sol. 18 (C) Moment of inertia of a disc is $(1/2)MR^2 = (1/2)\rho\pi wR^4$ where ρ is the iron density and w is the thickness of plate so by substituting the values of w and R we can see that option (C) is correct.

Sol. 19 (C) If cylinder moves at speed v then the plank will move at speed $2v$ as there is no slipping anywhere. The kinetic energy of the plank is $(1/2)M(2v)^2$ and that of cylinder in pure rolling is $(3/4)Mv^2$ thus option (C) is correct.

Sol. 20 (B) About the z-axis moment of inertia of the rod is MR^2 if R is the distance of rod from origin then about all points located at a distance R from the rod, its moment of inertia will be same which will lie on a circle.

Sol. 21 (B) Angular momentum of a particle moveing in a straight line is given by mvd and it remain constant about any fixed point.

Sol. 22 (B) For a body rotating with some angular acceleration, every point on the body will have a tangential acceleration as well as normal acceleration and the vector sum of the two will be horizontal and does not intersect with the axis of rotation.

Sol. 23 (C) For pure rolling on inclined plane the acceleration of body is given as $a = g \sin \theta/(1 + K^2/R^2)$ hence both solid spheres will reach the bottom together.

Sol. 24 (C) If friction is less then the sphere will roll down the incline with sliding so option (C) is correct.

Sol. 25 (C) When we rotate the raw sphere its shell will rotate and the inner fluid will rotate slightly due to the friction at inner wall of the shell whereas the boiled one is solid and will rotate fully hence will have greater moment of inertia.

Sol. 26 (D) As the scooter is moving on a smooth road, no external force is acting on it so internal forces cannot change the speed of center of mass of scooter.

Sol. 27 (B) A sphere cannot roll on a surface where no torque is present to provide the rotational motion in accordance with the linear motion of sphere due to gravity hence only option (B) is the case among other given cases where sphere cannot roll without sliding.

Sol. 28 (A) As the tube rotates, due to centrifugal force the water moves outward and its distance from the axis of rotation increases hence moment of inertia also increases.

Sol. 29 (C) According to parallel axes theorem option (C) is correct.

Sol. 30 (B) When the tortoise moves along the chord then its distance from center decreases and moment of inertia also decreases so angular velocity of the platform increases upto the point when tortoise reaches the mid point of the chord then it decreases to initial value when tortoise reaches the end of chord and stops.

Sol. 31 (B) When the axis of rotation is passing through A the moment of inertia will be higher compared to the case when axis of rotation is passing through B so for same torque angular acceleration will be less.

Sol. 32 (D) Due to change in G, the graviatinal force and energy changes but as the gravitational force is a central force, net torque on satellite about center of planet still remain zero hence angular momentum of the satellite will remain constant.

Sol. 33 (B) For a body in pure rolling its rotational energy is $(1/2)MK^2\omega^2$ and total energy is $(1/2)M(K^2+R^2)\omega^2$ and given that $K^2 = 0.4(K^2+R^2)$ which gives $K = (2/3)^{1/2}R$ which is the case of hollow sphere.

Sol. 34 (C) As the person walks toward the center of the rotating platform, its moment of inertia decreases so angular velocity increases as angular momentum is constant.

Sol. 35 (B) Torque on pencil is $\tau = \dfrac{mgl\sin\theta}{2} = \dfrac{ml^2}{3}\alpha$

$$\Rightarrow \quad \alpha = \frac{3g\sin\theta}{2l}$$

$$a_{tip} = l\alpha = \frac{3}{2}g\sin\theta$$

This we can see it exceeds g when $\sin\theta > \frac{2}{3}$

Sol. 36 (B) Solve the problem using μ as the coefficient of kinetic friction. Linear velocity radius to zero before angular velocity becomes zero.

Sol. 37 (D) All points mentioned in (A) (B) and (C) have acceleration so with respect to these points centre of mass of system will exerience a pseudo force so conservation law cannot be applied about these points.

Sol. 38 (D) The different forces on the block are shown in figure.

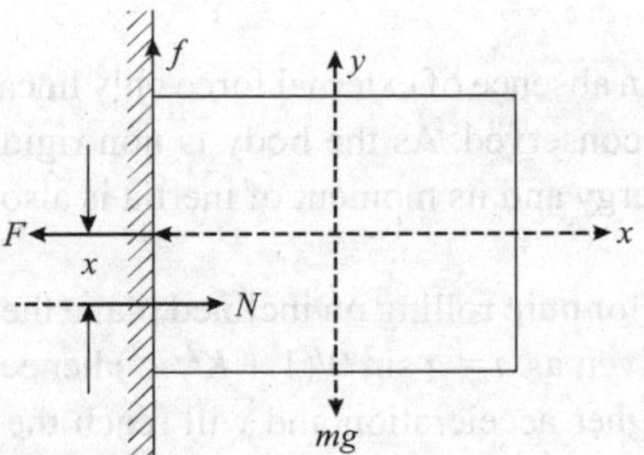

For equilibrium, $f = mg$

and normal reaction, $N = F$

torque due to $F = 0$ (F passes through centre)

As the body is in equilibrium and hence, torque due to friction about centre of mass is equal to torque due to normal reaction about centre of mass.

Sol. 39 (C) Torque of Internal force is always zero. All other quantities may vary in different situations.

Sol. 40 (A) It will continue rolling because the inclined plane and sphere are initially at rest with respect to the car as pseudo force on sphere $ma\cos\theta$ is balanced by $mg\sin\theta$.

Sol. 41 (A) Using impulse momentum theorem

$$J = mV_{cm} \Rightarrow V_{cm} = \frac{J}{m}$$

Using angular momentum theorem about centre of mass

$$J\frac{l}{2} = \left(\frac{ml^2}{12}\right)\omega$$

$$\omega = \frac{6J}{ml}$$

Speed of point A is $\dfrac{2J}{m}$

Solutions of NUMERICAL MCQS Single Option Correct

Sol. 1 (A) Using parallel axes theorem,

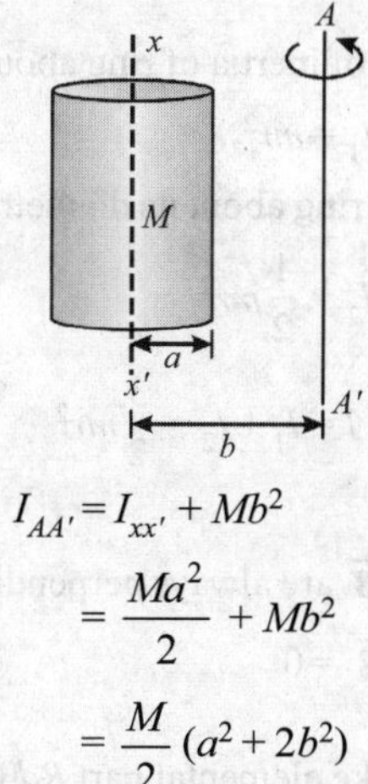

$$I_{AA'} = I_{xx'} + Mb^2$$

$$= \frac{Ma^2}{2} + Mb^2$$

$$= \frac{M}{2}(a^2 + 2b^2)$$

Sol. 2 (A) About an axis passing through point O and perpendicular to both rods moment of inertia is

$$I = 2 \times \frac{ML^2}{12} = \frac{ML^2}{6}$$

If we consider a line $X'Y'$ perpendicular to XY then moment of inertia of the two rods about both XY and $X'Y'$ will be same and we use

$$I_{XY} = I_{X'Y'} = \frac{1}{2}I = \frac{ML^2}{12}$$

Sol. 3 (D) For rotational motion, only friction is there which will exert a clockwise torque on it as torque of Mg and N will be zero.

$$fR = I\alpha$$

$$fr = \frac{mr^2}{2} \times \frac{a}{r}$$

$$f = \frac{ma}{2}$$

Sol. 4 (C) There will be two friction forces acting on sphere, one along $(-\hat{i})$ direction due to translation motion and along $(+\hat{k})$ direction due to rotational motion.

$$f = \frac{\mu mg}{\sqrt{2}}(\hat{k} - \hat{i})$$

Sol. 5 (C) $L = MvR + I\omega$

$$L = M(\omega R)R + \frac{MR^2}{2}\omega$$

$$L = M\omega R^2 + \frac{M\omega R^2}{2}$$

$$\Rightarrow \quad L = \frac{3MR^2\omega}{2}$$

Sol. 6 (C) B has double torque compared to A. Thus, B has double linear acceleration and thus double displacement compared to A.

Sol. 7 (C) $V_P = \sqrt{v_0^2 + v_0^2} = v_0\sqrt{2}$

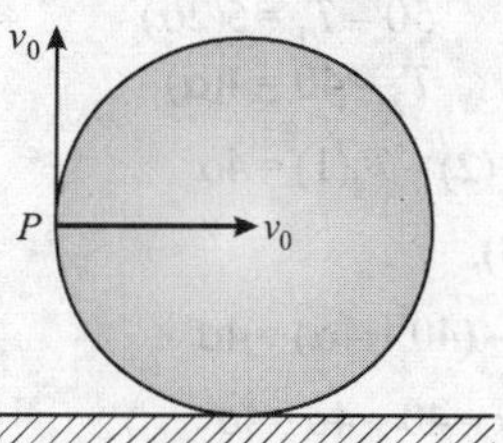

Sol. 8 (C) The curve traced by a point on the rim of the wheel rolls along a straight line without skidding is called cycloid. Path length of cycloid between two points on ground is

$$l_{AB} = \int_0^{2\pi R/v} v_P dt = \int_0^{2\pi R/v} 2v \sin\frac{\omega t}{2} dt = 8R$$

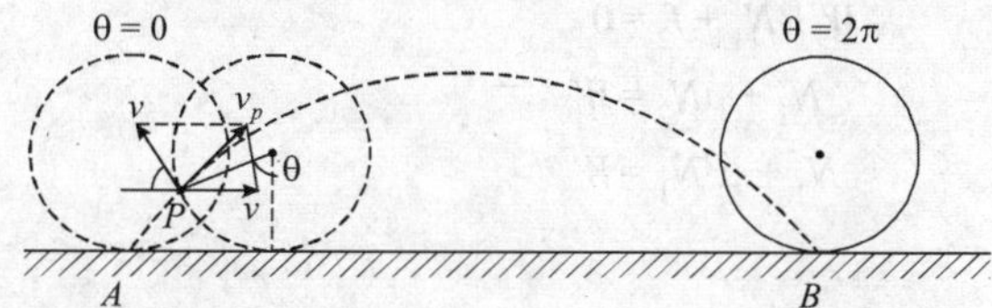

Sol. 9 (C) Using angular momentum conservation

$$2 \times \frac{m(2l)^2}{12}\omega_0 = I'\omega'$$

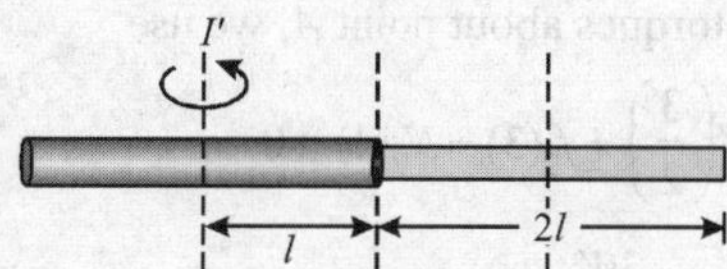

$$\frac{m(2l)^2}{12} + \frac{m(2l)^2}{12} + m(2l)^2$$

$$= \frac{ml^2}{3} + \frac{13ml^2}{3} = \frac{14ml^2}{3}$$

$$\frac{2}{3}ml^2\omega_0 = \frac{14}{3}ml^2\omega'$$

$$\Rightarrow \quad \omega' = \frac{\omega_0}{7}$$

Sol. 10 **(A)** From figure shown

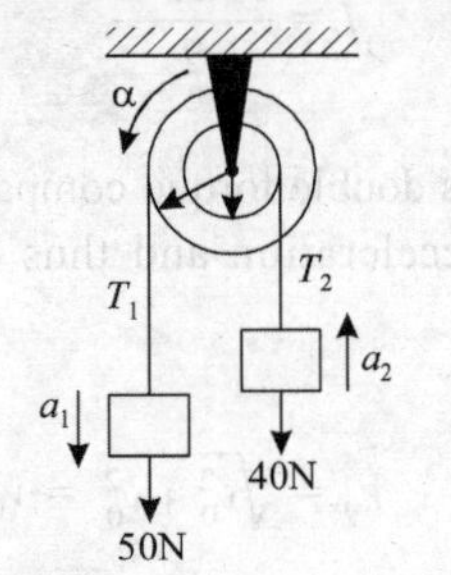

$$50 - T_1 = 5(2\alpha) \quad \ldots(1)$$

$$T_2 - 40 = 4(\alpha) \quad \ldots(2)$$

$$T_1(2) - T_2(1) = 4\alpha \quad \ldots(3)$$

From (1), (2) and (3),

$$2(50 - 10\alpha) - (40 + 4\alpha) = 4\alpha$$

$$\Rightarrow \quad 100 - 20\alpha - 40 - 4\alpha = 4\alpha$$

$$\Rightarrow \quad 28\alpha = 60$$

$$\Rightarrow \quad \alpha = \frac{60}{28} = 2.1 \text{ m/s}^2$$

Sol. 11 **(C)** For equilibrium of rod considering limiting friction we use

$$f_1 = N_2$$

$$\Rightarrow \quad \mu N_1 = N_2 \quad \ldots(1)$$

$$-W + N_1 + f_2 = 0$$

$$N_1 + \mu N_2 = W$$

$$N_1 + \mu^2 N_1 = W \quad \ldots(2)$$

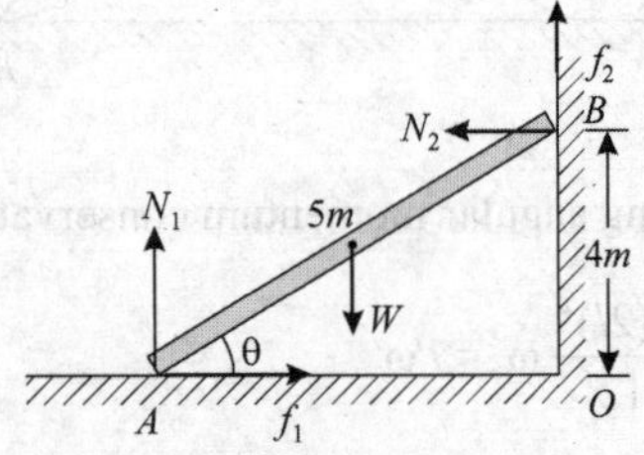

Balancing all torques about point *A*, we use

$$\Rightarrow \quad -W\left(\frac{3}{2}\right) + f_2(3) + N_2(4) = 0$$

$$\Rightarrow \quad \frac{-3W}{2} + 3f_2 + 4N_2 = 0$$

$$\Rightarrow \quad 3\mu N_2 + 4N_2 = \frac{3}{2}(W)$$

$$\Rightarrow \quad \mu N_1(3\mu + 4) = \frac{3}{2}N_1(1 + \mu^2)$$

$$\Rightarrow \quad 2(3\mu^2 + 4\mu) = 3 + 3\mu^2$$

$$\Rightarrow \quad 6\mu^2 + 8\mu = 3 + 3\mu^2$$

$$\Rightarrow \quad 3\mu^2 + 8\mu - 3 = 0$$

$$\Rightarrow \quad 3\mu^2 + 9\mu - \mu - 3 = 0$$

$$\Rightarrow \quad 3\mu(\mu + 3) - 1(\mu + 3) = 0$$

$$\Rightarrow \quad \mu = \frac{1}{3} \quad (\text{As } \mu \neq -3)$$

Sol. 12 **(C)** Moment of inertia of ring about central axis is

$$I_1 = mr^2$$

moment of inertia of a ring about its diametrical axis is

$$I_2 = \frac{1}{2}mr^2$$

$$I = I_1 + I_2 = \frac{3}{2}mr^2$$

Sol. 13 **(C)** $\vec{A}$ and $\vec{B}$ are always perpendicular to each other

$$\Rightarrow \quad \vec{A} \cdot \vec{B} = 0$$

Sol. 14 **(A)** Let us take elemental part $Rd\theta$ of mass *dm*, given as

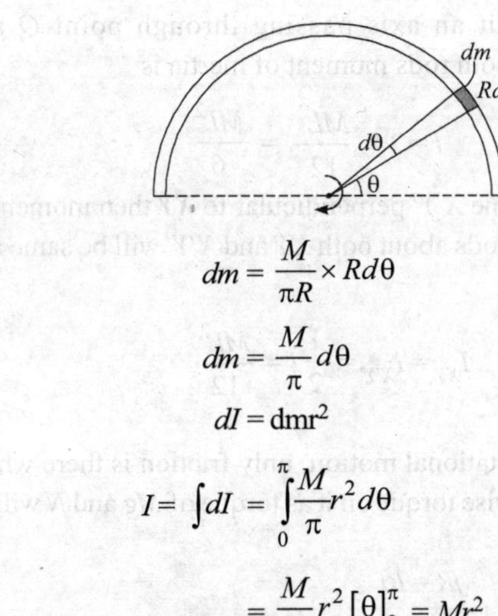

$$dm = \frac{M}{\pi R} \times Rd\theta$$

$$dm = \frac{M}{\pi} d\theta$$

$$dI = \text{dm}r^2$$

$$I = \int dI = \int_0^{\pi} \frac{M}{\pi} r^2 d\theta$$

$$= \frac{M}{\pi} r^2 [\theta]_0^{\pi} = Mr^2$$

Alternatively: Using mass distribution property, moment of inertia of a part of body having same mass distribution will be given by same expression as that of body.

Sol. 15 **(C)** We consider an element in rod as shown in figure of mass *dm* given as

$$dm = \frac{m}{l} dx$$

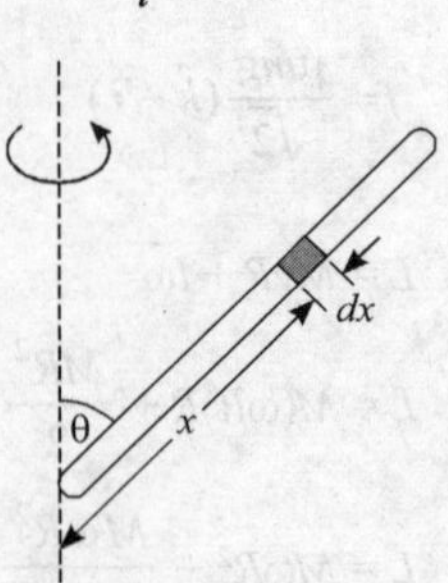

moment of inertia of this element is

$$I = \int dI = \int_0^l \frac{m}{l}\, dx \cdot x^2 \sin^2\theta$$

$$\Rightarrow \quad I = \frac{m}{l}\sin^2\theta\left(\frac{x^3}{3}\right)_0^l$$

$$\Rightarrow \quad I = \frac{m}{3l}\sin^2\theta(l^3)$$

$$\Rightarrow \quad I = \frac{1}{3}ml^2\sin^2\theta$$

Sol. 16 (D) Given that $T_A = 10W$

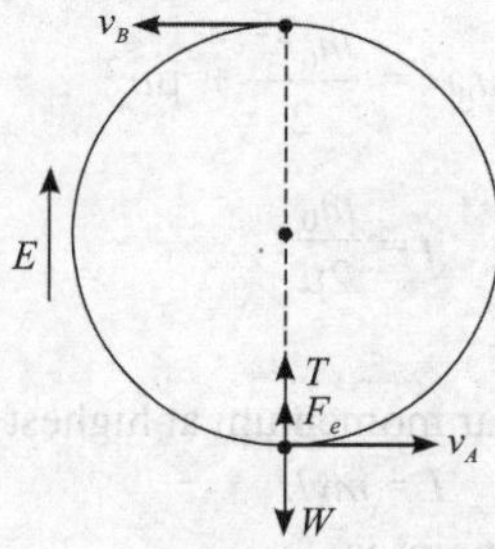

At point A $\quad F_e + T = W + \dfrac{mv_A^2}{R}$

$$QE + 10mg = mg + \frac{mv_A^2}{R}$$

$$\Rightarrow \quad \frac{QE}{m} + 9g = \frac{v_A^2}{l} \qquad \ldots(1)$$

Using work energy theorem,

$$\frac{1}{2}mv_B^2 + mg(2l) - QE(2l) = \frac{1}{2}mv_A^2$$

$$\Rightarrow \quad \frac{1}{2}mv_B^2 + 2mgl - 2QEl = \frac{1}{2}m\left[\frac{QEl}{m} + 9gl\right]$$

$$\Rightarrow \quad \frac{1}{2}mv_B^2 + 2mgl - 2QEl = \frac{1}{2}m\frac{QEl}{m} + \frac{9}{2}mgl$$

$$\Rightarrow \quad \frac{m}{2}v_B^2 = \frac{5mgl}{2} + \frac{mQEl}{2m} + 2QEl$$

$$\Rightarrow \quad \frac{m}{2}v_B^2 = \frac{5mgl}{2} + \frac{5QEl}{2}$$

$$\Rightarrow \quad v_B^2 = 5gl + \frac{5QEl}{m}$$

$$\Rightarrow \quad v_B = \sqrt{5l\left(g + \frac{QE}{m}\right)}$$

Sol. 17 (A) The particle is moving in a conical pendulum,

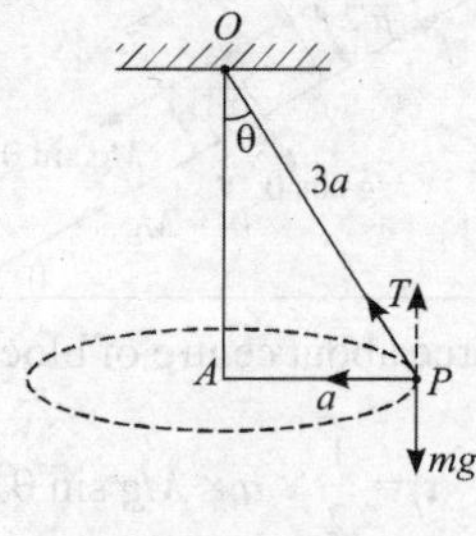

$$OA = \sqrt{9a^2 - a^2} = 2\sqrt{2}a$$

$$\cos\theta = \frac{2\sqrt{2}a}{3a} = \frac{2\sqrt{2}}{3}$$

When the particle is suddenly stopped and let go, then particle moves in a vertical circle as shown in figure

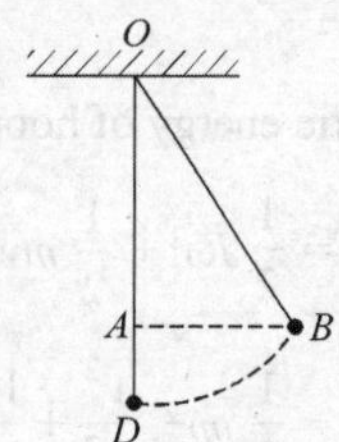

$$h = OD - OA = 3a - 2\sqrt{2}a$$

Velocity of particle at point D is

$$v = \sqrt{2gh}$$

$$\Rightarrow \quad v = \sqrt{2ag(3 - 2\sqrt{2})}$$

$$\Rightarrow \quad v = [2ga(3 - 2\sqrt{2})]^{1/2}$$

Sol. 18 (A) If after time t disc comes to rest, we use

$$t = \frac{V_0}{a} = \frac{\omega_0}{\alpha}$$

$$V_0 = \left(\frac{a}{\alpha}\right)\omega_0$$

$$\Rightarrow \quad V_0 = \frac{\mu g}{\mu mgr \Big/ \frac{mr^2}{2}} \cdot \omega_0$$

As $\quad V_0 = \dfrac{\omega_0 r}{2}$

$$\frac{V_0}{\omega_0 r} = \frac{1}{2}$$

Sol. 19 (D) The block is moving with uniform velocity

$$\Rightarrow \quad f = mg\sin\theta$$

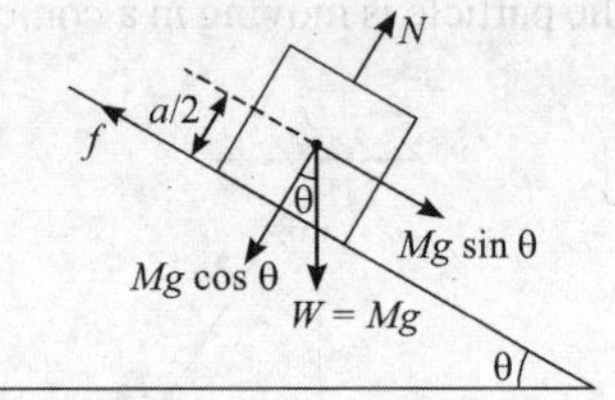

Torque of friction force about centre of block,

$$\tau_f = \frac{1}{2} \times a \times Mg \sin\theta$$

$$\tau_f = \frac{1}{2}(Mag \sin\theta)$$

As block is not rotating torque of normal reaction will balance torque of friction

$$\tau_N = \tau_f = \frac{1}{2}(Mga \sin\theta)$$

Sol. 20 **(B)** Total kinetic energy of hoop is

$$K = \frac{1}{2} I\omega^2 + \frac{1}{2} mv^2$$

$$\Rightarrow \quad K = \frac{1}{2} mr^2 . \frac{v^2}{r^2} + \frac{1}{2} mv^2$$

$$\Rightarrow \quad K = \frac{1}{2} mv^2 + \frac{1}{2} mv^2$$

$$\Rightarrow \quad K = mv^2$$

Thus, a work of mv^2 has to be done to stop it.

Sol. 21 **(C)** Applying conservation of angular momentum,

$$I\omega + mv\frac{l}{2} = \frac{ml^2}{3}\omega'$$

$$\frac{ml^2}{12}\omega + m\left(\frac{\omega l}{6}\right)\cdot\frac{l}{2} = \frac{ml^2}{3}\omega'$$

$$\Rightarrow \quad \frac{\omega}{12} + \frac{\omega}{12} = \frac{\omega'}{3}$$

$$\Rightarrow \quad \frac{\omega'}{3} = \frac{2\omega}{12}$$

$$\Rightarrow \quad \omega' = \frac{\omega}{2}$$

Sol. 22 **(A)** For pure rolling we use the cylinder will rotate about O as instantaneous axis of rotation, we use

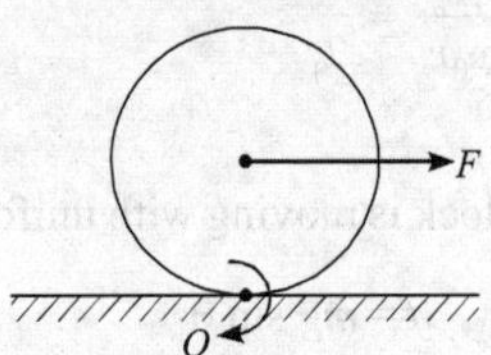

using $\quad Fr = I_0\alpha$

$$\Rightarrow \quad Fr = \frac{3Mr^2}{2}\alpha$$

$$\Rightarrow \quad \alpha = \frac{2F}{3Mr}$$

Sol. 23 **(D)** Mass of cotton pad after time t is

$$m = \mu t$$

By conservation of angular momentum,

$$\frac{m_0 r^2}{2}\omega = \left[\frac{m_0 r^2}{2} + \mu t r^2\right]\frac{\omega}{2}$$

$$\Rightarrow \quad m_0 r^2 = \frac{m_0 r^2}{2} + \mu t r^2$$

$$\Rightarrow \quad t = \frac{m_0}{2\mu}$$

Sol. 24 **(C)** Angular momentum at highest point is

$$L = mvH$$

Velocity at highest point is

$$v = u\cos\theta$$

Maximum height reached,

$$H = \frac{u^2 \sin^2\theta}{2g}$$

$$L = m(u\cos\theta)\left(\frac{u^2\sin^2\theta}{2g}\right)$$

$$\Rightarrow \quad L = \frac{mu^3 \sin^2\theta\cos\theta}{2g}$$

Sol. 25 **(D)** Angular velocity is independent of r.

Sol. 26 **(D)** Centripetal force required to maintain rod in rotational motion is

$$F = m\omega^2\frac{l}{2}$$

This force is provided by the clamp on rod.

Sol. 27 **(C)** Let speed of COM of cylindrical drum is v, then time taken by it to cover a distance of $\frac{l}{2}$

$$t = \frac{l}{2v} \quad \ldots(1)$$

Speed of plank = $2v$ [due to pure rolling of drum]

Distance travelled by plank is

$$s = 2v \times t$$

$$\Rightarrow \quad s = 2v \times \frac{l}{2v}$$

$$\Rightarrow \quad s = l$$

Sol. 28 (B) By conservation of angular momentum,

$$\frac{ML^2}{12}\omega_0 = \left(\frac{ML^2}{12} + \frac{2mL^2}{4}\right)\omega'$$

$$\Rightarrow \quad \frac{M\omega_0}{12} = \frac{M+6m}{12}\omega'$$

$$\Rightarrow \quad \omega' = \frac{M\omega_0}{M+6m}$$

Sol. 29 (A) Acceleration of a rolling body on inclined plane is

$$a = \frac{g\sin\theta}{1+\frac{k^2}{R^2}}$$

For two bodies time of rolling same length is

$$\frac{t_1}{t_2} = \sqrt{\frac{a_2}{a_1}}$$

$$= \sqrt{\frac{1+k_1^2/R^2}{1+k_2^2/R^2}}$$

For a solid sphere $\quad k_1^2 = \frac{2}{5}R^2$

and for disc $\quad k_2^2 = \frac{1}{2}R^2$

$$\Rightarrow \quad \frac{t_1}{t_2} = \sqrt{\frac{1+2/5}{1+1/2}}$$

$$= \sqrt{\frac{14}{15}}$$

Sol. 30 (B) In process A, tension in string = 5 N while it is less than 5 N in B.

Sol. 31 (B) Let speed of disc which rolls is v_A and that which slides is v_B. For equal kinetic energies, we use

$$\frac{1}{2}I\omega^2 + \frac{1}{2}Mv_A{}^2 = \frac{1}{2}Mv_B{}^2$$

$$\Rightarrow \quad \frac{1}{2}\frac{MR^2}{2} \times \frac{v_A^2}{R^2} + \frac{1}{2}Mv_A^2 = \frac{1}{2}Mv_B^2$$

$$\Rightarrow \quad \frac{v_A^2}{4} + \frac{v_A^2}{2} = \frac{v_B^2}{2}$$

$$\Rightarrow \quad 3v_A{}^2 = 2v_B{}^2$$

$$\Rightarrow \quad \frac{v_A}{v_B} = \frac{\sqrt{2}}{\sqrt{3}}$$

Sol. 32 (D) Velocity with which mud is detached at topmost point is

$$v' = v + r\omega = 2v$$

$$d = 2v \times t \quad \text{[where } t \rightarrow \text{time of flight]}$$

$$\Rightarrow \quad d = 2v \times \sqrt{\frac{4r}{g}}$$

$$\Rightarrow \quad d = \sqrt{\frac{16rv^2}{g}}$$

Sol. 33 (A) Let friction is acting in backward direction

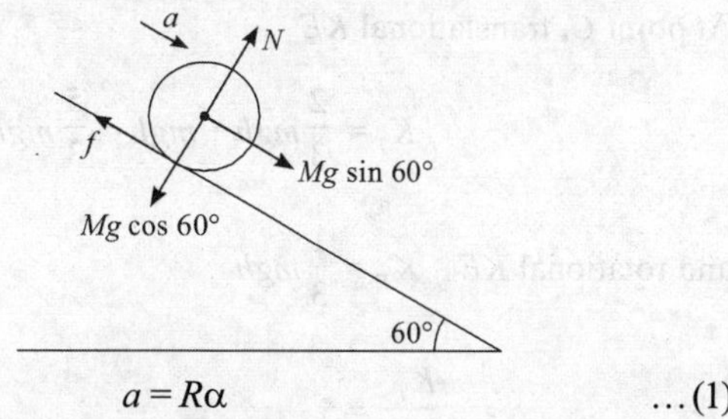

$$a = R\alpha \quad \ldots(1)$$

$$mg\sin 60° - f = Ma \quad \ldots(2)$$

$$fR = I\alpha$$

$$\Rightarrow \quad fR = \frac{MR^2}{2}\left(\frac{a}{R}\right)$$

$$\Rightarrow \quad f = \frac{Ma}{2} \quad \ldots(3)$$

$$Mg\sin 60° = \frac{3}{2}Ma$$

$$\Rightarrow \quad a = \frac{2}{3}g\sin 60° = \frac{g}{\sqrt{3}}$$

$$\Rightarrow \quad f = \frac{Mg}{2\sqrt{3}}$$

For sliding, $\quad f = \mu Mg\cos 60°$

$$\frac{Mg}{2\sqrt{3}} = \frac{2-3x}{\sqrt{3}} \times \frac{1}{2}$$

$\Rightarrow \quad 2 - 3x = 1$

$\Rightarrow \quad 3x = 1$

$\Rightarrow \quad x = \frac{1}{3} m$

Sol. 34 (B) Upto point B,

Translational KE $\quad K_T = \frac{2}{3} mgh$

Rotational KE $\quad K_R = \frac{1}{3} mgh$

After point B, rotational K.E. is constant, but translational K.E. increases.

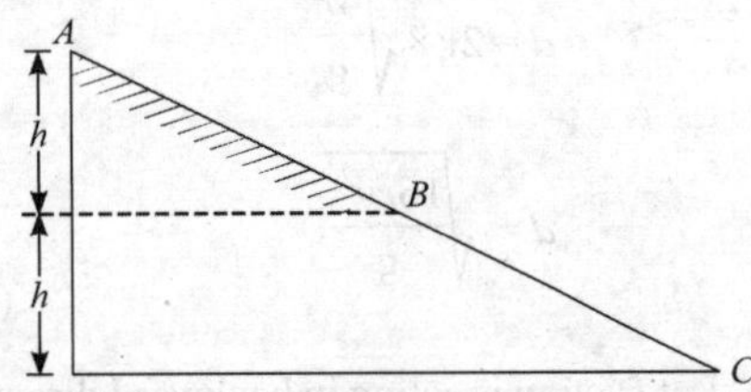

At point C, translational KE

$$K_T = \frac{2}{3} mgh + mgh = \frac{5}{3} mgh$$

and rotational KE $\quad K_R = \frac{1}{3} mgh$

$$\frac{K_T}{K_R} = 5$$

Sol. 35 (C) Friction on ball acts in backward direction which will decrease its linear speed and increase its angular velocity until it starts pure rolling after time t so we use

$$mv_0 - ft = mv \quad \ldots(1)$$

$$0 + fRt = I\frac{v}{R} \quad \ldots(2)$$

For sliding, $\quad f = \mu mg$

Dividing (1) by (2), we get

$$\frac{mv_0 - ft}{fRt} = \frac{mv}{\frac{2}{5}mR^2 \times \frac{v}{R}}$$

$$\Rightarrow \quad \frac{mv_0 - \mu mgt}{\mu mgt} = \frac{5}{2}$$

From (1) and (3), we get

$$mv_0 - \mu mg.\frac{2v_0}{7\mu g} = mv$$

$$\Rightarrow \quad v = \frac{5v_0}{7}$$

Sol. 36 (B) Let friction is acting in backward direction.

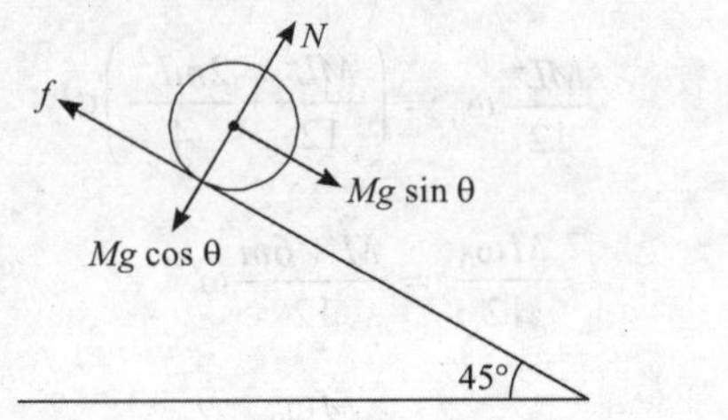

$$Mg \sin\theta - f = Ma \quad \ldots(1)$$

$$fR = I\alpha$$

$$\Rightarrow \quad fR = \frac{2}{5}MR^2 \times \frac{a}{R}$$

$$\Rightarrow \quad f = \frac{2}{2}Ma \quad \ldots(2)$$

$$Mg \sin\theta = Ma + \frac{2}{5}Ma = \frac{7}{5}Ma$$

$$\Rightarrow \quad a = \frac{5}{7} g\sin\theta$$

$$\Rightarrow \quad f = \frac{2}{5}M \times \frac{5}{7} g \sin\theta$$

$$\Rightarrow \quad f = \frac{2}{7} Mg \sin\theta$$

For pure rolling,

$$f \leq \mu Mg \cos\theta$$

$$\Rightarrow \quad \frac{2}{7} Mg \sin\theta \leq \mu Mg \cos\theta$$

$$\Rightarrow \quad \mu \geq \frac{2}{7}$$

Sol. 37 (A) According to principle of conservation of angular momentum,

$$I\omega = (I + I')\omega'$$

$$\Rightarrow \quad \frac{2}{5}MR^2 \times \frac{2\pi}{T} = \left(\frac{2}{5}MR^2 + \frac{2}{3}\Delta MR^2\right)\frac{2\pi}{T + \Delta T}$$

$$\Rightarrow \quad \frac{T + \Delta T}{T} = 1 + \frac{5}{3}\frac{\Delta M}{M}$$

$$\Rightarrow \quad 1+\frac{\Delta T}{T} = 1+\frac{5}{3}\frac{\Delta M}{M}$$

$$\Rightarrow \quad \Delta T = \frac{5}{3} T \times \frac{\Delta M}{M}$$

$$\Rightarrow \quad \Delta T = \frac{5}{3} \times 24 \times \frac{1}{5\times 10^{19}} hr$$

$$\Rightarrow \quad \Delta T \approx 8 \times 10^{-19}\ hr/\text{day}$$

Sol. 38 (A) The speed acquired by bob after bullet comes out is

$$v = \sqrt{5gl}$$

By conservation of linear momentum, we have

$$m_1 v_1 = m\sqrt{5gl} + m_1 \frac{v_1}{3}$$

$$\Rightarrow \quad \frac{2m_1 v_1}{3} = m\sqrt{5gl}$$

$$\Rightarrow \quad v_1 = \frac{3}{2}\left(\frac{m}{m_1}\right)\sqrt{5gl}$$

Sol. 39 (B) Let the sphere is released from height H and radius of gyration is k.

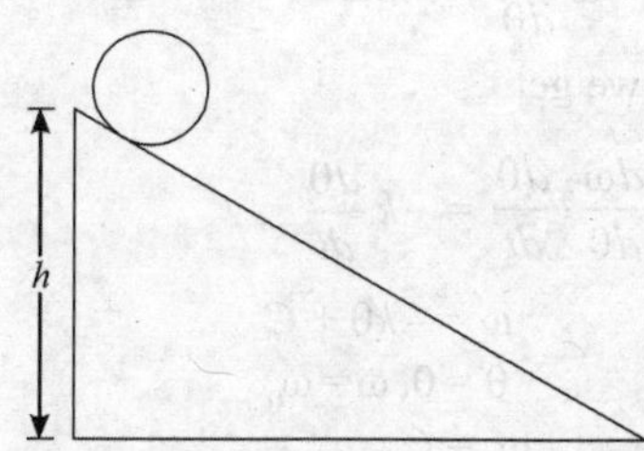

When the inclined plane is made smooth,

$$mgH = \frac{1}{2}m\left(\frac{5}{4}v_0\right)^2$$

$$\Rightarrow \quad gH = \frac{25}{32}v_0^{\,2} \quad \ldots(1)$$

When sphere is rolled down without slipping,

$$mgH = \frac{1}{2}I\omega^2 + \frac{1}{2}mv_0^{\,2}$$

$$\Rightarrow \quad mgH = \frac{1}{2}mk^2\frac{v_0^2}{R^2} + \frac{1}{2}mv_0^{\,2}$$

$$\Rightarrow \quad gH = \frac{k^2 v_0^2}{2R^2} + \frac{1}{2}v_0^{\,2} \quad \ldots(2)$$

From (1) and (2), we can write

$$\frac{25}{32}v_0^{\,2} = \frac{v_0^2}{2}\left[\frac{k^2}{R^2}+1\right]$$

$$\Rightarrow \quad k^2 = \left(\frac{25}{16}-1\right)R^2$$

$$\Rightarrow \quad k^2 = \frac{9}{16}R^2 \Rightarrow k = \frac{3R}{4}$$

Sol. 40 (B) By conservation of energy we use

$$\frac{1}{2}I\omega^2 = mg\frac{l}{2}$$

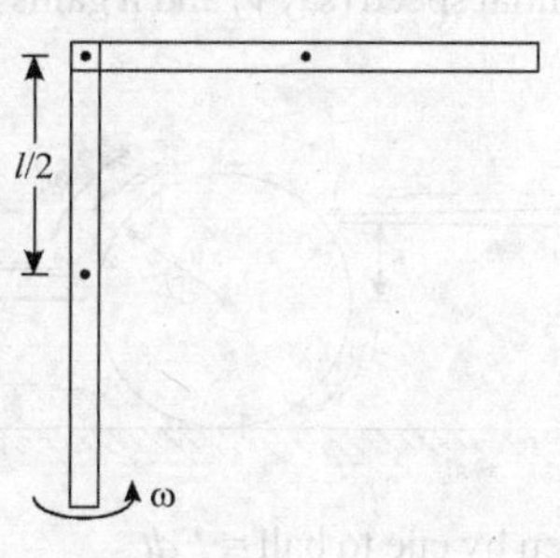

$$\frac{ml^2}{3}\omega^2 = mgl$$

$$\Rightarrow \quad \omega^2 = \frac{3g}{l}$$

$$\Rightarrow \quad \omega = \sqrt{\frac{3g}{l}}$$

Sol. 41 (C) Total kinetic energy = Rotational KE of sphere + Translational KE of sphere + Translation KE of water inside it.

$$K = \frac{1}{2}I\omega^2 + \frac{1}{2}mv^2 + \frac{1}{2}mv^2$$

$$\Rightarrow \quad K = \left(\frac{1}{2}\times\frac{2}{3}mR^2\times\frac{v^2}{R^2}\right) + \frac{1}{2}mv^2 + \frac{1}{2}mv^2$$

$$\Rightarrow \quad K = \frac{1}{3}mv^2 + mv^2$$

$$\Rightarrow \quad K = \frac{4}{3}mv^2$$

Angular momentum of sphere about a fixed point on ground,

$$L = (I\omega + mvR) + mvR$$

$$\Rightarrow \quad L = \frac{2}{3}mR^2 \times \frac{v}{R} + 2mvR$$

$\Rightarrow \quad L = \frac{2}{3}mvR + 2mvR$

$\Rightarrow \quad L = \frac{8mvR}{3}$

Sol. 42 (A) $\vec{\tau}$ is perpendicular to plane containing $\vec{F}$ and $\vec{r}$

$\Rightarrow \quad \vec{r}\cdot\vec{\tau} = 0$ and $\vec{F}\cdot\vec{\tau} = 0$

Sol. 43 (D) The moment of inertia cannot be determined from this information as data is insufficient.

Sol. 44 (A) If cue hits the ball h height above centre line, it shoots with an initial speed (say v) and it gains an initial angular speed (say ω_0)

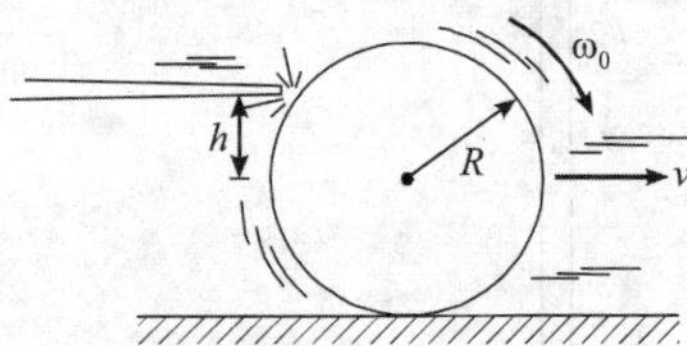

Let impulse given by cue to ball = Fdt

$$Fdt = mv \quad \ldots(1)$$

For rotational motion,

$$Fhdt = I\omega$$

$\Rightarrow \quad Fhdt = \frac{2}{5}mR^2.\frac{v}{R} \quad \ldots(2)$

Dividing (1) by (2), we get

$$\frac{1}{h} = \frac{1}{\frac{2}{5}R}$$

$\Rightarrow \quad h = \frac{2}{5}R$

Sol. 45 (B) Applying conservation of angular momentum,

$$I\omega = I'\omega'$$

$$Mr^2\omega = (Mr^2 + mr^2 + mr^2)\omega'$$

$\Rightarrow \quad \omega' = \frac{Mr^2\omega}{r^2(M+2m)}$

$\Rightarrow \quad \omega' = \frac{M\omega}{M+2m}$

Sol. 46 (D) Acceleration of sphere = μg(toward right)
Acceleration of plank = μg (toward left)
$\Rightarrow$ Acceleration of sphere relative to plank = $2\mu g$.

Sol. 47 (D) Angular momentum of particle moving in line AB is

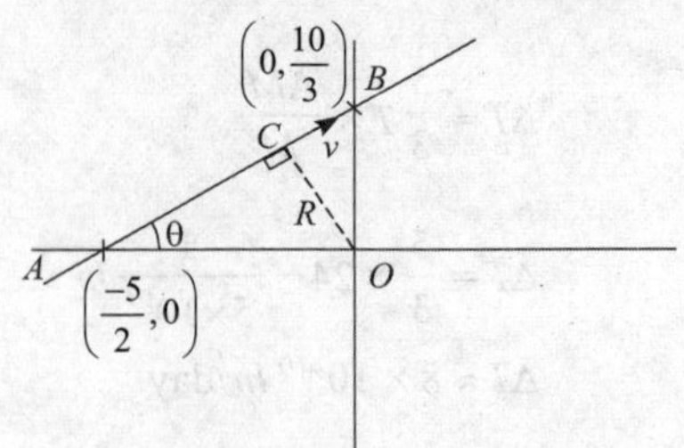

$$L = mvR$$

$$\tan\theta = \frac{10\times 2}{3\times 5} = \frac{4}{3}$$

$$\theta = 53°$$

In ΔOAC, $\quad \sin 53° = \frac{R}{\frac{5}{2}}$

$\Rightarrow \quad R = \frac{5}{2}\times\frac{4}{5} = 2$

$\Rightarrow \quad L = 10\times 6\times 2$

$\Rightarrow \quad L = 120 \text{ kg } m^2/\text{s}$

Sol. 48 (B) Given that $\alpha = -k\omega$

$$\omega\frac{d\omega}{d\theta} = -k\omega$$

On integrating we get

$$\frac{d\omega}{d\theta}\cdot\frac{d\theta}{dt} = -k\frac{d\theta}{dt}$$

$\Rightarrow \quad \omega = -k\theta + C$

Initially, $\quad \theta = 0, \omega = \omega_0$

$$\omega_0 = C$$

After n revolution,

$$\frac{\omega_0}{2} = -k(2n\pi) + \omega_0$$

$\Rightarrow \quad \frac{\omega_0}{2} = 2\,kn\pi$

$$k = \frac{\omega_0}{4n\pi} \quad \ldots(1)$$

For final stop, $\quad \omega = 0$

$$0 = \frac{-\omega_0}{4n\pi}(\theta) + \omega_0$$

$$\theta = 4n\pi$$

i.e. $2n$ revolution,

Number of revolutions that will further occur before flywheel stops

$$= 2n - n$$
$$= n$$

Sol. 49 (B) Revolution period of moon is

$$T_m = \frac{2\pi r_m}{v}$$

$$\Rightarrow \quad T_m = \frac{2\pi r_m}{\sqrt{\frac{GM}{r_m}}} \quad \left[\text{As orbital speed is } v = \sqrt{\frac{GM}{r_m}}\right]$$

$$\Rightarrow \quad T_m^2 = \frac{4\pi^2 r_m^3}{GM}$$

$$\Rightarrow \quad M = \frac{4\pi^2 r^3}{T_m^2 G}$$

Sol. 50 (C) When ring slides down the incline from height h,

$$mgh = \frac{1}{2}mv^2$$

$$\Rightarrow \quad v^2 = 2gh \quad \ldots(1)$$

Let velocity of ring at bottom is v' when it rolls down the same incline,

$$mgh = \frac{1}{2}I\omega^2 + \frac{1}{2}mv'^2$$

$$\Rightarrow \quad mgh = \frac{1}{2}mr^2.\frac{v'^2}{r^2} + \frac{1}{2}mv'^2$$

$$\Rightarrow \quad v'^2 = gh \quad \ldots(2)$$

Dividing (1) by (2), we get

$$\frac{v^2}{v'^2} = \frac{2}{1}$$

$$\Rightarrow \quad v' = \frac{v}{\sqrt{2}}$$

Sol. 51 (C) $K = \frac{1}{2}I\omega^2$

$$\Rightarrow \quad 360 = \frac{1}{2}I(30)^2$$

$$\Rightarrow \quad I = 0.8 \text{ kgm}^2$$

Sol. 52 (C) Angle of rotation in 1 sec is

$$\theta_1 = \frac{1}{2}\alpha(1)^2$$

$$\theta_1 = \frac{\alpha}{2}$$

$$\alpha = 2\theta_1 \quad \ldots(1)$$

$$\Rightarrow \quad \theta_1 + \theta_2 = \frac{1}{2}\alpha(2)^2$$

$$\Rightarrow \quad \theta_1 + \theta_2 = \frac{1}{2}(2\theta_1)(4)$$

$$\Rightarrow \quad \theta_1 + \theta_2 = 4\theta_1$$

$$3\theta_1 = \theta_2$$

$$\Rightarrow \quad \frac{\theta_2}{\theta_1} = 3$$

Sol. 53 (B) Using conservation of angular momentum

$$\frac{MR^2}{2}\omega = \left(\frac{MR^2}{2} + \frac{MR^2}{8}\right)\omega'$$

$$\Rightarrow \quad \frac{1}{2}\omega = \left(\frac{1}{2} + \frac{1}{8}\right)\omega'$$

$$\Rightarrow \quad \frac{\omega}{2} = \left(\frac{4+1}{8}\right)\omega'$$

$$\Rightarrow \quad \omega' = \frac{4}{5}\omega$$

Sol. 54 (C) Kinetic energy,

$$K = \frac{1}{2}I\omega^2$$

$$\Rightarrow \quad = \frac{1}{2}\frac{Ml^2}{3} \times \omega^2$$

$$\Rightarrow \quad = \frac{1}{6}Ml^2\omega^2$$

Sol. 55 (A) Force by liquid on other end is

$$F = M\omega^2\left(\frac{L}{2}\right)$$

Sol. 56 (C) Let radius of hollow sphere is R_1 and that of solid sphere is R_2

$$\frac{2}{3}MR_1^2 = \frac{2}{5}MR_2^2$$

$$\Rightarrow \quad \frac{R_1}{R_2} = \sqrt{\frac{3}{5}}$$

Sol. 57 (D) By conservation of energy,

$$\frac{1}{2}mv^2 = \frac{1}{2}M\left(\frac{mv}{M}\right)^2 + \frac{1}{2}\left(\frac{ML^2}{12}\right)(\omega)^2 \quad \ldots(1)$$

By conservation of momentum,

$$mv\frac{L}{2} = \frac{ML^2}{12}\omega$$

$$\Rightarrow \quad \omega = \frac{6mv}{ML} \quad \ldots(2)$$

From (1) and (2), we get

$$\frac{1}{2}mv^2 = \frac{1}{2}\frac{m^2v^2}{M} + \frac{1}{24}ML^2.\frac{36m^2v^2}{M^2L^2}$$

$$\Rightarrow \quad 1 = \frac{m}{M} + \frac{3m}{M}$$

$$\Rightarrow \quad 1 = \frac{4m}{M}$$

$$\Rightarrow \quad m = \frac{M}{4}$$

Sol. 58 (D) If a_C is initial acceleration of COM of disc and α is its initial angular acceleration, we use

$$T = 2\,ma_C$$

$$RT = \frac{2mR^2}{2}\alpha$$

$$\frac{m\left(\frac{J}{m}\right)^2}{2R} - T = m(a_c + R_\alpha)$$

$$T + \frac{T}{2} + T = \frac{J^2}{2mR}$$

FBD of disc FBD of particle

$$\Rightarrow \quad \frac{5T}{2} = \frac{J^2}{2mR}$$

$$\Rightarrow \quad T = \frac{J^2}{5mR}$$

$$\Rightarrow \quad a_C = \frac{T}{2m} = \frac{J^2}{5mR(2m)} = \frac{J^2}{10m^2R}$$

Putting all the values $a_c = 4\text{ m/s}^2$

Sol. 59 (A)

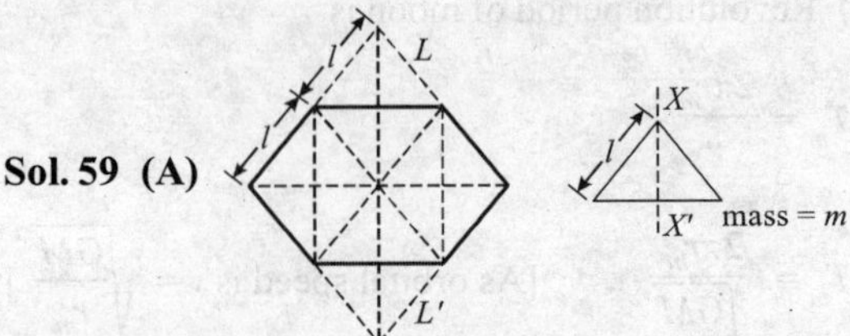

We divide hexgon in six equilateral triangles by dotted lines as shown in figure and added two more triangles to it to form a diamond. If moment of inertia of triangle about XX' is I_1 then we use

$$I + 2I_1 = 2\,[I_{1\,(m \leftarrow 4m\,\&\,l \leftarrow 2l)}]$$

$$I + 2I_1 = 32I_1$$

$$\Rightarrow \quad I_1 = \frac{I}{30}$$

Now as density of triangular plate is 3 times and thickness is double its moment of inertia will be

$$I_t = I_1 \times 3 \times 2 = \frac{I}{5}$$

Sol. 60 (A) If N_1 and N_2 are normal reaction on rear & front tyres, we have

$$N_1 + N_2 = Mg \quad \ldots(1)$$

$$\mu(N_1 + N_2) = Ma \quad \ldots(2)$$

As net torque about $C = 0$

$$\Rightarrow \quad \mu(N_1 + N_2)h + \frac{N_1W}{2} = \frac{N_2W}{2} \quad \ldots(3)$$

$$\Rightarrow \quad N_2 > N_1$$

Solving equation we get $N_1 = \frac{N}{2}\left\{g - \frac{2\mu gh}{W}\right\} \quad \ldots(4)$

For maintaning contact $N_1 > 0 \Rightarrow \mu = \frac{W}{2h}$

Sol. 61 (B) To maintain contact $N_1 > 0$ and maximum acceleration is

$$a = \mu g$$

$$\Rightarrow \quad a = \frac{Wg}{2h}$$

Sol. 62 (A) As hinges are smooth the disc continue to rotate at ω so by work energy theorem we use

$$\frac{1}{2}\left(\frac{1}{3}m(2R)^2\right)\omega^2 + \frac{1}{2}m\,(2R\omega)^2$$

$$= (mg\,(2R) + mgR)\,\frac{1}{2}$$

$$\Rightarrow \quad 2R^2\omega^2 + \frac{2R^2\omega^2}{3} = \frac{3gR}{2}$$

$$\Rightarrow \quad \frac{8R\omega^2}{3} = \frac{3g}{2}$$

$$\Rightarrow \quad \omega = \sqrt{\frac{9g}{16R}}$$

Sol. 63 (D) Relative velocity is

$$\left|\vec{V}_P - \vec{V}_Q\right| = 2\omega R\cos 30^\circ = \sqrt{3}\,\omega R$$

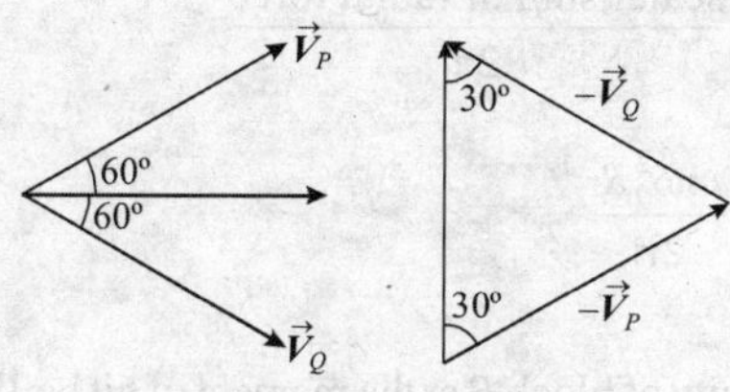

Sol. 64 (A) All maximum height when system is moving at speed v_1 by conservation of energy

$$P = 5mv_1 = mv$$

$$\frac{1}{2}mv^2 = \frac{1}{2}(5m)\,v_1^2 + mgh$$

$$\Rightarrow \quad \frac{P^2}{2m} = \frac{P^2}{10m} + mgh.$$

$$\Rightarrow \quad h = \frac{4P^2}{10m^2 g} = \frac{2P^2}{5m^2 g}$$

Sol. 65 (C) By inpulse equation we have

$$P(0.4\,r) = \frac{2}{5}mr^2.\omega \quad \Rightarrow \quad \omega_2 = \frac{P}{mr}$$

Final kinetic energy $\quad K = \frac{1}{2}(5m)\,v_1^2 + \frac{1}{2}I_{cm}\omega^2$

$$\Rightarrow \quad K = \frac{P^2}{10m} + \frac{1}{2}\left(\frac{2}{5}mr^2\right)\left(\frac{P}{mr}\right)^2$$

$$\Rightarrow \quad K = \frac{P^2}{10m} + \frac{P^2}{5m} = \frac{3P^2}{10m}$$

Sol. 66 (A) When sphere reaches flat portion again at speed v_3 and wedge is moving to right at v_2 we use

$$P = mV = 4mV_2 - mV_3$$

$$V_3 = (4V_2 - V)$$

by energy conservation

$$\frac{1}{2}mV^2 = \frac{1}{2}m\,(4V_2 - V)^2 + \frac{1}{2}4mV_2^2$$

$$V_2 = \frac{2P}{5m}$$

$$V_3 = \frac{3V}{5} = \frac{3P}{5m}$$

Sol. 67 (C) The speed is due to radial motion as well as due to angular motion so we use

$$v = \sqrt{\left(\frac{dR}{dt}\right)^2 + (R\omega)^2}$$

$$= \sqrt{\beta^2 + (R_0 - \beta t)^2}$$

Sol. 68 (C) By conserving angular momentum about vertical axis OP

$$mv_0 a = mv\sqrt{a^2 - h^2} \qquad \ldots(1)$$

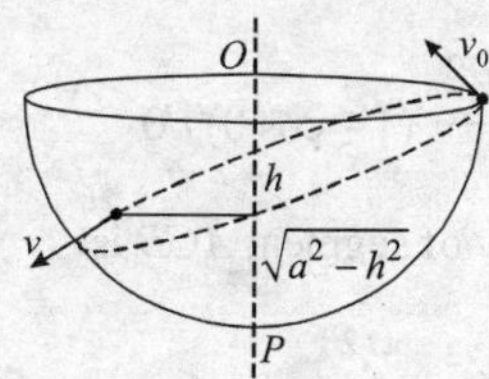

By conserving mechanical energy

$$\frac{1}{2}mv^2 = \frac{1}{2}mv_0^2 + mgh \qquad \ldots(2)$$

From equation (1) and (2) we get $h = \dfrac{a(\sqrt{5}-1)}{2}$

Sol. 69 (C) The acceleration of the point P is due to the axis and due to rotation about the axis

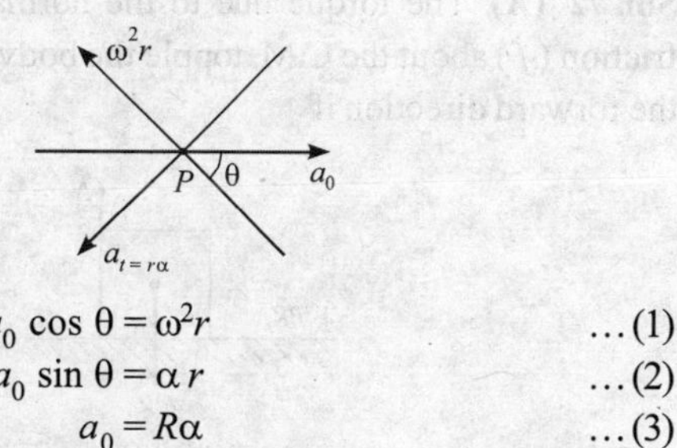

$$a_0 \cos\theta = \omega^2 r \qquad \ldots(1)$$

$$a_0 \sin\theta = \alpha\, r \qquad \ldots(2)$$

and $$a_0 = R\alpha \qquad \ldots(3)$$

from (2) and (3) $\sin\theta = \dfrac{r}{R}$

$$\Rightarrow \quad \theta = \sin^{-1}\left(\frac{r}{R}\right)$$

Sol. 70 (A) Considering an elemental mass dm on ring as shown in figure

$$dm = \left(\frac{m}{2\pi R}\right)(Rd\theta) = \frac{md\theta}{2\pi}$$

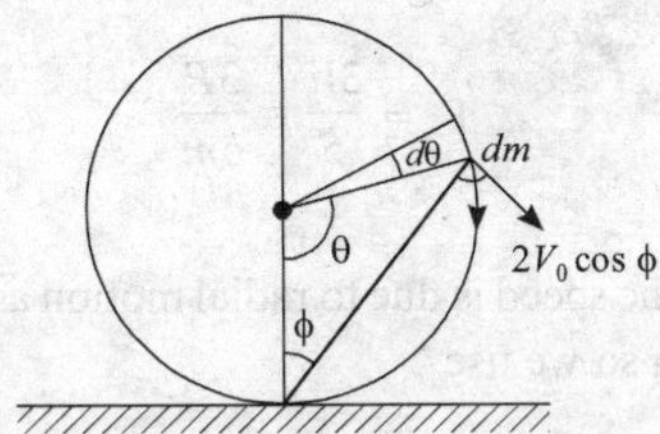

Velocity of elemental mass is $V = 2R\cos\phi\left(\frac{V_0}{R}\right)$

$$\Rightarrow \quad V = 2V_0\cos\phi = 2V_0\sin\frac{\theta}{2}$$

kinetic energy of element is

$$dK = \frac{1}{2}(dm)\times 4V_0^2 \times \sin^2\frac{\theta}{2}$$

$$\Rightarrow \quad dK = \frac{mV_0^2}{2\pi}(1-\cos\theta)\,d\theta$$

Total kinetic energy of segment ACB is

$$K_{ACB} = \frac{mV_0^2}{2\pi}\int_{-\pi/2}^{+\pi/2}(1-\cos\theta)d\theta = \frac{mV_0^2}{2} - \frac{mV_0^2}{\pi}$$

Sol. 71 (A) According to the perpendicular axes theorem

$$I_z = I_x + I_y$$

Since the plate is quite symmetrical about AB and CD we can use again perpendicular axes theorem

$$I_{AB} = I_{CD} = I$$

Sol. 72 (A) The torque due to the normal reaction (N) and friction (f) about the C.M. topple the body about front edge in the forward direction if

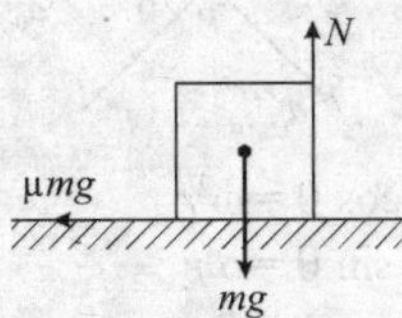

$$\Rightarrow \quad \mu mgh > \frac{Na}{2} \quad \mu > \frac{a}{2h} \quad [N = mg]$$

Sol. 73 (B) Vector force components are shown in figure

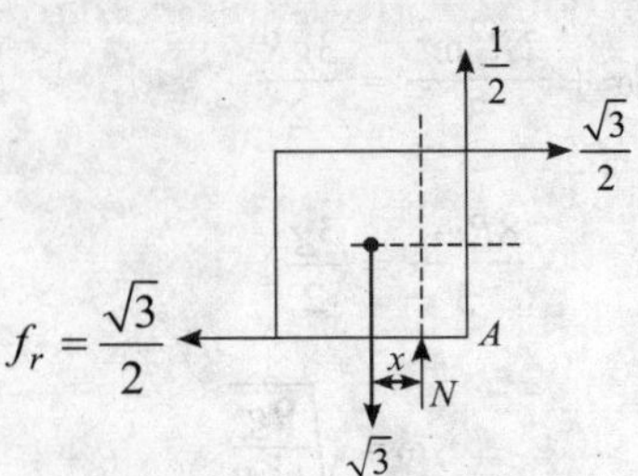

Torque about A due to all forces excluding normal force is found to be zero. Thus N must be passing through point A.

Sol. 74 (C) Tension is rotating rope is

$$T = \frac{\text{scaler sum of radial force}}{2\pi}$$

$$= \frac{m\omega_0^2 R}{2\pi}$$

Sol. 75 (D) Let velocity of block B at the moment of hit be V. So component of velocity of A along string at that instant is also V and component perpendicular to string is V', then using conservation of angular momentum about pulley we have

$$mV'2l = mV_0 l$$

$$\Rightarrow \quad V' = V_0/2$$

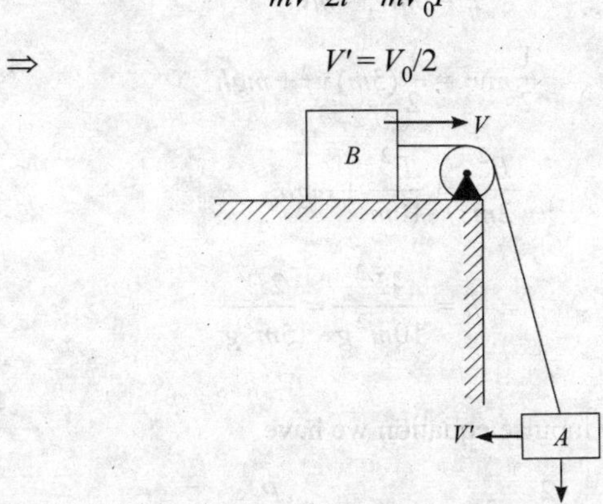

Using conservation of energy we have

Initial KE = Final KE

$$\frac{1}{2}mV^2 + \frac{1}{2}(V^2 + V'^2) = \frac{1}{2}mV_0^2 = \frac{1}{2}mV^2 + \frac{1}{2}m(V^2 + V'^2)$$

Solving $\quad V = V_0\sqrt{\frac{3}{8}}$

Sol. 76 (A) After B strikes pulley component velocities along string becomes zero and component perpendicular to string remains unchanged

$$V' = \frac{V_0}{2}$$

Solutions of ADVANCE MCQs One or More Option Correct

Sol. 1 (C, D) For pure rolling on inclined plane the acceleration of body is given as $a = g \sin \theta / (1+K^2/R^2)$ hence solid sphere will have higher acceleration and will reach the bottomfirst and ring will have least acceleration so will reach with least speed or liner momentum.

Sol. 2 (B, D) For rotation of a body axis of rotation may exist anywhere about which all particles of body will be in circular motion with all centers lying on the axis of rotation.

Sol. 3 (A, B, C) Due to engine friction on rear wheels act in forward direction due to which car accelerates forward and on front wheel in backward direction as axle at center pushes the front wheels in forward direction and as car is accelerating, forward friction must be more than backward friction.

Sol. 4 (B, C) Torque is given by cross product of position vector and the force.

Sol. 5 (A, C, D) For pure rolling the bottom most point will remain at rest hence option (A) is correct. In every point of wheel there will be two speeds v_0, one due to translational motion in forward direction and other due to rotational motion along tangential direction so speed of any point is the vector sum of these two hence option (C) and (D) is correct.

Sol. 6 (A) On a rough horizontal surface if a rolling body stops, it is due to rolling friction or air friction which tends to decrease the linear velocity.

Sol. 7 (B) As the sphere is rotating uniformly the tangential acceleratin of any particle on sphere will be zero and all particles will only have normal acceleration.

Sol. 8 (C, D) As all surfaces are smooth at the time of collision the impulse between the spheres due to the contact force will pass through their centers so it will not impart any angular impulse so angular speeds of the spheres will not change.

Sol. 9 (B, C, D) Angular momentum of a particle moveing in a straight line is given by mvd and it remain constant about any fixed point.

Sol. 10 (All) Due to impulse the rod attains an angular momentum Jl and the angular velocity attained will be Jl/I where moment of inertia $I = (1/3)Ml^2$ and the final kinetic enregy of the rod is $(1/2)I\omega^2$ and the linear velocity of the mid point will be $(l/2)\omega$.

Sol. 11 (B, C)

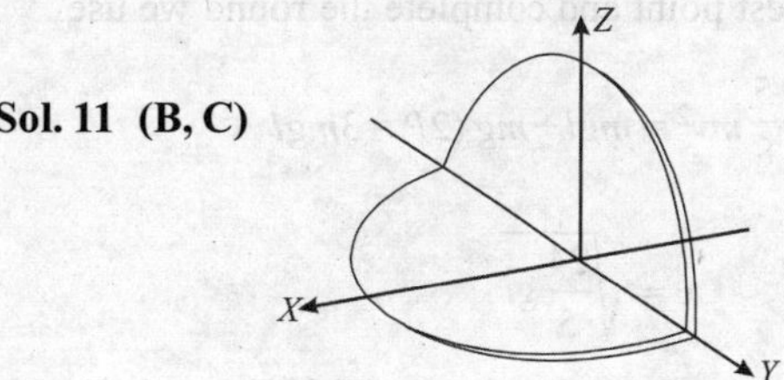

From figure we have

$$I_Y = \frac{1}{2}mR^2 \;\&\; I_X = I_Z = \frac{3}{4}mR^2$$

Sol. 12 (A, B, C) $v_0 = 2\text{m/s}$

$$\mu = 0.4$$

$$mv_0 - ft = mv \quad \ldots(1)$$

where v is velocity acquired by ring when slipping stops.

$$0 + fR\,t = I\frac{v}{R} \quad \ldots(2)$$

Dividing (1) by (2), we get,

$$\frac{mv_0 - ft}{fRt} = \frac{mv}{mR^2 \cdot \left(\frac{v}{R}\right)}$$

$$fRt = mv_0R - fRt$$

$$\mu mg\,Rt = mv_0R - \mu mg + R \qquad (\because\; f = \mu mg)$$

$$2\mu gt = v_0$$

$$t = \frac{v_0}{2\mu g} = \frac{2}{2\times 0.4\times 10} = 0.25\text{ s}$$

Thus, ring will start pure rolling after 0.25 s

From (1),

$$mv_0 - ft = mv$$

$$mv_0 - \mu mg\,t = mv$$

$$v = v_0 - \mu gt = 2 - (0.4)(10)(0.25)$$

$$v = 1\text{ m/s}$$

When ring will start pure rolling, its velocity is 1 m/s.

From 0.25 s to 0.5 s, i.e.,

$$t = 0.5 - 0.25 = 0.25\text{ s},$$

$$v' = v_0 - \mu gt$$

$$v' = 2 - 1 = 1\text{ m/s}$$

Sol. 13 (A, C, D) For different pivoted ends, moment of inertia is different torque is same and work by torque is same.

Sol. 14 (A, C) If v is speed imported to B, total kinetic energy of rod is

$$K = \frac{1}{2}mv^2 + \frac{1}{2}m\left(\frac{v}{2}\right)^2 = \frac{5}{8}mv^2$$

to reach the highest point and complete the round we use

$$\frac{5}{8}mv^2 = mgl + mg(2l) = 3mgl$$

$$\Rightarrow \qquad v = \sqrt{\frac{24}{5}gl}$$

At the highest point rod will be at rest and if T_{AC} and T_{BC} are tension in rod reactions AB and BC, we have

$$T_{BC} = mg \quad \text{and} \quad T_{AC} = 2gm \quad \Rightarrow \quad \frac{T_{AC}}{T_{BC}} = \frac{2}{1}$$

Sol. 15 (A, B, D) In the frame of rod the small vertical rods will experience centrifugal forces which forms a couple in clockwise direction in the state given in problem. To balance this couple force by hinge at A on the rod must be downword and the force by hinge at B must be upward.

The angular momenta of the vertical rod particles about point O will be inclined to rod hence option (D) is also correct.

Sol. 16 (A, C) When cylinder comes down, at the point where string leaves contact with the cylinder is point of instantaneous rest, thus string does zero work.

$$\frac{K_R}{K_T} = \frac{\frac{1}{2}I_C\omega^2}{\frac{1}{2}mv^2} = \frac{\frac{1}{2}\left(\frac{mR^2}{2}\right)\left(\frac{v}{R}\right)^2}{\frac{1}{2}mv^2} = \frac{1}{2}$$

* * * * *

ANSWERS & SOLUTIONS

CONCEPTUAL MCQS Single Option Correct

1	(A)	2	(B)	3	(B)
4	(C)	5	(D)	6	(B)
7	(D)	8	(D)	9	(A)
10	(C)	11	(B)	12	(D)
13	(A)	14	(B)	15	(A)
16	(A)	17	(D)	18	(C)
19	(B)	20	(B)	21	(C)
22	(A)	23	(B)	24	(B)
25	(A)	26	(B)	27	(C)
28	(C)	29	(A)	30	(B)
31	(D)	32	(C)	33	(B)
34	(D)	35	(C)	36	(D)
37	(A)	38	(D)	39	(C)

NUMERICAL MCQS Single Option Correct

1	(B)	2	(B)	3	(A)
4	(C)	5	(D)	6	(B)
7	(B)	8	(A)	9	(C)
10	(B)	11	(A)	12	(C)
13	(D)	14	(A)	15	(D)
16	(D)	17	(C)	18	(C)
19	(A)	20	(B)	21	(B)
22	(D)	23	(A)	24	(B)
25	(B)	26	(D)	27	(B)
28	(D)	29	(D)	30	(C)
31	(B)	32	(C)	33	(A)
34	(A)	35	(A)	36	(A)
37	(B)	38	(A)	39	(C)
40	(A)	41	(C)	42	(C)
43	(A)	44	(D)	45	(B)
46	(C)	47	(B)	48	(D)
49	(B)	50	(B)	51	(D)
52	(C)	53	(A)	54	(D)
55	(A)	56	(B)	57	(C)
58	(B)	59	(A)		

ADVANCE MCQs One or More Option Correct

1	(All)	2	(D)	3	(A, C)
4	(B, C)	5	(A, D)	6	(A, B, C)
7	(A, C)	8	(All)	9	(A, B, D)
10	(A)	11	(A, C, D)	12	(A, D)
13	(C, D)	14	(B, D)	15	(A, C, D)
16	(A, B D)	17	(A, D)		

Solutions of PRACTICE EXERCISE 6.1

(i) Force between balls is

$$F=\frac{Gm^2}{r^2}=\frac{6.674\times10^{-11}\times(10)^2}{(0.1)^2}$$
$$=6.674\times10^{-7}\,\text{N}$$

(ii) We use for circular motion

$$\frac{Gm^2}{(2R)^2}=\frac{mv^2}{R}$$

$$\Rightarrow \quad v=\sqrt{\frac{GM}{4R}}$$

(iii) Force on one mass due to other is

$$F_1=\frac{GM^2}{(\sqrt{2}R)^2}\text{ and }F_2=\frac{GM^2}{(2R)^2}$$

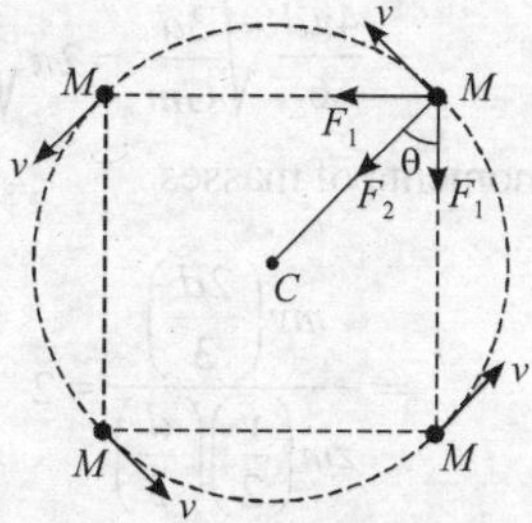

Net radial force is $F_c=F_2+\sqrt{2}F_1$

$$F_c=\frac{GM^2}{R^2}\left[\frac{1}{4}+\frac{1}{\sqrt{2}}\right]=\frac{mv^2}{R}$$

$$\Rightarrow \quad v=\sqrt{\frac{GM}{R}\left[\frac{2\sqrt{2}+1}{4}\right]}$$

(iv) Force between m and $(M-m)$ at separation r is

$$F=\frac{Gm(M-m)}{r^2}$$

F is maximum when

$$\frac{dF}{dm}=0$$

$$\Rightarrow \quad M-2m=0$$

$$\Rightarrow \quad \frac{m}{M}=\frac{1}{2}$$

(v) Gravitational force on masses is

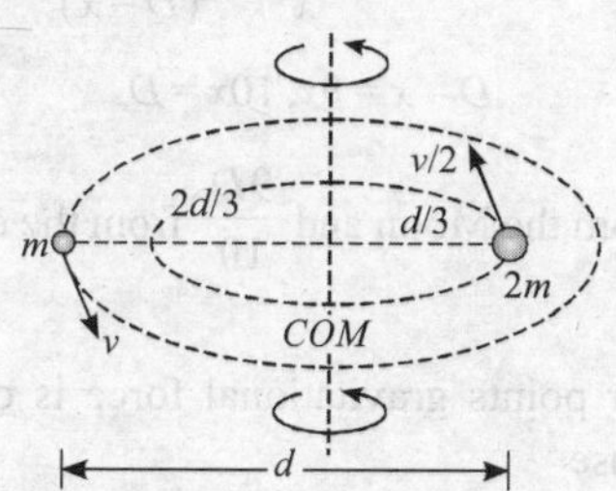

$$F = \frac{2Gm^2}{d^2}$$

for m we use $\frac{2Gm^2}{d^2} = \frac{mv^2}{2d/3}$

$\Rightarrow$ $$v = 2\sqrt{\frac{Gm}{3d}}$$

time period of revolution is

$$T = \frac{2\pi\left(\frac{2d}{3}\right)}{v}$$

$$= \frac{4\pi d}{6}\sqrt{\frac{3d}{Gm}} = 2\pi\sqrt{\frac{d^3}{3Gm}}$$

Ratio of angular momenta of masses

$$= \frac{mv\left(\frac{2d}{3}\right)}{zm\left(\frac{v}{2}\right)\left(\frac{d}{3}\right)} = 2$$

Ratio of kinetic energies of masses

$$= \frac{\frac{1}{2}mv^2}{\frac{1}{2}2m\left(\frac{v}{2}\right)^2} = 2$$

Solutions of PRACTICE EXERCISE 6.2

(i) Force on particle is only due to inner shell so it is given as

$$F = m\left(\frac{GM_1}{[(R_1+R_2)/2]^2}\right)$$

$$= \frac{4GM_1m}{(R_1+R_2)^2}$$

(ii) At a point P at a distance x from Moon, we have net gravitational field given by :

$$g = \frac{GM}{x^2} - \frac{G81M}{(D-x)^2} = 0$$

$\Rightarrow$ $$D - x = 9x;\ 10x = D$$

$x = \frac{D}{10}$ from the Moon and $\frac{9D}{10}$ from the earth.

(iii) At interior points gravitational force is only due to the sphere so we use

(a) $$F = \frac{Gmm'(x-r)}{r^3}$$

(b) $$F = \frac{Gmm'}{(x-r)^2}$$

(c) At exterior points it is due to both sphere and shell given as

$$F = \frac{GMm'}{(x-R)^2} + \frac{Gmm'}{(x-r)^2}$$

(iv) Work done by external agent is

$W = \vec{F}_{ext} \cdot \Delta\vec{r} = -\overrightarrow{mg} \cdot \overrightarrow{\Delta r}$ [for show shifting $\vec{F}_{ext} = -\overrightarrow{mg}$]

$= -10\,(2\hat{i} + 2\hat{j}) \cdot (5\hat{i} + 4\hat{j})$

$= -10 \times 18$

$= -180$ J

(v) At a point P inside the cavity gravitational field due to whole sphere is

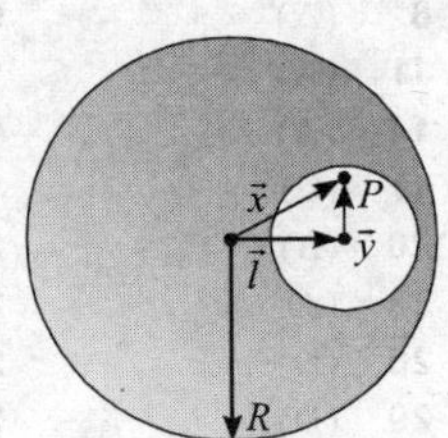

$$\vec{g}_{\text{sphere}} = -\frac{G\left(\rho \cdot \frac{4}{3}\pi R^3\right)\vec{x}}{R^3} = -\frac{4}{3}G\rho\pi\vec{x}$$

Similarly gravitational field at P due to mass in the volume of cavity is

$$\vec{g}_{\text{cavity}} = -\frac{4}{3}G\rho\pi\vec{y}$$

$$\vec{g}_{net} = \vec{g}_{sphere} - \vec{g}_{cavity}$$

$$= -\frac{4}{3}G\rho\pi(\vec{x} - \vec{y})$$

$$= -\frac{4}{3}G\rho\pi\vec{l}$$

$$|\vec{g}_{net\ at}\,P| = \frac{4}{3}G\rho\pi l$$

(vi) Force on mass is $F = mg = m\left(\frac{2G(3m)\sin\left(\frac{60}{2}\right)}{\frac{\pi}{3}R^2}\right)$

$$\left[\text{As } g \text{ due to arc is } \frac{2GM\sin\left(\frac{\phi}{2}\right)}{\phi R^2}\right]$$

$$\Rightarrow \quad = \frac{9Gm^2}{\pi R^2}$$

(vii) We use $m\left(\frac{2G\lambda}{x}\right) = \frac{mv^2}{x}$

here linear mass density

$$\lambda = \rho\,\pi\,R^2$$

$$\Rightarrow \quad 2G\rho\pi R^2 = v^2$$

$$\Rightarrow \quad v = R\sqrt{2G\rho\pi}$$

(viii) Gravitational field at m due to each rod is

$$g = \frac{GM}{l}\left[\frac{1}{l/2} - \frac{1}{3l/2}\right]$$

$$\Rightarrow \quad g = \frac{GM}{l^2}\left[2 - \frac{2}{3}\right] = \frac{4}{3}\frac{GM}{l^2}$$

Net gravitational field at m due to both rods is $\sqrt{2}g$

$$\Rightarrow \quad F = m(\sqrt{2}g) = \frac{4\sqrt{2}GMm}{3l^2}$$

Solutions of PRACTICE EXERCISE 6.3

(i) g due to earth and moon on surface are

$$g_{\text{earth}} = \frac{GM_e}{R_e^2} \text{ and } g_{\text{moon}} = \frac{GM_m}{R_m^2}$$

$$\Rightarrow \quad g_{\text{moon}} = \frac{g_{earth} : R_e^2 M_m}{M_e R_m^2}$$

$$= \frac{980 \times (6400)^2}{80 \times (1600)^2}$$

$$= 196 \text{ cm/s}^2$$

(ii) Acceleration due to gravity on the planet is

$$g_{\text{planet}} = \frac{G\left[\rho \cdot \frac{4}{3}\pi(4R)^3\right]}{(4R)^2}$$

$$= \frac{4G\left(\rho\frac{4}{3}\pi R^3\right)}{R^2} = 4g_{\text{earth}}$$

Time period of a seconds pendulum is

$$T_{\text{earth}} = 2\pi\sqrt{\frac{l}{g_{earth}}} = 2 \text{ sec}$$

$$T_{\text{planet}} = 2\pi\sqrt{\frac{l}{g_{planet}}} = 1 \text{ sec}$$

(iii) g on surface of a planet of mass M and radius R is given as

$$g = \frac{GM}{R^2} = \frac{G\rho\frac{4}{3}\pi R^3}{R^2}$$

$$\Rightarrow \quad g = \frac{4}{3}G\rho\pi R$$

$$\Rightarrow g \propto R \Rightarrow \frac{g}{g'} = \frac{R}{3R} \Rightarrow g' = 3g$$

(iv) At a height h above the Earth surface, acceleration due to gravity is

$$g' = g\left(1 - \frac{2h}{R}\right); \frac{\Delta g}{g} = \frac{2h}{R}$$

$$\Rightarrow \quad 1 = 2\frac{h}{R} \Rightarrow \frac{h}{R} = \frac{1}{2};$$

At a depth h below the Earth surface, acceleration due to gravity is

$$g' = g\left(1 - \frac{d}{R}\right)$$

$$\frac{\Delta g'}{g} = \frac{h}{R} \Rightarrow g \text{ decreases by } 0.5\%$$

(v) Force on particle is

$$F = mg = m\left(\frac{GM_e\sqrt{x^2 + \frac{R_e^2}{4}}}{R_e^3}\right)$$

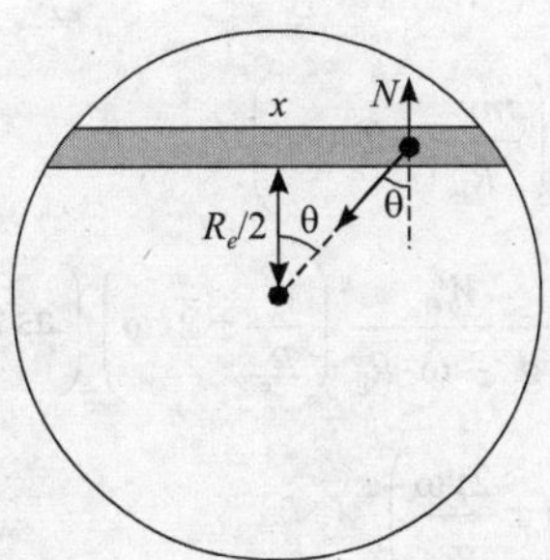

Normal force on particle is

$$N = F\cos\theta$$

$$= \frac{GmM_e}{R_e^3}\sqrt{x^2+\frac{R_e^2}{4}} \times \frac{R_e/2}{\sqrt{x^2+\frac{R_e^2}{4}}}$$

$$= \frac{GM_e m}{2R_e^2}$$

(vi) At a height h above the earth surface

$$g_h = \frac{gR_e^2}{(R_e+h)^2} = \frac{1}{2}g$$

$$\Rightarrow \quad 2R_e^{\,2} = R_e^{\,2} + h^2 + 2R_e h$$

$$\Rightarrow \quad h^2 + 2R_e h - R_e^2 = 0$$

$$\Rightarrow \quad h = \frac{-2R_e \pm \sqrt{4R_e^2+4R_e^2}}{2}$$

$$\Rightarrow \quad h = -R_e + \sqrt{2}R_e = (\sqrt{2}-1)R_e$$

(vii) $g_{\text{equator}} = g_{\text{pole}} - \omega^2 R_e$

$$g_{\text{pole}} - g_{\text{equator}} = \frac{4\pi^2}{(86400)^2} \times 6400 \times 10^3$$

$$= 0.0338 \text{ m/s}^2$$

$$g_{\text{equator}} = 9.830 - 0.0338$$

$$= 9.7962 \text{ m/s}^2$$

$$W_{\text{equator}} = W_{\text{pole}} \cdot \frac{g_{\text{equator}}}{g_{\text{pole}}} = 0.9966 \text{ kg}$$

(viii) When ship is at rest

$$W_0 = mg_s - m\omega^2 R_e$$

$$W = mg_s - \frac{m(v \pm R_e\omega)^2}{R_e}$$

When ship is sailing at speed v along equator in either direction

$$W = mg_s - \left(\frac{mv^2}{R_e} + m\omega^2 R_e \pm 2mv\omega\right)$$

$$\Rightarrow \quad W = W_0 - \left(\frac{mv^2}{R_e} \pm 2mv\omega\right)$$

$$\Rightarrow \quad = W_0 - \frac{W_0}{g_s - \omega^2 R_e}\left(\frac{v^2}{R_e} \pm 2v\omega\right)\left(\text{as } m = \frac{W_0}{g_s - \omega^2 R_e}\right)$$

$$\Rightarrow \quad \simeq W_0\left(1 \pm \frac{2v\omega}{g_s}\right)$$

[Here we neglect the term $\frac{v^2}{R_e}$ as $\frac{v^2}{R_e} << 2v\omega$ and considering $\omega^2 R_e << g_s$]

Solutions of PRACTICE EXERCISE 6.4

(i) For a body to escape its total energy ≥ 0

$$\Rightarrow \quad \frac{1}{2}mv^2 + mV_c \geq 0$$

$$\Rightarrow \quad KE \geq -mV_c$$

$$\Rightarrow \quad KE \geq -m\left(-\frac{GM}{R}\right) = \frac{GMm}{R}$$

(ii) As the given circle is equipotential, work done is zero.

(iii) If null point between stars is at point P at a distance x from $16\,M$ we use

$$\frac{G(16M)}{x^2} = \frac{GM}{(10a-x)^2}$$

$$\Rightarrow \quad \frac{x}{4} = 10a - x$$

$$\Rightarrow \quad \frac{5x}{4} = 10a$$

$$\Rightarrow \quad x = 8a$$

Potential at surface of large star is

$$V_1 = -\frac{G(16M)}{2a} - \frac{GM}{8a} = -\frac{65GM}{8a}$$

Potential at null point P is

$$V_P = -\frac{G(16M)}{8a} - \frac{GM}{2a} = -\frac{20GM}{8a}$$

If mass is thrown at speed v, it should be sufficient to cross the null point so we use

$$\frac{1}{2}mv^2 - \frac{65GMm}{8a} \geq -\frac{20GMm}{8a}$$

$$\Rightarrow \quad \frac{1}{2}mv^2 \geq \frac{45}{8}\frac{GMm}{a}$$

$$\Rightarrow \quad v \geq \sqrt{\frac{45}{4}\frac{GM}{a}} = \frac{3}{2}\sqrt{\frac{5GM}{a}}$$

(iv) As all mass of cup is at same distance R from centre we use

$$V_c = -\frac{GM}{R}$$

(v) Potential at origin

$$V_0 = -\frac{2GM}{a}$$

Potential at point $(0, 0, 2\sqrt{3}a)$ is

$$V_P = -\frac{2GM}{\sqrt{a^2 + 12a^2}} = -\frac{2}{\sqrt{13}}\frac{GM}{a}$$

By energy conservation we use

$$\frac{1}{2}\frac{M}{2}v^2 + \frac{M}{2}V_0 = \frac{M}{2}V_P$$

$$v = \sqrt{2(V_P - V_0)}$$

$$= \sqrt{2\left(\frac{2GM}{a} - \frac{2}{\sqrt{13}}\frac{GM}{a}\right)}$$

$$= 2\sqrt{\frac{GM}{a}\left(1 - \frac{1}{\sqrt{13}}\right)}$$

$$= 2\sqrt{\frac{GM}{a}\left(\frac{\sqrt{13}-1}{\sqrt{13}}\right)}$$

(vi) We can see that the direction of $\vec{g}$ is normal to given line so no work is done by gravitational force as forces perpendicular to displacement.

(vii) Considering an element of width dx as shown in figure we use its mass is

$$dm = \frac{M}{l}dx$$

Potential energy of dm and m is

$$dU = -\frac{Gmdm}{x} = -\frac{GMm}{l}\cdot\frac{1}{x}dx$$

Total energy in $\quad U = -\int_r^{r+l}\frac{GM}{l}\cdot\frac{1}{x}dx$

$$= -\frac{GM}{l}[\ln x]_r^{r+l}$$

$$= -\frac{GM}{l}\ln\left(\frac{r+l}{r}\right)$$

Solutions of PRACTICE EXERCISE 6.5

(i) $\quad KE_A = \frac{GM_em}{2R}$ and $KE_B = \frac{GM_em}{6R}$

$$PE_A = -\frac{GM_em}{R} \text{ and } PE_B = -\frac{GM_em}{3R}$$

$$\Rightarrow \quad \frac{KE_A + KE_B}{PE_A + PE_B} = \frac{1}{2}$$

(ii) (a) $\quad v = \sqrt{\frac{GM}{x}} = \sqrt{\frac{6.67\times10^{-11}\times6\times10^{24}}{8200\times10^3}}$

$$= 6.986\times10^3 \text{ m/s}$$

$$= 6.986 \text{ km/s}$$

(b) Kinetic energy

$$K = \frac{1}{2}mv^2 = \frac{1}{2}\times1000\times(6.986\times10^3)^2$$

$$= 2.44\times10^{10}\text{J}$$

(c) For a satellite

$$PE = -2KE = -4.88\times10^{10}\text{J}$$

(d) Time period $\quad T = \sqrt{\frac{4\pi^2}{GM_e}r^3}$

$$= \sqrt{\frac{4\times\left(\frac{22}{7}\right)^2\times(8\times10^6)^3}{6.67\times10^{-11}\times6\times10^{24}}}$$

$$= 7109.7 \text{ s}$$

$$= 1.975 \text{ hr}$$

(iii) Orbital speed $\quad v = \sqrt{\frac{GM_e}{r}} = \sqrt{\frac{gR_e^2}{r}}$

$$= \sqrt{\frac{9.8\times(6.4\times10^6)^2}{8\times10^6}}$$

$$= 7.08\times10^3 \text{ m/s}$$

$$= 7.08 \text{ km/s}$$

Time period $\quad T = \frac{2\pi r}{v} = \frac{2\times3.14\times8\times10^6}{7.08\times10^3}$

$$= 7.096\times10^6 \text{ s} = 118.26 \text{ min}$$

(iv) Radius of orbit $\quad r = 6400 + 1400 = 7800$ km

Revolution period of satellite is

$$T = \frac{2\pi r}{v} = \frac{2\pi r}{\sqrt{\frac{gR_e^2}{r}}}$$

$$= \frac{2\times3.14\times7.8\times10^6}{\sqrt{\frac{10\times(6.4\times10^6)^2}{7.8\times10^3}}}$$

$$= \frac{48.98\times10^6}{7.24\times10^3}$$

$$= 6.765\times10^3$$

$$= 1.88 \text{ hrs}$$

time after which satellite reappears above a point on earth is

$$\Delta t = \frac{2\pi}{\omega_s - \omega_e} = \frac{2\pi}{\frac{2\pi}{T_s} - \frac{2\pi}{T_e}}$$

$$= \frac{T_s T_e}{T_e - T_s} = \frac{1.88 \times 24}{24 - 1.188} = 2.038 \text{ hr}$$

(v) Initial energy of satellite

$$E_1 = -\frac{GM_e m}{4R}$$

Final energy of satellite

$$E_2 = -\frac{GM_e m}{6R}$$

Required energy $\quad \Delta E = E_2 - E_1 = \frac{GM_e m}{R}\left[\frac{1}{4} - \frac{1}{6}\right]$

$$= \frac{GM_e m}{12R}$$

$$= \frac{6.67 \times 10^{-11} \times 6 \times 10^{24} \times 2 \times 10^3}{12 \times 6.4 \times 10^6}$$

$$= 1.042 \times 10^{10} \text{ J}$$

(vi) Masses m_1 and m_2 move about their centre of mass in double star system and if their separation is l we use

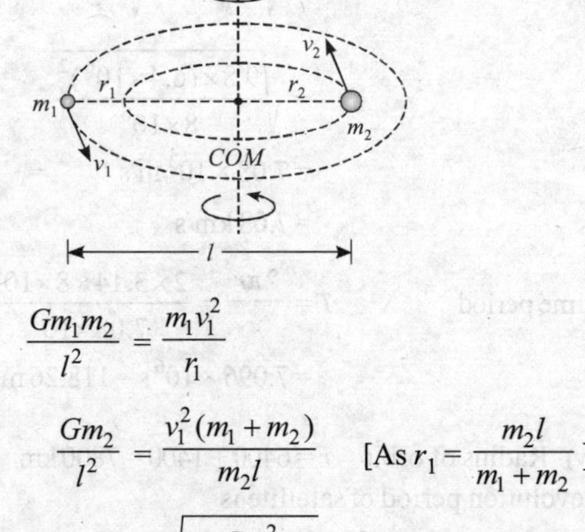

$$\frac{Gm_1 m_2}{l^2} = \frac{m_1 v_1^2}{r_1}$$

$$\Rightarrow \quad \frac{Gm_2}{l^2} = \frac{v_1^2(m_1 + m_2)}{m_2 l} \quad \left[\text{As } r_1 = \frac{m_2 l}{m_1 + m_2}\right]$$

$$\Rightarrow \quad v_1 = \sqrt{\frac{Gm_2^2}{l(m_1 + m_2)}}$$

Revolution period is

$$T = \frac{2\pi r_1}{v_1} = \frac{2\pi m_2 l}{(m_1 + m_2)} \cdot \sqrt{\frac{l(m_1 + m_2)}{Gm_2^2}}$$

$$\Rightarrow \quad l = \sqrt[3]{GM\left(\frac{T}{2\pi}\right)^2} \quad [\text{as } m_1 + m_2 = M]$$

(vii) Using concept of degenerated ellipse with zero minor axis, here major axis is equal to the separation between planet and Sun so by Kepler's law we use

$$t_1^2 = \frac{4\pi^2}{GM_s} \cdot \left(\frac{R}{2}\right)^3 \quad \ldots (1)$$

and we have revolution period of planet T as

$$T^2 = \frac{4\pi^2}{GM_s} \cdot R^3 \quad \ldots (2)$$

from (1) & (2) $\quad t_1 = \frac{T}{2\sqrt{2}}$

$\Rightarrow$ time to fall into Sun is

$$\frac{t_1}{2} = \frac{T}{4\sqrt{2}} = \frac{\sqrt{2}}{8} T$$

(viii) At a distance x from centre of earth acceleration of particle is

$$a = -\frac{GM_e x}{R_e^3} = -\frac{g}{R_e} x$$

as $a \propto x$ the particle is executing SHM with angular frequency ω such that

$$a = -\omega^2 x$$

$$\Rightarrow \quad \omega = \sqrt{\frac{g}{R_e}}$$

Time taken for one quarter oscillation (from surface to earth centre) is

$$t_1 = \frac{\pi}{2\omega} = \frac{\pi}{2}\sqrt{\frac{R_e}{g}} \quad \ldots (1)$$

if g is a constant, time taken is

$$t_2 = \sqrt{\frac{2R_e}{g}} \quad \ldots (2)$$

from (1) and (2) $\quad \frac{t_1}{t_2} = \frac{\pi}{2\sqrt{2}}$

Solutions of PRACTICE EXERCISE 6.6

(i) Semi major axis of elliptical orbit is

$$a = \frac{r + R}{2}$$

from Kepler's third law we use

$$T^2 = \frac{4\pi^2}{GM_s} a^3$$

$$\Rightarrow \quad T = \pi\sqrt{\frac{(r + R)^3}{2GM_s}}$$

(ii) From Kepler's third law we have

$$T^2 = \frac{4\pi^2}{GM_s}\cdot a^3$$

[where $a \to$ semi major axis of orbit]

if ρ is the density of Sun and R_s is its radius we use

$$T^2 = \frac{4\pi^2}{G\rho\left(\frac{4}{3}\pi R_s^3\right)}\cdot a^3$$

if both a and R_s are scaled down in same ratio, no effect on T.

(iii) Time period of two satellites are T_1 & T_2 given as

$$T_1 = \sqrt{\frac{4\pi^2}{GM_e}\cdot r^3}$$

and $$T_2 = \sqrt{\frac{4\pi^2}{GM_e}(r-\Delta r)^3}$$

time duration between their minimum distances is

$$\Delta t = \frac{2\pi}{\omega_2-\omega_1} = \frac{T_1T_2}{T_1-T_2}$$

$$\Rightarrow \quad \Delta t = \frac{2\pi\sqrt{\frac{r^3}{GM_e}}\times 2\pi\sqrt{\frac{(r-\Delta r)^3}{GM_e}}}{\frac{2\pi}{\sqrt{GM_e}}[r^{3/2}-(r-\Delta r)^{3/2}]}$$

$$\Rightarrow \quad \Delta t = \frac{2\pi}{\sqrt{GM_e}}r^{3/2}\left[\frac{(2-\Delta r)^{3/2}}{r^{3/2}-(r-\Delta r)^{3/2}}\right]$$

(iv) Using angular momentum conservation

$$m\sqrt{g_sR_e}\ \sqrt{3/2}\ .R_e = mv_fr_{max} \quad \ldots(1)$$

Using energy conservation

$$\frac{1}{2}m\left(\frac{3}{2}g_sR_e\right) - \frac{GM_em}{R_e} = \frac{1}{2}mv_f^2 - \frac{GM_em}{r_{max}} \quad \ldots(2)$$

$$\Rightarrow \quad \frac{3}{4}g_sR_e - g_sR_e = \frac{1}{2}v_f^2 - \frac{g_sR_e^2}{r_{max}}$$

from equation (1)

$$-\frac{1}{4}g_sR_e = \frac{1}{2}\left(\frac{\sqrt{3/2}\sqrt{g_sR_e^3}}{r_{max}}\right)^2 - \frac{g_sR_e^2}{r_{max}}$$

$$\Rightarrow \quad -\frac{1}{4}g_sR_e = \frac{3}{4}g_sR_e\left(\frac{R_e^2}{r_{max}{}^2}\right) - g_sR_e\left(\frac{R_e}{r_{max}}\right)$$

$$\frac{R_e^2}{r_{max}{}^2} - \frac{4}{3}\frac{R_e}{r_{max}} + \frac{1}{3} = 0$$

$$\Rightarrow \quad \frac{R_e}{r_{max}} = \frac{\frac{4}{3}\pm\sqrt{\frac{16}{9}-\frac{4}{3}}}{2} = \frac{\frac{4}{3}\pm\frac{2}{3}}{2} = \frac{2}{3}\pm\frac{1}{3}$$

$$\Rightarrow \quad = 1 \text{ or } \frac{1}{3}$$

$$\Rightarrow \quad r_{max} = 3R_e \qquad [\text{As } r_{max} \neq R_e]$$

Thus maximum distance of satellite from earth surface is

$$3R_e - R_e = 2R_e$$

(v) Using angular momentum conservation

$$mv_0d = mv_{max}r_{min} \quad \ldots(1)$$

by energy conservation

$$\frac{1}{2}mv_0^2 - 0 = \frac{1}{2}mv_{max}^2 - \frac{GMm}{r_{min}}$$

from equation-(1)

$$v_0^2 = \left(\frac{v_0d}{r_{min}}\right)^2 - \frac{2GM}{r_{min}}$$

$$\Rightarrow \quad r_{min}^2v_0^2 = v_0^2d^2 - 2GMr_{min}$$

$$\Rightarrow \quad r_{min}^2 + \frac{2GM}{v_0^2}r_{min} - d^2 = 0$$

$$\Rightarrow \quad r_{min} = \frac{-\frac{2GM}{v_0^2}\pm\sqrt{\frac{4G^2M^2}{v_0^4}+4d^2}}{2}$$

$$\Rightarrow \quad r_{min} = \frac{GM}{v_0^2}\left[\sqrt{\left(\frac{v_0^4d^2}{G^2M^2}+1\right)}-1\right]$$

(vi) When S_2 is closest to S_1 & they are moving at speeds v_2 and v_1

(a) Relative speed of S_2 wrt S_1 is :

$$v_{S_2S_1} = v_1 - v_2 \quad \ldots(1)$$

(b) Angular speed of S_2 w.r.t. S_1 is

$$\omega_{S_2S_1} = \frac{v_2-v_1}{r_2-r_1} \quad \ldots(2)$$

From kepler's third law

$$\left(\frac{T_1}{T_2}\right)^2 = \left(\frac{r_1}{r_2}\right)^3$$

$$\Rightarrow \qquad \left(\frac{1}{8}\right)^2 = \left(\frac{10^4}{r_2}\right)^3$$

$$\Rightarrow \qquad r_2 = 4 \times 10^4 \text{ km}$$

Also we use $\quad T_1 = \dfrac{2\pi r_1}{v_1}$ and $T_2 = \dfrac{2\pi r_2}{v_2}$

$\Rightarrow$ from equation (1)

$$v_{S_2S_1} = \frac{2\pi r_1}{T_1} - \frac{2\pi r_2}{T_2} = 2\pi\left(\frac{10^4}{1} - \frac{4\times 10^4}{8}\right)$$

$$= \pi \times 10^4 \text{ km/hr}$$

from equation-(2)

$$\omega_{S_2S_1} = \frac{\pi \times 10^4}{3\times 10^4} = \frac{\pi}{3} \text{ rad/hr}$$

(vii) In the figure shown

$$r_L = \frac{1}{2}\text{(latus rectum)}$$

$$r_L = \frac{1}{2}\left(\frac{2b^2}{a}\right) = \frac{b^2}{a} \qquad \ldots(1)$$

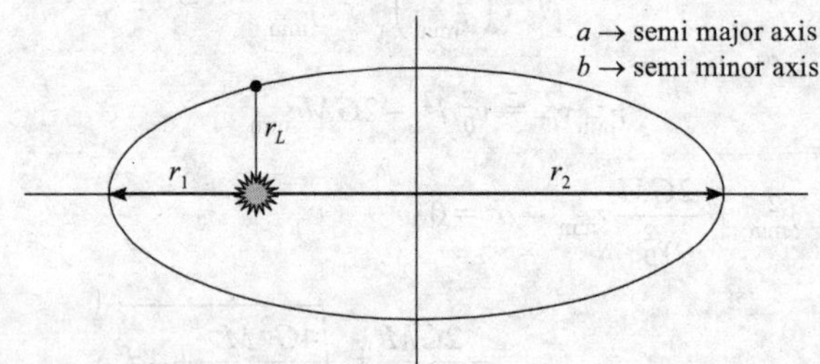

Here semi major axis is

$$a = \frac{r_1 + r_2}{2}$$

we have $\qquad b^2 = a^2(1 - e^2)$ and $a - r_1 = ae$

$$\Rightarrow \qquad b^2 = a^2 - (a - r_1)^2 = 2ar_1 - r_1^2$$

$$\Rightarrow \qquad b^2 = 2r_1\left(\frac{r_1 + r_2}{2}\right) - r_1^2 = r_2 r_1$$

from equation-(1)

$$r_L = \frac{b^2}{a} = \frac{2r_1 r_2}{r_1 + r_2}$$

Solutions of PRACTICE EXERCISE 6.7

(i) Period of satellite is

$$T = \sqrt{\frac{4\pi^2}{GM_p} \cdot r^3}$$

We use $\qquad M_P = \rho \cdot \dfrac{4}{3}\pi r_P^3$

$$\Rightarrow \qquad T = \sqrt{\frac{4\pi^2}{G\left(\rho \frac{4}{3}\pi r_P^3\right)} \cdot r^3}$$

as $r \simeq r_P$ we get

$$T = \sqrt{\frac{3\pi}{G\rho}}$$

(ii) Area left to be covered for satellite of orbit radius r as shown in figure is

$$A = 2 \times 2\pi\left(1 - \frac{\sqrt{r^2 - R^2}}{r}\right) \cdot R^2$$

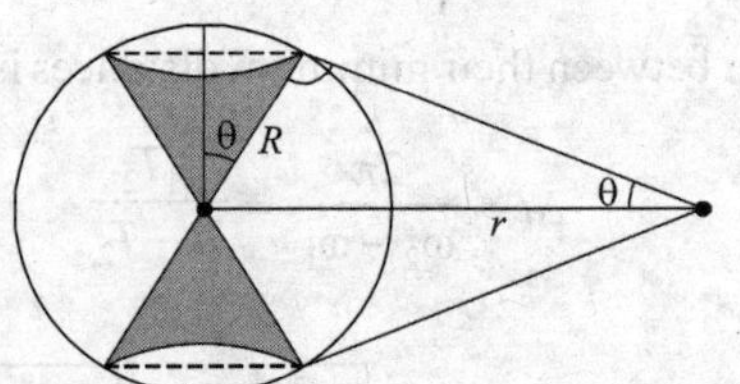

Given that $\qquad A = 0.25 \times 4\pi R^2$

$$\Rightarrow \qquad 1 - \frac{\sqrt{r^2 - R^2}}{r} = 0.25$$

$$\Rightarrow \qquad \frac{r^2 - R^2}{r^2} = \frac{9}{16}$$

$$\Rightarrow \qquad 16r^2 - 16R^2 = 9r^2$$

$$\Rightarrow \qquad r = \frac{4}{\sqrt{7}} R = 1.515\, R$$

(iii) Satellite period is

$$T = \sqrt{\frac{4\pi^2}{GM} \cdot R_2^3}$$

acceleration due to gravity on planet is

$$g_P = \frac{GM}{R_1^2}$$

$$\Rightarrow \qquad g_P = \frac{1}{R_1^2}\left(\frac{4\pi^2 R_2^3}{T^2}\right)$$

$$\Rightarrow \qquad g_P = \frac{4\pi^2 R_2^3}{R_1^2 T^2}$$

(iv) Let separation between stars is r and lighter one is revolving in a circle of radius $\frac{r}{3}$ then for heavier star, we use

$$\Rightarrow \frac{G\left(\frac{M_s}{3}\right)\left(\frac{2M_s}{3}\right)}{r^2} = \frac{\left(\frac{2M_s}{3}\right)V^2}{r/3}$$

$$V^2 = \frac{GM_s}{9r} \Rightarrow V = \sqrt{\frac{GM_s}{9r}}$$

$$\Rightarrow T = \frac{2\pi r/3}{V} \Rightarrow \frac{2\pi r/3}{\sqrt{\frac{GM_s}{9r}}} = \frac{2\pi r}{\sqrt{\frac{GM_s}{r}}}$$

Time period of earth when moving around sun is

$$T = \frac{2\pi R^{3/2}}{\sqrt{GM_s}} \quad \text{So} \quad r = R$$

(v) Angular speed are

$$\omega_1 = \frac{2\pi}{T_1} = \frac{\omega}{2\sqrt{2}}$$

$$\omega_2 = \frac{2\pi}{T_2} = \frac{\omega}{8}$$

(a) When revolving in same sence if after time t they become closest, we use

$$\Rightarrow t_1 = \frac{\theta}{\omega_2} = \frac{\theta + 2\pi}{\omega_1} = \frac{2\pi}{\omega_1 - \omega_2}$$

$$= \frac{2\pi}{\frac{2\pi}{T_1} - \frac{2\pi}{T_2}} = \frac{T_1T_2}{T_2 - T_1} = \frac{(2R)^{3/2}\cdot(4R)^{3/2}}{(4R)^{3/2} - (2R)^{3/2}}$$

$$= \frac{2\pi}{\sqrt{GM}}\frac{2\sqrt{2}\times 8}{8 - 2\sqrt{2}}\cdot R^{3/2}$$

$$= \frac{2\pi}{\sqrt{GM}}\frac{8}{2\sqrt{2} - 1}\cdot R^{3/2}$$

(b) When revolving in opposite sence, if after time t, they become closest, we use

$$t_2 = \frac{\theta}{\omega_1} = \frac{2\pi - \theta}{\omega_2} = \frac{2\pi}{\omega_1 + \omega_2} = \frac{T_1T_2}{T_1 + T_2}$$

$$= \frac{2\pi}{\sqrt{GM}}\cdot\frac{8}{2\sqrt{2} + 1}\cdot R^{3/2}$$

(vi) Using conservation of angular momentum

$$m(v_1\cos 60°)4R = mv_2R \Rightarrow \frac{v_2}{v_1} = 2$$

by conservation of energy system

$$-\frac{GMm}{4R} + \frac{1}{2}mv_1^2 = -\frac{GMm}{R} + \frac{1}{2}mv_2^2$$

$$\Rightarrow \frac{1}{2}v_2^2 - \frac{1}{2}v_1^2 = \frac{3}{4}\frac{GM}{R}$$

$$\Rightarrow v_1 = \frac{1}{\sqrt{2}}\sqrt{64\times 10^6} = \frac{8000}{\sqrt{2}}\text{ m/s}$$

(vii) Escape velocity is

$$v = \sqrt{\frac{2GM}{R}}$$

We use $$R = \frac{2GM}{v^2} = \frac{2\times 6.67\times 10^{-11}\times 6\times 10^{24}}{(3\times 10^8)^2}$$

$$= 8.893\times 10^{-3}\text{ m}$$

$$= 8.893\text{ mm}$$

Solutions of CONCEPTUAL MCQS Single Option Correct

Sol. 1 (A) If the gravitational force is inversely proportional to r then this force will provide the necessary centripetal force for circular motion of the particle and the radius r in denominator of both terms will cancel and the speed will be independent of r.

Sol. 2 (B) For small altitudes value of g decreases linearly with height above the earth surface and at a depth it is always varying linearly with depth h below the surface of earth.

Sol. 3 (B) Gravitational potential at the center of a uniform spherical shell is given as - GM/R where R is the radius of shell. If we use mass = surface mass density x area of shell ($4\pi R^2$) thus the potential comes out to be directly proportional to the radius of the shell hence option (B) is correct.

Sol. 4 (C) Acceleration due to gravity is given as $g = GM/R^2$ and on changing the mass to 0.99M and R to $0.99R$ the result will be changed as $g' = 1.01GM/R^2$ hence option (C) is correct.

Sol. 5 (D) Escape velocity is given as $(2gR)^{1/2}$ here g is increasing by 1% and R is decreasing by 1% so no change in escape velocity.

Sol. 6 (B) For a body revolving under force following inverse square law we know that $|TE| = |KE| = (1/2)|PE|$ hence option (B) is correct.

Sol. 7 (D) Gravitational potential at a distance r outside a uniformly charged solid sphere varies inversely with r and inside it is given by the expression $(KQ/2R^3)(3R^2 - r^2)$ hence option (D) is correct.

Sol. 8 (D) For n particles number of interaction each particle can have with all other particles are $(n-1)$ so total interactions by all particles with all remaining particles are n with one interaction for each particle accounted twice hence option (D) is correct.

Sol. 9 (A) As it looses some energy, it will be attracted toward the earth and distance decreases and due to work done by gravity its interaction energy decreases and kinetic energy increases hence option (A) is correct.

Sol. 10 (C) If a body has to escape from earth's surface its total mechanical energy in frame of earth with reference at infinite separation must be zero.

Sol. 11 (B) As $U = -GMm/r$ and weight is $W = GMm/r^2$ so option (B) is correct.

Sol. 12 (D) As inside of shell there is zero gravity so no force will act on the particle after release and it will stay just inside the surface after release.

Sol. 13 (A) As Train P is moving opposite to the direction of rotation of earth, its speed relative to earth's rotation axis is less and it experiences less centripetal force for its revolution along equator hence the normal reaction on this train by the track will be more compared to Train Q which is moving in the direction of rotation of earth.

Sol. 14 (B) Kinetic Energy of a satellite in circular orbit is inversely proportional to the orbit radius and in this case orbit radii of the two satellites are $4R$ and $2R$ respectively hence option (B) is correct.

Sol. 15 (A) Above the surface of earth for small altitudes gravitational potential varies linearly with height hence option (A) is correct.

Sol. 16 (A) A geostationary satellite must have an angular speed in circular orbit which is equal to that of earth's rotation in same direction and for it to appear at rest from earth surface it must be in equatorial plane hence option (A) is correct.

Sol. 17 (D) If the density of planet is equal to the average density of earth and mass is double then its radius must be $2^{1/3}R$ so that its volume is double that of earth. The value of acceleration due to gravity at the surface of the planet can be compared with that at earth as $g_P = G(2M)/(2^{1/3}R)^2 = 2^{1/3}\, g_E$ hence option (D) is correct.

Sol. 18 (C) The potential, kinetic and total energy of a satellite varies inversely with the orbit radius of the satellite and the relation we know is $TE = (1/2)\, PE = -KE$ hence option (C) is correct.

Sol. 19 (B) The values of acceleration due to gravity at a height and at a depth for small values of h and d are given as $g_h = g(1-2h/R)$ and $g_d = g(1-d/R)$ hence equating the two we get option (B) is correct.

Sol. 20 (B) For a conservative field we can check by the gradient relation $\vec{E}_g = -\text{grad}\, V$ and verify that the work done in displacement of a particle from one point to another is independent of path this gives option (B) is correct.

Sol. 21 (C) A ship which moves along the direction of rotation of earth will have more net speed relative to axis of rotation of earth so it will need more centripetal force for its circular motion so the normal reaction on it will be less or its effective weight will be less hence options (A) and (B) are true and option (D) is also true which has time period $2\pi(R/g)^{1/2}$ in both cases. Earth has retained its atmosphere because the value of most probable speed of molecules in atmosphere is less than the escape velocity.

Sol. 22 (A) For a revolving satellite by Kepler's Third Law we use $T^2 = (4\pi^2/GM)R^3$ and $M = (4\pi R^3/3)\rho$ we get option (A) is correct.

Sol. 23 (B) Total energy and angular momentum of a planet+sun system remain conserved hence option (B) is correct.

Sol. 24 (B) In gravity free space the water particles in surrounding of the two bubbles attracts due to gravity so bubbles will start moving away from each other.

Sol. 25 (A) Inside the shell there is zero gravity hence no force will act and outside the shell acceleration due to gravity varies inversely proportional to r^2 hence option (A) is correct.

Sol. 26 (B) Inside the cavity the acceleration due to gravity is zero and outside the shell it varies inversely proportional to r^2 and in the annular region it increase in some non liner manner hence option (B) is correct.

Sol. 27 (C) For a shell at all interior points the gravitational potential is constant and outside it varies inversely with the distance from center hence option (C) is correct.

Sol. 28 (C) As the separated part has same speed as that of satellite, it will continue to move in the same orbit.

Sol. 29 (A) As gravitational force passes through centre of earth option (A) is correct.

Sol. 30 (B) Total mechanical energy of a planet in elliptical orbit is given as $-\dfrac{GMm}{2a}$ where a is a semi major axis.

Sol. 31 (D) $$x = \frac{m_2 r}{m_1 + m_2}$$

Using the concept of centripetal force

$$\frac{Gm_1m_2}{r^2} = m_1\omega^2 x = \frac{m_1\omega^2 m_2 r}{m_1 + m_2}$$

$$\Rightarrow \quad \omega = \sqrt{\frac{G(m_1+m_2)}{r^3}}$$

$$\Rightarrow \quad T = 2\pi\sqrt{\frac{r^3}{G(m_1+m_2)}}$$

Sol. 32 (C) $$\omega' = \omega_s + \omega_E = \frac{2\pi}{6} + \frac{2\pi}{24} = \frac{10\pi}{24}$$

or, $$\omega'' = \omega_s - \omega_E = \frac{2\pi}{6} - \frac{2\pi}{24} = \frac{6\pi}{24}$$

Thus possible values of T are

$$\Rightarrow \quad T' = \frac{2\pi}{\omega'} = 4.8 \text{ hour}$$

$$\Rightarrow \quad T'' = \frac{2\pi}{\omega''} = 8 \text{ hour}$$

Sol. 33 (B) Angular momentum of the comet is conserved.

Sol. 34 (D) Kinetic energy is maximum at centre and potential energy is minimum.

Sol. 35 (C) Time taken by A and B can be obtained by energy conservation when particle is at a distance x from tunnel center as

$$t_A = \int_{\frac{\sqrt{15}R}{4}}^{0} \frac{dx}{\sqrt{\frac{g}{R}\left(\frac{15}{16}R^2 - x^2\right)}};$$

$$t_B = \int_{\frac{\sqrt{3}R}{2}}^{0} \frac{dx}{\sqrt{\frac{g}{R}\left(\frac{3R^2}{4} - x^2\right)}}$$

on solving the above expressions of integration we can see that $t_A = t_B$.

Sol. 36 (D) In all the options given, the term force is used. But gravitational potential at a point is defined in terms of the work done in displacing a unit mass from infinity to that point without change in kinetic energy.

Sol. 37 (A) Tidal waves in the sae are produced due to periodic approaches of moon at different locations above the see on earth due to the pull of gravitational attraction of moon.

Sol. 38 (D) As the mass of earth remain same, nothing would happen because all gravitational forces remain same.

Sol. 39 (C) Inside the shell due to the block gravitational potential and field both exist.

Solutions of NUMERICAL MCQS Single Option Correct

Sol. 1 (B) Time period of a simple pendulum of length l_0 is

$$t_1 = 2\pi\sqrt{\frac{l_0}{g}}$$

and time period of a simple pendulum of infinite length is

$$t_2 = 2\pi\sqrt{\frac{R}{g}} \qquad \text{[Refer topic of SHM]}$$

$$\Rightarrow \quad \frac{t_1}{t_2} = \sqrt{\frac{l_0}{R}}$$

Sol. 2 (B) At latitude 60°, $g_{\text{eff}} = 0$

$$\Rightarrow \quad 0 = g - R\omega^2\cos^2 60°$$

$$\Rightarrow \quad \frac{R^2\omega^2}{4} = g$$

$$\Rightarrow \quad \omega = 2\sqrt{\frac{g}{R}}$$

$$\Rightarrow \quad T = \frac{2\pi}{\omega} = 4\pi\sqrt{\frac{R}{g}}$$

Sol. 3 (A) g at a height h above earth surface is $g_n = \dfrac{gR^2}{(R+h)^2}$

$$\left(g - \frac{3g}{4}\right) = \frac{gR^2}{(R+h)^2}$$

$$\Rightarrow \quad h = R$$

Sol. 4 (C) We know that

$$g = -\frac{dV}{dr}$$

$$\Rightarrow \quad -\frac{k}{r} = -\frac{dV}{dr}$$

$$\Rightarrow \quad \int_{V_0}^{V} dv = K\int_{r_o}^{r}\frac{dr}{r}$$

$$\Rightarrow \quad V = K\ln\left(\frac{r}{r_o}\right) + V_0$$

Sol. 5 (D) g on planet surface is given as

$$g = \frac{GM}{R^2} = \frac{G\left(\frac{4\pi R^3}{3}\right)\rho}{R^2}$$

$$\Rightarrow \quad g = \frac{4\pi RG\rho}{3}$$

Sol. 6 (B) Force on a mass placed at a distance from centre of shell is

$$F = \begin{cases} \frac{GMm}{r^2} & r \geq R \text{ (outside and at surface)} \\ 0 & r < R \text{ (inside)} \end{cases}$$

Sol. 7 (B) We use $g_h = g_d$

$$g\left(1-\frac{2h}{R}\right) \cong g\left(1-\frac{d}{R}\right)$$

$$\Rightarrow \quad d = 2h$$

Sol. 8 (A) From Kepler's third law

$$T^2 = kr^3$$

$$\Rightarrow \quad 2\frac{\Delta T}{T} = 3\frac{\Delta r}{r}$$

$$\Rightarrow \quad \frac{\Delta T}{T} = \frac{3}{2}\frac{\Delta r}{r}$$

Sol. 9 (C) Use Gauss Theorem for Gravitation.

Sol. 10 (B)

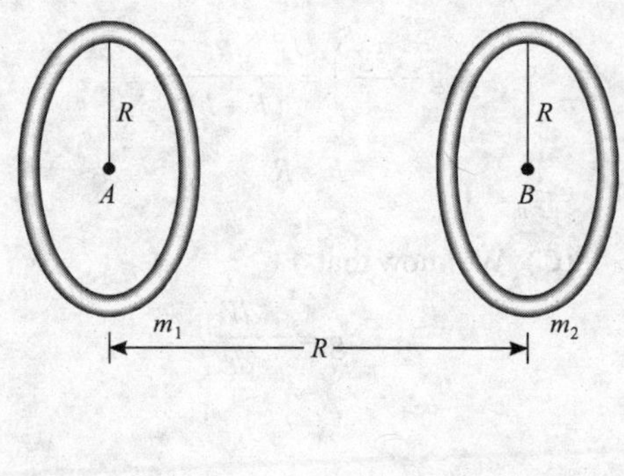

$$V_A = \left(\begin{array}{c}\text{Potential at} \\ A \text{ due to } A\end{array}\right) + \left(\begin{array}{c}\text{Potential at} \\ A \text{ due to } B\end{array}\right)$$

$$\Rightarrow \quad V_A = -\frac{Gm_1}{R} - \frac{Gm_2}{\sqrt{2}R} \text{ and}$$

Similarly, $$V_B = \left(\begin{array}{c}\text{Potential at} \\ B \text{ due to } A\end{array}\right) + \left(\begin{array}{c}\text{Potential at} \\ B \text{ due to } B\end{array}\right)$$

Work done in moving mass m from A to B is

$$W_{A\to B} = m(V_B - V_A)$$

$$\Rightarrow \quad W_{A\to B} = \frac{Gm(m_1 - m_2)(\sqrt{2}-1)}{\sqrt{2}R}$$

Sol. 11 (A) By energy conservation we use

$$\frac{1}{2}m(0)^2 - \frac{GMm}{\sqrt{\left(\sqrt{3}R\right)^2 + R^2}} = \frac{1}{2}mv^2 - \frac{GMm}{R}$$

$$\Rightarrow \quad -\frac{GMm}{2R} = \frac{1}{2}mv^2 - \frac{GMm}{R}$$

$$\Rightarrow \quad v = \sqrt{\frac{GM}{R}}$$

Sol. 12 (C) Kinetic and potential energies of a satellite are

$$\text{K.E.} = \frac{GMm}{2r} = -E_0,$$

and $$\text{P.E.} = -\frac{GMm}{r} = 2E_0$$

$$\Rightarrow \quad \text{T.E.} = \text{K.E.} + \text{P.E.} = -\frac{GMm}{2r} = E_0$$

Sol. 13 (D) By Kepler's second law we use

$$\text{Areal velocity} = \frac{\text{Area Swept}}{\text{Time for one Revolution of Earth about the sun}}$$

also we use $\text{Areal velocity} = \frac{L}{2M}$

$$\Rightarrow \quad \text{Area Swept} = \left(\frac{L}{2M}\right)\left(\begin{array}{c}\text{Time for one} \\ \text{Revolution of Earth} \\ \text{about the sun}\end{array}\right)$$

$$\Rightarrow \quad \text{Area Swept} = \frac{1}{2}(4.4\times10^{15})(365\times24\times60\times60)$$

$$\Rightarrow \quad \text{Area Swept} = 7\times10^{22}\ \text{m}^2$$

Sol. 14 (A) By Law of Conservation of Energy

Total surface energy = Potential energy at a height h

$$\Rightarrow \quad \frac{1}{2}\frac{GMm}{R_e}-\frac{GMm}{R_e}=0-\frac{GMm}{R_e+h}$$

As velocity at maximum height is zero

$$\Rightarrow \quad h=R_e$$

Sol. 15 (D) Given, $r=3.6\times10^7$ m,

$m=5000$ kg,

$v=4000$ m s^{-1},

$\phi=30°$

Angular momentum of satellite

$$L=mvr\sin\phi$$

$$=5000\times4000\times3.6\times10^7\times\sin30°$$

$$=3.6\times10^{14}\text{ J-s}$$

Sol. 16 (D) Energy of the satellite

$$E=\frac{1}{2}mv^2-\frac{GMm}{r}$$

$$=\frac{1}{2}\times500\times(4000)^2-\frac{(6.67\times10^{-11})\times(5.97\times10^{24})\times5000}{3.6\times10^7}$$

$$=-1.5\times10^{10}\text{ J}$$

Sol. 17 (C) Minimum distance

$$r_{min}=a(1-e)$$

$$=6.6\times10^7\times(1-0.804)$$

$$=1.29\times10^7\text{m}$$

(for eccentricity refer solution to Q.20)

Sol. 18 (C) Maximum distance

$$r_{max}=a(1+e)=6.6\times10^7\times(1+0.804)$$

$$=11.9\times10^7\text{m}$$

Sol. 19 (A) Now semi-major axis a

$$=\frac{-GMm}{2E}$$

$$=-\frac{6.67\times10^{-11}\times5.97\times10^{24}\times5000}{2\times(-1.5\times10^{10})}$$

$$=6.6\times10^7\text{m}$$

Sol. 20 (B) Eccentricity of the orbit

$$e=\left(1+\frac{2EL^2}{G^2M^2m^3}\right)$$

$$=1+\frac{2\times(-1.5\times10^{10})\times(3.6\times10^{14})^2}{(6.67\times10^{-11})^2\times(5.97\times10^{24})^2\times(5000)^3}$$

$$=0.804$$

Hence, semi-minor axis $b=a\sqrt{1-e^2}$

$$=6.6\times10^7\sqrt{1-(0.804)^2}$$

$$=3.92\times10^7\text{ m}$$

Sol. 21 (B) For stable circular orbit of planet we use

$$mR\omega^2\propto R^{-5/2}$$

$$\Rightarrow \quad T^2\propto R^{7/2}$$

Sol. 22 (D) By energy conservation we use

$$\Rightarrow \quad -\frac{GMm}{R}+\frac{1}{2}m(kv_e)^2=-\frac{GMm}{r}+0$$

where $\quad v_e=\sqrt{\frac{2GM}{R}}$

$$\Rightarrow \quad r=\frac{R}{1-k^2}$$

Sol. 23 (A) Since $\quad T^2\propto r^3$

$$\Rightarrow \quad \frac{r_1^3}{r_2^3}=\frac{T_1^2}{T_2^2}=\frac{1}{64}$$

$$\Rightarrow \quad \frac{r_1}{r_2}=\frac{1}{4}$$

$$\Rightarrow \quad r_2=4\times10^4\text{ km}$$

$$v_1=\frac{2\pi r_1}{T_1}\text{ and }v_2=\frac{2\pi r_2}{T_2}$$

$$\Rightarrow \quad v_1=\frac{2\pi\times10^4}{1}\text{ and}$$

$$v_2=\frac{2\pi\times4\times10^4}{8}\text{ (in } kmph)$$

$$\Rightarrow \quad v_1=2\pi\times10^4\text{ kmh}^{-1}$$

and $\quad v_2=\pi\times10^4\text{ kmh}^{-1}$

So, speed of S_2 with respect to S_1 is $\pi\times10^4$ kmh^{-1}. When they are closest.

Sol. 24 (B) Relative angular speed is

$$\omega=\left|\frac{v_2-v_1}{r_2-r_1}\right|$$

$$\Rightarrow \quad \omega=\left|\frac{10^4\pi}{3\times10^4}\right|$$

$$\Rightarrow \qquad \omega = \frac{\pi}{3}\ \text{rads}^{-1}$$

Sol. 25 (B) As only mutual interaction force is there we use concept of reduced mass.

Let m_1 be at rest we consider that m_2 has been replaced by μ and is moving with velocity v relative to m_1. Then by conservation of energy we use

$$\frac{1}{2}m_1(0)^2 + \frac{1}{2}\mu v^2 = -\frac{Gm_1m_2}{r} + 0$$

where, μ is considered as reduced mass, given as

$$\mu = \frac{m_1m_2}{m_1+m_2}$$

$$\Rightarrow \qquad v = \sqrt{\frac{2G(m_1+m_2)}{r}}$$

Sol. 26 (D) Already analysed the path of projected bodies in article 6.14.

Sol. 27 (B) For a body by in a bounded path around earth its speed must be more their orbital speed & less then escape speed.

$$v_0 < v < v_e$$

$$\Rightarrow \qquad \frac{v_e}{\sqrt{2}} < v < v_e \qquad \left\{\text{Here } v_0 = \sqrt{\frac{GM}{R_e}} \text{ and } v_e = \sqrt{\frac{2GM}{R_e}}\right\}$$

Sol. 28 (D) Let gravitational field be zero at a point lying at distance x from M. Then,

$$\frac{GM}{x^2} = \frac{Gm}{(d-x)^2}$$

$$\Rightarrow \qquad \frac{d-x}{x} = \sqrt{\frac{m}{M}}$$

$$\Rightarrow \qquad \frac{d}{x} - 1 = \sqrt{\frac{m}{M}}$$

$$\Rightarrow \qquad x = \left(\frac{\sqrt{M}}{\sqrt{M}+\sqrt{m}}\right)d \qquad \ldots(1)$$

$$\Rightarrow \qquad (d-x) = \left(\frac{\sqrt{m}}{\sqrt{M}+\sqrt{m}}\right)d \qquad \ldots(2)$$

Since, $$V_p = -\frac{Gm}{d-x} - \frac{GM}{x} \qquad \ldots(3)$$

Substituting (1) and (2) in (3), we get

$$V_p = -\frac{G}{d}(\sqrt{m}+\sqrt{M})^2$$

Sol. 29 (D) As from Kepler's law we have

$$T_0^2 = 4\pi^2\left(\frac{r^3}{GM}\right)$$

and $$T^2 = 4\pi^2\left[\frac{(\eta r)^3}{G\left(\rho \frac{4}{3}\pi(\eta R)^3\right)}\right]$$

$$= 4\pi^2\frac{r^3}{GM} = T_0$$

Sol. 30 (C) Speed of a satellite just above earth surface is

$$v = \sqrt{gR} = 7.9\ \text{kms}^{-1}, \text{ and}$$

$$T = \frac{2\pi R}{v} = \frac{2\pi 6400 \times 100}{7900}$$

$$= 84.79 \text{ minute}$$

is the time period of satellite revolving very close to earth's surface. So time period of spy satellite must be slightly greater and so C is the appropriate answer.

Sol. 31 (B) Let us consider the shell when a mass m is already there on it. If V is the potential on the shell, then

$$V = -\frac{Gm}{R}$$

To add a mass dm further work done in process is

$$dW = Vdm$$

$$\Rightarrow \qquad dW = -\frac{Gm}{R}dm$$

$$\Rightarrow \qquad W = -\frac{G}{R}\int_0^M m\,dm$$

$$\Rightarrow \qquad W = -\frac{1}{2}\frac{GM^2}{R}$$

= Potential Energy of Interaction

Sol. 32 (C) Considering an elemental shell of radius r and width dr as shown

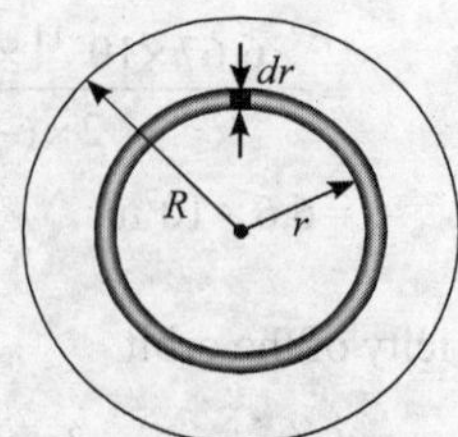

If inside mass is m then interaction energy of shell with mass is

$$dU = -\frac{Gmdm}{r}$$

$$\Rightarrow \quad dU = -\frac{G\left(\frac{4}{3}\pi r^3\rho\right)(4\pi r^2 dr\rho)}{r}$$

$$\Rightarrow \quad dU = -\frac{16\pi^2 G\rho^2}{3} r^4 dr$$

net interaction energy is

$$\Rightarrow \quad U = -\frac{16}{3}\pi^2 G\left(\frac{M}{\frac{4}{3}\pi R^3}\right)^2 \int_0^R r^4 dr$$

$$\Rightarrow \quad U = -\left(\frac{16}{3}\pi^2 G\right)\left(\frac{M^2}{\frac{16}{9}\pi^2 R^6}\right)\left(\frac{R^5}{5}\right)$$

$$\Rightarrow \quad U = -\frac{3}{5}\frac{GM^2}{R}$$

Sol. 33 (A) Effective gravity at equator is

$$g_e = g_0 - R\omega^2$$

$$\Rightarrow \quad g_0/2 = g_0 - R\omega^2$$

$$\Rightarrow \quad \omega^2 R = \frac{g_0}{2}$$

$$\Rightarrow \quad \omega = \sqrt{\frac{g_0}{2R}}$$

$\Rightarrow$ $T = 2$, putting $R = 6.4 \times 10^6\, m$

and $g_0 = 9.8$ m/sec^2, we obtain,

$T = 1.99$ hrs ≈ 2 hrs

Sol. 34 (A) The time period of satellite is given by

$$T^2 = \frac{4\pi^2}{GM}(R+h)^3 = \frac{4\pi^2}{g}\frac{(R+h)^3}{R^2}$$

$$\Rightarrow \quad T = \frac{2\pi}{R}\sqrt{\frac{(R+h)^3}{g}}$$

$$\Rightarrow \quad T = \frac{2\pi}{6400\times 10^3}\sqrt{\frac{10^{21}}{9.8}}$$

$$\Rightarrow \quad T = 31360.78 \text{ sec} = 8.71 \text{ hrs}$$

Sol. 35 (A) Orbital speed is

$$V_0 = \sqrt{\frac{GM}{(R+h)}} = \sqrt{\frac{gR^2}{(R+h)}}$$

$$= \frac{9.8\times(6400\times 10^3)^2}{10^7} \text{ m/s}$$

$$= 6335 \text{ m/s}$$

$$= 6.335 \text{ km/s}$$

Sol. 36 (A) Work required is

$$W = U_{\text{final}} - U_{\text{initial}}$$

$$= 3\left[-\left\{\frac{G(m)(m)}{r_f}\right\} - \left\{\frac{G(m)(m)}{r_i}\right\}\right]$$

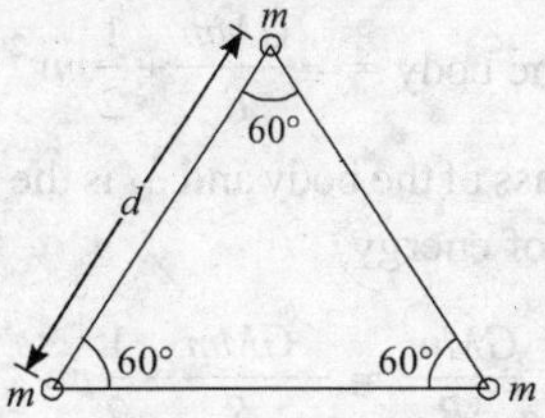

Putting $r_f = 0.4m, r_i = 0.2\, m$ and

$$G = 6.67\times 10^{-11}\frac{N-m^2}{kg^2}$$

and $m = 0.1$ kg

We get $W = 5.0 \times 10^{-12}$ J

Sol. 37 (B) Orbital velocity

$$v = \frac{2\pi r}{T}$$

Hence, $KE \propto \frac{1}{T^2}$

Sol. 38 (A) It is given that

$$T_s = 29.5\, T_e;$$

$$R_e = 1.5 \times 10^{11} \text{ m}$$

Now, according to Kepler's third law

$$\frac{T_S^2}{T_e^2} = \frac{R_S^3}{R_e^3}$$

$$\Rightarrow \quad R_s = R_e\left(\frac{T_S}{T_e}\right)^{\frac{2}{3}}$$

$$\Rightarrow \quad R_s = 1.5\times 10^{11}\left(\frac{29.5\,T_e}{T_e}\right)^{\frac{2}{3}}$$

$$\Rightarrow \quad R_s = 1.43\times 10^{12}\text{ m} = 1.43\times 10^9\text{ km}$$

Sol. 39 (C) Let g_0 to the acceleration due to gravity on surface, we use

$$mg_0 = \frac{GM_o m}{\left(\frac{D_o}{2}\right)^2}$$

$$g_0 = \frac{4GM_o}{D_o^2}$$

Sol. 40 (A) Initial energy of the body

$$= -\frac{GMm}{(R+2R)}$$

Final energy of the body $= -\frac{GMm}{R} + \frac{1}{2}mv^2$

where m is the mass of the body and M is the mass of the earth.

By conservation of energy

$$-\frac{GMm}{3R} = -\frac{GMm}{R} + \frac{1}{2}mv^2$$

$$\Rightarrow \quad \frac{1}{2}mv^2 = \frac{2GMm}{3R}$$

$$\Rightarrow \quad v^2 = \frac{4GM}{3R}$$

$$\Rightarrow \quad v = \sqrt{\frac{4GM}{3R}}$$

$$\Rightarrow \quad v = \sqrt{\frac{4GMR}{3R^2}} = \sqrt{\frac{4}{3}gR}$$

Sol. 41 (C) If time period of satellites are T_1 and T_2 we use

$$T_1 = 2\pi R/v$$

and

$$T_2 = 2\pi(3R)/v_B$$

$$\frac{T_1}{T_2} = \frac{1}{3}\left(\frac{v_B}{v}\right)$$

$$\left(\frac{T_1}{T_2}\right)^2 = \frac{1}{9}\left(\frac{v_B}{v}\right)^2$$

By Kepler's third law

$$\frac{T_1^2}{T_2^2} = \left(\frac{R_1}{R_2}\right)^3 = \left(\frac{1}{3}\right)^3$$

$$\left(\frac{1}{3}\right)^3 = \frac{1}{9}\left(\frac{v_B}{v}\right)^2$$

$$\Rightarrow \quad v_B = v/\sqrt{3}$$

Sol. 42 (C) Let M be the mass of the planet and m the mass of satellite

Then

$$mr\omega^2 = \frac{GMm}{r^2}$$

$$\Rightarrow \quad GM = r^3\omega^2$$

$$\Rightarrow \quad g = \frac{GM}{R^2} = \frac{r^3\omega^2}{R^2}$$

Sol. 43 (A) Work done will be zero when displacement is perpendicular to the field

The field makes an angle

$$\theta_1 = \tan^{-1}\left(\frac{1}{4}\right)$$

with positive x-axis

While the line $y + 4x = 2$ makes an angle

$$\theta_2 = \tan^{-1}(-4) \text{ with positive } x\text{-axis}$$

$$\theta_1 + \theta_2 = 90°$$

i.e. the line $y + 4x = 2$

is perpendicular to $\vec{g}$

Sol. 44 (D) As the gravitational field inside the shell is zero, the particle will remain stationary.

Sol. 45 (B) From the data given in orbital speed

$$v = 2 \times 10^5 \text{ m/s}$$

$$\frac{mv^2}{r} = \frac{GMm}{r^2}$$

Where M is mass of the massive object and m is mass of particle.

$$\Rightarrow \quad M = \frac{rv^2}{G}$$

$$= \frac{6 \times 9.5 \times 10^{15} \times 4 \times 10^{10}}{6.67 \times 10^{-11}} \simeq 10^{37} \text{ kg (order)}$$

Sol. 46 (C) $\frac{\text{Mass of the object}}{\text{Mass of sun}} \approx \frac{10^{37}}{10^{30}} = 10^7 > 50$

$\Rightarrow$ It is a black hole

Sol. 47 (B) $R_{EH} = \frac{2GM}{c^2}$

$$= \frac{2 \times 6.67 \times 10^{-11} \times 6 \times 10^{24}}{(3 \times 10^8)^2} \approx 10^{-3}$$

$\Rightarrow$ Radius compression factor $= \frac{10^{-3}}{6400 \times 10^3} \approx 10^{-9}$

Sol. 48 (D) $v_0 = \sqrt{gr}$

(for close to surface of earth)

$$v_e = \sqrt{2gr}$$

So, the speed of particle will be $\sqrt{gr} = \frac{v_e}{\sqrt{2}}$

Sol. 49 (B) Gravitational force between balls is

$$F = \frac{Gm^2}{(a-X)^2}$$

for equilibrium of each ball we use

$$T\sin\theta = \frac{Gm^2}{(a-X)^2} \qquad ...(1)$$

$$T\cos\theta = mg \qquad ...(2)$$

$$\frac{(1)}{(2)} \Rightarrow \tan\theta = \frac{Gm}{(a-X)^2 g}$$

Sol. 50 (B) At a displacement x from mean position, restoring force on m_s is

$$F_s = \frac{Gmm_s}{(x^2+d^2)} \cdot \sin\theta \times 2$$

$$F_s = \frac{2Gmm_s x}{(x^2+d^2)^{3/2}}$$

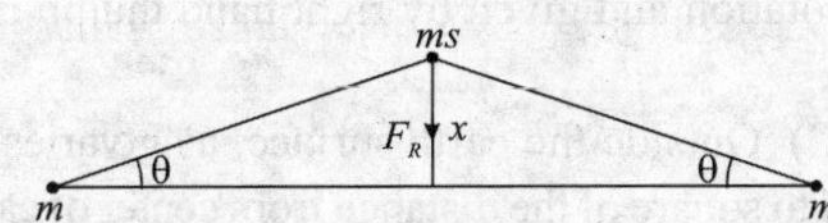

for $x << d$, we use

$$F_s = \frac{2Gmm_s}{d^3} \cdot x$$

acceleration of ball is

$$a = \frac{F_s}{m} = \frac{2Gm_s}{d^3} \cdot x$$

as a is opposite to x we use

$$a = -\frac{2Gm_s}{d^3} x$$

Comparing with $a = -\omega^2 x$ we get

$$\omega = \frac{2Gm_s}{d^3}$$

$\Rightarrow$ oscillation frequency of particle is

$$F_s = \frac{\omega}{2\pi} = \frac{1}{2\pi}\sqrt{\frac{2Gm_s}{d^3}}$$

Sol. 51 (D) In figure shown as we know at all points in the plane of base of a hemispherical shell gravitational field is normal to base hence the surface is equipotential.

Sol. 52 (C) At point P the gravitational field is such that it must be opposite in direction to that due to an inverted hemispherical shell which when placed on this shell to complete the spherical shell as at interior points net gravitational field is zero for a hollow sphere. Hence only (C) is the possible option.

Sol. 53 (A) Gravitational field due to element dx at origin is

$$dg = \frac{G(a+bx^2)dx}{x^2}$$

net field at O is $\quad g = \int dg = \int_{\alpha}^{l+\alpha} \left(\frac{Ga}{x^2} + Gb\right) dx$

$$\Rightarrow \quad g = \left[-\frac{Ga}{x}\right]_{\alpha}^{l+\alpha} + Gbl.$$

$$= Ga\left[\frac{1}{\alpha} - \frac{1}{l+\alpha}\right] + Gbl$$

Thus force on mass m is $F = mg = GM\left[a\left(\frac{1}{\alpha} - \frac{1}{l+\alpha}\right) + bl\right]$

Sol. 54 (D) Considering g to be constant, atmospheric pressure would be

$$p = \frac{mg}{4\pi R^2} \qquad \text{[taking } m \text{ to be atmospheric mass]}$$

$$\Rightarrow \quad \frac{p_1}{p_2} = \frac{m_1 R_2^2 g_1}{m_2 R_1^2 g_2}$$

$$\Rightarrow \quad \frac{m_1}{m_2} = \frac{p_1 R_1^2 g_2}{p_2 R_2^2 g_1}$$

$$\text{using } g = \frac{Gmp}{R^2} = \frac{G\rho\left(\frac{4}{3}\pi R^3\right)}{R^2} = \frac{4}{3}G\pi\rho t$$

$$\Rightarrow \quad \frac{m_1}{m_2} = \frac{p_1 R_1^2}{p_2 R_2^2} \times \frac{\rho_2 R_2}{\rho_1 R_1} = \frac{p_1 R_1 \rho_2}{p_2 R_2 \rho_1}$$

Sol. 55 (A) By Kepler's second law we use

$$\frac{L}{2M} = \frac{\pi ab}{T}$$

where a is semi major and b is semi minor axis of elliptical orbit.

$$\Rightarrow \quad L = \frac{m\pi(r_a + r_p)\sqrt{r_a r_p}}{T}$$

Sol. 56 (B) Force on element dx on rod is

$$dF = \left(\frac{m}{R}dx\right)\frac{GM}{x^2}$$

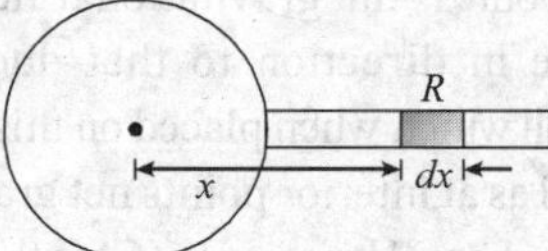

Total force on rod is

$$F = \int dF = \frac{GMm}{R}\int_R^{2R}\frac{1}{x^2}dx$$

$$= \frac{GMm}{R}\left[-\frac{1}{x}\right]_R^{2R}$$

$$= \frac{GMm}{2R^2}$$

Sol. 57 (C) As mass of body is $2M_e$ on releasing from rest if it moves at speed v at any instant earth will move at $2v$ and before hitting earth body will travel a distance $h/3$ with acceleration g thus time to hit earth surface is

$$t = \sqrt{\frac{2\left(h/3\right)}{g}} = \sqrt{\frac{2h}{3g}}$$

Sol. 58 (B) Surface integral is

$$\phi = \oint \vec{g}\cdot\overrightarrow{ds}$$

if we consider S is a symmetric sphere of radius R, we use

$$\phi = -\oint\frac{Gm_0}{R^2}\cdot ds = -\frac{Gm_0}{R^2}\cdot 4\pi R^2 = -4\pi Gm_0$$

As the result is independent of R, for all surfaces of any shape this result is valid and this is also called Gauss's law for gravitational field.

Sol. 59 (A) Initially force on particle P due to sphere is

$$F_1 = m\cdot\frac{GM}{(2R)^2} = \frac{GMm}{4R^2}$$

After capacity is created by removing mass

$$m_{cavity} = \frac{M}{\frac{4}{3}\pi R^3}\cdot\frac{4}{3}\pi\left(\frac{R}{2}\right)^3 = \frac{M}{8}$$

the force on particle P is

$$F_2 = F_1 - F_{cavity}$$

$$= \frac{GMm}{4R^2} - m\frac{G\left(M/8\right)}{\left(3R/2\right)^2}$$

$$= \frac{GMm}{R^2}\left[\frac{1}{4}-\frac{1}{18}\right]$$

$$= \frac{7}{36}\frac{GMm}{R^2}$$

$$\Rightarrow \quad \frac{F_1}{F_2} = \frac{9}{7}$$

Solutions of ADVANCE MCQs One or More Option Correct

Sol. 1 (All) As initial energy is zero by conservation of energy during motion of particles total energy will remain zero. At a separation r the potential energy of the particles can be given as $-4Gm^2/r$ hence the kinetic energy magnitude must be same for total energy to be zero and by kinetic energy we can calculate the velocity of approach as no external force or torque is present in the system total angular momentum of the system will remain conserved.

Sol. 2 (D) Areal velocity of the position vector of the planet is given as $L/2m$ where L is the angular momentum so option (D) is correct.

Sol. 3 (A, C) Areal velocity is considered as an angular vector of which direction is given in the plane normal to the plane of revolution/rotation and given by right hand thumb rule.

Sol. 4 (B, C) Outside the earth surface, as g varies inversely proportional to square of the distance from center of earth option (A) is correct and inside the earth as g varies as directly proportional to the distance option (C) is correct.

Sol. 5 (A, D) In elliptical orbit at the positions of aphelion and perihelion points the velocity of planet is perpendicular to the position vector so for small displacements at these points work done by gravitational force of sun is zero and in one complete revolution of planet it is also zero as gravitational field is a conservative field.

Sol. 6 (A, B, C) As the orbital speed of a satellite in a circular orbit around earth varies inversely proportional to the square root of the orbit radius, in this case as the orbit radius is minimum options (A), (B) and (C) are correct.

Sol. 7 (A, C) As G will decrease the time period of orbit will increase and orbital sped which depends upon square root of G will decrease hence options (A) and (C) are correct.

Sol. 8 (All) Comparing the velocity of projected body in different cases with orbital velocity as explained in article 6.14, all options are correct.

Sol. 9 (A, B, D) For a spherical shell inside $E = 0$ but $V = constant$ and outside both are non zero hence options (A) and (B) are correct. For a solid sphere inside E and V both are non zero and varies continuously with distance r from inside to outside hence option (D) is correct.

Sol. 10 (A) Gravitational field inside the cavity is

$$\vec{E} = \frac{4}{3}\pi\rho G\vec{r}$$

where ρ is mass density and $\vec{r}$ is separation between centre of sphere and centre of cavity. Escape velocity at point A is given as

$$\frac{1}{2}mV_{esc}^2 - \frac{GMm}{R} + \frac{G\left(M/9\right)m}{\left(5R/3\right)} = 0$$

$$\Rightarrow \quad V_{esc} = \sqrt{\frac{28}{15}\frac{GM}{R}}$$

Sol. 11 (A, C, D) By symmetry the gravitational field at center will be zero and the equation of circles given in options (C) and (D) are equipotential due to symmetry.

Sol. 12 (A, D) As the force along both the tunnels at a distance x from tunnel center are same, the angular frequency of oscillations of both the particles will be same hence $T_1 = T_2$ but the tunnel along the chord is shorter hence the maximum speed at center in this case will be less.

Sol. 13 (C, D) During elliptical path only at points where the position vector is normal to trajectory, gravitational force will be the centripetal force (normal force) on satellite at which the power of gravitational force will be zero.

Sol. 14 (B, D) As value of g is directly proportional to M/R^2 and as M is same for both we use ρR^3 = constant hence we get $R_1 : R_2 = 2 : 1$ thus $g_1 : g_2 = 1 : 4$ and escape velocity is $\sqrt{2gR}$ the ratio of escape velocities will be $1:\sqrt{2}$.

Sol. 15 (A, C, D) If G starts decreasing then the gravitational force starts decreasing due to which the satellite will start moving away from the earth because of inertia of its motion and the resulting path will be an outward spiral. As no external torque is there on the satellite, its angular momentum will remain constant.

Sol. 16 (A, B, D) Due to dust it experiences an opposition force due to which its speed will decrease and due to which it is attracted toward the earth by gravitational force and in this process gravitational force will do work on satellite and its kinetic energy will increase continuously more than the opposition work done and as it gets closer to earth center its potential energy will decrease. It will move in spiral path but due to torque of opposition force angular momentum will not be conserved. Due to dust friction it gets heated and may burn off before falling on earth surface.

Sol. 17 (A, D) The field inside the shell is zero and so potential inside the shell is constant and equal to the value that exists at the surface i.e. $-\frac{GM}{a}$.

* * * * *

ANSWERS & SOLUTIONS

CONCEPTUAL MCQS Single Option Correct

1	(A)	2	(B)	3	(A)
4	(D)	5	(C)	6	(D)
7	(B)	8	(A)	9	(C)
10	(C)	11	(B)	12	(C)
13	(B)	14	(C)	15	(B)
16	(A)	17	(B)		

NUMERICAL MCQS Single Option Correct

1	(C)	2	(C)	3	(A)
4	(B)	5	(A)	6	(A)
7	(B)	8	(B)	9	(B)
10	(C)	11	(B)	12	(D)
13	(B)	14	(A)	15	(D)
16	(C)	17	(D)	18	(B)
19	(B)	20	(A)	21	(B)
22	(C)	23	(A)	24	(B)
25	(D)	26	(A)	27	(C)
28	(C)	29	(C)	30	(D)
31	(D)	32	(A)	33	(A)
34	(C)	35	(C)	36	(B)

ADVANCE MCQs One or More Option Correct

1	(A, C, D)	2	(A, C, D)	3	(A, D)
4	(D)	5	(B, D)	6	(All)
7	(A, B, C)	8	(A, D)	9	(B, C, D)
10	(A, C)	11	(A, B, D)	12	(B, D)
13	(A, C, D)	14	(A, C)	15	(B, C)
16	(C, D)	17	(B, C)	18	(A, C)

Solutions of PRACTICE EXERCISE 7.1

(i) Force on bottom of vessel = weight of liquid

$$= \pi r^2 h\rho g$$

force on side walls of vessel

$$= \left(\frac{h}{2}\rho g\right) \times 2\pi rh$$

given that $\quad \pi r^2 \rho g = \frac{h}{2}\rho g \times 2\pi rh$

$\Rightarrow \quad h = r$

(ii) If cavity volume is V we use

$$\left(\frac{264}{8.8} + V\right)\rho_w = 43$$

$$V = 43 - \frac{264}{8.8} = 13 \text{ cm}^3$$

(iii) (a) Pressure of water at bottom of vessel is

$$P = h\rho g + P_{atm}$$
$$= 1 \times 10^5 + 0.2 \times 1000 \times 10$$
$$= 1.02 \times 10^5 \text{ N/m}^2$$

force on bottom $\quad P = 1.02 \times 10^5 \times 20 \times 10^{-4}$

$$= 204 \text{ N}$$

(b) Weight of water in vessel

$$= 0.5 \times 10^{-3} \times 1000 \times 10 = 5 \text{ N}$$

upward force on water by bottom

$$= 204 \text{ N}$$

downward force on water by atmosphere

$$= 1 \times 10^5 \times 20 \times 10^{-4} = 200 \text{ N}$$

If force by side walls is F_s upwards, for equilibrium of water we use

$$F_s + 204 = 200 + 5$$
$$F_s = 1 \text{ N upward}$$

(iv) For equilibrium of sphere we use

$$\frac{4}{3}\pi(10)^3 \times \frac{1}{2} \times 0.8 = \frac{4}{3}\pi((10)^3 - (9)^3) \times \rho$$

$$\rho = \frac{0.4 \times 1000}{1000 - 729} = \frac{400}{271}$$

$$= 1.476 \text{ gm/cm}^3$$

If ρ_L be the density of liquid in which sphere will just float then

$$\frac{4}{3}\pi(10)^3\rho_L = \frac{4}{3}\pi(10)^3 \times \frac{1}{2} \times 0.8$$

$\Rightarrow \quad \rho_L = 0.4 \text{ gm/cm}^3$

(v) If x *gm* copper is mixed in 36-x gm gold we use

$$\left(\frac{x}{\rho_{Cu}} + \frac{36 - x}{\rho_{gold}}\right)\rho_\omega = 2$$

$$\frac{x}{8.9} + \frac{36 - x}{19.3} = 2$$

$$19.3x + 8.9 \times 36 - 8.9x = 2 \times 8.9 \times 19.3$$

$\Rightarrow \quad 10.4x = 343.54 - 320.4 = 23.14$

$\Rightarrow \quad x = 2.225 \text{ gm}$

(vi) If V_c is volume of cavities we use

$$\left(V_c + \frac{36}{\rho_{Gold}}\right)\rho_w = 2$$

$\Rightarrow \quad V_c = \frac{2}{\rho_w} - \frac{36}{\rho_{Gold}}$

$$V_c = 2 - \frac{36}{19.3} = 0.135 \text{ cm}^3$$

(vii) If water is filled to a height h and l is length of tube is submerged in water we use

$$l\pi r^2\rho_\omega = 30 + \pi r^2 h\rho_w \quad \dots(1)$$

also it is given that

$$\frac{l}{2} = \frac{30\times 10 + \pi r^2 h\rho_w \times \frac{h}{2}}{30 + \pi r^2 h\rho_w}$$

$$\frac{1}{2}(30 + \pi r^2 h\rho_\omega)\left(\frac{30 + \pi r^2 h\rho_\omega}{\pi r^2 \rho_\omega}\right) = 300 + \frac{1}{2}\pi r^2 h^2 \rho_\omega$$

$$450 + \frac{1}{2}(\pi r^2 h\rho_\omega)^2 + 30(\pi r^2 h\rho_\omega) = 300\pi r^2\rho_\omega + \frac{1}{2}(\pi r^2\rho_\omega h)^2$$

$$h = \frac{300\pi r^2\rho_\omega - 450}{30\pi r^2\rho_\omega}$$

$$= 10 - \frac{450}{30\times 3.14\times (2)^2\times 1}$$

$$= 8.8 \text{ cm}$$

mass of water $m = \pi r^2 h\rho_\omega = 3.14\times(2)^2\times 8.8\times 1$

$$= 110.53\text{gm}$$

(viii) Buoyant force on submerged part of rod is

$$F_B = 2\times S\times \rho_\omega \times g \quad \dots(1)$$

Here we assume S is cross-sectional area of rod

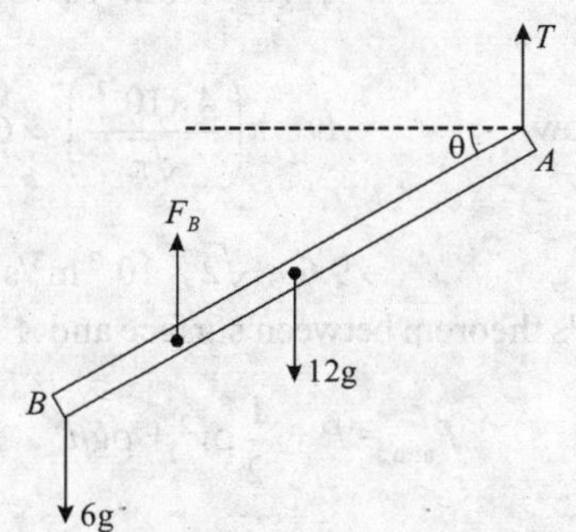

For equilibrium of rod we use

$$F_B + T = 18\text{g} \quad \dots(2)$$

Analyzing torque about point A, we get

$$12\text{g}\times 2\cos\theta + 6\text{g}\times 4\cos\theta = F_B\times 3\cos\theta$$

$$\Rightarrow \quad F_B = 16\text{g} = 160\text{ N} \quad \dots(3)$$

$$\Rightarrow \quad T = 18\text{g} - F_B = 2\text{g} = 20\text{ N}$$

from equation (1) we use

$$2S\times 10^4 = 160$$

$$S = 80\times 10^{-4}\text{ m}^2$$

Volume of rod is $V = Sl = 80\times 10^{-4}\times 4 = 3.2\times 10^{-2}\text{ m}^3$

(ix) (a) Force on a strip of length L and width dx at a depth x is

$$dF = x\rho g.Ldx$$

Let force on dam is $F = \int dF = \rho gL\int_0^H x dx = \frac{1}{2}\rho g L H^2$

(b) Torque on strip about point O is

$$d\tau = x\rho gLdx(H - x)$$

Net torque is $\tau = \int d\tau$

$$= \rho gL\int_0^H (Hx - x^2)dx$$

$$= \rho gL\left(\frac{H^3}{2} - \frac{H^3}{3}\right) = \frac{1}{6}\rho gLH^3$$

(c) If the moment arm of net force is at a height h_1 from O, we use

$$\frac{1}{2}\rho gLH^2\times h_1 = \frac{1}{6}\rho gLH^3$$

$$\Rightarrow \quad h_1 = \frac{1}{3}H$$

(x) Considering an atmospheric layer at a height y of width dy, the pressure due to this layer is

$$dP = dy\rho g$$

$$dP = \rho_0 e^{-Ay} gdy$$

Net pressure is $P = \int dP = \rho_0 g\int_0^\infty e^{-Ay}dy$

$$= \rho_0 g\left[\frac{1}{A}e^{-Ay}\right]_0^\infty$$

$$= \frac{\rho_0 g}{A} = \frac{1.3\times 9.8}{1.2\times 10^{-4}}$$

$$= 1.0616\times 10^5\text{ N/m}^2$$

Solutions of PRACTICE EXERCISE 7.2

(i) Density of ball $= \frac{10}{15} = \frac{2}{3}$ gm/cm^3

(a) At a depth 10m, acceleration of ball is $a = g\left(\frac{\rho_2}{\rho_3} - 1\right)$

$$= 9.8\left(\frac{3}{2} - 1\right) = 4.9\text{ m/s}^2$$

(b) Time taken to reach surface is $t = \sqrt{\frac{2h}{a}} = \sqrt{\frac{2\times 10}{4.9}} = 2.02\text{s}$

(ii) For liquid not to spill out

$$h\rho g = l\rho a$$

$$\Rightarrow \quad a = \frac{hg}{l}$$

(iii) (a) For equilibrium of sphere, we use

$$m(g+a)+T=\left(\frac{m}{\rho}\right)\rho_{\omega}(g+a)$$

$$\Rightarrow \quad T=(g+a)\left(\frac{\rho_{\omega}}{\rho}-1\right)$$

$$=2\times 12\left[\frac{1000}{500}-1\right]$$

$$=24\text{ N}$$

(b) As thread snaps acceleration of sphere is

$$a=(g+a)\left[\frac{\rho_{\omega}}{\rho}-1\right]$$

$$=12\text{ m/s}^2$$

(iv) Using pascal's equation we have

$$P_A+h\rho g+l\rho a=P_B$$
$$P_B-P_A=(hg+la)\rho$$

(v) Pressure at bottom of vessel is

$$P=P_{atm}+h\rho g+\frac{(mg-V\rho g)}{(0.04)^2}$$

$$P_{avg}=(P_{atm}+h\rho g)+\frac{(mg-V\rho g)}{A}$$

$$=10^5+0.04\times 1000\times 10+\frac{0.1\times 10-64\times 10^{-6}\times 1000\times 10}{16\times 10^{-4}}$$

$$=10^5+400+\frac{1-0.64}{16}\times 10^4$$

$$=10^5+400+225$$
$$=1.00625\times 10^5\ Pa$$

(vi) Pressure difference due to horizontal length of liquid is

$$\Delta P=\int_0^L dx\rho\omega^2 x$$

As liquid is at rest in frame of tube, we use

$$\Delta P=\frac{\rho\omega^2L^2}{2}=h\rho g$$

$$\Rightarrow \quad h=\frac{\omega^2L^2}{2g}$$

(vii) Using Pascal's equation we use

$$(l-x)\times 2\rho\times g\sin 60^\circ+x\times 3\rho\times g\times\sin 60^\circ$$
$$-(l-x)\times 3\rho\times g\times\sin 60^\circ-x\times\rho\times g\times\sin 60^\circ=0$$

$$\Rightarrow \quad 2(l-x)+3x-3(l-x)-x=0$$

$$\Rightarrow \quad 3x=l$$

$$\Rightarrow \quad x=\frac{l}{3}$$

Sol. (viii) In equilibrium

$$\frac{600\times 10}{800\times 10^{-4}}=\frac{F}{25\times 10^{-4}}+h\rho g$$

$$\Rightarrow \quad \frac{F}{25\times 10^{-4}}=\frac{60}{8}\times 10^4-8\times(0.75\times 10^3)\times 10$$

$$\frac{F}{25\times 10^{-4}}=1.5\times 10^4$$

$$\Rightarrow \quad F=37.5\text{ N}$$

Solutions of PRACTICE EXERCISE 7.3

(i) Using equation of continuity, we have

$$12\times 20+8\times 16=v\times 16$$

$$\Rightarrow \quad v=\frac{240+128}{16}=23\text{ kph}$$

(ii) **(a)** Velocity of flow

$$=\sqrt{2gh}=\sqrt{2\times 10\times 3.6}=6\sqrt{2}\text{ m/s}$$

(b) Rate of flow

$$=Av=\pi\left(\frac{4\times 10^{-2}}{\sqrt{\pi}}\right)^2\times 6\sqrt{2}$$

$$=9.6\times\sqrt{2}\times 10^{-3}\text{ m}^3\text{/s}$$

(c) Bernoulli's theorem between surface and A

$$P_{atm}=P+\frac{1}{2}\rho v^2+\rho gh$$

$$\Rightarrow \quad P=P_{atm}-\frac{1}{2}\rho v^2-\rho gh$$

$$=10^5-\frac{1}{2}\times 10^3(6\sqrt{2})^2-10^3\times 10\times 1.8$$

$$=4.6\times 10^4\text{ N/m}^2$$

(iii) Force of reaction due to ejection of fluid through a hole is

$$F=\rho Sv^2$$

Due to two opposite holes net force on vessel is

$$F=\rho S(v_1^2-v_2^2)$$

$$=\rho S((\sqrt{2g(h+\Delta h)})^2-(\sqrt{2gh})^2)$$

$$=2S\rho g\Delta h$$

(iv) Using Bernoulli's theorem for venturi tube, flow velocity is

$$v = \sqrt{\frac{2gh}{\frac{A_1^2}{A_2^2}-1}} = \sqrt{\frac{2\times10\times0.02}{\frac{(4)^2}{(2)^2}-1}}$$

$$= \sqrt{\frac{0.4}{3}} = 0.365\ \text{m/s}$$

$$\text{Flow rate} = Av = 4\times10^{-4}\times0.365$$
$$= 1.4605\times10^{-4}\ \text{m}^3/\text{s}$$
$$= 146.05\ \text{cm}^3/\text{s}$$

(v) Horizontal reaction on vessel due to ejection of liquid is

$$F = \rho S v^2$$

to slide $\rho S v^2 \geq \mu mg$

$$S \geq \frac{\mu mg}{\rho(2gh)}$$

$$S \geq \frac{0.4\times100}{2\times1000\times2} = 0.01\text{m}^2$$

if d is hole diameter $S = \dfrac{\pi d^2}{4}$

$$\Rightarrow \quad d = \sqrt{\frac{4S}{\pi}} = \sqrt{\frac{4\times0.01}{3.14}} = 0.1128\text{m}$$

(vi) Using Bernoulli's theorem

$$P_A + \frac{1}{2}\rho V_A^2 = P_B + \frac{1}{2}\rho V_B^2$$

and $\quad A_A V_A = A_B V_B$

$$P_B = P_A + \frac{1}{2}\rho V_A^2 - \frac{1}{2}\rho V_A^2\left(\frac{A_A}{A_B}\right)^2$$

$$= \text{P}_\text{A} + \frac{1}{2}\rho V_A^2\left[1-\left(\frac{d_A}{d_B}\right)^4\right]$$

$$= 2\times10^4 + \frac{1}{2}\times1000\times(4)^2\left[1-\left(\frac{1}{2}\right)^4\right]$$

$$= 2\times10^4 + 8000\times\frac{15}{16}$$

$$= 2.75\times10^4\ \text{N/m}^2$$

(vii) Using Bernoulli's theorem, we have

$$P_B = P_{\text{atm}} + \frac{1}{2}\rho v^2 \qquad \ldots(1)$$

and

$$P_B - P_{\text{atm}} = \int_{l-h}^{l} dr\cdot\rho\cdot\omega^2 x$$

$$= \frac{\rho\omega^2}{2}\left[l^2-(l-h)^2\right]$$

$$= \frac{1}{2}\rho\omega^2(2lh-h^2)$$

from equation (1)

$$\frac{1}{2}\rho\omega^2(2lh-h^2) = \frac{1}{2}\rho v^2$$

$$\Rightarrow \quad v = \omega h\sqrt{\left(\frac{2l}{h}-1\right)}$$

(viii) When liquid level is at a height h, ejection speed of water is

$$v = \sqrt{2gh} \qquad [\text{as } a \ll A]$$

Water jet crossed the wall when

$$x = v\sqrt{\frac{2y}{g}}$$

$$\Rightarrow \quad x = \sqrt{2gh}\sqrt{\frac{2y}{g}}$$

$$\Rightarrow \quad h = \frac{x^2}{4y}$$

by continuity equation we use

$$-\frac{dh}{dt}A = a\sqrt{2gh}$$

$$\Rightarrow \quad \int_H^h \frac{dh}{\sqrt{h}} = -\frac{a}{A}\sqrt{2g}\int_0^t dt$$

$$\Rightarrow \quad 2(\sqrt{H}-\sqrt{h}) = \frac{a}{A}\sqrt{2g}t$$

$$\Rightarrow \quad t = \frac{A}{A}\sqrt{\frac{2}{g}}\left(\sqrt{H}-\sqrt{\frac{x^2}{4y}}\right)$$

(ix) (a) Friction on plug

$$F \geq h\rho g\times\frac{\pi d^2}{4}$$

$$= 6\times1000\times1g\times\frac{3.14\times(0.04)^2}{4}$$

$$= 75.36\ \text{N}$$

(b) Ejection speed of water

$$= \sqrt{2gh}$$

$$\text{How rate} = \frac{\pi d^2}{4}\sqrt{2gh}$$

Water flows in time t is

$$= \frac{\pi d^2}{4}\sqrt{2gh} \times t$$

$$= \frac{3.14 \times (0.04)^2}{4}\sqrt{2 \times 10 \times 6} \times 3 \times 3600$$

$$= 148.59 \text{ m}^3$$

Solutions of CONCEPTUAL MCQS Single Option Correct

Sol. 1 (A) The upward buoyant force on the bady is equal to $V\sigma g$ where V is the volume of the body given as $V = m/\rho$ and in this case the density of liquid is more so buoyant force will be more than the weight of the body so it will accelerate up by an acceleration $(V\sigma g - mg)/m$ which gives option (A) is correct.

Sol. 2 (B) As the ice melts the stone which was floating till now will sink and the weight of liquid displaced is less than the weight of stone so compared to the floating state of stone hence the liquid level will fall

Sol. 3 (A) Bernoulli's theorem relates the total energy of a mass of a flowing ideal fluid body per unit volume and in absence of all external forces this energy remain constant.

Sol. 4 (D) When a floating coin falls in water the overall level of water in container will go down as earlier the coin was floating and displaced amount of water is equal to the weight of the coin where as when it falls in water displaced water is less than the weight hence l will decrease. As the total displaced water is due to the wooden block, after coin falls in the tank h will also decrease.

Sol. 5 (C) When the enclosure is in free fall the effective gravity is zero and buoyancy force will also be zero hence body can float with any part of its volume submerged hence option (C) is correct.

Sol. 6 (D) By continuity equations in narrow part area decreases, speed increases and by Bernoulli's theorem on increasing speed pressure decreases.

Sol. 7 (B) As $\rho_{iron} > \rho_{Al}$, iron ball is heavier and due to same size bouyant force is same on both so acceleration if iron ball is more and it will take less time in reaching bottom of lake.

Sol. 8 (A) As initially ice was floating so it was displacing the water equal to the weight of ice, and when it melts, the water thus obtained will have specific gravity 1 so it will have less volume than ice and will spread over the liquid of specific gravity 1.25

Sol. 9 (C) Initially when the stones are in the boat the total amount of water displaced is balancing the weight of boat and stones but when the stones are unloaded into the water the stones will sink and the water displaced will be less so the water level will fall.

Sol. 10 (C) Initially the body will have a volume submerged in liquid in the vessel. If vessel will starts falling then the effective gravity in the frame of vessel will be $(g - a)$ for both liquid and body and the submerged part remain same hence option (C) is correct.

Sol. 11 (B) In the bottle just after shaking the sediment will be falling down so as center of mass of the bottle and its contents is coming down total normal reaction on it must be less than its weight hence option (B) is correct.

Sol. 12 (C) As temperature rises liquid will expand and in A it will rise more compared to B as top cross section is less hence at the bottom pressure in A will increase more than that in B.

Sol. 13 (B) As air is filled in the bag its volume increases and due to which the force of buoyance also increases by the amount equal to weight of the air filled in it hence Vasu is correct.

Sol. 14 (C) As pressure at any point in the liquid will be affected by both g and a in vertical and horizontal direction hence it will be affected by both its x and y coordinates.

Sol. 15 (B) On wings of aeroplane due to the shape and motion in plane relative speed of air above and below the wing is different which creates a pressure difference at upper and lower surfaces of the wings and the force due to this pressure difference balances the weight of plane while flying.

Sol. 16 (A) Due to pseudo force on water pressure increases on the rear wall so maximum pressure will be at point B as due to gravity also it is increased at B. Similarly pressure due to acceleration is least on front face so minimum pressure is at point D.

Sol. 17 (B) Due to air pumping out from the jar, more liquid will evaporate as air pressure in the jar decreases. As liquid will evaporate liquid level will decrease and hence pressure at the bottom will also decrease.

Solutions of NUMERICAL MCQS Single Option Correct

Sol. 1 (C) Let v_1 and v_2 be the velocity of efflux from square and circular hole respectively. S_1 and S_2 be cross-section areas of square and circular holes

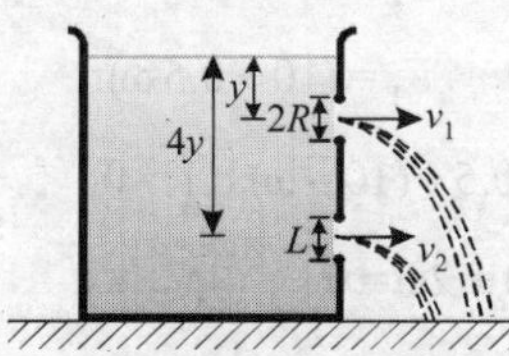

$$v_1 = \sqrt{8gy} \text{ and } v_2 = \sqrt{2gy}$$

The volume of water coming out of square and circular hole per second is

$$Q_1 = v_1 S_1 = \sqrt{8gy}\ L^2;$$

$$Q_2 = v_2 S_2 = \sqrt{2gy}\ \pi R^2$$

As $\quad Q_1 = Q_2$

$\Rightarrow \quad R = \sqrt{\frac{2}{\pi}} \cdot L$

Sol. 2 (C) Let h is the height to which water column is filled then we use

$$\rho_w gh + \rho_{Hg} g(10 - h) = \rho_{Cu} g(10)$$

$\Rightarrow \quad h + 13.6(10 - h) = 73$

$\Rightarrow \quad 63 = 12.6h$

$\Rightarrow \quad h = 5 \text{ cm}$

Sol. 3 (A) Let ρ_S, ρ_L be the density of silver and liquid. Also m and V be the mass and volume of silver block.

$\Rightarrow$ Tension in string = mg – bouyant force

$$T = \rho_S Vg - \rho_L Vg = (\rho_S - \rho_L)Vg$$

Also $\quad V = \frac{m}{\rho_s}$

$\Rightarrow \quad T = \left(\frac{\rho_S - \rho_L}{\rho_S}\right) mg$

$$mg = \frac{(10 - 0.72)}{10} \times 4 \times 10$$

$$= 37.12 \text{ N}$$

Sol. 4 (B) Pressure exerted by fluid at closed end B is

$$P = P_{atm} + \rho gl$$

$\Rightarrow$ force exerted by fluid at closed end B is

$$F = PA = (P_{atm} + \rho gl)A_0$$

Sol. 5 (A) The four piston are initially in equilibrium. As additional force F is applied to each piston, the pressure in fluid at each point must be increased by $\frac{F}{A}$ so that each piston retains the state of equilibrium.

Hence the bouyant force increases

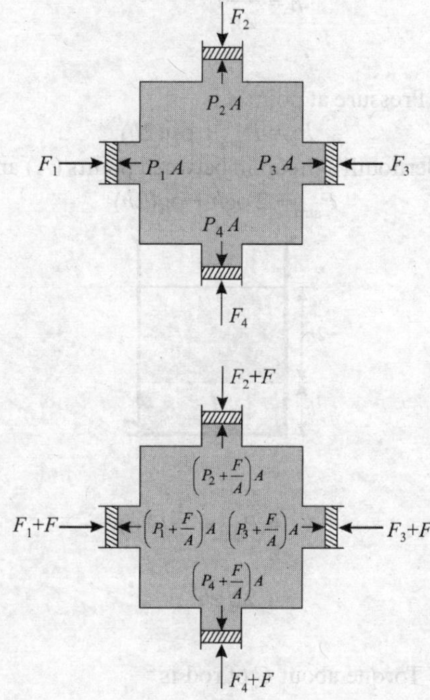

Thus the increment in pressure at each point is $\Delta P = \frac{F}{A}$.

Sol. 6 (A) Increasing the temperature of water from 2ºC to 3ºC increases its density while decreases the density of iron so Buoyant force will increase.

Sol. 7 (B) For the given situation, liquid of density 2ρ should be behind that of ρ as both liquids are at same level. From right limb pressure at point A is given as

$$P_A = P_{atm} + \rho gh$$

$$P_B = P_A + \rho a\frac{l}{2} = P_{atm} + \rho gh + \rho a\frac{l}{2}$$

$$P_C = P_B + (2\rho)a\frac{l}{2}$$

$$= P_{atm} + \rho gh + \frac{3}{2}\rho a l \quad \ldots(1)$$

And from left limb pressure at point C is given as

$$P_C = P_{atm} + (2\rho)gh \quad \ldots(2)$$

From (1) and (2):

$$P_{atm} + \rho gh + \frac{3}{2}\rho a l = P_{atm} + 2\rho gh$$

$$\Rightarrow \quad h = \frac{3a}{2g} l$$

Sol. 8 (B) Pressure at point A is

$$P_A = P_{atm} + \rho g(2h)$$

Applying Bernoulli's theorem between points (A) and (B)

$$P_{atm} + 2\rho gh + \rho g(2h)$$

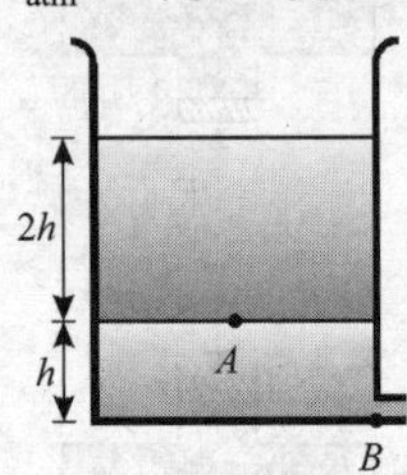

$$= P_{atm} + \frac{1}{2}(2\rho)v^2$$

$$\Rightarrow \quad v = 2\sqrt{gh}$$

Sol. 9 (B) Torque about C of rod is

$$F_b \cdot \frac{l}{4} = I\alpha$$

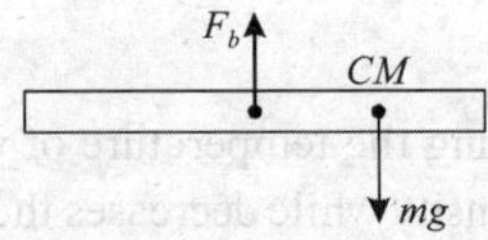

$$\Rightarrow \quad \alpha = (\pi r^2)(l)(\rho)(g) \cdot \frac{l}{4}$$

$$\Rightarrow \quad \alpha = \frac{\pi r^2 l^2 g\rho}{4I}$$

Sol. 10 (C) From equation of continuity,

$$(A \times 3) = (A \times 1.5) + (1.5 A \times V)$$

$$\Rightarrow \quad v = 1 \text{ m/s}^2$$

Sol. 11 (B) Given that relative to nozzle ejection speed is same

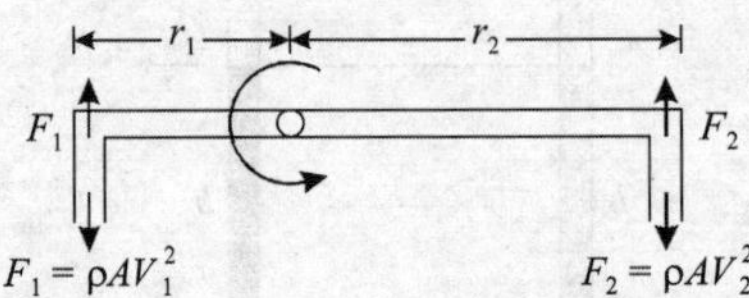

And as no external torque is acting as angular speed is constant we use

$$F_1 r_1 - F_2 r_2 = 0$$

$$\rho A V_1^2 r_1 - \rho A V_2^2 r_2 = 0$$

or $\quad V_1 r_1 - V_2 r_2 = 0$

here we use $\quad V_2 = 10 - \omega$

$$V_1 = (10 + 0.5\,\omega)$$

$$\Rightarrow \quad (10 + 0.5\,\omega) \times 0.5 - (10 - \omega) \times 1 = 0$$

$$\Rightarrow \quad 10 + 0.5\,\omega - 20 + 2\omega = 0$$

$$2.5\,\omega = 10$$

$$\omega = 4 \text{ radian/sec}$$

Sol. 12 (D) Centre of buoyancy of a floating object is the point where buoyant force is supposed to be acting which is located at the centre of gravity of the liquid displaced.

Sol. 13 (B) Weight of rod is

$$W = (0.012)(1)(2 \times 10^3)(10) = 240 \text{ N}$$

Buoyancy force on rod is

$$F_b = (0.012)(1)(10^3)(10) = 120 \text{ N}$$

Torque about O (For equilibrium) from FBD of rod is

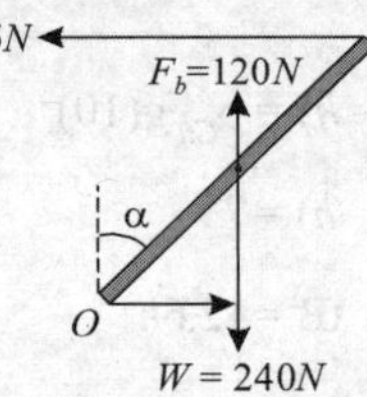

$$\tau = (240 - 120)\left(\frac{\sin\alpha}{2}\right) = 45(\cos\alpha)$$

$$\Rightarrow \quad \tan\alpha = \frac{90}{120} = \frac{3}{4}$$

$$\Rightarrow \quad \alpha = 37°$$

Sol. 14 (A) After oil is filled up, pressure at the depth of lower end should be equal if measured from inside and outside the tube. Suppose depth of oil is x cm then

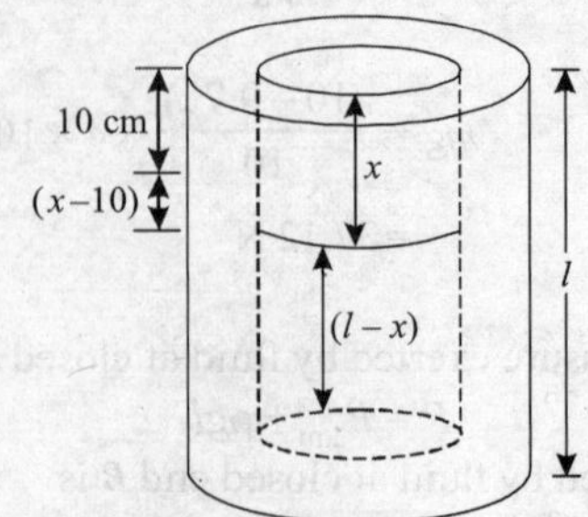

$$1000.g.\ [(l-10)\text{cm}] = 800\ g.(x\ \text{cm}) + 1000\ g[(l-x)\text{cm}]$$

$$\Rightarrow \quad x = 50\ \text{cm}$$

Sol. 15 (D) $F_b = V\rho_{\text{liquid}}g$

'g' is different on moon and on the earth.

Hence only (iii) is a correct statement rest all are related to factors other then $V_1\ \rho_0 rg$.

Hence (D)

Sol. 16 (C) Applying continuity equation

$$V_A A_A = V_B A_B$$

$$\Rightarrow \quad A_A = A_B \text{ so } V_A = V_B.$$

Applying Bernoulli's equation

$$P_A + \rho g h_A + 1/2\ \rho V_A^2 = P_B + \rho g h_B + 1/2\rho V_B^2$$

since $V_A = V_B$; and $h_A = h_B$

$$\Rightarrow \quad P_A = P_B$$

Sol. 17 (D) The velocity of fluid at the hole is

$$V_2 = \sqrt{\frac{2gh}{1+(a^2/A^2)}}$$

Using continuity equation at the two cross-sections A and B :

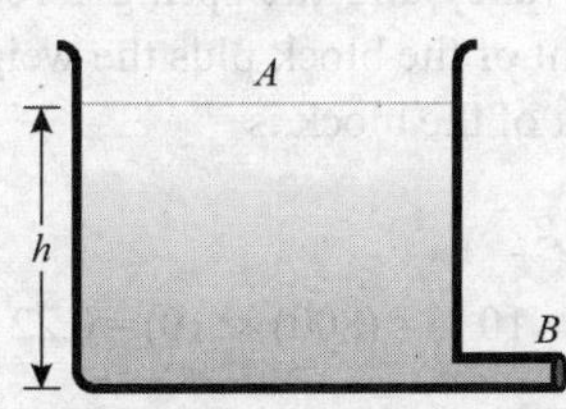

$$V_1 A = V_2 a$$

$$\Rightarrow \quad V_1 = \frac{a}{A} V_2$$

$\Rightarrow$ acceleration of top surface

$$= -V_1 \frac{dV_1}{dh} = -\left(\frac{a}{A}\right) V_2 \frac{d}{dh}\left(\frac{a}{A} V_2\right)$$

$$a_1 = -\frac{a^2}{A^2} V_2 \frac{dV_2}{dh}$$

$$= -\frac{a^2}{A^2}\sqrt{2gh}\sqrt{2g}.\frac{1}{2\sqrt{h}}$$

$$\Rightarrow \quad a_1 = -\frac{ga^2}{A^2}$$

Sol. 18 (B) Efflux velocity at holes X and Y

$$v_1 = \sqrt{2g(h - H/2)}$$

$$v_2 = \sqrt{2gh}$$

By continuity equation at top surface and holes we have

$$A\left(-\frac{dh}{dt}\right) = a(v_1 + v_2)$$

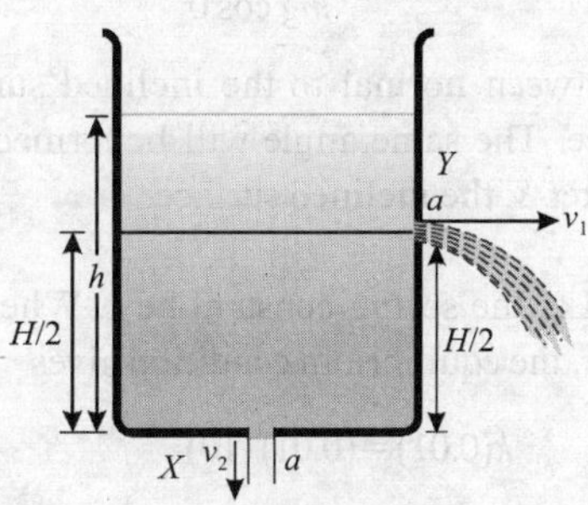

$$\Rightarrow \quad A\left(-\frac{dh}{dt}\right) = a\ \{\sqrt{2g(h-H/2)} + \sqrt{2gh}\}$$

$$\text{or} \quad -\frac{A}{a\sqrt{2g}} \int_H^{H/2} \frac{dh}{\sqrt{h} + \sqrt{h - H/2}} = \int_0^t dt$$

$$\Rightarrow \quad t = \frac{2A}{3a}(\sqrt{2}-1)\sqrt{\frac{H}{g}}$$

Sol. 19 (B) Using Pascal's equation from first to second tank surface

$$p_a + h_1\rho g - 40\rho_1 g + 40\rho g = p_a + h_2\rho g$$

$$h_2\rho g - h_1\rho g = 40\rho g - 40\rho_1 g$$

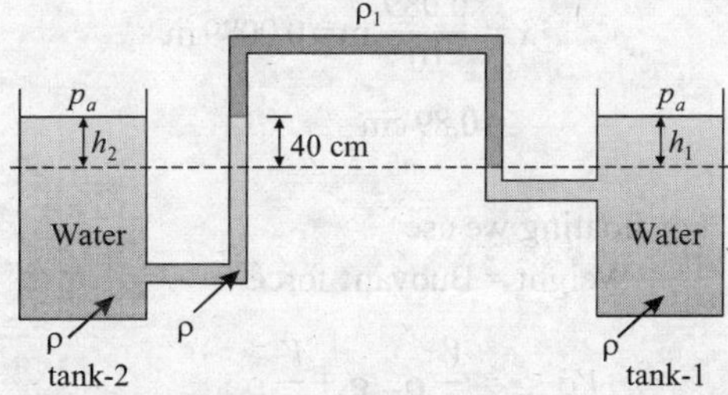

as $\quad \rho_1 = 0.9\rho$

$$(h_2 - h_1)\rho g = 40\rho g - 36\rho g$$

$$h_2 - h_1 = 4\ \text{cm}$$

Sol. 20 (A) Figure below shows forces acting on a 'particle' on the surface, with respect to vessel

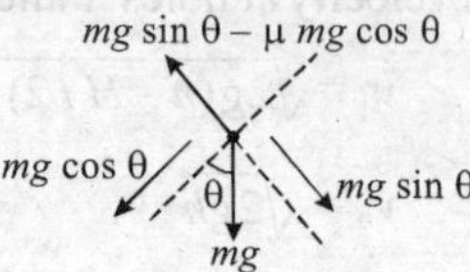

$mg \sin\theta - \mu\, mg \cos\theta$ is pseudo force

Here if ϕ is angle made by water surface with incline we use

$$\tan\phi = \frac{\mu mg\cos\theta}{mg\cos\theta} = \mu$$

ϕ is angle between normal to the inclined surface and the resultant force. The same angle will be formed between the surface of water & the inclined surface.

Sol. 21 (B) Let the spring constant be k. When the piece is hanging in air, the equilibrium condition gives

$$k(0.01) = (0.01)(10)$$

$$\Rightarrow \quad k(0.01) = 0.1\text{ N} \qquad \ldots(1)$$

$$\Rightarrow \quad k = 10\text{ Nm}$$

The volume of the copper piece

$$= \frac{0.01\text{ kg}}{9000\text{ kg/m}^3} = \frac{1}{9} \times 10^{-5}\text{ m}^3$$

This is also the volume of water displaced when the piece is immersed in water

$\Rightarrow$ The force of buoyancy = weight of the liquid displaced

$$= \frac{1}{9} \times 10^{-5} \times (1000) \times (10) = 0.011\text{ N}$$

If the elongation of the spring is x when the piece is immersed in water, the equilibrium condition of the piece gives,

$$kx = 0.1\text{ N} - 0.011\text{ N} = 0.089\text{ N} \qquad \ldots(2)$$

By (1) and (2),

$$x = \frac{0.089}{10}\text{ m} = 0.0089\text{ m}$$

$$= 0.89\text{ cm}$$

Sol 22 (C) For floating we use

Weight = Buoyant force

$$V\rho_m g = \frac{V}{2}\rho_{Hg} g + \frac{V}{2}\rho_{\text{oil}}$$

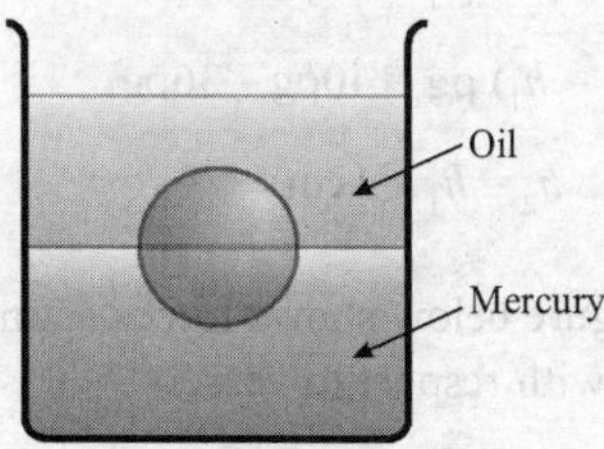

$$\rho_m = \frac{\rho_{Hg} + \rho_{oil}}{2} = \frac{13.6 + 0.8}{2}$$

$$= \frac{14.4}{2} = 7.2$$

Sol. 23 (A) Buoyant force

$$= F_b = V_{\text{sub}} \cdot \rho_l \cdot g$$

where, V_{sub}, ρ_l and g all are same w.r.t. O_1 and O_2

Sol. 24 (B) The specific gravity of the block = 0.8. Hence the height inside water is 3 cm × 0.8 = 2.4 cm. The height outside water is 3 cm – 2.4 = 0.6 cm. Suppose the maximum weight that can be put without wetting it is W. The block in this case is completely immersed in the water

The volume of the displaced water = volume of the bloc

$$= 27 \times 10^{-6}\text{ m}^3$$

The force of Buoyant on block is $V\rho g$

$$\Rightarrow \quad F_B = (27 \times 10^{-6}\text{ m}^3)(1000) \times (10) = 0.27\text{ N}$$

The spring is compressed by 0.6 cm and hence the upward force exerted by the spring is

$$F_S = 50\text{ N/m} \times 0.6\text{ cm} = 0.3\text{ N}$$

The force of buoyancy and the spring force taken together balance the weight of the block plus the weight W put on the block. The weight of the block is

$$W' = V\rho_\omega g$$

$$= (27 \times 10^{-6}) \times (800) \times (10) = 0.22\text{ N}$$

Thus for equilibrium we use

$$\Rightarrow \quad W = 0.27\text{ N} + 0.3\text{ N} - 0.22\text{ N} = 0.35\text{ N}$$

Sol. 25 (D) Let area of ice-cuboid excluding hole = A weight of ice block = weight of liquid displaced

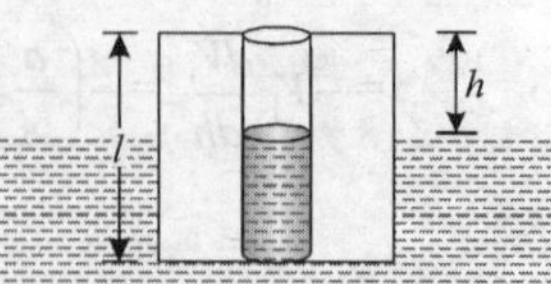

$$A\rho_{\text{ice}}\, lg = A\rho_\omega (l - h)\, g$$

$$\frac{9l}{10} = l - h$$

$$\Rightarrow \quad h = l - \frac{9l}{10} = \left(\frac{l}{10}\right)$$

Sol. 26 (A) From continuity equation, velocity at narrow cross-section is more than that at wide cross-section. So by Bernoulli's theorem we use $P_1 < P_2$. Thus liquid level in the tube at narrow cross section will be lower.

Sol. 27 (C) If h height of float is submerged in water, we use

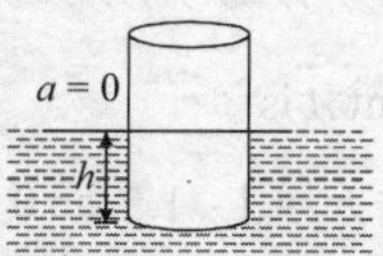

$$mg = F_B$$

$$\Rightarrow \quad dSH \times g = \rho_w Sh \times g$$

$$\Rightarrow \quad h = \frac{dH}{\rho}$$

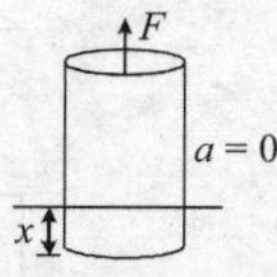

Now when force F is applied, for minimum work we slowly pull it out and when submerged length is x, we use

$$F - mg + \rho Sxg = 0$$

$$F = mg - \rho Sxg$$

$$W = \int F dx = \int (mg - \rho Sxg) dx$$

$$= mg \int dx - \rho Sg \int x dx$$

$$W = mgh - \frac{\rho Sgh^2}{2}$$

$$= (\rho Sh)\, gh - \frac{\rho Sgh^2}{2} = \frac{\rho Sgh^2}{2}$$

$$= \frac{\rho Sg}{2}\left(\frac{dH}{\rho}\right)^2 = \frac{Sgd^2H^2}{2\rho}$$

Sol. 28 (C) Area of bottom $= \pi r_0^2$

If r is radius of the exposed bottom, then

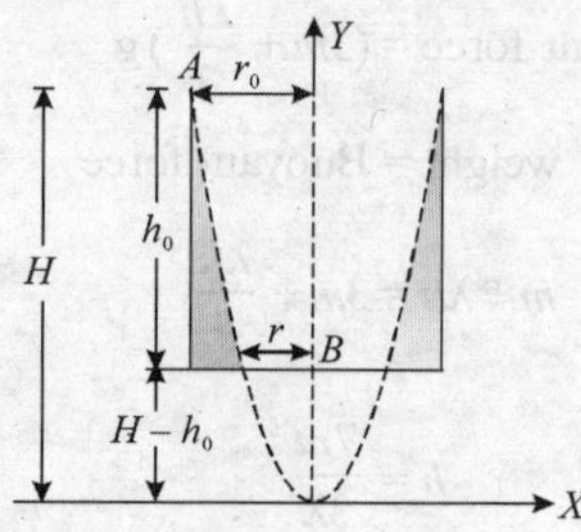

$$\pi r^2 = \frac{1}{2}\pi r_0^2$$

$$r = \frac{r_0}{\sqrt{2}}$$

Due to rotation of liquid surface profile has an equation given as

$$y = \frac{\omega^2 x^2}{2g}$$

here at $\quad y = H$, $\quad x = r_0$

and at $\quad y = H - h_0$, $\quad x = \frac{r_0}{\sqrt{2}}$

$$\Rightarrow \quad h_0 = \frac{\omega^2}{2g}\left(\frac{r_0^2}{2}\right)$$

$$\Rightarrow \quad \omega = 2\sqrt{\frac{gh_0}{r_0}}$$

$$= \frac{2\sqrt{10 \times 0.1}}{0.02}$$

$$= 100 \text{ rad/s}$$

Sol. 29 (C) Let the velocity at $A = v_A$ and that at $B = v_B$

By the equation of continuity,

$$\frac{v_B}{v_A} = \frac{30}{15} = 2$$

By Bernoulli's equation,

$$P_A + \frac{1}{2}\rho v_A^2 = P_B + \frac{1}{2}\rho v_B^2$$

or, $$P_A - P_B = \frac{1}{2}\rho(2v_A)^2 - \frac{1}{2}\rho v_A^2 = \frac{3}{2}\rho v_A^2$$

or, $$600 = \frac{3}{2}(1000)\, v_A^2$$

or, $$v_A = \sqrt{0.4} = 0.63 \text{ m/s}$$

The rate of flow = (30) (0.63) = 1800 cm³/s

Sol. 30 (D) Acceleration of container is

$$a = a_0(\hat{i} - \hat{j} + \hat{k})$$

As there is no gravity; the pressure difference will be only due to the acceleration. All points other than point 'H', are acted upon by a pseudo force. Hence, at point 'H' pressure developed is zero.

Sol. 31 (D) To measure the atmospheric pressure, same length of tubes containing mercury are required, no matter how many tubes are used as

$$P_{atm} = \rho_{Hg}\, gh$$

Sol. 32 (A) Figure shows the limiting state of oil surface in tank when just spilling starts from rear end

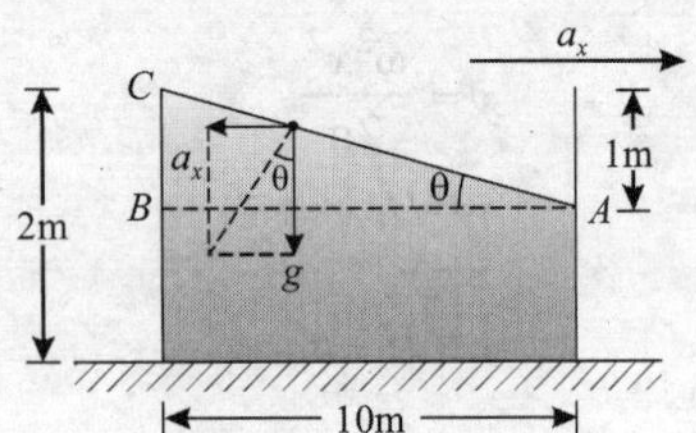

In frame of container for liquid surface, we use

$$\tan\theta = \frac{a_x}{g} = \frac{v}{tg} = \frac{1}{10}$$

$$\Rightarrow \qquad t = \frac{10 \times 20}{10} = 20 \text{ s}$$

Sol. 33 (A) Along x and y directions along in momentum of water is

$$|\overrightarrow{\Delta P}_x| = mv \sin 60° = \frac{\sqrt{3}}{2} mv$$

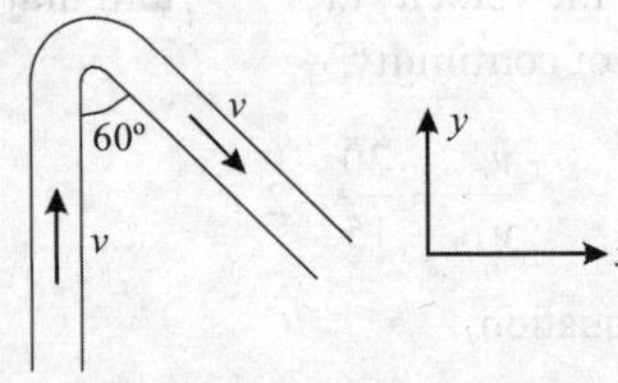

$$|\overrightarrow{\Delta P}_y| = \frac{mv}{2} + mv = \frac{3}{2} mv$$

$$\Rightarrow \qquad |\overrightarrow{\Delta P}_{net}| = \sqrt{\Delta P_x^2 + \Delta P_y^2} = \sqrt{\left(\frac{9}{4} + \frac{3}{4}\right)}\, mv$$

$$|\overrightarrow{\Delta P}_{net}| = \sqrt{3}\, mv$$

Force on bend is rate of change of momentum

$$\Rightarrow \qquad |\overrightarrow{\Delta F}_{net}| = \sqrt{3}\left(\frac{dm}{dt}\right).v = \sqrt{3}\,\rho A v^2$$

Sol. 34 (C) Figure shows the liquid state in equilibrium with respect to container. The angle θ is given as

$$\tan\theta = \frac{a}{g} = \frac{1}{3}$$

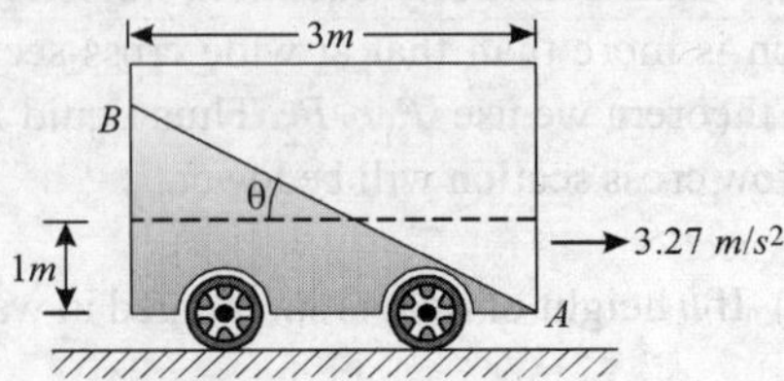

Depth of water at point A is

$$h_A = 1 - 1.5 \tan\theta$$

$$= 0.5 \text{ m}$$

Depth of water at point B is

$$h_B = 1 + 1.5 \tan\theta = 1.5 \text{ m}$$

Sol. 35 (C) Pressure in a liquid at same level is same, so we use Pascal's equation from open end

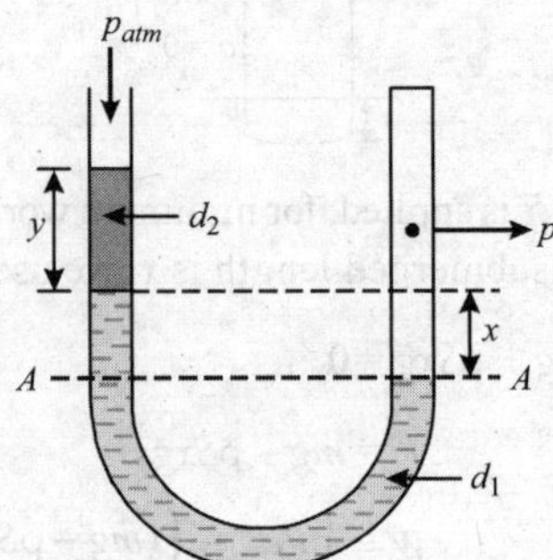

$$P_{atm} + d_2 y g + x d_1 g = p$$

In C.G.S.

$$P_{atm} + 13.6 \times 2 \times 25 \times g + 13.6 \times 26 \times g = p$$

$$P_{atm} + 13.6 \times g\,(50 + 26) = p$$

As $P_{atm} = 13.6 \times g \times 76$ so we use

$$2P_{atm} = p$$

$$\Rightarrow \qquad P_{atm} = \frac{p}{2}$$

Sol. 36 (B) Weight of sphere + chain = $(m + \lambda h)g$

$$\text{Buoyant force} = \left(3m + \frac{\lambda h}{7}\right)g$$

For equilibrium, weight = Buoyant force

or, $$m + \lambda h = 3m + \frac{\lambda h}{7}$$

or $$h = \frac{7m}{3\lambda}$$

Solutions of ADVANCE MCQs One or More Option Correct

Sol. 1 (A, C, D) For an ideal fluid the volume flow rate remains constant throughout the tube and is equal to the product of area of cross section and the flow velocity at any section of the tube hence option (A) is correct and if we use Barnoullie's theorem at the two points in the tube just below the vertical tubes we get option (C) correct. According to Barnoullie's theorem option (D) is correct

Sol. 2 (A, C, D) At the equator due to rotation of earth the effective gravity decreases but at poles it remain same. In case of a spring balance the weight is measured by the gravity and the reading of equator will be less but for a beam balance the weights reading will remain same.

Sol. 3 (A, D) In second case partly the ball's weight is also supported by weighing so here we use $W_1 > W_3$ hence option (A) is correct similarly machine option (D) is also correct.

Sol. 4 (D) For equilibrium of ball in the three cases we use

$$W_1 = W_2 = W_3 + W_4$$

hence none of the given option is correct.

Sol. 5 (B, D) For equilibrium of liquid, side walls of flask exert a force in downward direction on liquid due to which net force on base by liquid increase hence $W_1 > W_2$ and by Newton's third law option (D) is also correct.

Sol. 6 (All) Pressure at bottom of vessel is

$$P_B = 2h\rho g$$

Force at bottom is

$$F_B = P_B A_2 = 2h\rho g\, A_2$$

Pressure at level x is

$$P_x = h\rho g$$

Force on horizontal walls of container is

$$F_x = h\rho g\,(A_2 - A_1) \text{ upward}$$

hence walls will exert same downward force on liquid.

Sol. 7 (A, B, C) The efflux velocity of the flowing fluid is given by $(2gh)^{1/2}$ and the time of flight in reaching the ground taken by the efflux is $(2(H\text{-}y)/g)$ so the horizontal range x is obtained in such a way that at a specific value of y $(H/2)$ range x is getting maximum H so as y increases value of x first increase then start decreasing hence options (A), (B) and (C) are correct.

Sol. 8 (A, D) As the cross sectional area of the tube is same, flow velocity will remain same through out the tube and as point b is at a low height the gravitational potential energy of the flowing liquid is less hence at this point pressure energy will be more hence options (A) and (D) are correct.

Sol. 9 (B, C, D) The force due to continuous flow of liquid is equal to the change in momentum per second which is given as $F = \rho A v^2$ hence options (B), (C) and (D) are correct.

Sol. 10 (A, C) As density of ice is less then water and it displaces the same mass of water for floating if liquid is water, after melting the amount of water produced will be same so no change in level of liquid but if liquid is denser than water then the water produced will be more in volume than the liquid displaced by ice in floating state so after melting the level will rise.

Sol. 11 (A, B, D) As ice displaces the water of same amount as that of its mass, water level will not change if it melts. If ice cube contains some lead pieces then on melting ice lead pieces will sink and will not be able to displace the water equal to their weights so water level will fall. If some cork pieces are inside the ice cube then after melting cork pieces will remain in floating state so water level will not change.

Sol. 12 (B, D) Buoyant force on casting is

$$9_g = 90\text{ N} = V\rho_\omega g$$

$$\Rightarrow \quad V = 9000\text{ cm}^3$$

If the cavity volume if V_c we use

$$(V - V_c)\,\rho_{\text{iron}} = 27\text{ kg}$$

$$\Rightarrow \quad V_c = 9000 - \frac{27000}{7.8} = 5338\text{ cm}^3$$

Sol. 13 (A, C, D) In case of liquid if $\rho_L > \rho$ the buoyancy force will be more than the weight of the ball so it will retard upto certain depth then start rising up and finally reaches the original position in a longer time t_2 and during motion the acceleration of ball outside and inside the liquid remain constant so the motion cannot be simple harmonic. If $\rho_L = \rho$ then inside the liquid net force on ball will be zero so it will continue to move with same constant velocity.

Sol. 14 (A, C) Siphon will work only when the pressure inside the lower face of tube is more than atmospheric pressure for which $h_2 > h_1$. And to start the siphon the pressure due to column h_1 must be less than the atmospheric pressure otherwise it will stop hence option (C) is also correct.

Sol. 15 (B, C) As equal volume of the liquid is filled in all vessels, in case of vessel *C* the pressure at bottom is more than the weight of the liquid due to downward force exerted by the side walls hence option (B) is correct and net force by liquid in all the three vessels including side walls is equal to the weight of the liquid which is same in all cases.

Sol. 16 (C, D) If cross sectional area of the tube is uniform everywhere speed will remain same and hence pressure will also be same. If tube cross sectional area is non uniform then at different points of the cross section at different heights pressure may be same but not at points which are at same horizontal levels.

Sol. 17 (B, C) Siphon works only till the atmospheric pressure supports in flowing the liquid out of a vessel, hence (B) and (C) are correct.

Sol. 18 (A, C) To get the maximum range on the level at a depth h below the base of tank we use

$$\text{Range } x = [2(2h - y)/g]^{1/2} \, x \, [2gy]^{1/2}$$

For maximum range we use $dx/dy = 0$ which gives $y = h$ and $x_{max} = 2h$.

* * * * *